Quantitative Methods in Business

Audrey Curnock

Stanley Thornes (Publishers) Ltd

First published in 1996 by
Stanley Thornes Publishers Ltd
Ellenborough House
Wellington Street
Cheltenham
GL50 1YW
UK

96 97 98 99 00 / 10 9 8 7 6 5 4 3 2 1

A catalogue record for this book is available from The British Library.

ISBN 0 7487 2083 9

Typeset by Paston Press Ltd, Loddon, Norfolk
Printed and bound in Great Britain by Redwood Books, Trowbridge, Wiltshire

Contents

How to use this book

Quantitative Methods in Business has been written in response to various needs, particularly amongst students on business and related courses. At a time when universities and colleges are moving away from formal lectures towards a more student-centred learning environment, and are facing the demands of a semesterised, modular course structure, *Quantitative Methods in Business* provides the support lecturers need and a self-sufficient text to allow students to learn independently and constructively. It does so by providing:

- support in revising basic maths skills, in which many students lack confidence
- help in making best use of calculators, spreadsheet and statistical packages such as Excel and Minitab
- a rigorous, step-by-step approach to build skills and understanding progressive in what can seem a technical and demanding subject, and to allow students to learn more independently
- an applied approach emphasising practical business issues to motivate students and help them relate skills to their broader studies
- a comprehensive and flexible coverage suited to an introductory, modular course in quantitative methods
- the time-saving support hard-pressed lecturers need as work loads increase.

These needs are reflected in the following features of the text.

Building maths skills

Students face increasing difficulty with the maths skills required on a quantitative methods course. Chapter 3 enables students to revise core maths skills quickly and effectively before tackling more advanced applications in Chapter 5. To increase understanding and motivation, the chapter uses practical scenarios to illustrate points and there is a section applying skills leant to practical business problems. There are numerous exercises to reinforce skills. Answers to the odd-numbered questions are contained at the back of the book.

Detailed answers to the even numbered questions are contained in the accompanying lecturer's pack (see below).

The chapter also includes highlighted sections on using calculators. The reader is advised to buy a scientific calculator with a fraction button, SD and LR mode and nCr and nPr buttons, such as a Casio FX 570S. We shall use the statistical programs SD in chapters 4 and 9. The LR (linear regression) mode is a very useful facility to have and this is used in chapter 9. If, however, your model does not have an LR mode, there are longer methods, using the SD mode. Instructions are also given for older versions of the Casio scientific calculator.

Other manufacturers' models are broadly similar to the Casio (in particular, Sharp models), although the reader will need to refer to the manual for all calculators for additional information; this applies particularly to Texas calculators.

The structure of individual chapters

To assist learning, each chapter is focused around one or more scenarios designed to illuminate the skills learnt and their practical application. Chapters also use a clear, step-by-step approach to building skills, allowing students to think through problems systematically and independently. Practical exercises are included throughout chapters so students can consolidate skills as they proceed. Relevant chapters also include case-studies on the use of Minitab and Excel.

How the book is organised

The chapters in *Quantitative Methods in Business* are designed to provide a stepped course in business mathematics and statistics and can be read consecutively. However, the book has also been organised to allow chapters to be read in a different order to fit individual course or student needs. This section explains the role of each chapter and how they are related so that readers can choose a path appropriate to them. It should be read in conjunction with the following diagram which shows which chapters, particularly those covering maths skills, provide the underpinning skills for chapters which follow.

What do individual chapters cover?

Question	Topic	Chapter
How do I collect data?	Sampling	1
How do I present data?	Data representation	2
What maths skills do I need?	Revision maths	3
How can I build mathematical models to solve problems?	Linear and quadratic equations	5
	Linear programming	11
How do I calculate interest rates?	Simple and compound interest; depreciation	6
How can I use mathematical models to help me plan a project?	Critical path analysis	12
What is the average?	Averages	4
What is the chance of this occurring?	Probability	7,8
What is the relationship between these variables?	Correlation and regression	9
Is there a trend?	Index numbers and time series	10

Chapter interdependencies

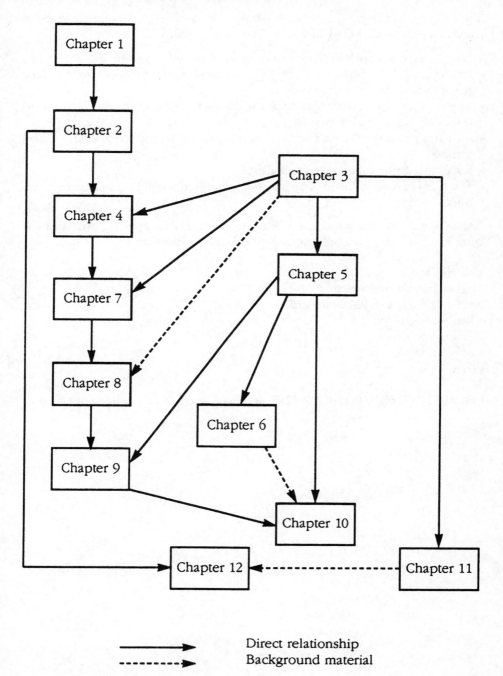

Direct relationship
Background material

The lecturer's pack

To support lecturers, *Quantitative Methods in Business* is accompanied by a lecturer's pack available to adopters. The pack contains:

- answers to even-numbered questions in the text
- step-by-step solutions to complex questions where students may need particular guidance though each step
- a bank of multiple-choice questions for relevant chapters to enable lecturers to test skills easily and effectively
- statistics projects to test a range of skills across the text in a practical business setting
- additional Excel exercises and solutions
- key diagrams and illustrations which can be used as OHTs or lecture hand-outs.

A free sample of the pack is available for lecturers to inspect. This and the complete pack available only to adopters can be obtained from:

Francis Dodds
Higher Education Publisher
Stanley Thornes (Publishers) Ltd
Ellenborough House
Wellington Street
Cheltenham
GL50 1YW

(Tel.: 01242 228888; fax: 01242 221914; e-mail: sthornes@rmplc.co.uk)

Acknowledgements

The author and publishers are grateful to the following organisations for permission to reproduce material: Casio Electronics for the use of model Casio FX 570S; Cambridge University Press for the t-tables in the Appendix, from Biometrika; Microsoft Corporation Ltd for reference to Excel version 5 and Minitab Inc, 3081 Enterprise Drive, State College, PA 16801, USA. Tel: 814 238 3280; fax: 814 238 3280; e-mail: Info@minitab.com. MINITAB is a registered trademark of Minitab Inc.

My warmest thanks to my colleagues and students at South Bank University. In particular I have very much valued the support and friendship of Bernard Chalk (and his mum, Ivy), Mike Parker and David Singmaster. I would also like to thank Jon Warwick, Sylvia Jennings, Val Flynn, Pat Spellacy and Chris Clare (for appointing me!). At Goldsmiths' I would like to thank Cho-Ho Chu, and at King's, Frank Jellett. Also thanks to Joe Rushton for all his support in the early years!

At Stanley Thornes I would like to thank Francis Dodds for all his patience and support, Sandy Marshall and Robert West, and all who worked on the production of the book.

Dedication

To my mum and family: Paul, Olwyn, John, Ron and Teresa;
and to the memory of my dear father.

Also to all the students I have taught.

1 What are statistics and what are their uses?

Objectives

- Understand where statistics are used;
- Understand what constitutes information and data and their distinction;
- Appreciate the difference between descriptive and inferential statistics;
- Recognise different data types and scales;
- Understand how to conduct a statistical investigation;
- Understand sampling techniques: simple random sampling, cluster sampling, stratified sampling, systematic sampling and quota sampling;
- Appreciating the *best* sampling technique for a given problem.

Scenario: the graduate employment survey

The Graduate Employment Agency has been asked to conduct a survey on trends in Graduate Employment in 1996. Its mandate is to advise the Government on current skills within the graduate pool and to determine whether employers are able to recruit the skilled staff they require. Important questions include: are there too few engineers graduating or too many scientists going into research posts or too few teachers entering the profession? It has also been asked to report on graduate salaries and training programmes. As a member of the project planning team undertaking this survey, your job is to consider how to undertake this survey and what information to gather to write the report.

Introduction

Statistics principally involves the collection and analysis of numerical data. In everyday life we are continually bombarded with statistical information, be it about the latest opinion poll on political parties, and in particular the popularity of the current Government, or data on the economy, inflation or some other attribute. The layperson is likely to think that statistics are 'facts and figures' and as such any argument based on statistical calculations must be entirely objective and irrefutable. Unfortunately this is not quite the whole picture. Experimental error may occur, for example, if the data were monthly sales of a product and some items are subsequently returned as faulty and the customer refunded. Thus this data will be subject to error. Clearly further errors may occur in the way the data has been collected: for example, if in collecting monthly sales figures only data from the two prime stores is chosen. This will not necessarily give the correct impression of sales in an average-sized store including smaller outlets.

Interpreting data is also an area which is very subjective: just because statistics are used to qualify statements it can only support the claim if it has been validly collected and analysed.

It is now clear that statistics can be misleading to the general public in a myriad of ways. The information presented may be based on some truth, but is sometimes removed from its original context so as to be no longer founded on anything other than hearsay. Statistics have many uses and abuses – there is even a book entitled *How to lie with statistics* (by D. Huff, Penguin 1991). To be uninformed of the uses and limitations of statistics leaves one open to being misled by advertisers, politicians, and even independent financial advisers. The layperson cannot ignore the information being presented to him or her, so it is important to have some understanding of such information and its various interpretations.

Statistics in business

From a business perspective, why do we need statistics? In almost every part of manufacture, design, management or marketing, statistics are a very useful tool. We list some areas of particular interest to illustrate this point.

Production and manufacture

Statistics are used in production control and management in such areas as measuring and determining quality. In the aeronautical industry precision components are a matter of life or death—Rolls Royce or any other aircraft supplier would simply not remain in the market place if their products failed to meet the highest quality assurance. Every component has a unique identifier and is made to an exact precision, be it dimension or breaking strength. In a general manufacturing company products would be routinely removed from the production line and tested against a set of criteria. If a certain proportion of any batch failed to meet these criteria the batch would be rejected. In warehouses, supermarkets and wholesalers stock-control models are used to determine the optimum time for re-ordering goods or the best size of an order to place for efficient running of the venture. In business efficiency such tools as time measurement for each jot within an organisation are used. From the promotional viewpoint, market research cannot be ignored if your product is going to do well. To launch a new product without studying market response and behaviour spells commercial disaster.

Forecasting

In economic forecasting, statistics are vital in predicting sales, economic growth, estimating the supply and demand of products, predicting the balance of payments, bank base rates, or unemployment figures. Predicting the weather can be equally important in the business world, and yes, it uses statistical models! For example, deciding the optimum time for a sale of your summer clothing before the weather turns wintry, or when to hire or not to hire large cranes in the building world, and of course when farmers should begin harvesting. For ice-cream manufacturers it is important to know when there will be a heat wave and so employ contract labour to boost production. Corporate strategic planning is increasingly used by go-ahead companies who want to stay one foot ahead of their competitors as well as building strong companies to withstand economic change. Statistical techniques for business forecasting are ever important in this respect.

Medical testing

In the pharmaceutical industry large scale testing of new drugs is an important part of safety and consumer confidence. It takes years for new drugs to pass through all the stages until fully licensed in either the UK or USA. Statistical trials are always set up when consultants are trying a new medical treatment. Results are later published in medical journals such as *The Lancet* and other teams will independently verify these results. It is often at this stage that some fundamental basic flaw is found in the scientific design or analysis of these trials. When large scale testings are carried out these results will tend to have more credibility—if the size of the group tested is too small it is unlikely to be validated or accepted as a new treatment.

Statistics in this text

In the subsequent chapters we shall use statistical techniques in the following situations.

Sampling

We shall look at ways in which the Graduate Employment Agency could collect the required information and data. The way in which data is collected is vital if the data is to be of any use in making inferences about what is happening in the graduate employment market. If for example we sampled only employed graduates our data would be distorted: it is likely that some graduates will not have found work at the time of survey or that they are employed in non-graduate type jobs. If our data is to be a reliable source of information the statistical investigation needs to be carefully designed.

Statistical analysis

We shall look at tabulating the amount spent on library resources across UK higher education and how such data can be represented pictorially. We shall compute typical values or averages and measure the variability within these spending figures.

Correlation

Correlation will be used to assess consistencies between respondents' preferences for a set of products. We shall also use correlation to assess if it is appropriate to predict a company's operating profit if we know its turnover. If this did seem appropriate, we could then use regression analysis to predict what we would expect the profit to be if the turnover was a particular figure.

Time series

Given a set of consecutive monthly figures for inflation, unemployment or base rates we can use time series analysis to investigate whether there is any evidence of an underlying trend in this data, and furthermore we could forecast what the coming months' figures might be.

Probability and probability distributions

We shall use probability to calculate the chance of winning on the National Lottery, and to compute expected profits. We shall use the binomial distribution to look at how many defective items we might expect from a production line. The Poisson distribution is used to look at the chance of a machine breaking down. The normal distribution is used to describe the typical life span of a consumer product. Moreover, if the manufacturer wishes to replace at most 1% of products whilst under guarantee, what the length of guarantee should be is calculated.

Hypothesis testing

Hypothesis testing is used to measure the significance of preferences in a market research survey, or the results of pharmaceutical trials of a drug. We shall look at claims about inner city crime to see if these are more alarming then the data which is used to support these claims indicates.

Information and data

In starting any collection of facts and figures, the most important thing to ask is: 'What information do I need to find to answer the questions I have in mind?' Knowing the topic of research, and the information of particular interest, will enable one to determine how best to collect data to provide this information. To understand this more clearly we shall firstly look at the distinction between information and data.

If we have some facts and figures which we have collected with no particular question in mind and in no specific order, then we would call these facts and figures *raw data*.

If we put our facts and figures into a semblance of order, perhaps arranged to scale (e.g. alphabetically, or according to size) then we might be able to see some pattern emerge. At this instance we could say that this data was information, but only if it could assist us in answering a question we wanted to ask.

Formally we would say that data becomes information when it helps us to answer a question or make a decision, or 'information is raw data converted into a form which will enable the user to make a decision in response to a business need'.

For example, in the graduate employment scenario, the data we collect might include the salaries of all graduate respondents together with their degree subject and classification and possibly gender. The information we should be able to deduce from this data would include:

- what the typical (average) graduate salary is in 1996;
- if there are any differences between different degree subjects or class and salary;
- if there are any gender differences between salaries.

If we also collected the name and location of the university of each graduate respondent we might be able to answer questions about geographical differences between graduate salaries or indeed between salaries and the academic reputation of a university.

After the data has been carefully collected in such a way that the data will be reliable and unlikely to have a large degree of error, this data is termed the *raw data* or raw material for collating, condensing and summarising. This usually involves tabulation and then visual display. Finally the data is analysed and interpreted in order that some conclusions may be drawn. Thus the data will provide the information to answer our specific questions.

Once the data has been collected it is usually difficult to see the overall situation, so it is important that the data is summarised and organised to display its principal features and so aid further analysis. We can see that there are two main processes going on here:

- The collection and summation of data
  This is known as *descriptive statistics* as it is concerned with describing the given situation and looking at what is happening in the given situation.
- Analysis and conclusions to be drawn or inferred
  This is known as the *inferential statistics*. As its name suggests, this is concerned with inferring what is likely to be happening on a larger scale—within the whole underlying situation, i.e. within all companies or all graduates or the whole country—the *population*, rather than just the companies or graduates selected, the *sample*. It is important to understand that collection and analysis of data go hand in hand. To simply collect data and stop there gives no understanding about the questions to be answered. To try to interpret a situation without having reliable representative data amounts to no less than guesswork. That is to say that having an understanding of the pitfalls of both activities is vital if your business, social or medical data are to have any credibility.

In the next section we take a look at what actually constitutes data.

Data types: levels of data measurement

When we conduct a survey of TV viewing or count the number of vehicles using a petrol station it is helpful to recognise the type of data being collected. More importantly this will assist in the development of data collection and questionnaires or studies being conducted. To understand the level of information stored in any particular collection of data we shall look at levels of data measurement. Firstly there are two broad categories for data: qualitative or quantitative data.

Qualitative data: this is when codes or labels have been assigned for categories of items. For example in employee records a company might use a code such as A for male and B for female. Such a code would be non-numeric. Equally if the code for employee jobs was 1 for administrator, 2 for accounts clerk, 3 for section manager, etc. Such a code would be numeric. It is qualitative as it measures a particular quality of attribute: here gender or employee description. If this data was recorded in a data base or spreadsheet it is more usually recorded as a numeric code. Qualitative data is sometimes referred to as non-metric data.

Quantitative data indicates 'how much' or 'how many'. For example, a company's records would store how many workers of each grade it employed, and how much each employee earned. Such data would by their nature by numeric: they are measuring quantity in some category. Quantitative data is sometimes referred to as metric data.

Within each of these two data types are sub-categories which enable us to see more clearly exactly what the data is depending on, what level of detail it contains and how we can process this data.

There are four main levels of measurement of data which we can consider. These are: nominal scale: ordinal scale: interval scale and ratio scale. Nominal and ordinal data are both examples of qualitative data, whilst interval and ratio data are examples of quantitative data. We shall consider each in turn.

The nominal level of measurement

This is the lowest level of data measurement. The key feature of a nominal data entries is that codes or labels are used to identify the particular characteristics measured. Examples of such data include:

National Insurance numbers	WB 12 34 56 D
Tax reference numbers	LP 838 p745
Telephone numbers	0171 815 3568
Vehicle registration numbers	M 874 WJX
Postal codes with house number	GL53 2RZ, 30

We can see that such data contains examples which are numeric and non-numeric (and a mixture). What uses can be made of such data? Well, take the postal codes: from this we can determine a particular area of the country—here usually the first two letters denote the nearest large town. Similarly with the phone number the first set of digits indicate the country code, London in this instance, with the next 3 digits indicating the part of inner or outer London where this number is. Can we manipulate such data, i.e. can we summarise it, or add or subtract these values? Generally no, although you could find, for example, the total number of cars registered in the UK with an M-registered car, or those registered in a particular area. Nominal scales are often used in market research where, for example, an interviewer might ask which age group the interviewee fell in:

Code	Age group
1	under 20
2	20 to 30
3	30 to 45
4	45 to 60
5	over 60

The ordinal level of measurement

An ordinal measurement is one which gives a code to categorise but also permits us to rank or order data. This is widely used in market research where preferences are sought. For example: which brand of butter/coffee/coca-cola did you prefer out of four products A, B, C and D? An interviewee would be asked to rank them in the order preferred: a rank of 1 would denote 'liked best', 2 would denote 'quite liked', 3 would denote 'did not really like' and 4 would denote 'least liked'. Similarly ordinal data would measure the rankings for how busy various photocopiers were in a university, or to rank productivity of sections of a production line, or popularity of holiday destinations for different age groups. Thus ordinal data could be numeric or non-numeric. Hotels, restaurants and tour operators often have a quality ratings card which customers are asked to complete. For example, on the return flight from Rhodes you might be asked to complete a form as follows:

Rhodesque flight questionnaire

1. Which resort did you stay at: _____

2. Was your stay (circle your answer):
   B&B   Half-board   Full-board

How would you rate the following aspects of your holiday (tick the most appropriate box):

	Excellent	Good	Satisfactory	Poor	V. Poor
3. The accommodation					
4. The connections to the airport/hotel					
5. The service of hotel staff					
6. The assistance of the courier					
7. The resort you stayed at					
8. The overall holiday					

9. How many organised excursions did you go on: 0   1   2   3 or more

	Excellent	Good	Satisfactory	Poor	V. Poor
10. The organised excursions were					

11. Would you return to Rhodes?   Y   N

12. Are there any improvements you would like to see?
   _____
   _____

The responses to questions 1 and 2, 9 and 11 would be nominal data entries, whilst the responses to 3–8 and 10 are ordinal as the customer ranks how they viewed their holiday. Once all the forms are collected the tour operator can find out the total number who thought the accommodation was poor or very poor and perhaps consider why. Notice that the difference between 'excellent' and 'good' may not be the same as the difference between 'poor' and 'very poor'. Thus with ordinal data it makes no sense to consider the differences or distances between rankings. In fact the range of what is 'good' may not be the same as the range of what is viewed 'satisfactory'. All that can be deduced from ordinal data is that 'good' is better than 'satisfactory' or that rank is inherent. Thus it would make no sense to carry out any arithmetic calculations on ordinal data. Notice that if we are entering these responses on a spreadsheet we might use a numeric code to denote 'good', 'satisfactory', etc. We can see that the response to question 12 is a datum but could not be entered on a spreadsheet in a numeric format but simply as a text field.

Interval scale

Interval scale is used when (i) data have the properties of ordinal data and (ii) the differences or range of values between observations have meaning. Such data is always numeric and examples include temperatures, air pressure, total marks awarded to any undergraduate for all units of a degree. To see that such data is ordinal consider the temperature on a day in May in the capitals of London, Paris and Brussels. Suppose it is 25 °C in London, 26 °C in Brussels and 27 °C in Paris. Then we can rank them as Paris being the warmest, then Brussels and then London. Moreover we can say that there is 1 °C between each of the cities in this order. It makes sense to rank them but furthermore the differences between the temperatures has meaning: the difference between Paris and Brussels is exactly the same as between London and Brussels. Thus this is more than just ordinal data, as there are equal distances or equal *interval* between two consecutive rankings, which is not so for ordinal data. Such data naturally lends itself to statistical calculations.

Ratio scale

Finally, the ratio scale of measurement of a variable is when (i) data have all the properties of interval data and (ii) the ratio between two observations has meaning. If we consider the cost of a family car (say £10 000) compared to a typical home (say £80 000), it makes sense to talk about the ratio of one to the other. The house costs is 8 times as much as the car. Other examples include the cost of one product (compared to another), distances (from one place compared to another), heights, time, weights, share prices, interest rates, etc. The distinguishing feature of this scale is the requirement that zero is inherent in its definition. This means a ratio measurement of absolute zero is the lowest reading possible on this scale and so there are no negative values. It is clear that it makes no sense to talk about negative heights, or distances. Similarly share prices are ratio data as we cannot have a negative share price: £0.00 is the lowest possible share price. However, if we look at the amount in a bank balance, this is in £ but it could be an overdrawn account and so is not in the ratio scale but the interval scale. With ratio data we can carry out any statistical analysis which can be performed on the three other levels of measurement, but there are some tools which would be exclusively suitable for ratio data.

Summary

We can see that the amount of information stored in our data varies according to the scale of measurement: qualitative data contains less information than quantitative data.

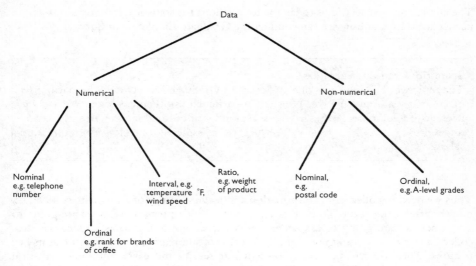

Figure 1.1

Nominal and ordinal contain the lowest levels of information, compared to interval and ratio scales which contain the highest levels of information. When we begin to summarise, represent and analyse data, the techniques we use depend on whether the data is qualitative or quantitative. A diagram summarising the levels of measurement is contained in figure 1.1.

Exercises 1.1 _____

Identify the scale of measurement used in the following examples:

1.1.1   The number of tickets sold in the National Lottery in a week.

1.1.2   The ranking of a person in a list of the best dressed people in 1996.

1.1.3   The age of your computer hardware.

1.1.4   The UK size of ladies clothes.

1.1.5   The volume of a can of cola in ml.

1.1.6   The number of hours children in a school watch TV each week.

1.1.7   The ranking of students in a lecture theatre according to A-level results.

1.1.8   The time taken to complete a crossword/100 m race/10 laps at Silverstone.

1.1.9   The countdown time to the launch of a space rocket.

1.1.10 Temperature in degrees Fahrenheit or Centigrade.

The aim of the next section is to lay the foundations for statistical investigations and in particular to look at how we can conduct the Graduate Employment Survey.

Scenario: Graduate earnings

The topic we shall look at is one aspect of the Graduate Employment Scenario, that of graduate earnings in 1996. We shall in particular ask the questions: 'What is the average graduate of 1996 earning six months after graduating? Are there any differences between degree subject/degree classification/gender/geography and salary?'

Thus we need to collect some information about the earnings of a graduate of 1996, six months after graduating. To do this we need to decide precisely who we are going to ask, when we are going to ask them, and what we are going to ask. Once we have collected this data we can then begin the process of summarising, and looking at its key features. Then we will be able to present our results and carry out some statistical analysis of it. This should give us the information to be able to answer the above questions.

Populations and samples

We would generally not ask every graduate in the UK who satisfied our criteria. This would constitute the *population* in this topic of investigation. If we decided to select the whole population we would be undertaking a *census*. This is time-consuming and costly and we might not get any clearer information on trends in graduate employment than if we asked a large collection of graduates—a *sample* or sub-collection from the whole graduate population. Generally we have an underlying population for our given investigation; this population may be very large or even infinite and our main aim is to find out some information about this population without actually going out and asking every one who satisfies the criteria for our investigation. We therefore select sub-collections or subsets from our population: samples which we can say represent the underlying population. We can describe the characteristics from these samples and then go on to analyse and make inferences about the population from our samples. Generally the larger the sample, the more weight we would give to inferences about the population. The picture to keep in mind is given by figure 1.2.

Given a particular investigation, the statistician will decide the criteria which will fix the population. A listing of all members of a population for a given statistical research is called a *sampling frame*. A sampling frame might be a listing of all entries in a telephone directory for a city, or a list of companies in a graduate directory, or a map of all cities in a country. Once a sampling frame is determined, the next stage will involve selecting samples. To begin this process, we shall outline the main steps in any statistical enquiry and then look at our chosen problem about graduate earnings. As with any scientific enquiry, conclusions will only carry credibility if the methods employed are soundly based. Statistical reasoning must be as logical as mathematical reasoning.

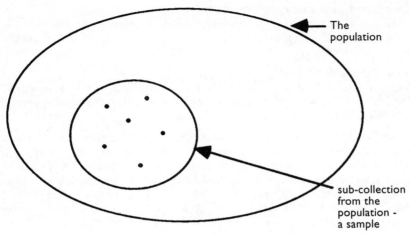

The population

sub-collection from the population - a sample

Figure 1.2

The statistical life cycle

Step 1: Identifying the problem
Start off with a particular topic in mind—for example a socio-economic theme, and formulate precisely what you want to investigate about this theme. Pose clear questions. This may include a claim or hypothesis you want to test. Notice that we need to specify precisely what we are going to ask in the survey.

Step 2: The sampling frame
Clearly we need to know exactly who belongs to the population, i.e. what precisely is the sampling frame. The sampling frame should correspond as closely as possible to the target population. If you are interested in the profitability of large companies in private and public ownership, you will need to decide what you mean by 'large', possibly in terms of turnover or number of employees.

Step 3: The data
Decide what data you will need to provide you with a solution to step 1. The place the data has originated from is known as the *source* of the data. Generally you may have two choices: collect your own data, a primary statistical source; or use some published source of information such as Government statistics, known as a secondary statistical source. We shall look at this in detail below.

Step 4: Decide how you will collect the data
Collecting the data will involve using a suitable sampling technique. There are many possible ways of selecting a sample (or samples) such as simple random sampling, cluster sampling, stratified sampling, systematic sampling and quota sampling. We shall discuss these in detail below. Different problems will require a different sampling technique.

Step 5: Describe and analyse the data

Collect the data, arrange it in a suitable format, tabulate it, present the data, visually display the data. Calculate certain values for central location and variation to focus the visual picture. Analyse the data.

Step 6: The inferences and conclusions

Decide what information the data conveys. Test the hypothesis as in step 1, make any inferences which are possible, draw conclusions. In particular does the data support or refute your hypothesis and with what chance of error?

These are guidelines only, and you may not always carry out the steps exactly as above. If your methodology is logically correct, then your conclusions are more likely to be valid. It is in this very process of validity of argument that statistics differs from mathematics. In the latter, statements are proved or disproved with absolute certainty. The emphasis in statistics is in what is likely to be true, or how confident we are about our conclusion—such as how likely we are to be wrong. Our terms of certainty are expressed in terms of chance or probability.

The graduate earnings life cycle

Step I: Identify the problem

Firstly, by a graduate we mean anyone who has been awarded a first degree from a university or college in the UK. We must decide when we will record the salary of the graduate, when, say, six months have passed since graduating? We will say that most students graduating in 1996 will have been awarded their BAs or BScs etc. by the end of August, and so we will want to know their earnings as at the end of February 1997. Do we choose gross salary, monthly or annual? We will choose gross salary per annum. Do we choose gross salary for the tax year 1996/1997 or the calendar year 1996? Whichever we choose we must be consistent and make sure that the questions are clear to the graduate.

Step 2: The sampling frame

The list of all graduates of all the universities will be the population for our problem. The likely size of this population is about 80 000. We now need to choose a sampling frame which closely resembles this population. This means that the graduates we choose to ask must be likely (in theory) to contain a whole range of graduates—from different parts of the country with different degree subjects and classes, from different social backgrounds, male and female, employed and unemployed or on a course.

Step 3: The data

Notice that we could simply collect the gross annual salary—but as we shall encounter the other details it makes sense to record them at this stage, as we may later decide to answer questions about the relationship between salary and degree subjects, gender, geographical location, etc. The specific data we shall collect is thus:

- the university or college awarding the degree;
- graduate name and address;
- gender;
- subject of degree;
- degree classification;
- annual gross salary of the graduate at 28/2/97.

Step 4: Decide how you will collect the data

It is most likely that here we would need to collect our own data—although there are some published sources which could be helpful. Universities publish 'first destinations' of all their graduates and this might give us some help. Another secondary source would be the national press which print listings of names of all graduates by university, with the class of their degree. Using either or these documents we need to decide how we will collect the data. Below are listed some possible options for collecting our own data, using various sampling techniques. With this in mind we must decide how large a sample we need to select. We could select one graduate and ask his/her salary and stop there. Clearly we could draw no conclusions from so small a sample. The larger the sample the smaller the chance of our conclusions being wrong, but obviously while selecting all 80 000 would be the best possible sample it would be cumbersome to deal with and we would undoubtedly go over budget! We will decide to use a sample 1% of the population. This will mean we have to sample 800 graduates, a reasonably large sample.

Step 5: Describe and analyse the data

Step 6: The inferences and conclusions

Sources of data: primary versus secondary sources

A *primary statistical source* is one which is collected by the statistician undertaking a particular investigation. Such data collections may be costly and time-consuming, but in many instances this is the only viable option. For example if you have just launched a new product and wish to undertake market research to test its commercial strength, it is unlikely anyone else will have already collected any information about this. *Secondary sources* are published sources of data which has been collected with some particular aim in mind. The use of such sources is economical but must be used with care. Obviously this information has been collected with the view to particular questions and you may be able to collect information for your own problem, but you may need to collect some data yourself so that you have a complete picture of the topic in question. For example, suppose you are using data produced by the Inland Revenue about the gross profits earned by companies in the UK in 1996. You are particularly interested in the ratio of gross turnover to number of employees. The published data may well be very comprehensive and properly collected, but it was collected to look at the amount of tax paid. You may well be able to extract the data you need from it, provided you bear in mind its limitations. Some small companies may have profits below the tax limit, and will not have paid tax in this year and so may not have been selected in the Inland Revenue data. Similarly, some companies may have been declared bankrupt and their taxes will not have been recorded. Using the Inland Revenue alone may therefore give an incomplete picture of what is happening in all companies. You could still use the data to extract data for your questions, provided you also sampled some small companies which did not pay tax and some that were declared bankrupt. Before we proceed to techniques for collecting and sampling data we take a look at the various different types that we are likely to encounter.

Strategies for collecting graduate data

We can see that our main options are to collect data from the company or the university and then the graduate. Which is a fairer, more representative sample? It is possible that some graduates are unemployed six months after graduating or that a graduate is not necessarily employed in a 'career' job using his/her graduate status. In this case we will not select any of these if we go to the companies employing graduates, possibly on graduate training programmes. For a fair or representative sample each member of the population must be equally likely to be selected. Clearly if we have some unemployed graduates in our population but we never select them, our sampling technique is biased. Why is being representative important? The underlying aim of our statistical work is to 'predict' the average salary of a typical graduate. If we cannot draw such inferences from our analysis then we are wasting our time. The only way we can be assured of making inferences with only a small chance of error is if the sample we choose to draw inferences from is representative of the population.

We list a few possibilities:

(i) We could go to one particular large employer organisation and interview all graduates of the class of 1996.

(ii) We could go to several companies of different types such as banks, insurance companies, retail companies, accountancy or law firms listed in graduate directories, etc. To do this we would need to choose these companies randomly and then interview or mail all graduates of the class of 1996 within these companies. (Exactly how we could choose 'randomly' will be discussed in detail below.) Then when we contact the company we are in effect conducting a census by contacting all members in the population.

(iii) We could go to several companies of one type—go to all banks, etc. again using a randomly drawn up list of banks and interview all graduates of 1996 employed there.

Are there any problems associated with these strategies? Firstly if we are looking for a large sample of 800 respondents any of these methods may be very time-consuming and costly—and may not yield the given sample size. Conducting the survey by post we would at best be likely to get a 40% response. More importantly, none of these sampling techniques satisfy the criteria of our sampling frame: we would not interview anyone who was unemployed. There is another possible error we could make here. Suppose we selected only ambitious, highly motivated graduates. We would unconsciously have introduced subjectivity to our data, or selected a biased sample. This would not give accurate inferences about the underlying population as a whole. We would need to build into our sampling method a strategy that would ensure we are able to select a cross section of graduates even if by chance we did select more ambitious graduates or more Oxbridge graduates than we might expect.

Sampling techniques

We now discuss some commonly used methods of sampling which are more likely to yield the sample we require.

Simple random sample

To conduct a simple random sample we would need to get a list of graduates from all universities and choose a sample of 800 at random from this list. If our sample is going to be of an real use for making inferences about the population then the sample must represent, or be typical of, the population. By this we mean that every member of the population is equally likely to be selected for our sample. For example if we are choosing a person to represent the student body on the board of governors of a university we must be sure that all student names are put into the pool of names for selection. If there are 10 000 students there will be a 1 in 10 000 chance of any student being chosen. Choosing at random means that we have no preconceived ideas about who or what item we will select—it is a bit like pulling a name out of a bag. If our population of graduates is 80 000 then each graduate has a 1 in 80 000 chance of being selected. Clearly if we are going to conduct our survey by post we might need to build a much larger sample, bearing in mind that at most 30–40% of graduates will respond.

Multi-stage sampling

For this sampling method we would need a list of all universities in the UK. We would then need to identify specific elements within the population for each stage of sampling. These are known as sampling units within the population. In our scenario these might be first the universities, then the departments, and then the individual graduates. We would need to choose a specific number of sampling units to generate the required sample size (or larger if some elements sampled fail to respond). Here to generate a sample of 800 we might choose say 20 universities at random. From each of these universities choose a number of departments at random, say 8 at each university. We could then decide to choose a number of graduates at random from each of the departments and contact these. This would mean we would contact 5 graduates from each of the 8 departments at each of the 20 universities. This would give us our sample of 800 students. (Again we might need to contact more graduates as some will not respond.) Such a sampling technique is known as *multi-stage sampling*. The stages are recorded in the table below:

Stage	Sampling unit	Number of selections
1	UK universities	20
2	Departments	8
3	Graduates	5
Total		800

Multi-stage sampling is most readily described as frequently sub-dividing your population until a sample of the size wanted is selected. Notice that the number at each sub-division is arbitrary. We have chosen sub-divisions which will give us our required sample size but such a choice is clearly not unique.

Stratified sampling

Here we divide the population into non-overlapping sub-populations. This methodology is better than simple random sampling when the underlying population is heterogeneous. By heterogeneous we mean a population which is of very different social class, geographical location, ethnicity, etc. which is quite likely here. Within each stratum there is a degree of homogeneity expected, that is, the variation within the stratum is less than within the population. By choosing a stratum for each degree classification one would expect that on average one would select each social group, ethnic group, geographical location, male and female, etc. To carry out the stratified sampling method we would require a list of all graduates from all universities, with graduate addresses and decide to contact the students in equal-sized groups depending on the class of their degree. That is, if we consider there are 5 possible pass grades a graduate can get, then our equal-sized groups would be $\frac{1}{5}$ of students who had a first-class honours degree, $\frac{1}{5}$ who gained an upper-second degree, etc. This would be a stratified sample. Notice that here we would randomly select our proportion of $\frac{1}{5}$ of each classification. Thus in fact we would choose 160 students for each classification of degree. In place of using $\frac{1}{5}$ as the proportion of each strata we might choose to use proportionate stratified random sampling where the percentage of the sample taken for each stratum is proportional to the percentage of that stratum in the population. That is, if we thought only 10% of graduates obtain a first-class degree, we might choose 10% of the sample (80 graduates), etc. trying to mimic the underlying proportion in the population.

Systematic sampling

Given a list of all graduates from all universities, with graduate addresses we would need to number the students from 1 to 80 000, say by alphabetical order. Then we might decide to select every kth graduate from this list where k is an integer determined by the formula:

$$k = \text{integer}\left(\frac{N}{n}\right)$$

where N = size of the population and n = the size of the sample required. Thus here we have $N = 80\,000$ and $n = 800$ thus $k = (80\,000/800) = 100$. Thus every 100th graduate is selected. This is known as systematic sampling. Where in the list of graduates do we start? Between 1 and k, a point which is chosen at random using random number tables (as described below). Suppose this was the 56th graduate, then we choose the 56th, the 156th, and 256th, etc.

Cluster sampling

We divide the population into non-overlapping areas, termed *clusters*. For example, each cluster could be a town, or county, or university. The basic idea is that each cluster is a mini-population or microcosm which closely resembles the sampling frame. From each chosen cluster a random selection of elements are chosen. Here if we decided to choose 1 university at random to be typical of all graduates, this might not be very close to our sampling frame, particularly if a very good or a very poor university was chosen.

Alternatively we could split the UK into counties where each county was a cluster. If we had 20 counties, we might randomly choose e.g. 5 clusters. This would be the first stage of our clustering—if we asked all graduates of all universities within these 5 counties this would be a 1-stage cluster. If we continued to subdivide each cluster into smaller clusters, and say the number of sub-divisions is k, then this would be a k-stage cluster and at this stage all elements of the cluster are interviewed. A more accurate picture of the population is obtained if more small clusters are chosen than a lesser number of clusters.

For our purposes it then makes sense to randomly choose, say, 2 universities within each of these clusters (counties). This would give use 10 institutions and we would need 80 graduates from each to complete our sample. We might choose 2 departments at random from the universities and interview all graduates. Note that we are unlikely to get a sample of exactly 800 but we could determine the likely size of the resulting sample and enlarge the number of clusters chosen at any stage of the process.

A random selection

In most of the methods of sampling outlined above we have used the words 'selecting at random'. How can we achieve this in practice?

We mention here that we have a list of 80 universities, in some order, probably alphabetical order. From this list we wish to select 20 universities. One way of randomly selecting these 20 universities would be to put all 80 names into a hat and simply pull out 20. Such a method is none too practical with larger data sets and so alternatives are necessary.

Consider the method outlined for multi-stage sampling. This means we wish to select one in every four universities. This leads us to one easy way of randomising a set of entries: number each university sequentially 1, 2, 3 and 4 in the order they appear on the list. For example if the list of universities started off as:

Aberdeen, Bath, Belgravia, Birkbeck, Birmingham, etc.,

we would number allocate numbers as follows:

University	Number allocated
Aberdeen	1
Bath	2
Belgravia	3
Birkbeck	4
Birmingham	1
Bradford	2
Bristol	3
etc.	

We have then subdivided the list of 80 universities into 4 groups at random, and we could simply select say—all universities allocated a number 2 as our randomly selected group of 20 universities. Equally any other group (1, 3 or 4) would also constitute a random sample of 20 from the 80 universities.

An alternative method would be to use random number tables, an extract of which is given below:

Extract from a random number table

83	30	92	39	18	40	03	00
99	27	69	48	85	32	16	46
18	26	36	67	68	47	31	69
26	71	47	94	32	71	72	91

Take the list of universities, say in alphabetical order, and number each sequentially from 1 to 80 depending on their position in the list. We would have:

University	Number allocated
Aberdeen	1
Bath	2
Belgravia	3
Birkbeck	4
Birmingham	5
Bradford	6
Bristol	7
etc.	

Now we wish to select 2-digit numbers from our table of random numbers and any number we choose (provided it is the required range from 01 to 80) would correspond to selecting one of the universities. We thus select twenty 2-digit numbers from the random number table in the required range. We can start at any point in the table (we can simply blindly choose a starting point with a pin) and reading along or down. We shall start at the second column third entry down: reading down the column until the bottom and then starting at the top of the next column. This would give us random numbers:

26 71 and 92 (which we discard as it is outside our range from 01 to 80) 69 36 47 39 48 67 94 (again this is discarded) etc.

until we have 20 numbers. Thus we have chosen the 26th, 71st, 69th university, etc.

Other sampling techniques

Census

It may sometimes be appropriate to conduct a census rather than select a sample, for example if our population was quite small—such as all Ferrari owners in the UK.

Quota sampling

This method of sampling does not in fact generate a truly random sample, but it is a fairly inexpensive method to employ and is widely used by market researchers. It is much cheaper and quicker than stratified sampling although it is somewhat similar. Firstly the population is divided into sub-classes according to some attribute such as age, location, social class, degree subject/classification. The market researcher then uses a non-random sampling method to collect data from 1 sub-class until the given quota is filled. If age is used to divide the population, for example into classes:

16 to 21 years
21 to 29 years
30 to 39 years
40 to 49 years
over 50 years

then if the interviewer is told to question 10% of the first group, 20% of the second, etc., then as soon as this quota is filled no more are questioned in that group. If the quota is chosen to mimic the proportion of that age group in the population (for example if we used degree classification and said a quota of 10% first class degrees, etc.) then we can see the similarities with stratified sampling. The difference being that the stratified methodology randomly selects each member of each stratum whilst the market researcher merely questions whoever passes by—if this is done in a shopping centre during early afternoon of a week-day this is likely to mean that mainly mothers/fathers with young children or the unemployed are surveyed.

Sampling techniques: advantages and disadvantages

Simple random sample

Advantage: generally the smaller the population the easier this is to do.

Disadvantage: for large populations simply numbering all elements of the population and using random numbers to select a random sample can be very cumbersome and time-consuming. Consequently costs rise and a cheaper methodology would be sought.

Stratified sampling

Advantage: one of the principal aims of stratified sampling is to reduce sampling error. With a large heterogeneous population this is often the most suitable method as a cross section of the population would be selected. Generally the benefits increase as the strata become more distinct.

Systematic sampling

Advantage: in fact systematic sampling works best when the population is ordered in a fairly random way with respect to the attribute being measured. This is used for its convenient methodology and easy administration rather than an attempt to reduce sampling error.

Disadvantage: it would be unsuitable if there was any periodicity in the data or the sampling interval was in phase with the periodicity of the data, for example if the list of all graduates of all 80 universities was in fact merged where within each university listing the graduates were ranked according to degree classification. Then if we decided to choose every 56th, 156th, 256th, ... person we might end up with a sample of all graduates with a third-class or unclassified degree.

Cluster sampling

Advantage: this is cheaper than stratified sampling and quicker. This methodology is better than simple random and stratified sampling if:

(a) the only sampling frame is in fact clusters (e.g. a set of companies, regional health authorities, or collection of local radio stations, etc.);
(b) the population is very spread out or it is difficult to obtain data on all individual members of the population.

Disadvantage: if all elements are very similar then sampling from 1 cluster may be no better than sampling 1 unit from the cluster.

Exercises 1.2 _____

1.2.1 Which method would you choose to sample graduates and why? Can you think of any other methods? Describe an alternative method of choosing a sample using the multi-stage method where universities are first placed into counties.

1.2.2 Why is the population non-homogeneous? Does geographical location or academic reputation have any bearing on this?

1.2.3 The tables below show clinics licensed by the Human Fertilisation and Embry-ology Authority during 1993–94. Table 1.1 shows 40 clinics where two treatments are given: Donor Insemination (DI) and In Vitro Fertilisation (IVF). The clinics in table 1.1 have been ranked according to their relative success, where success has been measured by their live birth rate for the IVF treatment. Table 1.2 lists 20 clinics (unranked) where only DI treatments are used. The live birth rates are adjusted to take into account the women's age, length of infertility, etc., and so have a degree of error, for example 23.4 ± 4; for simplicity these are omitted. Where an X is recorded, this treatment was not available.

(i) Using a suitable cycle of numbers choose 10 clinics at random from table 1.1. List the percentage of live births for these 10 clinics for the IVF treatments.
(ii) Using tables 1.1 and 1.2 and the table of random numbers, choose a random sample of 40 clinics which have DI treatments. List the percentage of live births for these clinics. Comment on your findings.

We shall use these results in chapter 2.

One of the best methods here would probably be the stratified sampling. There is no one 'best' method, but some are better than others!

Table 1.1

Hospital/cinic	IVF treatment		DI treatment	
	No. of treatments	Live birth rate %	No. of treatments	Live birth rate %
St James, Leeds	459	23.4	X	X
Royal Masonic	653	19.8	3	33.5
Lister, London	905	19.8	68	14.9
BUPA, Southampton	366	19.7	616	6.5
Leeds General	734	19.4	500	4.6
Hammersmith	1098	17.9	17	9.6
Chelsfield, Kent	90	17.7	44	17.8
BMI, Nottingham	647	17.6	110	6.2
Radcliffe Maternity, Oxford	613	16.9	X	X
Southmead, Bristol	74	16.8	263	3.2
Sheffield Clinic	507	16.3	5	34.4
St Thomas', London	351	16.2	X	X
Royal Maternity, Belfast	459	16.2	448	4.7
Midland Fertility Services	606	16.2	461	5.8
Walsgrave, Coventry	466	16.0	136	14.6
London Women's Clinic	577	15.3	597	14.9
Churchill, London	594	14.4	52	15.3
Bourn Hall, Cambridge	1501	13.8	185	17.4
Manchester Fertility Services	560	13.7	720	10.3
BMI, Birmingham	355	13.6	193	9.5
St Mary's, Manchester	821	13.6	573	13.8
University of Bristol IVF	446	13.5	23	42.6
Bridge Centre, London	458	13.5	563	12.2
Portland, London	148	13.5	10	34.3
University of Wales, Glamorgan	401	13.2	123	10.8
BUPA, Ilford	170	12.9	110	6.8
Esperance, Eastbourne	176	12.7	386	10.0
Royal, Edinburgh	344	12.7	528	4.1
Aberdeen	231	12.6	449	6.9
Chiltern, Bucks	70	12.2	19	24.5
Holly House, Essex	314	11.7	90	19.9
King's, London	1161	11.4	85	8.3
Ninewells, Dundee	312	11.3	236	2.1
Wirral Fertility Services	132	11.3	115	2.3
Middle England Leicester	76	10.9	81	9.0
University College London	278	10.4	95	14.5
St George's, London	143	10.3	133	13.2
London Gynaecological Centre	728	10.1	74	8.2
Nurture, Nottingham	720	10.1	1060	3.6
Royal Victoria, Newcastle	183	9.9	X	X

Table 1.2   Donor insemination treatment only

| Hospital/clinic | DI treatment | |
	No. of treatments	Live birth rate
Tower House, Bristol	311	5.8
Rosie Maternity, Cambridge	147	8.4
South Cleveland	103	7.5
Cleveland Fertility	134	15.5
Exeter Fertility Clinic	401	4.1
Nuffield, Plymouth	429	3.6
Winterbourne	86	5.5
Billinge, Manchester	16	5.1
Wessex Fertility Service	391	6.9
Watford General	39	3.1
Maidstone	41	2
Queen Mary's, Sidcup	6	0
Dr L. Hughes, Harley St	949	6.8
West Middlesex	68	10
Pregnancy Advisory Service	922	4.6
Middlesex, London	367	6.2
Newham General	69	14.3
Clinic of Rep Medicine, UCH	121	8.2
Rodney Fertility Clinic, Liverpool	528	3.7
Northampton Fertility Services	169	8

(Source: *Patient's Guide to DI and IVF Clinics* by the Human Fertilisation and Embryology Authority.)

Collecting the data

We will outline one way of collecting our graduate data using a stratified sampling technique, and then ask you to think of other ways.

The list of universities would give you, say, 80 universities to approach. (Here we shall use the term *university* for any college awarding a UK degree.) From each university you would require 100 student names and addresses who had graduated in 1996 and as we have 5 degree classes: 1st class, 2i, 2ii, 3rd and pass, we choose $\frac{1}{5}$ for each classification. Thus in 100 graduates we choose 20 with first class, 20 with upper-second class, etc. Now to rely on the universities to give you this information in the way you would like it is perhaps expecting too much. However, university results—names and degree classification are published in the newspapers, so collecting these would be easy. Then for each university you would make a list of all students who were awarded each class with the degree subject, and with surnames in alphabetical order. So for each class of degree at each university you will need to collect 20 names at random. As described above, the easiest way to do this is to number the graduates within each class with a number between 1 and 20, in that order, down the list. For example, suppose the students with a first-class degree from Belgravia University are:

Name	Number you assign
Abbott A	1
Ahmed S	2
Allott M	3
	.
etc.	.
Baljit S	20
Ball T	1
Bambe G	2
	.
etc.	.
Chung	20
Collins B	1
Cooper A	2
Crowther	3
etc.	

Now to select our 20 graduates from this class and university, we select all students with the same number assigned them. We could equally have chosen any other of the assigned numbers.

Continuing in this way we will have a list of 800 graduates and we can approach the universities for their addresses. Then the task of asking them their salary can be conducted. In an ideal world, everyone would reply to such a question, but don't rely on more then 30–40% replying—and that's even if you enclose a prepaid envelope! If too few reply, we might need to send letters to say all number 4s and number 10s on the list above. We shall look at what to do with this data in the next chapter.

Numeric data: a second look

Now we know what sort of information we want to collect and have briefly investigated various strategies for collecting this information and data, we need to take a closer look at what we shall find. We have already seen that the data we collect can be numeric or non-numeric. We now go on to look at how we categorise numeric data: this is arguably of greater importance than the scale of measurement of the data because the category of numeric data we have will affect the type of statistical analysis we carry out.

We can look at numeric data as one of two main types: discrete data and continuous data.

Discrete data

Definition: data is called *discrete* if it can only take a finite number of values between any two values within its range of possible values.

For example, if we are measuring the number of students doing any particular course at a UK college of higher education, realistically this is likely to be between about 40 and 200. Why is it discrete? Well, because it satisfies the criteria that this would be any value (finite number) which in theory could be between zero and say the total number of students at the largest such college, say 25 000. Similarly the number of people living in any house on an estate is a discrete number: its possible values are 0, 1, 2, 3, up to a probable maximum of say 12 (allowing for some large families which would today be unusual). You might think that a discrete number has to be a whole number (or integer) but this is not so: what is important is its possible values are spaced out and there is space between each possible value. Other examples include the shoe sizes: 3, $3\frac{1}{2}$, 4, $4\frac{1}{2}$, 5, $5\frac{1}{2}$, etc., of the number of people on a bus or in a train carriage at any time, the number of vehicles entering a petrol station, the number of faulty items in a batch. Prices are discrete data, for example the price of a company's shares, student's income, the value of sterling against the US dollar—this is continually changing and can be any value between say $1.40 on a bad day and $2.00 on a very good day. Notice that it could take the value of $1.40 and $1.41 but there is no possible value between these two, which is a characteristic of discrete data.

Continuous data

Definition: *continuous* data is very closely packed data, and its possible values are infinitely many over a particular range or interval, for example, weights of people in a lift, the time it takes a city office worker to walk to work, the height of product coming off a production line, etc. Why do the weights of people in a lift satisfy the criteria for being continuous? Well, if no one is in the lift, there is 0 kg. If say 1 person is in the lift this could be any weight from say 40 kg to 90 kg (or more); obviously we do not have a precise value for this weight: it could be any value from the least weight (of say a child) to the largest weight of say 300 kg (that's pretty heavy!). What we know is that a typical weight can be anywhere between these 2 extremes—and there are an infinite number of possibilities. Similarly if there are 2, 3, 4 or more in the lift. It is usually necessary to record continuous data to a certain degree of accuracy such as 1 (or 2 or more) decimal place(s) or 2 (or more) significant figures as we cannot usually measure a variable to a great degree of accuracy. It thus may sometimes appear that continuous data looks like discrete data but it is in fact continuous. For example, a set of heights of children might be 1.25 m, 1.46 m, 1.72 m, etc. which look as if they are recorded to 2 decimal places— but if we had more accurate measurements (e.g. using lasers) we might record to say 6 decimal places or more. The point is it might appear that the height of a child can be 1.72 m or 1.73 m but there are no children with height in between this value—it thus might appear to be discrete. It is not—it is continuous but recorded as discrete due to measuring constraints. Similarly age: if we record the age of a person in years then this is continuous data recorded as discrete (20, 21, 22 years, etc.) whereas a person's age is really continuous as it is a number of years, months, weeks, days, etc.

Summary

Discrete data

Ages in years: 0, 1, ...18, 19, 20, 22, ... up to about 120

Number of children in a family: 0, 1, 2, 3, ...say about 12

Number of people on a bus: 0, 1, 2, 3, ...80/90

Shoe sizes (children's): 8, $8\frac{1}{2}$, 9, $9\frac{1}{2}$, 10, $10\frac{1}{2}$, 11, . . . ,13, $13\frac{1}{2}$, 1, $1\frac{1}{2}$, 2, . . . up to about 4

Number of people entering a supermarket: 1, 2, 3, ...

Number of phone calls arriving at a busy office each day: 0, 1, 2, ..., 500, ...

Value of shares: the value is continually changing through the day but there will be a base value below which the shares are not traded—and the value is unlikely to go beyond a certain value.

Annual gross salary of a graduate: any possible value between £9 000 to £80 000!

Continuous data

Height of a kitchen unit coming off production: any value between the stated tolerance allowed: say 496 mm to 504 mm. (Nominal height should be 500 mm.)

Time taken to complete a crossword: from a matter of a few minutes to several hours.

Exercises 1.3

1.3.1 Give some examples of discrete data and list their possible range of values.

1.3.2 Give some examples of continuous data and list their possible range of values.

1.3.3 Give some examples of continuous data which have been recorded as discrete data and list their possible range of values.

1.3.4 Give some examples of qualitative discrete and continuous data.

1.3.5 Give some examples of quantitative discrete and continuous data.

Before we close this chapter we give a word of caution about data that we may be trying to collect: are we in fact actually doing so?

Caution: collecting the right data

Generally if we are collecting data we can say this data comes from one of two ways: either data is *observational*: we observe a set of outcomes and record the results, e.g. counting traffic flows, conducting questionnaires, counting the number of defectives in a batch, etc. Here no attempt is made to control or influence the outcome of the variables being counted, although 'dummy' questions are often built into a questionnaire to see how consistent the respondent is.

Or the data is *experimental*: we conduct trials—e.g. medical trials for a new drug, trials for a new model of car, etc. In this latter data collection we are measuring some attribute—such as the fuel consumption at a steady speed, braking distances, or blood pressure under moderate exercise, cholesterol level/blood viscosity when taking a certain drug. With experimental data we can see that there are usually many variables which can be measured and it is important when we design our trial that we are in fact going to measure the data we think we are. The design of statistical experiments is a very specialised branch of statistics and we will not attempt to cover this in any detail, merely attempt to highlight the difficulties.

Consider measuring the effect of a new drug on a heart patient: in particular we are interested in the viscosity of a sample of blood when the patient is taking this drug. The viscosity is the variable of interest. There are other variables which we need to control in some way so that our measurements are for viscosity alone and any other variable is as far as possible not being counted. This is clearly not easy to achieve! Other variables include different cholesterol levels, different blood groups, different diets, different blood pressures: it is these variables which we aim to control so that we can see the effect of the new drug on the blood's viscosity. It is only then that we shall be clear about the value of this drug as a treatment.

How is this achieved? Firstly a large sample will be needed. This sample will be divided into groups: each group will be a control for one of the variables we are trying to exclude. For example, one group will be those with high blood pressure, another with reasonably normal blood pressure, another will be those who have high cholesterol levels, etc. A *control group* will also be used: a group with each attribute (e.g. high BP) will be observed when either a placebo (a tablet containing no drug) is given or no treatment at all is given to see if there are any differences between this 'no drug group' and the corresponding 'drug' group. The dosage of the drug will be fixed for any one group: the different groups will be given different levels of the drug. Data on the viscosity will then be collected for each group and analysed. By careful design of this trial the statistician is confident that any changes in the viscosity of the controlled group and the 'drug' group are then likely to be due to the drug and not another attribute. In fact medical trials often use a process of 'double-blind' trials. This is when neither the doctor nor the patient knows whether the group is the control or the drug-group, or what level of the drug is being tested.

2 Presenting data

Objectives

- Understand why we wish to summarise data and how this can be achieved;
- Understand how to tabulate data;
- Understand how to present data pictorially;
- Be able to draw a dot plot, bar chart, pie chart, line chart, histogram, and frequency polygon;
- Understand what is the most suitable graphical representation;
- Be able to draw and interpret a cumulative frequency graph;
- Be able to change from relative frequency to frequency and vice versa;
- Understand how some pictorial representations can be misleading.

Introduction

We have collected the following data using one of the techniques outlined in chapter 1. In this chapter we shall consider how to proceed firstly to summarise this data and secondly to graphically represent this data. One of the main reasons for collecting data is to gather information on a particular topic and so once we have actually gathered this information we need to order it and decide what it tells us. A graphical representation has the benefit of telling us at a glance what sort of pattern, shape and variation there might be in this data and from this we can deduce trends and patterns in the underlying population from which the data was extracted. We shall consider three data sets: a simple one and two larger ones.

Data set 2.1

The following are net monthly line rental charges (in £) for mobile phones on the vodafone and cellnet networks:

12.47	15.50	11.80	12.80	16.25	10.18

Data set 2.2

The following are the typical number of A-level points required by 36 UK universities for entrance to one particular course, where 10 points are awarded for an A grade, 8 for a B, 6 for a C, 4 for a D and 2 for an E grade:

30	28	26	24	24	24	24	22	22	22	22	22
22	22	20	20	20	20	20	20	20	18	18	18
18	18	18	18	18	16	16	16	16	16	14	14

(Source: *Times Higher Education Supplement* May 1995)

Data set 2.3

The following table of data shows the amount spent (in £) on library resources per student by 80 UK universities and colleges of higher education during 1992/93. This includes spending on books, periodicals and staff per full-time equivalent student (excluding the buildings costs):

210	180	204	226	247	272	284	312
248	274	301	314	157	180	207	230
162	184	148	250	275	301	315	363
232	251	275	301	322	383	162	215
185	220	232	256	304	325	428	312
165	191	235	257	276	305	563	613
195	225	237	259	279	330	1040	165
306	326	170	200	225	238	260	280
306	175	200	225	283	311	330	334
178	200	225	244	265	284	359	343

(Source: *Times Higher Education Supplement* May 1995)

How to summarise a data set

Data set 2.1

Step 1: Data recognition

Consider data set 2.1. We shall call this a *simple* data set as there are only a few observations and there is no frequency: none of the items occur with any particular repetition. This data is discrete as it is monetary. To see this consider the consecutive values of £12.47 and £12.48. There is no real monetary value between these values and this is a characteristic of discrete data. It is in fact on the ratio scale of measurement. The data is recorded to 2 decimal places.

Step 2: Describing the data

What can we deduce from looking at this raw data? Here we have only 6 items of data and it is clear that we can do little to summarise such a data set as it can be summarised at almost a glance. We can see that the charges vary from a minimum of £10.18 to a maximum of £16.25. This gives us a range of £16.25 − £10.18 = £6.07, where the *range* is the difference between the maximum and minimum values.

We can see that the values are reasonably spread out between these values. If summarising such data is not necessary, can we display small data sets graphically and so avoid looking at the detailed figures? The most suitable method of representation is possibly the simplest form of a graphical plot: the dot plot. As its name suggests, it is a horizontal axis (with a scale and label) and each monthly rental charge is displayed as a dot above the horizontal line. The resulting graphical display is given in figure 2.1.

From this graph we can deduce something that we may not have noticed from the raw data: the majority of values are clustered at the lower end of the axis. This might suggest that the upper two values (£15.50 and £16.25) are a little higher than the majority of charges. In chapter 4 we shall carry out some further statistical analysis to confirm or negate this.

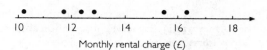

Figure 2.1

Tabulation

As we can see from data sets 2.2 and 2.3, when we have a larger set of data it is not easy simply to look at a collection of data and decide that this conveys certain meanings or conclusions. In fact it could be argued that this is nigh impossible. Given a data set, we must firstly put it into some meaningful order, or summarise it. This is usually done by tabulating the data: writing it into tabular form. (It is sometimes more suitable to enter a large data collection onto a spreadsheet or statistical package.) Notice that this data set is unordered. It might make the following tasks easier if the data was presented in order, such as in ascending order. This is particularly easy if you have entered the data into a computer package as we shall see later.

Data set 2.2

Step 1: Data recognition
What type of data is this? We can see the figures are recorded as integers taking even values. This is in fact a discrete data set as there are no observable values between 20 and 22, or 18 and 20, etc. Its level of measurement is on the ordinal scale.

Step 2: Find the range of the data set
The largest number of A-level points required is 30 and the least is 14. This gives us a range of $30 - 14 = 16$.

Step 3: Observable values recorded
Taking a look at the data we see that the values recorded are 30, 28, 26, 24, 22, 20, 18, 16 and 14 each with various frequencies. To summarise this data we now proceed to determine how many universities require each of these A-level scores, that is, we construct a frequency table. To do this we simply count up the number of each A-level score.

Step 4: Construct a frequency table

A-level points	Number of universities (requiring this score)
14	2
16	5
18	8
20	7
22	7
24	4
26	1
28	1
30	1
Total	36

Our column headings will be 'A-level points' and 'Number of universities requiring this A-level score'. The former will be the actual observation and this latter column will be the frequency each observation occurs. We shall arrange the first column in ascending order.

Step 5: Observations

From the table we can see a clearer pattern of the number of A-level points required by the universities which was not possible from simply scanning the raw data. We can see that there is a peak at 18: the largest number of universities selected require 18 points for entrance. This might be an A-level grade combination of A and 2 Ds, or 3 Cs, or an A and B, etc. The data is fairly evenly spread around this peak, although we might be inclined to think that there are more universities that require less than this peak number of points. We shall look at graphical representation in the next section.

Data set 2.3

Step 1: Data recognition

What type of data is this? We can see the figures are recorded to the nearest pound. It is in fact discrete data. Generally money (e.g. in the UK) is counted to the nearest penny as mentioned for data set 2.1.

Step 2: Find the range of the data set

Here by careful observation we can see that the amount spent on libraries varies from a minimum of £148 per student to a maximum of £1040. This is the range of the data set; here this is £892. The advantage of ordering the data is that such values can simply be read off from the data set. We shall now set about tabulating this data.

Question: Is it appropriate to set about tabulating this data as data set 2.2? A careful scan through the data shows that there are few (if any) amounts which occur with any regularity and so a different approach is called for: compiling a grouped frequency table.

Step 3: Decide how many classes to have

We wish to divide or group these 80 observations into a set of non-overlapping intervals known as class intervals. Suppose this number is k classes. This will mean in place of the 80 raw items we will have condensed the data into these k classes. Within each class will lie a number of the individual items. The number of data entries in any particular class is the frequency for that class. The total of all the individual class frequencies will come to the total number of data: 80 here. How many class intervals do we need? Consider choosing 2. This means that we have condensed the data into 2 classes. Is this a good idea? In doing so we have lost a great deal of detail of this data set and so any further statistical calculations will be imprecise. Thus concentrating the data into 2 classes reduces the data too much. At the other extreme, if we chose to divide the data into 20 class intervals we can see that in place of the 80 raw items we have 20 classes. This is hardly much of a summary. There is no 'right' number of classes but somewhere between these 2 extremes, usually between 5 and 20. Basically the larger the data set the more intervals you can allow.

As a rough rule of thumb $k \approx \dfrac{\text{total frequency}}{5}$

Here this would give us 16 classes which is perhaps a bit too detailed for our purposes. For this data set 10 or 12 would be sufficient and we shall choose 12. Notice there is no 'right' number.

Step 4: Determine the class bounds

Given the range and an idea of k, the number of classes, we can choose the actual class intervals. Usually a class interval has boundaries: there is a lower value, a Lower Class Bound (LCB), which is the minimal value in the interval, and an upper value which is the cut-off point for this interval, the Upper Class Bound (UCB). There are exceptions which we shall discuss shortly. To do this we bear in mind the following:

(i)   try not to choose class bounds which coincide with observed values;
(ii) class limits should be unambiguous and non-overlapping.

Here our data starts as 148 and goes up to 1040, and the range is 892. For any class the difference between the LCB and UCB divided by the number of classes is the class width. Here we shall be using a constant or fixed class width throughout the problem, but it is not unusual to have various class widths for a data set. Here the class width can be found by dividing the range 892 by k (12 here), and choosing a suitable near integer.

This would give us a formula for the class width of:

$$\text{range} \approx \frac{\text{Class width}}{k}$$

Here $\frac{892}{12} \approx 74.33$. We shall choose a class width of 75 for simplicity. (We could equally decide that a class width of 100 was better to work with.)

Thus our classes must start at a value so that 148 is included in this interval. A suitable choice would be 125. Thus for class 1, the LCB is 125 and to find its UCB we need to add the class width, i.e. 75. Thus the first class has bounds 125 to 200 and then by repeatedly adding the class width we will get the next class.

The second class interval is 200 to 275, the third is 275 to 350, etc. until we have reached 1040. The list of class intervals is:

Class number	Class interval
1	125 to 200
2	200 to 275
3	275 to 350
4	350 to 425
5	425 to 500
6	500 to 575
7	575 to 650
8	650 to 725
9	725 to 800
10	800 to 875
11	875 to 950
12	950 to 1025
13	1025 to 1100

Notice that we aimed to have about 12 class intervals, but as we did not actually start at 148 and we chose a suitable number for the class width (near to $\frac{892}{12}$) we do not have exactly 12 class intervals.

Now it would appear that our class intervals are overlapping: take the first and second classes; at present 200 appears in both classes and so where do we actually put any observed values of 200? We must ensure our class intervals are disjoint and as such we simply decide that 200 lies in one of the intervals but not both, and we do this consistently for all the classes. We shall put 200 in the first class, and so this class is actually up to and including the boundary point 200. Similarly the second class must be any value greater than 200 and up to and including 275. For consistency we carry this out for each of the intervals and use the signs $<$ (less than) and $\leqslant$ (less than or equal to) to express this formally. If we write L to mean the library spending, then the second class would be written:

Class	Bounds	Formal bounds
Class 2	200 to 275	$200 < L \leqslant 275$

This formally means that the amount spend on a library lies between 200 and 275 but excludes 200 yet could equal (includes) 275. Notice that the tip of the point of the inequality sign points to the smaller quantity: 200 is smaller than L, i.e. L is greater than 200. We shall meet such symbols in more detail later in the book.

Hence our classes are in fact:

Class	Bounds	Formal bounds
Class 2	200 to 275	$200 < L \leqslant 275$
Class 3	275 to 350	$275 < L \leqslant 350$
Class 4	350 to 425	$350 < L \leqslant 425$
etc.		

The last class is $1025 < L \leqslant 1100$. What about the first class? For consistency we have excluded the LCB point from the interval and so this should be $125 < L \leqslant 200$.

If we look at the data we can see that in fact some of the observations do indeed coincide with the class bounds. This did not cause a problem as we ensured that the class bounds were non-overlapping. An alternative approach is to use an extra decimal place (0.5) after the recorded data. Here this could, for example, result in class intervals:

Classes	Formal bounds
124.5 to 200.5	$124.5 \leqslant L \leqslant 200.5$
200.5 to 275.5	$200.5 \leqslant L \leqslant 275.5$
etc.	

This has the immediate effect of ensuring that none of the recorded data can lie at the end points of a class as the data has fewer decimal places.

(If the classes were 10.9 to 20.9, and 20.9 to 30.9 we would add an extra 0.5 after the last decimal place, giving us:

10.95 to 20.95
20.95 to 30.95
etc.

As with many of the above decisions, no one is 'right', we would generally choose bounds which are easier to work with.

Step 5: Grouping the data to construct a tally chart

We now need to put the data into these classes. As for data set 2.2 this is done by putting a tally mark (|) into a class which contains the first, second, third, etc. up to 80th item of data. When we get 5 tally marks in any class we put the fifth mark horizontally across the first 4 to make the tally marks distinct. That is, $\cancel{||||}$.

Here we begin reading each of the above columns of data, and the tally chart would start off as follows:

Class	Formal bounds	Tally marks
Class 1	$125 < L \leqslant 200$	$\cancel{||||}$
Class 2	$200 < L \leqslant 275$	|||
Class 3	$275 < L \leqslant 350$	||

This would take us to the end of the first column.

The final tally chart would be:

Class number	Class interval	Tally	Frequency
1	$125 < L \leqslant 200$	$\cancel{||||}$ $\cancel{||||}$ $\cancel{||||}$ $\cancel{||||}$ |||	18
2	$200 < L \leqslant 275$	$\cancel{||||}$ $\cancel{||||}$ $\cancel{||||}$ $\cancel{||||}$ $\cancel{||||}$ $\cancel{||||}$	30
3	$275 < L \leqslant 350$	$\cancel{||||}$ $\cancel{||||}$ $\cancel{||||}$ $\cancel{||||}$ $\cancel{||||}$	25
4	$350 < L \leqslant 425$	|||	3
5	$425 < L \leqslant 500$			1
6	$500 < L \leqslant 575$			1
7	$575 < L \leqslant 650$			1
8	$650 < L \leqslant 725$		
9	$725 < L \leqslant 800$		
10	$800 < L \leqslant 875$		
11	$875 < L \leqslant 950$		
12	$950 < L \leqslant 1025$		
13	$1025 < L \leqslant 1100$			1

We can see that in fact this tally is a record of the frequency, that is, the number of items occurring in each class interval. We thus place a final column in the tally chart for the frequency which is found by summing the tally for each class. For example the first class has 18 tally marks, the second class, 30, etc. Notice that the 8th class to the 12th class have no entries recorded in them. This could be presented by simply combining them into the class $L > 650$.

Step 6: Observations

Firstly we can see that as we have summarised the data we can see more clearly where the data lies: we can say that the majority of the 80 items lie at the lower end of the scale, the classes 1–3. This tells us that it is more common for a university to spend a small amount per capita than a relatively large amount. Higher spending universities are few and far between. We shall see in the next section ways of pictorially representing this data so that these conclusions can be drawn without the need to show the actual data or table.

Step 7: Conclusion

We can see that the list of 80 items have been summarised into a concise format: a table. This is now known as grouped data as we have grouped our 80 observations into classes with a corresponding frequency.

Caution

Think carefully about what sort of data you are tabulating. Notice that this was in fact discrete data that we have grouped. Sometimes it is more natural to tabulate discrete data similar to data set 2.2—it depends on how many observed outcomes there are. As for data set 2.3 we had a large number of distinct observations and so it was only really appropriate to group the data into class intervals. Just because it looks discrete it may not be and even if it is discrete it is sometimes more suitable to use a seemingly continuous tabulation into class intervals.

We would generally use a grouped data table for continuous data with a frequency. This is natural given the definition of continuous data: where a dense range or interval of values is observable.

Exercises 2.1 _____

2.1.1 Use class bounds 100 to 200, 200 to 300, etc. for the above data set 2.3 and see whether this has any noticeable difference to the above table. Make a comment to summarise your findings from this table.

2.1.2 Pear PLC is undertaking a time measurement exercise in its finance department. During this exercise 30 members of staff of similar grade undertake to input, process and report on a given set of information and data.

The times taken to complete this exercise are recorded below in minutes to 1 decimal place:

49.0	62.3	52.1
49.4	59.3	65.2
46.4	75.4	56.9
51.5	76.7	64.2
57.1	74.6	46.7
67.4	67.0	45.3
52.7	68.6	52.3
47.5	54.8	66.8
72.9	51.1	60.5
50.2	45.7	57.3

(i)   What type of data is this and what is the level of measurement?
(ii)   Decide upon the range of the data.
(iii)   What number of classes would you choose? Justify.

(iv)   What class width would you use? Justify. State the class intervals this would give.

(v)   Use a tally chart to construct a frequency table using the class intervals you have chosen. For example you may have chosen the following class intervals:

45.0 and under 50.0

50.0 and under 55.0

55.0 and under 60.0

etc.

(vi)   What is the main purpose of tabulation?

(vii) Write a brief memo to a director of Pear PLC to summarise your findings and perceptions about the performance of this department, in particular drawing on your findings in part (i) and (v).

(viii) What other choice of class intervals could you use? Explain why you have suggested these.

2.1.3 The following data is the percentage of first class degrees awarded by a sample of 36 UK Universities in 1992/93:

16	14	14	13	12	12	12	12	12	11	11	11
11	11	11	10	10	10	10	10	10	10	10	9
9	9	9	9	9	9	9	8	8	8	8	8

(Source: *Times Higher Education Supplement* May 1995)

Explain why this data is continuous data which has been recorded to the nearest integer value. What are the class intervals? Draw up a tally chart to summarise this data.

2.1.4 Using the table in exercise 1.2.3 for fertility treatment compile a grouped frequency table for:

(i)   the percentage of live births from IVF treatment;
(ii) the percentage of live births from DI treatment.

Representation of data

We now proceed to look at pictorial representation of data. In broad terms the type of data we have determines how it is graphically represented. For example nominal and ordinal data can only really be represented using a bar chart or pie chart, whereas interval and ratio data are naturally represented using a histogram. We shall look at various methods of data representation including: pictograms, bar charts, pie charts, dual bar charts, histograms, frequency polygons, cumulative frequency graphs and time series graphs. We shall discuss each in turn using examples.

Example 2.1
The following data has been collected using the secondary source, the Cadbury Schweppes PLC company report for 1991.

The number of employees in each country in 1991 were:

Country	Number employed
UK	16198
Europe	5945
Americas	1961
Pacific Rim	6412
Africa and others	4856
Total	35372

What information does this data contain? We can see that it has been tabulated and summarised and by studying the figures we can see that the largest group of employees is found in the UK. One of the aims of pictorial representation is to give the reader a summary of a collection of figures at a glance: the picture must emerge without the use of words. It must be informative in a second and convey the full detail of the data but without the reader needing necessarily to know the exact data or even see the data: the picture used to represent the data must make a strong enough statement to the reader about the key features of the data, so that actually showing the data is superfluous. As we shall see later, there are instances when in fact a different impression can be gained from using a certain type of representation and so it is hoped that some of the main pitfalls here can be avoided.

Pictograms

Notice that the data in example 2.1 is nominal data: we have information about employees of this company and we have collected the total for various locations. Thus one common way advertisers use to display such information is to use a picture—here a matchstick person would be most likely as we are counting the number of people. The height of the matchstick person would represent (be proportional to) a number of employees. For example as the figures are in thousands, one matchstick person might represent 1000 employees. There would then be 16 matchstick people for the UK, 6 for Europe, etc. A pictogram (also called a pictograph) is shown in Figure 2.2.

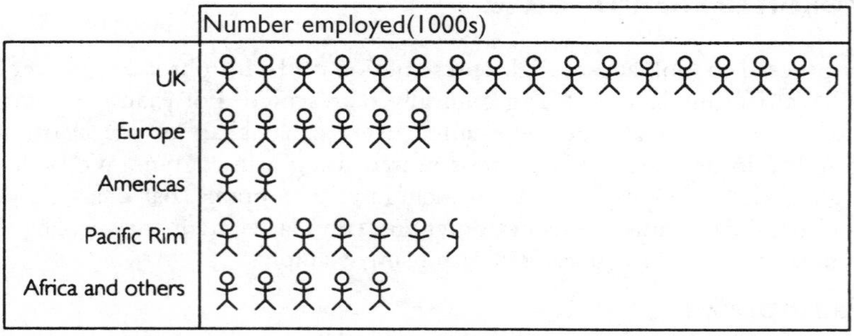

Figure 2.2

The type of picture used to denote the characteristic measured is one that suitably resembles the characteristic. For example different sized bottles would be used to denote the demand for a certain product such as drink/shampoo/beer, etc. although there are dangers involved here as the area rather than simply the height would be used to represent the level of demand. We shall discuss this notion further when we consider histograms.

There are two other ways we can display this type of data: either using a vertical (or horizontal) bar chart or using a circular pie chart.

Bar charts

A bar is used to represent each area of employment. These could be arranged either horizontally, or, more usually, vertically. If we chose to use a vertical bar, then our horizontal axis would look as follows:

UK	Europe	America	Pacific rim	Africa and others

A bar would then be drawn above each location—bars of equal width. We generally leave a gap between each of the bars to distinguish between each of the locations. The actual width of the bar has no significance although it would be misleading if some were wider than others. The vertical axis would indicate the numerical scale to show the number employed in each location. The height of the bar would thus represent how many were employed by Cadbury Schweppes at each location. Formally we would say that the height of each bar is proportional to the frequency occurring in each location. This would mean that if one location had twice as many as another, the height of the bar should be twice as long as the other.

What scale would be used? Really the best thing to do is to ask: How large a diagram is required? If we wish a diagram of say 5 cm high we would need to fit each of the bars into this size or scale. The largest bar will be the bar for the UK as this is where the largest number of employees are and so it is natural that the diagram should display this as the largest bar. To work out a suitable scale we look at how many people need to be included in this bar: here 16 198. There are now two choices: either say as we have 5 cm to represent about 15 000, each centimetre on the vertical scale would represent 3000 employees. This means that in fact our diagram will be a little more than 5 cm tall as there are 16 198 people rather than 15 000. Alternatively we could say that the 16 198 people are nearly 20 000 and choose a scale that fits into the 5 cm. This would give us 1 cm represents 4000 employees and our diagram would be less than 5 cm tall. We shall go for the first option. Thus our vertical scale would be:

15 000

10 000

5000

0

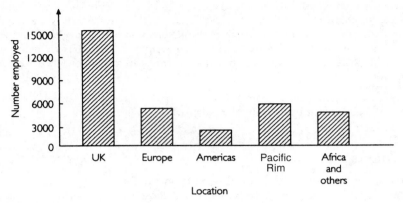

Figure 2.3

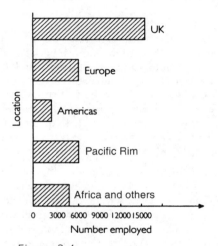

Figure 2.4

If we now put these two axes together we can draw the bars for each location, and it is good practice to label the characteristic on each axis (see figure 2.3).

Similarly we could plot each bar horizontally and interchange the two axes. Notice that it is convenient to write the labels for the bars actually along the bar (see figure 2.4).

What do these bar charts tell us? How would we interpret them? Firstly we would see that there are more UK employees than in other locations. This is possibly to be expected as it is a UK company. We can also see that there is a comparable number of employees in the Pacific region, Europe and Africa. The least number of employees is to be found in the Americas.

Line charts

In place of a bar, when the horizontal axis is a numerical scale, we sometimes use a vertical line in place of a vertical bar, where the height of the line represents (or is proportional to) the frequency. Such a representation is called a *line chart*. Line charts are commonly used to represent discrete data (for example data set 2.2) with each outcome having a certain frequency.

Frequency and relative frequency

Whenever we have a frequency table—for either discrete or grouped data, we can decide to convert the frequency into a percentage—*relative frequency*. This is particularly useful if the total frequency is large or the frequencies are fairly clumsy figures, as in the above scenario. To convert a frequency to a relative frequency we simply divide each individual frequency by the total frequency and multiply this by 100, and this is then a percentage. That is:

$$\text{relative frequency} = \frac{\text{actual frequency}}{\text{total frequency}}$$

For example, for the UK number of employees this would give us:

$$\frac{16\,198}{35\,372} \times 100\% = 45.8\%$$

Exercises 2.2

2.2.1 Plot a relative frequency bar chart for the number of Cadbury Schweppes employees in the given locations in 1991. What are the advantages of using relative frequency here?

2.2.2 Using data set 2 construct a line chart to represent the data and describe what this tells you about the data.

2.2.3 A recent survey of road transport emissions in London has shown the following levels of nitrogen oxides during 1993 from various types of motor vehicle:

Motor vehicle	Percentage of total emission (%)
Motorcycles	6
Cars	68
Taxis	1
Light goods vehicles	10
Medium goods vehicles	9
Heavy goods vehicles	4
Buses	2
Total emission (in thousands of tonnes)	112 512

(Source: London Energy Study)

Construct a bar chart to represent this information. If you were presented with evidence that levels of nitrogen oxide were particularly dangerous to general public health, what would your recommendation to the minister for transport be to reduce these levels?

Pie charts

We now consider how to represent the above example 2.1 pictorially using a circular chart: a *pie chart*. Here we have a circle divided into sectors, rather like slicing a cake into pieces. Each sector will represent one of the locations, giving us a total of 5 sectors. The sector is defined by an angle at the centre of the circle: the *sector angle*, and so to decide where to inscribe each of the locations on the circle we need to calculate the sector angle.

Step 1: Total number (or frequency) must equal the total number of degrees, 360°

Firstly recall that there are 360° in the circle and so we can see that this total number of degrees must represent the total number of employees: 360° is comparable to 35 372 employees.

Step 2: Determine a formula for calculating the sector angles

We need to find the number of degrees for an employee. To find this formula we shall firstly use a very natural approximate figure for the number of employees: say there are 36 000. Thus if 36 000 employees are represented by 360° then 1000 employees must be represented by 10°. (This is found by dividing both numbers by 36.) In fact as all our employee figures are in thousands this would be sufficient to give a formula for calculating each of the sector angles.

Every thousand employees is equivalent to 10° at the centre of the circle which gives us more generally: every n thousand employees $= n \times 10°$. Using this same approach we can find a more accurate formula, although as a rough one this is reasonable.

How can we be more precise? We can say that 35 372 employees must be represented by 360°. Notice that this is almost 36 thousand employees, but in fact 35.372 thousand employees. Thus if we divide 35 372 by 35.372 we will arrive at 1000 employees. Thus 1000 employees would be represented by 360/35.372 degrees, that is 10.18° to 2 decimal places.

(Previously we divided by 36, but we get a more exact formula by dividing by 35.372—the exact number of thousands of employees.)

A general formula for n thousand employees would be $= n \times 10.18°$.

Step 3: Determine each of the sector angles

UK sector angle

Here there are approximately 16 000 employees, i.e. 16 thousand which will be represented by $16 \times 10.18° = 163°$ to the nearest degree.

(We can give a more exact answer using 16.198 thousand, i.e. $16.198 \times 10.18° = 164.9°$. The degree of accuracy used will improve as mathematical skills and confidence are developed, and for our purposes this will not unduly affect the accuracy of the drawing.) Thus the UK sector angle will be represented by 163°.

Europe sector angle
Here there are approximately 6000 employees giving us a sector angle of $6 \times 10.18° = 61°$.

Americas sector angle
Here there are approximately 2000 employees giving us a sector angle of $2 \times 10.18° = 20°$.

Pacific Rim sector angle
Here there are approximately 6500 employees giving us a sector angle of $6.5 \times 10.18° = 66°$.

Africa and others sector angle
Here there are approximately 5000 employees giving us a sector angle of $5 \times 10.18° = 51°$.

A quick tally will confirm that the total number of degrees allocated for each sector does come to 360°. This may not be exactly 360 as we have done some rounding of values to be realistic about what can be drawn. (Check: $163° + 61° + 20° + 66° + 51° = 361$ and which is close enough to say it is as accurate as can be drawn.)

We now need to either use a package to draw this pie chart (such as Excel or MacDraw) or use a compass and protractor to measure the angles. The result is shown in figure 2.5.

We can label each of the sectors and shade each a different type of shading to distinguish between the locations. A key might be used in place of labelling each of the sectors.

Notice that a bar chart or pie chart is most suitable when the data is nominal or ordinal data.

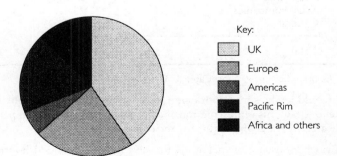

Figure 2.5

Exercises 2.3

2.3.1 The following data is an analysis of the turnover by product for the store British Home Stores (BhS) during 1992

Product	Turnover (%)
Womenswear	30
Menswear	15
Footwear and accessories	18
Household	19
Restaurant	8
Franchises	5

(Source: *Company report* Storehouse 1992)

Draw   (i)   a bar chart
       (ii) a pie chart

to represent this data and comment on your findings and the differences between these representations. If the total turnover for BhS was £634.7 m, what is the actual turnover for each product?

2.3.2 The following table shows the distribution of shares for Cable & Wireless PLC amongst various financial institutions during 1993:

Type of shareholder	Percentage of shares held (%)
Investment companies	0.2
Nominee companies	14.3
Limited companies	0.8
Banks	0.9
Insurance companies	0.5
Pension Funds	0.1
Public bodies	0.4
Trust companies	1.3
Others	81.5
Total	100

(Source: *Company report* Cable & Wireless PLC 1993)

What would be the simplest drawing to represent this information? Explain why and hence draw this representation and comment on its shape. In particular what is indicated by the shape of this for the company?

2.3.3 The British Household Panel Study for 1991 interviewed 5511 households in the UK and tabulated the following data for the number of earners in the households as:

Number of earners	Number of households
0	1874
1	1708
2	1598
more than 2	331
Total	5511

(Sources: *BHPS* 1991 and *Employment Gazette* October 1994)

Draw a pie chart to represent this information and describe what this tells you about this data.

2.3.4 The table below shows the highest qualification of people of various age groups for both male and female in the UK in 1993. The total number of people sampled was 33 699 and all figures are percentages:

Highest qualification	Age group				
	16–24 (%)	25–29 (%)	30–39 (%)	40–49 (%)	50–59 (%)
Degree	5	14	15	13	9
HE below degree	4	8	8	8	7
A-level	23	16	15	13	11
GCSE/O-level	37	31	26	21	17
Other qualification	13	15	13	13	12
No qualification	19	17	22	32	44
Total percentage	100	100	100	100	100
Total number of people	7017	4667	8262	7739	6014

(Source: *Education statistics for the UK* 1994 Edition)

(i) Compare the two age groups 25–29 and 40–49. Comment on any differences between the qualifications held.

(ii) Repeat part (i) for the age groups 16–24 and 30–39.

(iii) Draw bar charts to represent the qualifications for each of the age groups. Comment on what these show.

(iv) To some extent this data can be used to look at changes in the level of qualifications held over the last 25–30 years. What patterns do you notice? Why and how would you need to be careful about making such comments?

Dual bar charts

Suppose we have data about the number of employees at Cadbury Schweppes over two years and we wished to graphically compare these sets of data to see what changes if any have occurred. One natural graphical representation would be to compare the data using a *dual bar chart* (also called a component bar chart). The data is as follows:

Location	Number employed	
	1991	1990
UK	16 198	16 021
Europe	5945	6008
Americas	1961	1827
Pacific Rim	6412	6456
Africa and others	4856	5341
Total	35 372	35 653

(Source: *Company report* Cadbury Schweppes PLC 1991)

There are two ways of drawing such graphs.

Method 1
Imagine drawing two bar charts for each of the years concerned and then placing corresponding bars next to each other on a new graph as in figure 2.6.

Notice that the bars for each year are shaded differently to distinguish between them, and a key must be used to explain what each bar represents. Here the shading would not be used to distinguish between the locations but simply the years: the gap between the locations is sufficient to separate the information.

Method 2
Instead of placing the two corresponding bars next to each other we consider placing them on top of each other—in figure 2.7 we place the smaller bar on the bottom and then increase for the second year on top—here shading is crucial because it does not

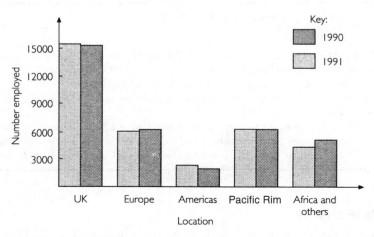

Figure 2.6

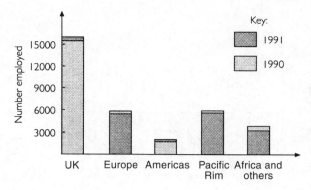

Figure 2.7

automatically follow that all the lower bars are the earlier year: it depends on which bar is smaller.

Notice that the second method could lead to misinterpretation if the reader has not noticed that the different shadings are of great significance. The resulting dual bar chart is more difficult to correctly interpret using this latter method of representation, and in fact method 1 is perhaps more fail-safe!

Representing negative values on a bar chart

There are instances when the information we wish to represent contains some negative values, for example when profits are in fact a loss—or the data is a record of differences between two data sets which may be negative. We can represent such data on a bar chart but must have a positive and negative range of values on a vertical axis.

Example 2.2

The following are the recorded profits for the Storehouse group in £ millions for 1991 and 1992:

Profit from retail operations	Year 1992
BhS	22.1
Habitat Group	(8.8)
Mothercare	(3.9)
Other retail	0.6
Total	10.0

(Source: *Company reports* Storehouse PLC 1992)

Represent this information on a suitable bar chart.

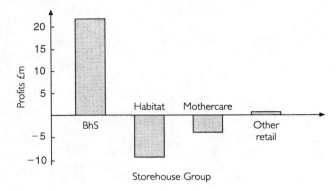

Figure 2.8

Solution

Notice that the figures which appear in brackets are typical of accountancy use to display negative values. Here a negative profit would mean the company has incurred a loss. We need a vertical axis to range from −9 to 22. On the horizontal axis we will plot a bar for each of the Storehouse outlets. The resulting bar chart is shown in figure 2.8.

Exercises 2.4 _____

2.4.1 The unit costs per full-time equivalent student in £ are recorded in the table below for the two sectors of higher education: the old universities; and the new universities (former polytechnics).

Academic year	Old university	New university
1979/80	7600	5990
1983/84	8050	4850
1987/88	8000	4500
1989/90	7550	4650
1990/91	6950	4200
1991/92	6700	3900

(i)   Outline the possible ways you could represent this data.
(ii) Draw 2 separate bar charts to represent the unit costs per student in each of the types of British university over the periods recorded.
(iii) Draw a dual bar chart to represent this information.

2.4.2 Using the data in the example above for recorded profits for the Storehouse Group in £ millions in 1992 and the table below for profits for 1991, draw a dual bar chart to compare the profits for each group over this period.

Profit from retail operations	Year 1991
Bhs	22.6
Habitat Group	(11.9)
Mothercare	6.8
Other retail	1.7
Total	18.2

(Source: *Company report* Storehouse PLC 1992)

Histograms

A histogram is a very special type of bar chart. It has two main distinguishing features:

(i)   the area of each bar represents the frequency;
(ii) there are no gaps between the bars—the data is assumed to be a continuum.

In fact a histogram is only suitable for data of interval or ratio level and is only really appropriate for grouped data. Such data is generally continuous, but as for data set 2.3 above, grouped data could be discrete data with a large number of possible observable outcomes.

Example 2.3
Draw a histogram to represent data set 2.3.

Solution
From the above discussion we tabulated data set 2.3 as:

Class interval	Frequency
$125 < L \leqslant 200$	18
$200 < L \leqslant 275$	30
$275 < L \leqslant 350$	25
$350 < L \leqslant 425$	3
$425 < L \leqslant 500$	1
$500 < L \leqslant 575$	1
$575 < L \leqslant 650$	1
$650 < L \leqslant 725$	0
$725 < L \leqslant 800$	0
$800 < L \leqslant 875$	0
$875 < L \leqslant 950$	0
$950 < L \leqslant 1025$	0
$1025 < L \leqslant 1100$	1
Total	80

Step 1: Decide on the horizontal scale

Here the amount spent per capita on library facilities will be plotted on the horizontal axis and this ranges from £125 to over £1100. Assuming that the graph paper is about 22 cm by 30 cm, we will use this 'landscape' and plot the horizontal axis on the longer side. Thus we will need a scale of say 2 cm represents £75. (This will allow us a range of up to £75 × 15 = £1125.)

Step 2: Decide on vertical axis

Here we have been given frequency (number of universities) with a peak of 30. Thus a scale might be 1 cm for 5 universities.

Step 3: Close the gaps between the adjacent classes

This task has already been completed in the tabulation section above. Another example is also discussed below.

Step 4: Consider the class widths

If the class width is constant for each class, then we can simply plot the given frequency or relative frequency and the bar against each class interval. In this instance the area of each bar will represent the frequency. Finally all axes are labelled and a scale is given on the graph for each axis. The resulting histogram is shown in figure 2.9.

Step 5: Comments on its shape

As was noted in the earlier discussion on this data set, we can see very clearly that the majority of the data lies in the early classes, showing that most universities spend a small amount per capita on library materials. There is just one university which spends a large amount, as is shown by the blip at the right-hand side of the histogram (figure 2.9). This point is called an *outlier* and the university might be identified for commendation of its library spending.

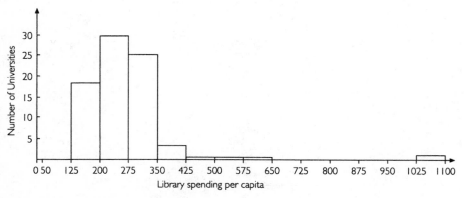

Figure 2.9

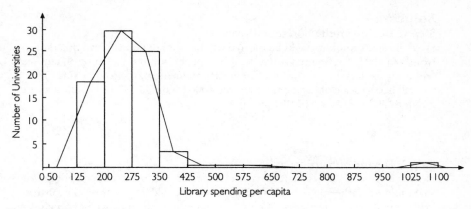

Figure 2.10

Frequency polygons

To plot a frequency polygon—which can be drawn over the histogram we simply put a dot on the top of each bar at the mid-points of the bar and adjacent dots are joined by a straight line. This represents the area contained within the histogram. Figure 2.10 shows this for the library spending example.

The next example is when class intervals are not of equal size and further calculations must be done before a histogram can be plotted.

Example 2.4

The table below shows the number of shares held and by what percentage of shareholders for Cadbury Schweppes PLC at 28 December 1991.

Size of holding	Percentage of shareholders (to 1 decimal place)
1 to 100	6.0
101 to 500	22.4
501 to 1000	23.5
1001 to 2000	24.9
2001 to 5000	16.2
5001 to 50 000	5.5
50 001 to 100 000	0.5
100 001 and above	1.0
Total	100

(Source: *Company report* Cadbury Schweppes PLC 1991)

Plot a histogram for this data, using graph paper.

Solution
Step 1: Decide on the horizontal scale
Here the size of holding will be plotted on the horizontal axis, and this ranges from 1 to 100 000. Assuming that the graph paper is about 22 cm by 30 cm, we will use this 'landscape' and plot the horizontal axis on the longer side. Thus we will need a scale of say 1 cm represents 4000 holdings. (This will allow us to go up to 4000 × 30 = 120 000 holdings.)

Step 2: Decide on vertical axis
Here we have been given relative frequency in the form of 'percentage of shareholders' rather than actual numbers of shareholders. Thus on the vertical axis we will plot percentages. We cannot state the scale until we have a closer look at the class widths.

Step 3: Close the gaps between the adjacent classes
There are several ways of closing the gaps between the class widths; the important thing is to be consistent throughout the data set.

Method 1
We can put half of the gap into adjacent classes. For example, take the first and second classes:

1 to 100   101 to 500

Here there is a gap between 100 and 101. The mid-point is 100.5 and so we could say the first class ends at 100.5 and the second class begins at 100.5. This clearly does not alter the way a given data entry would be put into the table. We would carry on doing this for all the classes and simply need to take another look at the LCB of class 1 and the open final class. For consistency we would start the first class at 0.5. We would also extend the UCB of the final class by 0.5 if it were a closed class. Here we need to decide on a suitable end point for the final class in order to be able to draw a final bar. As our paper will run out after 120 000 holdings, this would seem a suitable UCB (Note: to be consistent this should be 120 000.5, but with this scale we cannot draw to such a degree of accuracy).

Method 2
Alternatively you could keep to integer values for the class bounds and use inequalities as for data set 3. Thus we might say if H was the number of holdings, then class 1 is defined as $0 < H \leqslant 100$, and class 2 would be $100 < H \leqslant 500$ (or equally $0 < H < 101$ and $101 \leqslant H < 501$ etc.). We shall choose method 2 and so our true classes are:

Size of holding	Percentage of shareholders (to 1 decimal place)
$0 < H \leqslant 100$	6.0
$100 < H \leqslant 500$	22.4
$500 < H \leqslant 1000$	23.5
$1000 < H \leqslant 2000$	24.9
$2000 < H \leqslant 5000$	16.2
$5000 < H \leqslant 50\,000$	5.5
$50\,000 < H \leqslant 100\,000$	0.5
$100\,000 < H \leqslant 120\,000$	1.0
Total	100

Step 4: Consider the class widths

If the class width is constant for each class, then we can simply plot the given frequency or relative frequency and the bar against each class interval. In this instance the area of each bar will represent the relative frequency.

If, however, we have unequal class widths, as is the case here, then simply plotting the relative frequency will be a bar chart but not a histogram. This is because if we take two bars, which, say, have similar heights of, say, 10 cm where 1 cm represents 5% of shareholders, suppose one has a width of 2 cm and one has a width of 4 cm. A quick calculation will reveal that one bar has an area of 20 cm^2 and the other 40 cm^2. But if this is a histogram, area must be proportional to relative frequency, that is similar areas should represent similar relative frequencies. Both bars have a relative frequency of 10% of shareholders, but one has twice the area of the other due to the width of the bar. Thus to correct this we need to plot the relative frequency density which is the actual relative frequency divided by the class width:

$$\text{relative frequency density} = \frac{\text{class relative frequency}}{\text{class width}}$$

For example, class 1 has a class width of 100, and so its relative frequency density is $\frac{6}{100} = 0.06$. The class widths ($= \text{UCB} - \text{LCB}$) and relative frequency densities are in the table below:

Size of holding	Percentage of shareholders	Class width	Relative frequency density
$0 < H \leqslant 100$	6.0	100	0.06
$100 < H \leqslant 500$	22.4	400	0.056
$500 < H \leqslant 1000$	23.5	500	0.047
$1000 < H \leqslant 2000$	24.9	1000	0.025
$2000 < H \leqslant 5000$	16.2	3000	0.0054
$5000 < H \leqslant 50\,000$	5.5	4500	0.00012
$50\,000 < H \leqslant 100\,000$	0.5	50\,000	0.00001
$100\,000 < H \leqslant 120\,000$	1.0	20\,000	0.00005
Total	100		

Step 5: Determine the vertical scale

The values of the relative frequency density are very small and so it is important to choose a suitable scale. If all the frequencies were in 100 000s (such as 250 000, and 460 000) we would pull out a factor of 100 000 and plot the data as 2.5 and 4.6 and label the scale in 100 000s. Similarly here if we multiply all the relative frequency densities by 100 we could say the vertical scale is scaled by a factor of 10^{-2}. This gives us a more sensible data set to plot.

Size of holding	Relative frequency density $\times 10^{-2}$
$0 < H \leqslant 100$	6
$100 < H \leqslant 500$	5.6
$500 < H \leqslant 1000$	4.7
$1000 < H \leqslant 2000$	2.5
$2000 < H \leqslant 5000$	0.54
$5000 < H \leqslant 50\,000$	0.0012
$50\,000 < H \leqslant 100\,000$	0.001
$100\,000 < H \leqslant 120\,000$	0.005

A sensible scale on the vertical axis would be 2 cm for 1 unit of relative frequency density. Notice that the relative frequency densities (RFD) in the last 3 classes are very small (compared to the other classes) and in total come to *0.018*. This means that share holdings over 5000 shares are rare. Now our horizontal scale goes from 1 to 120 000 but after 5000 there is almost a zero r.f.d. Thus for a more suitable histogram we shall combine the last 3 classes and the resulting histogram is given in figure 2.11.

Notice that the last class is simply a heavy line carrying on after 5000.

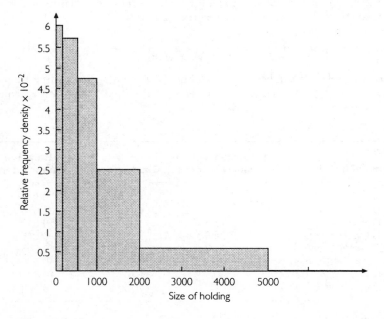

Figure 2.11

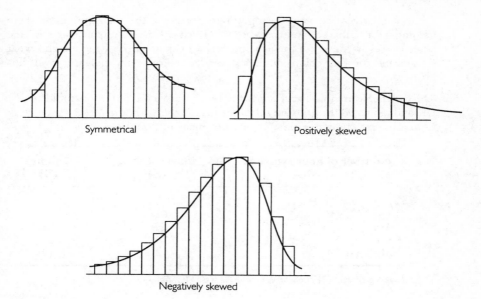

Figure 2.12

Step 6: Comment on its shape

We can see that the histogram is skewed: most of the data lies in the first few classes telling us that the majority of shareholders hold only a small number of shares. There are a very few shareholders who own the vast majority of shares. We would say the histogram is skewed to the right or positively skewed (as the right tail is the longest tail).

Typical shapes of histograms are shown in figure 2.12.

Exercises 2.5

2.5.1 The table below shows the distribution of ordinary shares for Cable & Wireless PLC at 31 March 1993.

Size of holding	Number of holdings
1 to 250	43 495
251 to 500	45 644
501 to 1000	31 401
1001 to 10 000	34 976
10 001 to 100 000	2018
100 001 to 999 999	776
1 000 000 and above	171
Total	158 481

(Source: *Company report* Cable & Wireless 1993)

Draw a relative frequency histogram to represent the distribution of share holdings for Cable & Wireless at 31 March 1993. (Combine some of the latter classes if you think this is appropriate.) Comment on its shape and what this means for this company. Draw a relative frequency polygon over this histogram.

2.5.2 The British Household Panel Study for 1991 interviewed 5511 households in the UK and tabulated the following data for the number of hours worked each week in all jobs (excluding overtime) by married men and couples.

Number of hours worked	Married men (%)	Couples (%)
1 to 30	5.5	9
31 to 40	62	21
41 to 60	27	23
61 to 80	4	32
81 +	2	13

(Source *BHPS* 1991 and *Employment Gazette* October 1994)

Draw two histograms to represent each of the data sets for the married men and for couples. Comment on their differences.

2.5.3 Plot relative frequency histograms for the IVF data tabulated in exercise 2.1.4 for both IVF and DI treatments. Comment on the similarities and differences you find.

2.5.4 Consider the table of highest qualifications in exercise 2.3.4 above. Look at the percentage of people (across the spectrum of age groups) whose highest qualification is a degree. Plot a histogram to represent this data and comment on what this indicates.

2.5.5 How would frequency density be found for data set 2.3? Plot the resulting histogram. How does it compare with figure 2.9?

Cumulative frequency graphs

Example 2.5

An educational researcher was investigating the amount of time a typical student spends revising a single topic in business in preparation for a written 30-minute test. One thousand first-year students were selected at random from a British university and were given the topic strategic management planning to prepare for a test the following day. They were asked to indicate how long they would spend preparing for this test, in minutes. The times they indicated were collated into a grouped frequency table as below:

Time (minutes)	Frequency
under an hour	191
60–69	158
70–79	204
80–89	270
90–99	51
100–119	98
2 hours or more	28
Total	1000

What percentage of students take less than 1 hour and 45 minutes to complete this revision? Within what time do 50% of students complete this revision?

To find percentiles as mentioned in these questions we form a running total of the frequency: the *cumulative frequency*. This is then plotted on a graph which is used to read off these and other solutions.

Solution
Step 1: Class boundaries
We need to locate the true class boundaries, as for histograms, except that we can leave any open intervals as open (namely the first and last classes).

One way of doing this is as follows:

Class number	Time T (minutes)	Frequency
1	$T < 60$	191
2	$60 \leqslant T < 70$	158
3	$70 \leqslant T < 80$	204
4	$80 \leqslant T < 90$	270
5	$90 \leqslant T < 99$	51
6	$100 \leqslant T < 119$	98
7	$T \geqslant 120$	28
Total		1000

Step 2: Form the cumulative frequency for each class
We shall form two new columns alongside the frequency column. Firstly the cumulative frequency (CF) column. To this end we write in the CF for class 1 as just the first frequency, 191. This is interpreted as meaning that by the end of the first class all 191 items have occurred. We cannot be sure exactly where in the class they lie, but by the end of the class they have all occurred. We form the CF for class 2 by adding the frequency for class 2 to the CF for the previous class. That is the CF for class 2 = 191 + 158 = 349. Again this means by the end of the second class 349 items have occurred. For this reason a cumulative frequency graph is also known as a 'less than' graph, or an ogive. We continue adding the next frequency to form the CF for class 3. We arrive at the table below:

Class number	Time T (minutes)	Frequency	Cumulative frequency
1	$T < 60$	191	191
2	$60 \leqslant T < 70$	158	349
3	$70 \leqslant T < 80$	204	553
4	$80 \leqslant T < 90$	270	823
5	$90 \leqslant T < 99$	51	874
6	$100 \leqslant T < 119$	98	972
7	$T \geqslant 120$	28	1000
Total		1000	

Notice that by the end of the final class all 1000 items will have occurred.

Step 3: Form the relative cumulative frequency

As we wish to read off the percentiles it is more easily done if we plot the percentage cumulative frequency, that is, the relative cumulative frequency. This means we must convert the CF values to percentages. Here this can be achieved by dividing our CFs by 10. Alternatively for each class interval we have

$$\text{relative CF } \% = \frac{\text{CF}}{\text{total frequency}} \times 100\%$$

Thus we add a final column to our table to show these figures: 19.1%, 34.9%, 55.3%, etc.

Step 4: Plot the relative cumulative frequency graph

Plot the relative cumulative frequency against the upper class bounds—this is due to the way we have interpreted the cumulative frequency. The relative cumulative frequency is plotted on the vertical axis and class intervals (to scale) on the horizontal axis. We join adjacent points by a smooth curve. (Joining adjacent points by a straight line is known as a (relative) cumulative frequency polygon.) The axes are then duly labelled as shown in figure 2.13.

Notice that on the horizontal axis we have a jagged line to indicate this starts at a value other than zero.

Step 5: Reading off the values and percentiles

Using the graph we can see that the percentage of students taking less than 1 hour and 45 minutes to complete this revision is found by reading off the 105 minutes time on the horizontal axis and drawing a vertical line at this point. Read the corresponding percentage on the vertical axis—where this line cuts the graph.

Similarly we can read off the time that 50% of students complete this revision in by finding 50% on the vertical axis and drawing a horizontal line on the graph and where this cuts the graph read down to the time. This is in fact called the median time (50% point). We also have the quartile times Q1 and Q3 (Q1 = 25% point and Q3 = 75% point). We shall meet these terms later in the book.

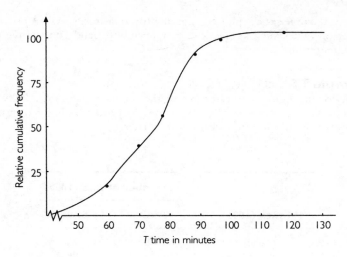

Figure 2.13

Exercises 2.6

The table below shows the duration of 40 office telephone calls from an office via the company switchboard:

Duration in minutes	Number of calls
⩽1	6
1–2	10
2–3	15
3–5	5
5–10	4
⩾10	0

(i)   What type of data is this and what is its level of measurement? Justify.
(ii) Represent this data on a histogram and describe its shape.
(iii) Plot a frequency polygon on your histogram.
(iv) Plot a relative cumulative frequency graph and read off the median and quartile values.
(v)   How would a 'greater than' CF graph be plotted?

Time series graphs

Whenever we have a characteristic measured over time we can plot a line graph to show the changes. On the vertical axis is the scale for the characteristics (mm for rainfall, degrees Celsius for temperatures, percentage rates for inflation, etc.) and along the horizontal axis the time scale is plotted (e.g. months, quarters, years). A point is plotted for each pair of values such as (percentage rate, month) and consecutive points are joined by a straight line.

Example 2.6

The following figures are estimates of the number of cars (in 1000s) taken across the Channel (Dover to Calais) on one-way journeys in 5 months during 1995 on Le Shuttle and P&O European Ferries:

	Number of cars (1000s)	
Month (1995)	P&O	Le Shuttle
March	138	75
April	156	94
May	144	83
June	158	100
July	175	112

Draw a time series graph to compare these two sets of data.

Solution

Here we use a horizontal axis with the 5 months: March to July and on the vertical axis the number of cars (in 1000s). Here we can see all the figures are greater than 50 and so instead of starting our vertical scale from 0, it would be more appropriate to start from 50. In doing so we are effectively breaking off the bottom of the vertical axis and to denote this on the graph we put a jagged line on the vertical axis to inform the reader.

The resulting time series graph is given in figure 2.14.

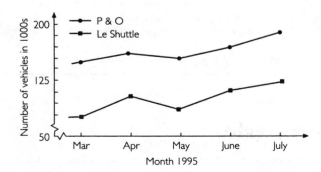

Figure 2.14

Summary

Dot plots are always used to represent a small number of data (both discrete and continuous) where there is no frequency.

Bar charts and pie charts are always used to represent nominal and ordinal data.

Line charts (or bar charts) are always used to represent ratio or interval data that is discrete data with a frequency.

Histograms are always used to represent ratio or interval data that is continuous data with a frequency.

A frequency polygon can be plotted either over a histogram or using the mid-points of a grouped data set.

A cumulative frequency graph is particularly useful when we have open class intervals or if we want to find what percentages are less than or more than some value.

Time series graphs are used when we are measuring an attribute over time.

Misrepresentation of data

Suppose a company's profits for the sale of line rental on mobile phones rose in 3 consecutive years from £1.2m to £2.5m as below:

£1.2m   in 1993
£1.8m   in 1994
£2.5m   in 1995

In the company's report to shareholders for 1995 a picture of a mobile phone might be used to represent the increase pictorially. As the height of the mobile phone would represent the profits, then the phone to represent 1995 would be approximately double the height of the mobile phone depicting 1993 profits. Figure 2.15 gives an indication of what the pictogram might look like.

We can see that the height of the first mobile is about 3 cm, the second 4.5 cm and the third is 6 cm. So far so good then, as the heights do indeed represent profits. What, however, do we notice about the overall size of each mobile? The width of the first mobile is about 2 cm, the second is about 3 cm and the third is about 4 cm. Does that mean there is a problem? Yes it does: the area of each diagram is increasing by more than the factor change in height, it is also increasing by the factor change in width. Thus the area of the first mobile is 6 cm^2 whilst the third one is 24 cm^2, which is 4 times the area of the first mobile. This means that the final mobile is giving the reader the impression that profits for 1995 are 4 times those of 1993. (Area always has a greater impact on the eye than a line chart.) This was something we noted about histograms: to draw correct histograms we must ensure that area does actually represent the frequency (i.e. the area is proportional to the frequency). Thus care is needed in interpreting pictograms—and advertisers in particular are rather known for their unfair tricks!

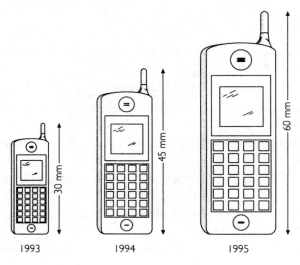

1993   1994   1995

Figure 2.15

Exercises 2.6 _____

2.6.1 Draw a dual bar chart to compare the percentage of pollutants emitted from cars
and heavy goods vehicles in a recent road transport report for London:

	Percentage of the pollutant	
Type of pollutant	**Motor car**	**Heavy goods vehicle**
Carbon dioxide	56	9
Sulphur dioxide	32	18
Black smoke	11	27
Carbon monoxide	87	1
Nitrogen oxides	68	4
Volatile organic compounds	52	14

(Source: London Energy Study)

Comment on the shape of this chart and on the differences between these two
types of vehicle.

2.6.2 As analysis of university income during 1990 has shown that the proportion of
total revenue from tuition fees was as follows:

Country	Percentage of total revenue from tuition fees
USA	25
Japan	34
Great Britain	21
The Netherlands	6
France	4
Germany	0
Sweden	0

(Source: *Times Higher Educational Supplement* October 1994)

Represent this information on a bar chart and comment on what this shows.

2.6.3 The following figures show the number of men and women awarded places to study dentistry at UK universities, from 1985 to 1995:

Year	Men	Women
1985	496	380
1986	500	394
1987	513	380
1988	505	401
1989	475	392
1990	442	411
1991	434	392
1992	428	436
1993	437	432
1994	460	452
1995	408	460

(Source: *Times Higher Educational Supplement* January 1996)

Plot this data as a time series graph and comment on what it shows.

3   Review of mathematical tools

Objectives

- Understand the key rules in addition and subtraction;
- Understand the key rules in multiplication and division;
- Understand the key rules in using fractions and decimals;
- Understand the key rules in using percentages;
- Understand the key rules in using powers and roots;
- Be able to tackle the end-of-section exercises and business examples included in the chapter.

Introduction

You are likely to come to this chapter with mixed feelings:

- You may think, I've done all this at school. If so, look at the exercises at the end of each section. If there is anything you feel uncertain about, concentrate on revising the relevant section.
- You may think, I've got a calculator/spreadsheet package and this will do all the work for me. However, you *do* need a grasp of the basic principles. If not, you may not spot if you are going wrong or, indeed, what the problem is if you do. The chapter includes boxed sections on calculator applications to help you once you are clear on the basics.
- On the other hand, your response may be one of trepidation. Many people find maths intimidating. This chapter builds step-by-step from a basic level and includes plenty of exercises to consolidate your knowledge. It also shows how maths helps with practical problems. After all, maths is just one tool we can use in decision-making and a very helpful and time-saving tool it can be.

Depending on your level of confidence, read through the relevant section and try out the exercises. Solutions are provided at the end of the book. Once you feel happy with your range of skills, try one of the business exercises (exercises 3.5).

The reader is advised to buy a scientific calculator such as a Casio FX 570S, with a fraction button, SD mode, nCr and nPr buttons.

Addition and subtraction

Scenario: the bank statement
The bank statement, whether monthly or quarterly, arrives on the doormat and must be dealt with—filed, binned or checked by varying degrees. Any transaction which is credited to your account can be regarded as an arithmetic addition to your balance; similarly a debit is an arithmetic subtraction. Understanding how these interact should help to avoid confusion with plus and minus signs: it does not guarantee you will always be in credit, but without it, you are unlikely to know.

How can we best understand addition and subtraction? First we need to see that all numbers are either positive or negative—they have a sign or lie in a certain direction from zero. Think of a number line as:

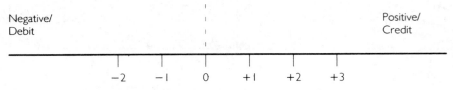

Right of zero is positive or a credit, left is negative or a debit.

If a number has no sign we say it is positive. Note that we do not need to say $+2$ if we are £2 in credit; if we write no sign, everyone knows it is positive. If it were negative, or overdrawn, we have to say so! Now, let's see what happens when we add or subtract two numbers.

Example 3.1

a) $1 + 3$ gives us 4 (think of having £1 in the bank and you credit a further £3, giving you a balance of £4. Notice that you are in credit by £4, or $+4$ but we simply write $1 + 3 = 4$ and do not need to specify this is positive.)

b) $2 - 1$ gives us 1 (think of £2 in the bank and you withdraw £1.)

c) Similarly, if you are overdrawn by £12 and you add £5 to your account, you would still be overdrawn by £7. We would write this as: $-12 + 5 = -7$. Notice that we are still on the left of zero on the above line.

d) If you are in credit by £20 and you withdraw £30, you go overdrawn by £10: $20 - 30 = -10$.

e) If you are overdrawn by £10 and credit your account with £25, your balance would be £15 in credit, or $-10 + 25 = 15$.

Note that the signs immediately preceding a term belong to it. We are allowed to move terms around in the expression but must move a term with all its signs. So in example 3.1 **(c)** could read $5 - 12 = -7$, meaning you start off in credit by £5, withdraw £12, and end up overdrawn by £7. We can write $+5 - 12 = -7$ for this, or more naturally, $5 - 12 = -7$. From the above example we can see that $-12 + 5 = -7$ is the same as $5 - 12 = -7$.

In actual fact, we can begin to see that signs are used in two ways: they are the sign belonging to a term (in example (**c**), being overdrawn by £12 is −12) and also a sign to connect two terms (in example (**c**) adding £5). Even though we are using these signs in slightly different ways, we use a + for being in credit as well as for adding to our account, and a − for being overdrawn and for withdrawing from our account. This leads us naturally to ask: what really happens when we credit a positive sum, or withdraw a positive sum, i.e. what happens if there are two signs? For simplicity, we use a rule for signs:

$$\left.\begin{array}{c} -\ - \\ +\ + \end{array}\right\} \text{ are positive} \qquad \left.\begin{array}{c} -\ + \\ +\ - \end{array}\right\} \text{ are negative}$$

This means that whenever we see two signs, we immediately tidy up to avoid confusion and mistakes. So for example:

  a) + −3 is −3 (debit)
  b) − +3 is −3 (debit)
  c) − −4 is +4 or simply 4 (credit)
  d) + +2 is +2 or simply 2 (credit)

Some authors use a bracket around the inside sign, i.e. − +3 would be −(+3). We will take a closer look at brackets later in the chapter. How do we add or subtract positive or negative numbers?

Example 3.2
a) $3 - -2 + 4 - +6 - 1$

Solution
Step 1
Well, first tidy up! Get rid of places where there are two signs, using our rule for signs. This expression becomes: $3 + 2 + 4 - 6 - 1$

Step 2
Now collect up 'adding terms' and collect 'subtracting terms'.
Adding $3 + 2 + 4 = 9$
Subtracting -6 and $-1 = -7$

If this is unclear, think of it as banking transactions. Here you withdraw £6 and then another £1 giving a total of £7 withdrawn, i.e. you subtract 7 in total.

Step 3
Finally we have $9 - 7$ which gives us 2.

Now try a few simple examples yourself:

Exercise 3.1 _____

a) $7 - +6$

b) $-5 - -6$

c) $-10 + -4$

d) $8 - +6$

(Solutions can be found at the end of the book.) **Note that + and − are equally powerful.** You can do either the adding or the subtraction first in step 2. We'll find later that other signs are more powerful and need to be dealt with first.

Multiplication and division

What about multiplication, ×, and division, ÷, of two numbers?

Example 3.3
a) 2×6

b) $14 \div 2$

c) $2 \times 10 \div 5$

Solution
Note: The signs × and ÷ are simpler to use than + and −, as they can only be use in one way: to connect two terms.

a) Here we are multiplying 2 by 6 giving us 12. Notice that we could equally think of this as multiplying 6 by 2, or doubling 6.

b) Here 14 is being divided by 2, or halved. This gives us 7. Notice here that this, unlike ×, can only be read in one direction: **in division the first term is divided by the second.** Division can also be represented vertically by the use of a line. In this example $14 \div 2$ can be shown as $\frac{14}{2}$. The second number, which does the dividing, is always shown below the line.

c) Here all signs are equally powerful, so we can take any pair with the connecting sign. That is, we can say 2×10, then divide this answer by 5. This gives us 4. Similarly we could take $10 \div 5$, giving us 2, and then multiply this by 2, which also gives us 4.

A key point to note is that × **and** ÷ **take precedence over a + or − sign**. If you come across any calculation with both in, you need to do the × and/or ÷ first and then the + and/or −. We shall clarify this relationship when we discuss brackets below.

The need for brackets

When we are likely to get confused or the mathematical statement could be ambiguous, we might choose to clarify the situation by using brackets to denote the order in which we expect the calculation to be done. In part **c)** of Example 3.3, if we had wanted the 2 to multiply the 10 first, we could have put it in brackets to tell the reader that this must be executed first. Thus, we could have written: **c)** $(2 \times 10) \div 5$. Note how this is then read: multiply the 2 by 10 first, then divide this answer by 5. As the signs × and ÷ do not take precedence over each other, we could equally have written part **c)** as $2 \times (10 \div 5)$. Notice again how this would be read: divide 10 by 5, and then multiply this answer by 2. This takes practice, but in time the eye will naturally read the expression in the mathematical sense. Brackets are especially useful in clarifying the order of precedence between × and ÷, and + and −, as we shall see below.

Example 3.4

a) $7 + 4 \times 3$

b) $8 \times 5 - 15 - 10 \div 2 + 7 + 5$

c) $\dfrac{11 - 12 \div 6 + 3 \times (8 - -3)}{7}$

Solution

How do you start? If there are brackets we would read this part first. If there are no brackets you might like to insert them to help decide which should be calculated first. How do we know where brackets should be inserted? A rough rule of thumb is to note whether the expression uses signs which are equally powerful (i.e., all $+$ and $-$, or all $\times$ and $\div$). If they are equally powerful we can simply group the numbers in pairs to make the arithmetic easiest. For example: $2 + 3 - 7$. Here we could put brackets in two ways: grouping the 2 and 3, $(2 + 3) - 7$ which would give us $5 - 7$ which is -2. Equally we could group the 3 and 7, i.e. $2 + (3 - 7)$. This would give us $2 + -4$ which is $2 - 4$ and finally this gives us -2 as before. Generally if you are worried that you have the brackets in the wrong place but get the same answer if you re-group, then you were probably right in the first place. In example 3.3(c) we saw an expression with $\times$ and $\div$ and noticed that we could put the brackets around any of the two pairs of numbers provided it made sense.

a) Here notice that the signs are not all equally powerful, and as such we ought to (but do not absolutely need to) put brackets around the more powerful sign and the numbers it connects to let the reader know (but mostly to remind ourselves!) that the brackets should be executed first. Thus the question could be written with a bracket around the 4 and 3 as:

$7 + (\mathbf{4 \times 3})$ or $7 + 12$ which equals 19.

It would change the sense of the problem if we grouped differently. If we were to put the bracket around the 7 and 4 this would be wrong, as it would mean that we would add the 7 to the 4 getting 11, and then multiply this by 3, giving us 33. We would only do this if the writer of the equation had specifically put the brackets here in the first place: we would then follow his/her order.

Using brackets when not absolutely necessary makes it easier to read for the beginner, since we always do the brackets first. The important thing to remember is we **always** do $\times$ or $\div$ first. If there are signs of different power, then putting brackets around these will mean we execute them first.

b) Again, you may feel easier rewriting using brackets. Where exactly are these put?

Step 1

Simply put brackets around the terms connected by the most powerful signs, here $\times$ and $\div$. We put these brackets around the pairs which are being multiplied and divided, i.e. the 8 and 5, and then the 10 and 2. If these were meant to be grouped in any way other than simple pairing then we would need to be told, and the brackets would already be in place. Thus $8 \times 5 - 15 - 10 \div 2 + 7 + 5$ becomes $(\mathbf{8 \times 5}) - 15 - (\mathbf{10 \div 2}) + 7 + 5$

Step 2

Executing the brackets first will give us: $8 \times 5 = 40$ and $10 \div 2 = 5$

Step 3

So the question is immediately rewritten as: $40 - 15 - 5 + 7 + 5$

Step 4

Collecting up 'adding terms', and 'subtracting' terms, we get

Adding: $40 + 7 + 5 = 52$ }
Subtracting: $-15 - 5 = -20$ } Thus $52 - 20$ yields 32

c) In this calculation, we need to do the top line first, before doing the division below the line last. There are some brackets already in place which help to get us started. At each stage rewriting the expression will help, as we will see it gradually reduce.

Step 1

Since there is already one pair of brackets, we can do this first, remembering the rule for tidying up signs. $(8 - -3)$ becomes $(8 + 3) = 11$

Step 2

A quick glance at the equation shows the need for more brackets to connect the most powerful signs, here $(12 \div 6)$ and (3×11) as the numerator.

Step 3

Executing the bracket first gives us $(12 \div 6) = 2$ and $(3 \times 11) = 33$

Thus the question is:

$$\frac{11 - 2 + 33}{7}$$

Step 4

On the numerator we can now group the $+$ and $-$ figures:

Adding: $11 + 33 = 44$ }
Subtracting: -2 } thus $44 - 2 = 42$

Step 5

Finally, we have the last calculation of $\frac{42}{7}$ which is 6

Now, try a few exercises yourself. Answers will be found at the end of the book. You will find these skills invaluable when tackling later chapters in the book.

Exercise 3.2 _____

a) $10 \div 5 \times 7 - -1$

b) $(3 + 2) \div 5 + 4$

c) $\dfrac{30 \div 2 + - 3}{3 \times 2}$

It takes time to develop the range of our mathematical language. If we wish a calculation or expression to be read in a certain way we must employ the full range of the language to do so. The language of mathematics should be thought of in the same way as any other language: emphasis is placed on different parts of the sentence by various positions of words and punctuation. It is exactly the same with mathematics: different positioning of brackets will have different meaning. The beauty of mathematical language is that it is precise and unambiguous and has a natural elegance of its own.

Fractions

So far, we have dealt with whole numbers (or *integers*, as mathematicians call them). How do we deal with fractions? If you use a calculator, you will already be familiar with decimals, which we will discuss later in this chapter. Why worry about fractions? It is important to understand fractions because you will come across them in a business context. Knowing about them also helps you to appreciate the way decimals work and will be important when we discuss probability.

We have already come across the use of lines in representing $\div$. Fractions follow the same principle. Consider the fraction $\frac{1}{4}$. This means 1 whole number divided into 4 parts, or if we take a whole circle and split it into 4 equal portions (like slices of a cake), 1 portion is a quarter, $\frac{1}{4}$. The diagram below is a helpful way of representing this.

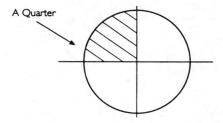

Similarly, the fraction $\frac{5}{8}$ means 5 divided by 8. Thinking of a circle divided into 8 equal portions, 5 of these would equal $\frac{5}{8}$. More generally:

$\dfrac{x}{y}$ **means** x **divided by** y **or** $x \div y$

x **is called the numerator, and** y **the denominator.**

How do we do calculations with fractions? There are differing rules for addition/subtraction, multiplication and division.

Addition/subtraction

The key rule here is to ensure that each fraction has a common **denominator** (the bottom figure in the fraction) so that we can compare like with like. Let us take a simple example to illustrate: $\frac{1}{2} + \frac{1}{4}$.

Here we need to find a common denominator for 2 and 4 (i.e. a common figure we can convert both numbers into). The simplest way is to multiply the two denominators together to produce 8, but here it is easy to see that both 2 and 4 will divide 4. Here 4 is the **lowest common denominator**. We can then convert the first fraction as follows:

$$\frac{1\ (\times 2)}{2\ (\times 2)} = \frac{2}{4}$$

Now we have two like fractions, the calculation is much easier:

$$\frac{2}{4} + \frac{1}{4} = \frac{3}{4}$$

To see this, think of a circle divided into quarters. We have two plus one quarter totalling three quarters. Once fractions are in 'common denominator', they can be added or subtracted.

Example 3.5

$$\frac{5}{6} - \frac{2}{7}$$

Solution

Step 1
Find the lowest common denominator. In this case, multiply denominators:
$6 \times 7 = 42$

Step 2
Multiply each of the denominators by either 6 or 7 to convert it to 42, remembering that whatever we do to the bottom of a fraction, we must also do to the top.

$$\frac{5\ (\times 7)}{6\ (\times 7)} = \frac{35}{42} \qquad \frac{2\ (\times 6)}{7\ (\times 6)} = \frac{12}{42}$$

Step 3
Subtract: $\dfrac{35}{42} - \dfrac{12}{42} = \dfrac{35 - 12}{42} = \dfrac{23}{42}$

Step 4
See if we can **cancel** to get a simpler fraction. In this case we cannot as there is no integer that divides both the numerator and the denominator so we leave the fraction as it is.

If you know how, check your answer on a calculator. There are notes on using the fraction button on our calculator in this chapter.

Multiplication

Fortunately, this is very easy. Simply multiply the two numerators and the two denominators. If you can, remember to cancel.

Example 3.6

$$\frac{2}{5} \times \frac{3}{4}$$

Solution

Step 1

$$\frac{2 \times 3}{5 \times 4} = \frac{6}{20}$$

Step 2

See if we can cancel to get a simpler fraction. In this case, both the numerator and denominator have 2 in common, so divide by 2:

$$\frac{6\,(\div 2)}{20\,(\div 2)} = \frac{3}{10}$$

Division

The basic rule here is to isolate the fraction doing the dividing, known as the **divisor**. The **divisor** is always the second fraction in the equation. So, when we see:

$$\frac{2}{5} \div \frac{4}{7} \qquad \tfrac{4}{7} \text{ is the } \textbf{divisor.}$$

Once the divisor is identified, it should be turned upside down

$$\frac{4}{7} \to \frac{7}{4}$$

It can then be **multiplied** with the first fraction.

$$\frac{2}{5} \times \frac{7}{4} = \frac{14}{20}$$

Finally, the fraction can be cancelled, in this case to $\frac{7}{10}$

Example 3.7

$$\frac{3}{4} \div \frac{4}{5}$$

Solution

Step 1

Isolate the divisor: $\frac{4}{5}$

Step 2

Turn it upside down: $\frac{4}{5} \to \frac{5}{4}$

Step 3

Multiply the new fraction with the first

$$\frac{3}{4} \times \frac{5}{4} = \frac{15}{16}$$

Step 4

Cancel, if appropriate. No further cancelling can be done in this case.

A fraction whose numerator is greater than its denominator is called an **improper fraction**. It is usual to convert to a whole number and the remaining fraction. As an example:

$\frac{5}{4}$ may be converted to $1\frac{1}{4}$

Calculator note: using the fraction button

The previous discussion helps you to understand some of the principles involved and allows you to check your calculations. Once you are clear on the approach, you can make use of the calculator. To tap in a fraction on a calculator, you need the:

$\boxed{a\frac{b}{c}}$ button

Example 3.8

$\frac{3}{5} \times 6$

Solution

To enter $\frac{3}{5}$ simply press 3 $\boxed{a\frac{b}{c}}$ 5.

On your display you will see $3 \perp 5$: this is how fractions are written by the calculator. Now to carry out the product press: $\times 6$. On the display you will have $3 \perp 3 \perp 5$. The first number here is the whole number and the rest is the fraction and so it is read $3\frac{3}{5}$.

If we simply had two numbers such as $3 \perp 7$ on the display, this would be read as $\frac{3}{7}$.

Example 3.9

$1\frac{1}{3} \div \frac{4}{5}$

Solution

To divide two fractions we turn both fractions into complete fractions (improper fractions) so including the whole number within the fraction. Thus $1\frac{1}{3}$ is 1 whole number which is 3 thirds (think of a circle divided into three equal parts) plus one third. Thus $1\frac{1}{3} = \frac{3}{3} + \frac{1}{3}$ giving us $\frac{4}{3}$. Thus the problem is $\frac{4}{3} \div \frac{4}{5}$. To find this, we turn the second fraction upside down and multiply the fractions. Thus $1\frac{1}{3} \div \frac{4}{5} = \frac{4}{3} \times \frac{5}{4}$ and cancelling the common 4, we have $\frac{4 \div 4}{3} \times \frac{5}{4 \div 4} = \frac{1}{3} \times \frac{5}{1} = \frac{5}{3}$. Now, as at the start, we saw that 1 whole number is $\frac{3}{3}$, $\frac{5}{3}$ is $\frac{3}{3} + \frac{2}{3}$ giving us $1\frac{2}{3}$. Again using the calculator:

1 $\boxed{a\frac{b}{c}}$ 1 $\boxed{a\frac{b}{c}}$ 3 $\div$ 4 $\boxed{a\frac{b}{c}}$ 5 $=$

giving $1 \perp 2 \perp 3$ on the display, or $1\frac{2}{3}$.

Example 3.10

$$\frac{2}{9} + 1\frac{1}{3}$$

Solution

Using your fraction button enter the following:

2 $\boxed{a\dfrac{b}{c}}$ 9 + 1 $\boxed{a\dfrac{b}{c}}$ 1 $\boxed{a\dfrac{b}{c}}$ 3 =

On the display you should have $1 \perp 5 \perp 9$ or $1\frac{5}{9}$.

Example 3.11

Cosy Carpets are advertising their carpet charges as $\frac{1}{3}$ off the normal price. If for an average room of 3 metres by 3 metres the charges are usually £18, what is the reduced charge?

Solution

Here we need to work out $\frac{1}{3}$ of £18 and this will give us the reduced price. Thus $\frac{1}{3}$ of £18 $= \frac{1}{3} \times$ £18. Using our calculator, this is

1 $\boxed{a\dfrac{b}{c}}$ 3 × 18 =

The result on the display will be 6. The reduced price is £18 less the discount of £6, which is £12.

Now try some calculations for your self using the fraction button on your calculator, if you have one. (Answers are at the end of the book.)

Exercise 3.3 _____

a) $2\dfrac{2}{3} + \dfrac{7}{8}$

b) $1\dfrac{3}{4} \times \dfrac{5}{6}$

c) $3\dfrac{1}{7} \div 2\dfrac{1}{4}$

Decimals

Fractions are a helpful way of introducing decimals, since fractions are a form of decimal. We can see decimals in our bank statement. We know that £1.25 means £1 and 25 pence. The decimal point separates the whole numbers (whole pounds) from the part of a number (pence). If we write £1.25, we say that 2 is in the first decimal place, meaning 2 tenths of a pound (or two tens of a pound) or 20p. Similarly the 5 is in the second decimal place meaning 5 hundredths of a pound and, as there are 100 pence in a pound, this must be 5p. If we separate the whole number (integer) and decimal, we can see more clearly: £1.25 = £1 + £0.25 = £1 + 20p + 5p. As £1 is 100p, we could also write 125p.

Decimals work in these groups of ten. If we set aside currency and think of numbers, decimals can be seen as strung along a number line divided into groups of 10. The decimal point divides numbers of 1 or more from fractional parts which are less than 1.

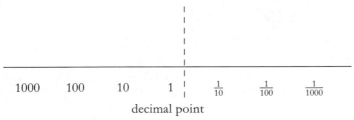

236.394 is $2 \times 100 + 3 \times 10 + 6 \times 1 + 3 \times \frac{1}{10} + 9 \times \frac{1}{100} + 4 \times \frac{1}{1000}$

The essential rule is to see the decimal point as the central point from which to work with any set of figures. Starting with the decimal point, we know that numbers grow by multiples of tens on the left of the line and get smaller by multiples of 10ths on the right.

How do we calculate with decimals?

You will already be familiar with calculations using decimals since calculators operate on a decimal system. This section is, therefore, relatively brief. Its value is to help you understand how an answer is arrived at, in order that you have a better chance of spotting errors in your work.

We perform addition and subtraction on decimal numbers in the same way as whole numbers, noting that we align both numbers, so that numbers in the same decimal position are added or subtracted.

Addition

Example 3.12
£13.27 + £139.35

Solution
Step 1
Remember the essential rule of using the decimal point as the central point for reading figures. Here we align the figures so that the decimal points are in the same position:

  13.27
139.35

Step 2
We can now add up numbers in the same decimal position, starting with the column on the furthest right and working towards the left. Here we start with

7 and 5. In this case, the answer comes to 12. When a number reaches double figures, it affects the next column along:

13.27
139.<u>35</u>
<u>2</u>
1

We add the extra into the next column so that our calculation for the next column becomes $2 + 3 + \mathbf{1} = 6$.

Step 3
We complete the calculation, including adding any 'extra' numbers into the next column along:

13.27
$+$ <u>139.35</u>
152.62

Subtraction

Example 3.13
$28.38 - 13.291$

Solution
Step 1
First align the 2 figures. Notice that here we must first make both numbers the same number of decimal places, here by adding an extra zero to the end of the first number:

23.380
13.291

Step 2
Begin the subtraction. Immediately we can see that we can't subtract 1 from 0. In this case, we need to borrow 1 from the next column so we have 10 from which we can subtract 1 to leave 9.

Step 3
We then reduce the next number along, so that 8 becomes 7. Again, we have the same problem so we borrow 1 from the next column so that we have $17 - 9$ is 8. Don't forget to reduce the next number along so that 3 becomes 2.

Step 4
Complete the calculation:

28.380
$-$ <u>13.291</u>
15.089

Multiplication

Example 3.14
0.2×0.027

Solution

Step 1
Remove all the decimal points and consider numbers alone. Here we'd have 2×27 which gives us 54.

Step 2
Now we count the number of decimal places in the question. There are four in total and so we must have four in the answer. Thus we have 0.0054.

Division

Example 3.15
$0.2 \div 0.05$

Solution
Step 1
Get rid of the decimal point altogether by multiplying each figure by the same amount. In this case, we would need to multiply 0.05 by 100 to make 5. We multiply 0.2 by 100 as well to produce 20.

Step 2
We then have a much easier calculation to understand $\frac{20}{5} = 4$.

Converting fractions into decimals and decimals into fractions

We have seen that the line in a fraction means 'divide'. We can use this idea to convert a fraction into a decimal. As an example $\frac{1}{4}$ means 1 divided by 4. Using our calculator we can do this division: press $1 \div 4$ and, on the display, we would have 0.25. Similarly, $\frac{5}{8}$ means 5 divided by 8, giving us 0.625 using a calculator. Thus any fraction can be written as a decimal. If we consider the fraction $\frac{1}{3}$ as a decimal ($1 \div 3$ using a calculator), we would get 0.333333333. We can immediately see that dealing with the fractional form $\frac{1}{3}$ is often preferable to its decimal form! It is also true that some decimals can be written as a fraction, but there are many decimals which cannot be, for example π. Press EXP and you will get π on the display to 9 decimal places. You have probably used the fraction $\frac{22}{7}$ for π, but this is only an approximate fraction, as we cannot find an exact fraction.

Example 3.16
Express 0.35 as a fraction.

Solution
0.35 is $0.3 + 0.05 = \frac{3}{10} + \frac{5}{100}$ or $\frac{30}{100} + \frac{5}{100} = \frac{35}{100}$. As before we generally leave fractions in their lowest form. To reduce this latter fraction we see that its numerator and denominator both have 5 in common, and so we can divide the top and bottom by 5: $\frac{35}{100} = \frac{35 \div 5}{100 \div 5} = \frac{7}{20}$. We could check our answer by calculator, evaluating $7 \div 20$ which should be 0.35!

Percentages

> **Scenario: discounts—are they fooling you?**
> Products are often sold with attractive 'so-much per cent extra free' or 'so-much percentage reduction'. These are not always quite what they seem. For example, when marketing a new formulation of shampoo, an advertisement might say: 'a third extra is free'. This is technically true but rather misleading. In fact a third of the original size, a smaller size than is being sold, is what is free. The advertiser is suggesting that in fact a third of the whole larger bottle is free. Yes it's sneaky!

A percentage (shown as %) is a quantity expressed as a number out of 100. For example:

50% means 50 out of 100 or $\frac{50}{100}$ (cancelled to $\frac{1}{2}$) or 0.5

5% means 5 out of 100 or $\frac{5}{100}$ (cancelled to $\frac{1}{20}$) or 0.05

0.5% means $\frac{5}{10ths}$ out of 100 or $\frac{5}{1000}$ (cancelled to $\frac{1}{200}$) or 0.005

As you can see, a percentage can be expressed as a fraction or a decimal. Since a percentage is a number out of 100, all you need to do to convert it into a decimal is divide by 100. Similarly, to convert a decimal to a percentage, simply multiply by 100.

How do we use percentages? Let us go back to the bank statement. The bank tells us we will receive 5% interest on our deposit account of £200. What does this mean?

$$5\% \text{ of } £200 = \frac{5}{100} \times £200 = 0.05 \times £200 = £10$$

so we will get an extra £10. Let's try some examples using percentages, to reinforce our understanding:

Example 3.17
a) What is 25% as a fraction?

b) What is the decimal 0.008 as a percentage?

c) What is $\frac{5}{8}$ as a percentage?

d) What is 8% of £36?

e) Write $33\frac{1}{3}\%$ in fractional and decimal form.

Solution
a) Convert a number out of 100 $= \frac{25}{100}$. Cancel to $\frac{1}{4}$

b) Remember, percentages represent a figure out of 100. All we need to do to convert is multiply the decimal by 100. So, $0.008 \times 100 = 0.8\%$

c) First, convert into decimals by dividing 5 by 8 = 0.625. Then, multiply by 100 to produce a percentage $0.625 \times 100 = 62.5\%$

d) First, convert percentage into a decimal; 8% is $\frac{8}{100} = 0.08$. Here 8% of 36 means $8\% \times 36$ ('of' generally means 'multiply')—thus $0.08 \times 36 = £2.88$

e) The shortest and easiest way of doing this is using your calculator:

Enter 33 $\boxed{a\frac{b}{c}}$ 1 $\boxed{a\frac{b}{c}}$ 3 ÷ 100 =

and you will arrive at $1 \perp 3$ or $\frac{1}{3}$.

Using the definition of the fraction is more tricky, but once you know the answer it seems so obvious that you tend to know the answer without working it out. You probably would not work through the problem like this but, by tackling the most awful looking expressions, you will learn never to be intimidated by a mathematical expression! Well hopefully! Firstly express the percentage as a fraction, which gives us

$$\frac{33\frac{1}{3}}{100}$$

The easiest way to tidy this up is to see that there are three $33\frac{1}{3}$ in 100, and so if we cancel down the fraction by dividing top and bottom by $33\frac{1}{3}$ we have

$$\frac{33\frac{1}{3} \div 33\frac{1}{3}}{100 \div 33\frac{1}{3}}$$

and we arrive at 1 on the top and 3 on the bottom or $\frac{1}{3}$. Phew! There's something to be said for the calculator! To convert into a decimal, remember to divide by 100. $33\frac{1}{3} \div 100$ on the calculator produces 0.333333333.

Now try the following exercises using decimals on your calculator and check your answers at the end of the book. If you have any problems, look through the section again.

Exercise 3.4 _____

a) £189.36 + £97.87 − £237.20

b) 0.07 × 3.003 ÷ 7.9

c) Find 20% of 58 expressed as a fraction and a decimal.

Using your skills: some business examples

Once you have read this part of the chapter, you will have the essential skills for many day-to-day mathematical operations. This will be much of your toolkit for the rest of the book. Before we go on to look at additional maths skills let us show the value of the skills learnt so far on some business examples.

You'll find you need separate analytical skills for dealing with these cases. The key thing is to divide each case into separate steps as we have already done for particular mathematical skills. To do this, isolate the key issues and then plan out the steps from there using your mathematical skills to help with each step.

Example 3.18

You have just been appointed as a Marketing Executive for a range of products, including product 'x'. Your boss tells you that last year's budget was £7000, but this year it's been cut by $5\frac{1}{4}$%. He's not sure of the exact figures, but $\frac{3}{4}$ of the budget is spent on advertising and direct mail, the rest on exhibitions. There are two regular exhibitions the company attends costing £500 each. A further exhibition is coming up which will cost £800. An alternative would be to spend any surplus on a mailing. He has a quote for leaflets at £250 for 3000.

a) Can we afford the extra exhibition?
b) If we don't go to the exhibition, how many leaflets could we mail instead?

Solution

Step 1
Isolate the key issues. Here, we need to establish what our budget is for this year, then take off all other expenses to get the relevant surplus. We can then answer the two questions.

Step 2
What is our budget for the year? £7000 less $5\frac{1}{4}$%, so what is $5\frac{1}{4}$% of £7000? First, convert $5\frac{1}{4}$% into a decimal. Recall that $\frac{1}{4}$ is 0.25 and so $5\frac{1}{4}$ is 5.25. To write 5.25% as a decimal we divide by 100. $\frac{5.25}{100}$ is 0.0525. $5\frac{1}{4}$% of £7000 = 5.25% × £7000 = 0.0525 × £7000 = £367.50.

Our budget is £7000 less this amount, i.e.

£7000 − £367.50 = £6632.50

Step 3
We know that $\frac{3}{4}$ of the budget is spent on advertising and direct mail, so we need to remove this. We could use the fraction button on our calculator or, as here, convert the fraction into decimal.

So, 3 ÷ 4 = 0.75

0.75 × £6632.50 is £4974.38 (rounding up to the nearest pence). Our budget for exhibitors is £6632.50 less this amount.

6632.50
4974.38
1658.12

Step 4
We now know what our exhibitions budget is. We can take the cost of the two regular exhibitions off:

£1658.12 − (2 × £500) = £1658.12 − £1000.00 = £658.12

We can now answer question **a)**—no, we haven't got the money to attend the extra exhibition.

Step 5
We can now turn to question **b)**. The most obvious step is to divide £658.12 by £250 to see how many leaflets we could produce. £658.12 ÷ £250 is 2.6 (rounded up to the nearest decimal point). We can spend 2.6 lots of £250 to

produce 2.6 lots of 3000. The answer to **b)** is 3000 × 2.6 or 7800 leaflets (we would still be left with £8.12).

Example 3.19

A wine merchant buys wine by the case (twelve bottles) from the wholesaler at £20 per case. She decides that to meet her overheads and make a reasonable profit, she must sell each case by 23% more than she buys them for (10% for her overheads and the rest for profit). At Christmas, she decides that due to increased competition from a new wine store she should offer a 20% discount on each case. Does she break even in doing this? How much discount should she offer so that she does not make a loss?

Solution
Step 1
Isolate the key issues. We need to know what the wine merchant's breakeven point on each case is. We can then compare this with the impact of a 20% discount.

Step 2
The wine merchant's breakeven point per case is £20 plus 10% for her overheads. We need to find out what 10% of £20 is and then add it on to the original £20. To do the calculations, we divide 10 by 100 to produce a decimal = 0.10; 0.10 × £20 = £2. Adding this to £20 produces a breakeven price of £22.00 per case.

Step 3
We can now consider the impact of the 20% discount. First, we know that the wine merchant normally sells her wine at £20 per case plus 23%. We use the same approach as Step 2 to find the normal selling price:

£20 × 0.23 = £4.60 plus original £20 = £24.60 per case.

Step 4
Now we can remove the 20% discount. £24.60 × 0.2 = £4.92. Subtracting the discount from the original price gives: £24.60 − £4.92 + £19.68.

Step 5
We can subtract the discounted price from the breakeven price. If she does discount at 20%, the wine merchant will lose £2.32 per case. Whoops!

Step 6
To establish what discount the wine merchant could get away with, and still cover her costs, we need to establish the difference between her normal price and her breakeven price, i.e. £24.60 − £22.00 = £2.60. The wine merchant could, therefore, get away with £2.60 off. We can express this as a percentage by dividing £2.60 by £24.60 and multiplying by 100. This gives a discount of 10.6% (rounded up). If she really does need to discount by up to 20%, she has a problem on her hands!

Example 3.20

A supermarket has a new product, Timotosa Hair Shampoo. A 200 millilitre bottle is enticingly advertised at $33\frac{1}{3}$% *extra free*. How much is really free? What is the usual size of the bottle when there is no promotion? How misleading is the promotion?

Solution

Step 1

Isolate the key issues. In this case, the key word is *extra*. This shows that the bottle is, in fact, $33\frac{1}{3}\%$ larger than its *usual* size. It is this proportion of the original bottle that is actually free and *not* $33\frac{1}{3}\%$ of 200 ml. The offer is misleading to the unwary!

Step 2

We need to find out the usual size of the bottle. 200 ml represents the usual size plus $33\frac{1}{3}\%$, i.e. it is 100% plus an extra $33\frac{1}{3}\%$ or $133\frac{1}{3}\%$ of the original size.

Step 3

A first step is to make $133\frac{1}{3}\%$ more manageable since it mixes up fractions and percentages. Let us convert it into a fraction. To do this, remember to divide $133\frac{1}{3}$ by 100. The easiest way is to use the fraction button on your calculator.

Enter 133 $\boxed{a\dfrac{b}{c}}$ 1 $\boxed{a\dfrac{b}{c}}$ 3 ÷ 100

and you will arrive at $1 \perp 1 \perp 3$ or $4 \perp 3$ or $\frac{4}{3}$

Step 4

Now we know 200 ml is $\frac{4}{3}$ of the original size. If $\frac{4}{3}$ represents 200 ml, then $\frac{1}{3}$ represents 50 ml (if we divide both by 4). Thus $\frac{3}{3}$ or $\frac{1}{1}$ represents $3 \times 50 = 150$ ml (multiplying both by 3). Hence the original bottle was 150 ml.

Step 5

We know that 50 ml is actually free, compared to the assumption many people would make that $\frac{1}{3}$ of 200 ml or 67 ml is free!

Now try these exercises using the skills you have learnt and the step-by-step approach to identify key issues and the stages to follow. Answers are at the end of the book.

Exercises 3.5 _____

3.5.1 If the cost of manufacturing an AppleMac is £1000 and Apple wish to make a profit of $12\frac{1}{2}\%$, what will be the selling price of each computer? If they then offer a 5% discount on the selling price as an incentive for bulk purchase, what price will they charge and what profit will they make on each computer sold as part of a bulk deal?

3.5.2 In a test, a student on a BA Business Studies Course scores 52 marks out of 80. The percentage needed to pass the test is 40% and to gain a distinction 70%. What is the pass mark and how well did the student do?

3.5.3 An A4 pad is advertised as 20% extra free. If the pad is 300 pp., how much is really free?

3.5.4 A cheese importer buys French brie at a price of £2.60 per kg. She sells it to a local delicatessen at a profit of 32%. In the summer months, she always offers a discount. How much should this discount be in order that she does not make a loss?

Powers

Consider 3^2. Here 2 is the *power* or *exponent*. This is read as '3 raised to the power 2'. How do we understand this? We say this means 3 multiplied by itself twice. Raising to the power 2 means multiplying a term by itself twice. So raising a number to the power 3 means multiply the number by itself 3 times, etc. Thus 3^2 is 3×3 or 9. If we have a different power, say 4, 3^4 would mean 3 multiplied by itself 4 times. Thus $3^4 = 3 \times 3 \times 3 \times 3 = 81$. The following examples explain how to use the calculator to work out powers.

Example 3.21
Calculate

a) $(1.29)^3$

b) $(0.36)^7$

c) $2^{1.02}$

Solution
a) This would read '1.29 raised to the power 3'. We could simply do the following calculation: $1.29 \times 1.29 \times 1.29$. Alternatively, we would use the x^y button (or y^x on some calculators). These are the operations:

Calculator note: powers or exponents

$(1.29)^3 = 1.29$ $\boxed{x^y}$ $3 =$

Here 1.29 is understood to be the x and 3 is the y. Notice that as you push the $\boxed{x^y}$ the symbol x^y appears on the display.

On the display you should have 2.146689.

b) This reads '0.36 raised to the power of 7'. This means $0.36 \times 0.36 \times 0.36 \times 0.36 \times 0.36 \times 0.36 \times 0.36$. These are the operations on the calculator:

Calculator note

0.36 $\boxed{x^y}$ $7 =$

On the display you would have: 7.83641641^{-04}. How would we interpret this? This in fact should be read as: $7.83641641^{-41} = 7.83641641 \times 10^{-4}$ and is known as *standard index form*. The actual answer should be 0.000783641. We must move the decimal point 4 places to the left to get the actual answer. The calculator uses this notation because your display has only 10 digits, and so it saves space by not printing all the zeros and merely says that you must move the decimal point 4 places. If it is negative 4, as here, you make the number smaller or move to the left. If it was $+4$ you make the number larger or move to the right.

c) Here the question reads '2 raised to the power 1.02'. To do this:

Calculator note

2   $\boxed{x^y}$ 1.02 = 2.027919896

Example 3.22

a) What numbers are the following Standard Index forms used on the calculator:

   i) 5.2345^{06}

   ii) 3.209^{-03}

b) Express the following in Standard Index form:

   i)   320 001.6

   ii)   0.001 45

   iii)   987.32

Solution

a) i) 5.2345^{06}

This would be written in standard index form as 5.2345×10^{06}.

This means we must move the decimal point 6 places, making the number larger as the index 06 is positive. Thus we move the point to the right. As we move from the right to the left we see that after we have moved 4 places we have run out of figures but still need to move the point two more places, and so we need to put in some zeros to allow us to do this.

This gives us

$5.2345^{06} = 5.2345 \times 10^{06} = 5\ 234\ 500$

Notice that the number is comparatively large because the index of 10 is positive.

ii) 3.209^{-03}

This would be written in standard index form as 3.209×10^{-03}

This means we must move the decimal 3 places, making the number smaller as the index 03 is negative. Thus we move the point to the left. As we move from the left to the right we see that after we have moved 1 place we have run out of figures but still need to move the point two more places, and so we need to put in some zeros to allow us to do this.

This gives us

$3.209^{-03} = 3.209 \times 10^{-03} = 0.003\ 209$

Notice that the number is comparatively small because the index of 10 is negative.

b) For each of the numbers we must express them in the form $a \times 10^n$ where a is a number between 1 and 10, and n is an integer (positive or negative whole number). Here a is called the mantissa and n the exponent.

   i) 320 001.6

   As a number between 1 and 10 this would be 3. something. Thus we must move the decimal point to the left until it lies between the 3 and

2. We have moved it 5 places, and as the number is a large number the power must be $+5$.

Thus

$$320\ 001.6 = 3.200\ 016 \times 10^5$$

ii) 0.001 45 as a number between 1 and 10, but less than 10, would be 1. something. Thus we must move the decimal point 3 places to the right. Thus $0.001\ 45 = 1.45 \times 10^n$, where n must be 3.

What about the sign of n? Well, as we have made a small number larger, we must multiply it by a small number to get back to the original. Thus if we multiply it by 10^3, which is 1000, we are clearly not going to get back to 0.001 45. However, if we multiply by 10^{-3} which is $1/1000$, we are obviously doing the right thing. Thus

$$0.001\ 45 = 1.45 \times 10^{-3}$$

iii) $987.32 = 9.8732 \times 10^n$

As we have moved the decimal point 2 places to the left, this will be a positive index. That is, $987.32 = 9.8732 \times 10^2$

Roots

Take the number 3. If we square 3, 3^2 is 9. The opposite operation to squaring is square rooting. Thus the square root of 9, written $\sqrt{9}$, is the number which when squared gives us 9. Thus $\sqrt{9} = 3$. Similarly the square root of 25 is a number which when squared gave us 25. Thus $\sqrt{25} = 5$. For most numbers we cannot easily find a square root, and need to use our calculator.

A notion comparable to the square root is the cube root. To see this, we consider the number 2. If we cube 2 we have: $2^3 = 2 \times 2 \times 2 = 8$. The cube root of 8 is the number which when cubed gives us 8. Thus the cube root of 8, written $\sqrt[3]{8} = 2$. Similarly, the cube root of 27 is a number which when cubed gives us 27. This is 3, and so $\sqrt[3]{27} = 3$. As with square roots, we usually have to use our calculator. Note in the symbol for square root we could write $\sqrt[2]{}$, but the 2 is understood to be there. For a cube root we need to explicitly say that it is a *cube* root.

Example 3.23
Find the square root and cube root of

a) 125

b) 81

Solution
a) The square root of $125 = \sqrt{125} = 11.180\ 339\ 89$

Calculator note

| $\sqrt{}$ | 125 $=$ |

Notice that as you push the square root button, a root sign $\sqrt{}$ will appear on the display.

On the display is 11.18034. To check your answer you can square 11.18033989 and you should get 125. (Either use the x^2 button or the x^y button with y as 2. Using the x^2 button we have: 11.183033989 $\boxed{x^2}$ = and you should get 125 on the display.)

Similarly, the cube root is $\sqrt[3]{125} = 5$

Calculator note

$\boxed{\sqrt[3]{}}$ 125 =

To arrive at the cube root, you will need to use the shift button as the cube root symbol is written in brown over the $\boxed{\pm}$. Again you will see cube root symbol appear on the display. Thus

$\boxed{\text{shift}}$ $\boxed{\pm}$ 125 =

Note that buttons are pressed sequentially, never simultaneously.
The display reads 5. (To check this you can compute $5 \times 5 \times 5$.)

---

b) The square root of 81 = $\sqrt{81}$ = 9

Calculator note

$\boxed{\sqrt{}}$ 81 =

On the display is 9.

Similarly, the cube root is $\sqrt[3]{81} = 4.326\,748\,711$

Calculator note

$\boxed{\sqrt[3]{}}$ 81 =

Again you will need to do:

$\boxed{\text{shift}}$ $\boxed{\pm}$ 81 =

The display reads 4.326748711.

Exercises 3.6 _____

3.6.1 Compute the following using your calculator:

a) 3.5^2

b) 4.8^4

c) 0.15^6

3.6.2 Compute the following using your calculator:

a) $\sqrt{10\,000}$

   b) $\sqrt{0.4}$

   c) $\sqrt[3]{243}$

3.6.3 Determine what the calculator means by the following standard index forms:

   a) 3.245^7

   b) 8.042^{-5}

Laws of indices

Consider the term a^2. Here the 2 is called the index, power or exponent, and a is called the base. We interpret them as follows:

a^2 means $a \times a$ (i.e. a multiplied by itself twice)

and a^3 means $a \times a \times a$ and so on. How would we multiply such terms?

$a^2 \times a^3 = a \times a \times a \times a \times a = a^5$

Similarly

$a^3 \times a^4 = a \times a \times a \times a \times a \times a \times a = a^7$

We can see that in fact we could have simply added the indices. In general, we have

Law I $\boldsymbol{a^m \times a^n = a^{m+n}}$

Note that the base must be the same in order to apply the law. If we try to use the law for the product of $3^2 \times 2^4$ this would be wrong!

Division of such expressions is handled similarly.

For example, take

$$\frac{a^4}{a^2} = \frac{a \times a \times a \times a}{a \times a}$$

and by cancelling common terms which appear on both the numerator and denominator we arrive at:

$$\frac{a^4}{a^2} = \frac{a \times a \times \cancel{a} \times \cancel{a}}{\cancel{a} \times \cancel{a}} = a^2$$

Analogously to Law I, we can obtain this by subtracting the indices. This gives us Law II:

Law II $\boldsymbol{\dfrac{a^m}{a^n} = a^{m-n}}$

In fact Law II gives some other useful results concerning negative indices.

Consider applying Law II to the problem $\dfrac{a^3}{a^4}$

We would get a^{-1}. Now by using the cancellation approach we would get:

$$\frac{a^3}{a^4} = \frac{\cancel{a} \times \cancel{a} \times \cancel{a}}{a \times \cancel{a} \times \cancel{a} \times \cancel{a}} = \frac{1}{a}$$

Comparing these two answers, we must have that $a^{-1} = \dfrac{1}{a}$.

This latter form is called the reciprocal of a. It appears that reciprocals are negative indices. We had better check this works for other samples.

$$\text{Take } \frac{a^2}{a^4} = \frac{a \times a}{a \times a \times a \times a}$$
$$= \frac{\cancel{a} \times \cancel{a}}{a \times \cancel{a} \times \cancel{a} \times a}$$
$$= \frac{1}{a^2}$$

If we had used Law II we would have $a^{2-4} = a^{-2}$. Thus we must have $a^{-2} = \dfrac{1}{a^2}$.

Generally we could say:

$$\frac{1}{a^n} = a^{-n}$$

What would happen if $n = 0$? If we take a look at Law I with $n = 0$, we would have $a^m \times a^0 = a^m$.

Now this can only be true if $a^0 = 1$, and so we simply define it as that: $a^0 = 1$

Notice that in the examples the powers were whole numbers—integers. In fact the above remarks hold for all real numbers. We shall see later in the chapter how to interpret fractional (rational) indices.

Example 3.24
Check that the definition of a^0 does not contradict Law II.

Solution
Take the case $m = n$ in Law II. For example let $m = n = 5$. Then

$$\frac{a^5}{a^5} = \frac{a \times a \times a \times a \times a}{a \times a \times a \times a \times a}$$
$$= \frac{\cancel{a} \times \cancel{a} \times \cancel{a} \times \cancel{a} \times \cancel{a}}{\cancel{a} \times \cancel{a} \times \cancel{a} \times \cancel{a} \times \cancel{a}}$$
$$= 1$$

Applying Law II would give us $a^{5-5} = a^0$ and so comparing these two answers we see that $a^0 = 1$ which does not contradict our definition.

Finally, noting that $(a^3)^2$ means $a^3 \times a^3 = a^6$ by Law I, we can state

Law III $(a^m)^n = a^{mn}$

Verify that this indeed works by trying a few examples with different numbers.

Exercises 3.7 _____

3.7.1 Evaluate the following indices:

    a) $10^4 \times 10^7$

    b) $\dfrac{10^8}{10^2}$

    c) $2^4 \times 2^{-4}$

    d) $\dfrac{3^6}{3^7}$

Brackets and more complex calculations

We have already seen how brackets are used to help to clarify how calculations should be tackled, i.e. in what order we do the calculation. We shall now see how these ideas extend to deal with abstract expressions involving variables such as x and y, or a and b, etc.

A bracket is a way of saying 'multiply everything outside by everything within'. To see how they are used we need some examples:

Example 3.25
Write $3(x - 5)$ without using brackets.

Solution
This is the same as writing $3 \times (x - 5)$, namely the 3 multiplies the x and the -5. The final answer is the sum of these two parts. Arrows are helpful.

3    $(x - 5)$

Thus we get $3 \times x + 3 \times -5$

$$= 3x + -15$$

$$= 3x - 15$$

Example 3.26
Find the product of $2x(3x + 1)$

Solution
Again using arrows we would have

2x $(3x + 1)$

From this we can see that our answer would be:

$2x \times 3x + 2x \times 1$ which would tidy up to give us $6x^2 + 2x$.

Example 3.27

Remove the brackets in $(x - 2)(x + 4)$

Solution

Here each of the terms in the first bracket multiplies the second bracket. By this we mean that every term in the first bracket multiplies every term in the second bracket. Making a quick tally of the final number of terms we would see that this would be 2×2 or 4 terms. If we build on the ideas from the example above, we could think of this product of two brackets as the first term of the first bracket multiplying the second bracket, added to the second term in the first bracket multiplying the second bracket. That is $x \times (x + 4)$ added to $-2 \times (x + 4)$. Using arrows for each of these would give us:

x   (x + 4)   added to   –2   (x + 4)

and from this we would have:

$x \times x + 4 \times x$ added to $-2 \times x + -2 \times 4$

We can tidy this up to arrive at $x^2 + 4x + -2x - 8$ which are the 4 terms we anticipated—the danger is to forget to do 4 products. Thus we can combine the x terms giving us a final answer of $x^2 + 2x - 8$.

In fact we tend to use a modified form of the arrows to enable us to carry out the brackets procedure in one step. We use the following display of arrow—really just indicating that the first term multiplies both terms in the second bracket, and the second term in the first bracket does likewise.

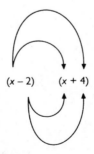

(x – 2)   (x + 4)

From the top set of arrows, we form the product $x \times (x + 4)$ and from the bottom set of arrows we form $-2 \times (x + 4)$.

Thus we get $x^2 + 4x$ and $-2x - 8$ and adding these we get the final solution of

$x^2 + 4x + -2x - 8$

giving $x^2 + 2x - 8$.

An expression of the form $ax^2 + bx + c$ is generally called a quadratic. We shall meet these again in later chapters.

How would we multiply 3 brackets? To see how we would naturally do this consider multiplying three numbers: take 2, 3 and 8. We would multiply any two and take the answer and multiply this by the third number. We do precisely this for 3 or more brackets.

Example 3.28

Find the product of $(x - 1)(x + 4)(2x + 3)$

Solution

First find the product of $(x - 1)(x + 4)$. From Example 3.27 we can see that this would be $x^2 + 4x + -x - 4$ giving us $x^2 + 3x - 4$.

Now we need to find the product of

$(x^2 + 3x - 4)(2x + 3)$

The method discussed in Example 3.27 would be used, simply noting that we have an extra term in the first bracket, so giving an extra two terms.

Taking each term in the first bracket we get:

$x^2 \times (2x + 3) + 3x \times (2x + 3) + -4 \times (2x + 3)$

Which is $2x^2 + 3x^2 + 6x^2 + 9x - 8x - 12$

Tidied, this is: $2x^2 + 9x^2 + x - 12$

Exercises 3.8 _____

3.8.1 Remove the brackets in the following expressions:

    a) $8(a + 2b)$

    b) $3a(a - b)$

    c) $2xy(3x + y)$

3.8.2 Find the product of:

    a) $(x + 4)(x - 3)$

    b) $(x + 3)(x - 3)$

    c) $(x + 5)(2 - x)$

    d) $(3x + 1)(2x - 1)$

3.8.3 Find the product of:

    a) $(2x - 1)(x - 5)(x + 3)$

    b) $(2x + 1)(x + 6)(1 - x)$

Are brackets ever unnecessary? We shall look at several examples to make the answer to this clear.

Example 3.29

In each of the following decide whether brackets are necessary or can be deleted:

a) $(3) + (x + y) + 2x$

b) $4 + (3 \div 2)$

c) $(3 \times x) + (3 - 2x)$

d) $5 \times (x - 2) + 4$

Solution

a) Clearly we never need a bracket around a single term so we may delete the brackets around the 3. The brackets around $x + y$ are not playing any useful role—nothing outside is multiplying these terms, all the signs within and without the brackets are equally powerful, and so these too can be safely removed.

Thus we would write $3 + x + y + 2x$ or $3 + 3x + y$.

b) Here the brackets are not necessary as not all terms are being divided by 2. Thus the answer to this would be $4 + 1.5$ or 5.5.

c) As with part **b)** the brackets, possibly helpful to the beginner, are not vital. The answer here would be $3x + 3 - 2x$ or $x + 3$.

d) Here the brackets are vital. Without them the 5 would be multiplying the x alone. With the brackets, the 5 multiplies both the x and the -2, giving $5x - 10 + 4$ and finally $5x - 6$.

Factorisation

So far we have only been concerned with removing brackets. Now we shall perform the opposite manoeuvre: factorisation.

Consider the expression $5x + 10y$.

The numbers 5 and 10 have a common multiple or factor. First, we must understand the term 'multiple'. Consider the numbers 3, 6, 9, 12 ... each of these are multiples of 3, in the sense that they are an integer multiplied by 3. Of course, 0, -3, -6, -9, ... are also multiples of 3. What are the multiples of 5? Clearly these are -15, -10, -5, 0, 5, 10, ..., etc.

In the above expression, we can write $10 = 1 \times 2 \times 5$ and would say that 1, 2, and 5 are factors (or divisors) of 10. That is, a factor of a term is an element which forms part of the product of the term. Notice that trivially we can always state that 1 is a factor of every number, this may seem slightly redundant, but is sometimes necessary. All will be made clear shortly!

Example 3.30

List the factors of:

a) 24   **b)** x **c)** $3x$

d) $6x^2$ **e)** $10x^3$

Solution

a) $24 = 1 \times 24 = 1 \times 2 \times 12 = 1 \times 2 \times 2 \times 6$
$= 1 \times 4 \times 6 = 1 \times 3 \times 8 = 1 \times 2 \times 3 \times 4$
$= 1 \times 2 \times 2 \times 2 \times 3$

We can see that there are many ways of expressing 24 in terms of its factors. The last way is a unique factorisation in terms of prime factors. (A number is prime if the only numbers which divide it are itself and 1. We exclude 1 from the set of primes.) To conclude we would say that the (positive) factors of 24 are 1, 2, 3, 4, 6, 8, 12, 24.

b) $x = 1 \times x$ so the factors of x are 1 and x.

c) $3x = 3 \times x = 1 \times 3 \times x$ and so the factors of $3x$ are 1, 3 and x, and any combination of 'coefficient factor' with the 'variable factor', so for example, $3x$ or $1x$ are also factors.

d) $6x^2 = 1 \times 6 \times x \times x \times x = 1 \times 2 \times 3 \times x \times x$

and so the factors of $6x^2$ are 1, 2, 3, 6, x and x^2, and any combination of the 'coefficient factor' with the 'variable factor', so for example $3x$, $2x$, $3x^2$ or $1x^2$.

Note: We simply take the factors of the coefficient and of the variable.

e) $10x^3$

Firstly we note that the factors of 10 are 1, 2, 5, and 10, and the factors of x^3 are x, x^2 and x^3. Thus the factors of $10x^3$ are 1, 2, 5, 10, x, x^2, x^3 and any combination of the coefficient factors with the variable factors.

Example 3.31

Factorise $15b - 30$

Method

Step 1

We rewrite the expression in terms of factors of each element and then look for common factors to each of the elements. We usually only include 1 being a factor if we need to.

Step 2

We 'pull out' the highest common factor (also called the greatest common divisor), namely a product of the largest coefficient factors and the largest variable factor, and put the remaining terms inside a bracket, together with any signs, all multiplied by the highest common factor.

Solution

Step 1

Thus we have $15b - 10 = 3 \times 5 \times b - 2 \times 5$.

If we circle the terms which are common to both expressions we would have

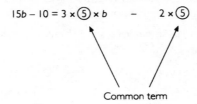

Step 2
We can see that 5 is common to both, so this is the highest common factor (HCF) as here the variable b and 3 are not common to both terms. Thus the HCF is 5, and we can pull this out of each of the terms and put the remaining terms inside a bracket (including any signs), which is multiplied by this HCF.

Thus we arrive at:

$$15b - 10 = 5(3b - 2)$$

We could always check that our factorisation is indeed correct by multiplying out the brackets. If you need convincing, try it!

Example 3.32
Factorise $20mn + 5m^2$

Solution
Step 1

$$20mn + 5m^2 = 4 \times 5 \times m \times n + 5 \times m \times m$$

If we circle the terms which are common to both expressions we would have:

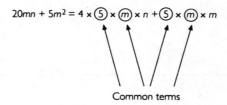

Step 2: The common factors are 5, and m and so the product of these is the HCF, namely $5m$. We pull these out and leave the remaining terms in a bracket:

$$20mn + 5m^2 = 5m(4n + m)$$

Example 3.33
Factorise $3pq + p$

Solution
$$3pq + p = 3 \times p \times q + 1 \times p$$

We see that p is common to both terms, and thus we have:

$$3pq + p = p(3q + 1)$$

Note here that if we had omitted to put the 1 as a factor, the second term would disappear as there would be nothing to write inside the bracket. Here we see that 1 being a hidden factor is vital.

We could have a situation where a whole bracket is a common factor.

Example 3.34

Factorise $9a(a - b) + 3(a - b)^2$

Solution

Rewriting this in terms of its factors gives us:

$$3 \times 3 \times a \times (a - b) + 3 \times (a - b) \times (a - b)$$

We can see that 3 and $(a - b)$ are the common factors and so the HCF is $3(a - b)$. The remaining terms will go into a bracket. Notice that it is often helpful to use square brackets when brackets are nested.

Thus $9a(a - b) + 3(a - b)^2 = 3(a - b)[3a + (a - b)]$

Tidying up inside the square brackets we see that there is a pair of brackets around $a - b$ playing no useful role and so these can be removed to give:

$$\begin{aligned}9a(a - b) + 3(a - b)^2 &= 3(a - b)[3a + a - b] \\ &= 3(a - b)[4a - b]\end{aligned}$$

and now we can use the usual brackets around $4a - b$ to give us:

$$9a(a - b) + 3(a - b)^2 = 3(a - b)(4a - b)$$

Exercises 3.9 _____

Factorise:

3.9.1 $8x + 32xy$

3.9.2 $3x^2 + 27x^4$

3.9.3 $4x(x - y) + 16(x - y)^2$

The basis of all algebraic manipulation rests on the above. Understanding the rules of arithmetic should give you confidence to tackle the rest of the book. Good luck! If you need further practice consult a GCSE book such as A. Greer's *A Complete GCSE Mathematics – Higher Course* (Stanley Thornes Publishers Ltd, 1992). Before we proceed to some applications in later chapters we complete this chapter with an introduction to fractional indices.

Fractional indices

We shall now consider powers which are fractions, or rational numbers. In fact these are familiar faces with a new name. We shall not need to go into great detail and so give only the key points.

Result 1

$$\sqrt{x} = x^{\frac{1}{2}}$$

Proof

The idea here is to find two ways of writing the same thing.

$x = \sqrt{x^2}$ as $\sqrt{}$ is the opposite operation to squaring, and so

$$x = \sqrt{x^2} = \sqrt{x \times x} = \sqrt{x} \times \sqrt{x} \qquad (1)$$

But $x = x^1 = x^{\frac{1}{2}} \times x^{\frac{1}{2}}$ \qquad (2)

by Law 1 of indices.

Now (1) and (2) both represent x and so must be equivalent. Thus we have the result
$\sqrt{x} = x^{\frac{1}{2}}$

Calculator note

We could simply just use the square root button. For example, to find the square root of 9, press $\boxed{\sqrt{}}$ 9. The answer should of course be 3.

Alternatively look at the symbol over $\boxed{x^{-y}}$ and you will see $x\sqrt{}$. This in fact means the xth root. To get this symbol we use the shift button before we push $[x^{-y}]$. So if we want to use this button to find the square root of a number we enter a 2 where the x is. For example finding the square root of 9 would be entered as:

2 $\boxed{\text{shift}}$ $\boxed{x^{-y}}$ 9 $=$

meaning that we have pushed $\boxed{2\sqrt{}}$ where x is 2.

For the following examples the $\boxed{x\sqrt{}}$ button is necessary.

Result 2

$$\sqrt[3]{x} = x^{\frac{1}{3}}$$

Exercise 3.10 _____

Prove result 2 in a similar way to result 1.

Example 3.35

Calculate the cube root of 85.

Solution

We wish to find $\sqrt[3]{85}$ which we know can be written $85^{\frac{1}{3}}$. To enter this on the calculator there are two methods, shown in the Calculator note below.

Result 3

$$\sqrt[n]{x} = x^{\frac{1}{n}}$$

Generally, how do we interpret fractional indices such as $x^{\frac{p}{q}}$?

The diagram below summarises this situation.

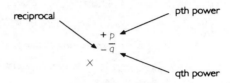

Example 3.36

Interpret the meaning of $x^{-\frac{2}{3}}$

Solution

The first step is to eliminate the negative in the index, so giving a reciprocal:

$$x^{-\frac{2}{3}} = \frac{1}{x^{\frac{2}{3}}} = \frac{1}{\sqrt[3]{x^2}}$$

and so this means the reciprocal of the cube root of the square of x.

Example 3.37

Interpret $x^{\frac{5}{2}}$

Solution

This would simply mean the square root of the fifth power of x, or equally the fifth power of the square root of x, i.e. $\sqrt{x^5}$.

Note: It is not a good style to write $x^{2\frac{1}{2}}$ as this has no direct interpretation.

Exercises 3.11

3.11.1 Interpret the following indices:

    a) $x^{-\frac{3}{2}}$

    b) $x^{\frac{4}{3}}$

3.11.2 Express the following in index form:

a) $\dfrac{1}{\sqrt{x}}$

b) $\sqrt[4]{x^5}$

Summary

You will now have had a chance to test most of the basic mathematical tools you will use and to try out a range of them on some actual business examples. Some of the later skills seem more abstract, but will be vital to later chapters on, for example, regression. These skills will also be important to chapter 5 when we will build further maths skills in the discussion of linear and quadratic equations. The key point is to remember the step-by-step approach which we have used throughout the text.

To complete this chapter we take a brief look at sequences and series which we shall need to calculate loan payments in chapter 6.

Sequences and series

We shall first take a brief look at sequences and then how to sum such sequences as well as a special type of sequence called a geometric progression.

Definition: A *sequence* is a list of items. For example:

Sequence 1: 1, 2, 3, 4, ...

Sequence 2: 1, -1, 1, -1, 1, ...

Sequence 3: 1, $\frac{1}{2}$, $\frac{1}{4}$, $\frac{1}{8}$, $\frac{1}{16}$, ...

Sequence 4: 5, 5.25, 5.5, 5.75, 6, ...

We denote the nth term of a sequence by a_n and usually write $\{a_n\}$ or (a_n) for the sequence whose terms are a_n for $n = 1, 2, 3, \ldots$ i.e. a_1, a_2, a_3, etc. Equally we might start the sequence with $n = 0$ and write a_0, a_1, a_2, a_3, etc. Notice that the n is a counter or counts the terms through the list.

Example 3.38
If the terms of a sequence a_n are defined by $a_n = 5^n$ for all $n \geqslant 0$, find the first 4 terms of this sequence. Hence find the sum of the first 4 terms of this sequence.

Solution
If $a_n = 5^n$ for all $n \geqslant 0$ then putting values for n into this formula gives us the first, second etc. terms of this sequence.

Thus if $n = 0$, we have $a_0 = 5^0$. Now 5^0 is 1, but if this is unclear, using our calculator we have 5 $\boxed{x^{-y}}$ 0 = and this will be 1. Thus the first term, $a_0 = 1$.

Now putting $n = 1$ we have $a_1 = 5^1$, thus the second term is 5, i.e. $a_1 = 5$.

Now if $n = 2$, we have $a_2 = 5^2$, giving us $a_2 = 25$.

Finally putting $n = 3$ we have $a_3 = 5^3$, and using our calculator we arrive at

$5 \boxed{x^y} 3 =$

and this will be 125.

Thus the terms in this sequence listed as a set are:

$\{a_n\} = \{5^0, \ 5^1, \ 5^2, \ 5^3 \ ...\} = \{1, \ 5, \ 25, \ 125 \ ...\}$ which we might call the sequence of ascending powers of 5. We are simply multiplying any term by 5 to arrive at the next term in the list. If we sum the first 4 terms we have sum (4 terms) which we denote by $S_4 = 1 + 5 + 25 + 125 = 156$.

Example 3.39

(i) If $a_n = \dfrac{1}{3^{n-1}}$ list the first 5 terms of the sequence. If S_n denotes the sum of the first n terms, find S_5.

(ii) For each of the four sequences listed above, find a_n.

Solution

(i) Here we have the nth term is $a_n = \dfrac{1}{3^{n-1}}$.

Here we are not given any starting value for n, so we could choose any suitable number, usually $n = 0$ or $n = 1$. We would generally choose a value of n such that a_0 or a_1 was non-zero. Here if we put $n = 1$ we have $a_1 = \dfrac{1}{3^{1-1}}$ which is $\dfrac{1}{3^0}$. Now 3^0 is 1, but again if we used our calculator we would have

$3 \boxed{x^y} 0 =$ and this will be 1. Thus the first term, $a_1 = 1$.

Now putting $n = 2$, we have $a_2 = \dfrac{1}{3^{2-1}} = \dfrac{1}{3^1} = \dfrac{1}{3}$.

Similarly putting $n = 3$ gives $a_3 = \dfrac{1}{3^{3-1}} = \dfrac{1}{3^2} = \dfrac{1}{9}$.

Hence $a_4 = \dfrac{1}{3^{4-1}} = \dfrac{1}{3^3} = \dfrac{1}{27}$ and $a_5 = \dfrac{1}{3^{5-1}} = \dfrac{1}{3^4} = \dfrac{1}{81}$.

Hence $\{a_n\} = \left\{\dfrac{1}{3^0}, \dfrac{1}{3^1}, \dfrac{1}{3^2}, \dfrac{1}{3^3}, \dfrac{1}{3^4}\right\} = \left\{1, \dfrac{1}{3}, \dfrac{1}{9}, \dfrac{1}{27}, \dfrac{1}{81}\right\}$. We can see the pattern is to multiply each term by $\frac{1}{3}$ to get the following term.

and $S_5 = 1 + \frac{1}{3} + \frac{1}{9} + \frac{1}{27} + \frac{1}{81}$ here using our fraction button $\boxed{a\frac{b}{c}}$ this gives us $1\frac{40}{81}$.

[Notice that if we had started the sequence putting $n = 0$ the first terms would have been $a_0 = \dfrac{1}{3^{0-1}} = \dfrac{1}{3^{-1}} = 3$. We can see that this does not quite fit in with our sequence which is in powers of $\frac{1}{3}$ and this is why we chose to start from $n = 1$].

(ii) Sequence 1

1, 2, 3, 4, ... here the first term is 1, the second 2, the third 3, and these are the counting or natural numbers. We can simply write $\{a_n\} = \{n\}$ for $n \geqslant 1$. Notice that here we add 1 to any term to get the successive term.

Sequence 2

1, −1, 1, −1, 1, ...

This sequence is an alternating sequence; its sign alternates between plus and minus. We would write $(-1)^n$ for $n \geqslant 0$ for this sequence. To check this works put $n = 0$, and $a_0 = (-1)^0 = 1$. (We can say this as any value to the power 0 is 1; again if not convinced check using your calculator:

1 $\boxed{\pm}$ $\boxed{x^y}$ 0 =)

Then putting $n = 1$ we have $a_1 = (-1)^1 = -1$.

Similarly $a_2 = (-1)^2 = -1 \times -1 = 1$.

Also $a_3 = (-1)^3 = -1 \times -1 \times -1 = -1$.

We can see that the sign is alternating between plus and minus depending on the power: an even number in the power would give an even number of negative signs which would be a positive. An odd number in the power would give an odd number of negative signs which would leave pairs of minus signs, and 1 remaining sign; overall this would be negative. Thus

$$\{a_n\} = \{(-1)^n\} \quad \text{for } n \geqslant 0.$$

Sequence 3

$$1, \frac{1}{2}, \frac{1}{4}, \frac{1}{8}, \frac{1}{16}, \ldots$$

Here this is a sequence of powers of $\frac{1}{2}$, and as the first term is 1 we see that we have started with $n = 0$. Thus $a_n = \left\{\frac{1}{2^n}\right\} = \left\{\frac{1}{2^0}, \frac{1}{2^1}, \frac{1}{2^2}, \frac{1}{2^3}, \frac{1}{2^4}, \ldots\right\}$. Notice that here we multiply any term by $\frac{1}{2}$ to get the next term in the list. Equally we can divide any term by $\frac{1}{2}$ to get the preceding term.

Sequence 4

5, 5.25, 5.5, 5.75, 6 ...

Here the first term is 5, and the next term is $5 + 0.25$. The following term is $5 + 0.5$ or $5 + 2 \times 0.25$, etc. Notice that we are adding 0.25 to a term to get the next term in the sequence.

We could write this as $a_0 = 5$, $a_1 = 5 + 0.25$, $a_2 = 5 + 2 \times 0.25$, $a_3 = 5 + 3 \times 0.25$, etc. Notice that the term is the sequence of the number of 0.25s we add to 5. Thus we could write $a_n = 5 + n \times 0.25$ or $a_n = 5 + n0.25$.

Geometric progressions

For the above sequences you will have noticed that there is usually a pattern for finding the next term or the nth term in a sequence, and usually this can be deduced from looking at how the term changes as you go along the list in the sequence. In fact some sequences have a special form which allows them to be manipulated easily. Take, for example, the list of powers of $\frac{1}{2}$. This sequence was $a_n =$ $\left\{\frac{1}{2^n}\right\} = \left\{\frac{1}{2^0}, \frac{1}{2^1}, \frac{1}{2^2}, \frac{1}{2^3}, \frac{1}{2^4}, \ldots\right\}$ Notice that if you have any term in this sequence

we simply had to multiply by $\frac{1}{2}$ to get to the next term. We would say that a $\frac{1}{2}$ was the common multiplier (or ratio) for this sequence. With a sequence of this form we need to know the starting term and what the common multiplier is and then the sequence is completely defined—we know the pattern to be able to list the sequence.

For example, if the first term in a sequence is 6 and the common multiplier is $-\frac{1}{4}$ we can list the terms as follows:

$a_0 = 6$

$a_1 = a_0 \times -\frac{1}{4} = 6 \times -\frac{1}{4} = -\frac{3}{2}$

$a_2 = a_1 \times -\frac{1}{4} = -\frac{3}{2} \times -\frac{1}{4} = +\frac{3}{8}$

$a_3 = a_2 \times -\frac{1}{4} = \frac{3}{8} \times -\frac{1}{4} = -\frac{3}{32}$ etc.

The pattern in the sequence is less obvious than some of the other sequences, but if we take two successive terms and divide the later term by the earlier (as in the order of the listing) then we will get the common multiplier. The only prerequisite is that this multiplier is common to any and every pair of terms in the sequence. What would a_n be in this example? Well, looking for the pattern we can see the first term is 6 and it is not multiplied by any $-\frac{1}{4}$, while the second term is multiplied by one $(-\frac{1}{4})$; similarly the third term is multiplied by two $(-\frac{1}{4})$s, the fourth by three $(-\frac{1}{4})$s, and so the nth term must be multiplied by $(n-1)(-\frac{1}{4})$s, that is

$a_n = a_0 \times -\frac{1}{4}(n-1)$

or $a_n = 6 \times -\frac{1}{4}(n-1)$

Definition

A geometric progression (GP for short) is a sequence of terms which has a common ratio between successive terms. Let us denote the first term by a and the common multiplier by r; then

A GP has the form $\{a, ar, ar^2, ar^3, ar^4, ar^5, \ldots, ar^{n-1} \ldots\}$

We can find the sum of any number of terms in the GP using the following formula.

The sum to n terms of a GP is

$$S_n = a\frac{(1-r^n)}{(1-r)}$$

where a is the first term and r is the common multiplier.

Example 3.40

Use the formula to sum the GP where:

 (i) $a = 5$, $r = 5$ and $n = 8$

 (ii) $a = 6$ and $r = -\frac{1}{4}$ and $n = 10$

 (iii) $a = 1$, $r = \frac{1}{2}$ and $n = 15$

Solution

 (i) $a = 5$, $r = 5$ and $n = 8$

Using $S_n = a\dfrac{(1 - r^n)}{(1 - r)}$, with $n = 8$ and $r = 5$ we have

$S_8 = 5 \times \dfrac{(1 - (5)^8)}{(1 - 5)}$. Here the denominator is -4, and the numerator is $1 - 390\,625$. Thus

$S_8 = 5 \times \dfrac{-390\,624}{-4}$ which gives us $5 \times 97\,656 = 488\,280$

 (ii) Here $S_n = a\dfrac{(1 - r^n)}{(1 - r)}$, with $n = 10$ and $r = -0.25$ we have

$S_{10} = 6 \times \dfrac{(1 - (-0.25)^{10})}{(1 - -0.25)}$

The denominator simplifies to $1 + 0.25 = 1.25$. To simplify the numerator we must use a calculator:

0.25 $\boxed{\pm}$ $\boxed{x^{-y}}$ $10 =$ and on the display you will have 9.536743164^{-07} which means $9.536743164 \times 10^{-07}$. Save this value in the memory on the calculator: the Min on this model is in the frame over the $\boxed{MR}$ and so press $\boxed{shift}$ $\boxed{MR}$ and you will seen an m appear on the display to show the memory is being used. This deletes any values previously stored in memory and stores this new value.

Thus our calculation so far is: $S_{10} = 6 \times \dfrac{1 - 9.536743164 \times 10^{-07}}{(1.25)}$

Now to work out the numerator we need to put 1 onto the display, and then to recall the value in the calculator's memory, using $\boxed{MR}$ button, Memory Recall.

That is we press: 1 $\boxed{-}$ $\boxed{MR}$ $=$ which means we are subtracting the value in the memory from 1. This will give us $0.999\,999\,046$. Thus

$S_{10} = 6 \times \dfrac{0.999\,999\,046}{1.25}$

now keeping the value $0.999\,999\,046$ on the display we multiply this by 6 and divide by 1.25 (in any order as they are equally powerful signs). Thus $S_{10} = 4.799\,995\,422$.

(iii) Here $a = 1$, $r = \frac{1}{2}$ and $n = 15$, and using $S_n = a\dfrac{(1 - r^n)}{(1 - r)}$, with $n = 15$ and $r = 0.5$ we have $S_{15} = 1 \times \dfrac{(1 - (0.5)^{15})}{(1 - 0.5)}$. Now evaluating the denominator will give us 0.5. Using our calculator on the numerator we will start with: 0.5 $\boxed{x^y}$ 15 $=$ which will be $3.051\,757\,813^{-05}$ meaning $3.051\,757\,813 \times 10^{-05}$. Thus

$$S_{15} = 1 \times \frac{1 - 3.051\,757\,813 \times 10^{-05}}{0.5}$$

Now to tidy the numerator we store the value on the display $3.051\,757\,813^{-05}$ in the memory ($\boxed{\text{shift}}$ $\boxed{\text{MR}}$). Then press 1 $\boxed{-}$ $\boxed{\text{MR}}$ $=$ which will give us 0.999\,969\,482 and thus $S_{15} = 1 \times \dfrac{0.999\,969\,482}{0.5}$ which will be 1.999\,938\,965

From this last example part (i) we saw that when the common ratio was 5 and there were 8 terms the sum was very large: 488 280. If we were to sum this sequence with a common ratio of 5 indefinitely, we would not get a finite answer; it would grow indefinitely large. For this reason, we restrict to small r values when summing indefinite sequences. Namely, the sum to infinity of a GP is $S_\infty = \dfrac{a}{1 - r}$

Exercises 3.14

3.14.1 Find the nth term in the sequence

(i) $1, 5, 9, 13 \ldots$

(ii) $3, 2.25, 1.5, 0.75, 0, -0.75 \ldots$

(iii) $2, 6, 18, 54, 162 \ldots$

(iv) $2, -\frac{2}{3}, \frac{2}{9}, -\frac{2}{27}, \frac{2}{81} \ldots$

3.14.2 Decide which of the above sequences are geometric progressions, and justify your answer.

3.14.3 For those which are GPs, find the sum to 15 terms.

4   Assessing averages

Objectives

For each of the three types of data:

- Raw data (small number of values)
- Discrete data tabulated with a frequency
- Continuous data (or grouped data) tabulated with a frequency,

the reader should be able to:

- Calculate a central value for a data set—mean, median, mode;
- Calculate a value to measure dispersion or spread within a data set;
- Be able to interpret what the values for central location and dispersion mean for a data set;
- Understand when a particular value for central location is most appropriate.

Measures of central location

Scenario: graduate earnings
A newspaper article appeared in 1996 suggesting that the earnings of a graduate with three years experience in full-time employment could be on average £24 500 per annum. Is it fair to say that this 'average' gives an indication of a student's earning potential? It could be that the majority of graduates did earn close to this figure, but it could be that this average was inflated by a small minority who were earning well above this figure. Another 'average' may give a fairer representation, or a measure of how variable or dispersed the data was: we could be given the variance (or standard deviation).

Data set 4.0: data type 1: raw data (small number of values)

Consider the following data, the earnings of 7 business studies graduates from Southern Town University 6 months after graduating in June 1996:

Graduate 1: £25 000
Graduate 2: £13 000
Graduate 3: £15 000
Graduate 4: £11 000
Graduate 5: £17 000
Graduate 6: £49 000
Graduate 7: £17 000

We shall use this data to find three types of averages, or centres of location, namely the mean, median and mode.

Mathematical language

We generally use some shorthand to denote either the above wage or graduate. It is obviously cumbersome to say graduate 3, or wage 5. Thus we might write $g1$ for graduate 1, $g2$ for graduate 2, etc. Here it is not uncommon to write the 1 and 2 following the g as subscripts, just below the line, as g_1 and g_2. As the number of graduates could be any number we like to have a way of denoting this: we might say g_i for the ith graduate, and so we think of the i as a counter—counting its way through the graduates. We shall often write g_i, where i goes from 1 to 7 to mean g_1, g_2, down to g_7. As we often use x and y to mean a variable in mathematics, we might write x_1 for wage 1, and x_2 for wage 2 etc. Equally we could have used y_1 for graduate 1, or any other character for the graduate. We generally start off by letting the reader know what we mean by any character, x or y, etc. so that there is no confusion. It is also good practice to do so when you are answering problems.

Means, medians and modes

Given a data set, such as the graduate earnings data, we can see there is some degree of variation in the values. It is usually helpful to have some idea of a typical salary, particularly if we had a large number of salaries, so that we can have some under-standing of the whole data set at once. It is useful for comparison of values within a data set or between different data sets. We could take any salary and say this is a typical salary, but as we can see there is a good deal of fluctuation in the salaries, and so we might wonder, how typical is any individual value? To 'objectively' choose a typical salary we look at values which lie centrally within the data set to give us some typical information about the overall data. We now show how to calculate three such measures of centrality and discuss their merits and weaknesses using data set 4.0.

Definition 1: The *arithmetic mean* (or *mean* or *average*) of a set of values is the sum (or weighted sum) of the values divided by the total number of values, usually denoted by $\overline{x}$.

$$\overline{x} = \frac{\text{sum of values}}{\text{total number of items}}$$

To write this mathematically we adopt some shorthand. Each of the values is denoted by x_i (the first item being x_1, the second x_2 and so on as we are allowing for any number of values, the nth term is the last, x_n). Then we need to write: sum all x_i. We use the Greek symbol for S, Σ (pronounced sigma) to denote *sum*. So the top part of the above fraction 'sum all x_i', would be written Σx_i. To be more precise we could say 'sum x_i for $i = 1$, $i = 2$, $i = 3$, ... up to $i = n$, and write

$$\sum_{i=1}^{n} x_i$$

Mathematical notation

$$\bar{x} = \frac{\text{sum of values}}{\text{total number of items}} = \frac{\sum_{i=1}^{n} x_i}{n} \quad \text{or} \quad \frac{\sum x}{n} \quad \text{for short}$$

We now use this in an example.

Example 4.1

Find the average (mean) graduate wage for the data set 4.0 above.

Solution

We could simply say, the average wage $= \dfrac{\text{sum of all the wages}}{\text{number of graduates}}$. Now there are 7 graduates and so the mean is

$$\frac{£25\,000 + £13\,000 + £15\,000 + £11\,000 + £17\,000 + £49\,000 + £17\,000}{7}$$

$$= \frac{£147\,000}{7}$$

giving us £21 000. More formally we could say the mean

$$\bar{x} = \frac{x_1 + x_2 + x_3 + x_4 + x_5 + x_6 + x_7}{7} = \frac{£147\,000}{7}$$

If we want to use the statistical programme on the calculator (any calculator with an SD mode has one) then we would enter the data as shown in the following Calculator note.

Calculator note

Firstly put your calculator in SD mode. To do this on the fx-570 you press the Mode button and on the display appears 4 modes:

COMP	SD	LR	CMPLX
1	2	3	4

Usual computational mode is 1, and this is likely to be the mode you are presently in, so pressing 2 will take you into the statistical mode (SD), standing for standard deviation. In chapter 9 we shall use mode 3, the LR mode, which stands for linear regression.

(On other calculators you may have a mode panel on the top of your calculator, and reading along the list of modes at the top of the calculator:

Mode	.	0	1	2	3	4	5	etc.
Key	SD	DEC	BIN	OCT	HEX	DEG	RAD	

Here we need the stats programme, so press ☐ mode ☐ . ☐, the decimal point.)

You should now see a small SD come up in the middle of your display. Notice the colour coding of the calculator. Brown for the shift keys (such as taking the x root and cube root), and blue frame surrounding brown characters for the stats keys. Once we are in the stats mode, the blue frames now operate. To call up the brown characters within the blue we use the shift button. (If you have a KOUT button then you will also have a black colour coding on keys, and you use the KOUT button to call up values colour coded black.)

Entering the data

Now we need to enter the data one at a time using the 'DATA' button, in blue, written on, but below the M+ button (or xd on some). To enter we press the following:

25 000 ☐ M+ ☐ enters the first salary.

Notice that DATA appears on the display as you press M+.

It is not necessary to clear the display, just enter the next value in the same way.

13 000 ☐ M+ ☐ enters the second salary.

15 000 ☐ M+ ☐ enters the third salary,

and so on. Stop once they are all entered.

If you make a mistake entering the data you will need to clear the stats memory and start again. To do this press ☐ SHIFT ☐ ☐ C ☐ which will operate the frame above the clear button, C, labelled Scl in a blue frame. (This stands for Statistical clear.) We use the shift key as the letters Scl are in brown, which means we need to press the Shift button to use this.

Look at the keys

$\bar{y}$	$y\sigma_n$	$y\sigma_{n-1}$
☐ 4 ☐	☐ 5 ☐	☐ 6 ☐

$\bar{x}$	$x\sigma_n$	$x\sigma_{n-1}$
☐ 1 ☐	☐ 2 ☐	☐ 3 ☐

As we have only entered one set of values, x_i, the frames above 1, 2 and 3 become active. Later, in chapter 9 we shall enter pairs of data and so call them x_i and y_i and so use buttons 4, 5 and 6 as well.

Consider these expressions written in blue frames above the 1, 2 and 3 buttons.

To find the value for $\bar{x}$ we simply press ☐ SHIFT ☐ ☐ 1 ☐.

It is never necessary to press buttons together but rather sequentially, the one followed by the other. As before, this should give us 21 000. Similarly pressing ☐ SHIFT ☐ ☐ 2 ☐ and ☐ 3 ☐ will give us the sample standard deviations, as we shall see later. From our calculator we can also check the *n* value (number of items entered) and the Σ*x* total, namely the sum of all the *x* values entered. To call up these refer to the reference card with your calculator, that is the RCL button followed by a number.

RCL 2 gives Σ*x* which should be 147 000,

RCL 3 gives *n* which should be 7.

We shall use the other RCL functions later in this chapter and in chapter 9.

We should always check the *n* value first as a useful error-detecting tool, as if we have entered the wrong number of items, we will need to start again.

Example 4.2
Recall data set 2.1 from chapter 2:

The following are net monthly line rental charges for mobile phones on the Vodafone and Cellnet networks, in £:

12.47   15.50   11.80   12.80   16.25   10.18

Calculate the mean monthly rental charge.

Solution
We could simply add up all the values and divide by 6. This would give us $\bar{x} = \dfrac{79.00}{6} = £13.17$ to the nearest penny. Alternatively, use the SD mode on the calculator and simply just enter the data. To do this firstly put your calculator in SD mode.

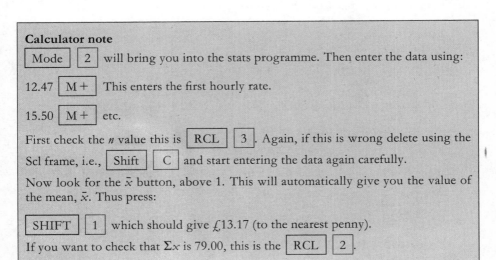

Calculator note

Mode 2 will bring you into the stats programme. Then enter the data using:

12.47 M+ This enters the first hourly rate.

15.50 M+ etc.

First check the *n* value this is RCL 3 . Again, if this is wrong delete using the Scl frame, i.e., Shift C and start entering the data again carefully.

Now look for the $\bar{x}$ button, above 1. This will automatically give you the value of the mean, $\bar{x}$. Thus press:

SHIFT 1 which should give £13.17 (to the nearest penny).

If you want to check that Σ*x* is 79.00, this is the RCL 2 .

There are other 'averages' which we shall move on to now: the median and the mode. Finally we will consider when each average should be used.

Definition 2: The *median* is the middle value in a list of data which has been arranged in ascending (or descending) order.

Example 4.3
Find the median graduate wage for the data set 4.0.

Solution
We firstly arrange the salaries in ascending order:

Graduate 1: £25 000
Graduate 2: £13 000
Graduate 3: £15 000
Graduate 4: £11 000
Graduate 5: £17 000
Graduate 6: £49 000
Graduate 7: £17 000

becomes:

£11 000　£13 000　£15 000　£17 000　£17 000　£25 000　£49 000

If we pair off the data from each end we see that the middle one left is £17 000. Thus the median (or middle) salary is £17 000. How else could we have found this? We could say that the middle value within n items always occurs at the $\dfrac{n+1}{2}$ position provided the items are written in ascending (or descending) order. Here $n = 7$, and $\dfrac{n+1}{2} = \dfrac{7+1}{2} = $ 4th position. The first salary taken in order is £11 000. The second is £13 000, and the fourth is £17 000. Thus the median wage is £17 000.

Example 4.4
Find the median for data set 2.1 from chapter 2.

Solution
Arranging the data in ascending order we have:

10.18　11.80　12.47　12.80　15.50　16.25

We can see that there is no one middle value (as n is even) but we have two middle values: the third and the fourth item: 12.47 and 12.80. We take the average (arithmetic mean) of these two values: $\dfrac{12.47 + 12.80}{2} = \dfrac{25.27}{2} = $ £12.64 to the nearest penny. We can see that this corresponds to taking the average of the third and the fourth item, i.e. the 3.5th item which is the item given by $\dfrac{n+1}{2}$ formula with $n = 6$.

Definition 3: The *mode* is the most frequently occurring value.

Example 4.5
Find the modal graduate wage for the data set 4.0.

Solution

Most salaries occur only once in this data set, but notice that £17 000 occurs twice. Thus this is the most frequently occurring value, and so the mode is £17 000. This data set is called *unimodal* as it has one mode. If the data set had been

£11 000   £13 000   £15 000   £15 000   £17 000   £17 000   £17 000
£25 000   £49 000

then here two values have replications. That is £15 000 and £17 000 are modes and the data is called *bimodal*. We can see that data set 2.1 has no mode as all values occur only once.

Exercises 4.1

4.1.1 The hourly wages of a group of students working part-time were found to be:

£3.50, £2.95, £3.18, £2.40, £4.32. Find the mean hourly wage.

4.1.2 Find the mean, median and mode for the following rates of sterling against the US dollar over a 1-week period:

1.54   1.56   1.60   1.64   1.40   1.54   1.46

Why would you want to calculate an average?

4.1.3 Enter each of the data sets on your calculator, in turn, clearing the programme at the end of the first calculation. Check the values for $\bar{x}$, n, and Σx.

Uses of measures of central tendency

What are their different uses? Consider the graduate earnings, data set 4.0. The mean was £21 000, the median and mode were £17 000. Let's take another look at the data set in order:

£11 000   £13 000   £15 000   £17 000   £17 000   £25 000   £49 000.

To help to understand the values we shall plot them on a number line drawn to scale (that is a dot plot), where the scale is in £1000s:

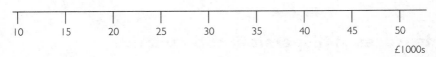

For each salary we draw a dot above the line at approximately the place where it lies. As there are two 17 000s we draw one dot slightly above the other, over the 17 on the line.

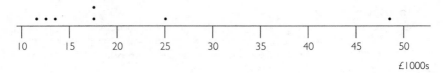

£1000s

As we saw in Chapter 2 such a diagram is called a *dot plot*. We can see that most of the values lie at the lower end of the scale. We can draw lines on for the mean, median and mode:

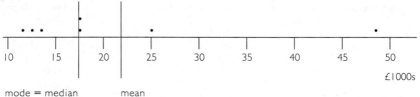

mode = median   mean

£1000s

Which values are more *central* to this data set? The mean, median or mode? Here we would undoubtedly agree that the median and mode were more central and thus better represent that typical salary. To see why the mean does not represent the data set well, notice that 5 values lie to left of it, where as only two lie to the right. It is not as central as the mode or median, but we might like to calculate the mean of a smaller data set excluding the large salary £49 000. This would give us $\dfrac{98\,000}{6}$ which is £16 333 and this is certainly more central than the mean of all 7 salaries. Here the one large salary of £49 000 is considerably larger than the other values and so we might say that the mean is somewhat inflated by its presence.

Definition 4: A data set is called *symmetrical* if the mean, median and mode are all the same value. This would, as its name suggests usually be where an equal number of values were lying on either side of the mean. A data set which is not symmetric may be slightly weighted to one side (as in the data set 4.0 more values were on the left of the mean); we would call it *skewed*. Our data set 4.0 is *positively skewed*, as the value mean–median is positive. We shall return to these ideas later in the book.

Exercise 4.2 _____

Plot the data 2.1 and for all questions in Exercise 4.1 on a dot plot and label the mean, median and mode. Which value is most central? Justify your answer. Is the data symmetrical?

Measures of dispersion: the variance

We now turn from looking at central values to looking at variation within a data set: measures of dispersion. To investigate the most important measure of dispersion (or spread), the variance, we use the following data set:

Data set 4.1

The following are values of sterling against the Deutsche Mark on eight consecutive days in August 1995:

Day 1	2.423	Day 2	2.437
Day 3	2.445	Day 4	2.434
Day 5	2.418	Day 6	2.435
Day 7	2.429	Day 8	2.323

Definition 5: The *variance* of a collection of data is, as its name suggests, a measure of the variability in the data set or how widely dispersed the data is. The variance is an estimate of how far each value of the data set lies away from the mean. Why the mean? This is because when we are taking samples to make inferences about the underlying population, it is known that measuring distances from the mean is a 'good' estimator of the variation within the sample, and so population. The variance is in fact the average squared distance of each value from the mean.

Formula

Take each element of the data set, x_i. If we measure its distance from the mean $\bar{x}$ we would calculate $x_i - \bar{x}$. Some values will be larger than the mean, and so this will be positive, and some will be smaller and so this will be negative. We then square all these values as all we are looking for is a measure of the distance each value lies from the mean (rather than which values are smaller or larger than the mean). Finally we find the average of these squared distances.

Example 4.6

Calculate the mean and variance for data set 4.1.

Solution

$$\bar{x} = \frac{2.423 + 2.437 + 2.445 + 2.434 + 2.418 + 2.435 + 2.429 + 2.323}{8}$$

Thus $\bar{x} = \dfrac{19.344}{8} = 2.418$ DM.

To calculate the variance we put the values in ascending order and in a table:

x_i
2.323
2.418
2.423
2.429
2.434
2.435
2.437
2.445

Now we need to calculate the distance of each point away from the mean, 2.418. We thus calculate for each value in the table $x_i - \bar{x}$ which here is $x_i - 2.418$. These are placed in the table below:

x_i	$x_i - \overline{x}$
2.323	$2.323 - 2.418 = -0.095$
2.418	$2.418 - 2.418 = 0$
2.423	$2.423 - 2.418 = 0.005$
2.429	$2.429 - 2.418 = 0.011$
2.434	$2.434 - 2.418 = 0.016$
2.435	$2.435 - 2.418 = 0.017$
2.437	$2.437 - 2.418 = 0.019$
2.445	$2.445 - 2.418 = 0.027$

The next step is to square each of the values $(x_i - \overline{x})$, and so form $(x_i - \overline{x})^2$. Again we put this into the above table:

x_i	$x_i - \overline{x}$	$(x_i - \overline{x})^2$
2.323	-0.095	$(-0.095)^2 = 0.009025$
2.418	0	$(0)^2 = 0$ etc.
2.423	0.005	0.000025
2.429	0.011	0.000121
2.434	0.016	0.000256
2.435	0.017	0.000289
2.437	0.019	0.000361
2.445	0.027	0.000729

This final column, $(x_i - \overline{x})^2$, we now sum. Using a calculator we have 0.010806. Now we define the variance to be

$$\text{Variance} = \frac{\text{sum of all } (x_i - \overline{x})^2}{n}$$

and so here the variance is $\dfrac{0.010\,806}{8}$ which is 0.00135 to 5 decimal places.

Note: mathematical language

1. In the formula we found the squared distances of each point from the mean, and then we averaged these: we added them up and divided by the total number. How could we write the above formula using mathematical shorthand? Recall that for 'sum of' we use a capital sigma, Σ. Thus a formula for the variance is

$$\text{variance} = \frac{\Sigma(x_i - \overline{x})^2}{n}$$

2. We would use σ^2 (lower case sigma) to denote the population variance and s^2 for the sample variance. As we rarely ever know all the population values normally we are computing s^2.

3. There are shortcuts, for example the numerator of the above can be simplified to $\Sigma x_i^2 - n\bar{x}^2$ and so

$$\text{sample variance} = \frac{\Sigma(x_i - \bar{x})^2}{n} = \frac{\Sigma x_i^2 - n\bar{x}^2}{n}$$

If we place the n under each part of this numerator we can cancel one of the ns to give us a more user-friendly formula:

$$\text{sample variance} = s^2 = \frac{\Sigma(x_1 - \bar{x})^2}{n} = \frac{\Sigma x_i^2}{n} - \bar{x}^2$$

We shall compare these two calculations in the next example. This shortcut is important as it allows us to check our values when using the calculator's SD programme.

4. If we take the square root of the variance, we arrive at s which is called the Standard Deviation. In example 4.6 the standard deviation

$$s = \sqrt{\frac{0.010\,806}{8}} = \sqrt{0.001\,350\,75} = 0.036\,752\,55$$

Use all the figures for the variance, not just 5 decimal places or we will have an inaccurate answer—we will have introduced so called *rounding error*.

We shall discuss the interpretation of the variance after the following example.

Example 4.7
Find the mean, variance and standard deviation of the following data set:

3.21, 3.25, 3.18, 3.29, 3.17, 3.14, 3.23

Solution
First, the mean is:

$$\bar{x} = \frac{3.21 + 3.25 + 3.18 + 3.29 + 3.17 + 3.14 + 3.23}{7} = \frac{22.47}{7} = 3.21$$

To calculate the variance we will use a table, putting the values in ascending order. Again we first compute the column $x_i - \bar{x}$ and then square these values, to form the $(x_i - \bar{x})^2$. This column is then summed.

x_i	$x_i - \bar{x}$	$(x_i - \bar{x})^2$
3.14	$3.14 - 3.21 = -0.07$	0.0049
3.17	$3.17 - 3.21 = -0.04$	0.0016
3.18	$3.18 - 3.21 = -0.03$	0.0009
3.21	$3.21 - 3.21 = 0$	0
3.23	$3.23 - 3.21 = 0.02$	0.0004
3.25	$3.25 - 3.21 = 0.04$	0.0016
3.29	$3.29 - 3.21 = 0.08$	0.0064
Total		0.0158

Thus the sample variance, $s^2 = \dfrac{\Sigma(x_i - \overline{x})^2}{n} = \dfrac{0.0158}{7} = 0.002\,26$ to three significant figures or five decimal places.

The standard deviation, s, is the square root of the variance; here this is $\sqrt{0.002\,26} = 0.0475$ to 4 decimal places; again we use all the decimal places before rooting, to avoid rounding errors.

Remarks

Notice that we could have used the alternative form of the variance

$$s^2 = \frac{\Sigma x_i^2}{n} - \overline{x}^2$$

and so we need to form a column of x_i^2.

x_i	x_i^2
3.14	$(3.14)^2 = 9.8596$
3.17	$(3.17)^2 = 10.0489$
3.18	$(3.18)^2$ etc.
3.21	$(3.21)^2$
3.23	$(3.23)^2$
3.25	$(3.25)^2$
3.29	$(3.29)^2$
Total	72.1445

Thus $s^2 = \dfrac{\sum x_i^2}{n} - \overline{x}^2 = \dfrac{72.1445}{7} - (3.21)^2 = 0.00226$

as we would have hoped for.

The standard deviation, s, is $\sqrt{\text{variance}}$ which is 0.0475 to four decimal places.

Calculator note

Finally as a check, enter the data on your calculator using the SD mode and entering the data as described above:

| mode | | 2 | for SD mode

then 3.14 | M + |

3.17 | M + | etc to enter the data.

Read off n by pressing | RCL | | 3 |. This should be 7.

Next read off the mean $\overline{x}$ by pressing | SHIFT | | 1 |—this should be 3.21. Check also the Σx button (| RCL | | 2 |).

To check the standard deviation, notice that there are two frames for this: $x\sigma_n$ above $\boxed{2}$ and $x\sigma_{n-1}$ above $\boxed{3}$. We shall use the frame $x\sigma_n$ and in the following calculation explain how the other frame is used. The $x\sigma_n$ refers to the standard deviation when we have n on the denominator, and is the sample standard deviation, i.e.:

$$x\sigma_n = \sqrt{\frac{\Sigma(x_i - \bar{x})^2}{n}}$$

Pressing $\boxed{\text{SHIFT}}$ $\boxed{2}$ should give us 0.0475093976. This does indeed agree with our earlier calculation and is a reassuring way of checking that the table does give us the correct standard deviation. If we square the value on the display, we get 0.002257142857 (probably written in standard form as $2.25714\ldots \times 10^{-3}$) which is the variance.

How can we do a further check on the table, or how can we calculate the standard deviation using the above algebraic shortcut? We saw above that

$$x\sigma_n = \sqrt{\frac{\Sigma(x_i - \bar{x})^2}{n}} = \sqrt{\frac{\Sigma x_i^2}{n} - \bar{x}^2}$$

and so if we read off the Σx_i^2 button we can check that this formulation is sound.

To call up the value for Σx_i^2 we use $\boxed{\text{RCL}}$ $\boxed{1}$, which should give us 72.1445. Notice that on the calculator there is no room for the subscript i on the x values. We have the $\bar{x}$ value already, from $\boxed{\text{SHIFT}}$ $\boxed{1}$. Thus

$$x\sigma_n = \sqrt{\frac{\Sigma(x_i - \bar{x})^2}{n}} = 0.004\,750\,939\,7$$

using $\boxed{\text{SHIFT}}$ $\boxed{2}$ and also

$$x\sigma_n = \sqrt{\frac{72.1445}{7} - (3.21)^2} = \sqrt{10.306\,357\,14 - 10.3041} = \sqrt{0.022\,571\,428}$$

$$= 0.047\,509\,396$$

as before, by using the workings given on the calculator.

A better standard deviation

You will sometimes see $n - 1$ in place of n in the denominator of the above sample variance, namely $s_{n-1}^2 = \dfrac{\Sigma(x_i - \bar{x})^2}{n - 1}$. This is so that we have a better statistical estimator. As a standard deviation we would write s_{n-1} and in fact this is denoted by the $x\sigma_{n-1}$ frame above $\boxed{3}$. This standard deviation with $n - 1$ on the denominator is the best estimate of the underlying population standard deviation. We shall now check the calculation of this. On all statistical packages, this is the standard deviation formula which is used, that is, in Minitab and Excel.

Mathematical notation

As we noted above the numerator of this expression, $\Sigma(x_i - \overline{x})^2$, can be written as: $\Sigma x_i^2 - n\overline{x}^2$ and so we can simplify our variance formula to:

$$s_{n-1}^2 = \frac{\Sigma(x_1 - \overline{x})^2}{n-1} = \frac{\Sigma x_i^2 - n\overline{x}}{n-1}$$

As before we take the denominator $n-1$ under both parts of the numerator separately to give us:

$$s_{n-1}^2 = \frac{\Sigma(x_i - \overline{x})^2}{n-1} = \frac{\Sigma x_i^2}{n-1} - \frac{n\overline{x}^2}{n-1}$$

In fact in the following chapters whenever we calculate a standard deviation we shall always use this formula as we shall in general be dealing with a sample and from the sample be estimating the population variance. It is in terms of estimation that s_{n-1}^2 is a better estimator than s_n^2.

Taking the square root of the s_{n-1}^2 value gives us an alternative standard deviation, s_{n-1}. As we tackle more topics we shall see that these two definitions of variance have a role to play, and we will know when to use either. In fact some statisticians might argue that you rarely ever use the definition with n on the denominator and so might even omit to mention it!

Calculating s_{n-1}^2

We have all the values required: n, Σx^2, $\overline{x}$ and xσn-1. These should be:

$n = 7$

$\overline{x} = 3.21$

$\Sigma x^2 = 72.1445,$

and xσn-1 $= 0.051\,316\,014$

$$s_{n-1}^2 = \frac{\Sigma(x_i - \overline{x})^2}{n-1} = \frac{\Sigma x_i^2}{n-1} - \frac{n\overline{x}^2}{n-1}$$

Thus $s_{n-1}^2 = \dfrac{72.1445}{6} - \dfrac{7 \times 3.21^2}{6} = 12.024\,083\,33 - 12.021\,45 = 0.026\,333\,333$

which gives us the population standard deviation, s_{n-1}, of $\sqrt{0.026\,333\,333} = 0.051\,316\,014$ as expected.

How do we interpret the variance or standard deviation?

As its name suggests the variance measures variability within the data, or gives us an indication as to how dispersed or spread out the data is. Here as we have seen we use the mean, $\bar{x}$ to measure our distances from, so the variance or standard deviation gives us an indication of how widely the data varies from the mean. We shall see later in the book that in fact we can say that 68% of the data lies within one standard deviation of the mean, and that 95% of the data lies within 2 standard deviations either side of the mean.

Exercises 4.3

4.3.1 The average hourly wage of 10 cashiers working part-time were found to be: £3.25, £3.05, £2.80, £3.40, £5.20, £3.15, £3.33, £2.76, £2.90, £3.40. Find the mean hourly wage and the variance of the hourly wages. Check these values using your SD programme.

4.3.2 Find the mean, median and mode of the following set of graduate earnings:

£17 500, £16 300, £30 000, £17 000, £32 500, £18 250, £16 300, £22 000, £50 850, £24 300.

Plot the data on a dot plot and label the position of the mean, median and mode. Is the data skewed? Which average represents the data best? Calculate the variance and standard deviation and check these using your SD programme.

4.3.3 Find the mean, median mode and standard deviation of the following data sets:
  (i) 13.24, 23.08, 22.80, 33.40, 25.20, 23.15, 13.33, 22.46.

  (ii) 0.140, 0.113, 0.123, 0.212, 0.289, 0.265, 0.113, 0.123.

4.3.4 Repeat the above exercises using the following formulations of the variance (the unbiased estimate of the population variance):

$$s_{n-1}^2 = \frac{\Sigma(x_i - \bar{x})^2}{n - 1} = \frac{\Sigma x_i^2}{n - 1} - \frac{n\bar{x}^2}{n - 1}$$

4.3.5 Repeat exercise 4.3.4 for data set 4.0 and data set 2.1.

We shall now take a brief look at how to enter small data sets into the statistical package, Minitab. In the case study following this chapter we shall look at this in more detail.

Using Minitab

Example 4.8
Enter data set 4.0 into the Minitab package.

Step 1: Getting into the package
Either open the application by double clicking on the Minitab icon (if using a windows version such as on the Apple Macintosh or a PC). Alternatively if you are using a mainframe version simply log-on in the usual way and at the mainframe prompt ($) type MINITAB.

The package is not case sensitive so you can use upper or lower case. In fact you can simply use the first four characters of any command.

Once in the package a standard worksheet appears (rather like a spreadsheet worksheet if using a windows version). The cells do not appear on the mainframe version but you can imagine these once you have given the commands to enter data.

Step 2: Entering a small data set
Once we are in the package, we read the data as a column, column 1 say. We do this using the command SET (or READ):

```
MTB>  Set c1  (return)
```

We would get the data prompt, Data > and enter each value on a line, each time pressing the return key.

```
Data>  25000 (leave no spaces between the numbers)
Data>  13000
Data>  15000
Data>  11000
Data>  17000
Data>  49000
Data>  17000
Data>  End
MTB>
```

Let's name column 1 'Gradearn' (we are allowed a maximum of 8 characters):

```
MTB>  name c1 'Gradearn'
```

Now we want to check we've entered the data correctly, and so ask it to print column 1.

```
MTB>  print c1
MTB>
```

    Gradearn

25 000   13 000   15 000   11 000   17 000   49 000   17 000

    7 items entered

This would appear on a single line simply because this is easier for the package/ screen set up. We can now go through the processes we have done above, namely the mean, median, and dot plot. (There is no command for mode). The commands are:

```
MTB>  mean c1
```

You would get the result above (21 000)

Repeat for median. The maximum and minimum values can also be found. Thus using the commands: Median Cl, Maximum Cl and Minimum Cl we should have 17 000, 49 000 and 11 000.

For the dot plot:

```
MTB>  plot c1
```

Finally for the standard deviation:

```
MTB>  stdev C1
```

The standard deviation used in this package is the one with $n-1$ in the denominator!

In the case study we shall see how to save and print our Minitab work.

Exercises 4.4

4.4.1 Repeat example 4.8 for data set 4.1.

4.4.2 Enter exercises 4.3.3 and repeat the Minitab example.

Larger data sets

We now look at calculating measures of central tendency and dispersion for larger data sets and in particular in the two cases where the data is tabulated with a frequency:

- discrete data tabulated with a frequency;
- continuous data (or grouped data) tabulated with a frequency.

To this end we need to modify the above formulae for mean and variance to include a frequency.

Example 4.9 data type 2: discrete data tabulated with a frequency
Recall data set 2.2.

The following are the typical number of A-level points required by 36 UK universities for entrance to one particular course, where 10 points are awarded for an A grade, 8 for a B, 6 for a C, 4 for a D and 2 for an E grade:

30	28	26	24	24	24	24	22	22	22	22	22
22	22	20	20	20	20	20	20	20	18	18	18
18	18	18	18	18	16	16	16	16	16	14	14

(Source: *The Times Higher Education Supplement*, May 1995)

Find the mean, mode, median, variance and standard deviation for this data set.

Solution
First we really need to tabulate this. In chapter 2 we tabulated this to give us the following frequency table:

A-level points	Number of universities (requiring this score)
14	2
16	5
18	8
20	7
22	7
24	4
26	1
28	1
30	1
Total	36

Step 1: Mathematical notation

Let x denote the observed A-level score and f denote the frequency for this that is, the number of universities requiring this A-level score). Thus the above columns will now simply have labels x and f. Notice that the sum of the frequency column is 36, which can be written $\sum_{i=1}^{n} f_i$ but for short we write Σf.

Step 2: Sample mean

If we consider precisely what the table tells us we will see that the score 14 occurs twice, and the score 16 occurs 5 times. If we used the above ideas on calculating the mean we would simply add all the A-level scores, i.e. $14 + 14 + 16 + \ldots + 16$ etc., until we had summed all 36 scores. This is fairly tedious and so we use a table to help us: if we form the product of each x by its frequency (i.e. A-level score multiplied by the number of times this occurs) we will see that these totalled will be exactly the same as summing the individual 36 scores. Thus we need a column of $f \times x$, usually written fx. We sum this column and then average this sum over all 36 universities, that is, we define:

$$\overline{x} = \frac{\Sigma fx}{\Sigma f}$$

for discrete data with a frequency.

Our table above becomes:

x	f	fx
14	2	28
16	5	80
18	8	144
20	7	140
22	7	154
24	4	96
26	1	26
28	1	28
30	1	30
Total	$\Sigma f = 36$	$\Sigma fx = 726$

Thus $\bar{x} = \dfrac{\Sigma fx}{\Sigma f} = \dfrac{726}{36} = 20.16666$ or 20.17 to 2 decimal places.

Step 3: Sample variance ($x\sigma$n-1 on the calculator)
Recall that the sample variance can be written

$$s^2 = \frac{\Sigma(x - \bar{x})^2}{n - 1} = \frac{\Sigma x^2 - n\bar{x}^2}{n - 1} \quad \text{for } n \text{ values.}$$

Now we need to rewrite these to include a frequency. The denominator is easy: in place of n we have the total frequency: Σf.

Thus $s^2 = \dfrac{\Sigma(x - \bar{x})^2}{\Sigma f - 1} = \dfrac{\Sigma x^2 - \Sigma f \times \bar{x}^2}{\Sigma f - 1}$

We need to be careful when calculating that there is no ambiguity: the term $\Sigma f \times \bar{x}^2$ could be misread. It means 'sum the frequency and then multiply this by the mean squared'. The mean is not summed over all the frequency: it is thus better to write $\bar{x}^2 \times \Sigma f$. This gives us

$$s^2 = \frac{\Sigma(x - \bar{x})^2}{\Sigma f - 1} = \frac{\Sigma x^2 - \bar{x}^2 \times \Sigma f}{\Sigma f - 1}$$

So far in this formula we know that $\Sigma f = 36$, $\bar{x} = 20.1\dot{6}$. (the dot means recurring), and so $\bar{x}^2 = 406.6944444$. We now need to consider what Σx^2 will become.

Note that $(x_i - \bar{x})^2$ occurs with a frequency and so we have $f_i \times (x_i - \bar{x})^2$ and we sum this over all i. This gives us Σfx^2 in place of Σx^2

$$s^2 = \frac{\Sigma f(x - \bar{x})^2}{\Sigma f - 1} = \frac{\Sigma fx^2 - \bar{x}^2 \times \Sigma f}{\Sigma f - 1}$$

We shall use this latter formula as it is easier to check using the calculator.

This means we need a final column of $f \times x^2$ to complete this calculation. This is most readily found by multiplying the column fx by x. Thus our table above becomes:

x	f	fx	fx²
14	2	28	392
16	5	80	1280
18	8	144	2592
20	7	140	2800
22	7	154	3388
24	4	96	2304
26	1	26	676
28	1	28	784
30	1	30	900
Total	$\Sigma f = 36$	$\Sigma fx = 726$	$\Sigma fx^2 = 15116$

Thus the sample variance is

$$s^2 = \frac{\Sigma fx^2 - \bar{x}^2 \times \Sigma f}{\Sigma f - 1} = \frac{15\,116 - (20.1\dot{6})^2 \times 36}{35}$$

$$= \frac{15\,116 - 14\,641}{35} = \frac{475}{35} = 13.571\,428\,57$$

This gives us a standard deviation of $\sqrt{13.571\,428\,57} = 3.683941988$

Step 4: Using the calculator

Putting the calculator into SD mode (mode 2), we enter the data as before using the data frame (i.e. the M+ button). The only difference here is that we have a frequency and so we simply use the $\boxed{\times}$ button to enter the observed value however many times it occurs. That is:

14 $\boxed{\times}$ 2 $\boxed{\text{M}+}$

This means you are entering 14 in twice.

As before data will appear on the display, and your display will return to the observation, i.e. 14 will be left on the display.

Repeating this we will have:

16 $\boxed{\times}$ 5 $\boxed{\text{M}+}$

18 $\boxed{\times}$ 8 $\boxed{\text{M}+}$

etc., and we can read off the mean using $\boxed{\text{SHIFT}}$ $\boxed{1}$, and standard deviation using $\boxed{\text{SHIFT}}$ $\boxed{3}$. We can check each of the values of Σf (using the n button i.e. $\boxed{\text{RCL}}$ $\boxed{3}$ etc., remembering that the calculator does not mention the frequency in the formula for Σfx etc.).

Step 5: The mode

We can look at the table to see which A-level score occurred most frequently. This will be the modal A-level score for admission. This in fact is 18 points at A-level.

Step 6: The median

We can calculate the median by firstly forming the Cumulative Frequency (CF) as described in Chapter 2. This is formed for each A-level score by writing down the first frequency: 2 for the A-level score of 14 points, and then adding the next frequency 5 to give a cumulative frequency of 7 for the A-level score of 16 points. This would be interpreted as meaning that 7 universities require A-level scores of 16 points or less. In this way we form the table:

x	14	16	18	20	22	24	26	28	30
CF	2	7	15	22	29	33	34	35	36

Notice that in fact this tells us the A-level scores in order: it is a condensed way of writing:

14, 14,   16.16,16, ...   16   18,18
(first item)   (third item)   (7th item)   (8th item) etc.

Thus the median occurs in 36 items listed in order at the middle value, which is

the mean of the 18th and 19th items (the $\dfrac{\Sigma f + 1}{2}$ item which would be the

18.5th item). Now the 18th item must be score of 20 A-level points, and the
19th would also be 20 points, which would clearly average out at 20. Thus the
median A-level score is 20 points.

Example 4.10

Continuous data (or grouped data) tabulated with a frequency: recall data set
2.3. The following table of data shows the amount spent (in £) on library
resources per student by 80 UK universities and colleges of higher education
during 1992/93. This includes spending on books, periodicals and staff per
full-time equivalent student (excluding the building costs):

210	180	204	226	247	272	284	312
248	274	301	314	157	180	207	230
162	184	148	250	275	301	315	363
232	251	275	301	322	383	162	215
185	220	232	256	304	325	428	312
165	191	235	257	276	305	563	613
195	225	237	259	279	330	1040	165
306	326	170	200	225	238	260	280
306	175	200	225	283	311	330	334
178	200	225	244	265	284	359	343

(Source: *The Times Higher Education Supplement*, May 1995)

Find the mean, mode, median, variance and standard deviation for this data
set.

Solution
Step 1: Tabulation
Firstly we really need to tabulate this. In Chapter 2 we tabulated this to give us
the following frequency table:

Class number	Class interval	Frequency
1	$125 < L \leqslant 200$	18
2	$200 < L \leqslant 275$	30
3	$275 < L \leqslant 350$	25
4	$350 < L \leqslant 425$	3
5	$425 < L \leqslant 500$	1
6	$500 < L \leqslant 575$	1
7	$575 < L \leqslant 650$	1
13	$1025 < L \leqslant 1100$	1
Total	$\Sigma f = 80$	

For convenience we omit classes 8–12 with zero frequency.

Step 2: A representative for each class interval

If we consider precisely what the table tells us we will see that there are 18 universities which spend between £125 and £200 per capita on library resources. Similarly there are 30 universities spending between £200 and £275 per capita on library resources. If we look back at the raw data we can see that the observed values are spread out over each interval. Now to be able to calculate the mean and variance we need to have some point to represent each class interval: a value which is typical of the class interval. We can then use this value in all of the above formulae (in example 4.9) to calculate the mean and variance. In fact we choose the mid-point of each class interval to be representative of the class. By this we are saying that the first 18 values occur somewhere between £125 and £200 but we shall assume that they all occur uniformly over the interval and so the mid-point of the interval is a suitable point to consider as a candidate for the whole class.

Step 3: Formula for sample mean

Thus we form a column of mid-points in our table of calculations where x_i denotes the midpoint given by

$$x_i = \frac{\text{UCB} + \text{LCB}}{2} \text{ for the } i\text{th class}$$

as we discussed in Chapter 2, where UCB means (true) Upper Class Boundary, and LCB means (true) Lower Class Boundary.

Thus for the first class, $x_1 = \dfrac{200 + 125}{2} = 162.5$. For the second class we have $x_2 = \dfrac{275 + 200}{2} = 237.5$ etc. As in example 4.9 we can then use the formula, without the subscripts:

$$\text{sample mean} = \overline{x} = \frac{\Sigma fx}{\Sigma f}$$

for grouped data with a frequency where x denotes the mid-point of the class interval.

Step 4: Formula for sample variance ($x\sigma$n-1 on the calculator)

As in Example 4.9 we can then use the formula, without the subscripts:

$$s^2 = \frac{\Sigma f(x - \overline{x})^2}{\Sigma f - 1} = \frac{\Sigma fx^2 - \overline{x}^2 \times \Sigma f}{\Sigma f - 1}$$

for grouped data with a frequency where x denotes the mid-point of the class interval.

As before we shall use this second formulation as it is easier to check on the calculator. To this end we need a column of $f \times x^2$, which can be found by multiplying the fx column by the x column. Thus our table becomes:

Class number	Class interval	Frequency	Mid-point x	fx	fx²
1	$125 < L \leqslant 200$	18	162.5	2925	475 312.5
2	$200 < L \leqslant 275$	30	237.5	7125	1 692 187.5
3	$275 < L \leqslant 350$	25	312.5	7812.5	2 441 406.25
4	$350 < L \leqslant 425$	3	387.5	1162.5	450 468.75
5	$425 < L \leqslant 500$	1	462.5	462.5	213 906.25
6	$500 < L \leqslant 575$	1	537.5	537.5	288 906.25
7	$575 < L \leqslant 650$	1	612.5	612.5	375 156.25
13	$1025 < L \leqslant 1100$	1	1062.5	1062.5	1 128 906.25
Total		$\Sigma f = 80$		$\Sigma fx = 21\,700$	$\Sigma fx^2 = 7\,066\,250$

Step 5: Calculations using the table

$$\text{Sample mean} = \overline{x} = \frac{\Sigma fx}{\Sigma f} = \frac{21\,700}{80} = £271.25$$

Sample variance

$$s^2 = \frac{\Sigma f(x - \overline{x})^2}{\Sigma f - 1} = \frac{\Sigma fx^2 - \overline{x}^2 \times \Sigma F}{\Sigma f - 1} = \frac{7\,066\,250 - (271.25)^2 \times 80}{79}$$

$$= \frac{7\,066\,250 - 5\,886\,125}{79} = \frac{1\,180\,125}{79} = 14\,938.291\,14$$

Thus the standard deviation $= \sqrt{14\,938.291\,14} = 122.222\,302\,1 = £122.22$ to the nearest penny.

Step 6: Using the calculator

We enter the data on the calculator in a similar way to discrete data, using the mid-points and multiplying by the corresponding frequency:

Getting into statistical mode, Mode 2:

Clear the stats programme $\boxed{\text{SHIFT}}$ $\boxed{\text{C}}$ —this is necessary as even if you turn the calculator off; the previous statistical data is still stored in the stats memory.

Enter the data:

162.5 $\boxed{\times}$ 18 $\boxed{\text{M}+}$ 162.5 returns to the display, also DATA appears on display.

237.5 $\boxed{\times}$ 30 $\boxed{\text{M}+}$ 237.5 returns to the display

etc.

Check the totals in the table and check $\overline{x}$ and s (the xσn-1 button)

Step 7: Median, modal class and mode

Median: plot a cumulative frequency graph and read off the x value corresponding to the CF of 50%. (Refer to Chapter 2 for details on how to draw such a graph).

Modal class: this is the class interval with the largest frequency.

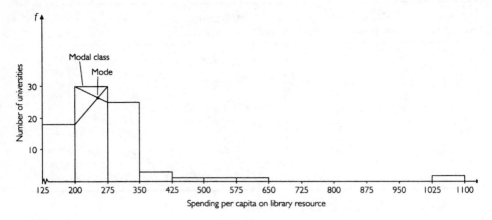

Figure 4.1

Mode: this can be found by plotting the histogram on graph paper and using interpolation. Let M be the modal class. Consider the classes either side of the modal class which we shall denote by class M − 1 and M + 1. On the modal bar two diagonals are drawn: one to connect the LCB corner of class M + 1 to the LCB corner of class M, and one to connect the UCB corner of class M − 1 to the UCB corner of class M. Where these two diagonals meet is the mode. This is shown in figure 4.1.

Exercises 4.5

4.5.1 Compare your answers for the mean and variance in Examples 4.9 and 4.10 by entering the raw data into the statistical programme on your calculator. Check these values by entering the data into a Minitab worksheet.

4.5.2 Calculate the mean, median, mode, variance and standard deviation for each question in Exercises 2.1 from Chapter 2. For some questions you will need to have tabulated the data first.

4.5.3 The following data was given in Example 2.5 in Chapter 2. An educational researcher was investigating the amount of time a typical student spends revising a single topic in business in preparation for a written 30-minute test. 1000 first-year students were selected at random from a British university and were given the topic *Strategic Management Planning* to prepare for a test the following day. They were asked to indicate how long they would spend preparing for this test in minutes. The times they indicated were collated into a grouped frequency table as below:

Time (minutes)	Frequency
under an hour	191
60–69	158
70–79	204
80–89	270
90–99	51
100–119	98
2 hours or more	28
Total	1000

Find the mean, median, modal class and mode. Calculate also the variance and standard deviation.

4.5.5 Repeat question 4.5.1 using the data given in Chapter 2, Exercises 2.6.

Summary

Raw data: no frequency table

$$\overline{x} = \frac{\text{sum of values}}{\text{total number of items}} = \frac{\sum\limits_{i=1}^{n} x_i}{n} \quad \text{or} \quad \frac{\sum x}{n} \quad \text{for short.}$$

Median: $\dfrac{n+1}{2}$ th item in a list of n items.

Mode: most frequently occurring item.

Using the identity $\Sigma(x_i - \overline{x})^2 = \Sigma x_i^2 - n\overline{x}^2$ we can simplify the formula for the variance:

$$\text{sample variance} = s_n^2 = \frac{\Sigma(x_1 - \overline{x})^2}{n} = \frac{\Sigma x_1^2}{n} - \overline{x}^2$$

$$\text{standard deviation} = \sqrt{\text{variance}}$$

$$\text{sample standard deviation} = s_n = \sqrt{\frac{\Sigma(x_i - \overline{x})^2}{n}} = \sqrt{\frac{\Sigma x_i^2}{n} - \overline{x}^2}$$

On the calculator this is denoted by $x\sigma_n$.

A better estimate of the population variance is given by:

$$s_{n-1}^2 = \frac{\Sigma(x_i - \overline{x})^2}{n-1} = \frac{\Sigma x_i^2 - n\overline{x}}{n-1} = \frac{\Sigma x_i^2}{n-1} - \frac{n\overline{x}^2}{n-1}$$

On the calculator this is denoted by $x\sigma_{n-1}$ and is the form of variance used by statistical packages. We shall use this form henceforth.

Discrete data tabulated with a frequency

Sample mean $= \bar{x} = \dfrac{\Sigma fx}{\Sigma f}$ for discrete data with a frequency where x denotes the observed value.

Median: $\dfrac{\Sigma f + 1}{2}$ th item in a list of Σf items.

Mode: Most frequently occurring item (value x where f is the largest)

$$s^2 = \frac{\Sigma f(x - \bar{x})^2}{\Sigma f - 1} = \frac{\Sigma fx^2 - \bar{x}^2 \times \Sigma f}{\Sigma f - 1}$$

for discrete data with a frequency where x denotes the observed value.

Grouped data (or continuous data tabulated with a frequency)

Sample mean $= \bar{x} = \dfrac{\Sigma fx}{\Sigma f}$ for grouped data with a frequency where x denotes the mid-point of the class interval.

Median: plot a cumulative frequency graph and read off the x value corresponding to the CF of 50%.

Modal class: class interval with the largest frequency.

Mode: can be found by plotting the histogram on graph paper and using interpolation. Let M be the modal class. Consider the classes either side of the modal class which we shall denote by class M − 1 and M + 1. On the modal bar two diagonals are drawn: one to connect the LCB corner of class M + 1 to the LCB corner of class M, and one to connect the UCB corner of class M − 1 to the UCB corner of class M. Where these two diagonals meet is the mode.

$$s^2 = \frac{\Sigma f(x - \bar{x})^2}{\Sigma f - 1} = \frac{\Sigma fx^2 - \bar{x}^2 \times \Sigma f}{\Sigma f - 1}$$

for grouped data with a frequency where x denotes the mid-point of the class interval.

Case study: using a computer application—Minitab

Objectives

- Understand how to enter data in a Minitab worksheet;
- Understand how to describe this data using Minitab;
- Understand the beginnings of statistical analysis using Minitab;
- Understand how to draw information and conclusions from this analysis.

Topic of investigation

We are going to investigate the final degree percentage and classification awarded to students taking a BA (Honours) degree in business and finance at a British university in 1996. In particular we are interested in:

- the distribution of marks awarded on this type of degree;
- the average degree percentage and classification for a student;
- the amount of variation in the final degree percentage awarded to students.

We are also interested in trying to draw comparisons with other percentage marks awarded to such students, in particular for their level of literacy and numeracy. For numeracy and literacy we shall ask the same questions as in the list above. In chapter 9 we shall investigate whether there is some relationship between these three marks. For example, we shall ask whether students gaining high degree percentages have correspondingly high marks for literacy and numeracy. In this case study we shall concentrate on how we can use a statistical package, Minitab, to help with this kind of analysis. As you can see, the case study draws on a range of skills developed in earlier chapters. We shall build further Minitab skills later in the book.

The version of Minitab being used here is 9.1.

Data for use in this case study

The following data was obtained from Belgravia University, from 30 students completing their studies in 1996 on the BA (Honours) degree course in business and finance. Tests for literacy and numeracy were devised by the educational research unit attached to the university. These tests were taken by all students at the end of their final examination papers.

Numeracy	Literacy	Final degree %
42	61	59
22	4	21
51	68	56
59	55	74
48	55	49
28	42	27
32	37	68
29	19	43
65	57	73
30	61	51
40	44	47
29	39	42
55	62	79
11	42	30
63	71	73
73	88	88
63	59	67

Continued

Numeracy	Literacy	Final degree %
31	43	48
67	48	45
32	21	47
69	66	70
45	59	57
22	39	55
67	62	11
53	42	63
55	71	73
90	88	63
71	59	31
43	43	67
38	48	32

The following are general guidelines used for classifying degrees:

70% and above	First class honours
60–69%	Upper second class honours
50–59%	Lower second class honours
40–49%	Third class honours
35–39%	Pass—unclassified
Under 35%	Fail—no degree is awarded.

Using Minitab

First we give instructions on how to get into the Minitab package for a mainframe computer—such as VAX/VMS^{TM} system. The basic Minitab commands are almost identical for Apple Macintosh and PC versions. If you are using a Macintosh or PC, your usual commands for opening, saving and printing files will work.

Once you have selected the VAX system (your menu may also allow entry to UNIX or Janet, etc.), you will probably need to enter your user name and your password. A dollar prompt ($) will appear on the screen to inform you that you are in the VAX/VMS operating system.

Now to enter the statistical package Minitab, you type MINITAB (notice that you can use lower or upper case). In fact you only need to type in the first four letters of this. Then the Minitab prompt (MTB>) will come onto the screen.

Now you are ready to enter data. The Minitab package has a very comprehensive Help menu, so you might like to have a look to see what it says. Type Help after the prompt:

MTB>Help (press the Return key)

After some introductory material, you will be asked if you want help on a particular topic. If you type **Y** (Yes) and then the Return key, it will ask you which topic. If you type **N** (No) with a return, it will take you back to the main menu and the Minitab prompt MTB>

Entering the data

As the data is presented in columns, we shall enter it as columns (columns go down, rows go across). For simplicity we will first enter the following five items which we are calling Column 1: these are the numbers 10 to 14.

Column 1
10
11
12
13
14

To enter one column you would type the following commands after your prompt:

MTB>Read C1

This informs the program that you intend to enter one column, called C1. The next line will automatically appear on screen:

Data>

This is expecting you to enter your data. You can enter each value as follows:

Data> 10   (Return)
Data> 11   (Return)
Data> 12   (Return)
Data> 13   (Return)
Data> 14   (Return)

Data>END   (Return)

Typing END shows that you have finished entering the data, and you would be told how many items have been entered: 5 rows read. At the end of each line a return is expected. To check that all the data has been entered properly type:

MTB>Print C1

The program then displays what has been entered. This will print in the sense that the data is displayed on the screen. It will not be sent to the printer!

MTB>Print C1

C1
            10   11   12   13   14

Notice that it is displayed as a single row and there is no confusion as there is only one set of data. This is simply quicker for the package to display on the screen.

Let us now consider how to enter three columns of data. First of all, type the following:

MTB>Read C1,C2,C3

This command tells the package that we are going to enter three columns of data. (You could type Read C1-C3 and it would have the same result.) Notice that this overrides what has previously been called C1, and we do not need to mention this to the program.

The simplest thing here is to enter the data in triples, each triple for a line in the above table, separated by commas or tabs. As before, when we are in entering data mode, we have the data prompt. We use the tab key to separate entries.

```
Data> 41 (Tab)    61 (Tab)    59 (Return)
Data> 22 (Tab)     4 (Tab)    21 (Return)
Data> 51 (Tab)    68 (Tab)    56 (Return)
```

. . . and so on.

After the final row is entered press Return to get the data prompt Data> and type End (and Return). You will be told how many rows have been entered: in this case there are 30. The MTB> prompt returns, waiting for your next instruction. To check that the columns are correct, ask the program to print C1–C3:

```
MTB>Print C1-C3
```

Now you will have four columns printed: Column 0 is the row number that the program inserts, Columns 1, 2 and 3 contain the data we have entered. You will always be given a count of the number of rows:

```
MTB>
```

Row	C1	C2	C3
1	42	61	59
2	22	4	21
3	51	68	56

. . . and so on.

```
30 rows read
MTB>
```

There are many other ways of entering data, for example from spreadsheets or other data files. For example, to enter data from another data file (suppose the file is called Belgravia.dat (the suffix .dat means that it is a data file), type:

```
MTB>Read from 'Belgravia.dat' into C1-C3
```

Another way of doing this is to use a cut and paste command, such as copying the data file, for example in a spreadsheet form. To do this in your spreadsheet, copy the data (⌘ C on the Macintosh) then return to the Minitab package. Ask for three columns in Minitab by typing Read C1-C3 and at the data prompt simply paste (⌘ V on the Macintosh) the data in, typing End at the final data prompt.

Column headings

We can assign names to the columns so that they are more easily recognised. Here we will call Column 1 Numeracy, Column 2 Literacy and Column 3 Final%. The command for this is as follows:

```
MTB>Name C1 'Numeracy', C2 'Literacy', C3 'Final%'
```

If you then repeat the command to print C1–C3, you will see the new column names appear:

```
MTB>Print C1-C3
Row      Numeracy     Literacy     Final%
1           42           61           59
2           22           4            21
3           51           68           56
```

.. and so on.

Now whenever you wish to refer to Column 1 you can just type 'Numeracy'. Here we shall continue to use C1, C2, etc. for convenience.

Saving and printing your Minitab work

We shall be using this data in the following chapters, so we will need to save it and print it out.

An important point about Minitab is that all the data you enter and use at any moment is only saved for that particular screen. Once your data has disappeared over the top of the screen it is lost forever. There are two ways in which you can save your work.

- You can send it all to the printer, using the command paper:

MTB>**Paper**

and when you have finished your calculations, graphs etc., end by:

MTB>**Nopaper**

The worksheets are no longer sent to the printer.

- An alternative, and probably more satisfactory, way is to go through all the exercises to make sure you can use the package, and then to start afresh, and send all your workings to a file with the suffix .LIS, meaning that it is a listings file or list of your exercises.

Using this method, we might decide to use the file name degree.lis (degree listings). The commands are:

MTB>**Outfile** 'degree.lis'

You then enter your data and do all the necessary exercises, graphs, etc., and when you have finished, type:

MTB>**Nooutfile**

A message telling you what file has just been saved will now appear on screen. All the work you do is then sent to the file, which could, of course, be edited and then printed. This file is saved in your space on the VAX. Most workers on a mainframe are allocated a certain quota of storage space, so if you are going to do a great deal of work, you may need to have your disk quota extended.

Data plots: dot plots and histograms

We shall now begin to look at the distribution of marks for each of the three characteristics. Firstly we shall plot a dotplot for each attribute. We simply enter the following commands:

MTB>**Dotplot C1**

We now see three horizontal graphs where each dot represents a single entry of data. This graph broadly resembles a bar chart but with more classes along the horizontal axis.

```
Numeracy

                  .         .   .                    .         .
      .           .     ......    . ....  .  .  .  .  .  .....  .  .           .
   ─────────────────────────────────────────────────────────────────────────
      10          25          40          55          70          85
```

Repeating this for Columns 2 and 3 we type in:

MTB>**Dotplot C2, C3**

and plots similar to the one above are printed on the screen. We can see some detail of the overall shape of the distribution of marks for each of the three characteristics, but the data has not been summarised or collated into a more concise form. A summary of the data into class intervals and a histogram plot would provide us with a more useful tool in this example, as there is quite a large number of items (30) in each column.

Now we shall plot a histogram for each column of data. The command is Histogram C1 for a histogram of Column 1. As we previously noted we could simply use the first four letters of Histogram:

MTB>**Hist C1**

When Minitab is asked to produce a histogram, it will do exactly as you would do by hand: it tabulates the data into suitable class widths. It would then find the mid-point of each class width and plot the histogram against this mid-point. The histogram produced would be a row of asterisks ****** printed horizontally to indicate the number of observations in the class. The following type of histogram would appear on your screen after the command for histogram:

```
Histogram of Numeracy    N = 30

Midpoint      Count

10            *
20            * *
30            * * * * * * *
40            * * * *
50            * * * *
60            * * * * *
70            * * * * * *
80
90            *
```

Exercises 4.6

4.6.1 What do you think are the true class intervals being used?

4.6.2 What is the interval width of each class interval?

4.6.3 Tabulate the data for column 1 by hand to check the above histogram plot.

4.6.4 Why is a histogram preferable to a dot plot in this case?

4.6.5 Comment on the shape of this histogram and what it tells you about the distribution of marks in numeracy.

4.6.6 Plot the histogram for the other columns: for example use:

```
MTB>Hist C1-C3
```

Here we are asking for three separate histograms of columns 1, 2 and 3.

4.6.7 Repeat questions 1 to 5 for columns 2 and 3.

Subcommands

We could use a subcommand to make the package use a particular midpoint and interval. To do this we use a semicolon at the end of the command line when we have asked for a histogram plot.

```
MTB>Hist C1;
```

The next prompt which would appear would be SUBC which stands for subcommand. You would therefore have:

```
MTB>Hist C1;
SUBC>
```

We now need to enter two subcommands: after the initial command for histogram we need to specify the first mid-point and then the interval length of each class width (which needs to be the same for each class interval of the histogram). After you enter each subcommand use a semicolon and press Return until the penultimate subcommand. After the last subcommand there is no need to use a semicolon; Simply press Return and then enter End and you will return to the usual Minitab prompt when the command has been executed. For example:

```
MTB>Hist C1;
SUBC>Start 15;
SUBC>Increment 10
SUBC>END (Return)
```

A new histogram appears with midpoints 15, 25, 35, etc.

If the subcommand routine goes wrong, simply type **Abort** which will cancel the whole subcommand.

Exercises 4.7 _____

4.7.1 What would be the true classes now?

4.7.2 Repeat this for the other columns.

4.7.3 Comment on the shape of each of the histograms and compare the plots.

4.7.4 Use other midpoints and interval widths to plot the histograms for C1–C3. What would be the best mid-points and interval width to use?

4.7.5 Use the command Describe to get a summary of various calculations for each column. For example:

```
MTB>Describe C1
```

You will be given the following values:

```
N (number in the column)
Mean
Median
TRMean (5% trimmed mean)
STDEV (standard deviation)
SEMEAN (standard error of the means, which we
        shall use in Chapter 8)
MIN (minimum value)
MAX (maximum)
Q1 (first quartile)
Q3 (3rd quartile).
```

Any of these commands will work on their own. For example, if we want the median of Column 3, simply type in:

```
MTB>Median C3
```

and you will be given this value. (Notice that the mode is omitted by the package).

4.7.6 Comment on the average mark for each column, and the variation (standard deviation) for each column.

4.7.7 On your printout for each of the histograms, describe each, and plot a horizontal line for the mean of each data set.

4.7.8 Decide how many students were awarded each class of degree and plot a histogram for this.

Leaving Minitab

To leave the Minitab package, type STOP

```
MTB>STOP
```

The dollar prompt will return:

```
$>
```

Now you can print your file degree.lis

Finally, you can log out by typing either logout or lg

```
$>lg
```

A message on the screen will confirm that your session has terminated, and give the time.

5 Mathematical model building

Objectives

- Understand how to build a linear model;
- Understand cost functions, supply and demand;
- Be able to change the subject of an expression;
- Be able to interpret a graph;
- Be able to plot a line and find an equation through 2 points;
- Be able to sketch and shade linear inequalities;
- Be able to plot general non-linear models using Excel and the ChartWizard facility;
- Understand quadratics and their uses in business.

Building linear models

Scenario : organising a party
It is your birthday and you have decided to spend a certain amount on throwing a party. The catering company will charge you per head—for food and drink. There will also be a charge for hiring the hall or band. If you know how much you want to spend in total, how would you work out how many people you could invite? If you wanted to increase this number to say ten more, how much less would you need to spend either per head or for the hall without stretching your budget?

To solve problems such as the above, we need to know how to build and solve equations. We begin this process using the scenario as a starting point. If you invite no-one you will have the cost of the hall or band to pay. Suppose this cost is £250. If you invite 1 person you will have to pay for the hall plus the catering cost for the guest. Most caterers' charges are stated per head; suppose this is £15. The total cost now is the hall plus the catering which is the beginning of an equation:

total cost = hall cost + catering cost.

We now have the basis of a model, a way of describing the cost of the party, although we have to build into it how the cost will very depending on the number of people invited. In mathematical language we would give each of the costs a label, a short-hand. For example we might call the catering cost per head 'c' by taking the first letter of the word and the hall cost 'h', then the total cost of the party might be 'p'. Notice that you could use any character to stand for each of the costs, but by using the first character of each letter it helps you to remember what the character stood for. Thus our equation is written $p = h + c$.

Here replacing the values of h and c by the given figures above, we have $p = £250 + £15$, giving us the party bill of $p = £265$.

If you invite 2 people this bill would increase by another caterer's charge, £15. Thus $p = £265 + £15$, that is, $p = £280$.

How would the equation now look? Mathematically this would be $p = h + c + c$, giving us $p = h + 2c$ for the total bill for inviting two people. We can begin to see the pattern now. If we invite 3 people, the cost of the party would be $p =$ cost of hall + cost of inviting 2 people + the catering cost for 1 extra person. This gives us $p = h + 2c + c$, namely $p = h + 3c$.

Can you see the party bill for inviting an arbitrary number of people?

Well, $p =$ hall cost + caterer's cost $\times$ number of people invited. Written formally using x to denote the number of people invited we have:

$p = h + c \times x$, and we would tidy up this expression to $p = h + cx$.

Party model:
total cost of the party = hall cost + caterer's cost $\times$ number of people invited written as $p = h + cx$.

This would be the general expression for inviting x people to a party where the hall or band cost h and the cost per head for food and drink was c. Here we have 4 unknown quantities: $p, h, c,$ and x. In the above scenario we are given these costs for this particular party and so we could write these into our equation which would give us: $p = 250 + 15 \times x$, or tidying up:

$p = 250 + 15x$

Points to remember when forming models (or equations):

- there is only one equals sign;
- each character has a unique definition, for example c doesn't stand for the cost both of the hall and the catering;
- generally x or y is used as a variable, which measures some attribute which is changing.

General terms

Take the equation: $p = 250 + 15x$

Subject: p is called the *subject* of this equation, since it stands alone on one side.

Side of an equation: the left of an equals sign is called the *left-hand side* of an equation, written LHS for short. Similarly the right side is written RHS.

Variables: there are two unknowns in our equation, p and x. These are the variables in our party bill model as they could be changing, representing the number of people we invite and the total budget.

Coefficients: the value of c (the cost per head) is called the coefficient of x, i.e. 15 is the coefficient of x here. Similarly the coefficients of p is 1, a coefficient of 1 is not usually explicitly written.

Units: the units in the equation are not usually written to avoid unnecessary clutter. However we would always use units when we were calculating any particular values of x or p.

Example 5.1

(i)   How much does it cost to invite 200 people to your party?

(ii) If you have £600 to spend, how many at most can you invite?

Solution

(i) Step 1: Identify the problem

We start with the linear model we have built: $p = 250 + 15x$.

Here we know the value for $x = 200$ people.

Step 2: Do the calculation

Putting this into the equation gives us $p = 250 + 15 \times 200$.

The only unknown in this equation is p and so we can use this equation to calculate p.

This gives us $p = 250 + 3000$ giving us finally that $p = £3250$.

Step 3: Conclude

Thus to conclude, it costs £3250 to invite 200 people to the party.

(ii) Step 1: Identify the problem

The linear model we have built is $p = 250 + 15x$.

We can see that we have a value for p and so putting this into the model

$p = 250 + 15x$ gives us

$600 = 250 + 15x$

Step 2: Solve the problem

We can see that there is only 1 unknown; we can solve the equation to find x. Now x is not yet the subject of the equation, and so we must rearrange the equation to get it into this form. A detailed strategy will be developed as we proceed, but let's taker a close look at our equation $600 = 250 + 15x$.

We need to get the x alone on one side of the equals sign. We could collect up all the money that stands alone onto one side of the equation. This means we could move the 600 to the RHS, or move the 250 to the left. We can not yet move the 15 as it is attached to the x. As we want the x on one side, by default we must want all the other terms, money here, on the other side, and so it is best to move the 250 to the LHS.

If we think of the equals sign as being a pivotal point in the equation, or the balancing point where each side is a scale, we can see that at the start the equation is in equilibrium: it is perfectly balanced. If we move the 250 we would tip the balance and the only way we preserve the status quo is to remove 250 from both sides. It would disappear on the RHS only if it was subtracted. This then is what we shall do:

$600 - 250 = 250 - 250 + 15x$

Tidying gives us: $350 = 15x$.

What does this equation mean? Translating it back into the party bill, this is the catering cost. In fact it says: the cost per head of x number of people at £15 per head comes to £350. How do we find the number of people? Well 1 person costs £15, 2 cost £30, etc. and so we need to know how many times 15 will go into £350. We must therefore divide 350 by 15. Again to preserve this balance in our equation we must divide both sides by 15:

$$\frac{350}{15} = \frac{15x}{15}$$

The RHS becomes x and using our calculator we get 23.3333333 for the LHS. This means $x = 23.3333$.

Step 3: Conclude
Translating this into the given situation tells us that you could invite 23.3 people and stay within your budget of £600. Clearly you would not invite 0.3 of a person; you would either spend under the £600 and invite 23 people, or decide to spend extra and invite 24. The party for 23 people would cost: $250 + 15 \times 23 = £595$. You would therefore go over budget by £10 if you decided to invite another person.

General equations

The simplest type of equation is the one we have already met and is of the form

$$y = mx + c$$

where y is the subject. We would always regard the x and y as variables and m and c would usually be given specific values. We would use the term parameter to describe m and c, meaning they are fixed values for any question, but vary between questions. Such an equation is called a linear equation, which comes from the word line. It is linear as there are no powers to the variables xs and ys. As its name suggests, if we were to draw the expression as a graph, which we shall do later in this chapter, we would get a straight line.

Change of subject of the formula

In the above example we needed to make x the subject. Here we look at this problem of changing the subject in more detail.

Strategy
In order to move terms around the equation, we need some rules—do's and don'ts. Basically we perform the opposite operation to both sides. Later you will realise a shorter way: we do the opposite operation to the side we want the given term moved to. Firstly what is *opposite* or *inverse* operation? Well, we can use the table:

Operation	Opposite operation
+	−
−	+
×	÷
÷	×
square	square root ($\sqrt{}$)
cube	cube-root ($\sqrt[3]{}$)
more advanced $\left\{ \begin{array}{l} \dfrac{dy}{dx} \\ L \end{array} \right.$	$\displaystyle\int y\,dx$ L^{-1}

Example 5.2

If $y = mx + c$, make x the subject.

Method

Basic step

We need to collect all terms involving x on one side, moving everything else to the other side (using 'opposite operation'). We tend to think of this as collecting 'like' terms together.

Does it matter in which order you move terms? Well, if a term has no xs, then you can move these first. If xs are present, you need to leave those all on one side, including their coefficient, m here.

Other steps are given in the next example.

Solution

Method 1: Long way

Step 1: Moving the c term

Using the opposite operation, $+ c$ becomes $- c$ which gives us

$$y - c = mx + c - c$$

Tidying up the cs cancel on the RHS: c has moved, which was the principal aim.

This gives us: $y - c = mx$

Step 2: Move the m

To remove the m we observe that m multiplies the x, and so the opposite operation is to $\div$ both sides by m. Thus

Thus $\dfrac{y - c}{m} = \dfrac{mx}{m}$

We can see that on the RHS we can now cancel the ms, and so they have indeed moved from this side as required. Thus $\dfrac{y - c}{m} = x$

Method 2: Direct way (preferred)

Step 1: Moving the c term

$(-c) \Rightarrow y - c = mx$

Notice that the symbol $\Rightarrow$ means 'it follows that' or 'it implies that'. This is a very useful symbol when moving from one line to another whilst performing some algebraic/numeric change.

Step 2: Moving the m term
Next we move the m

$$(\div m) \Rightarrow \frac{y - c}{m} = x$$

Notice that in the direct way we simply write down the operation—usually brackets in the margin—and then simply move the term to the new side, deleting it from its previous place. This does take practice!

Exercises 5.1 _____

5.1.1 Given the general party model of $p = b + cx$ find an expression for the number of people you can invite to the party in terms of b and c.

5.1.2 Make x the subject in the following:

(i) $3x + 2y + 5 = 0$

(ii) $4x + 7y - 3 = -5x + 6$

(iii) $2y - 7x + 21 = 0$

Example 5.3

Make x the subject in $a = \dfrac{b(x + 1)}{2x - 1}$

The following principles may be helpful:

Method: General order of operations

Step 1: Remove fractions.

Step 2: Remove brackets (if the elements you require are inside these).
Remove roots (again if elements you require are therein).

Step 3: Then repeat the basic step as outlined above.

Solution

We shall firstly use a long method and then display the more concise method.

Method 1: Long method

Step 1: Remove fraction
To remove the fractional part, the $2x - 1$ is dividing and so we multiply by it. Thus we shall need brackets around it. Hence multiplying both sides by $(2x - 1)$ we have:

$$a \times (2x - 1) = \frac{b(x + 1)}{(2x - 1)} \times (2x - 1)$$

Now we can cancel the $(2x - 1)$ on the RHS as this is a common factor on the numerator and the denominator. Thus

$$a(2x - 1) = b(x + 1)$$

Step 2: Remove brackets
Now removing the brackets we have:

$$2ax - a = bx + b$$

Step 3: Collecting up like terms
Collecting the xs to one side (either side here, we will choose the LHS) this means subtracting bx from both sides:

$$2ax - a - bx = bx + b - bx$$

which now cancel the bxs on the RHS to give us: $2ax - a - bx = b$

We now collect the constant terms to the other side (all the as and bs with no xs move to the RHS here) which means moving the $-a$, i.e. adding a to both sides:

$$2ax - a - bx + a = b + a$$

Tidying we have $2ax - bx = a + b$

Step 4: Isolate the x
Now to be able to isolate the x, we will need to factorise the LHS, giving us $x(2a - b) = a + b$

Step 5: Make x the subject
Finally, dividing both sides by the coefficient of x, $(2a - b)$ we arrive at:

$$\frac{x(2a - b)}{(2a - b)} = \frac{a + b}{(2a - b)}$$

we can again cancel the common factor $(2a - b)$ on the LHS to give us

$$x = \frac{a + b}{2a - b}$$

Method 2: Direct method

Step 1: Remove fraction
To remove the fractional part, the $2x - 1$ is dividing and so we multiply by it.

$$\Rightarrow a(2x - 1) = b(x + 1)$$

Step 2: Remove brackets
Now removing the brackets:

$$\Rightarrow 2ax - a = bx + b$$

Step 3: Collecting up like terms
Collecting the xs on LHS and the other terms on the RHS:

$$\Rightarrow 2ax - bx = a + b$$

Step 4: Isolate the x

Factorising the LHS

$$\Rightarrow x(2a - b) = a + b$$

Step 5: Make x the subject

Finally, dividing by $(2a - b)$

$$\Rightarrow x = \frac{a + b}{2a - b}$$

Exercise 5.2 _____

Make x the subject in each of the following (in terms of any of the other terms given in the question):

(i) $3x - 2 + a = 4x - -3x + b$

(ii) $y = 3 - \dfrac{5}{x}$

(iii) $\dfrac{5}{2ax} = \dfrac{a}{16}$ where $a > 0$

(iv) $y = \dfrac{3x}{x - 5}$

Scenario: building models of production costs

Cam UK is a British manufacturer of camcorders. Its production manager has been asked to look at the total cost of production. To see how such a cost function could be built, we first notice that there are two types of costs—fixed costs—the overheads—including such things as rent, rates, utilities and equipment. There are also variable costs—or the unit cost, which is the cost of producing 1 item usually known as a unit. These costs might include labour costs, and component or raw material costs. Combining these costs enables us to build a model for the production of Cam UK's products. Such a model is sometimes referred to as a *cost function*.

Example 5.4

Cam UK's unit cost for 1 camcorder (or variable cost) is made up of labour and component costs. Labour costs are £5.75 per hour and each camcorder takes 4 hours to assemble. The raw materials—components cost £185 for 1 unit of production. If the fixed overheads are £2000 per day, find

(i)   an expression for the total daily production costs;

(ii) the cost of producing 300 camcorders;

(iii) an expression for the quantity made in terms of the total cost.

Solution

(i) Step 1: Unit cost

There are two elements to the unit cost here: labour and components. If we find the unit cost for labour and the unit cost for the components then we can sum these to give the unit cost for 1 camcorder.

Labour costs per unit = cost per hour × number of hours it takes to make a unit = £5.75 × 4. This gives us £23 each.

Components for 1 unit = £185, giving us a unit production cost of £23 + 185 = £208.

Step 2: Total cost function

The total cost, C for q camcorders = unit cost × quantity + overheads.

Hence $C = 208q + 2000$ in £ per day.

Thus a linear model for the daily cost of production is given by:

$C = 208q + 2000$ where q is the number of units of production.

Sometimes we might write $C(q)$ in place of C to show that this cost depends on how many units are produced. Thus $C(q) = 208q + 2000$.

Generally a linear model for a cost function is given by $C(q) = a q + b$ where a is the unit cost, b is the fixed cost and q is the quantity produced.

(ii) If $q = 300$ then the cost of production would be found by replacing q by 300 in the cost function. Thus $C(300) = 208 × 300 + 2000$.

That is, the cost = £62 400 + £2000 = £64 400.

(iii) Making q the subject will give us the quantity made:

$C - 2000 = 208q$

$$\Rightarrow q = \frac{C - 2000}{208}$$

Exercise 5.3 _____

5.3.1 Make x the subject in each of the following:

(i) $3y + 5x - 3 = 8 + 7x - 15$

(ii) $\dfrac{y}{x + 1} = 7$

5.3.2 PC First LTD is a manufacturer of PCs. One of its models takes 15 hours to make and skilled labour is costed at £14 an hour. The raw materials are bought from local suppliers at a cost of £395 per unit of production. If the daily overheads are £450 find a model for the cost of production. By rearranging your equation, find an expression for the unit cost of a PC. Define any variables you use.

5.3.3 You have been asked to organise the Christmas party for your office. A local restaurant charges £15 per head for a vegetarian set meal and £22 per head for a non-vegetarian meal. Find a model for the total cost of this office party depending on the number of people who are vegetarian and non-vegetarian. Define any variables you use.

Solving equations with one unknown

So far we have looked at rearranging equations with several variables in them. In the special case where an equation has only one variable in it and all the other terms are numeric, then to make this variable, usually x, the subject would amount to finding the precise value for x. Under such circumstances we would say we solve for x.

Example 5.5
Thirty items are bought from a stationer. Some items cost 15p whilst others cost 11p. If a total of £3.98 is spent how many of each are purchased?

Solution

Step 1: Mathematical language
We need some notation for the number of items of each type purchased. Let x be the number of items purchased at 15p each. We can see that the total number of items purchased is 30 and so if y items are purchased at 11p each then $x + y$ must total 30. In fact we have $x + y = 30$ and so $y = x - 30$.

Step 2: Total bill
If our total bill in pence is 398p then

total bill = the cost of x items at 15p each + the cost of $(30 - x)$ items at 11p each. This gives us

$$398 = x \times 15 + (30 - x) \times 11$$

This would tidy up to give

$$398 = 15x + 11(30 - x)$$

In fact this would be a linear model for this scenario.

Step 3: Make x the subject
Rearranging this expression we first need to remove the brackets. Thus $398 = 15x + 11 \times 30 - 11 \times x$

$\Rightarrow 398 = 15x + 330 - 11x$
$\Rightarrow 398 = 4x + 330$ (collecting up the xs)
$\Rightarrow 398 - 330 = 4x$ (subtracting 330)
$\Rightarrow 68 = 4x$ (dividing by 4)
$\Rightarrow x = \frac{68}{4} = 17$

Step 4: Conclusion
Thus if $x = 17$, then 17 items at 15p each would be purchased together with $30 - x = 30 - 17 = 13$ items at 11p each.

Example 5.6
Solve for x where (i) $\sqrt{x} = 5$;   (ii) $x^2 = 25$.

Solution

(i) Step 1: Opposite operation

Here we need to do the opposite operation to both sides. The opposite of a square root is to raise to the power 2. Thus we must square both sides, and this will eliminate the root from the left-hand side.

This is written

$(\sqrt{x})^2 = 5^2$

Step 2: Tidy the expression

This reduces to $x = 25$.

(ii) Step 1: Opposite operation

Well we would again perform the opposite operation to both sides. The opposite of squaring is square rooting. Thus we would arrive at

$\sqrt{x^2} = \sqrt{25}$

Step 2: Tidy the expression

This would give us $x = \sqrt{25}$.

Step 3: Check signs if roots are used

Note that the square root of 25 is 5. Thus $x = 5$. But hold on there! If we start off with $+5$ and square it we indeed arrive at 25. But if we also start off with -5 and square this we also get 25. Clearly squaring a term ignores the sign of the term, so when we square root we must take into account that the answer could have either sign.

We should therefore always write a plus and minus when we have rooted:

$\sqrt{x^2} = \pm \sqrt{25}$

Would it matter which side of the equation we wrote the $\pm$? No, either side, but as we are finding x, it makes sense to put it on the side where the answer will be. Thus $x = \pm 5$, or $x = +5$, and $x = -5$.

Exercises 5.4 _____

5.4.1 Solve for x in the following equations:

(i) $3x + 2 - 5x - 1 = -3 + x$

(ii) $\sqrt{x} = 6$

(iii) $x^2 = 9$

5.4.2 Solve for x where $\dfrac{3p + 2q}{2x} = 3 + p - q$ given that $p = 2$, and $q = 7$.

5.4.3 Solve for a when $\frac{1}{3}(a + 2) - \frac{1}{4}(a - 3) = 1$.

5.4.4 Solve the equation for $\dfrac{5x + 3}{2x - 1} = \dfrac{16}{3}$.

5.4.5 Make x the subject in each of the following: (in terms of any of the other terms given in the question), solve for x where appropriate:

(i) $y = 4 - \dfrac{5}{3x - 1}$

(ii) $y = x^2$

(iii) $x^{2/3} = \frac{125}{16}$ where $a > 0$

(Hint: the opposite raising to the power $\dfrac{a}{b}$ is to raise to the power $\dfrac{b}{a}$. Why is this so? Explain using Law III of indices.)

5.4.6 The unit cost for a product involves labour and raw material costs. Labour costs are £4.80 per hour and each unit takes 4.5 hours to make. Raw materials (wood) costs £8.50 per kilogram (kg) and each unit takes 4 kg of wood. The overheads for production are £900 per week. Find an expression for the total cost of production.

5.4.7 A candidate running for parliament has a certain budget for launching a publicity campaign. The overheads of running the campaign office are £220 per week, and the cost of publicity material is £0.45 per leaflet. If the campaign lasts three weeks and the candidate has a total budget of £2500, how many leaflets could be produced? If her ward has 5000 people, does she run short of funds?

Linear models in business

Scenario: The supply and demand of labour to the market
We shall consider that the wage paid for any particular grade of job is dependent on the number of people available or skilled to undertake that job. In so doing we can plot the changes in salaries depending on the scarcity or surplus of suitably qualified people. There are two viewpoints to consider: the employer's perspective and the employees' perspective. The employer generates jobs and so is able to demand certain grades of workers at certain salaries. From the employees' perspective, they are supplying the market place with labour, and during recessions unemployment may be high or during a boom employment may be high. Accordingly if there is a surplus of workforce, wages will be constrained. There are a great many factors affecting both the supply and demand of labour, including the make-up of the underlying population, government and trade union policies as well as levels of training and education. We shall look at various simple models and their graphs which describe these situations.

Linear equations represented graphically

We have two axes—the horizontal, usually called the x-axis, and the vertical, usually called the y-axis. In setting up our axes we are indicating that the vertical axis depends on the horizontal. In our supply and demand of labour we would plot the wage on the y-

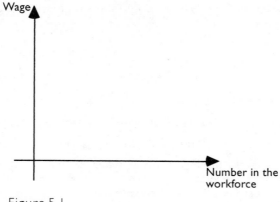

Figure 5.1

axis and the number in the labour force on the *x*-axis. In so doing we are saying that the wage paid to staff will depend on the number of people seeking such posts (figure 5.1).

We outline how both equations come about and then discuss their interaction.

The supply of labour

What happens if there is a minimum wage? All wages must be above this minimum which would be a cut-off point. This would say that irrespective of the number in the labour force available for such work, the wage had to be at least this. In fact it would be a horizontal line (figure 5.2). This would be indicating that there was a precondition to labour entering the labour place—there is a constraint to the supply of labour.

This situation would be modelled by the equation: wage = minimum wage, or using w for wage, and if the minimum wage was £200 per week for a certain trade, then $w = 200$ would be the equation (figure 5.3).

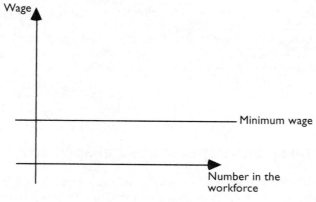

Figure 5.2

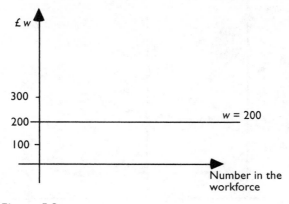

Figure 5.3

What happens if for a certain skilled workforce the number of people entering the workforce is equal to the number of people leaving? This would indicate that irrespective of the wages involved the size of the workforce did not expand. If the wage can be any value but the number in the workforce is fixed, this would be a vertical line on our graph (figure 5.4).

This would be modelled by: number in labour force = fixed value. If n denotes the number in the workforce in thousands, and suppose the fixed size of the workforce was 3000, then this situation would be modelled by the equation: $n = 3$. Note that because the unit for labour force is already in thousands; when we write the model we put the number of the workforce in thousands into the equation, that is, 3 here rather than 3000, see figure 5.5.

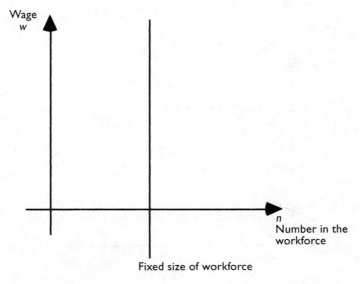

Figure 5.4

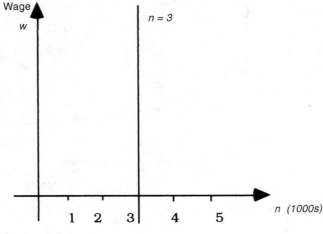

Figure 5.5

In general the supply equation for a particular occupation would be a line inclined to the axes. Generally as the supply of labour to the workforce increased, the respective wage would also increase (up to a certain point). The higher the wage, the greater the number of employees that will aspire to this salary. This would be a line pointing up, as shown in figure 5.6.

We would say that the steepness of this graph was positive as it is pointing up. It would be modelled by an equation of the form:

$aw + bn = c$

where a, b and c are constants. We can always rearrange this equation to make w the subject:

$aw = c - bn$

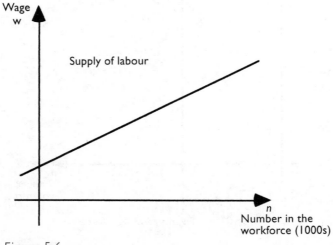

Figure 5.6

and

$$w = \frac{c - bn}{a}$$

That is $w = -\frac{b}{a}n + \frac{c}{a}$ (figure 5.7).

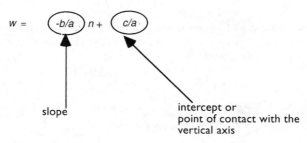

Figure 5.7

As we know the slope is positive, the value $\frac{b}{a}$ must also be negative in order that $-\frac{b}{a}$ is positive.

The demand for labour

In general the demand equation for a particular occupation would be a line inclined to the axes. Generally as the demand for labour to the workforce decreased, the respective wage would also increase: the rarer the worker the greater the value. This would be a line pointing down as in figure 5.8.

Again it would have the same type of model as for the supply equation, but its slope would be negative as it is sloping down.

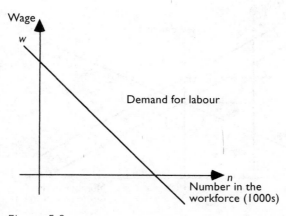

Figure 5.8

How does the supply and demand for labour interact?

First we can see there would be a balance between the two perspectives in terms of salary. The employer would not pay an indefinitely large salary and the supply of labour would not increase indefinitely. There would be a balance between what the employer would be prepared to pay and how much of an incentive this was to the workforce. There is a compromise wage: the wage at which the employer is prepared to employ this number of people, and this is exactly the wage that this number of the labour force are prepared to accept in this particular occupation and economic circumstances (figure 5.9).

Notice that if the supply of labour is fixed and the demand for labour increased, such as when there are changes in the economy, we can see that the demand equation would move to the right as in figure 5.10.

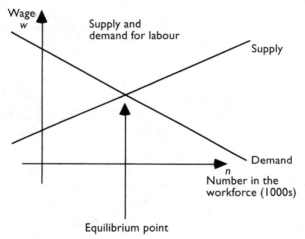

Figure 5.9

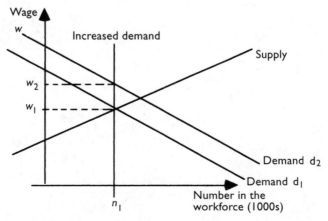

Figure 5.10

This would indicate that the wage an employer would be prepared to pay to maintain the workforce would be higher. In times of economic boom we can see that in order to retain its skilled workforce, employers would need to increase incentives to stop staff being head-hunted. The wage for this size of workforce n_1 would increase from wage 1 (w_1) to wage 2 (w_2).

An analogous set of circumstances would occur if the supply of labour increased.

The mathematics of linear models

Definition: A *linear* expression is one of the general form $y = mx + c$ where m and c are constants and y and x are variables. Note: y and x could be given other labels, as we have seen above, for example, in terms of wages, w, and labour size, n, this would be $w = mn + c$ which is a linear model where w and n are the variables. A linear graph is a straight line where m represents the gradient or slope, and the c represents the intercept, or point of contact with the y-axis.

The term gradient could be interpreted as the number of units ascended or descended for one unit moved in the horizontal direction. Clearly a gradient is positive if, as you move horizontally, you ascend, and negative if you descend. Any point on the line has an x and y coordinate, written as an ordered pair, (x, y).

Example 5.6
If $3x + 2y - 4 = 0$, find the gradient and intercept, and sketch this line.

Solution

Step 1: We first make y the subject
$\Rightarrow 3x + 2y = 4$ (adding 4)
$\Rightarrow 2y = 4 - 3x$ (subtracting $3x$)
$\Rightarrow 2y = -3x + 4$ (writing in standard form)
Thus $y = \dfrac{-3}{2}x + 2$ (dividing by 2)

Step 2: Read off the gradient and intercept
If $y = -\frac{3}{2}x + 2$ then the gradient $m = -3/2$ and the intercept $c = 2$. Thus the graph cuts the y-axis at $y = 2$ and so by default $x = 0$ here.

Step 3: Sketching a line
To sketch this line, we simply need to find two points which lie on it, as there is a unique line through any pair of points. We could choose two x values and use the equation to calculate the corresponding y values, or vice-versa.

As we already know the intercept, this gives us one point immediately: $x = 0$ and $y = 2$, that is, $(0,2)$.

Choose any x value. We will take $x = 2$, and find y.

If $x = 2$, then $y = -\frac{3}{2} \times 2 + 2 = -1$.

Hence two points are: $(0, 2)$ and $(2, -1)$.

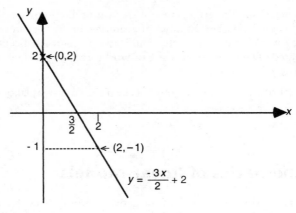

Figure 5.11

Step 4: Join the two points

Notice that if we sketch such a line, we do not need necessarily to use graph paper, unless specifically asked to. A sketch simply means a freehand diagram with any points of contact with the x and y axes clearly labelled (figure 5.11).

Special cases: horizontal and vertical lines

What happens in the case $m = 0$? We would have $y = c$, a constant. For example, $y = 1$. Any point on this line would be an arbitrary x value and a y value of 1. This would describe a horizontal line (figure 5.12).

From this we can easily see that we could equally call the x-axis the line $y = 0$. Notice that any such line $y = c$ has a zero gradient: for one unit along you do not go up or down. What happens if there is no y present in the equation? For example, $x = 5$. Here any point on the line would have an x value of 5 and an arbitrary y value. This would give us a vertical line (figure 5.13).

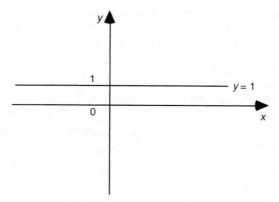

Figure 5.12

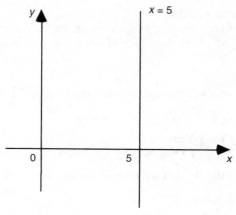

Figure 5.13

It is natural to ask what the gradient of such a line would be. We tend to think of it having an infinite gradient. Consider being at a point on the line. If we move one unit along from this we would not remain on the line. So without moving horizontally, we continue to go up indefinitely.

Notice that to draw a line we found two points which lay on the line. A natural question is to ask 'what would be the linear model through two known points?' For example if we know two wages and the number of staff with these wages, could we find a linear model to represent this situation?

Finding the linear model through two known points

Given two points we have a unique line through these points. We now show how the equation of such a line can be found.

Method

Step 1: Identify the two points, A and B
Suppose we call their coordinates $A = (x_1, y_1)$ and $B = (x_2, y_2)$.

Step 2: Identify the linear model: here $y = mx + c$.

Step 3: Find the gradient
To find the gradient we use

$$m = \frac{y_1 - y_2}{x_1 - x_2}$$

Step 4: Find the intercept
To find the intercept, we use $y = mx + c$ with the value of m now known (step 3), replacing x and y with the values of one of the points, either A or B (from step 1).

Example 5.7
Find the equation given that two points lying on it are $(1, 1)$ and $(-3, 4)$

Solution

Step 1: Identify the points
Let $A = (1, 1) = (x_1, y_1)$ and $B = (-3, 4) = (x_2, y_2)$

Step 2: Identify the linear model: here $y = mx + c$.

Step 3: Find the gradient
$$m = \frac{y_1 - y_2}{x_1 - x_2} = \frac{1 - 4}{1 - -3} = -\frac{3}{4}$$

Thus

$$y = -\tfrac{3}{4}x + c \tag{*}$$

Step 4: Find the intercept
Using $(1, 1)$ to find c we put $x = 1$ and $y = 1$ into eqn (*)
$$\Rightarrow 1 = -\tfrac{3}{4} \times 1 + c$$
$$\Rightarrow 1 = -\tfrac{3}{4} + c$$

Making c the subject we arive at $c = \tfrac{7}{4}$. Hence the equation of the line is $y = -\tfrac{3}{4}x + \tfrac{7}{4}$.

In this form we can read off the gradient and intercept: the gradient is $-\tfrac{3}{4}$ and the intercept is at $y = \tfrac{7}{4}$. Alternatively we might tidy up the equation of the line—using principles of basic algebra and remove the fractions. To do this we need to multiply each term in the equation by 4, so arriving at $4y + 3x - 7 = 0$.

Example 5.8: Application to cost functions
A printer produces leaflets for a course from camera-ready-copies. Find the cost function for the production of leaflets given that it costs £480 to print 100 leaflets and £960 to print 500 leaflets.

Solution

Step 1: Identify the two points
For this problem points are not in the form (x, y) but are in the form $(q, C(q))$.

Here we have $C(100) = £480$ which would mean if the quantity $q = 100$, then the cost is £480. Thus a point in the form $(q, C(q)) = (100, 480)$. We might write $(q_1, C(q_1)) = (100, 480)$.

Similarly $C(500) = £960$ which would mean if the quantity $q = 500$, then the cost is £960. Thus a point in the form $(q_2, C(q_2)) = (500, 960)$. Thus Let $A = (100, 480)$ and $B = (500, 960)$.

Notice that it is simpler to drop the units during the workings.

Step 2: Identify the linear model
Recall that in example 5.4 the linear model for a cost function was given by
$C(q) = $ unit cost $\times q + $ overheads, or

$$C(q) = aq + b$$

where a is the unit cost (ie the gradient) and b is the fixed cost (ie the intercept).
Thus we need to find a and b.

Step 3: Find the gradient
This is denoted by a in our model:

$$a = \frac{y_1 - y_2}{x_1 - x_2} = \frac{C(q_1) - C(q_2)}{q_1 - q_2} = \frac{480 - 960}{100 - 500} = \frac{-480}{-400} = 1.2$$

Thus the gradient is 1.2 or in pounds, £1.20, which is also the unit cost.

Thus $a = 1.2$ or £1.20 is the gradient of the cost function. This gives us a cost
function of $C(q) = 1.2q + b$

Step 4: Find the intercept
This is labelled b in our model. Using one of the points, say (100, 480) to find b
we have:

$480 = 1.2 \times 100 + b$ and rearranging to make b the subject we arrive at
$b = 360$.

Hence the equation of the cost function is

$$C(q) = 1.2q + 360$$

where all units are in £.

Exercises 5.5

5.5.1 State the gradient and intercept of the following lines and sketch them:

(i) $y = 2x - 5$

(ii) $3x - 2y + 8 = 0$

(iii) $y = -2$

(iv) $x = -1$

5.5.2 Find the equation of the line through each of the following pairs of points:

(i) $(1, -1)$ and $(-\frac{3}{5}, 3)$

(ii) $(11, 1)$ and $(7, 2)$

5.5.3 If the supply equation has two known points: wage $=$ £300 when labour $= 3000$,
and wage $=$ £450 when labour $= 5000$, sketch the supply equation using graph
paper. If the demand equation has two known points, wage $=$ £500 when
labour $= 3000$, and wage $=$ £200 when labour $= 5000$, sketch this on the same

axes as the supply equation. From your graph read off the equilibrium point and describe what it means.

This is known as solving equations simultaneously.

5.5.4 Sketch the lines in question 5.5.2 and graphically find where these two lines meet, or intersect. There are algebraic methods (not discussed here).

5.5.5 The cost of producing promotional leaflets for the Ideal Home Exhibition at Olympia is £1285 for 200 leaflets and £2535 for 450 leaflets. Find the linear cost model for this production and determine how many can be produced for £6000. Sketch the graph of this cost function (q is placed on the horizontal axis and $C(q)$ is placed on the vertical axis).

Linear inequalities

We shall only need to deal with linear inequalities, that is, expressions of the form $ax + by \leqslant c$ or $ax + by \geqslant c$. For inequalities involving general polynomials, see a standard A-level text. How do we interpret an inequality sign? Well, in fact there are two inequality signs, $\leqslant$ and $<$. The former is read 'less than or equal to' and the latter 'strictly less than'. For example, $1 \leqslant 1$ but $1 < 2$. Notice that the tip of the inequality points to the smaller object. We could equally write either of the above examples with the inequality facing the other way and interchanging the terms: $1 \geqslant 1$ and $2 > 1$. Generally we treat inequalities in the same way as equalities (and so apply all the tools mentioned in the above section) with one exception.

Inequality rule

If we multiply or divide by a negative value, we reverse the inequality.

Example 5.9
Sketch the area in the x–y plane satisfied by the inequality $x \leqslant 3$.

Solution

Step 1: Sketch the corresponding line
We first sketch the line $x = 3$ given in figure 5.14.

Step 2: Use a test point
We now decide which side of the line satisfies the inequality by taking a test point, usually the origin $(0, 0)$. We see that at our test point $(0, 0)$, $x = 0$ and putting this into our line give us $0 \leqslant 3$. Thus the origin lies in the required region and the area required is to the left of the line (figure 5.15).

Example 5.10
Sketch the area in the x–y plane satisfied by the inequality $2x + y > 1$.

Solution

Step 1: Sketch the corresponding line
Again we sketch the line representing this inequality, replacing the inequality with an equality. That is, $2x + y = 1$.

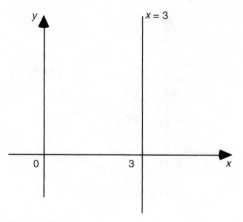

Figure 5.14

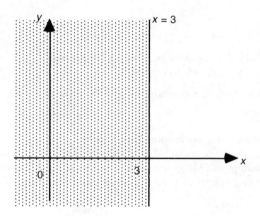

Figure 5.15

To sketch the line, choose two x-values. We choose $x = 0$ and $x = 2$. Thus we arrive at $(0, 1)$ and $(2, -3)$.

When we sketch the line in this example, we will use a broken line as points on the line do not satisfy $2x + y > 1$.

Step 2: Use a test point
Using a test point of $(0, 0)$ we see that $0 \not> 1$ and so we shade the area to the right of the line (figure 5.16).

Example 5.11
Solve the inequality

$-3x + 2 \leqslant -x + 1 - 2y$, and sketch the required region in the x–y plane.

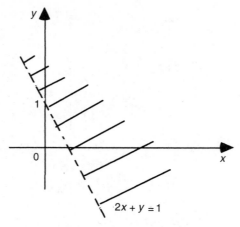

Figure 5.16

Solution

Step 1: Tidy the inequality (collect like terms)
Collecting up terms we have:

$-2x + 1 \leqslant -2y$ and dividing by -2 we have to reverse the inequality:

$x - \frac{1}{2} \geq y$.

Step 2: Sketch the corresponding line
Sketching the line $x - 1/2 = y$, we use $x = 0$ and $x = 2$ and find the corresponding y. This gives us two points $(0, -1/2)$ and $(2, 3/2)$ and so we join these two points to give us the required line (figure 5.17).

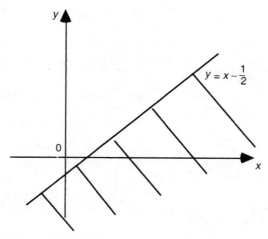

Figure 5.17

Step 3: Take a test point
Taking $(0, 0)$ as a test point, we see that $-1/2 \not\geq 0$ and so we shade to the right of the line.

Exercises 5.6

5.6.1 Sketch the area in the x–y plane satisfied by each of the following inequalities:

(i) $x \geq -2$

(ii) $y \leq 3$

(iii) $2x + 5y \geq 0$

(iv) $8x - 2y < 13$

(v) $-3 < x < 1$

5.6.2 Shade area is contained within the following bounds:

$$x \geq 0, \quad y \geq 0, \quad x + y \leq 1, \quad 2y - x \leq 1.$$

5.6.3 Shade the area contained within the bounds

$$x \geq 0, \quad y \geq 0, \quad 3x + 2y \leq 60, \quad 12y + 5x \leq 250.$$

5.6.4 Shade the area contained by the lines:

$$x \geq 0, \quad y \geq 0, \quad x + 2y \leq 6, \quad 2x + y \leq 12, \quad -x + y \leq 1, \quad y \leq 2.$$

Other mathematical models

Scenario: the state of play in the economy
Inflation is still rising, but steadily: unemployment is soaring; confidence in the economy is declining. How would we depict such situations graphically? What model would be appropriate? Similarly, a company's production costs are usually linear for a small number of batches, but as the number of batches increases it gets slightly cheaper to make each batch and so the costs increase at a slower rate than for the initial batches. Similarly for selling prices (that is, demand functions) discounts are offered on the larger the number of items purchased. Such models are unlikely to be simple linear models. These and many other situations gives rise to more complex models than the linear ones expressed so far. We briefly indicate the suitable type of model for each of these situations and plot these using Excel. We shall then go on to discuss one model in greater detail.

The exponential model: unemployment is soaring

As time goes by, the number of people supplied to the workforce increases rapidly. Similarly population growth in third world countries tends to rise rapidly, or exponentially. A graph for this model is shown in figure 5.18.

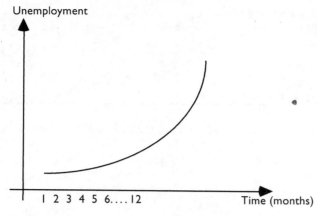

Figure 5.18

Mathematically we would say this would be of the form $y = e^x$, or $y = a^x$ for some constant a. Here the variables y would denote the number unemployed at a time x in months/years (from a particular year). This is an *exponential model* with e a special number between 2 and 3. (To find e on your calculator look at the e^x button and press this $\boxed{e^x}$ followed by 1 = which will be 2.7182818 . . . This is the exponential function programmed into your calculator.)

The logarithmic model: inflation is rising steadily

A model for this is shown in figure 5.19.

Such a mathematical model would be described as a *logarithmic model*, $y = \log x$. Here $y =$ the rate of inflation at time x (in months from a given starting time). Equally a

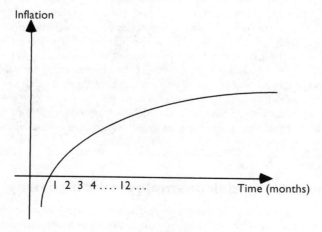

Figure 5.19

model would be $y = \dfrac{a}{x^b}$ where a and b are constants with $a > 0$ and b is between 0 and 1 $(0 < b < 1)$.

We shall see later in this chapter how such graphs are formed with the help of a spreadsheet package such as Excel. The important thing here is to be able to interpret the information the graph is telling us. This really all depends to a large extent on its shape and gradient. In particular a graph's shape and steepness will tell us what type of increase or decrease is happening.

A constant model: inflation is steady

If, for example, we have a horizontal line with time along the horizontal axis, this would say that over time there is no increase or decrease. For example, inflation remaining fairly constant over a time period would be depicted as figure 5.20.

Similarly we might interpret the graphs of figures 5.21, 5.22 and 5.23.

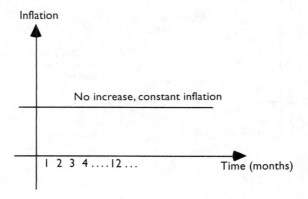

Figure 5.20

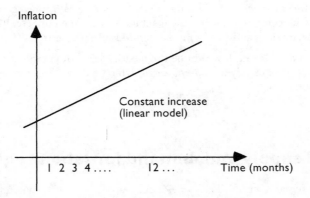

Figure 5.21

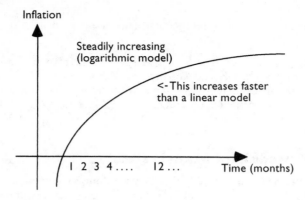

Figure 5.22

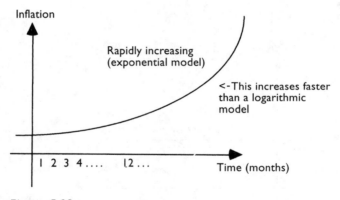

Figure 5.23

A quadratic model: production costs

Production costs usually start out linearly, being made up of the overheads and a unit or batch cost. After production has been underway for a certain time economies are often made: staff are working to capacity, the machinery is warmed up, etc. The cost per item usually starts reducing, and such a model would look like figure 5.24.

In fact as a model this graph would be the next in order of complexity from the linear model and is approximately a *quadratic model*, which will be discussed in more detail in the next section.

General supply and demand for labour equations

Models for demand could be $y = \dfrac{b}{x^a}$ and supply $y = ax^b$, where $y =$ wage and $x =$ number in the workforce (figure 5.25) for suitable choice of a and b.

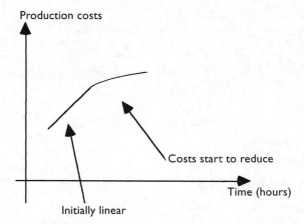

Figure 5.24

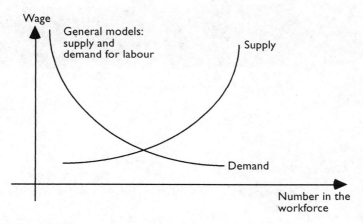

Figure 5.25

We now look at how to plot these models using a spreadsheet package, such as Excel. The commands below are similar for a PC version or Macintosh version of Excel, although the diagrams are actually from Macintosh Excel version 4.0. (version 5.0 is very similar—we shall be using the ChartWizard—although the menu and tool bars are slightly different in versions 4.0 and 5.0.)

Using Excel

First you should familiarise yourself with using the mouse and be able to move around a document and menus using this, for example on a word-processing package.

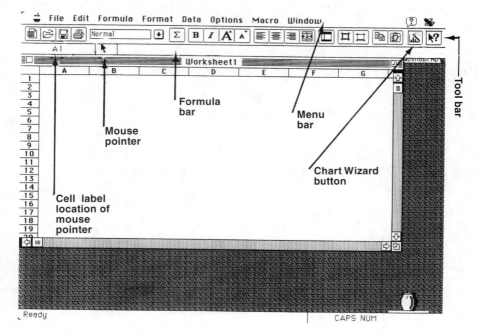

Figure 5.26

Cells in the spreadsheet

Once you have opened the Excel folder and application (the icon is

Microsoft Excel), a worksheet appears on your screen as figure 5.26.

This is basically a large table with columns labelled A, B, C etc. and rows labelled 1, 2, 3, 4, etc. Any one position in this table is called a cell and is given a position depending on which row and column it lies in. For example D7 would denote the cell in the D column (4th across from the left) and in the 7th row down. The default name for any worksheet is simply worksheet 1 (or sheet 1), worksheet 2, etc.

The menu bar

The menu bar at the top of your screen will appear with names like File, Edit, Formula, Format, etc. Each of these menus are called pull-down menus, because if you click on any of them you will see a list of items appear below this menu. For example, pull down the file menu to see what it says: to do this simply click on the word File at the top of your screen (menu bar) and you will see a screen such as that shown in figure 5.27.

By simply letting go of the mouse this will close.

We shall find out how to use Excel as a mathematical tool as we progress.

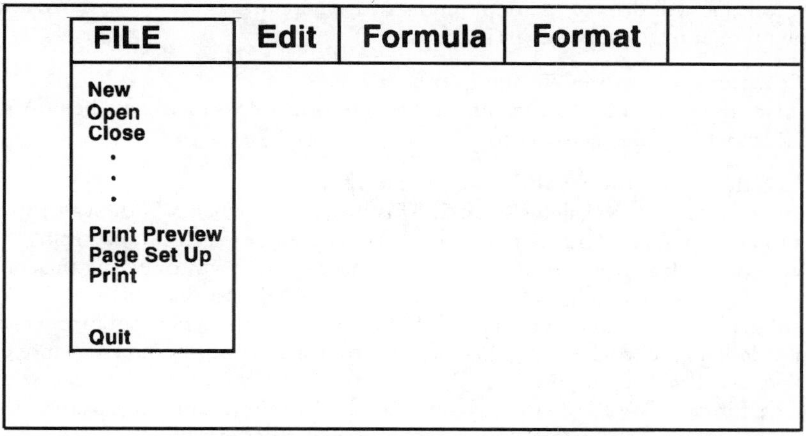

FILE	Edit	Formula	Format	
New Open Close • • • Print Preview Page Set Up Print Quit				

Figure 5.27

Tool bar

The tool bar is the set of tools which can be used simply by clicking onto them. We shall not discuss in any detail how to use them but simply use the ones we require. As you become more familiar with this package you will soon discover how useful this kit is. (Note that your worksheet 1 may look slightly different to figure 5.26 depending on whether you have closed down some parts of the tool bar.)

Tabulating the function for 'Unemployment is soaring'

The above model for this was: $y = e^x$ where y = number unemployed and x = time in months (for example month 1, month 2 after December 1995). W shall now calculate a table of values for this function using Excel.

Step 1: Enter the column headings
Enter the following column headings in worksheet 1: x = time/months, and $y = \exp\hat{\ }(x)$. To this end, place the mouse pointer (arrow head) in cell A1. You will see the A1 appears in the left section of the Formula Bar (which indicates location in the spreadsheet) and the mouse pointer is now in the right of the formula bar (now as a blinking cursor rather like an I). When the cursor is in the formula bar text or formulae can be entered. Type in the formula bar: x = time/months. Press Return or click on the Tick in the Formula bar separating the cell location from the text/formula you have inserted.

Press Tab and your mouse pointer will move to the next cell: B1, Type in y = exp^(x) and press return.

(Using Formula Menu: Note that we could have found the mathematical function using the Formula menu and PASTE FUNCTION. On the screen would appear the various functions and the necessary format for the spreadsheet: click onto Mathematical and Statistical functions. Use the arrow to search down this list and you will see EXP. If clicked on this will display the required format—here it says use ^ for superscript and put the number in the superscript in a bracket.)

Step 2: Enter the *x* values for the graph
Now place the pointer in A2 and enter 1, press return and you will now be in A3. Enter 2 and then 3,4,5,...12 in cells A4 to A13.

Step 3: Calculating the *y* values for the graph
The first cell we wish to calculate is B2. This means that when *x* is the value in A2 we wish *y* to be Exp^(A2). This is done by placing the pointer in cell B2 and typing =. You will see = in the Formula Bar. Placing = first in a cell is the way of giving the command 'now do this calculation'. Here we type in = exp^(A2) and press return. As A2 = 1, you will see e^1 is calculated (which is 2.718281828). (The package is not case sensitive so upper or lower case work equally.) Now press return and your pointer will move to the next line, cell B3. Type in = exp^(A3). Here would be 7.389056099 (which you could check, that is calculate e^2). Now we could move down the column B repeating this, but we have the tools of the spreadsheet which can be further exploited.

Step 4: Using the Edit menu
Highlight the last cell calculated so far in your B column—B3.

Using the Edit Menu select Copy. (A shortcut is ⌘ C).

Then select the cells where you want not this value but this formula applied: drag the mouse from B4 to B13.

Then use the Edit menu to select Paste Special.

A small window now opens and you will see the following paste options as in figure 5.28.

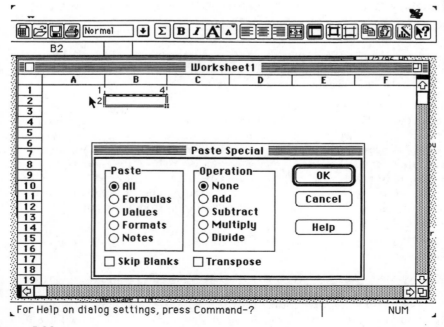

Figure 5.28

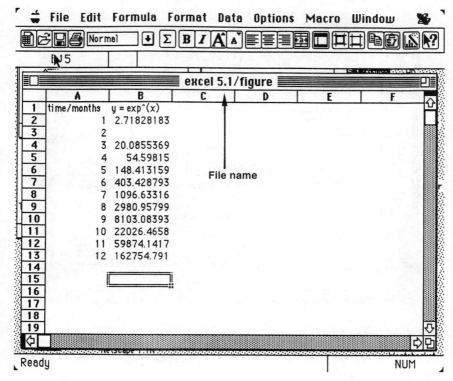

Figure 5.29

Use the pointer to select 'formulas'. Then press the OK button on the screen—this can be done by either clicking on the OK button with the mouse or simply pressing return. The contents of cells B4–B13 will be as shown in figure 5.29.

In effect this means that in B4 we have the formula $= \exp^\wedge(A4)$, and so on.

Save this spreadsheet— use the File menu and click on the save (s for short)—I have used the name excel 5.1/figure—which you will see in the file name location.

Step 5: Using the ChartWizard facility in the Tool Bar
Now use the mouse to select all the cells that you have created: A1 to B13.

Click onto the ChartWizard button in the Tool Bar. Now place the mouse back on your spreadsheet and drag the cursor into a rectangular box shape—this will be the area where your chart (graph) will appear. Now the ChartWizard facility produces step 1– step 5—after each window press Return (that is, press the Next button).

Now you will have figure 5.30 on screen.

Notice that the range of data that you have selected will be given (A1: B13). Click on the Next button.

You will then have a screen such as figure 5.31.

Here you will have many types of graphing facilities: select the XY (Scatter)

Press the Next button and select graph type 2 to produce a screen such as figure 5.32.

On Screen will now appear a sample chart (figure 5.33).

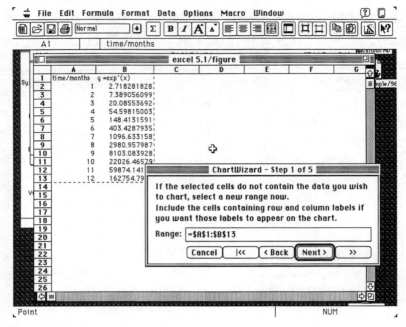

Figure 5.30

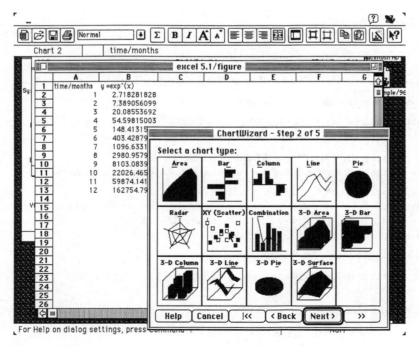

Figure 5.31

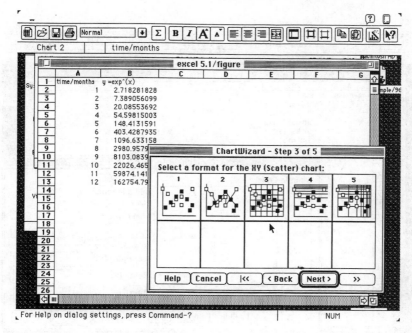

Figure 5.32

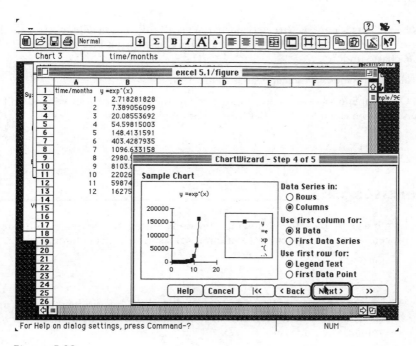

Figure 5.33

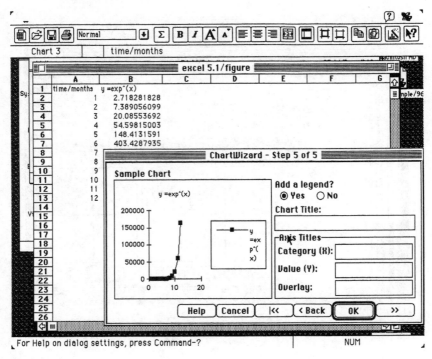

Figure 5.34

Press Next. This is now the last step in ChartWizard and you can enter a name and label the axes. Note that here we have added a legend (this is the box in the right of the sample chart window).

The following windows then appear as figure 5.34.

Press OK to obtain a screen such as figure 5.35. At the bottom of your window in Excel 4 you will see an extended Tool Bar for further graphing tools.

Exercises 5.7 _____

Use Excel to plot the following functions (using the above step-by-step procedure) and the given range of input values for the first column.

5.7.1 $y = \log x$

for $x = 0.1, 0.2, 0.5, 0.8, 1, 2, 3, 4, 5, \ldots, 10$.

Hint: you could use the Formula Menu and find the logarithmic function under the Paste Function item. Note that in your column for y you would enter at row 2 (assuming the x value is in A2, A3, A4, etc, ...)

$= \log(a2)$.

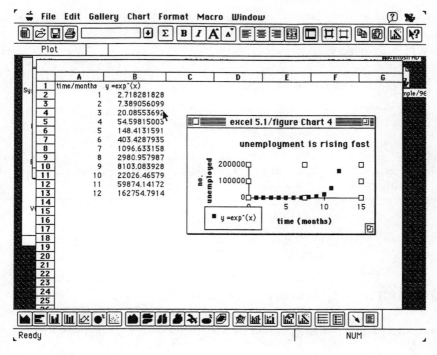

Figure 5.35

5.7.2 $y = \dfrac{b}{x^a}$

for any chosen b value ($b > 0$)

for $a = 0, \frac{1}{2}, 1$ and 2

taking x values 0.1, 0.2, 0.5, 1, 2, 3, ... 20.

(Hint: Here if $b = 2$ and $a = \frac{1}{2}$ then at the second entry in the column for y you would enter $= 2/(A2^0.5)$ etc.)

Why is this a suitable model for a demand function (for example demand for labour)?

5.7.3 $y = bx^a$

for any chosen b value ($b > 0$)

for $a = 0, \frac{1}{2}, 1, 2$ and 3

taking x values 0, 0.1, 0.2, 0.5, 1, 2, 3, ... 20.

Compare this model with your answer to question 5.7.2.

Notice that you can hide a column in your spreadsheet using the Format Menu. Select the Format Menu and scan down this for Column—a small window opens allowing you to change the column width from standard 10 points to Best Fit or Hide (which would conceal this column). Unhide would then bring this back. By hiding a column you can re-use the same x input values and plot your graph for these same x and new y values.

5.7.4 Plotting quadratics: models of the form $y = ax^2 + bx + c$. Taking x values of x = 6, -5, -4, -3, ...0, 1, 2, 3,....., 10

choose all possible combinations of different signs for a, b and c.

For example   (i)   let $a = +2$, $b = +3$ and $c = +6$,
               (ii) let $a = +2$, $b = -3$ and $c = +6$
              (iii) let $a = +2$, $b = -3$ and $c = -6$, etc.

This graph is a quadratic and is always a U shape (or an upturned U). Try other values for a, b and c and, discuss their role in determining the shape and position of this graph in the plane.

We now take a closer look at quadratic equations using business applications.

Quadratic equations in business

Scenario: supply and demand for consumer goods
The demand, or price, equation for a product can be regarded as a function of the quantity of items the consumer is prepared to buy at this price. When the price is high, generally the consumer demand is limited, but as the price reduces, the demand increases. Similarly, the supply or selling price equation for a product can be regarded as a function of the quantity a manufacturer or supplier is prepared to put into the market at that price. Generally the lower the price, the less the manufacturer will be prepared to supply at that price (as profits will be low), but as the price rises, so will the quantity that the manufacturer will supply to the market. Clearly there has to be equilibrium—a balance between what the consumer is prepared to pay and the manufacturer to supply.

Example 5.12
A product is released onto the market and the consumer price (demand) equation, D, is given by $D = \dfrac{15}{q}$ for q in 1000s of units. The manufacturer will supply q units (1000s) at a selling price, S, where $S = \dfrac{2q - 6}{q + 3}$. S and D are prices in £100s. Find the equilibrium price and quantity for this product.

Solution
First we could plot both of these curves—they will be curves as there are reciprocals in the equations. Here we would plot price on the y axis—both selling price and the purchasing price, and on the x-axis we would plot the quantity of goods. Notice that here we might call the x-axis the q-axis for quantity and the y-axis the p-axis for price. The graph would look very similar to the general supply and demand for labour graph sketched in figure 5.25. We shall sketch these graphs below using Excel. When the supply is equal to the demand, there is an equilibrium between the two prices.

Using Excel

Step 1: Inputting the q values

Firstly let us enter in the first column of this spreadsheet the q values for our graph. Here q is the number of units and is the input value for our pricing functions. In the first entry in column 1, (cell A1) enter the label q. We have no prior knowledge of a suitable range of values for q other than q must be positive. Notice in the denominator for demand q is present and so if $q = 0$, we will have $\frac{15}{0}$ which is infinite. Thus we must not allow denominators of graphs to be zero—the spreadsheet may not pick this up but try to join up points—so it is important to notice suitable values. The spreadsheet will do all the tedious calculations but you must apply the brains! Thus for the demand function, $q > 0$ and for the supply curve $q > -3$. Thus a range of positive values will suffice. We thus choose $q = 1, 2, 3, \ldots, 15$. Enter this into column A.

Step 2: Entering the demand function

Enter Demand in cell B1. Then in B2 enter the formula for demand, namely $= 15/A2$.

Similarly for B3 enter $= 15/A3$. Use the copy command in the Edit menu and copy cell B3. Drag the cursor down from cell B4 to B16. Then again from the Edit Menu select Paste Special and paste the formula by clicking on Formulas.

You should now see the values for $D = \dfrac{15}{q}$ computed.

Step 3: Entering the supply function

Repeat step 2 for the supply function: $S = \dfrac{2q - 6}{q + 3}$. Be careful to use sufficient parentheses. Namely, B2 $= (2*A2 - 6)/(A2 + 3)$ etc.

Step 4: Plotting the demand and supply functions on the same graph

Select the cells A1–C16 by dragging the cursor. Then touch the ChartWizard button with the mouse and drag an area on the spreadsheet where you would like the chart to be. Then step 1 of 5 will commence. (Proceed as the earlier section on Excel, pressing Next button at each stage.) We use the XY scatterplot to sketch these graphs. Notice that the q values (that is, the x-axis) appear in the first column—as noted in step 2 of the ChartWizard facility. (This has been saved as Excel 5.10 figure). The resulting graph and spreadsheet will be as shown in figure 5.36.

By double clicking onto the chart it will expand to the whole screen and this will display the details more clearly.

The two graphs merge—and equilibrium occurs—near $q = 10$, that is, near 10 000 items. We shall now proceed to find this exact value and price using algebra.

Algebraically find (q, P) at the equilibrium

Step 1: Equate S and D

To do this we must find where the two graphs $D = \dfrac{15}{q}$ and $S = \dfrac{2q - 6}{q + 3}$ meet,

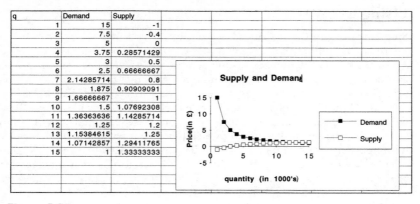

Figure 5.36

that is, we equate them. This gives us:

$$\frac{15}{q} = \frac{2q - 6}{q + 3}$$

Step 2: Rearrange to find q

We really are trying to make q the subject. This in fact involves further algebraic techniques than currently met, but the procedures on 'changing the subject' do work to some extent. Firstly we remove all fractions. To do this we firstly cross-multiply both sides by q:

$$\Rightarrow q \times \frac{15}{q} = \frac{2q - 6}{q + 3} \times q$$

$$\Rightarrow 15 = \frac{(2q - 6) \times q}{q + 3}$$

Now we cross-multiply by $(q + 3)$:

$$\Rightarrow 15 \times (q + 3) = \frac{(2q - 6) \times q}{q + 3} \times (q + 3).$$

This now leaves us with:

$$15 \times (q + 3) = (2q - 6) \times q$$

We now remove brackets: $\Rightarrow 15q + 45 = 2q^2 - 6q$.

If we collect all the terms on one side we now see that:

$$\Rightarrow 2q^2 - 6q - 15q - 45 = 0$$
$$\Rightarrow 2q^2 - 21q - 45 = 0$$

This is now a standard model: a quadratic model. The standard model being:

$$ax^2 + bx + c = 0, \text{ which occurs when } x = \frac{-b \pm \sqrt{b^2 - 4ac}}{2a}$$

To solve this we must either factorise into two brackets or use the above formula (which we shall do here): although here we have qs rather than xs. Thus $a = 2$, $b = -21$ and $c = -45$.

Thus $q = \dfrac{--21 \pm \sqrt{(-21)^2 - 4 \times 2 - 45}}{2 \times 2}$.

This tidies up to give us:

$$\Rightarrow q = \frac{21 \pm \sqrt{441 + 360}}{4}$$

$$\Rightarrow q = \frac{21 \pm \sqrt{801}}{4}$$

$$\Rightarrow q = \frac{21 \pm 28.3019434}{4}$$

$$\Rightarrow q = \frac{21 + 28.3019434}{4} \quad \text{or} \quad q = \frac{21 - 28.3019434}{4}$$

$$\Rightarrow q = 12.232548585 \quad \text{or} \quad q = -1.825485849$$

Step 3: Interpretation

Now this tells us that the actual number of units is either 12.233 thousand (to 3 decimal places) or a negative value. Clearly we discard the negative solution as inappropriate here for our problem.

Thus $q = 12.233$ (in thousands). Now we need to compute the corresponding price—using either of the two pricing functions—they will both give us the same answer as at this value of q the two graphs coincide.

Thus using $D = \dfrac{15}{q} = \dfrac{15}{12.233} = 1.226\,191\,449$ in £100s.

Step 4: Conclusion

Thus the equilibrium price is 1.2261914 (in £100s) or £122.62 each. That is at a price of £122.62 per unit the supplier will supply to the market place 12 233 units. At this price of £122.62 each, the consumer is prepared to buy 12 233 units.

Exercises 5.8 _____

5.8.1 Using the formula $x = \dfrac{-b \pm \sqrt{b^2 - 4ac}}{2a}$ find the values of x where

(i) $3x^2 - 3x - 1 = 0$

(iii) $-x^2 - x + 4 = 0$

(iii) $4x^2 + 3x - 5 = 0$

(iv) $-5x^2 + 3x + 5 = 0$

(v) $-5x^2 + 3x - 5 = 0$

Plot each of the graphs $y = 3x^2 - 3x - 1$, $y = -x^2 - x + 4$ etc. using Excel. The points you have just found are called the roots of the quadratic. Label these on each of your Excel charts.

In (v) we can see that the formula fails—can you see why? Consider the Excel chart for an idea.

5.8.2 Find the equilibrium points for the following demand equations, D, and supply equations, S where $D = \dfrac{3000}{q}$ and $S = \dfrac{5q + 1}{20q - 3}$

5.8.3 Plot the following supply and demand function using Excel:

$$S = \frac{q}{3} + 15$$

$$D = \frac{5.6}{q}$$

Label the equilibrium point and hence find this point algebraically.

Applications of quadratics: profits, revenue and cost functions

Example 5.16

Juno Research Limited is a manufacturer of power PCs. It has been estimated that if q power PCs are manufactured each week then the cost of production is given by:

$C(q) = 30q - 0.01\,q^2 - 200$

The maximum weekly production is 2000 power PCs. Sketch this cost function using Excel and explain why it is a suitable model.

Solution

Step 1: Use a suitable range of q values
If the maximum weekly production is 2000 then we need to go no further than this on our horizontal axis (where q the quantity manufactured will be displayed). To this end it is probably best to have a start of 0 units and go up in steps of 100, i.e. $q = 0, 100, 200, 300$, up to 2000. These values will go in column A.

Step 2: Compute the cost function
In cell B2 enter $= 30*$ A2 $- (0.01\,*$A2$*$A2$) - 200$

Copy and Paste this down the column.

Drag the cursor over this data and touch the ChartWizard button in the Tool Bar.

Notice that by dragging the cursor over the column labels this will mean a legend will be automatically added to the chart for this range of costs.

Step 3: Plot the cost function
Now go through the five-step ChartWizard routine (as outlined above).

You screen should look like figure 5.37.

Step 4: Interpreting your graph
We can see that as the number of items increases so does the (total) cost of production. This is as we would expect. Notice also that after 1500 items have been produced the total cost starts to reduce. This would mean that after the production has been running for some time the costs start to reduce, due to savings such as staff working to capacity, machinery being fully used, etc. Notice from your table of values that at $q = 0$ the cost is $-£200$. What does this mean? Well at $q = 0$ no items are being made—yet costs are still being incurred. This is natural as overheads would still need to be paid.

Exercises 5.9

5.9.1 Use Excel to plot the following function:

The costs, C, in a month for a certain production process can be expressed in the form $C = 12.3 + 5.6x - 2.1x^2$,

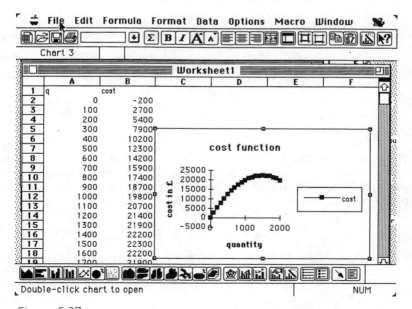

Figure 5.37

where C is in £1000, and x is the number of units produced in 100s. The company never makes more than 225 units in a month due to staffing levels.

(i) Plot this graph. To work out a table of values, choose x values between $x = 0$ and $x = 2.25$ with steps of 0.25.

(ii) Interpret the graph. Estimate the initial costs and label this point on your graph. Estimate the maximum cost, and find the level of production in order to achieve this. Label the point where the maximum cost occurs. What is the unit cost at this point?

What sort of monthly production run would you advise?

Note: the unit cost at this point would be found by subtracting the initial costs (overheads) from the maximum cost and then dividing this remaining value by the quantity of production, 1500. Thus the unit

$$\text{cost} = \frac{15\,975 - 12\,300}{150} = £24.50.$$

5.9.2 A new furniture removals company has been set up and it is estimated that this business can support up to 8 vans, with average running costs, $\bar{C}$, in £ per week per van given by $\bar{C} = \dfrac{215}{x} + 125 + 4.6x$,

where x is the number of vans.

Plot the graph $y = \bar{C}$, using x-values from 0.5 (with steps of 0.5). What is the largest value of x you should choose? Decide from the values in your Excel worksheet.

Find an expression for the total cost of running an arbitrary number of vans (x say). If the company decides to run 3 vans for the first 6 months, and 5 vans for the rest of the year, what would be the company's total cost for running this business?

5.9.3 Using Excel tabulate the following graphs, taking any suitable range of values for x:

(i) $y = 2x^2 - 4x + 9$

(ii) $y = \dfrac{4}{x}$

(iii) $y = 3x - \dfrac{2.3}{x}$

5.9.4 A business consortium is interested in purchasing a regional railway when the railway network is privatised. The consortium's financial planning director has been modelling the cost of running the Network Wessex Railway and has produced the following models for the revenue R and the costs C, where

$$R = 80 + 0.4q$$

and

$$C = \frac{48\,000}{q + 3}$$

where q is the number of units of travel bought in thousands, where a unit is a journey of one mile or under;

where both R and C are expressed in £1000s.

Determine

(i) An expression for the total monthly profit that Network Wessex Railway can expect to receive.

(ii) At what level of rail usage does the company break even?

(iii) Using Excel tabulate values for the profit function for values of q from in intervals of 50 up to $q = 500$. Hence plot this graph and use it to estimate the rail usage that would give the maximum profit. What would this profit be?

Hint: profit is the difference between income and expenditure, and so is the difference in revenue and cost functions.

That is if $P =$ profit, then $P = R - C$.

The consortium can expect to break even when revenue equals cost, or profit is zero.

Basically this means there is no loss but no profit.

5.9.5 The cost of producing x terms of a product is modelled by the expression $C(x) = 1050 + 100x - 0.15x^2$. Determine when the cost is maximal and sketch the graph of $y = C(x)$.

The cost per item is $\dfrac{C(x)}{x}$. Does this have a maximum?

5.9.6 Nike's Parcels Express has franchised a delivery route, which is a route of 600 miles. The driver is given instructions to drive at a constant speed of x miles per hour. Diesel costs £1.65 per gallon and is consumed at a rate of $1.4 + \dfrac{x^2}{840}$ gallons per hour. The driver's salary is £6.95 per hour.

(i) Explain how you would find an expression for the total fuel bill, F, for this journey. Check that the units of your formulation are indeed £.

(ii) Hence find this expression for total expenses encurred by Nike's Parcels Express in operating this route.

(iii) Using Excel plot the graph for the company's expenses function. Use your graph to estimate the minimum total expenses incurred by the company.

What would be the speed the driver should travel at in order to minimise the company's expenses?

How long does the journey take and what gross salary does the driver receive?

(Recall: speed $= \dfrac{\text{distance}}{\text{time}}$)

6   Financial options

Objectives

- Be able to calculate simple and compound interest and to understand their difference;
- Be able to compare monthly interest rates with the effective annual rate;
- Be able to compute depreciation (straight line and reducing balance depreciation);
- Understand the meaning of present and future values;
- Be able to compute loan repayments and a loan figure, given a regular payment;
- Be able to compute the value of a savings plan on maturity;
- Understand how to compute a pension income, given a life expectancy.

Scenario: interest rates—are they fooling you?

In the commercial world, investors and borrowers are always paid or pay interest. Banks will lend money, but at a price—the amount you pay back is always considerably more than you borrow. Credit card companies and store cards often advertise in a more subtle way—quoting their lending rates as monthly percentage rates. They are obviously much lower than the effective annual percentage rate and are designed to look very attractive. When analysed, however, they may not be quite as favourable as they seem. If you think that the annual percentage rate is simply 12 times the monthly rate then I am afraid you are in fact paying more than you realise. The important thing to keep in mind is never rush to conclusions—always work out rates so that you can compare like with like.

Interest

Simple interest

When we invest or borrow money (capital), there is an interest rate involved. Simple interest means the same amount of interest is paid each period (e.g. at the end of the period) and this is kept separate from the sum invested or borrowed, that is, in future periods interest is paid on the capital alone. The money invested or borrowed is usually called the *principal* and the percentage return is called the Annual Percentage Rate (APR). We often call this simple rate of interest the nominal rate, which means it makes no mention of when interest is added to the principal.

Example 6.1

The sum of £1500 is borrowed at 12% per annum simple interest.

(i)   How much interest is paid at the end of one year?

(ii) How much will the interest be at the end of five years? Assuming that no repayments were made, what will be the outstanding debt?

Solution

(i) Interest will be 12% of £1500. Thus 12% × £1500 i.e. $\frac{12}{100}$ × £1500 = £180

(ii) Each year the amount of interest is the same, so after

> 1 year   1 × £180
> 2 years   2 × £180
> 3 years   3 × £180

then after 5 years, 5 × £180 or £900.

This gives us a total outstanding debt of £1,500 plus interest of £900, which is £2,400.

Formally we might write:

$$\text{simple interest} = \text{principal} \times \frac{\text{interest rate}}{100} \times \text{time period}$$

that is, the amount borrowed/saved is worth

$$A_n = P + P \times \frac{i}{100} \times n = P\left(1 + \frac{i}{100} \times n\right)$$

where P is the amount borrowed or invested, i is the percentage rate of interest, n is the number of time periods and A_n is the value of the investment after interest has been added for n periods.

Exercise 6.1

Check that using this formula with $n = 5$, $P = £1500$ and $i = 12$ that A_5 is indeed £2400.

Compound interest

With compound interest, the interest is added to the principal at the end of each time period (year, month, etc.), and so after each period interest is paid or earned on the interest as well as the original sum borrowed or invested. In the business world, interest is almost always in the form of compound interest. We could have the loan/saving annually compounded or monthly compounded—or more likely, compounded daily. Notice that the interest rates published by building societies and banks must always state the annual percentage rate, that is the nominal rate, and then qualify the rate by stating how often interest is added—how often it is compounded. We adopt this same convention.

Example 6.2

Compare the interest found in example 6.1 with the interest payable if £1500 is borrowed over 5 years at 12% per annum compounded annually (again assuming that no repayments are made).

Solution

(All figures are rounded to the nearest penny)

The principal: £1500

1st year's interest: (12% of £1500 = $\frac{12}{100}$ × £1500) = £180
Total amount owing at the end of year 1 = £1680

(This is the principal plus the interest.)

2nd year's interest: (12% of £1680 = $\frac{12}{100}$ × £1680) = £201.60
Total amount owing at end of year 2 = £1881.60

3rd year's interest: (12% of £1881.60 = $\frac{12}{100}$ × £1881.60) = £225.79
Total amount owing at end of year 3 = £2107.39

4th year's interest: (12% of £2107.39 = $\frac{12}{100}$ × £2107.39) = £252.89
Total amount owing at end of year 4 = £2360.28

5th year's interest: (12% of £2360.28 = $\frac{12}{100}$ × £2360.28) = £283.23

Finally the total amount owing at end of year 5 = £2643.51

The total interest paid over 5 years with simple interest was £900, but with compound interest the interest is £1143.51. We can see that with simple interest the amount is fixed each time period, but with compound interest the interest grows. From a banker's point of view it is clear why rates are compounded!

Example 6.3

£6000 is invested for 2 years at a 3% interest rate per annum compounded quarterly. Calculate the value of the investment at the end of this period.

Solution

The principal: £6000. The annual interest rate is 3%. Thus the nominal rate per quarter is a quarter of this, or $\frac{1}{4}$ of 3% = $\frac{3}{4}$% or $\frac{1}{4}$ × $\frac{3}{100}$ = $\frac{3}{400}$

1st quarter's interest: ($\frac{3}{4}$% of £6000 = $\frac{3}{400}$ × £6000) = £45

Value of investment at the end of 1st quarter = £6045

2nd quarter's interest: ($\frac{3}{4}$% of £6045 = $\frac{3}{400}$ × £6045) = £45.34

Value of investment at end of 2nd quarter = £6090.34

Exercise 6.2 _____

Work out the total amount earned after 2 years, on the above investment.

You can see it gets a bit tedious working out the compound interest, say after 20 periods, so mathematicians resort to finding a shortcut—devising a formula. This is derived later in this chapter. Here we simply state the result.

Let P denote the principal sum invested/borrowed, for a term of n periods (years, quarters or months) at i percent rate of interest compounded at the end of each period. Then the amount at the end of the term, A_n is given by the formula:

$$A_n = P\left(1 + \frac{i}{100}\right)^n$$

Example 6.4

Check this works using example 6.2.

Solution

Let $n = 5$, $P = £1500$, $i = 12$ and so

$$A_5 = 1500\left(1 + \frac{12}{100}\right)^5$$

First work out the inside of the brackets: $1 + \frac{12}{100} = 1.12$

So $A_5 = 1500\,(1.12)^5$

Next calculate $(1.12)^5$. This means raise 1.12 to the power of 5. (Recall that raising to the power 2 means multiplying a term by itself twice. Raising to the power 3, means multiply a term by itself 3 times, etc.)

This is the x^y button (or y^x on some calculators). These are the operations:

$$1.12 \quad \boxed{\begin{array}{c} x^y \\ \text{button} \end{array}} \quad 5 =$$

You would see 1.762 341 683 displayed (or more if you have more decimal places than me!)

Now finally $A_5 = 1500 \times 1.762\,341\,683 = £2643.51$. Good, it works!

Example 6.5

A pensions company decides to invest £3 million in the futures market. They are able to invest it for a period of 4 years and are informed that the best rates they can expect to receive are 5.2% compounded annually, or 4.8% compounded quarterly. Which would be the best investment?

Solution

The principal is £3 000 000, and the nominal rate for the investment if compounded annually is 5.2%. Thus after a term of 4 years, that is, $n = 4$ the investment would have grown to:

$$A_4 = 3\,000\,000 \times \left(1 + \frac{5.2}{100}\right)^4$$

Calculating the inside of the bracket first we have $\frac{5.2}{100} = 0.052$, and thus we add the 1 to give $1 + \frac{5.2}{100} = 1.052$.

Now raising this to the power 4: is $1.052 \quad \boxed{\begin{array}{c} x^y \\ \text{button} \end{array}} \quad 4 = 1.222\,479\,374\,4$ and

multiplying this by 3 million will give us the value of $= £3\,674\,381.23$.

This is in effect a profit of just over £674 000.

The second investment would be at a lower rate but interest would be added more often, and so it might work out as favourably as the first rate. If the annual rate is 4.8% compounded quarterly, then we need to work out the nominal quarterly rate, or here $\frac{1}{4}$. This is $\frac{4.8}{4}$% which is 1.2%. Now our term is measured in quarters, and as there are 4 quarters in each year and 4 years, in total we have 16 terms. Thus the quantity we require is

$$A_{16} = 3\,000\,000 \times \left(1 + \frac{1.2}{100}\right)^{16}$$

Again calculating the inside of the bracket, we have $\frac{1.2}{100} = 0.012$, and thus we add the 1 to give $1 + \frac{1.2}{100} = 1.012$. This raised to the power 16 is 1.210 286 531, which gives us a final value of the investment as $A_{16} = 3\,000\,000 \times 1.210\,286\,531 = £3\,630\,859.60$. This is in fact slightly less than the first investment, less by £43 521.61, and so the company should choose the first investment deal.

A natural question is: what does the quarterly compounded rate have to be to match the annually compounded rate? The answer is in fact an APR of 5.1%. To demonstrate this we need some further basic algebra, which we shall cover shortly. Furthermore, when we know how to rearrange these formulas we will be able to calculate n the term of the investment or loan given the rate, initial and final values of the capital.

Exercise 6.3

If the pensions company received 5.1% per annum for investing the same sum as above for 4 years, what is the difference in interest if this sum is compounded annually, or quarterly?

Example 6.6

A self-employed person decides to invest £12 000 in a high interest account in order that he can have new capital to invest in the future. The rate of interest most favourably offered is 6.2% (gross) compounded annually. If he must pay income tax at 25% on the interest earned, what would the net value of the investment in three years (assuming that tax is paid at the end of each year)? How much is actually paid in tax? If the rate of interest was quoted as a net figure, what would this be?

Solution

Every time interest is paid (i) he will only receive 75% of this interest, or 75% of i. As a decimal this is written $0.75 \times i$. Thus in the formula for compound interest we replace i by $0.75i$.

$A_n = P\left(1 + \frac{0.75i}{100}\right)^n$. Alternatively $A_n = P\left(1 + \frac{3i}{400}\right)^n$ as 75% of i is the

same as $\frac{3}{4}$ of i%, and $\frac{3}{4} \times i$% is $\frac{3}{4} \times \frac{i}{100} = \frac{3i}{400}$.

Thus

$$A_3 = 12\,000\left(1 + \frac{3 \times 6.2}{400}\right)^3 = 12\,000(1.0465)^3 = £13\,753.05$$

to the nearest penny. If the gross figure was calculated, we would have

$$A_3 = 12\,000\left(1 + \frac{6.2}{100}\right)^3 = 12\,000(1.062)^3 = £14\,373.24$$

and the difference of these two figures is the tax: £620.19. As a net figure, the nominal rate of interest would be $\frac{3}{4}i = 4.65\%$.

It is often helpful to see what is happening by presenting the various values in a table:

Year	Interest gross	Interest nett	Tax	Investment gross	Investment nett
0				12 000.00	12 000.00
1	744.00	558.00	186.00	12 744.00	12 558.00
2	778.60	583.95	194.65	13 534.13	13 141.95
3	814.80	611.10	203.70	14 373.24	13 753.05

Example 6.7

Four teenagers each inherit £2000 from their grandmothers' estates. Assuming that the interest rate is 14% per annum, who has gained the most:

Samuel decides to leave his in an account for 2 years, gaining interest compounded annually.

Kameljeet spends £1000 and leaves the rest in her account for 15 months.

Natasha spends her inheritance as soon as she receives it.

Jason spends £500 and leaves the rest in an account for 2 years.

Justify your conclusions.

Solution

We need to calculate the value of each of the sums—at the end of each of the periods.

Samuel: his inheritance will be worth $A_2 = 2000 \times (1 + 0.14)^2 = £2599.20$

Kameljeet: her inheritance is worth £1000 + the amount invested with interest. £1000 is invested over 1 and 1/4 of a year and is worth $1000 \times (1 + 0.14)^{1.25} = £1177.96$, giving a total of £2177.96.

Natasha spends her inheritance and so it is worth £2000.

Jason invests £1500 for 2 years and so his total assets are valued at:

$$A_2 = 1500 \times (1 + 0.14)^2 + £500 \text{ cash} = £2449.40.$$

We can see that Samuel gains most.

Effective APR

Example 6.8

BetterCredit Ltd is a credit card company that advertises its interest rate as 1.85% compounded monthly. What is the equivalent annual percentage rate and how does this compare with the nominal rate?

Solution

Here we need to modify the above formula for annually compounded rate.

The equivalent annual percentage rate or effective annual percentage rate is given by

$$\text{effective APR} = \left(\left(1 + \frac{i}{100}\right)^n - 1\right) \times 100\%$$

where n is the number of periods.

Thus if $i = 1.85$, and $1 + i$ gives us $1 + \frac{1.85}{100} = 1 + 0.0185 = 1.0185$. Now there are 12 months in a year and so $n = 12$. Thus for the effective APR we have APR $= ((1.0185)^{12} - 1) \times 100$. Working out the inside of the bracket namely $(1.0185)^{12}$ which is 1.0185 $\boxed{\begin{array}{c} x^y \\ \text{button} \end{array}}$ 12 $= 1.246\,041\,193$. Thus the APR $= (1.246\,041\,193 - 1) \times 100\% = 0.246\,041\,193 \times 100\%$ which is 24.6%.

The nominal rate is the monthly percentage rate $\times\ 12 = 22.2\%$. This can be regarded as the simple rate if the monthly rate is constant over the year with no interest added until the end of the year. It's not difficult to see why lenders advertise using monthly rates. The layperson will think the actual rate they pay is simply 12 times the monthly rate—now you know it's more! The higher the monthly rate the more misleading the figure is!

Example 6.9

Debrums store card for the large department store are advertising their store card as being cheaper than a rival store card, at only 2.3% per month. What does this give as the effective APR? How does this compare with the nominal rate?

Solution

Again we use the effective APR $= \left(\left(1 + \frac{i}{100}\right)^n = 1\right) \times 100\%$

where n is the number of periods which is here 12. Thus if $i = 2.3$ and $1 + i$ gives us $1 + \frac{2.3}{100} = 1 + 0.023 = 1.023$. Thus for the effective APR we have APR $= ((1.023)^{12} - 1) \times 100\%$.

Working out the inside of the bracket $(1.023)^{12}$ using the calculator is 1.023 $\boxed{\begin{array}{c} x^y \\ \text{button} \end{array}}$ 12 $= 1.313\,734\,498$. Thus the APR $= (1.313\,734\,498 - 1) \times 100\% = 0.313\,734\,498 \times 100\%$ which is 31.4% to 1 decimal place. This compares with 2.3% $\times$ 12 which gives us a nominal APR of 27.6%.

Depreciation

In order for a business to calculate the value of its capital assets and so know what the whole business is worth if it were to be realised, it must take into account that all its equipment depreciates each year. Similarly when buying consumer items, these will all depreciate once bought. In the same way as there is simple interest and compound interest we can have two types of depreciation: *simple depreciation*—usually called straight line depreciation—and *depreciation* (also called reducing balance depreciation). To arrive at a formula for each of these we simply modify the ones for interest.

Straight line depreciation

Value of assets initially valued at £P depreciating by $i\%$ per annum is valued at:

$$A_n = P\left(1 - \frac{i}{100} \times n\right) \ n \text{ years later.}$$

Reducing balance depreciation

Similarly appealing to the formulation for compound interest and note that in place of an accumulation of interest we subtract an equivalent amount:

If goods have an initial value of £P, and depreciate at a percentage rate of $i\%$ per annum, then the value at the end of n years, A_n is

$$A_n = P\left(1 - \frac{i}{100}\right)^n$$

We shall refer to this latter formula simply as depreciation.

Example 6.10
On 1 August 1993 you decide to buy a new L registration Pigout 305 at a cost of £15 000. In the first two years it depreciates by 30% per annum; what is it worth at the end of this period using

(i)   straight line depreciation,

(ii) depreciation (regarded as compounded)?

Solution
(i)   Using straight line depreciation we can see that from the graph below that the initial value of £15 000 is plotted on the vertical axis against the time period $n = 0$ on the horizontal axis. The slope will represent the rate of depreciation which will be for each time period 30% of the initial value. Thus at time period 1, the value of the car is 30% less than it initially was: thus it has a value of

$$A_1 = P\left(1 - \frac{i}{100} \times 1\right) \ 1 \text{ year later, which is:}$$

$A_1 = £15\,000(1 - \frac{30}{100} \times 1) = £10\,500$. This is a decrease of £4500. At the end of year 2 it will have decreased by the same amount, i.e. £4500.

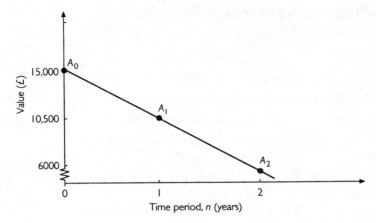

Figure 6.1

Thus at the end of year 2 it has a value of $A_2 = £15\,000(1 - \frac{30}{100} \times 2) = £6000$. Thus on the graph of figure 6.1, when $n = 2$, $A_2 = £6000$.

(ii) At the end of two years, $A_2 = £15\,000 \times (1 - \frac{30}{100})^2 = £7350$.

Example 6.11

Sacks Merchant Bank PLC are preparing their annual report to present to shareholders. Part of their auditing involves deciding on the value of their capital assets—computer hardware, telecommunications equipment, as well as the furniture. The lease on the building is also taken into account. The chief financial controller estimates that over the next few years 5% of the capital assets should be written off due to depreciation. If the assets are estimated at £5.3 million, what will they be estimated to be worth in three years time?

Solution

The value of the assets here gives us P, which is £5.3 million. To make the calculation easier we will leave the magnitude of the figure until the end of the problem. That is, we will omit the million on the value of P, and at the end say that A_n is measured in millions. The percentage rate $i = 5\%$ and the term is 3 years, so $n = 3$. Putting this into A_n here we are finding A_3. Thus

$$A_3 = 5.3 \times \left(1 - \frac{5}{100}\right)^3$$

The inside of the bracket gives us $1 - 0.05 = 0.95$. Thus we have $A_3 = 5.3 \times (0.95)^3$. Using the calculator we perform 0.95 $\boxed{\begin{array}{c} x^y \\ \text{button} \end{array}}$ 3 which gives us 0.857 375, and so finally $A_3 = £4.544\,087\,5$ which is in millions. This is approximately £4.5 million. To get a more precise figure we multiply this figure by 1 000 000, and arrive at the capital assets being realised at £4 544 087.50, which is £755 912.50 less. That's three quarters of a million!

Compound interest formula derived

Recall that earlier in the chapter we stated the formula:

$$A_n = A_0(i + 1)^n$$

Here the value of the principal or loan is A_0.

At the end of the 1st period the total value (borrowed or invested), is denoted by A_1.

Let A_1 be the interest on the principal plus the principal.

Thus $A_1 = i \times A_0 + A_0 = A_0(i + 1)$ b factorising.

At the end of the 2nd period, A_2, will be the interest on the amount at the end of period 1, plus the value of the investment at the end of period 1. Thus $A_2 = i \times A_1 + A_1 = A_1(i + 1)$ by factorising. Thus

$$A_2 = A_0(i + 1)(i + 1) \text{ using the expression for } A_1 \text{ above}$$
$$= A_0(i + 1)^2 \text{ by laws of indices.}$$

Similarly at the end of the third period

$$A_3 = i \times A_2 + A_2$$
$$= A_2(i + 1)$$
$$= A_0(i + 1)^2 \times (i + 1) \text{ using } A_2 \text{ from above.}$$
$$= A_0(i + 1)^3.$$

Thus if we continue in this way for all values of n, $n = 4$, $n = 5$, etc., generally known as deriving the expression inductively, we could show that the value of the investment/loan at the end of the nth period, A_n, was

$$A_n = i \times A_{n-1} + A_{n-1} = A_{n-1}(i + 1)$$
$$= A_0(i + 1)^{n-1} \times (i + 1)$$
$$= A_0(i + 1)^n, \text{ as required.}$$

Present value and future value of an investment

Recall the value of a capital sum (A_0) invested at a percentage rate of $i\%$ compounded for n periods:

$$A_n = A_0\left(1 + \frac{i}{100}\right)^n$$

We can regard this (A_n) as the future value of the investment, that is, at the end of the term. If we invest a sum today, at some future time it will be worth a greater value, its future value. Similarly if we withdraw funds from an account after it has been on deposit for some time, the sum initially deposited would be called the present value of the investment. Here the present value is A_0. We can rearrange the formula to make A_0 the subject, giving us the present value of an investment.

To make A_0 the subject we must move the bracketed term to the other side. This would simply involve a division:

$$A_0 = \frac{A_n}{\left(1 + \dfrac{i}{100}\right)^n} \quad \text{or} \quad A_n\left(1 + \frac{i}{100}\right)^{-n}$$

The factor $\dfrac{1}{\left(1 + \dfrac{i}{100}\right)^n}$ is sometimes known as the present value factor or discount factor.

Example 6.12

If the value of an investment is worth £25 700 after being invested at a rate of 5.4% compounded semi-annually, what was the initial sum invested?

Solution

If the annual rate of interest is 5.4% the semi-annual rate is 2.7% and in 5 years there are 10 half-years. Thus $i = 2.7$ and $n = 10$. Now putting these into the expression for A_0 we have

$$A_0 = \frac{A_n}{\left(1 + \dfrac{i}{100}\right)^n} \quad \text{giving us } A_0 = \frac{25\,700}{\left(1 + \dfrac{2.7}{100}\right)^{10}}$$

To calculate this we need a calculator! Firstly, the denominator:

the inside of the bracket gives us $1 + \frac{2.7}{100} = 1 + 0.027 = 1.027$. That is $A_0 = \frac{25\,700}{(1.027)^{10}}$. Now we raise 1.027 to the power 10. That is

1.027 $\boxed{x^y}$ 10 =

On your display you should have 1.305 282 261. We now need to complete the calculation by dividing 25 700 by this answer. Thus £25 700 ÷ 1.305 282 261 = £19 689.23 to 2 decimal places.

Summary

Simple interest $A_n = P\left(1 + \dfrac{i}{100} \times n\right)$

Compound interest $A_n = P\left(1 + \dfrac{i}{100}\right)^n$

Effective APR $= \left(\left(1 + \dfrac{i}{100}\right)^n - 1\right) \times 100\%$

Straight line depreciation $A_n = P\left(1 - \dfrac{i}{100} \times n\right)$

Depreciation $A_n = P\left(1 - \dfrac{i}{100}\right)^n$

The future value of an initial investment A_0 is given by $A_n = A_0\left(1 + \dfrac{i}{100}\right)^n$ and the

present value of an accumulated investment A_n is given by $A_0 = \dfrac{A_n}{\left(1 + \dfrac{i}{100}\right)^n}$ or

$A_n\left(1 + \dfrac{i}{100}\right)^{-n}$

Exercises 6.4 _____

6.4.1 The sum of £800 is invested for 8 years at a rate of 7.5% compounded annually. How much is the investment worth at the end of this time?

6.4.2 Compare the total amount of interest gained at the end of 7 years if £50 000 is invested at:

(i)   a simple interest rate of 5.6% for the term;

(ii)   an interest rate of 4.9% compounded annually;

(iii) an interest rate of 4.75% compounded quarterly.

6.4.3 A company's capital assets depreciate by 2.4% per annum. If they are valued at £102 000 in 1991, what will they be worth in 1995? If straight line depreciation is used, what would the value be?

6.4.4 If £2.5 million is invested for 6 years at an annual interest rate of 4.3%, what is the difference in interest earned if it is compounded annually or monthly?

6.4.5 Find the present value of an investment worth £3600 after being invested for 8 years at an interest rate of 3.8% compounded quarterly.

6.4.6 How much is borrowed if I repay a total of £5780 having made 48 repayments at a nominal rate of 7.5% per annum compounded monthly?

6.4.7 Complete example 6.3 using the compound interest formula.

_____

So far we have considered interest accumulating on a loan or an investment but not taken into account that either repayments are made to clear the loan, or that instead of making a one-off deposit we might choose to make a regular savings. We shall look at these types of problems in the following section on annuities.

Scenario: loans and savings plans
Power Plus is an electrical store selling household electrical products. They are offering what appears to be reasonable credit terms for the purchase of a new TV and video recorder. What would the monthly repayment be if 18 monthly payments are made? If a customer could afford to pay it back more quickly what would the repayments be? What would the savings be for paying back early? Similarly, how long would it take to pay back a car loan if monthly repayments are quoted? Or how

much should be invested in a Personal Equity Plan, if someone planned to retire in 15 years with a certain lump sum? If a first-time buyer can afford to make a certain repayment each month on a repayment mortgage, how much would the building society be prepared to forward for a new home? These questions can all be answered by applying compound interest to a sequence of payments, a so-called *annuity*.

Annuities

Definition: An *annuity* is a sequence of repayments or investments made at a fixed period over a given time span. Traditionally annuities were an income for life bought with a lump sum, such as an inheritance. Jane Austen wrote that annuities were 'a serious business'. Today they mean more than just an income. For example monthly payments made for a loan/mortgage would be an annuity, also a monthly savings/pension plan made for a number of years would be an annuity. In the first case the building society or loan company buy the annuity and you make regular payments to them. Here the total amount paid is to repay a fixed initial advance, that is, a fixed present value.

Making regular payments into a savings/pension plan can be thought of in a similar way, but here the final amount the policy matures to has a value in the future, a future value, which depends on the interest rate during the life span of the plan. The periodic payment is often called the premium.

One different type of annuity would be a two-stage annuity which is commonly used in the pensions market. In this case, an employee pays an annuity into the company pension plan for a number of years and on retirement receives a lump sum. The lump sum is then used to buy an annuity which would give an assured (usually fixed) income for a certain time or life (a perpetual annuity). The income from such annuity depends very much on the prevailing base rate at the time the annuity is bought. If rates are very low it may be worth waiting a certain time before purchasing.

Loan accounts: using present values

The time span for the mortgage/loan account/savings plan is called the *term*. Unless otherwise stated we shall assume that the periodic payment is in arrears and made at the end of each time period. This means that interest is compounded at the end of the period. Usually a loan is *amortised*. This means that each repayment is part capital and part interest. As the term of the loan proceeds the amount of interest reduces and the amount of capital increases.

Example 6.13
Power Plus electrical store are offering credit terms of 18 months at a nominal interest rate of 12% per annum, compounded monthly on all purchases over £500. Currently they have a special offer of a TV and video recorder for £500. The company quote you a monthly figure of £30.49. Is it correct for this annual percentage rate? How is it evaluated? What is the total interest you pay at the end of this credit agreement?

Solution

Firstly we shall take a look at the calculations and then try to analyse them to find the formula for an annuity. Notice that it is an annuity by definition as a sequence of payments are being made. The first thing we shall note is that the amount of the loan advanced is the present value. You buy the TV today, and £500 is its cost. Thus for a loan sum, the amount advanced is known as a present value. As we shall see in the following calculations, the final total amount paid is the sum of all the monthly present values.

At the beginning of the loan the initial sum advanced, $A_0 = £500$. This the present value of the loan.

The nominal rate of interest is $i\%$ per annum, which is a monthly nominal rate of $\frac{i}{12}\%$. Here $i = 12\%$ and so the monthly rate is 1%.

At the end of month 1:

The first repayment R is made. Here $R = £30.49$.

What part of this payment is interest? The first month's interest is 1% of the loan, that is $1\% \times 500 = £5$.

Thus the repayment $R = £5$ (interest) and £25.49 (capital).

The capital outstanding is the initial loan plus the first month's interest less the repayment.

Thus present capital $= £500 + £5 - £30.49 = £474.51$.

At the end of month 2:

Another repayment of $R = £30.49$ is made.

The interest paid will be 1% of the balance outstanding at the end of the previous month: $1\% \times 474.51 = £4.75$ to the nearest penny.

Thus the repayment $R = £4.75$ (interest) and £25.74 (capital).

The capital outstanding is the previous month's capital balance plus the second month's interest less the second repayment.

Hence the capital outstanding is $£474.51 + £4.75 - £30.49 = £448.77$

At the end of month 3:

A third repayment of $R = £30.49$ is made.

The interest paid will be 1% of the balance outstanding at the end of the previous month: $1\% \times 448.77 = £4.49$ to the nearest penny.

Thus the repayment $R = £4.49$ (interest) and £26 (capital).

The capital outstanding is the previous month's capital balance plus the third month's interest less the third repayment.

Hence the capital outstanding is $£448.77 + £4.49 - £30.49 = £422.77$

In a table we can see this more clearly:

End of period	Repayment	Repayment interest	Breakdown of capital	Capital outstanding
1	£30.49	£5	£25.49	474.51
2	£30.49	£4.75	£24.74	448.77
3	£30.49	£4.49	£26.00	422.77
.				
.				
.				
18	£30.49			0
Total	£548.82	48.82	500.00	0

We can see that the interest does indeed decrease each month and the capital repaid increases. The total repaid is the sum of the 18 monthly repayments which is $18 \times £30.49 = £548.82$. Thus the total interest paid is £48.82.

Exercises 6.5

6.5.1 For the 4th and 5th periods calculate the entries in the above table in the same way as in the example above.

6.5.2 Use a spreadsheet (such as Excel) to enter the above information and set up the columns to calculate each of the columns in the above table.

6.5.3 Use this spreadsheet and change the value of r to 16%.

Derivation of the formula for an annuity for a loan account

Now we need to find the formula for the loan/annuity.

As we have already stated, we shall denote the initial advance by A_0, which is the present value of the loan.

At the end of month 1:

The amount of the loan outstanding at the end of the 1st month is given by A_1. We can see from the above example that this was

$A_1 = £500$ (loan A_0) + £5 (interest) − £30.49 (repayment R)

Notice that the interest was given by the monthly rate $\times A_0$. For ease we shall denote the monthly rate by i where i in fact stands for $\dfrac{\text{annual rate as percentage}}{12}$

Thus $A_1 = A_0 + (i \times A_0) - R$ which we can tidy up to arrive at:

$A_1 = A_0 + iA_0 - R$ which we would factorise to give $A_1 = A_0(1 + i) - R$

To check this is correct put in the values: $i = 0.01$, $A_0 = £500$ and $R = £30.49$. We arrive at $A_1 = £500 \times (1 + 0.01) - £30.49 = £500 \times 1.01 - £30.49$ which is indeed £474.51 as expected. Proceeding in this manner we can see that

At the end of month 2:

The amount of the loan outstanding at the end of the 2nd month is given by A_2. We can see from the above example that this was

$A_2 = £474.51$ (balance of loan at the end of month 1) $+ £4.75$ (interest for month 2) $- £30.49$ (repayment R)

Notice that the interest was given by the monthly rate $\times A_1$.

Thus $A_2 = A_1 + (i \times A_1) - R$ which we can tidy up to arrive at:

$A_2 = A_1 + iA_1 - R$ which we would factorise to give $A_2 = A_1(1 + i) - R$. Now from the previous calculation we had $A_1 = A_0(1 + i) - R$ and so we can substitute this into A_2 to find A_2 in terms of A_0, R and i alone. Thus

$A_2 = A_1(1 + i) - R = \{A_0(1 + i) - R\}(1 + i) - R$. Now if we multiply this out we arrive at

$A_2 = A_0(1 + i)^2 - R(1 + i) - R.$

A similar expression for $A_3 = A_2 + iA_2 - R = A_2(1 + i) - R$ and hence

$$A_3 = A_0(1 + i)^3 - R(1 + i)^2 - R(1 + i) - R. \tag{6.1}$$

Consider the last three terms of this expression for A_3. If we factorise the $(-R)$ out and write in the reverse order we see that we have

$$- R(1 + i)^2 - R(1 + i) - R = -R[1 + (1 + i) + (1 + i)^2]$$

which is a GP with the first term $a = 1$ and the common multiplier $(1 + i)$ with 3 terms. Thus its sum for the first three terms (denoted by S_3) will be

$$- R(1 + i)^2 - R(1 + i) - R = -R \times S_3$$

where $S_3 = a\dfrac{(1 - \text{ratio}^3)}{(1 - \text{ratio})}$ being a GP.

Thus $S_3 = 1 \times \dfrac{(1 - (1 + i)^3)}{1 - (1 + i)} = \dfrac{(1 - (1 + i)^3)}{-i}$ which can be written as

$S_3 = \dfrac{(1 + i)^3 - 1}{i}$ if multiply top and bottom by (-1).

Putting this back into line (6.1) above we have:

$$A_3 = A_0(1 + i)^3 - R(1 + i)^2 - R(1 + i) - R = A_0(1 + i)^3 - R \times S_3$$

$$\Rightarrow A_3 = A_0(1 + i)^3 - R \times \dfrac{(1 + i)^3 - 1}{i}$$

Continuing in this fashion we would find that we would replace 3 by n in the above. That is

$$A_n = A_0(1 + i)^n - R \times \dfrac{(1 + i)^n - 1}{i}$$

Now at the end of the term of the loan all the capital is cleared, and so A_n is zero. Thus

$$A_0(1 + i)^n = R \times \frac{(1 + i)^n - 1}{i} \tag{6.2}$$

We can now find an expression for the amount the loan would be, A_0, if periodic repayments of £R are made. This is found by dividing (6.2) by $(1 + i)^n$ which would give us:

$$A_0 = R \times \frac{(1 + i)^n - 1}{i} \div (1 + i)^n \text{ which could be written}$$

$$A_0 = R \times \frac{(1 + i)^n - 1}{i(1 + i)^n} \text{ or equivalently } A_0 = \frac{R}{i}\{1 - (1 + i)^{-n}\}$$

Similarly if we divide (6.2) by $\dfrac{(1 + i)^n - 1}{i}$ we would arrive at an expression for the periodic repayment R.

This is:

$$R = A_0(1 + i)^n \div \frac{(1 + i)^n - 1}{i}$$

which is equivalent to

$$R = \frac{A_0(1 + i)^n}{1} \times \frac{i}{(1 + i)^n - 1} = \frac{i \times A_0(1 + i)^n}{(1 + i)^n - 1}$$

Now if we divide top and bottom of the fraction by the bracket $(1 + i)^n$ this will simplify the expression for R.

Thus

$$R = \frac{i \times A_0}{1 - (1 + i)^{-n}}$$

Example 6.14

Use the above formula for finding the monthly repayment for the store's credit facilities on the TV and video recorder purchased for £500.

Solution

Here the periodic payment is made each month for 18 months. Thus $n = 18$, the annual rate is 12% and so the monthly rate i is 1% = 0.01 and A_0 is £500.

Thus using

$$R = \frac{iA_0}{1 - (1 + i)^{-n}} = \frac{0.01 \times 500}{1 - (1 + 0.01)^{-18}}$$

The numerator reduces to 5 whilst the denominator becomes

$$1 - (1 + 0.01)^{-18} = 1 - (1.01)^{-18}$$

Taking the bracket first we need to press 1.01 $\boxed{x^{-y}}$ 18 $\boxed{\pm}$ = and this would give us 0.836 017 314. Store this value in the memory by pressing $\boxed{\text{M in}}$. Now we need to find $1 - 0.836\,017\,314$ which we do by pressing $1 - \boxed{\text{MR}}$ = and on the display we would have 0.163 982 685. Finally

$R = \frac{5}{0.163\,982\,685} = \pounds 30.49$. We can thus see that the monthly charge quoted by the store was indeed correct.

Example 6.15

Mortgages: if you can afford to make a monthly net repayment on your mortgage of £670 and wish to take out a 100% 25 year repayment mortgage with the Haliflux Building Society who are offering a rate of 8% per annum, what price house could you afford to purchase?

Solution

Here we can use the above formula for an annuity—which in this case Haliflux are buying on your behalf. You will make monthly repayments to them. If you are taking out a 100% mortgage this means that you are borrowing the full amount of the house purchase and are not advancing any deposit. The term of the loan is 25 years, which is 25×12 months and so $n = 300$. The repayment is $R = \pounds 670$, and the monthly rate is $i = \frac{8\%}{12} = \frac{0.08}{12} = 0.006\,666\,667$. Here we need to find A_0 which is the present value of the annuity: that is the amount the building society will forward.

Thus using $A_0 = \dfrac{R[1 - (1 + i)^{-n}]}{i}$ we have

$$A_0 = \frac{670[1 - (1 + 0.006\,666\,667)^{-300}]}{0.006\,666\,667}$$

Looking at the numerator we first tidy the inside bracket:

$(1 + 0.006\,666\,667)^{-300} = (1.006\,666\,667)^{-300}$; using the calculator this is:

$1.006\,666\,667$ $\boxed{x^y}$ 300 $\boxed{\pm}$ = this will give you 0.136 236 516. Store this value in the memory using $\boxed{\text{M in}}$. Returning to the overall calculation we now have:

$$A_0 = \frac{670[1 - 0.136\,236\,516]}{0.006\,666\,667}$$

Again tidying the numerator we will have $1 - \boxed{\text{MR}}$ which is 0.863 763 483. We now multiply this latter value by 670. This gives us 578.721 534 1 for the numerator. Thus

$$A_0 = \frac{578.721\,534\,1}{0.006\,666\,667} = \pounds 86\,808.24;$$ thus Haliflux would be prepared to lend you at most £87 000 for your house purchase. The only proviso is that your income could support such a mortgage!

Example 6.16

You are about to retire at the age of 60. Your company pension plan has matured to give you a sum of £100 000. Royalty Life are offering the sale of annuities at a rate of 10% compounded annually. They quote a guaranteed annual income of £11 257 for a woman and £12 782 for a man. These figures are based on average life expectancy of 83 years for a woman and 76 years for a man. How are these incomes calculated? (This would be the second stage of the two-stage annuity type.)

Solution

If the sum invested $A_0 = 100\,000$, and $i = 0.1$ then for a woman, assuming she lives for 23 years, $n = 23$. Thus the annual income would be

$$R = \frac{iA_0}{(1 - (1 + i)^{-n}} = \frac{0.1 \times 100\,000}{1 - (1 + 0.1)^{-23}} = \frac{10\,000}{0.888\,321\,842} = £11\,257.18$$

Similarly for a man, his life expectancy is 16 years beyond the age of 60, and thus you would expect his annual income to be more than the woman's, as it would be paid on average for fewer years. Thus

$$R = \frac{iA_0}{1 - (1 + i)^{-n}} = \frac{0.1 \times 100\,000}{1 - (1 + 0.1)^{-16}} = \frac{10\,000}{0.782\,370\,864} = 12\,781.66$$

Exercises 6.6

6.6.1 Derive the loan account formula using the present values as follows:

(i)   At the time of the advance of the loan, the present value of the first repayment made at the end of period 1 is $[R/(1 + i)]$. Explain why this is so.

(ii) The present value of the second repayment has a value of $[R/(1 + i)^2]$. Similarly the value when the loan is advanced of the final nth repayment will be $[R/(1 + i)^n]$. Explain why this is so.

(iii) Explain why these present values form a GP.

(iv) By summing each of these present values find an expression for the sum of the present values, which will be the total advance.

6.6.2 What would the monthly repayment be on a car loan of £5000 if it is repaid over 3 years at a nominal interest rate of 15% per annum?

6.6.3 If the monthly repayment of a hire purchase agreement is £150 per quarter, what would the loan have been if it was repaid over 2 years at a nominal rate of 8% per annum?

6.6.4 What mortgage could a person take out if they could afford to pay £900 per month over 25 years and are offered a rate of 6.4% per annum?

6.6.5 You are about to retire at the age of 65. Your company pension plan has matured to give you a sum of £350 000. Pro-Life are offering the sale of annuities at a rate of 7.5% compounded annually. They quote a guaranteed annual income for a woman and for a man. These figures are based on average life expectancy of 85 years for a woman and 78 years for a man. How much would this guaranteed income be?

Savings plan or sinking fund

Example 6.17

I wish to invest £1000 each year into a savings plan, which will mature in 5 years' time. The Boston Assurance Company are advertising such plans at a nominal rate of 4% per annum, compounded annually. If I make payments at the beginning of each year, what would my savings plan be worth at maturity?

Solution

Year 1: At the beginning of year 1, I pay £1000 into the plan. This will then be accruing interest for the whole term, here 5 years. Thus the future value of this first payment can be calculated using the future value formula, as each premium, P, matures in the future, namely at the end of the term of the savings plan. The future value for P using the compound interest formula is:

$$A_n = P\left(1 + \frac{i}{100}\right)^n$$

Thus here $n = 5$, $i = 4$ and $P = £1000$ which gives us:

$$A_5 = £1000 \times \left(1 + \frac{4}{100}\right)^5$$

which gives us:

$$A_5 = £1000 \times (1.04)^5$$
$$= £1000 \times 1.216\,652\,902$$
$$= £1216.65$$

Year 2: At the beginning of year 2, another £1000 is deposited, and this will be accruing interest for the remaining 4 years. Thus at the end of the term of the plan this will have a future value of:

$$A_4 = £1000 \times \left(1 + \frac{4}{100}\right)^4$$

which gives us:

$$A_4 = £1000 \times (1.04)^4$$
$$= £1000 \times 1.169\,858\,56$$
$$= £1169.86$$

Year 3: Similarly at the start of year 3, a further £1000 is paid into the plan, and this will be on deposit for the remaining 3 years of the plan. Thus its future value will be worth $A_3 = £1000 \times (1.04)^3 = £1124.86$.

Continuing in this way we would have:

Year 4: Future value would be: $A_2 = £1000 \times (1.04)^2 = £1081.60$

Year 5: Future value would be: $A_1 = £1000 \times (1.04)^1 = £1040$

Notice that this final payment is only on deposit for 1 year.

Thus the total value of the savings plan at maturity is the sum of each of these future values $= A_1 + A_2 + A_3 + A_4 + A_5 = £1040 + £1081.60 + £1124.86 + £1169.86 + £1216.65 = £5632.97$

which would be £5000 payments into the plan and interest earned to the value of £632.97.

Mathematical formulation of this sinking fund/savings plan

For simplicity we write i in place of $\dfrac{i}{100}$; thus i is the percentage rate of interest. Notice that in fact the total value of the sinking fund is the sum of future values of:

sinking fund $= A_1 + A_2 + A_3 + A_4 + A_5$

and as each of these terms has an exact formulation we can write this as:

sinking fund $= A_1 + A_2 + A_3 + A_4 + A_5$
$= P(1+i)^1 + P(1+i)^2 + P(1+i)^3 + P(1+i)^4 + P(1+i)^5$

Now this is a geometric progression with a common ratio of $(1 + i)$ and a first term of $P(1 + i)$. Thus we are finding the sum to 5 terms of this GP which would be calculated using the sum to n terms of a GP is:

$$S_n = a\frac{(1 - r^n)}{(1 - r)}$$

where a is the first term. r is the common multiplier. Hence

$$\text{sinking fund} = A_1 + A_2 + A_3 + A_4 + A_5 = a\frac{(1 - r^n)}{(1 - r)}$$

$$S = \text{sinking fund} = P(1+i) \times \left(\frac{1 - (1+i)^5}{1 - (1+i)}\right) = P(1+i) \times \left(\frac{1 - (1+i)^5}{-i}\right)$$

which can be written as:

$$S = P(1+i) \times \left(\frac{(1+i)^5 - 1}{i}\right)$$

if we divide the top and bottom fraction by (-1).

Thus the general formula for a savings plan/sinking fund for n periods at a nominal rate of $i\%$ compounded each period with a periodic investment of $£P$ is S where:

$$S = P(1+i) \times \left(\frac{(1+i)^n - 1}{i}\right)$$

Example 6.18
Check that this does indeed agree with the above calculation.

Solution
We need to evaluate

$$S = P(1+i) \times \left(\frac{(1+i)^5 - 1}{i}\right)$$

using $i = 4$ and $P = £1000$. Thus

$$\text{sinking fund} = P(1 + i) \times \left(\frac{(1 + i)^5 - 1}{i} \right)$$

$$= £1000 \left(1 + \frac{4}{100} \right) \times \left(\frac{\left(1 + \frac{4}{100} \right)^5 - 1}{\frac{4}{100}} \right)$$

$$= £1000 \times 1.04 \times \left(\frac{(1.04)^5 - 1}{0.04} \right)$$

$$= £1040 \times \left(\frac{1.216\,652\,902 - 1}{0.04} \right)$$

$$= £1040 \times \frac{0.216\,652\,902}{0.04} = £5632.98.$$

which does indeed agree.

Exercises 6.7

6.7.1 Mr and Mrs Jones wish to set up a sinking fund for their child's education. They can afford to pay premiums of £250 per month for 7 years, which is when their child goes to preparatory school. What would their savings mature to if a favourable rate of 6.2% is offered, compounded monthly?

6.7.2 Re-arrange the formula for S to make P the subject. Use this to answer the following problem.

In 10 years the 30 year lease on a company's headquarters in London expires. This is likely to be sold for £1.3 million. What would the premium on a savings plan need to be to meet this future commitment if an annuity can be bought at a rate of 9% per annum compounded monthly?

Summary

Loan account

If an annuity is purchased for a sum of A_0 at a rate of $i\%$ compounded each period then the periodic repayment is

$$R = \frac{iA_0}{1 - (1 + i)^{-n}}$$

and the present value of the annuity A_0 (the loan) is

$$A_0 = R \times \frac{(1+i)^n - 1}{i(1+i)^n} \quad \text{or equivalently } A_0 = \frac{R[1 - (1+i)^{-n}]}{i}$$

Savings account

A savings plan/sinking fund invested for n periods at a nominal rate of $i\%$ compounded each period with a periodic investment of $£P$ matures to S where

$$S = P(1+i) \times \left(\frac{(1+i)^n - 1}{i}\right)$$

Exercises 6.8 _____

6.8.1 A car loan is offered on all new Romer cars. If a Romer Golf is currently sold at £6900, and the loan over 3 years is at a rate of 8.25% per annum, what would your quarterly payment be? What would a monthly payment be? How much interest would you pay for each method of repayment?

6.8.2 Bradfield Building Society are currently offering a repayment mortgage for 15-year terms at an annual fixed interest rate of 11.2%. If you want to buy a country cottage for £48 000, what would your monthly repayment be?

6.8.3 Standardise Life are offering the sale of an annuity for a lump sum of £100 000 at a rate of 9% per annum. What would your expected annual income be if you purchased this annuity with your matured pension plan, if you are expected to live for 25 years if a woman and 17 if a man?

6.8.4 What would monthly savings of £40 be worth in 15 years' time if interest accrues at a nominal rate of 5.5% compounded quarterly?

7 What's the chance?

Objectives

- Understand the concepts of probability and conditional probability;
- Be able to use and interpret a Venn diagram and a tree diagram;
- Understand the notion of expected value;
- Use discrete probability models: binomial and Poisson.

Probability

Scenario

- You are asked to look at whether a die used in a casino is fair. How would you check this or how would you know if it was not fair? If two die are thrown simultaneously and the sum of the two die is 10, what is the likelihood that one of the die shows an even number? If you are playing cards with a friend and a spade has just been dealt, what's the chance that this card is the queen of spades?
- A survey of holidays by an agency called EuroTours gives information on what type of holiday is preferred by which age group. What proportion of the 21 to 30 age group prefer beach holidays? If this survey shows that one age group spends on average more than any other, what sort of holiday should this company be marketing to this age group for optimum sales? Would this affect the promotional material for different types of holiday?

These problems in the scenario relating to chance are investigated within the topic of probability and we shall answer these and other problems below.

Probability: empirical versus theoretical

Consider the problem of a fair die in the casino. A regular die has 6 faces, numbered from 1 to 6. If we throw the die it would be considered fair if there was an equal chance of the die landing on any one of its faces. One way of investigating the problem would be to carry out an experiment and throw the die a large number of times and count the number of times it landed on any particular face. For example, we might throw the die 60 times and during this trial we would expect to get roughly ten 1s, ten 2s, etc. We might not get exactly 10 of each face but we would perhaps get 9 1s and 12 2s and 10 3s etc. The result of this experiment would clearly be different each time we carried out the experiment. We would call this *empirical* data, and from this we can calculate empirical probability—these are only relevant to this particular experiment. Performing this experiment would not formally prove that the die was indeed fair (although this could be done with other statistical tools) but it would certainly highlight if one side of the die were weighted!

We would define the probability of face n turning up on any throw to be the number of times such a face occurred on the die divided by the total number of trials—here this would be the total number of throws of the die. We could write this using shorthand (and in fact more formally) by saying P(some event) denotes the probability of 'some event' happening. Thus we could define empirical probability as:

$$P(\text{scoring a face } n) = \frac{\text{number of times } n \text{ occurs}}{\text{total number of trials}}$$

where n could be 1, or 2, or 3, ... 6. Here as we noted above there were 9 1s in 60 throws of the dice. This would give us a probability:

$$P(\text{scoring a face } 1) = \frac{\text{number of 1s}}{\text{number of trials}} = \frac{9}{60}$$

and if we reduced this fraction to its lowest form we would have P(scoring a 1) $= \frac{3}{20}$ as a decimal this is 0.15. In fact we might call this the *relative frequency* of scoring a 1.

Similarly scoring a 2 would have a probability of P(scoring a 2) $= \frac{12}{60} = \frac{1}{5}$ or 0.2.

It is clear that if each time you wanted to work out a probability you had first to conduct the experiment, then the theory would progress very slowly, and each time you carried out the experiment you would be likely to get different values for such probabilities.

If each time we had thrown the die 60 times we observed the exact same number of 1s, 2s, ... 6s we would be rather suspicious, although it is just possible that it could happen. Thus empirical probability is the starting point, but we move on to a more concrete fixed value probability: *theoretical probability*.

Definition: The probability of an event A occurring is the chance or likelihood of this event occurring. It is defined to be the number of ways such an event can occur divided by the total number of possible outcomes for the problem. We would write this as:

$$P(\text{Event A}) = \frac{\text{number of times A can occur}}{\text{total number of outcomes}}$$

For the die there are 6 possible outcomes: scoring 1, 2, 3, 4, 5, 6. This set of all possible outcomes is often referred to as the *sample space*. Thus the denominator for the above definition would be:

$$P(\text{scoring a value } n \text{ on the die}) = \frac{\text{number of times } n \text{ occurs on die}}{6}$$

Hence P(scoring 1) $= \frac{1}{6}$, as there is only 1 face numbered 1 on a regular die. Similarly the P(scoring 2) $= \frac{1}{6}$, and P(scoring 3) $= \frac{1}{6}$, ... P(scoring 6) $= \frac{1}{6}$.

We can immediately see that the values on the faces are fixed and so the theoretical probability will always be fixed for this 6-sided die. It is clear that if we want to build a theory for calculating probabilities, being sure of the probability for any particular event is very convenient and avoids all the experimentation and all the various possible values of probability. Thus theoretical probabilities are soundly based and do not depend on the results of this particular experiment. For this reason, we always use the theoretical probability on which to build our theory of probability.

What is the relationship between theoretical and empirical probability? It is simply this: if we allow the number of repetitions of our experiment to increase indefinitely, for example instead of throwing the die 60 times we keep throwing the die, then the value of the empirical probability (or relative frequency) approaches the theoretical probability and gets closer as the number of repetitions increases. We could say that as the number of trials increase *ad infinitum* then the empirical probability coincides with the theoretical probability.

Example 7.1

In a pack of 52 cards, there are four suits: hearts, diamonds, clubs and spades. Each suit contains 13 cards. A card is selected at random: what is the chance of this being a heart?

Solution

Using our definition of probability we can say:

$$P(\text{heart}) = \frac{\text{number of hearts in the pack}}{\text{total number of cards in the pack}}$$

We can see that there are 13 hearts and so $P(\text{heart}) = \frac{13}{52} = \frac{1}{4}$.

This is natural if we think that a quarter of the pack is made up of hearts and so there is a 1 in 4 chance that the card chosen at random will be of any particular suit. We could equally express the probability as a percentage and say that there is a 25% chance of selecting a heart. Notice that a probability is also a proportion: here the proportion which are hearts.

Absolute certainty and impossibility

Notice that probabilities have a certain range of possible values: if an event is impossible it has no chance of occurring, and so the probability is zero. No probability can be less than this value. Similarly there is an upper bound on the values probabilities can take: if an absolute certain event occurs it has 100% chance of happening and so the largest possible value for probability is 1. This is useful—if you get silly answers such as negative or values larger than 1 you must have made an error either in your underlying assumptions or in your calculations (see figure 7.1).

Example 7.2

Today is Thursday. What's the chance of today being Thursday? What's the chance of tomorrow being Sunday?

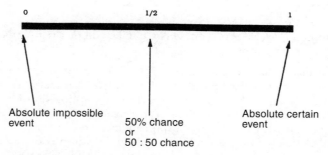

Figure 7.1

Solution

We can see that if today is Thursday, then P(today is Thursday) = 1. Clearly tomorrow is Friday and so it is not possible for it to be Sunday, and so P(tomorrow is Sunday) = 0.

Example 7.3

Two die are thrown simultaneously and their sum is recorded. Find the probability that the sum is 8 and the probability that the sum is divisible by 3.

Solution

We need to think about all the possible outcomes on finding the sum of two die: clearly the minimum sum is when a 1 is on both die and the maximum when there is a 6 on both die. In fact putting all the outcomes into a table is helpful: it means we will not forget any outcomes and we can simply use this to read off the solutions. For example, the first row of the table below is found by finding the sum when a 1 is on the one die and any value 1 to 6 is on the other die.

Die 1						
6	7	8	9	10	11	12
5	6	7	8	9	10	11
4	5	6	7	8	9	10
3	4	5	6	7	8	9
2	3	4	5	6	7	8
1	2	3	4	5	6	7

| Sum | 1 | 2 | 3 | 4 | 5 | 6 |

Die 2

We can see that there are a total of 36 possible outcomes.

The sum of 8 occurs as a diagonal row in the table—that is 5 times, when such combinations as a 2 and 6, or 3 and 5, etc. occur. Thus the probability of the sum of two die being 8 is

$$P(\text{sum} = 8) = \frac{\text{number of sums being 8}}{\text{total number of outcomes}} = \frac{5}{36}$$

Similarly the total number of sums being divisible by 3 is 12 out of 36, that is

P(sum is divisible by 3) = $\frac{12}{36} = \frac{1}{3}$

Exercises 7.1 _____

In the above example find the probability of the sum of two die is:

7.1.1 six;

7.1.2 five;

7.1.3 divisible by 4;

7.1.4 even.

7.1.5 Describe the terms event, sample space and trial.

Notice that if we know the chance of the sum of the two die is 8, then immediately we also know the chance that the sum will not be 8. As there are 36 outcomes and 5 are when the sum is 8, the remaining 31 are when the sum is not 8. This gives us a probability: P(sum is not 8) = $\frac{31}{36}$. That is we have a law of probability. There are three laws of probability that govern the way events interact or exclude other events.

Basic laws of probability

Law I: addition law—A OR B

Example 7.4

In the pack of 52 cards what is the chance that a card will be a heart or a queen?

Solution

In 52 cards we know that 13 are hearts and 4 are queens. Thus if we simply added these together we would have all the possible ways of a card being a heart or a queen—and in terms of probability this would give us $\frac{13}{52} + \frac{4}{52}$.

Is there any problem here? In fact we have counted some events twice! There are 13 hearts—this includes the queen of hearts; then we added this to the 4 queens—again this included the queen of hearts. We simply need to count all possible events once only to arrive at the answer: here we correct our sum by subtracting off the event we have counted twice:

P(heart or a queen) = P(heart) + P(queen) − P(heart and a queen), i.e. the queen of hearts.

Thus P(heart or a queen) = $\frac{13}{52} + \frac{4}{52} - \frac{1}{52}$

We could represent this on a diagram called a Venn diagram. This involves using a circle to represent each event; we would then have two overlapping circles for the possible outcomes as shown in figure 7.2.

The shaded area denotes where both events occur—the card is a heart and a queen—the card is the queen of hearts. There are in fact 4 distinct areas in this Venn diagram: outside the two circles where the card is not a heart or queen. (There are 36 cards which remain when we have selected all the hearts and queens.) In the centre there is only 1 card which is in both the set of hearts and queens. In the area representing the hearts but not in the queens there are 12

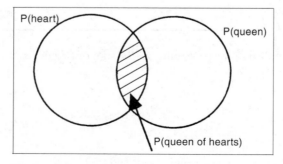

Figure 7.2

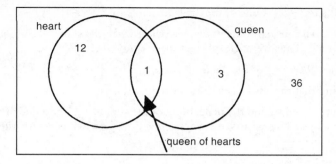

Figure 7.3

cards, and in the circle for the queens but not in the hearts there are 3 possible cards. Thus we could put these figures on the Venn diagram—in terms of possible outcomes or probability—but number of outcomes is most useful. This gives figure 7.3.

Notice that all possible sectors add up to 52—the total number of outcomes. Such diagrams which evolved in set theory are very helpful when we move to more complex probabilities—and can easily be extended to 3 events.

Let A denote the event the card is a heart and B denote the event the card is a queen then this in fact gives us the law for A OR B:

$$P(A \text{ OR } B) = P(A) + P(B) - P(A \text{ AND } B)$$

Example 7.5
In the sum of two die example what would be the probability of the sum being 9 or one of the die is divisible by 3? Check that the above law does indeed hold here.

Solution
Using the table of the sum of two die, we could count the number of times the sum is 9. This can occur in 4 ways. The number of times one of the die is divisible by 3 is when the die is either a 3 or a 6 which occurs in 20 of the outcomes. These are outlined in figure 7.4.

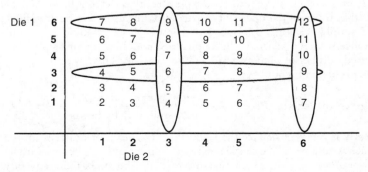

Figure 7.4

Thus P(sum = 9 OR one of the die is divisible by 3) = $\frac{24}{36}$

But we have counted some outcomes twice: when the sum is 9 and the one die is a 3 or a 6. Thus we must subtract these 2 outcomes:

P(sum) = 9 OR one of the die is divisible by 3) = $\frac{24}{36} - \frac{2}{36} = \frac{22}{36} = \frac{11}{18}$

Checking that the above law does indeed hold here:

We simply need to find the probability of the sum being 9 and one of the die is divisible by 3. This occurs in 2 ways and is thus $\frac{2}{36}$, which is exactly the amount subtracted.

Example 7.6

In the sum of two die example what would be the probability of the sum being 8 or the sum being divisible by 3?

Solution

Using the table of the sum of two die, we could count the number of times the sum is 8 or the sum is divisible by 3 and arrive at 5, for the sum is 8 and 12 for the sum being divisible by 3. Thus the probability P(sum = 8 OR sum is divisible by 3) = $\frac{17}{36}$.

Notice that if the sum is 8 it cannot be divisible by 3: they cannot both occur simultaneously. Such events are called *mutually exclusive*. Thus we do not need to subtract off where both events occur as this is zero.

For mutually exclusive events the law of addition is simply:

P(A OR B) = P(A) + P(B)

A Venn diagram here would be two disjoint circles.

Notice in each of the above examples we have calculated the chance of *both* events occurring simultaneously without needing to refer to any formal method of calculation. In order to proceed to formulate a law for A AND B we need to look at conditional events first.

Conditional probability

Suppose from the pack of 52 cards you have already selected a heart. What would the chance be that this was the queen of hearts? Would this in fact be any different to the chance of simply selecting the queen of hearts? Yes it would: we would argue as follows. Once we have selected a heart this card could be any of 13 possible cards. So now the total number of outcomes is 13 rather than 52. There is only 1 queen of hearts and so the probability would be:

$$P(\text{queen given that the card is a heart}) = \frac{\text{number of queen of hearts}}{\text{number of hearts}} = \frac{1}{13}$$

which clearly is a higher chance than selecting the queen of hearts from a pack of 52 cards, which would be $\frac{1}{52}$. We can see that selecting the queen when we know the card is a heart is *conditional* on the event that the card is a heart. Is there any other way of calculating this which would lead to a formula? Well, if we took the P(queen of hearts) and divided this by the chance of selecting a heart, $\frac{1}{4}$ we would arrive at $\frac{1}{52} \div \frac{1}{4}$ which gives us $\frac{1}{13}$.

Formally we would write P(queen given the card is a heart) $= \dfrac{\text{P(queen of hearts)}}{\text{P(heart)}}$

We usually use the notation for 'given that' and write a vertical line |.

Thus if selecting a queen is event A and selecting a heart is event B we would write the law for conditional probability as:

$$P(A \mid B) = \frac{P(A \text{ AND } B)}{P(B)}$$

By interchanging A and B we would also have $P(B \mid A) = \dfrac{P(A \text{ AND } B)}{P(B)}$. Notice that we divide by the second event's probability. In terms of a Venn diagram we would say that $P(A \mid B)$ is the fraction of the shaded $P(A \text{ AND } B)$ which lies in the area $P(B)$, see figure 7.5.

We take the proportion in B because B has definitely occurred.

Not all probabilities are conditional. Whenever the outcome of one event does not affect the chance of another event occurring then we say such events are independent. For example, if each time we throw the pair of die we select a card from the pack, clearly these events are independent: whatever the sum of the two die this does not make it any more or less likely that we will select a heart.

This leads us naturally to the law for the AND of two events which we shall treat in two cases: firstly when events are conditional, and secondly the special case when events are independent.

Law 2: multiplication law—A AND B

Example 7.7 Conditional Events
In the sum of two die what is the chance that the sum is 9 and one of the die is divisible by 6?

Solution
Let A be the event the sum is 9 and B be the event one die is divisible by 6.

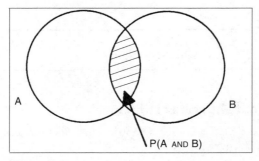

Figure 7.5

In the table of the sum of two die we are thus looking at the top row and far right column and observing when one of these outcomes gives a sum of 9. There are 2 such outcomes and so the probability is $\frac{2}{36}$ or $\frac{1}{18}$.

More formally we need to calculate P(A AND B) which is found by re-arranging the rule for conditional probability, which stated: $P(A \mid B) = \dfrac{P(A \ \text{AND} \ B)}{P(B)}$. Multiplying through by P(B) we arrive at:

Law 2: P(A AND B) where A and B are conditional events

$$P(A \ \text{AND} \ B) = P(A \mid B) \times P(B) \tag{7.1}$$

Thus we need to find the probability of A | B which means the sum is 9 given that one die is a 6. In the table of the sum of two die we are thus looking at the top row and far right column which means when one die is a 6. There are 11 possible outcomes here. Two of these outcomes give us when the sum is 9. Thus $P(A \mid B) = \frac{2}{11}$. Now $P(B) = \frac{11}{36}$ and so combining these we have

$$P(A \ \text{AND} \ B) = P(A \mid B) \times P(B) = \frac{2}{11} \times \frac{11}{36} = \frac{2}{36} \ \text{or} \ \frac{1}{18}$$

Are these two events conditional or are they independent?

If two events are independent then using the definition of conditional probability $P(A \mid B) = \dfrac{P(A \ \text{AND} \ B)}{P(B)}$ we can see that if the chance of A occurring does not depend on B then $P(A \mid B)$ is simply the probability of A. Similarity $P(B \mid A) = P(B)$. Now putting this into the Law 2 above 7.1 we have

Law 2': P(A AND B) where A and B are independent events

$P(A \ \text{AND} \ B) = P(A) \times P(B)$.

We can see that in this example $P(A) = \frac{4}{36}$ or $\frac{1}{9}$ and thus if A and B were independent $P(A \ \text{AND} \ B) = P(A) \times P(B) = \frac{1}{9} \times \frac{11}{36} = \frac{11}{324}$ which is clearly not $\frac{1}{18}$.

Thus we not only have a law for computing the AND of conditional and independent events we also have a way of checking whether two events are independent or not: we simply need to compute P(A AND B) as if they were conditional and then compute P(A) × P(B), and if these are not equal the events are not independent but conditional.

Exercise 7.2 _____

Draw a Venn diagram to represent these events.

Law 3: law of total probability

P(event A or not event A) = 1. Either A happens or A does not with absolute certainty. Using law 1 we could re-write this as

P(event A) + P(not event A) = 1. Using $\overline{A}$ (or A') for not A this would be written:

$P(A) + P(\overline{A}) = 1.$

In the sum of the two die we saw that the sum being 8 was $\frac{5}{36}$ and the sum being not 8 was $\frac{31}{36}$ and it is clear that this gives us 1. In terms of the Venn diagram this means that the numbers in each sector add up to the total number of outcomes.

Summary

Probability $P(\text{Event A}) = \dfrac{\text{number of times A can occur}}{\text{Total number of outcomes}}$

Conditional Probability

The probability of A occurring given that B has occurred is given by

$P(A \mid B) = \dfrac{P(A \text{ AND } B)}{P(B)}$

Events A and B are Mutually Exclusive if $P(A \text{ AND } B) = 0$

Events A and B are Independent if $P(A \mid B) = P(A)$

Basic laws of probability

Law 1: Addition Law — A OR B
$P(A \text{ OR } B) = P(A) + P(B) - P(A \text{ AND } B)$

Law 2: $P(A \text{ AND } B)$ where A and B are Conditional Events
$P(A \text{ AND } B) = P(A \mid B) \times P(B)$

Law 2′: $P(A \text{ AND } B)$ where A and B are Independent Events
$P(A \text{ AND } B) = P(A) \times P(B)$

Law 3: Law of total probability
$P(A) + P(\overline{A}) = 1$

Exercise 7.3 _____

A survey of 115 chartered accountants was conducted to determine the principal hobbies of a typical accountant. The following information was produced:

52 played golf;
36 enjoyed gardening;
26 restored vintage cars;

18 played golf and restored vintage cars;
10 played golf and enjoyed gardening;
5 enjoyed gardening and restoring vintage cars;

27 did not undertake any of these activities.

Represent this information on a Venn diagram. (Notice that if you add all individual sectors of the Venn diagram you will have 115, the total number surveyed.) Using the Venn diagram determine the probability that an accountant chosen at random from the group of 115 surveyed:

(i)   did not enjoy any of the three activities;
(ii)   enjoyed all three activities;
(iii) enjoyed golf and gardening but not vintage cars.

Example 7.8

EuroTours, the holiday agency, conducted a survey of 160 of its previous customers to assist in the marketing of its holidays. The agency wanted to know what type of summer holiday was preferred by which age group. The age groups were divided into 5 groups: under 21, 21 to 30, 31 to 40, 41 to 50 and the over 50s. The results of the survey were put into a table below (sometimes called a contingency table):

	Type of holiday		
Age of person	**Water sports**	**Beach**	**Walking**
under 21	8	15	2
21–30	17	16	10
31–40	9	14	17
41–50	5	13	13
over 50	1	9	11

A person is selected at random from this group of 160 people. Find the probability that such a person is (i) aged under 21, (ii) prefers a beach holiday.

Solution

How to use the contingency table to calculate probabilities:

We simply total each of the rows and columns to give us the total number in (a) each age group, (b) preferring each type of holiday. For example, there are a total of $8 + 15 + 2$ people in this survey aged under 21. Similarly there are a total of $8 + 17 + 9 + 5 + 1$ which is 40 who prefer water sports holidays.

(i) The probability that a person is aged under 21 would be $=$

$$\frac{\text{number of people aged under 21}}{\text{total number of people}} = \frac{8 + 15 + 2}{160} = \frac{25}{160}$$

which can be reduced to $\frac{5}{32}$ or 0.156 to 3 decimal places.

(ii) Similarly to find the probability that a person of any age prefers a beach holiday we would need to find the total number of people in the beach holidays column (irrespective of age) which is 67. Then the probability that any one person prefers a beach holiday is $\frac{67}{160}$ which is 0.41875 or approximately 42%. We shall use this example in the following exercise—the solution appears at the back of the book.

Exercises 7.4

7.4.1 In the sum of two die example above calculate the following probabilities:
(i)   the sum of one die is 10 or one of the die is even;
(ii) one die is even given that the sum of the two die is 10.

7.4.2 In a room of 20 people 8 are graduates. Twelve work in the city in banking and finance 3 of whom are graduates. Represent this information on a Venn diagram. What is the probability that someone selected at random in the room is a graduate and a banker/financier? If the person selected is a graduate, what is the chance that this person is not in banking/finance.

7.4.3 In the EuroTours example above (example 7.8), a person is selected at random from the 160 people surveyed.

Calculate the following probability that this person would be:
(i)   aged between 21 and 30;
(ii)   aged between 31 and 40;
(iii)   aged between 41 and 50;
(iv)   will prefer water sports and be aged between 31 and 40;
(v)   prefers any holiday but a beach holiday;
(vi)   given that this person prefers walking holidays, the person is aged over 50:
(vii)   either the person is under 21 or prefers a beach holiday;
(viii) Are the events age and holiday independent? Check by computing law 2.

If the age group 41 to 50 spent on average more than any other age group, what holiday would you target at this group? In your adverts for beach holidays, what age group would be best used in the adverts to attract this said group?

Tree diagrams

Example 7.9
A recent Romi survey of a large number of households in the UK showed that 10% of households had no car, 75% had one car, 15% had two or more cars. Two households were selected at random. Using a tree diagram or otherwise, find the probability that:

(i)   both households had no car:
(ii)   one household had no car, one had one car;
(iii) the two households combined had a total of three or more cars.

Solution
First we must construct a diagram to represent this situation. Once we have such a pictorial representation—a *tree diagram* with branches rather like a tree representing each possible event, we shall then be able to answer the above problems by going along the branches and reading off the answer. Figure 7.6 gives the tree diagram for this example.

First notice that there are two sets of branches, the first set to represent the first chosen household and the second set to represent the second household. As we go along the branches we would be saying 'This happens for the first household and this happens for the second': accordingly we use law 2 and multiply the probabilities. (Why are these events independent?) If we go along several different routes in the tree (from start to the outer branch) then we would be saying 'this happens ... or this happens' and so would add the final

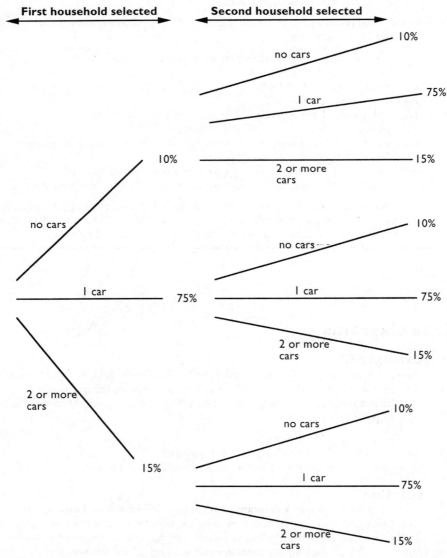

Figure 7.6

probabilities from each route applying law 1 of probability. (A moot point is simply to say that only two households are selected and so only 1 route through the tree can hold—that is, both routes cannot hold so law 1 is for mutually exclusive events.) Observe that all the probabilities are percentages which we could easily convert to decimals.

(i) For example P(both households had no car) would mean going along the topmost branch on the first household (probability of 0.1), and then following the topmost branch in the upper set of branches (again with a probability of 0.1), i.e.

no car 0.1   no car 0.1

As we want BOTH these events to happen (and they are chosen at random without affecting the other outcome) we can thus multiply the probabilities. Thus P(both households have no car) = 0.1 × 0.1 = 0.01

or 1% chance of happening.

(ii) P(one household had no car, one had one car) can happen in two ways: there are two routes through the tree.

Either the first household has no car (0.1 chance) and the second has 1 (0.75 chance). We would multiply these probabilities as both must happen = 0.1 × 0.75 = 0.075.

OR

the first household has 1 car (0.75) and the second has no car (0.1). As before this would be 0.075.

As we wish either the first outcome OR the second we simply add the probabilities, which is 0.15 or 15%.

(iii) P(the two households combined had a total of three or more cars) which can occur in several ways:

1 car and then 2 or more	probability = 0.75 × 0.15 = 0.1125
2 or more cars and 1 car	probability = 0.15 × 0.75 = 0.1125
2 or more cars and 2 or more cars	probability = 0.15 × 0.15 = 0.0225

As we want either of these 3 possible combinations we add the probabilities, which gives us 0.2475 or approximately a 25% chance.

Mathematical expectation

The expectation of an event occurring is the probability of the event multiplied by the total number of outcomes. For example in a village fete a game of die is played where three dice are thrown together and players win depending on the number of sixes thrown. If you throw three sixes you win 50p, if you throw 2 sixes you win 25p, and if you throw 1 six you win 10p. What can any player expect to win in 1 play of the game? To calculate the expected winnings, we would need to calculate the probability of throwing 1 six, or 2 sixes or 3 sixes using three dice and then we would multiply each probability by the winnings. The chance of throwing 1 six means 1 die has a six with a chance of $\frac{1}{6}$ and the other 2 dice have any number but a six, with a chance of $\frac{5}{6}$. We multiply these probabilities and so P(1 six) $= \frac{1}{6} \times \frac{5}{6} \times \frac{5}{6} = \frac{25}{216}$. Formally we define:

The *mathematical expectation* of an event A occurring $=$ P(A) $\times$ total number of outcomes.

If A is a single event, or if A consists of a series of trials, A_i, then

expected value of A $= \Sigma$ P(A_i) $\times$ total number of outcomes for A_i

Thus the expected winnings is P(1 six) $\times$ total winnings $= \frac{25}{216} \times 10p = 1.15p$ in 1 play of the game. We shall calculate the other expected winnings in the exercise below.

One use of expectation in business is for calculating expected profits (or losses). This is interpreted to mean the average profits/losses in the long term. There will be fluctuations but this is what the company could expect on average in the long run.

Example 7.10

In a sample of businesses surveyed by a magazine, *Computer Weekly*, 28% of senior managers were found to be wary of introducing new computer systems into their organizations. If a sample of 20 senior managers were selected at random from this group, what number would you expect to be happy to introduce new computer technology?

Solution

If 28% are unhappy to introduce new technology, then 72% are reasonably happy to, and so P(happy for new technology) $= 0.72$. Thus in a group of 20 we would expect $0.72 \times 20 =$ approximately 14 managers.

Example 7.11

A company wishes to determine the level of demand for its cold drinks during August 1996. The marketing manager suggests that the demand is closely related to the weather and to calculate the expected demand in August 1996 the company needs to seek advice on the weather. The results are given in the table below: where demand (in 1000s of cans) together with the probability of the given weather prevailing:

Demand	Weather	Chance of this weather
100	Cool	0.1
250	Warm	0.4
350	Hot	0.45
500	Heat wave	0.05

Find the expected demand for cold drinks during August 1996.

Solution

Step 1: Identify the problem

Here the expected demand depends on the weather: if it's cool it will have a low demand, but if a heat wave occurs, a very high demand will be required. Thus the expected demand is weighted by the chance of these weather conditions, that is, the level of demand is multiplied by the chance of the prevailing weather condition occurring: (Ai) $\times$ P(Ai).

The expected demand for cold drinks in August 1996 will then be the sum of these weighted demand figures.

Step 2: Find the expected demands for each type of weather:

Cool $\quad\quad$ EV = 100 × 0.1 $\quad$ = 10

Warm $\quad\quad$ EV = 250 × 0.4 $\quad$ = 100

Hot $\quad\quad\quad$ EV = 350 × 0.45 = 157.5

Heat wave $\quad$ EV = 500 × 0.05 = 25

Step 3: Find the EV of the demand (for whatever weather occurs)

Summing the EVs we have

Expected Value (EV) of the demand = 10 + 100 + 157.5 + 25 = 292.5 (ie 292 500 cans).

Exercises 7.4

7.4.1 Three architects, A, B and C, share one personal assistant. The probability of an incoming phone call for each of them is 0.3 for A, 0.4 for B and 0.3 for C. The likelihood that A will be out when a call is taken for him is 0.85. The corresponding probabilities for B and C are 0.6 and 0.75 respectively. Assuming that all probabilities are independent, use a tree diagram to represent these probabilities. Using the tree diagram find the probability that:

(i)   none of the architects is in to take the call;

(ii) the call is for B and B is in the office;

(iii) the call is for C and C is the only one of the three not in.

7.4.2 A company manufactures two models of calculator, model FX and FD. The manufacturing director has to determine which model would be most likely to produce a good return in the medium- to long-term period. To enable this decision to be quantified, the design team are asked to submit annual projected profits and the chance of such profits being realised. The following data is presented:

	Model FX		Model FD	
	Profit (£1000s)	**Probability**	**Profit (£1000s)**	**Probability**
Optimistic outcome	72	0.3	75	0.15
Most likely outcome	48	0.6	50	0.7
Pessimistic outcome	34	0.1	12	0.15

Calculate the expected value for each model and determine the most likely decision the manufacturing director would make, assuming such a decision was taken using this information alone.

7.4.3 To play the National Lottery a player chooses 6 numbers within the range 01 to 49. What is the chance that one number comes up when the lottery is drawn? Using a tree diagram or otherwise, what is the chance that two numbers come up when the lottery is drawn?

Probability distributions

Scenario

You are running the local draw at a village fair and are using a digital machine to generate the winning number. How would you test that the machine was fair?

The number 53 bus is timetabled to arrive every 10 minutes during the peak rush hour.

Unfortunately you have just seen two go by but have missed them. Is it likely you will have to wait more than 10 minutes for the next one? Such problems involve looking at a more general view of probability and trying to model a given situation. The above examples follow two important models which we shall now look at.

The uniform distribution

You are testing the village electronic machine for generating the winning ticket number (or equally the National Lottery machine). After setting the machine to generate numbers in the range 01 to 10, you then ask it to give you twenty numbers. How would you know the machine was fair? Well, you would expect approximately that the machine would give you equal numbers of 1 to 10. This would mean that we would expect about 2 of each number in twenty goes. We would expect something like the following table:

Number	Frequency occurred (theoretically)
1	2
2	2
3	2
4	2
5	etc.
6	
7	
8	
9	
10	

What would the probability of each number occurring be? This would be

$$P(\text{number } n) = \frac{\text{frequency } n \text{ occurs}}{\text{total number of goes}} = \frac{2}{20} = \frac{1}{10} = 0.1$$

We could put this into the above table and we would have:

Frequency and probability table

Number	Frequency occurred (theoretically)	Probability (theoretical)
1	2	0.1
2	2	0.1
3	2	0.1
4	2	0.1
5	2	0.1
6	2	0.1
7	2	0.1
8	2	0.1
9	2	0.1
10	2	0.1
Total	20	1

We could sum each of the frequencies and probabilities—notice that the probability has a total of 1. This means that this is a complete listing of all possible probabilities for this machine. In fact we would say this table gave us the probability model for this experiment, and so would call it the probability distribution for this experiment. We could plot the distribution of this using a line chart or a bar chart as shown in figure 7.7.

Here we have only set the machine to run 20 times and might want to test 100 or more outcomes to know if the machine really was fair or biased. In twenty outcomes the observed number would probably not be exactly two for each number, but would be about two. If we had number 10 occurring 7 times we would know our machine was fixed—we simply would not expect such a high frequency of one number to occur in twenty goes of the machine. We could plot the observed probabilities and would hope to get a rectangular type shape, although not as perfect as the theoretical shape.

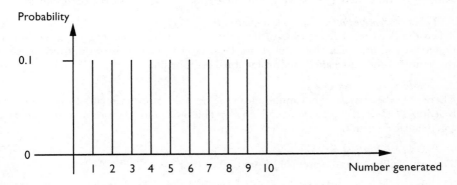

Figure 7.7 Probability distribution for the numbers generated by the draw machine.

Exercise 7.5 _____

You are asked to design a test to see if the machine which generates the winning number for the National Lottery is fair. If there are 49 balls in the machine, numbered from 01 to 49, how would you test the machine and what sort of shape would this line chart have?

The binomial distribution

Scenario
A barrister, specialising in criminal defence law, advertises that 80% of the cases she takes on are won on either the first trial or on subsequent appeals. If five clients from her list of recent cases are chosen at random, what is the chance that all five have been acquitted? Is it possible that all five would have been convicted?

Such cases involving 'success' and 'failure' are modelled by a probability distribution: the *binomial distribution*.

The key features of a binomial model
There are four main factors which determine whether a model follows a binomial distribution. An experiment is repeated a number of times; each time the conditions of the experiment are the same. Then the four factors are:

1. Success or failure
At each trial of the experiment there are two possible outcomes to the trial: an event which can be termed *success* and an event that can be termed *failure*. There are only two possible outcomes—they are mutually exclusive. For example, in terms of the legal case either the defendant wins or loses (assuming that all appeals have been completed). The chance of success must be known—with a probability p. The chance of failure is q where:

$p + q = 1$

as there are only these two possible outcomes. Such a trial is called a Bernoulli trial.

2. Trials are repeated independently and identically
When the barrister defends each of the trials she uses the same level of commitment, undertakes all the research and does not let personal judgement of guilt/innocence or the nature of the crime affect her professional responsibility.

3. Fixed number of trials
There must be n trials: you cannot allow the number of experiments to be continued indefinitely. (If trials do continue indefinitely a binomial model is not representative but a geometric distribution—see the exercises.)

4. Fixed probability of success
The probabilities p and q are fixed from trial to trial.

The chance of success/failure at each trial must be the same. If the barrister was an expert in criminal law but rarely defended a case regarding commercial law then the likelihood of success might not be the same as each trial if some cases were criminal work and some commercial work. If this were so the binomial model would not be appropriate, but first principles would be needed—see the exercise below.

The binomial distribution counts the number of successes in n trials. For example, the barrister has 5 cases and so $n = 5$. There could be no successes and so 5 failures, or 1 success and 4 failures, or 2 successes and 3 failures, etc., up to 5 successes and no failures. This is the set of all possible outcomes, the sample space. We use a formula to compute the likelihood of each possible outcome. Notice that we could use a counter for the number of successes: either there are 0 successes, or 1 or 2 or ... up to n successes. We usually use r as this counter for the number of successes. Before we move to the formula we look at some typical binomial models.

The multiple-choice test

An applicant for a job with a large bank is asked to do a multiple-choice test with 30 questions. Each question has 4 possible answers, one of which is correct and the rest are wrong. Here the candidate's answer to any given question is either right or wrong. Right is 'success' and wrong is 'failure' and so a binomial model is indicated. There is a 1 in 4 chance of the answer being correct and a 3 in 4 chance of being wrong. There are fixed number of possible answers to give—30 in total. We must assume there are no disruptions to the candidate during the test—the conditions are the same for each question answered.

The biological experiment

A biological experiment is undertaken—for example looking at the number of seeds which germinate. For example a parsley seed which has been genetically altered to make it easier to germinate is undergoing horticultural tests. A hundred seeds are planted under identical conditions—same light, soil, fertilisers, water, etc. The number that germinate are then observed. Some will grow (germinate)—success; some may not—failure. The horticulturist will only claim a new seed if say, 75% of the seeds germinate. This experiment indicates a Binomial model.

Quality on the production line

A manufacturer of an electrical product—such as light bulbs, 3-pin plugs, digital clocks, etc. will have a quality control section which inspects batches before release onto the market. One of the inspection team will take a batch at random from the production line every hour to inspect the product for quality. The same features of the inspection are checked each time and recorded in a report. In a batch of say 20 items the company will have a certain quota which can be defective, say 2 in each batch, and up to this level the batch will pass the inspection provided not more than 2 defectives are found. The batch passes—success if there are 0, 1 or 2 defective; but fails if there are more than 2. Such a situation is indicative of a binomial model.

Exercise 7.6 _____

For each of the above binomial models determine the values for n, p and q and decide what is success and what the binomial distribution will count in this case.

Example 7.12 Formulation of the first scenario (the legal case)

Assuming that the eventual outcome of such cases follows a binomial distribution, find the probability that five of the barrister's clients chosen at random will include

(i)   5 wins;

(ii) only one win.

In this case $n = 5$ as there are 5 cases. The chance of success, p, is 80% or 0.8, and the chance of failure q is $1 - p$ and therefore 0.2. These values are called the parameters of the binomial distribution—they change from question to question but are fixed in this question. Before we proceed we need a brief note on using an important calculator button: the nCr button for the binomial coefficients.

Calculator note: The binomial coefficients, nCr

Find the nCr button on your calculator—on our calculator this is over the ÷ button. To use this we must therefore use the shift button.

Example 7.13

Calculate 5C2

Solution

In nCr this means we put $n = 5$ and $r = 2$ in this expression. Using the calculator we are then going to evaluate 5C2. Enter 5 on the display then ⎡Shift⎤ ⎡÷⎤ 2 = you will have 20 on your display.

Alternative method: using the factorial button x!

An alternative way to evaluate 5C2 is to use the Factorial button x! over ⎡Yx⎤. For example 5! means $5 \times 4 \times 3 \times 2 \times 1$ which is 120. Check this using the factorial button: enter 5 ⎡Shift⎤ ⎡Yx⎤ and this should be 120. Note that 0! is 1 and so factorials are well defined (we may sometimes need to divide by 0! which would be undefined if 0! was 0).

We thus define 5C2 using factorials to be: $\dfrac{5!}{2! \times 3!}$. Here the top number is the one to the left of the C and the button numbers are the one to the right of the C multiplied by the difference of these numbers ($5 - 2$ here). If we now either use the factorial button or by hand we will see that

$$5C2 = \frac{5!}{2! \times 3!} = \frac{5 \times 4 \times 3 \times 2 \times 1}{2 \times 1 \times 3 \times 2 \times 1}$$

which cancels down to 20.

Example 7.14

Repeat the above to evaluate 7C4

Solution

Calculating 7C4 would be entered as 7 ⎡Shift⎤ ⎡÷⎤ 4 which should be 35.

Using factorials

$$7C4 = \frac{7!}{4! \times 3!} = \frac{7 \times 6 \times 5 \times 4 \times 3 \times 2 \times 1}{4 \times 3 \times 2 \times 1 \times 3 \times 2 \times 1}$$

which cancels down to 35.

Notice that if we require nCr we put $n!$ on the top of the fraction, then divide this by $r!$ and $(n - r)!$, that is

$$nCr = \frac{n!}{r! \times (n - r)!}$$

The binomial formula

Once we know n, p and q the formula for calculating the number r successes is given by

$$P(r) = nCr \times p^r \times q^{n-r}$$

where the values for n, p and q are always known for the given question, nCr is a button on the calculator and r can take the values for all possible number of successes ie $r = 0$, 1, 2, ... n. (It is more formally correct to denote the values of r as a random variable, X, and so write $P(X = r)$ and we would write $X \sim B(n, p)$ to mean X has a binomial model with parameters n and p. We shall adopt a less formal approach.)

Solution to the first scenario (Example 7.12)
We require the probability of 5 wins and then the probability of one win.

Step 1:
Firstly we put in the values of n (5), p (0.8) and q (0.2) into the binomial model:

$$P(r) = 5Cr \times (0.8)^r \times (0.2)^{5-r} \text{ where } r \text{ can be 0, 1 2, 3, 4 or 5}$$

Step 2: The value for r
If we require the chance of 5 successes we put $r = 5$. If we require the probability of one success we put $r = 1$, etc. and r can be any value between 0 and 5.

When $r = 5$

$$P(r = 5) = 5C5 \times (0.8)^5 \times (0.2)^{5-5}$$

Step 3: Calculate each part of this and then multiply each of the three parts together

Now $5C5 = \dfrac{5!}{5! \times 0!}$ as $0! = 1$, and we have $\dfrac{5!}{5!}$ which cancels to give 1. Thus $5C5 = 1$. In fact kCk is always 1 for any positive integer k.

To calculate $(0.8)^5$ enter this using the x^y button on the calculator (this means 0.8 multiplied by itself 5 times): 0.8 $\boxed{x^y}$ 5 = and on the display you will have 0.32768.

Also $(0.2)^{5-5} = (0.2)^0$ which if we recall (from chapter 3) any value to the power zero is 1 (check using the $\boxed{x^y}$ button if you are unsure).

Step 4: The product of all 3 terms
$$P(r = 5) = 5C5 \times (0.8)^5 \times (0.2)^{5-5} = 1 \times 0.32768 \times 1 = 0.32768$$

Step 5: interpreting the result

In 5 cases the chance that all defendants will be acquitted is approximately 0.33 or about 33%.

We now repeat steps 2, 3, 4 and 5 using $r = 1$.

Step 2: $r = 1$

Thus $P(r = 1) = 5C1 \times (0.8)^1 \times (0.2)^{5-1}$

Step 3: Calculate each part of this and then multiply each of the three parts together

We have $5C1 = \dfrac{5!}{1! \times 4!} = \dfrac{5 \times 4!}{1 \times 4!}$ and the 4! will cancel leaving 5 on the top. Thus 5C1 is 5.

Also $(0.8)^1$ this means 0.8 multiplied by itself once which is simply 0.8.

And $(0.2)^{5-1} = (0.2)^4$ which is entered as 0.2 $\boxed{x^y}$ 4 = and the answer displayed in standard index form as 1.6^{-03} which means $1.6 \times 10^{-03} = 0.0016$.

Step 4: The product of all 3

$P(r = 1) = 5C1 \times (0.8)^1 \times (0.2)^4 = 5 \times 0.8 \times 0.0016 = 0.0064$

Step 5: Interpreting the result

In 5 cases the chance that only 1 defendant will be acquitted and so 4 will be convicted is approximately 0.0064 or about 0.64%. This is a very small chance and we can see it is much more likely that all 5 will be acquitted!

Notice that if we write out each of the probabilities in terms of n (5), p and q we would have the following table:

r	$P(r)$	Interpretation
0	q^5	This means no successes and so 5 failures (q and q and q and q and q) probabilities which we can multiply as the cases are independent.
1	$5pq^4$	This means 1 success (probability p) and 4 failures (q and q and q and q) probabilities which we can multiply as the cases are independent. There are 5 ways of arranging these cases (*pqqqq. qpqqq. qqpqq. qqqpq.* or *qqqqp*).
2	$10p^2q^3$	This means 2 successes (probability p and p) and 3 failures (q and q and q) probabilities which we can multiply as the cases are independent. There are 10 ways of arranging these cases.
3	$10p^3q^2$	This means 3 successes (probability p and p and p) and 2 failures (q and q) probabilities which we can multiply as the cases are independent. There are 10 ways of arranging these cases.
4	$5p^4q^1$	This means 4 successes (probability p and p and p and p) and 1 failure (q) probabilities which we can multiply as the cases are independent. There are 5 ways of arranging these cases.
5	p^5	This means 5 successes (probability p and p and p and p and p) and no failures probabilities which we can multiply as the cases are independent. There is only 1 way of arranging these 5 successful cases (*ppppp*).

We can plot the probabilities for each value of r on a line chart as shown in figure 7.8.

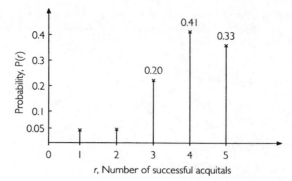

Figure 7.8

The mean of a binomial distribution is np and its variance is npq.

Example 7.15

Batch acceptance sampling: this is a method of accepting a large batch from the production line given that only a small proportion or less of a random sample of the batch is defective.

The quality control manager for Sparks & Pencer's examines the quality of all ladies' shoes as they leave the production line. Every three hours 20 pairs of shoes are taken from a large batch from the production line and closely examined according to a standard checklist. If 10% are found to be below standard the whole batch is returned to the factory for improvement or disposal. What is the chance that in 20 pairs more than 2 pairs will be faulty? How likely is it that a batch will be accepted?

Solution

Here we have a success/failure situation where the total number of possible pairs selected (the total number of trials) is 20. Thus it appears to have the characteristics of a binomial model. In this example we want to count the number of defectives in 20 pairs chosen at random from the large batch, that is, defective is our event 'success' where there can be 0, 1, 2 ... 20 defectives. The chance of any batch being rejected will be if more than 2 pairs are defective. Thus the probability of success will be 10% or 0.1. Thus $n = 20$, $p = 0.1$ and $q = 0.9$. We can thus apply the binomial model.

Step 1: Isolate the problem

We need to find the chance of 2 or more defectives. That is, $P(r \geqslant 2)$. This means we need to calculate the chance of 2, or 3, or 4, or any number of defectives up to 20. This will clearly be time-consuming and a little thought will enable a quicker and very useful approach using the laws of probability. Recall that for any probability distribution the sum of all the probabilities sum to 1, by the law of total probability: the batch of 20 items can have 0, or 1 or 2, or up to 20 defectives with a probability of 1 because one of these must happen. Thus the chance of 2 or more will be 1 less the chance of 0, or 1, written as

$$P(r \geqslant 2) = 1 - P(r = 0) - P(r = 1)$$

Notice that we are also appealing to law 1 (A or B), but do not need to consider the chance of 0 and 1 defective occurring simultaneously as the events are mutually exclusive.

Step 2

Now we need to use

$P(r) = nCr \times p^r \times q^{n-r}$ where r can be 0, 1, 2, ... , 20

with $n = 20$, $p = 0.1$ and $q = 0.9$. Thus

$P(r) = 20Cr \times (0.1)^r \times (0.9)^{20-r}$

We need to put $r = 0$ and $r = 1$.

Step 3: If $r = 0$

then $P(0) = 20C0 \times (0.1)^0 \times (0.9)^{20-0}$

We now calculate each part of this and then multiply each of the three parts together.

$20C0 = 1$, as $20C0 = \dfrac{20!}{0! \times 20!} = \dfrac{20!}{1 \times 20!}$ which is 1.

$(0.1)^0$ is 1 by the laws of indices (or use the calculator).

$(0.9)^{20-0} = (0.9)^{20}$ which is entered as 0.9 $\boxed{x^y}$ 20 = and the display will read 0.121576654.

Step 4: The product of all 3

$P(r = 1) = 20C0 \times (0.1)^0 \times (0.9)^{20-0} = 1 \times 1 \times 0.121576654$
$\qquad\qquad = 0.121576654$

We now repeat step 3 and 4 with $r = 1$ and arrive at:

$P(1) = 20 \times 0.1 \times 0.135085171$ which is 0.270170343

Step 5:

Putting these two results together we have $P(r \geqslant 2) = 1 - 0.121576654 - 0.270170343 = 0.608253002$.

Step 6: Interpreting the result

The quality manager of Sparks & Pencer's will accept the whole production for that period provided the sample of 20 has less than two defectives. In approximately 61% of batches there are 2 or more defectives and so 61% of batches are rejected. There is approximately a 39% chance that any batch will be accepted. That's high quality shoes!

Cumulative binomial tables

Note: tables of cumulative binomial probabilities are widely used for certain values of n and p. For example

$n = 1, 2, \ldots 10, 20, 50, 100$ and

$p = 0.01, 0.02$, with increments of 0.01 up to 0.10, then 0.15, 0.20, 0.25 with increments of 0.05 up to $p = 0.5$.

(By interchanging p and q we can use the tables for larger values of p). These are extremely useful and save a great deal of time as well as allowing us to answer problems such as questions 5 and 6 below.

Summary

The uniform distribution

If X takes the values $r = 0, 1, 2, \ldots n$ with a uniform distribution then $P(X = r) = \dfrac{1}{n}$.

The binomial probability distribution

If $X \sim B(n, p)$ where X counts the number of successes, then the probability of r successes is given by $P(X = r) = nCr \times p^r \times q^{n-r}$ where $r = 0, 1, 2, \ldots n$.

Exercises 7.7 _____

7.7.1 In example 7.12 what is the chance that (i) none, (ii) 2, (iii) 3, (iv) 4 are acquitted? If a number of her cases are selected at random, what is the chance these will contain 5 acquittals? Why is this no longer a binomial model?

7.7.2 In example 7.15, calculate P(2), P(3), P(4), P(5), using parameters $n = 20, p = 0.1$, and $q = 0.9$. Plot a line chart with the values for r along the horizontal axis, and the probabilities along the vertical axis.

7.7.3 In example 7.15, what is the chance of accepting a batch when in fact 15% of the sample of 20 are defective? A technique to analyse a sampling plan in greater detail involves plotting a curve of the chance of accepting a batch (on the vertical axis) against different values of the proportion of defectives, p on the x axis. Such a graph is called the Operating Characteristic curve (OC curve). Plot the OC for example 7.15.

7.7.4 Delloit—Librand is a large accountancy firm in the city of Birmingham. It has three main buildings in Birmingham: the Archway, Brasswear, and Cornhill. A large number of employees are selected from the company's central database. If every two out of five employees are based at the Archway, find the probability that out of 8 people selected at random from the employee database, 4 of them will be based at the Archway. If the company has 900 employees, how many would you expect to be based at each building?

7.7.5 A team of horticulturists conducted tests for a new parsley seed which has been genetically altered to make it easier to germinate. The team claims that 75% of the seeds germinate. During independent trials by the Ministry of Agriculture 50 seeds were planted under identical conditions—same light, soil, fertilizers, water, etc. The number that germinate are then observed. As accurately as the cumulative binomial tables allow, calculate the probability of 30, or 31 or 32 seeds germinating. What is the chance that more than half will germinate? In the batch of 50 how many would you expect to germinate ($n \times p$)? What is the variation in this sample?

7.7.6 A box contains 12 PC disks; 5 are high density and 7 are double density. A disk is removed from the box without replacement. A second disk is removed without replacement. What is the chance that these two disks selected at random will both be double density disks? Why is this not a binomial model? Which properties fail to hold?

7.7.7 The geometric distribution
If each trial of an experiment is a Bernoulli trial with probability of success being p, and trials are repeated identically and independently, then the chance that the first success is observed on the rth trial is given by:

$$P(X = r) = p \times (1 - p)^{r-1}$$

(Note: This means that we have $r - 1$ failures on the first $r - 1$ trials and then a success occurs on the rth trial).

Using the geometric distribution, find the chance that if a fair coin is tossed the first head occurs on the 5th throw. How does this model differ from the binomial model?

7.7.8 Minitab exercise
Enter the following commands in the Minitab package:

```
MTB> Binomial n = 10 p = 0.2 put in C2
```

This command is asking the package to compute the binomial probabilities for a model B(10, 0.2) and to put these probabilities in C2. In C1 we will expect to have the value for K, that is the number of successes in 10 trials. Minitab uses K as a counter.

The output we should get would be the following:

```
BINOMIAL PROBABILITIES FOR N= 10 AND P = 0.2000

K       P(X = K)              P(X LESS OR =K)
0       0.10737               0.10737
1       0.26844               0.37581
2       0.30199               0.6778
3       0.20133               0.87913

etc.
```

(i) Plot a graph of C2 against C1. Comment on its shape.

(ii) Repeat this Minitab exercise using $n = 20$ and $p = 0.1, 0.2, 0.5$. Plot a graph for each set of outcomes. What do you notice about these graphs as p increases?

(iii) Use the cumulative binomial tables to find the chance of 0, 1, 2, 3, ... 9 successes when $p = 0.5$ and $n = 10$. Multiplying each of these probabilities by 200 will give the expected number of successes in 200 trials.

7.7.9 Minitab exercise: generating a binomial population
Enter the following commands:

`MTB> random 200 C1;`	(This means put 200 random numbers in column 1 followed by a subcommand.)
`SUBC> binomial n=10 and p=0.5.`	(The full stop indicates an end to the subcommand. This statement is saying that the 200 random numbers chosen must be values 1, 2, up to $n = 10$, with the probability of success being 0.5.)
`MTB> tally C1`	(This is indicating that the tally or count for the random exercise should be put in C1 overriding the previous allocation for C1.)

The printout will be 200 observations which fit a binomial model B(10, 0.5). Using the data generated, plot a line chart for this exercise by hand. Why are these values different from your answer to 7.7.8 (iii)?

The Poisson distribution

There are instances when a binomial model seems appropriate but we do not exactly have the characteristics to be able to evaluate the parameters n, p and q. For example, on a certain stretch of the M25 there are a number of accidents reported each month, on average 3. We do not know the total number of potential accidents (n), but we can see that from all the traffic 3 out of a large traffic flow is in fact a very small proportion (p). Under these circumstances, when the proportion is very small—the event is termed 'rare' and n is very large, we appeal to an approximation to the binomial model, namely the *Poisson model*.

There are classic examples of when a Poisson is suitable, one of the main characteristics being if we are counting the number of times an event occurs randomly in a fixed time interval/fixed area/fixed volume. For example.

Where a fixed time interval is used:
the number of cars entering a petrol station in a 10 minute period;
the number of telephone calls received by directory enquiries during a 15 minute period;
the number of breakdowns of a photocopier in a weekly interval;
the number of 53 busses passing a stop in a 10 minute interval.

Where a fixed area is used:
the number of typos on an A4 page;
the number of flaws on a metre of fine silk material;
the number of African elephants in a square kilometre of Kenya.

Where a fixed volume is used:
the number of erythrocytes in a millimetre of blood;
the number of bacteria growing in a standard sized culture.

As for the binomial model there are key characteristics for a Poisson model, namely:

1. The average occurrence of the event is proportional to the interval (time, area, or volume). This in fact means that the probability of an event is constant over any interval of the same length. For example if on average 5 cars enter the petrol station in a 10-minute interval, then we would expect 10 to enter in a 20-minute interval, and 15 in a 30-minute interval. We denote this mean number of occurrences of an event by μ in the given interval.

2. No two events can happen simultaneously: two phone calls cannot get through at exactly the same time (a queue is formed).

3. Events must be independent: occurrence of breakdowns of the photocopier in 1 week must not affect the outcome of events (breakdowns) in the following week, or such outcomes are unaffected by what has previously happened. (There are instances when this may not be the case but we shall not consider these.)

Poisson model formula

Formally we would write that if X counted the number of randomly occurring events in a given interval of time, area or volume then $X \sim P(\mu)$ meaning that X is distributed as a Poisson random variable with mean μ (which is also in fact its variance) where the probability that X takes any value r is

$$P(X = r) = \frac{e^{-\mu} \times \mu^r}{r!} \text{ where } r \text{ takes values } 0, 1, 2, \ldots$$

We shall as before simply write $P(r)$ in place of $P(X = r)$.

Example 7.16
The Health and Safety Executive undertook a study of the reported fatalities in the construction industry in 1994. One of its findings was that on average in the UK in 1994 there were 3 fatalities per week. What is the chance that in any 1-week period there were: (i) no fatalities, (ii) at least 3 fatalities.

Solution

Step 1: Model recognition
If we let r be the counter for the number of fatalities where here the time interval is a 1-week period, and the average number of fatalities in a week is 3. Thus $\mu = 3$. We can see this is a classic Poisson model and as such the probability of r occurring is given by

$$P(r) = \frac{e^{-\mu} \times \mu^r}{r!} \text{ with } \mu = 3, \text{ that is } P(r) = \frac{e^{-3} \times 3^r}{r!}.$$

Step 2: Probability formula
$$P(r) = \frac{e^{-3} \times 3^r}{r!} \text{ where } r = 0, 1, 2, \ldots$$

Notice that e^{-3} can be found using the $\boxed{e^x}$ button on our calculator which is over one of the logarithm buttons, $\boxed{\ln}$ button. We need to enter 3 on the display and then to make this negative press $\boxed{\pm}$, that is: $\boxed{\text{Shift}}$ $\boxed{\ln}$ 3 $\boxed{\pm}$ = which will give us $\boxed{e^x}$ with x as -3. On the display we will have 0.049 787 068 which should be stored in the memory, $\boxed{\text{M in}}$.

Thus $P(r) = \dfrac{e^{-3} \times 3^r}{r!} = \dfrac{0.049\,787\,068 \times 3^r}{r!}$ where $r = 0, 1, 2, \ldots$

Now we can solve part (i)

Step 3: Calculation
We require the probability of no fatalities in a week, or P(0), that is put $r = 0$.

Hence $P(0) = \dfrac{e^{-3} \times 3^0}{0!} = \dfrac{0.049\,787\,068 \times 1}{1} = 0.049\,787\,068.$

Step 4: Interpretation
Approximately there is a 0.05 chance of no fatalities in any week in 1994, or multiplying by 100 for a percentage, a 5% chance there will be no deaths in the construction industry, which is rather too small for comfort.

For part (ii) repeat steps 2, 3 and 4.

Step 2: Probability formula
The chance of at least three fatalities means 3, or 4, or 5 or an indefinite number of fatalities. We cannot know how many we should compute until we stop, but common sense should dictate that we stop when the chance becomes very small. Alternatively, a quicker solution can be obtained using the laws of probability:

$P(0) + P(1) + P(2) + \ldots = 1$ (clearly such events are mutually exclusive).

Hence $P(\text{At least } 3) = P(r \geqslant 3) = 1 - P(r \leqslant 2) = 1 - P(0) - P(1) - P(2).$

Step 3: Calculation
Hence we need to evaluate the formula when $r = 0$, $r = 1$, and $r = 2$.

The case $r = 0$ is already known from (i) as 0.049 787 068.

If $r = 1$

$P(r) = \dfrac{0.049\,787\,068 \times 3^r}{r!}$ with $r = 1$ gives us:

$P(1) = \dfrac{0.049\,787\,068 \times 3^1}{1!} = 0.048\,787\,068 \times 3 = 0.149\,361\,205$

If $r = 2$, $P(2) = \dfrac{0.049\,787\,068 \times 3^2}{2!} = \dfrac{0.048\,787\,068 \times 3 \times 3}{2}$

$= \dfrac{0.149\,361\,205 \times 3}{2} = 0.224\,041\,807$

Hence subtracting each of these from 1 will give us

P(At least three fatalities) $= 1 - 0.049\,787\,068 - 0.149\,361\,205$
$$- 0.224\,041\,807 = 1 - 0.423\,190\,081$$

which is $0.576\,809\,918$

Step 4: Interpretation
If we multiply the probability by 100, we will arrive at an approximately 58% chance of at least 3 fatalities occurring in any week in the construction industry—an alarmingly high chance!

Recurrence formula for the calculator
Once we have e^{-3} on the display, which was in fact the P(0), we can arrive at each of the subsequent probabilities by using facilities on the calculator, a so-called recurrence formula. To see this, consider

$$P(0) = \frac{e^{-3} \times 3^0}{0!} = e^{-3} \text{ as the other terms are 1}$$

Then $P(1) = \dfrac{e^{-3} \times 3^1}{1!} = e^{-3} \times 3 = P(0) \times 3$

So once we have the probability of no fatalities on our calculator we can store this value and simply multiply it by 3 to get the probability of 1 fatality.

Similarly $P(2) = \dfrac{e^{-3} \times 3^2}{2!} = \dfrac{e^{-3} \times 3 \times 3}{2} = P(1) \times \dfrac{3}{2}$

So to get P(2) we store P(1) on the calculator and then multiply this by $\frac{3}{2}$. This is a recurrence formula because we have the probability for a certain number, say k fatalities and we can use this—it recurs—to give the following probability of $k + 1$ fatalities.

Similarly $P(3) = \dfrac{e^{-3} \times 3^3}{3!} = \dfrac{e^{-3} \times 3 \times 3 \times 3}{3 \times 2} = P(2) \times \dfrac{3}{3} = P(2)$

Similarly $P(4) = \dfrac{e^{-3} \times 3^4}{4!} = \dfrac{e^{-3} \times 3 \times 3 \times 3 \times 3}{4 \times 3 \times 2} = P(3) \times \dfrac{3}{4}$

if we cancel one pair of 3s.

Cumulative Poisson tables

As for binomial probabilities, tables of cumulative Poisson probabilities are widely used for certain values of μ, such as 0.1, with increments of 0.1 up to 10.0 and from there 12, 14, 16, 18, 20. These are extremely useful and save a great deal of time as well as allowing us to answer problems such as question 7.8.3(ii) below.

Summary

Poisson probability distribution

If X counts the number of observations occurring randomly in a fixed time interval/ fixed area/fixed volume with a constant mean μ then the probability of r observations is given by

$$P(X = r) = \frac{e^{-\mu} \times \mu^r}{r!} \text{ with } r = 0, 1, 2, \ldots$$

Exercises 7.8 _____

7.8.1 Generalise the recurrence formula for the probability of $k + 1$ fatalities if we have the chance of k fatalities is $\dfrac{e^{-3} \times 3^k}{k!}$.

7.8.2 Your secretary is an excellent typist and on average the number of typos he is known to make on an A4 page of typing is 0.4. Find the probability of:
(i)   no typos;
(ii) at least 2 typos;
(iii) less than 4 typos.

If a document has 120 pages, on how many pages would you expect to find no typos? On how many pages would you expect to find 1 typo?

7.8.3 A small bus company has 4 coaches available for hire each day. Assuming the daily demand for coaches is approximately modelled by a Poisson model with a mean of 2.5:
(i) find the demands for one and two coaches each day;
(ii) use cumulative Poisson tables find the chance that exactly no coaches, one coach, two coaches, three and four coaches will be hired per day.

7.8.4 (i)   Carry out the following Minitab exercises

```
MTB> Poisson mean = 1 put in C2
```

This will give a list of Poisson probabilities for each possible value of $K = 0, 1, 2, \ldots$ (K the counter will be automatically placed in C1) with the probabilities assigned to C2.

```
MTB> Plot C2 vs C1
```

will give a scatterdiagram of these probabilities. Comment on the shape of this graph.

(ii) Repeat this Minitab exercise with the mean value of $\mu = 2, 3, 5, 10$, and 20.

(iii) Compare the values for the probabilities given by the binomial and Poisson probabilities when

(a) binomial $n = 25$ and $p = 0.1$
     Poisson mean $= 2.5$

(b) Binomial $n = 40$ and $p = 0.05$
    Poisson mean $= 2$.

7.8.5 Generating a Poisson population

Enter the following commands:

```
MTB>   Random 100 cl;
SUBC> Poisson mean = 3.
MTB>   tally C1
```

Explain what this routine generates and plot a line chart by hand.

The binomial and Poisson models are probability models for discrete random variables: the set of possible outcomes for each experiment is a set of numbers such as $(0, 1, 2, 3, \ldots n, \ldots)$ stopping at n successes for the binomial model. In the next chapter we look at the most important probability model for a continuous data set. The normal model. Here the normal model is a model where the set of observable values takes an interval or range of values.

8 What's the chance and what's the evidence?

Objectives

- Be able to use the normal probability model;
- Understand when to use an approximation to a probability model;
- Be able to use approximations to probability models to ease calculations;
- Understand the concept of a sampling distribution;
- Be able to use Minitab to generate a sampling distribution of the mean;
- Be able to test a claim about the average of some population using a Z or t test.

We now move on to a model for a continuous data set, the normal model. Here the normal model is a model where the set of observable values take an interval or range of values.

The normal probability model

Scenario: A weighty problem for airlines
Airlines across the globe have recently been investigating the weight of passengers boarding a typical aircraft. From 1998 airlines in Europe will assume that the average passenger, male or female, weighs 84 kg (13 st 3 lb), compared to the currently used notational weights of 75 kg for men (11 st 11 lb) and 65 kg for women (10 st 3 lb). There are safety factors involved in adjusting the notional weight of a passenger as an aeroplane will be designed to carry a certain maximum load, and may well be overloaded if estimates are out of date. Alternatively they may be forced to remove seats from aircrafts and so lose revenue if their estimates of a typical passenger are wrong.

If we plotted a histogram for the weights of a randomly selected group of people boarding a flight at Heathrow, there would be some weight that was typical or average for the group, which we might call a central value or the mean. There would be variation from this central value: some people would weigh more than the average whilst some would weigh less. The number of people weighing very much more or less than this central value would be few. A measure of how spread out or dispersed the weights were would be measured by the standard deviation. Figure 8.1 gives two typical histograms for a particular mean (65 kg here) but with different standard deviations.

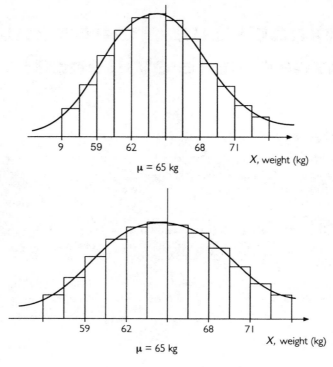

Figure 8.1

We can see in the first graph that weights are peaked around the average, 65 kg, but the variation is less than on the second graph as the first graph is more peaked. The second graph is more spread out—there is more variation.

The normal model is a model for data whose histogram is approximately symmetrical, about a central value, the mean, μ, and with a standard deviation σ. Many data sets are of this nature: for example weights where a certain age group and gender are given.

In fact the area under each of the histograms can represent probability if we plot relative frequency, and so the area under the histogram is 1. Moreover if the histogram had unequal class widths we would plot relative frequency density. Such a histogram is called a probability density function. We can then use the area between any two values on the x axis to represent the chance that someone has a weight between these two values, or what proportion of this data set lies between these values. A model for such a histogram was developed by Gauss and is sometimes referred to as the Gaussian distribution. Such graphs are bell-shaped and symmetrical. The normal density model for mean μ and standard deviation σ is given by a very complicated function

$$f(x) = \frac{1}{\sqrt{2\pi} \times \sigma} e^{-\frac{1}{2}\left(\frac{x-\mu}{\sigma}\right)^2}$$

We do not actually use this expression as its integral has no exact form and so we use numerical integration to estimate the area under the graph. In fact tables have already

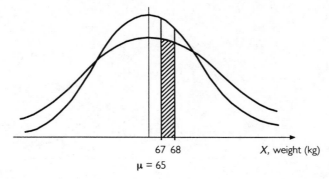

67 68

μ = 65

X, weight (kg)

Figure 8.2

been calculated to spare us the labour! Notice that in the above graphs, we had different peaks, the height of each being $\dfrac{1}{\sqrt{2\pi} \times \sigma}$. If we superimpose them and look at the area between 67 kg and 68 kg on the graphs, we can see a slightly different area would sit under each graph because of the different spread.

Our tables must model any normal model and this could be a problem. As the shape of the normal histogram changes as μ and σ change, the area between two values will be different for different values of μ and σ. Thus, in theory we would need an infinite number of normal tables for all possible combinations of μ and σ. In fact this is overcome by *standardising* our weights (or variable X) so that only one table is needed. We can imagine this standardisation as a squashing process which squashes any given histogram into a standard shape, and so a standard area lies between any two points.

Standardisation:
We transform X into a Z value by:

$Z = \dfrac{X - \mu}{\sigma}$ and Z has a normal distribution (is of the form $e^{-\frac{1}{2}x^2}$) with a mean of 0 and a standard deviation of 1.

Mathematical language:
We write $X \sim N(\mu, \sigma^2)$ for the statement

X is distributed normally with a mean μ, and a variance σ^2.

A graph of the probability density function for X is given in figure 8.3.

Similarly we write $Z \sim N(0, 1)$ for the statement

Z is distributed normally with a mean 0, and a variance 1.

A graph of the probability density function for Z is given in figure 8.4.

Example 8.1
Using the 1998 Airlines in Europe regulations, assuming that the weights of passengers are approximately normally distributed, if the standard deviation of the typical passenger is 4 kg, what proportion of passengers are estimated to be (i) over 88 kg, or (ii) over 91 kg? How does this compare with the current

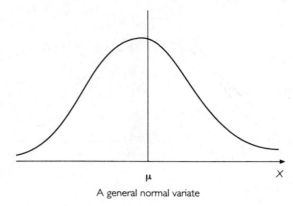

A general normal variate

Figure 8.3

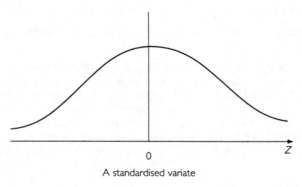

A standardised variate

Figure 8.4

assumptions for say male passengers with a standard deviation of 5 kg and female passengers with a standard deviation of 6 kg?

Solution

(i) Step 1: Identify the area required

Let X denote the notional weight of a typical passenger (in 1998), with a mean of 84 kg and a standard deviation of 4 kg, ie $\mu = 84$ and $\sigma = 4$. As X is normally distributed we can write $X \sim N(84 \text{ kg}, 4^2 \text{ kg}^2)$. Such a histogram (probability density function) for X is shown in figure 8.5.

We wish to find the area to the right of the weight 88 kg as this will represent the proportion of passengers over 88 kg. Such an area would be the shaded area of figure 8.6.

We shall refer to this as an X diagram, as X is plotted along the horizontal axis.

Step 2: Compare this with the corresponding Z area

We now need to standardise our area, i.e. press it into a standard Z area and so calculate the area using the tables. By converting $X = 88$ into a Z value, we use

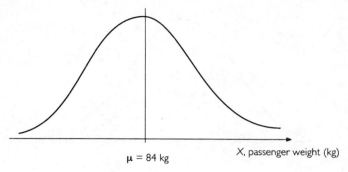

μ = 84 kg   X, passenger weight (kg)

Figure 8.5

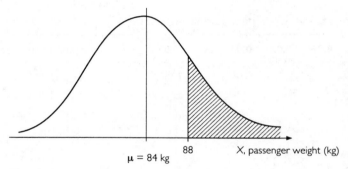

88   X, passenger weight (kg)
μ = 84 kg

Figure 8.6

the formula

$$Z = \frac{X - \mu}{\sigma}$$

Thus using $\mu = 84$ kg, and $\sigma = 4$ kg and $X = 88$ kg, the corresponding Z value is

$$Z = \frac{X - \mu}{\sigma} = \frac{88 - 84}{4} = \frac{4}{4} = 1$$

that is $Z = 1$ and so the corresponding Z area is given in figure 8.7.

We shall refer to this as a Z diagram. Notice that this is equivalent to the above figure 8.6.

Step 3: Using the normal tables: Table 1 Areas of the standardised normal distribution

If we take a look at the normal tables, Table 1 in the Appendix, the area tabulated is the area to the right of any (positive) Z values. We might refer to this as the right tail of the Z distribution. A glance at the normal tables would give us

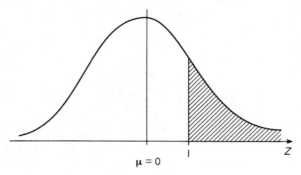

Figure 8.7

Table 1: Areas of the standardised normal distribution

Z	0.00	0.01	0.02	0.03	...	0.09	← This is the second decimal place
0.0	0.50000						
0.1	0.46017						
0.2	0.42074						
0.3							
.							
.							
1.0	0.15866						
1.1							
1.2							
...							
3.9							

If we glance down the first column we see the Z value to 1 decimal place tabulated. To find Z to 2 decimal places we need to move across to which ever column is the digit in the second decimal place of our Z value. Here $Z = 1$, and we simply look down the first column and read across under the 0.00 column as this will give us the area to the right of 1.00. The value we see is 0.15866.

Notice that the Z values are only tabulated for Z values up to $+4$, and by symmetry as the Z distribution has a mean of 0, the Z values in the left half of the distribution must be negative Z values down to -4. We use the symmetry of the graph to find areas in the left tail—notice that these areas will be positive; it is the Z value that is negative. Our standardised Z histogram would be that given in figure 8.8.

Step 4: Interpretation
If we multiply the proportion by 100% we will have 15.866% or approximately 16% of passengers over 88 kg. Notice that this would also tell us that we have approximately 84% of passengers under 88 kg.

(ii) We now repeat the above steps with $X = 91$ kg.

Step 1: Identify the area required
As before we can write $X \sim N(84 \text{ kg}, 4^2 \text{ kg}^2)$.

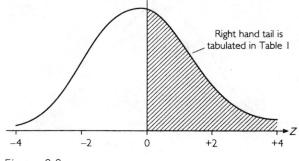

Right hand tail is
tabulated in Table I

Figure 8.8

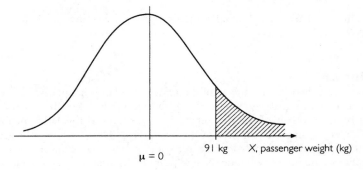

$\mu = 0$ 91 kg   X, passenger weight (kg)

Figure 8.9

We wish to find the area to the right of the weight 91 kg as this will represent the proportion of passengers over 91 kg. Such an area would be the shaded area of figure 8.9.

Step 2: Compare with the corresponding Z area

We now need to standardise our area, i.e. press it into a standard Z area and so calculate the area using the tables by converting $X = 91$ into a Z value.

Here the values of μ and σ are unchanged at 84 kg, and 4 kg respectively. Thus if $X = 91$ kg, the corresponding Z value is

$$Z = \frac{X - \mu}{\sigma} = \frac{91 - 84}{4} = \frac{7}{4} = 1.75$$

that is $Z = 1.75$ and so the corresponding Z diagram is given in figure 8.10.

Step 3: Using the normal tables

Here $Z = 1.75$, and we simply look down the first column for 1.7 and read across under the 0.05 column as this will give us the area to the right of $Z = 1.75$. The value we see is 0.04006.

Step 4: Interpretation

If we multiply the proportion by 100% we will have approximately 4% of passengers over 91 kg.

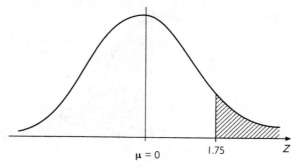

Figure 8.10

Question: Is there any difference in computing the chance of $X > 91$ kg or $X \geqslant 91$ kg?

Solution

In a discrete distribution this would matter as the latter inequality includes the chance that $X = 91$ kg, whilst the former excludes this. In a continuous distribution both probabilities represent areas and so the latter probability $P(X \geqslant 91$ kg) includes the area of the line $P(X = 91$ kg). Clearly the area of a line is negligible or approximately zero, and so for a continuous distribution whether we include or exclude the end point of an interval does not change the probability. Namely:

$P(X > k) = P(X \geqslant k)$ for any finite value k of the random variable X.

How do these figures compare with those estimates currently used by Airlines in Europe?

Case 1 Male passengers $X \sim N(75 \text{ kg}, 5^2 \text{ kg}^2)$
(The reader might choose to write X_M for the random variable denoting the weight of a male passenger.)

Here the proportion greater than 88 kg will be the shaded area of figure 8.11.

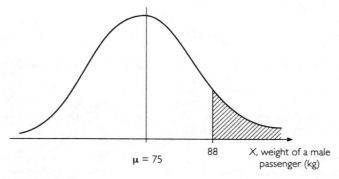

Figure 8.11

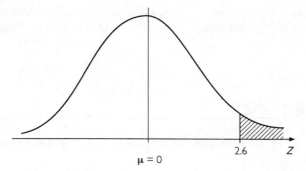

Figure 8.12

Standardising $Z = \dfrac{X - \mu}{\sigma} = \dfrac{88 - 75}{5} = \dfrac{13}{5} = 2.6$, that is $Z = 2.6$ and so the corresponding Z diagram is figure 8.12.

The area to the right is 0.01970, or approximately 2% of male passengers.

Case 2 Female passengers $X \sim N(65 \text{ kg}, 6^2 \text{ kg}^2)$
(Again the reader might choose to write X_F for the random variable denoting the weight of a female passenger.)

Here the proportion greater than 88 kg will be the shaded area of figure 8.13.

Standardising

$$Z = \frac{X - \mu}{\sigma} = \frac{88 - 65}{6} = \frac{23}{6} = 3.83$$

that is $Z = 3.83$ and so the corresponding Z area is 0.00006. That is 6 female passengers in every 100 000.

Conclusion
Under the new regulations 16% of passengers are estimated to exceed 88 kg. Under current regulations, 2% of males and 0.006% of females exceed this weight. Current research shows that people are on average heavier than

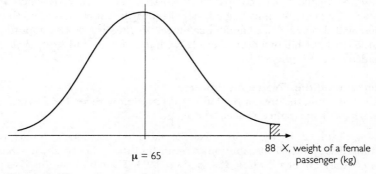

Figure 8.13

previous studies have shown, and possibly new regulations, which are already in place in the USA, should be more quickly adopted in Europe. Happy flying!

Exercises 8.1

8.1.1 Find the Z values that correspond to the following X values assuming $X \sim \text{N}(14, 10.24)$:
(i) $X = 20.88$;
(ii) $X = 10.8$;
(iii) $X = 8.816$.

8.1.2 Find the area to the right of each of the X values in question 8.1.1 and shade corresponding X diagrams and Z diagrams. (Hint: you may need to use the law of total probability; the total area under the graph is 1.)

8.1.3 Find the area to the left of each of the X values in question 8.1.1 and shade corresponding X diagrams and Z diagrams. (Hint: you may need to use the law of total probability; the total area under the graph is 1.)

Example 8.2
The life of a typical Amsran PC keyboard is 4 years with a variance of 1.69 years. A new marketing manager suggests that the company should replace, free of charge, all keyboards that fail whilst under the guarantee. Assuming that a keyboard life is normally distributed, how long should the guarantee be, to the nearest month, if the company replaces no more than 3% of the keyboards sold?

Solution

Step 1: Outline the problem
Here let X denote the time in years a keyboard is likely to last, which is normally distributed with a mean $\mu = 4$ years and variance $\sigma^2 = 1.69$, and so $\sigma = 1.3$ years. We are interested in the proportion of keyboards which do not last a certain length of time, T say. Note that T is a particular value of the random variable X. The company will replace 3% of keyboards which last this value (T) or less. We must include here keyboards that fail less than T years as these will also be replaced under guarantee. We thus are looking at putting 3% in the left-hand tail of a normal model with $\mu = 4$ years and $\sigma = 1.3$ years, the shaded area of figure 8.14.

Step 2: Find the Z value for this area
Here we know the area in the tail but do not know the value T which is the length of the guarantee Amsran should give.

Using Table 2 in the Appendix, the table of percentage points of the standardised normal distribution, we can find the value of Z for which the area to the right of a Z value, α%, is 3% or 0.03. The table calls this Z value Z_α. Below is an extract from this table:

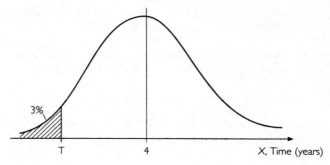

Figure 8.14

Table 2: Percentage points of the standardised normal distribution

α	Z_α	α	Z_α	α	$Z_\alpha \ldots$
0.50	0.00000	0.24	0.70630		
0.49	0.02507	0.23			
0.48	0.05015	.			
.		.			
.		.			
.		0.03	1.88079		
0.25					

[Alternatively we can use the previous normal tables but look for an area of 0.03 and read off the closest Z value. (We can see that it is easier to use the percentage points table!)]

Here the if area to the right of a Z value is 0.03, then the corresponding Z value is 1.88079.

Putting this onto a Z diagram we get figure 8.15.

The area required is in the left tail and so by symmetry this Z value must be negative. Thus we have $Z = -1.88079$ and we need to find the time X that

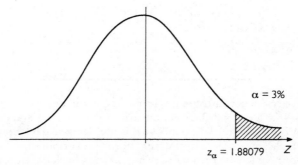

Figure 8.15

corresponds to this Z value. (This X value will be the specific T value we require and so we now use T in place of X.)

Step 3: Find the value for T that corresponds to this Z value

Here we know the equation linking Z and T is

$Z = \dfrac{T - \mu}{\sigma}$, now putting in the values we have:

$Z = -1.88079$, $\mu = 4$ and $\sigma = 1.3$ and T which is unknown (all variables are measured in years), that is:

$$-1.88079 = \dfrac{T - 4}{1.3}$$

Now re-arranging the equation to find T we multiply first by 1.3:

$$-1.88079 \times 1.3 = T - 4$$

Then add 4 to both sides to give us

$$T = -1.88079 \times 1.3 + 4$$

That is $T = -2.445027 + 4$ which gives us $T = 1.554973$

This is 1 year and 0.554973 of a year, which if we multiply by 12 will be in months: 6.65 months. Thus the marketing director should decide that the guarantee could by anything up to 1 year and 7 months and approximately only 3% of all keyboards would be replaced under guarantee. He will probably choose an 18 month guarantee.

Exercises 8.2

8.2.1 The results of a survey of 150 people contain details of their income levels and are summarised in the table below:

Weekly income	Number of people
under £100	10
£100 but under £200	40
£200 but under £300	65
£300 but under £500	20
£500 but under £900	10
over £900	5

Plot a relative frequency histogram for this sample and describe its shape. Does it appear to follow a normal distribution that is symmetrical about some central value? What is this central value, and what is the standard deviation? Using these values to 1 decimal place, apply the normal distribution to estimate the proportion of people who earn more than £350 per week. What proportion earn between £320 and £470 per week?

8.2.2 On a typical day the time taken to deliver mail to the High Street is approximately normally distributed with a mean of 25 minutes and a standard deviation of 4 minutes. Find the probability that it takes:

    (i)   more then 31 minutes;
    (ii)   less than 16.2 minutes;
    (iii) between 18.6 and 29.4 minutes;

to deliver the mail.

8.2.3 Packages of sugar from a machine have a weight which is normally distributed with a mean of 1 kg and a variance of 0.15 kg^2. Find the probability that a packet of sugar chosen at random from this machine's output weighs:

    (i)   more than 1.195 kg;
    (ii)   more than 1.225 kg;
    (iii) between 1.195 kg and 1.225 kg.

8.2.4 Heights of boys at a particular age follow a normal distribution, N(150 cm, 25 cm^2). A boy is selected at random from this age group. Find the probability that he is:

    (i)   taller than 158 cm;
    (ii)   shorter than 153 cm;
    (iii) shorter than 148 cm;
    (iv) taller than 144 cm;
    (v)   between 150 and 158 cm;
    (vi) between 147 and 149.5 cm.

8.2.5 Marks in a part I British Banking Examination were normally distributed with a mean mark of μ% and a standard deviation of σ%. If 10% of the candidates score more than 75% and 20% score less than 40%, find the values of μ, and σ. (Hint: label these areas and X values for a diagram and find the corresponding Z.) Hence find the values for μ and σ using simultaneous equations.

8.2.6 Cornflakes are sold in boxes marked 300 g. The weights of the boxes are normally distributed with a mean of 340 g and a standard deviation of 12 g. Find the percentage of packs which are underweight.

8.2.7 Research workers hope to diagnose, by means of a screening test, a certain disease in babies. The test consists of measuring the concentration level of a certain protein in the blood. Extensive study has shown that the distribution of the protein, in mg/ml, is N(18, 9) for babies not having the disease. For babies having the disease the corresponding distribution of the protein present is N(28, 16).

It is decided that any baby whose level of the protein is greater than 24 mg/ml will be sent for further tests, whilst all the others will be classified as not having the disease.

Find the probability to 3 decimal places that:

    (i)   a baby having the disease will be classified as not having the disease;
    (ii) a baby not having the disease will be sent for further tests.

Approximations

Under certain conditions it becomes infeasible to use the binomial model. An approximation such as the Poisson or normal models are easier to use and give approximately the correct answer. Similarly for the Poisson model there are circumstances when it is more convenient to use the normal. The following rules of thumb apply.

Approximations for the binomial distribution

(i) Poisson approximation to the binomial model

If n is large ($n > 20$) and p is small ($p < 0.1$), that is the event success is a rare event, then computing binomial probabilities is time-consuming and so the Poisson model is suitable and easier to compute. We add the extra proviso $np < 5$. These are rough rules of thumb and authors differ as to what range of parameters are best.

(ii) Normal approximation to the binomial

Here there are two cases:

if p is approximately 0.5 and n is not too small, say $n > 10$;

or

if p is in the range 0.2 to 0.8 and n is large, $n > 30$ say.

(iii) Normal approximation to the Poisson model

If μ, the mean and variance of a Poisson model is large, say $\mu > 20$, then a normal approximation is suitable.

(See the exercises 8.3 below on Minitab to justify these approximations.)

When we are approximating a discrete model by a continuous one we need to apply a continuity correction, as shown in the example below.

Example 8.3

A newsagent sells on average 45 local newspapers a day. How many papers should he order at the beginning of each day so that he has a 5% chance of not meeting the demand?

Solution

Step 1: The underlying model

The number of newspapers sold each day could be 0, 1, 2, ... , up to an indefinite number depending on the availability of supply. This is then a discrete model counting the number of sales. The number sold each day occurs randomly throughout the day with an average of 45. These are characteristics of the Poisson model. Here we have $\mu = 45$ per day where the Poisson formula for r sales would be:

$$P(r) = \frac{e^{-\mu} \times \mu^r}{r!} = \frac{e^{-45} \times 45^r}{r!}$$

To answer the problem we would need to find r sales which occurs when the newsagent has sold out, and so cannot meet demand, that is such that the chance of r or more sales would be 5%. We could only do this using cumulative Poisson tables which are not generally computed for such a large μ.

Step 2: Using an approximation
Here we must use the only approximation to the Poisson we have: the normal distribution.

If X is the number of sales per day, then under the Poisson the mean is 45 and the variance are equal to μ, thus σ^2 is 45 and so $\sigma = 6.708$. Hence $X \sim P(45)$ and now approximately $X \sim N(45, 45)$ using the normal approximation to the Poisson model.

Step 3: Locate and label the area required
We need to find r or more sales (this will be the area to the right of r) which gives a probability of 5%. This is shown in figure 8.16.

Step 4: Find the Z value
Here we standardise $Z = \dfrac{X - \mu}{\sigma}$ where X is the value r and $\mu = 45$ and $\sigma = 6.708$.

Thus $Z = \dfrac{r - 45}{6.708}$

Now we know Z is the value which has an area of 5% to the right of it; thus we need to find Z_α for $\alpha = 0.05$, using Table 2 in the Appendix. We arrive at $Z = 1.64485$, so that

Thus

$$1.64485 = \dfrac{r - 45}{6.708}$$

Step 5: Applying the continuity correction
Here we are looking at the chance of r or more sales. Under a continuous distribution, whether we include the end point of the interval or not will not affect the area concerned as we will be adding or withdrawing the area of a line which is negligible. However, we are really looking at a discrete distribution and as such are using the normal approximation to facilitate this. Now for a discrete distribution it does make a difference if we say, for example, the chance of more than 5 sales or the chance or 5 or more sales. In the first instance we

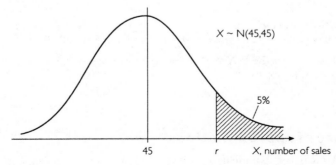

Figure 8.16

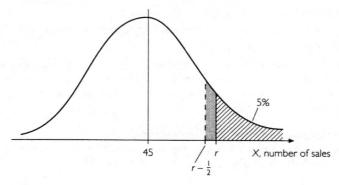

Figure 8.17

exclude 5 and so have 6, 7, 8, etc. sales, whereas in the latter case we include 5 and count 5, 6, 7 ... sales.

To build this into our above expression for the P($\geqslant r$ sales) we must be sure to include the value of r and so go to the left of r by a half, and so use $r - 0.5$. Our diagram above becomes figure 8.17.

Thus $1.64485 = \dfrac{r - 0.5 - 45}{6.708}$

Step 6: Find r

By re-arranging $1.64485 = \dfrac{r - 0.5 - 45}{6.708}$ we will find the value of r. Firstly cross multiply by 6.708 and to give us

$r - 0.5 - 45 = 1.644865 \times 6.708$

and so $r = 11.03365 + 45 + 0.5$ which gives us $r = 56.53$.

Step 7: Conclusion

The newsagent should order at least 57 local papers a day if he is to have a less than 5% chance of not meeting demand.

Note: Continuity corrections

If we have P($X > r$) we use $r + 0.5$, as shown in figure 8.18

and if we require the P($X = r$) we use the interval $r - 0.5$ to $r + 0.5$. The area is shown in figure 18.19.

Summary of approximations

Let N = normal, b = binomial, and P = Poisson, then figure 8.20 summarises the situations in which we can use approximations.

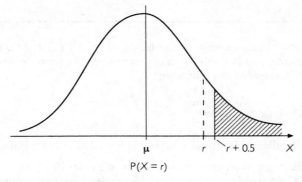

$P(X = r)$

Figure 8.18

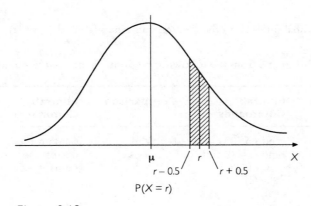

$P(X = r)$

Figure 8.19

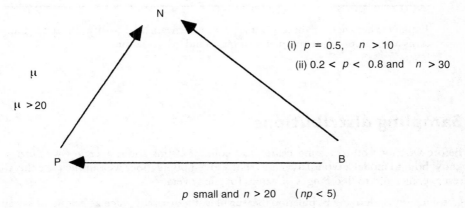

(i) $p = 0.5$, $n > 10$

(ii) $0.2 < p < 0.8$ and $n > 30$

p small and $n > 20$ ($np < 5$)

Figure 8.20

Exercises 8.3

8.3.1 Assuming a normal approximation to the binomial model B(10, 0.6), find the value of the mean and standard deviation of this model. Use these values to find the Z value corresponding to the following:

(i) $P(X > 7)$;
(ii) $P(X = 8)$;
(iii) $P(X \leqslant 6)$.

Compare the probabilities from the normal and binomial models for this example.

8.3.2 Assuming a Poisson approximation to the binomial model B(80, 0.05) find the value of the mean and standard deviation of this model. Use these values to find the corresponding Poisson probabilities for the following:

(i) $P(X = 3)$;
(ii) $P(X < 4)$;
(iii) $P(X \leqslant 4)$.

Compare the probabilities from the Poisson and binomial models for (i).

8.3.3 Minitab exercise
Compare the histograms from the following randomly generated populations:

Population	Minitab Commands	Comparison	Minitab Commands
(i) B(10, 0.5)	random 100 c1; Bino n = 10 and p = 0.5 Tally C1 Hist c1	N(5, 2.5)	random 100 C1; normal mean = 5 sigma = 1.58 Hist c1
(ii) P(25)	random 100 c1; poiss mean = 25 tally c1 Hist c1	N(25, 25)	random 100 C1 normal mean = 25, sigma = 5. Hist c1

Explain what each of these Minitab routines means and justify the approximations and values of the mean and sigma (standard deviation).

Sampling distributions

Before we move on to testing claims and counter-claims about averages we need to know how to model a typical average from a given population; we can then use this to test averages and to find ranges of values for such averages.

Consider any underlying population measuring some attribute, such as height, of say all people (male/female) aged over 18 in the UK. If we took one sample of size n from this population, then the mean of this sample, $\bar{x}$, would be a reasonable estimate for the true population mean, μ, (which we would be unlikely to know). We would say $\bar{x}$ is a point estimate for μ. If the same way the sample standard deviation, s (unbiased $\text{x}\sigma_{n-1}$) is an estimator of the population standard deviation, σ, where any sample statistic is an estimator for a population parameter. (Recall that calculations using sample data are called statistics whilst calculations using population data are called parameters.)

If we took a different sample of size n, we would be unlikely to get the same $\bar{x}$, but this value would be equally good an estimator for μ. If we continue taking many samples of the same size from the underlying population we would get an $\bar{x}$ for each sample, so giving us a set of means $\{\bar{x}_1, \bar{x}_2, \bar{x}_3 \ldots \text{etc.}\}$. Collating these mean values into a grouped frequency table we could then plot this frequency distribution for the means. In particular, if plotted as a relative frequency density histogram this would be called the sampling distribution of the means. We could consider the shape, the mean and variation for this set of means. If we took all possible random samples of some fixed size, we can form a probability model known as the sampling distribution for that estimator, the mean here (or equally the standard deviation). Below we shall consider the probability model for such a sampling distribution. Computer simulations will quite easily verify this model—see the Minitab exercise and the case study at the end of this section.

Selecting samples of various sizes

Consider a population $\sim N(\mu, \sigma^2)$ and suppose we are selecting samples from this population. A distribution for this population might look like figure 8.21.

From this underlying population we are going to select samples of various sizes to see what happens to the set of means of such samples, and in particular see to what degree there is less variation than in the population. By finding the shape and spread of the sampling distribution of the means we will be able to calculate differences in averages and compare values of a sample mean with the underlying population mean.

Case 1: samples of size 1
If we were to select every possible sample of size 1 from the population, we would just obtain the original population with the same mean μ and variance σ^2.

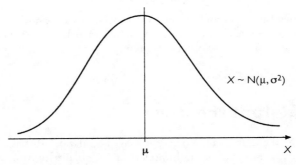

Figure 8.21

Case 2: samples of size 2

If we now select a sample of size two from this population, we are more likely to obtain values lying close to the population mean, μ, than values a long way off from μ, simply because there are more of these in the population. Thus the probability that the mean $\bar{x}$ of our sample will be closer to μ will be considerably higher than the probability that $\bar{x}$ is a long way off from μ. Now taking all possible samples of size two, and considering calculating the mean for each sample, many of these sample means will be closer to the population mean than they were in the original population (as one small value and one large value will give a mean closer to the centre of the distribution). We can now think of forming a new distribution from the means of these samples. This will have the same centre as the population but will be more peaked—will have slightly less variation than the population.

If we continue in this way, we would see that the mean of all the sample means will be the population mean, μ. Since the distribution becomes more peaked—extremes are slightly less likely to occur—there will be a reduction in the variance of the sample of means.

General case: samples of size n

As we increase the sample size, the probability of sample values (and hence the sample mean) lying in the extreme tail of the original population becomes extremely small, whilst the probability of the sample mean being close to the original population mean increases. In fact we can show that as the sample size increases the distribution of the sample means remains a normal distribution with mean μ. However, the variance of the distribution decreases as the sample size increases—there is less variability in the means of the samples than in the population itself. It can be shown that the random variable for the sample means, $\bar{X}$, has the following distribution: $\bar{X} \sim N\left(\mu, \dfrac{\sigma^2}{n}\right)$

We call the standard deviation of the sampling distribution of the means the *standard error* of the means, $\dfrac{\sigma}{\sqrt{n}}$. The Z transformation for standardisation of sample mean is:

$$Z = \frac{\bar{X} - \mu}{\dfrac{\sigma}{\sqrt{n}}}$$

Notice that this is exactly comparable with our previous standardised Z value $Z = \dfrac{X - \mu}{\sigma}$, but in place of X we have the sample mean $\bar{X}$ and in place of σ we have the standard deviation of $\bar{X}$, namely $\dfrac{\sigma}{\sqrt{n}}$.

What happens when the underlying population is not normal or not even symmetrical? Can we deduce some characteristics that its sampling distribution of means is likely to have? In fact we can apply the following theorem.

The central limit theorem

The central limit theorem states that for any population distribution (discrete, continuous, skewed, uniform or multimodel, etc.) the distribution of the sample means will become approximately normal provided the sample size is sufficiently large.

By sufficiently large we generally mean greater than 30. The mean of this distribution of means will be μ and its variance will be $\dfrac{\sigma^2}{n}$. Thus $\bar{X} \sim N\left(\mu, \dfrac{\sigma^2}{n}\right)$. If σ is unknown we can estimate it by s (the best estimate for σ), namely the $x\sigma_{n-1}$ button on the calculator computed using a formula of the form: $\sqrt{\dfrac{\Sigma(x - \bar{x})^2}{n - 1}}$

We now present a case study and a Minitab exercise on the sampling distribution of the mean.

Case study: sampling distribution of the mean

Class exercise 8.4

This exercise should be used in a class of any size over about 30 students. A suitable characteristic is measured—here age is chosen, but it could equally be unit mark for a certain subject, part-time income, and so on.

Task 1:
Your class is the population for the following exercise. It is a finite population, and we should adjust for that, but for simplicity we will not.

We will tabulate the population values and calculate the mean μ and standard deviation σ. This information is collected on a tally chart by a show of hands and tabulated as below. (Other class intervals or smaller widths may be more suitable.)

Class interval (age)	Mid-points	Frequency
under 20		
20 and under 23		
23 and under 26		
26 and under 29		
29 and under 32		
32 and over		

8.4.1 Calculate the mean μ and the standard deviation σ.

8.4.2 Plot a histogram for the above population distribution. Label μ on the histogram.

8.4.3 Describe the shape of the histogram.

(The larger the class the more symmetrical the histogram, but a skewed histogram will perhaps show the value of sampling distributions.)

Task 2
Get into groups of 5—say each row in the lecture theatre.

Choose one member of your group as the leader. This person asks each group member to write down their age on a piece of paper, and then records these for your group, and works out the mean age for this group. This means we are selecting samples of size 5 from our population.

If the class is small, asking the group leaders to remain fixed and getting all other students to rotate will generate many more samples. This can be done several times.

When this is complete the tutor then collects this data as below:

Group	Mean
1	
2	
3	
4	
5	
6	
7	
8	
9	
10	
11	
12	
13	
14	
15	
16	

8.4.4 Tabulate this into class intervals as above and plot a histogram for the sample means. For simplicity, use the same classes as in the population histogram. Label the mean on the histogram. Comment on the shape of this histogram and the shape relative to the population histogram.

8.4.5 Calculate mean $\bar{X}$ of the means and SE, the standard error (standard deviation) of the means.

8.4.6 Compare the values $\bar{X}$ with μ and SE with $\dfrac{\sigma}{\sqrt{5}}$.

Minitab exercise 8.5 _____

Carry out the following Minitab simulation which will generate samples of size 10 and 30 from an underlying binomial population B(20, 0.2).

First the underlying population is plotted to investigate the shape of the distribution.

Generating the population:

```
MTB>    random 1000 c1;
SUBC>   Binomial n = 20 p = 0.2
MTB>    Tally C1
MTB>    Histogram C1
```

The histogram will be skewed.

It is thus necessary to appeal to the central limit theorem to say that the sampling distribution of means for samples of $n = 30$ from this underlying population will be approximately normally distributed with mean $\mu = np$ and standard error $= \dfrac{\sigma}{\sqrt{n}} = \dfrac{\sqrt{npq}}{\sqrt{n}}$. We should notice that for the samples of size 10 the sampling distribution will not be very normal like. As n increases the sampling distribution becomes more normal like.

Generating samples and calculating their means:

	Interpretation
`MTB>    Let K2=1`	Ki is the counter
`MTB>    store`	store the following
`STOR>   random 10 observations,`	sample size = 10
`        put into C1;`	(subcommand)
`STOR>   Binomial n=20 p=0.2`	underlying population
`STOR>   mean data in C1, put in K1`	store $\bar{x}$ in K1 (constant cell)
`STOR>   Let C2=K1`	
`STOR>   Let K2=K1+1`	
`STOR>   END`	
`MTB>    Execute 50 times`	generate 50 sample means

Repeat this for $n = 30$.

Repeat this for a Poisson population $X \sim P(5)$.

Hypothesis testing

Scenario

A crime reporter was told by a neighbourhood watch group that on average 4000 burglaries were recorded per month in a certain city. Before going to press, the reporter wanted to check the story, by examining past reported burglaries. She noted that in 36 months, the average number of burglaries was in fact 3480 with a standard deviation of 960 per month. Does this provide evidence to support the claim of the neighbourhood watch group at the 5% level of significance, or would it appear that the neighbourhood watch group was exaggerating the level of burglaries?

Background

Mathematicians like to prove statements—hypotheses or conjectures. Statisticians never *prove conclusively* any statement; they say what chance it has of occurring, or not occurring. This is carried out within the framework of an hypothesis test. It is possible to test the validity of various parameters and use one or more samples, but we shall restrict out attention to testing claims about averages. (For tests on variances the reader is encouraged to read about F tests.)

We shall consider the following two main categories:

Case 1   Large samples, $n \geqslant 30$
Case 2   Small samples, $n < 30$.

Case I: Large samples $n \geqslant 30$

To test whether or not the neighbourhood watch group is justified we need to look at a model for a typical average number of burglaries per month. In our scenario we had data from a sample of 36 months, that is our sample size n is 36. The mean for the sample $\bar{x}$ is 3480 and the standard deviation is 960. Thus we have $n = 36$, $\bar{x}$ is 3480 and $s = 960$ with a claim that the true monthly average is in fact 4000, that is $\mu = 4000$. This is thus the claim that we will test and we shall see use evidence from the sample to see if it supports or negates this claim. We follow the subsequent step-by-step procedure:

Step 1: Set up a null hypothesis, H_0
This is a statement about an underlying claim relating to the distribution of some observations (given in the problem). This must be a precise statement which includes an underlying model for these observations. Here we are testing the average number of burglaries per month, and we are told that $\mu = 4000$. This will form our H_0:

$H_0 : \mu = 4000$, that is to say the claim of the neighbourhood watch group is valid.

We do not allow statements such as $\mu > 4000$ or $\mu \neq 4000$ for H_0. The null hypothesis is always stated in terms of the population parameter.

The underlying probability model
Do we know a model for the average number of burglaries? We cannot be sure as to what the underlying typical pattern of burglaries is, that is our population is of an unknown model, but we know its mean is $\mu = 4000$ and we can estimate its standard deviation by $s = 960$. As our sample size is 36 months, that is, it is a large sample, we can use the central limit theorem to tell us that the average of such a population will have approximately a normal distribution with a mean μ and variance $\dfrac{\sigma^2}{n}$, but we use s in place of σ. Thus the average number of burglaries per months is $\bar{X} \sim N\left(4000, \dfrac{(960)^2}{36}\right)$.

Step 2: Set up an alternative hypothesis, H_1
This is our counter-claim. If we are testing whether H_0 is consistent with certain data, some alternative is naturally implied. Here the reporter has found that the average over 36 months was 3480, considerably less than the statement from the neighbourhood watch. What we need to decide is, is it significantly less than 4000 or is it due simply to random variation which we would expect? Here our counter-claim is $H_1 : \mu < 4000$.

Other forms could be $H_1 : \mu > 4000$, if we suspected the observed data suggested that there had been an increase in the mean or $H_1 : \mu \neq 4000$ if we were looking for differences from the stated mean value.

The form of H_1 will tell us if we are conducting a one-tailed or two-tailed test.

Conducting a one-tailed test: if in our H_1 we are looking at the option that the observed data provides evidence of an increase or decrease from the stated value in H_0, then we are conducting a one-tailed test as we are looking for changes in one direction. For example:

$H_1 : \mu < 4000$
$H_1 : \mu > 4000$

would both be 1 tailed tests, whereas

$H_1 : \mu \neq 4000$

would indicate that we were looking for differences from the stated mean value, which could be an increase or a decrease. This would be a two-tailed test.

Step 3: Calculate a test statistic

This is computable using H_0, the underlying probability model and the test data. Here our test is based on a normal distribution and so we use:

$$Z = \frac{\bar{X} - \mu}{\frac{\sigma}{\sqrt{n}}} \text{ or if we have s rather than } \sigma, \text{ then } Z = \frac{\bar{X} - \mu}{\frac{s}{\sqrt{n}}}$$

This is known as a Z test.

Putting in the values we will have:

$$Z = \frac{3480 - 4000}{\frac{960}{\sqrt{36}}} = \frac{-520}{\frac{960}{6}} = \frac{-520}{160} = -3.25$$

Step 4: Level of significance

This is usually given in the problem. It can be interpreted as the chance of the value of the test statistic (or greater or smaller values) occurring by chance alone, under the supposition that H_0 is true. This is in fact the margin of error we allow, or one type of error: the chance of rejecting H_0 when in fact it is true. There is another type of error: accepting H_1 when in fact it is false. The percentage we attach to the level of significance indicates how sure we are in either accepting H_0 or in saying we cannot accept H_0. If the test is significant at a certain level this would roughly be interpreted as follows.

We would use a 1% level of significance if we were examining data for which it was very important that we were sure about our conclusion, for example if we were examining medical data. In such trials the margin of error we allow for must be small. A level of 1% means almost conclusive evidence against H_0. The chance of the observed data occurring whilst H_0 is true is so small that we conclude H_0 cannot be true (it could be … if we are wrong).

When we are less sensitive about the outcome we might adopt a 5% level of significance. A level of 5% would mean there is moderate evidence against H_0's validity.

Not significant at 5% would indicate that the observed data provided no evidence against H_0.

If our test is a one-tailed test, the level of significance is the probability in the tail (right tail if we are looking for increases or left tail if we are looking for decreases). If we are conducting a two-tailed test we put half of the level of significance value in each tail.

Step 5: Label the critical region, label your test statistic

Here our test (due to H_1) is a one-tailed test and as we are looking for decreases from a stated mean we are looking at the left tail, and so our 5% level of significance is the area in the left tail. Our diagram is labelled as figure 8.22.

On our diagram we need to find the Z value that corresponds to the area of 5% to the left. By symmetry from Table 2 in the appendix we see that the positive Z value is 1.64485. Thus the negative Z value will be -1.64485. The critical zone is labelled and corresponds to the area containing the level of significance. The Z value of -1.64485 is known as our critical Z value. This zone is critical in the sense that if our test statistics falls in this zone then it provides evidence critical to H_0 and in fact evidence against H_0 being true. Thus this is the zone where we would reject H_0, since here our observed data is significantly less than (less then due to H_1) the value given under H_0 and so does not support H_0. As the observed data has been found, this cannot be a false premise, and so it must be that H_0 is negated. We thus accept our alternative hypothesis, H_1. Notice that the region containing 95% of the area under our Z diagram is the zone where we accept the validity of H_0 if our test statistic lies here.

Labelling our test statistic on the diagram we see that $Z = -3.25$ and lies far to the left of our critical Z value of -1.64485.

Thus our diagram is given by figure 8.23.

Hence we must reject H_0 and accept H_1. As this value is quite some way inside the critical zone, we say this is strong evidence against H_0. Here we are really comparing out test statistic with the critical Z value. An alternative way of thinking of this is to compare the area to the left of the test statistic and decide if this is smaller than the critical zone. If we carry out a test using Minitab we will be given the area— probability—to the left of our test statistic. (Here we compare the area to the left of our test statistic because our H_1 is considering the possibility that our parameter is less than the one claimed.)

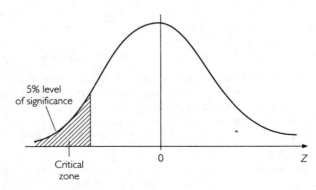

5% level
of significance

Critical
zone

0

Z

Figure 8.22

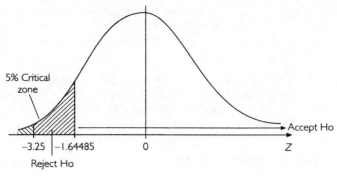

Figure 8.23

Step 6: Conclusion
We have strong evidence at the 5% level of significance to reject the claim of the neighbourhood watch group and support the careful research of the journalist that the average level of burglaries is in fact less then 4000 per month. Notice we have not disproved the claim of the neighbourhood watch. We have evidence to dispute their claim with a 5% margin of error.

We usually combine steps 5 and 6, thus giving us a five-step routine.

Notice that $\bar{X}$ denotes the random variable for any sample mean and $\bar{x}$ denotes some particular observation of the random variable $\bar{X}$.

Exercises 8.6 _____

For each of the following questions state clearly the null and alternative hypotheses (N.B. In H_0 give the distribution of the test statistic you decide to use.) Set up each problem using the five-step routine.

8.6.1 Durarun batteries are advertised as lasting for 600 hours on average. You are appointed manager of the quality assurance department and need to examine this more closely. If in fact they last less then 600 hours on average, you could end up having to replace many or have problems with The Trades Description Act. If, however, they last longer than 600 hours on average, then you should revise your advertising! To check the claim, you test 100 batteries under similar conditions and get the following results: $\bar{x} = 615$ hours and $s = 52.5$ hours. What conclusion would you reach at the 1% level of significance?

8.6.2 A market research analyst is employed to advise the Swank organisation whether or not it is economically feasible to open a new cinema complex near London Bridge. From past studies, the cinema complex would be viable if the typical household within a radius of 3 miles of London Bridge spent at least 18 hours on average at the cinema each year. The market researcher selects a random sample of 80 households living within the given radius; they were found to spend on average 20.8 hours per year at the cinema with a standard deviation of 7.5 hours.

How should the analyst advise the Swank organisation at the 5% level of significance? Is this sufficient evidence for building a new cinema?

We shall generally carry out two tests: a Z test using the normal distribution and a t test using the t distribution. Which test we use depends on two factors: whether the sample is small or large, and whether the underlying population variance, σ^2, is known or unknown.

Case 2: Small samples $n < 30$

We now proceed to consider a test for small samples based on a population mean where the underlying population is a normal distribution. (For large samples we did not need this extra restriction of the population being normal because of the central limit theorem.)

We need to consider small samples in two cases:

Case 2A: σ is known

Here we can use the additive property of the normal distribution:

If X_1, X_2, ... X_n are normally distributed samples then the sum of them is also distributed normally and so is its average, $\bar{X}$. That is $\bar{X} \sim N\left(\mu, \dfrac{\sigma^2}{n}\right)$ and the test statistic

is as above: $Z = \dfrac{\bar{X} - \mu}{\dfrac{\sigma}{\sqrt{n}}}$.

Example 8.4

PowerGemm Electricity Company supply the county of Wessex with electricity. Over the last few years the average consumption of electricity for the month of February has been 850 kilowatt-hours (kWh) per residential customer in Wessex with a standard deviation of 64.2 kWh. PowerGemm have made a request to the Government that they be allowed to build a new power station in Wessex to meet a perceived increased demand: they argue that by February 1997 the power usage will be considerably higher.

To demonstrate this they have called in your consulting firm to examine a random sample of customer accounts. Twenty customers were selected and the mean consumption of electricity for February 1996, $\bar{x}$, was found to be 880 kWh. What would you advise PowerGemm? Is the average consumption during this February significantly higher than previous findings at the 1% level? State clearly the hypotheses you are testing. Assume that the usage of electricity follows an approximate normal distribution.

Solution

Notice that the consumption of electricity in February 1996 is indeed higher than a typical February: what we need to determine if this is simply larger due to random variation in average usage or if it is significantly higher. We follow the five-step routine as above.

Step 1: Null hypothesis
H_0: $\mu = 850$; the average consumption of electricity in Wessex for a typical February is 850 kWh. The distribution of the average consumption for any 20 residential users is approximately normal with a mean of $\mu = 850$ and a standard error of $\dfrac{\sigma}{\sqrt{n}} = \dfrac{64.2}{\sqrt{20}}$.

Formally $\bar{X} \sim N\left(850, \left(\dfrac{64.2}{\sqrt{20}}\right)^2\right)$.

Step 2: Alternative hypothesis
$H_1 : \mu > 850$, the average consumption for 1996 is greater than a typical February. This is a one-tailed test with the right tail the critical region.

Step 3: Test statistic

Here $Z = \dfrac{\bar{X} - \mu}{\dfrac{\sigma}{\sqrt{n}}}$

thus $Z = \dfrac{880 - 850}{\dfrac{64.2}{\sqrt{20}}} = \dfrac{30}{14.35555642} = 2.090$ to 3 decimal places.

Step 4: Level of significance
Here we are given a 1% level of significance. This is really because if the decision is wrong and a new power station is not needed the company could have extreme cash flow problems.

Step 5: Label a critical zone, critical Z value and conclude
The critical Z is where the area to right is 0.01 and we see this is 2.32635 using Table 2. Labelling a diagram with all the above information we have figure 8.24.

We see that our test statistics lie in the acceptance region for H_0; thus we should advise PowerGemm not to request to build a new power station based on the present levels of demand, at the 1% level of significance.

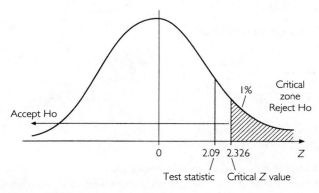

Figure 8.24

Case 2B: σ is unknown

Here we must use another distribution, namely the t distribution on $(n-1)$ degrees of freedom. We use s as the best estimate of σ. Our test statistic is $t = \dfrac{\bar{X} - \mu}{\frac{s}{\sqrt{n}}}$. The t distribution is of a similar shape to the normal distribution in that it is symmetrical about 0 but its values depend on the size of the sample. Its tails are wider in general, although as n becomes large (greater than 100) the t distribution approaches the normal. To understand what the degrees of freedom means, consider a sample with a fixed mean $\bar{x}$. Then any of the values of the sample up to $n-1$ values can vary freely: its nth value is completely determined by the other $n-1$ values and $\bar{x}$. There are precisely $n-1$ degrees of freedom.

We carry out a t test in exactly the same five-step routine as for a Z test.

Example 8.5

At the peak of the last housing boom in the UK, in 1988, the average number of days that a home stayed on the market in London was 100. An estate agent believed that in Richmond the average number of days a house stayed on the market before selling was in fact less than this. To test this claim, he decided that 15 homes that sold in 1988 from Richmond's housing market would be selected at random and for each the number of days on the market before sale was recorded. This is given below:

105   110   83   82   115   75   120   91   95   88   119   73   103   60   83

Is the estate agent justified in his premise, at the 5% level of significance?

Solution

For this sample we can calculate $\bar{x}$ and s and then perform the five-step routine as above. In doing so we have:

$\bar{x} = 95.87$ and $s = 15.55$ and a standard error of $\dfrac{s}{\sqrt{15}} = 4.02$ (to 2 decimal places).

Step 1: Null hypothesis
$H_0 : \mu = 100$

where $\bar{X}$ has a t distribution on 14 degrees of freedom with a mean $\mu = 100$, and a standard error of 4.02.

Step 2: Alternative hypothesis
$H_1 : \mu < 100$

Step 3: Test statistic

The test statistic of $t = \dfrac{95.87 - 100}{4.02} = -1.03$ on 14 degrees of freedom.

Step 4: Level of significance
We are given a 5% level of significance.

Step 5: Label the critical zone and conclude
We shall use Table 3 for the critical values of the t distribution and its corresponding percentage points.

Table 3 Percentage points of the t distribution

v	$\alpha = 0.4$ $2\alpha = 0.8$	0.25 0.5	0.1 0.2	0.05 ... 0.1 ...
1				
2				
3				
4				
.				
.				
14	0.258	0.692	1.345	1.761

Notice that the values down the first column of Table 3 are the degrees of freedom, v (pronounced nu). Along the first row of Table 3 we have two options: either a percentage of α in the right tail, or a percentage of 2α giving us α in both tails. As for the normal distribution, only positive t values are published and by symmetry we arrive at negative t values.

Drawing a diagram of a t distribution on $(n - 1) = 14$ degrees of freedom (see figure 18.25) we have $\alpha = 0.05$ in the left tail (as under H_1 we are considering values of $\mu < 100$); a critical t value is 1.761 if we were in the right tail, but in the left it will be $t = -1.761$.

We accept H_0, that there is no evidence that houses sold is under the London regional average in Richmond in the 1988 housing boom.

We can confirm these values using Minitab by entering the following commands:

```
MTB>   Read C1
Data>  105
Data>  110
```

and enter all the 15 items

```
Data>  END
MTB>   Mean C1
MTB>   StDev C1
```

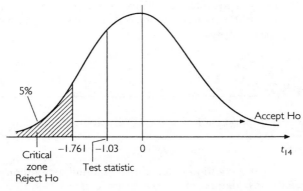

Figure 8.25

These values should agree with the above values.

Now to carry out the t test:

```
MTB>   TTest of mu=100 using C1;
SUBC>  Alternative=-1.
```

(Here we are testing mu $= 100$ against an alternative of two types:

Alternative $= 1$ means $H_1 : \mu > 100$
Alternative $= -1$ means $H_1 : \mu < 100$

Simply omit the subcommand semi-colon—if a two-tailed test is required.)

The printout you get should give you a test of μ versus greater than μ and a p value will be included. This will be the area to the left of the test statistic. If the value for p is less then the level of significance we reject H_0 and accept H_1.

Similar Minitab commands can be used for a Z test replacing the line TTest with ZTest.

Summary of Z and t tests

	Category	Test
Case 1	Large samples, $n \geqslant 30$	Z test
If the population is a normal model:		
Case 2	Small samples ($n < 30$) and σ is known	Z test
Case 3	Small samples ($n < 30$) and σ is unknown	t test

There are two types of error associated with a test conclusion:

Type I error $= \alpha\% =$ the chance of rejecting H_0 when in fact it is valid (this is the level of significance of a test).

Type II error $= \beta\% =$ the chance of accepting H_1 (and thus rejecting H_0) when in fact it is invalid. The power of a statistical test is $1 - \beta$ which we hope is large (and so β is small). Notice that $1 - \beta$ represents the probability of making a correct decision: if H_0 is false we should reject it! For a discussion on how to compute the power of a test you should read an advanced statistical book.

Exercises 8.7

8.7.1 If the underlying population is a normal distribution, explain when you would use a t test and when you would use a Z test to test if the average of a sample is comparable with the population average.

For each of the following questions state clearly the null and alternative hypotheses (N.B. In H_0 give the distribution of the test statistic you decide to use.) Set up each problem using the five-step routine.

8.7.2 Thamesborough Health Authority recently advised all their doctors (GPs) to try to prescribe cheaper generic drugs rather than the expensive brand-name drugs. A health review body was set up to investigate the total bill for drugs given on prescription by one particular GP who was opposed to this cost cutting policy. They decided to compare the total price of each of the brand-named drug with the similar generic drug for 12 prescriptions chosen at random from this GP's many prescriptions. The differences in price for each prescription were calculated to the nearest £ and recorded as:

35, 31, 50, 42, 56, 23, 27, 38, 25, 43, 45, 20

   (i)   Calculate the mean and standard deviation of this sample to 2 decimal places.
   (ii) The Health Authority are particularly concerned when the average difference in the two prices exceeds £25. Form a test statistic to see whether or not the average difference does exceed £25. State clearly the hypotheses under consideration and also the distribution of the sample means. Assume that the underlying differences are normally distributed.
   (iii) Does this sample provide evidence at the 5% level of significance that the advice from the Health Authority was being adhered to?
   (iv) Use Minitab to confirm your results.

8.7.3 A manufacturing process for engineering components produces components whose weights when packed are approximately normally distributed with a mean of 45 kg and a standard deviation of 2.3 kg. A modification is introduced by the design team which is intended to reduce costs without increasing the mean weight of the components—rather it is hoped to decrease the mean weight. This modification is not expected to modify the standard deviation of items from the production line.

To test whether the mean weight is appreciably smaller under the modified design, a sample of 9 components were selected from the production line at random. Their weights in kg were tested and were as follows:

44.6, 40.2, 45.9, 41.4, 39.1, 39.6, 42.6, 41.8, 43.6

Does this sample provide evidence to support the claim of the design team at the 5% level of significance?

Confirm your answer by entering the data into Minitab and performing a Z test (with commands as in example 8.5 but changing the TTest command to ZTest).

8.7.4 A senior executive of a publishing house decides to train its employees to read faster than 1000 words per minute. A random sample of 21 employees underwent the special speed-reading course. This sample had a mean reading speed of 1012 words per minute with a standard deviation of 30 words per minute. Does this data provide evidence to support the belief that the speed reading course will enable employees to read more than 1000 words per minute at a level of significance of 5%? Assume that the reading speeds of persons who have taken the course are normally distributed.

8.7.5 You are an employee from auditing firm sent out to an electronics company to determine if it was overstating the value of its inventory. Customary practice is that 15 items should be randomly selected from the company's record. For each item the recorded amount, the audited amount (true value), with the difference between these amounts (recorded — audited) were determined. Of particular interest was whether you could demonstrate that the average difference exceeded £30, in which case the electronics company would be subject to a loss of contracts and legal penalties. The following differences were recorded:

19, 37, 34, 22, 50, 42, 56, 26, 27, 48, 20, 25, 43, 45, 29

Calculate $\bar{x}$ and s. At the 5% level are the differences significant?

What would be your report to the company director?

Confirm your answer by entering this data in Minitab and performing a suitable test.

8.7.6 An Indian take-away company decide to set up a free delivery service if the average order in a small suburban area is over £15. A random sample of 23 orders resulted in an average price of £17 with a standard deviation of £2.50. Test at the 5% level of significance that the mean take-away order is greater than £15.

8.7.7 A 95% confidence interval for μ where the sample averages

$$\bar{X} \sim \mathrm{N}\left(\mu, \frac{\sigma^2}{n}\right)$$

is given by

$$\bar{X} - \frac{\sigma}{\sqrt{n}} \times 1.96 \leqslant \mu \leqslant \bar{X} + \frac{\sigma}{\sqrt{n}} \times 1.96$$

If we replace 1.96 by 2.33 we have a 99% confidence interval. If $\bar{X}$ has a t distribution then we use the corresponding t_{n-1} values in place of 1.96 and 2.33 with $\alpha = 0.025$ and $\alpha = 0.005$ respectively.

A 95% confidence interval would be interpreted as follows:

If many samples of size n were selected from the population $\mathrm{N}(\mu, \sigma^2)$ and a confidence interval of the above form calculated for μ, then for 95% of these confidence intervals μ the true population mean would lie in this interval, and in 5% of intervals it would not be contained.

Compute such intervals for questions 8.7.7 and 8.7.5. How could a two-tailed test be carried out using such an interval? Use the Minitab help menu to compute a confidence interval using Minitab.

9 Spotting relationships— correlation and regression

Objectives

- Understanding linear association between two attributes;
- Understanding the most appropriate measures of linear correlation;
- Be able to compute appropriate measures of linear correlation;
- Understanding how to measure a linear relationship between two variables;
- Be able to compute an equation of linear regression;
- Understand interpolation and extrapolation;
- Be able to interpret a Minitab printout for linear regression.

Correlation

Scenario

A TV producer of children's programmes has undertaken research into children's preferences for week-time TV viewing. After questioning many children she has found two very typical responses. The respondents were asked to rank in order of preference ten prime TV shows, with a 1 for the most like and 10 for least liked. The results are recorded in the data set 9.1. This information can then be used to help develop new TV programmes. If a new TV show was to be designed is there any show which could be a model? Are there any shows which are generally unpopular? Is there any agreement between the two responses? Is there disagreement between the two responses?

Such questions can be studied within the framework of correlation.

Data set 9.1

Two typical responses to the TV producer's questions were:

TV programme	Child 1	Child 2
A Grange Hill	2	1
B Blue Peter	1	8
C After 5 with a Star	5	6
D Byker Grove	3	2
E Countdown	4	4
F Newsround	7	5
G Neighbours	9	7
H Reactive	6	3
I Telecartoons	10	10
J Home and away	8	9

Bivariate data

Notice that for each programme we have a pair of responses. Whenever we are measuring a response or observation consisting of two variables, such pairs of data are referred to as *bivariate* data. For example we might be recording weights/heights, salary/age for a set of people, or turnover/profit, profit/earnings per share etc, for a collection of companies. We can represent such pairs of data as points in a suitable pair of co-ordinates. For example, in data set 9.1 we would place one child's response on a horizontal (x) axis, and the other child's response on a vertical (y) axis. Each point would be plotted as an ordered pair (child 1, child 2) on a diagram known as a *scatter diagram*. This is plotted below in figure 9.1.

Deductions from the scatter diagram

We can see that there is broad agreement between the two children: they both like programme A (Grange Hill) and they both dislike programme I (Telecartoons). On the other programmes D, E, H, etc. they are broadly in agreement: the rank assigned by the one child is fairly similar, although not usually identical to the other child. There is one programme they disagree about programme B (Blue Peter) is strongly favoured by child 1 but not well liked by child 2. If you were the producer what would you determine from these typical responses? Programmes such as A (Grange Hill), D (Byker Grove) and even E (Countdown) are popular with children and new types of programmes along these lines would be most likely to be successful. Making programmes like J (Home and away), G (Neighbours) and I (Telecartoons) is generally not very popular.

Formally we would say that the scatter diagram provides evidence that there is some degree of linear association between the two children's responses; the graph does appear to indicate that as the ranking given by child 1 increases so does the ranking allocated by child 2 (with the exception of one programme). Evidence of linear association is apparent from the graph as the pairs of rankings form a trend along a line. Such linear association is formally called linear correlation. Given some evidence from a scatter diagram of the existence of linear association, we can now proceed to measure if there is indeed statistical evidence to confirm this correlation between the two children's responses. To this end we measure a correlation coefficient. Here the data

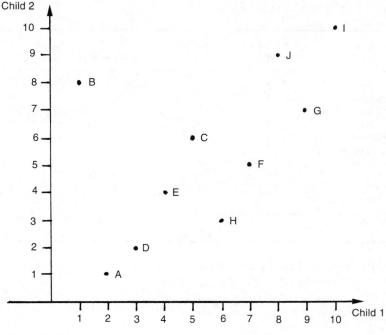

Figure 9.1

is ranked data and one of correlation can be obtained using a rank correlation coefficient; one we discuss is due to Spearman.

Spearman's rank correlation coefficient

Step 1: Assign the ranks
In this problem the children have already done this by ranking their favourite programmes in order of merit. Here we have 10 pairs of data, or 10 pairs of rankings. This means n, the number of rankings is 10. If we need to allocate ranks we assign rank 1 for the most liked/best preferred and 10 (or n) for the least liked. Let child 1's rankings be denoted by R_1, and child 2's rankings be denoted by R_2.

Step 2: Differences in the rankings
We then form the difference in the child's rankings, namely $R_1 - R_2$. This is placed in a column in the table below. This column is denoted by d_i where i is the position of the row in the table. That is, d_1 is the difference between the children's ranking for the first programme, Grange Hill. We next form a column for the squared differences, d_i^2. We then form the total of the squared differences in the ranks, written $\sum d_i^2$.

Our table will then look like the following:

TV programme	Child 1 R_1	Child 2 R_2	$d_i = R_1 - R_2$	$d_i^2 = (R_1 - R_2)^2$
A Grange Hill	2	1	1	1
B Blue Peter	1	8	−7	49
C After 5 with a Star	5	6	−1	1
D Byker Grove	3	2	1	1
E Countdown	4	4	0	0
F Newsround	7	5	2	4
G Neighbours	9	7	2	4
H Reactive	6	3	3	9
I Telecartoons	10	10	0	0
J Home and away	8	9	−1	1
Total				70

Step 3: Calculate the rank correlation coefficient

Spearman's rank correlation coefficient, r_s, is given by:

$$r_s = 1 - \frac{6 \times \sum d_i^2}{n \times (n^2 - 1)}$$ where n is the number of pairs of rankings.

Thus putting $n = 10$, and $\sum d_i^2 = 70$ this will give us:

$$r = 1 - \frac{6 \times 70}{10 \times (10^2 - 1)} = 1 - \frac{420}{990} = 1 - 0.4242 = 0.5758$$

to four decimal places.

Thus the degree of agreement between the two rankings is reasonably good. Exactly how good depends on the number of pairs of observations and we shall see later in this chapter how to carry out a test of hypothesis on the value of r_s.

Observations about r_s

The largest value of r_s is $+1$ which will occur when all the ranks agree, that is $\sum d_i^2 = 0$. This would mean complete agreement in the preferences of the two children for all programmes selected. The smallest value of r_s would be -1 which would indicate that the ranking given by 1 child was in complete reverse order to that of the other child. This would mean that if the favourite programme for child 1 was Grange Hill, with a rank of 1, then the worst programme would be Grange Hill for child 2 given a rank of 10, and a difference of 9 between the ranks. (We shall consider this in the exercises below.) A value of $r_s = 0$ would indicate no agreement between the rankings. This would occur when $\sum d_i^2 \approx \frac{n}{6}(n^2 - 1)$. Thus critically we are looking for values of r_s close to $+1$ or -1 for correlation to be statistically significant. This explains the earlier comment that the value of $r_s \approx 0.6$ was reasonable evidence for correlation between the two children's preferences, without carrying out a test of its significance.

Uses of rank correlation coefficients

Notice that the above data about children's preference for certain TV programmes is in fact qualitative data: it simply measures a consumer's response. Here correlation could only be measured using a rank correlation coefficient. Using a rank correlation coefficient for quantitative data is possible, as the next example shows.

Example 9.1

Two judges at the recent World Athletics Championship awarded the following marks out of 6 to the given country for their team's gymnastics floor exercises:

Country	Judge 1	Judge 2
Canada	5.4	5.4
China	5.7	5.6
France	4.5	5.0
GB	4.3	4.8
Germany	5.6	5.7
Russia	5.8	5.9
Ukraine	5.9	5.8
USA	5.6	5.8

Is there evidence of agreement between the two judges?

Solution
Step 1: Allocating the rankings
Notice that there are 8 pairs of data, and so $n = 8$. This data needs to be ranked with a 1 for the highest score from the judge and an 8 for the lowest score from the judge. As in the above example, we call judge 1's ranks R_1, and judge 2's rankings R_2.

Starting with judge 1:
We assign ranks 1, 2 and 3 as expected to Ukraine (5.9), Russia (5.8) and China (5.7). A problem occurs when we are to assign ranks 4 and 5 as there are two countries (Germany and USA) which both score the next largest score of 5.6. To overcome this problem we assign the average of these ranks to both countries, giving us a rank $= \dfrac{4+5}{2} = 4.5$. We then proceed to allocate the next rank, rank 6, to the next highest mark, here Canada with 5.4. The ranks are given in the table below.

Judge 2's rankings:
We assign rank 1 to Russia which has the highest mark (5.9). We thus have to assign ranks 2 and 3 to Ukraine (5.8) and USA (5.8). As before we assign the average of these ranks to both countries, giving us a rank $= \dfrac{2+3}{2} = 2.5$. We then proceed to allocate the next rank, rank 4, to the next highest mark, here Germany with 5.7. We continue until both judges' marks have been ranked.

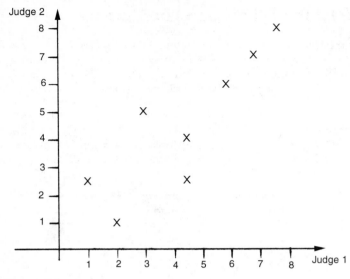

Figure 9.2

Step 2: Plotting the scatter diagram
Plotting judge 1's marks on the x axis and judge 2's marks on the y axis we have the scatter diagram given by figure 9.2.

We can see that there is some evidence for agreement between the two judges. They both highly rate Russia and Ukraine. We now go to see if there is statistically any evidence for linear association between the two judges.

Step 3: Differences in the rankings
We then form the difference in the judges' rankings, namely $R_1 - R_2$. This is placed in a column in the table below, denoted by d_i, where i is the position of the row in the table. Next to this column we form a column for the squared differences, d_i^2. We then form the total of the squared differences in the ranks, written $\sum d_i^2$.

Our table will then look like the following:

Country	Judge 1 Mark	R_1	Judge 2 Mark	R_2	$d_i = R_1 - R_2$	$d_i^2 = (R_1 - R_2)^2$
Canada	5.4	6	5.4	6	0	0
China	5.7	3	5.6	5	−2	4
France	4.5	7	5.0	7	0	0
GB	4.3	8	4.8	8	0	0
Germany	5.6	4.5	5.7	4	0.5	0.25
Russia	5.8	2	5.9	1	1	1
Ukraine	5.9	1	5.8	2.5	−1.5	2.25
USA	5.6	4.5	5.8	2.5	2	4
Total						11.5

Step 4: Calculate the rank correlation coefficient

Spearman's rank correlation coefficient, r_s, is given by:

$$r_s = 1 - \frac{6 \times \sum d_i^2}{n \times (n^2 - 1)}$$ where $n = 8$, the number of pairs of rankings.

Putting $\sum d_i^2 = 11.5$ this will give us:

$$r_s = 1 - \frac{6 \times 11.5}{8 \times (8^2 - 1)} = 1 - \frac{69}{504} = 1 - 0.1369 = 0.8631$$

to four decimal places.

Thus the degree of agreement between the two judges is quite strong, as r_s is close to $+1$.

Exercise 9.1 _____

9.1.1 Two wine connoisseurs gave their judgements on ten newly released wines. For each wine they allocated a score from 1 to 10 for their preference. Their opinions were recorded as follows:

Wine	Wine expert 1	Wine expert 2
A	1	1
B	2	9
C	6	5
D	4	4
E	3	2
F	7	7
G	10	8
H	5	3
I	8	6
J	9	10

Plot a scatter diagram and decide if there is any evidence of agreement between the two experts. If you were to stock some wines which would you choose on their advice? Are there any wines both experts viewed sceptically and you might avoid? Are there any wines the experts disagree on? Calculate Spearman's rank correlation coefficient to measure the degree of linear association between the two experts.

9.1.2 If $n = 10$, what value of $\sum d_i^2$ would give us $r_s = -1$? What ranks would this give for each of the two examples above? Confirm that this does give approximately a value of -1 for r_s. What sort of scatter diagram would this give? Plot this and comment on its appearance.

9.1.3 A value of $r_s = 0$ would indicate no agreement between the rankings. This would occur when $\sum d_i^2 \approx \frac{n}{6}(n^2 - 1)$. Confirm that if $n = 10$ this would give approximately an average squared difference between the two rankings of 16, and so an average difference between the ranks of 4. Determine suitable ranks that satisfy this and confirm this does give $r_s \approx 0$. Plot the scatter diagram concerned and comment on its appearance.

9.1.4 Compare the answer to question 1 by computing Kendall's rank correlation coefficient:

Step 1: Assign ranks as previously discussed, if necessary.

Step 2: Look at the list of pairs of ranks. If two ranks agree (that is both ranks are the same—for example wine A has a 1 in both ranks) then allocate a score of $+1$ to this pair. If the two ranks are different allocate a -1 to this pair. Sum these scores and call this S.

Step 3: Calculate r_k, Kendall's rank correlation coefficient:

$$r_k = \frac{S}{\frac{n}{2}(n-1)} \text{ where } n \text{ is the number of pairs of ranks.}$$

9.1.5 Compare the answers to data set 9.1 and example 9.1 using Kendall's correlation coefficient.

9.1.6 Explain why the largest value for r_k is $+1$ and when $r_k \approx 0$.

Product moment correlation coefficient

Given a set of quantitative bivariate data a natural question is to ask if there is any evidence of a linear relationship between the two variables. A scatter diagram will aid in this: we plot one variable (the independent variable) on the x-axis and the other variable (the dependent variable) on the y-axis where each pair of data is a point on this x–y plane. (These terms are explained fully below.) Statistically we can determine whether this graphical evidence is significant by calculating a correlation coefficient known as the *product moment correlation coefficient*, also sometimes called Pearson's correlation coefficient.

Scenario
Is there any evidence to suggest that if a company's turnover is large, its operating profit will be large? Or, if a turnover is large, is it unlikely that the operating profit will be low? To investigate these questions we need to collect appropriate data (given in data set 9.2) and carry out an analysis using a correlation coefficient.

Data set 9.2

The following figures show the annual turnover (in £m) and the gross operating profits (in £m) of various companies in several countries over the period 1990 to 1993:

Company	Turnover £m	Operating profit £m
A	708	80
B	1368	168
C	597	100
D	1075	121
E	1506	162
F	656	76
G	438	43
H	491	65
I	1258	100
J	480	59
K	1412	487

(*Source*: various company reports)

Correlation analysis

Step 1: Determining the axes of the scatter diagram

A scatter diagram will allow us to see if there is any evidence of linear association between turnover and operating profit. We shall call the turnover X and regard this as the independent variable. Here we can see that the company's turnover is independent of the company's profit. In fact it is the company's profit which is to some extent determined by the company's turnover. Thus we can see a natural interdependency: this leads us to the definitions of independent and dependent variable.

Types of bivariate data: independent and dependent

When both variables recorded as a bivariate data collection are randomly varying then it generally does not matter which variable we plot on the x- or y-axis. For example, if we have weights/heights or systolic blood pressure/pulse, both variables randomly vary and so we could plot either as X or Y. When we proceed to linear regression, which involves finding a linear model to fit a particular bivariate data set, then we would call the Y value the variable which we would be interested in predicting or estimating. The X would then be the *predictor* variable.

In some cases both variables do not randomly vary and so it is important that careful choice is made as to which is labelled X and which Y. We give some examples:

Consider an experiment where we are measuring an outcome (such as a bank's base rate) for a given pre-assigned set of values (here a time interval, such as each month). Each pair of values will form a set of bivariate data which we would write as an ordered pair (month, base rate). Here there is a control placed on one of the inputs: the month is preselected. It is known as a *non-stochastic* variable. We record the randomly varying base rate (a *stochastic* variable), but we can see that time is not subject to a random variation. Thus our bivariate data collection consists of a controlled variable known as the *independent variable*, or *predictor*, (or *explanatory*) variable and is usually given the code X and plotted on the x-axis. This would be month 1, 2, 3, etc. The measured response depends on which month is being recorded and is the base rate, denoted by Y, which would be plotted on the y-axis. Here we can see that the base rate depends on which month we have, and so Y is the *dependent* or *response* variable. As we shall investigate later in linear regression, it is only for a given month that we would be able to *predict* the corresponding base rate. Given any base rate it would be inappropriate to try to estimate which month is was for, as we are controlling the inputs for the time factor. These points are summarised below.

Independent variable/controlled variable/explanatory X
Whenever an experiment has a variable which is to some extent controlled, such as measuring a result every hour, day or when a particular fixed amount of insulin is given in doses such as 10 ml, 20 ml, 30 ml...etc, to a set of patients.

Dependent variable/uncontrolled or response variable Y
Whenever we are recording a patient's systolic blood pressure (every hour) or the value of a company's shares (every day), or the amount of glucose in the blood a given time after a set dose of insulin has been given.

In cases where both variables are stochastic (randomly varying) we can generally call either one the dependent/independent variable.

In this example (data set 9.2) the variable which is controlled is the company's turnover and for each company's turnover (X) we observe or record the operating profit (Y), the dependent variable.

Step 2: The scatter diagram
We can see that as the turnover increases, so does the gross operating profit. In fact most of the data are close to an imaginary line through the data (see figure 9.3), the so-called line of best fit, by eye.

There is one observation which lies quite a long way off from the majority of the data, the pair (1412, 487). This value might be called an *outlier* as it lies a long way from the majority of the data. (Some statistical packages might call it a *rogue value*.) We can either decide to leave it in the data set, or it could be argued that this is not typical of the other data and it could be discarded from the analysis. We shall in fact take the latter course to make the calculations easier. In the exercises it can be determined what difference adding this pair back into the calculations makes.

Recall that a measure of the variability in X was given by its standard deviation, s_x where s_x was the average sum of squares of each value from the mean:

$$s_x = \sqrt{\frac{\sum_{i=1}^{n}(x_i - \bar{x})^2}{n}}$$

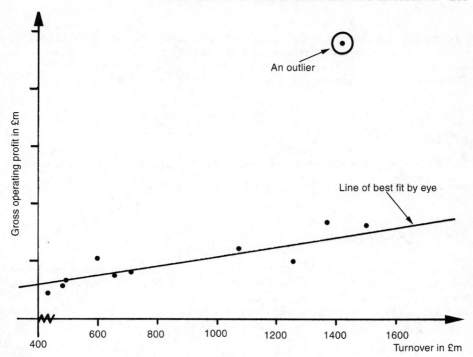

Figure 9.3

Putting $n - 1$ on the denominator gave us a better estimate of the underlying population standard deviation. The numerator is known as the sum of squares of X, SSx where

$$SSx = \sum_{i=1}^{n}(x_i - \bar{x})^2$$

From chapter 4 we saw that this in fact simplifies to give us:

$$SSx = \sum_{i=1}^{n}(x_i - \bar{x})^2 = \sum x^2 - n\bar{x}^2$$

Similarly the sum of squares of Y is written:

$$SSy = \sum_{i=1}^{n}(y_i - \bar{y})^2 = \sum y^2 - n\bar{y}^2$$

Remark
Notice that we call the variable by a capital letter X or Y, but for any particular value of X we write x_i where i is a counter for the position this value is in the list of all x_i, ie x_1 for the first item (708 above), x_2 for the second item, (1368 above) etc. As on the calculator, you will recall that we tend to drop the subscript i and write x where in fact we mean x_i and so $\sum x$ where we really mean $\sum_{i=1}^{n} x_i$.

Definition: Covariance of X *and* Y

The covariance between two variables, here X and Y, is a measure of the interdependence of the two variables and is found by computing the average product of the differences between each variable and its mean: that is the average of $(x_i - \bar{x})(y_i - \bar{y})$ for each x_i, y_i where i ranges from 1 to n, the number of pairs of data. That is,

$$\text{Covariance } (X, Y) = \text{Cov}(X, Y) = \frac{\sum_{i=1}^{n}(x_i - \bar{x})(y_i - \bar{y})}{n}$$

In fact on the denominator we can use $n - 1$ as a better approximator for the population covariance. The numerator $\sum_{i=1}^{n}(x_i - \bar{x})(y_i - \bar{y})$ is known as the Sum of Squares of X and Y, $SSxy$:

$$SSxy = \sum_{i=1}^{n}(x_i - \bar{x})(y_i - \bar{y})$$

The covariance depends on the scales in which X and Y are measured (as we shall see in the calculation below), and so we eliminate this by putting the covariance with the standard deviations to give a measure of the dependence of X and Y whilst cancelling the effect of magnitude of the values of either X or Y. Thus we have:

Definition

The product moment correlation coefficient, r, is given by

$$r = \frac{\text{Cov}(X, Y)}{s_x \times s_y}$$

where $\text{Cov}(X,Y)$ is the covariance of X and Y and s_x is the sample standard deviation of X variable and s_y is the sample standard deviation of the Y variable. In fact we can use n or $n - 1$ in the denominators of $\text{Cov}(X,Y)$ and s_x, s_x, obviously being consistent.

Thus we can write

$$r = \frac{\text{Cov}(X, Y)}{s_x \times s_y} = \frac{\dfrac{\sum_{i=1}^{n}(x_i - \bar{x})(y_i - \bar{y})}{n}}{\sqrt{\dfrac{\sum_{i=1}^{n}(x_i - \bar{x})^2}{n}} \times \sqrt{\dfrac{\sum_{i=1}^{n}(y_i - \bar{y})^2}{n}}}$$

or with $n - 1$ in the denominators. By careful cancellation in fact we can remove the need to use n or $n - 1$ in the denominators and use the sum of squares, as described earlier to give us:

$$r = \frac{SSxy}{\sqrt{SSx \times SSy}}$$

where $SSxy$ are the sum of squares of XY, SSx and SSy are the sum of squares of X and Y respectively.

This can be simplified to give us a working formula for the product moment correlation coefficient, r, given by

$$r = \frac{\sum xy - n\bar{x}\bar{y}}{\sqrt{(\sum x^2 - n\bar{x}^2)(\sum y^2 - n\bar{y}^2)}}$$

In fact as we are dealing with sample data, r is the sample product moment correlation coefficient, being an estimate for ρ, the population correlation coefficient.

Step 3: Calculating the sum of squares of X and Y and XY

From above we decided that turnover was the independent variable, which we shall denote by X, and operating profit is the dependent variable, Y.

We now need to form the sum of squares of X, which is

$$SSx = \sum_{i=1}^{n} (x_i - \bar{x})^2 = \sum x^2 - n\bar{x}^2$$

This means that we need a column for X^2. Similarly for the sum of squares of Y:

$$SSx = \sum_{i=1}^{n} (y_i - \bar{y})^2 = \sum y^2 - n\bar{y}^2$$

we need a column of Y^2. Also for the $SSxy$ we need a column of the product of each pair of X and Y, i.e. a column for XY. Our table becomes:

Company	Turnover £m	Profit £m			
	X	Y	X²	Y²	XY
A	708	80	501 264	6400	56 640
B	1368	168	1 871 424	28 224	229 824
C	597	100			59 700
D	1075	121			130 075
E	1506	162			243 972
F	656	76			49 856
G	438	43			18 834
H	491	65			31 915
I	1258	100			125 800
J	480	59			28 320
Total	8577	974	8 828 983	110 840	974 936

Notice that we have left to the reader to complete the calculations for X^2 and Y^2 and to confirm the sums of each of the columns.

Step 4: Compute the means, $\bar{x}$ and $\bar{y}$

Recall that $\bar{x} = \dfrac{\sum x}{n} = \dfrac{8577}{10} = 857.7$ using the total for xs, $\sum x$ from the table.

Similarly $\bar{y} = \dfrac{\sum y}{n} = \dfrac{974}{10} = 97.4$. Squaring the means will give us $\bar{x}^2 = 735\,649.29$ and $\bar{y}^2 = 9486.76$.

Step 5: Compute r

Using the totals from the above table we have:

$\sum x^2 = 8828983$, $\sum y^2 = 110\,840$, and $\sum xy = 974936$.

Thus

$$
\begin{aligned}
r &= \frac{SSxy}{\sqrt{SSx \times SSy}} = \frac{\sum xy - n\bar{x}\bar{y}}{\sqrt{\left(\sum x^2 - n\bar{x}^2\right)\left(\sum y^2 - n\bar{y}^2\right)}} \\[2mm]
&= \frac{974\,936 - 10 \times 857.7 \times 97.4}{\sqrt{8\,828\,983 - 10 \times (857.7)^2} \times \sqrt{110\,840 - 10 \times (97.4)^2}} \\[2mm]
&= \frac{974\,936 - 835\,399.8}{\sqrt{8\,828\,983 - 7\,356\,492.9} \times \sqrt{110\,840 - 94\,867.6}} \\[2mm]
&= \frac{139\,536.2}{\sqrt{1\,472\,490.1} \times \sqrt{15\,972.4}} = \frac{139\,536.2}{1213.462\,031 \times 126.381\,96} = \frac{139\,536.2}{153\,359.7107} \\[2mm]
&= 0.9099 \text{ to 4 decimal places}
\end{aligned}
$$

Step 6: Using the calculator programme

We shall now use the LR programme on the calculator to check our calculation of r as well as the totals on the above table. To this end:

Mode 3 will take us into the LR programme. Clear the stats memory just as good practice. We enter pairs of data using the blue frame below the parenthesis button $[(\ldots]$ You will see a point labelled in blue (x_d, y_d) on this frame standing for the pair of x and y values. Consult your reference card or book for other models.

Here we enter:

708   $[(\ldots]$ or (x_d, y_d) You will see a comma appear on the display to indicate that the first value, x, of the pair has been recognised.

80   $M+$ or Data button   This is entering the corresponding y value (data will also appear on the display).

1368 $[(\ldots]$ 168 $M+$

597   $[(\ldots]$ 100 $M+$

1075 $[(\ldots]$ 121 $M+$

etc until

480   $[(\ldots]$ 59 $M+$

We can then check the value for r: $SHIFT$ 9

We can also check the workings from our table—consult your reference card or book for other models. For our models these are:

n RCL 3 $\sum x^2$ RCL 1

Σx | RCL | | 2 | Σy^2 | RCL | | 4

Σy | RCL | | 5

Σxy | RCL | | 6

Using the shift button we can call up the values for $\bar{x}$, $\bar{y}$, etc as depicted on the blue frame for each button numbered 1–6. These checks are very useful, as it is so easy in statistics to mis-calculate something and not realise!

Step 7: Conclusion
The value of r is fairly close to $+1$ and this indicates that there is a strong linear association or correlation between the two variables. Being positive this suggests that as the turnover increases so does the operating profit. If this value for r were negative it would indicate that as the turnover increased the profit decreased.

There are further tests we can do to see exactly what is the chance of this value of r occurring quite by chance, and we shall do this later using statistical tables to carry out a test of hypothesis.

Note: The covariance $= \dfrac{974\,936 - 835\,399.8}{10} = 139\,536.2$

We can see that this is large because the values in X and Y are themselves large. We can also see that by dividing the covariance by the standard deviations of X and Y, we cancel out this dependence of the covariance on the scale of the values for X and Y; this gives us r which will always be within a fixed range, as we shall now see.

Observations about r

Generally we would say that if our correlation coefficients have the following properties

(i) $r \approx +1$ indicates a direct correlation. This means as one variable increases so does the other (not necessarily by the same amount) but a proportional increase.

(ii) $r \approx -1$ indicates an inverse correlation. This means that as 1 variable increases the other variable decreases, by some proportionate amount.

(iii)   If $r = +1$ or -1 we would describe this as *perfect* correlation.

(iv) $r \approx 0$ generally indicates no correlation is present. Such a scatter diagram is described as *spurious*. Thus critically we are looking at a range of values for r between -1 and $+1$. The closer to the edges of this band, the stronger the evidence for correlation between the pairs of data.

(v)   The larger the number of pairs of observations, the lower the value of r can be and still be statistically highly significant.

The corresponding scatter diagram is given below in figure 9.4 for each of the above cases.

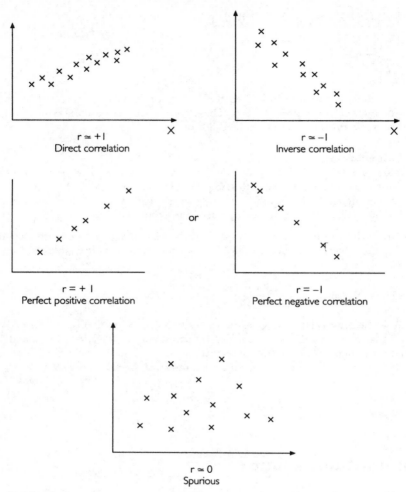

Figure 9.4

Exercise 9.2

Replace the last observation

K	1412	487

in the above calculations and re-calculate the correlation coefficient.

Caution: cause and effect

The existence of evidence of linear correlation between two variables does not imply a deterministic relationship between the two variables concerned (turnover and operating profit here): one does not necessarily *cause* an *effect* in the other. It just means that in the companies where there was a high turnover there was a corresponding large operating profit. It could well be that both are affected by other factors which have not been measured, for example the value of sterling, underlying base rates, confidence in the economy, etc. Whenever we carry out a correlation analysis we must be clear that we are saying there is evidence of a linear relationship but we are not saying one variable causes an increase or decrease in the other. Both could be the effects of a common cause. A linear relationship is a simple model to describe an underlying relationship between two attributes, and it could well be that the whole picture is much more complex and many other variables are affecting the bivariate data set.

For example, if we were to look at data for the life expectancy of adults (male or female) over the last 50 years we would see a steady increase. If we were to look at the number of marriages over the same period, we would be likely to see a steady decrease. Coupling these results we would arrive at a fairly negative linear association between these data. We might even be tempted to say that because people live longer, they are less inclined to marry. Moreover, someone may even be tempted to say one causes the other! This is extremely tenuous, and highly unlikely! The point is that just because a set of data can be plotted to give a certain credibility to an association between the variables, does not necessarily mean they are in any way related and the very fact that one variable increases in no way causes and effects the other to either increase or decrease! Correlation implies nothing about causation! Both variables may be affected by other attributes.

Data set 9.3

The table below gives the percentage increase in average earnings from January 1990 during 1993/94 together with the retail prices index for the period (with January 1990 as base year).

Date	% increase in average earnings (from January 1990)	RPI% (January 1990 base)
1993		
April	17.6	17.7
May	18.3	18.1
June	17.8	18.0
July	18.3	17.7
August	18.9	18.2
September	18.8	18.7
October	19.4	18.7
November	19.7	18.5
December	19.6	18.7
1994		
January	21.2	18.2

(Source: *Employment Gazette*, March 1994, and *Monthly Digest of Statistics*, March 1994, CSO)

Example 9.2
Are salaries keeping in line with price increases over this period?

Solution
Step 1: Scatter diagram
Notice here both variables are stochastic: they are both subject to random variation (and possible errors) and thus either could be the dependent or independent variable. We shall plot RPI on the x-axis and increase in average earnings on the y-axis. The scatter diagram is given in figure 9.5.

We can see that as the RPI increases, there seems to be a steady increase in the average increase in salary. There is one value which appears to be a considerable way away from the majority of values: the pair for January 1994 (18.2, 21.2). This value might be called an *outlier* but we shall leave it in the data set. To some extent the scale we have used to draw the graph has exaggerated the differences between the values. From the scatter diagram we get the impression that the percentage increase in average salary does indeed seem to keep pace with the RPI over this period 93/94.

Step 2: Correlation coefficient
Here it is natural to determine whether the evidence from the scatter diagram is statistically valid by calculating a correlation coefficient, the product moment coefficient, as all the data is quantitative. In the table for our

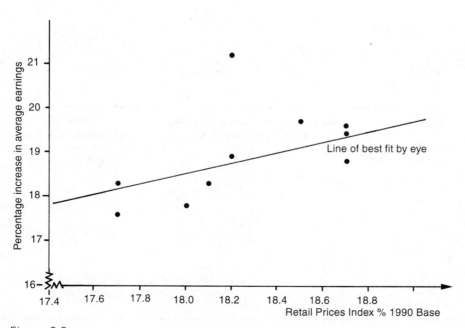

Figure 9.5

calculations we need a column for X, Y, and XY. This time we shall use our calculator to find the means, $\bar{x}$ and $\bar{y}$ and the sum of X^2 and Y^2.

Step 3: Compute the means, $\bar{x}$, $\bar{y}$ and $\sum x^2$, $\sum y^2$ and $\sum xy$

As described earlier in data set 9.2, we need to enter the data using the LR programme on the calculator. (If your calculator does not allow you to enter pairs of data we can simply enter the x data, read off the values, clear and then enter y as described in chapter 4, using the SD programme alone. The value for $\sum xy$ will need to be found using the table below.)

Entering the data on the calculator
Putting the calculator into Mode LR, i.e. Mode 3, for Linear Regression work, we first clear the stats memory using $\boxed{\text{SHIFT}}$ $\boxed{\text{C}}$. We then enter each value for x into the programme using the $\boxed{[(\ldots}$ button. A comma will then appear on the display to show the calculator is now ready for the y value, which is entered using the data button, $\boxed{\text{M}+}$. When each value has been entered, check the n value; this should be 10. Read off the buttons for $\sum x$ and $\sum x^2$ and $\bar{x}$, etc. These should be:

$n = 10$, $\sum = 182.5$, $\sum y^2 = 3331.99$ and $\bar{y} = 18.25$.

$\sum x = 189.6$, $\sum x^2 = 3605.08$ and $\bar{x} = 18.96$, $\sum xy = 3462.19$

Now in our table we shall confirm the value of XY, although this is just a secondary check.

% increase in average earnings (from Jan 1990)	RPI% (January 1990 base)	
X	**Y**	**XY**
17.6	17.7	311.52
18.3	18.1	331.23
17.8	18.0	320.4
18.3	17.7	323.91
18.9	18.2	343.98
18.8	18.7	351.56
19.4	18.7	362.78
19.7	18.5	364.45
19.6	18.7	366.52
21.2	18.2	385.84
Total		3462.19

Step 4: Compute r
Using the above values we have:

where $\sum y^2 = 3331.99$, $\sum x^2 = 3605.08$, and $\sum xy = 3462.19$

$$r = \frac{SSxy}{\sqrt{SSx \times SSy}} = \frac{\sum xy - n\bar{x}\bar{y}}{\sqrt{\left(\sum x^2 - n\bar{x}^2\right)\left(\sum y^2 - n\bar{y}^2\right)}}$$

$$= \frac{3462.19 - 10 \times 18.96 \times 18.25}{\sqrt{3605.08 - 10 \times (18.96)^2} \times \sqrt{3331.99 - 10 \times (18.25)^2}}$$

$$= \frac{3462.19 - 3460.2}{\sqrt{3605.08 - 3594.816} \times \sqrt{3331.99 - 3330.625}}$$

$$= \frac{1.99}{\sqrt{1.365} \times \sqrt{10.264}} = \frac{1.99}{1.168\,332\,145 \times 3.203\,747\,805} = \frac{1.99}{3.743\,041\,544}$$

$$= 0.5317 \text{ to 4 decimal places.}$$

We can also confirm this value from our calculator: $\boxed{\text{SHIFT}}$ $\boxed{9}$.

Step 5: Conclusion

The value of r is reasonably close to $+1$ and this indicates that there is some degree of linear association or correlation between the two variables. Being positive this suggests that as the RPI increases so does the percentage increase in average earnings.

This value does not, however, on first appearance provide very conclusive evidence that there is some association between the two variables. We shall now carry out a further test to give us a degree of confidence in our results, to see exactly what is the chance of this value of r occurring quite by chance. We shall use statistical tables to carry out a test of hypothesis.

Test of hypothesis on r

Our (population) parameter is in fact ρ and so we use this in our hypotheses. Firstly we must assume that there is no underlying linear correlation between the two variables, X and Y. This gives us a null hypothesis of

H_0: $\rho = 0$. No correlation between X and Y.

We now must decide what an acceptable alternative hypothesis is: we can see from the scatter diagram that there is evidence of a positive association between X and Y, which naturally leads us to:

$H_1 : \rho > 0$. Positive correlation between X and Y.

We shall adopt a 5% level of significance. There are $n - 1$ degrees of freedom, as we have estimated one parameter (ρ). That is, $v = n - 1$. There this gives us $v = 9$.

An extract of the table of critical values of the product moment correlation coefficient for one-tailed and two-tailed tests for specific levels of significance is given below (Table 4).

Interpreting the table

The first column contains the degrees of freedom; here we have 9, which means we go to the 9th row. The other columns to the right of v are the level of significance for a one-tailed test and two-tailed test. Thus the first column is a critical value for r when we have 5% in one tail (for a one-tailed test) or 5% in a left and right tail (giving us a total

Table 4   Critical values of the product moment correlation coefficient

v		0.05	0.025	0.01	0.005	0.000 5
	One-tailed	**0.05**	**0.025**	**0.01**	**0.005**	**0.000 5**
	Two-tailed	**0.1**	**0.05**	**0.02**	**0.01**	**0.001**
1		0.987 69	0.996 92	0.999 507	0.999 877	0.999 998 8
2		0.900 00	0.950 00	0.980 00		
3		etc.				
4						
.						
9		0.521 4	0.602 1	0.685 1	0.734 8	0.847 1
10						
.						
.						

of 10%) for a two-tailed test. We can illustrate this on a diagram as we have for other test statistics during tests of hypotheses.

Two-tailed test
For example a two-tailed test, our alternative hypothesis would be

$H_1 : \rho \neq 0$

with a 10% level of significance for $v = 9$ gives us a critical value of $r = +0.5214$. We would also have a negative critical value for $r = -0.5214$. A diagram for a two-tailed test is given in figure 9.6.

We then observe where our calculated value of r lies, which here was 0.5317. If our test value of r lies in the critical zone, we reject H_0 and accept H_1, at the 10% level of significance. Here we can see that our value does indeed lie in the critical zone and thus for a two-tailed test we accept H_1 which means there is evidence of linear correlation between X and Y.

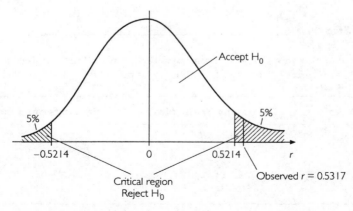

Figure 9.6

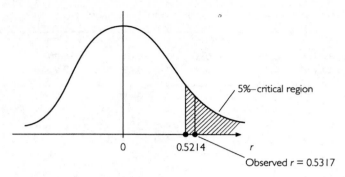

Figure 9.7

One-tailed test
We do exactly as we have above:

$H_1: \rho > 0$

with a 5% level of significance for $v = 9$ (5% will lie in the right-hand tail as we are looking for increases from $\rho = 0$) which gives us a critical value of $r = +0.5214$. A diagram for a one-tailed test is given in figure 9.7.

As before, we locate our observed value of r which here was 0.5317. If our test value of r lies in the critical zone, we reject H_0 and accept H_1, at the 5% level of significance. Here we can see that our value does indeed lie in the critical zone and thus for a one-tailed test we accept H_1 which means there is evidence of positive linear correlation between X and Y.

(If we had a negative value of r, we might use $H_1 : \rho < 0$ giving us a negative critical value for $r = -0.5214$. On a diagram for a one-tailed test this would be exactly as figure 9.7 but in the left tail.)

Exercises 9.3

9.3.1 The data below shows the operating profits (in £m) and the earnings per share (in pence) for Cable & Wireless PLC in the 5 year period from 1989 to 1993 inclusive.

Year	Operating Profit (£m)	Earnings per share (p)
1989	366.7	40.5
1990	533.5	77.9
1991	563.0	28.5
1992	656.6	30.1
1993	771.0	47.5

(Source: Company report Cable & Wireless PLC 1993)

Is there any association between this data? Is it true that as the operating profits increase generally the earnings per share increases? Carry out a test of hypothesis to conclude your answer using a 5% level of significance.

9.3.2 The data below gives the average gross hourly earnings (excluding overtime) for male and female full-time employees aged between 21 and 24, from 1987 to 1994:

Year	Male	Female
1987	3.83	3.36
1988	4.18	3.72
1989	4.64	4.15
1990	5.03	4.57
1991	5.41	4.97
1992	5.67	5.18
1993	5.66	5.28
1994	5.90	5.38

(Source: *Monthly digest of statistics*, Central Statistical Office, August 1995)

Draw a scatter diagram of one variable against another. Is either variable the independent/dependent? Is there any linear association between this data? Calculate a correlation coefficient to measure this.

9.3.3 The data below relates to overseas travel and tourism during 1994/95. This includes the amount spent in the UK by overseas visitors, and the amount spent overseas by UK residents, in £m, at current prices (not seasonally adjusted):

Date	Expenditure in UK by overseas visitors (£m)	Expenditure overseas by UK residents (£m)
1994		
April	678	1018
May	829	1106
June	871	1429
July	1182	1563
August	1431	2052
September	1084	1774
October	833	1425
November	560	813
December	741	737
1995		
January	715	860
February	530	725
March	790	975
April	840	1085
May	895	1235

(Source: Monthly Digest of Statistics, Central Statistical Office, August 1995).

Are both variables stochastic? Explain. Hence plot a suitable scatter diagram and comment on what this tells you. Calculate a correlation coefficient and determine its significance at the 5% level of significance.

9.3.4 Enter data set 9.2 into Minitab: using the command Read:

```
MTB>    read C1, C2
```

The data prompt will than allow you to enter the pairs;

```
Data>
```

and so enter

```
Data> 708   80
Data> 1368 168
```

etc.

```
Data> End
```

Now plot a scatter diagram of Y versus X using the Plot command:

```
MTB>    Plot C2 vs C1
```

Then use the DESCRIBE command to find various calculations about X and Y, and then use the Correlation command to arrive at the product moment correlation coefficient:

```
MTB>    Correlation between C1, C2
```

Repeat this for exercises 9.3.1 and 9.3.2 above.

9.3.5 Look at the value of the covariance for each of the questions 9.3.1–9.3.3 and comment on how this is affected by the scale of values for X and Y. Hence explain how we eliminate the magnitude of the factors for X and Y in our calculation of r.

9.3.6 If X and Y are independent then $r = 0$ and X and Y are uncorrelated. Can you explain why? If we have $r = 0$ for a set of data does this mean that they are independent?

9.3.7 Use table 5, critical values of the Spearman rank correlation coefficient, to determine whether the values of r_s for data set 9.1 and example 9.1 are significant at the 5% level of significance.

9.3.8 Repeat question 9.3.7 for exercises 9.1.

Linear regression

Recall the scenarios for data sets 9.2 and 9.3. We investigated whether there was firstly any graphical evidence of a linear association or dependence between the pairs of variables, (turnover, profit) in data set 9.2 and (RPI, percentage increase in average earnings) in data set 9.3. A natural consequence from this is to investigate exactly what form this linear relationship takes. This is in effect finding the equation of the line that connects two variables. This opens a wealth of further analysis: we can then begin to predict values of one variable (the dependent variable) from the independent variable.

Example 9.3

Find a linear relationship to model data set 9.2.

Solution

Notice that we could draw a line through the scatter diagram for data set 9.2 without doing any calculations but simply drawing the line that looks closest to all the points, a so-called line of best fit, by eye, as in figure 9.5. We could then work out an approximate equation for this line using the graph to find its slope and intercept. As a first model this would be a reasonable attempt. We now move to a more satisfactory method which ensures the best line.

Method

Step 1: Determine which is the independent (X)/dependent (Y) variable

Our linear model will always be known as a linear model for regressing Y on X. This means that we are assuming Y depends on X and if we find this relationship we can use this to predict a value of Y for given X. If both variables are stochastic and neither is in any way controlled then it is likely to be meaningful to regress Y on X or X on Y. In the case however where X is controlled and non-stochastic, then a regression of Y on X is the only permissible form of regression analysis.

Step 2: Form of the linear model

Let each pair of data be a pair of the form: (x_i, y_i) for $i = 1, \ldots, n$. It is assumed that there are no (or negligible errors) in measuring X, but there are some errors in measuring the response for the corresponding Y. Such errors will be denoted by e_i for $i = 1, \ldots, n$.

A linear model for any y_i value given any x_i value is then of the form:

$$y_i = \alpha + \beta x_i + e_i$$

where α and β are the parameters of the line through this data set. The coefficient α is the intercept and the slope of this line is β.

A method known as the *least squares method* is then used to find best estimates for α and β which are a and b, given by the formulae:

$$b = \frac{SSxy}{SSx} = \frac{\sum xy - n\bar{x}\bar{y}}{\sum x^2 - n\bar{x}^2}$$

$$a = \bar{y} - b\bar{x}$$

The regression line $y = a + bx$ is known as the regression line of Y on X or the line of best fit through the data.

Notice that α and β are called parameters as there are many possible lines through the given data set. The best line is found by finding a and b such that the line is closest to all the points. This in effect means that the errors are minimal. (In fact the coefficients for the line a and b, are found by finding the minimal sum of squared errors of each point from the line.) The error term is in y_i and thus the errors must be the vertical length from each point (x_i, y_i) to the line. The error is also known as the residual. Figure 9.8 shows these residuals.

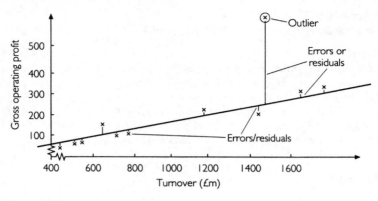

Figure 9.8

Step 3: Calculation of linear model

We now calculate the line through data set 9.2.

From the above calculations we have already found all the values to put into our formulas for a and b:

Recall that $\bar{x} = \dfrac{\sum x}{n} = \dfrac{8577}{10} = 857.7$ and $\bar{y} = \dfrac{\sum y}{n} = \dfrac{974}{10} = 97.4$. Squaring the means will give us $\bar{x}^2 = 735\,649.29$. We also have previously found $\sum x^2 = 8\,828\,983$ and $\sum xy = 974\,936$ and $n = 10$.

Thus

$$b = \frac{SSxy}{SSx} = \frac{\sum xy - n\bar{x}\bar{y}}{sum\ x^2 - n\bar{x}^2}$$

$$= \frac{974\,936 - 10 \times 857.7 \times 97.4}{8\,828\,983 - 10 \times (857.7)^2}$$

$$= \frac{974\,936 - 835\,399.8}{8\,828\,983 - 17\,356\,492.9} = \frac{139\,536.2}{1\,472\,490.1} = 0.094\,762\,063$$

We use all the figures for b and round at the end of the calculation.

Similarly for $a = \bar{y} - bx = 97.4 - (0.094\,762\,063 \times 857.7)$

giving us $\quad a = 97.4 - 81.277\,421\,65 = 16.122\,578\,35$.

Thus to 2 decimal places our linear model is:

$y \approx 16.12 + 0.09x$

Step 4: Interpretation of the linear model

In terms of the variables, the equation would read:

Operating profit $\approx 16.12 + 0.09 \times$ turnover

(all units are in £m).

If we now consider the slope of this line we have a slope of 0.09. This means that if we go along 1 unit on the x-axis, we go up 0.09 units on the y-axis. As the units are in millions of pounds this would more naturally be read as saying that for every increase in turnover of £1m, there corresponds an increase in operating profit of £0.09 m, this is £0.09 × 10^6 = £90 000.

Uses of the linear model: prediction

If we have regressed Y on X we can use the regression equation $y = a + bx$ to predict a value of y for a given x.

Firstly, consider the range of values for X in data set 9.2: the turnover ranges from £480m to £1506m. This is the range of validity of our regression equation. We can thus use this range to predict any value of Y for an X value lying within this range. This is usually known as *interpolation*. It makes sense to use the regression equation to predict values in this way as if we step a long way from these observed x-values it may be entirely inappropriate to predict a value of Y. To predict a value for Y outside the range of validity of the regression line for X is known as *extrapolation*, and this should only be done with extreme caution. A simple example is if we have age (of a young child) on the horizontal axis and weight on the vertical axis, then it is clear that as the child grows, so its weight increases. But if you wanted to use this model to extrapolate the weight of an adult, then this would be likely to give an extraordinary large weight.

Example 9.4
Use the above regression line $y \approx 16.12 + 0.09x$ to estimate a company's operating profit when its turnover is £1000 m.

Solution
We have the regression line to two decimal places, but we should use all available decimal places to evaluate points on the regression line, so we use: $y = 16.122\,578\,35 + 0.094\,762\,063\,5x$.

Putting $x = 1000$ we need to find y. Notice that as x lies in the observed range: £480m ⩽ 1000 ⩽ £1506m, we are interpolating.

Thus $y = 16.122\,578\,35 + 0.094\,762\,063 \times 1000$ giving us $y = 110.88$ to 2 decimal places. Thus the corresponding operating profit would be approximately £110.88 m.

(Notice that if we had used the rounded coefficients: $y \approx 16.12 + 0.09x$ we would arrive at $y = 106.5$ m in which would be a slight under-estimate.)

Exercises 9.4

9.4.1 For example 9.2 (data set 9.3) calculate a regression line for the percentage increase in average earnings (Y) on RPI (X).

Use this regression line to predict the value of Y when $X = 18.6\%$.

9.4.2 How would we regress X on Y? We could simply interchange the labels for X and Y in our original table and use the coefficients as defined above.

Interchange the X and Y in question 9.4.1 and calculate the regression line for RPI (X) on percentage increase in average earnings (Y). Discuss whether you think this is an appropriate equation to find.

9.4.3 Enter data set 9.3 into Minitab (as in exercise 9.3) and use the following regression commands (assuming C1 - average percentage increase in earnings (Y) and C2 = RPI (X)).

```
MTB> Plot C2 vs C1      (to give a scatter plot)
MTB> Regress C1 on 1 predictor in C2
                        (to derive a regression equation).
```

(The general Minitab model for linear regression on one variable is $y = b_0 + b_1 x_1$).

This latter command will in fact give you further analysis which we shall discuss in the following section.

Further analysis of the linear regression model

There are many factors which can be checked on completing the initial regression analysis. The types of procedures are:

- Check the assumptions of the linear regression model;
- Carry out a test of hypothesis/find a confidence interval for α and β;
- Calculate the r^2 percentage, the coefficient of determination.

We shall not discuss these in any great detail but outline the kinds of procedures which can be employed. All these procedures can be carried out using Minitab, and so we shall interpret this printout rather than discuss theoretical statistics, for which the reader is encouraged to consult a specialised statistics text.

Assumptions of the linear model: regression of **Y** on **X**

1) There are errors in the response variable (Y), which we denote by e_i. There are no or negligible errors in the explanatory variable (X).

2) The errors e_i are approximately normally distributed with a mean of 0 and a constant variance of σ^2. That is, $e_i \sim N(0, \sigma^2)$. Generally we assume that y_i are approximately normally distributed. We shall also assume they are independently distributed. The least squares estimates of α and β are found by minimising $\sum e_i^2$. The errors are also known as residuals, and the sum of residuals should be zero.

3) For each value (x_i, y_i) the point (x_i, y_{Ri}) is the point corresponding to x_i on the regression line. Thus the $e_i = (y_i - y_{Ri})$ and so minimising $\sum e_i^2$ corresponds to minimising $\sum e_i^2 = \sum (y_i - y_{Ri})^2$.

The residuals

The residuals are important for checking some of the assumptions of the linear model. We shall now proceed to calculate these from first principles.

Example 9.5

Calculate the residuals for example 9.3 (data set 9.2)

Solution

Notice that the residual (error/deviation) is the vertical distance of any y_i to the regression line. Let this y value on the regression line be y_{Ri}. Notice that y_i and y_{Ri} have the same x value x_i. We thus put x_i into the regression equation to find the value y_{Ri} and then subtract y_{Ri} from y_i to get the error, e_i.

We use the exact regression equation:

$y = 16.122\,578\,35 + 0.094\,862\,063x$

Putting $x = 708$ we need to find y.

(This in fact is really $x_1 = 708$ we need to find y_{R1}).

Thus $y = 16.122\,578\,35 + 0.094\,726\,063 \times 708$ giving us $y = 83.189$ to 3 decimal places. We shall work to 3 decimal places in the following.

Similarly for the second point, $x = 1368$ and so $y = 16.122\,578\,35 + 0.094\,726\,063 \times 1368$ giving us $y = 145.811$ (to 3 dp). This is y_{R2}. Continuing in this way we put these values in a table.

Co	Turnover £m X_i	Profit £m Y_i	Y_{Ri}	Residuals/ Errors $Y_i - Y_{Ri}$	(Residuals)^2 $(Y_i - Y_{Ri})^2$
A	708	80	83.189	−3.189	10.170
B	1368	168	145.811	22.189	492.352
C	597	100	72.777	27.223	741.092
D	1075	121	117.953	3.047	9.248
E	1506	162	158.780	3.220	10.368
F	656	76	78.263	−2.263	5.121
G	438	43	57.613	−14.613	213.540
H	491	65	62.633	2.367	5.603
I	1258	100	135.288	−35.288	1245.243
J	480	59	61.591	−2.591	6.713
Total	8577	974		0.102	2739.486

Do the residuals sum to zero? That is $\sum e_i = \sum (y_i - y_{Ri}) = 0$? Well almost (0.102), which is due to rounding errors, which cannot really be avoided here.

The residuals can be plotted, against each corresponding x value, to look for patterns and trends. This is done in figure 9.9.

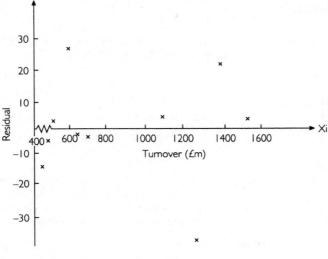

Figure 9.9

Here we can see no definite pattern and so we can assume that the assumptions about $\sum e_i^2$ of a constant variance and normality may be justified here. In fact this can be done more readily using Minitab, where the command FITS is used to calculate the y_{R_i}:

The Minitab command is: (assuming Y is in C1 and X is in C2)

```
MTB>   Regress C1 on 1 predictor in C2;
                (the semi-colon sets up the subcommand)
SUBC> FITS in C3.    (The full stop ends the routine)
MTB>   Print C1-C3
```

You will then see the fitted Y values for the linear model in C3 (given the X values in C2). A scatter diagram would then be:

```
MTB> Plot C3 vs C2
```

Patterns in the residuals to look for include:

1. Any patterns may indicate that successive observations of y may not be independent, or there is a trend over time.
2. If there are patterns, such as a funnelling effect in the residuals, this may indicate that there is not a constant variance in the errors.
3. If we order the residuals by the x values we can see if there is evidence that a linear model is inappropriate. Again we are looking for randomness.
4. We could look for non-normality in the residuals by plotting standardised residuals, which is most easily done using Minitab where

$$Z_i = \frac{e_i - 0}{\text{stdev}(e_i)}$$

where $(e_i) = \sqrt{\text{MSE} - \text{Var}(Y_R)}$ (see below).

The Minitab command combining the FITS and standardised residuals is (assuming Y is in C1 and X is in C2):

```
MTB>   Regress C1 on 1 predictor in C2;
SUBC>  Fits in C3;      (semi-colon to continue routine)
SUBC>  Sres in C4.      (The full stop ends the routine)
```

This will put the standardised residuals in C4.

```
MTB>   Print C1-C4
MTB>   Plot C4 vs C2
```

will produce a scatter diagram of the standardised residuals against the X values.

Tests of significance on α and β

These are automatically done if you use Minitab, and are part of the printout after the 'regress' command.

We now use $\sum e_i^2$ (which was 2739.486 above) to estimate σ^2 which we shall call s^2. This will enable us to test values for α and β. We shall use a t-test to test specific values of α and β which can be used provided $y \approx$ normally distributed (as then α and β will be normal being the sum of normal random variables). To this end, we need the degrees of freedom for the squared errors.

The degrees of freedom
Notice that when we calculated the $\sum e_i^2$ we used estimates for α and β. Thus there are n less the number of estimates (2 here) degrees of freedom remaining when we estimate $\sum e_i^2$. This will then give use an estimate for σ^2, which we shall call s^2. Thus we have:

The Mean Square for the Errors, MSE, from the regression line is given by

$$\text{MSE} = \sigma^2 = \text{variance of } e_i = \frac{\sum e_i^2}{\text{degrees of freedom}} = \frac{\sum e_i^2}{n-2} \approx s^2.$$

Here we have $\text{MSE} \approx s^2 = \dfrac{2739.486}{10-2} = 342.436$, giving us $s = 18.505$ to 3 decimal places.

The value for s gives us an indication of the variation in y about the regression line.

Now we can test:

Significance test for α
$H_0: \alpha = \alpha_0$

$H_1: \alpha > \alpha_0$ (or $\alpha < \alpha_0$)

Using a t-test $t = \dfrac{a - \alpha_0}{\dfrac{s}{\sqrt{n}}}$ on $n - 2$ degrees of freedom.

Significance test for β

$H_0: \beta = \beta_0$

$H_1: \beta > \beta_0$ (or $\beta < \beta_0$)

Using a t-test $t = \dfrac{b - \beta_0}{\frac{s}{\sqrt{SSx}}}$ on $n - 2$ degrees of freedom.

(If we test $\beta = 0$ this is in effect saying there is no regression: Y does not depend on X but Y is constant for all X. In fact the Minitab package automatically tests for $\alpha = 0$ and $\beta = 0$.)

The Minitab printout for regression analysis

Suppose we have used the command

```
MTB> Regress C2 using 1 predictor in C1
```

The following output would be on the screen:

Regression equation is: y = a + bx (with a and be given)

Two tables would follow: we insert the formulas whereas Minitab would insert the numerical results.

Predictor	Coefficient	StDEV	t-Ratio	p
(Y)	a	$s_a = \dfrac{s}{\sqrt{n}}$	$t = \dfrac{a - 0}{\frac{s}{\sqrt{n}}}$	$P\left(t > \dfrac{a - 0}{\frac{s}{\sqrt{n}}}\right)$, or $<$
(X)	b	$s_b = \dfrac{s}{\sqrt{SSx}}$	$t = \dfrac{b - 0}{\frac{s}{\sqrt{SSx}}}$	$P\left(t > \dfrac{b - 0}{\frac{s}{\sqrt{SSx}}}\right)$, or $<$
$s =$	R-sq =	R-sq(adj)		

Analysis of variance

Source	Degrees of freedom	SS	MS
Regress	1	$SSR = \dfrac{(SS_{xy})^2}{SS_x}$	$MSR = \dfrac{SSR}{1}$
Error	$n - 2$	$SSE = \sum e_i^2$	$MSE = \dfrac{SSE}{n - 2}$
Total	$n - 1$	SSy	

Notice that the columns in the last table do indeed sum to the given total. This tells us that the total variation in Y, SSy is divided into two parts: one due to the regression line and one due to the errors. We would also have two final columns in the analysis of variance table giving us an F ratio of MSR/MSE and the chance of this or greater values occurring (p).

A typical Minitab printout for regression from our statistical case study

Suppose we have regressed literacy on numeracy, we would have the following printout:

The regression equation is: literacy $= 17.0 + 0.732$ numeracy

Predictor	Coefficient	StDEV	t-Ratio	p
constant	17.033	6.218	2.74	0.011
numeracy	0.7323	0.1221	6.0	0.000

Analysis of variance

Source	Degrees of freedom	SS	MS	F	p
Regression	1	5504.5	5504.5	35.95	0.000
Error	28	4286.9	153.1		
Total	29	9791.4			

Using the r^2 percentage, the coefficient of determination

The value for the r^2 percentage is a measure of how good a fit the regression line is to the given data set. It tells us what proportion of the variation in the data set is explained by the regression model. Firstly we find the ratio of SSE to SSy. If there is a perfect fit then, $SSE = 0$ and this ratio will be zero tells us that the regression model explains all the data, that is 100% of the Y values. In fact $SSE : SSy$ tells us the proportion of variation in Y which is unexplained by the regression model. Thus one minus this ratio tells us how much of the variation in Y is explained by the regression line. It turns out that one minus this ratio is r^2.

That is $r^2 = 1 - \dfrac{SSE}{SSy}$ which is usually written as a percentage.

This can also be used in multiple linear regression (see below).

In example 9.3 (data set 9.2) we had a value of $r^2 = (0.9099)^2 \approx 0.82$ or 82%. This in fact is extremely good as it tells us that 82% of the variation in the operating profit is explained by the regression line of profit versus turnover. Thus the regression line is a very good fit for this data set.

Exercises 9.5 _____

9.5.1 Confirm that the values in the above Minitab printout do indeed agree with the above formula and interpretation.

9.5.2 Using data set 9.3 carry out a Minitab regression analysis. Interpret the printout in the light of the earlier discussion. Check the results by hand. Perform the tests of significance on α and β by hand. Calculate by hand the table of residuals and squared residuals. Plot the residuals on a scatter diagram.

9.5.3 Use the FITS and SRES subcommands to continue your Minitab analysis of data set 9.3. Plot the standardised residuals to see if there is any pattern.

9.5.4 Repeat questions 9.5.2 and 9.5.3 for data sets given in questions 9.3.1, 9.3.2 and 9.3.3.

9.5.5 For the statistical case study on comparing degree results with literacy and numeracy results, perform a regression analysis on the data set you have previously stored : regressing C3 on C2, and C3 on C1. Comment on your findings. Repeat question 9.5.3 for this data set using Minitab.

9.5.6 Great West Packaging have been looking at their closing monthly share prices (Y) in pence, and monthly turnover figures (X) in £1000s for 9 months during 1994. The results were as follows:

Turnover: X	20.09	21.30	24.14	25.86	23.95	30.1	29.4	26.14	31.86	35.25
Share price: Y	112	115	125	109	113	118	116	113	121	122

(i)   Plot this data on a scatter diagram and comment on your findings.

(ii) Find the line of regression of the share price on the quarterly earnings. Show clearly each step of your calculation.

(iii) Perform an analysis using Minitab, including finding the fits and standardised residuals.

(iv) Using your regression line, estimate the share price if the month's turnover has been £30 000.

Multiple linear regression

Before we close the chapter we take a brief look at regression where the dependent variable Y does not simply depend linearly on one variable, but on several variables. We do this using Minitab. Consider the statistical case study earlier in the book. Here we have regressed C3 on C2 and C3 on C1 where C1 = numeracy, C2 was literacy and C3 was final degree mark (all are percentages).

Minitab printout (scatter diagrams, etc.) would indicate a reasonable degree of linear association between C3 and C2, and C3 and C1: thus we have evidence for a linear model where the final degree percentage depends on literacy, and for the final degree percentage depending on numeracy.

We thus can ask the question, does the final degree percentage depend not just on literacy, or numeracy, but both? To investigate this we use a model of the form:

$$y = b_0 + b_1 x_1 + b_2 x_2$$

Where y = dependent variable (final degree percentage) and we are using two explanatory variables to describe y, namely x_1, literacy and x_2 numeracy.

The Minitab command is similar to before, but with two predictors:

`MTB> Regress C3 on 2 predictors in C1 and C2`

(The general Minitab model for linear regression with no n variables is $y = b_0 + b_1 x_1 + b_2 x_2 + b_3 x_3 + \ldots + b_n x_n$.)

As before, the assumptions are that there are errors in the stochastic variable y but none or negligible errors in the (non-stochastic/stochastic) x_i.

The b_i for $i = 1$ to n are called the *partial regression coefficients* and represent the increase in y due to a unit increase in x_i when all the other variables (x_j, $j \neq i$) are fixed.

Exercise 9.6

Complete this Minitab exercise and comment on your findings. Interpret the b_i for this model. Interpret the value of r^2.

10 Changes over time: index numbers and time series

Objectives

- Understanding changes of attributes over time;
- Understanding how to compute indices to measure changes over time;
- Understanding the most appropriate index for a given situation;
- Understanding how the retail prices index is computed;
- Understanding how to use a sequence of data measured at successive points in time;
- Understanding the key features of a time series;
- Be able to generate forecasts and projections.

Index numbers

Scenario: the rate of inflation is soaring; how is it calculated?
In business and economics, how could we compare the price of, for example, mortgage costs over a certain time period, or the cost of leasing commercial property over various locations, or measure the effect of a wage increase on manufacturing costs, or compare manufacturing costs in one part of the UK compared to another? Similarly, in education, how could we compare A-level grades from one year to another or the performance of 7, 11 and 14 year olds in their standard attainment tests (SATs) from one local education authority to another? All of these can be dealt with by calculating an appropriate index number. The best known index number is the Retail Prices Index, used by economists and the government to measure monthly changes in the retail price of various domestic commodities.

Definition

An *index number* is a mathematical tool for calculating price or cost changes over a time period, or between locations, or with respect to a given characteristic (such as income, or gender, or profession, etc.). Index numbers are always expressed as percentages.

Different forms of index numbers are used depending on whether we are comparing a single item with another, or a set of prices with another, or if prices or costs depend on the quantities used. In this last case we can see that the effect of a small increase in the price of a raw component used in the manufacture of your product will have less of an impact on your overall costs than the same price increase but in your most frequently used components. Clearly we must take this into account in the way we build our index numbers. We shall look at each of these cases in turn as well as taking a closer look at the Retail Prices Index.

Data set 10.1: mortgage repayments

The following sums are the net monthly repayments quoted by New Town Building Society for a typical £50 000 repayment mortgage. The interest rates were variable, but payments were fixed for each year.

Year	Repayment
1988	£434
1989	£560
1990	£620
1991	£575
1992	£470
1993	£390
1994	£340

We shall use this data to illustrate the first type of index number, the price relative index.

Example 10.1: price relative index number (one commodity)

This index number is used when we wish to compare the price of a single commodity in a given time period/location/characteristic to its price in another period/location/characteristic. In the following example we are going to compare the cost of a typical mortgage over the period 1988 to 1994.

Method
Step 1: Choose the time/location/characteristic to make the focus of comparison

We use this as a yardstick to measure changes from. This is the base of our calculations, and when we are measuring changes over time is aptly called the *base year*. Similarly it could be called the base location if comparing regional changes. We denote the price in the base year by P_0, meaning price at the start.

Here we might choose two possible candidates for the base year, depending on whether we were speaking from the lender's or the borrower's perspective. The lender would want to say mortgages were much more expensive in previous years, and so choose 1990 as the base year to compare changes from. Whereas the borrower would probably say that the interest rates have fluctuated quite significantly in this 7-year period, and to measure change in the cost of a mortgage in the depths of a slump is not very representative; it is likely the borrower would compare from the 1988 figure, the cost at the end of the housing boom. We will compute both. It is often easier to use notation that fits the situation, so we will use P_{1990} for the price in 1990 and P_{1988} for the price in 1988.

Step 2: What do you want to compare with your base year?
We call this P_n to indicate price now. The most likely answer is what is the more recent situation, that is in 1994. We might use the notation P_{1994} for easy recognition.

Step 3: Calculate the price relative index
To do this form the quotient of the price now with the price at base, i.e. $\dfrac{P_n}{P_0}$. On the calculator this is simply $P_n \div P_0$. We then have a decimal, which we convert to a percentage by multiplying by 100.

Formally the Price Relative Index $= \dfrac{P_n}{P_0} \times 100\%$.

Step 4: Interpret the index number
If the index number is 100%, it would indicate that there has been no change from the base year to now. This is unusual. If the index number is more than 100%, the value it exceeds 100 by is the percentage increase from the base year to the present time. If the index is less than 100%, the amount is less by the decrease in the price now compared with the base year.

Solution

From the mortgagor's viewpoint
Here first comparing 1994 against base year of 1990. Thus we need to calculate the quotient of $P_{1994} + P_{1990}$, i.e. $\dfrac{P_{1994}}{P_{1990}}$. This is $\dfrac{£340}{£620} = 340 \div 620$ which is 0.548 to 3 decimal places. Hence multiplying by 100 for a percentage gives us 54.8%. Thus the Price Relative Index $= \dfrac{P_{1994}}{P_{1990}} \times 100\% = 54.8\%$.

How would this be interpreted? As there is a decrease from 100% we know that the cost of a mortgage in 1994 has decreased since 1990. It has in fact decreased by $100\% - 54.8\% = 45.2\%$.

From the mortgagee's viewpoint
Comparing the price relative index with 1988 as the base year, we would arrive at: $\dfrac{P_{1994}}{P_{1988}} \times 100$. Thus we need to find $\dfrac{£340}{£434} \times 100\%$. Using a calculator this is $£340 \div £434$ which gives us 0.783 to 3 decimal places. Finally multiplying by 100 gives us 78.3 which is now a percentage. Thus the Price Relative Index is 78.3%. This again would be interpreted as a decrease in the cost a mortgage from 1994 compared to 1988, a decrease of $100\% - 78.3\% = 21.7\%$.

Data set 10.2: the cost of leasing office space

The following are the average prices of leasing office space per square foot in various locations:

Location	Price
City of London	£13.50
Cardiff	£10
Leeds	£9.50
Middlesbrough	£7
Canary Wharf	£8

We shall use this to illustrate a price relative index where the scale of comparison is not time but location.

Example 10.2

An enterprising estate agent is looking at a new advertising slogan for increasing the amount of office space leased in Canary Wharf. She decided to collect data from each of its offices leasing office space of a similar standard to the Canary Wharf location. She wanted to show that the average cost of leasing property around the country varies considerably and in particular is keen to use this to show that leasing office space in Canary Wharf is considerably cheaper than some locations.

(i)   What would she use as the base location?

(ii)   What is the price relative index of The City of London compared to the base location?

(iii)   What is the price relative index of each of the other locations?

Solution

(i)   Here we are measuring the price of office space relative to office space in Canary Wharf. For this reason we will measure increases/decreases from the Canary Wharf price. Thus our base location here is Canary Wharf.

(ii)   Here Canary Wharf is the base location with a rental at £8 per square foot. The City of London costs £13.50 per square foot for a similar office let. Thus for the City of London the price relative index is $\frac{£13.50}{£8} \times 100 = 168.75\%$. This means that the rental at the City of London is 68.75% more than the cost of renting office space in Canary Wharf.

(iii)   The price relative of Cardiff compared to our base location, Canary Wharf, is $\frac{£10}{£8} \times 100\%$ which is 125%, meaning that in Cardiff the office space costs 25% more than at Canary Wharf.

Similarly the price relative for Leeds is $\frac{£9.50}{8} \times 100\% = 118.75$, 18.75% more than at Canary Wharf. Finally for Middlesbrough the price relative is $\frac{£7}{£8} \times 100\% = 87.5\%$ which would be interpreted as meaning office space in Middlesbrough costs 12.5% less than in Canary Wharf.

This index number is of rather limited use as it compares one price/location/ characteristic compared to another or over time. As we shall see with the following type of index number, quantifying changes of a group of prices, etc. over time is of greater use.

Exercises 10.1

10.1.1 The retail price of a typical undergraduate set text book over period of 4 years is listed below:

Year	Price
1990	£14.50
1991	£15.25
1992	£15.95
1993	£16.40

If you want to measure the price change of the typical text in 1993 what would you use as a base year? Using this year, compute a price relative index for 1993 compared to the base year.

10.1.2 The total number of GCSEs being taken in 1994 in the UK was 2.2 million, where most candidates took 8 or 9. The number of passes awarded to male and female candidates gaining grades A to C was 739 200 and 827 200 respectively. What is the pass rate index number for the female candidates compared to the male candidates? What are you taking as the base characteristic?

Scenario
What is the price change of a typical basket of shopping over time? How can we compare graduate salaries with non-graduate salaries? Or how can we measure changes in graduate earnings with, say, changes in the cost of living? How would changes in the price of various raw materials and wage increases affect the total cost of production?

Data set 10.3: a student's shopping basket

The following are two sets of retail prices of a typical student's shopping basket. The items were on sale in a London supermarket during the autumn in 1993 and 1995:

Item	1993 price	1995 price
I pizza	£2.09	£2.59
I loaf	£0.69	£1.00
I pint of milk	£0.35	£0.48
4 pack of lager	£2.65	£2.40
Can of baked beans	£0.32	£0.34
I lb of apples	£0.45	£0.67

We shall use this data to illustrate the following type of index number, the simple aggregate index number.

Simple aggregate index number

The *simple aggregate index number* (also called the simple average index number) is used when we wish to compare a collection of retail prices or production costs (called *commodities* in general). Usually we would express one year's commodities as a percentage of the commodities in another year. As before we could also compare locational and characteristic changes.

Example 10.3
Compare the price changes of a basket of shopping over the two-year period from 1993 to 1995.

Method
Step 1: Decide what time/location/characteristic is to be the focus
This will form the base of our calculation, i.e. the base year. As we are looking at price changes from 1993 and measure either increases or decreases from this year, i.e. 1993, we could call these prices P_0 meaning 'price at zero time' or price at the beginning of our study, or the initial price. With a base year of 1993 we might write P_{1993}.

Step 2: What are we going to compare with this base year?
Usually this is the current year. This will be the prices in 1995. Again we might use some notation, such as P_n for price now, or more naturally, P_{1995}.

Step 3: Sum the prices
Sum all the prices in the base year: sum all the prices in the year you are comparing, that is the prices now.

Step 4: Form the index
Divide the two values, i.e. (sum of prices of current year) ÷ (sum of base year prices). To convert this into a percentage we multiply this by 100. As before, if there have been no changes from the base year to the current year, our index number would be 100%. Any increase from 100% is interpreted as an increase from the base period, and any decreases from 100% would mean a decrease from the base period.

Mathematical language

If the prices in the year of interest are P_n and the prices in the base year are P_0, then the sum of each of these prices would be written $\sum P_n$ and $\sum P_0$. Thus the simple aggregate index number, $I = \dfrac{\sum P_n}{\sum P_0} \times 100\%$

where P_n is the price in the year of particular interest and P_0 is the price in the base year.

Solution to example 10.3

Step 1

1993 is the base year.

Step 2

1995 is the year of comparison.

Step 3

We must sum the prices in both of these years from the table above.

The sum of the base year prices $\sum P_0$ or $\sum P_{1993} = £2.09 + £0.69 + £0.35 + £2.65 + £0.32 + £0.45 = £6.55$.

The sum of prices for the current period $\sum P_n$ or $\sum P_{1995} = £2.59 + £1 + £0.48 + £2.40 + £0.34 + £0.67 = £7.48$.

Step 4: Divide the two totals

That is find $\dfrac{\sum P_n}{\sum P_0}$ which is $\dfrac{\sum P_{1995}}{\sum P_{1993}}$ here. This is $\dfrac{£7.48}{£6.55} = 1.14$. Convert this to a percentage by multiplying by 100, and thus

The simple aggregate index number,

$$I = \frac{\sum P_{1995}}{\sum P_{1993}} \times 100\% = \frac{£7.48}{£6.55} \times 100\% = 1.14 \times 100\% = 114\%.$$

We could conclude by saying that the cost of a typical basket of student shopping has risen by 14% in the two years from 1993.

Data set 10.4: graduate and non-graduate earnings

Six companies from within the UK were selected at random from a directory of graduate employers. The following are the graduate and non-graduate earnings in 1995 from these companies; each employee has been in the company between two and three years.

Location	Graduate earning	Non-graduate earning
Company 1	£18 000	£13 500
Company 2	£24 000	£15 000
Company 3	£14 500	£18 800
Company 4	£46 000	£30 000
Company 5	£19 000	£14 000
Company 6	£22 000	£16 000

Example 10.4

Find a simple aggregate index number to compare graduate with non-graduate earnings in 1995. Such an index number would also be a measure of the companies salaries bill for 1995.

Solution

Here we are comparing salaries, i.e. a characteristic.

Step 1: The base characteristic

As the base characteristic we will take the non-graduate earning. We could call each salary P_{ng} where ng stands for non-graduate.

Step 2: Characteristic of comparison

We are comparing graduate salaries, which we could denote by P_g.

Step 3

We need to sum each of the columns of earnings, that is find $\sum P_{ng}$ and $\sum P_g$. The total non-graduate earnings $= \sum P_{ng} = £13\,500 + £15\,000 + £18\,800 + £30\,000 + £14\,000 + £16\,000 = £107\,300$.

The total graduate earnings $= £18\,000 + £24\,000 + £14\,500 + £46\,000 + £19\,000 + £22\,000 = £143\,500$.

Step 4: Dividing the two totals

Thus the simple aggregate index number, $I = \dfrac{\sum P_g}{\sum P_{ng}} \times 100\% = \dfrac{£143\,500}{£107\,300}$ $\times 100\% = 133.7\%$. Thus we might conclude that the typical graduate could expect to earn 33.7% more than a non-graduate in 1995. Equally we might say that a companies salary bill is 33.7% more for graduates than for non-graduates.

Remark

This index number has the disadvantage in that it is sensitive to the units used (e.g. £ per kg, or pence per gram) as we shall see in the exercises to follow. A perhaps more serious drawback is that it places no importance on the commodities—all are equally important or equally weighted. This would mean in the shopping basket example above that we would place equal importance to bread and a pack of lager—that is not the case. Similarly the second example makes no mention of how many graduates and non-graduates earn this salary. This makes it difficult to place much weight on the outcome as it is difficult to justify it as a truly representative measure of salaries. We can overcome this by using a weight to prices or commodities, thereby making some more important.

To overcome this latter problem, generally we would use one of the following *weighted aggregate index numbers* where we choose a weighting factor for each commodity to be the quantity or volume used during either the base year Q_0 or in the given year Q_n.

Exercises 10.2 _____

10.2.1 The following data is the British consumer's expenditure on vehicles in each of the four quarters of the year for 1991 and 1993; all figures are to the nearest £ million.

Consumer's expenditure on vehicle	1991	1993
1st quarter	4501	4466
2nd quarter	3502	3811
3rd quarter	5561	6150
4th quarter	2885	3619

(Source: Central Statistical Office: Monthly Digest of Statistics, Oct 1994)

Calculate a simple aggregate index number to measure the change in consumer expenditure on vehicles over this time period.

10.2.2 The Department of Transport (DoT) collect data concerning the type and amount of freight transported by British Rail over set time periods. Below is an extract from a report by the DoT comparing the amount of coal and coke transported by BR compared to its total freight carried during the period 1988 to 1993. All figures are expressed in millions net tonnes per km.

Year	Type of freight	
	Coal and coke	Total
1988	78.8	150.6
1989	76.5	143.4
1990	74.9	140.3
1991	74.8	134.8
1992	68.8	125.2
1993	54.8	108.6

(Source: Central Statistical Office: Monthly Digest of Statistics, Oct 1994)

10.2.3 Powerfuse Electricity PLC uses coal and oil to generate electricity for the south-west grid. The following were prices paid for oil and coal in 1992 and 1994:

Fuel	1992	1994
Coal per tonne	£350	£440
Oil per barrel	£62	£85

Find a simple average index number to estimate the price increase in Powerfuse's costs from 1992 to 1994.

Convert the prices for coal to £ per kg by dividing each of the coal prices by 1000. Show that using the cost of coal in £ per kg significantly increases the index of production costs for Powerfuse to 37%.

Scenario A
You have recently been appointed as the human resources manager for Modern Starlight, an insurance company in Birmingham. Currently it employs 154 members of staff with grades from junior assistant (grade 1) to the senior management scale (grades 7, 8, 9 and 10). You have been asked to advise the managing director what would be the overall effect of implementing a two-tier pay rise for the annual pay review for the coming year, 1995. The lower grades are set to receive 2.2% and the higher grades a 3% increase. The table below shows how many staff are employed at each grade:

Grade	1	2	3	7	8	9	10
Number of staff	20	40	38	22	17	12	5

The salary for each grade during 1994 was:
the lower grades (grades 1, 2 and 3) are paid £10 000, £12 500 and £14 000, respectively. The higher management grades (grades 7, 8, 9 and 10) are paid £25 000, £26 500, £28 000 and £38 000 respectively.

Weighted aggregate index number

Such index numbers are used when a weighting factor for each commodity is used to show the relative importance of each commodity in the production, staffing or characteristic. The weight is usually taken to be the quantity or volume used (number of staff employed) during either the base year or in the current year. We would write Q for quantity and so denote quantity in the base year by Q_0 and for the current year by Q_n.

There are numerous types of index numbers of this sort; we name three types, but from a statistician's point of view this is only the tip of the iceberg.

Solution to scenario A

Step 1: Type of index number
We have staff of different grades and a quantity of staff of each grade. Thus to have a realistic measure of the change in the staff budget for 1995 we must make use of the said quantities. This in effect means we must calculate a weighted aggregate index number.

Step 2: Base year
We are measuring the change in total staff budget from 1994. Thus 1994 is the focus or base of the calculation, and as before we denote the salaries in 1994 by P_0 or P_{1994}, the pay at base. Measuring changes in 1995, the current pay rise which we could denote by P_n or P_{1995}. In effect we are calculating changes in 1995 compared to the base year.

Step 3: Choice of weights
The number of staff employed in 1994 is set to remain the same in 1995 for the calculation of the weighted aggregate index number. The weights we choose to use in fact give rise to several weighted aggregate index numbers. When we use the same quantity in the base year as in the current year, that is we are using

the base year weights, Q_0, then we call this index number the base year index number (or Laspeyre's index).

The base year method

Here the quantities stated in the base year remain fixed, and so this would give a measure of the total costs in any given year compared to the base year; thus this is sometimes referred to as a *prices index*.

For scenario A we are calculating a staffing budget we could call it a staff budget index.

Step 4: Finding the two staff bills
Calculate the total salary bill in both years of interest, 1994 and 1995.

Staff bill for 1994
If 20 staff earn £10 000 each, the total bill for these staff is $20 \times £10\,000 = £200\,000$. Similarly if 40 staff earn £12 500 each, their total earned is $40 \times £12\,500 = £500\,000$. Thus we take the quantity of staff Q_0 and multiply this by the salary of that grade P_0. This would be written $Q_0 \times P_0$. We find the total staff bill for 1994 by summing these, so finding $\Sigma P_0 Q_0$. Here this would be as shown in the following table.

Number of staff	Salary £	Number of staff × salary £
Q_0	P_0	$Q_0 \times P_0$
20	10 000	200 000
40	12 500	500 000
38	14 000	532 000
22	25 000	550 000
17	26 500	450 500
12	28 000	336 000
5	38 000	190 000
	Total	£2 758 500

Thus $\sum P_0 Q_0 = £2\,758\,500$.

Staff bill for 1995
First we must calculate the pay increase for each grade. Thus for grade 1s, we need to find 2.2% of £10 000, which is $\dfrac{2.2}{100} \times 10\,000 = 0.022 \times 10\,000 = £220$. Thus the new salary will be £10 220. Notice that a short cut would be to say that the new salary is 100% + 2.2% or 102.2% of the original salary. As a decimal, $\dfrac{102.2}{100} = 1.022$. If we multiply each of the old salary (for the lower grades) by this we would get the new salary quickly. To check, we could calculate $1.022 \times £10\,000 = £10\,220$ as we would hope!

Thus for the grade 2 employee the new salary will be $1.022 \times 12\,500 = £12\,775$, and for a grade 3 it would be $1.02 \times 14\,000 = £14\,308$. For the higher grades a 3% pay rise is anticipated giving a new salary of $100\% + 3\%$ of the original. This is 103% or 1.03 and so we would multiply the old salary by 1.03. The results are in the table below.

Number of staff	Salary £ 1994	Salary £ 1995	Number of staff × salary £
Q_0	P_0	P_n	$Q_0 \times P_0$
20	10 000	10 220	204 400
40	12 500	12 775	511 000
38	14 000	14 308	543 704
22	25 000	25 750	566 500
17	26 500	27 295	464 015
12	28 000	28 840	346 080
5	38 000	39 140	195 700
		Total	£2 831 399

Step 5: Divide the two staff bills
Finally find the quotient of these two totals, the salary bill for 1995 divided by the salary bill of 1994. This is written $\dfrac{\sum P_n Q_0}{\sum P_0 Q_0}$. To find the base year index number we now convert this into a percentage by multiplying by 100, that is we find

$$I_1 = \frac{\sum P_n Q_0}{\sum P_0 Q_0} \times 100\%$$

which is the base year index number, or Laspeyre's index. As we have already said it would be more naturally labelled a staffing budget index here. Thus

$$I_1 = \frac{\sum P_n Q_0}{\sum P_0 Q_0} \times 100\% = \frac{£2\,831\,399}{£2\,758\,500} \times 100\% = 102.6\%$$

This would be interpreted as the budget for the staffing budget for 1995 represents a 2.6% increase from 1994.

Scenario (continued) B
The MD of Modern Starlight PLC has asked you to advise him on streamlining its middle management ranks in order to be more competitive once the recession is over. He would like to see the levels of the higher grades (7, 8, 9 and 10) reduced to 20, 14, 9 and 4 respectively. Given that the previous pay rise is still on offer to all staff, what effect would the new staffing levels have on the index calculated in the first part of the scenario?

Solution B

In the above scenario we used the base year quantities for both the current and base year staffing levels. Now we must re-think this.

Step 1: Type of index number

As before we must calculate a weighted aggregate index number as the number of each grade of staff varies.

Step 2: Base year

As before we are measuring the change in total staff budget from 1994; this is the base year. We denote the salaries in 1994 by P_0 or P_{1994}, the pay at base. Measuring changes in 1995, the current pay rise which we could denote by P_n or P_{1995}.

Step 3: Choice of weights

The number of staff employed in 1994 is set as above. For 1995 a reduction in some of the staffing levels is envisaged, and so it is natural to take into account the new staffing levels for the calculation of the weighted aggregate index number. This gives rise to another weighted aggregate index number. We might call it a staff savings index number. Let us denote the staffing level in the base period by Q_0 and the quantity in the current period, 1995 by Q_n. The table of staffing levels is shown below:

Grade	Number of staff 1994	Number of staff 1995
	Q_0	Q_n
1	20	20
2	40	40
3	38	38
7	22	20
8	17	14
9	12	9
10	5	4

Step 4: Finding the staff bills

Calculate the total salary bill for both years of interest (1994 and 1995), using the staffing levels for each year.

Staff bill for 1994

This will be the same as above, giving us a total bill of £2 758 500. As before we could write $\sum P_0 Q_0 = £2\,758\,500$.

Staff bill for 1995

We can use the pay increases as from the table above for 1995. This can be seen in the first two columns in the table below. The number of the lower grades has not changed and so the first few entries in the third column will also be unchanged.

Number of staff	Salary £ 1995	Number of staff × salary £	
Q_n	P_n	$Q_n \times P_n$	
20	10 220	204 400	Unchanged
40	12 775	511 000	Unchanged
38	14 308	543 704	Unchanged
20	25 750	515 500	
14	27 295	382 130	
9	28 840	259 560	
4	39 140	156 560	
	Total	£2 572 854	

Step 5: Dividing the two staff bills

Finally find the quotient of these two totals, the salary bill for 1995 divided by the salary bill for 1994. This is written $\dfrac{\sum P_n Q_n}{\sum P_0 Q_0}$. To find the staff savings index number we now convert this into a percentage, that is

$$\frac{\sum P_n Q_n}{\sum P_0 Q_0} \times 100\% = \frac{£2\,572\,854}{£2\,758\,500} \times 100\% = 93.3\%.$$

This would be interpreted as the reduction in middle management staffing levels having resulted in a saving of 6.7% of the 1994 staffing budget, or the salaries bill for 1995 being 6.7% less than in 1994. This index number here is often known as the industrial/consumer confidence index.

Formally the industrial/consumer confidence index,; I_c is given by:

$I_c = \dfrac{\sum P_n Q_n}{\sum P_0 Q_0} \times 100$. It is known by this name as it is a realistic measure of how industry or the consumer is acting today—what quantities are being manufactured/bought in the current situation compared to a previous time period.

Scenario (continued) C

You are asked to measure the effect of the pay rise due in 1995 on the staffing levels which have been anticipated in this year, but this time your MD has asked what the difference in the last index number would have been if the staff reductions had taken place in 1994, the previous year. What would have been the saving if redundancies had been made a year earlier? Would it have helped to ease the pressure of cash-flow difficulties?

Solution C

Steps 1 and 2 remain the same as for B above.

Step 3: The weights

The number of staff employed in 1994 is the reduced level, denoted by Q_n. The same staffing levels are used for 1995, Q_n. This gives rise to another weighted aggregate index number: the *given year index number* (or Paasche's index).

Step 4: The salaries bill

As before we calculate the staffing bill for 1994 and 1995.

The bill for 1995 will be the same as for B above as these included the pay rise and the lower levels of staff. Thus the total bill for 1995 is $\sum P_n Q_n = £2\,572\,854$.

We must recalculate the bill for 1994 using the reduced levels of staff and before the pay rise took effect. Notice that the lower grades are unaffected by the changes and so the first 3 entries in the final column are unchanged from the salary bill for 1994 as for cases A and B above. The figures are in the table below:

Number of staff	Salary £ 1994	Number of staff × salary £	
Q_n	P_0	$Q_n \times P_0$	
20	10 000	204 400	Unchanged
40	12 500	511 000	Unchanged
38	14 000	543 704	Unchanged
20	25 000	500 000	
14	26 500	371 000	
9	28 000	252 000	
4	38 000	152 000	
	Total	£2 534 104	

Step 5: Divide the two total staffing bills

Finally find the quotient of these two totals, the salary bill for 1995 divided by the salary bill for 1994. This is written $\dfrac{\sum P_n Q_n}{\sum P_0 Q_n}$. To find the index number we now convert this into a percentage, that is

$\dfrac{\sum P_n Q_n}{\sum P_0 Q_n} \times 100\% = \dfrac{£2\,572\,854}{£2\,534\,104} \times 100\% = 101.5\%$. This would mean that if the lower staffing levels were brought in earlier the effect of giving a pay rise of 2.2% to the lower grades and 3% to the higher grades would result in an overall staff budget increase of 1.5% in 1995. If the staffing levels are unchanged (case A above) we saw that the index number showed a 2.6% increase in the staffing budget. This gives the MD the option of keeping morale reasonably intact by awarding pay increases whilst minimising the overall cost to the company by streamlining middle management.

This index number here is often known as the given year index number, or Paasche's index.

Formally Paasche's index, I_p is given by:

$$I_p = \frac{\sum P_n Q_n}{\sum P_0 Q_n} \times 100\%$$

This gives a measure of the total cost of commodities relative to what the cost would have been if these had been made in the base year.

This index number is particularly useful if you want to look at the effect future changes would have on the economic outlook of a company if those changes were implemented earlier, and so aid decision-making by giving the optimal time scale. Having various strategies open to a staff resourcing team can make the difference between surviving in a difficult economic condition and going under. It does have one disadvantage in that this index requires all the latest prices and quantities. This might be a costly data collection exercise— particularly for government departments that look at figures for all companies.

Finally what would you advise the MD? Let's compare the total staffing bill for each year and for each level of staffing. The figures are in the table below:

Staffing level	1994	1995	Difference in 94/95 budget
Full staff quota	£2 758 500	£2 831 399	£72 899
Reduced staff level	£2 534 104	£2 572 854	£38 750
Difference in the year with two staffing levels	£224 396	£258 545	

If the company was struggling it is clear that by cutting staffing levels a year earlier would save it £1/4 million in 1994 and a similar figure in 1995. This would be a total saving of approximately 20% of the staffing budget over two years. Also the total increase to the staffing budget is only £38 750 if the lower staffing levels are introduced earlier.

Exercises 10.3

10.3.1 The following show some typical average monthly household costs in 1993 and 1995. Calculate a simple aggregate index number to measure the rise in household expenses from 1993 to 1995.

Household expense	1993	1995
Electricity	£11.50	£15
Gas	£25	£30
Telephone	£40	£43
Rates	£36	£49
Insurance	£24	£39

10.3.2 The following table shows the weekly costs of running a car in 1992 and 1994. Each cost has a weight associated with it to show how much of each item is purchased each week. For example, road taxation is bought for the year and so 1 week the weight is 1 in 52, or as a fraction $\frac{1}{52}$. Assume that the weights are fixed for 1992 and are used continuously through to 1994.

Motor expense	Weight	Costs 1992	Costs 1994
Road taxation	1/52	£125.00	£150.00
Petrol (gallons)	10	£2.09	£2.55
Oil (litres)	1/5	£2.80	£3.20
Insurance	1/52	£450.00	£530.00

Calculate a suitable weighted aggregate index number to measure the cost of running a car in 1992 compared with running a similar vehicle in 1994.

Finally we introduce the most important of all index numbers, the Retail Prices Index.

Retail Prices Index

The Retail Prices Index is the average weighted index number of a set of typical household expenditures taking into account the proportion of income spent on various types of goods and services. To do this, each month the Government needs to collect information about two main subjects: they need to record actual prices of typical goods and services, as well as how much of the average householder's income is being spent on each of these types of commodity. To do this they conduct a monthly prices survey, which is carried out by the Department of Education and Employment (DoEE). Secondly, each month they conduct The Family Expenditure Survey which looks at the income and expenditure of an average UK household, including pensioner householders. This is carried out on behalf of the DoEE by the Office of Population Censuses and Surveys. The results of these surveys are published monthly by the Central Statistical Office publications: Monthly Digest of Statistics and The Retail Prices Index (Business Monitor MM23). The source for all the following data is this publication.

Overview of the calculations

All price changes are measured from 13th January 1987. This is the *base date*. The typical household expenses are divided into 14 sections: food, catering, alcoholic drinks, tobacco, housing, fuel and light, household goods, household services, clothing and footwear, personal goods and services, motoring expenditure, fares and other travel costs, leisure goods, and finally leisure services. Each section is then sub-divided to form 83 sub-groups. For any given month for the 83 sub-groups, the *price relative* for each is formed and then weighted for each sub-group. These are then averaged to produce the index number for each section. Finally these are weighted and summed to form the Retail Prices Index for the given month. The details of how the weights are chosen and the price relatives are formed are briefly outlined with examples below.

The Family Expenditure Survey

This supplies the detailed information of what a typical household buys and also what their incomes are. Approximately 10 000 households are selected randomly from an electoral register. Interviewers then call at these selected households across the United Kingdom and ask for their assistance. These households give details, in the strictest confidence, about their total income and record all payments over a 14-day period. They are also asked about other payments which may occur regularly but did not fall in the specific 14-day cycle, such as mortgage payments, water rates, TV licence, etc. The information is then compiled, with all details about the client removed, before the data is forwarded to the government department, The Central Statistical Office. The primary use of this information is to provide the weights for calculating the Retail Prices Index. It is clear that the Government can readily collect information about prices and price changes over any given month, but this is of limited use unless they can assess how important each of the consumer items and services is to the average household, be they a two-earner household or a pensioner household. These weights are fixed for any one year, but are annually adjusted to show changes in consumer spending patterns. The weights are calculated using the previous 12-month cycle of average household expenditure (a three-year cycle is used for a pensioner household). For example, during 1994, the weights used are those calculated from the typical expenditure of a household in 1993. It is clear that in times of recession the average household spends less on leisure items such as CD players, and camcorders and more on the essentials such as food and fuel. Thus the weights must be adjusted each year if the RPI is to have any relevance to UK expenditure/income patterns.

The average basket of goods

To collect the price of every householder's shopping basket and services each week or month would be a huge task and would undoubtedly mean that the Retail Prices Index would never be published on a monthly basis. A more manageable and realistic attempt to monitor price changes is done by selecting some 350 items, which are then combined into 83 sections which are themselves then collated into 14 areas of expenditure (these are as stated earlier on page 326).

How the price relatives are formed

The prices of 350 different items are collected, on the Tuesday nearest the middle of the month, by offices of The Department of Education and Employment (DoEE) around the country. The DoEE contacts various retailers and service outlets and housing specialists in their specific area and records the prices of the 350 items each month. Altogether about 150 000 prices are collected. As far as possible prices are chosen which are most representative of the given sub-group. The prices for each commodity are then averaged and a sub-group price is formed. The price relative for this subgroup is then calculated by dividing the current monthly (average) price by the base price and multiplying by 100 to form a percentage.

For example, consider the price relative for restaurant meals for July 1994. The price relative for this sub-group of the catering section is quoted as 162.2%. How was this calculated? We give an example of how it might have been calculated, although the prices of the 150 000 items selected each month are never published, so we can only estimate what they might have been.

Recall that a price relative is defined to be $P_n/P_0 \times 100\%$ where P_n is the current price and P_0 is the base price.

Firstly the base figure was known—this would be the average amount spent on restaurant meals by a typical household during 1993. Suppose that was in fact £22.37. This will be P_0. Now we need to calculate the current price, that would be the average amount spent on restaurant meals during the selected two-week period in July 1994 around the country. Suppose that seven households selected stated that their restaurant bills were:

£35, £52, £48, £13, £10, £75, and £21.

(Obviously many more households were selected.) We need to find the average amount spent on restaurant meals. Thus we form the sum of the given amounts and divide by the number of households, 7 here. This gives us £35 + £52 + ... + £21 = £254. The average bill is therefore £254/7 = £36.29. This would be our P_n value.

The price relative for July 1994 $= \dfrac{P_n}{P_0} \times 100\% = \dfrac{£36.29}{£22.37} \times 100\%$. This gives us $1.622 \times 100\%$ which is the published figure of 162.2%.

Exercise 10.4

Show that the price relative for the subgroup rail fares of fares and other travel costs for May 1994, is 168.5%, given that the base price for 1993 was £25.89 and using the following 8 householder's expenses:

£12, £6, £48, £39, £0, £76, £52, £123.

How the weights are formed

For 1994 the weights are taken from the spending patterns of the typical household in 1993. This is done by calculating the average percentage for 1993 that each household has said they spent on each of the 83 sub-groups. For greater accuracy these percentages are then multiplied by 10 so that the total weight for all expenditure comes to 1000.

During 1994 the following weights are used for each of these areas of expenditure:

Table: weightings for 1994

Item of expenditure	Weight
Food	142
Catering	45
Alcoholic drinks	76
Tobacco	35
Housing	158
Fuel and light	45
Household goods	76
Household services	47
Clothing and footwear	58
Personal goods and services	37
Motoring expenditure	142
Fares and other travel costs	20
Leisure goods	48
Leisure services	71
Total weight	1000

(Source: Central Statistical Office: Monthly Digest of Statistics)

This means that the typical household spends $158 \div 1000$ (15.8 as percentage) of their income on housing, 14.2% on food, 3.5% on tobacco, etc.

Example 10.4

Consider the housing section. This is split into 7 sub-groups: rent, mortgage interest payments, council tax, water and other charges, repairs and maintenance, do-it-yourself materials, household insurance and ground rent. Weightings for each of these sub-groups depend on how much the average household spent on them during 1993. Then the price relatives for each sub-group are calculated for any given month. We first consider February 1994. The weights and price relatives for each sub-group of the housing section are given in the table below:

Housing section

	Weight 1994	Price relative Feb 1994
Rent	42	183.3
Mortgage interest payments	44	141.3
Council tax	30	124.5
Water and other charges	10	207.7
Repairs and maintenance	11	148.9
Do-it-yourself materials	14	143.1
Household insurance and ground rent	7	194.2
Total weight	158	

(Source: Central Statistical Office: Monthly Digest of Statistics)

Calculate the weighted aggregate prices index for housing in February 1994 (using the base date of January 13th, 1987).

Solution
Step 1: Form a sum of the weighted price relatives
We need to find a weighted aggregate for the price relative for February 1994 using the weights which will give us the consumer's proportion of expenditure in each area. This means we need to multiply the price relative by the weight (to give a weighted price relative) and by summing these we will arrive at the weighted aggregate price relative.

This gives us: $42 \times 183.3 + 44 \times 141.3 + ... + 7 \times 194.2 = 7698.6 + 6217.2 + 3735 + 2077 + 1637.9 + 2003.4 + 1345.4 = 23\,076.6$.

Step 2: Average the weighted aggregate price relative for housing

We now divide the weighted aggregate price relative by the total proportion for housing: 158. Thus $\dfrac{23\,076.6}{158} = 146.05$.

This will give us the index number for housing. Thus in February 1994, the amount of income spent on housing is 46.5% more than the value of income spent on housing in 1987.

The Retail Prices Index

The index number so calculated for housing would be repeated for each of the remaining 13 sections. These 14 index numbers are then weighted by the weight given to each section for 1994 (i.e. 14.2/1000 for food = 0.142, 0.045 for catering, etc.) and then summed to give the Retail Prices Index for the given month relative to January 1987.

Here one component of the RPI for the housing section would be $0.158 \times 146.05 = 23.0759$. This would then be added to each of the other sections to give the RPI.

The exercises below explore such calculations more fully.

Exercises 10.5 _____

10.5.1 Calculate the Retail Price Index for leisure goods using the following weightings and price relatives for June 1994:

Leisure goods	Weight	Price relative
Audio-visual equipment	10	75.4
CD's and tapes	6	113.4
Toys, photographic and sports equipment	12	120.9
Books and newspapers	14	159.2
Gardening products	6	141.2
Total weight	48	

(Source: Central Statistical Office: Monthly Digest of Statistics, Oct 1994)

10.5.2 Calculate a Retail Prices Index for food using the following weightings and price relatives for August 1994:

Food	Weight	Price relative
Bread	7	135.9
Cereals	4	137.7
Biscuits and cake	9	144.8
Beef	7	131.9
Lamb	3	125.0
Pork	2	118.8
Bacon	3	132.3
Poultry	6	109.2
Other meat	8	123.0
Fish	7	125.5
Butter	1	134.7
Oils and fats	2	131.4
Cheese	4	142.8
Eggs	2	126.9
Milk	10	144.8
Milk products	3	138.5
Tea	2	147.4
Coffee and other hot drinks	2	113.0
Soft drinks	10	155.8
Sugar and preserves	2	143.5
Sweets and chocolates	13	134.7
Potatoes	7	179.6
Vegetables	17	102.8
Fruit	13	121.7
Other foods	16	135.9
Total	**142**	

(Source: Central Statistical Office: Monthly Digest of Statistics, Oct. 1994)

10.5.3 Using Table: weightings for 1994 for the 14 groups, calculate a Retail Prices Index for July 1994 using the following price relatives calculated with 13 January 1987 as the base date:

Food	132.3
Catering	162.2
Alcoholic drinks	159.1
Tobacco	168.5
Housing	156.8
Fuel and light	133.9
Household goods	126.3
Household services	142.3
Clothing and footwear	116.0
Personal goods and services	152.4
Motoring expenditure	150.0
Fares and other travel costs	155.6
Leisure goods	120.7
Leisure services	162.6

(Source: Central Statistical Office: Monthly Digest of Statistics, Oct. 1994)

The published figure for this month is 144.0. Why is your figure slightly different? If the RPI for June 1994 was 144.7, what is the percentage change between the two months?

Internal purchasing power of the pound

It is difficult to measure the real value of money over a time interval, as, for example interest rates change, sterling has at times been devalued, inflation varies from one month to the next. Economists have devised a way of measuring the value of the pound in your pocket today with what you could have bought with it had you been purchasing the items in previous years. This is the so-called *purchasing power of the pound* which is calculated using the RPI of successive years.

Example 10.5

Consider the table below of annual average RPIs from 1987 to 1993 using 13 January 1987 as the base date:

Year	RPI	Value of 100p
1987	101.9	100
1988	106.9	
1989	115.2	
1990	126.1	
1991	133.5	
1992	138.5	
1993	140.7	

(Source: Central Statistical Office: Monthly Digest of Statistics, Oct. 1994)

Calculate the value of the pound for each year from 1987.

Solution

To calculate the value of the pound in 1988 compared to 1987 we find the quotient of the two RPIs (all figures are calculated to the nearest penny):

The pound is worth $\dfrac{101.9}{106.9}$ in 1988 = 95 p to the nearest penny.

In 1989 the pound is worth $\dfrac{101.9}{115.2}$ = 88 p

For 1990, £1 = $\dfrac{101.9}{126.1}$ = 81 p. The remaining figures are 76p, 74p, 72p.

Exercise 10.5

10.5.1 The following data set 10.5 shows the annual average RPIs for 1974 to 1986 using 15 January 1974 as the base date. Calculate the internal purchasing power of the pound for each year from 1974, taking 15 January 1974's value to be 100 p.

Data set 10.5

Year	RPI	Value of 100 p
1974	108.5	100
1975	134.8	
1976	157.1	
1977	182.0	
1978	197.1	
1979	223.5	
1980	263.7	
1981	295.0	
1982	320.4	
1983	335.1	
1984	351.8	
1985	373.2	
1986	385.9	

(Source: Central Statistical Office: Monthly Digest of Statistics, Oct. 1994)

Why do you think a new base year was taken for the RPI after 1986?

The rate of inflation

One of the most important uses of the RPI is that it is used to calculate the rate of inflation—a crucial economic factor for any government minister. Often a government will base its whole economic policy on controlling inflation. Within the European Union countries are allied to each other by keeping their rate of inflation within a narrow band of each other. The Bundesbank will often take corrective action on its interest rates if it even looks as if the German economy has rising inflation. Today in the UK the rate of inflation is running at about 2.4% per annum which is very healthy and indicates that prices and household costs are rising at a very slow rate. In some economies around the world, particularly Third World economics, inflation can be running at 100% or 200% or more per annum.

How the rate of inflation is calculated

Data set 10.6: monthly figures for the RPI for 1990

Taking the base date as 13/1/87 the following figures are the published monthly indices for all retail prices during 1990:

January	119.5%
February	120.2%
March	121.4%
April	125.1%
May	126.2%
June	126.7%
July	126.8%
August	128.1%
September	129.3%
October	130.3%
November	130.0%
December	129.9%

(Source: Central Statistical Office: Monthly Digest of Statistics)

Example 10.6

Calculate the rate of inflation for each month during 1990 and for the year as a whole.

Solution

Step 1: Monthly change in RPI

We simply subtract any two consecutive months and divide by the earlier month for a monthly figure for inflation. Using mathematical language, we would write RPI Month i to denote the RPI for any month in 1990. Once a month is chosen, we know what will be looking at the consecutive month which we shall denote by month $i + 1$. Notice that we are really using i for a counter to take us through the months from the first month, January, through to the twelfth month.

Thus the rate of inflation for month $i + 1 =$

$$\frac{\text{RPI month } i + 1 - \text{RPI month } i}{\text{RPI month } i} \times 100\%.$$

Step 2: Calculations for each month

The rate of inflation for February 1990 $= \dfrac{\text{RPI Feb} - \text{RPI Jan}}{\text{RPI Jan}} \times 100\%.$

Inserting the figures we have rate for February 1990

$$= \frac{120.2 - 119.5}{119.5} \times 100\%$$

$$= \frac{0.7}{119.5} \times 100\% = 0.00586 \times 100\% = 0.59\% \text{ to 2 decimal places.}$$

Similarly for April 1990 the rate of inflation

$$= \frac{\text{RPI Apr} - \text{RPI Mar}}{\text{RPI Mar}} \times 100\%$$

$$= \frac{125.1 - 121.4}{121.4} \times 100\%$$

This gives us $\dfrac{3.7}{121.4} \times 100\% = 3.05\%.$

Similar calculations hold for each of the other months. Notice that for January 1990 we can see that we would need the previous month's RPI, which is for December 1989, which is 118.8.

Step 3: The annual rate of inflation

To find the annual rate of inflation we calculate the rate of inflation for December 1990 using January 1990 as the previous month. That is

$$\text{The annual rate of inflation} = \frac{\text{RPI Dec} - \text{RPI Jan}}{\text{RPI Jan}} \times 100\%.$$

Thus for 1990 inflation was running at: $\dfrac{129.9 - 119.5}{119.5} \times 100\%$

$= \dfrac{10.4}{119.5} \times 100\% = 8.7\%.$

Exercises 10.6 _____

10.6.1 Find the monthly rate of inflation for each of the other months using data set 10.5 above.

10.6.2 Calculate the rate of inflation for each of the twelve months June 1993 to July 1994 using the following RPIs:

June 1993	141.0	Dec 1993	141.9
July 1993	140.7	Jan 1994	141.3
Aug 1993	141.3	Feb 1994	142.1
Sept 1993	141.9	Mar 1994	142.5
Oct 1993	141.9	Apr 1994	144.2
Nov 1993	141.6	May 1994	144.7

(Source: Central Statistical Office: Monthly Digest of Statistics)

What is the annual figure running at for this period?

10.6.3 Using data set 10.5 in exercise 10.5 above estimate the annual rate of inflation for each of the years from 1974 to 1986.

Time series

Scenario: consumer expenditure is soaring—new confidence in the High Street

The above headline appears in the London Evening Standard in July 1994. Is it justified, and how was this economic picture determined? To be able to say whether or not a rate is going down or up or simply staying steady, we need to look at the pattern of monthly or quarterly expenditure figures. Such analysis involves drawing a *time series*: a series of points to denote consumer expenditure at successive months/ quarters plotted on a graph.

Introduction

Whenever we have a set of bivariate data where the dependent/uncontrolled variable is measured over time, we have previously considered regression analysis to study its behaviour. A more systematic approach is to use a time series to analyse this type of data. Generally any data measured over time would be subject to random variation or fluctuation. In being able to model such historical data we could then move to predict its future behaviour or forecast its future values. This is of vital economic importance for any business or economy.

Data set 10.7

The following is an extract from Gross Domestic Product (GDP) figures showing the quarterly consumer expenditure over 14 successive quarters:

		Consumers' expenditure (in £ millions × 10^3)
1991	Q1	84.922
	Q2	88.617
	Q3	93.830
	Q4	97.603
1992	Q1	89.465
	Q2	93.308
	Q3	98.060
	Q4	101.407
1993	Q1	94.992
	Q2	98.548
	Q3	104.447
	Q4	107.652
1994	Q1	100.931
	Q2	103.395

(Source: Central Statistical Office: Monthly Digest of Statistics, Oct. 1994)

By allocating a number to the time period, we then have a set of bivariate data where the time period T is the independent variable and the recorded expenditure is the Y variable. Given this we can look for patterns in the Y variable's behaviour, and the aim of our analysis is to use past data to predict future Y values, that is to *forecast* the future consumer expenditure. It is likely that the Y variable does not solely depend on time; other factors will effect the changes in expenditure such as the value of sterling, government policy on borrowing, job security, strength of the British/European economies, etc. We can see that a time series model can be quite a complex model, and to deal with this in our analysis of the time series we isolate key features of the series, and from this build up a picture of how and where future changes in the time series are likely to be.

We shall analyse a typical time series data set by looking at the four principle features of time series analysis, which are:

seasonal component;
trend component;
cyclical component;
irregular component.

The aim is then to analyse the time series by estimating the various components that constitute the particular time series.

A time series graph

Recall that in Chapter 2 we plotted such data as a time series (T, Y) where on the horizontal axis is the time period (here, in quarters) and on the vertical axis the consumers' expenditure is plotted. (Note that as all the expenditures exceed $\pounds 80$ m $\times 10^3$ we shall truncate the vertical axis and commence at 80.)

Each point is joined to its predecessor and successor by a straight line and a time series graph is formed. We shall plot this by hand (or using Excel); the resulting graph is found in figure 10.1.

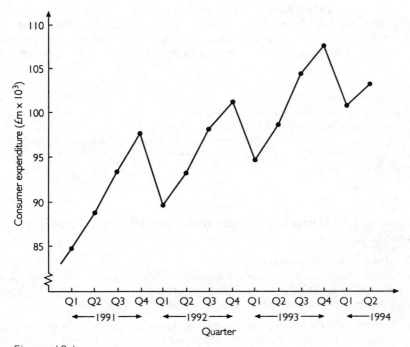

Figure 10.1

Overview of the components of a time series

We shall briefly describe each of the components of a times series and then go on to discuss how we can develop a model for a given time series to enable us to forecast.

Seasonal component
Whenever we see a regular pattern of variation within a year's data we could attribute this to a seasonal effect. For example, sales would be likely to peak in the 4th quarter of a year, as this includes Christmas. Similarly unemployment figures would portray a seasonal effect: a peak would occur in the autumn of a year when all the new school and college leavers seek employment. A similar trough would occur in December as employers take on 'seasonal labour'. With a 1-day period transport networks (rail/tube/road) would display a peak during the rush hours and a trough after and before. Notice that we could not use annual data to look at seasonal effects as by this we mean variation within the year.

Trend component
The trend component of a time series is largely due to long-term factors affecting the data. Within a time series graph this would be observed as a gradual upward or downward shift. We might say that the time series follows an underlying trend—such as inflation steadily declining. This might be due to such factors as economic policy, or changes in the workplace or population. We shall consider linear trends below and how we can model such linear trends.

Cyclical component
A time series graph will often show an alternating sequence of values above and below the trend line. Any regular pattern in such a sequence lasting for longer than 1 year could be attributed to a cyclical component. Meteorologists might suggest that drought years in the UK may occur every n years (and may even estimate n). Cycles in rainfall data are well recorded.

Irregular component
Any other variation in the time series not due to the above three factors would be termed irregular. This amounts to saying that residual variation (i.e. random variation) in the time series which is not explained by seasonal, trend and cyclical factors would be attributed to an irregular component. Such factors are unpredictable and most likely due to short-term factors.

Analysing the time series for data set 10.7: smoothing techniques

Step 1: Observations from the graph
The first thing to notice is the typical zig-zag shape of the time series. The indications of peaks and troughs are familiar in data which is subject to seasonal variation. We shall now look at what to do about this.

We shall consider two smoothing techniques (moving averages and linear trend analysis) and then put these two together and see how to use both to predict future values in our time series.

Smoothing techniques: moving averages

Step 2: Removing the seasonal component

Generally a seasonal component is present when there is a periodic increase and decrease regularly occurring, in data. Once we can recognise a pattern we can begin to predict the future occurrences which are due to seasonality.

One way of removing seasonal variation is to use an averaging process such as to calculate the 4-quarterly moving averages (or 12-month moving average for monthly data). As its name suggests, a 4-quarter average is found for groups of 4 successive quarters and then this average is plotted in the middle of the range used.

Step 3: Calculate the first 4-quarter moving average

For example, the quarters are allocated numbers 1, 2, ... 14, giving us bivariate data:

(1, 84.922)
(2, 88.617)
(3, 93.830)
$\vdots$
(14, 103.395)

We take the first 4 quarterly figures.

The 4-quarter moving average (for the first set of quarters)

$$= \frac{Q1 + Q2 + Q3 + Q4 \text{ figures}}{4}$$

This amounts to averaging the expenditures for times periods 1 to 4. This will give us

The 4-quarter moving average (for the first set of quarters)

$$= \frac{88.922 + 88.617 + 93.830 + 97.603}{4}$$

$$= \frac{364.972}{4} = 91.243$$

This is a moving average. It amounts to saying that this is the average for the year Q1 to Q4 and as such it can be said to occur in the middle of the year, which is mid-way between Q2 and Q3. Thus we plot the moving average on our time series graph at (2.5, 91.243). (If we took the 3-quarter moving average then this would always be observed at a quarter—as we are taking the middle of an odd number of quarters.)

Step 4: Calculate the second 4-quarter moving average

To calculate the moving average for periods 2 to 5 inclusive we can again sum the 4 expenditures and average these giving us 92.379. This is plotted mid-way between periods 3 and 4. In fact we can continue in this fashion, but using a spreadsheet is far quicker. If we are calculating by hand we can notice a short-cut.

If we take the difference in expenditure between periods 1 and 5, we have 4.543. If we take a quarter of this difference and add it to the first moving average we get the second moving average. In the table below we have continued in this way to find the 4-quarterly moving averages:

Table of 4-quarterly moving averages (in £ millions × 10^3)

Quarter	Time period	Consumer expenditure	Difference	Difference 4	Moving average
1991					
Q1	1	84.922			
Q2	2	88.617			
Q3	3	93.830			91.243
Q4	4	97.603	4.543	1.136	92.379
1992					93.552
Q1	5	89.465	4.691	1.173	
Q2	6	93.308	4.23	1.058	94.610
Q3	7	98.060	3.804	0.951	95.561
Q4	8	101.407	5.527	1.382	96.943
1993					98.253
Q1	9	94.992	5.24	1.31	99.849
Q2	10	98.548	6.387	1.597	101.411
Q3	11	104.447	6.245	1.561	102.895
Q4	12	107.652	5.939	1.485	104.107
1994					
Q1	13	100.931	4.847	1.212	
Q2	14	103.395			

Now plotting the moving averages over the original time series we have figure 10.2

We can see that the net effect of plotting the moving averages is to smooth the jagged shape of the time series. It is then that we can see that there is a steady increase of consumer expenditure over the 14 quarters from 1991. Thus we can see that the moving average technique has helped to reveal this general trend. Reducing the impact of the zig-zag nature of the time series allows us to see the clear underlying behaviour of the data.

Step 5: Forecasting
We can see a general trend now and so we could try to extend the line of moving averages by eye. This would enable us to forecast the next 4-quarter moving average. From my time series figure this would be approximately £105.8 m × 10^3.

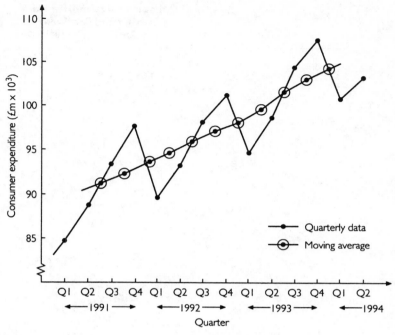

Figure 10.2

Step 6: Accuracy of forecasts
How accurate would forecasts be from such a smoothing process?

One way of assessing forecasting errors is to compute the differences of observed values the times series (which are here slightly below the moving average) with the moving average. This should sum to zero if the errors in the time series are random). Similarly the squared sum of these differences can be computed to give

$$\text{mean squared error} = \frac{\text{sum of squared errors}}{\text{number of errors}}$$

Exercises 10.7 _____

10.7.1 Plot a time series for consumer expenditure on clothing and footwear (prefer-ably using a spreadsheet), for quarters from 1987 to 1994:

		Consumer expenditure on clothing and footwear (in £ millions $\times 10^3$)
1987	Q1	3.570
	Q2	4.085
	Q3	4.300
	Q4	5.893
1988	Q1	3.838
	Q2	4.366
	Q3	4.566
	Q4	6.253
1989	Q1	4.151
	Q2	4.657
	Q3	4.729
	Q4	6.310
1990	Q1	4.412
	Q2	4.961
	Q3	5.084
	Q4	6.419
1991	Q1	4.448
	Q2	5.012
	Q3	5.183
	Q4	6.769
1992	Q1	4.391
	Q2	5.135
	Q3	5.352
	Q4	7.207
1993	Q1	4.666
	Q2	5.349
	Q3	5.613
	Q4	7.694
1994	Q1	5.032
	Q2	5.668

(Source: Central Statistical Office: Monthly Digest of Statistics, Oct. 1994)

Smooth the time series by calculating 4-quarter moving averages for the period and plotting the resulting time series. Comment on your findings. Can you explain any particular peaks?

10.7.2 Calculate the mean squared error for data set 10.7 and exercise 10.7.1.

We now look at some of the other features. Notice that once we eliminated the seasonal effect on the time series a general trend becomes apparent. We shall look at estimating this linear trend using statistical techniques learnt in the previous chapter. When we have modelled any linear trend in a time series, the next stage will be to put together these two forecasting techniques together and look at the impact of both seasonal and trend factors together.

Forecasting: linear trend projections

If a time series exhibits a long-term linear trend then we can model this using linear regression techniques.

Data set 10.8

The following are the monthly rates of interest as published by New Town Building Society for 1991:

January	14.82	July	12.28
February	14.70	August	11.91
March	14.24	September	11.82
April	13.86	October	11.47
May	12.84	November	11.41
June	12.75	December	11.39

Plot a time series for this data set and consider the result.

Solution

The resulting time series is displayed in figure 10.3.

We can see that the overall pattern of the graph is a general decline. There appears to be a steady downward movement in the interest rate. We can call such a movement a trend. If no such general movement is apparent then the time series has no trend. A trend generally reflects a long-term decline or growth—here in the housing market lending rates were steadily declining after a peak following major crisis in the housing market of 1990 (probably attributable to Government policy and the overheating of the British economy). Trends often appear due to inflation, changes in personal income, or

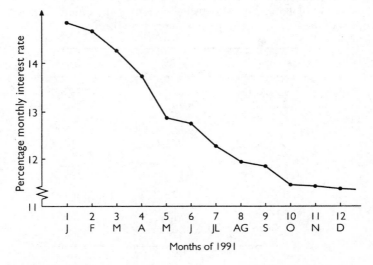

Figure 10.3

population changes. Trends can take a variety of shapes, the simplest of which is a linear trend. Other trends include quadratic trends, exponential trends, logarithmic trends, etc. We shall restrict our attention to linear trends. Formally a trend is linear if the rate of change between successive time periods is approximately constant. Given this, we can use linear regression to estimate a model for the trend.

Model for linear trend in *y*

A linear model has:

$y \approx a + bx$

where x is the time period and:

$$b = \frac{\sum xy - n\bar{x}\bar{y}}{\sum x^2 - n\bar{x}^2};$$

$$a = \bar{y} - b\bar{x}.$$

Notice that we can adopt some aids to our calculations. We can assume that the sum of integers $1 + 2 + 3 + \dots + n = \dfrac{n(n + 1)}{2}$ and the sum of squared integers $= 1^2 + 2^2 + 3^2 + \dots + n^2 = \dfrac{n(n + 1)(2n + 1)}{6}$.

Example 10.6

Find an equation for the trend in the above time series of interest rates for 1991.

Solution

Step 1: Construct a table of *x*, *y* and *xy*

We construct a table to carry out the calculations for the regression coefficients b and a: with columns for x (the time period), y the interest rate and xy the product of these two, and for each column form the total.

x	*y*	*xy*
1	14.82	14.82
2	14.70	29.4
3	14.24	42.72
4	13.86	55.44
5	12.84	64.2
6	12.75	76.5
7	12.28	85.96
8	11.91	95.28
9	11.82	106.38
10	11.47	114.7
11	11.41	125.51
12	11.39	136.59
78	153.49	947.59

Step 2: Calculate the sum of x and the sum of x^2

Notice we can use the aid to sum the time periods:

$$1 + 2 + 3 + ... + n = \frac{n(n+1)}{2} \text{ putting } n = 12 \text{ gives us}$$

$$1 + 2 + 3 + ... + 12 = \frac{12(12+1)}{2} = \frac{12 \times 13}{2} = 78$$

Similarly we can find the sum of squared x using:

sum of squared integers $= 1^2 + 2^2 + 3^2 + ... + n^2 = \dfrac{n(n+1)(2n+1)}{6}$ with $n = 12$.

This gives us:

sum of squared integers $= 1^2 + 2^2 + 3^2 + ... + 12^2$

$$= \frac{12(12+1)(24+1)}{6} = \frac{78}{3} \times 25 = 650.$$

Step 3: Compute a and b: the linear model coefficients

$$b = \frac{\sum xy - n\bar{x}\bar{y}}{\sum x^2 - n\bar{x}^2} = \frac{947.59 - 12 \times 6.5 \times 12.79083333}{650 - 12 \times (6.5)^2}$$

$$= \frac{947.59 - 997.685}{650 - 507} = \frac{-50.095}{143}$$

$$= -0.350314685 \approx -0.35 \text{ to 2 decimal places.}$$

Finally $a = \bar{y} - b\bar{x} = \dfrac{153.49}{12} - -0.3503146 \times 6.5$ which gives us $a = 15.07$ to 2 decimal places.

Hence the equation for the trend in interest rates is given by:

$$y \approx 15.07 - 0.35x$$

The linear trend model: here we are saying that the value of the interest rate y depends on a factor of time (x) and a constant value.

(Computing this using your calculator's LR mode is much the quickest way. A check of r gives us $r = -0.97127$ which results in a coefficient of determination of $r^2\%$ of 94%. That's very good—only 6% of the variation in the interest rates is unexplained by the trend model.)

Step 4: Forecasting

Use the regression line to predict the interest rate for January 1992.

Here this would mean $x = 13$. Thus $y = 15.07 - 0.35 \times 13$ giving us $y = 10.514\%$.

Exercises 10.8 _____

10.8.1 Use the above regression equation in example 10.6 to forecast the rate of interest in January and February 1992. Could you use this trend to forecast the interest rate for January 1995?

10.8.2 The following are monthly figures for the retail prices index (base 100% January 13 1987):

1993		1994	
Jan	137.9	Jan	141.3
Feb	138.8	Feb	142.1
Mar	139.3	Mar	142.5
Apr	140.6	Apr	144.2
May	141.1	May	144.7
June	141.0	June	144.7
Jul	140.7		
Aug	141.3		
Sep	141.9		
Oct	141.8		
Nov	141.6		
Dec	141.9		

Plot a time series for this 18-month period and decide if there appears to be any general trend. If there does appear to be, find an equation for this trend using linear regression techniques. Check your answers using Minitab.

Seasonal and component trend within a time series

If we take another look at figure 10.2 for the consumer expenditure from 1991 to 1994 we can see that once we have smoothed the figures using the 4-quarterly moving averages, we can then see a linear upward trend: the expenditure appears to be steadily increasing. Thus it is clear that this time series is affected by two factors—seasonality and trend. How do we generally deal with such data when we can see a steady increase as well as regular 'seasonal peaks and dips'?

Method

We adopt a step-by-step method using data set 10.7:

Step 1: Calculate the moving averages
This amounts to removing some of the seasonal effect

Step 2: Calculate the centred moving averages
One way of adjusting the trend projections is to use a seasonal index. This is formed from the moving averages. To this end we first compute centred moving averages.

Consider the 4 quarter moving averages for data set 10.7. Looking at the first 4-quarter moving average we can see this provides an estimate for the mid-point between Q2 and Q3. We could thus say that this is an average for the latter half of Q3. Taking the second 4-quarter moving average we can see that this is plotted mid-way between Q3 and Q4. Thus this provides an average for consumer expenditure for the latter half of Q3. By taking these two 4-quarter moving averages for Q3, 91.243 and 92.379, we could find one average for this quarter by averaging these two moving averages. This is called a *centred moving average*.

Here a centred moving average for Q3

$$= \frac{\text{moving average Q1 : Q4} + \text{moving average Q2 : Q5}}{2}$$

$$= \frac{91.243 + 92.379}{2} = 91.811.$$

We can continue in this way by averaging successive 4-quarter moving averages as in the table below:

Table of centred moving averages

Quarter	Time period	Consumers' expenditure (in £ millions × 10³)	Moving average	Centred moving average
1991				
Q1	1	84.922		
Q2	2	88.617		
			91.243	
Q3	3	93.830		91.811
			92.379	
Q4	4	97.603		92.966
			93.552	
1992				
Q1	5	89.465		94.081
			94.610	
Q2	6	93.308		95.086
			95.561	
Q3	7	98.060		96.252
			96.943	
Q4	8	101.407		97.598
			98.253	
1993				
Q1	9	94.992		99.051
			99.849	
Q2	10	98.548		100.63
			101.411	
Q3	11	104.447		102.153
			102.895	
Q4	12	107.652		103.501
			104.107	
1994				
Q1	13	100.931		
Q2	14	103.395		

We can now plot these centred moving averages over our original times series (figure 10.1) to arrive at figure 10.4.

From this graph we can see how the time series has become very smooth. As we have computed 4-quarterly centred moving averages they are not influenced by seasonal effects. Thus each centred moving average estimates the time series as if there were no seasonal or irregular effect.

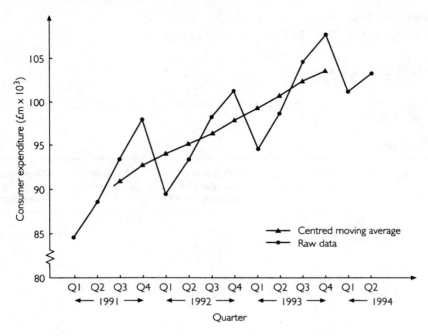

Figure 10.4

Step 4: Compute the seasonal index

Forming the ratio of the time series observations to the centred moving averages gives us a measure of the seasonal effect. This is called the *seasonal index* for the quarter:

$$\text{seasonal index} = \frac{y \text{ value in time series}}{\text{centred moving average}}$$

A value of 1.0 would say there is no difference between this quarter's consumer expenditure and the quarterly average. A value of 0.7 would mean a 30% decrease and 1.45 would mean a 45% increase.

For example take the figures for Q1 in 1991. The ratio $= \dfrac{93.830}{91.811} = 1.022$. We call this the seasonal index for the third quarter. This value would suggest that the times series value for Q3 is 2.2% greater than the average quarterly consumer expenditure.

The real use of seasonal indices is that if we divide the time series observation by the corresponding seasonal index we have removed the seasonal factor. You will notice that Government data such as unemployment figures are always 'seasonally adjusted'. This process of removing the seasonal component is also sometimes referred to as deseasonalising the time series.

Step 5: Use linear trend projection

This amounts to finding the line of regression: $y = a + bx$ for the data. This can then be used to forecast.

The final two factors of a time series we shall not consider in any great detail.

Cyclical component

Any gradual movement about the general trend is known as a *cyclical component* in the time series. The length of time from a peak to a trough is called the *cycle length* or *periodicity* of the time series. Such cyclical activity is common amount weather data and in financial indices where periods of financial depression can be for a period of 2 to 10 or more years, followed by a period of economic recovery. The main difference between cyclical and seasonal factors is the length of time. Seasonal effects tend to take place within a year, whereas cyclical activity is usually associated between years. Cycles in business time series most generally represent prevailing economic conditions: the boom and bust of the 80s.

Irregular component

After a time series has been analysed for seasonal, trend and cyclical effects, any remaining effects are called irregular activity, which is somewhat similar to the error term in a linear regression model. Generally irregular activity is a random movement within the time series and tends to represent the unexpected occurrences, such as large fluctuations in a currency, or a financial disaster (such as Barings).

Exercises 10.9 _____

10.9.1 Compute the seasonal indices for data set 10.7. Hence de-seasonalise this time series.

10.9.2 Carry out a regression analysis to determine the linear trend in the 4-quarterly moving average data in data set 10.7 before centred moving averages were computed.

10.9.3 The following quarterly data shows index numbers for the output of manufacturing industries from 1991 to 1994 (with 1990 as base year).

		Percentage output for the mining industries (1990 = 100%)
1991	Q1	97.0
	Q2	94.9
	Q3	91.2
	Q4	95.7
1992	Q1	94.8
	Q2	93.9
	Q3	91.5
	Q4	96.3
1993	Q1	96.2
	Q2	95.4
	Q3	92.7
	Q4	97.1
1994	Q1	98.1
	Q2	99.1

(Source: Central Statistical Office: Monthly Digest of Statistics, Oct. 1994)

(i)   Plot a time series for this data.
(ii) Compute the 4-quarter moving averages and the centred moving averages.
(iii) Plot each of these on your initial time series and comment.
(iv) Compute the seasonal indices for each quarter. What do these show?
(v)   Determine if there is any evidence of a linear trend within the data. If so, determine a suitable model for this trend.
(vi) Use this model to forecast the percentage output in Q3 and Q4 of 1994.

11 Making decisions— what's the best mix: linear programming

Objectives

- Be able to formulate a linear programming problem;
- Be able to graphically solve the linear programming problem;
- Have an understanding of the simplex algorithm.

Introduction to the problem

The objective of *linear programming* is to optimise (that is maximise or minimise) some particular function, such as profit or costs, subject to certain restrictions on your production or budget or even given some environmental restrictions. Such restrictions are known as constraints, and these are what bind a solution or give us a set of all possible solutions to our problem. As its name suggests, such problems are restricted to all the constraints and optimal function—known as the *objective function*—being concerned with linear functions.

Formulation

Example 11.1: the objective function

Pilldrug Foundation produce two types of anti-inflammatory drugs—Eezit and Ridopane. Each drug is made in tablets of 500 mg each and batches of 20 tablets are foil wrapped and boxed ready for sale. Each box of twenty tablets of Eezit costs £1.50 to produce, whilst a similar quantity of Ridopane costs £2.20. What would it cost to make 500 boxes of Eezit and 400 boxes of Ridopane? What about the cost of producing any number of boxes of each drug?

Solution

We can see that producing 1 box of twenty tablets of Eezit costs £1.50. Thus making 100 boxes would cost 100 times this amount, which is £150. Thus 500 boxes would cost 5 times this sum, or 5 × £150 which is £750.

Similarly the cost of 100 boxes of Ridopane would be 100 times £2.20 or £220. Thus 400 boxes would cost 4 times this, that is £880. Together this would give us a total production cost of £750 + £880 = £1,630.

The general case would be to use some notation for any number of boxes of each drug, and we would usually use the first letter of each product. Let E denote the number of boxes of Eezit produced and R the number of boxes of Ridopane produced. The cost function C, is then the sum of costs for each drug which would be $E \times £1.50$ and $R \times £2.20$. Combining these we would write $C = E \times £1.50 + R \times £2.20$, or more naturally $C = 1.5E + 2.2R$.

Example 11.2: the constraints

The Pilldrug laboratory employs 50 scientists and 20 non-specialist staff. Each works a 40-hour week. The time to produce each of its main brands in boxes of twenty 500 mg tablets is given in the table below, taking into account when the scientists and non-specialist staff are used in the production:

	Product	
	Eezit	**Ridopane**
Scientist hours	2	3
Non-specialist hours	1	0.5

Summarise the problem: that is, formulate it.

Solution

Step 1: Recognition

In fact we can see that the number of labour hours available for production is a major constraint on the amount of any manufacturing process. Thus the above problem is in fact the constraints to a problem which we need to formulate.

Step 2: The total number of hours available

Here we can see that if there are 50 scientists and each works a 40 hour week, we have a total number of available hours as $50 \times 40 = 2000$ hours per week. Similarly for the non-specialists we have 20 staff and each works 40 hours, giving us 800 hours per week.

Step 3: The variables

Here we are looking at how many batches of each drug can be made per week within the number of available hours. We can see there are two drugs, and as before it is natural to use the first letter of each to denote the number of units of each made: here E denotes the number of boxes (20 × 500 mg tablets) of Eezit, R for the number of boxes of Ridopane.

Step 4: The constraints

There are two totals for each different type of worker and so we will have two constraints: one on the productivity of the scientists and one on the productivity of the non-specialists.

If we manufactured 1 box of E and 1 box of R, just looking at the number of scientist hours employed we would arrive at $2 + 3$, or 5 hours in total. Similarly if we made 2 of E and 3 of R we would need to employ $2 \times 2 + 2 \times 3$ giving us 10 hours. Our dilemma is that we do not really know how many of each drug should be produced to use the available scientist hours. All we can say is that if we make E kg of Eezit it would use $2 \times E$

scientist hours and if we made R kgs of Ridopane we would use $3 \times R$ hours. All together this must be less than the total hours worked by the scientists in a week, namely:

$$2E + 3R \leqslant 2000$$

Similarly for the non-specialist staff we would use $1 \times E$ hours for Eezit, $0.5 \times R$ for Ridopane. Thus our constraint on the number of non-specialist labour hours available would be:

$$E + 0.5R \leqslant 800$$

Step 5: The next stage
Now we have a cost function and we have some restrictions on how many boxes of each drug we can make, we are in the enviable position of being able to ask: what is the best production mix to minimise our costs? This is one way of asking how we can use our staff most efficiently to minimise our operating costs. We shall return to this to solve it shortly.

Example 11.3
Petro UK manufactures agricultural fertilisers: Magi Growmore and Betternate. There are two chemicals, 1 and 2, used in the manufacture of each of these liquid fertilisers. The composition of each of the fertilisers, by volume excluding water, in terms of the chemicals 1 and 2 are given below:

	Chemical 1	**Chemical 2**
Magi Growmore	10%	20%
Betternate	40%	30%

where chemicals 1 and 2 are manufactured on site by Petro UK.

The maximum monthly production capacities for each chemical (in litres per month) and their costs (in £ per litre) are given below:

	Maximum production capacity	**Production costs**
Chemical 1	12 000	7.80
Chemical 2	14 000	9.20

Production costs for manufacturing the fertiliser from the two main chemicals are:

Magi Growmore: £6.50 per hour, taking 30 minutes per litre;
Betternate: £4.20 per hour, taking 45 minutes per litre.

The current market price of the two fertilisers, per litre, are:

Magi Growmore £8.37
Betternate   £12.43

For environmental reasons the Ministry of Agriculture has imposed a restriction on the number of litres of Magi Growmore that the company can manufacture, and set an upper bound of at most 50 000 litres per month.

Formulate this problem as a set of linear constraints and an objective function (a *linear programming problem*).

Solution
Step 1: Determine the variables
Petro UK are manufacturing 2 liquid fertilisers and we are interested in determining the number of litres of each product it should manufacture each month. Using mathematical notation we shall let:

M be the number of litres of Magi Growmore produced each month;
B the number of litres of Betternate produced each month.

Step 2: Determine the objective function
Here we are considering costs of each of the constituent chemicals, and the cost of manufacturing the fertilisers from the chemicals, together with selling prices of the finished fertilisers. If we consider the income from the sale of a product we have revenue, and if we have the production costs for the fertilisers we have the variable costs of producing the fertiliser. Thus subtracting variable costs from selling prices will give us contribution to profit from each of the fertilisers—contribution to profit is profit excluding the overhead or fixed costs of production. We thus need to find the production costs for 1 litre of Magi Growmore and Betternate respectively.

Magi Growmore uses 10% of chemical 1 which cost £7.80 per litre to produce. Thus the cost for Magi Growmore is 10% of £7.80 = £0.78. Similarly Magi Growmore uses 20% of chemical 2 which costs £9.20 per litre and so this increases the costs for Magi Growmore by 20% × £9.20 = £1.84.

The cost of manufacturing 1 litre of fertiliser from the 2 chemicals is £6.50 per hour, with the production time of 30 minutes. This gives us a cost of £3.25.

This gives us a total production cost of £0.78 + £1.84 + £3.25 = £5.87 for 1 litre of Magi Growmore.

Similarly, Betternate uses 40% of chemical 1 which costs £7.80 per litre to produce. Thus the cost for Betternate is 40% of £7.80 = £3.12. Similarly Betternate uses 30% of chemical 2 which costs £9.20 per litre and so this increases the costs by 30% × £9.20 = £2.76. The cost of manufacturing 1 litre of fertiliser from the 2 chemicals is £4.20 per hour, with the production time of 45 minutes. This gives us a cost of £3.15. Hence we have a total production cost of £3.12 + £2.76 + £3.15 = £9.03 for 1 litre of Betternate.

Now if we know the selling price per litre of Magi Growmore is £8.37, then the contribution to profit from Magi Growmore is £8.37 − £5.87 = £2.50 per litre. For M litres this would give us £2.50 × M or 2.5M. Similarly for Betternate the contribution to profit is £12.43 − £9.03 = £3.40 per litre. For B litres this would give us £3.40 × B or 3.4B.

Combining these would give us a total contribution to profit from these 2 fertilisers as:

$$2.5M + 3.4B$$

This is then our objective function: $Z = 2.5M + 3.4B$.

Step 3: Determine the constraints

Here we need to look at the total amount of variables available: here there are totals for chemical 1 and 2, together with an environmental restriction. These will form our 3 constraints together with the obvious ones of: $M \geqslant 0$ and $B \geqslant 0$.

Constraint on chemical 1

There are 12 000 litres of chemical 1 that can be produced each month. This means that 10% of this is used in 1 litre of Magi Growmore and 10% in 1 litre of Betternate. Thus if we make M litres of Magi Growmore we use 10% $\times$ M of chemical 1 and B litres of Betternate will use 40% $\times$ B of chemical 1 and together we can use at most 12 000 litres of chemical 1.

Combining these facts gives us:

10% $\times$ M + 40% $\times$ $B \leqslant 12\,000$.

Tidying this gives us $0.1M + 0.4B \leqslant 12\,000$.

Constraint on chemical 2

There are 14 000 litres of chemical 2 that can be produced each month. This means that 20% of this is used in 1 litre of Magi Growmore and 30% in 1 litre of Betternate. Thus if we make M litres of Magi Growmore we use 20% $\times$ M of chemical 2 and B litres of Betternate will use 30% $\times$ B of chemical 2 and together we can use at most 14 000 litres of chemical 2.

Combining these facts gives us:

20% $\times$ M + 30% $\times$ $B \leqslant 14\,000$.

Tidying this gives us $0.2M + 0.3B \leqslant 14\,000$.

It is more natural to write these two equations without the decimal point, that is by multiplying by 10 throughout both equations to give us:

$M + 4B \leqslant 120\,000$
$2M + 3B \leqslant 140\,000$.

The environmental constraint

The Government has imposed a restriction on the production of at most 50 000 litres of Magi Growmore per month. This gives us a constraint of:

$M \leqslant 50\,000$.

The problem is thus formulated. In the next section we shall consider a graphical solution to optimise this type of problem: that is, finding the right mix of fertilisers to manufacture each month to maximise the contribution of profit.

Notice that all the constraints are linear equations, and the objective function is a linear expression. This type of problem: optimising an objective function subject to a set of linear constraints is the classical linear programming problem.

Exercises 11.1

Formulate the following problems.

11.1.1 The library plans to buy three main types of new books for business computing students at Southern County University from its 1996/97 budget:

- accounting books,
- business information technology (BIT) books,
- law books.

The library needs to determine how best to distribute its budget so that the books with the greatest demand are bought.

The table below shows the average cost of such books together with the 96/97 budget for books of £60 000. In the last two rows of this table is the pattern of average daily readership over the autumn and spring terms 1995/96 session. The average daily readership was measured by taking the daily total number of books on loan each term to business computing students. The total number of books on each of these three topics was 1400 in the autumn term and 1700 in the spring term 95/96.

	Accounting books	BIT books	Law books	Totals
Average costs (£)	16	8	9	60 000
Autumn '95 average daily readership	8	5	2	1400
Spring '96 average daily readership	2	9	4	1700

Set up this problem as a system of linear inequalities, so that the library can determine some guidelines on the number of books of each of these three categories which should be purchased to supply the books which have the greatest demand. Define any variables being used.

11.1.2 A small electronics manufacturer produces three models of calculator: a business calculator, a scientific calculator and a programmable calculator.

Each calculator goes through three departments: wiring, assembly and testing. The labour hours involved for the production of one calculator for each of the three types in each department are given in the table below:

Model	Business calculator	Scientific calculator	Programmable calculator
Wiring	1	4	3
Assembly	3	1	2
Testing	1	1	2

The number of labour hours available per day in each department is: 240 for wiring, 210 for assembly and 120 for testing. Set up this problem as a system of linear inequalities. Define any variables being used.

Solution to the linear programming problem

Graphical solution: 2 variables

Example 11.4
Consider the following problem.

Maximise $Z = 10x - 6y$ by subject to:

$2x + y \leqslant 6$
$5x + 3y \geqslant 4$

$x \geqslant 0$ and $y \geqslant 0$.

Solve this problem using a graphical solution.

Solution
Here our constraints are $2x + y \leqslant 6$ and $5x + 3y \geqslant 4$ and $x \geqslant 0$ and $y \geqslant 0$. As x and y are both positive we are only interested in the first quadrant. The set of all points which satisfy these four inequalities is known as the *feasible region*. Here our objective function is $Z = 10x - 6y$.

The problem is to find all points which are feasible for our objective function, that is, all points lying in the feasible region. Thus the first stage is to sketch the feasible region: here as we have two variables x and y are feasible region is a two-dimensional subset of the plane.

Step 1: Sketching the feasible region
We first change all the inequalities to equalities and so each constraint represents a line and the inequality will be an area to one side of this line.

That is our 4 inequalities:

$2x + y \leqslant 6$
$5x + 3y \geqslant 4$

$x \geqslant 4$ and $y \geqslant 0$

become:

$2x + y = 6$
$5x + 3y = 4$

$x = 0$ and $y = 0$.

Notice that the line $x = 0$ is the y-axis and the line $y = 0$ is the x-axis. Thus the areas $x \geqslant 0$ and $y \geqslant 0$ will be above the x-axis and to the right of the y axis that is the first quadrant.

We now sketch line 1: $2x + y = 6$.

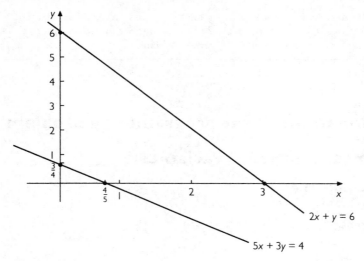

Figure 11.1

Recall that from chapter 5 we used two points to sketch a line.

Here is $x = 0$ then $y = 6$ and we have 1 point $(0, 6)$. Similarly if $y = 0$ then $2x = 6$ and $x = 3$, giving us our second point $(3, 0)$.

Line 2: $5x + 3y = 4$

If $x = 0$ then $y = \frac{3}{4}$ and if $y = 0$ then $5x = 4$ and $x = \frac{4}{5}$, giving us our points $(0, \frac{3}{4})$ and $(\frac{4}{5}, 0)$.

We can now plot these to lines in figure 11.1.

Our feasible region is now bounded by these lines and lying in the first quadrant.

Step 2: Shading the area of the feasible region

We now need to locate the area that satisfies each inequality. This will be one side of the line and we need to use a test point, something easy like the origin (provided the origin does not lie on the given line). Take inequality 1:

$2x + y \leqslant 6$ we put $(0, 0)$ into this to test whether the origin lies in the required area. This in effect means we are saying is this inequality true.

Thus $2 \times 0 + 0 \leqslant 6$: is this true? Here this gives us $0 \leqslant 6$ which is true and so the area required lies to the left of line 1 (containing the origin).

Similarly for inequality 2: $5 \times 0 + 3 \times 0 \geqslant 4$ which is false and so the origin does not lie in the area required by the second inequality, that is the area must be the area to the right of line 2.

The feasible region is the set of points that satisfy *all* the constraints and so is where both areas intersect: where they *both* lie. This will result in the area between the lines shown in figure 11.2.

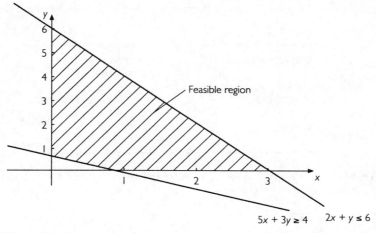

Figure 11.2

Step 3: Locating the extreme points

Where any two constraints meet is called an *extreme point* or a *vertex* of the feasible region. Thus if the graph is plotted using graph paper we can simply read off the extreme points. In this case it is where the 2 lines meet the co-ordinate axes. Labelling these A, B, C and D gives us figure 11.3, where A = $(\frac{4}{5}, 0)$, B = (3, 0), C = (0, 6) and D = $(0, \frac{3}{4})$.

Step 4: Evaluating the objective function

We now evaluate the objective function at each extreme point: there is an important theorem in mathematical analysis which tells us that the optimal solution to a linear programming problem occurs at an extreme point on the

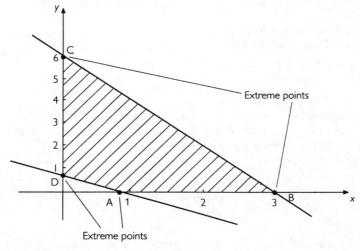

Figure 11.3

convex feasible region. Putting these points into a table we evaluate Z at each vertex:

Extreme point	Objective function: $Z = 10x - 6y$
$A = (\frac{4}{5}, 0)$	$Z = 10 \times \frac{4}{5} - 6 \times 0 = 8$
$B = (3, 0)$	$Z = 10 \times 3 - 6 \times 0 = 30$
$C = (0, 6)$	$Z = 10 \times 0 - 6 \times 6 = -36$
$D = (0, \frac{4}{5})$	$Z = 10 \times 0 - 6 \times \frac{3}{4} = -4\frac{1}{2}$

We can see that the maximum value for Z occurs at B ie when $x = 3$ and $y = 0$. The maximal value of Z is 30.

Example 11.5

Consider the Magi Growmore and Betternate fertiliser problem in example 11.2 above. The constraints were:

$M \geqslant 0$;
$B \geqslant 0$;
$M + 4B \leqslant 120\,000$;
$2M + 3B \leqslant 140\,000$;
$M \leqslant 50\,000$.

The objective function was: the contribution to profit from each fertiliser:

$Z = 2.5M + 3.4B$ which we need to maximise.

Solve this problem graphically.

Solution
Step 1: Choose the axes
Firstly we need to decide which variable we plot on which axis. Here either is suitable, and we choose to plot M on the x-axis and B on the y-axis.

Step 2: Plot the constraints
Turning all the constraints into equalities we will need to plot 3 lines:

Line 1 $M + 4B = 120\,000$;
Line 2 $2M + 3B = 140\,000$;
Line 3 $M = 50\,000$.

Line 3 will be easiest: here M is constant and this will be a vertical line: B can be any value along this line, but M is always 50 000. Thus on our axes we need to choose a suitable scale to plot this. We shall plot in units of a thousand on each axis.

Line 1: Let $M = 0$ and we will have $B = 30\,000$. Similarly letting $B = 0$ will give us $M = 120\,000$ which is likely to go off our scale. It is probably best to choose an additional point. We shall let $M = 40\,000$ and this gives us $B = 20\,000$.

Thus 2 points will be (0, 50 000) and (40 000, 20 000). On our graph these will be: (0, 50) and (40, 20) as we shall be plotting in 1000s.

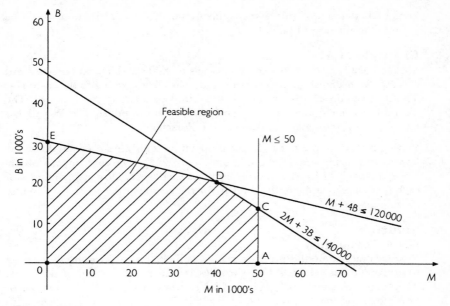

Figure 11.4

Line 2: Let $M = 0$ and we have $B = 46\,666$. If $B = 0$, $M = 70\,000$. Thus we have $(0, 46.666)$ and $70, 0)$.

The 3 lines are plotted in the figure 11.4.

We shade each side of the line required: to the left as all our inequalities are $\leqslant$. The region satisfied by all the constraints is the feasible region: any point lying in this region is a possible solution to the problem of optimising the contribution to profit.

Step 3: Find the extreme points of the feasible region
Here we have labelled them O, A, C, D and E. Their coordinates are in the table below together with an evaluation of $Z = 2.5M + 3.4B$ at each extreme point. For example take $D = (40\,000, 20\,000)$ then $Z = £2.50M + £3.40B = 2.5 \times 40\,000 + 3.4 \times 20\,000 = £168\,000$.

Extreme point	$Z = 2.5M + 3.4B$
O (0, 0)	0
A (50 000, 0)	£125 000
C = (50 000, 13 333)	£170 332
D = (40 000, 20 000)	£168 000
E = (0, 30 000)	£102 000

Step 4: The best solution
We can see that the maximum contribution to profit would occur when the company policy was to produce 50 000 litres of Magi Growmore and 13 333

litres of Betternate. If this is the company policy, its contribution would be £170 332 to the nearest pound.

Example 11.6

Speedo Car Company produce two models of XJTs and Turbo Porsches. All cars are given a finishing coat of paint and polish before going to the customer. The XJT requires 1 labour hour to spray, and $\frac{1}{2}$ a labour hour to polish. The Turbo Porsche requires 1 hour to spray and 1 hour to polish. It costs £250 to finish an XJT and £400 to finish a Turbo Porsche.

During each week the assembly line is operating there are a total of 100 labour hours for spraying and 80 labour hours for polishing. The company has orders placed for 20 XJTs and 30 Turbo Porsches each week. How many models of each type of car can be finished ready for the customer per week to minimise finishing costs?

Solution

Step 1: Formulation

First we must set up this problem as a set of linear inequalities and so we need to determine our variables. Our variables are: the number of car of each type. That is, let x denote the number of XJTs sprayed and y for the number of Porsches sprayed, where $x \geqslant 0$ and $y \geqslant 0$. The aim of this problem is to minimise a cost function: the objective function.

Step 2: The objective function

Here we have the cost of finishing an XJT as £250 giving us a total of $250x$ for finishing x cars. Similarly the cost of finishing a Porsche is £400 and so to finish y cars costs $400y$. This gives us a total cost function of

$$Z = 250x + 400y$$

Step 3: The constraints

Firstly, consider the constraints on the number of hours for spraying. If we spray one XJT and spray one Porsche, we have used a total of 2 hours. Similarly spraying 2 XJTs and 2 Porsches, uses $1 \times 2 + 1 \times 2 = 4$ labour hours. There are a total of 100 hours available. We need to determine how many of each model we should spray to use all the labour hours. Thus we could let x denote the number of XJTs sprayed and y for the number of Porsches sprayed. Thus to spray x XJTs takes $1 \times x$ and y Porsches takes $1 \times y$, and so we have an inequality:

$$1x + 1y \leqslant 100$$

Now consider the constraints on the number of models which can be polished in the available hours. If we polish 1 XJT and 1 Porsche, this will take 1.5 hours. Similarly polishing 2 of each would use $0.5 \times 2 + 1 \times 2$ giving us a total of 3 hours used. Hence using x and y for the hours used on the XJTs and Porsches as above, we have

$$0.5x + 1y \leqslant 80$$

Now the company has two fixed orders: it must satisfy these each week. Thus it must make at least 20 xs and at least 30 ys. This gives us two inequalities:

$$x \geqslant 20 \text{ and } y \geqslant 30$$

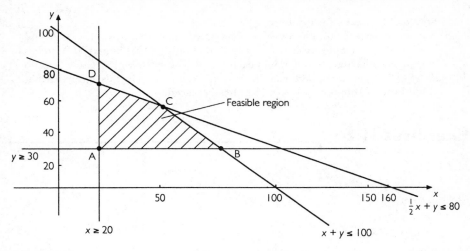

Figure 11.5

Thus we have a feasible region bounded by:

$x + y \leqslant 100$
$0.5x + y \leqslant 80$
$x \geqslant 20$
$y \geqslant 30.$

Step 4: Graphical solution
The feasible region is bounded by the lines:

Line 1: $x + y = 100$
Line 2: $0.5x + y = 80$

and the lines $x = 20$ and $y = 30$.

Two points on line 1 are $(0, 100)$ and $(100, 0)$. For line 2 we have $(160, 0)$ and $(0, 80)$. We now sketch the feasible region shading to the left of both lines. The lines $x = 20$ and $y = 30$ are vertical and horizontal lines, giving us figure 11.5.

The extreme points of the feasible region labelled A, B, C and D are:

A $(20, 30)$, B $(70, 30)$, C $(40, 60)$ and D $(20, 70)$.

Step 5: Evaluating the objective function
We now evaluate the objective function at each extreme point. Putting these points into a table we evaluate Z at each vertex:

Extreme point	Objective function $Z = 250x + 400y$
A = (20, 30)	$Z = 250 \times 20 + 400 \times 30 + 17\,000$
B = (70, 30)	$Z = 250 \times 70 + 400 \times 30 + 29\,500$
C = (40, 60)	$Z = 250 \times 40 + 400 \times 60 + 34\,000$
D = (20, 70)	$Z = 250 \times 20 + 400 \times 70 + 33\,000$

Step 6: The best solution here

We can see that the minimum value for Z occurs at A, that is when $x = 20$ and $y = 30$. Thus the Speedo Car Company should finish 20 XJTs and 30 Porsches within the available labour hours each week. The finishing costs for Speedo are £17 000 per week. We can see that for the company this means that it should stick to supplying the orders already placed.

Exercises 11.2

11.2.1 Maximise $Z = x + 3y$ subject to

$x + 4y \leqslant 20$
$x \leqslant 12$
$x + y \geqslant 1$
x and $y \geqslant 0$.

11.2.2 Formulate and solve this problem graphically:

Great Western Packaging manufacture two types of packaging:
A: a quality packaging for fragile goods;
B: a cheaper packaging for more robust goods.

For 1 unit of production of each product the following resources are required:

Product	Raw materials (kgs)	Machine time (hrs)	Labour time (hrs)
A	3	2	1
B	1	1	1.5

The weekly total availability of these resources is:

raw materials: 180 kgs;
machine hours: 140 hours;
labour hours: 80 hours.

The contribution to profit from product A is £5 per unit, and £6 for each unit of B. (Contribution is the profit excluding overheads). Determine the weekly production of each product to maximise contribution to profit.

11.2.3 Find the graphical solution to example 11.1 above.

11.2.4 In example 11.5 are there any resources unused? This would be called slack in the system (for an inequality constraint of the form $\leqslant$).

11.2.5 In example 11.4 are there any unused resources: Are there any surplus products? (A surplus would occur in a $\geqslant$ inequality.)

11.2.6 In example 11.5, if the company had an order of 35 000 litres of Magi Growmore to supply, would this change the optimal solution? If the environmental constraint were dropped and this order was required would this change the optimal production mix? Are there any changes to the spare resources or surplus litres of each fertiliser?

Solution to the linear programming problem: 2 or more variables

When we have more than two variables it is not possible to draw accurately the feasible region and find the extreme points. In such cases we use an algorithm to evaluate a solution. This is known as the *simplex algorithm*.

Example 11.7

Consider the problem which is to maximise $Z = x_1 + 2x_2 - 3x_3$ subject to

$$x_1 + 2x_2 - 4x_3 \leqslant 400$$
$$2x_1 + x_3 \leqslant 180$$
$$x_1 + x_3 \leqslant 300$$

$x_1, x_2, x_3 \geqslant 0$.

Solve this problem using the simplex algorithm.

Method

Step 1: Write the inequalities as equalities, adding slack variables

The first stage is to remove the inequality signs. To do this take first the inequality:

$$x_1 + 2x_2 - 4x_3 \leqslant 400.$$

This means that LHS is either less than or equal to 400. If we add some positive number to the LHS we can balance the equation. We must add either a positive or zero number and it will change depending on what values x, y and z take. We call such an additional variable a SLACK variable. For equation 1 we add S_1 as the slack variable, and for equation 2 we add S_2, and for equation 3, S_3. This gives us:

$$x_1 + 2x_2 - 4x_3 + S_1 = 400$$
$$2x_1 + x_3 + S_2 = 180$$
$$x_1 + x_3 + S_3 = 300$$

where $S_1, S_2,$ and $S_3 \geqslant 0$.

Step 2: Set up a tableau with the constraints

We now put this system of equations into a special tableau which always has the same format:

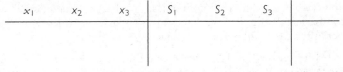

x_1	x_2	x_3	S_1	S_2	S_3	

Each equation becomes a row in the tableau. We put the coefficient for each variable in the given column: that is, all the x_1 coefficients are put in column 1, etc. This gives us:

x_1	x_2	x_3	S_1	S_2	S_3	RHS
1	2	−4	1	0	0	400
2	0	1	0	1	0	180
1	0	1	0	0	1	300

In the final row of the tableau we put the objective function: Here $Z = x_1 + 2x_2 - 3x_3$ can be written:

$Z - x_1 - 2x_2 + 3x_3 = 0$ and this form goes into the tableau.

	x_1	x_2	x_3	S_1	S_2	S_3	RHS
	1	2	−4	1	0	0	400
	2	0	1	0	1	0	180
	1	0	1	0	0	1	300
Z	−1	−2	3	0	0	0	0

Before we proceed to solve this problem we need to use some mathematical notation to locate entries in this tableau.

Mathematical notation

We use a_{ij} to denote the entry in the tableau whose position is in the ith row and jth column. For example a_{32} is the entry in row 3, and the second column, that is 0 here. We shall call the entries in the Z row, c_j, (where j stands for the column) and the entries in the RHS column b_i (where i stands for the row).

Step 3: An initial basic feasible solution
The solution we require is feasible in that it does satisfy all the constraints. We start the solution by putting $x_1 = 0$, $x_2 = 0$ and $x_3 = 0$. If this is the case then we can read off the solution to the slack variables from simply reading across each row, recalling that each row is in fact an equation and equated to the RHS.

Thus $S_1 = 400$, $S_2 = 180$, and $S_3 = 300$.

Thus $x_1 = 0$, $x_2 = 0$ and $x_3 = 0$, and so $Z = 0$, and $S_1 = 400$, $S_2 = 180$, $S_3 = 300$. Notice that the variables which have a solution are in fact the slack variables. If we look at their form we can see that each is in fact a *unit vector*. They are columns which contain one 1 and several 0s. The variables x_1, x_2 and x_3 we have put equal to zero. In fact we call the variables which form a unit vector a basic variable, and any other variables, non-basic. Thus here x_1, x_2 and x_3 are non-basic and the slack variables are the basic variables. We shall record this fact in the first column of our tableau.

What does this solution for the slack variables mean? If we assume that each row represents a constraint on certain types of raw materials then this is saying there is a slack of components for row 1 of 400, that is 400 are unused, and a slack of components of 180 for row 2, and 300 for row 3. Clearly as all the variables x_1, x_2 and x_3 are zero this is not surprising, as we are not using any resources if we are not manufacturing any products. Thus our tableau is:

Tableau I

Basic variable	x_1	x_2	x_3	S_1	S_2	S_3	b_i
S_1	1	2	-4	1	0	0	400
S_2	2	0	1	0	1	0	180
S_3	1	0	1	0	0	1	300
Z	-1	-2	3	0	0	0	0

In order to solve this problem we need to carry out some pivoting: making non-basic variables into basic variables. This is done using Gauss-Jordan elimination.

Tableau manipulation: Gauss-Jordan elimination

Gauss-Jordan elimination is performed using *elementary row operations* to transform this pivotal column into a unit column. The type of operations which constitute elementary operations are:

Elementary row operations
We are allowed to perform any one or combination of the following:

1. Interchange any row with any other row;
2. Multiply any row by a non-zero scalar;
3. Add or subtract R_i to R_j replacing R_j by the resulting row.

Note: firstly, we are *not* allowed to perform any of the above operations on columns, as each column represents a particular distinct variable. To interchange columns would amount to interchanging variables which would be nonsensical. Secondly, we cannot multiply any row by a variable or multiply one row by another, as this would change our linear system into a non-linear system and so introduce new solutions, as well as a new problem.

In fact any of the above operations are precisely what would be used if we were solving any number of simultaneous (linear) equations without appealing to the linear algebra. They simply amount to adding one row of the table to another, that is, one equation to another or multiplying one equation through by a constant.

We are now ready to apply the simplex algorithm which uses Gauss-Jordan elimination to solve this problem.

Simplex algorithm

Step 1
Apply the optimality test: are all the c_j (the entries in the Z row) positive?

If no, go to step 2. If yes, stop and read off solution from the tableau.

Step 2
Choose pivotal column—the column with the smallest Z value. This column becomes the new basic variable in this iteration. Call the entries in this column of the tableau a_{ip} where p stands for pivotal column.

Step 3

Choose a pivotal row—the minimum of $\dfrac{b_i}{a_{ip}}$ (where a_{ip} is chosen as the non-negative and non-zero entries in the pivotal column).

This deletes a slack variable replacing it with the basic variable of the pivotal row.

This element min $\dfrac{b_i}{a_{ip}}$ is now called the pivotal element.

Step 4

Use Gauss-Jordan elimination (explained below) to get a 1 in the pivotal element position and zeros elsewhere in the pivotal column (that is transform this pivotal column into a unit vector).

Step 5

Return to step 1.

Application of the simplex algorithm (continuation of example 11.6)

We now use the simplex algorithm to solve the above problem.

Step 1: Optimality test

Are all the c_j positive? No, only c_3 is positive. Go to step 2 then.

Step 2: Choose the pivotal column

Take the smallest Z value: here this is -2, that is c_2. (Note -2 is smaller than -1). Thus the second column is our pivotal column. The a_{ip} here is then

$$\begin{array}{r} 2 \\ 0 \\ 0 \\ -2 \end{array}$$

Step 3: Choose a pivotal row

We need to calculate the $\dfrac{b_i}{a_{ip}}$ where a_{ip} is chosen as the non-negative and non-zero entries in the pivotal column. We choose the minimum of

from row 1 $\dfrac{400}{2}$ or

from row 2 $\dfrac{180}{0}$ or

from row 3 $\dfrac{300}{0}$

As the latter two values are infinite, we must take the first value as the minimum which means we have chosen the first row as our pivotal row. In fact we can see that the entries a_{2p} and a_{3p} are zero; we have no choice but must take the entry in the first row, the a_{1p} entry, namely 2.

Thus the pivotal row is the first row. This element 2 is called the pivotal element. This means we delete a slack variable in row 1 (S_1) and replacing it with the basic variable of the pivotal row, which is x_2.

Step 4: Gauss-Jordan elimination

We use Gauss-Jordan elimination to make column 2 into

1
0
0
0

form, that is a unit vector. Row 1 is the pivotal row and we must make the pivotal element 2 into a 1. We do this by dividing row 1 by 2. This gives us our first row operation:

$$R_1 \rightarrow \frac{R_1}{2}$$

Now we can see that the entries in the 2nd column are already zero except for the entry in the final row (Zs row). To make this zero using the pivotal element we must perform the addition: $-2 + 2$. Thus we must add 2 × the pivotal element from row 4. In fact we need to perform this calculation for the whole of row 4. This gives us our final row operation:

$$R_4 \rightarrow R_4 + 2R_1$$

This gives us:

Tableau 2

Basic variable	x_1	x_2	x_3	S_1	S_2	S_3	b_i
x_2	1/2	1	−2	1/2	0	0	200
S_2	2	0	1	0	1	0	180
S_3	1	0	1	0	0	1	300
Z	0	0	−1	1	0	0	400

Here our basic variables are x_2, S_2 and S_3 (as these are the unit vectors and so have the solution, and all the non-basic variables are put to zero).

Thus $x_1 = 0$, $x_3 = 0$ and $S_1 = 0$.

Then reading across each line we have $x_2 = 200$, $S_2 = 180$, and $S_3 = 300$.

This means we should manufacture 200 of product x_2, and we have a slack (unused capacity) of 180 units of raw material 2, and 300 for raw material 3.

How do we read off the value for Z? We understand this to be:

$Z + 0x_1 + 0x_2 + x_3 + S_1 = 400$

Thus $Z = 400$

(The variables x_3 and S_1 in this row can be ignored here as we have equated them to zero.)

We can check this value of Z using $Z = x_1 + 2x_2 - 3x_3$ and the values found at this iteration. This would give: $Z = 0 + 2 \times 200 - 0 = 400$ as expected.

We now apply the simplex algorithm again.

Optimality test: no not all the c_j are positive.

The pivotal column will be column 3: this corresponds to replacing the basic variable in equation 3 (S_3) by x_3. We now evaluate the b_i/a_{ip}.

We choose the minimum of

From row 1 $\frac{200}{-2}$ or

from row 2 $\frac{180}{1}$ or

from row 3 $\frac{300}{1}$

We ignore the negative value (in fact this corresponds to ensuring that the b_i are always positive) and the minimum will be 180, which gives us row 2 as the pivotal row. The element 1 is called the pivotal element.

We now use Gauss-Jordan elimination to make column 3 into:

0

1

0

0

form, that is a unit vector. Row 2 is the pivotal row and this is unchanged as it is already a 1.

Now we need to make the entries in the 3rd column into a zero except for the 1 in the position a_{23} (the pivotal element).

Take row 1: the entry in the pivotal column is -2 and we need to add something to this to get 0. This will be 2. We can get a 2 by multiplying the pivotal element by 2 and adding this to the -2. This is done for the whole row 1 giving us a row operation of:

$$R_1 \rightarrow R_1 + 2R_2$$

Similarly we subtract the pivotal row from row 3 to get a zero entry in this position giving us:

$$R_3 \rightarrow R_3 - R_2$$

Finally the same argument holds for row 4: $R_4 \rightarrow R_4 + R_2$

Notice that in all these row operations we are using row 2 to pivot, this is to get zeros in the other entries: it is precisely because it is chosen as the pivotal row that we do this.

This gives us:

Tableau 3

Basic variable	x_1	x_2	x_3	S_1	S_2	S_3	b_i
x_2	4.5	1	0	1/2	2	0	560
x_3	2	0	1	0	1	0	180
S_3	-1	0	0	0	-1	1	120
Z	2	0	0	1	1	0	580

Here our basic variables are x_2, x_3 and S_3 (as these are the unit vectors and so these have the solution, and all the non-basic variables are put to zero).

Thus $x_1 = 0$, $S_1 = 0$ and $S_2 = 0$.

Then reading across each line we have $x_2 = 560$, $x_3 = 180$, and $S_3 = 120$.

This means we should manufacture 560 of product x_2, and 180 of product x_3 but no product x_1. We have a slack (unused capacity) of 120 units of raw material 3.

We now apply the simplex algorithm again.

Optimality test: are all the c_j positive?

Yes, and so the algorithm draws to a halt.

How do we read off the final row of the table? As before this is read as

$Z + 2x_1 + S_1 + S_2 = 580$

As before we can check this value of Z using the objective function and the values for x_1, x_2 and x_3 found at this iteration.

(The variables x_1, S_1 and S_2 in this row can be ignored here when we are evaluating the maximal value of Z as we have equated them to zero.) In fact the appearance of these variables in the objective function does have a meaning.

Firstly the negative x_1: $-2x_1$ (found by taking $2x_i$ to RHS).

This means that for every unit of product x_1 made, this yields a loss of $2x_1$ to the objective function: in commercial terms, manufacturing x_1 is not really an economically viable decision, although if there is a market for the goods, a manufacturer might be prepared to carry the loss if other profits were assured.

Shadow prices

Re-arrange the final row for Z into the form:

$Z = -S_1 - S_2 + 580$

In fact the values for S_1 and S_2 appearing in this final row of the tableau are known as the *shadow prices* corresponding to the resources for x_1 and x_2. Shadow price: for x_1 (S_1) = 1 and for x_2 (S_2) = 1.

Here putting $S_1 = 1$ (its shadow price) would correspond to reducing the value of Z. Similarly for S_2. In fact whenever shadow prices are negative when on the RHS of the objective equation, this corresponds to a decrease in the objective function. If they were negative, it would correspond to an increase. For example, if $Z = S_1 + S_2 + 580$, and $S_1 = 1$ and $S_2 = 1$ then this means that we should consider paying up to £1 for an extra unit of resource x_1 and x_2. Thus if we do, the value of Z will rise by this amount extra.

(If S_3 were also present this would be a shadow price for x_3.)

Additional comments

1: The primal and dual

The above form of the algorithm is used for solving the maximal problem. If we solve the maximum problem, this is known as the *primal* problem. Corresponding to a primal problem is a dual problem, which is a minimal problem (not necessarily of the same format as the maximal problem). The solution to the dual problem can be read off from the shadow prices. The corresponding minimal value for Z would be minus the maximal value.

2: Using $\geqslant$ inequalities, artificial variables

What happens is one of the inequalities is in fact a greater than or equal to? that is suppose equation 3 above was in fact

$$x_1 \quad + \quad x_3 \qquad\qquad \geqslant 300$$

The RHS is here less than or equal to the left and so to balance the equation we need to add a positive variable to the RHS, say S_3. This would give us:

$$x_1 \quad + \quad x_3 \qquad\qquad = 300 + S_3.$$

If we write all three equations in a similar format it makes sense to put all the slacks on the same side, and so we will re-arrange equation 3 to get:

$$x_1 \quad + \quad x_3 \qquad\qquad - S_3 = 300.$$

Thus our system of constraints has become the three equations:

$$
\begin{aligned}
x_1 + 2x_2 - 4x_3 + S_1 \qquad\qquad &= 400 \\
2x_1 \qquad + \quad x_3 \quad + S_2 \qquad &= 180 \\
x_1 \qquad + \quad x_3 \qquad - S_3 &= 300
\end{aligned}
$$

where S_1, S_2, and $S_3 \geqslant 0$.

S_3 could be called a *surplus* variable.

3: Initial basic feasibility solution

What does this solution for the slack variables mean? As before we assume that each row represents a constraint on certain types of raw materials; this is saying there is a slack of components for row 1 of 400, that is 400 are unused, and a slack of components of 180 for row 2. Clearly as all the variables x_1, x_2 and x_3 are zero this is not surprising.

This latter solution of $S_3 = -400$ is in fact not feasible as we started off by saying that the slack variables were all positive. Thus to correct this we can add an artificial variable to equation 3, and so equation 3 is re-written:

$$x_1 + x_3 - S_3 + A = 400$$

and so $A = -400$, and $S_3 = 0$. We should now continue to use A in our tableau, although it is formally correct to do so using an extra column. As A has no meaning in the final solution, it would not be terribly wrong to omit it. An artificial variable is exactly as its name suggests: it is simply to form an initial basic feasible solution. If there are a number of resources unused from a $\geqslant$ constraint, this is called a surplus.

4: Computer solution

There are many computer applications for solving linear programming problems. These are extremely useful as they contain additional information on post-optimality analysis: sensitivity analysis. This involves looking at the coefficients c_j and b_i and seeing how sensitive to change the optimal solution is for small changes in c_j and b_i. In the commercial world this is extremely useful to know as an organisation can consider increasing resources/staff/raw materials or increasing profit margins and consider how this effects profits/costs, etc.

Exercises 11.3

11.3.1 Repeat example 11.7 using the artificial variable outlined above. What do you notice?

11.3.2 Read off the results from the final tableau:

	x_1	x_2	x_3	x_4	S_1	S_2	S_3	S_4	b_i
	1	0	0	−3	3	0	7	2	25
	0	1	0	2	1	0	−4	−1	425
	0	0	1	5					150
	0	0	0	−1	−2	1	5	−4	25
Z	0	0	0	−45	−3	0	−60	−17	−48 450

Interpret the shadow prices, and slack or surpluses for each variable. What does the value of −£45 mean for x_4 (sometimes called a reduced cost)?

11.3.3 Use the simplex algorithm to solve the following:

(i) Maximise $x_1 + 3x_2$ subject to

$$x_1 + x_2 \geqslant 5$$
$$x_1 - x_2 \leqslant 10$$
$$x_1 - 2x_2 \leqslant 0$$

with $x_1 \geqslant 0$ and $x_2 \geqslant 0$

(ii) Maximise $5x + 6y$ subject to

$$x + y \leqslant 5$$
$$x - y \leqslant 10$$
$$x \geqslant y$$

with $x \geqslant 0$ and $y \geqslant 0$

(iii) Maximise $x_1 + 2x_2 + x_3$ subject to:

$$x_1 \leqslant 20$$
$$x_2 \leqslant 20$$
$$x_3 \leqslant 20$$
$$x_1 + x_2 + x_3 \leqslant 35 \text{ and}$$
$$x_1 \geqslant 0, x_2 \geqslant 0, x_3 \geqslant 0.$$

(iv) Solve examples 11.4 and 11.6 using the simplex algorithm. Interpret the shadow prices and determine if there is any unused capacity.

12 Project planning decisions—what's the best time/cost?

Objectives

- Be able to draw a network to represent a project;
- Be able to calculate the cost and duration of a project;
- Be able to determine which activities are critical to the on-time completion of this project;
- Determine whether or not a project duration can be reduced;
- Be able to reduce the project time where appropriate;
- Be able to draw and interpret a Gantt chart.

Scenario

A developer has just placed a bid for an old hospital site, subject to planning permission, to build a superstore. Provided the local planning department accept the architectural plans for the redevelopment of this site the sale of land will be completed.

There are many activities involved in the preparation for the new superstore. These include demolishing the former building, clearing the site, commissioning architectural drawings, preparing planning submission, submitting plans to contractors for tenure, and finally selecting the contractor and constructing the building. Once the building has been completed the developer will lease the building to a supermarket chain.

Introduction to critical path analysis

This is a tool for organising and planning large scale projects which consist of a list of smaller tasks that need to be completed at various stages in order for the project to progress. Such projects might be for example:

- the construction of a transport link (such as the M11, the Channel Tunnel, the Jubilee Line extension);
- preparing a dinner party (or organising a wedding);
- launching a new product (or launching an election campaign).

Each of these projects involves a large number of activities, which all need to be completed in a certain order before the whole project is finished. Some activities can be performed simultaneously, whilst others can only be tackled once other activities have finished. If you are planning a building, clearly the plastering of the internal walls can be undertaken at the same time as the grounds are landscaped. However, the walls cannot be built until the foundations are laid, and so on. Here we can see a natural precedence relation between activities, and as each activity can only be completed in a certain time scale, the project manager faces the dilemma of carrying out all the activities in the best time and at reasonable cost so that the project completes on time and meets the budget constraints. We can see that certain activities are *critical* to the on-time completion of the project; for example, if you are planning a dinner party and spend all your time setting the table and forget to put the main dish in the oven, the dinner will be late! This also means that other activities have slack time or *float* available, such as laying the table. We shall use a network technique known as Critical Path Analysis (CPA) to enable us to look at the order of the activities in a project and to plan the time scale involved. (CPA can be thought of as an application of graph theory.) In fact large scale projects would make use of a computerised tool such as the PC-based Microsoft project.

Other examples include

- taking a HND or a BA programme;
- developing a management information system.

Background

Project planning techniques were first developed during the Second World War for military purposes. In the late 50s the US Navy set up a team to devise a method for controlling the planning of complex projects. The outcome was the network technique called PERT (Programme Evaluation and Review Technique). This technique was used to plan and develop the Polaris missile and is said to have reduced the development time by two years. In the UK the electricity company CEGB (Central Electricity Generating Board) also developed this method to reduce the overhaul time at a power station. Today there are many variations of this method handling factors such as time, cost, resources, probabilities, etc. For example:

CPP	Critical Path Planning
CPA	Critical Path Analysis
CPS	Critical Path Scheduling
CPM	Critical Path Method
PERT,PERT/COST	Programme Evaluation and Review Technique

Such techniques have been applied to almost every commercial and industrial activity: accountancy & finance, construction, the study of organisations (for example managing change), as well as the original military uses.

The main objectives of the critical path method are:

1. to locate the critical activities;
2. to allocate the timing of other activities to obtain the most efficient use of labour and resources;
3. to consider ways of reducing the total project time by speeding up the activities on the critical path, while monitoring the overall project to ensure that the critical activities remain critical or, if there are changes, to act on this.

Example 12.1

A developer has just placed a bid for an old hospital site, subject to planning permission, to build a superstore. Provided the local planning department accept the architectural plans for the redevelopment of this site the sale of land will be completed. Below is a list of activities for this work together with their prerequisites.

Activity	Prerequisite
A Demolishing the former building	F, H
B Clearing the site	A
C Commissioning architectural drawings	None
D Preparing planning submission	C
E Submitting plans to contractors for tenure	C
F Selecting the contractor	E
G Obtaining planning permission	C, D
H Completing the purchase	G
I Construction of the building	B
J Leasing the building to a supermarket chain	I

We shall proceed to analyse this project, firstly by representing the project as a network graph which will indicate the order in which the various activities should be executed.

Representing a project: network graphs

We represent the project as a digraph (a directed graph)—the so called project network. This is a type of graph with nodes connected by arrows. To visualise this, think of a map with the major towns (nodes) linked by motorways and primary routes (some of which will be one-way roads), that is, arrows. Generally the arrow (or edge) represents the activity (demolishing the building) whilst the node (or vertex) represents an event or a particular point in the project (the building is demolished). We use a node to represent the start of the project and a node for the finish. As the length of the arrow has no meaning, there is no scale to the drawing. We say that an event is completed if all activities directed into it have been completely executed. This type of representation is often referred to as activity between the nodes.

Drawing the network

Step 1: Draw the start node and starting activities

Drawing a node to depict the start node we obtain figure 12.1. We then look at the table to see which activities we can commence with. These will be the activities with no prerequisites—they can begin because it is not necessary to wait for any other activity to

Start ◯

Figure 12.1

be completed. Here we can see that activity C: commissioning architectural drawings, has no pre-requisite and so this activity can commence the project. We represent this by drawing an arrow labelled C from the start node. Our network is drawn from the left of the page horizontally to the right of the page, as in figure 12.2.

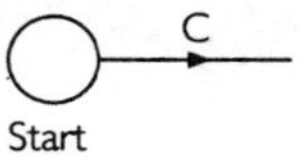

Figure 12.2

Step 2: Drawing the next level of activities

We now look at the table of activities to see which activities require the completion of C before they can commence. This will give us:

D   Preparing planning submission;
E   Submitting plans to contractors for tenure.

Once the event 'the architectural plans' have been drawn up, D and E can commence. We depict this by drawing a node at the end of the arrow for C to show this activity is complete and the next activities can begin: D and E here. We thus draw two arrows from the node after C and label them D and E (figure 12.3).

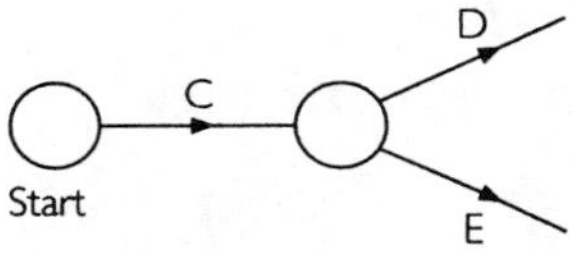

Figure 12.3

We also see that activity G, obtain planning permission, has C and D as prerequisites. At this stage we cannot add G unless both C and D have been completed. Thus we can see we shall add G after the event 'planning submission prepared' is complete. In fact this tells us that from the list of prerequisites, C is superfluous as a prerequisite for G as D can only commence once C has been completed. We call C *redundant* from the list of prerequisites for G. This gives us figure 12.4.

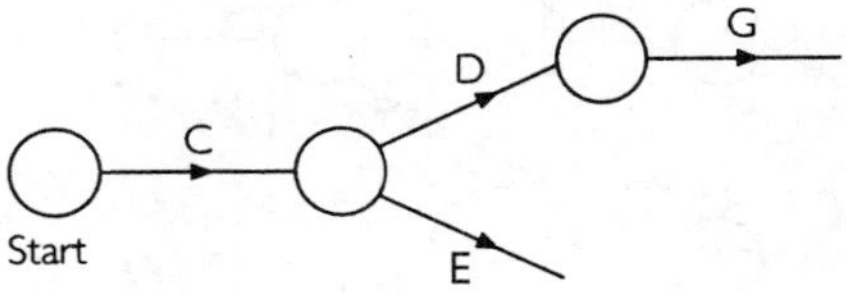

Figure 12.4

Step 3: Completing the network

We continue to add arrows for each of the remaining activities, in the order depending on the completion of the necessary prerequisites. To this end we next add H after G. Notice that as E has been completed we can also add F to the network. In fact from this we can see that several activities can be executed simultaneously: here DG and H (planning permission and purchase) can be carried out whilst E and F (finding the contractor) are also being executed. This gives us figure 12.5.

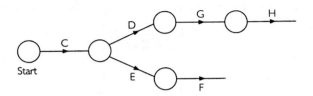

Figure 12.5

Once F and H are through, we can begin demolition and site clearance. This means we need a node to indicate F and H are finished, and as we need them both finished before A can commence we will represent this using a node with F and H feeding into the node and A coming out of the node. This gives us figure 12.6.

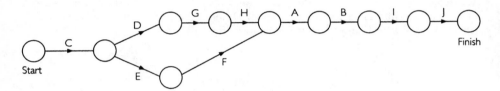

Figure 12.6

Finally we add I, J and the finish node to indicate that all activities required for the project are completed.

Step 4: Number the nodes
We number the nodes sequentially, starting at 1 for the start node, numbering from left to right 2, 3, 4, etc. for the 2nd, 3rd, etc. node added. The nodes are numbered sequentially simply to allow us to discuss position within the network (in fact there are numbering algorithms—see the summary below). This gives us figure 12.7.

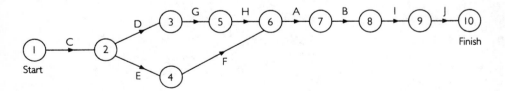

Figure 12.7

Step 5: Head and tail events
If we look at activity C, node 2 is known as its *head event*, and node 1 is known as its *tail event*. Similarly node 2 is the tail event for activities D and E, and nodes 3 and 4 are the head events for D and E respectively.

Step 6: Understanding the network
There are a total of 10 nodes and we can see that the arrows of the graph are all focused from the start towards the finish: this indicates that the network is concerned with the order of activities. All activities going into a node must be completed before any activity coming out of a node can commence.

Graph-theoretic language

Formally we would say that the network is constructed by taking each activity and representing it by an arrow $(i\,j)$ where i and j are nodes. Taking the graph above we can see H is represented by arrow (5,6) and F is represented by (4,6). We can see that the only activities to immediately precede A (6,7) are incident at node 6. Thus the network is formed by arranging the arrows so that the only activities which immediately precede an activity represented by arrow (i,j) are incident at node j for any i.

The first node is called the *start* (here the number of arrows going into the node is zero and we say it has in-degree $= 0$) and the last node is called the *finish* (here we say the number of arrows going out of the node are 0, or out-degree $= 0$).

There is another way of representing projects known as activity on the nodes, which we shall not discuss. There are rules for the construction of a network which we shall outline and discuss using an example.

In general for each network we require:

- a list of each activity in the project with an associated time (hours/weeks);
- a list of the immediate pre-requisite activities for each activity.

Example 12.2: Construction of a new home
The following schedule is used by a major construction company for the building of a residential property.

Activity	Prerequisites
Clear land	None
Lay foundations	Clear land
Build walls	Lay foundations
Electrical wiring	Build walls
Plastering	Wiring, Roof
Landscaping	Lay foundations
Interior work	Plastering, Roof
Roof	Build walls

Draw a network to represent the project

Solution
Firstly notice that we can label each of the activities by a letter and these will be written on the arrows of our network. Observe: the interior work requires the plastering and roofing as prerequisites. The roofing, however, is also an activity required before the plastering. It is thus redundant to list roofing as a prerequisite for the interior work, so we shall delete this.

The list of activities and prerequisites can thus be rewritten as:

Activity	Prerequisites
A	None
B	A
C	B
D	C
E	D,H
F	B
G	E
H	C

Step 1: Draw the start node and starting activities

Drawing a node to the start node, we have A as the first activity as it has no prerequisites. After A is completed, we can commence B. Then C and F follow after B, as shown in figure 12.8.

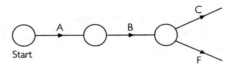

Figure 12.8

Step 2: Drawing the next level of activities

We now look at the table of activities to see which activities require the completion of C and F before they can commence. This shows us that D and H follow after C but there are no activities which require F as a prerequisite so for the moment we shall leave this branch open (see figure 12.9).

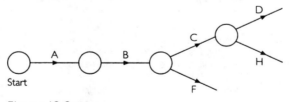

Figure 12.9

Step 3: Completing the drawing

We continue to add arrows for each of the remaining activities, in the order depending on the completion of the necessary prerequisites. To this end we next add E. To do this we see that both D and H must be completed before E commences and so we need one event to signify that D and H are completed. Thus we have figure 12.10.

We call D and H *parallel activities* and in fact we must modify this network to clarify the precedence relationship between D and H. We shall need to use a

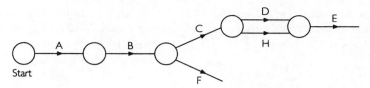

Figure 12.10

dummy activity, as we see later. Activity G follows after E. There are no more activities to add to this network as the list is exhausted, and so once F and G are completed the project is completed. Thus the arrows for F and G both go into the finish node.

Finally we number the nodes sequentially which gives us figure 12.11.

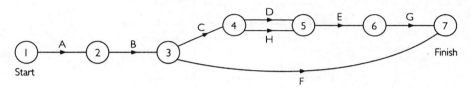

Figure 12.11

Step 4: Using a dummy activity

Note that there are two parallel arrows between nodes 4 and 5. We shall generally not use this but insert a dummy activity. We call activities D and H parallel, meaning that the order between them is unclear: we do not know which precedes E first. The aim of the network is to show precedence and we can see that with parallel activities, this fails. To correct this we disconnect either D or H from node 5 and insert a new event (node) at the end of the disconnected one. We then insert a dummy arrow—a dashed arrow to connect the dummy event to node 5. We now renumber the nodes, which gives us figure 12.12.

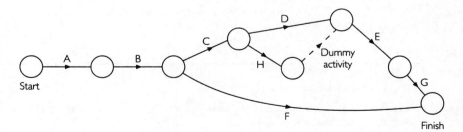

Figure 12.12

This would be interpreted as saying that H waits for D to finish before E can commence and so we have established a definitive order between D and H.

Here we could equally have inserted a dummy after D. In fact when we have times allocated to our nodes, we can insert the dummy activity more clearly and it will be either after D or H, but not usually both, depending on the time each takes to complete.

Exercise 12.1

12.1.1 Draw the network to represent the following project:

Activity	Prerequisite
A	NONE
B	A
C	A
D	A
E	B,C
F	D
G	E,F

12.1.2 Before launching a new product a manufacturer has to undertake the following activities:

Activity	Description	Predecessor
A	Design new product	None
B	Undertake review of current market	None
C	Build new prototype	A
D	Market testing of new product	C
E	Cost estimates and sales forecasting	C,D
F	Develop advertising for new product	A
G	Modify prototype	D
H	Launch new product	G

Draw a network to represent this project

12.1.3 A student must complete units in various areas in order to obtain a HND in Computing. He/she must study:

Computing Maths (CM)
Management Information Systems (MIS)
Modula-2
C++
Databases (DB).

The following table shows the prerequisites:

Activity	Prerequisite
CM1	None
CM2	CM1
Mod-2	None
DB1	CM1
DB2	DB1,CM2
DB3	DB2
C++	Mod-2,CM1
MIS	DB3,CM2,Mod-2

Draw the network to represent this project, indicating why you need any dummy activities.

Summary for drawing a network: some do's and don'ts

1 A network has only one start and one finish node.
2 Every activity must have one preceding event (tail) and one succeeding event (head). Note that many activities may use the same tail event (figure 12.13).

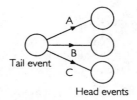

Figure 12.13

Many activities may use the same head event (figure 12.14).

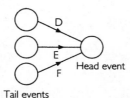

Figure 12.14

An activity cannot share the same tail event and the same head event (instead we use a dummy to establish order), see figure 12.15 which is correctly drawn as figure 12.16.

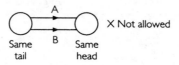

Figure 12.15

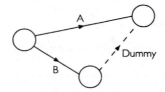

Figure 12.16

3 A network cannot contain a circuit (figure 12.17).

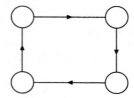

Figure 12.17

Why? From the figure it is clear that the network never reaches the finish node and the start is none too clear. In terms of the project it means that it would go on indefinitely.

As there are no circuits the events can be numbered sequentially 1,2, ... , such that for any activity (i,j) $i < j$.

4 Don't use a dangler—figure 12.18.

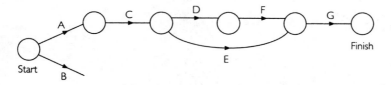

Figure 12.18

Here B is disconnected at one end—it is called a *dangler*. As such it must be completed if the project is to finish and so it is most likely connected to the finish node.

5 Numbering algorithm

Step 1   Start event = 1

Step 2   Give the next number to the unnumbered event whose predecessor events are each already completed (exists as there are no circuits).

Repeat step 2 until all the events are numbered. The finish event is the highest number.

Allocating times and costs

Example 12.3

Consider example 12.2 above with the following times and costs allocated:

Activity	Time (weeks)	Prerequisites	Normal cost
A	2	None	£2000
B	4	A	£3000
C	6	B	£4000
D	3	C	£1000
E	3	D,H	£1500
F	4	B	£1000
G	5	E	£5000
H	2	C	£2500

Find the project duration and total cost.

Solution

Step 1: Project cost

The total cost of the project is the sum of all the costs for each activity, since the project is deemed complete when all activities have been completed.

This gives us:

Project cost = Sum of the costs of all activities (at normal costs)
$$= £2000 + £3000 + £4000 + \ldots + £2500$$
$$= £20\,000.$$

Step 2: Inserting new nodes

Redraw the above network for example 12.2 using the following node with three sectors: Earliest Starting Time (EST), Latest Starting Time (LST) and node number (see figure 12.19).

Insert the numbers for each of the nodes in the bottom sector as in example 12.2. Definition: here we define the EST to be the soonest the next activity can begin. The LST is the latest time at which the preceding activity can finish without increasing the project duration. This will be clearer when we have inserted these times onto our network.

On each arrow on the network write the number of weeks this activity takes.

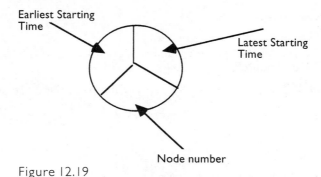

Earliest Starting Time

Latest Starting Time

Node number

Figure 12.19

Step 3: Calculating the ESTs

To calculate the ESTs we put 0 in the first node. By definition this is saying that the earliest starting time for the next activity (A) is 0 weeks, i.e. A is at the start of the project. We now move to node 2 and here insert the previous node's EST, plus the duration of the activity which is incident at node 2, i.e. this is 0 + A's duration, which gives a total EST of 2 in node 2. This means that the EST for B is 2 weeks after the start of the project. For node 3 we add the previous EST (2) plus the duration for B, giving an EST of 6. We continue in this way working in the direction of the arrows, adding the next value on an arrow together with the tail's EST to form the EST of the head node. If two or more routes lead to the same node, the maximum value is inserted in the EST sector. For example for node 6 we have a choice of 12 + 3 or 14 + 0; the maximum, being 15, is chosen. We select the maximum because we need to be certain that all preceding activities are completed before the subsequent activity can commence. Here this means that even though activity H is finished by the end of the 14th week, E cannot begin until D is finished which takes an extra week. Thus E cannot commence until both D and H are completed and so E's EST is 15 weeks.

Note than any dummy activity is given a zero duration. We can also see from this that the dummy activity is doing exactly as we required: it tells us the correct order between D and H. If at this stage H's EST was greater than the EST for node 4 plus D's duration then we would need to interchange D and H on the network (see step 4 in example 12.2). We place the dummy activity on H precisely because it is shorter than D.

The value in the finish node EST is the total time for the project. This gives us figure 12.20. Here the project duration is 23 weeks.

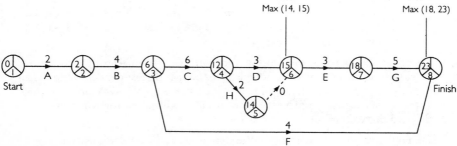

Figure 12.20

Step 4: Calculating the LSTs

For the latest starting times, we work backwards through the network (in the opposite direction of the arrow) from the finish node LST sector, placing the project duration as the finish node LST and subtracting the activity duration at each stage. For example, consider node 5. Here the LST is 15 weeks. This is telling us that the latest time activity H can finish is week 15—any later and it will delay the completion of the project. If two or more routes lead to the same node, we take the minimum value as the LST. To see this take node 4; here we have a choice of 12 weeks (from node 6) and 13 weeks from node 5. This is telling us the latest time activity C can finish is either 12 or 13 weeks. It is, however, the minimum value of 12 we choose because if C finishes later than 12 weeks the project will overrun. Eventually this will give us a LST of 0 at the start node.

This would give us figure 12.21.

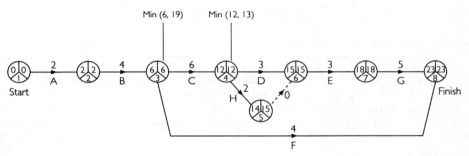

Figure 12.21

Exercises 12.2

12.2.1 Draw the network for the following project.

Activity	Duration	Previous activity
A	13	None
B	3	A
C	5	A
D	4	B
E	2	B
F	5	B
G	2	C
H	3	D
I	1	E, F
J	2	I
K	1	G, H
L	3	K

12.2.2 On April 1st of each year, Sagesales Ltd begins the task of preparing budgets for the coming year. The various stages in the budgeting process have been identified as follows:

Activity	Prerequisite	Time (days)
A Estimate total payroll	None	3
B Develop a market forecast	None	10
C Estimate selling prices	None	3
D Estimate client orders	B	4
E Prepare sales (revenue) budget	C,D	2
F Prepare marketing budget	A,B,D	3
G Prepare production quantities	D	6
H Prepare overhead budget	A	4
I Prepare transport budget	A,D	5
J Prepare materials budget	G	4
K Prepare plant and equipment budget	G	5
L Produce overall profit forecast	E,F,I,J,K	5
M Prepare final report	L	3

Draw a network to represent this set of tasks, calculating the EST and LST. If the budgeting team work a 5-day week, what date is it likely that the final report will be ready for the directors?

Backward and forward pass

Moving through the network from the start towards the finish, so calculating the ESTs—the earliest time a succeeding activity can start—is termed making a *forward pass* through the network. Similarly, calculating the LSTs—the latest possible time at which the preceding activity can finish without increasing the duration of the project—and moving through the network from the finish backwards towards the start is termed making a *backward pass* through the network.

Critical paths

Are there certain activities which ought not to be delayed? Can other activities be late without affecting the overall times to complete the project? There questions are answered within the framework of a critical path.

A simple definition of a *critical path* is a chain of activities through the network from the starting node to the finishing node where each node along this path has equal ESTs and LSTs. This is in fact sometimes not quite sufficient and we shall need to use a tighter definition, as below. Each activity on the critical path is critical to the on-time completion of the project.

In example 12.3 the critical path was: A, B, C, D, E and G. To confirm this we sum the duration of these activities and this should give us the project duration which was 23 weeks. Here we have $2 + 4 + 6 + 3 + 3 + 5 = 23$. We can also see an alternative definition of a critical path: it is the longest path from the start to finish through the network. To see this consider other paths through the network:

A, B, F which takes $2 + 4 + 4 = 10$ weeks

or

A, B, C, H, (Dummy), E and G which is $2 + 4 + 6 + 2 + 0 + 3 + 5 = 22$ weeks.

From this we can see that the longest path is 23 weeks.

A network could have several critical paths, but they would all need to be the same length (the project duration). For simple networks, the critical path is easily found by inspection. Any delays in one of these activities on the critical path would lead to a delay in the project. There could be a delay of one time period elsewhere in the project without affecting the total time of the project. For example, if H was delayed until week 15, this would not delay the project. Similarly we can see that F can start after week 6 but does not need to be completed until the end of the project, week 23. Such activities are non-critical and have spare time or *float* available. We shall look at this float in the following section.

Float or slack time in the project

We shall use one type of float—total float— which is concerned with the slack time in the overall project.

For any activity,

total float = LST(head) − EST(tail) − activity duration
= amount of time a path of activities could be delayed without delaying the overall project. We shall use float unqualified to mean total float.

Definition: a chain of activities from the start node to the finish node is called a critical path when the total float along the path is zero. This is exactly what we mean by critical: there is no slack time. The float at each critical activity is zero.

Non-critical activities have spare time or float available.

Example 12.4
Calculate a table of total floats for each activity in example 12.3.

Solution
From the network shown in figure 12.21 we can see the ESTs and LSTs for each head and tail of an activity, which are given in the table below:

Activity	Time (weeks)	LST(head)	EST(tail)	Total float = LST(head) − EST(tail) − activity duration
A	2	2	0	0
B	4	6	2	0
C	6	12	6	0
D	3	15	12	0
E	3	18	15	0
F	4	23	6	13
G	5	23	18	0
H	2	15	12	1

This confirms that A, B, C, D, E and G are critical activities and F and H have some spare time available.

Exercise 12.3

Calculate a table of floats for the questions in exercises 12.2. What is the project duration and what is the critical path for each question?

Reduction in project time

If we are to use network analysis to aid project planning and project management, one way in which this can be done is in the reduction of project time. In the commercial world project planners will receive huge bonuses for their companies if they can complete early—for example the rebuilding of the San Francisco freeway after the earthquake in 1994. On the down side, any contractor is likely to have to forfeit huge penalties if the project is delayed—it is clear that the delays on completing the UK access to the Channel Tunnel had a great impact on commercial confidence in this project.

Gantt charts

You will remember that the network was drawn to represent the precedence relationship between activities within the project. The length of the arrow did not represent time. If, however, we are going to consider how reducing the time of activities affects the overall project we need to have a way of assessing time changes within our network. One way of doing this is to draw a type of horizontal bar chart where the length of the bar represents the time an activity takes, whilst at the same time mimicking the overall order of activities in the project. There are many ways of drawing such a Gantt chart, and we show one such representation.

Example 12.5
Draw a Gantt chart to represent the time factor in the project in example 12.3.

Solution

Firstly we start with the network as in figure 12.21. Here we use the ESTs to draw the Gantt chart. The vertical axis of the Gantt chart will contain the activities (we can see there are three main chains through the network:

(1) A, B, C, D, E, G;
(2) A, B, F;
(3) A, B, C, H, (Dummy), E, G.

Therefore our vertical axis must contain room for three horizontal bars. The horizontal axis displays the time element, which will need to be from 0 to 23 (weeks). Using graph paper the diagram of figure 12.22 will emerge.

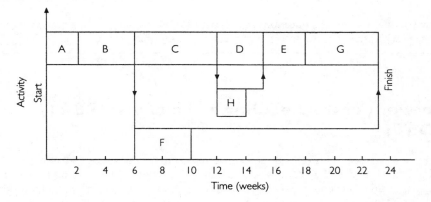

Figure 12.22

We can see that this bar chart is not quite complete: there is the float time which is evident from the bars but which we have not yet added. To do this we use a shaded bar after each of the activities with float—shown in figure 12.23.

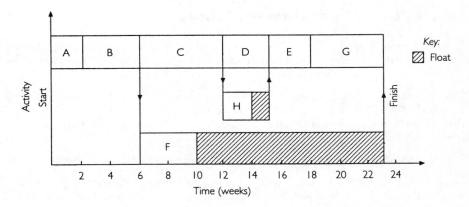

Figure 12.23

It is clear now that H has a float of 1 week and F has a float of 13 weeks. In fact we do not need to use the ESTs for drawing the Gantt chart—but it does make our work consistent. We can see that activity F, for example, could be delayed until the 19th week and then completed. This would mean that the float would be a shaded bar before F. Similarly for H. In this example it is clear that the float for F and H are for this particular activity, but as we have said earlier in the definition of total float, there are instances when the float for an activity is in fact for the chain through this activity. Together with floats and Gantt charts we are now in a position to begin to reduce the project duration.

Exercises 12.4

Draw Gantt charts for the questions in exercises 12.2. Clearly label the floats. Are there instances when the float for an activity is in fact for the chain through this activity?

Network cost scheduling and analysis (PERT/COST)

If we are to reduce the project duration, we must reduce the time of activities on the critical path. It may be that some activities cannot be reduced (e.g. waiting for paint to dry, baking time, a chemical process) but in most cases the duration can be reduced at some cost. Typical costs incurred will be overtime payments to staff, or paying contract staff, buying new machinery (better computers, printers, copiers), renting a larger building, etc. When we begin to consider the cost of an activity we have the normal cost for the activity. We shall see below that if we do choose to speed up certain activities this will bring in additional costs.

Least cost scheduling—crashing

Least cost scheduling (LCS), also called crashing, is the method for finding the least cost for reducing the overall project duration, time period by time period. The method for this is shown in the following examples.

The minimum possible duration of an activity is known as the crash duration. Care is always needed: when reducing the time of activities in the network it is vital to ensure that the time is not reduced by so much that it is no longer a critical activity. New critical paths will arise in this process.

Before we begin to consider crashing activities we need some basic definitions.

Crash costs: these are the more expensive costs for running an activity, for example using extra staff or overtime payments or purchasing additional machinery or space. So for each activity we will have the normal cost together with the crash cost, which is the cost we would budget for if we speeded up the activity.

Crash time: this is the minimum time an activity can take. Some activities cannot be reduced and so the crash time is the same as the normal time.

Cost slope: is the cost per unit of time in reducing an activity by 1 time unit. This is the difference in the crash and normal costs divided by the difference in the crash and normal time. That is

$$\text{cost slope} = \frac{\text{crash cost} - \text{normal cost}}{\text{normal time} - \text{crash time}}$$

If we decide to crash an activity (which must be on the critical path if it is to achieve its aim of reducing the project duration) then the cost slope will inform us how much the total project costs will increase by per unit time of crashing. Thus the total cost of the project will increase by the time reduction multiplied by the cost slope.

Example 12.6: Simple crashing
Consider the following project:

Activity	Preceding activity	Activity times (days)		Total cost (£)	
		Normal	**Crash**	**Normal**	**Crash**
A	—	5	4	500	620
B	—	2	2	300	300
C	A	9	6	650	770
D	A	5	2	400	490
E	B,C	6	3	850	1000
F	C,D	4	2	500	700

Find the normal time and cost for this project and determine if it can be speeded up. Can it be completed in 14 days? At what cost?

Solution
Step 1: Draw a network
Construct a Network for this project as in figure 12.24. Notice here that we have used a dummy activity in a slightly different way: we needed a dummy to

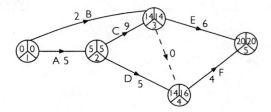

Figure 12.24

show precedence. Activity F cannot commence until both C and D have been executed and so we needed a dummy to show that F is dependent on C (as well as to avoid the parallel activities of C and D). This network is not unique: we could have a dummy from D to node 3 and then F coming off node 3 (although this would have meant using another dummy to avoid E and F being parallel). The project takes 20 days.

Step 2: Calculate floats, cost slopes and project cost. Draw a Gantt chart
A table of floats and costs slopes is:

Activity	Float	Cost slope (£ per day)
A	0	120
B	12	—
C	0	40
D	6	30
E	0	50
F	2	100

The total cost of the project is the sum of normal costs which is £3200. Notice that activity B cannot be reduced, probably because of the nature of this activity.

From the table of floats we can see that the critical path is A, C, E (check: $5 + 9 + 6 = 20$) whilst B, D and F have spare time available.

A Gantt chart is given in figure 12.25.

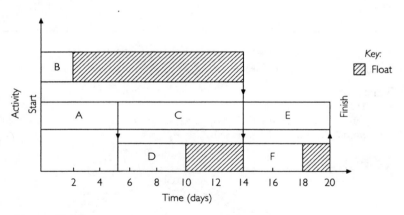

Figure 12.25

Notice from the Gantt chart that the float for D is in two places: the total float of 6 days is partly after D and the remaining 2 days after F. It is for this reason that total float refers to float along a chain of activities.

Step 3: Method for LCS/crashing activities
Can we reduce the project time to 14 days? If so, at what total cost?

We obviously need to reduce the time of the activities on the critical path in order to reduce the overall project duration. We reduce the time of such an activity with the lowest cost slope as this will mean the minimal increase in the overall project expenses. Progressively this is repeated until the desired reduction in time is achieved. Complications occur when time reductions cause several paths to become critical simultaneously. In this instance it is necessary to crash several activities at the same time. If at any stage all activities on one critical path are crashed then this is the minimum amount of time that the project can be reduced and so is the minimum total duration of the project.

We shall be able to use a trial-and-error method for deciding which activities to crash as we usually only encounter smaller networks. There are other methods using linear programming (which is outside the scope of this book) and in large-scale networks it is preferable to use specialised software, for example CA-Super Project for Microsoft Windows.

Crashing step 3.1
We can crash either A, C or E. As C has the least cost slope (is cheapest), this is the desired option. The difference in crash and normal times for C is 3 days and so we can crash C by at most 3 days. This will increase the project costs to $£3200 + 3 \times £40 = £3320$ and takes the project duration to 17 days. To confirm that this is satisfactory we need to either redraw the network and check the floats (to confirm that A, C, E are still critical) or we redraw the Gantt chart. We shall adopt this latter strategy as we can then watch what happens to the float in the overall project as we reduce the project duration.

The Gantt chart would be given by figure 12.26. Notice that we write C* to indicate that C has been crashed to its minimal duration. From the Gantt we can see that the float for B is 9, for F is 2 and for D is 3. This means that they have all reduced: the slack has been used up in the speeding-up process. We need to check which activities are critical: these are still A, C and E as this is the longest path.

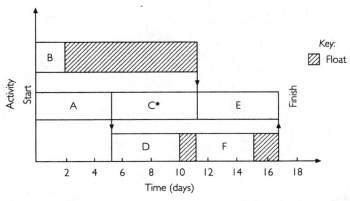

Figure 12.26

Crashing step 3.2
The next stage is to crash either A or E. Activity E is cheaper, so this is the best option. We can reduce E from 8 days to 3 days at a cost of £50 per day. This

will bring the total project cost to £3470 and a project duration of 14 days, which would seem to be as required. We need to check using the Gantt chart which is given by figure 12.27.

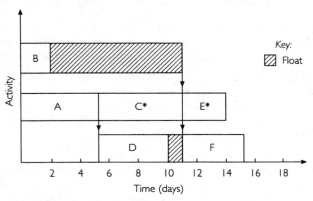

Figure 12.27

We can now see that there is a problem in reducing E to 3 days: A, C, E is no longer the longest (critical) path. The path A, C, F is longer at 15 days. This in effect means that the final day we have spent £50 reducing E has been a waste of money as the project still takes 15, not 14, days. Thus in fact we can only reduce E by 2 days and we need to redraw the Gantt chart as figure 12.28. The project now takes 15 days and costs £3420.

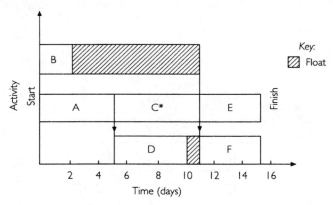

Figure 12.28

Crashing step 3.3
We can see that the floats are 9 for B and 1 for D. We can also see that there are two critical paths: A, C, E and A, C, F. To reduce the project time we must crash both paths. We have already crashed C and cannot reduce E further without making it non-critical. This same argument would mean that F should not be reduced. Thus it makes sense to crash A—especially as this will

simultaneously reduce the duration along both critical paths. We can reduce A by 1 day at most at a cost of £120, giving us a project duration of 14 days and a total cost of £3540. Note: we could crash both E and F by 1 day, but this would cost £150 and is a more expensive option.

Finally, checking the Gantt chart (figure 12.29) will confirm that we now have 2 critical paths: A C E and A C F.

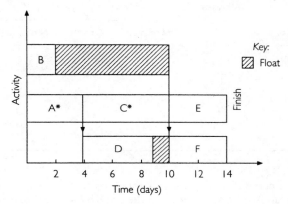

Figure 12.29

Additional notes

1 The usual assumption that the cost slope is linear is not always so. This should not be assumed if circumstances point to some other conclusion.

2 Dummy activities have zero cost slopes and so cannot be crashed.

3 Always use a Gantt chart to see what is happening when you crash activities—this will allow you to see the floats and see them reduce as you crash a critical activity.

4 If there are several independent critical paths then several activities must be crashed simultaneously. These are selected as above: activities with the least cost slope. If they are not independent but share common activities then it may be cost effective to crash the shared activities even though they may not have the lowest cost slopes.

5 Always look for the possibility of increasing the duration of a previously crashed activity when subsequent crashing renders it non-critical (with float).

6 A common feature of many real projects is a liability clause (penalty) for delayed completion and/or a bonus for earlier completion. We can be left with a situation of deciding whether to pay extra to complete the project on time, and so save a penalty, or avoid the extra cost and pay the penalty (but possibly discredit your business name).

Exercises 12.5

12.5.1 Consider the project times and costs as given in the table below:

Activity	Preceding activity	Activity times (days)		Total cost (£)	
		Normal	Crash	Normal	Crash
A	—	10	8	300	500
B	—	4	2	200	350
C	A	2	1	150	190
D	B	10	5	100	400
E	B	5	1	100	200
F	C,E	3	1	80	100
G	D,F	5	3	250	350

Construct a network that represents this project. Identify the critical path and find the duration of the project using the normal duration for each activity. Find the cost of completing the project in the shortest possible time and state its cost. At each stage draw a Gantt chart.

12.5.2 Consider the project outlined in the following table:

Activity	Preceding activity	Activity times (days)		Total cost (£)	
		Normal	Crash	Normal	Crash
A	—	3	2	1200	1500
B	—	2	1	1250	1300
C	A	6	4	1000	1800
D	A	5	3	1500	2800
E	C,D	5	4	1800	3000
F	B,D	3	1	500	1000
G	F	2	1	500	1000

Draw the network for this project, find the project time, project cost and the critical path. Can the project duration be reduced? What activities should be crashed? What then would be the total cost of the project? What is the cost of completing in this time scale?

12.5.3 An organisation has determined that to complete one of its projects the following activities must be completed, with associated costs, times and crash details:

Activity	Preceding activity	Activity times (days)		Total cost (£)	
		Normal	Crash	Normal	Crash
A	—	4	3	25	37
B	A	4	4	16	16
C	—	5	2	35	75
D	A,C	8	7	49	95
E	B,C	8	4	60	130
F	D,E	6	3	41	76
G	E,F	5	3	23	45
H	G	4	3	40	65

(i) Calculate and state the critical path(s) and the cost of completion in the normal time.

(ii) Calculate and state the critical path(s) and the cost of completion in the crash time.

(iii) Calculate and state the minimum cost of completion and associated critical path(s) and time.

12.5.4 Julia Burbage is in charge of planning and co-ordinating the annual sales management training programme for the Institute of Sales Management. She has ordered the activities in the following way where times are measured in weeks:

Activity	Description	Predecessor	Normal time	Crash time	Normal cost (£)	Crash cost (£)
A	Plan course	—	6	3	700	1000
B	Invite speakers	A	3	2	300	500
C	Determine possible venues	—	2	1	250	400
D	Book the venue	C	2	2	800	800
E	Finalise speaker travel plans	B,D	2	1	270	300
F	Make final check with speakers	E	2	1	200	280
G	Prepare and send brochure	B,D	4	3	750	900
H	Take reservations	E,G	4	3	400	500

(i) Draw a PERT network for this project. What does this network represent?

(ii) Determine its normal duration and cost and list the critical path for this project.

(iii) Explain the terms EST, LST and float for a non-critical activity.

(iv) Draw an initial Gantt chart for this network and explain what this represents.

(v) If the conference starts in the second week of September, when does Ms Burbage need to commence organising this? Can her project duration be reduced by three weeks so that the team can have a holiday before the planning starts? What extra cost would there be to the Institute of Sales Management?

12.5.5 An environmental group is planning to refurbish part of a London office block during the summer vacation 1995. This block has two floors: a ground floor and a basement garage, but within the basement garage space a new research laboratory is planned. The office is ready for works to commence on Monday 17th July 1995 and all works must be completed by Monday September 11th 1995 when its annual conference begins. A calendar for 1995 is shown in table Table 12.1: assume that work continues on bank holidays.

Table 12.1

Calendar for Summer 1995

July								**August**				
Monday			3	10	17	24	31		7	14	21	28
Tuesday			4	11	18	25		1	8	15	22	29
Wednesday			5	12	19	26		2	9	16	23	30
Thursday			6	13	20	27		3	10	17	24	31
Friday			7	14	21	28		4	11	18	25	
Saturday		1	8	15	22	29		5	12	19	26	
Sunday		2	9	16	23	30		6	13	20	27	

September					
Monday		4	11	18	25
Tuesday		5	12	19	26
Wednesday		6	13	20	27
Thursday		7	14	21	28
Friday	1	8	15	22	29
Saturday	2	9	16	23	30
Sunday	3	10	17	24	

The proposed works have gone to tender and the groups governing body have agreed to accept the bid from Great Western Building Contractors Ltd. The schedule of work is listed below with the times in days and preceding tasks and the normal costs. The contractors work a 6-day week and work can be carried out on the ground and basement simultaneously.

A table of all the planned refurbishment including times and costs are in Table 12.2.

In the contract the group have inserted a penalty clause: if the contractors delay and do not complete on time they must pay £1500 per day over the agreed time.

Explain the main purpose of project planning for this example.
(i)   How much is this refurbishment going to cost?
(ii) Draw a network to represent this project and determine how many days it should take to execute. Are the contractors going to finish on time? What activities are critical to the on-time completion?
(iii) Draw a Gantt chart for the above network and briefly explain why it is useful.

Table 12.2

Building tasks	Preceding Task	Normal		Crash	
		Duration in days	Costs	Duration in days	Costs
Ground floor					
A Remove 2 internal walls	None	12	12 000	10	15 000
B Build archways to connect rooms	A	7	8 000	4	10 000
C Replastering	B,H	13	3 000	10	7 200
D Rewiring	C	8	2 000	7	3 000
E Redecoration	D	10	7 000	10	7 000
F Build storage cupboards	D	6	2 000	4	5 000
G Install new telephone exchange	D	5	10 000	5	10 000
H Reconstruct reception	None	20	35 000	17	40 000
Basement					
I Install air conditioning	N	12	30 000	10	36 000
J Install wall partitions	K	5	5 000	4	6 500
K Put in suspended ceilings	I	4	3 000	3	4 500
L Redecoration	J	10	7 000	10	7 000
M Install fixtures and fittings	L	11	22 000	9	27 000
N Electrical wiring	None	7	2 000	6	3 500
P Install plumbing	None	1	8 000	1	8 000

(iv) If the contractors can speed up certain activities, which should they try, and how much would each cost per day?

(v) By crashing suitable activities, can you reduce the project duration and avoid paying any penalties? Might it be cheaper to pay the penalty for 1 or 2 days? Advise the contractor as to the best option.

Solutions to the odd-numbered questions

Chapter 1

Exercises 1.1

1.1.1 Nominal

1.1.3 Ratio

1.1.5 Ratio

1.1.7 Ordinal

1.1.9 Interval

Exercises 1.2

1.2.1 Probably multi-stage sampling.

Exercises 1.3

1.3.1 **(i)** The number of people in a cinema (say between 0 and the capacity of the cinema, around 250 say).

(ii) The number of times a photocopier breaks down in a week (between 0 and say 10).

(iii) The number of seeds which germinate in a pack of 200 seeds (between 0 and 200).

1.3.3 Heights would generally be recorded as discrete random variables: 1.50 m, 1.65 m, 1.87 m, here to 2 decimal places). The range likely to be observed: 0.30 m to, say 2.50 m.

1.3.5 Quantitative discrete: how many students registered at a university, how much money students spent in the refectory in a term, how much they spent on accommodation or fees in a year.

Quantitative continuous: how long you wait for a bus or a train, how much time you spend watching TV in a typical month, how much shares rise or decline in a day.

Chapter 2

Exercises 2.1

2.1.1

L	f
$100 < L \leqslant 200$	18
$200 < L \leqslant 300$	36
$300 < L \leqslant 400$	22
$400 < L \leqslant 500$	1
$500 < L \leqslant 600$	1
$600 < L \leqslant 700$	1
$L > 700$	1
Total	80

2.1.3 In any one university, if say 2000 students graduate and 165 gain 1st class degrees, then this would be 8.25%, or 8% recorded to the nearest integer. Therefore 8% could mean any value from 7.50% up to 8.49%, or strictly less than 8.50%. This then gives us a guideline for finding the true class intervals.

True Classes	f
$7.50 \leqslant p < 8.50$	5
$8.50 \leqslant p < 9.50$	8
$9.50 \leqslant p < 10.50$	8
$10.50 \leqslant p < 11.50$	6
$11.50 \leqslant p < 12.50$	5
$12.50 \leqslant p < 13.50$	1
$13.50 \leqslant p < 14.50$	2
$14.50 \leqslant p < 16.50$	1
Total	36

Exercises 2.2

2.2.1 Shows proportions more clearly where the totals are irregular.

2.2.3 Reduce the number of cars immediately and place some restriction on the number of light and medium goods vehicles.

Exercises 2.3

2.3.1 Actual turnovers in millions to 2 decimal places are: £190.41; £95.21; £114.25; £120.59; £50.78; £31.74.

2.3.2 The pie chart would show more clearly than the raw data that there were similar numbers of households with no 1 and 2 earners but very few households with more than 2 earners.

Exercises 2.4

2.4.1 Dual bar charts 2 pie charts, time series or 2 separate bar charts.

Exercises 2.5

2.5.1 Relative frequencies: 27.4%; 28.8%; 19.8%; 22.1%; 1.3%; 0.5%; 0.1%. Here plotting relative frequency density would be necessary. NB: This would not then be a percentage. The histogram would be positively skewed with the majority of shareholders owning less than 10 000 shares each.

Exercises 2.6

2.6.1 **(i)** Continuous data, quantitative, on the ratio scale. (This is because all calls must be of longer duration than 0 minutes and one call could be twice as long as another; it makes sense to discuss the ratio of length of one call to another.)

(ii) Fairly symmetrical

(iv) Median $\approx$ 2.27 mins, Q1 $\approx$ 1.4 mins and Q3 $\approx$ 2.93 mins.

Exercises 2.7

2.7.1 Clearly the motor car produces a higher percentage of pollutants than heavy goods vehicles in all categories other than black smoke.

Chapter 3

Exercise 3.1

3.1 a) 1

3.1 b) 1

3.1 c) -14

3.1 d) 2

Exercise 3.2

3.2 a) 15

3.2 b) 5

3.2 c) 2

Exercise 3.3

3.3 a) $3\frac{13}{24}$

3.3 b) $1\frac{11}{24}$

3.3 c) $1\frac{25}{63}$

Exercise 3.4

3.4 a) £50.03
3.4 b) 0.0266
3.4 c) 11.6 or $11\frac{3}{5}$

Exercises 3.5

3.5.1 £1125; 5% discount = £1068.75, making a £68.75 profit or 6.875% profit per machine.

3.5.3 50 pages are really free.

Exercises 3.6

3.6.1 a) 12.25
b) 530.8416
c) $1.139\,062\,5 \times 10^{-5}$ or 0.000 011 39

3.6.3 a) $3.245 \times 10^7 = 32\,450\,000$
b) $8.042 \times 10^{-5} = 0.000\,080\,42$

Exercises 3.7

3.7.1 a) $10^{11} = 100\,000\,000\,000$
b) 100
c) 1
d) 1/3 or 3^{-1}

Exercises 3.8

3.8.1 a) $8a + 16b$
b) $3a^2 - 3ab$
c) $6x^2y + 2xy^2$

3.8.3 a) $2x^3 - 5x^2 + 38x + 15$
b) $6 + 7x - 11x^2 - 2x^3$

Exercises 3.9

3.9.1 $8x(1 + 4y)$
3.9.3 $4(x - y)(5x - 4y)$

Exercise 3.10

$x^1 = x^{\frac{1}{3}+\frac{1}{3}+\frac{1}{3}} = x^{\frac{1}{3}} \times x^{\frac{1}{3}} \times x^{\frac{1}{3}}$ by law I.

$x^1 = \sqrt[3]{x^3} = \sqrt[3]{x \times x \times x} = \sqrt[3]{x} \times \sqrt[3]{x} \times \sqrt[3]{x}$

and so $x^{\frac{1}{3}} = \sqrt[3]{x}$.

Exercises 3.11

3.11.1 **a)** $\dfrac{1}{x^{3/2}} = \dfrac{1}{\sqrt{x^3}}$

b) $\sqrt[3]{x^4}$

Exercises 3.12

3.12.1 **(i)** $1 + 4(n - 1)$
(ii) $3 - \frac{3}{4}(n - 1)$
(iii) $2 \times 3^{n-1}$
(iv) $2 \times (-1)^{n-1} \times \left(\frac{1}{3}\right)^{n-1}$ or $2 \times \left(\frac{-1}{3}\right)^{n-1}$

3.12.3 **(iii)** $S_{15} = 14348906$
(iv) $S_{15} = 1.500000105$

Chapter 4

Exercises 4.1

4.1.1 £3.27

Exercise 4.2

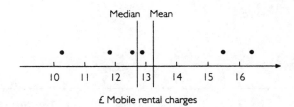

Median is most central (no mode). Not symmetrical.

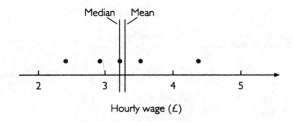

Median is most central. (No mode). Data fairly symmetrical.

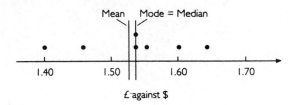

£ against $

Mean = 1.53, mode = 1.54, median = 1.54; fairly symmetrical. As values for all are quite close, mean, median and mode are central values.

Exercises 4.3

4.3.1 $\bar{x} = £3.32$, $S_n^2 = £0.44$, $S_{n-1}^2 = £0.49$ to 2 decimal places.

4.3.3 (i) $\bar{x} = 22.0825$, $S_n = 6.076\,517\,815$
Median = 23.3. No mode.

4.3.3 (ii) $\bar{x} = 0.172\,25$, $S_n = 0.067\,754\,612$
mode = 0.123 $\Big\}$ median = 0.1315
    = 0.113
data is Bi-modal.

4.3.5 $S_{n-1}^2 = \dfrac{4\,119\,000\,000}{6} - \dfrac{7 \times (21\,000)^2}{6}$

$= 172\,000\,000$

$S_{n-1}^2 = \dfrac{1066.5258}{5} - \dfrac{6 \times (13.166\,666\,67)^2}{5}$

$= \underline{5.271\,826\,668}$

Exercises 4.4

4.4.3

Time	f	True classes	x Mid-points	cf
<60	191	49.5–59.5	54.5	191
60–69	158	59.5–69.5	64.5	349
70–79	204	69.5–79.5	74.5	553
80–89	270	79.5–89.5	84.5	823
90–99	51	89.5–99.5	94.5	874
100–119	98	99.5–119.5	109.5	972
⩾2 hrs	28	119.5–139.5	129.5	1000
	1000			

$\bar{x} = 77.79$ minutes, $S_n = 18.262\,691\,48$
$S_{n-1} = 18.271\,829\,68$
Median $\simeq 76.9$ mins (from a cf graph)
Modal class = 80–89 Mode = 82 (from histogram)

Chapter 5

Exercises 5.1

5.1.1 $x = \dfrac{p - h}{c}$

Exercises 5.2

5.2.2 (i) $x = \dfrac{a - b - 2}{4}$

(ii) $x = \dfrac{5}{3 - y}$

(iii) $x = \dfrac{40}{a^2}$

(iv) $x = \dfrac{5y}{y - 3}$

Exercises 5.3

5.3.1 i) $x = 2 + \frac{3}{2}y$

(ii) $x = \dfrac{y - 7}{7}$

5.3.3 Let v = number of vegetarians and c = number of carnivors. Total cost of office party = $15v + 22c$ in £.

Exercises 5.4

5.4.1 (i) $x = \frac{4}{3}$
(ii) $x = 36$
(iii) $x = \pm 3$

5.4.3 $a = -5$

5.4.5 (i) $x = \dfrac{9 - y}{3(4 - y)}$

(ii) $x = \pm\sqrt{y}$

(iii) $x = \left(\dfrac{125}{16}\right)^{3/2} = \dfrac{\sqrt{1\,953\,125}}{64}$

$= 21.836\,601\,34$

5.4.7 Campaign costs model:

$2500 = 3 \times 220 + 0.45q$

where q = number of leaflets

$q = 4088.89 \simeq 4089$ leaflets. Yes!

Exercises 5.5

5.5.1 (i) $m = 2, c = -5$
(ii) $m = \frac{3}{2}, c = 4$
(iii) $m = 0, c = -2$
(iv) $m = \infty$, never crosses y-axis.

5.5.3

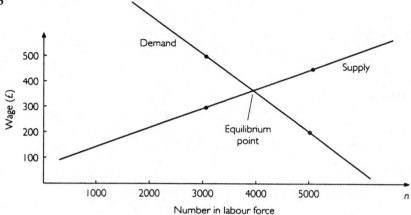

Equilibrun point $= (3800, £360)$. At a wage of £360 the employers will employ 3800 people; at this wage 3800 employees enter the labour force.

5.5.5 $C = 5q + 285$

where C = cost of production, q = number of leaflets.

For C = 6000, $q = 1143$

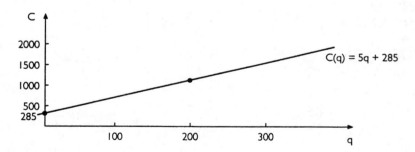

Exercises 5.6

5.6.1 (i)

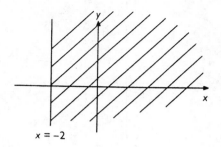

$x = -2$

(ii)

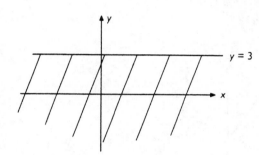

$y = 3$

(iii)

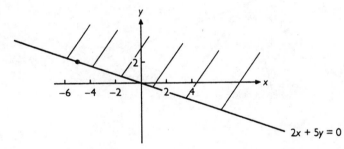

$2x + 5y = 0$

(iv)

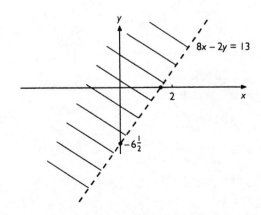

$8x - 2y = 13$

$-6\frac{1}{2}$

5.6.1 (v)

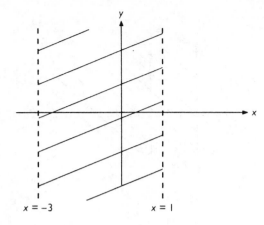

$x = -3$ $x = 1$

5.6.3

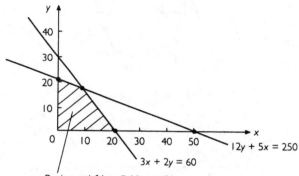

$12y + 5x = 250$

$3x + 2y = 60$

Region satisfying all 4 inequalities

Exercises 5.8

5.8.1 (i) $a = 3, b = -3, c = -1$
  $x = \underline{1.2638}$, or $x = \underline{-0.2638}$ to 4 decimal places

  (ii) $a = -1, b = -1, c = 4$
  $x = \underline{-2.5616}$, or $x = \underline{1.5616}$ to 4 decimal places

  (iii) $a = 4, b = 3, c = -5$
  $x = \underline{0.8042}$, or $x = \underline{-1.5542}$ to 4 decimal places

  (iv) $x = -0.7440$, or $x = 1.3440$

  (v) cannot evaluate; root of a negative value is not a real number.

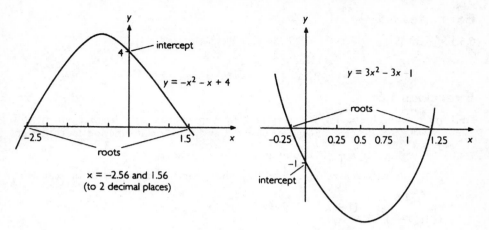

Graph (v) has 'imaginary roots'; this graph does not actually cross the x-axis.

Each graph has a line of symmetry about $x = -b/2a$ which is the mid-point of the roots.

5.8.3

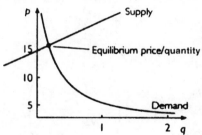

Equilibrium = (0.37, 15.123).

Chapter 6

Exercise 6.2

£6369.59

Exercise 6.3

Annually: £3.66 m
Quarterly: £3.67 m
An extra £13,723.29 if interest is added quarterly.

Exercises 6.4

6.4.1 £1426.78

6.4.3 £92 554.91; straight line depreciation would give £92 208.

6.4.5 £2660.11

Exercises 6.5

6.5.1 4 £30.49   £4.23   £26.26   £396.51
       5 £30.49   £3.97   £26.52   £369.99

Exercises 6.6

6.6.1 (i) The value at time 0 (when the loan is advanced) of the first repayment will be less than the repayment worth R at the end of time period 1. Its present value is thus $\dfrac{R}{1+i}$ assuming that interest is at $i\%$.

(ii) Similarly the value at time 0 of the second repayment will be scaled by $(1+i)^2$ ie $\dfrac{R}{(1+i)^2}$.

(iii) The present values are:

$$\frac{R}{1+i}, \frac{R}{(1+i)^2}, \frac{R}{(1+i)^3}, \ldots, \frac{R}{(1+i)^n}$$

which form a G.P. with first term $a = \dfrac{R}{1+i}$ and common ratio $r = \dfrac{1}{1+i}$.

(iv) Loan = sum of values of all present values of repayments.

= sum of a G.P. $a = \dfrac{R}{1+i}$, $r = \dfrac{1}{1+i}$, n periods.

Thus loan $= S_n = \dfrac{a(1-r^n)}{1-r}$

$$= \left(\frac{R}{1+i}\right)\left(\frac{1 - \left(\frac{1}{1+i}\right)^n}{1 - \frac{1}{1+i}}\right)$$

$$= \frac{R}{i}\left(1 - \left(\frac{1}{1+i}\right)^n\right)$$

or $\dfrac{R}{i}(1 - (1+i)^{-n})$

6.6.3 £2036.66

6.6.5 Woman: £31 398.74
       Man: £36 060.14 (assuming retirement ages of 60 for both men and women).

Exercises 6.7

6.7.1 £26 346.49

Exercises 6.8

6.8.1 £654.97; £217.01; £7859.64; £7812.36

6.8.3 Woman: £10 180.63
       Man: £11 704.62

Chapter 7

Exercises 7.1

7.1.1 $\frac{5}{36}$

7.1.3 $\frac{1}{12}$

7.1.5 Event: the outcome observed from a particular experiment.
Sample space: set of all outcomes for an experiment.
Trial: one go of the experiment.

Exercises 7.2

7.2.1

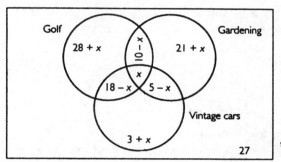

Adding up all
the sectors gives
$x = 3$

    (i) $\frac{27}{115}$

    (ii) $\frac{3}{115}$

    (iii) $\frac{7}{115}$

Exercises 7.3

7.3.1 (i) $\frac{28}{36}$ or $\frac{7}{9}$

    ii) $\frac{2}{3}$

7.3.3 (i) $\frac{43}{160}$

    (ii) $\frac{40}{160}$ or $\frac{1}{4}$

    (iii) $\frac{31}{160}$

    (iv) $\frac{9}{160}$

    (v) $\frac{93}{160}$

    (vi) $\frac{11}{53}$

    (vii) $\frac{77}{160}$

    (viii) No. For example if true, then p (under 21 and preferring a beach holiday) $= p$ (under 21) $\times p$ (prefers a beach holiday)
              $= \frac{25}{160} \times \frac{67}{160} = \underline{0.0654}$

        But from the table, p (under 21 and preferring a beach holiday) $= \frac{15}{160} = \underline{0.0938}$ and these values are clearly not equal.

Target beach and walking holidays to 41–50. Use 41–50 group in adverts too.

Exercises 7.4

7.4.1 (i) 0.72
 (ii) 0.16
 (iii) 0.225

7.4.3 (i) $\frac{5}{216} \times 25p = 0.6p$ in 1 play
 (ii) $\frac{1}{216} \times 50p = 0.2p$ in 1 play

Exercises 7.5

7.5.1 (i) 0.000 32
 (ii) 0.0512
 (iii) 0.2048
 (iv) 0.4096
Not binomial as n is not fixed 0.327 68

7.5.3 $B(20, 0.15)$; $P(\times \geqslant 2) = 1 - 0.1756$
$\qquad\qquad\qquad\quad = 82.44\%$ chance of rejecting batch when in fact 15% are faulty, and so a 17.6% chance of accepting the batch.

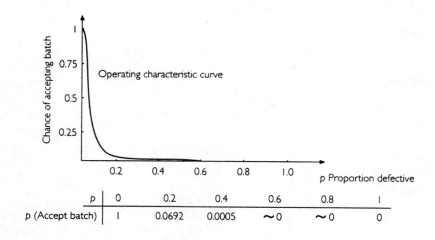

p	0	0.2	0.4	0.6	0.8	1
p (Accept batch)	1	0.0692	0.0005	~ 0	~ 0	0

7.5.5 0.0076
0.0148
0.0264
$\simeq 1.000$
$np = 37.5$, Variance $= npq = 9.375$

7.5.7 $\frac{1}{32}$

Here n, the number of trials is unknown.

```
MTB > random 200c1;
SUBC> binomial n = 10 p = 0.5.
MTB > tally c1
         C1    COUNT
          0      1
          1      1
          2     10
          3     22
          4     35
          5     52
          6     41
          7     25
          8      9
          9      3
         10      1
         N=    200

MTB > hist c1

Histogram of C1  N = 200
Each * represents 2 obs.

Midpoint   Count
       0      1  *
       1      1  *
       2     10  *****
       3     22  **********
       4     35  *****************
       5     52  *************************
       6     41  ********************
       7     25  *************
       8      9  *****
       9      3  **
      10      1  *
```

Exercises 7.6

7.6.1 $p(x = k + 1) = \dfrac{3}{k+1} \times p(x = k)$

$$= \dfrac{3}{k+1} \times \dfrac{e^{-3} \times 3^k}{k!}$$

7.6.3 **(i)** $p(1 \text{ coach demanded}) = 0.2052$
$p(2 \text{ coaches demanded}) = 0.2565$

  (ii) $p(x = 10) = 0.082\,08$
$p(x = 1) = 0.205\,22$ and $p(x = 2) = 0.256\,51$
$p(x = 3) = 0.213\,77$
$p(x = 4) = 0.1336$

```
MTB > random 100 cl;
SUBC> poisson mean = 3.
MTB > tally cl

      C1   COUNT
      0     7
      1    16
      2    22
      3    24
      4    21
      5     6
      6     3
      7     1
      N=   100

MTB > hist cl

Histograms of C1 N = 100

Midpoint   Count
      0      7    *******
      1     16    ****************
      2     22    **********************
      3     24    ************************
      4     21    *********************
      5      6    ******
      6      3    ***
      7      1    *
```

Chapter 8

Exercises 8.1

8.1.1 (i) $z = 0.67$ to 2 decimal places
(ii) $z = -0.31$ to 2 decimal places
(iii) $z = -0.51$ to 2 decimal places

8.1.3 (i)

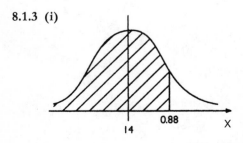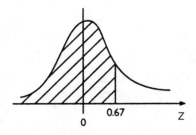

$p(z \le 0.67) = 0.74857$

(ii)

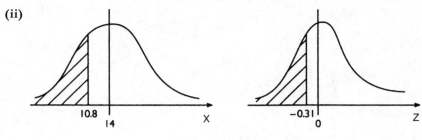

$$p(z \leqslant -0.31) = 0.37828$$

(iii)

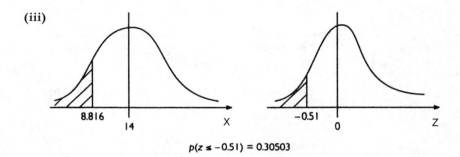

$$p(z \leqslant -0.51) = 0.30503$$

Exercises 8.2

8.2.1

Relative frequency	Class width	Relative frequency density RFD	RFD $\times 10^3$
30/150 = 20%	100	0.002	2
40/150 = 27%	100	0.0027	2.7
45/150 = 30%	100	0.003	3
20/150 = 13%	200	0.0065	6.5
10/150 = 7%	400	0.000 175	0.18
5/150 = 3%	200	0.000 15	0.15
Total 100%			

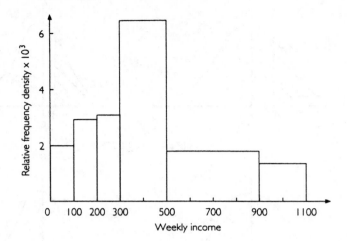

Weekly income slightly skewed, but we could say it is approximately symmetrical.

Mean, $\bar{x} = £263.33$, and $s_{n-1} = £210.14$.

Using these to 1 decimal place,

p (someone earns $< £350$) $= p(Z < 0.41) = 0.6591$
$= 66\%$

$p(320 < \text{wage} < 470) = p(0.27 < Z < 0.98)$
$= 0.230\,04$ or 23%.

8.2.3 (i)   0.308 54
(ii) 0.280 96
(iii) 0.027 58

8.2.5

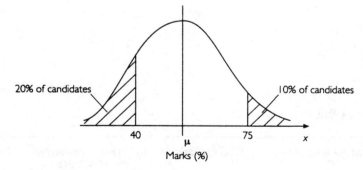

Corresponding Z values are -0.84 and 1.28 to two decimal places.

Thus $-0.84 = \dfrac{40 \min \mu}{\sigma}$ and $1.28 = \dfrac{75 - \mu}{\sigma}$

Solving simultaneously gives $\mu = 53.9\%$ and $\sigma = 16.5\%$ to 1 decimal place.

8.2.7 (i) 0.15866
(ii) 0.02275

Exercises 8.3

8.3.1 $\mu = 6$, $\sigma = 1.55$ to 2 decimal places.

(i) 0.098 53	**(i)** 0.167 29
(ii) 0.112 232 Using normal	**(ii)** 0.120 95 Using binomial
(iii) 0.625 53	**(iii)** 0.617 72

Values are reasonably close.

Minitab exercise on sampling distributions

```
MTB > random 1000 c1;
SUBC> bino n = 20 p = 0.2.
MTB > tally c1
      C1   COUNT
       0     18
       1     57
       2    142
       3    208
       4    206
       5    170
       6    105
       7     61
       8     20
       9      7
      10      5
      11      1
      N=   1000

MTB > hist c1

Histogram of C1 N = 1000
Each * represents 5 obs.
Midpoint   Count
       0     19   ****
       1     57   ************
       2    142   ****************************
       3    208   ******************************************
       4    206   ******************************************
       5    170   **********************************
       6    105   ********************
       7     61   *************
       8     20   ****
       9      7   **
      10      5   *
      11      1   *

MTB > let K2 = 1
MTB > store
Storing in file: MINITAB.MTB
STOR> random 10 observations, put into c1;
STOR> bino n = 20 p = 0.2.
STOR> mean data in c1, put in k1
STOR> let c2 = k1
STOR> let k2 = k1 + 1
```

```
STOR> end
MTB > execute 50 times
Executing from file: MINITAB.MTB
   MEAN     =      4.5000
   MEAN     =      4.6000
   MEAN     =      3.3000
   MEAN     =      4.1000
   MEAN     =      4.1000
   MEAN     =      4.5000
   MEAN     =      4.2000
   MEAN     =      3.3000
   MEAN     =      4.0000
   MEAN     =      4.4000
   MEAN     =      3.7000
   MEAN     =      4.2000
   MEAN     =      4.1000
   MEAN     =      3.8000
   MEAN     =      4.0000
   MEAN     =      4.5000
   MEAN     =      3.6000
   MEAN     =      3.5000
   MEAN     =      3.5000
   MEAN     =      3.6000
   MEAN     =      3.3000
   MEAN     =      4.1000
   MEAN     =      2.8000
   MEAN     =      2.9000
   MEAN     =      3.6000
   MEAN     =      4.3000
   MEAN     =      3.1000
   MEAN     =      4.5000
   MEAN     =      5.1000
   MEAN     =      4.8000
   MEAN     =      3.9000
   MEAN     =      3.8000
   MEAN     =      4.5000
   MEAN     =      4.4000
   MEAN     =      4.5000
   MEAN     =      3.6000
   MEAN     =      3.8000
   MEAN     =      4.4000
   MEAN     =      4.8000
   MEAN     =      4.5000
   MEAN     =      4.6000
   MEAN     =      4.4000
   MEAN     =      3.2000
   MEAN     =      3.5000
   MEAN     =      3.4000
   MEAN     =      3.4000
   MEAN     =      3.4000
   MEAN     =      4.6000
```

```
MEAN    =    3.7000
MEAN    =    4.7000
```

Exercises 8.4

8.4.1 Reject H_0; bulbs last longer than 600 hours on average—change advertising.

Exercises 8.5

8.5.1 z test: large sample, σ known or unknown.
small sample, σ known, population normal.

t test: small sample, σ unknown, population normal.

8.5.3 $\bar{x} = 42.089$, Mean is significantly reduced at the 5% level.

8.5.5 $\bar{x} = 34.87$, $S_{n-1} = 11.90$.

Accept H_0, no significant difference at 5% level.

8.5.7 For question 3, a 95% C.I. for μ is:

$40.59 \leqslant \mu \leqslant 43.59$

For question 5, a 95% C.I. for μ is $28.85 \leqslant \mu \leqslant 40.89$.

If $\bar{x}$ lies in the C.I. for μ, we would accept H_0: μ is true, $\bar{x}$ supports the value of μ claimed.

Chapter 9

Exercises 9.1

9.1.1 Both judges are sceptical about wine G.

They seem to disagree over wine B.

$r_s = 0.6121$

9.1.3 If $\sum d^2 = 165$, average squared difference in the ranks is 16.5

d^2	16	16	16	16	...	16
d_i	−4	−4	4	4	...	4
r_1	1	2	10	7	...	6
r_2	5	6	4	3	...	2

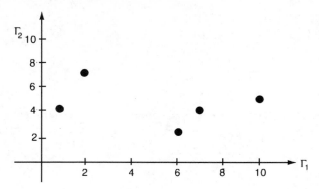

9.1.5 $S = -6, r_k = -0.133$
$S = -6, r_k = -0.214$

Exercises 9.3

9.3.1 $r = -0.079$, not a large enough value to conclude that there is statistical evidence of linear association.

9.3.3 Yes, both randomly varying.
$r = 0.9213$, strong evidence that as 1 variable increases, so does the other.

9.3.5 Consider $r = 0.9213$.

$$\text{Here covariance } (x, y) = \frac{\Sigma xy - n\bar{x}\bar{y}}{n - 1}$$
$$= \frac{15\,533\,178 - 15 \times 855.64 \times 1199.79}{14}$$
$$= \underline{134\,356.85}$$

The joint variation is large as the values for X and Y are large. This is why we divide covariance by the variation in X and Y to eliminate the effect of the magnitude of either variable.

9.3.7 $r_s(\text{critical}) = 0.564$. Thus at 5% level, $r_s = 0.5758$ is critical. For example 9.1, $r_s(\text{critical}) = 0.643$, thus $r_s = 0.8631$ is critical at the 5% and even 1% levels.

Exercises 9.4

9.4.1 $y = 14.5740 + 0.1939x$

If $x = 18.6\%, y = 18.18$.

$(r^2 = 28\%)$.

Exercises 9.5

9.5.3 `MTB > c1-c2`
`DATA> 708          80`
`DATA> DATA> 1368        168`
`DATA> DATA> 597         100`

```
DATA> DATA> 1075      121
DATA> DATA> 1506      162
DATA> DATA> 656       76
DATA> DATA> 438       43
DATA> DATA> 491       65
DATA> DATA> 1258      100
DATA> DATA> 480       59
DATA> end
     10 rows read.

MTB > regress c2 on 1 predictor in c1;
SUBC> fits in C3;
SUBC> sres in c4
* NOTE * Subcommand does not end in. or ; (; assumed).
SUBC> end

The regression equation is
C2 = 16.1 + 0.0948 C1

Predictor       Coef      Stdev     t-ratio        p
Constant        16.12     14.36       1.12     0.294
C1             0.09476   0.01528      6.20     0.000

s = 18.54      R-sq = 82.8%      R-sq(adj) = 80.6%

Analysis of Variance

SOURCE        DF       SS       MS       F        P
Regression     1     13223    13223    38.47   0.000
Error          8      2750      344
Total          9     15972

Unusual Observations
Obs.     C1         C2       Fit    Stdev.Fit   Residual   St.Resid
9       1258     100.00    135.33      8.47      -35.33     -2.14R

R denotes an obs. with a large st. resid.
MTB > print c1-c4

ROW     C1      C2        C3          C4

  1     708     80      83.214     -0.18431
  2    1368    168     145.757      1.41085
  3     597    100      72.696      1.59386
  4    1075    121     117.992      0.17417
  5    1506    162     158.834      0.21782
  6     656     76      78.286     -0.13205
  7     438     43      57.628     -0.89320
  8     491     65      62.651      0.14091
  9    1258    100     135.333     -2.14265
 10     480     59      61.608     -0.15699
```

Chapter 10

Exercises 10.1

10.1.1 Use 1990; 13% increase.

Exercises 10.2

10.2.1 9.7% increase from 1991 to 1993.

10.2.3 27.4% increase from 1992 to 1994.

$$I = \frac{85.44}{62.35} \times 100\% = 137\% \text{ or a } 37\% \text{ increase.}$$

Exercises 10.3

10.3.1 $I = 128.9$ or a 28.9% increase.

Exercises 10.4

10.4.1 $\dfrac{5961.2}{48} = 124.19$

10.4.3 $\dfrac{145\,239.5}{1000} = 145.24$

Differences are due to rounding errors. 0.7% decrease.

Exercises 10.5

10.5.1 80.48, 69.06, 59.62p, 55.05p, 48.55p, 41.15p, 36.78p, 33.86p, 32.38p, 30.84p, 29.07p, 28.12p.

Base year changed as RPI shows 285.9% increase in 1986!

Exercises 10.6

10.6.1 0.998%, 3.0%, 0.88%, 0.40%, 0.08%, 1%, 0.94%, 0.77%, prices decrease by 0.23%, and by 0.77%.

10.6.3 24.2%, 16.5%, 15.8%, 8.3%, 13.3%, 18.0%, 11.9%, 8.6%, 4.6%, 5.0% 6.1%, 3.4%.

Exercises 10.7

10.7.1 4.462, 4.529, 4.849, 4.666, 4.756, 4.834, 4.9068, 4.948, etc.

Peaks occur in 4th quarter—possibly explained by Christmas.

Chapter 11

Exercises 11.1

11.1.1 Let A = number of accounting books
$\quad\quad\quad B$ = number of BIT books
$\quad\quad\quad L$ = number of law books.

$$16A + 8B + 9L \leqslant 60\,000$$
$$8A + 5B + 2L \leqslant 1400$$
$$2A + 9B + 4L \leqslant 1700$$

Exercises 11.2

11.2.1

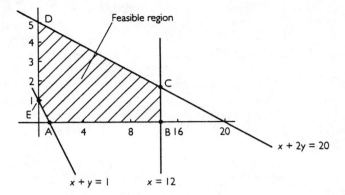

Extreme points	$z = x + 3y$
A (1, 0)	1
B (12, 0)	12
C (12, 4)	24 ← Maximum
D (0, 5)	15
E (0, 1)	3

11.2.3 Minimise $C = 1.5I + 2.2N$

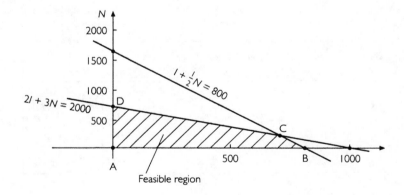

Extreme point	$C = 1.5I + 2.2N$
A (0, 0)	0
B (800, 0)	1200
C (700, 200)	1490
D (0, 666.67)	1466.67

Minimum costs occur when no items are made.

Also solutions occur when only 1 drug is manufactured. As the company has a market for both drugs, most realistic option is C, $I = 700$, $N = 200$ boxes costing £1490.

11.2.5 In constraints $y \geqslant 30$ and $x \geqslant 20$, as exactly $y = 30$ and $x = 20$ is optimal, there is no surplus of either variable manufactured.

Exercises 11.3

11.3.1 $x + y + S_1 = 100$
$0.5x + y + S_2 = 80$
$x - S_3 + A_1 = 20$
$y - S_4 + A_2 = 30$

Initial tableau:

Basic variable	x	y	S_1	S_2	S_3	S_4	A_1	A_2	b_i
S_1	1	1	1	0	0	0	0	0	100
S_2	$\frac{1}{2}$	1	0	1	0	0	0	0	80
S_3	1	0	0	0	-1	0	1	0	20
S_4	0	1	0	0	0	-1	0	1	30
z	-250	-400	0	0	0	0	0	0	0

Initial basic feasible solution:
$x = y = 0$, $S_1 = 100$, $S_2 = 80$, $S_3 = A_1 - 20$, $S_4 = A_2 - 30$, $z = 0$.
(We use A_1 and A_2 so that S_3 and S_4 are non-negative). Pivotal element is a_{42}.

Tableau 2:

Basic variable	x	y	S_1	S_2	S_3	S_4	A_1	A_2	b_i
S_1	1	0	1	0	0	1	0	-1	70
S_2	$\frac{1}{2}$	0	0	1	0	1	0	-1	50
S_3	1	0	0	0	-1	0	1	0	20
y	0	1	0	0	0	-1	0	1	30
z	-250	0	0	0	0	-400	0	400	120 000

Basic feasible solution $y = 30$, $S_1 = 70$, $S_2 = 50$, $S_3 = A_1 - 20$, $S_4 = 0 = x$, $z = 120\,000$.

Basic variable	x	y	S_1	S_2	S_3	S_4	A_1	A_2	b_i
S_1	0	0	1	0	1	1	-1	-1	50
S_2	0	0	0	1	$\frac{1}{2}$	1	$-\frac{1}{2}$	-1	40
x	1	0	0	0	-1	0	1	0	20
y	0	1	0	0	0	-1	0	1	30
z	0	0	0	0	-250	-400	250	400	170 000

Basic feasible solution:

$$x = 20 \atop y = 30 \Big\} \quad z = 17\,000.$$

$$S_1 = 50 \atop S_2 = 40 \Big\} \quad \text{Slack in 1st and 2nd constraints.}$$

This means unused 50 hours in the spraying department, and 40 unused hours in the polishing department.

$S_3 = S_4 = 0$ (non-basic variables) are set to zero.

Shadow prices: $S_3 = -250$, $S_4 = -400$ (from the final row of the tableau).

If the company choose to make 1 more x (XJT) it would make a loss of £250, and a similar loss of £400 for any y (Porsche). S_3 is shadow price for constraint 3 (x here). Similarly $S4$ is shadow price for constraint 4, y here. Set $A_1 = A_2 = 0$; these have no meaning in the solution.

Chapter 12

Exercises 12.1

12.1.1

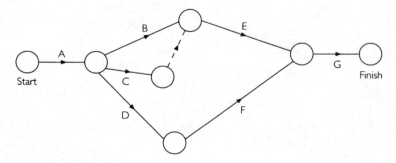

12.1.3

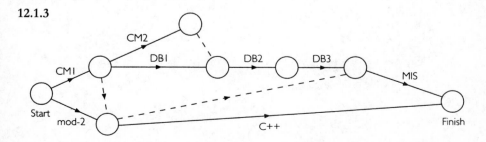

Exercises 12.2

12.2.1

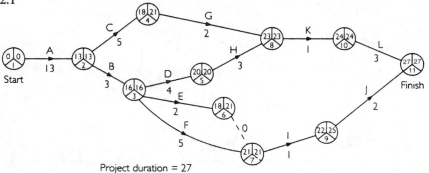

Project duration = 27

Exercises 12.3

12.3.1 Floats for Exercise 12.2.1

Activity	A	B	C	D	E	F	G	H	I	J	K	L
Float	0	0	3	0	3	0	3	0	3	3	0	0

Exercises 12.4

12.4.1 Gantt chart for Exercise 12.2.1

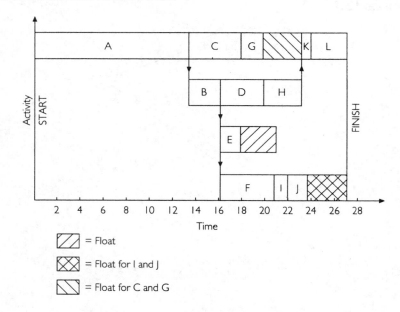

= Float

= Float for I and J

= Float for C and G

Critical path: A, B, D, H, K, L

We can see the float after G is in fact float for a path along C, G; similarly for I and J.

Exercises 12.5

12.5.1

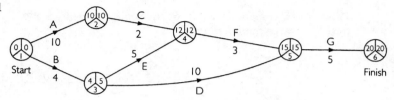

Critical path: A, C, F, G = 20 days.

Cost of completing project = £1180.

Initial Gantt chart:

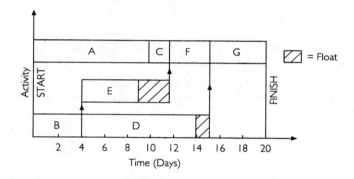

Activity	Cost slopes £/day
A	£100
B	£75
C	£40
D	£60
E	£25
F	£10
G	£50

Step 1 Crash F @ £10 per day. Crash by 1 day.
Now 2 critical paths: A, C, F, G and B, D, G. project takes 19 days. Costs £1190.

Step 2 Crash G by 2 days, @ £50 per day.
Project takes 17 days. Costs £1290.

Step 3 Crash F and D simultaneously costing £10 + £60, by 1 day. Project takes 16 days, costs £1350.
F and G are now at minimum time.

Step 4 Crash C & D simultaneously, by 1 day, costing £100. Thus the project takes 15 days and costs £1450.
C now minimum time.

Step 5 Crash A and D simultaneously by 2 days, costing £320. Thus the project now takes 13 days and costs £1770.
This is the minimum duration for the project as A, C, F and G are all crashed i.e. at minimum duration.

12.5.3

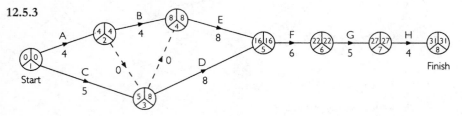

(i)   Critical path: A, B, E, F, G, H.
Costs = £289
Takes 31 days.

(ii) Crash G by 2 days, then F by 3 days, then A by 1 day. Crash E by 2 days. Project costs £393.01 and takes 23 days.

(iii) Crash H by 1 day and then E by a further 2 days simultaneously as you crash C by 2 days. This is the minimal project duration: 20 days and costs a total of £479.67.

Appendix

Table I   Areas of the standardised normal distribution

The function tabulated is $\dfrac{1}{\sqrt{2\pi}}\displaystyle\int_{z}^{\infty} e^{-x^2/2}\,dx,$

the probability that $Z > z$, where $Z \sim N(0, 1)$.

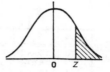

z	0.00	0.01	0.02	0.03	0.04	0.05	0.06	0.07	0.08	0.09
0.0	0.50000	0.49601	0.49202	0.48803	0.48405	0.48006	0.47608	0.47210	0.46812	0.46414
0.1	0.46017	0.45620	0.45224	0.44828	0.44433	0.44038	0.43644	0.43250	0.42858	0.42465
0.2	0.42074	0.41683	0.41294	0.40905	0.40517	0.40129	0.39743	0.39358	0.38974	0.38591
0.3	0.38209	0.37828	0.37448	0.37070	0.36693	0.36317	0.35942	0.35569	0.35197	0.34827
0.4	0.34458	0.34090	0.33724	0.33360	0.32997	0.32636	0.32276	0.31918	0.31561	0.31207
0.5	0.30854	0.30503	0.30153	0.29806	0.29460	0.29116	0.28774	0.28434	0.28096	0.27760
0.6	0.27425	0.27093	0.26763	0.26435	0.26109	0.25785	0.25463	0.25143	0.24825	0.24510
0.7	0.24196	0.23885	0.23576	0.23269	0.22965	0.22663	0.22363	0.22065	0.21770	0.21476
0.8	0.21186	0.20897	0.20611	0.20327	0.20045	0.19766	0.19489	0.19215	0.18943	0.18673
0.9	0.18406	0.18141	0.17879	0.17619	0.17361	0.17106	0.16853	0.16602	0.16354	0.16109
1.0	0.15866	0.15625	0.15386	0.15150	0.14917	0.14686	0.14457	0.14231	0.14007	0.13786
1.1	0.13567	0.13350	0.13136	0.12924	0.12714	0.12507	0.12302	0.12100	0.11900	0.11702
1.2	0.11507	0.11314	0.11123	0.10935	0.10749	0.10565	0.10383	0.10204	0.10027	0.09853
1.3	0.09680	0.09510	0.09342	0.09176	0.09012	0.08851	0.08692	0.08534	0.08379	0.08226
1.4	0.08076	0.07927	0.07780	0.07636	0.07493	0.07353	0.07215	0.07078	0.06944	0.06811
1.5	0.06681	0.06552	0.06426	0.06301	0.06178	0.06057	0.05938	0.05821	0.05705	0.05592
1.6	0.05480	0.05370	0.05262	0.05155	0.05050	0.04947	0.04846	0.04746	0.04648	0.04551
1.7	0.04457	0.04363	0.04272	0.04182	0.04093	0.04006	0.03920	0.03836	0.03754	0.03673
1.8	0.03593	0.03515	0.03438	0.03362	0.03288	0.03216	0.03144	0.03074	0.03005	0.02938
1.9	0.02872	0.02807	0.02743	0.02680	0.02619	0.02559	0.02500	0.02442	0.02385	0.02330
2.0	0.02275	0.02222	0.02169	0.02118	0.02068	0.02018	0.01970	0.01923	0.01876	0.01831
2.1	0.01786	0.01743	0.01700	0.01659	0.01618	0.01578	0.01539	0.01500	0.01463	0.01426
2.2	0.01390	0.01355	0.01321	0.01287	0.01255	0.01222	0.01191	0.01160	0.01130	0.01101
2.3	0.01072	0.01044	0.01017	0.00990	0.00964	0.00939	0.00914	0.00889	0.00866	0.00842
2.4	0.00820	0.00798	0.00776	0.00755	0.00734	0.00714	0.00695	0.00676	0.00657	0.00639
2.5	0.00621	0.00604	0.00587	0.00570	0.00554	0.00539	0.00523	0.00508	0.00494	0.00480
2.6	0.00466	0.00453	0.00440	0.00427	0.00415	0.00402	0.00391	0.00379	0.00368	0.00357
2.7	0.00347	0.00336	0.00326	0.00317	0.00307	0.00298	0.00289	0.00280	0.00272	0.00264
2.8	0.00256	0.00248	0.00240	0.00233	0.00226	0.00219	0.00212	0.00205	0.00199	0.00193
2.9	0.00187	0.00181	0.00175	0.00169	0.00164	0.00159	0.00154	0.00149	0.00144	0.00139
3.0	0.00135	0.00131	0.00126	0.00122	0.00118	0.00114	0.00111	0.00107	0.00104	0.00100
3.1	0.00097	0.00094	0.00090	0.00087	0.00084	0.00082	0.00079	0.00076	0.00074	0.00071
3.2	0.00069	0.00066	0.00064	0.00062	0.00060	0.00058	0.00056	0.00054	0.00052	0.00050
3.3	0.00048	0.00047	0.00045	0.00043	0.00042	0.00040	0.00039	0.00038	0.00036	0.00035
3.4	0.00034	0.00032	0.00031	0.00030	0.00029	0.00028	0.00027	0.00026	0.00025	0.00024
3.5	0.00023	0.00022	0.00022	0.00021	0.00020	0.00019	0.00019	0.00018	0.00017	0.00017
3.6	0.00016	0.00015	0.00015	0.00014	0.00014	0.00013	0.00013	0.00012	0.00012	0.00011
3.7	0.00011	0.00010	0.00010	0.00010	0.00009	0.00009	0.00008	0.00008	0.00008	0.00008
3.8	0.00007	0.00007	0.00007	0.00006	0.00006	0.00006	0.00006	0.00005	0.00005	0.00005
3.9	0.00005	0.00005	0.00004	0.00004	0.00004	0.00004	0.00004	0.00004	0.00003	0.00003

Table 2   Percentage points of the standardised normal distribution

The z_α values tabulated are such that $\Pr(Z > z_\alpha) = \alpha$, where $Z \sim N(0, 1)$

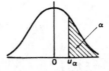

α	z_α	α	z_α	α	z_α	α	z_α
0.50	0.00000	0.34	0.41246	0.18	0.91537	0.025	1.96000
0.49	0.02507	0.33	0.43991	0.17	0.95416	0.020	2.05375
0.48	0.05015	0.32	0.46770	0.16	0.99446	0.010	2.32635
0.47	0.07527	0.31	9.49585	0.15	1.03643	0.009	2.36562
0.46	0.10004	0.30	0.52440	0.14	1.08032	0.008	2.40891
0.45	0.12566	0.29	0.55338	0.13	1.12639	0.007	2.45726
0.44	0.15097	0.28	0.58284	0.12	1.17499	0.006	2.51214
0.43	0.17637	0.27	0.61281	0.11	1.22653	0.005	2.57583
0.42	0.20189	0.26	0.64335	0.10	1.28155	0.004	2.65207
0.41	0.22754	0.25	0.67449	0.09	1.34076	0.003	2.74778
0.40	0.25335	0.24	0.70630	0.08	1.40507	0.002	2.87816
0.39	0.27932	0.23	0.73885	0.07	1.47579	0.001	3.09023
0.38	0.30548	0.22	0.77219	0.06	1.55477	0.0005	3.29053
0.37	0.33185	0.21	0.80642	0.05	1.64485	0.0001	3.71902
0.36	0.35846	0.20	0.84162	0.04	1.75069	0.00005	3.89060
0.35	0.38532	0.19	0.87790	0.03	1.88079	0.00001	4.26489

6

EDITION

Cognition

The Un

Cognition

ROBERT J. STERNBERG
Oklahoma State University

KARIN STERNBERG
Oklahoma State University

with contributions of the
Investigating Cognitive Psychology boxes by

JEFF MIO
California State University–Pomona

WADSWORTH
CENGAGE Learning

Australia • Brazil • Japan • Korea • Mexico • Singapore • Spain • United Kingdom • United States

Cognition, Sixth Edition, International Edition
Robert J. Sternberg and Karin Sternberg

Acquisitions Editor: Jaime Perkins

Development Editor: Tangelique Williams

Production Manager: Matthew Ballantyne

Compositor/Production Service: PreMediaGlobal

Marketing Manager: Elisabeth Rhoden

Marketing Program Manager: Sean Foy

Marketing Communications Manager: Talia Wise

Content Project Management: PreMediaGlobal

Design Director: Rob Hugel

Art Director: Vernon Boes

Print Buyer: Mary Beth Hennebury

Rights Acquisitions Specialist: Roberta Broyer

Rights Acquisitions Director: Bob Kauser

Photo Researcher: PreMediaGlobal

Text Researcher: Karyn Morrison

Cover Designer: Denise Davidson

Cover Image: Russell Illig/Getty Images; Digital Vision

Library of Congress Control Number: 2010935207

International Edition:

ISBN-13: 978-1-111-34539-6

ISBN-10: 1-111-34539-2

Cengage Learning International Offices

Asia
www.cengageasia.com
tel: (65) 6410 1200

Australia/New Zealand
www.cengage.com.au
tel: (61) 3 9685 4111

Brazil
www.cengage.com.br
tel: (55) 11 3665 9900

India
www.cengage.co.in
tel: (91) 11 4364 1111

Latin America
www.cengage.com.mx
tel: (52) 55 1500 6000

UK/Europe/Middle East/Africa
www.cengage.co.uk
tel: (44) 0 1264 332 424

Represented in Canada by Nelson Education, Ltd.
www.nelson.com
tel: (416) 752 9100 / (800) 668 0671

Cengage Learning is a leading provider of customized learning solutions with office locations around the globe, including Singapore, the United Kingdom, Australia, Mexico, Brazil, and Japan. Locate your local office at: **www.cengage.com/global**

For product information and free companion resources: **www.cengage.com/international**

Visit your local office: **www.cengage.com/global**

Visit our corporate website: **www.cengage.com**

Printed in Canada
2 3 4 5 15 14 13 12

Contents in Brief

Contents

To the Instructor

Welcome to the Sixth Edition of *Cognition*. This edition is now coauthored by Karin Sternberg, PhD. As you will see, this edition underwent a major revision. We reorganized and meticulously revised all chapters with the goal of providing an even more comprehensible text that integrates the latest research but also retains students' interest by providing more examples from other areas of research and from the real world.

What Are the Goals of this Book?

Cognitive psychologists study a wide range of psychological phenomena, such as perception, learning, memory, and thinking. In addition, cognitive psychologists study seemingly less cognitively oriented phenomena, such as emotion and motivation. In fact, almost any topic of psychological interest may be studied from a cognitive perspective. In this textbook, we describe some of the preliminary answers to questions asked by researchers in the main areas of cognitive psychology. The goals of this book are to:

- present the field of cognitive psychology in a comprehensive but engaging manner;
- integrate the presentation of the field under the general banner of human intelligence; and
- interweave throughout the text key themes and key ideas that permeate cognitive psychology.

Our Mission in Revising the Text

A number of goals guided us through revising *Cognition*. In particular we decided to:

- make the text more accessible and understandable;
- make cognitive psychology more fascinating and less intimidating;
- increase coverage of applications in other areas of psychology as well as in the real world; and
- better integrate coverage of human intelligence and cognitive neuroscience in each chapter.

Key Themes and Ideas

The key themes of this book, discussed in greater detail in Chapter 1, are:

1. nature versus nurture;
2. rationalism versus empiricism;

3. structures versus processes;
4. domain generality versus domain specificity;
5. validity of causal inferences versus ecological validity;
6. applied versus basic research; and
7. biological versus behavioral methods.

The key ideas of this book, also discussed at more length in Chapter 1, are as follows:

1. Empirical data and theories are both important. Data in cognitive psychology can be fully understood only in the context of an explanatory theory, but theories are empty without empirical data.
2. Cognition is generally adaptive but not in all specific instances.
3. Cognitive processes interact with each other and with non-cognitive processes.
4. Cognition needs to be studied through a variety of scientific methods.
5. All basic research in cognitive psychology may lead to applications, and all applied research may lead to basic understandings.

Major Organizing and Special Pedagogical Features

Special features, some new and some established, characterize *Cognition*, 6th Edition. Here are the new features:

- *Believe It or Not* feature boxes present incredible and exciting information and facts from the world of cognitive psychology.
- A "Neuroscience and ..." section in every chapter.
- An "Intelligence and ..." section in every chapter integrates the theme of intelligence with the chapter topic at hand. The separate intelligence chapter, formerly Chapter 13, has been eliminated.
- *Concept Checks* follow each major section to encourage students to quickly check their comprehension.

And here are some of the established features:

- *Practical Applications of Cognitive Psychology* feature boxes help students think about applications of cognitive psychology in their own lives.
- *Investigating Cognitive Psychology* features present mini-experiments and tasks that students can complete on their own.

What's New to the 6ᵗʰ Edition

Cognition, 6th Edition underwent a major revision to make the book more comprehensible, accessible, and interesting to students. Revision highlights include:

- Revised *In the Lab* features, including new profiles of Henry Roediger, III in Chapter 1; Marvin Chun in Chapter 2; Martha Farah in Chapter 3; and Keith Rayner in Chapter 10.
- *Believe It or Not* boxes now appear in every chapter to make cognitive psychology more fascinating and less intimidating to students and to show it can be fun and surprising.

- The *Practical Applications* boxes now conclude with a critical thinking question.
- Concept Checks now appear after each major section.
- Updated Suggested Readings are now preceded by headings so students can quickly find what they are interested in.
- Key experiments are now clearly highlighted in *Investigating Cognitive Psychology* boxes.
- Thoroughly integrated intelligence coverage now appears throughout the 6th edition.
- Advance organizers added to improve the reading flow and students' understanding of how things fit together into a larger context.
- Updated chapter organization for greater comprehensibility.
- Reduced coverage of cognitive development and other non-cognitive topics more accurately reflect the focus of cognitive psychology courses.
- New subheadings increase understanding of content matter and larger context.

Chapter-specific revisions include:

Chapter 1

1. An all new introduction to intelligence in Chapter 1 discusses what intelligence is, how intelligence relates to cognition, and three cognitive models of intelligence (Carroll, Gardner, Sternberg).
2. New everyday examples include analyzing why companies spend so much money on advertising products that students use, for example, Apple iPhone and Windows 7.
3. New example in section on why learning about psychology's history is important: a discussion on newspapers' coverage of the success of educational programs, hardly any which use control groups.
4. New example of how nurture influences cognition by comparing Western and Asian cultures.
5. Expanded discussion of rationalism vs. empiricism now includes Plato and Aristotle.
6. Expanded explanation of Descartes' views.
7. Enhanced introduction to section on early dialectics and explanation of what dialectics are.
8. Expanded explanation of what being a structuralist means in terms of psychology.
9. Expanded discussion of introspection.
10. Explanation of Ebbinghaus's experiment and new Ebbinghaus's forgetting curve figure.
11. New example from contemporary times has been added to the section on behaviorism explaining how reward and punishment are used in modern psychotherapy.
12. New section on criticisms of behaviorism.
13. New *Believe It or Not* box on scientific "progress" in the first half of the 20th century and the introduction of prefrontal lobotomies.
14. New explanation of why behaviorists regarded the mind as a "black box".
15. New *In the Lab of Henry L. Roediger, III* feature.
16. New coverage of control variables.
17. New explanation of why control over experimental conditions is important.

18. Expanded section on when to use correlational studies and discuss their potential shortcomings.
19. New section on how other professions and fields benefit from findings in cognitive psychology.

Chapter 2

1. New "hands-on" activity now opens chapter by asking students to look out of the window to see for themselves how objects that are farther away look small, even if they are huge.
2. Reorganized chapter first presents basics of perception, perceptual illusions, and how our visual system works; then, the theories of perception, perception of objects and forms, perceptual constancies; and last, deficits in perception.
3. New introduction to "From Sensation to Perception" discussion illustrates with two examples how complex perception can be.
4. New *In the Lab of Marvin Chun* feature box.
5. New coverage of the Ganzfeld effect and experiment to experience the Ganzfeld effect.
6. New discussion of light as a precondition for vision, and about the spectrum of light waves and which ones humans can see.
7. Reorganized coverage of how our visual system works.
8. Visual pathways discussion expanded, updated, and now appears near the beginning of the chapter.
9. New introduction to approaches to perception (that is, the part about theories), and a more thorough explanation of what bottom-up and top-down approaches are.
10. Direct perception is now discussed as part of bottom-up theories discussion.
11. New sections on the everyday importance of neuroscience and direct perception.
12. New section discusses template theory as an example of a chunk-based theory and connects visual perception with long-term memory.
13. New section on neuroscience and template theories.
14. New discussion of why it is so hard for computers to read handwriting.
15. Updated coverage of pandemonium model and updated coverage of the local-precedence effect.
16. Expanded coverage of neuroscience and feature-matching theories.
17. New section on neuroscience and recognition-by-components theory.
18. Top-down theories section now includes discussion of intelligence and perception.
19. Expanded coverage of elaboration/explanation of object-centered versus viewer-centered representation.
20. Reorganized discussion of Gestalt approach section.
21. Reorganized discussion of the neuroscience of recognizing faces and patterns.
22. New neuropsychological research on perceptual constancies.
23. New coverage of stereoscopic seeing with just one eye in strabismic eyes.
24. Expanded coverage of neuroscience and depth perception, with new research results.
25. Reorganized discussion of ataxias and agnosias separately discusses "difficulties in perceiving the what" and "difficulties in knowing the how".
26. New section on perception in practice with respect to traffic and accidents.

Chapter 3

1. New organization: Now a section on the anatomy and mechanisms of the brain discusses the structure of the brain first before going into details regarding neuronal structure and function; a second section then discusses research methods/methods of viewing the brain; a third section discusses brain disorders; and a fourth (new) section covers intelligence and neuroscience.
2. New *In the Lab of Martha Farah* box.
3. Updated discussion of the function of brain parts reflects the latest literature.
4. Expanded explanation of how autism relates to the function of the amygdala.
5. Reorganized discussion of the hippocampus.
6. Updated and expanded information on the function of the hypothalamus.
7. New coverage of the evolution of the human brain.
8. Updated and expanded coverage of the lateralization of function.
9. New explanation of vocabulary frequently used to describe brain regions: dorsal, caudal, rostral, ventral.
10. The concept of "action potential" is now discussed.
11. Expanded coverage of myelin and Nodes of Ranvier.
12. Updated coverage of neurotransmitters to reflect current status of knowledge.
13. New coverage of genetic knockout studies and neurochemical ways to induce particular lesions in the section on animal studies.
14. New coverage of "noise" in EEG recordings, and how this noise can be dealt with by averaging recordings.
15. New detailed example of a study using ERP to help students understand the technique.
16. New explanation of the N400 effect.
17. Updated discussion of research and imaging methods, including new references.
18. Expanded information on CT scans, angiography, and MRIs.
19. More detailed explanation of the subtraction method.
20. New explanation of how DTI works.
21. Expanded section on TMS and introduced concept of rTMS.
22. Brain disorders discussion now begins by explaining why brain disorders are of importance to finding out how the brain works.
23. New section on intelligence and neuroscience that discusses the connection between intelligence and (a) brain size, (b) neurons, (c) brain metabolism as well as biological bases of intelligence testing and the P-FIT theory of intelligence.

Chapter 4

1. Reorganized chapter first presents attention (signal detection, vigilance, search, selective attention, and divided attention), then discusses what happens when attentional processes fail; habituation and adaptation, as well as automatic and controlled processes in attention are explored; and last, consciousness.
2. Included new introductory example for introduction to signal detection and vigilance: lifeguard on beach and research psychologist.
3. Expanded coverage of neuroscience and vigilance.
4. New research on feature integration theory.
5. Expanded coverage of the neuroscience of visual search and aging.
6. Updated discussion of selective attention.
7. Expanded discussion of neuroscience and selective attention.

8. Divided attention now integrates information regarding human intelligence.
9. Updated and reorganized coverage of theories of divided attention.
10. Revised network model discussion in "Neuroscience and Attention" section.
11. New section on intelligence and attention includes discussion of reaction time and inspection time.
12. Reorganized and updated discussion of section "When our attention fails us" includes a discussion of Gardner's theory of intelligence as potentially relevant to ADHD treatment.
13. Updated discussion of change blindness and inattentional blindness.
14. Updated coverage of "extinction" in spatial neglect as well as updated information on neuroscience research in spatial neglect.
15. "Controlled and Automatic Processes" section has been reorganized and updated.
16. Sternberg's triarchic theory of intelligence now connected to controlled and automatic processes.
17. The Stroop effect is now featured in "automatization in daily life".
18. Updated discussion of consciousness.

Chapter 5

1. New discussion of intelligence testing and culture that describes problems of culture-fair testing and how memory abilities may differ across different cultural groups.
2. New coverage of long-term store and new techniques that are being developed to help students transfer learned facts into long-term memory.
3. Expanded coverage of how experiments were conducted on the levels-of-processing approach and what their results mean (in particular, why people with schizophrenia have memory problems).
4. Fisher & Craik (1977) experiment about the effectiveness of acoustic and semantic retrieval has been elaborated more, with examples to make clear the differences between the different kinds of retrieval.
5. Expanded coverage of the phonological loop.
6. New section on intelligence and working memory.
7. New discussion of neuropsychological coverage added to the section on amnesia.
8. New explanation of double dissociation.
9. Updated coverage in section on how memories are stored.
10. Expanded explanation of the term long-term potentiation.

Chapter 6

1. Updated research on long-term storage.
2. Expanded neuropsychological coverage of section on long-term storage.
3. New section explaining the difference between interference and decay.
4. Expanded coverage of the spacing effect.
5. Expanded coverage of organization of information.
6. Expanded coverage of forcing functions and their use in hospitals.
7. Expanded coverage and new figure on neuropsychological experiments on retrieval from long-term memory.
8. Expanded coverage of the "recent-probes task".

9. Expanded coverage of flashbulb memory and the effect of mood on memory.
10. Updated research on memory distortions.
11. Updated research on eyewitness testimony; expanded coverage and new introduction of the *post-identification feedback effect*.
12. Expanded coverage of children as eyewitnesses and lineups.
13. Updated research on context effects.

Chapter 7

1. Revised coverage of internal and external representations.
2. Updated research on mental imagery.
3. New research on mental rotations.
4. Updated coverage of gender and mental rotation.
5. Updated coverage of research on image scanning.
6. Updated research on section "synthesizing images and propositions".
7. Updated coverage of demand characteristics.
8. Updated discussion of Johnson-Laird's mental models.
9. Updated discussion of mental shortcuts.

Chapter 8

1. Updated research on concepts.
2. Updated research on prototypes.
3. New coverage of VAM (varying abstraction model) theory in the exemplars discussion.
4. New discussion of concepts in different cultures.
5. Updated research on scripts, ACT-R, and the PDP model.
6. Expanded section on criticism of connectionist models.

Chapter 9

1. New discussion of reading and discourse have been added to this chapter.
2. New introduction to section "What is language" discusses how many languages there are in the world, that still new languages are being discovered, etc.
3. Updated research on basic components of words.
4. New introduction to the section on processes of language comprehension.
5. Updated research on section "the view of speech perception as ordinary".
6. New coverage of new research to explain the phenomenon of phonemic restoration.
7. Updated discussion of the motor theory of speech perception.
8. Updated section on the McGurk effect with the latest neuropsychological research.
9. Updated coverage of semantics.
10. Updated research in the section on syntactical priming.
11. More in-depth description of the Luka & Barsalou (2005) experiment.
12. Expanded explanations of phrase-structure grammar.
13. Expanded explanation of the critique of Chomsky's theory.
14. Updated research on dyslexia.

15. Updated research on lexical processes in reading.
16. New section on intelligence and lexical access speed.
17. Updated research on propositional representations.
18. Updated research on "Representing the Text in Mental Models."

Chapter 10

1. New coverage of animal language (formerly in Chapter 9).
2. Reorganized discussion of the neuropsychology of language.
3. New *In the Lab of Keith Rayner* boxed feature.
4. New coverage in colors discussion includes recent research and demonstrates how one's language can influence color perception.
5. New research in section on verbs and grammatical gender features description of new research experiments on grammatical gender and prepositions.
6. New neuropsychological research on bilinguals.
7. Updated research on second language acquisition.
8. Expanded discussion of Meinzer et al. (2007) study.
9. Updated research on language mixtures and change.
10. Extended coverage of neuroscience and bilingualism.
11. Updated research on slips of the tongue.
12. New coverage of Steven Pinker's new theory of indirect speech.
13. Updated research on gender and language.
14. Updated and revised coverage of animal language.
15. New coverage of the brain and word recognition.
16. New coverage of the brain and semantic processing.
17. Expanded and updated coverage on the brain and syntax.
18. Updated and extended coverage of the brain and language acquisition.
19. Updated and extended coverage on the plasticity of the brain.
20. New and updated research on the brain and gender difference in language processing.
21. Updated research on autism.

Chapter 11

1. Reorganized discussion of judgment and decision making for improved comprehension.
2. New explanation of the difference between the model of economic man and woman and subjective expected utility theory.
3. Streamlined discussion of subjective expected utility theory.
4. Streamlined and updated coverage of satisficing now includes a comparison with classical decision theory.
5. Updated discussion of framing effects.
6. Updated coverage of gambler's fallacy and hot hand.
7. Updated discussion of the evaluation of heuristics.
8. Updated section on naturalistic decision making.
9. Expanded discussion of evolution and reasoning.
10. Updated and streamlined coverage of syllogisms.
11. Streamlined discussion of inductive reasoning.

12. Streamlined section on reaching causal inferences.
13. Updated section on categorical inferences.
14. Updated coverage of an alternative view of reasoning.
15. Updated and expanded section on the neuroscience of reasoning.

Chapter 12

1. Reorganized discussion of the problem-solving cycle.
2. Streamlined discussion of well-structured problems.
3. Updated section on problem representation.
4. Streamlined discussion of insight.
5. Streamlined discussion of the early Gestaltist view.
6. Expanded discussion of the Metcalfe (1986) experiment covered in the section on the neo-Gestaltist view.
7. Coverage of neuroscience and insight aggregated into a neuroscience section, expanded, and updated.
8. Streamlined discussion of intentional transfer.
9. Revised discussion of incubation includes new coverage of a meta-analysis.
10. New discussion of intelligence and complex solving (formerly chapter 13).
11. Section on expertise has been updated and an experiment on beer tasting in experts and novices has been added.
12. Updated discussion of automatic expert processes.
13. Updated coverage of innate talent and acquired skill.
14. New and updated coverage of artificial intelligence and expertise (formerly chapter 13).
15. Updated and streamlined coverage of creativity.
16. Updated discussion of neuroscience and creativity.

Ancillaries

As an instructor, you have a multitude of resources available to you to assist you in the teaching of your class. Student ancillaries are also offered. Available resources include:

Instructor's Manual with Test Bank—Written by Donna Dahlgren of Indiana University Southeast. The Instructor's Manual portion contains chapter outlines, in-class demonstrations, discussion topics, and suggested websites. The Test Bank portion consists of approximately 75 multiple choice and 20 short-answer questions per chapter. Each multiple-choice item is labeled with the page reference and level of difficulty.

PowerLecture with ExamView—With the one-stop digital library and presentation tool, instructors can assemble, edit, and present custom lectures with ease. The PowerLecture, contains a selection of digital media from Wadsworth's latest titles in introductory psychology, including figures and tables. Create, deliver, and customize printed and online tests and study guides in minutes with Exam-View's easy-to-use assessment and tutorial system. Also included are animations, video clips, and preassembled Microsoft PowerPoint lecture slides, written by

Lise Abrams of University of Florida, based on each specific text. Instructors can use the material or add their own material for a truly customized lecture presentation.

CogLab 2.0—CogLab 2.0 lets students do more than just think about cognition. CogLab 2.0 uses the power of the web to teach concepts using important classic and current experiments that demonstrate how the mind works. Nothing is more powerful for students than seeing the effects of these experiments for themselves! It includes features such as simplified student registration, a global database that combines data from students all around the world, between-subject designs that allow for new kinds of experiments, and a "quick display" of student summaries. Also included are trial-by-trial data, standard deviations, and improved instructions.

And when you adopt Sternberg's *Cognition*, you and your students will have access to a rich array of online teaching and learning resources that you won't find anywhere else. The outstanding site features tutorial quizzes, a glossary, weblinks, flashcards, and more!

Acknowledgments

We are grateful to a number of reviewers who have contributed to the development of this book:

Jane L. Pixley, Radford University

Martha J. Hubertz, Florida Atlantic University

Jeffrey S. Anastasi, Sam Houston State University

Robert J. Crutcher, University of Dayton

Eric C. Odgaard, University of South Florida

Takashi Yamauchi, Texas A & M University

David C. Somers, Boston University

Michael J. McGuire, Washburn University

Kimberly Rynearson, Tarleton State University

A special thank you goes to Gerd Gigerenzer and Julian Marewski for their helpful review of, and comments on, Chapter 11.

We would also like to thank Ann Greenberger, developmental editor, as well as all members of our Wadsworth/Cengage Learning editorial and production teams: Jaime Perkins, Acquisitions Editor; Paige Leeds, Assistant Editor; Lauren Keyes, Media Editor; Beth Kluckhohn, Senior Project Manager for PreMedia Global; Tangelique Williams, Developmental Editor; Matt Ballantyne, Senior Content Project Manager; and Jessica Alderman, Editorial Assistant.

To the Student

Why do we remember people whom we met years ago, but sometimes seem to forget what we learned in a course shortly after we take the final exam (or worse, sometimes right before)? How do we manage to carry on a conversation with one person at a party and simultaneously eavesdrop on another more interesting conversation taking place nearby? Why are people so often certain that they are correct in answering a question when in fact they are not? These are just three of the many questions that are addressed by the field of cognitive psychology.

Cognitive psychologists study how people perceive, learn, remember, and think. Although cognitive psychology is a unified field, it draws on many other fields, most notably neuroscience, computer science, linguistics, anthropology, and philosophy. Thus, you will find some of the thinking of all these fields represented in this book. Moreover, cognitive psychology interacts with other fields within psychology, such as psychobiology, developmental psychology, social psychology, and clinical psychology.

For example, it is difficult to be a clinical psychologist today without a solid knowledge of developments in cognitive psychology because so much of the thinking in the clinical field draws on cognitive ideas, both in diagnosis and in therapy. Cognitive psychology has also provided a means for psychologists to investigate experimentally some of the exciting ideas that have emerged from clinical theory and practice, such as notions of unconscious thought.

Cognitive psychology will be important to you not only in its own right, but also in helping you in all of your work. For example, knowledge of cognitive psychology can help you better understand how best to study for tests, how to read effectively, and how to remember difficult-to-learn material.

Cognitive psychologists study a wide range of psychological phenomena such as perception, learning, memory, and thinking. In addition, cognitive psychologists study seemingly less cognitively oriented phenomena, such as emotion and motivation. In fact, almost any topic of psychological interest may be studied from a cognitive perspective. In this textbook we describe some of the preliminary answers to questions asked by researchers in the main areas of cognitive psychology.

- Chapter 1, *Introduction to Cognitive Psychology*: What are the origins of cognitive psychology, and how do people do research in this field?
- Chapter 2, *Perception*: How does the human mind perceive what the senses receive? How does the human mind perceive forms and patterns?
- Chapter 3, *Cognitive Neuroscience*: What structures and processes of the human brain underlie the structures and processes of human cognition?
- Chapter 4, *Attention and Consciousness*: What basic processes of the mind govern how information enters our minds, our awareness, and our high-level processes of information handling?
- Chapter 5, *Memory: Models and Research Methods*: How are different kinds of information (e.g., our experiences related to a traumatic event, the names of U.S. presidents, or the procedure for riding a bicycle) represented in memory?

- Chapter 6, *Memory Processes:* How do we move information into memory, keep it there, and retrieve it from memory when needed?
- Chapter 7, *Representation and Manipulation of Knowledge in Memory: Images and Propositions:* How do we mentally represent information in our minds? Do we do so in words, in pictures, or in some other form representing meaning? Do we have multiple forms of representation?
- Chapter 8, *Representation and Organization of Knowledge in Memory: Concepts, Categories, Networks, and Schemas:* How do we mentally organize what we know?
- Chapter 9, *Language: Nature and Acquisition:* How do we derive and produce meaning through language?
- Chapter 10, *Language in Context:* How does our use of language interact with our ways of thinking? How does our social world interact with our use of language?
- Chapter 11, *Decision Making and Reasoning:* How do we reach important decisions? How do we draw reasonable conclusions from the information we have available? Why and how do we so often make inappropriate decisions and reach inaccurate conclusions?
- Chapter 12, *Problem Solving and Creativity:* How do we solve problems? What processes aid and impede us in reaching solutions to problems? Why are some of us more creative than others? How do we become and remain creative?

To acquire the knowledge outlined above, we suggest you make use of the following pedagogical features of this book:

1. *Chapter outlines,* beginning each chapter, summarize the main topics covered and thus give you an advance overview of what is to be covered in that chapter.
2. *Opening questions* emphasize the main questions each chapter addresses.
3. *Boldface terms,* indexed at ends of chapters and defined in the glossary, help you acquire the vocabulary of cognitive psychology.
4. *End-of-chapter summaries* return to the questions at the opening of each chapter and show our current state of knowledge with regard to these questions.
5. *End-of-chapter questions* help you ensure both that you have learned the basic material and that you can think in a variety of ways (factual, analytical, creative, and practical) with this material.
6. *Suggested readings* refer you to other sources that you can consult for further information on the topics covered in each chapter.
7. *Investigating Cognitive Psychology* demonstrations, appearing throughout the chapters, help you see how cognitive psychology can be used to demonstrate various psychological phenomena.
8. *Practical Applications of Cognitive Psychology* demonstrations show how you and others can apply cognitive psychology to your everyday lives.
9. *In the Lab of ...* boxes tell you what it really is like to do research in cognitive psychology. Prominent researchers speak in their own words about their research—what research problems excite them most and what they are doing to address these problems.
10. *Believe It or Not* boxes present incredible and exciting information and facts from the world of cognitive psychology.
11. *Key Themes* sections, near the end of each chapter, relate the content of the chapters to the key themes expressed in Chapter 1. These sections will help

you see the continuity of the main ideas of cognitive psychology across its various subfields.

12. *CogLab*, an exciting series of laboratory demonstrations in cognitive psychology provided by the publisher of this textbook (Wadsworth), is available for purchase with this text. You can actively participate in these demonstrations and thereby learn firsthand what it is like to be involved in cognitive-psychological research.

This book contains an overriding theme that unifies all the diverse topics found in the various chapters: Human cognition has evolved over time as a means of adapting to our environment, and we can call this ability to adapt to the environment *intelligence*. Through intelligence, we cope in an integrated and adaptive way with the many challenges with which the environment presents us.

Although cognitive psychologists disagree about many issues, there is one issue about which almost all of them agree; namely, cognition enables us to successfully adapt to the environments in which we find ourselves. Thus, we need a construct such as that of *human intelligence*, if only to provide a shorthand way of expressing this fundamental unity of adaptive skill. We can see this unity at all levels in the study of cognitive psychology. For example, diverse measures of the psychophysiological functioning of the human brain show correlations with scores on a variety of tests of intelligence. Selective attention, the ability to tune in certain stimuli and tune out others, is also related to intelligence, and it has even been proposed that an intelligent person is one who knows what information to attend to and what information to ignore. Various language and problem-solving skills are also related to intelligence, pretty much without regard to how it is measured. In brief, then, human intelligence can be seen as an entity that unifies and provides direction to the workings of the human cognitive system.

We hope you enjoy this book, and we hope you see why we are enthusiastic about cognitive psychology and proud to be cognitive psychologists.

About the Authors

Robert J. Sternberg is Provost and Senior Vice President as well as Professor of Psychology at Oklahoma State University. Prior to that, he was Dean of the School of Arts and Sciences and Professor of Psychology at Tufts University, and before that, IBM Professor of Psychology and Education in the Department of Psychology at Yale University.

Dr. Sternberg received his B.A. from Yale and his Ph.D. in Psychology from Stanford University. He also holds 11 honorary doctorates.

He has received numerous awards, including the James McKeen Cattell Award from the American Psychological Society; the Early Career and McCandless Awards from the APA; and the Outstanding Book, Research Review, Sylvia Scribner and Palmer O. Johnson Awards from the AERA.

Dr. Sternberg has served as President of the American Psychological Association and of the Eastern Psychological Association and is currently President-elect of the Federation of Associations of Brain and Behavioral Sciences. In addition, he has been editor of the *Psychological Bulletin* and of the *APA Review of Books: Contemporary Psychology* and is a member of the Society of Experimental Psychologists. He was the director of the Center for the Psychology of Abilities, Competencies, and Expertise at Yale University and then Tufts University.

Karin Sternberg is Adjunct Assistant Professor at Oklahoma State University. She has a PhD in psychology from the University of Heidelberg, Germany, as well as an MBA with a specialization in banking from the University of Cooperative Education in Karlsruhe, Germany. Karin did some of her doctoral research at Yale and her postdoctoral work in psychology at the University of Connecticut. Afterwards, she worked as a research associate at Harvard University's Kennedy School of Government and School of Public Health. In 2008, together with her husband, Robert J. Sternberg, she founded Sternberg Consulting. The company's focus is on applying in practice their theories of intelligence, wisdom, creativity, and leadership, among others. This has led to consulting work and product development based on their theories (e.g., admissions tests for higher education institutions and schools, training programs, etc.).

1 CHAPTER

Introduction to Cognitive Psychology

Here are some of the questions we will explore in this chapter:

1. What is cognitive psychology?
2. How did psychology develop as a science?
3. How did cognitive psychology develop from psychology?
4. How have other disciplines contributed to the development of theory and research in cognitive psychology?
5. What methods do cognitive psychologists use to study how people think?
6. What are the current issues and various fields of study within cognitive psychology?

■ **BELIEVE IT OR NOT**

Now You See It, Now You Don't!

Cognitive psychology yields all kinds of surprising findings. Dan Simons of the University of Illinois is a master of surprises (see Simons, 2007; Simons & Ambinder, 2005; Simons & Rensink, 2005). Try it out yourself! Watch the following videos and see if you have any comments on them.

http://viscog.beckman.illinois.edu/flashmovie/23.php

Note: Do not read on before you have watched the video.

Did you notice that the person who answers the phone is not the same as the one who was at the desk? Note that they are wearing distinctively different clothing. You have just seen an example of *change blindness*—our occasional inability to recognize changes. You will learn more about this concept in Chapter 2.

Now view the following video. Your task will be to count the number of times that students in *white shirts* pass the basketball. You must not count passes by students wearing black shirts:

http://viscog.beckman.illinois.edu/flashmovie/15.php

Note: Do not read on before you have watched the video.

Well, it doesn't really matter how many passes there were. Did you notice the person in the gorilla outfit walk across the video as the students were throwing the balls? Most people don't notice. This video demonstrates a phenomenon called *inattentional blindness*. You will learn more about this concept in Chapter 4. Throughout this book, we will explore these and many other phenomena.

Think back to the last time you went to a party or social gathering. There were probably tens and maybe hundreds of students in a relatively small room. Maybe music played in the background, and you could hear chatter all around. Yet, when you talked to your friends, you were able to figure out and even concentrate on what they said, filtering out all the other conversations that were going on in the background. Suddenly, however, your attention might have shifted because you heard someone in another conversation nearby mention your name. What processes would have been at work in this situation? How were you able to filter out irrelevant voices in your mind and focus your attention on just one of the many voices you heard? And why did you notice your name being mentioned, even though you did

When you are at a party, you are usually able to filter out many irrelevant voice streams in order to concentrate on the conversation you are leading. However, you will likely notice somebody saying your name in another conversation even if you were not listening intently to that conversation.

not purposefully listen to the conversations around you? Our ability to focus on one out of many voices is one of the most striking phenomena in cognitive psychology, and is known as the "cocktail party effect."

Cognitive processes are continuously taking place in your mind and in the minds of the people around you. Whether you pay attention to a conversation, estimate the speed of an approaching car when crossing the street, or memorize information for a test at school, you are perceiving information, processing it, and remembering or thinking about it. This book is about those cognitive processes that are often hidden in plain sight and that we take for granted because they seem so automatic to us. This chapter will introduce you to some of the people who helped form the field of cognitive psychology and make it what it is today. The chapter also will discuss methods used in cognitive-psychological research.

Cognitive Psychology Defined

What will you study in a textbook about cognitive psychology?

Cognitive psychology is the study of how people perceive, learn, remember, and think about information. A cognitive psychologist might study how people perceive various shapes, why they remember some facts but forget others, or how they learn language. Consider some examples:

- Why do objects look farther away on foggy days than they really are? The discrepancy can be dangerous, even deceiving drivers into having car accidents.
- Why do many people remember a particular experience (e.g., a very happy moment or an embarrassment during childhood), yet they forget the names of people whom they have known for many years?

- Why are many people more afraid of traveling in planes than in automobiles? After all, the chances of injury or death are much higher in an automobile than in a plane.
- Why do you often well remember people you met in your childhood but not people you met a week ago?
- Why do marketing executives in large companies spend so much company money on advertisements?

These are some of the kinds of questions that we can answer through the study of cognitive psychology.

Consider just the last of these questions: Why does Apple, for example, spend so much money on advertisements for its iPhone? After all, how many people remember the functional details of the iPhone, or how those functions are distinguished from the functions of other phones? One reason Apple spends so much is because of the *availability heuristic*, which you will study in Chapter 11. Using this heuristic, we make judgments on the basis of how easily we can call to mind what we perceive as relevant instances of a phenomenon (Tversky & Kahneman, 1973). One such judgment is the question of which phone you should buy when you need a new cell phone. We are much more likely to buy a brand and model of a phone that is familiar. Similarly, Microsoft paid huge amounts of money to market its roll-out of Windows 7 in order to make the product cognitively available to potential customers and thus increase the chances that the potential customers would become actual ones. The bottom line is that understanding cognitive psychology can help us understand much of what goes on in our everyday lives.

Why study the history of cognitive psychology? If we know where we came from, we may have a better understanding of where we are heading. In addition, we can learn from past mistakes. For example, there are numerous newspaper stories about how one educational program or another has resulted in particular gains in student achievement. However, it is relatively rare to read that a control group has been used. A control group would tell us about the achievement of students who did not have that educational program or who maybe were in an alternative program. It may be that these students also would show a gain. We need to compare the students in the experimental group to those in the control group to determine whether the gain of the students in the experimental group was greater than the gain of those in the control group. We can learn from the history of our field that it is important to include control groups, but not everyone learns this fact.

In cognitive psychology, the ways of addressing fundamental issues have changed, but many of the fundamental questions remain much the same. Ultimately, cognitive psychologists hope to learn how people think by studying how people have thoughts about thinking.

The progression of ideas often involves a *dialectic*. A dialectic is a developmental process where ideas evolve over time through a pattern of transformation. What is this pattern? In a dialectic:

- **A thesis is proposed.** A *thesis* is a statement of belief. For example, some people believe that human nature governs many aspects of human behavior (e.g., intelligence or personality; Sternberg, 1999). After a while, however, certain individuals notice apparent flaws in the thesis.

- **An antithesis emerges.** Eventually, or perhaps even quite soon, an antithesis emerges. An *antithesis* is a statement that counters a previous statement of belief. For example, an alternative view is that our nurture (the environmental contexts in which we are reared) almost entirely determines many aspects of human behavior.
- **A synthesis integrates the viewpoints.** Sooner or later, the debate between the thesis and the antithesis leads to a synthesis. A *synthesis* integrates the most credible features of each of two (or more) views. For example, in the debate over nature versus nurture, the interaction between our innate (inborn) nature and environmental nurture may govern human nature.

The dialectic is important because we may be tempted to think that if one view is right, another seemingly contrasting view must be wrong. For example, in the field of intelligence, there has been a tendency to believe that intelligence is either all or mostly genetically determined, or else all or mostly environmentally determined. A similar debate has raged in the field of language acquisition. Often, we are better off posing such issues not as either/or questions, but rather as examinations of how different forces covary and interact with each other. Indeed, the most widely accepted current contention is that the "nature or nurture" view is incomplete. Nature and nurture work together in our development.

Nurture can work in different ways in different cultures. Some cultures, especially Asian cultures, tend to be more dialectical in their thinking, whereas other cultures, such as European and North American ones, tend to be more linear (Nisbett, 2003). In other words, Asians are more likely to be tolerant of holding beliefs that are contradictory, seeking a synthesis over time that resolves the contradiction. Europeans and Americans expect their belief systems to be consistent with each other.

Similarly, people from Asian cultures tend to take a different viewpoint than Westerners when approaching a new object (e.g., a movie of fish in an ocean; Nisbett & Masuda, 2003). In general, people from Western cultures tend to process objects independently of the context, whereas people from many Eastern cultures process objects in conjunction with the surrounding context (Nisbett & Miyamoto, 2005). Asians may emphasize the context more than the objects embedded in those contexts. So if people see a movie of fish swimming around in the ocean, Europeans or Americans will tend to pay more attention to the fish, and Asians may attend to the surround of the ocean in which the fish are swimming. The evidence suggests that culture influences many cognitive processes, including intelligence (Lehman, Chiu, & Schaller, 2004).

If a synthesis seems to advance our understanding of a subject, it then serves as a new thesis. A new antithesis then follows it, then a new synthesis, and so on. Georg Hegel (1770–1831) observed this dialectical progression of ideas. He was a German philosopher who came to his ideas by his own dialectic. He synthesized some of the views of his intellectual predecessors and contemporaries. You will see in this chapter that psychology also evolved as a result of dialectics: Psychologists had ideas about how the mind works and pursued their line of research; then other psychologists pointed out weaknesses and developed alternatives as a reaction to the earlier ideas. Eventually, characteristics of the different approaches are often integrated into a newer and more encompassing approach.

Philosophical Antecedents of Psychology: Rationalism versus Empiricism

Where and when did the study of cognitive psychology begin? Historians of psychology usually trace the earliest roots of psychology to two approaches to understanding the human mind:

- *Philosophy* seeks to understand the general nature of many aspects of the world, in part through *introspection*, the examination of inner ideas and experiences (from *intro-*, "inward, within," and *-spect*, "look");
- *Physiology* seeks a scientific study of life-sustaining functions in living matter, primarily through *empirical* (observation-based) methods.

Two Greek philosophers, Plato (ca. 428–348 B.C.) and his student Aristotle (384–322 B.C.), have profoundly affected modern thinking in psychology and many other fields. Plato and Aristotle disagreed regarding how to investigate ideas.

Plato was a rationalist. A **rationalist** believes that the route to knowledge is through thinking and logical analysis. That is, a rationalist does not need any experiments to develop new knowledge. A rationalist who is interested in cognitive processes would appeal to reason as a source of knowledge or justification.

In contrast, Aristotle (a naturalist and biologist as well as a philosopher) was an empiricist. An **empiricist** believes that we acquire knowledge via empirical evidence—that is, we obtain evidence through experience and observation (Figure 1.1). In order to explore how the human mind works, empiricists would design experiments and conduct studies in which they could observe the behavior and processes of interest to them. Empiricism therefore leads directly to empirical investigations of psychology.

In contrast, rationalism is important in theory development. Rationalist theories without any connection to observations gained through empiricist methods may not be valid; but mountains of observational data without an organizing theoretical framework may not be meaningful. We might see the rationalist view of the world as a thesis and the empirical view as an antithesis. Most psychologists today seek a synthesis of the two. They base empirical observations on theory in order to explain

(a)   (b)

Figure 1.1   (a) According to the rationalist, the only route to truth is reasoned contemplation; (b) according to the empiricist, the only route to truth is meticulous observation. Cognitive psychology, like other sciences, depends on the work of both rationalists and empiricists.

what they have observed in their experiments. In turn, they use these observations to revise their theories when they find that the theories cannot account for their real-world observations.

The contrasting ideas of rationalism and empiricism became prominent with the French rationalist René Descartes (1596–1650) and the British empiricist John Locke (1632–1704). Descartes viewed the introspective, reflective method as being superior to empirical methods for finding truth. The famous expression "cogito, ergo sum" (I think, therefore I am) stems from Descartes. He maintained that the only proof of his existence is that he was thinking and doubting. Descartes felt that one could not rely on one's senses because those very senses have often proven to be deceptive (think of optical illusions, for example). Locke, in contrast, had more enthusiasm for empirical observation (Leahey, 2003). Locke believed that humans are born without knowledge and therefore must seek knowledge through empirical observation. Locke's term for this view was *tabula rasa* (meaning "blank slate" in Latin). The idea is that life and experience "write" knowledge on us. For Locke, then, the study of learning was the key to understanding the human mind. He believed that there are no innate ideas.

In the eighteenth century, German philosopher Immanuel Kant (1724–1804) dialectically synthesized the views of Descartes and Locke, arguing that both rationalism and empiricism have their place. Both must work together in the quest for truth. Most psychologists today accept Kant's synthesis.

Psychological Antecedents of Cognitive Psychology

Cognitive psychology has roots in many different ideas and approaches. The approaches that will be examined include early approaches such as structuralism and functionalism, followed by a discussion of associationism, behaviorism, and Gestalt psychology.

Early Dialectics in the Psychology of Cognition

Only in recent times did psychology emerge as a new and independent field of study. It developed in a dialectical way. Typically, an approach to studying the mind would be developed; people then would use it to explore the human psyche. At some point, however, researchers would find that the approach they learned to use had some weaknesses, or they would disagree with some fundamental assumptions of that approach. They then would develop a new approach. Future approaches might integrate the best features of past approaches or reject some or even most of those characteristics. In the following section, we will explore some of the ways of thinking early psychologists employed and trace the development of psychology through the various schools of thinking.

Understanding the Structure of the Mind: Structuralism

An early dialectic in the history of psychology is that between structuralism and functionalism (Leahey, 2003; Morawski, 2000). Structuralism was the first major school of thought in psychology. **Structuralism** seeks to understand the structure (configuration of elements) of the mind and its perceptions by analyzing those perceptions into their constituent components (affection, attention, memory, sensation, etc.).

Archives of the History of American Psychology—University of Akron

Wilhelm Wundt was no great success in school, failing time and again and frequently finding himself subject to the ridicule of others. However, Wundt later showed that school performance does not always predict career success because he is considered to be among the most influential psychologists of all time.

Consider, for example, the perception of a flower. Structuralists would analyze this perception in terms of its constituent colors, geometric forms, size relations, and so on. In terms of the human mind, structuralists sought to deconstruct the mind into its elementary components; they were also interested in how those elementary components work together to create the mind.

Wilhelm Wundt (1832–1920) was a German psychologist whose ideas contributed to the development of structuralism. Wundt is often viewed as the founder of structuralism in psychology (Structuralism, 2009). Wundt used a variety of methods in his research. One of these methods was introspection. **Introspection** is a deliberate looking inward at pieces of information passing through consciousness. The aim of introspection is to look at the elementary components of an object or process.

The introduction of introspection as an experimental method was an important change in the field because the main emphasis in the study of the mind shifted from a rationalist approach to the empiricist approach of trying to observe behavior in order to draw conclusions about the subject of study. In experiments involving introspection, individuals reported on their thoughts as they were working on a given task. Researchers interested in problem solving could ask their participants to think aloud while they were working on a puzzle so the researchers could gain insight into the thoughts that go on in the participants' minds. In introspection, then, we can analyze our own perceptions.

The method of introspection has some challenges associated with it. First, people may not always be able to say exactly what goes through their mind or may not be able to put it into adequate words. Second, what they say may not be accurate. Third, the fact that people are asked to pay attention to their thoughts or to speak out loud while they are working on a task may itself alter the processes that are going on.

Wundt had many followers. One was an American student, Edward Titchener (1867–1927). Titchener (1910) is sometimes viewed as the first full-fledged structuralist. In any case, he certainly helped bring structuralism to the United States. His experiments relied solely on the use of introspection, exploring psychology from the vantage point of the experiencing individual. Other early psychologists criticized both the method (introspection) and the focus (elementary structures of sensation) of structuralism. These critiques gave rise to a new movement—functionalism.

Understanding the Processes of the Mind: Functionalism

An alternative that developed to counter structuralism, functionalism suggested that psychologists should focus on the *processes* of thought rather than on its contents. **Functionalism** seeks to understand what people *do* and *why* they do it. This principal question about processes was in contrast to that of the structuralists, who had asked what the elementary contents (structures) of the human mind are. Functionalists held that the key to understanding the human mind and behavior was to study the processes of how and why the mind works as it does, rather than to study the

Many cognitive psychologists regard William James, a physician, philosopher, and brother of author Henry James, as among the greatest psychologists ever, although James himself seems to have rejected psychology later in his life.

structural contents and elements of the mind. They were particularly interested in the practical applications of their research.

Functionalists were unified by the kinds of questions they asked but not necessarily by the answers they found or by the methods they used for finding those answers. Because functionalists believed in using whichever methods best answered a given researcher's questions, it seems natural for functionalism to have led to pragmatism. **Pragmatists** believe that knowledge is validated by its usefulness: What can you *do* with it? Pragmatists are concerned not only with knowing what people do; they also want to know what we can do with our knowledge of what people do. For example, pragmatists believe in the importance of the psychology of learning and memory. Why? Because it can help us improve the performance of children in school. It can also help us learn to remember the names of people we meet.

A leader in guiding functionalism toward pragmatism was William James (1842–1910). His chief functional contribution to the field of psychology was a single book: his landmark *Principles of Psychology* (1890/1970). Even today, cognitive psychologists frequently point to the writings of James in discussions of core topics in the field, such as attention, consciousness, and perception. John Dewey (1859–1952) was another early pragmatist who profoundly influenced contemporary thinking in cognitive psychology. Dewey is remembered primarily for his pragmatic approach to thinking and schooling.

Although functionalists were interested in how people learn, they did not really specify a mechanism by which learning takes place. This task was taken up by another group, Associationists.

An Integrative Synthesis: Associationism

Associationism, like functionalism, was more of an influential way of thinking than a rigid school of psychology. **Associationism** examines how elements of the mind,

PRACTICAL APPLICATIONS OF COGNITIVE PSYCHOLOGY

PRAGMATISM

Take a moment right now to put the idea of pragmatism into use. Think about ways to make the information you are learning in this course more useful to you. Notice that the chapter begins with questions that make the information more coherent and useful, and the chapter summary returns to those questions. Come up with your own questions and try organizing your notes in the form of answers to your questions.

Also, try relating this material to other courses or activities you participate in. For example, you may be called on to explain to a friend how to use a new computer program. A good way to start would be to ask your friend, "Do you have any questions?" That way, the information you provide is more directly useful to your friend rather than forcing your friend to search for the information by listening to a long, one-sided lecture.

How can pragmatism be useful in your life (other than in your college coursework)?

like events or ideas, can become associated with one another in the mind to result in a form of learning. For example, associations may result from:

- *contiguity* (associating things that tend to occur together at about the same time);
- *similarity* (associating things with similar features or properties); or
- *contrast* (associating things that show polarities, such as hot/cold, light/dark, day/night).

In the late 1800s, associationist Hermann Ebbinghaus (1850–1909) was the first experimenter to apply associationist principles systematically. Specifically, Ebbinghaus studied his own mental processes. He made up lists of nonsense syllables that consisted of a consonant and a vowel followed by another consonant (e.g., zax). He then took careful note of how long it took him to memorize those lists. He counted his errors and recorded his response times. Through his self-observations, Ebbinghaus studied how people learn and remember material through *rehearsal*, the conscious repetition of material to be learned (Figure 1.2). Among other things, he found that frequent repetition can fix mental associations more firmly in memory. Thus, repetition aids in learning (see Chapter 6).

Another influential associationist, Edward Lee Thorndike (1874–1949), held that the role of "satisfaction" is the key to forming associations. Thorndike termed this principle the *law of effect* (1905): A stimulus will tend to produce a certain response over time if an organism is rewarded for that response. Thorndike believed that an organism learns to respond in a given way (the *effect*) in a given situation if it is rewarded repeatedly for doing so (the *satisfaction*, which serves as a stimulus to future actions). Thus, a child given treats for solving arithmetic problems learns to solve arithmetic problems accurately because the child forms associations between valid solutions and treats. These ideas were the predecessors of the development of behaviorism.

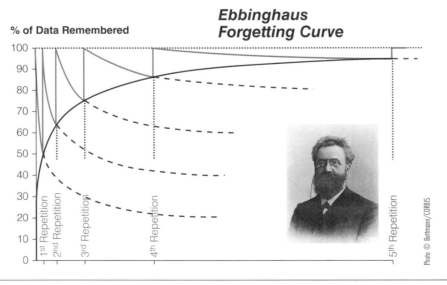

Figure 1.2   The Ebbinghaus Forgetting Curve shows that the first few repetitions result in a steep learning curve. Later repetitions result in a slower increase of remembered words.

It's Only What You Can See That Counts: From Associationism to Behaviorism

Other researchers who were contemporaries of Thorndike used animal experiments to probe stimulus–response relationships in ways that differed from those of Thorndike and his fellow associationists. These researchers straddled the line between associationism and the emerging field of behaviorism. **Behaviorism** focuses only on the relation between observable behavior and environmental events or stimuli. The idea was to make physical whatever others might have called "mental" (Lycan, 2003). Some of these researchers, like Thorndike and other associationists, studied responses that were voluntary (although perhaps lacking any conscious thought, as in Thorndike's work). Other researchers studied responses that were involuntarily triggered in response to what appear to be unrelated external events.

In Russia, Nobel Prize–winning physiologist Ivan Pavlov (1849–1936) studied involuntary learning behavior of this sort. He began with the observation that dogs salivated in response to the sight of the lab technician who fed them. This response occurred before the dogs even saw whether the technician had food. To Pavlov, this response indicated a form of learning (classically conditioned learning), over which the dogs had no conscious control. In the dogs' minds, some type of involuntary learning linked the technician to the food (Pavlov, 1955). Pavlov's landmark work paved the way for the development of behaviorism. His ideas were made known in the United States especially through the work of John B. Watson (see next section). Classical conditioning involves more than just an association based on temporal contiguity (e.g., the food and the conditioned stimulus occurring at about the same time; Ginns, 2006; Rescorla, 1967). Effective conditioning requires *contingency* (e.g., the presentation of food being contingent on the presentation of the conditioned stimulus; Rescorla & Wagner, 1972; Wagner & Rescorla, 1972). Contingencies in the form of reward and punishment are still used today, for example, in the treatment of substance abuse (Cameron & Ritter, 2007).

Behaviorism may be considered an extreme version of associationism. It focuses entirely on the association between the environment and an observable behavior. According to strict, extreme ("radical") behaviorists, any hypotheses about internal thoughts and ways of thinking are nothing more than speculation.

Proponents of Behaviorism

The "father" of radical behaviorism is John Watson (1878–1958). Watson had no use for internal mental contents or mechanisms. He believed that psychologists should concentrate only on the study of observable behavior (Doyle, 2000). He dismissed thinking as nothing more than subvocalized speech. Behaviorism also differed from previous movements in psychology by shifting the emphasis of experimental research from human to animal participants. Historically, much behaviorist work has been conducted (and still is) with laboratory animals, such as rats or pigeons, because these animals allow for much greater behavioral control of relationships between the environment and the behavior emitted in reaction to it (although behaviorists also have conducted experiments with humans). One problem with using nonhuman animals, however, is determining whether the research can be *generalized* to humans (i.e., applied more generally to humans instead of just to the kinds of nonhuman animals that were studied).

B. F. Skinner (1904–1990), a radical behaviorist, believed that virtually all forms of human behavior, not just learning, could be explained by behavior emitted in reaction to the environment. Skinner conducted research primarily with non-human animals. He rejected mental mechanisms. He believed instead that *operant conditioning*—involving the strengthening or weakening of behavior, contingent on the presence or absence of reinforcement (rewards) or punishments—could explain all forms of human behavior. Skinner applied his experimental analysis of behavior to many psychological phenomena, such as learning, language acquisition, and problem solving. Largely because of Skinner's towering presence, behaviorism dominated the discipline of psychology for several decades.

Criticisms of Behaviorism

Behaviorism was challenged on many fronts like language acquisition, production, and comprehension. First, although it seemed to work well to account for certain kinds of learning, behaviorism did not account as well for complex mental activities such as language learning and problem solving. Second, more than understanding people's behavior, some psychologists wanted to know what went on inside the head. Third, it often proved easier to use the techniques of behaviorism in studying nonhuman animals than in studying human ones. Nonetheless, behaviorism continues as a school of psychology, although not one that is particularly sympathetic to the cognitive approach, which involves metaphorically and sometimes literally peering inside people's heads to understand how they learn, remember, think, and reason. Other criticisms emerged as well, as discussed in the next section.

Behaviorists Daring to Peek into the Black Box

Some psychologists rejected radical behaviorism. They were curious about the contents of the mysterious *black box*. Behaviorists regarded the mind as a black box that is best understood in terms of its input and output, but whose internal processes cannot be accurately described because they are not observable. For example, a critic, Edward Tolman (1886–1959), thought that understanding behavior required taking into account the purpose of, and the plan for, the behavior. Tolman (1932) believed

■ **BELIEVE IT OR NOT**

SCIENTIFIC PROGRESS!?

The progress of science can take quite unbelievable turns at times. From the early 1930s to the 1960s, lobotomies were a popular and accepted means of treating mental disorders. A lobotomy involves cutting the connections between the frontal lobes of the brain and the thalamus. Psychiatrist Walter Freeman developed a particular kind of lobotomy in 1946—the transorbital or "ice pick" lobotomy. In this procedure, he used an instrument that looked like an ice pick and inserted it through the orbit of the eyes into the frontal lobes where it was moved back and forth. The patient had been previously rendered unconscious by means of a strong electrical shock. By the late 1950s, tens of thousands of Americans had been subjected to this "psychosurgery." According to some accounts, people felt reduced tension and anxiety after the surgery; however, there were many people who died or were permanently incapacitated after the lobotomy. Famous lobotomy patients include John F. Kennedy's sister Rosemary. Unbelievably, lobotomy was even performed on patients who were not aware they were receiving the surgery. The shocking story of Howard Dully, who was lobotomized at age 12 and did not find out about the procedure until much later in life, can be found at

http://www.npr.org/templates/story/story
.php?storyId=5014080 (Helmes & Velamoor,
2009; MSNBC, 2005).

that all behavior is directed toward a goal. For example, the goal of a rat in a maze may be to try to find food in that maze. Tolman is sometimes viewed as a forefather of modern cognitive psychology.

Bandura (1977b) noted that learning appears to result not merely from direct rewards for behavior, but it also can be social, resulting from observations of the rewards or punishments given to others. The ability to learn through observation is well documented and can be seen in humans, monkeys, dogs, birds, and even fish (Brown & Laland, 2001; Laland, 2004). In humans, this ability spans all ages; it is observed in both infants and adults (Mejia-Arauz, Rogoff, & Paradise, 2005). This view emphasizes how we observe and model our own behavior after the behavior of others. We learn by example. This consideration of social learning opens the way to considering what is happening inside the mind of the individual.

The Whole Is More Than the Sum of Its Parts: Gestalt Psychology

Of the many critics of behaviorism, Gestalt psychologists may have been among the most avid. **Gestalt psychology** states that we best understand psychological phenomena when we view them as organized, structured wholes. According to this view, we cannot fully understand behavior when we only break phenomena down into smaller parts. For example, behaviorists tended to study problem solving by looking for subvocal processing—they were looking for the observable behavior through which problem solving can be understood. Gestaltists, in contrast, studied insight, seeking to understand the unobservable mental event by which someone goes from having no idea about how to solve a problem to understanding it fully in what seems a mere moment of time.

The maxim "the whole is more than the sum of its parts" aptly sums up the Gestalt perspective. To understand the perception of a flower, for example, we would have to take into account the whole of the experience. We could not understand such a perception merely in terms of a description of forms, colors, sizes, and so on. Similarly, as noted in the previous paragraph, we could not understand problem solving merely by looking at minute elements of observable behavior (Köhler, 1927, 1940; Wertheimer, 1945/1959). We will have a closer look at Gestalt principles in Chapter 2.

Emergence of Cognitive Psychology

In the early 1950s, a movement called the "cognitive revolution" took place in response to behaviorism. **Cognitivism** is the belief that much of human behavior can be understood in terms of how people think. It rejects the notion that psychologists should avoid studying mental processes because they are unobservable. Cognitivism is, in part, a synthesis of earlier forms of analysis, such as behaviorism and Gestaltism. Like behaviorism, it adopts precise quantitative analysis to study how people learn and think; like Gestaltism, it emphasizes internal mental processes.

Early Role of Psychobiology

Ironically, one of Watson's former students, Karl Spencer Lashley (1890–1958), brashly challenged the behaviorist view that the human brain is a passive organ merely responding to environmental contingencies outside the individual (Gardner, 1985). Instead, Lashley considered the brain to be an active, dynamic organizer of behavior. Lashley sought to understand how the macro-organization of the human brain made possible such complex, planned activities as musical performance, game playing, and using language. None of these activities were, in his view, readily explicable in terms of simple conditioning.

In the same vein, but at a different level of analysis, Donald Hebb (1949) proposed the concept of cell assemblies as the basis for learning in the brain. Cell assemblies are coordinated neural structures that develop through frequent stimulation. They develop over time as the ability of one neuron (nerve cell) to stimulate firing in a connected neuron increases. Behaviorists did not jump at the opportunity to agree with theorists like Lashley and Hebb. In fact, behaviorist B. F. Skinner (1957) wrote an entire book describing how language acquisition and usage could be explained purely in terms of environmental contingencies. This work stretched Skinner's framework too far, leaving Skinner open to attack. An attack was indeed forthcoming. Linguist Noam Chomsky (1959) wrote a scathing review of Skinner's ideas. In his article, Chomsky stressed both the biological basis and the creative potential of language. He pointed out the infinite numbers of sentences we can produce with ease. He thereby defied behaviorist notions that we learn language by reinforcement. Even young children continually are producing novel sentences for which they could not have been reinforced in the past.

Add a Dash of Technology: Engineering, Computation, and Applied Cognitive Psychology

By the end of the 1950s, some psychologists were intrigued by the tantalizing notion that machines could be programmed to demonstrate the intelligent processing of information (Rychlak & Struckman, 2000). Turing (1950) suggested that soon it would be hard to distinguish the communication of machines from that of humans. He suggested a test, now called the "Turing test," by which a computer program would be judged as successful to the extent that its output was indistinguishable, by humans, from the output of humans (Cummins & Cummins, 2000). In other words, suppose you communicated with a computer and you could not tell that it was a computer. The computer then passed the Turing test (Schonbein & Bechtel, 2003).

By 1956 a new phrase had entered our vocabulary. **Artificial intelligence (AI)** is the attempt by humans to construct systems that show intelligence and, particularly, the intelligent processing of information (*Merriam-Webster's Collegiate Dictionary*, 2003). Chess-playing programs, which now can beat most humans, are examples of artificial intelligence. However, experts greatly underestimated how difficult it would be to develop a computer that can think like a human being. Even today, computers have trouble reading handwriting and understanding and responding to spoken language with the ease that humans do.

Many of the early cognitive psychologists became interested in cognitive psychology through applied problems. For example, according to Berry (2002), Donald Broadbent (1926–1993) claimed to have developed an interest in cognitive

"This problem had been my life's work. I planned to devote my remaining years to it. It's just been solved in four seconds."

psychology through a puzzle regarding AT6 aircraft. The planes had two almost identical levers under the seat. One lever was to pull up the wheels and the other to pull up the flaps. Pilots apparently regularly mistook one for the other, thereby crashing expensive planes upon take-off. During World War II, many cognitive psychologists, including one of the senior author's advisors, Wendell Garner, consulted with the military in solving practical problems of aviation and other fields that arose out of warfare against enemy forces. Information theory, which sought to understand people's behavior in terms of how they process the kinds of bits of information processed by computers (Shannon & Weaver, 1963), also grew out of problems in engineering and informatics.

Applied cognitive psychology also has had great use in advertising. John Watson, after he left Johns Hopkins University as a professor, became an extremely successful executive in an advertising firm and applied his knowledge of psychology to reach his success. Indeed, much of advertising has directly used principles from cognitive psychology to attract customers to products (Benjamin & Baker, 2004).

By the early 1960s, developments in psychobiology, linguistics, anthropology, and artificial intelligence, as well as the reactions against behaviorism by many mainstream psychologists, converged to create an atmosphere ripe for revolution.

Early cognitivists (e.g., Miller, Galanter, & Pribram, 1960; Newell, Shaw, & Simon, 1957b) argued that traditional behaviorist accounts of behavior were inadequate precisely because they said nothing about how people think. One of the most famous early articles in cognitive psychology was, oddly enough, on "the magic number seven." George Miller (1956) noted that the number seven appeared in many different places in cognitive psychology, such as in the literature on perception and memory, and he wondered whether there was some hidden meaning in its frequent reappearance. For example, he found that most people can remember about seven items of information. In this work, Miller also introduced the concept of *channel capacity*, the upper limit with which an observer can match a response to information given to him or her. For example, if you can remember seven digits presented to you sequentially, your channel capacity for remembering digits is seven. Ulric Neisser's book *Cognitive Psychology* (Neisser, 1967) was especially critical in bringing cognitivism to prominence by informing undergraduates, graduate students, and academics about the newly developing field.

Neisser defined *cognitive psychology* as the study of how people learn, structure, store, and use knowledge. Subsequently, Allen Newell and Herbert Simon (1972) proposed detailed models of human thinking and problem solving from the most basic levels to the most complex. By the 1970s cognitive psychology was recognized widely as a major field of psychological study with a distinctive set of research methods.

In the 1970s, Jerry Fodor (1973) popularized the concept of the modularity of mind. He argued that the mind has distinct modules, or special-purpose systems, to deal with linguistic and, possibly, other kinds of information. Modularity implies that the processes that are used in one domain of processing, such as the linguistic (Fodor, 1973) or the perceptual domain (Marr, 1982), operate independently of processes in other domains. An opposing view would be one of domain-general processing, according to which the processes that apply in one domain, such as perception or language, apply in many other domains as well. Modular approaches are useful in studying some cognitive phenomena, such as language, but have proven less useful in studying other phenomena, such as intelligence, which seems to draw upon many different areas of the brain in complex interrelationships.

Curiously, the idea of the mind as modular goes back at least to phrenologist Franz-Joseph Gall (see Boring, 1950), who in the late eighteenth century believed that the pattern of bumps and swells on the skull was directly associated with one's pattern of cognitive skills. Although phrenology itself was not a scientifically valid technique, the practice of mental cartography lingered and eventually gave rise to ideas of modularity based on modern scientific techniques.

✔ CONCEPT CHECK

1. What is pragmatism, and how is it related to functionalism?
2. How are associationism and behaviorism both similar and different?
3. What is the fundamental idea behind Gestalt psychology?
4. What is the meaning of modularity of mind?
5. How does cognitivism incorporate elements of the schools that preceded it?

Cognition and Intelligence

Human intelligence can be viewed as an integrating, or "umbrella" psychological construct for a great deal of theory and research in cognitive psychology. **Intelligence** is the capacity to learn from experience, using metacognitive processes to enhance learning, and the ability to adapt to the surrounding environment. It may require different adaptations within different social and cultural contexts. People who are more intelligent tend to be superior in processes such as divided and selective attention, working memory, reasoning, problem solving, decision making, and concept formation. So when we come to understand the mental processes involved in each of these cognitive functions, we also better understand the bases of individual differences in human intelligence.

What Is Intelligence?

Before you read about how cognitive psychologists view intelligence, test your own intelligence with the tasks in *Investigating Cognitive Psychology: Intelligence*.

Each of the tasks in *Investigating Cognitive Psychology* is believed, at least by some cognitive psychologists, to require some degree of intelligence. (The answers are at the end of this section.) Intelligence is a concept that can be viewed as tying together all of cognitive psychology. Just what is intelligence, beyond the basic definition? In a recent article, researchers identified approximately 70 different definitions of intelligence (Legg & Hutter, 2007). In 1921, when the editors of the *Journal of*

INVESTIGATING COGNITIVE PSYCHOLOGY
Intelligence

1. Candle is to tallow as tire is to (a) automobile, (b) round, (c) rubber, (d) hollow.
2. Complete this series: 100%, 0.75, 1/2; (a) whole, (b) one eighth, (c) one fourth.
3. The first three items form one series. Complete the analogous second series that starts with the fourth item:

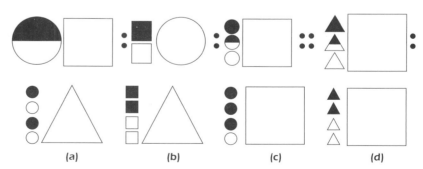

4. You are at a party of truth-tellers and liars. The truth-tellers always tell the truth, and the liars always lie. You meet someone new. He tells you that he just heard a conversation in which a girl said she was a liar. Is the person you met a liar or a truth-teller?

Educational Psychology asked 14 famous psychologists that question, the responses varied but generally embraced these two themes. Intelligence involves:

1. the capacity to learn from experience, and
2. the ability to adapt to the surrounding environment.

Sixty-five years later, 24 cognitive psychologists with expertise in intelligence research were asked the same question (Sternberg & Detterman, 1986). They, too, underscored the importance of learning from experience and adapting to the environment. They also broadened the definition to emphasize the importance of *metacognition*—people's understanding and control of their own thinking processes. Contemporary experts also more heavily emphasized the role of culture. They pointed out that what is considered intelligent in one culture may be considered stupid in another culture (Serpell, 2000).

There are actually a number of cultural differences in the definition of intelligence. These differences have led to a field of study within intelligence research that examines understanding of cultural differences in the definition of intelligence. This field explores what is termed *cultural intelligence*, or CQ. This term is used to describe a person's ability to adapt to a variety of challenges in diverse cultures (Ang et al., 2010; Sternberg & Grigorenko, 2006; Triandis, 2006). Research also shows that personality variables are related to intelligence (Ackerman, 1996, 2010). Taken together, this evidence suggests that a comprehensive definition of intelligence incorporates many facets of intellect.

Definitions of intelligence also frequently take on an assessment-oriented focus. In fact, some psychologists have been content to define intelligence as whatever it is that the tests measure (Boring, 1923). This definition, unfortunately, is circular. According to it, the nature of intelligence is what is tested. But what is tested must necessarily be determined by the nature of intelligence. Moreover, what different tests of intelligence measure is not always the same thing. Different tests measure somewhat different constructs (Daniel, 1997, 2000; Kaufman, 2000; Kaufman & Lichtenberger, 1998). So it is not feasible to define intelligence by what tests measure, as though they all measured the same thing. By the way, the answers to the questions in *Investigating Cognitive Psychology: Intelligence* are:

1. Rubber. Candles are frequently made of tallow, just as tires are frequently made of (c) rubber.
2. 100%, 0.75, and 1/2 are quantities that successively decrease by 1/4; to complete the series, the answer is (c) one fourth, which is a further decrease by 1/4.
3. The first series was a circle and a square, followed by two squares and a circle, followed by three circles and a square; the second series was three triangles and a square, which would be followed by (b), four squares and a triangle.
4. The person you met is clearly a liar. If the girl about whom this person was talking were a truth-teller, she would have said that she was a truth-teller. If she were a liar, she would have lied and said that she was a truth-teller also. Thus, regardless of whether the girl was a truth-teller or a liar, she would have said that she was a truth-teller. Because the man you met has said that she said she was a liar, he must be lying and hence must be a liar.

Three Cognitive Models of Intelligence

There have been many models of intelligence. Three models are particularly useful when linking human intelligence to cognition: the three-stratum model, the theory of multiple intelligences, and the triarchic theory of intelligence.

Carroll: Three-Stratum Model of Intelligence

According to the **three-stratum model of intelligence**, intelligence comprises a hierarchy of cognitive abilities comprising three strata (Carroll, 1993):

- Stratum I includes many narrow, specific abilities (e.g., spelling ability, speed of reasoning).
- Stratum II includes various broad abilities (e.g., fluid intelligence, crystallized intelligence, short-term memory, long-term storage and retrieval, information-processing speed).
- Stratum III is just a single general intelligence (sometimes called *g*).

Of these strata, the most interesting is the middle stratum, which is neither too narrow nor too all-encompassing.

In the middle stratum are fluid ability and crystallized ability. *Fluid ability* is speed and accuracy of abstract reasoning, especially for novel problems. *Crystallized ability* is accumulated knowledge and vocabulary (Cattell, 1971). In addition to fluid intelligence and crystallized intelligence, Carroll includes several other abilities in the middle stratum. They are learning and memory processes, visual perception, auditory perception, facile production of ideas (similar to verbal fluency), and speed (which includes both sheer speed of response and speed of accurate responding). Carroll's model is probably the most widely accepted of the measurement-based models of intelligence. You will learn about these processes in later chapters.

Gardner: Theory of Multiple Intelligences

Howard Gardner (1983, 1993b, 1999, 2006) has proposed a **theory of multiple intelligences**, in which intelligence comprises multiple independent constructs, not just a single, unitary construct. However, instead of speaking of multiple abilities that together constitute intelligence (e.g., Thurstone, 1938), this theory distinguishes eight distinct intelligences that are relatively independent of each other (Table 1.1). Each is a separate system of functioning, although these systems can interact to produce what we see as intelligent performance. Looking at Gardner's list of intelligences, you might want to evaluate your own intelligences, perhaps rank ordering your strengths in each.

Gardner does not entirely dismiss the use of psychometric tests. But the base of evidence used by Gardner (e.g., the existence of exceptional individuals in one area, brain lesions that destroy a particular kind of intelligence, or core operations that are essential to performance of a particular intelligence) does not rely on the factor analysis of various psychometric tests alone. Take a moment to reflect:

- In thinking about your own intelligences, how fully integrated do you believe them to be?
- How much do you perceive each type of intelligence as depending on any of the others?

Gardner's view of the mind is modular. Modularity theorists believe that different abilities—such as Gardner's intelligences—can be isolated as emanating from distinct portions or modules of the brain. Thus, a major task of existing and future research on intelligence is to isolate the portions of the brain responsible for each of the intelligences. Gardner has speculated as to at least some of these locales, but hard evidence for the existence of these separate intelligences has yet to be produced. Furthermore, some scientists question the strict modularity of Gardner's theory (Nettelbeck & Young, 1996). Consider the phenomenon of preserved specific

Table 1.1 Gardner's Eight Intelligences

On which of Howard Gardner's eight intelligences do you show the greatest ability? In what contexts can you use your intelligences most effectively? (After Gardner, 1999.)

Type of Intelligence	Tasks Reflecting This Type of Intelligence
Linguistic intelligence	Used in reading a book; writing a paper, a novel, or a poem; and understanding spoken words
Logical-mathematical intelligence	Used in solving math problems, in balancing a checkbook, in solving a mathematical proof, and in logical reasoning
Spatial intelligence	Used in getting from one place to another, in reading a map, and in packing suitcases in the trunk of a car so that they all fit into a compact space
Musical intelligence	Used in singing a song, composing a sonata, playing a trumpet, or even appreciating the structure of a piece of music
Bodily-kinesthetic intelligence	Used in dancing, playing basketball, running a mile, or throwing a javelin
Interpersonal intelligence	Used in relating to other people, such as when we try to understand another person's behavior, motives, or emotions
Intrapersonal intelligence	Used in understanding ourselves—the basis for understanding who we are, what makes us tick, and how we can change ourselves, given our existing constraints on our abilities and our interests
Naturalist intelligence	Used in understanding patterns in nature

From *Multiple Intelligences* by Howard Gardner. Copyright © 1993 by Howard Gardner. Reprinted by permission of Basic Books, a member of Perseus Books, L.L.C.

cognitive functioning in autistic savants. Savants are people with severe social and cognitive deficits but with corresponding high ability in a narrow domain. They suggest that such preservation fails as evidence for modular intelligences. The narrow long-term memory and specific aptitudes of savants may not really be intelligent (Nettelbeck & Young, 1996). Thus, there may be reason to question the intelligence of inflexible modules.

Sternberg: The Triarchic Theory of Intelligence

Whereas Gardner emphasizes the separateness of the various aspects of intelligence, Robert Sternberg tends to emphasize the extent to which they work together in his triarchic theory of human intelligence (Sternberg, 1985a, 1988, 1996b, 1999). According to the **triarchic theory of human intelligence**, intelligence comprises three aspects: creative, analytical, and practical.

- *Creative abilities* are used to generate novel ideas.
- *Analytical abilities* ascertain whether your ideas (and those of others) are good ones.

- *Practical abilities* are used to implement the ideas and persuade others of their value.

Figure 1.3 illustrates the parts of the theory and the interrelationships of the three parts.

According to the theory, cognition is at the center of intelligence. Information processing in cognition can be viewed in terms of three different kinds of components. First are metacomponents—higher-order executive processes (i.e., metacognition) used to plan, monitor, and evaluate problem solving. Second are performance components—lower-order processes used for implementing the commands of the metacomponents. And third are knowledge-acquisition components—the processes used for learning how to solve the problems in the first place. The components are highly interdependent.

Suppose that you were asked to write a term paper. You would use metacomponents for higher-order decisions. Thus, you would use them to decide on a topic, plan the paper, monitor the writing, and evaluate how well your finished product succeeds in accomplishing your goals for it. You would use knowledge-acquisition components for research to learn about the topic. You would use performance components for the actual writing.

Sternberg and his colleagues performed a comprehensive study testing the validity of the triarchic theory and its usefulness in improving performance. They predicted that matching students' instruction and assessment to their abilities would lead to improved performance (Sternberg et al., 1996; Sternberg et al., 1999). Students were selected for one of five ability patterns: high only in analytical ability, high only in creative ability, high only in practical ability, high in all three abilities, or not high in any of the three abilities. Then students were assigned at random to one of four instructional groups. Instruction in the groups emphasized either memory-based, analytical, creative, or practical learning. Then the memory-based, analytical, creative, and practical achievement of all students was

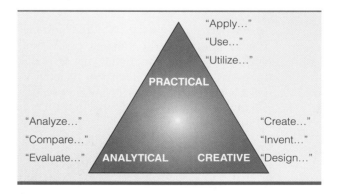

Figure 1.3 According to Robert Sternberg, intelligence comprises analytical, creative, and practical abilities. In analytical thinking, we solve familiar problems by using strategies that manipulate the elements of a problem or the relationships among the elements (e.g., comparing, analyzing). In creative thinking, we solve new kinds of problems that require us to think about the problem and its elements in a new way (e.g., inventing, designing). In practical thinking, we solve problems that apply what we know to everyday contexts (i.e., applying, using).

assessed. The researchers found that students who were placed in an instructional condition that matched their strength in terms of pattern of ability outperformed students who were mismatched. Thus, the prediction of the experiment was confirmed. For example, a high-analytical student being placed in an instructional condition that emphasized analytical thinking outperformed a high-analytical student being placed in an instructional condition that emphasized practical thinking.

Teaching students to use all of their analytic, creative, and practical abilities has resulted in improved school achievement for every student, whatever their ability pattern (Grigorenko, Jarvin, & Sternberg, 2002; Sternberg & Grigorenko, 2004; Sternberg, Torff, & Grigorenko, 1998). One important consideration in light of such findings is the need for changes in the assessment of intelligence (Sternberg & Kaufman, 1996). Current measures of intelligence are somewhat one-sided. They measure mostly analytical abilities. They involve little or no assessment of creative and practical aspects of intelligence (Sternberg et al., 2000; Wagner, 2000). A more well-rounded assessment and instruction system could lead to greater benefits of education for a wider variety of students—a nominal goal of education.

One attempt to accomplish this goal can be seen through the Rainbow Project. In the Rainbow Project, students completed the SAT and additional assessments. These additional assessments included measures of creative and practical as well as of analytical abilities (Sternberg & the Rainbow Project Collaborators, 2006). The addition of these supplemental assessments resulted in superior prediction of college grade point average (GPA) as compared with scores on the SAT and high school GPA. In fact, the new tests doubled the prediction of first-year college GPA obtained just by the SAT. Moreover, the new assessments substantially reduced differences in scores among members of diverse ethnic groups.

We have discussed how human intelligence provides a conceptual base for understanding phenomena in cognitive psychology. What methods do we use to study these phenomena?

Research Methods in Cognitive Psychology

Researchers employ a variety of research methods. These methods include laboratory or other controlled experiments, psychobiological research, self-reports, case studies, naturalistic observation, and computer simulations and artificial intelligence. Each of these methods will be discussed in detail in this section. To better understand the specific methods used by cognitive psychologists, one must first grasp the goals of research in cognitive psychology.

Goals of Research

Briefly, research goals include data gathering, data analysis, theory development, hypothesis formulation, hypothesis testing, and perhaps even application to settings outside the research environment. Often researchers simply seek to gather as much information as possible about a particular phenomenon. They may or may not have preconceived notions regarding what they may find while gathering the data. Their research focuses on describing particular cognitive phenomena, such as how people recognize faces or how they develop expertise.

Data gathering reflects an empirical aspect of the scientific enterprise. Once there are sufficient data on the cognitive phenomenon of interest, cognitive psychologists use various methods for drawing inferences from the data. Ideally, they use multiple converging types of evidence to support their hypotheses. Sometimes, just a quick glance at the data leads to intuitive inferences regarding patterns that emerge from those data. More commonly, however, researchers use various statistical means of analyzing the data.

Data gathering and statistical analysis aid researchers in describing cognitive phenomena. No scientific pursuit could get far without such descriptions. However, most cognitive psychologists want to understand more than the *what* of cognition; most also seek to understand the *how* and the *why* of thinking. That is, researchers seek ways to explain cognition as well as to describe it. To move beyond descriptions, cognitive psychologists must leap from what is observed directly to what can be inferred regarding observations.

Suppose that we wish to study one particular aspect of cognition. An example would be how people comprehend information in textbooks. We usually start with a theory. A **theory** is an organized body of general explanatory principles regarding a phenomenon, usually based on observations. We seek to test a theory and thereby to see whether it has the power to predict certain aspects of the phenomena with which it deals. In other words, our thought process is, "If our theory is correct, then whenever x occurs, outcome y should result." This process results in the generation of **hypotheses**, tentative proposals regarding expected empirical consequences of the theory, such as the outcomes of research.

Next, we test our hypotheses through experimentation. Even if particular findings appear to confirm a given hypothesis, the findings must be subjected to statistical analysis to determine their statistical significance. **Statistical significance** indicates the likelihood that a given set of results would be obtained if only chance factors were in operation. For example, a statistical significance level of .05 would mean that the likelihood of a given set of data would be a mere 5% if only chance factors were operating. Therefore, the results are not likely to be due merely to chance. Through this method we can decide to retain or reject hypotheses.

Once our hypothetical predictions have been experimentally tested and statistically analyzed, the findings from those experiments may lead to further work. For example, the psychologist may engage in further data gathering, data analysis, theory development, hypothesis formulation, and hypothesis testing. Based on the hypotheses that were retained and/or rejected, the theory may have to be revised. In addition, many cognitive psychologists hope to use insights gained from research to help people use cognition in real-life situations. Some research in cognitive psychology is applied from the start. It seeks to help people improve their lives and the conditions under which they live their lives. Thus, basic research may lead to everyday applications. For each of these purposes, different research methods offer different advantages and disadvantages.

Distinctive Research Methods

Cognitive psychologists use various methods to explore how humans think. These methods include (a) laboratory or other controlled experiments, (b) psychobiological research, (c) self-reports, (d) case studies, (e) naturalistic observation, and (f) computer simulations and artificial intelligence. See Table 1.2 for descriptions and examples of each method. As the table shows, each method offers distinctive advantages and disadvantages.

IN THE LAB OF HENRY L. ROEDIGER

The Science of the Mind

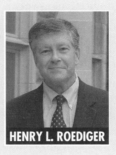

HENRY L. ROEDIGER

In 1620 Sir Francis Bacon wrote: "If you read a piece of text through twenty times, you will not learn it by heart so easily as if you read it ten times while attempting to recite from time to time and consulting the text when your memory fails." How did he know that? The answer is that he did not know, for sure, but based his judgment on his own personal experience. The case is interesting because Bacon was one of the originators of the scientific method and laid out the framework for experimental science.

Science in Bacon's time was applied to the natural world, what today would be called the physical sciences (chiefly, physics and chemistry). The idea that scientific methods could be applied to people was not even dreamt of and, had the notion been raised, it would have been hooted down. Human beings were not dross stuff; they had souls, they had free will—surely they could not be studied scientifically! It took another 250 years before pioneers would question this assumption and take the brave step to create a science of psychology, the study of the mind. The date usually given is 1879, when Wilhelm Wundt founded the first psychology laboratory in Leipzig, Germany.

Edwin G. Boring, the great historian of psychology, wrote that the "application of the experimental method to the problem of mind is the great outstanding event in the study of the mind, an event to which no other is comparable" (1929, p. 659). Boring is right, and the textbook you hold relates the fascinating story of cognitive psychology, today's experimental study of mind.

But what about Bacon's assertion? Does reciting material really help one learn it more than studying it? This idea seems odd, because in education we think of studying as being how we learn; and of testing as only measuring what has been learned.

My students and I have been studying the possible validity of Bacon's claim in a variety of experimental contexts (although, truth be told, we found the quotation after the studies were well under way). In our experiments, students learn materials (either simple sets of words or more complex textbook passages—the material does not matter) by various combinations of studying and testing the material. The general finding is that retrieval (or reciting, as Bacon called it) during a test provides a great boost to later retention, much more so than repeated studying (Roediger & Karpicke, 2006).

Let's consider just one experiment here to make the point. Zaromb and Roediger (2011) gave students lists of words to remember in preparation for a test that would be given two days later. Students in one condition studied the material eight times with short breaks, but students in two other conditions received either two or four tests in place of some of the study trials. If S denotes a study trial and T denotes a test (or recitation), the three conditions can be labeled $SSSSSSSS$, $STSSSTSS$, or $STSTSTSTST$. If studying determines later recall, then the three conditions just listed should be ordered in terms of decreasing effectiveness (from eight to six to four study trials). However, if Bacon is right, the conditions should be ordered in increasing effectiveness for later retention (from zero to two to four test trials). The result: the proportion recalled two days later was .17, .25 and .39 for the three conditions in the order listed above.

Sir Francis Bacon was right: Reciting is more effective than studying (although of course some studying is required). To my knowledge, no one has done the actual experiment he suggested (20 trials), but it would make a fine class project with 20 study trials for one condition or 10 study and 10 test trials for the other. By the way, self-testing on material is a good way to study for your courses (Roediger, McDermott & McDaniel, 2011).

Experiments on Human Behavior

In controlled experimental designs, an experimenter will usually conduct research in a laboratory setting. The experimenter controls as many aspects of the experimental situation as possible. There are basically two kinds of variables in any given experiment. **Independent variables** are aspects of an investigation that are individually *manipulated*, or carefully regulated, by the experimenter, while other aspects of the investigation are held constant (i.e., not subject to variation). **Dependent variables** are outcome responses, the values of which depend on how one or more independent variables influence or affect the participants in the experiment. When you tell some student research participants that they will do very well on a task, but you do not say anything to other participants, the independent variable is the amount of information that the students are given about their expected task performance. The dependent variable is how well both groups actually perform the task—that is, their score on the math test.

When the experimenter manipulates the independent variables, he or she controls for the effects of irrelevant variables and observes the effects on the dependent variables (outcomes). These irrelevant variables that are held constant are called *control variables*. For example, when you conduct an experiment on people's ability to concentrate when subjected to different kinds of background music, you should make sure that the lighting in the room is always the same, and not sometimes extremely bright and other times dim. The variable of light needs to be held constant.

Another type of variable is the confounding variable. *Confounding variables* are a type of irrelevant variable that has been left uncontrolled in a study. For example, imagine you want to examine the effectiveness of two problem-solving techniques. You train and test one group under the first strategy at 6 A.M. and a second group under the second strategy at 6 P.M. In this experiment, time of day would be a confounding variable. In other words, time of day may be causing differences in performance that have nothing to do with the problem-solving strategy. Obviously, when conducting research, we must be careful to avoid the influence of confounding variables.

In implementing the experimental method, experimenters must use a representative and random sample of the population of interest. They must exert rigorous control over the experimental conditions so that they know that the observed effects can be attributed to variations in the independent variable and nothing else. For example, in the above mentioned experiment, people's ability to concentrate did not depend on the general lighting conditions in the room, per se, because during a few sessions, the sun shone directly into the eyes of the subjects so that they had trouble seeing.

The experimenter also must randomly assign participants to the treatment and control conditions. For example, you would not want to end up in an experiment on concentration with lots of people with ADD—Attention Deficit Disorder—in your experimental group, but no such people in your control group. If those requisites for the experimental method are fulfilled, the experimenter may be able to infer probable causality. This inference is of the effects of the independent variable or variables (the treatment) on the dependent variable (the outcome) for the given population.

Many different dependent variables are used in cognitive-psychological research. Two common variables are percent correct (or its additive inverse, error rate) and reaction time. These measures are popular because they can tell the investigator, respectively, the accuracy and speed of mental processing. Independent and dependent variables must be chosen with great care, because no matter what processes one is observing, what is learned from an experiment will depend almost exclusively on the variables one chooses to isolate from the often complex behavior one is observing.

Table 1.2   Research Methods

Cognitive psychologists use controlled experiments, psychobiological research, self-reports, case studies, naturalistic observation, and computer simulations and artificial intelligence when studying cognitive phenomena.

Method	Controlled Laboratory Experiments	Psychobiological Research	Self-Reports, such as Verbal Protocols, Self-Rating, Diaries
Description of method	Obtain samples of performance at a particular time and place	Study animal brains and human brains, using postmortem studies and various psychobiological measures or imaging techniques (see Chapter 3)	Obtain participants' reports of own cognition in progress or as recollected
Random assignment of subjects	Usually	Not usually	Not applicable
Experimental control of independent variables	Usually	Varies widely, depending on the particular technique	Probably not
Sample size	May be any size	Often small	Probably small
Sample representativeness	May be representative	Often not representative	May be representative
Ecological validity	Not unlikely; depends on the task and the context to which it is being applied	Unlikely under some circumstances	Maybe; see strengths and weaknesses
Information about individual differences	Usually de-emphasized	Yes	Yes
Strengths	• Easy to administer, score, and do statistical analyses • High probability of drawing valid causal inferences	• "Hard" evidence of cognitive functions through physiological activity • Alternative view of cognitive processes • Possibility to develop treatments for cognitive deficits	• Access to introspective insights from participants' point of view
Weaknesses	• Difficulty in generalizing results beyond a specific place, time, and task setting • Discrepancies between behavior in real life and in the laboratory	• Limited accessibility for most researchers (need appropriate subjects and expensive equipment) • Small samples • Decreased generalizability when abnormal brains or animal brains are investigated	• Inability to report on processes occurring outside conscious awareness • **Verbal protocols & self-ratings:** May influence cognitive process being reported • **Recollections:** Discrepancies between actual cognition and recollected cognitive processes and products
Examples	Karpicke (2009) developed a laboratory task in which participants had to learn and recall Swahili-English word pairs. After subjects first recalled the meaning of a word, that pair was either dropped, presented twice more in a study period, or presented twice more in test periods. Subjects took a final recall test one week later.	New and colleagues (New et al., 2009) have found that Borderline patients with Intermittent Explosive Disorder responded more aggressively to a provocation than did normal control subjects. The patients particularly showed an increase in glucose consumption in brain areas associated with emotion like the amygdala and less activity in dorsal brain regions that serve to control aggression.	In a study about the relation between cortisol levels (which are stress-dependent) and sleep, self-rated health, and stress, participants kept diaries and collected saliva samples over four weeks (Dahlgren et al., 2009).

Case Studies	Naturalistic Observations	Computer Simulations and Artificial Intelligence
Engage in intensive study of single individuals, drawing general conclusions about behavior	Observe real-life situations, as in classrooms, work settings, or homes	**Simulations:** Attempt to make computers simulate human cognitive performance on various tasks **AI:** Attempt to make computers demonstrate intelligent cognitive performance, regardless of whether the process resembles human cognitive processing
Highly unlikely	Not applicable	Not applicable
Highly unlikely	No	Full control of variables of interest
Almost certain to be small	Probably small	Not applicable
Not likely to be representative	May be representative	Not applicable
High ecological validity for individual cases; lower generalizability to others	Yes	Not applicable
Yes; richly detailed information regarding individuals	Possible, but emphasis is on environmental distinctions, not on individual differences	Not applicable
• Access to detailed information about individuals, including historical and current contexts • May lead to specialized applications for special groups (e.g., prodigies, persons with brain damage)	• Access to rich contextual information	• Exploration of possibilities for modeling cognitive processes • Allows clear hypothesis testing • Wide range of practical applications (e.g., robotics for performing dangerous tasks)
• Applicability to other persons • Limited generalizability due to small sample size and nonrepresentativeness of sample	• Lack of experimental control • Possible influence on behavior due to presence of observer	• Limitations imposed by the hardware (i.e., the computer circuitry) and the software (i.e., the programs written by the researchers) • Simulations may imperfectly model the way that the human brain thinks
A case study with a breast cancer patient showed that a new technique (problem-solving therapy) can reduce anxiety and depression in cancer patients (Carvalho & Hopko, 2009).	A study using questionnaires and observation found that Mexicans on average consider themselves less sociable than U.S. Americans consider themselves; however, Mexicans behave much more sociably than U.S. Americans in their everyday lives (Ramirez-Esparza et al., 2009).	**Simulations:** Through detailed computations, David Marr (1982) attempted to simulate human visual perception and proposed a theory of visual perception based on his computer models. **AI:** Various AI programs have been written that can demonstrate expertise (e.g., playing chess), but they probably do so via different processes than those used by human experts.

Psychologists who study cognitive processes with reaction time often use the *subtraction method*, which involves estimating the time a cognitive process takes by subtracting the amount of time information processing takes with the process from the time it takes without the process (Donders, 1868/1869). If you are asked to scan the words *dog, cat, mouse, hamster, chipmunk* and to say whether the word *chipmunk* appears in it, and then are asked to scan *dog, cat, mouse, hamster, chipmunk, lion* and to say whether *lion* appears, the difference in the reaction times might be taken, by some models of mental processing, roughly to indicate the amount of time it takes to process each stimulus.

Suppose the outcomes in the treatment condition show a statistically significant difference from the outcomes in the control condition. The experimenter then can infer the likelihood of a causal link between the independent variable(s) and the dependent variable. Because the researcher can establish a likely causal link between the given independent variables and the dependent variables, controlled laboratory experiments offer an excellent means of testing hypotheses.

Suppose that we wanted to see whether loud, distracting noises influence the ability to perform well on a particular cognitive task (e.g., reading a passage from a textbook and responding to comprehension questions). Ideally, we first would select a random sample of participants from within our total population of interest. We then would randomly assign each participant to a treatment condition or a control condition. Then we would introduce some distracting loud noises to the participants in our treatment condition. The participants in our control condition would not receive this treatment. We would present the cognitive task to participants in both the treatment condition and the control condition and then measure their performance by some means (e.g., speed and accuracy of responses to comprehension questions). Finally, we would analyze our results statistically. We thereby would examine whether the difference between the two groups reached statistical significance.

Suppose the participants in the treatment condition showed poorer performance at a statistically significant level than the participants in the control condition. We might infer that loud, distracting noises influenced the ability to perform well on this particular cognitive task.

In cognitive-psychological research, though the dependent variables may be quite diverse, they often involve various outcome measures of accuracy (e.g., frequency of errors), of response times, or of both. Among the myriad possibilities for independent variables are characteristics of the situation, of the task, or of the participants. For example, characteristics of the situation may involve the presence versus the absence of particular stimuli or hints during a problem-solving task. Characteristics of the task may involve reading versus listening to a series of words and then responding to comprehension questions. Characteristics of the participants may include age differences, differences in educational status, or differences based on test scores.

On the one hand, characteristics of the situation or task may be manipulated through random assignment of participants to either the treatment or the control group. On the other hand, characteristics of the participant are not easily manipulated experimentally. For example, suppose the experimenter wants to study the effects of aging on speed and accuracy of problem solving. The researcher cannot randomly assign participants to various age groups because people's ages cannot be manipulated (although participants of various age groups can be assigned at random to various experimental conditions). In such situations, researchers often use other kinds of studies, for example, studies involving *correlation* (a statistical relationship between two or more attributes, such as characteristics of the participants or of a situation). Correlations are usually expressed through a correlation coefficient known as Pearson's r. Pearson's r is a number that can range from -1.00 (a negative correlation) to 0 (no correlation) to 1.00 (a positive correlation).

A correlation is a description of a relationship. The correlation coefficient describes the strength of the relationship. The closer the coefficient is to 1 (either positive or negative), the stronger the relationship between the variables is. The sign (positive or negative) of the coefficient describes the direction of the relationship. A positive relationship indicates that as one variable increases (e.g., vocabulary size), another variable also increases (e.g., reading comprehension). A negative relationship indicates that as the measure of one variable increases (e.g., fatigue), the measure of another decreases (e.g., alertness). No correlation—that is, when the coefficient is 0—indicates that there is no pattern or relationship in the change of two variables (e.g., intelligence and earlobe length). In this final case, both variables may change, but the variables do not vary together in a consistent pattern.

Correlational studies are often the method of choice when researchers do not want to deceive their subjects by using manipulations in an experiment or when they are interested in factors that cannot be manipulated ethically (e.g., lesions in specific parts of the human brain). However, because researchers do not have any control over the experimental conditions, causality cannot be inferred from correlational studies.

Findings of statistical relationships are highly informative. Their value should not be underrated. Also, because correlational studies do not require the random assignment of participants to treatment and control conditions, these methods may

"He's pretty good at rote categorization and single-object relational tasks, but he's not so hot at differentiating between representational and associational signs, and he's very weak on syntax."

be applied flexibly. However, correlational studies generally do not permit unequiv-ocal inferences regarding causality. As a result, many cognitive psychologists strongly prefer experimental data to correlational data.

Psychobiological Research

Through *psychobiological research*, investigators study the relationship between cogni-tive performance and cerebral events and structures. Chapter 3 describes various spe-cific techniques used in psychobiological research. These techniques generally fall into three categories:

- techniques for studying an individual's brain *postmortem* (after the death of an individual), relating the individual's cognitive function prior to death to observ-able features of the brain;
- techniques for studying images showing structures of or activities in the brain of an individual who is known to have a particular cognitive deficit;
- techniques for obtaining information about cerebral processes during the normal performance of a cognitive activity.

Postmortem studies offered some of the first insights into how specific *lesions* (areas of injury in the brain) may be associated with particular cognitive deficits. Such studies continue to provide useful insights into how the brain influences cogni-tive function. Recent technological developments also increasingly enable research-ers to study individuals with known cognitive deficits *in vivo* (while the individual is alive). The study of individuals with abnormal cognitive functions linked to cerebral damage often enhances our understanding of normal cognitive functions.

Psychobiological researchers also study normal cognitive functioning by studying cerebral activity in animal participants. Researchers often use animals for experi-ments involving neurosurgical procedures that cannot be performed on humans because such procedures would be difficult, unethical, or impractical. For example, studies mapping neural activity in the cortex have been conducted on cats and monkeys (e.g., psychobiological research on how the brain responds to visual stimuli; see Chapter 2).

Can cognitive and cerebral functioning of animals and of abnormal humans be generalized to apply to the cognitive and cerebral functioning of normal humans? Psychobiologists have responded to these questions in various ways. For some kinds of cognitive activity, the available technology permits researchers to study the dynamic cerebral activity of normal human participants during cognitive processing (see the brain-imaging techniques described in Chapter 3).

Self-Reports, Case Studies, and Naturalistic Observation

Individual experiments and psychobiological studies often focus on precise specifica-tion of discrete aspects of cognition across individuals. To obtain richly textured information about how particular individuals think in a broad range of contexts, researchers may use other methods. These methods include:

- *self-reports* (an individual's own account of cognitive processes);
- *case studies* (in-depth studies of individuals); and
- *naturalistic observation* (detailed studies of cognitive performance in everyday situations and nonlaboratory contexts).

Experimental research is most useful for testing hypotheses; however, research based on self-reports, case studies, and naturalistic observation is often particularly useful for the formulation of hypotheses. These methods are also useful to generate descriptions of rare events or processes that we have no other way to measure.

In very specific circumstances, these methods may provide the only way to gather information. An example is the case of Genie, a girl who was locked in a room until the age of 13 and thus provided with severely limited social and sensory experiences. As a result of her imprisonment, Genie had severe physical impairments and no language skills. Through case-study methods, information was collected about how she later began to learn language (Fromkin et al., 1974; Jones, 1995; LaPointe, 2005). It would have been unethical experimentally to deny a person any language experience for the first 13 years of life. Therefore, case-study methods are the only reasonable way to examine the results of someone being denied language and social exposure.

Similarly, traumatic brain injury cannot be manipulated in humans in the laboratory. Therefore, when traumatic brain injury occurs, case studies are the only way to gather information. For example, consider the case of Phineas Gage, a railroad worker who, in 1848, had a large metal spike driven through his frontal lobes in a freak accident (Torregrossa, Quinn, & Taylor, 2008; see also Figure 1.4). Surprisingly, Mr. Gage survived. His behavior and mental processes were drastically changed by the accident, however. Obviously, we cannot insert large metal rods into the brains of experimental participants. Therefore, in the case of traumatic brain injury, we must rely on case-study methods to gather information.

The reliability of data based on self-reports depends on the candor of the participants. A participant may misreport information about his or her cognitive processes for a variety of reasons. These reasons can be intentional or unintentional. Intentional misreports can include trying to edit out unflattering information.

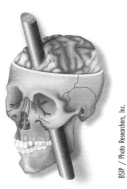

BSIP / Photo Researchers, Inc.

Figure 1.4   When an explosion forced an iron rod through his head, Phineas Gage sustained frontal lobe damage. Gage was the subject of case studies both during his life and after his death.

Unintentional misreports may involve not understanding the question or not remembering the information accurately. For example, when a participant is asked about the problem-solving strategies he or she used in high school, the participant may not remember. The participant may try to be completely truthful in his or her reports. But reports involving recollected information (e.g., diaries, retrospective accounts, questionnaires, and surveys) are notably less reliable than reports provided during the cognitive processing under investigation. The reason is that participants sometimes forget what they did.

In studying complex cognitive processes, such as problem solving or decision making, researchers often use a verbal protocol. In a *verbal protocol*, the participants describe aloud all their thoughts and ideas during the performance of a given cognitive task (e.g., "I like the apartment with the swimming pool better, but I can't really afford it, so I might have to choose the one without the swimming pool.").

An alternative to a verbal protocol is for participants to report specific information regarding a particular aspect of their cognitive processing. For example, consider a study of insightful problem solving (see Chapter 12). Participants were asked at 15-second intervals to report numerical ratings indicating how close they felt they were to reaching a solution to a given problem. Unfortunately, even these methods of self-reporting have their limitations. What kind of limitations? Cognitive processes may be altered by the act of giving the report (e.g., processes involving brief forms of memory; see Chapter 5). Or, cognitive processes may occur outside of conscious awareness (e.g., processes that do not require conscious attention or that take place so rapidly that we fail to notice them; see Chapter 4). To get an idea of some of the difficulties with self-reports, carry out the following *Investigating Cognitive Psychology: Self-Reports* tasks. Reflect on your experiences with self-reports.

Case studies (e.g., an in-depth study of individuals who are exceptionally gifted) and naturalistic observations (such as detailed observations of the performance of employees operating in nuclear power plants) may be used to complement findings from laboratory experiments. These two methods of cognitive research offer high **ecological validity**, the degree to which particular findings in one environmental

---

 INVESTIGATING COGNITIVE PSYCHOLOGY
Self-Reports

1. Without looking at your shoes, try reporting aloud the various steps involved in tying your shoe.

2. Recall aloud what you did on your last birthday.

3. Now, actually tie your shoe (or something else, such as a string tied around a table leg), reporting aloud the steps you take. Do you notice any differences between task 1 and task 3?

4. Report aloud how you pulled into consciousness the steps involved in tying your shoe or your memories of your last birthday. Can you report exactly how you pulled the information into conscious awareness? Can you report which part of your brain was most active during each of these tasks?

context may be considered relevant outside of that context. As you probably know, *ecology* is the study of the interactive relationship between an organism (or organisms) and its environment. Many cognitive psychologists seek to understand the interactive relationship between human thought processes and the environments in which humans are thinking. Sometimes, cognitive processes that are commonly observed in one setting (e.g., in a laboratory) are not identical to those observed in another setting (e.g., in an air-traffic control tower or a classroom).

Computer Simulations and Artificial Intelligence

Digital computers played a fundamental role in the emergence of the study of cognitive psychology. One kind of influence is indirect—through models of human cognition based on models of how computers process information. Another kind is direct—through computer simulations and artificial intelligence.

In *computer simulations*, researchers program computers to imitate a given human function or process. Examples are performance on particular cognitive tasks (e.g., manipulating objects within three-dimensional space) and performance of particular cognitive processes (e.g., pattern recognition). Some researchers have attempted to create computer models of the entire cognitive architecture of the human mind. Their models have stimulated heated discussions regarding how the human mind may function as a whole (see Chapter 8). Sometimes the distinction between simulation and artificial intelligence is blurred. For example, certain programs are designed to simulate human performance and to maximize functioning simultaneously.

Consider a computer program that plays chess. There are two entirely different ways to conceptualize how to write such a program. One is known as brute force: A researcher constructs an algorithm that considers extremely large numbers of moves in a very short time, potentially beating human players simply by virtue of the number of moves it considers and the future potential consequences of these moves. The program would be viewed as successful to the extent that it beat the best humans. This kind of artificial intelligence does not seek to represent how humans function, but done well, it can produce a program that plays chess at the highest possible level.

An alternative approach, simulation, looks at how chess grand masters solve chess problems and then seeks to function the way they do. The program would be successful if it chose, in a sequence of moves in a game, the same moves that the grand master would choose. It is also possible to combine the two approaches, producing a program that generally simulates human performance but can use brute force as necessary to win games.

Putting It All Together

Cognitive psychologists often broaden and deepen their understanding of cognition through research in cognitive science. **Cognitive science** is a cross-disciplinary field that uses ideas and methods from cognitive psychology, psychobiology, artificial intelligence, philosophy, linguistics, and anthropology (Nickerson, 2005; Von Eckardt, 2005). Cognitive scientists use these ideas and methods to focus on the study of how humans acquire and use knowledge.

Cognitive psychologists also profit from collaborations with other kinds of psychologists. Examples are social psychologists (e.g., in the cross-disciplinary field of social cognition), psychologists who study motivation and emotion, and engineering psychologists (i.e., psychologists who study human-machine interactions), but also clinical psychologists who are interested in psychological disorders. There is also close exchange and collaboration with a number of other related fields. Psychiatrists are interested in how the brain works and how it influences our thinking, feeling, and reasoning. Anthropologists in turn may explore how reasoning and perception processes differ from one culture to the next. Computer specialists try to develop computer interfaces that are highly efficient, given the way humans perceive and process information. Traffic planners can use information from cognitive psychology to plan and construct traffic situations that result in a maximal overview for traffic participants and therefore, hopefully, fewer accidents.

✔ CONCEPT CHECK

1. What is the meaning of "statistical significance"?
2. How do independent and dependent variables differ?
3. Why is the experimental method uniquely suited to drawing causal inferences?
4. What are some of the advantages and disadvantages of the case-study method?
5. How does a theory differ from a hypothesis?

Fundamental Ideas in Cognitive Psychology

Certain fundamental ideas keep emerging in cognitive psychology, regardless of the particular phenomenon one studies. Here are what might be considered five fundamental ideas. These ideas crosscut some of the Key Themes listed at the end of this chapter.

1. *Empirical data and theories are both important—data in cognitive psychology can be fully understood only in the context of an explanatory theory, and theories are empty without empirical data.*

    Theories give meaning to data. Suppose that we know that people's ability to recognize information that they have seen is better than their ability to recall such information. As an example, they are better at recognizing whether they heard a word said on a list than they are at recalling the word without the word being given. This is an interesting empirical generalization, but it does not, in the absence of an underlying theory, provide *explanation*. Another important goal of science is also *prediction*. Theory can suggest under which circumstances limitations to the generalization should occur. Theory thus assists both in explanation and in prediction.

    At the same time, theory without data is empty. Almost anyone can sit in an armchair and propose a theory—even a plausible-sounding one. Science, however, requires empirical testing of such theories. Thus, theories and data depend on each other. Theories generate data collections, which help correct theories, which then lead to further data collections, and so forth.

2. *Cognition is generally adaptive, but not in all specific instances.*

    We can perceive, learn, remember, reason, and solve problems with great accuracy. And we do so even though we are constantly distracted by a plethora of stimuli. The same processes, however, that lead us to perceive, remember, and reason accurately in most situations also can lead us astray. Our memories and reasoning processes, for example, are susceptible to certain well-identified, systematic errors. For example, we tend to overvalue information that is easily available to us. While this tendency generally helps us to make cognitive processes more efficient, we do this even when this information is not optimally relevant to the problem at hand.

3. *Cognitive processes interact with each other and with noncognitive processes.*
Although cognitive psychologists try to study and often to isolate the functioning of specific cognitive processes, they know that these processes work together. For example, memory processes depend on perceptual processes. What you remember depends in part on what you perceive. But noncognitive processes also interact with cognitive ones. For example, you learn better when you are motivated to learn. Cognitive psychologists therefore seek to study cognitive processes not only in isolation but also in their interactions with each other and with noncognitive processes.

One of the most exciting areas of cognitive psychology today is at the interface between cognitive and biological levels of analysis. In recent years, it has become possible to localize activity in the brain associated with various kinds of cognitive processes. However, one has to be careful about assuming that the biological activity is causal of the cognitive activity. Research shows that learning that causes changes in the brain—in other words, cognitive processes—can affect biological structures just as biological structures can affect cognitive processes. The cognitive system does not operate in isolation. It works in interaction with other systems.

4. *Cognition needs to be studied through a variety of scientific methods.*
There is no one right way to study cognition. All cognitive processes need to be studied through a variety of methods. The more different kinds of techniques that lead to the same conclusion, the higher the confidence one can have in that conclusion. For example, suppose studies of reaction times, error rates, and patterns of individual differences all lead to the same conclusion. Then one can have much more confidence in the conclusion than if only one method led to that conclusion.

All these methods, however, must be *scientific*. They enable us to disconfirm our expectations when those expectations are wrong. Nonscientific methods do not have this feature. For example, methods of inquiry that simply rely on faith or authority to determine truth may have value in our lives, but they are not scientific.

5. *All basic research in cognitive psychology may lead to applications, and all applied research may lead to basic understandings.*
But the truth is, the distinction between basic and applied research often is not clear at all. Research that seems like it will be basic often leads to immediate applications. Similarly, research that seems like it will be applied sometimes leads quickly to basic understandings. For example, a basic finding from research on memory is that learning is superior when it is spaced out over time rather than crammed into a short time interval. This basic finding has an immediate application to study strategies. At the same time, research on eyewitness testimony, which seems on its face to be very applied, has enhanced our basic understanding of memory systems and of the extent to which humans construct their own memories.

In this book, we emphasize the underlying common ideas and organizing themes across cognitive psychology, rather than simply to state the facts. We follow this path to help you perceive large, meaningful patterns within the domain of cognitive psychology. We also try to give you some idea of how cognitive psychologists think and how they structure their field in their day-to-day work. We hope that this approach will help you to contemplate problems in cognitive psychology at a deeper level than might otherwise be possible. Ultimately, the goal of cognitive psychologists is to understand not only how people may think in their laboratories but also how they think in their everyday lives.

Key Themes in Cognitive Psychology

If we review the important ideas in this chapter, we discover some of the major themes that underlie cognitive psychology, such as nature vs. nurture and rationalism vs. empiricism. These, and the other key themes listed here, address the core of the nature of the human mind. These themes appear again and again in the study of cognitive psychology.

As you read each chapter, think of the topics in terms of how they relate to the major themes in cognitive psychology. You will be encountering these themes throughout this text and can review them in each chapter's *Key Themes* section.

Note that these questions can be posed in the "either/or" form of thesis/antithesis or in the "both/and" form of a synthesis of views or methods. The synthesis view often proves more useful than one extreme position or another. For example, our nature may provide an inherited framework for our distinctive characteristics and patterns of thinking and acting. But our nurture may shape the specific ways in which we flesh out that framework.

We may use empirical methods for gathering data and for testing hypotheses. But we may use rationalist methods for interpreting data, constructing theories, and formulating hypotheses based on theories. Our understanding of cognition deepens when we consider both basic research into fundamental cognitive processes and applied research regarding effective uses of cognition in real-world settings. Syntheses are constantly evolving. What today may be viewed as a synthesis may be viewed tomorrow as an extreme position or vice versa.

Remember, each of the topics in this text (perception, memory, and so on) can be examined using these seven major themes in cognitive psychology:

1. ***Nature versus nurture***
   Thesis/Antithesis: Which is more influential in human cognition—nature or nurture? If we believe that innate characteristics of human cognition are more important, we might focus our research on studying innate characteristics of cognition. If we believe that the environment plays an important role in cognition, we might conduct research exploring how distinctive characteristics of the environment seem to influence cognition.
   Synthesis: We can explore how covariations and interactions in the environment (e.g., an impoverished environment) adversely affect someone whose genes otherwise might have led to success in a variety of tasks.

2. ***Rationalism versus empiricism***
   Thesis/Antithesis: How should we discover the truth about ourselves and about the world around us? Should we do so by trying to reason logically, based on

**Well, you walk like a duck, you quack like a duck...
May I ask who brought you up?**

Nature vs. nurture: Both our genes and our environment may influence what we are, how we behave, and how we think.

what we already know? Or should we do so by observing and testing our observations of what we can perceive through our senses?

Synthesis: We can combine theory with empirical methods to learn the most we can about cognitive phenomena.

3. **Structures versus processes**

   Thesis/Antithesis: Should we study the structures (contents, attributes, and products) of the human mind? Or should we focus on the processes of human thinking?

   Synthesis: We can explore how mental processes operate on mental structures.

4. **Domain generality versus domain specificity**

   Thesis/Antithesis: Are the processes we observe limited to single domains, or are they general across a variety of domains? Do observations in one domain apply also to all domains, or do they apply only to the specific domains observed?

   Synthesis: We can explore which processes might be domain-general and which might be domain-specific.

5. **Validity of causal inferences versus ecological validity**

   Thesis/Antithesis: Should we study cognition by using highly controlled experiments that increase the probability of valid inferences regarding causality? Or should we use more naturalistic techniques, which increase the likelihood of obtaining ecologically valid findings but possibly at the expense of experimental control?

Synthesis: We can combine a variety of methods, including laboratory methods and more naturalistic ones, so as to converge on findings that hold up, regardless of the method of study.

6. ***Applied versus basic research***
   Thesis/Antithesis: Should we conduct research into fundamental cognitive processes? Or should we study ways in which to help people use cognition effectively in practical situations?
   Synthesis: We can combine the two kinds of research dialectically so that basic research leads to applied research, which leads to further basic research, and so on.

7. ***Biological versus behavioral methods***
   Thesis/Antithesis: Should we study the brain and its functioning directly, perhaps even scanning the brain while people are performing cognitive tasks? Or should we study people's behavior in cognitive tasks, looking at measures such as percent correct and reaction time?
   Synthesis: We can try to synthesize biological and behavioral methods so that we understand cognitive phenomena at multiple levels of analysis.

Summary

1. **What is cognitive psychology?** Cognitive psychology is the study of how people perceive, learn, remember, and think about information.

2. **How did psychology develop as a science?** Beginning with Plato and Aristotle, people have contemplated how to gain understanding of the truth. Plato held that rationalism offers the clear path to truth, whereas Aristotle espoused empiricism as the route to knowledge. Centuries later, Descartes extended Plato's rationalism, whereas Locke elaborated on Aristotle's empiricism. Kant offered a synthesis of these apparent opposites. Decades after Kant proposed his synthesis, Hegel observed how the history of ideas seems to progress through a *dialectical* process.

3. **How did cognitive psychology develop from psychology?** By the twentieth century, psychology had emerged as a distinct field of study. Wundt focused on the structures of the mind (leading to *structuralism*), whereas James and Dewey focused on the processes of the mind (*functionalism*).

   Emerging from this dialectic was *associationism*, espoused by Ebbinghaus and Thorndike. It

paved the way for behaviorism by underscoring the importance of mental associations. Another step toward behaviorism was Pavlov's discovery of the principles of classical conditioning. Watson, and later Skinner, were the chief proponents of *behaviorism*. It focused entirely on observable links between an organism's behavior and particular environmental contingencies that strengthen or weaken the likelihood that particular behaviors will be repeated. Most behaviorists dismissed entirely the notion that there is merit in psychologists trying to understand what is going on in the mind of the individual engaging in the behavior.

However, Tolman and subsequent behaviorist researchers noted the role of cognitive processes in influencing behavior. A convergence of developments across many fields led to the emergence of *cognitive psychology* as a discrete discipline, spearheaded by such notables as Neisser.

4. **How have other disciplines contributed to the development of theory and research in cognitive psychology?** Cognitive psychology has

roots in philosophy and physiology. They merged to form the mainstream of psychology. As a discrete field of psychological study, cognitive psychology also profited from cross-disciplinary investigations.

Relevant fields include linguistics (e.g., How do language and thought interact?), biological psychology (e.g., What are the physiological bases for cognition?), anthropology (e.g., What is the importance of the cultural context for cognition?), and technological advances like artificial intelligence (e.g., How do computers process information?).

5. **What methods do cognitive psychologists use to study how people think?** Cognitive psychologists use a broad range of methods, including experiments, psychobiological techniques, self-reports, case studies, naturalistic observation, and computer simulations and artificial intelligence.

6. **What are the current issues and various fields of study within cognitive psychology?** Some of the major issues in the field have centered on how to pursue knowledge. Psychological work can be done:

- by using both *rationalism* (which is the basis for theory development) and *empiricism* (which is the basis for gathering data);

- by underscoring the importance of cognitive structures and of cognitive processes;
- by emphasizing the study of domain-general and of domain-specific processing;
- by striving for a high degree of experimental control (which better permits causal inferences) and for a high degree of *ecological validity* (which better allows generalization of findings to settings outside of the laboratory);
- by conducting basic research seeking fundamental insights about cognition and applied research seeking effective uses of cognition in real-world settings.

Although positions on these issues may appear to be diametrical opposites, often apparently antithetical views may be synthesized into a form that offers the best of each of the opposing viewpoints.

Cognitive psychologists study biological bases of cognition as well as attention, consciousness, perception, memory, mental imagery, language, problem solving, creativity, decision making, reasoning, developmental changes in cognition across the life span, human intelligence, artificial intelligence, and various other aspects of human thinking.

Thinking about Thinking: Analytical, Creative, and Practical Questions

1. Describe the major historical schools of psychological thought leading up to the development of cognitive psychology.
2. Describe some of the ways in which philosophy, linguistics, and artificial intelligence have contributed to the development of cognitive psychology.
3. Compare and contrast the influences of Plato and Aristotle on psychology.
4. Analyze how various research methods in cognitive psychology reflect empiricist and rationalist approaches to gaining knowledge.
5. Design a rough sketch of a cognitive-psychological investigation involving one of the research methods described in this chapter. Highlight both the advantages and the disadvantages of using this particular method for your investigation.
6. This chapter describes cognitive psychology as the field is at present. How might you speculate that the field will change in the next 50 years?
7. How might an insight gained from basic research lead to practical uses in an everyday setting?
8. How might an insight gained from applied research lead to a deepened understanding of the fundamental features of cognition?

Key Terms

artificial intelligence (AI), *p. 14*
associationism, *p. 9*
behaviorism, *p. 11*
cognitive psychology, *p. 3*
cognitive science, *p. 33*
cognitivism, *p. 13*
dependent variables, *p. 25*
ecological validity, *p. 32*
empiricist, *p. 6*

functionalism, *p. 8*
Gestalt psychology, *p. 13*
hypotheses, *p. 23*
independent variables, *p. 24*
intelligence, *p. 17*
introspection, *p. 8*
pragmatists, *p. 9*
rationalist, *p. 6*
statistical significance, *p. 23*

structuralism, *p. 7*
theory, *p. 23*
theory of multiple intelligences, *p. 19*
three-stratum model of intelligence, *p. 19*
triarchic theory of human intelligence, *p. 20*

Media Resources

Visit the companion website—**www.cengagebrain.com**—for quizzes, research articles, chapter outlines and, more.

Perception

Here are some of the questions we will explore in this chapter:

1. How can we perceive an object like a chair as having a stable form, given that the image of the chair on our retina changes as we look at it from different directions?

2. What are two fundamental approaches to explaining perception?

3. What happens when people with normal visual sensations cannot perceive visual stimuli?

■ **BELIEVE IT OR NOT**

IF YOU ENCOUNTERED TYRANNOSAURUS REX, WOULD STANDING STILL SAVE YOU?

Have you seen the movie *Jurassic Park*? In this movie, one protagonist tells another while facing a Tyrannosaurus Rex that they will be safe as long as they don't move, because the T. Rex can detect his prey only when it is moving. Well, he could not have been more wrong. As it now turns out, T. Rex had excellent binocular vision (i.e., the vision fields of both eyes are combined to achieve depth perception). Researchers had the heads of several dinosaur species reconstructed and found that T. Rex probably could see 13 times better than humans (for comparison, eagles can only see 3.6 times better than humans). Its excellent vision is due to the big binocular range, which is the area that can be seen by both eyes at the same time. In addition, over time T. Rex's snout became longer, its cheeks grew thinner so as not to obstruct the view, and its eyeballs became bigger. These changes all helped T. Rex to have excellent three-dimensional (3-D) vision (Jaffe, 2006; Stevens, 2006). This chapter will introduce you to the basics of visual perception for humans—and sometimes for other species as well.

As we are writing this chapter, we can look out of the window onto the city of Boston. The high-rise buildings that are less than a mile away look about as small as our computer screen. Yet we know that they are actually much bigger than our screen—they only appear to be small. Try it out yourself. Look out of your window. Can you see how things that are farther away seem much smaller than you know they are? This is just one example of the complex process of perception.

Have you ever been told that you "can't see something that's right under your nose"? How about that you "can't see the forest for the trees"? Have you ever listened to your favorite song over and over, trying to decipher the lyrics? In each of these situations, we call on the complex construct of perception. **Perception** is the set of processes by which we recognize, organize, and make sense of the sensations we receive from environmental stimuli (Goodale, 2000a, 2000b; Kosslyn & Osherson, 1995; Marr, 1982; Pomerantz, 2003). Perception encompasses many psychological phenomena. In this chapter, we focus primarily on visual perception. It is the most widely recognized and the most widely studied perceptual modality (i.e., system for a particular sense, such as touch or smell). First, we will get to know a few basic terms and concepts of perception. We will then consider optical illusions that illustrate some of the intricacies of human perception. Next, we will have a look at the biology of the visual system. We will consider some approaches to explain perception, and afterward have a closer look at some details of the perceptual process, namely the perception of objects and forms, and how the environment provides cues to help you perceive your surroundings. We will also explore what happens when people have difficulties in perception.

INVESTIGATING COGNITIVE PSYCHOLOGY
Perception

Stand at one end of a room and hold your thumb up to your eye so that it is the same size as the door on the opposite side of the room. Do you *really* think that your thumb is as large as a door? No. You know that your thumb is close to you, so it just *looks* as large as the door. There are numerous cues in the room to tell you that the door is farther away from you than your thumb is. In your mind, you make the door much larger to compensate for the distance away from you. Knowledge is a key to perception. You know that your thumb and the door are not the same size, so you are able to use this knowledge to correct for what you know is not so.

From Sensation to Representation

We do not perceive the world exactly as our eyes see it. Instead, our brain actively tries to make sense of the many stimuli that enter our eyes and fall on our retina. Take a look at Figure 2.1. You can see two high-rise buildings in the city of Boston. (We live in one of them!) In the right photo, the right tower seems to be substantially higher than the left one. The left picture, however, shows that the towers actually are in fact exactly the same height. Depending on your viewpoint, objects can look quite different, revealing different details. Thus, perception does not consist of

(a)   (b)

Figure 2.1 Objects Look Different Depending on the Perspective.
The pictures show the same two high-rise buildings in Boston from two different perspectives. In (a) they look about the same size, as they in fact are. In (b), their image on the retina makes them seem to be of different heights, and it is only through further processing that we can pinpoint they are the same size.

© Karin Sternberg

Figure 2.2   Reality or Reflection?

This picture shows the reflection of a church in a skyscraper. What is easy for us to perceive constitutes a big problem for computers. Where does one building end and the next one start? Which part of the percept belongs to which object? What distinguishes the real person on the street from his or her reflection in the building so that a computer can recognize which one is the reflection?

just seeing what is being projected onto your retina; the process is much more complex. Your brain processes the visual stimuli, giving the stimuli meaning and interpreting them.

How difficult it is to interpret what we see has become clear in recent years as researchers have tried to teach computers to "see"; but computers are still lagging behind humans in object recognition. Can you recognize what is shown in Figure 2.2? The picture shows a church that is reflected in a high-rise building. It might have taken you a few moments to figure out what is depicted in the photo, but for computers, this is an extremely difficult task. It is not immediately clear in this picture what is reflection, what is the building, and what is surrounding. Furthermore, the borders of the church are blurred so that it becomes very challenging to see where the object ends and what it really is. So, while it may not take you a lot of effort to identify the objects in this photo, it does take a lot of processing to perceive them, as the stimuli are very ambiguous.

This chapter focuses on the processes of visual perception and the processes we use to make sense of the visual stimuli that are focused on our retina. We start our exploration by familiarizing ourselves with some basic concepts. To illustrate the intricacies of perception, we then look at some optical illusions. And finally we learn how the eye receives impressions of stimuli and sends signals to the brain.

Some Basic Concepts of Perception

In his influential and controversial work, James Gibson (1966, 1979) provided a useful framework for studying perception. He introduced the concepts of distal (external) object, informational medium, proximal stimulation, and perceptual object. Let's examine each of these.

The *distal* (far) *object* is the object in the external world (e.g., a falling tree). The event of the tree falling creates a pattern on an *informational medium*. The informational medium could be sound waves, as in the sound of the falling tree. The informational medium might also be reflected light, chemical molecules, or tactile information coming from the environment. For example, when the information from light waves come into contact with the appropriate sensory receptors of the eyes, *proximal* (near) *stimulation* occurs (i.e., the cells in your retina absorb the light waves). Perception occurs when a *perceptual object* (i.e., what you see) is created in you that reflects the properties of the external world. That is, an image of a falling tree is created on your retina that reflects the falling tree that is in front of you.

Table 2.1 lists the various properties of distal objects, informational media, proximal stimuli, and perceptual objects for five different senses (sight, sound, smell, taste, and touch). The processes of perception vary tremendously across the different senses.

Table 2.1 Perceptual Continuum

Perception occurs when the informational medium carries information about a distal object to a person. When the person's sense receptors pick up on the information, proximal stimulation occurs, which results in the person's perceiving an object.

Modality	Distal Object	Informational Medium	Proximal Stimulation	Perceptual Object
Vision—sight	Grandma's face	Reflected light from Grandma's face (visible electromagnetic waves)	Photon absorption in the rod and cone cells of the retina, the receptor surface in the back of the eye	Grandma's face
Audition—sound	A falling tree	Sound waves generated by the tree's fall	Sound-wave conduction to the basilar membrane, the receptor surface within the cochlea of the inner ear	A falling tree
Olfaction—smell	Bacon being fried	Molecules released by frying bacon	Molecular absorption in the cells of the olfactory epithelium, the receptor surface in the nasal cavity	Bacon
Gustation—taste	Ice cream	Molecules of ice cream both released into the air and dissolved in water	Molecular contact with taste buds, the receptor cells on the tongue and soft palate, combined with olfactory stimulation	Ice cream
Touch	A computer keyboard	Mechanical pressure and vibration at the point of contact between the surface of the skin and the keyboard	Stimulation of various receptor cells within the dermis, the innermost layer of skin	Computer keys

So, if a tree falls in the forest and no one is around to hear it, does it make a sound? It makes no perceived sound. But it does make a sound by creating sound waves. So the answer is "yes" or "no," depending on how you look at the question. "Yes" if you believe that the existence of sound waves is all that's needed to confirm the existence of a sound. But you would answer "no" if you believe the sound needs to be perceived (for the sound waves to have landed on the receptors in someone's ears).

The question of where to draw the line between perception and cognition, or even between sensation and perception, arouses much debate with no ready resolution. Instead, to be more productive in moving toward answerable questions, we should view these processes as part of a continuum. Information flows through the system. Different processes address different questions. Questions of *sensation* focus on qualities of stimulation. Is that shade of red brighter than the red of an apple? Is the sound of that falling tree louder than the sound of thunder? How well do one person's impressions of colors or sounds match someone else's impressions of those same colors or sounds?

This same color or sound information answers different questions for *perception*. These are typically questions of identity and of form, pattern, and movement. Is that red thing an apple? Did I just hear a tree falling? Finally, *cognition* occurs as this information is used to serve further goals. Is that apple edible? Should I get out of this forest?

We never can experience through vision, hearing, taste, smell, or touch exactly the same set of stimulus properties we have experienced before. Every apple casts a somewhat different image on our retina; no falling tree sounds exactly like another; and even the faces of our relatives and friends look quite different, depending on whether they are smiling, enraged, or sad. Likewise, the voice of any person sounds somewhat different, depending on whether he or she is sick, out of breath, tired, happy, or sad. Therefore, one fundamental question for perception is "How do we achieve perceptual stability in the face of this utter instability at the level of sensory receptors?" Actually, given the nature of our sensory receptors, variation seems even necessary for perception! In the phenomenon of *sensory adaptation*, receptor cells adapt to constant stimulation by ceasing to fire until there is a change in stimulation. Through sensory adaptation, we may stop detecting the presence of a stimulus.

To study visual perception, scientists devised a way to create stabilized images. Such images do not move across the retina because they actually follow the eye movements. The use of this technique has confirmed the hypothesis that constant stimulation of the cells of the retina gives the impression that the image disappears (Ditchburn, 1980; Martinez-Conde, Macknik, & Hybel, 2004; Riggs et al., 1953).

The word "Ganzfeld" is German and means "complete field." It refers to an unstructured visual field (Metzger, 1930). When your eyes are exposed to a uniform field of stimulation (e.g., a red surface area without any shades, a clear blue sky, or dense fog), you will stop perceiving that stimulus after a few minutes and see just a gray field instead. This is because your eyes have adapted to the stimulus.

The mechanism of sensory adaptation ensures that sensory information is changing constantly. Because of the dulling effect of sensory adaptation in the retina (the receptor surface of the eye), our eyes constantly are making tiny rapid movements. These movements create constant changes in the location of the projected image inside the eye. Thus, stimulus variation is an essential attribute for perception. It paradoxically makes the task of explaining perception more difficult.

INVESTIGATING COGNITIVE PSYCHOLOGY
The Ganzfeld Effect

Cut a Ping-Pong ball in two halves or use two plastic spoons. Paint them uniformly in red, for example, making sure there are no streaks so that you really have one uniform field of color. Put the ball halves or the spoons over your eyes so that your eyes are completely covered. Then gaze toward a light source for a few minutes. At some point, your perception will change from the color red to gray because your cells have adapted to the constant stimulus. Some people also perceive hallucinations and experience altered states of consciousness when exposed to a Ganzfeld (Wackermann, Puetz, & Allefeld, 2008).

Seeing Things That Aren't There, or Are They?

To find out about some of the phenomena of perception, psychologists often study situations that pose problems in making sense of our sensations. Consider, for example, the image displayed in Figure 2.3. To most people, the figure initially looks like a blur of meaningless shadings. A recognizable creature is staring them in the face, but they may not see it. When people finally realize what is in the figure, they rightfully feel "cowed." The figure of the cow is hidden within the continuous gradations of shading that constitute the picture. Before you recognized the figure as a cow, you correctly sensed all aspects of the figure. But you had not yet organized those sensations to form a mental **percept**—that is, a mental representation of a stimulus that is perceived. Without such a percept of the cow, you could not meaningfully grasp what you previously had sensed.

The preceding examples show that sometimes we cannot perceive what does exist. At other times, however, we perceive things that do not exist. For example, notice the black triangle in the center of the left panel of Figure 2.4. Also note the white triangle in the center of the right panel of Figure 2.4. They jump right out at

Figure 2.3   Dallenbach's Cow.

What do you learn about your own perception by trying to identify the object staring at you from this photo?

Source: From Dallenbach, K. M. (1951). A puzzle-picture with a new principle of concealment. *American Journal of Psychology, 54,* 431–433.

Figure 2.4   Elusive Triangles: Real or Illusions?

You easily can see the triangles in this figure—or are the triangles just an illusion?

Source: From *In Search of the Human Mind* by Robert J. Sternberg, © 1995 by Harcourt Brace & Company. Reproduced by permission of the publisher.

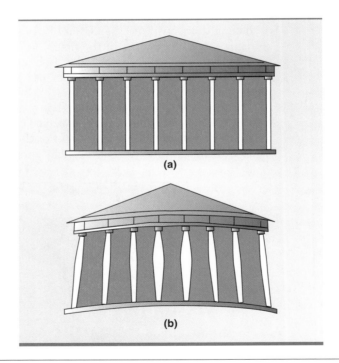

Figure 2.5   The Parthenon.

The columns of the Parthenon in Greece actually bulge slightly in the middle (b) to compensate for the visual tendency to perceive that straight parallel lines (a) seem to curve inward. Similarly, the horizontal lines of the beams crossing the top of the columns and the top step of the porch bulge slightly upward to counteract the tendency to perceive that they curve slightly downward. In addition, the columns lean ever so slightly inward at the top to compensate for the tendency to perceive them as spreading out as we gaze upward at them. Architects consider these distortions of visual perception in their designs today.

you. Now look very closely at each of the panels. You will see that the triangles are not really all there. The black that constitutes the center triangle in the left panel looks darker, or blacker, than the surrounding black. But it is not. Nor is the white central triangle in the right panel any brighter, or whiter, than the surrounding white. Both central triangles are optical illusions. They involve the perception of visual information not physically present in the visual sensory stimulus.

So, sometimes we perceive what is not there. Other times, we do not perceive what is there. And at still other times, we perceive what cannot be there.

The existence of perceptual illusions suggests that what we sense (in our sensory organs) is not necessarily what we perceive (in our minds). Our minds must be taking the available sensory information and manipulating that information somehow to create mental representations of objects, properties, and spatial relationships within our environments (Peterson, 1999). The way we represent these objects will depend in part on our viewpoint in perceiving the objects (Edelman & Weinshall, 1991; Poggio & Edelman, 1990; Tarr, 1995; Tarr & Bülthoff, 1998). An example in architecture is the use of optical illusions in the construction of the Parthenon (Figure 2.5). Were the Parthenon actually constructed the way it appears to us perceptually (with strictly rectilinear form), its appearance would be bizarre.

Architects are not the only ones to have recognized some fundamental principles of perception. For centuries, artists have known how to lead us to perceive 3-D percepts when viewing two-dimensional (2-D) images. What are some of the principles that guide our perceptions of both real and illusory percepts? We will explore the answer to this question as we move through the chapter. We begin with examining our visual system.

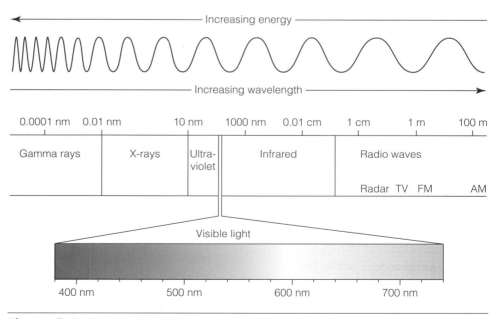

Figure 2.6 **The Electromagnetic Spectrum.**
This image shows the different wavelengths that light comes in, and the small array of wavelengths that is actually visible to humans.

How Does Our Visual System Work?

The precondition for vision is the existence of light. Light is electromagnetic radiation that can be described in terms of wavelength. Humans can perceive only a small range of the wavelengths that exist; the visible wavelengths are from 380 to 750 nanometers (Figure 2.6; Starr, Evers, & Starr, 2007).

Vision begins when light passes through the protective covering of the eye (Figure 2.7). This covering, the *cornea,* is a clear dome that protects the eye. The light then passes through the *pupil,* the opening in the center of the *iris.* It continues through the *crystalline lens* and the *vitreous humor.* The vitreous humor is a gel-like substance that comprises the majority of the eye.

Eventually, the light focuses on the **retina** where electromagnetic light energy is transduced—that is, converted—into neural electrochemical impulses (Blake, 2000). Vision is most acute in the **fovea,** which is a small, thin region of the retina, the size of the head of a pin. When you look straight at an object, your eyes rotate so that the image falls directly onto the fovea. Although the retina is only about as thick as a single page in this book, it consists of three main layers of neuronal tissue (Figure 2.8).

The first layer of neuronal tissue—closest to the front, outward-facing surface of the eye—is the layer of **ganglion cells,** whose axons constitute the **optic nerve.** The second layer consists of three kinds of interneuron cells. **Amacrine cells** and **horizontal cells**

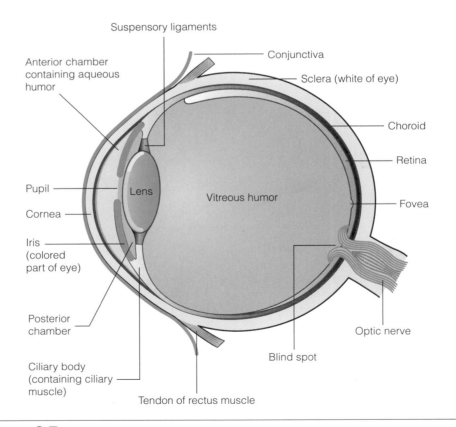

Figure 2.7 The Human Eye.

The composition of the human eye.

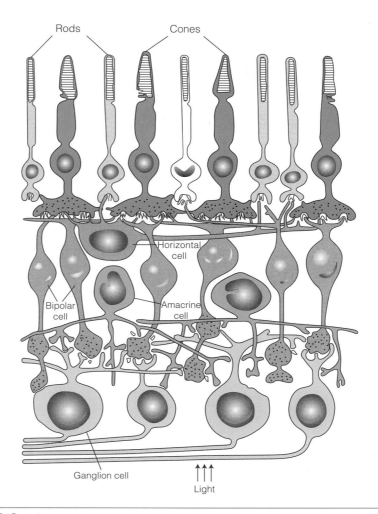

Rods   Cones

Horizontal cell

Bipolar cell

Amacrine cell

Ganglion cell

Light

Figure 2.8   The Retina.

The retina is made up of rods and cones, horizontal cells, bipolar cells, amacrine cells, and ganglion cells.

make single lateral (i.e., horizontal) connections among adjacent areas of the retina in the middle layer of cells. **Bipolar cells** make dual connections forward and outward to the ganglion cells, as well as backward and inward to the third layer of retinal cells.

The third layer of the retina contains the **photoreceptors,** which convert light energy into electrochemical energy that is transmitted by neurons to the brain. There are two kinds of photoreceptors—rods and cones. Each eye contains roughly 120 million rods and 8 million cones. Rods and cones differ not only in shape but also in their compositions, locations, and responses to light. Within the rods and cones are **photopigments,** chemical substances that react to light and transform physical electromagnetic energy into an electrochemical neural impulse that can be understood by the brain. The **rods** are long and thin photoreceptors. They are more highly concentrated in the periphery of the retina than in the foveal region. The rods are responsible for night vision and are sensitive to light and dark stimuli.

The **cones** are short and thick photoreceptors and allow for the perception of color. They are more highly concentrated in the foveal region than in the periphery of the retina (Durgin, 2000).

The rods, cones, and photopigments could not do their work were they not somehow hooked up to the brain. The neurochemical messages processed by the rods and cones of the retina travel via the bipolar cells to the ganglion cells (see Goodale, 2000a, 2000b). The axons of the ganglion cells in the eye collectively form the optic nerve for that eye. The optic nerves of the two eyes join at the base of the brain to form the *optic chiasma* (see Figure 3.8 in Chapter 3). At this point, the ganglion cells from the inward, or nasal, part of the retina—the part closer to your nose—cross through the optic chiasma and extend to the opposite hemisphere of the brain. The ganglion cells from the outward, or temporal area of the retina closer to your temple go to the hemisphere on the same side of the body. The lens of each eye naturally inverts the image of the world as it projects the image onto the retina. In this way, the message sent to your brain is literally upside-down and backward.

After being routed via the optic chiasma, about 90% of the ganglion cells then go to the lateral geniculate nucleus of the *thalamus*. From the thalamus, neurons carry information to the primary visual cortex (V1 or striate cortex) in the occipital lobe of the brain. The *visual cortex* contains several processing areas. Each area handles different kinds of visual information relating to intensity and quality, including color, location, depth, pattern, and form.

Pathways to Perceive the What and the Where

What are the visual pathways in the brain? A pathway in general is the path the visual information takes from its entering the human perceptual system through the eyes to its being completely processed. Generally, researchers agree that there are two pathways. Work on visual perception has identified separate neural pathways in the cerebral cortex for processing different aspects of the same stimuli (De Yoe & Van Essen, 1988; Köhler et al., 1995). Perception deficits like ataxia and agnosia that are covered later in this chapter also point toward the existence of different pathways.

Why are there two pathways? It is because the information from the primary visual cortex in the occipital lobe is forwarded through two fasciculi (fiber bundles): One ascends toward the parietal lobe (along the dorsal pathway), and one descends to the temporal lobe (along the ventral pathway). The dorsal pathway is also called the *where pathway* and is responsible for processing location and motion information; the ventral pathway is called the *what pathway* because it is mainly responsible for processing the color, shape, and identity of visual stimuli (Ungerleider & Haxby, 1994; Ungerleider & Mishkin, 1982).

This general view is referred to as the *what/where hypothesis*. Most of the research in this area has been carried out with monkeys. In particular, a group of monkeys with lesions in the temporal lobe were able to indicate *where* things were but seemed unable to recognize *what* they were. In contrast, monkeys with lesions in the parietal lobe were able to recognize *what* things were but not *where* they were.

An alternative interpretation of the visual pathways has been suggested. This interpretation is that the two pathways refer not to what things are and to where they are, but rather, to what they are and to how they function. This view is known as the *what/how hypothesis* (Goodale & Milner, 2004; Goodale & Westwood, 2004). This hypothesis argues that spatial information about where something is located in space is always present in visual information processing. What differs between the two pathways is whether the emphasis is on identifying what an object is or, instead, on how we can situate ourselves so as to grasp the object.

The *what pathway* can be found in the ventral stream and is responsible for the identification of objects. The *how pathway* is located in the dorsal stream and controls movements in relation to the objects that have been identified through the "what" pathway. Ventral and dorsal streams both arise from the same early visual areas (Milner & Goodale, 2008).

The what/how hypothesis is best supported by evidence of processing deficits: There are deficits that impair people's ability to recognize *what* they see and there are distinct deficits that impair people's ability to reach for what they see (*how*).

✔ CONCEPT CHECK

1. What is the difference between sensation and perception?
2. What is the difference between the distal and the perceptual object?
3. How are rods and cones both similar to and different from each other?
4. What are some of the major parts of the eye and what are their functions?
5. What is the "what/where" hypothesis?

Approaches to Perception: How Do We Make Sense of What We See?

Now that we know how a light stimulus that enters our eye is processed and routed to the brain, the question still remains as to *how* we actually perceive what we see. Do we just perceive whatever is being projected on our retina, or is there more to perception? Does our knowledge, and other rules we have learned throughout our life, maybe influence our perception of the world? Going back to our view out of the window, the image on our retina suggests that the buildings we see in the distance are very small. However, we do see other buildings, trees, and streets in front of them that suggest that those buildings are in fact quite large and just appear small because they are far away from our office. In this case, our experience and knowledge about perception and the world allows us to perceive those buildings as tall ones even though they do not look larger than does our hand in front of us on our desk.

There are different views on how we perceive the world. These views can be summarized as bottom-up theories and top-down theories. **Bottom-up theories** describe approaches where perception starts with the stimuli whose appearance you take in through your eye. You look out onto the cityscape, and perception happens when the light information is transported to your brain. Therefore, they are data-driven (i.e., stimulus-driven) theories.

Not all theorists focus on the sensory data of the perceptual stimulus. Many theorists prefer **top-down theories,** according to which perception is driven by high-level cognitive processes, existing knowledge, and the prior expectations that influence perception (Clark, 2003). These theories then work their way down to considering the sensory data, such as the perceptual stimulus. You perceive buildings as big in the background of the city scene because you know these buildings are far away and therefore must be bigger than they appear. From this viewpoint, expectations are important. When people expect to see something, they may see it even if it is not there or is no longer there. For example, suppose people expect to see a certain person in a certain location. They may think they see that person, even if they are actually seeing someone else who looks only vaguely similar (Simons, 1996).

Top-down and bottom-up approaches have been applied to virtually every aspect of cognition. Bottom-up and top-down approaches usually are presented as being in opposition to each other. But to some extent, they deal with different aspects of the same phenomenon. Ultimately, a complete theory of perception will need to encompass both bottom-up and top-down processes.

Bottom-Up Theories

The four main bottom-up theories of form and pattern perception are direct perception, template theories, feature theories, and recognition-by-components theory.

Direct Perception

How do you know the letter *A* when you see it? Easy to ask, hard to answer. Of course, it's an *A* because it looks like an *A*. What makes it look like an *A*, though, instead of like an *H*? Just how difficult it is to answer this question becomes apparent when you look at Figure 2.9. You probably will see the image in Figure 2.9 as the words "THE CAT." Yet the *H* of "THE" is identical to the *A* of "CAT." What subjectively feels like a simple process of pattern recognition is almost certainly quite complex.

Gibson's Theory of Direct Perception   How do we connect what we perceive to what we have stored in our minds? Gestalt psychologists referred to this problem as the *Hoffding function* (Köhler, 1940). It was named after 19th-century Danish psychologist Harald Hoffding. He questioned whether perception is such a simple process that all it takes is to associate what is seen with what is remembered (associationism). An influential and controversial theorist who questioned associationism is James J. Gibson (1904–1980).

According to Gibson's theory of **direct perception,** the information in our sensory receptors, including the sensory context, is all we need to perceive anything. As the environment supplies us with all the information we need for perception, this view is sometimes also called *ecological perception.* In other words, we do not need higher cognitive processes or anything else to mediate between our sensory experiences and our perceptions. Existing beliefs or higher-level inferential thought processes are not necessary for perception.

Figure 2.9   *Can You Read These Words?*
When you read these words, you probably have no difficulty differentiating the *A* from the *H.* Look more closely at each of these two letters. What features differentiate them?

Gibson believed that, in the real world, sufficient contextual information usually exists to make perceptual judgments. He claimed that we need not appeal to higher-level intelligent processes to explain perception. Gibson (1979) believed that we use this contextual information directly. In essence, we are biologically tuned to respond to it. According to Gibson, we use texture gradients as cues for depth and distance. Those cues aid us to perceive directly the relative proximity or distance of objects and of parts of objects.

In Figure 2.10, you can see different rock formations at the sea coast. For the rocks that are closest to the photographer, you can see many details, like notches, holes, and variations in color. The farther away the objects on the picture are, the fewer the details you can see. You are using texture gradients as an indicator of how far away the rocks are. And because some of the rocks cover up parts of other rocks, you infer from that information that the rocks that are partly covered must be farther away than the rocks that cover them. Based on our analysis of the stable relationships among features of objects and settings in the real world, we directly perceive our environment (Gibson, 1950, 1954/1994; Mace, 1986). We do not need the aid of complex thought processes.

Such contextual information might not be readily controlled in a laboratory experiment. But such information is likely to be available in a real-world setting.

Figure 2.10 Cues Used in Depth Perception.
The farther away an object is, the fewer details you can see. You can see small holes and the rough texture of the rock in the foreground whereas the rocks in the background look much smoother. The rock that is partly obscured is located behind the rock that obscures it. We use these cues to aid us in depth perception.

Therefore, as noted above, Gibson's model sometimes is referred to as an ecological model (Turvey, 2003). This reference is a result of Gibson's concern with perception as it occurs in the everyday world (the ecological environment) rather than in laboratory situations, where less contextual information is available.

Ecological constraints apply not only to initial perceptions but also to the ultimate internal representations (such as concepts) that are formed from those perceptions (Hubbard, 1995; Shepard, 1984). Continuing to wave the Gibsonian banner was Eleanor Gibson (1991, 1992), James' wife. She conducted landmark research in infant perception. She observed that infants (who certainly lack much prior knowledge and experience) quickly develop many aspects of perceptual awareness, including depth perception.

Direct perception may also play a role in interpersonal situations when we try to make sense of others' emotions and intentions (Gallagher, 2008). After all, we can recognize emotion in faces as such; we do not see facial expressions that we then try to piece together to result in the perception of an emotion (Wittgenstein, 1980).

Neuroscience and Direct Perception   Neuroscience also indicates that direct perception may be involved in person perception. About 30 to 100 milliseconds after a visual stimulus, mirror neurons start firing. Mirror neurons are active both when a person acts and when he or she observes that same act performed by somebody else. So before we even have time to form hypotheses about what we are perceiving, we may already be able to understand the expressions, emotions, and movements of the person we observe (Gallagher, 2008).

Furthermore, studies indicate that there are separate neural pathways (*what pathways*) in the lateral occipital area for the processing of form, color, and texture in objects. When asked to judge the length of an object, for example, people cannot ignore the width. However, they can judge the color, form, and texture of an object independently of the other qualities (Cant & Goodale, 2007; Cant, Large, McCall, & Goodale, 2008).

Template Theories

Template theories suggest that we have stored in our minds myriad sets of templates. **Templates** are highly detailed models for patterns we potentially might recognize. We recognize a pattern by comparing it with our set of templates. We then choose the exact template that perfectly matches what we observe (Selfridge & Neisser, 1960). We see examples of template matching in our everyday lives. Fingerprints are matched in this way. Machines rapidly process imprinted numerals on checks by comparing them to templates. Increasingly, products of all kinds are identified with universal product codes (UPCs or "bar codes"). They can be scanned and identified by computers at the time of purchase. Chess players who have knowledge of many games use a matching strategy in line with template theory to recall previous games (Gobet & Jackson, 2002). Template matching theories belong to the group of chunk-based theories that suggest that expertise is attained by acquiring chunks of knowledge in long-term memory that can later be accessed for fast recognition. Studies with chess players have shown that the temporal lobe is indeed activated when the players access the stored chunks in their long-term memory (Campitelli, Gobet, Head, Buckley, & Parker, 2007).

In each of the aforementioned instances, the goal of finding one perfect match and disregarding imperfect matches suits the task. You would be alarmed to find that your bank's numeral-recognition system failed to register a deposit to your account.

Such failure might occur because it was programmed to accept an ambiguous character according to what seemed to be a best guess. For template matching, only an exact match will do. This is exactly what you want from a bank computer. However, consider your perceptual system at work in everyday situations. It rarely would work if you required exact matches for every stimulus you were to recognize. Imagine, for example, needing mental templates for every possible percept of the face of someone you love. Imagine one for each facial expression, each angle of viewing, each addition or removal of makeup, each hairdo, and so on.

Template-matching theories fail to explain some aspects of the perception of letters. For one thing, such theories cannot easily account for our perception of the letters and words in Figure 2.9. We identify two different letters (A and H) from only one physical form. Hoffding (1891) noted other problems. We can recognize an A as an A despite variations in the size, orientation, and form in which the letter is written. Are we to believe that we have mental templates for each possible size, orientation, and form of a letter? Storing, organizing, and retrieving so many templates in memory would be unwieldy. How could we possibly anticipate and create so many templates for every conceivable object of perception (Figure 2.11)?

Neuroscience and Template Theories   Letters of the alphabet are simpler than faces and other complex stimuli. But how do we recognize letters? And does it make a difference to our brain whether we perceive letters or digits? Experiments suggest that there is indeed a difference between letters and digits. There is an area on or near the left fusiform gyrus that is activated significantly more when a person is presented with letters than with digits. It is not clear if this "letter area" only processes letters or if it also plays a more minor role in the processing of digits (Polk et al., 2002). The notion of the visual cortex specializing in different stimuli is not new; other areas have been found that specialize in faces, for example (see Kanwisher et al., 1997; McCarthy et al., 1997). Later in this chapter we will consider in more detail the structures of the brain that enable us to recognize faces.

Why Computers Have Trouble Reading Handwriting   Think about how easy it is for you to perceive and understand someone's handwriting. In handwriting, everybody's numbers and letters look a bit different. You can still distinguish them without any problems (at least in most cases). This is something computers do not do very well at all. For computers, the reading of handwriting is an incredibly difficult process that's prone to mistakes. When you deposit a check at an ATM machine, it "reads" your check automatically. In fact, the numbers at the bottom of your check that are written in a strange-looking font are so distinct that a machine cannot mistake them for one another. However, it is much harder for a machine to decipher handwriting. Similarly, a machine also will have trouble determining that all the letters in the right of Figure 2.11 are As (unless it has a template for each one of the As). Therefore, some computers work with algorithms that consider the context in which the word is presented, the angular positions of the written letters (e.g., upright or tilted), and other factors.

Given the sophistication of current-day robots, what is the source of human superiority? There may be several, but one is certainly knowledge. We simply know much more about the environment and sources of regularity in the environment than do robots. Our knowledge gives us a great advantage that robots, at least of the current day, are still unable to bridge.

Figure 2.11   Template Matching in Barcodes and Letters.
A particular barcode will always look exactly the same way, making it easy for computers to read. Letters, to the contrary, can look very differently although they depict the same letter. Template matching will distinguish between different bar codes but will not recognize that different versions of the letter *A* written in different scripts are indeed both *A*s.

Feature-Matching Theories

Yet another alternative explanation of pattern and form perception may be found in **feature-matching theories**. According to these theories, we attempt to match features of a pattern to features stored in memory, rather than to match a whole pattern to a template or a prototype (Stankiewicz, 2003).

The Pandemonium Model   One such feature-matching model has been called *Pandemonium* ("pandemonium" refers to a very noisy, chaotic place and hell). In it, metaphorical "demons" with specific duties receive and analyze the features of a stimulus (Selfridge, 1959).

In Oliver Selfridge's Pandemonium Model, there are four kinds of demons: image demons, feature demons, cognitive demons, and decision demons. Figure 2.12 shows

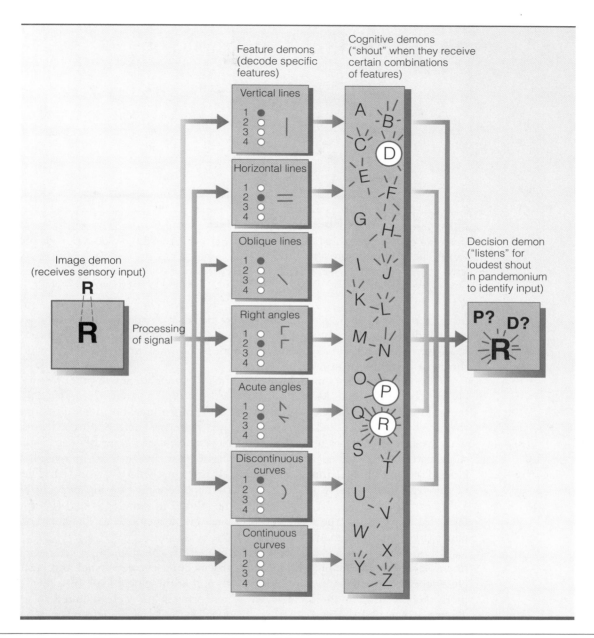

Figure 2.12 Selfridge's Feature-Matching Model.
According to Oliver Selfridge's feature-matching model, we recognize patterns by matching observed features to features already stored in memory. We recognize the patterns for which we have found the greatest number of matches.

this model. The "image demons" receive a retinal image and pass it on to "feature demons." Each feature demon calls out when there are matches between the stimulus and the given feature. These matches are yelled out at demons at the next level of the hierarchy, the "cognitive (thinking) demons." The cognitive demons in turn shout out possible patterns stored in memory that conform to one or

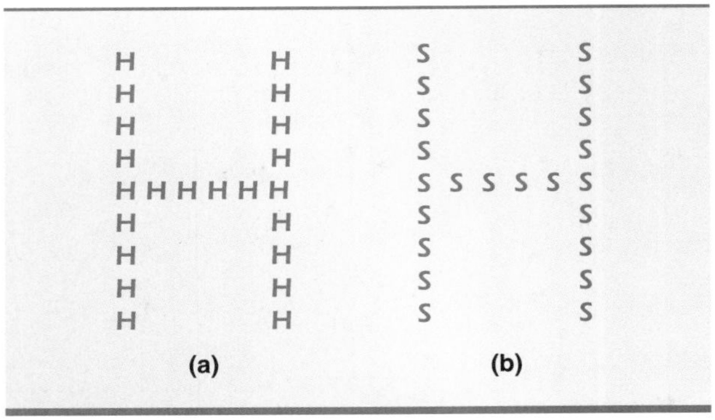

Figure 2.13 **The Global Precedence Effect.**

Compare panel (a) (a global *H* made of local *H*s) with panel (b) (a global *H* made of local *S*s). All the local letters are tightly spaced.

Source: From D. Navon, "Forest before Trees: The Precedence to Global Features in Visual Perception," *Cognitive Psychology*, July 1977, Vol. 9, No. 3, pp. 353–382. Reprinted by permission of Elsevier.

more of the features noticed by the feature demons. A "decision demon" listens to the pandemonium of the cognitive demons. It decides on what has been seen, based on which cognitive demon is shouting the most frequently (i.e., which has the most matching features).

Although Selfridge's model is one of the most widely known, other feature models have been proposed. Most also distinguish not only different features but also different kinds of features, such as global versus local features. Local features constitute the small-scale or detailed aspects of a given pattern. There is no consensus as to what exactly constitutes a local feature. Nevertheless, we generally can distinguish such features from global features, the features that give a form its overall shape. Consider, for example, the stimuli depicted in Figure 2.13 (a) and (b). These are of the type used in some research on pattern perception (see for example Navon, 1977, or Olesen et al., 2007). Globally, the stimuli in panels (a) and (b) form the letter *H*. In panel (a), the local features (small *H*s) correspond to the global ones. In panel (b), comprising many local letter *S*s, they do not.

In one study, participants were asked to identify the stimuli at either the global or the local level (Navon, 1977). When the local letters were small and positioned close together, participants could identify stimuli at the global level (the "big" letter) more quickly than at the local level. When participants were required to identify stimuli at the global level, whether the local features (small letters) matched the global one (big letter) did not matter. They responded equally rapidly whether the global *H* was made up of local *H*s or of local *S*s. However, when the participants were asked to identify the "small" local letters, they responded more quickly if the global features agreed with the local ones. In other words, they were slowed down if they had to identify local (small) *S*s combining to form a global (big) *H* instead of identifying local (small) *H*s combining to form a global (big) *H*. This pattern of results is called the *global precedence effect* (see also Kimchi, 1992). Experiments have showed that global information dominates over local information even in infants (Cassia, Simion, Milani, & Umiltà, 2002).

In contrast, when letters are more widely spaced, as in panels (a) and (b) of Figure 2.14, the effect is reversed. Then a *local precedence* effect appears. That is,

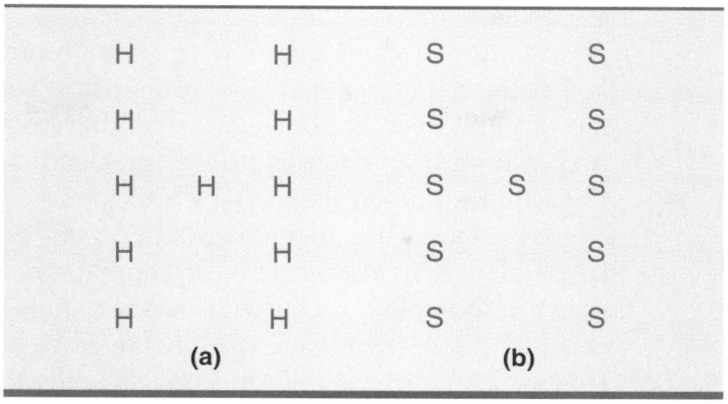

H	H	S	S
H	H	S	S
H H H		S S S	
H	H	S	S
H	H	S	S
(a)		(b)	

Figure 2.14 **The Local Precedence Effect.**

Compare panels (a) and (b), in which the local letters are widely spaced. Why does Figure 2.13 show the global precedence effect, and why does Figure 2.14 show the local precedence effect?

Source: D. Navon, "Forest before Trees: The Precedence to Global Features in Visual Perception," *Cognitive Psychology*, July 1977, Vol. 9, No. 3, pp. 353–382. Reprinted by permission of Elsevier.

the participants more quickly identify the local features of the individual letters than the global ones, and the local features interfere with the global recognition in cases of contradictory stimuli (Martin, 1979). So when the letters are close together at the local level, people have problems identifying the local stimuli (small letters) if they are not concordant with the global stimulus (big letter). When the letters on the local level are relatively far apart from each other, it is harder for people to identify the global stimulus (big letter) if it is not concordant with the local stimuli (small letters). Other limitations (e.g., the size of the stimuli) besides special proximity of the local stimuli hold as well, and other kinds of features also influence perception.

Neuroscience and Feature-Matching Theories   Some support for feature theories comes from neurological and physiological research. Researchers used single-cell recording techniques with animals (Hubel & Wiesel, 1963, 1968, 1979). They carefully measured the responses of individual neurons to visual stimuli in the visual cortex. Then they mapped those neurons to corresponding visual stimuli for particular locations in the visual field (see Chapter 3). Their research showed that the visual cortex contains specific neurons that respond only to a particular kind of stimulus (e.g., a horizontal line), and only if that stimulus fell onto a specific region of the retina. Each individual cortical neuron, therefore, can be mapped to a specific receptive field on the retina. A disproportionately large amount of the visual cortex is devoted to neurons mapped to receptive fields in the foveal region of the retina, which is the area of the most acute vision.

Most of the cells in the cortex do not respond simply to spots of light. Rather, they respond to "specifically oriented line segments" (Hubel & Wiesel, 1979, p. 9). What's more, these cells seem to show a hierarchical structure in the degree of complexity of the stimuli to which they respond, somewhat in line with the ideas behind the Pandemonium Model. That means that the outputs of the cells are combined to create higher-order detectors that can identify increasingly more complex features. At the lowest level, cells respond to lines, at a higher level they respond to corners and edges, then to shapes, and so forth. Neurons that can recognize a complex object are called *gnostic units* or "grandmother cells" because they imply that there is a neuron that is capable of recognizing your grandmother. None of those neurons are quite so specific, however, that they respond to just one person's head. Even at such a high level there is still some selectivity involved that allows cells to generally fire when a human face comes into view.

Consider what happens as the stimulus proceeds through the visual system to higher levels in the cortex. In general, the size of the receptive field increases, as does the complexity of the stimulus required to prompt a response. As evidence of this hierarchy, there were once believed to be just two kinds of visual cortex neurons (Figure 2.15), *simple cells* and *complex cells* (Hubel & Wiesel, 1979), which were believed to differ in the complexity of the information about stimuli they processed. This view proved to be oversimplified.

Based on Hubel and Wiesel's work, other investigators have found feature detectors that respond to corners, angles, stars, or triangles (DeValois & DeValois, 1980; Shapley & Lennie, 1985; Tanaka, 1993). In some areas of the cortex, highly sophisticated complex cells fire maximally only in response to very specific shapes, regardless of the size of the given stimulus. Examples would be a hand or a face. As the stimulus decreasingly resembles the optimal shape, these cells are decreasingly likely to fire.

We now know the picture is more complex than Hubel and Wiesel imagined. Cells can serve multiple functions. These cells operate partially in parallel, although we are not conscious of their operation. For example, spatial information about locations of perceived objects was found to be processed simultaneously with information about the contours of the object. Quite complex judgments about what is perceived are made quite early in information processing, and in parallel (Dakin & Hess, 1999).

But once discrete features have been analyzed according to their orientations, how are they integrated into a form we can recognize as particular objects? The recognition-by-components theory we will consider next sheds some light on this question.

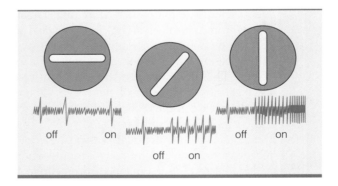

Figure 2.15 **Line Orientation and Cell Activation.**

David Hubel and Torsten Wiesel discovered that cells in our visual cortex become activated only when they detect the sensation of line segments of particular orientations. As you can see, there is hardly any activation when the cell is presented with a horizontal line segment. There is more activation when the line is diagonally oriented, and when the line is vertical, the cell reacts with even more activation.

Source: From *In Search of the Human Mind* by Robert J. Sternberg, copyright © 1995 by Harcourt Brace & Company. Reproduced by permission of the publisher.

Recognition-by-Components Theory

How do we form stable 3-D mental representations of objects? The recognition-by-components theory explains our ability to perceive 3-D objects with the help of simple geometric shapes.

Seeing with the Help of Geons   Irving Biederman (1987) suggested that we achieve this by manipulating a number of simple 3-D geometric shapes called geons (for geometrical ions). They include objects such as bricks, cylinders, wedges, cones, and their curved axis counterparts (Biederman, 1990/1993b). According to Biederman's **recognition-by-components (RBC) theory,** we quickly recognize objects by observing the edges of them and then decomposing the objects into geons. The geons also can be recomposed into alternative arrangements. You know that a small set of letters can be manipulated to compose countless words and sentences. Similarly, a small number of geons can be used to build up many basic shapes and then /myriad/ basic objects (Figure 2.16).

The geons are simple and are viewpoint-invariant (i.e., distinct from various viewpoints). The objects constructed from geons thus are recognized easily from many perspectives, despite visual noise. According to Biederman (1993a, 2001), his RBC theory parsimoniously explains how we recognize the general classification for multitudinous objects quickly, automatically, and accurately. This recognition occurs despite changes in viewpoint. It occurs even under many situations in which the stimulus object is degraded in some way. For example, if you see a car, you perceive it as being made up of a number of different geons. You can recognize the car even if you can't see all of the geons because the car is partly obscured by another object in front of it. Because the geons are viewpoint-invariant, you will also recognize the car even if you look at it from the side or from behind. Cells in the inferior temporal cortex (i.e., the lower part of the temporal cortex) react stronger to changes in geons (which are viewpoint-invariant) than to changes in other geometrical properties (e.g., changes in the size or diameter of a cylinder; Vogels, Biederman, Bar, & Lorincz, 2001).

Biederman's RBC theory explains how we may recognize general instances of chairs, lamps, and faces, but it does not adequately explain how we recognize particular chairs or particular faces. An example would be your own face or your best friend's face. They are both made up of geons that constitute your mouth, eyes, nose, eyebrows, and so forth. But these geons are the same for both your and your friend's faces. So RBC theory cannot explain how we can distinguish one face from the next.

Biederman recognized that aspects of his theory require further work, such as how the relations among the parts of an object can be described (Biederman, 1990/1993b). Another problem with Biederman's approach, and the bottom-up approach in general, is how to account for the effects of prior expectations and environmental context on some phenomena of pattern perception.

Neuroscience and Recognition-by-Components Theory   What results would we expect if we were to confirm Biederman's theory? Geons are viewpoint-invariant, so studies should show that neurons exist that react to properties of an object that stay the same, no matter whether you look at them from the front or the side. And indeed, there are studies that have found neurons in the inferior temporal cortex that are sensitive to just those viewpoint-invariant properties (Vogels et al., 2001). However, many neurons respond primarily to one view of an object and decrease their response gradually the more the object is rotated (Logothetis, Pauls, & Poggio,

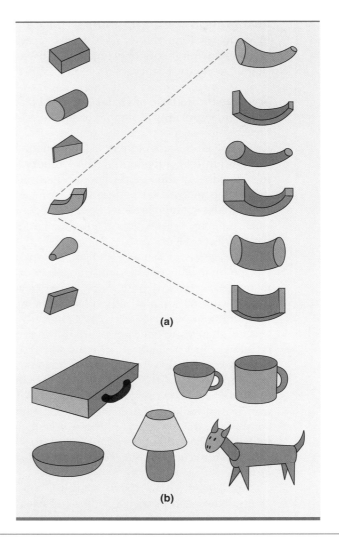

Figure 2.16   Geons.

Irving Biederman amplified feature-matching theory by proposing a set of elementary components of patterns (a), which he based on variations in 3-D shapes derived in large part from a cone (b).

1995). This finding contradicts the notion of Biederman's theory that we recognize objects by means of viewpoint-invariant geons. As a result, it is not clear at this point whether Biederman's theory is correct.

Top-Down Theories

In contrast to the bottom-up approach to perception is the top-down, constructive approach (Bruner, 1957; Gregory, 1980; Rock, 1983; von Helmholtz, 1909/1962). In **constructive perception,** the perceiver builds (constructs) a cognitive understanding (perception) of a stimulus. The concepts of the perceiver and his or her cognitive processes influence what he or she sees. The perceiver uses sensory information as the foundation for the structure but also uses other sources of information to build the perception. This viewpoint also is known as *intelligent perception* because it states that higher-order thinking plays an important role in perception. It also emphasizes the role of learning in perception (Fahle, 2003). Some investigators have pointed out that not only does the world affect our perception but also the world we experience is actually formed by our perception (Goldstone, 2003). In other words, perception is reciprocal with the world we experience. Perception both affects and is affected by the world as we experience it.

An interesting feature of the theory of constructive perception is that it links human intelligence even to fairly basic processes of perception. According to this theory, perception comprises not merely a low-level set of cognitive processes, but actually a quite sophisticated set of processes that interact with and are guided by human intelligence. When you look out your window, you "see" many things, but what you recognize yourself as seeing is highly processed by your intelligence. Interestingly, Titchener's structuralist approach (described in Chapter 1) ultimately failed because despite the efforts of Titchener and his followers to engage in introspection independently of their prior knowledge, they and others found this, in the end, to be impossible. What you perceive is shaped, at some level, by what you know and what you think.

For example, picture yourself driving down a road you have never traveled before. As you approach a blind intersection, you see an octagonal red sign with white lettering. It bears the letters "ST_P." An overgrown vine cuts between the *T* and the *P*. Chances are, you will construct from your sensations a perception of a stop sign. You thus will respond appropriately. Perceptual constancies are another example (see below). When you see a car approaching you on the street, its image on your retina gets bigger as the car comes closer. And yet, you perceive the car to stay the same size. This suggests that high-level constructive processes are at work during perception. In color constancy, we perceive that the color of an object remains the same despite changes in lighting that alter the hue. Even in lighting that becomes so dim that color sensations are virtually absent, we still perceive bananas as yellow, plums as purple, and so on.

According to constructivists, during perception we quickly form and test various hypotheses regarding percepts. The percepts are based on three things:

- what we sense (the sensory data),
- what we know (knowledge stored in memory), and
- what we can infer (using high-level cognitive processes).

In perception, we consider prior expectations. You'll be fast to recognize your friend from far away on the street when you have arranged a meeting. We also use what we know about the context. When you see something approaching on rail tracks you infer that it must be a train. And we also may use what we reasonably can infer, based both on what the data are and on what we know about the data. According to constructivists, we usually make the correct attributions regarding our visual sensations. The reason is that we perform unconscious inference, the process by which we unconsciously assimilate information from a number of sources to create a perception (Snow & Mattingley, 2003). In other words, using more than one source of information, we make judgments that we are not even aware of making.

In the stop-sign example, sensory information implies that the sign is a meaningless assortment of oddly spaced consonants. However, your prior learning tells you something important—that a sign of this shape and color posted at an intersection of roadways and containing these three letters in this sequence probably means that you should stop thinking about the odd letters. Instead, you should start slamming on the brakes. Successful constructive perception requires intelligence and thought in combining sensory information with knowledge gained from previous experience.

One reason for favoring the constructive approach is that bottom-up (data-driven) theories of perception do not fully explain context effects. **Context effects** are the influences of the surrounding environment on perception (e.g., our perception of "THE CAT" in Figure 2.9). Fairly dramatic context effects can be demonstrated experimentally (Biederman, 1972; Biederman et al., 1974; Biederman, Glass, & Stacy, 1973; De Graef, Christiaens, & D'Ydewalle, 1990). In one study, people were asked to identify objects after they had viewed the objects in either an appropriate or an inappropriate context for the items (Palmer, 1975). For example, participants might see a scene of a kitchen followed by stimuli such as a loaf of bread, a mailbox, and a drum. Objects that were appropriate to the established context, such as the loaf of bread in this example, were recognized more rapidly than were objects that were inappropriate to the established context. The strength of the context also plays a role in object recognition (Bar, 2004).

Perhaps even more striking is a context effect known as the *configural-superiority effect* (Bar, 2004; Pomerantz, 1981), by which objects presented in certain configurations are easier to recognize than the objects presented in isolation, even if the objects in the configurations are more complex than those in isolation. Suppose you show a participant four stimuli, all of them diagonal lines [see Figure 2.17 (a)]. Three of the lines are slanting one way, and one line is slanting the other way. The participant's task is to identify which stimulus is unlike the others. Now suppose that you show participants four stimuli that are comprised of three lines each [Figure 2.17 (c)]. Three of the stimuli are shaped like triangles, and one is not. In each case, the stimulus is a diagonal line [Figure 2.17 (a)] plus other lines [Figure 2.17 (b)]. Thus, the stimuli in this second condition are more complex variations of the stimuli in the first condition. However, participants can more quickly spot which of the three-sided, more complicated figures is different from the others than they can spot which of the lines is different from the others.

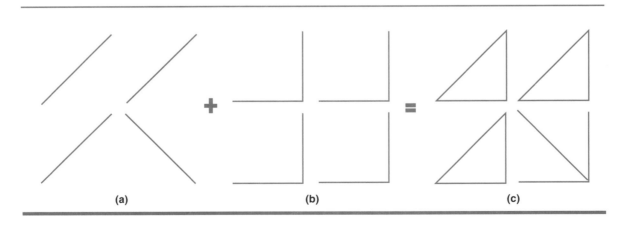

(a)   (b)   (c)

Figure 2.17   The Configural-Superiority Effect.

Subjects more readily perceive differences among integrated configurations comprising multiple lines (c) than they do solitary lines (a). In this figure, the lines in panel (b) are added to the lines in panel (a) to form shapes in panel (c), thereby making panel (c) more complex than panel (a).

In a similar vein, there is an _object-superiority effect_, in which a target line that forms a part of a drawing of a 3-D object is identified more accurately than a target that forms a part of a disconnected 2-D pattern (Lanze, Weisstein, & Harris, 1982; Weisstein & Harris, 1974). These findings parallel findings in the study of letter and word recognition: The _word-superiority effect_ indicates that when people are presented with strings of letters, it is easier for them to identify a single letter if the string makes sense and forms a word instead of being just a nonsense sequel of letters. For example, it is easier to recognize the letter "o" in the word "house" than in the word "huseo" (Reicher, 1969).

The viewpoint of constructive or intelligent perception shows the central relation between perception and intelligence. According to this viewpoint, intelligence is an integral part of our perceptual processing. We do not perceive simply in terms of what is "out there in the world." Rather, we perceive in terms of the expectations and other cognitions we bring to our interaction with the world. In this view, intelligence and perceptual processes interact in the formation of our beliefs about what it is that we are encountering in our everyday contacts with the world at large.

An extreme top-down position would drastically underestimate the importance of sensory data. If it were correct, we would be susceptible to gross inaccuracies of perception. We frequently would form hypotheses and expectancies that inadequately evaluated the sensory data available. For example, if we expected to see a friend and someone else came into view, we might inadequately consider the perceptible differences between the friend and a stranger and mistake the stranger for the friend. Thus, an extreme constructivist view of perception would be highly error-prone and inefficient. However, an extreme bottom-up position would not allow for any influence of past experience or knowledge on perception. Why store knowledge that has no use for the perceiver? Neither extreme is ideal for explaining perception. It is more fruitful to consider ways in which bottom-up and top-down processes interact to form meaningful percepts.

How Do Bottom-Up Theories and Top-Down Theories Go Together?

Both theoretical approaches have garnered empirical support (cf. Cutting & Kozlowski, 1977, vs. Palmer, 1975). So how do we decide between the two? On one level, the constructive-perception theory, which is more top-down, seems to contradict direct-perception theory, which is more bottom-up. Constructivists emphasize the importance of prior knowledge in combination with relatively simple and ambiguous information from the sensory receptors. In contrast, direct-perception theorists emphasize the completeness of the information in the receptors themselves. They suggest that perception occurs simply and directly. Thus, there is little need for complex information processing.

Instead of viewing these theoretical approaches as incompatible, we may gain deeper insight into perception by considering the approaches to be complementary. Sensory information may be more richly informative and less ambiguous in interpreting experiences than the constructivists would suggest. But it may be less informative than the direct-perception theorists would assert. Similarly, perceptual processes may be more complex than hypothesized by Gibsonian theorists. This would be particularly true under conditions in which the sensory stimuli appear only briefly or are degraded. Degraded stimuli are less informative for various reasons. For example, the stimuli may be partially obscured or weakened by poor lighting. Or they may be incomplete, or distorted by illusory cues or other visual "noise" (distracting visual stimulation analogous to audible noise). We likely use a combination of information from the sensory receptors and our past knowledge to make sense of what we perceive. Some experimental evidence supports this integrated view (Treue, 2003; van Zoest & Donk, 2004; Wolfe et al., 2003).

Recent work suggests that, whereas the very first stage of the visual pathway represents only what is in the retinal image of an object, very soon, color, orientation, motion, depth, spatial frequency, and temporal frequency are represented. Later-stage representations emphasize the viewer's current interest or attention. In other words, the later-stage representations are not independent of our attentional focus. On the contrary, they are directly affected by it (Maunsell, 1995). Moreover, vision for different things can take different forms. Visual control of action is mediated by cortical pathways that are different from those involved in visual control of perception (Ganel & Goodale, 2003). In other words, when we merely see an object, such as a cell phone, we process it differently than if we intend also to pick up the object. In general, according to Ganel and Goodale (2003), we perceive objects holistically. But if we plan to act on them, we perceive them more analytically so that we can act in an effective way.

To summarize, current theories concerning the ways we perceive patterns explain some, but not all, of the phenomena we encounter in the study of form and pattern perception. Given the complexity of the process, it is impressive that we understand as much as we do. At the same time, clearly a comprehensive theory is still forthcoming. Such a theory would need to account fully for the kinds of context effects, such as the configural-superiority effect, described in this section.

Perception of Objects and Forms

Do we perceive objects in a viewer-centered or in an object-centered way? When we gaze at any object in the space around us, do we perceive it in relation to us rather than its actual structure, or do we perceive it in a more objective way that is independent of how it appears to us right this moment? We'll examine this question in the next section. Then, we look at Gestalt principles for perception, which explain why we perceive some objects as in groups but others as not so grouped (what is it that makes some birds flying in the afternoon sky appear to be in a group whereas others do not?). Finally, we will consider the question of how we perceive patterns, for example faces.

Viewer-Centered vs. Object-Centered Perception

Right now one of your authors is looking at the computer on which he is typing this text. He depicts the results of what he sees as a mental representation. What form does this mental representation take? There are two common positions regarding the answer to this question.

One position, **viewer-centered representation,** is that the individual stores the way the object looks to him or her. Thus, what matters is the appearance of the object to the viewer (in this case, the appearance of the computer to the author), not the actual structure of the object. The shape of the object changes, depending on the angle from which we look at it. A number of views of the object are stored, and when we try to recognize an object, we have to rotate that object in our mind until it fits one of the stored images.

The second position, **object-centered representation,** is that the individual stores a representation of the object, independent of its appearance to the viewer. In this case, the shape of the object will stay stable across different orientations

DEPTH CUES IN PHOTOGRAPHY

Models and actors often use these depth cues of perception to their advantage while being photographed. For example, some models only allow certain angles or orientations to be photographed. A long nose can appear shorter when photographed from slightly below the facial midline (just look closely at some pictures of Barbara Streisand from different angles) because the bridge of the nose recedes slightly into the distance. Also, leaning forward a little can make the upper body appear slightly larger than the lower body, and vice versa for leaning backward. In group pictures, standing slightly behind another person makes you appear smaller; standing slightly in front makes you appear larger. Women's swimsuit designers create optical-illusion swimsuits to enhance different features of the body, making legs appear longer or waists appear smaller and either enhancing or de-emphasizing bustlines. Some of these processes to alter perceptions are so basic that many animals have special adaptations designed to make them appear larger (e.g., the fanning peacock tail) or to disguise their identity from predators.

How could you apply perceptual processes to your advantage when having a photo taken or when dressing for a party?

(McMullen & Farah, 1991). This stability can be achieved by means of establishing the major and minor axes of the object, which then serve as a basis for defining further properties of the object.

Both positions can account for how the author represents a given object and its parts. The key difference is in whether he represents the object and its parts in relation to him (viewer-centered) or in relation to the entirety of the object itself, independent of his own position (object-centered).

Consider, for example, the computer on which this text is being written. It has different parts: a screen, a keyboard, a mouse, and so forth. Suppose the author represents the computer in terms of viewer-centered representation. Then its various parts are stored in terms of their relation to him. He sees the screen as facing him at perhaps a 20-degree angle. He sees the keyboard facing him horizontally. He sees the mouse off to the right side and in front of him. Suppose, instead, that he uses an object-centered representation. Then he would see the screen at a 70-degree angle relative to the keyboard. And the mouse is directly to the right side of the keyboard, neither in front of it nor in back of it.

One potential reconciliation of these two approaches to mental representation suggests that people may use both kinds of representations. According to this approach, recognition of objects occurs on a continuum (Burgund & Marsolek, 2000; Tarr, 2000; Tarr & Bülthoff, 1995). At one end of this continuum are cognitive mechanisms that are more viewpoint-centered. At the other end of the continuum are cognitive mechanisms that are more object-centered. For example, suppose you see a picture of a car that is inverted. How do you know it is a car? Object-centered mechanisms would recognize the object as a car, but viewpoint-centered mechanisms would recognize the car as inverted.

A third orientation in representation is **landmark-centered**. In landmark-centered representation, information is characterized by its relation to a well-known or prominent item. Imagine visiting a new city. Each day you leave your hotel and go on short trips. It is easy to imagine that you would represent the area you explore in relation to your hotel.

Evidence indicates that, in the laboratory, participants can switch between these three strategies. There are, however, differences in brain activation among these strategies (Committeri et al., 2004).

The Perception of Groups—Gestalt Laws

Perception helps us make sense of the confusing stimuli that we perceive in the world. One way to bring order and coherence into our perception is our ability to group similar things. This way, we can reduce the number of things that need to be processed. We can also better decide which things belong together or to the same object. In other words, we organize objects in a visual array into coherent groups.

The **Gestalt approach to form perception** that was developed in Germany in the early 20th century is useful particularly for understanding how we perceive groups of objects or even parts of objects to form integral wholes (Palmer, 1999a, 1999b, 2000; Palmer & Rock, 1994; Prinzmetal, 1995). It was founded by Kurt Koffka (1886–1941), Wolfgang Köhler (1887–1968), and Max Wertheimer (1880–1943) and was based on the notion that the whole differs from the sum of its individual parts (see Chapter 1).

The overarching law is the **law of Prägnanz.** We tend to perceive any given visual array in a way that most simply organizes the different elements into a stable and coherent form. Thus, we do not merely experience a jumble of unintelligible, disorganized sensations. For example, we tend to perceive a focal figure and other sensations as forming a background for the figure on which we focus.

Other Gestalt principles include *figure-ground perception, proximity, similarity, continuity, closure,* and *symmetry* (Figure 2.18; see also Table 2.2). Each of these principles supports the overarching law of Prägnanz. Each illustrates how we tend to

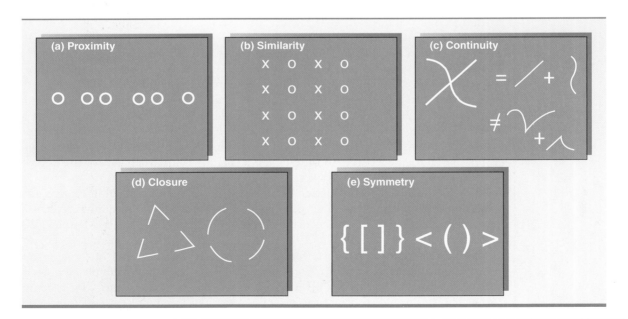

Figure 2.18   The Gestalt Principles of Form Perception.

The Gestalt principles of form perception include perception of figure-ground, (a) proximity, (b) similarity, (c) continuity, (d) closure, and (e) symmetry. Each principle demonstrates the fundamental law of law of Prägnanz, which suggests that through perception, we unify disparate visual stimuli into a coherent and stable whole.

perceive visual arrays in ways that most simply organize the disparate elements into a stable and coherent form. Stop for a moment and look at your environment. You will perceive a coherent, complete, and continuous array of figures and background. You do not perceive holes in objects where your textbook covers up your view of them. If your book obscures part of the edge of a table, you still perceive the table as a continuous entity. In viewing the environment, we tend to perceive groupings. We see groupings of nearby objects (proximity) or of like objects (similarity). We also perceive objects as complete even though we may only see a part of them (closure), continuous lines rather than broken ones (continuity), and symmetrical patterns rather than asymmetrical ones.

Let's have a closer look at some of the Gestalt principles. Consider what happens when you walk into a familiar room. You perceive that some things stand out (e.g., faces in photographs or posters). Others fade into the background (e.g., undecorated walls and floors). A figure is any object perceived as being highlighted. It is almost always perceived against or in contrast to some kind of receding, unhighlighted (back)ground. Figure 2.19 (a) illustrates the concept of **figure-ground**—

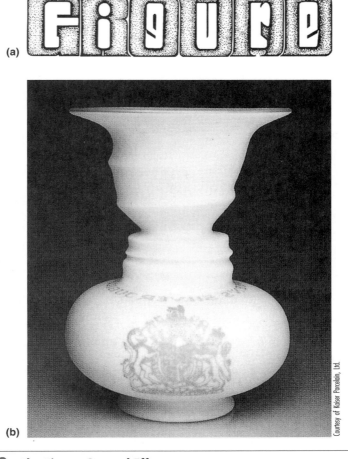

(a)

(b)

Courtesy of Kaiser Porcelain, Ltd.

Figure 2.19 The Figure-Ground Effect.

In these two Gestalt images, (a) and (b), find which is the figure and which is the ground.

what stands out from, versus what recedes into, the background. You probably first will notice the light-colored lettering of the word *figure*. We perceive this light-colored lettering as the figure against the darker ground. But if you take a closer look, you can see that the darker surrounding actually depicts the word "ground."

Similarly, in Figure 2.19 (b), you can see either a white vase against a black background or two silhouetted faces peering at each other against a white ground. It is virtually impossible to see both sets of objects simultaneously. Although you may switch rapidly back and forth between the vase and the faces, you cannot see them both at the same time. One of the reasons suggested as to why each figure makes sense is that both figures conform to the Gestalt principle of *symmetry*. Symmetry requires that features appear to have balanced proportions around a central axis or a central point.

People tend to use Gestalt principles even when they are confronted with novel stimuli. Palmer (1977) showed participants novel geometric shapes that served as targets. He then showed them fragments of the shapes. For each fragment, the participants had to say whether it was part of the original novel geometric shape. Participants were quicker to recognize the fragments as part of the original target if they conformed to Gestalt principles. For example, a triangle exhibits *closure,* in that its three sides form a complete, closed object. A triangle was recognized more quickly as part of the original novel figure than were three line segments that were comparable to the triangle except that they were not closed. They thus did not conform to the Gestalt principle. In sum, we seem to use Gestalt principles in our everyday perception. We use them, whether the figures to which we apply the principles are familiar or not.

Table 2.2 Gestalt Principles of Visual Perception

The Gestalt principles of proximity, similarity, continuity, closure, and symmetry aid in our perception of forms.

Gestalt Principles	Principle	Figure Illustrating the Principle
Figure-ground	When perceiving a visual field, some objects (figures) seem prominent, and other aspects of the field recede into the background (ground).	Figure 2.19 shows a figure-ground vase, in which one way of perceiving the figures brings one perspective or object to the fore, and another way of perceiving the figures brings a different object or perspective to the fore and relegates the former foreground to the background.
Proximity	When we perceive an assortment of objects, we tend to see objects that are close to each other as forming a group.	In Figure 2.18 (a), we tend to see the middle four circles as two pairs of circles.
Similarity	We tend to group objects on the basis of their similarity.	In Figure 2.18 (b), we tend to see four columns of xs and os, not four rows of alternating letters.
Continuity	We tend to perceive smoothly flowing or continuous forms rather than disrupted or discontinuous ones.	Figure 2.18 (c) shows two fragmented curves bisecting, which we perceive as two smooth curves, rather than as disjointed curves.
Closure	We tend to perceptually close up, or complete, objects that are not, in fact, complete.	Figure 2.18 (d) shows only disjointed, jumbled line segments, which you close up to see a triangle and a circle.
Symmetry	We tend to perceive objects as forming mirror images about their center.	For example, when viewing Figure 2.18 (e), a configuration of assorted brackets, we see the assortment as forming four sets of brackets, rather than eight individual items, because we integrate the symmetrical elements into coherent objects.

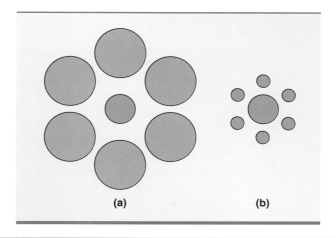

(a)   (b)

Figure 2.20 **Ebbinghaus Illusion.**

Guess which center circle is larger (a or b) and then measure the diameter of each one.

The Gestalt principles of form perception are remarkably simple. Yet they characterize much of our perceptual organization (Palmer, 1992). Even young infants organize visual stimuli by means of the Gestalt law of proximity (Quinn, Bhatt, & Hayden, 2008). Interestingly, the Gestalt principles appear to apply only to humans and not to other primates. An experiment by Parron and Fagot (2007) showed that only humans misjudged the size of the central circle in the Ebbinghaus illusion (Figure 2.20), whereas baboons did not. Maybe this difference is because a result of humans' paying more attention to the surrounding stimuli, whereas baboons concentrated their attention on the central circle.

The Gestalt principles provide valuable descriptive insights into form and pattern perception. But they offer few or no explanations of these phenomena. To understand how or why we perceive forms and patterns, we need to consider explanatory theories of perception.

Recognizing Patterns and Faces

How do we recognize patterns when we look at objects? And are faces a special form of pattern, or is there a special mechanism just for faces? In the next section we explore these and other questions.

Two Different Pattern Recognition Systems

Martha Farah suggests that humans have two systems for recognizing patterns (Farah, 1992, 1995; Farah et al., 1998). The first system specializes in recognition of parts of objects and in assembling those parts into distinctive wholes (*feature analysis system*). For example, when you are in a biology class and notice the elements of a tulip—the stamen, the pistil, and so forth—you look at the flower through this first system. The second system (*configurational system*) specializes in recognizing larger configurations. It is not well equipped to analyze parts of objects or the construction of the objects. But it is especially well equipped to recognize configurations. For example, if you look at a tulip in a garden and admire its distinctive beauty and form, you look at the flower through the second system.

The second system is most relevant to the recognition of faces. When you spot a friend whom you see on a daily basis, you recognize him or her using the configurational system. So dependent are you on this system in everyday life that you might not even notice some major change in your friend's appearance, such as his or her having longer hair or having put on new glasses.

The feature analysis system can also be used in face recognition. Suppose you see someone whose face looks vaguely familiar, but you are not sure who it is. You start analyzing features and then realize it is a friend you have not seen for 10 years. In this case, you were able to make the facial recognition only after you analyzed the face by its features. In the end, both configurational and feature analysis may help in making difficult recognitions and discriminations.

Face recognition occurs, at least in part, in the *fusiform gyrus* of the temporal lobe (Gauthier et al., 2003; Kanwisher, McDermott, & Chun, 1997; Tarr & Cheng, 2003). This brain area responds intensely when we look at faces but not when we look at other objects. There is good evidence that there is something special about recognition of faces, even from an early age. For example, infants track movements of a photograph of a human face more rapidly than they track movements of stimuli of similar complexity that are not, however, faces (Farah, 2000a). In one study, experimental participants were shown sketches of two kinds of objects, faces, and houses (Farah et al., 1998). In each case, the face was paired with the name of the person whom the face represented and the house was paired with the name of the house owner. There were six pairings per trial. After learning the six pairings,

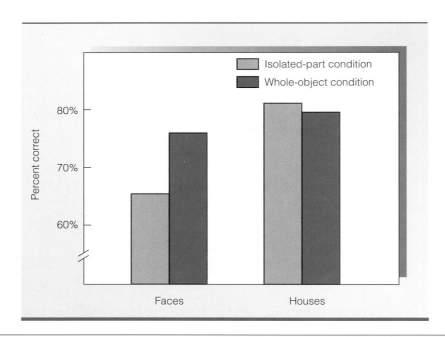

Figure 2.21   Recognition of Faces and Houses.

People have more trouble recognizing parts of faces than whole faces. They recognize parts of houses about as well as they recognize whole houses, however.

Source: From J. W. Tanaka and M. J. Farah, "Parts and Wholes in Face Recognition," *Quarterly Journal of Experimental Psychology*, 46A, pp. 225–245, Fig. 6. Reprinted by permission of the Experimental Psychology Society.

participants were asked to recognize parts of either the faces or the houses or to recognize the faces or houses as a whole. For example, they might see just a nose or ear, or just a window or a doorway. Or they might see a whole face or house.

If face recognition is somehow special and especially dependent on the second, configurational system, then people should have more difficulty recognizing parts of faces than parts of houses. And this is what the data showed (Figure 2.21): People generally were better at recognizing houses, whether they were presented in parts or in wholes. But more importantly, people had relatively more difficulty in recognizing parts of faces than they had in recognizing whole faces. In contrast, they recognized parts of houses just as well as whole houses. Face recognition, therefore, appears to be special. Presumably, it is especially dependent on the configurational system.

An interesting example of a configurational effect in face recognition occurs when people stare at distorted faces. If you stare at a distorted face for a while and then stare at a normal face, the normal face will look distorted in the opposite direction.

When you look at the faces in Figure 2.22, you will notice that the face in the middle looks normal, whereas the faces to the right and left are gradually more distorted. If you stare at the face to the very left, where the eyes are too close together, for example, and then look back to the normal face in the middle, the eyes in that face will appear too far apart (Leopold et al., 2001; Webster et al., 2004; Zhao & Chubb, 2001). Your knowledge of faces normally tells you what is a normal face and what is a distorted one, but in this case, that knowledge is very briefly overridden by your having accustomed yourself to the distorted face.

Cognitive processing of faces and the emotions of the face can interact. Indeed, there is some evidence of an age-related "face positivity" effect. In one study, older but not younger adults were found to show a preference for looking at happy faces and away from sad or angry faces (Isaacowitz et al., 2006a, 2006b). Furthermore, happy faces are rated as more familiar than are either neutral or negative faces (Lander & Metcalfe, 2007). But can you choose to ignore the emotion that another person is displaying? Studies indicate that, at least in the case of some negative emotions, like fear, your amygdala processes the emotion automatically, at least when you do not have to pay much attention to anything else. It is also possible that there is a difference between highly anxious and less anxious individuals: Highly anxious people's amygdalas always process fear automatically, but less anxious people's do not (Palermo & Rhodes, 2007).

Figure 2.22   Normal and Distorted Faces.
Normal (center) and distorted faces.

IN THE LAB OF MARVIN CHUN

What Happens to Unattended Information?

Apollo Robins, the gentleman thief, can pick your pockets clean without your noticing it, even after telling you that he will be stealing from you, or even if you are on security detail for the Secret Service. Magicians and illusionists are not just deft with their hands, but have the more magical ability to control your attention. Because perception is a construction of the mind, whoever can control your attention governs what you perceive. Most of we see, hear, feel, smell, taste, and even remember depends on what we select and attend to. Unattended information slips by—gorillas go unnoticed, pockets get picked, or traffic signals missed by distracted observers focused elsewhere. What happens to the rivers of unattended information that pass by us all the time? My laboratory uses both behavioral methods and functional magnetic resonance imaging to study the fate of unattended, ignored events.

Consider a lab task of searching for two letters among digits presented sequentially at a blindingly fast rate of 10 items per second, MTV style. People have a fleeting sense of what's going by and can pick out the first letter around 90% of the time. However, if the second letter appears about 200–300 milliseconds after the first letter target, it is missed up to 70% of the time. This phenomenon, known as the attentional blink (Raymond et al., 1992), is a form of inattentional blindness that highlights fundamental limitations regarding how much you can attend.

But what happens to the missed target? We proposed that missed targets are identified, but then get lost or forgotten while waiting for the first target to be encoded (Chun and Potter, 1995, *JEP:HPP*). However, it was difficult to prove unconscious identification with behavioral methods alone. Hence, we used functional magnetic resonance imaging (fMRI) to investigate

MARVIN CHUN

subliminal processing during the attentional blink. FMRI can directly probe how information is processed in different brain areas, even when subjects cannot report them. A region of the brain called the parahippocampal gyrus is devoted to scene processing; this "place area" is more active when scenes are viewed.

Our experiment presented scenes as second targets to be missed during the attentional blink. First, we measured the fMRI signal in the place area to scenes that were presented and consciously detected by the subject (the experiment was designed so that about half would be detected probabilistically). We also measured the lower boundary of activity in the place area for trials when no scenes were presented.

The focus of the study was then to ask how the place area responds to scenes that were missed. When subjects said they could not see the scene, did the place area unconsciously see the scene? If so, the fMRI signal in the place area to unseen scenes should be higher than the lower bound baseline when no scene was presented. Indeed, the place area produced significantly higher fMRI signals, suggesting that subliminal perception occurs to a high level (scene detection), and that fMRI can be used to measure such unconscious processing (Marois et al., 2004).

Attention modulates not just ongoing perception, but also your ability to remember. Simply looking at or reading something does not ensure you will encode it, as you may know all too well while studying for exams. You must attend to the information you're trying to learn, or memory traces of the information will not be formed reliably in brain circuits important for memory. In fact, using fMRI we demonstrated that attention is important both during encoding and when trying to retrieve information (Yi and Chun, 2005). Unfortunately, for students, learning without attention seems unlikely!

The Neuroscience of Recognizing Faces and Patterns

There is evidence that emotion increases activation within the fusiform gyrus when people are processing faces. In one study, participants were shown a face and asked either to name the person or to name the expression. When asked to name the expression, participants show increased activation of the fusiform gyrus compared with when the participants were asked to name the person (Ganel et al., 2005). Examination of patients with autism provides additional evidence for the processing of emotion within the fusiform gyrus. Patients with autism have impaired emotional recognition. Scanning the brains of persons with autism reveals that the fusiform gyrus is less active than in nonautistic populations.

Patients with autism can learn to identify emotions through an effortful process. However, this training does not allow identification of emotion to become an automatic process in this population, nor does it increase the activation within the fusiform gyrus (Bolte et al., 2006; Hall, Szechtman, & Nahmias, 2003).

Researchers do not all agree that the fusiform gyrus is specialized for face perception, in contrast to other forms of perception. Another point of view is that this area is that of greatest activation in face perception, but that other areas also show activation, but at lower levels. Similarly, this or other brain areas that respond maximally to faces or anything else may still show some activation when perceiving other objects. In this view, areas of the brain are not all-or-none in what they perceive, but rather, may be differentially activated, in greater or lesser degrees, depending on what is perceived (Haxby et al., 2001; Haxby, Gobbini, & Montgomery, 2004; O'Toole et al., 2005).

Another theory concerning the role of the fusiform gyrus is called the *expert-individuation hypothesis*. According to this theory, the fusiform gyrus is activated when one examines items with which one has visual expertise. Imagine that you are an expert on birds and spend much of your time studying birds. It is expected that you could differentiate among very similar birds and would have much practice at such differentiation. As a result, if you are shown five robins, you would likely be able to tell birds apart. It is unlikely that a person without this expertise could discern among these birds. If your brain were scanned during this activity, activation in the fusiform gyrus, specifically the right one, would be seen. Such activation is seen in persons who are experts concerning cars and birds. Even when people are taught to differentiate among very similar abstract figures, activation of the fusiform gyrus is observed (Gauthier et al., 1999, 2000; Rhodes et al., 2004; Xu, 2005). This theory is able to account for the activation of the fusiform gyrus when people view faces because we are, in effect, experts at identifying and examining faces.

■ BELIEVE IT OR NOT

DO TWO DIFFERENT FACES EVER LOOK THE SAME TO YOU?

Have you ever noticed that it is easier to recognize faces of people that belong to your own ethnic group? For example, if you are of African-American descent, it is likely easier for you to recognize and differentiate between black faces than between white or Asian faces. Maybe you thought that this is just because you are more familiar with the faces you happen to see most often around you and that it is this familiarity that makes it easier for you to discriminate faces that are similar to your own. But now imagine being told you have a "red" personality. Do you think knowing this would make it easier for you to recognize people who also have a "red" personality as opposed to a "green" personality (even if they all are of the same race)? Studies have shown that indeed social categorization plays a role in how easy it is for you to recognize faces. As soon as you perceive somebody as an out-group member, it will be harder for you to recognize that person's face. This effect is so stable that it can be elicited by imaginary differences like "red" or "green" personalities, or just by adding an African-American or Latino hairdo to a white face (Bernstein et al., 2007; MacLin & Malpass, 2001, 2003; Ge et al., 2009).

Prosopagnosia—the inability to recognize faces—would imply damage of some kind to the configurational system (Damasio, Tranel, & Damasio, 1990; De Renzi Faglioni, Grossi, & Nichelli, 1991; Farah, 2004). Somebody with prosopagnosia can see the face of another person and even recognize if that person is sad, happy, or angry. But what he fails to recognize is whether that person being observed is a stranger, his friend, or his own mother. The ability to recognize faces is especially influenced by lesions of the right fusiform gyrus, either unilateral or bilateral. Facial memories are affected, in particular, when the bilateral lesions include the right anterior temporal lobe (Barton, 2008).

Other disabilities, such as an early reading disability in which a beginning reader has difficulty in recognizing the features that comprise unique words, might stem from damage to the first, element-based system. Moreover, processing can move from one system to another. A typical reader may learn the appearances of words through the first system—element by element—and then come to recognize the words as wholes. Indeed, some forms of reading disability might stem from the inability of the second system to take over from the first.

✔ CONCEPT CHECK

1. What are the major Gestalt principles?
2. What is the "recognition by components" theory?
3. What is the difference between top-down and bottom-up theories of perception?
4. What is the difference between viewer-centered and object-centered perception?
5. What is prosopagnosia?

The Environment Helps You See

As we have seen, perceptual processes are not so easily completed that the image on your retina can be taken as is without further interpretation. Our brain needs to interpret the stimuli it receives and make sense of them. The environment provides cues that aid in the analysis of the retinal image and facilitate the construction of a perception that is as close as possible to what is out there in the world—at least, to the extent we can ascertain what is out there! The following part of this chapter explains how we use environmental cues to perceive the world.

Perceptual Constancies

Picture yourself walking to your cognitive psychology class. Two students are standing outside the classroom door. They are chatting as you approach. As you get closer to the door, the amount of space on your retina devoted to images of those students becomes increasingly large. On the one hand, this proximal sensory evidence suggests that the students are becoming larger. On the other hand, you perceive that the students have remained the same size. Why?

The perceptual system deals with variability by performing a rather remarkable analysis regarding the objects in the perceptual field. Your classmates' perceived constancy in size is an example of perceptual constancy. **Perceptual constancy** occurs when our perception of an object remains the same even when our proximal sensation of the distal object changes (Gillam, 2000). The physical characteristics of the external distal object are probably not changing. But because we must be able to deal effectively with the external world, our perceptual system has mechanisms that adjust our perception of the proximal stimulus. Thus, the perception remains constant although the proximal sensation changes. Here we consider two of the main constancies: size and shape constancies.

Size constancy is the perception that an object maintains the same size despite changes in the size of the proximal stimulus. The size of an image on the retina depends directly on the distance of that object from the eye. The same object at two different distances projects different-sized images on the retina. Some striking illusions can be achieved when our sensory and perceptual systems are misled by the very same information that usually helps us to achieve size constancy.

An example of size constancy is the Müller-Lyer illusion (Figure 2.23). Here, two line segments that are of the same length appear to be of different lengths. We use shapes and angles from our everyday experience to draw conclusions about the relative sizes of objects. Equivalent image sizes at different depths usually indicate different-sized objects.

Studies indicate that the right posterior parietal cortex (involved in the manipulation of mental images) and the right temporo-occipital cortex are activated when people are asked to judge the length of the lines in the Müller-Lyer illusion. The strength of the illusion can be changed by adjusting the angles of the arrows that delimit the horizontal line—the sharper the angles, the more pronounced the illusion. The strength of the illusion is associated with bilateral (on both sides) activation in the lateral (i.e., located on the side of) occipital cortex and the right superior parietal cortex. As the right intraparietal sulcus (furrow) is activated as well, it seems like there is an interaction of the illusory information with the top-down processes in the right parietal cortex that are responsible for visuo-spatial judgments (Weidner & Fink, 2007).

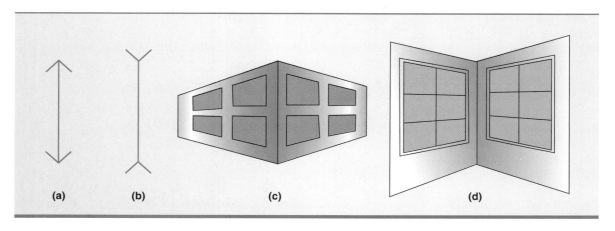

Figure 2.23 **The Müller-Lyer Illusion.**

In this illusion, we tend to view two equally long line segments as being of different lengths. The vertical line segments in panels (a) and (c) appear shorter than the line segments in panels (b) and (d), although they are the same size. Oddly enough, we are not certain why such a simple illusion occurs. Sometimes, the illusion we see in the abstract line segments (panels (a) and (b)) is explained in terms of the diagonal lines at the ends of the vertical segments which may be implicit depth cues similar to the ones we would see in our perceptions of the exterior and interior of a building (panels (c) and (d)) (Coren & Girgus, 1978).

Finally, compare the two center circles in the pair of circle patterns in Figure 2.20. Both center circles are actually the same size. But the size of the center circle relative to the surrounding circles affects perception of the center circle's size.

Like size constancy, shape constancy relates to the perception of distances but in a different way. *Shape constancy* is the perception that an object maintains the same shape despite changes in the shape of the proximal stimulus (Figure 2.24). An object's perceived shape remains the same despite changes in its orientation and hence

Figure 2.24 Shape Constancy.
Here, you see a rectangular door and door frame, showing the door as closed, slightly opened, more fully opened, or wide open. Of course, the door does not appear to be a different shape in each panel. Indeed, it would be odd if you perceived a door to be changing shapes as you opened it. Yet, the shape of the image of the door sensed by your retinas does change as you open the door. If you look at the figure, you will see that the drawn shape of the door is different in each panel.

in the shape of its retinal image. As the actual shape of the pictured door changes, some parts of the door seem to be changing differentially in their distance from us. It is possible to use neuropsychological imaging to localize parts of the brain that are used in this shape analysis. They are in the extrastriate cortex (Kanwisher et al., 1996, 1997). Points near the outer edge of the door seem to move more quickly toward us than do points near the inner edge. Nonetheless, we perceive that the door remains the same shape.

Depth Perception

Consider what happens when you reach for a cup of tea, or throw a baseball. You must use information regarding depth. **Depth** is the distance from a surface, usually using your own body as a reference surface when speaking in terms of depth perception. This use of depth information extends beyond the range of your body's reach. When you drive, you use depth to assess the distance of an approaching automobile. When you decide to call out to a friend walking down the street, you determine how loudly to call. Your decision is based on how far away you perceive your friend to be. How do you manage to perceive 3-D space when the proximal stimuli on your retinas comprise only a 2-D projection of what you see? You have to rely on depth cues. The next section explores what depth cues are and how we use them.

Depth Cues

Look at the impossible configurations in Figure 2.25. They are confusing because there is contradictory depth information in different sections of the picture. Small segments of these impossible figures look reasonable to us because there is no inconsistency in their individual depth cues (Hochberg, 1978). However, it is difficult to make sense of the figure as a whole. The reason is that the cues providing depth information in various segments of the picture are in conflict.

Generally, depth cues are either monocular (mon-, "one"; ocular, "related to the eyes") or binocular (bin-, "both," "two"). **Monocular depth cues** can be represented in just two dimensions and observed with just one eye. Figure 2.26 illustrates several of the monocular depth cues defined in Table 2.3. They include texture gradients, relative size, interposition, linear perspective, aerial perspective, location in the picture plane, and motion parallax. Before you read about the cues in either the table or the figure caption, look just at the figure. See how many depth cues you can decipher simply by observing the figure carefully.

Table 2.3 also describes motion parallax, the only monocular depth cue not shown in the figure. Motion parallax requires movement. It thus cannot be used

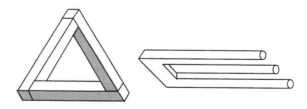

Figure 2.25 Impossible Figures.
What cues may lead you to perceive these impossible figures as entirely plausible?

to judge depth within a stationary image, such as a picture. Another means of judging depth involves **binocular depth cues,** based on the receipt of sensory information in three dimensions from both eyes (Parker, Cumming, & Dodd, 2000). Table 2.3 also summarizes some of the binocular cues used in perceiving depth.

Binocular depth cues use the relative positioning of your eyes. Your two eyes are positioned far enough apart to provide two kinds of information to your brain: binocular disparity and binocular convergence. In *binocular disparity*, your two eyes send increasingly disparate (differing) images to your brain as objects approach you. Your brain interprets the degree of disparity as an indication of distance from you. In addition, for objects we view at relatively close locations, we use depth cues based on binocular convergence. In *binocular convergence*, your two eyes increasingly turn

Crivelli, Carlo (c. 1430/35–1495) / National Gallery, London, UK / The Bridgeman Art Library

© 2007 The M.C. Escher Company–Holland. www.mcescher.com.

Figure 2.26 Depth Cues.

In *The Annunciation* (left), Carlo Crivelli masterfully illustrated at least five monocular depth cues: (1, 2) Texture gradients and relative size: The floor tiles appear similar both in front of and behind the figures in the forefront of the corridor, but the tiles at the front of the corridor are larger and are spread farther apart than the tiles at the rear. (3) Interposition: The peacock partially blocks our view of the frieze on the wall to the right of the corridor. (4) Linear perspective: The sides of the wall seem to converge inward toward the rear of the corridor. (5) Location in the picture plane: The figures at the rear of the corridor are depicted higher in the picture plane than are the figures at the front of the corridor. M. C. Escher used his mastery of visual perception to create paradoxical depictions such as in his drawing "Waterfall" (right). Make a list of the various monocular depth cues in the Waterfall that lead us to perceive the impossible.

Table 2.3 Monocular and Binocular Cues for Depth Perception

Various perceptual cues aid in our perception of the 3-D world. Some of these cues can be observed by one eye alone; other cues require the use of both eyes.

Cues for Depth Perception	Appears Closer	Appears Farther Away
Monocular Depth Cues		
Texture gradients	Larger grains, farther apart	Smaller grains, closer together
Relative size	Bigger	Smaller
Interposition	Partially obscures other object	Is partially obscured by other object
Linear perspective	Apparently parallel lines seem to diverge as they move away from the horizon	Apparently parallel lines seem to converge as they approach the horizon
Aerial perspective	Images seem crisper, more clearly delineated	Images seem fuzzier, less clearly delineated
Location in the picture plane	Above the horizon, objects are higher in the picture plane; below the horizon, objects are lower in the picture plane	Above the horizon, objects are lower in the picture plane; below the horizon, objects are higher in the picture plane
Motion parallax	Objects approaching get larger at an ever-increasing speed (i.e., big and moving quickly closer)	Objects departing get smaller at an ever-decreasing speed (i.e., small and moving slowly farther away)
Binocular Depth Cues		
Binocular convergence	Eyes feel tug inward toward nose	Eyes relax outward toward ears
Binocular disparity	Huge discrepancy between image seen by left eye and image seen by right eye	Minuscule discrepancy between image seen by left eye and image seen by right eye

inward as objects approach you. Your brain interprets these muscular movements as indications of distance from you.

In about 8% of people whose eyes are not aligned properly (strabismic eyes), depth perception can occur even with just one eye. Usually people with strabismic eyes have a sensitive zone in their retina other than the fovea that captures a part of the space that should have been captured were the eyes properly aligned. This capacity normally goes along with a partial inhibition of signals from the fovea. If the fovea stays sensitive, however, those people produce double images, which can be fused and result in stereoscopic vision with just one eye (Rychkova & Ninio, 2009).

Depth perception may depend upon more than just the distance or depth at which an object is located relative to oneself. The perceived distance to a target is influenced by the effort required to walk to the location of the target (Proffitt et al., 2003, 2006). People with a heavy backpack perceive the distance to a target location as farther than those not wearing a heavy backpack. In other words, there can be an interaction between the perceptual result and the perceived effort required to reach the object perceived (Wilt, Proffitt, & Epstein, 2004). The more effort one requires to reach something, the farther away it is perceived to be.

Depth perception is a good example of how cues facilitate our perception. When we see an object that appears small, there is no automatic reason to believe it is

INVESTIGATING COGNITIVE PSYCHOLOGY
Binocular Depth Cues

You can test the differing perspectives in binocular disparity by holding your finger about an inch from the tip of your nose. Look at it first with one eye covered, then the other: It will appear to jump back and forth. Now do the same for an object 20 feet away, then 100 yards away. The apparent jumping, which indicates the amount of binocular disparity, will decrease with distance. Your brain interprets the information regarding disparity as a cue indicating depth.

farther away. Rather, the brain uses this contextual information to conclude that the smaller object is farther away.

The Neuroscience of Depth Perception

Figure 2.27 illustrates how binocular disparity and binocular convergence work. The brain contains neurons that specialize in the perception of depth. These neurons are, as one might expect, referred to as *binocular neurons*. The neurons integrate incoming information from both eyes to form information about depth. The binocular neurons are found in the visual cortex (Parker, 2007).

Research on both nonhuman animals and humans has shown that visual shape is processed in the ventral visual stream as well as important visual areas such as the lateral occipital cortex and the ventral temporal cortex. After the initial processing in the primary visual cortex, moving 3-D shapes are processed in the human motion complex (hMT), an area that is concerned with motion processing. Next to be processed are depth and shape information. This processing occurs mainly in the V5 region of the visual cortex; the medial parietal cortex may also participate in the processing to some extent. In the next step, different features of the stimulus are analyzed in the lateral occipital cortex in order to infer the shape from the moving object. The shape that was inferred is then compared with the shape representation in the ventral occipital and ventral temporal areas of the cortex. The process ends with activation in the parietal cortex and primary visual cortex which suggests that the parietal cortex is involved in top-down processes that influence the areas in the primary visual cortex where the visual stimuli are being processed in the beginning (Jiang et al., 2008; Orban et al., 2003).

Deficits in Perception

Clearly, cognitive psychologists learn a great deal about normal perceptual processes by studying perception in normal participants. However, we also often gain understanding of perception by studying people whose perceptual processes differ from the norm (Farah, 1990; Weiskrantz, 1994).

Agnosias and Ataxias

Perceptual deficits provide an excellent way to test hypotheses with regard to how the perceptual system works. Remember that there are two distinct visual pathways,

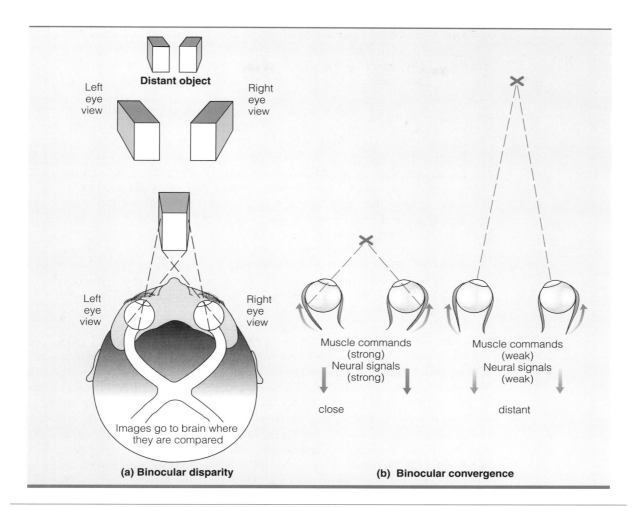

Figure 2.27 **Binocular Disparity and Convergence.**

(a) Binocular disparity: The closer an object is to you, the greater the disparity between the views of it as sensed in each of your eyes. (b) Binocular convergence: Because your two eyes are in slightly different places on your head, when you rotate your eyes so that an image falls directly on the central part of your eye, in which you have the greatest visual acuity, each eye must turn inward slightly to register the same image. The closer the object you are trying to see, the more your eyes must turn inward. Your muscles send messages to your brain regarding the degree to which your eyes are turning inward, and these messages are interpreted as cues indicating depth.

one for identifying objects ("*what*"), the other for pinpointing where objects are located in space and how to manipulate them ("*where*" or "*how*").

The *what/how hypothesis* is best supported by evidence of processing deficits: There are both deficits that impair people's ability to recognize *what* they see, and deficits that impair people's ability to reach for what they see (*how*).

Difficulties Perceiving the "What"

Consider first the "what." People who suffer from an **agnosia** have trouble to perceive sensory information (Moscovitch, Winocur, & Behrmann, 1997). Agnosias often are caused by damage to the border of the temporal and occipital lobes (Farah, 1990, 1999) or restricted oxygen flow to areas of the brain, sometimes as a result of traumatic brain injury (Zoltan, 1996). There are many kinds of agnosias. Not all of them are visual. Here we focus on a few specific inabilities to see forms and patterns in space.

Generally, people with agnosia have normal sensations of what is in front of them. They can perceive the colors and shapes of objects and persons but they cannot recognize what the objects are—they have trouble with the "what" pathway.

People who suffer from visual-object agnosia can see all parts of the visual field, but the objects they see do not mean anything to them (Kolb & Whishaw, 1985). For example, one agnosic patient, on seeing a pair of eyeglasses, noted first that there was a circle, then that there was another circle, then that there was a crossbar, and finally guessed that he was looking at a bicycle. A bicycle does, indeed, comprise two circles and a crossbar (Luria, 1973).

Disturbance in the temporal region of the cortex can lead to *simultagnosia*. In simultagnosia, an individual is unable to pay attention to more than one object at a time. A person with simultagnosia would not see each of the objects depicted in Figure 2.28. Rather, the person might report seeing the hammer but not the other objects (Williams, 1970).

Prosopagnosia results in a severely impaired ability to recognize human faces (Farah et al., 1995; Feinberg et al., 1994; McNeil & Warrington, 1993; Young, 2003). A person with prosopagnosia might not recognize her or his own face in the mirror. This fascinating disorder has spawned much research on face identification, a "hot topic" in visual perception (Damasio, 1985; Farah et al., 1995; Farah, Levinson, & Klein, 1995; Haxby et al., 1996). The functioning of the right-hemisphere fusiform gyrus is strongly implicated in prosopagnosia. In particular, the disorder is associated with damage to the right temporal lobe of the brain. Prosopagnosia, in particular, and agnosia, in general, are obstacles that persist over time. In one particular case, a woman who sustained carbon-monoxide toxicity began to suffer from agnosia, including prosopagnosia. After 40 years, this woman was reevaluated

Figure 2.28   Simultagnosia.

When you view this figure, you see various objects overlapping. People with simultagnosia cannot see more than one of these objects at any one time.

Source: From *Sensation and Perception* by Stanley Coren and Lawrence M. Ward, copyright © 1989 by Harcourt Brace & Company. Reproduced by permission of the publisher.

and still demonstrated these deficits. These findings reveal the lasting nature of agnosia (Sparr et al., 1991).

Difficulties in Knowing the "How"

A different kind of perceptual deficit is associated with damage to the "how" pathway. This deficit is **optic ataxia,** which is an impairment in the ability to use the visual system to guide movement (Himmelbach & Karnath, 2005). People with this deficit have trouble reaching for things. All of us have had the experience of coming home at night and trying to find the keyhole in the front door. It's too dark to see, and we have to grope with our key for the keyhole, often taking quite a while to find it. Someone with optic ataxia has this problem even with a fully lit visual field. The "how" pathway is impaired.

Ataxia results from a processing failure in the posterior parietal cortex, where sensorimotor information is processed. It is assumed that higher order processes are involved because most patients' disorders are complex and they can indeed grasp objects under certain circumstances (Jackson et al., 2009). People with ataxia can improve their movements toward a visible aim when they hold off with their movements for a few seconds. Immediate movements are executed through dorsal-stream processing, while delayed movements make use of the ventral system, comprising the occipito-temporal and temporo-parietal areas (Milner et al., 2003; Milner & Goodale, 2008; Himmelbach et al., 2009).

Are Perceptual Processes Independent of Each Other?

When we consider the different kinds of perceptual deficits, it is stunning to see how specific they are. Some people cannot name colors; others cannot recognize movement or faces. Others can see a mug on the table in front of them, yet cannot grasp the mug. This kind of extreme specificity of deficits leads to questions about specialization (modular processes). Specifically, are there distinct processing centers or modules for particular perceptual tasks, such as for color or face recognition? This question goes beyond the separation of perceptual processes along different sensory modalities (e.g., the differences between visual and auditory perception). Modular processes are those that are specialized for particular tasks. They may involve only visual processes (as in color perception), or they may involve an integration of visual and auditory processes (as in certain aspects of speech perception that are discussed in Chapter 10). For face perception (or any perceptual process) to be considered a truly modular process, we would need to have further evidence that the process is domain-specific and therefore only uses specific kinds of information, and that information does not freely flow across different modules. That is, other perceptual processes should not contribute to, interfere with, or share information with face perception.

Anomalies in Color Perception

Color perception deficits are much more common in men than in women, and they are genetically linked. However, they can also result from lesions to the ventro-medial occipital and temporal lobes.

There are several kinds of color deficiency, which are sometimes referred to as kinds of "color blindness." Least common is *rod monochromacy*, also called *achromacy*. People with this condition have no color vision at all. It is thus the only true form of pure color blindness. People with this condition have cones that are nonfunctional. They see only shades of gray, as a function of their vision through the rods of the eye.

Most people who suffer from deficits in color perception can still see some color, despite the name "color blindness." In *dichromacy*, only two of the mechanisms for color perception work, and one is malfunctioning. The result of this malfunction is one of three types of color blindness (color-perception deficits). The most common is red-green color blindness. People with this form of color-blindness have difficulty in distinguishing red from green, although they may be able to distinguish, for example, dark red from light green (*Visual disabilities: Color-blindness*, 2004). The extreme form of red-green color blindness is called *protanopia*. The other types of color blindness are: *deuteranopia* (trouble seeing greens), and *tritanopia* (blues and greens can be confused, but yellows also can seem to disappear or to appear as light shades of reds).

See the companion website for a picture showing a rainbow as seen by a person with normal color vision and by persons suffering from the three kinds of dichromacy.

✔ CONCEPT CHECK

1. What is shape constancy?
2. What are the main cues for depth perception?
3. What is visual agnosia?
4. To what does "modularity" refer?
5. What is the difference between monochromacy and dichromacy?

Why Does It Matter? Perception in Practice

Perceptual processes and change blindness play a significant role in accidents and efforts at accident prevention. About 50% of all collision accidents are a result of missing or delayed perception (Nakayama, 1978). Especially two-wheeled vehicles are often involved in "looked-but-failed-to-see" accidents, where the driver of the involved car states that he did indeed look in the direction of the cyclist, but failed to see the approaching motorcycle. It is possible that drivers develop a certain "scanning" strategy that they use in complex situations, such as at crossroads. The scanning strategy concentrates on the most common and dangerous threats but fails to recognize small deviations, or more uncommon objects like two-wheeled vehicles. In addition, people tend to fail to recognize new objects after blinking and saccades (fast movements of both eyes in one direction).

Generally, people are not aware of the danger of change blindness and believe that they will be able to see all obstacles when looking in a particular direction ("change blindness blindness", Simons & Rensink, 2005; Davis et al., 2008). This tendency has implications for the education of drivers with regard to their perceptual abilities. It also has implications for the design of traffic environments, which should be laid out in a way that facilitates complex traffic flow and makes drivers aware of unexpected obstacles, like bicycles (Galpin et al., 2009; Koustanai, Boloix, Van Elslande, & Bastien, 2008).

Key Themes

Several key themes, as outlined in Chapter 1, emerge in our study of perception.

Rationalism versus empiricism. How much of the way we perceive can be understood as due to some kind of order in the environment that is relatively independent of our perceptual mechanisms? In the Gibsonian view, much of what we perceive derives from the structure of the stimulus, independent of our experience with it. In contrast, in the view of constructive perception, we construct what we perceive. We build up mechanisms for perceiving based on our experience with the environment. As a result, our perception is influenced at least as much by our intelligence (rationalism) as it is by the structure of the stimuli we perceive (empiricism).

Basic versus applied research. Research on perception has many applications, such as in understanding how we can construct machines that perceive. The U.S. Postal Service relies heavily on machines that read zip codes. To the extent that the machines are inaccurate, mail risks going astray. These machines cannot rely on strict template matching because people write numbers in different ways. So the machines must do at least some feature analysis.

Another application of perception research is in human factors. Human-factors researchers design machines and user interfaces to be user-friendly. An automobile driver or airplane pilot sometimes needs to make split-second decisions. The cockpits thus must have instrument panels that are well-lit, easy to read, and accessible for quick action. Basic research on human perception can inform developers what user-friendly means.

Domain generality versus domain specificity. Perhaps nowhere is this theme better illustrated than in research on face recognition. Is there something special about face recognition? It appears so. Yet many of the mechanisms that are used for face recognition are used for other kinds of perception as well. Thus, it appears that perceptual mechanisms may be mixed—some general across domains, others specific to domains such as face recognition.

Summary

1. **How can we perceive an object like a chair as having a stable form, given that the image of the chair on our retina changes as we look at it from different directions?** Perceptual experience involves four elements: distal object, informational medium, proximal stimulation, and perceptual object. Proximal stimulation is constantly changing because of the variable nature of the environment and physiological processes designed to overcome sensory adaptation. Perception therefore must address the fundamental question of constancy.

Perceptual constancies (e.g., size and shape constancy) result when our perceptions of objects tend to remain constant. That is, we see constancies even as the stimuli registered by our senses change. Some perceptual constancies may be governed by what we know about the world. For example, we have expectations regarding how rectilinear structures usually appear. But constancies also are influenced by invariant relationships among objects in their environmental context.

One reason we can perceive 3-D space is the use of binocular depth cues. Two such cues are binocular disparity and binocular convergence. Binocular disparity is based on the fact that each of two eyes receives a slightly different image of the same object as it is being viewed. Binocular convergence is based on the degree to which our two eyes must turn inward toward each other as objects get closer to us. We also are aided in perceiving depth by monocular depth cues. These cues include texture gradients, relative size, interposition, linear perspective, aerial perspective, height in the picture plane, and motion parallax. One of the earliest approaches to form and pattern perception is the Gestalt approach to form perception. The Gestalt law of Prägnanz has led to the explication of several principles of form perception. These principles include figure-ground, proximity, similarity, closure, continuity, and symmetry. They characterize how we perceptually group together various objects and parts of objects.

2. **What are two fundamental approaches to explaining perception?** Perception is the set of processes by which we recognize, organize, and make sense of stimuli in our environment. It may be viewed from either of two basic theoretical approaches: constructive or direct-perception. The viewpoint of constructive (or intelligent) perception asserts that the perceiver essentially constructs or builds up the stimulus that is perceived. He or she does so by using prior knowledge, contextual information, and sensory information. In contrast, the viewpoint of direct perception asserts that all the information we need to perceive is in the sensory input (such as from the retina) that we receive.

An alternative to both these approaches integrates features of each. It suggests that perception may be more complex than direct-perception theorists have suggested, yet perception also may involve more efficient use of sensory data than constructive-perception theorists have suggested. Specifically, a computational approach to perception suggests that our brains compute 3-D perceptual models of the environment based on information from the 2-D sensory receptors in our retinas.

The main bottom-up theoretical approaches to pattern perception include template-matching theories and feature-matching theories. Some support for feature-matching theories comes from neurophysiological studies identifying what are called "feature detectors" in the brain. It appears that various cortical neurons can be mapped to specific receptive fields on the retina. Differing cortical neurons respond to different features. Examples of such features are line segments or edges in various spatial orientations. Visual perception seems to depend on three levels of complexity in the cortical neurons. Each level of complexity seems to be further removed from the incoming information from the sensory receptors. Another bottom-up approach, the recognition-by-components (RBC) theory, more specifically delineates a set of features involved in form and pattern perception.

Bottom-up approaches explain some aspects of form and pattern perception. Other aspects require approaches that suggest at least some degree of top-down processing of perceptual information. For example, top-down approaches better but incompletely explain such phenomena as context effects, including the object-superiority effect and the word-superiority effect.

3. **What happens when people with normal visual sensations cannot perceive visual stimuli?** Agnosias, which are usually associated with brain lesions, are deficits of form and pattern perception. They cause afflicted people to be insufficiently able to recognize objects that are in their visual fields, despite normal sensory abilities. People who suffer from visual-object agnosia can sense all parts of the visual field. But the objects they see do not mean anything to them. Individuals with simultagnosia are unable to pay attention to more than one object at a time. People with spatial agnosia have severe difficulty in comprehending and handling the relationship between their bodies and the spatial configurations of the world around them. People with prosopagnosia have severe impairment in their ability to recognize human faces, including their own. These deficits lead to the question of whether specific perceptual processes are modular—specialized for particular tasks. Color blindness is another type of perceptual deficit.

Thinking about Thinking: Analytical, Creative, and Practical Questions

1. Briefly describe each of the monocular and binocular depth cues listed in this chapter.
2. Describe bottom-up and top-down approaches to perception.
3. How might deficits of perception, such as agnosia, offer insight into normal perceptual processes?
4. Compare and contrast the Gestalt approach to form perception and the theory of direct perception.
5. Design a demonstration that would illustrate the phenomenon of perceptual constancy.
6. Design an experiment to test the feature-matching theory.
7. To what extent does perception involve learning? Why?

Key Terms

agnosia, p. 85
amacrine cells, p. 50
binocular depth cues, p. 82
bipolar cells, p. 51
bottom-up theories, p. 53
cones, p. 52
constructive perception, p. 64
context effects, p. 66
depth, p. 81
direct perception, p. 54
feature-matching theories, p. 58
figure-ground, p. 71
fovea, p. 50

ganglion cells, p. 50
Gestalt approach to form perception, p. 70
horizontal cells, p. 50
landmark-centered, p. 69
law of Prägnanz, p. 70
monocular depth cues, p. 81
object-centered representation, p. 68
optic ataxia, p. 87
optic nerve, p. 50
percept, p. 47
perception, p. 42

perceptual constancy, p. 78
photopigments, p. 51
photoreceptors, p. 51
recognition-by-components (RBC) theory, p. 63
retina, p. 50
rods, p. 51
templates, p. 56
top-down theories, p. 53
viewer-centered representation, p. 68

Media Resources

Visit the companion website—**www.cengagebrain.com**—for quizzes, research articles, chapter outlines, and more.

CogLab

Explore CogLab by going to **http://coglab.wadsworth.com.** To learn more, examine the following experiments:

Mapping the Blind Spot

Receptive Fields

Apparent Motion

Metacontrast Masking

Müller-Lyer Illusion

Signal Detection

Visual Search

Lexical Decision

Cognitive Neuroscience

Here are some of the questions we will explore in this chapter:

1. What are the fundamental structures and processes within the brain?
2. How do researchers study the major structures and processes of the brain?
3. What have researchers found as a result of studying the brain?

■ BELIEVE IT OR NOT

DOES YOUR BRAIN USE LESS POWER THAN YOUR DESK LAMP?

The brain is one of the premier users of energy in the human body. As much as 20% of the energy in your body is consumed by your brain, although it accounts only for about 2% of your body mass. This may come as no surprise, given that you need your brain for almost anything you do, from moving your legs to walk to reading this book, to talking to your friend on the phone. Even seeing what is right in front of your eyes takes a huge amount of processing by the brain, as you have seen in Chapter 2. And yet, for all the amazing things your brain achieves, it does not use much more energy than your computer and monitor when they are "asleep." It is estimated that your brain uses about 12–20 watts of power. Your sleeping computer consumes about 10 watts when it's on, and 150 watts together with its monitor or even more. Even the lamp on your desk uses more power than your brain. Your brain performs many more tasks than your desk lamp or computer. Just think about all you'd have to eat if your brain consumed as much energy as those devices (Drubach, 1999). You'll learn more about how your brain works in this chapter.

Our brains are a central processing unit for everything we do. But how do our brains relate to our bodies? Are they connected or separate? Do our brains define who we are? An ancient legend from India (Rosenzweig & Leiman, 1989) tells of Sita. She marries one man but is attracted to another. These two frustrated men behead themselves. Sita, bereft of them both, desperately prays to the goddess Kali to bring the men back to life. Sita is granted her wish. She is allowed to reattach the heads to the bodies. In her rush to bring the two men back to life, Sita mistakenly switches their heads. She attaches them to the wrong bodies. Now, to whom is she married? Who is who?

The mind–body issue has long interested philosophers and scientists. Where is the mind located in the body, if at all? How do the mind and body interact? How are we able to think, speak, plan, reason, learn, and remember? What are the physical bases for our cognitive abilities? These questions all probe the relationship between cognitive psychology and neurobiology. Some cognitive psychologists seek to answer such questions by studying the biological bases of cognition. Cognitive psychologists are especially concerned with how the anatomy (physical structures of the body) and the physiology (functions and processes of the body) of the nervous system affect and are affected by human cognition.

Cognitive neuroscience is the field of study linking the brain and other aspects of the nervous system to cognitive processing and, ultimately, to behavior. The **brain** is the organ in our bodies that most directly controls our thoughts, emotions, and motivations (Gloor, 1997; Rockland, 2000; Shepherd, 1998). Figure 3.1 shows photos of what the brain actually looks like. We usually think of the brain as being at the top of the body's hierarchy—as the boss, with various other organs responding to it. Like any good boss, however, it listens to and is influenced by its subordinates, the other organs of the body. Thus, the brain is reactive as well as directive.

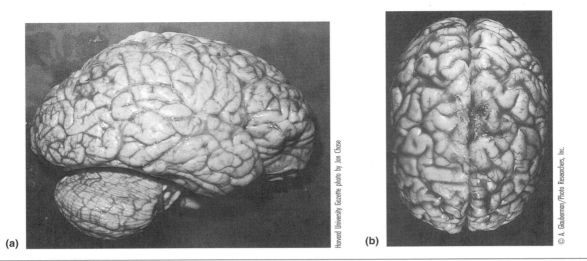

(a)

Harvard University Gazette photo by Jon Chase

(b)

© A. Glauberman/Photo Researchers, Inc.

Figure 3.1 The Brain.
What does a brain actually look like? Here you can see side (a) and top (b) views of a human brain. Subsequent figures and schematic pictures (i.e., simplified diagrams) point out in more detail some of the main features of the brain.

A major goal of present research on the brain is to study localization of function. **Localization of function** refers to the specific areas of the brain that control specific skills or behaviors. Facts about particular brain areas and their function are interspersed throughout this chapter and also throughout the whole book.

Our exploration of the brain starts with the anatomy of the brain. We will look at the gross anatomy of the brain as well as at neurons and the ways in which information is transmitted in the brain. Then we will explore the methods scientists use to examine the brain, its structures, and functions. And finally, we will learn about brain disorders and how they inform cognitive psychology.

Cognition in the Brain: The Anatomy and Mechanisms of the Brain

The **nervous system** is the basis for our ability to perceive, adapt to, and interact with the world around us (Gazzaniga, 1995, 2000; Gazzaniga, Ivry, & Mangun, 1998). Through this system we receive, process, and then respond to information from the environment (Pinker, 1997a; Rugg, 1997). In the following section, we will focus on the supreme organ of the nervous system—the brain—paying special attention to the cerebral cortex, which controls many of our thought processes. In a later section, we consider the basic building block of the nervous system—the neuron. We will examine in detail how information moves through the nervous system at the cellular level. Then we will consider the various levels of organization within the nervous system and how drugs interact with the nervous system. For now, let's look at the structure of the brain.

Gross Anatomy of the Brain: Forebrain, Midbrain, Hindbrain

What have scientists discovered about the human brain? The brain has three major regions: forebrain, midbrain, and hindbrain. These labels do not correspond exactly to locations of regions in an adult or even a child's head. Rather, the terms come from the front-to-back physical arrangement of these parts in the nervous system of a developing embryo. Initially, the *forebrain* is generally the farthest forward, toward what becomes the face. The *midbrain* is next in line. And the *hindbrain* is generally farthest from the forebrain, near the back of the neck [Figure 3.2 (a)]. In development, the relative orientations change so that the forebrain is almost a cap on top of the midbrain and hindbrain. Nonetheless, the terms still are used to designate areas

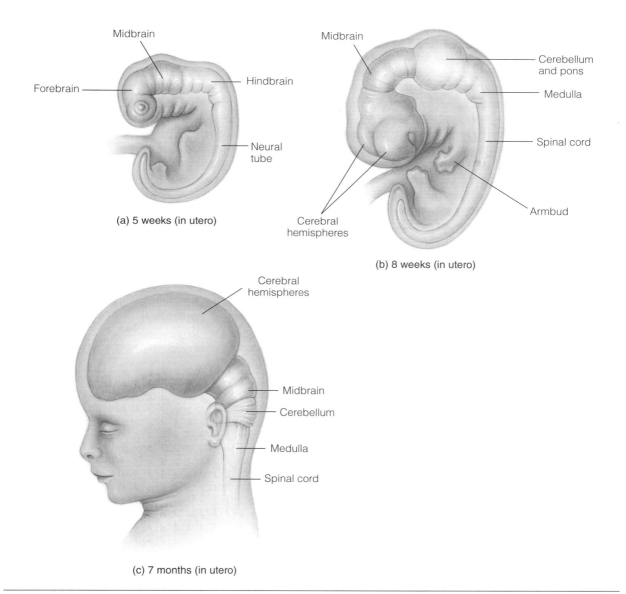

(a) 5 weeks (in utero)

(b) 8 weeks (in utero)

(c) 7 months (in utero)

Figure 3.2   Fetal Brain Development.

Over the course of embryonic and fetal development, the brain becomes more highly specialized and the locations and relative positions of the hindbrain, the midbrain, and the forebrain change from conception to term.

Source: From *In Search of the Human Mind* by Robert J. Sternberg, copyright © 1995 by Harcourt Brace & Company. Reproduced by permission of the publisher.

of the fully developed brain. Figures 2.2 (b) and (c) show the changing locations and relationships of the forebrain, the midbrain, and the hindbrain over the course of development of the brain. You can see how they develop, from an embryo a few weeks after conception to a fetus of seven months of age.

The Forebrain

The forebrain is the region of the brain located toward the top and front of the brain. It comprises the cerebral cortex, the basal ganglia, the limbic system, the thalamus, and the hypothalamus (Figure 3.3). The cerebral cortex is the outer layer of the cerebral hemispheres. It plays a vital role in our thinking and other mental processes. It therefore merits a special section in this chapter, which follows the present

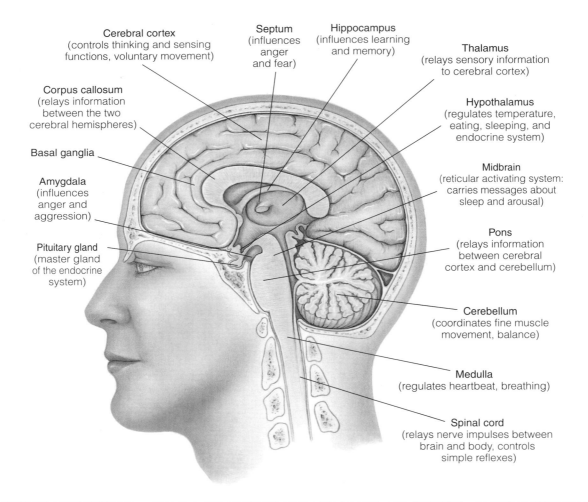

Figure 3.3   Structures of the Brain.

The forebrain, the midbrain, and the hindbrain contain structures that perform essential functions for survival and for high-level thinking and feeling.

Source: From *Psychology: In Search of the Human Mind* by Robert J. Sternberg, copyright © 2000 by Harcourt Brace & Company, reproduced by permission of the publisher.

discussion of the major structures and functions of the brain. The *basal ganglia* (singular: ganglion) are collections of neurons crucial to motor function. Dysfunction of the basal ganglia can result in motor deficits. These deficits include tremors, involuntary movements, changes in posture and muscle tone, and slowness of movement. Deficits are observed in Parkinson's disease and Huntington's disease. Both these diseases entail severe motor symptoms (Rockland, 2000; Lerner & Riley, 2008; Lewis & Barker, 2009).

The **limbic system** is important to emotion, motivation, memory, and learning. Animals such as fish and reptiles, which have relatively undeveloped limbic systems, respond to the environment almost exclusively by instinct. Mammals and especially humans have relatively more developed limbic systems. Our limbic system allows us to suppress instinctive responses (e.g., the impulse to strike someone who accidentally causes us pain). Our limbic systems help us to adapt our behaviors flexibly in response to our changing environment. The limbic system comprises three central interconnected cerebral structures: the septum, the amygdala, and the hippocampus.

The **septum** is involved in anger and fear. The **amygdala** plays an important role in emotion as well, especially in anger and aggression (Adolphs, 2003; Derntl et al., 2009). Stimulation of the amygdala commonly results in fear. It can be evidenced in various ways, such as through palpitations, fearful hallucinations, or frightening flashbacks in memory (Engin & Treit, 2008; Gloor, 1997; Rockland, 2000).

Damage to (lesions in) or removal of the amygdala can result in maladaptive lack of fear. In the case of lesions to the animal brain, the animal approaches potentially dangerous objects without hesitation or fear (Adolphs et al., 1994; Frackowiak et al., 1997). The amygdala also has an enhancing effect for the perception of emotional stimuli. In humans, lesions to the amygdala prevent this enhancement (Anderson & Phelps, 2001; Tottenham, Hare, & Casey, 2009). Additionally, persons with autism display limited activation in the amygdala. A well-known theory of autism suggests that the disorder involves dysfunction of the amygdala, which leads to the social impairment that is typical of persons with autism, for example, difficulties in evaluating people's trustworthiness or recognizing emotions in faces (Adolphs, Sears, & Piven, 2001; Baron-Cohen et al., 2000; Howard et al., 2000; Kleinhans et al., 2009) Two other effects of lesions to the amygdala can be visual agnosia (inability to recognize objects) and hypersexuality (Steffanaci, 1999).

The **hippocampus** plays an essential role in memory formation (Eichenbaum, 1999, 2002; Gluck, 1996; Manns & Eichenbaum, 2006; O'Keefe, 2003). It gets its name from the Greek word for "seahorse," its approximate shape. The hippocampus is essential for flexible learning and for seeing the relations among items learned as well as for spatial memory (Eichenbaum, 1997; Squire, 1992). The hippocampus also appears to keep track of where things are and how these things are spatially related to each other. In other words, it monitors what is where (Cain, Boon, & Corcoran, 2006; Howland et al., 2008; McClelland et al., 1995; Tulving & Schacter, 1994). We return to the role of the hippocampus in Chapter 5.

People who have suffered damage to or removal of the hippocampus still can recall existing memories—for example, they can recognize old friends and places—but they are unable to form new memories (relative to the time of the brain damage). New information—new situations, people, and places—remain forever new. A disease that produces loss of memory function is **Korsakoff's syndrome**. Other symptoms include apathy, paralysis of muscles controlling the eye, and tremor.

IN THE LAB OF MARTHA FARAH

Cognitive Neuroscience and Childhood Poverty

MARTHA FARAH

Around the time I had my daughter, I shifted my research focus to developmental cognitive neuroscience. People naturally assumed that these two life changes were related, and they were—but not in the way people thought. What captured my interest in brain development was not principally watching my daughter grow, as wondrous a process as that was. Rather, it was getting to know the babysitters who entered our lives, and learning about theirs.

These babysitters were young women of low socioeconomic status (SES), who grew up in families dependent on welfare and supported their own young children with a combination of state assistance supplemented with cash wages from babysitting. As caregivers for my child, they were not merely hired help; they were people I liked, trusted, and grew to care about. And as we became closer, and I spent more time with their families, I learned about a world very different from my own.

The children of these inner-city families started life with the same evident potential as my own child, learning words, playing games, asking questions, and grappling with the challenges of cooperation, discipline, and self-control. But they soon found their way onto the same dispiriting life trajectories as their parents, with limited skills, options, hope. As a mother, I found it heart-breaking. As a scientist, I wanted to understand.

This led to a series of studies in which my collaborators and I tried first to simply document the effects of childhood poverty in terms of cognitive neuroscience's description of the mind, and then to explain the effects of poverty in terms of more specific, mechanistic causes. With Kim Noble, then a graduate student in my lab, we assessed the functioning of five different neurocognitive systems in kindergarteners of low and middle SES. We found the most pronounced effects in language and executive function systems. These results were replicated and expanded upon in additional studies with Noble and with Hallam Hurt, a pediatrician

collaborator. In first graders and in middle-school students, we again found striking SES disparities in language and executive function, as well as in declarative memory. Assuming that these disparities are the result of different early life experiences, what is it about growing up poor that would interfere with the development of these specific systems?

In one study, we made use of data collected earlier on the middle-school children just mentioned. We found that their language ability in middle school was predicted by the amount of cognitive stimulation they experienced as four-year olds—being read to, taken on trips, and so on. In contrast, we found that their declarative memory ability in middle school was predicted by the quality of parental nurturance that they received as young children—being held close, being paid attention to, and so on. The latter finding might seem an odd association. Why would affectionate parenting have anything to do with memory? Yet research with animals shows that when a young animal is stressed, the resulting stress hormones can damage the hippocampus, a brain area important for both stress regulation and memory. This research has also shown that more nurturing maternal behavior can buffer the young animal's hippocampus against the effects of stress. It would appear that children living in the stressful environment of poverty benefit in a similar way from attentive and affectionate parenting.

Our most recent work, with graduate student Daniel Hackman and radiology colleague Hengyi Rao, has tested these hypothesized mechanisms more directly. Brain imaging has confirmed that hippocampal size is affected by early life parental nurturance in low SES individuals, and direct measures of hormonal responses to stress indicate that both SES and parenting in early childhood program later life stress response. Our ultimate goal is to understand the complex web of social, psychological and physiological influences that act upon children in low SES families and to use that understanding to help them achieve their true potential.

This loss is believed to be associated with deterioration of the hippocampus and is caused by a lack of thiamine (Vitamin B-1) in the brain. The syndrome can result from excessive alcohol use, dietary deficiencies, or eating disorders.

There is a renowned case of a patient known as H.M., who after brain surgery retained his memory for events that transpired before the surgery but had no memory for events after the surgery. This case is another illustration of the resulting problems with memory formation due to hippocampus damage (see Chapter 5 for more on H.M.). Disruption in the hippocampus appears to result in deficits in declarative memory (i.e., memory for pieces of information), but it does not result in deficits in procedural memory (i.e., memory for courses of action) (Rockland, 2000).

The **thalamus** relays incoming sensory information through groups of neurons that project to the appropriate region in the cortex. Most of the sensory input into the brain passes through the thalamus, which is approximately in the center of the brain, at about eye level. To accommodate all the types of information that must be sorted out, the thalamus is divided into a number of nuclei (groups of neurons of similar function). Each nucleus receives information from specific senses. The information is then relayed to corresponding specific areas in the cerebral cortex. The thalamus also helps in the control of sleep and waking. When the thalamus malfunctions, the result can be pain, tremor, amnesia, impairment of language, and disruptions in waking and sleeping (Rockland, 2000; Steriade, Jones, & McCormick, 1997). In cases of schizophrenia, imaging and *in vivo* studies reveal abnormal changes in the thalamus (Clinton & Meador-Woodruff, 2004). These abnormalities result in difficulties in filtering stimuli and focusing attention, which in turn can explain why people suffering from schizophrenia experience symptoms such as hallucinations and delusions.

The **hypothalamus** regulates behavior related to species survival: fighting, feeding, fleeing, and mating. The hypothalamus also is active in regulating emotions and reactions to stress (Malsbury, 2003). It interacts with the limbic system. The small size of the hypothalamus (from Greek *hypo-*, "under"; located at the base of the forebrain, beneath the thalamus) belies its importance in controlling many bodily functions (Table 3.1). The hypothalamus plays a role in sleep: Dysfunction and neural loss within the hypothalamus are noted in cases of narcolepsy, whereby a person falls asleep often and at unpredictable times (Lodi et al., 2004; Mignot, Taheri, & Nishino, 2002). The hypothalamus also is important for the functioning of the endocrine system. It is involved in the stimulation of the pituitary glands, through which a range of hormones are produced and released. These hormones include growth hormones and oxytocin (which is involved in bonding processes and sexual arousal; Gazzaniga, Ivry, & Mangun, 2009).

The forebrain, midbrain, and hindbrain contain structures that perform essential functions for survival as well as for high-level thinking and feeling. For a summary of the major structures and functions of the brain, as discussed in this section, see Table 3.1.

The Midbrain

The midbrain helps to control eye movement and coordination. The midbrain is more important in nonmammals where it is the main source of control for visual and auditory information. In mammals these functions are dominated by the forebrain. Table 3.1 lists several structures and corresponding functions of the midbrain. By far the most indispensable of these structures is the **reticular activating system (RAS**; also called the "reticular formation"), a network of neurons essential to the

Table 3.1   Major Structures and Functions of the Brain

Region of the Brain	Major Structures within the Regions	Functions of the Structures
Forebrain	Cerebral cortex (outer layer of the cerebral hemispheres)	Involved in receiving and processing sensory information, thinking, other cognitive processing, and planning and sending motor information
	Basal ganglia (collections of nuclei and neural fibers)	Crucial to the function of the motor system
	Limbic systems (hippocampus, amygdala, and septum)	Involved in learning, emotions, and motivation (in particular, the hippocampus influences learning and memory, the amygdala influences anger and aggression, and the septum influences anger and fear)
	Thalamus	Primary relay station for sensory information coming into the brain; transmits information to the correct regions of the cerebral cortex through projection fibers that extend from the thalamus to specific regions of the cortex; comprises several nuclei (groups of neurons) that receive specific kinds of sensory information and project that information to specific regions of the cerebral cortex, including four key nuclei for sensory information: (1) from the visual receptors, via optic nerves, to the visual cortex, permitting us to see; (2) from the auditory receptors, via auditory nerves, to the auditory cortex, permitting us to hear; (3) from sensory receptors in the somatic nervous system, to the primary somatosensory cortex, permitting us to sense pressure and pain; and (4) from the cerebellum (in the hindbrain) to the primary motor cortex, permitting us to sense physical balance and equilibrium
	Hypothalamus	Controls the endocrine system; controls the autonomic nervous system, such as internal temperature regulation, appetite and thirst regulation, and other key functions; involved in regulation of behavior related to species survival (in particular, fighting, feeding, fleeing, and mating); plays a role in controlling consciousness (see reticular activating system); involved in emotions, pleasure, pain, and stress reactions
Midbrain	Superior colliculi (on top)	Involved in vision (especially visual reflexes)
	Inferior colliculi (below)	Involved in hearing

(continued)

Table 3.1   Continued

Region of the Brain	Major Structures within the Regions	Functions of the Structures
	Reticular activating system (also extends into the hindbrain)	Important in controlling consciousness (sleep arousal), attention, cardiorespiratory function, and movement
	Gray matter, red nucleus, substantia nigra, ventral region	Important in controlling movement
Hindbrain	Cerebellum	Essential to balance, coordination, and muscle tone
	Pons (also contains part of the RAS)	Involved in consciousness (sleep and arousal); bridges neural transmissions from one part of the brain to another; involved with facial nerves
	Medulla oblongata	Serves as juncture at which nerves cross from one side of the body to opposite side of the brain; involved in cardiorespiratory function, digestion, and swallowing

regulation of consciousness (sleep; wakefulness; arousal; attention to some extent; and vital functions such as heartbeat and breathing; Sarter, Bruno, & Berntson, 2003).

The RAS also extends into the hindbrain. Both the RAS and the thalamus are essential to our having any conscious awareness of or control over our existence. The **brainstem** connects the forebrain to the spinal cord. It comprises the hypothalamus, the thalamus, the midbrain, and the hindbrain. A structure called the *periaqueductal gray* (PAG) is in the brainstem. This region seems to be essential for certain kinds of adaptive behaviors. Injections of small amounts of excitatory amino acids or, alternatively, electrical stimulation of this area results in any of several responses: an aggressive, confrontational response; avoidance or flight response; heightened defensive reactivity; or reduced reactivity as is experienced after a defeat, when one feels hopeless (Bandler & Shipley, 1994; Rockland, 2000).

Physicians make a determination of brain death based on the function of the brainstem. Specifically, a physician must determine that the brainstem has been damaged so severely that various reflexes of the head (e.g., the pupillary reflex) are absent for more than 12 hours, or the brain must show no electrical activity or cerebral circulation of blood (Berkow, 1992).

The Hindbrain

The hindbrain comprises the medulla oblongata, the pons, and the cerebellum.

The **medulla oblongata** controls heart activity and largely controls breathing, swallowing, and digestion. The medulla is also the place at which nerves from the right side of the body cross over to the left side of the brain and nerves from the left side of the body cross over to the right side of the brain. The medulla oblongata is an elongated interior structure located at the point where the spinal cord enters the skull and joins with the brain. The medulla oblongata, which contains part of the RAS, helps to keep us alive.

The **pons** serves as a kind of relay station because it contains neural fibers that pass signals from one part of the brain to another. Its name derives from the Latin for "bridge," as it serves a bridging function. The pons also contains a portion of the RAS and nerves serving parts of the head and face. The **cerebellum** (from Latin, "little brain") controls bodily coordination, balance, and muscle tone, as well as some aspects of memory involving procedure-related movements (see Chapters 7 and 8) (Middleton & Helms Tillery, 2003). The prenatal development of the human brain within each individual roughly corresponds to the evolutionary development of the human brain within the species as a whole. Specifically, the hindbrain is evolutionarily the oldest and most primitive part of the brain. It also is the first part of the brain to develop prenatally. The midbrain is a relatively newer addition to the brain in evolutionary terms. It is the next part of the brain to develop prenatally. Finally, the forebrain is the most recent evolutionary addition to the brain. It is the last of the three portions of the brain to develop prenatally.

Additionally, across the evolutionary development of our species, humans have shown an increasingly greater proportion of brain weight in relation to body weight. However, across the span of development after birth, the proportion of brain weight to body weight declines. For cognitive psychologists, the most important of these evolutionary trends is the increasing neural complexity of the brain. The evolution of the human brain has offered us the enhanced ability to exercise voluntary control over behavior. It has also strengthened our ability to plan and to contemplate alternative courses of action. These ideas are discussed in the next section with respect to the cerebral cortex.

Cerebral Cortex and Localization of Function

The **cerebral cortex** plays an extremely important role in human cognition. It forms a 1- to 3-millimeter layer that wraps the surface of the brain somewhat like the bark of a tree wraps around the trunk. In human beings, the many convolutions, or creases, of the cerebral cortex comprise three elements. *Sulci* (singular, sulcus) are small grooves. *Fissures* are large grooves. And *gyri* (singular, gyrus) are bulges between adjacent sulci or fissures. These folds greatly increase the surface area of the cortex. If the wrinkly human cortex were smoothed out, it would take up about 2 square feet. The cortex comprises 80% of the human brain (Kolb & Whishaw, 1990).

The volume of the human skull has more than doubled over the past 2 million years, allowing for the expansion of the brain, and especially the cortex (Toro et al., 2008). The complexity of brain function increases with the cortical area. The human cerebral cortex enables us to think. Because of it, we can plan, coordinate thoughts and actions, perceive visual and sound patterns, and use language. Without it, we would not be human. The surface of the cerebral cortex is grayish. It is sometimes referred to as *gray matter*. This is because it primarily comprises the grayish neural-cell bodies that process the information that the brain receives and sends. In contrast, the underlying *white matter* of the brain's interior comprises mostly white, myelinated axons.

The cerebral cortex forms the outer layer of the two halves of the brain—the left and right cerebral hemispheres (Davidson & Hugdahl, 1995; Galaburda & Rosen, 2003; Gazzaniga & Hutsler, 1999; Levy, 2000). Although the two hemispheres appear to be quite similar, they function differently. The left cerebral hemisphere is specialized for some kinds of activity whereas the right cerebral hemisphere is specialized for other kinds. For example, receptors in the skin on the right side of the body generally send information through the medulla to areas in the left hemisphere in the brain. The receptors on the left side generally transmit information to the right hemisphere. Similarly, the left hemisphere of the brain directs the motor responses on the right side of the body. The right hemisphere directs responses on the left side of the body.

However, not all information transmission is **contralateral**—from one side to another (contra-, "opposite"; lateral, "side"). Some **ipsilateral** transmission—on the same side—occurs as well. For example, odor information from the right nostril goes primarily to the right side of the brain. About half the information from the right eye goes to the right side of the brain, the other half goes to the left side of the brain. In addition to this general tendency for contralateral specialization, the hemispheres also communicate directly with one another. The **corpus callosum** is a dense aggregate of neural fibers connecting the two cerebral hemispheres (Witelson, Kigar, & Walter, 2003). It allows transmission of information back and forth. Once information has reached one hemisphere, the corpus callosum transfers it to the other hemisphere. If the corpus callosum is cut, the two **cerebral hemispheres**—the two halves of the brain—cannot communicate with each other (Glickstein & Berlucchi, 2008). Although some functioning, like language, is highly lateralized, most functioning—even language—depends in large part on integration of the two hemispheres of the brain.

Hemispheric Specialization

How did psychologists find out that the two hemispheres have different responsibilities? The study of hemispheric specialization in the human brain can be traced back to Marc Dax, a country doctor in France. By 1836, Dax had treated more than 40 patients suffering from *aphasia*—loss of speech—as a result of brain damage. Dax noticed a relationship between the loss of speech and the side of the brain in which damage had occurred. In studying his patients' brains after death, Dax saw that in every case there had been damage to the left hemisphere of the brain. He was not able to find even one case of speech loss resulting from damage to the right hemisphere only.

In 1861, French scientist Paul Broca claimed that an autopsy revealed that an aphasic stroke patient had a lesion in the left cerebral hemisphere of the brain. By 1864, Broca was convinced that the left hemisphere of the brain is critical in speech, a view that has held up over time. The specific part of the brain that Broca identified, now called *Broca's area*, contributes to speech (Figure 3.4).

Another important early researcher, German neurologist Carl Wernicke, studied language-deficient patients who could speak but whose speech made no sense. Like Broca, he traced language ability to the left hemisphere. He studied a different precise location, now known as *Wernicke's area*, which contributes to language comprehension (Figure 3.4).

Karl Spencer Lashley, often described as the father of neuropsychology, started studying localization in 1915. He found that implantations of crudely built electrodes in apparently identical locations in the brain yielded different results. Different locations sometimes paradoxically yielded the same results (e.g., see Lashley, 1950). Subsequent researchers, using more sophisticated electrodes and measurement procedures, have found that specific locations do correlate with specific motor

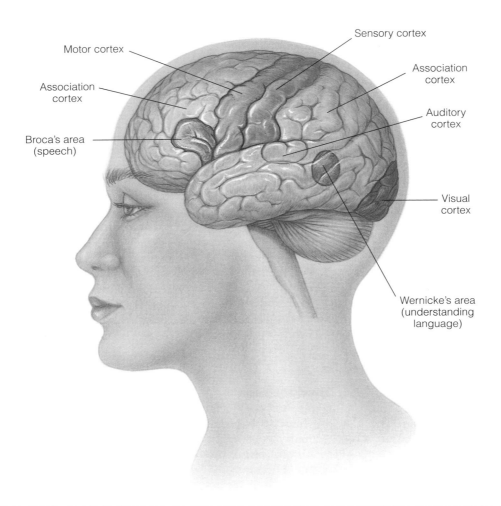

Motor cortex

Sensory cortex

Association
cortex

Association
cortex

Auditory
cortex

Broca's area
(speech)

Visual
cortex

Wernicke's area
(understanding
language)

Figure 3.4   Functional Areas of the Cortex.

Strangely, although people with lesions in Broca's area cannot speak fluently, they can use their voices to sing or shout.

Source: From *Introduction to Psychology*, 11/e, by Richard Atkinson, Rita Atkinson, Daryl Bem, Ed Smith, and Susan Nolen Hoeksema, copyright © 1995 by Harcourt Brace & Company, reproduced by permission of the publisher.

responses across many test sessions. Apparently, Lashley's research was limited by the technology available to him at the time.

Despite the valuable early contributions by Broca, Wernicke, and others, the individual most responsible for modern theory and research on hemispheric specialization was Nobel Prize–winning psychologist Roger Sperry. Sperry (1964) argued that each hemisphere behaves in many respects like a separate brain. In a classic experiment that supports this contention, Sperry and his colleagues severed the corpus callosum connecting the two hemispheres of a cat's brain. They then proved that information presented visually to one cerebral hemisphere of the cat was not recognizable to the other hemisphere. Similar work on monkeys indicated the same discrete performance of each hemisphere (Sperry, 1964).

Some of the most interesting information about how the human brain works, and especially about the respective roles of the hemispheres, has emerged from studies of humans with epilepsy in whom the corpus callosum has been severed. Surgically severing this neurological bridge prevents epileptic seizures from spreading from one hemisphere to another. This procedure thereby drastically reduces the severity of the seizures. However, this procedure also results in a loss of communication between the two hemispheres. It is as if the person has two separate specialized brains processing different information and performing separate functions.

Split-brain patients are people who have undergone operations severing the corpus callosum. Split-brain research reveals fascinating possibilities regarding the ways we think. Many in the field have argued that language is localized in the left hemisphere. Spatial visualization ability appears to be largely localized in the right hemisphere (Farah, 1988a, 1988b; Gazzaniga, 1985). Spatial-orientation tasks also seem to be localized in the right hemisphere (Vogel, Bowers, & Vogel, 2003). It appears that roughly 90% of the adult population has language functions that are predominantly localized within the left hemisphere. There are indications, however, that the lateralization of left-handers differs from that of right-handers, and that for females, the lateralization may not be as pronounced as for males (Vogel, Bowers, & Vogel, 2003). More than 95% of right-handers and about 70% of left-handers have left-hemisphere dominance for language. In people who lack left-hemisphere processing, language development in the right hemisphere retains phonemic and semantic abilities, but it is deficient in syntactic competence (Gazzaniga & Hutsler, 1999).

The left hemisphere is important not only in language but also in movement. People with *apraxia*—disorders of skilled movements—often have had damage to the left hemisphere. Such people have lost the ability to carry out familiar purposeful movements like forming letters when writing by hand (Gazzaniga & Hutsler, 1999; Heilman, Coenen, & Kluger, 2008). Another role of the left hemisphere is to examine past experiences to find patterns. Finding patterns is an important step in the generation of hypotheses (Wolford, Miller, & Gazzaniga, 2000). For example, while observing an airport, you may notice that planes often approach the landing strip from different directions. However, you may soon find that at any given time, all planes approach from the same direction. You then might hypothesize that the direction of their approach may have to do with the wind direction and speed. Thus, you have observed a pattern and generated ideas about what causes this pattern with the help of your left hemisphere.

The right hemisphere is largely "mute" (Levy, 2000). It has little grammatical or phonetic understanding. But it does have very good semantic knowledge. It also is involved in practical language use. People with right-hemisphere damage tend to have deficits in following conversations or stories. They also have difficulties in making inferences from context and in understanding metaphorical or humorous speech (Levy, 2000). The right hemisphere also plays a primary role in self-recognition. In particular, the right hemisphere seems to be responsible for the identification of one's own face (Platek et al., 2004).

In studies of split-brain patients, the patient is presented with a composite photograph that shows a face that is made up of the left and right side of the faces of two different persons (Figure 3.5). They are typically unaware that they saw conflicting information in the two halves of the picture. When asked to give an answer about what they saw in words, they report that they saw the image in the right half of the picture. When they are asked to use the fingers of the left hand (which contralaterally sends and receives information to and from the right hemisphere) to point to what they saw, participants choose the image from the left half of the

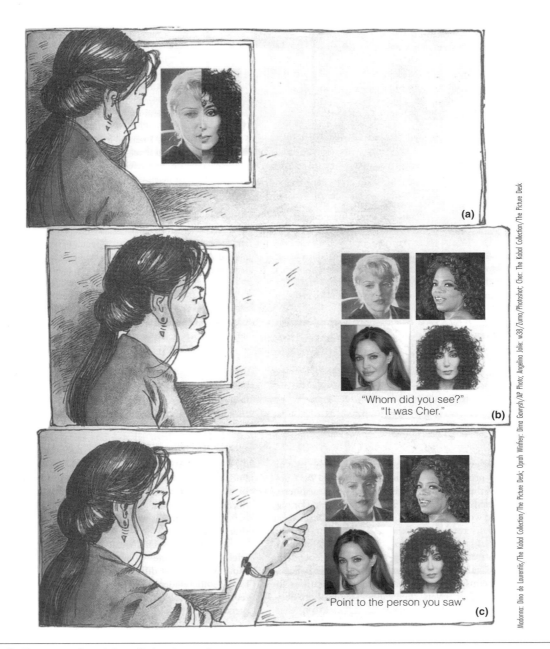

"Whom did you see?"
"It was Cher."   (b)

"Point to the person you saw"   (c)

Figure 3.5   A Study with Split-brain Patients.
In one study, the participant is asked to focus his or her gaze on the center of the screen. Then a chimeric face (a face showing the left side of the face of one person and the right side of another) is flashed on the screen. The participant then is asked to identify what he or she saw, either by speaking or by pointing to one of several normal (not chimeric) faces.

picture. Recall the contralateral association between hemisphere and side of the body. Given this, it seems that the left hemisphere is controlling their verbal processing (speaking) of visual information. The right hemisphere appears to control spatial processing (pointing) of visual information. Thus, the task that the participants are asked to perform is crucial in determining what image the participant thinks was shown.

Gazzaniga (Gazzaniga & LeDoux, 1978) does not believe that the two hemispheres function completely independently but rather that they serve complementary roles. For instance, there is no language processing in the right hemisphere (except in rare cases of early brain damage to the left hemisphere). Rather, only visuospatial processing occurs in the right hemisphere. As an example, Gazzaniga has found that before split-brain surgery, people can draw three-dimensional representations of cubes with each hand (Gazzaniga & LeDoux, 1978). After surgery, however, they can draw a reasonable-looking cube only with the left hand. In each patient, the right hand draws pictures unrecognizable either as cubes or as three-dimensional objects. This finding is important because of the contralateral association between each side of the body and the opposite hemisphere of the brain. Recall that the right hemisphere controls the left hand. The left hand is the only one that a split-brain patient can use for drawing recognizable figures. This experiment thus supports the contention that the right hemisphere is dominant in our comprehension and exploration of spatial relations.

Gazzaniga (1985) argues that the brain, and especially the right hemisphere of the brain, is organized into relatively independent functioning units that work in parallel. According to Gazzaniga, each of the many discrete units of the mind operates relatively independently of the others. These operations are often outside of conscious awareness. While these various independent and often subconscious operations are taking place, the left hemisphere tries to assign interpretations to these operations. Sometimes the left hemisphere perceives that the individual is behaving in a way that does not intrinsically make any particular sense. For example, if you see an adult staggering along a sidewalk at night in a way that does not initially make sense, you may conclude he is drunk or otherwise not in full control of his senses. The brain thus finds a way to assign some meaning to that behavior.

In addition to studying hemispheric differences in language and spatial relations, researchers have tried to determine whether the two hemispheres think in ways that differ from one another. Levy (1974) has found some evidence that the left hemisphere tends to process information analytically (piece-by-piece, usually in a sequence). She argues that the right hemisphere tends to process it holistically (as a whole).

Lobes of the Cerebral Hemispheres

For practical purposes, four **lobes** divide the cerebral hemispheres and cortex into four parts. They are not distinct units. Rather, they are largely arbitrary anatomical regions divided by fissures. Particular functions have been identified with each lobe, but the lobes also interact. The four lobes, named after the bones of the skull lying directly over them (Figure 3.6), are the frontal, parietal, temporal, and occipital lobes. The lobes are involved in numerous functions. Our discussion of them here describes only part of what they do.

The **frontal lobe**, toward the front of the brain, is associated with motor processing and higher thought processes, such as abstract reasoning, problem solving, planning, and judgment (Stuss & Floden, 2003). It tends to be involved when sequences of thoughts or actions are called for. It is critical in producing speech. The *prefrontal cortex*, the region toward the front of the frontal lobe, is involved in complex motor control and tasks that require integration of information over time (Gazzaniga, Ivry, & Mangun, 2002).

The **parietal lobe**, at the upper back portion of the brain, is associated with somatosensory processing. It receives inputs from the neurons regarding touch, pain, temperature sense, and limb position when you are perceiving space and your

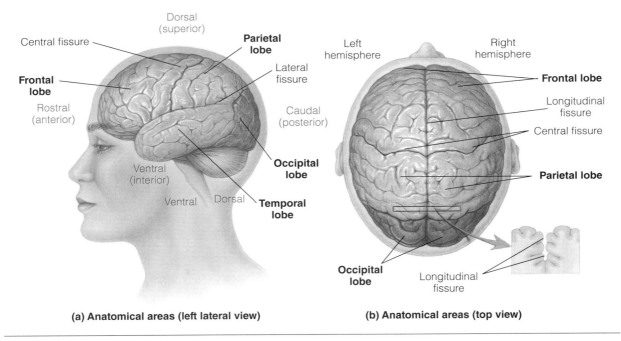

(a) Anatomical areas (left lateral view)   **(b) Anatomical areas (top view)**

Figure 3.6   Four Lobes of the Brain.
The cortex is divided into the frontal, parietal, temporal, and occipital lobes. The lobes have specific functions but also interact to perform complex processes.
Source: From Psychology: *In Search of the Human Mind* by Robert J. Sternberg, copyright © 2000 by Harcourt Brace & Company, reproduced by permission of the publisher.

relationship to it—how you are situated relative to the space you are occupying (Culham, 2003; Gazzaniga, Ivry, & Mangun, 2002). The parietal lobe is also involved in consciousness and paying attention. If you are paying attention to what you are reading, your parietal lobe is activated.

The **temporal lobe**, directly under your temples, is associated with auditory processing (Murray, 2003) and comprehending language. It is also involved in your retention of visual memories. For example, if you are trying to keep in memory Figure 3.6, then your temporal lobe is involved. The temporal lobe also matches new things you see to what you have retained in visual memory.

The **occipital lobe** is associated with visual processing (De Weerd, 2003b). The occipital lobe contains numerous visual areas, each specialized to analyze specific aspects of a scene, including color, motion, location, and form (Gazzaniga, Ivry, & Mangun, 2002). When you go to pick strawberries, your occipital lobe is involved in helping you find the red strawberries in between the green leaves.

Projection areas are the areas in the lobes in which sensory processing occurs. These areas are referred to as projection areas because the nerves contain sensory information going to (projecting to) the thalamus. It is from here that the sensory information is communicated to the appropriate area in the relevant lobe. Similarly, the projection areas communicate motor information downward through the spinal cord to the appropriate muscles via the peripheral nervous system (PNS). Now let us consider the lobes, and especially the frontal lobe in more detail.

The frontal lobe, located toward the front of the head (the face), plays a role in judgment, problem solving, personality, and intentional movement. It contains the **primary motor cortex**, which specializes in the planning, control, and execution of movement, particularly of movement involving any kind of delayed response. If your motor cortex were electrically stimulated, you would react by moving a corresponding body part. The nature of the movement would depend on where in the motor cortex your brain had been stimulated. Control of the various kinds of body movements is located contralaterally on the primary motor cortex. A similar inverse mapping occurs from top to bottom. The lower extremities of the body are represented on the upper (toward the top of the head) side of the motor cortex, and the upper part of the body is represented on the lower side of the motor cortex.

Information going to neighboring parts of the body also comes from neighboring parts of the motor cortex. Thus, the motor cortex can be mapped to show where and in what proportions different parts of the body are represented in the brain (Figure 3.7). Maps of this kind are called "homunculi" (homunculus is Latin for "little person") because they depict the body parts of a person mapped on the brain.

The three other lobes are located farther away from the front of the head. These lobes specialize in sensory and perceptual activity. For example, in the parietal lobe, the **primary somatosensory cortex** receives information from the senses about pressure, texture, temperature, and pain. It is located right behind the frontal lobe's primary motor cortex. If your somatosensory cortex were electrically stimulated, you probably would report feeling as if you had been touched.

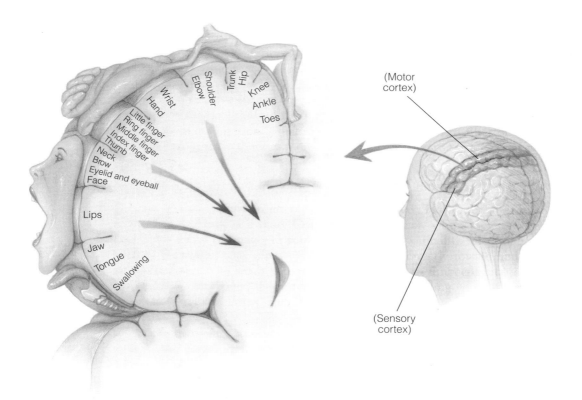

Figure 3.7 (part 1)   Homunculus of the Primary Motor Cortex.
This map of the primary motor cortex is often termed a homunculus (from Latin, "little person") because it is drawn as a cross section of the cortex surrounded by the figure of a small upside-down person whose body parts map out a proportionate correspondence to the parts of the cortex.

From looking at the homunculus (see Figure 3.7), you can see that the relationship of function to form applies in the development of the motor cortex. The same holds true for the somatosensory cortex regions. The more need we have for use, sensitivity, and fine control in a particular body part, the larger the area of cortex generally devoted to that part. For example, we humans are tremendously reliant on our hands and faces in our interactions with the world. We show correspondingly large proportions of the cerebral cortex devoted to sensation in, and motor response by, our hands and face. Conversely, we rely relatively little on our toes for both movement and information gathering. As a result, the toes represent a relatively small area on both the primary motor and somatosensory cortices.

The region of the cerebral cortex pertaining to hearing is located in the temporal lobe, below the parietal lobe. This lobe performs complex auditory analysis. This kind of analysis is needed in understanding human speech or listening to a symphony. The lobe also is specialized—some parts are more sensitive to sounds of higher pitch, others to sounds of lower pitch. The auditory region is primarily contralateral, although both sides of the auditory area have at least some representation from each ear. If your auditory cortex were stimulated electrically, you would report having heard some sort of sound.

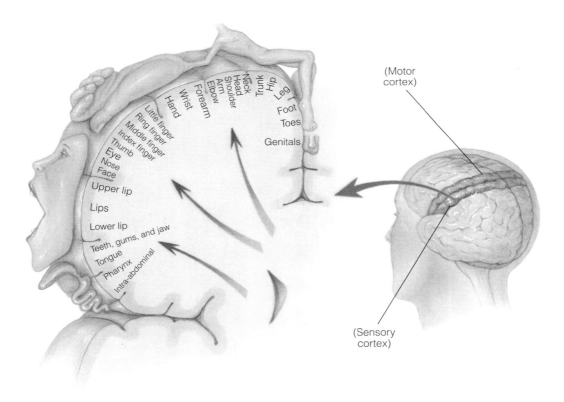

Figure 3.7 (part 2)   Homunculus of the Somatosensory Cortex.

As with the primary motor cortex in the frontal lobe, a homunculs of the somatosensory cortex maps, in inverted form, the parts of the body from which the cortex receives information.

Source: From *In Search of the Human Mind* by Robert J. Sternberg, Copyright © 1995 by Harcourt Brace & Company, reproduced by permission of the publisher.

The **visual cortex** is primarily in the occipital lobe. Some neural fibers carrying visual information travel ipsilaterally from the left eye to the left cerebral hemisphere and from the right eye to the right cerebral hemisphere. Other fibers cross over the *optic chiasma* (from Greek, "visual X" or "visual intersection") and go contralaterally to the opposite hemisphere (Figure 3.8). In particular, neural fibers go from the left side of the visual field for each eye to the right side of the visual cortex. Complementarily, the nerves from the right side of each eye's visual field send information to the left side of the visual cortex.

The brain is a very complex structure, and researchers use a variety of expressions to describe which part of the brain they are speaking of. Figure 3.6 explains some other words that are frequently used to describe different brain regions. These

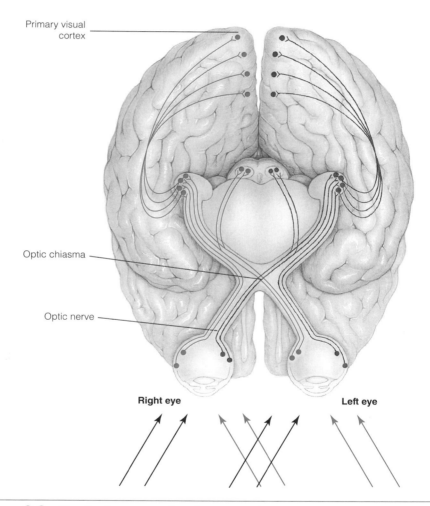

Primary visual cortex

Optic chiasma

Optic nerve

Right eye　　　　　　　　**Left eye**

Figure 3.8　**The Optic Tract and Pathways to the Primary Visual Cortex.**
Some nerve fibers carry visual information ipsilaterally from each eye to each cerebral hemisphere; other fibers cross the optic chiasma and carry visual information contralaterally to the opposite hemisphere.

Source: From *Psychology: In Search of the Human Mind* by Robert J. Sternberg, copyright © 2000 by Harcourt Brace & Company, reproduced by permission of the publisher.

are the words *rostral*, *ventral*, *caudal*, and *dorsal*. They are all derived from Latin words and indicate the part of the brain with respect to other body parts.

- *Rostral* refers to the front part of the brain (literally the "nasal region").
- *Ventral* refers to the bottom surface of the body/brain (the side of the stomach).
- *Caudal* literally means "tail" and refers to the back part of the body/brain.
- *Dorsal* refers to the upside of the brain (it literally means "back," and in animals the back is on the upside of the body).

The brain typically makes up only one fortieth of the weight of an adult human body. Nevertheless, it uses about one fifth of the circulating blood, one fifth of the available glucose, and one fifth of the available oxygen. It is, however, the supreme organ of cognition. Understanding both its structure and function, from the neural to the cerebral levels of organization, is vital to an understanding of cognitive psychology. The recent development of the field of cognitive neuroscience, with its focus on localization of function, reconceptualizes the mind–body question discussed in the beginning of this chapter. The question has changed from "Where is the mind located in the body?" to "Where are particular cognitive operations located in the nervous system?" Throughout the text, we return to these questions in reference to particular cognitive operations and discuss these operations in more detail.

Neuronal Structure and Function

To understand how the entire nervous system processes information, we need to examine the structure and function of the cells that constitute the nervous system. Individual neural cells, called **neurons**, transmit electrical signals from one location to another in the nervous system (Carlson, 2006; Shepherd, 2004). The greatest concentration of neurons is in the neocortex of the brain. The neocortex is the part of the brain associated with complex cognition. This tissue can contain as many as 100,000 neurons per cubic millimeter (Churchland & Sejnowski, 2004). The neurons tend to be arranged in the form of networks, which provide information and feedback to each other within various kinds of information processing (Vogels, Rajan, & Abbott, 2005).

Neurons vary in their structure, but almost all neurons have four basic parts, as illustrated in Figure 3.9. These include a soma (cell body), dendrites, an axon, and terminal buttons.

The **soma**, which contains the nucleus of the cell (the center portion that performs metabolic and reproductive functions for the cell), is responsible for the life of the neuron and connects the dendrites to the axon. The many **dendrites** are branch-like structures that receive information from other neurons, and the soma integrates the information. Learning is associated with the formation of new neuronal connections. Hence, it occurs in conjunction with increased complexity or ramification in the branching structure of dendrites in the brain. The single **axon** is a long, thin tube that extends (and sometimes splits) from the soma and responds to the information, when appropriate, by transmitting an electrochemical signal, which travels to the terminus (end), where the signal can be transmitted to other neurons.

Axons are of two basic, roughly equally occurring kinds, distinguished by the presence or absence of myelin. **Myelin** is a white, fatty substance that surrounds some of the axons of the nervous system, which accounts for some of the whiteness of the white matter of the brain. Some axons are myelinated (in that they are surrounded by a myelin sheath). This sheath, which insulates and protects longer axons from electrical interference by other neurons in the area, also speeds up the

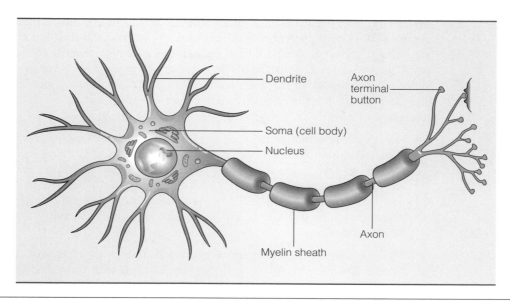

Figure 3.9 **The Composition of a Neuron.**
The image shows a neuron with its various components. The information arrives at the dendrites and then is transferred through the axon to the terminal buttons.

conduction of information. In fact, transmission in myelinated axons can reach 100 meters per second (equal to about 224 miles per hour). Moreover, myelin is not distributed continuously along the axon. It is distributed in segments broken up by nodes of Ranvier. **Nodes of Ranvier** are small gaps in the myelin coating along the axon, which serve to increase conduction speed even more by helping to create electrical signals, also called *action potentials*, which are then conducted down the axon. The degeneration of myelin sheaths along axons in certain nerves is associated with multiple sclerosis, an autoimmune disease. It results in impairments of coordination and balance. In severe cases this disease is fatal. The second kind of axon lacks the myelin coat altogether. Typically, these unmyelinated axons are smaller and shorter (as well as slower) than the myelinated axons. As a result, they do not need the increased conduction velocity myelin provides for longer axons (Giuliodori & DiCarlo, 2004).

The **terminal buttons** are small knobs found at the ends of the branches of an axon that do not directly touch the dendrites of the next neuron. Rather, there is a very small gap, the synapse. The **synapse** serves as a juncture between the terminal buttons of one or more neurons and the dendrites (or sometimes the soma) of one or more other neurons (Carlson, 2006). Synapses are important in cognition. Rats show increases in both the size and the number of synapses in the brain as a result of learning (Federmeier, Kleim & Greenough, 2002). Decreased cognitive functioning, as in Alzheimer's disease, is associated with reduced efficiency of synaptic transmission of nerve impulses (Selkoe, 2002). Signal transmission between neurons occurs when the terminal buttons release one or more neurotransmitters at the synapse. These **neurotransmitters** are chemical messengers for transmission of information across the synaptic gap to the receiving dendrites of the next neuron (von Bohlen und Halbach & Dermietzel, 2006).

Although scientists have identified more than 100 transmitter substances, it seems likely that more remain to be discovered. Medical and psychological researchers are working to discover and understand neurotransmitters. In particular, they wish to understand how the neurotransmitters interact with drugs, moods, abilities, and perceptions. We know much about the mechanics of impulse transmission in nerves. But we know relatively little about how the nervous system's chemical activity relates to psychological states. Despite the limits on present knowledge, we have gained some insight into how several of these substances affect our psychological functioning.

At present, it appears that three types of chemical substances are involved in neurotransmission:

- *monoamine neurotransmitters* are synthesized by the nervous system through enzymatic actions on one of the amino acids (constituents of proteins, such as choline, tyrosine, and tryptophan) in our diet (e.g., acetylcholine, dopamine, and serotonin);
- *amino-acid neurotransmitters* are obtained directly from the amino acids in our diet without further synthesis (e.g., gamma-aminobutyric acid, or GABA);
- *neuropeptides* are peptide chains (molecules made from the parts of two or more amino acids).

Table 3.2 lists some examples of neurotransmitters, together with their typical functions in the nervous system and their associations with cognitive processing.

Table 3.2   Neurotransmitters

Neurotransmitters	Description	General Function	Specific Examples
Acetylcholine (Ach)	Monoamine neurotransmitter synthesized from choline	Excitatory in brain and either excitatory (at skeletal muscles) or inhibitory (at heart muscles) elsewhere in the body	Believed to be involved in memory because of high concentration found in the hippocampus (McIntyre et al., 2002)
Dopamine (DA)	Monoamine neurotransmitter synthesized from tyrosine	Influences movement, attention, and learning; mostly inhibitory but some excitatory effects	Parkinson's disease, characterized by tremors and limb rigidity, results from too little DA; some schizophrenia symptoms are associated with too much DA
Epinephrine and norepinephrine	Monoamine neurotransmitter synthesized from tyrosine	Hormones (also known as adrenaline and noradrenaline) involved in regulation of alertness	Involved in diverse effects on body related to fight-or-flight reactions, anger, and fear
Serotonin	Monoamine neurotransmitter synthesized from tryptophan	Involved in arousal, sleep and dreaming, and mood; usually inhibitory but some excitatory effects	Normally inhibits dreaming; defects in serotonin system are linked to severe depression
GABA (gamma-aminobutyric acid)	Amino acid neurotransmitter	General neuromodulatory effects resulting from inhibitory influences on presynaptic axons	Currently believed to influence certain mechanisms for learning and memory (Izquierdo & Medina, 1997)
Glutamate	Amino acid neurotransmitter	General neuromodulatory effects resulting from excitatory influences on presynaptic axons	Currently believed to influence certain mechanisms for learning and memory (Riedel, Platt, & Micheau, 2003)
Neuropeptides	Peptide chains serving as neurotransmitters	General neuromodulatory effects resulting from influences on postsynaptic membranes	Endorphins play a role in pain relief. Neuromodulating neuropeptides sometimes are released to enhance the effects of Ach

Acetylcholine is associated with memory functions, and the loss of acetylcholine through Alzheimer's disease has been linked to impaired memory functioning in Alzheimer's patients (Hasselmo, 2006). Acetylcholine also plays an important role in sleep and arousal. When someone awakens, there is an increase in the activity of so-called cholinergic neurons in the basal forebrain and the brainstem (Rockland, 2000).

Dopamine is associated with attention, learning, and movement coordination. Dopamine also is involved in motivational processes, such as reward and reinforcement. Schizophrenics show very high levels of dopamine. This fact has led to the "dopamine theory of schizophrenia" which suggests that high levels of dopamine may be partially responsible for schizophrenic conditions. Drugs used to combat schizophrenia often inhibit dopamine activity (von Bohlen und Halbach & Dermietzel, 2006).

In contrast, patients with Parkinson's disease show very low dopamine levels, which leads to the typical trembling and movement problems associated with Parkinson's. When patients receive medication that increases their dopamine level, they (as well as healthy people who receive dopamine) sometimes show an increase in pathological gambling. Gambling is a compulsive disorder that results from impaired impulse control. When dopamine treatment is suspended, these patients no longer exhibit this behavior (Drapier et al., 2006; Voon et al., 2007; Abler et al., 2009). These findings support the role of dopamine in motivational processes and impulse control.

Serotonin plays an important role in eating behavior and body-weight regulation. High serotonin levels play a role in some types of anorexia. Specifically, serotonin seems to play a role in the types of anorexia resulting from illness or treatment of illness. For example, patients suffering from cancer or undergoing dialysis often experience a severe loss of appetite (Agulera et al., 2000; Davis et al., 2004). This loss of appetite is related, in both cases, to high serotonin levels. Serotonin is also involved in aggression and regulation of impulsivity (Rockland, 2000). Drugs that block serotonin tend to result in an increase in aggressive behavior.

The preceding description drastically oversimplifies the intricacies of constant neuronal communication. Such complexities make it difficult to understand what is happening in the normal brain when we are thinking, feeling, and interacting with our environment. Many researchers seek to understand the normal information processes of the brain by investigating what is going wrong in the brains of people affected by neurological and psychological disorders. In the case of depression, for example, in the early 1950s a drug (iproniazid, a monoamine oxidase inhibitor) intended to treat tuberculosis was found to have a mood-improving effect. This finding led to some early research on the chemical causes of depression. Perhaps if we can understand what has gone awry—what chemicals are out of balance—we can figure out how processes normally work and how to put things back into balance. One way of doing so might be by providing needed neurotransmitters or by inhibiting the effects of overabundant neurotransmitters.

Receptors and Drugs

Receptors in the brain that normally are occupied by the standard neurotransmitters can be hijacked by psychopharmacologically active drugs, legal or illegal. In such cases, the molecules of the drugs enter into receptors that normally would be for neurotransmitter substances endogenous in (originating in) the body.

When people stop using the drugs, withdrawal symptoms arise. Once a user has formed narcotic dependence, for example, the form of treatment differs for *acute toxicity* (the damage done from a particular overdose) versus *chronic toxicity* (the damage done by long-term drug addiction). Acute toxicity is often treated with naloxone or related drugs. Naloxone (as well as a related drug, naltrexone) occupies opiate receptors in the brain better than the opiates themselves occupy those sites; thus, it blocks all effects of narcotics. In fact, naloxone has such a strong affinity for the endorphin receptors in the brain that it actually displaces molecules of narcotics already in these receptors and then moves into the receptors. Naloxone is not addictive, however. Even though it binds to receptors, it does not activate them. Although naloxone can be a life-saving drug for someone who has overdosed on opiates, its effects are short-lived. Thus, it is a poor long-term treatment for drug addiction.

In narcotic detoxification, methadone often is substituted for the narcotic (typically, heroin). Methadone binds to endorphin receptor sites in a similar way to naloxone and reduces the heroin cravings and withdrawal symptoms of addicted persons. After the substitution, gradually decreasing dosages are administered to the patient until he or she is drug-free. Unfortunately, the usefulness of methadone is limited by the fact that it is addictive.

✔ CONCEPT CHECK

1. Name some of the major structures in each part of the brain (forebrain, midbrain, and hindbrain) and their functions.
2. What does *localization of function* mean?
3. Why do researchers believe that the brain exhibits some level of hemispheric specialization?
4. What are the four lobes of the brain and some of the functions associated with them?
5. How do neurons transmit information?

Viewing the Structures and Functions of the Brain

Scientists can use many methods for studying the human brain. These methods include both *postmortem* (from Latin, "after death") studies and *in vivo* (from Latin, "living") techniques on both humans and animals. Each technique provides important information about the structure and function of the human brain. Even some of the earliest postmortem studies still influence our thinking about how the brain performs certain functions. However, the recent trend is to focus on techniques that provide information about human mental functioning as it is occurring. This trend is in contrast to the earlier trend of waiting to find people with disorders and then studying their brains after they died. Because postmortem studies are the foundation for later work, we discuss them first. We then move on to the more modern in vivo techniques.

Postmortem Studies

Postmortem studies and the dissection of brains have been done for centuries. Even today, researchers often use dissection to study the relation between the brain and behavior. In the ideal case, studies start during the lifetime of a person. Researchers observe and document the behavior of people who show signs of brain damage while they are alive (Wilson, 2003). Later, after the patients die, the researchers examine the patients' brains for *lesions*—areas where body tissue has been damaged, such as from injury or disease. Then the researchers infer that the lesioned locations may be related to the behavior that was affected. The case of Phineas Gage, discussed in Chapter 1, was explored through these methods.

Through such investigations, researchers may be able to trace a link between an observed type of behavior and anomalies in a particular location in the brain. An early example is Paul Broca's (1824–1880) famous patient, Tan (so named because that was the only syllable he was capable of uttering). Tan had severe speech problems. These problems were linked to lesions in an area of the frontal lobe (Broca's area). This area is involved in certain functions of speech production. In more recent times, postmortem examinations of victims of Alzheimer's disease (an illness that causes devastating losses of memory; see Chapter 5) have led researchers to identify some of the brain structures involved in memory (e.g., the hippocampus, described earlier in this chapter). These examinations also have identified some of the microscopic aberrations associated with the disease process (e.g., distinctive tangled fibers in the brain tissue). Although lesioning techniques provide the basic foundation for understanding the relation of the brain to behavior, they are limited in that they cannot be performed on the living brain. As a result, they do not offer insights into more specific physiological processes of the brain. For this kind of information, we need to study live nonhuman animals.

Studying Live Nonhuman Animals

Scientists also want to understand the physiological processes and functions of the living brain. To study the changing activity of the living brain, scientists must use in vivo research. Many early in vivo techniques were performed exclusively on animals. For example, Nobel Prize–winning research on visual perception arose from in vivo studies investigating the electrical activity of individual cells in particular regions of the brains of animals (Hubel & Wiesel, 1963, 1968, 1979; see Chapter 2).

To obtain *single-cell recordings*, researchers insert a very thin electrode next to a single neuron in the brain of an animal (usually a monkey or a cat). They then record the changes in electrical activity that occur in the cell when the animal is exposed to a stimulus. In this way, scientists can measure the effects of certain kinds of stimuli, such as visually presented lines, on the activity of individual neurons. Neurons fire constantly, even if no stimuli are present, so the task of the researcher is to find stimuli that produce a consistent change in the activity of the neuron. This technique can be used only in laboratory animals, not in humans, because no safe way has yet been devised to perform such recordings in humans.

A second group of animal studies includes selective *lesioning*—surgically removing or damaging part of the brain—to observe resulting functional deficits (Al'bertin, Mulder, & Wiener, 2003; Mohammed, Jonsson, & Archer, 1986). In recent years, researchers have found neurochemical ways to induce lesions in animals' brains by administering drugs that destroy only cells that use a particular neurotransmitter. Some drugs' effects are reversible, so that conductivity in the brain is disrupted only for a limited amount of time (Gazzaniga, Ivry, & Mangun, 2009).

A third way of doing research with animals is by employing genetic knockout procedures. By using genetic manipulations, animals can be created that lack certain kinds of cells or receptors in the brain. Comparisons with normal animals then indicate what the function of the missing receptors or cells may be.

Studying Live Humans

Obviously, many of the techniques used to study live animals cannot be used on human participants. Generalizations to humans based on these studies are therefore somewhat limited. However, an array of less invasive imaging techniques for use with humans has been developed. These techniques—electrical recordings, static imaging, and metabolic imaging—are described in this section.

Electrical Recordings

The transmission of signals in the brain occurs through electrical potentials. When recorded, this activity appears as waves of various widths (frequencies) and heights (intensities). **Electroencephalograms (EEGs)** are recordings of the electrical frequencies and intensities of the living brain, typically recorded over relatively long periods (Picton & Mazaheri, 2003). Through EEGs, it is possible to study brain-wave activity indicative of changing mental states such as deep sleep or dreaming. To obtain EEG recordings, electrodes are placed at various points along the surface of the scalp. The electrical activity of underlying brain areas is then recorded. Therefore, the information is not localized to specific cells. However, the EEG is very sensitive to changes over time. For example, EEG recordings taken during sleep reveal changing patterns of electrical activity involving the whole brain. Different patterns emerge during dreaming versus deep sleep. EEGs are also used as a tool in the diagnosis of epilepsy because they can indicate whether seizures appear in both sides of the brain at the same time, or whether they originate in one part of the brain and then spread.

To relate electrical activity to a particular event or task (e.g., seeing a flash of light or listening to sentences), EEG waves can be measured when participants are exposed to a particular stimulus. An **event-related potential (ERP)** is the record of a small change in the brain's electrical activity in response to a stimulating event. The fluctuation typically lasts a mere fraction of a second. ERPs provide very good information about the time-course of task-related brain activity. In any one EEG recording, there is a great deal of "noise"—that is, irrelevant electrical activity going on in the brain. ERPs cancel out the effects of noise by averaging out activity that is not task-related. Therefore, the EEG waves are averaged over a large number (e.g., 100) of trials to reveal the event-related potentials (ERPs). The resulting wave forms show characteristic spikes related to the timing of electrical activity, but they reveal only very general information about the location of that activity (because of low spatial resolution as a result of the placement of scalp electrodes).

The ERP technique has been used in a wide variety of studies. Some studies of mental abilities like selective attention have investigated individual differences by using event-related potentials (e.g., Troche et al., 2009). ERP methods are also used to examine language processing. One study examined children who suffered from developmental language impairment and compared them with those who did not. The children were presented with pictures and a sound or word, and then had to decide whether the picture, on the one hand, and the sound or word, on the other, matched. For example, in a matching pair, a picture of a rooster would be presented with either the sound "cockadoodledoo" or the spoken word "crowing." A mismatch would be the picture of the rooster presented with the sound "ding dong" or the spoken word "chiming." There was no difference between the two groups when they had to match the picture with the sound. The children with language impairment had greater difficulty matching the picture with the spoken word and exhibited a delayed N400 effect (the N400 is a component of ERPs that occurs especially when people are presented with meaningful stimuli). The results confirmed the hypothesis that the language networks of the children with language impairment may be weakened (Cummings & Ceponiene, 2010).

ERP can be used to examine developmental changes in cognitive abilities. These experiments provide a more complete understanding of the relationship between brain and cognitive development (Taylor & Baldeweg, 2002).

The high degree of temporal resolution afforded by ERPs can be used to complement other techniques. For example, ERPs and positron emission tomography (PET) were used to pinpoint areas involved in word association (Posner & Raichle, 1994). Using ERPs, the investigators found that participants showed increased activity in certain parts of the brain (left lateral frontal cortex, left posterior cortex, and right insular cortex) when they made rapid associations to given words. Another study showed that decreases in electrical potentials are twice as great for tones that are attended to as for tones that are ignored (see Phelps, 1999). As with any technique, EEGs and ERPs provide only a glimpse of brain activity. They are most helpful when used in conjunction with other techniques to identify particular brain areas involved in cognition.

Static Imaging Techniques

Psychologists use still images to reveal the structures of the brain (see Figure 3.10 and Table 3.3). The techniques include angiograms, computed tomography (CT) scans, and magnetic resonance imaging scans (MRI). The X-ray–based techniques (angiogram and CT scan) allow for the observation of large abnormalities of the brain, such as damage resulting from strokes or tumors. However, they are limited

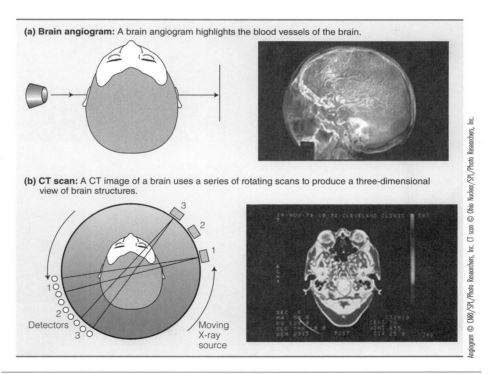

(a) Brain angiogram: A brain angiogram highlights the blood vessels of the brain.

(b) CT scan: A CT image of a brain uses a series of rotating scans to produce a three-dimensional view of brain structures.

Detectors

Moving X-ray source

Figure 3.10   Brain Imaging Techniques.

Various techniques have been developed to picture the structures—and sometimes the processes—of the brain.

in their resolution and cannot provide much information about smaller lesions and aberrations.

Computed tomography (CT or CAT). Unlike conventional X-ray methods that only allow a two-dimensional view of an object, a CT scan consists of several X-ray images of the brain taken from different vantage points that, when combined, result in a three-dimensional image.

The aim of an *angiography* is not to look at the structures in the brain, but rather to examine the blood flow. When the brain is active, it needs energy, which is

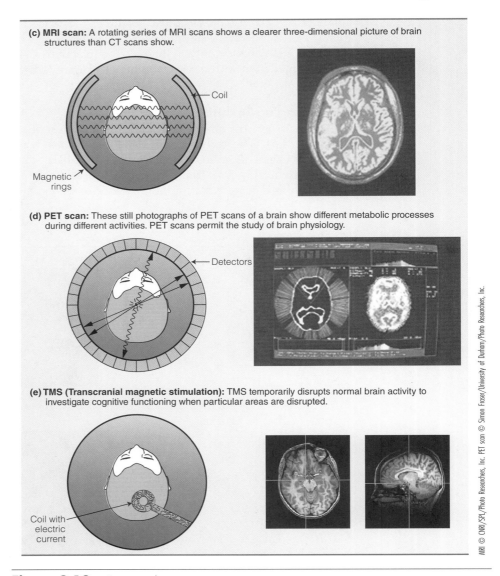

(c) MRI scan: A rotating series of MRI scans shows a clearer three-dimensional picture of brain structures than CT scans show.

Coil

Magnetic rings

(d) PET scan: These still photographs of PET scans of a brain show different metabolic processes during different activities. PET scans permit the study of brain physiology.

Detectors

(e) TMS (Transcranial magnetic stimulation): TMS temporarily disrupts normal brain activity to investigate cognitive functioning when particular areas are disrupted.

Coil with electric current

Figure 3.10   Continued

Table 3.3   Cognitive Neuropsychological Methods for Studying Brain Functioning

Method	Procedure	Suitable for Humans?	Advantages	Disadvantages
Single-cell recording	Very thin electrode is inserted next to a single neuron. Changes in electrical activity occurring in the cell are then recorded.	No	Rather precise recording of electrical activity	Cannot be used with humans
EEG	Changes in electrical potentials are recorded via electrodes attached to scalp.	Yes	Relatively noninvasive	Imprecise
ERP	Changes in electrical potentials are recorded via electrodes attached to scalp.	Yes	Relatively noninvasive	Does not show actual brain images
PET	Participants ingest a mildly radioactive form of oxygen that emits positrons as it is metabolized. Changes in concentration of positrons in targeted areas of the brain are then measured.	Yes	Shows images of the brain in action	Less useful for fast processes
fMRI	Creates magnetic field that induces changes in the particles of oxygen atoms. More active areas draw more oxygenated blood than do less active areas in the brain. The differences in the amounts of oxygen consumed form the basis for fMRI measurements.	Yes	Shows images of the brain in action; more precise than PET	Requires individual to be placed in uncomfortable scanner for some time
TMS	Involves placing a coil on a person's head and then allowing an electrical current to pass through it. The current generates a magnetic field. This field disrupts the small area (usually no more than a cubic centimeter) beneath it. The researcher can then look at cognitive functioning when the particular area is disrupted.	Yes	Enables researcher to pinpoint how disruption of a particular area of brain affects cognitive functioning	Potentially dangerous if misused
MEG	Involves measuring brain activity through detection of magnetic fields by placing a device over the head.	Yes	Extremely precise spatial and temporal resolution	Requires expensive machine not readily available to researchers

transported to the brain in the form of oxygen and glucose by means of the blood. In angiography, a dye is injected into an artery that leads to the brain, and then an X-ray image is taken. The image shows the circulatory system, and it is possible to detect strokes (disruption of the blood flow often caused by the blockage of the arteries through a foreign substance) or aneurysms (abnormal ballooning of an artery), or arteriosclerosis (a hardening of arteries that makes them inflexible and narrow).

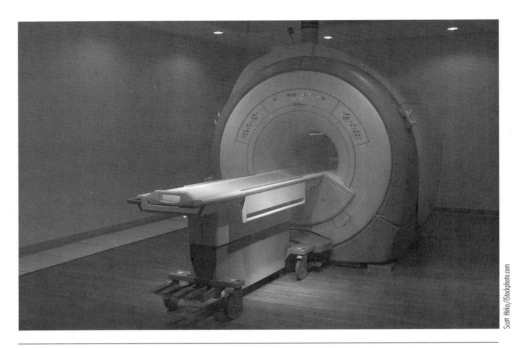

Scott Hitko/iStockphoto.com

Figure 3.11 Magnetic Resonance Imaging (MRI).
An MRI machine can provide data that show what areas of the brain are involved in different kinds of cognitive processing.

The **magnetic resonance imaging (MRI)** scan is of great interest to cognitive psychologists (Figure 3.11). The MRI reveals high-resolution images of the structure of the living brain by computing and analyzing magnetic changes in the energy of the orbits of nuclear particles in the molecules of the body. There are two kinds of MRIs—structural MRIs and functional MRIs. Structural MRIs provide images of the brain's size and shape whereas functional MRIs visualize the parts of the brain that are activated when a person is engaged in a particular task. MRIs allow for a much clearer picture of the brain than CT scans. A strong magnetic field is passed through the brain of a patient. A scanner detects various patterns of electromagnetic changes in the atoms of the brain. These molecular changes are analyzed by a computer to produce a three-dimensional picture of the brain. This picture includes detailed information about brain structures. For example, MRI has been used to show that musicians who play string instruments such as the violin or the cello tend to have an expansion of the brain in an area of the right hemisphere that controls left-hand movement (because control of hands is contralateral, with the right side of the brain controlling the left hand, and vice versa; Münte, Altenmüller, & Jäncke, 2002). We tend to view the brain as controlling what we can do. This study is a good example of how what we do—our experience—can affect the development of the brain. MRI also facilitates the detection of lesions, such as lesions associated with particular disorders of language use, but does not provide much information about physiological processes. However, the two techniques discussed in the following section do provide such information.

Metabolic Imaging

Metabolic imaging techniques rely on changes that take place within the brain as a result of increased consumption of glucose and oxygen in active areas of the brain. The basic idea is that active areas in the brain consume more glucose and oxygen than do inactive areas during some tasks. An area specifically required by one task ought to be more active during that task than during more generalized processing and thus should require more glucose and oxygen. Scientists attempt to pinpoint specialized areas for a task by using the *subtraction method.* This method uses two different measurements: one that was taken while the subject was involved in a more general or control activity, and one that was taken when the subject was engaged in the task of interest. The difference between these two measurements equals the additional activation recorded while the subject is engaged in the target task as opposed to the control task. The subtraction method thus involves subtracting activity during the control task from activity during the task of interest. The resulting difference in activity is analyzed statistically. This analysis determines which areas are responsible for performance of a particular task above and beyond the more general activity. For example, suppose the experimenter wishes to determine which area of the brain is most important for retrieval of word meanings. The experimenter might subtract activity during a task involving reading of words from activity during a task involving the physical recognition of the letters of the words. The difference in activity would be presumed to reflect the additional resources used in retrieval of meaning.

There is one important caveat to remember about these techniques: Scientists have no way of determining whether the net effect of this difference in activity is excitatory or inhibitory (because some neurons are activated by, and some are inhibited by, other neurons' neurotransmitters). Therefore, the subtraction technique reveals net brain activity for particular areas. It cannot show whether the area's effect is positive or negative. Moreover, the method assumes that activation is purely additive—that it can be discovered through a subtraction method without taking into account interactions among elements.

This description greatly oversimplifies the subtraction method. But it shows at a general level how scientists assess physiological functioning of particular areas using imaging techniques.

Positron emission tomography (PET) scans measure increases in oxygen consumption in active brain areas during particular kinds of information processing (O'Leary et al., 2007; Raichle, 1998, 1999). To track their use of oxygen, participants are given a mildly radioactive form of oxygen that emits positrons as it is metabolized (positrons are particles that have roughly the same size and mass as electrons, but that are positively rather than negatively charged). Next, the brain is scanned to detect positrons. A computer analyzes the data to produce images of the physiological functioning of the brain in action.

PET scans can assist in the diagnosis of disorders of cognitive decline like Alzheimer's by searching for abnormalities in the brain (Patterson et al., 2009). PET scans have been used to show that blood flow increases to the occipital lobe of the brain during visual processing (Posner et al., 1988). PET scans also are used for comparatively studying the brains of people who score high versus low on intelligence tests. When high-scoring people are engaged in cognitively demanding tasks, their brains seem to use glucose more efficiently—in highly task-specific areas of the brain. The brains of people with lower scores appear to use glucose more diffusely, across larger regions of the brain (Haier et al., 1992). Likewise, a study has shown that Broca's area as well as the left anterior temporal area and the cerebellum are involved in the learning of new words (Groenholm et al., 2005).

PET scans have been used to illustrate the integration of information from various parts of the cortex (Castelli et al, 2005; Posner et al., 1988). Specifically, PET scans were used to study regional cerebral blood flow during several activities involving the reading of single words. When participants looked at a word on a screen, areas of their visual cortex showed high levels of activity. When they spoke a word, their motor cortex was highly active. When they heard a word spoken, their auditory cortex was activated. When they produced words related to the words they saw (requiring high-level integration of visual, auditory, and motor information), the relevant areas of the cortex showed the greatest amount of activity.

PET scans are not highly precise because they require a minimum of about half a minute to produce data regarding glucose consumption. If an area of the brain shows different amounts of activity over the course of time measurement, the activity levels are averaged, potentially leading to conclusions that are less than precise.

Functional magnetic resonance imaging (fMRI) is a neuroimaging technique that uses magnetic fields to construct a detailed representation in three dimensions of levels of activity in various parts of the brain at a given moment in time. This technique builds on MRI, but it uses increases in oxygen consumption to construct images of brain activity. The basic idea is the same as in PET scans. However, the fMRI technique does not require the use of radioactive particles. Rather, the participant performs a task while placed inside an MRI machine. This machine typically looks like a tunnel. When someone is wholly or partially inserted in the tunnel, he or she is surrounded by a donut-shaped magnet. Functional MRI creates a magnetic field that induces changes in the particles of oxygen atoms. More active areas draw more oxygenated blood than do less active areas in the brain. So shortly after a brain area has been active, a reduced amount of oxygen should be detectable in this area. This observation forms the basis for fMRI measurements. These measurements then are computer analyzed to provide the most precise information currently available about the physiological functioning of the brain's activity during task performance.

This technique is less invasive than PET. It also has higher temporal resolution—measurements can be taken for activity lasting fractions of a second, rather than only for activity lasting minutes to hours. One major drawback is the expense of fMRI. Relatively few researchers have access to the required machinery and testing of participants is very time consuming.

The fMRI technique can identify regions of the brain active in many areas, such as vision (Engel et al., 1994; Kitada et al., 2010), attention (Cohen et al.; 1994; Samanez-Larkin et al., 2009), language (Gaillard et al., 2003; Stein et al., 2009), and memory (Gabrieli et al., 1996; Wolf, 2009). For example, fMRI has shown that the lateral prefrontal cortex is essential for working memory. This is a part of memory that processes information that is actively in use at a given time (McCarthy et al., 1994). Also, fMRI methods have been applied to the examination of brain changes in patient populations, including persons with schizophrenia and epilepsy (Detre, 2004; Weinberger et al., 1996).

A related procedure is *pharmacological MRI* (phMRI). The phMRI combines fMRI methods with the study of psychopharmacological agents. These studies examine the influence and role of particular psychopharmacological agents on the brain. They have allowed the examination of the role of agonists (which strengthen responses) and antagonists (which weaken responses) on the same receptor cells. These studies have allowed for the examination of drugs used for treatment. The investigators can predict the responses of patients to neurochemical treatments through examination of the person's brain makeup. Overall, these methods aid in the understanding of brain areas and the effects of psychopharmacological agents on brain functioning (Baliki et al., 2005; Easton et al., 2007; Honey & Bullmore, 2004; Kalisch et al., 2004).

Another procedure related to fMRI is *diffusion tensor imaging* (DTI). Diffusion tensor imaging examines the restricted dispersion of water in tissue and, of special interest, in axons. Water in the brain cannot move freely, but rather, its movement is restricted by the axons and their myelin sheaths. DTI measures how far protons have moved in a particular direction within a specific time interval. This technique has been useful in the mapping of the white matter of the brain and in examining neural circuits. Some applications of this technique include examination of traumatic brain injury, schizophrenia, brain maturation, and multiple sclerosis (Ardekani et al., 2003; Beyer, Ranga, & Krishnan, 2002; Ramachandra et al., 2003; Sotak, 2002; Sundgren et al., 2004).

A recently developed technique for studying brain activity bypasses some of the problems with other techniques (Walsh & Pascual-Leone, 2005). **Transcranial magnetic stimulation (TMS)** temporarily disrupts the normal activity of the brain in a limited area. Therefore, it can imitate lesions in the brain or stimulate brain regions. TMS requires placing a coil on a person's head and then allowing an electrical current to pass through it (Figure 3.10). The current generates a magnetic field. This field disrupts the small area (usually no more than a cubic centimeter) beneath it. The researcher can then look at cognitive functioning when the particular area is disrupted. This method is restricted to brain regions that lie close to the surface of the head. An advantage to TMS is that it is possible to examine causal relationships with this method because the brain activity in a particular area is disrupted and then its influence on task-performance is observed; most other methods allow the investigator to examine only correlational relationships by the observation of brain function (Gazzaniga, Ivry, & Mangun, 2009). TMS has been used, for example, to produce "virtual lesions" and investigate which areas of the brain are involved when people grasp or reach for an object (Koch & Rothwell, 2009). It is even hypothesized that repeated magnetic impulses (rTMS) can serve as a therapeutic means in the treatment of neuropsychological disorders like depression or anxiety disorders (Pallanti & Bernardi, 2009).

Magnetoencephalography (MEG) measures activity of the brain from outside the head (similar to EEG) by picking up magnetic fields emitted by changes in brain activity. This technique allows localization of brain signals so that it is possible to know what different parts of the brain are doing at different times. It is one of the most precise of the measuring methods. MEG is used to help surgeons locate pathological structures in the brain (Baumgartner, 2000). A recent application of

MEG involved patients who reported phantom limb pain. In cases of phantom limb pain, a patient reports pain in a body part that has been removed, for example, a missing foot. When certain areas of the brain are stimulated, phantom limb pain is reduced. MEG has been used to examine the changes in brain activity before, during, and after electrical stimulation. These changes in brain activity corresponded with changes in the experience of phantom limb pain (Kringelbach et al., 2007).

Current techniques still do not provide unambiguous mappings of particular functions to particular brain structures, regions, or even processes. Rather, some discrete structures, regions, or processes of the brain appear to be involved in particular cognitive functions. Our current understanding of how particular cognitive functions are linked to particular brain structures or processes allows us only to infer suggestive indications of some kind of relationship. Through sophisticated analyses, we can infer increasingly precise relationships. But we are not yet at a point where we can determine the specific cause–effect relationship between a given brain structure or process and a particular cognitive function because particular functions may be influenced by multiple structures, regions, or processes of the brain. Finally, these techniques provide the best information only in conjunction with other experimental techniques for understanding the complexities of cognitive functioning. These combinations generally are completed with human participants, although some researchers have combined in vivo studies in animals with brain-imaging techniques (Dedeogle et al., 2004; Kornblum et al., 2000; Logothetis, 2004).

✔ CONCEPT CHECK

1. In the investigation of the structure and functions of the brain, what methods of study can be used only in nonhuman animals, and what methods can be used in humans?
2. What are typical questions that are investigated with EEGs, PETs, and fMRIs?
3. Why is it useful to have imaging methods that display the metabolism of the brain?
4. What are the advantages and disadvantages of in vivo techniques compared to postmortem studies?

Brain Disorders

A number of brain disorders can impair cognitive functioning. Brain disorders can give us valuable insight into the functioning of the brain. As mentioned above, scientists often write detailed notes about the condition of a patient and analyze the brain of a patient once the patient has died to see which areas in the brain may have caused the symptoms the patient experienced. Furthermore, with the in vivo techniques that have been developed over the past decades, many tests and diagnostic procedures can be executed during the lifetime of a patient to help ease patient symptoms and to gain new insight into how the brain works.

Stroke

Vascular disorder is a brain disorder caused by a stroke. Strokes occur when the flow of blood to the brain undergoes a sudden disruption. People who experience stroke typically show marked loss of cognitive functioning. The nature of the loss depends on the area of the brain that is affected by the stroke. There may be paralysis, pain, numbness, a loss of speech, a loss of language comprehension, impairments in thought processes, a loss of movement in parts of the body, or other symptoms.

Two kinds of stroke may occur (*NINDS stroke information page, 2009*). An *ischemic stroke* usually occurs when a buildup of fatty tissue occurs in blood vessels over a period of years, and a piece of this tissue breaks off and gets lodged in arteries of the brain. Ischemic strokes can be treated by clot-busting drugs. The second kind of stroke, a *hemorrhagic stroke*, occurs when a blood vessel in the brain suddenly breaks. Blood then spills into surrounding tissue. As the blood spills over, brain cells in the affected areas begin to die. This death is either from the lack of oxygen and nutrients or from the rupture of the vessel and the sudden spilling of blood. The prognosis for stroke victims depends on the type and severity of damage. Symptoms of stroke appear immediately on the occurrence of stroke.

Typical symptoms include (*NINDS stroke information page, 2009*):

- numbness or weakness in the face, arms, or legs (especially on one side of the body)
- confusion, difficulty speaking or understanding speech
- vision disturbances in one or both eyes
- dizziness, trouble walking, loss of balance or coordination
- severe headache with no known cause

Brain Tumors

Brain tumors, also called *neoplasms*, can affect cognitive functioning in very serious ways. Tumors can occur in either the gray or the white matter of the brain. Tumors of the white matter are more common (Gazzaniga, Ivry, & Mangun, 2009).

Two types of brain tumors can occur. Primary brain tumors start in the brain. Most childhood brain tumors are of this type. Secondary brain tumors start as tumors somewhere else in the body, such as in the lungs. Brain tumors can be either benign or malignant. Benign tumors do not contain cancer cells. They typically can be removed and will not grow back. Cells from benign tumors do not invade surrounding cells or spread to other parts of the body. However, if they press against sensitive areas of the brain, they can result in serious cognitive impairments. They also can be life-threatening, unlike benign tumors in most other parts of the body. Malignant brain tumors, unlike benign ones, contain cancer cells. They are more serious and usually threaten the victim's life. They often grow quickly. They also tend to invade surrounding healthy brain tissue. In rare instances, malignant cells may break away and cause cancer in other parts of the body. Following are the most common symptoms of brain tumors (*What you need to know about brain tumors, 2009*):

- headaches (usually worse in the morning)
- nausea or vomiting
- changes in speech, vision, or hearing
- problems balancing or walking
- changes in mood, personality, or ability to concentrate
- problems with memory
- muscle jerking or twitching (seizures or convulsions)
- numbness or tingling in the arms or legs

■ **BELIEVE IT OR NOT**

BRAIN SURGERY CAN BE PERFORMED WHILE YOU ARE AWAKE!

Can you imagine having major surgery performed on you while you are awake? It's possible, and indeed sometimes it is done. When patients who have brain tumors or who suffer from epilepsy receive brain surgery, they are often woken up from the anesthesia after the surgeons have opened their skull and exposed the brain. This way the surgeons can talk to the patient and perform tests by stimulating the patient's brain in order to map the different areas of the brain that control important functions

like vision or memory. The brain itself does not contain any pain receptors, and when doctors stimulate a patient's brain during open-brain surgery while the patient is awake, the patient does not feel any pain. You can nevertheless get a headache, but that is because the tissue and nerves that surround the brain are sensitive to pain, not the brain itself. The communication with the patient enhances the safety and precision of the procedure as compared with brain surgery that is performed solely on the basis of brain scans that were performed using imaging technologies discussed in this chapter.

The diagnosis of brain tumor is typically made through neurological examination, CT scan, and/or MRI. The most common form of treatment is a combination of surgery, radiation, and chemotherapy.

Head Injuries

Head injuries result from many causes, such as a car accident, contact with a hard object, or a bullet wound. Head injuries are of two types. In *closed-head injuries*, the skull remains intact but there is damage to the brain, typically from the mechanical force of a blow to the head. Slamming one's head against a windshield in a car accident might result in such an injury. In *open-head injuries*, the skull does not remain intact but rather is penetrated, for example, by a bullet.

Head injuries are surprisingly common. Roughly 1.4 million North Americans suffer such injuries each year. About 50,000 of them die, and 235,000 need to be hospitalized. About 2% of the American population needs long-term assistance in their daily living due to head injuries (*What is traumatic brain injury, 2009*).

Loss of consciousness is a sign that there has been some degree of damage to the brain as a result of the injury. Damage resulting from head injury can include spastic movements, difficulty in swallowing, and slurring of speech, among many other cognitive problems. Immediate symptoms of a head injury include (*Signs and symptoms, 2009*):

- unconsciousness
- abnormal breathing
- obvious serious wound or fracture
- bleeding or clear fluid from the nose, ear, or mouth
- disturbance of speech or vision
- pupils of unequal size
- weakness or paralysis
- dizziness
- neck pain or stiffness
- seizure
- vomiting more than two to three times
- loss of bladder or bowel control

Generally, brain damage can result from many causes. When brain damage occurs, it always should be treated by a medical specialist at the earliest possible time. A neuropsychologist may be called in to assist in diagnosis, and rehabilitation psychologists can be helpful in bringing the patient to the optimal level of psychological functioning possible under the circumstances.

✔ CONCEPT CHECK

1. Why is the study of brain disorders useful for cognitive psychologists?
2. What are brain tumors, and how are they diagnosed?
3. What are the causes of strokes?
4. What are the symptoms of head injuries?

Intelligence and Neuroscience

The human brain is clearly the organ that serves as a biological basis for human intelligence. Early studies, such as those of Karl Lashley, studied the brain to find biological indices of intelligence and other aspects of mental processes. They were a resounding failure, despite great efforts. As tools for studying the brain have become more sophisticated, however, we are beginning to see the possibility of finding physiological indicators of intelligence. Some investigators believe that at some point we will have clinically useful psychophysiological indices of intelligence (e.g., Matarazzo, 1992). But widely applicable indices will be much longer in coming. In the meantime, the biological studies we now have are largely correlational. They show statistical associations between biological and psychometric or other measures of intelligence. They do not establish causal relations.

Intelligence and Brain Size

One line of research looks at the relationship of brain size or volume to intelligence (see Jerison, 2000; Vernon et al., 2000; Witelson, Beresh, & Kiga, 2006). The evidence suggests that, for humans, there is a modest but significant statistical relationship between brain size and intelligence (Gignac, Vernon, & Wickett, 2003; McDaniel, 2005). The amount of gray matter in the brain is strongly correlated with IQ in many areas of the frontal and temporal lobes (Haier, Jung, Yeo, Head, & Alkire, 2004). However, the brain areas that are correlated with IQ appear to differ in men versus women. Frontal areas are of relatively more importance in women, whereas posterior areas are of relatively more importance in men, even if both genders are matched for intelligence (Haier, Jung, Yeo, Head, & Alkire, 2005). This finding opens the question of whether there are two different brain architectures in men versus women that both result in roughly equal levels of intelligence (Haier, 2010). It is important to note that the relationship between brain size and intelligence does not hold across species (Jerison, 2000). Rather, what holds seems to be a relationship between intelligence and brain size, relative to the rough general size of the organism.

Intelligence and Neurons

The development of electrical recording and imaging techniques offers some appealing possibilities. For example, complex patterns of electrical activity in the brain, which are prompted by specific stimuli, appear to correlate with scores on IQ tests (Barrett & Eysenck, 1992). Several studies initially suggested that speed of conduction of neural impulses may correlate with intelligence, as measured by IQ tests (McGarry-Roberts, Stelmack, & Campbell, 1992; Vernon & Mori, 1992). A follow-up study, however, failed to find a strong relation between neural-conduction velocity and intelligence (Wickett & Vernon, 1994). In this study, conduction velocity was measured by neural-conduction speeds in a main nerve of the arm. Intelligence was measured by a Multidimensional Aptitude Battery. Surprisingly, neural-conduction velocity appears to be a more powerful predictor of IQ scores for men than for women. So gender differences may account for some of the differences in the data (Wickett & Vernon, 1994). As of now, the results are inconsistent (Haier, 2010).

Intelligence and Brain Metabolism

More recent work suggests that the flexibility of neural circuitry, rather than speed of conduction, is key (Newman & Just, 2005). Hence, we would want to study not just speed but neural circuitry. An alternative approach to studying the brain suggests that neural efficiency may be related to intelligence. Such an approach is based on studies of how the brain metabolizes glucose (a simple sugar required for brain activity) during mental activities. Higher intelligence correlates with reduced levels of glucose metabolism during problem-solving tasks (Haier et al., 1992; Haier & Jung, 2007). That is, smarter brains consume less sugar and therefore expend less effort than less smart brains doing the same task. Furthermore, cerebral efficiency increases as a result of learning on a relatively complex task involving visuospatial manipulations, for example, the computer game Tetris (Haier et al., 1992). As a result of practice, more intelligent participants not only show lower cerebral glucose metabolism overall but also show more specifically localized metabolism of glucose. In most areas of their brains, smarter participants show less glucose metabolism. But in selected areas of their brains, believed to be important to the task at hand, they show higher levels of glucose metabolism. Thus, more intelligent participants may have learned how to use their brains more efficiently. They carefully focus their thought processes on a given task.

Other research, however, suggests that the relationship between glucose metabolism and intelligence may be more complex (Haier et al., 1995; Larson et al., 1995). On the one hand, one study confirmed the earlier findings of increased glucose metabolism in less smart participants, in this case, participants who had mild mental retardation (Haier et al., 1995). On the other hand, another study found, contrary to the earlier findings, that smarter participants had increased glucose metabolism relative to their average comparison group (Larson et al., 1995).

There was a problem with earlier studies—the tasks participants received were not matched for difficulty level across groups of smart and average individuals. The study by Larson and colleagues used tasks that were matched to the ability levels of the smarter and average participants. They found that the smarter participants used more glucose. Moreover, the glucose metabolism was highest in the right hemisphere of the more intelligent participants performing the hard task. These results again suggest selectivity of brain areas. What could be driving the increases in glucose metabolism? Currently, the key factor appears to be subjective task difficulty. In earlier studies, smarter participants simply found the tasks to be too easy. Matching task difficulty to participants' abilities seems to indicate that smarter participants increase glucose metabolism when the task demands it. The preliminary findings in this area will need to be investigated further before any conclusive answers arise.

Biological Bases of Intelligence Testing

Some neuropsychological research suggests that performance on intelligence tests may not indicate a crucial aspect of intelligence—the ability to set goals, to plan how to meet them, and to execute those plans (Dempster, 1991). Specifically, people with lesions on the frontal lobe of the brain frequently perform quite well on standardized IQ tests. These tests require responses to questions within a highly structured situation. But they do not require much in the way of goal setting or planning. These tests frequently use what could be classified as crystallized intelligence. Damage to the posterior regions of the brain seems to have negative effects on measures of crystallized intelligence (Gray & Thompson, 2004; Kolb & Whishaw, 1996; Piercy, 1964). In patients with frontal lobe damage, impairments in fluid intelligence are observed (Duncan, Burgess, & Emslie, 1995; Gray, Chabris, & Braver, 2003; Gray & Thompson, 2004). This result should come as no surprise, given that the frontal lobes are involved in reasoning, decision making, and problem solving (see Chapters 11 and 12). Other research highlights the importance of the parietal regions for performance on general and fluid intelligence tasks (Lee et al., 2006; see also Glaescher et al., 2009). Intelligence involves the ability to learn from experience and to adapt to the surrounding environment. Thus, the ability to set goals and to design and implement plans cannot be ignored. An essential aspect of goal setting and planning is the ability to attend appropriately to relevant stimuli. Another related ability is that of ignoring or discounting irrelevant stimuli.

The P-FIT Theory of Intelligence

The discovered importance of the frontal and parietal regions in intelligence tasks has led to the development of an integrated theory of intelligence that highlights the importance of these areas. This theory, called the parietal-frontal integration theory (P-FIT), stresses the importance of interconnected brain regions in determining differences in intelligence. The regions this theory focuses on are the prefrontal cortex, the inferior and superior parietal lobe, the anterior cingulated cortex, and portions of the temporal and occipital lobes (Colom et al., 2009; Jung & Haier, 2007). P-FIT theory describes patterns of brain activity in people with different levels of intelligence; it cannot, however, explain what makes a person intelligent or what intelligence is.

We cannot realistically study a brain or its contents and processes in isolation without also considering the entire human being. We must consider the interactions of that human being with the entire environmental context within which the person acts intelligently. Many researchers and theorists urge us to take a more contextual view of intelligence. Furthermore, some alternative views of intelligence attempt to broaden the definition of intelligence to be more inclusive of people's varied abilities.

✔ CONCEPT CHECK

1. Is there a relationship between brain size and intelligence?

2. Why does higher intelligence in many instances correlate with reduced levels of glucose metabolism during problem-solving tasks?

3. What is the P-FIT theory of intelligence?

Key Themes

In Chapter 1, we reviewed seven key themes that pervade cognitive psychology. Several of them are relevant here.

Biological versus behavioral methods. The mechanisms and methods described in this chapter are primarily biological. And yet, a major goal of biological researchers is to discover how cognition and behavior relate to these biological mechanisms. For example, they study how the hippocampus enables learning. Thus, biology, cognition, and behavior work together. They are not in any way mutually exclusive.

Nature versus nurture. One comes into the world with many biological structures and mechanisms in place. But nurture acts to develop them and enable them to reach their potential. The existence of the cerebral cortex is a result of nature, but the memories stored in it derive from nurture. As stated in Chapter 1, nature does not act alone. Rather, its marvels unfold through the interventions of nurture.

Applied versus basic research. Much of the research in biological approaches to cognition is basic. But this basic research later enables us, as cognitive psychologists, to make applied discoveries. For example, to understand how to treat and, hopefully, help individuals with brain damage, cognitive neuropsychologists first must understand the nature of the damage and its pervasiveness. Many modern antidepressants, for example, affect the reuptake of serotonin in the nervous system. By inhibiting reuptake, they increase serotonin concentrations and ultimately increase feelings of well-being. Interestingly, applied research can help basic research as much as basic research can help applied research. In the case of antidepressants, scientists knew the drugs worked before they knew exactly how they worked. Applied research in creating the drugs helped the scientists understand the biological mechanisms underlying the success of the drugs in relieving symptoms of depression.

Summary

1. **What are the fundamental structures and processes within the brain?** The nervous system, governed by the brain, is divided into two main parts: the central nervous system, consisting of the brain and the spinal cord, and the peripheral nervous system, consisting of the rest of the nervous system (e.g., the nerves in the face, legs, arms, and viscera).

2. **How do researchers study the major structures and processes of the brain?** For centuries scientists have viewed the brain by dissecting it. Modern dissection techniques include the use of electron microscopes and sophisticated chemical analyses to probe the mysteries of individual cells of the brain. Additionally, surgical techniques on animals (e.g., the use of selective lesioning and single-cell recording) often are used. On humans, studies have included electrical analyses (e.g., electroencephalograms and event-related potentials), studies based on the use of X-ray techniques (e.g., angiograms and computed tomograms), studies based on computer analyses of magnetic fields within the brain (magnetic resonance imaging), and

studies based on computer analyses of blood flow and metabolism within the brain (positron emission tomography and functional magnetic resonance imaging).

3. **What have researchers found as a result of studying the brain?** The major structures of the brain may be categorized as those in the forebrain (e.g., the all-important cerebral cortex and the thalamus, the hypothalamus, and the limbic system, including the hippocampus), the midbrain (including a portion of the brainstem), and the hindbrain (including the medulla oblongata, the pons, and the cerebellum). The highly convoluted cerebral cortex surrounds the interior of the brain and is the basis for much of human cognition. The cortex covers the left and right hemispheres of the brain. They are connected by the corpus callosum. In general, each hemisphere contralaterally controls the opposite side of the body. Based on extensive split-brain research, many investigators believe that the two hemispheres are specialized: In most people, the left hemisphere primarily controls language. The right hemisphere primarily controls visuospatial processing. The two hemispheres also may process information differently.

Another way to view the cortex is to identify differences among four lobes. Roughly speaking, higher thought and motor processing occur in the frontal lobe. Somatosensory processing occurs in the parietal lobe. Auditory processing occurs in the temporal lobe, and visual processing occurs in the occipital lobe. Within the frontal lobe, the primary motor cortex controls the planning, control, and execution of movement. Within the parietal lobe, the primary somatosensory cortex is responsible for sensations in our muscles and skin. Specific regions of these two cortices can be mapped to particular regions of the body.

Thinking about Thinking: Analytical, Creative, and Practical Questions

1. How have views of the nature of the relation between brain and cognition changed over time?
2. Briefly summarize the main structures and functions of the brain.
3. What are some of the reasons that researchers are interested in finding out the localization of function in the human brain?
4. In your opinion, why have the hindbrain, the midbrain, and the forebrain evolved (across the human species) and developed (across human prenatal development) in the sequence mentioned in this chapter? Include the main functions of each in your comments.
5. Researchers already are aware that a deficit of a neurotransmitter, acetylcholine, in the hippocampus is linked to Alzheimer's disease. Given the difficulty of reaching the hippocampus without causing other kinds of brain damage, how might researchers try to treat Alzheimer's disease?
6. In your opinion, why is it that some discoveries, such as that of Marc Dax, go unnoticed? What can be done to maximize the possibility that key discoveries will be noticed?
7. Given the functions of each of the cortical lobes, how might a lesion in one of the lobes be discovered?
8. What is an area of cognition that could be studied effectively by viewing the structure or function of the human brain? Describe how a researcher might use one of the techniques mentioned in this chapter to study that area of cognition.

Key Terms

amygdala, *p. 97*
axon, *p. 112*
brain, *p. 93*
brainstem, *p. 101*

cerebellum, *p. 102*
cerebral cortex, *p. 102*
cerebral hemispheres, *p. 103*
cognitive neuroscience, *p. 93*

contralateral, *p. 103*
corpus callosum, *p. 103*
dendrites, *p. 112*

Media Resources

Visit the companion website—www.cengagebrain.com—for quizzes, research articles, chapter outlines, and more.

CogLab

Explore CogLab by going to http://coglab.wadsworth.com. To learn more, examine the following experiments:

Brain Asymmetry

4 CHAPTER

Attention and Consciousness

135

Here are some of the questions we will explore in this chapter:

1. Can we actively process information even if we are not aware of doing so? If so, what do we do, and how do we do it?

2. What are some of the functions of attention?

3. What are some theories cognitive psychologists have developed to explain attentional processes?

4. What have cognitive psychologists learned about attention by studying the human brain?

■ **BELIEVE IT OR NOT**

DOES PAYING ATTENTION ENABLE YOU TO MAKE BETTER DECISIONS?

So you've got an important decision to make? People are usually taught to deliberate carefully upon the more complex decisions in their lives. Sometimes, however, unconsciously made decisions can be better than carefully deliberated ones.

Ap Dijksterhuis and colleagues (2006) conducted experiments in which participants had to choose the best from four cars and other objects like toothpaste. The complexity of the decision depended on the number of important attributes that described the object. Participants were best able to make a simple decision, like the one for toothpaste (which was based on two attributes), when they deliberated about their choices. However, when participants had to choose the best of four cars (described by 12 attributes each), they fared much better when they were not given the chance consciously to think about their choices.

Conscious choices can be flawed because we do not have unlimited mental capacity. At some point, we have to cut down on the amount of information we will consider. Also, when consciously thinking about alternatives, we sometimes attach more importance to less relevant attributes, which can lead to suboptimal choices. So next time you have a complex decision to make, it may be best to just sit back, relax, and let the decision come to you. This chapter introduces you to attention and consciousness and how cognitive psychologists approach them (See also the description of the work of Gerd Gigerenzer on fast and frugal heuristics in Chapter 11).

Let's examine what it means to pay attention in an everyday situation. Imagine driving in rush hour, near a major sports stadium where an event is about to start. The streets are filled with cars, some of them honking. At some intersections the police are regulating the traffic, but not quite in synchrony with the traffic lights. This asynchronicity—with the traffic light signaling one thing and the police signaling another—divides your attention. Some cars are stranded in the middle of an intersection. Also, there are thousands of people streaming through the streets to attend the sports event. You need to pay close attention to the traffic light as well as the officer on the road, the cars passing by, and the pedestrians that might unexpectedly cross the street. What is it that lets us pay attention to so many different moving parts in traffic? What lets us shift attention if a pedestrian suddenly walks out into the street without notice? And why does our attention sometimes fail us, occasionally with drastic consequences such as a car accident? This chapter will explore our amazing capability to pay attention, divide our attention, and select stimuli to which to pay attention in detail.

The Nature of Attention and Consciousness

*[Attention] is the taking possession of the mind, in clear and vivid form,
of one out of what seem several simultaneously possible objects or trains
of thoughts. ... It implies withdrawal from some things in order to deal
effectively with others.*

—William James, *Principles of Psychology*

It can be difficult to clearly describe in words what we mean when we talk about
attention (or any other psychological phenomenon). So what do we refer to exactly,
when we talk about attention in this chapter? **Attention** is the means by which we
actively process a limited amount of information from the enormous amount of information available through our senses, our stored memories, and our other cognitive
processes (De Weerd, 2003a; Rao, 2003). It includes both conscious and unconscious processes. In many cases, conscious processes are relatively easy to study. Unconscious processes are harder to study, simply because you are not conscious of
them (Jacoby, Lindsay, & Toth, 1992; Merikle, 2000). For example, you always
have a wealth of information available to you that you are not even aware of until
you retrieve that information from your memory or shift your attention toward it.
You probably can remember where you slept when you were ten years old or where
you ate your breakfasts when you were 12. At any given time, you also have available a dazzling array of sensory information to which you just do not attend. After
all, if you attended to each and every detail of your environment, you would feel
overwhelmed pretty fast (Figure 4.1). You also have very little reliable information
about what happens when you sleep. Therefore, it is hard to study processes that are
hidden somewhere in your unconsciousness, and of which you are not aware.

Attention allows us to use our limited mental resources judiciously. By dimming
the lights on many stimuli from outside (sensations) and inside (thoughts and memories), we can highlight the stimuli that interest us. This heightened focus increases
the likelihood that we can respond speedily and accurately to interesting stimuli.

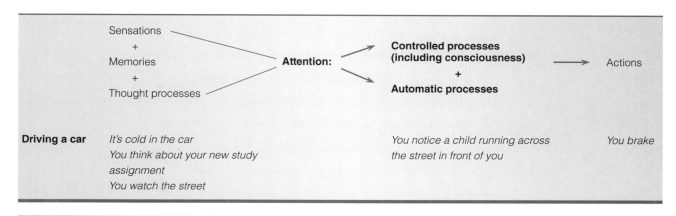

Figure 4.1   How Does Attention Work?

At any point in time, we perceive a lot of sensory information. Through attentional processes (which can be automatic
or controlled), we filter out the information that is relevant to us and that we want to attend to. Eventually, this leads to
our taking action on the basis of the information we attended to.

Heightened attention also paves the way for memory processes. We are more likely to remember information to which we paid attention than information we ignored.

At one time, psychologists believed that attention was the same thing as consciousness. Now, however, they acknowledge that some active attentional processing of sensory and of remembered information proceeds without our conscious awareness (Bahrami et al., 2008; Shear, 1997). For example, writing your name requires little conscious awareness. You may write it while consciously engaged in other activities. In contrast, writing a name that you have never encountered requires attention to the sequence of letters.

Consciousness includes both the feeling of awareness and the content of awareness, some of which may be under the focus of attention (Bourguignon, 2000; Farthing, 1992, 2000; Taylor, 2002). Therefore, attention and consciousness form two partially overlapping sets (Srinivasan, 2008; DiGirolamo & Griffin, 2003).

Conscious attention serves three purposes in playing a causal role for cognition. First, it helps in monitoring our interactions with the environment. Through such monitoring, we maintain our awareness of how well we are adapting to the situation in which we find ourselves. Second, it assists us in linking our past (memories) and our present (sensations) to give us a sense of continuity of experience. Such continuity may even serve as the basis for personal identity. Third, it helps us in controlling and planning for our future actions. We can do so based on the information from monitoring and from the links between past memories and present sensations.

In this chapter, we will first explore different kinds of attention like vigilance, search, selective attention, and divided attention. Afterward, we will consider what happens when our attention does not work properly, and what strategies we use in order not to get overwhelmed in a world that is full of sensory stimuli. Then, we will explore the nature of automatic processes, which help humans to make the best use of their attentional resources. Last but not least, we will consider the topic of consciousness in more detail.

Attention

In this section, we will explore the four main functions of attention as well as theories to explain them (see also Table 4.1):

Here are the four main functions of attention:

1. **Signal detection and vigilance:** We try to detect the appearance of a particular stimulus. Air traffic controllers, for example, keep an eye on all traffic near and over the airport.
2. **Search:** We try to find a signal amidst distracters, for example, when we are looking for our lost cell phone on an autumn leaf-filled hiking path.
3. **Selective attention:** We choose to attend to some stimuli and ignore others, as when we are involved in a conversation at a party.
4. **Divided attention:** We prudently allocate our available attentional resources to coordinate our performance of more than one task at a time, as when we are cooking and engaged in a phone conversation at the same time.

We will also have a look at a number of neuroscientific studies and explanatory models. Lastly, we will turn our attention to situations and conditions when our attention fails us.

Table 4.1   Four Main Functions of Attention

Function	Description	Example
Signal detection and vigilance	On many occasions, we vigilantly try to detect whether we did or did not sense a signal—a particular target stimulus of interest. Through vigilant attention to detecting signals, we are primed to take speedy action when we do detect signal stimuli.	In a research submarine, we may watch for unusual sonar blips; on a dark street, we may try to detect unwelcome sights or sounds; or following an earthquake, we may be wary of the smell of leaking gas or of smoke.
Search	We often engage in an active search for particular stimuli.	If we detect smoke (as a result of our vigilance), we may engage in an active search for the source of the smoke. In addition, some of us are often in search of missing keys, sunglasses, and other objects.
Selective attention	We constantly are making choices regarding the stimuli to which we will pay attention and the stimuli that we will ignore. By ignoring or at least deemphasizing some stimuli, we thereby highlight particularly salient stimuli. The concentrated focus of attention on particular informational stimuli enhances our ability to manipulate those stimuli for other cognitive processes, such as verbal comprehension or problem solving.	We may pay attention to reading a textbook or to listening to a lecture while ignoring such stimuli as a nearby radio or television or latecomers to the lecture.
Divided attention	We often manage to engage in more than one task at a time, and we shift our attentional resources to allocate them prudently, as needed.	Experienced drivers easily can talk while driving under most circumstances, but if another vehicle seems to be swerving toward their car, they quickly switch all their attention away from talking and toward driving.

Attending to Signals over the Short and Long Terms

Have you ever spent a hot summer day at an overcrowded beach? People are lying side by side on the sand, lined up like sardines in a tin. And though a trip to the water might bring some relief from the heat, it does not provide any relief from the crowding on the beach—people are standing thronged in the water with little space to move unless you move out considerably further into the water. The lifeguards on duty have to be constantly monitoring the crowds in the water to detect anything that seems unusual. In this way, they can act fast enough in case there is an emergency. In the short term, they have to detect a crucial stimulus among the mass of stimuli on the beach (*signal detection*), for example, making sure no one is drowning; but they also have to maintain their attention over a long period of time (*vigilance*) to make sure nothing is amiss during their entire working period. What factors contribute to their ability to detect events that might be emergencies? How do they search the beaches and shorelines to detect important stimuli? Understanding this function of attention has immediate practical importance. Occupations requiring vigilance include those involving communications and warning systems and quality control, as well as the work of police detectives, physicians. Also, research psychologists must search out from among a diverse array of items those that are

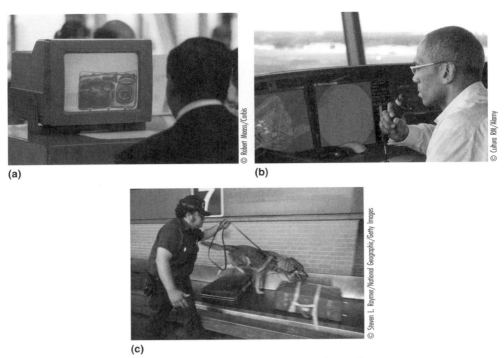

(a) (b)

(c)

Signal Detection, Vigilance, and Search in Everyday Life.
(a) **Signal detection.** Luggage screeners learn techniques to enable them to maximize
"hits" and "correct rejections" and to minimize "false alarms" and "misses." (b) **Vigilance.**
For air traffic controllers, vigilance is a matter of life and death. (c) **Search.** These trained
police dogs are actively seeking out a target, such as bombs or drugs.

more important. In each of these settings, people must remain alert to detect the
appearance of a stimulus. But each setting also involves the presence of distracters,
as well as prolonged periods during which the stimulus is absent. In the following
sections, we will first explore how people detect a target stimulus out of a wealth of
stimuli (i.e., how they detect signals). Once we know how people discriminate
between target signals and distracters, we will turn to the maintenance of attention
over a prolonged period of time (vigilance) in order to detect important stimuli.

Signal Detection: Finding Important Stimuli in a Crowd

Signal-detection theory (SDT) is a framework to explain how people pick out the
few important stimuli when they are embedded in a wealth of irrelevant, distracting
stimuli. SDT often is used to measure sensitivity to a target's presence. When we try
to detect a target stimulus (**signal**), there are four possible outcomes (Table 4.2).
Let's stay with our example of the lifeguard. First, in *hits* (also called "true positives"), the lifeguard correctly identifies the presence of a target (i.e., somebody
drowning). Second, in *false alarms* (also called "false positives"), he or she incorrectly
identifies the presence of a target that is actually absent (i.e., the lifeguard thinks
somebody is drowning who actually isn't). Third, in *misses* (also called "false negatives"), the lifeguard fails to observe the presence of a target (i.e., the lifeguard does
not see the drowning person). Fourth, in *correct rejections* (also called "true negatives"), the lifeguard correctly identifies the absence of a target (i.e., nobody is
drowning, and he or she knows that nobody is in trouble).

Table 4.2 Signal Detection Matrix Used in Signal-Detection Theory

Signal-detection theory was one of the first theories to suggest an interaction between the physical sensation of a stimulus and cognitive processes such as decision making. Think about the work of airport screeners. They need to be capable of perceiving objects like a box cutter in hand-carried luggage.

Signal	Detect a Signal	Do Not Detect a Signal
Present	Hit *The screener recognizes a box cutter in the luggage.*	Miss *The screener fails to see the box cutter in the luggage.*
Absent	False alarm *The screener thinks there is a box cutter in the luggage when there is none.*	Correct rejection *The screener recognizes that there is no box cutter in the luggage, and there is indeed none.*

Usually, the presence of a target is difficult to detect. Thus, we make detection judgments based on inconclusive information with some criteria for target detections. The number of hits is influenced by where you place your criteria for considering something a hit. In other words, how willing are you to make false alarms? For example, in the case of the lifeguard, the consequences of a miss are so grave that the lifeguard lowers the criteria for considering something as a hit. In this way, he or she increases the number of false alarms to boost hits (correct detections).

This trade-off often occurs with medical diagnoses as well. For example, it might occur with highly sensitive screening tests where positive results lead to further tests. Thus, overall sensitivity to targets must reflect a flexible criterion for declaring the detection of a signal. If the criterion for detection is too high, then the doctor will miss illnesses (misses). If the criterion is too low, the doctor will falsely detect illnesses that do not exist (false alarms). Sensitivity is measured in terms of hits minus false alarms.

Signal-detection theory can be discussed in the context of attention, perception, or memory:

- attention—paying enough attention to perceive objects that are there;
- perception—perceiving faint signals that may or may not be beyond your perceptual range (such as a very high-pitched tone);
- memory—indicating whether you have/have not been exposed to a stimulus before, such as whether the word "champagne" appeared on a list that was to be memorized.

Disturbingly, on September 11, 2001, when terrorists crashed two airliners into the Twin Towers in New York City, the 9/11 hijackers were screened at airports as they prepared to board their flights. Several of them were pulled aside because they set off metal detectors. After further screening, they were allowed onto their planes anyway, even though they were carrying box cutters. The results of what constituted a "miss" for the screeners were disastrous. As a result of this fiasco, the rules for screening were tightened up considerably. But the tightening of rules created many false alarms. Babies, grandmothers, and other relatively low-risk passengers started to get second and sometimes even third screenings. So the rules were modified to profile passengers by computer. For example, those who bought one-way tickets or changed their flight plans at the last moment became more likely to be subjected to extra screening. This procedure, in turn, has inconvenienced those travelers who need to change their travel plans frequently, such as business travelers. The system for screening passengers is constantly evolving in order to minimize both misses and false alarms.

Vigilance: Waiting to Detect a Signal

When you have to pay attention in order to detect a stimulus that can occur at any time over a long period of time, you need to be vigilant.

What is Vigilance?   **Vigilance** refers to a person's ability to attend to a field of stimulation over a prolonged period, during which the person seeks to detect the appearance of a particular target stimulus of interest. When being vigilant, the individual watchfully waits to detect a signal stimulus that may appear at an unknown time. Typically, vigilance is needed in settings where a given stimulus occurs only rarely but requires immediate attention as soon as it does occur. Military officers watching for a sneak attack are engaged in a high-stakes vigilance task.

In an early study, participants watched a visual display that looked like the face of a clock (Mackworth, 1948). A clock hand moved in continuous steps except that sometimes it would take a double step, which needed to be detected by the participants. Participants' performance began to deteriorate substantially after just half an hour of observation (see MacLean et al., 2009, for a more recent study). To relate these findings to SDT, over time it appears that participants become less willing to risk reporting false alarms. They err instead by failing to report the presence of the signal stimulus when they are not sure they detect it, showing higher rates of misses. Training can help to increase vigilance, but to counteract fatigue, nothing but taking a break really helps much (Fisk & Schneider, 1981).

In vigilance tasks, expectations regarding stimulus location strongly affect response efficiency (LaBerge, Carter, & Brown, 1992; Motter, 1999). Thus, a busy lifeguard or air-traffic controller may respond quickly to a signal within a narrow radius of where a signal is expected to appear. But signals appearing outside the concentrated range of vigilant attention may not be detected as quickly or as accurately. However, the abrupt onset of a stimulus (i.e., the sudden appearance of a stimulus) captures our attention (Yantis, 1993). Thus, we seem to be predisposed to notice the sudden appearance of stimuli in our visual field. We might speculate about the adaptive advantage this feature of attention may have offered to our ancestral hunter-gatherer forebears. They presumably needed to avoid predators and had to catch prey.

Vigilance is extremely important during scans at airports in detecting abandoned bags or suspect items that may pose a security risk. Medical workers interpreting results like MRI scans or X-rays need to be vigilant as well, watching for any abnormalities in the results they are interpreting, even if they are very small. The costs of failure of vigilance, in today's world, can be great loss of life as well as of property.

Neuroscience and Vigilance   Increased vigilance is seen in cases where emotional stimuli are used (e.g., when somebody is confronted with a threatening stimulus). The amygdala plays a pivotal role in the recognition of emotional stimuli. Thus, the amygdala appears to be an important brain structure in the regulation of vigilance (Phelps, 2004, 2006; van Marle et al., 2009). The thalamus is involved in vigilance as well. Two specific activation states play a role in vigilance: bursts and the tonic state. A burst is the result of relative hyperpolarization of the resting membrane potential (i.e., polarity of the membrane increases relative to its surrounding), and a tonic state results from relative depolarization. During sleep, when people are less responsive to stimuli, the neurons are hyperpolarized and in burst mode higher levels of vigilance are associated with tonic discharges. Also, the less vigilance a person displays, the more low-frequency activity and smaller event-related potentials can be detected through EEG measurement (Llinas & Steriade, 2006; Oken et al., 2006).

Search: Actively Looking

Have you ever picked up your parents or friends at a crowded airport and tried to locate them among the masses of people streaming out of the terminals? Search involves actively and often skillfully seeking out a target (Cisler et al., 2007; Posner & DiGirolamo, 1998). Specifically, **search** refers to a scan of the environment for particular features—actively looking for something when you are not sure where it will appear. As with vigilance, when we are searching for something, we may respond by making false alarms. The police actively search an area where a crime like a bank robbery has occurred, trying to find the robbers before they can escape. Search is made more difficult by **distracters**, nontarget stimuli that divert our attention away from the target stimulus. In the case of search, false alarms usually arise when we encounter such distracters while searching for the target stimulus. For instance, consider searching for a product in the grocery store. We often see several distracting items that look something like the item we hope to find. Package designers take advantage of the effectiveness of distracters when creating packaging for products. For example, if a container looks like a box of Cheerios, you may pick it up without realizing that it's really Tastee-O's.

The number of targets and distracters affects the difficulty of the task. This is illustrated in Figure 4.2. Try to find the *T* in panel (a). Then try to find the *T* in panel (b) of Figure 4.2. *Display size* is the number of items in a given visual array. (It does not refer to the size of the items or even the size of the field on which the array is displayed.) The display-size effect is the degree to which the number of items in

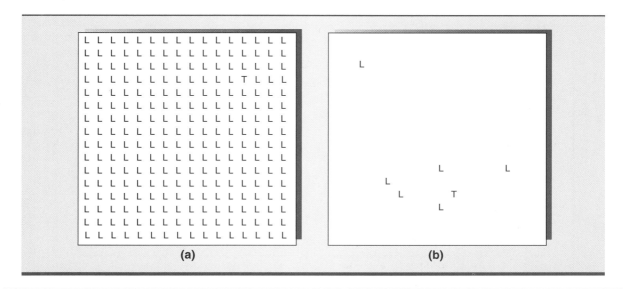

Figure 4.2   Display Size.

Compare the relative difficulty in finding the T in panels (a) and (b). The display size affects your ease of performing the task.

a display hinders (slows down) the search process. When studying visual-search phenomena, investigators often manipulate the display size. They then observe how various contributing factors increase or decrease the display-size effect.

Distracters cause more trouble under some conditions than under others. Suppose we look for an item with a distinct feature like color or shape. We conduct a **feature search**, in which we simply scan the environment for that feature (Treisman, 1993; Weidner & Mueller, 2009). Distracters play little role in slowing our search in that case. For example, try to find the O in panel (c) of Figure 4.3. The O has a distinctive form as compared with the L distracters in the display. The O thus seems to pop out of the display. Featural singletons, which are items with distinctive features, stand out in the display (Yantis, 1993). When featural singletons are targets, they seem to grab our attention. Unfortunately, any featural singletons grab our attention. This includes featural singletons that are distracters that can distract us from finding the target (Navalpakkam & Itti, 2007). For example, find the T in panel (d) of Figure 4.3. The T is a featural singleton. But the presence of the black (filled) circle probably slows you down in your search.

A problem arises, however, when the target stimulus has no unique or even distinctive features, like a particular boxed or canned item in a grocery aisle. In these situations, the only way we can find it is to conduct a conjunction search (Treisman, 1991). In a **conjunction search**, we look for a particular combination (conjunction—joining together) of features. For example, the only difference between a T and an L is the particular integration (conjunction) of the line segments. The difference is not a property of any single distinctive feature of either letter. Both letters comprise a horizontal line and a vertical line. So a search looking for either of these features would provide no distinguishing information. In panels (a) and (b), you had to perform a conjunction search to find the T. So it probably took you longer to find it than to find the O in panel (c). The dorsolateral prefrontal cortex as well as both

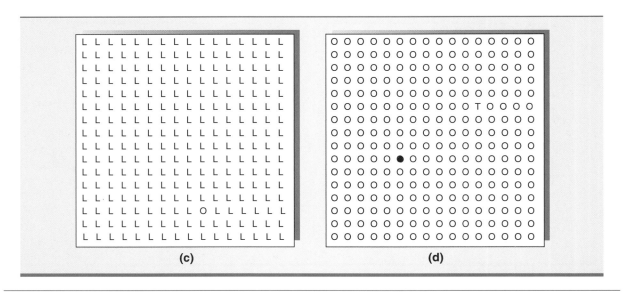

(c)   (d)

Figure 4.3 Feature Search.

In panel (c), find the O, and in panel (d), find the T.

frontal eye fields and the posterior parietal cortex play a role only in conjunction searches, but not so in feature searches (Kalla et al., 2009).

In the following section, we explore three theories that try to explain search processes. These theories have developed in a dialectical way as responses to each other: feature-integration theory, similarity theory, and guided search theory.

Feature-Integration Theory

Feature-integration theory explains the relative ease of conducting feature searches and the relative difficulty of conducting conjunction searches. Consider Treisman's (1986) model of how our minds conduct visual searches. For each possible feature of a stimulus, each of us has a mental map for representing the given feature across the visual field. For example, there is a map for every color, size, shape, or orientation (e.g., p, q, b, d) of each stimulus in our visual field. For every stimulus, the features are represented in the feature maps immediately. There is no added time required for additional cognitive processing. Thus, during feature searches, we monitor the relevant feature map for the presence of any activation anywhere in the visual field. This monitoring process can be done in parallel (all at once). It therefore shows no display-size effects. However, during conjunction searches, an additional stage of processing is needed. During this stage, we must use our attentional resources as a sort of mental "glue." This additional stage conjoins two or more features into an object representation at a particular location. In this stage, we can conjoin the features only one object at a time. This stage must be carried out sequentially, conjoining each object one by one. Effects of display size (i.e., a larger number of objects with features to be conjoined) therefore appear.

There is some neuropsychological support for Treisman's model. For example, Nobel laureates David Hubel and Torsten Wiesel (1979) identified specific neural feature detectors. These are cortical neurons that respond differentially to visual stimuli of particular orientations (e.g., vertical, horizontal, or diagonal). More recent research has indicated that the best search strategy is not for the brain to increase the activity of neurons that respond to the particular target stimuli; in fact, the brain seems to use the more nearly optimal strategy of activating neurons that best distinguish between the target and distracters while at the same time ignoring the neurons that are tuned best to the target (Navalpakkam & Itti, 2007; Pouget & Bavelier, 2007).

Similarity Theory

Not everyone agrees with Treisman's model, however. According to *similarity theory*, Treisman's data can be reinterpreted. In this view, the data are a result of the fact that as the similarity between target and distracter stimuli increases, so does the difficulty in detecting the target stimuli (Duncan & Humphreys, 1992; Watson et al., 2007). Thus, targets that are highly similar to distracters are relatively hard to detect. Targets that are highly disparate from distracters are relatively easy to detect. For example, try to find the black (filled) circle in Figure 4.4, panel (e). The target is highly similar to the distracters (black squares or white circles). Therefore it is very difficult to find. Furthermore, the difficulty of search tasks depends on the degree of disparity among the distracters. But it does not depend on the number of features to be integrated. For instance, one reason that it is easier to read long strings of text written in lowercase letters than text written in capital letters is that capital letters tend to be more similar to one another in appearance. Lowercase letters, in contrast, have more

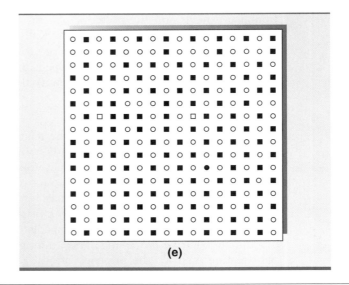

(e)

Figure 4.4 Similarity Theory.

In panel (e), find the black circle.

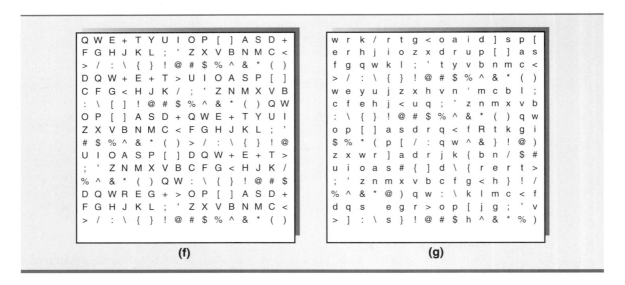

Figure 4.5 Similarity Theory.

In panels (f) and (g), find the R.

distinguishing features. Try to find the capital letter *R* in panels (f) and (g) of Figure 4.5 to get an idea of how highly dissimilar distracters impede visual search.

Guided Search Theory

In response to these and other findings, investigators have proposed an alternative to Treisman's model. They call it *guided search* (Cave & Wolfe, 1990; Wolfe, 2007). The guided-search model suggests that all searches, whether feature searches or

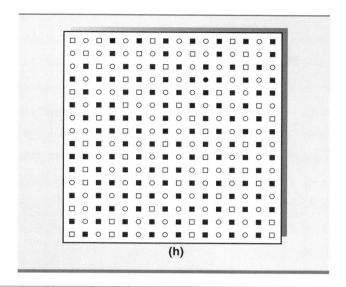

(h)

Figure 4.6   Guided Search Theory.

In panel (h), find the black circle.

conjunction searches, involve two consecutive stages. The first is a parallel stage: the individual simultaneously activates a mental representation of all the potential targets. The representation is based on the simultaneous activation of each of the features of the target. In a subsequent serial stage, the individual sequentially evaluates each of the activated elements, according to the degree of activation. Then, the person chooses the true targets from the activated elements. According to this model, the activation process of the parallel initial stage helps to guide the evaluation and selection process of the serial second stage of the search.

Let's see how guided search might work. Look at panel (h) of Figure 4.6. Try to find the black circle. The parallel stage will activate a mental map that contains all the features of the target (circle, black). Thus, black circles, white circles, and black squares will be activated. During the serial stage, you first will evaluate the black circle, which was highly activated. But then you will evaluate the black squares and the white circles, which were less highly activated. You then will dismiss them as distracters.

Neuroscience: Aging and Visual Search

An interesting study investigated the effect of aging on visual search capabilities (Madden et al., 2002; Madden, 2007). The researchers had two groups of participants—one in their 20s and one between 60 and 77 years of age—conduct a variety of visual searches of various difficulties for a black upright L: a feature search, where participants had to find the black upright L between white, partly rotated Ls; a guided search, where the target had to be found in between white Ls as well as three black Ls of various rotation; and a conjunction search where the black L had to be found in between a variety of rotated Ls that were either black or white (Figure 4.7).

Younger adults' searches were more accurate and faster than the searches of the older adults. Also, participants were slower by approximately 300 milliseconds when doing guided searches as compared with feature searches. Older adults' cortical

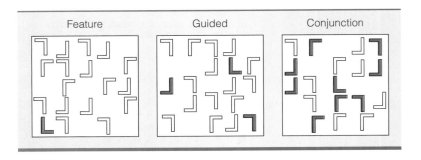

Figure 4.7 **Search Tasks in an Experiment.**

Here are examples for feature search, guided search, and conjunction search. In all three cases, participants were instructed to look for the upright black L.

Source: Madden, D. J., Turkington, T. G., Provenzale, J. M., Denny, L. L., Langley, L. K., Hawk, T. C., et al. (2002). Aging and attentional guidance during visual search: Funtional neuroanatomy by positron emission tomography. *Psychology and Aging, 17*(1), 24–43.

volume was lower than that of the younger adults, which is consistent with an approximate decline in volume of 2% per decade. The most difficult search (conjunction search) led to activation in the dorsal and ventral visual pathways as well as the prefrontal cortex in both young and older adults. Although there was less activation in the right occipital cortex in older adults, the activation was about the same in both age groups in the prefrontal and superior parietal regions. The more difficult a search task was, the more the occipito-temporal cortex was activated in younger adults but not in older adults. The older adults seem to have this brain region activated at a higher level even during easier search tasks, apparently trying to compensate for the age-related decline; but they did not recruit other brain regions outside the visual pathways to compensate for age-related decline.

Selective Attention

We explored the first two functions of attention—signal detection and search. Now, let's examine another function of attention—selective attention.

What Is Selective Attention?

Suppose you are at a dinner party. It is just your luck that you are sitting next to a salesman. He sells 110 brands of vacuum cleaners. He describes to you in excruciating detail the relative merits of each brand. As you are listening to this blatherer, who happens to be on your right, you become aware of the conversation of the two diners sitting on your left. Their exchange is much more interesting. It contains juicy information you had not known about one of your acquaintances. You find yourself trying to keep up the semblance of a conversation with the blabbermouth on your right, but you are also tuning in to the dialogue on your left.

Colin Cherry (1953, see also Bee & Micheyl, 2008) referred to this phenomenon as the **cocktail party problem**, the process of tracking one conversation in the face of the distraction of other conversations. He observed that cocktail parties are often settings in which selective attention is salient. Cherry did not actually hang out at numerous cocktail parties to study conversations. He studied selective attention in a more carefully controlled experimental setting. He devised a task known as shadowing.

Figure 4.8 **Dichotic Presentation.**

In dichotic presentation, each ear is presented a separate message.

In *shadowing*, you listen to two different messages. Cherry presented a separate message to each ear, known as **dichotic presentation**. Figure 4.8 illustrates how these listening tasks might be presented. You are required to repeat back only one of the messages as soon as possible after you hear it. In other words, you are to follow one message (think of a detective "shadowing" a suspect) but ignore the other.

Cherry's participants were quite successful in shadowing distinct messages in dichotic-listening tasks, although such shadowing required a significant amount of concentration. The participants were also able to notice physical, sensory changes in the unattended message—for example, when the message was changed to a tone or the voice changed from a male to a female speaker. However, they did not notice semantic changes in the unattended message. They failed to notice even when the unattended message shifted from English to German or was played backward. Conversely, about one third of people, when their name is presented during these situations, will switch their attention to their name. Some researchers have noted that those who hear their name in the unattended message tend to have limited working-memory capacity. As a result, they are easily distracted (Conway, Cowan, & Bunting, 2001). Infants will also shift their attention to one of two messages if their name is said (Newman, 2005).

Think of being in a noisy restaurant. Three factors help you to selectively attend only to the message of the target speaker to whom you wish to listen:

1. Distinctive sensory characteristics of the target's speech. Examples of such characteristics are high versus low pitch, pacing, and rhythmicity.
2. Sound intensity (loudness).
3. Location of the sound source (Brungard & Simpson, 2007).

Attending to the physical properties of the target speaker's voice has its advantages. You can avoid being distracted by the semantic content of messages from non-target speakers in the area. Clearly, the sound intensity of the target also helps. In addition, you probably turn one ear toward and the other ear away from the target speaker. Note that this method offers no greater total sound intensity. The reason is that with one ear closer to the speaker, the other is farther away. The key advantage is the difference in volume. It allows you to locate the source of the target sound. Recent psychophysical studies have found, however, that spatial cues are less important than factors like how harmonious and rhythmic the target sounds (Darwin, 2008; Muente et al., 2010).

Theories of Selective Attention

In the following section, we will discuss several theories of selective attention. Note how dialectical processes influenced the development of subsequent theories. The theories described here belong to the group of filter and bottleneck theories. A filter blocks some of the information going through and thereby selects only a part of the total of information to pass through to the next stage. A bottleneck slows down information passing through. The models differ in two ways. First, do they have a distinct "filter" for incoming information? Second, if they do, where in the processing of information does the filter occur (early or late)?

Broadbent's Model   According to one of the earliest theories of attention, we filter information right after we notice it at the sensory level (Broadbent, 1958; Figure 4.9). Multiple channels of sensory input reach an attentional filter. Those channels can be distinguished by their characteristics like loudness, pitch, or accent. The filter permits only one channel of sensory information to proceed and reach the processes of perception. We thereby assign meaning to our sensations. Other stimuli

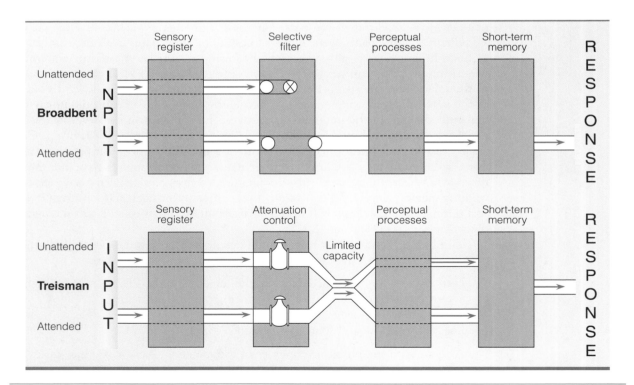

Figure 4.9   Broadbent and Treisman's Models of Attention.
Various mechanisms have been proposed suggesting a means by which incoming sensory information passes through the attentional system to reach high-level perceptual processes.

will be filtered out at the sensory level and may never reach the level of perception. Broadbent's theory was supported by Colin Cherry's findings that sensory information sometimes may be noticed by an unattended ear if it does not have to be processed elaborately (e.g., you may notice that the voice in your unattended ear switches to a tone). But information requiring higher perceptual processes is not noticed if not attended to (e.g., you would likely not notice that the language in your unattended ear switches from English to German).

Selective Filter Model   Not long after Broadbent's theory, evidence began to suggest that Broadbent's model must be wrong (e.g., Gray & Wedderburn, 1960). Moray found that even when participants ignore most other high-level (e.g., semantic) aspects of an unattended message, they frequently still recognize their names in an unattended ear (Moray, 1959; Wood & Cowan, 1995). He suggested that the reason for this effect is that messages that are of high importance to a person may break through the filter of selective attention (e.g., Koivisto & Revonsuo, 2007; Marsh et al., 2007). But other messages may not. To modify Broadbent's metaphor, one could say that, according to Moray, the selective filter blocks out most information at the sensory level. But some personally important messages are so powerful that they burst through the filtering mechanism.

Attenuation Model   To explore why some unattended messages pass through the filter, Anne Treisman conducted some experiments. She had participants shadowing coherent messages, and at some point switched the remainder of the coherent message from the attended to the unattended ear. Participants picked up the first few words of the message they had been shadowing in the unattended ear (Treisman, 1960), so they must have been somehow processing the content of the unattended message. Moreover, if the unattended message was identical to the attended one, all participants noticed it. They noticed even if one of the messages was slightly out of temporal synchronization with the other (Treisman, 1964a, 1964b). Treisman also observed that some fluently bilingual participants noticed the identity of messages if the unattended message was a translated version of the attended one.

Moray's modification of Broadbent's filtering mechanism was clearly not sufficient to explain Treisman's (1960, 1964a, 1964b) findings. Her findings suggested that at least some information about unattended signals is being analyzed. Treisman proposed a theory of selective attention that involves a later filtering mechanism (Figure 4.9). Instead of blocking stimuli out, the filter merely weakens (attenuates) the strength of

INVESTIGATING COGNITIVE PSYCHOLOGY
Attenuation Model

Get two friends to help you with this experiment. Ask one friend to read something very softly into your other friend's ear (it can be anything—a joke, a greeting card, or a cognitive psychology textbook), and have your other friend try to "shadow" what the other friend is saying. (Shadowing is repeating all the words that another person is saying.) In your friend's other ear, say "animal" very softly. Later, ask your friend what you said. Is your friend able to identify what you said? Probably not. Try this again, but this time say your friend's name. Your friend will most likely be able to recall that you said his or her name. This finding demonstrates Treisman's attenuation model.

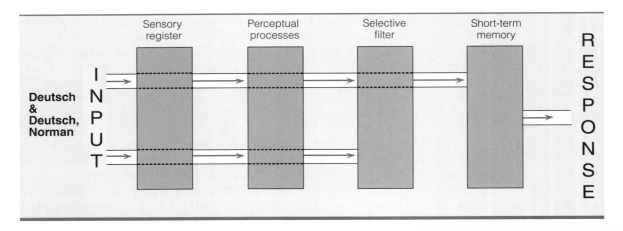

Figure 4.10   **Deutsch & Deutsch's Late-Filter Model.**
According to some cognitive psychologists, the attentional filtering mechanisms follow, rather than precede, preliminary perceptual processes.

stimuli other than the target stimulus. So when the stimuli reach us, we analyze them at a low level for target properties like loudness and pitch. You may listen for the voice of the person you are talking to in a noisy bar, for example. If the stimuli possess those target properties, we pass the signal on to the next stage; if they do not possess those target properties, we pass on a weakened version of the stimulus. In a next step, we perceptually analyze the meaning of the stimuli and their relevance to us, so that even a message from the unattended ear that is supposedly irrelevant can come into consciousness and influence our subsequent actions if it has some meaning for us.

Late-Filter Model   Deutsch and Deutsch (1963; Norman, 1968) developed a model in which the location of the filter is even later (Figure 4.10). They suggested that stimuli are filtered out only after they have been analyzed for both their physical properties and their meaning. This later filtering would allow people to recognize information entering the unattended ear. For example, they might recognize the sound of their own names or a translation of attended input (for bilinguals). Note that proponents of both the early and the late-filtering mechanisms propose that there is an attentional bottleneck through which only a single source of information can pass. The two models differ only in terms of where they hypothesize the bottleneck to be positioned.

A Synthesis of Early-Filter and Late-Filter Models   Both early and late selection theories have data to support them. So what is a researcher to do? In 1967, Ulric Neisser synthesized the early-filter and the late-filter models and proposed that there are two processes governing attention:

- *Preattentive processes:* These automatic processes are rapid and occur in parallel. They can be used to notice only physical sensory characteristics of the unattended message. But they do not discern meaning or relationships.
- *Attentive, controlled processes:* These processes occur later. They are executed serially and consume time and attentional resources, such as working memory. They also can be used to observe relationships among features. They serve to synthesize fragments into a mental representation of an object.

A two-step model could account for Cherry's, Moray's, and Treisman's data. The model also nicely incorporates aspects of Treisman's signal-attenuation theory and of her subsequent feature-integration theory. According to Treisman's theory, discrete processes for feature detection and for feature integration occur during searches. The feature-detection process may be linked to the former of the two processes (i.e., speedy, automatic processing). Her feature-integration process may be linked to the latter of the two processes (i.e., slower, controlled processing). Unfortunately, however, the two-step model does not do a good job of explaining the continuum of processes from fully automatic ones to fully controlled ones. Recall, for example, that fully controlled processes appear to be at least partially automatized (Spelke, Hirst, & Neisser, 1976). How does the two-process model explain the automatization of processes in divided-attention phenomena? For example, how can one read for comprehension while writing dictated, categorized words? We will discuss this in the section on divided attention.

Neuroscience and Selective Attention

As early as in the 1970s, researchers employed event-related potentials (ERPs) to study attention. A groundbreaking study was conducted by Hillyard and his colleagues (1973), when they exposed their participants to two streams of tones, one in each ear (the streams differed in pitch). The participants had to detect occasionally occurring target stimuli. When the target stimuli occurred in the attended ear, the first negative component of the ERP was larger than when the target occurred in the unattended ear. N1 is a negative wave that appears about 90 milliseconds after the onset of the target stimulus. The researchers hypothesized that the N1 wave was a result of the enhancement of the target stimulus. At the same time, there was a suppression of the other stimuli. This result is consistent with filter theories. Later studies (Woldorff & Hillyard, 1991) found an even earlier reaction to the target stimulus in the form of a positive wave that occurs about 20–50 milliseconds after the onset of a target. The wave originates in the Heschl's gyri, which are located in the auditory cortex (Woldorff et al., 1993). Studies still use these methods today to explore topics as diverse as the influence of mothers' socio-economic status on children's selective attention (Stevens et al., 2009). They have found that children of mothers with lower levels of education show reduced effects of selective attention on neural processing.

Similar effects also have been found for visual attention. If a target stimulus appears in an attended region of the visual field, the occipital P1 (a wave of positive polarity) is larger than when the target appears in an unattended region (Eason et al., 1969; Van Voorhis & Hillyard, 1977). The P1 effect also occurs when participants' attention is drawn to a particular location by a sensory cue, and the target subsequently appears in just that location. If the interval between the appearance of the cue and the target is very small, the P1 wave is enlarged and the reaction time is faster than for targets that appear with a significant delay after the cue. In fact, a delay between cue and target can even lead to a delay in reaction time and decreased size of P1 wave (Hopfinger & Mangun, 1998, 2001).

Divided Attention

Have you ever been driving with a friend and the two of you were engaged in an exciting conversation? Or have made dinner while on the phone with a friend? Anytime you are engaged in two or more tasks at the same time, your attention is divided between those tasks.

Failure of Divided Attention

Investigating Divided Attention in the Lab

Early work in the area of divided attention had participants view a videotape in which the display of a basketball game was superimposed on the display of a hand-slapping game. Participants could successfully monitor one activity and ignore the other. However, they had great difficulty in monitoring both activities at once, even if the basketball game was viewed by one eye and the hand-slapping game was watched separately by the other eye (Neisser & Becklen, 1975).

Neisser and Becklen hypothesized that improvements in performance eventually would have occurred as a result of practice. They also hypothesized that the performance of multiple tasks was based on skill resulting from practice. They believed it not to be based on special cognitive mechanisms.

The following year, investigators used a dual-task paradigm to study divided attention during the simultaneous performance of two activities: reading short stories and writing down dictated words (Spelke, Hirst, & Neisser, 1976). The researchers would compare and contrast the response time (latency) and accuracy of performance in each of the three conditions. Of course, higher latencies mean slower responses. As expected, initial performance was quite poor for the two tasks when the tasks had to be performed at the same time. However, Spelke and her colleagues had their participants practice to perform these two tasks 5 days a week for many weeks (85 sessions in all). To the surprise of many, given enough practice, the participants' performance improved on both tasks. They showed improvements in their speed of reading and accuracy of reading comprehension, as measured by comprehension tests. They also showed increases in their recognition memory for words they had written during dictation. Eventually, participants' performance on both tasks reached the same levels that the participants previously had shown for each task alone.

When the dictated words were related in some way (e.g., they rhymed or formed a sentence), participants first did not notice the relationship. After repeated practice, however, the participants started to notice that the words were related to

INVESTIGATING COGNITIVE PSYCHOLOGY
Dividing Your Attention

Repeatedly write your name on a piece of paper while you picture everything you can remember about the room in which you slept when you were 10 years old. While continuing to write your name and picturing your old bedroom, take a mental journey of awareness to notice your bodily sensations, starting from one of your big toes and proceeding up your leg, across your torso, to the opposite shoulder, and down your arm. What sensations do you feel—pressure from the ground, your shoes, or your clothing or even pain anywhere? Are you still managing to write your name while retrieving remembered images from memory and continuing to pay attention to your current sensations? Either task would have been easier done by itself than when done in parallel. Were you able to divide your attention successfully?

each other in various ways. They soon could perform both tasks at the same time without a loss in performance. Spelke and her colleagues suggested that these findings showed that controlled tasks can be automatized so that they consume fewer attentional resources. Furthermore, two discrete controlled tasks may be automatized to function together as a unit. The tasks do not, however, become fully automatic. For one thing, they continue to be intentional and conscious. For another, they involve relatively high levels of cognitive processing.

An entirely different approach to studying divided attention has focused on extremely simple tasks that require speedy responses. When people try to perform two overlapping speeded tasks, the responses for one or both tasks are almost always slower (Pashler, 1994). When a second task begins soon after the first task has started, speed of performance usually suffers. The slowing resulting from simultaneous engagement in speeded tasks, as mentioned earlier in the chapter, is the PRP (psychological refractory period) effect, also called *attentional blink*. Findings from PRP studies indicate that people can accommodate fairly easily perceptual processing of the physical properties of sensory stimuli while engaged in a second speeded task (Miller et al., 2009; Pashler, 1994). However, they cannot readily accomplish more than one cognitive task requiring them to choose a response, retrieve information from memory, or engage in various other cognitive operations. When both tasks require performance of any of these cognitive operations, one or both tasks will show the PRP effect.

How well people can divide their attention also has to do with their intelligence (Hunt & Lansman, 1982). For example, suppose that participants are asked to solve mathematical problems and simultaneously to listen for a tone and press a button as soon as they hear it. We can expect that they both would solve the math problems effectively and respond quickly to hearing the tone. According to Hunt and Lansman, more intelligent people are better able to timeshare between two tasks and to perform both effectively.

Theories of Divided Attention

In order to understand our ability to divide our attention, researchers have developed capacity models of attention. These models help to explain how we can perform more than one attention-demanding task at a time. They posit that people

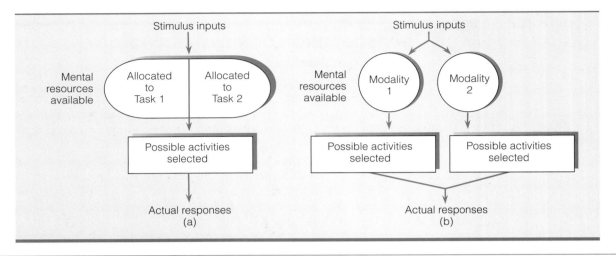

Figure 4.11   Allocation of Attentional Resources.
Attentional resources may involve either a single pool or a multiplicity of modality-specific pools. Although the attentional resources theory has been criticized for its imprecision, it seems to complement filter theories in explaining some aspects of attention.

have a fixed amount of attention that they can choose to allocate according to what the task requires. There are two different kinds: One kind of model suggests that there is one single pool of attentional resources that can be divided freely, and the other model suggests that there are multiple sources of attention (McDowd, 2007). Figure 4.11 shows examples of the two kinds of models. In panel (a), the system has a single pool of resources that can be divided up, say, among multiple tasks (Kahneman, 1973).

It now appears that such a model represents an oversimplification. People are much better at dividing their attention when competing tasks are in different modalities. At least some attentional resources may be specific to the modality (e.g., verbal or visual) in which a task is presented. For example, most people easily can listen to music and concentrate on writing simultaneously. But it is harder to listen to the news station and concentrate on writing at the same time. The reason is that both are verbal tasks. The words from the news interfere with the words you are thinking about. Similarly, two visual tasks are more likely to interfere with each other than are a visual task coupled with an auditory one. Panel (b) of Figure 4.11 shows a model that allows for attentional resources to be specific to a given modality (Navon & Gopher, 1979).

Attentional-resources theory has been criticized severely as overly broad and vague (e.g., Navon, 1984; S. Yantis, personal communication, December 1994). Indeed, it may not stand alone in explaining all aspects of attention, but it complements filter theories quite well. Filter and bottleneck theories of attention seem to be more suitable metaphors for competing tasks that appear to be attentionally incompatible, like selective-attention tasks or simple divided-attention tasks.

Consider the psychological refractory period (PRP) effect, for example. To obtain this effect, participants are asked to respond to stimuli once they appear, and if a second stimulus follows a first one immediately, the second response is delayed. For these kinds of tasks, it appears that processes requiring attention must be handled

■ BELIEVE IT OR NOT

ARE YOU PRODUCTIVE WHEN YOU'RE MULTITASKING?

You're working on your term paper, you're texting with your best friend, and are having a little snack while listening to some music in the background. And you think you're productive? Researcher David Meyer and colleagues (2007) have found that working on more than one task at the same time not only makes you slower but also increases your chances of making mistakes. Your reaction time goes down by up to one second when you do two things at once. While this may not be so crucially important while you sit at your desk working, it can save or risk lives when you drive your car and text or make a call at the same time. However, even your learning capabilities

are impaired. A study by Foerde and colleagues (2006) found that the formation of declarative memory (which is essential for successful learning) is hampered even by little distractions like a sound in the background. This is because when we perform complex tasks, we keep a lot of information activated in our memory. The required concentration can easily be broken by external disturbances. If you want to try out how well you can text and drive at the same time, here's a little game for you:

http://www.nytimes.com/interactive/2009/
07/19/technology/20090719-driving-game
.html

sequentially, as if passing one-by-one through an attentional bottleneck (Olivers & Meeter, 2008).

Resource theory seems to be a better metaphor for explaining phenomena of divided attention (see *Believe It or Not*) on complex tasks. In these tasks, practice effects may be observed. According to this metaphor, as each of the complex tasks becomes increasingly automatized, performance of each task makes fewer demands on limited-capacity attentional resources. Additionally, for explaining search-related phenomena, theories specific to visual search (e.g., models proposing guided search [Cave & Wolfe, 1990; Wolfe, 2007] or similarity [Duncan & Humphreys, 1989]) seem to have stronger explanatory power than do filter or resource theories. However, these two kinds of theories are not altogether incompatible. Although the findings from research on visual search do not conflict with filter or resource theories, the task-specific theories more specifically describe the processes at work during visual search.

Divided Attention in Everyday Life

Divided attention plays an important role in our lives. How often are you engaged in more than one task at a time? Consider driving a car, for example. You need to be constantly aware of threats to your safety. Suppose you fail to select one such threat, such as a car that runs a red light and is headed directly toward you as you enter an intersection. The result is that you may become an innocent victim of a horrible car accident. Moreover, if you are unsuccessful in dividing your attention, you may cause an accident. Most automobile accidents are caused by failures in divided attention.

Some intriguing studies are based on our own set of everyday experiences. One widely used paradigm makes use of a simulation of the driving situation (Strayer & Johnston, 2001, see also Fisher & Pollatsek, 2007). Researchers had participants perform a tracking task. The participants had control of a joystick, which moved a cursor on a computer screen. The participants needed to keep the cursor in position on a moving target. At various times, the target would flash either green or red. If the color was green, the participants were to ignore the signal. If the color was red, however, the participants were to push a simulated brake. The simulated brake was a button on the joystick. In one condition, participants only had to accomplish this one task. In another condition, participants were involved in a second task. This procedure created a dual-task situation. The participants either listened to a radio broadcast while doing the task or talked on a cell phone to an experimental confederate (a collaborator of the experimenter). Participants talked roughly half the time and also listened roughly half the time. Two different topics were used to ensure that the results were not a result of the topic of conversation.

As shown in Figure 4.12, the probability of a miss in the face of the red signal increased substantially in the cell-phone dual-task condition relative to the

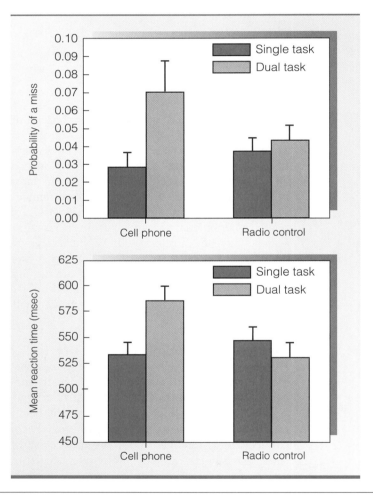

Figure 4.12 Dual-Task Performance During Driving.

Top panel: Dual-task performance significantly increased the probability of a miss in the cell-phone condition but not in the radio-control condition.

Bottom panel: Reaction time increased significantly for a dual task in the cell-phone condition but not in the radio-control condition.

Source: From Strayer, D. L., & Johnston, W. A. (2001). Driven to distraction: Dual-task studies of simulated driving and conversing on a cellular telephone. *Psychological Science, 12,* 463. Reprinted by permission of Blackwell Publishing.

single-task condition. Reaction times were also substantially slower in this condition than in the single-task condition. In contrast, there was no significant difference between probabilities of a miss in the single-task and radio dual-task condition, nor was there a significant difference in reaction time in this condition. Thus, use of cell phones appears to be substantially more risky than listening to the radio while driving (see also Charltona, 2009; Drews, 2008). So when you are driving, you are better off not using your cell phone.

There are also studies that analyze data from real-world incidents. A study of 2700 crashes in the state of Virginia between June and November of 2002 investigated causes of accidents (Warner, 2004). Here are some of the main factors that resulted in accidents, with the percentage of accidents for which each was responsible:

- rubbernecking (viewing accidents that have already occurred), 16%;
- driver fatigue, 12%;
- looking at scenery or landmarks, 10%;
- distractions caused by passengers or children, 9%;
- adjusting a radio, tape, or CD player, 7%; and
- cell phone use, 5%.

On an average, distractions occurring inside the vehicle accounted for 62% of the distractions reported. Distractions outside the vehicle accounted for 35%. The other 3% were of undetermined cause. The causes of accidents differed somewhat for rural versus urban areas. Accidents in rural areas were more likely to be due to driver fatigue, insects entering or striking the vehicle, or pet distractions. In urban areas, crashes were more likely to result from rubbernecking, traffic, or cell-phone use (Cohen & Graham, 2003; Figure 4.13).

As many as 21% of accidents and near-accidents involve at least one driver talking on a cell phone, although the conversation may or may not have been the cause of the accident (Seo & Torabi, 2004). Other research has indicated that, when time on task and driving conditions are controlled for, the effects of talking on a cell phone can be as detrimental as driving while intoxicated (Strayer, Drews, & Crouch, 2006). Still other research has found that, compared with people not on a cell phone, people talking on a cell phone exhibit more anger, through honking and facial expressions, when presented with a frustrating situation (McGarva, Ramsey, & Shear, 2006). Increased aggression has been linked with increased accidents (Deffenbacher et al., 2003). Therefore, it is likely that people who talk on the phone while driving are more prone to anger and, as a result, more accidents. These findings, combined with those on the effects of divided attention, help to explain why an increase in accidents is seen when cell phones are involved.

Factors That Influence Our Ability to Pay Attention

The existing theoretical models of attention may be too simplistic and mechanistic to explain the complexities of attention. There are many other variables that have an impact on our ability to concentrate and pay attention. Here are some of them:

- **Anxiety:** Being anxious, either by nature (trait-based anxiety) or by situation (state-based anxiety), places constraints on attention (Eysenck & Byrne, 1992; Reinholdt-Dunne et al., 2009).

Figure 4.13 **Divided Attention: Driving and Talking on the Cell Phone.**
Illustrating a failure of divided attention, accidents often happen because drivers are engaged in other activities like cell phone conversations. Drivers who rubberneck at the scene of an accident are another major cause of further accidents.

- **Arousal:** Your overall state of arousal affects attention as well. You may be tired, drowsy, or drugged, which may limit attention. Being excited sometimes enhances attention (MacLean et al., 2009).
- **Task difficulty:** If you are working on a task that is very difficult or novel for you, you'll need more attentional resources than when you work on an easy or highly familiar task. Task difficulty particularly influences performance during divided attention.
- **Skills:** The more practiced and skilled you are in performing a task, the more your attention is enhanced (Spelke, Hirst, & Neisser, 1976).

In sum, certain attentional processes occur outside our conscious awareness. Others are subject to conscious control. The psychological study of attention has included diverse phenomena, such as vigilance, search, selective attention, and divided attention during the simultaneous performance of multiple tasks. To explain this diversity of attentional phenomena, current theories emphasize that a filtering mechanism appears to govern some aspects of attention. Limited modality-specific attentional resources appear to influence other aspects of attention. Clearly, findings from cognitive research have yielded many insights into attention, but additional understanding also has been gained through the study of attentional processes in the brain.

Neuroscience and Attention: A Network Model

Imagine how hard it is to synthesize all those diverse studies investigating the full range of attentional processes in the brain. Is attention a function of the entire brain, or is it a function of discrete attention-governing modules in the brain? According to Michael Posner, the attentional system in the brain "is neither a property of a single brain area nor of the entire brain" (Posner & Dehaene, 1994, p. 75). In 2007, Posner teamed up with Mary Rothbart and they conducted a review of neuroimaging studies in the area of attention to investigate whether the many diverse results of studies conducted pointed to a common direction. They found that what at first seemed like an unclear pattern of activation could be effectively organized into areas associated with the three subfunctions of attention: alerting, orienting, and executive attention. The researchers organized the findings to describe each of these functions in terms of the brain areas involved, the neurotransmitters that modulate the changes, and the results of dysfunction within this system.

Alerting: *Alerting* is defined as being prepared to attend to some incoming event, and maintaining this attention. Alerting also includes the process of getting to this state of preparedness. The brain areas involved in alerting are the right frontal and parietal cortexes as well as the locus coeruleus. The neurotransmitter norepinephrine is involved in the maintenance of alertness. If the alerting system does not work properly, people develop symptoms of ADHD; in the process of regular aging, dysfunctions of the alerting system may develop as well.

Orienting: *Orienting* is defined as the selection of stimuli to attend to. This kind of attention is needed when we perform a visual search. You may be able to observe this process by means of a person's eye movements, but sometimes attention is covert and cannot be observed from the outside. The orienting network develops during the first year of life. The brain areas involved in the orienting function are the superior parietal lobe, the temporal parietal junction, the frontal eye fields, and the superior colliculus. The modulating neurotransmitter for orienting is acetylcholine. Dysfunction within this system can be associated with autism.

Executive Attention: Executive attention includes processes for monitoring and resolving conflicts that arise among internal processes. These processes include thoughts, feelings, and responses. The brain areas involved in this final and highest order of attentional process are the anterior cingulate, lateral ventral, and prefrontal cortex as well as the basal ganglia. The neurotransmitter most involved in the executive attention process is dopamine. Dysfunction within this system is associated with Alzheimer's disease, borderline personality disorder, and schizophrenia.

Intelligence and Attention

Attention also plays a role in intelligence (Hunt, 2005; Stankov, 2005). One model of intelligence that takes attention into account is the Planning, Attention, and Simultaneous–Successive Process Model of Human Cognition (PASS; Das, Naglieri, & Kirby, 1994; see also Davidson & Kemp, 2010). Based on Luria's (1973) theory of intelligence, it assumes that intelligence consists of an assortment of functional units that are the basis for specific actions (Naglieri & Kaufman, 2001). According to the PASS model, there are three distinct processing units and each is associated with specific areas of the brain: *arousal* and *attention*, *simultaneous and successive processing*, and *planning* (Das et al., 1994; Naglieri & Kaufman, 2001). The first unit, *arousal* and *attention*, is primarily attributed to the brainstem, diencephalon, and medial cortical regions of the brain. The researchers suggest that arousal is an essential antecedent to selective and divided attention.

Researchers have considered both the speed and the accuracy of information processing to be important factors in intelligence. Attention always plays a role because people must pay attention to a stimulus and then decide how to react to it. Let's look at how attention influences processing time and accuracy of responses.

Inspection Time

Inspection time is the amount of time it takes you to inspect items and make a decision about them (Gregory, Nettelbeck & Wilson, 2009; Neubauer & Fink, 2005). Essentially, the task requires concentrated bursts of focused attention. Here is a typical way researchers measure inspection time: For each of a number of trials, a computer monitor displays a fixation cue (a dot in the area where a target figure will appear) for half a second. Then there is a short pause. Afterward, the computer presents the target stimulus—two lines of differing lengths joined by a vertical bar at the top—for a particular interval of time. Finally, the computer presents a visual mask (a stimulus that erases the trace in iconic memory). The task of the participant is to decide which of the two lines is longer. The answer is indicated by pressing a left-hand or right-hand button on a keypad. The key variable here is actually the length of time for the presentation of the target stimulus, not the speed of responding by pressing the button. The inspection time is the length of time for presentation of the target stimulus after which the participant still responds with at least 90% accuracy. Nettelbeck found that shorter inspection times correlate with higher scores on intelligence tests (e.g., various subscales of the Wechsler Adult Intelligence Scale) among differing populations of participants (Nettelbeck, 1987; Williams et al., 2009).

Reaction Time

Some investigators have proposed that intelligence can be understood in terms of speed of neuronal conduction (e.g., Jensen, 1979, 1998). In other words, the smart person is someone whose neural circuits conduct information rapidly. When Arthur Jensen proposed this notion, direct measures of neural-conduction velocity were not readily available. So Jensen primarily studied a proposed proxy for measuring neural-processing speed. The proxy was *choice reaction time*—the time it takes to select one answer from among several possibilities. In such a task, one needs to attend in a focused and concentrated way on visual displays. Consider a typical choice-reaction-time paradigm.

The participant is seated in front of a set of lights on a board. When one of the lights flashes, he or she extinguishes it by pressing as rapidly as possible a button beneath the correct light. The experimenter would then measure the participant's speed in performing this task.

Participants with higher IQs are faster than participants with lower IQs in their choice reaction time (CRT) (Jensen, 1982; Schmiedek et al., 2007). These findings may be a function of increased central nerve-conduction velocity, although at present this proposal remains speculative (Budak et al., 2005; Reed & Jensen, 1991, 1993; see also Rostad et al., 2007). Interestingly, a study has found even the speed of the patellar reflex (knee-jerk response) to be significantly correlated with intelligence, although this reflex does not necessitate any conscious thought (McRorie & Cooper, 2001).

When Our Attention Fails Us

The real importance of attention becomes clear in situations in which we cannot concentrate. Many studies involve normal participants. But cognitive neuropsychologists also have learned a great deal about attentional processes in the brain by studying people who do not show normal attentional processes, such as people who show specific attentional deficits and who are found to have either lesions or inadequate blood flow in key areas of the brain. Overall, attention deficits have been linked to lesions in the frontal lobe and in the basal ganglia (Lou, Henriksen, & Bruhn, 1984); visual attentional deficits have been linked to the posterior parietal cortex and the thalamus, as well as to areas of the midbrain related to eye movements (Posner & Petersen, 1990; Posner et al., 1988). Work with split-brain patients (e.g., Ladavas et al., 1994; Luck et al., 1989) also has led to some interesting findings regarding attention and brain function, such as the observation that the right hemisphere seems to be dominant for maintaining alertness and that the attentional systems involved in visual search seem to be distinct from other aspects of visual attention.

In the following sections, we will consider two examples of failing attention: attention deficit hyperactivity disorder and change/inattentional blindness.

Attention Deficit Hyperactivity Disorder (ADHD)

Most of us take for granted our ability to pay attention and to divide our attention in adaptive ways. But not everyone can do so. People with *attention deficit hyperactivity disorder* (ADHD) have difficulties in focusing their attention in ways that enable them to adapt in optimal ways to their environment (*Attention deficit hyperactivity disorder*, 2009; see also Swanson et al., 2003).

The condition was first described by Dr. Heinrich Hoffman in 1845. Today, it has been widely investigated. No one knows for sure the cause of ADHD. It may be a partially heritable condition. There is some evidence of a link to maternal smoking and drinking of alcohol during pregnancy (Hausknecht et al., 2005; Obel et al., 2009; Rodriguez & Bohlin, 2005). Lead exposure on the part of the child may also be associated with ADHD. Brain injury is another possible cause, as are food additives—in particular, sugar and certain dyes (Cruz & Bahna, 2006; Nigg et al., 2008). There are noted differences in the frontal-subcortical cerebellar catecholaminergic circuits and in dopamine regulation in people with ADHD (Biederman & Faraone, 2005).

The three primary symptoms of ADHD are inattention, hyperactivity (i.e., levels of activity that exceed what is normally shown by children of a given age), and impulsiveness. There are three main types of ADHD, depending on which symptoms are predominant: (a) hyperactive-impulsive, (b) inattentive, and (c) a combination of hyperactive-impulsive and inattentive behavior. We will focus on the inattentive type here because it is most relevant to the topic of this chapter.

Children with the inattentive type of ADHD show several distinctive symptoms:

- They are easily distracted by irrelevant sights and sounds.
- They often fail to pay attention to details.
- They are susceptible to making careless mistakes in their work.
- They often fail to read instructions completely or carefully.
- They are susceptible to forgetting or losing things they need for tasks, such as pencils or books.
- They tend to jump from one incomplete task to another.

Bacall, Aaron/www.CartoonStock.com

**"It wasn't me jumping up and down and
yelling in class. It was the sugar talking."**

Up to 20% of all children worldwide may be affected by ADHD (attention deficit hyperactivity disorder).

Studies have shown that children with ADHD exhibit slower and more variable reaction times than their siblings who are not affected by the disorder (Andreou, 2007).

ADHD typically first displays itself during the preschool or early school years. It is estimated that about 5% of children worldwide have the disorder, though estimates range widely from less than 3% to more than 20% (Polanczyk & Jensen, 2008). The disorder does not typically end in adulthood, although it may vary in its severity, becoming either more or less severe. There is some evidence that the incidence of ADHD has increased in recent years. During the period from 2000 to 2005, the prevalence of medicinal treatment increased by more than 11% each year (Castle et al., 2007). The reasons for this increase are not clear. Various hypotheses have been put forward, including increased watching of fast-paced television shows, use of fast-paced video games, additives in foods, and increases in unknown toxins in the environment.

ADHD is most often treated with a combination of psychotherapy and drugs. Some of the drugs currently used to treat ADHD are Ritalin (methylphenidate), Metadate (methylphenidate), and Strattera (atomoxetine). This last drug differs from other drugs used to treat ADHD in that it is not a stimulant. Rather, it affects the neurotransmitter norepinephrine. The stimulants, in contrast, affect the neurotransmitter dopamine. Interestingly, in children, the rate of boys who are given medication for treatment of ADHD is more than double that of girls. However, in adults, the use of ADHD medication is approximately equal for both sexes (Castle et al., 2007). A number of studies have noted that, although medication is a useful tool in the treatment of ADHD, it is best used in combination with behavioral interventions (Corcoran & Dattalo, 2006; Rostain & Tamsay, 2006).

The theory of multiple intelligences (Gardner, 1985) has proven to be especially helpful in the treatment and support of children with ADHD. Gardner has suggested that intelligence comprises multiple independent constructs, not just a single, unitary construct. However, instead of speaking of multiple abilities that together constitute intelligence (e.g., Thurstone, 1938), this theory distinguishes eight distinct intelligences that are relatively independent of each other: linguistic, logical-mathematical, naturalist, interpersonal, intrapersonal, spatial, musical, and bodily-kinesthetic intelligences. Each intelligence is alleged to form a separate system of functioning, although these systems can interact to produce what we see as intelligent performance. By concentrating on the students' abilities (or predominant intelligences) in educational interventions, the achievements of students with ADHD can be increased and their strengths can be emphasized (Davidson & Kemp, 2010; Schirduan & Case, 2004).

Change Blindness and Inattentional Blindness

Evolutionarily, our ability to spot predators as well as to detect food sources has been a great advantage for our survival. Adaptive behavior requires us to be attentive to changes in our environment because changes cue us to both opportunities and dangers. It thus may be surprising to discover that people can show remarkable levels of **change blindness**, an inability to detect changes in objects or scenes that are being viewed (Galpin et al., 2009; O'Regan, 2003). Closely related to change blindness is inattentional blindness, which is a phenomenon in which people are not able to see things that are actually there (Bressan & Pizzighello, 2008). You can find some examples for change blindness and inattentional blindness in *Believe It or Not* at the very beginning of Chapter 1. Change and inattentional blindness are of major importance in traffic situations or during medical screenings, for example, where an overlooked motorcycle or a mass in the body can have potentially fatal consequences. For more on change blindness, see Chapter 2.

Spatial Neglect—One Half of the World Goes Amiss

Imagine you are in a zoo with an acquaintance and you both look at the cages containing animals. Meanwhile, you are making comments to each other about the animals' behavior. However, you soon notice that your friend is not aware of anything that is occurring in the left side of your visual fields. It is not only that he does not see the animals there; he is not even aware of their being there.

This condition is called *spatial neglect* or *hemi-neglect*. It is an attentional dysfunction in which participants ignore the half of their visual field that is contralateral to (on the opposite side of) the hemisphere of the brain that has a lesion. It is a result mainly of unilateral lesions in the parietal and frontal lobes, most often in the right hemisphere. One way to test for neglect is to give patients who are suspected of suffering from neglect a sheet of paper with a number of horizontal lines. Patients are then asked to bisect the lines precisely in the middle of each. Patients with lesions in the right hemisphere tend to bisect the lines to the right of the midline. Patients with lesions in the left hemisphere tend to bisect the lines to the left of the midline. The reason is that the former group of patients does not see all of the lines to the left, whereas the latter group does not see all of the lines to the right. Sometimes patients miss the lines altogether (i.e., patients who neglect the entire visual field). If patients are asked to copy little pictures they are presented with, they often draw only one side of the picture (Figure 4.14).

Figure 4.14 **Drawing by a Person with Hemispatial Neglect.**
This drawing is from a patient who is suffering from neglect. As you can see, he ignores part of the clock.

Interestingly, when patients are presented with stimuli only to their right or their left side, they often can perceive the stimuli, no matter which side they are on. This means that they have no major visual-field defects. However, when stimuli are present in both sides of the visual field, people with hemi-neglect suddenly ignore the stimuli that are contralateral to their lesion (i.e., if the lesion is in the right hemisphere, they neglect stimuli in the left visual field). This phenomenon is called "*extinction.*" The reason for extinction may be that patients are not able to disengage their attention from the stimulus in the ipsilateral field (the part of the visual field where the lesion is) in order then to shift their attention to the contralateral visual field. Their attention gets "stuck" on the ipsilateral object so that they cannot shift attention to stimuli that appear on the contralateral side. Fascinatingly, this finding holds true not only for people's perceptions in the external world, but also for their memories.

In a 1977 study conducted by Bisiach and Luzzatti, participants with neglect were asked to describe the main square in their town. They described only one side of the square, although when asked to describe it from opposite ends they demonstrated that they knew how both sides of the square looked.

There is no full consensus regarding which part of the brain is responsible for the symptoms of neglect. Recent studies indicate that the posterior superior temporal gyrus, insula, and basal ganglia, as well as the superior longitudinal fasciculus in the parietal lobe are most likely connected with spatial neglect (Hillis, 2005, 2006; Karnath et al., 2004; Shinoura et al., 2009).

✔ CONCEPT CHECK

1. Why is attention important for humans?
2. What are the mistakes we can make when trying to detect a signal?
3. What is vigilance?
4. What is a feature search, and how does it differ from a conjunction search?
5. What is the difference between divided and selective attention?
6. What are filter theories of attention?

Dealing with an Overwhelming World—Habituation and Adaptation

Crossing a street, we need to see that suddenly there is a car racing around the corner and in our direction. When we interact with our family and friends, we want to be aware of changes in their emotions and behavior so we can respond to them adequately. And yet, if we responded to every little change and stimulus in our environment, we would be quickly and completely overwhelmed.

The authors live close to a major hospital in Boston, and our ability to filter out the noise of the many ambulances that are coming in, day and night, helps us preserve our good night's sleep. So in a way, it is sometimes a blessing if there are stimuli to which we habituate (i.e., to which we get accustomed) so that we do not notice them anymore.

Habituation involves our becoming accustomed to a stimulus so that we gradually pay less and less attention to it. The counterpart to habituation is dishabituation. In **dishabituation**, a change in a familiar stimulus prompts us to start noticing the stimulus again. Both processes occur automatically. The processes involve no conscious effort. The relative stability and familiarity of the stimulus govern these processes. Any aspects of the stimulus that seem different or novel (unfamiliar)

PRACTICAL APPLICATIONS OF COGNITIVE PSYCHOLOGY

OVERCOMING BOREDOM

Habituation is not without faults. Becoming bored during a lecture or while reading a textbook is a sign of habituation. Your attention may start to wander to the background noises, or you may find that you have read a paragraph or two with no recollection of the content. Fortunately, you can dishabituate yourself with very little effort. Here are a few tips on how to overcome the negative effects of boredom.

1. **Take a break or alternate between different tasks.** If you do not remember the last few paragraphs you read in your text, it is time to stop for a few minutes. Go back and mark the last place in the text you do remember and put the book down. If you feel like a break is a waste of valuable time, do some other work for a while.

2. **Take notes while reading or listening.** Note-taking focuses attention on the material more than simply listening or reading. If necessary, try switching from script to printed handwriting to make the task more interesting.

3. **Adjust your attentional focus to increase stimulus variability.** Is the instructor's voice droning on endlessly so that you cannot take a break during lecture? Try noticing other aspects of your instructor, like hand gestures or body movements, while still paying attention to the content. Create a break in the flow by asking a question—even just raising your hand can make a change in a lecturer's speaking pattern. If all else fails, you may have to force yourself to be interested in the material. Think about how you can use the material in your everyday life. Also, sometimes just taking a few deep breaths or closing your eyes for a few seconds can change your internal arousal levels.

What other tasks in your life tend to be boring? How can you use the tips above to benefit more from these tasks?

either prompt dishabituation or make habituation less likely to occur in the first place. For example, suppose that a radio is playing instrumental music while you study your cognitive psychology textbook. At first the sound might distract you. But after a while you become habituated to the sound and scarcely notice it. If the loudness of the noise were suddenly to change drastically, however, immediately you would dishabituate to it. The once familiar sound to which you had been habituated would become unfamiliar. It thus would enter your awareness. Habituation is not limited to humans. It is found in organisms as simple as the mollusk *Aplysia* (Castellucci & Kandel, 1976).

We usually exert no effort to become habituated to our sensations of stimuli in the environment. Nonetheless, although we usually do not consciously control habituation, we can do so. In this way, habituation is an attentional phenomenon that differs from the physiological phenomenon of sensory adaptation. **Sensory adaptation** is a lessening of attention to a stimulus that is not subject to conscious control. It occurs directly in the sense organ, not in the brain. We can exert some conscious control over whether we notice something to which we have become habituated, but we have no conscious control over sensory adaptation. For example, we cannot consciously force ourselves to smell an odor to which our senses have become adapted. Nor can we consciously force our pupils to adapt—or not adapt—to differing degrees of brightness or darkness. In contrast, if someone asked us, "Who's the lead guitarist in that song?" we can once again notice background music. Table 4.3 provides some of the other distinctions between sensory adaptation and habituation.

Two factors that influence habituation are internal variation within a stimulus and subjective arousal. Some stimuli involve more internal variation than do others. For example, background music contains more internal variation (changing melodies, harmonies, and rhythms) than does the steady drone of an air conditioner. The relative complexity of the stimulus (e.g., an ornate, intricate oriental rug versus

Table 4.3   Differences between Sensory Adaptation and Habituation

Responses involving physiological adaptation take place mostly in our sense organs, whereas responses involving cognitive habituation take place mostly in our brains (and relate to learning).

Adaptation	Habituation
Not accessible to conscious control Example: You cannot decide how quickly to adapt to a particular smell or a particular change in light intensity.	*Accessible to conscious control* Example: You can decide to become aware of background conversations to which you had become habituated.
Tied closely to stimulus intensity Example: The more the intensity of a bright light increases, the more strongly your senses will adapt to the light.	*Not tied very closely to stimulus intensity* Example: Your level of habituation will not differ much in your response to the sound of a loud fan and to that of a quiet air conditioner.
Unrelated to the number, length, and recency of prior exposures Example: The sense receptors in your skin will respond to changes in temperature in basically the same way no matter how many times you have been exposed to such changes and no matter how recently you have experienced such changes.	*Tied very closely to the number, length, and recency of prior exposures* Example: You will become more quickly habituated to the sound of a chiming clock when you have been exposed to the sound more often, for longer times, and on more recent occasions.

a gray carpet) does not seem to be important to habituation. Rather, what matters is the amount of change within the stimulus over time. For example, a mobile involves more change than does an ornate but rigid sculpture. Thus, it is also relatively difficult to remain continually habituated to the frequently changing noises coming from a television. But it is relatively easy to become habituated to a constantly running fan. The reason is that the voices typically speak animatedly and with great inflectional expression. They are constantly changing, whereas the sound a fan makes remains constant with little to no variation.

Psychologists can observe habituation occurring at the physiological level by measuring our degree of arousal. **Arousal** is a degree of physiological excitation, responsivity, and readiness for action, relative to a baseline. Arousal often is measured in terms of heart rate, blood pressure, electroencephalograph (EEG) patterns, and other physiological signs. Consider what happens, for example, when an unchanging visual stimulus remains in our visual field for a long time. Our neural activity (as shown on an EEG) in response to that stimulus decreases. Both neural activity and other physiological responses (e.g., heart rate) can be measured. These measurements detect heightened arousal in response to perceived novelty or diminished arousal in response to perceived familiarity.

Psychologists in many fields use physiological indications of habituation to study a wide array of psychological phenomena in people (e.g., infants, or comatose patients) who cannot provide verbal reports of their responses. Physiological indicators of habituation tell the researcher whether the person notices changes in the stimulus. Such changes might occur in the color, pattern, size, or form of a stimulus. These indicators signal whether the person notices the changes at all, as well as what specific changes the person notices in the stimulus.

Without habituation, our attentional system would be much more greatly taxed. How easily would we function in our highly stimulating environments if we could not habituate to familiar stimuli? Imagine trying to listen to a lecture if you could not habituate to the sounds of your own breathing, the rustling of papers and books, or the faint buzzing of fluorescent lights.

An example of the failure to habituate can be seen in persons who suffer from tinnitus (ringing in the ears). People who complain of having tinnitus seem to have problems habituating to auditory stimuli. Many people have ringing in their ears, and if they are placed in a quiet room, will report a buzzing or other sounds. However, people who chronically suffer from tinnitus have difficulty adapting to the noise (Bessman et al., 2009; Walpurger et al., 2003). Evidence also indicates that people with attention deficit hyperactivity disorder (ADHD) have difficulty habituating to many types of stimuli. This difficulty helps to explain why ordinary stimuli, such as the buzzing of fluorescent lights, can be distracting to a person with ADHD (Jansiewicz et al., 2004).

Automatic and Controlled Processes in Attention

As we have seen, our attention is capable of processing only so many things at once. There are attentional filters that filter out irrelevant stimuli to enable us to process in depth what is important to us. To help us navigate our environment more successfully, we automatize many processes so that we can execute them without using up resources that then can be spent on other processes. Therefore, it is useful to differentiate cognitive processes in terms of whether they do or do not require conscious control (Schneider & Shiffrin, 1977; Shiffrin & Schneider, 1977).

Automatic and Controlled Processes

Automatic processes like writing your name involve no conscious control (Palmeri, 2003). For the most part, they are performed without conscious awareness. Nevertheless, you may be aware that you are performing them. They demand little or no effort or even intention. Multiple automatic processes may occur at once, or at least very quickly, and in no particular sequence. Thus, they are termed *parallel processes*. You are able to read this text while at the same time sharpening your pencil and scratching your leg with your foot.

In contrast, **controlled processes** are accessible to conscious control and even require it. Such processes are performed serially, for example, when you want to compute the total cost of a trip you are about to book online. In other words, controlled processes occur sequentially, one step at a time. They take a relatively long time to execute, at least as compared with automatic processes.

Three attributes characterize automatic processes (Posner & Snyder, 1975). First, they are concealed from consciousness. Second, they are unintentional. Third, they consume few attentional resources.

An alternative view of attention suggests a continuum of processes between fully automatic processes and fully controlled processes. For one thing, the range of controlled processes is so wide and diverse that it would be difficult to characterize all the controlled processes in the same way (Logan, 1988). Also, some automatic processes are easy to retrieve into consciousness and can be controlled intentionally, whereas others are not accessible to consciousness and/or cannot be controlled intentionally. Table 4.4 summarizes the characteristics of controlled versus automatic processes.

Many tasks that start off as controlled processes eventually become automatic ones as a result of practice (LaBerge, 1975, 1990; Raz, 2007). This process is called **automatization** (also termed *proceduralization*). For example, driving a car is initially a controlled process. Once we master driving, however, it becomes automatic under normal driving conditions. Such conditions involve familiar roads, fair weather, and little or no traffic. Similarly, when you first learn to speak a foreign language, you need to translate word-for-word from your native tongue. Eventually, however, you begin to think in the second language. This thinking enables you to bypass the intermediate-translation stage. It also allows the process of speaking to become automatic. Your conscious attention can revert to the content, rather than the process, of speaking. A similar shift from conscious control to automatic processing occurs when acquiring the skill of reading. However, when conditions change, the same activity may again require conscious control. In the driving example, if the roads become icy, you will likely need to pay attention to when you need to brake or accelerate. Both tasks usually are automatic when driving.

According to Sternberg's theory of triarchic intelligence (1999), relatively novel tasks that have not been automatized—such as visiting a foreign country, mastering a new subject, or acquiring a foreign language—make more demands on intelligence than do tasks for which automatic procedures have been developed. A completely unfamiliar task may demand so much of the person as to be overwhelming.

IN THE LAB OF JOHN F. KIHLSTROM

Posthypnotic Amnesia

Hypnosis is a special state of consciousness in which subjects may see things that aren't there, fail to see things that are there, and respond to posthypnotic suggestions without knowing what they are doing or why (Kihlstrom, 2007, 2008). Afterward, they may be unable to remember the things they did while they were hypnotized—a phenomenon known as posthypnotic amnesia, which has been a major focus of my work.

JOHN F. KIHLSTROM

First, however, we have to find the right subjects. Unfortunately, there is no way to predict in advance who can experience hypnosis and who cannot. The only way to find out is to try hypnosis and see if it works. For this purpose, we rely on a set of standardized scales of hypnotic susceptibility. These are performance-based tests structured much like tests of intelligence. Each scale begins with an induction of hypnosis, followed by a series of suggestions for various hypnotic experiences. Response to each suggestion is evaluated according to standardized, behavioral criteria, yielding a total score representing the person's ability to experience hypnosis.

From this point on, however, our experiments on cognition look just like anyone else's—except that our subjects are hypnotized. In one study using a familiar verbal-learning paradigm (Kihlstrom, 1980), the subjects memorized a list of 15 familiar words, such as *girl* or *chair*, and then received a suggestion that "You will not be able to remember that you learned any words while you were hypnotized … until I say to you, 'Now you can remember everything.'" After coming out of hypnosis, highly hypnotizable subjects remembered virtually none of the study list, whereas insusceptible subjects, who had gone through the same procedures, remembered it almost perfectly. This shows that the occurrence of posthypnotic amnesia is highly correlated with hypnotizability.

Then, we presented the subjects with a word association test, in which they were asked to report the first word that came to mind. Some of the cues were words like *boy* or *chair*, which were likely to elicit items from the study list.

Others were equally likely to elicit control words that had not been studied. Despite their inability to remember the words they had just studied, the hypnotizable, amnesic subjects produced items from the study list at the same rate as the insusceptible, nonamnesic subjects. This shows that posthypnotic amnesia is a disruption of episodic, but not semantic, memory. Even more important, the subjects showed semantic priming, responding with items from the study list more often compared to other items that they had not previously studied. The magnitude of the priming effect was the same in the hypnotizable, amnesic subjects as it was in the insusceptible, nonamnesic subjects. In other words, posthypnotic amnesia entails a dissociation between explicit and implicit expressions of episodic memory (Schacter, 1987).

While explicit and implicit memory is dissociated in other forms of amnesia, the dissociation observed in posthypnotic amnesia has some features that make it special. Most studies of implicit memory in neurologically intact subjects employ highly degraded encoding conditions, such as shallow processing, to impair explicit memory. But in our experiments, the subjects deliberately memorized the list to a strict criterion of learning before the amnesia suggestion was given, and they remembered the list perfectly well after the amnesia suggestion was canceled. Thus, implicit memory can be dissociated from explicit memory even under deep processing conditions.

More important, most studies of implicit memory in amnesia focus on repetition priming, which can be mediated by a perception-based representation of the prime. Accordingly, some of the most popular theories of implicit memory focus on perceptual representation systems in the brain. But in our original study, the priming was semantic in nature and must have been mediated by a meaning-based representation of the prime. In this way, studies of hypnosis remind us that a comprehensive theory of implicit memory is going to have to go beyond repetition priming and beyond perceptual representation systems.

Table 4.4   Controlled versus Automatic Processes

There is probably a continuum of cognitive processes, from fully controlled processes to fully automatic ones; these features characterize the polar extremes of each.

Characteristics	Controlled Processes	Automatic Processes
Amount of intentional effort	Require intentional effort	Require little or no intention or effort (and intentional effort may even be required to avoid automatic behaviors)
Degree of conscious awareness	Require full conscious awareness	Generally occur outside of conscious awareness, although some automatic processes may be available to consciousness
Use of attentional resources	Consume many attentional resources	Consume negligible attentional resources
Type of processing	Performed serially (one step at a time)	Performed by parallel processing (i.e., with many operations occurring simultaneously or at least in no particular sequential order)
Speed of processing	Relatively time-consuming execution, as compared with automatic processes	Relatively fast
Relative novelty of tasks	Novel and unpracticed tasks or tasks with many variable features	Familiar and highly practiced tasks, with largely stable task characteristics
Level of processing	Relatively high levels of cognitive processing (requiring analysis or synthesis)	Relatively low levels of cognitive processing (minimal analysis or synthesis)
Difficulty of tasks	Usually difficult tasks	Usually relatively easy tasks, but even relatively complex tasks may be automatized, given sufficient practice
Process of acquisition	With sufficient practice, many routine and relatively stable procedures may become automatized, such that highly controlled processes may become partly or even wholly automatic; naturally, the amount of practice required for automatization increases dramatically for highly complex tasks	

Suppose, for example, you were visiting a foreign country. You probably would not profit from enrolling in a course with unfamiliar abstract subject matter taught in a language you do not understand. The most intellectually stimulating tasks are those that are challenging and demanding but not overwhelming.

How Does Automatization Occur?

How do processes become automatized? A widely accepted view has been that during the course of practice, implementation of the various steps becomes more efficient. The individual gradually combines individual effortful steps into integrated components that are further integrated until the whole process is one single operation (Anderson, 1983; Raz, 2007). This operation requires few or no cognitive resources, such as attention. This view of automatization seems to be supported by one of the earliest studies of automatization (Bryan & Harter, 1899). This study investigated how telegraph operators gradually automatized the task of sending and receiving messages. Initially, new operators automatized the transmission of individual letters. However, once the operators had made the transmission of letters automatic, they automatized the transmission of words, phrases, and then other groups of words.

An alternative explanation, called "instance theory," has been proposed by Logan (1988). Logan suggested that automatization occurs because we gradually accumulate knowledge about specific responses to specific stimuli. For example, when a child first learns to add or subtract, he or she applies a general procedure—counting—for handling each pair of numbers. Following repeated practice, the child gradually stores knowledge about particular pairs of particular numbers. Eventually, the child can retrieve from memory the specific answers to specific combinations of numbers. Nevertheless, he or she still can fall back on the general procedure (counting) as needed. Similarly, when learning to drive, the person can draw on an accumulated wealth of specific experiences. These experiences form a knowledge base from which the person quickly can retrieve specific procedures for responding to specific stimuli, such as oncoming cars or stoplights. Preliminary findings suggest that Logan's instance theory may better explain specific responses to specific stimuli, such as calculating arithmetic combinations (Logan, 1988).

The effects of practice on automatization show a negatively accelerated curve. In such a curve, early practice effects are great. Later practice effects make less and less difference in the degree of automatization. A graph of improvement in performance would show a steeply rising curve early on, and the curve would eventually level off (Figure 4.15). Clearly, automatic processes generally govern familiar, well-practiced as well as easy tasks. Controlled processes govern relatively novel as well as difficult tasks. Because highly automatized behaviors require little effort or conscious control, we often can engage in multiple automatic behaviors. But we rarely can engage in more than one labor-intensive controlled behavior.

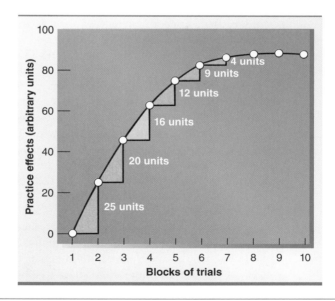

Figure 4.15   **The Practice Effect.**

The rate of improvement caused by practice effects shows a pattern of negative acceleration. The negative acceleration curve attributed to practice effects is similar to the curve shown here, indicating that the rate of learning slows down as the amount of learning increases, until eventually learning peaks at a stable level.

Automatization in Everyday Life

Automatization of tasks like reading is not guaranteed, even with practice. In the case of dyslexia, for example, automatization is impaired. Persons who have dyslexia frequently have difficulty completing tasks, in addition to reading, that are normally automated (Brambati et al., 2006; Ramus et al., 2003; van der Leij, de Jong, & Rijswijk-Prins, 2001).

Sometimes, automatization in reading can work against us, however. One demonstration of this is the **Stroop effect**, which is named after John Ridley Stroop (1935). The task works as follows: Quickly read aloud the following words: brown, blue, green, red, purple. Easy, isn't it? Now quickly name aloud the colors shown in part (a) of the top figure on the back endpaper of this book. In this figure, the colored ink matches the name of the color word. This task, too, is easy. Now, look at part (c) of the same figure. Here, the colors of the inks differ from the color names that are printed with them. Again, name the ink colors you see, out loud, as quickly as possible.

You probably will find the task very difficult: Each of the written words interferes with your naming the color of the ink. The Stroop effect demonstrates the psychological difficulty in selectively attending to the color of the ink and trying to ignore the word that is printed with the ink of that color. One explanation of why the Stroop test may be particularly difficult is that, for you and most other adults, reading is now an automatic process. It is not readily subject to your conscious control (MacLeod, 1996, 2005). For that reason, you find it difficult intentionally to refrain from reading and instead to concentrate on identifying the color of the ink, disregarding the word printed in that ink color. An alternative explanation is that the output of a response occurs when the mental pathways for producing the response are activated sufficiently (MacLeod, 1991). In the Stroop test, the color word activates a cortical pathway for saying the word. In contrast, the ink-color name activates a pathway for naming the color. But the former pathway interferes with the latter. In this situation, it takes longer to gather sufficient strength of activation to produce the color-naming response and not the word-reading response.

A number of variations of the Stroop effect exist, including the number Stroop, the directional Stroop, the animal Stroop, and the emotional Stroop. Theses tasks are very similar to the standard Stroop. For example, in the number Stroop, number words are used. Thus, the word *two* might be written three times, *two two two*, and the participant be asked to count the number of words. As with the standard Stroop task, reading sometimes interferes with the counting task (Girelli et al., 2001; Kaufmann & Nuerk, 2006). One of the most extensively used Stroop variations is the emotional Stroop. In this task, the standard task is modified so that the color words are replaced with either emotional or neutral words. Participants are asked to name the colors of the words. Researchers find that there is a longer delay in color naming for emotional words as compared with neutral words. These findings suggest that the automatic reading of emotional words causes more interference than reading of neutral words (Bertsch et al., 2009; Phaf & Kan, 2007; Thomas, Johnstone, & Gonsalvez, 2007).

In some situations, however, automatic processes may be life saving. Therefore, it is important to automate safety practices (Norman, 1976). This is particularly true for people engaging in high-risk occupations, such as pilots, undersea divers, and firefighters. For example, novice divers often complain about the frequent repetition of various safety procedures within the confines of a swimming pool, like releasing a cumbersome weight belt. However, the practice is important so the divers can rely on automatic processes in the face of potential panic should they confront a life-threatening deep-sea emergency.

But there are other situations where automatization may result in "mindlessness" and may be life threatening (Kontogiannis & Malakis, 2009; Krieger, 2005; Langer, 1989, 1997): In 1982, a pilot and copilot went through a routine checklist prior to takeoff. They mindlessly noted that the anti-icer was "off," as it should be under most circumstances. But it should not have been off under the icy conditions in which they were preparing to fly. The flight ended in a crash that killed 74 passengers. Typically, our absentminded implementation of automatic processes has far less lethal consequences. For example, when driving, we may end up routinely driving home instead of stopping by the store, as we had intended to do. Or we may pour a glass of milk and then start to put the carton of milk in the cupboard rather than in the refrigerator.

Mistakes We Make in Automatic Processes

An extensive analysis of human error shows that errors can be classified either as mistakes or as slips (Reason, 1990). *Mistakes* are errors in choosing an objective or in specifying a means of achieving it. *Slips* are errors in carrying out an intended means for reaching an objective. Suppose you decided that you did not need to study for an examination. Thus, you purposely left your textbook behind when leaving for a long weekend. But then you discovered at the time of the exam that you should have studied. In Reason's terms, you made a mistake. However, suppose instead you fully intended to bring your textbook with you. You had planned to study extensively over the long weekend, but in your haste to leave, you accidentally left the textbook behind. That would be a slip. In sum, mistakes involve errors in intentional, controlled processes. Slips often involve errors in automatic processes (Reason, 1990).

There are several kinds of slips (Norman, 1988; Reason, 1990; see Table 4.5). In general, slips are most likely to occur when two circumstances occur. First, when we must deviate from a routine and automatic processes inappropriately override intentional, controlled processes. Second, when our automatic processes are interrupted. Such interruptions are usually a result of external events or data, but sometimes they are a result of internal events, such as highly distracting thoughts. Imagine that you are typing a paper after an argument with a friend. You may find yourself pausing in your typing as thoughts about what you should have said interrupt your normally automatic process of typing. Automatic processes are helpful to us under many circumstances. They save us from needlessly focusing attention on routine tasks, such as tying our shoes or dialing a familiar phone number. We are thus unlikely to forgo them just to avoid occasional slips. Instead, we should attempt to minimize the costs of these slips.

How can we minimize the potential for negative consequences of slips? In everyday situations, we are less likely to slip when we receive appropriate feedback from the environment. For example, the milk carton may be too tall for the cupboard shelf, or a passenger may say, "I thought you were stopping at the store before going home." If we can find ways to obtain useful feedback, we may be able to reduce the likelihood that harmful consequences will result from slips. A particularly helpful kind of feedback involves forcing functions. These are physical constraints that make it difficult or impossible to carry out an automatic behavior that may lead to

Table 4.5   Slips Associated with Automatic Processes

Occasionally, when we are distracted or interrupted during implementation of an automatic process, slips occur. However, in proportion to the number of times we engage in automatic processes each day, slips are relatively rare events (Reason, 1990).

Type of Error	Description of Error	Example of Error
Capture errors	We intend to deviate from a routine activity we are implementing in familiar surroundings, but at a point where we should depart from the routine we fail to pay attention and to regain control of the process; hence, the automatic process captures our behavior, and we fail to deviate from the routine.	Psychologist William James (1890/1970, cited in Langer, 1989) gave an example in which he automatically followed his usual routine, undressing from his work clothes, then putting on his pajamas and climbing into bed—only to realize that he had intended to remove his work clothes to dress to go out to dinner.
Omissions*	An interruption of a routine activity may cause us to skip a step or two in implementing the remaining portion of the routine.	When going to another room to retrieve something, if a distraction (e.g., a phone call) interrupts you, you may return to the first room without having retrieved the item.
Perseverations*	After an automatic procedure has been completed, one or more steps of the procedure may be repeated.	If, after starting a car, you become distracted, you may turn the ignition switch again.
Description errors	An internal description of the intended behavior leads to performing the correct action on the wrong object.	When putting away groceries, you may end up putting the ice cream in the cupboard and a can of soup in the freezer.
Data-driven errors	Incoming sensory information may end up overriding the intended variables in an automatic action sequence.	While intending to dial a familiar phone number, if you overhear someone call out another series of numbers, you may end up dialing some of those numbers instead of the ones you intended to dial.
Associative-activation errors	Strong associations may trigger the wrong automatic routine.	When expecting someone to arrive at the door, if the phone rings, you may call out, "Come in!"
Loss-of-activation errors	The activation of a routine may be insufficient to carry it through to completion.	All too often, each of us has experienced the feeling of going to another room to do something and getting there only to ask ourselves, "What am I doing here?" Perhaps even worse is the nagging feeling, "I know I should be doing something, but I can't remember what." Until something in the environment triggers our recollection, we may feel extremely frustrated.

*Omissions and perseverations may be considered examples of errors in the sequencing of automatic processes. Related errors include inappropriately sequencing the steps, as in trying to remove socks before taking off shoes.

a slip (Norman, 1988). For example, some modern cars make it difficult or impossible to drive the car without wearing a seatbelt. You can devise your own forcing functions. You may post a small sign on your steering wheel as a reminder to run an errand on the way home. Or you may put items in front of the door to block your exit so that you cannot leave without the items you want.

Over a lifetime, we automatize countless everyday tasks. However, one of the most helpful pairs of automatic processes first appears within hours after birth: habituation and its complementary opposite, dishabituation.

Consciousness

Not everything we do, reason, and perceive is necessarily conscious. We may be unaware of stimuli that alter our perceptions and judgments or unable to come up with the right word in a sentence even though we know that we know the right word. This section will explore the consciousness of mental processes and how preconscious processing can influence our mind.

The Consciousness of Mental Processes

No serious investigator of cognition believes that people have conscious access to very simple mental processes. For example, none of us has a good idea of the means by which we recognize whether a printed letter such as A is an uppercase or lowercase one. But now consider more complex processing. How conscious are we of our complex mental processes? Cognitive psychologists have differing views on how this question is best answered.

One view (Ericsson & Simon, 1984) is that people have quite good access to their complex mental processes. Simon and his colleagues, for example, have used *protocol analysis* in analyzing people's solving of problems, such as chess problems and so-called cryptarithmetic problems, in which one has to figure out what numbers substitute for letters in a mathematical computation problem. These investigations have suggested to Simon and his colleagues that people have quite good conscious access to their complex information processes.

A second view is that people's access to their complex mental processes is not very good (e.g., Nisbett & Wilson, 1977). In this view, people may think they know how they solve complex problems, but their thoughts are frequently erroneous. According to Nisbett and Wilson, we typically are conscious of the products of our thinking, but only vaguely conscious, if at all, of the processes of thinking. For example, suppose you decide to buy one model of bicycle over another. You certainly will know the product of the decision—which model you bought. But you may have only a vague idea of how you arrived at that decision. Indeed, according to this view, you may believe you know why you made the decision, but that belief is likely to be flawed. Advertisers depend on this second view. They try to manipulate your thoughts and feelings toward a product so that, whatever your conscious thoughts may be, your unconscious ones will lead you to buy their product over that of a competitor. The essence of the second view is that people's conscious access to their thought processes, and even their control over their thought processes, is quite minimal (Levin, 2004; Wegner, 2002; Wilson, 2002). Consider the problem of getting over someone who has terminated an intimate relationship with you. One technique that is sometimes used to get over someone is thought suppression. As soon as you think of the person, you try to put the individual out of your mind. There is one problem with this technique, but it is a major one: It often does not work. Indeed, the more you try not to think about the person, the more you may end up thinking about him or her and having trouble getting the person off your mind. Research has actually shown that trying not to think about something usually does not work (Tomlinson et al., 2009; Wegner, 1997a, 1997b). Ironically, the more you try not to think about someone or something, the more "obsessed" you may become with the person or object.

Preconscious Processing

Some information that currently is outside our conscious awareness still may be available to consciousness or at least to cognitive processes. For example, when you comb your hair while getting ready for a first date, you are still able to do the combing although your mind in all likelihood will be completely elsewhere, namely, on the date. The information about how to comb your hair is available to you even if you are not consciously combing. Information that is available for cognitive processing but that currently lies outside conscious awareness exists at the preconscious level of awareness. Preconscious information includes stored memories that we are not using at a given time but that we could summon when needed. For example, when prompted, you can remember what your bedroom looks like. But obviously you are not always consciously thinking about your bedroom (unless, perhaps, you are extremely tired). Sensations, too, may be pulled from preconscious to conscious awareness. For example, before you read this sentence, were you highly aware of the sensations in your right foot? Probably not. However, those sensations were available to you.

Studying the Preconscious—Priming

How can we study things that currently lie outside conscious awareness? Psychologists have solved this problem by studying a phenomenon known as priming. In **priming**, participants are presented with a first stimulus (the prime), followed by a break that can range from milliseconds to weeks or months. Then, the participants are presented with a second stimulus and make a judgment (e.g., are both the first and the second stimulus the same?) to see whether the presentation of the first stimulus affected the perception of the second (Neely, 2003). The thought behind this procedure is that the presentation of the first stimulus may activate related concepts in memory that are then more easily accessible. Suppose, for example, someone is talking to you about how much he has enjoyed watching television since buying a satellite dish. He speaks at length about the virtues of satellite dishes. Later, you hear the word *dish*. You are probably more likely to think of a satellite dish, as opposed to a dish served at dinner, than is someone who did not hear the prior conversation about satellite dishes. Most priming is positive in that the first stimulus facilitates later recognition. But priming on occasion may be negative and impede later recognition. For example, if you are asked to solve several algebra problems that can be solved by the same formula, and then you are asked to solve another problem that requires another formula, you may be negatively primed relative to someone who did not solve the first set of problems with the now-irrelevant formula.

Sometimes we are aware of the priming stimuli. However, priming occurs even when the priming stimulus is presented in a way that does not permit its entry into conscious awareness (e.g., it is presented too briefly to be registered consciously).

Let us look at some studies that have used priming. Marcel (1983a, 1983b), for example, observed processing of stimuli that were presented too briefly to be detected in conscious awareness (Marcel, 1983a, 1983b). In one study, Marcel presented participants with a prime that had two different meanings. One such prime could be the word *palm* which can refer both to a body part and a plant. Afterward, participants were presented with another word that they were asked to classify into various categories. For participants who had *consciously* seen the prime, the mental pathway to one of the two meanings (e.g., plant) became activated and facilitated (speeded up) the classification of a subsequent *related* word. The pathway to the other meaning (e.g., body part) showed a negative priming effect in that it inhibited (slowed down) the classification of a subsequent *unrelated* word. For example, if the word *palm* was presented, the word either facilitated or inhibited the classification of the word *wrist*, depending on whether the participant associated *palm* with *hand* or with *tree*. In contrast, if the word *palm* was presented so briefly that the person was unaware of seeing the word, both meanings of the word appeared to be activated.

Another example of possible priming effects and preconscious processing can be found in a study described as a test of intuition. This study used a "dyad of triads" task (Bowers et al., 1990). Participants were presented with pairs (dyads) of three-word groups (triads). One of the triads in each dyad was a potentially coherent grouping. The other triad contained random and unrelated words. For example, the words in Group A, a coherent triad, might have been *playing, credit,* and *report*. The words in Group B, an incoherent triad, might have been *still, pages,* and *music*. (The words in Group A can be meaningfully paired with a fourth word—*card* [playing card, credit card, report card]; the words in Group B bear no such relationship.) After presentation of the dyad of triads, participants were shown various possible choices for a fourth word related to one of the two triads. The participants then were asked to identify which of the two triads was coherent and related to a fourth word, and which fourth word linked the coherent triad. Some participants could not figure out the unifying fourth word for a given pair of triads. They were nevertheless asked to indicate which of the two triads was coherent. When participants could not ascertain the unifying word, they still were able to identify the coherent triad at a level well above chance. They seemed to have some preconscious information available to them. This information led them to select one triad over the other. They did so even though they did not consciously know what word unified that triad.

The examples described here involve visual priming. Priming, however, does not have to be visual. Priming effects can be demonstrated using aural material as well. Experiments exploring auditory priming reveal the same behavioral effects as visual priming. Using neuroimaging methods, investigators have discovered that similar brain areas are involved in both types of priming (Badgaiyan, Schacter, & Alpert, 1999; Bergerbest, Ghahremani, & Gabrieli, 2004).

An interesting application of auditory priming was used with patients under anesthesia. While under anesthesia, these patients were presented lists of words. After awakening from anesthesia, the patients were asked yes/no questions and word-stem completion questions about the words they heard. The patients performed at chance on the yes/no questions. They reported no conscious knowledge of the words. However, on the word-stem completion task, patients showed evidence of priming. The patients frequently completed the word-stems with the items they were presented while they were under anesthesia. These findings reveal that, even when the patient has absolutely no recollection of an aural event, that event still can affect performance (Deeprose et al., 2005).

What's That Word Again? The Tip-of-the-Tongue Phenomenon

Unfortunately, sometimes pulling preconscious information into conscious awareness is not easy. Most of you probably have experienced the **tip-of-the-tongue**

phenomenon, in which you try to remember something that is stored in memory but that cannot readily be retrieved. Psychologists have tried to generate experiments that measure this phenomenon (see Hanley & Chapman, 2008, for example). In one classic study (Brown & McNeill, 1966), participants were read a large number of dictionary definitions. For example, they might have been given the clue, "an instrument used by navigators to measure the angle between a heavenly body and a horizon." The subjects then were asked to identify the corresponding words having these meanings. This procedure constituted a game similar to the television show *Jeopardy*. Some participants could not come up with the word but thought they knew it. Still, they often could identify the first letter, the number of syllables, or approximate the word's sounds. For example, it begins with an *s*, has two syllables, and sounds like *sextet*. Eventually, some participants realized that the sought-after word was *sextant*. These results indicate that particular preconscious information, although not fully accessible to conscious thinking, is still available to attentional processes.

The tip-of-the-tongue phenomenon is apparently universal. It is seen in speakers of many different languages. Bilingual people experience more tip-of-the-tongues than monolingual speakers which may be because bilinguals use either one of their languages less frequently than do monolinguals (Pyers et al., 2009). It is also seen in people with limited or no ability to read (Brennen, Vikan, & Dybdahl, 2007). Older adults have more tip-of-the-tongue experiences compared with younger adults (Galdo-Alvarez et al., 2009; Gollan & Brown, 2006). The anterior cingulate-prefrontal cortices are involved when one is experiencing the tip-of-the-tongue

I can't remember it right now,
but it's on the tips of my tongue...

In the tip-of-the-tongue phenomenon, you cannot think of a word or phrase that is stored in your memory and usually easily accessible.

phenomenon. This is likely due to high-level cognitive mechanisms being activated in order to resolve the retrieval failure (Maril, Wagner, & Schacter, 2001).

When Blind People Can See

Preconscious perception also has been observed in people who have lesions in some areas of the visual cortex (Rees, 2008; Ro & Rafal, 2006). Typically, the patients are blind in areas of the visual field that correspond to the lesioned areas of the cortex. Some of these patients, however, seem to show **blindsight**—traces of visual perceptual ability in blind areas (Kentridge, 2003). When forced to guess about a stimulus in the "blind" region, they correctly guess locations and orientations of objects at above-chance levels (Weiskrantz, 1994, 2009). Similarly, when forced to reach for objects in the blind area, "cortically blind participants ... will nonetheless preadjust their hands appropriately to size, shape, orientation and 3-D location of that object in the blind field" (Marcel, 1986, p. 41). Yet they fail to show voluntary behavior, such as reaching for a glass of water in the blind region, even when they are thirsty. Some visual processing seems to occur even when participants have no conscious awareness of visual sensations.

An interesting example of blindsight can be found in a case study of a patient called D. B. (Weiskrantz, 2009). The patient was blind on the left side of his visual field as an unfortunate result of an operation. That is, each eye had a blind spot on the left side of its visual field. Consistent with this damage, D. B. reported no awareness of any objects placed on his left side or of any events that took place on this side. But despite his unawareness of vision on this side, there was evidence of vision. The investigator would present objects to the left side of the visual field and then present D. B. with a forced-choice test in which the patient had to indicate which of two objects had been presented to this side. D. B. performed at levels that were significantly better than chance. In other words, he "saw" despite his unawareness of seeing.

Another study paired presentations of a visual stimulus with electric shocks (Hamm et al., 2003). After multiple pairings, the patient began to experience fear when the visual stimulus was presented, even though he could not explain why he was afraid. Thus, the patient was processing visual information, although he could not see.

One explanation for blindsight is the following: The information from the retina is forwarded to the visual cortex which is damaged in cortically blind people. It seems, however, that a part of the visual information bypasses the visual cortex and is sent to other locations in the cortex. The information from these locations is unconsciously accessible, although it seems to be conscious only when it is processed in the visual cortex (Weiskrantz, 2007).

The preceding examples show that at least some cognitive functions can occur outside of conscious awareness. We appear able to sense, perceive, and even respond to many stimuli that never enter our conscious awareness (Marcel, 1983a). Just what kinds of processes do or do not require conscious awareness?

✔ CONCEPT CHECK

1. Why is habituation important?

2. How do we become habituated to stimuli?

3. How do mental processes become automated?

4. What is priming and how can it be studied?

5. What symptoms do patients have who exhibit blindsight?

Key Themes

The study of attention and consciousness highlights several key themes in cognitive psychology.

Structures versus processes. The brain contains various structures and systems of structures, such as the reticular activating system, that generate the processes that contribute to attention. Sometimes, the relationship between structure and process is not entirely clear, and it is the job of cognitive psychologists to better understand it. For example, blindsight is a phenomenon in which a process occurs—sight—in the absence of the structures in the brain that would seem to be necessary for the sight to take place.

Validity of causal inferences versus ecological validity. Should research on vigilance be conducted in a laboratory to achieve careful experimental control? Or should the research of high-stakes vigilance situations be studied ecologically? For example, a study in which military officers are examining radar screens for possible attacks against the country must have a high degree of ecological validity to ensure that the results apply to the actual situation in which the military officers find themselves. The stakes are too high to allow slippage. Yet, when vigilance in the actual-life situation is studied, one cannot and would not want to make attacks against the country happen. Therefore, it is necessary to use simulations that are as realistic as possible. In this way, the ecological validity of conclusions drawn can be ensured.

Biological versus behavioral methods. Blindsight is a case of a curious and as yet poorly understood link. The biology does not appear to be there to generate the behavior. Another interesting example is attention deficit hyperactivity disorder. Physicians now have available a number of drugs that treat ADHD. These treatments enable children as well as adults to focus better on tasks that they need to get done. But the mechanisms by which the drugs work are still poorly understood. Indeed, somewhat paradoxically, most of the drugs used to treat ADHD are stimulants, which, when given to children with ADHD, appear to calm them down.

Summary

1. **Can we actively process information even if we are not aware of doing so? If so, what do we do, and how do we do it?** Whereas attention embraces all the information that an individual is manipulating (a portion of the information available from memory, sensation, and other cognitive processes), consciousness comprises only the narrower range of information that the individual is aware of manipulating. Attention allows us to use our limited active cognitive resources (e.g., because of the limits of working memory) judiciously, to respond quickly and accurately to interesting stimuli, and to remember salient information.

Conscious awareness allows us to monitor our interactions with the environment, to link our past and present experiences and thereby sense a continuous thread of experience, and to control and plan for future actions.

We actively can process information at the preconscious level without being aware of doing so. For example, researchers have studied the phenomenon of priming, in which a given stimulus increases the likelihood that a subsequent related (or identical) stimulus will be readily processed (e.g., retrieval from long-term memory). In contrast, in the tip-of-the-tongue phenomenon, another example of preconscious processing, retrieval of desired information from memory does not occur, despite an ability to retrieve related information.

Cognitive psychologists also observe distinctions in conscious versus preconscious attention by distinguishing between controlled and automatic processing in task performance. Controlled processes are relatively slow, sequential in nature, intentional (requiring effort), and under conscious control. Automatic processes are relatively fast, parallel in nature, and for the most part outside of conscious awareness. Actually, a continuum of processing appears to exist, from fully automatic to fully controlled processes. Two automatic processes that support our attentional system are habituation and dishabituation, which affect our responses to familiar versus novel stimuli.

2. **What are some of the functions of attention?** One main function involved in attention is identifying important objects and events in the environment. Researchers use measures from signal-detection theory to determine an observer's sensitivity to targets in various tasks. For example, vigilance refers to a person's ability to attend to a field of stimulation over a prolonged period, usually with the stimulus to be detected occurring only infrequently. Whereas vigilance involves passively waiting for an event to occur, search involves actively seeking out a stimulus.

People use selective attention to track one message and simultaneously to ignore others. Auditory selective attention (such as in the cocktail party problem) may be observed by asking participants to shadow information presented dichotically. Visual selective attention may be observed in tasks involving the Stroop effect. Attentional processes also are involved during divided attention, when people attempt to handle more than one task at once; generally, the simultaneous performance of more than one automatized task is easier to handle than the simultaneous performance of more than one controlled task. However, with practice, individuals appear to be capable of handling more than one controlled

task at a time, even engaging in tasks requiring comprehension and decision making.

3. **What are some theories cognitive psychologists have developed to explain attentional processes?** Some theories of attention involve an attentional filter or bottleneck, according to which information is selectively blocked out or attenuated as it passes from one level of processing to the next. Of the bottleneck theories, some suggest that the signal-blocking or signal-attenuating mechanism occurs just after sensation and prior to any perceptual processing; others propose a later mechanism, after at least some perceptual processing has occurred.

Attentional-resource theories offer an alternative way of explaining attention; according to these theories, people have a fixed amount of attentional resources (perhaps modulated by sensory modalities) that they allocate according to the perceived task requirements. Resource theories and bottleneck theories actually may be complementary. In addition to these general theories of attention, some task-specific theories (e.g., feature-integration theory, guided-search theory, and similarity theory) have attempted to explain search phenomena in particular.

4. **What have cognitive psychologists learned about attention by studying the human brain?** Early neuropsychological research led to the discovery of feature detectors, and subsequent work has explored other aspects of feature detection and integration processes that may be involved in visual search. In addition, extensive research on attentional processes in the brain seems to suggest that the attentional system primarily involves two regions of the cortex, as well as the thalamus and some other subcortical structures; the attentional system also governs various specific processes that occur in many areas of the brain, particularly in the cerebral cortex. Attentional processes may be a result of heightened activation in some areas of the brain, of inhibited activity in other areas of the brain, or perhaps of some combination of activation and inhibition. Studies of responsivity to particular stimuli show that even when an individual is focused on a primary task and is not consciously aware of processing other stimuli, the brain of the individual automatically

responds to infrequent, deviant stimuli (e.g., an odd tone). By using various approaches to the study of the brain (e.g., PET, ERP, lesion studies, and psychopharmacological studies), researchers are gaining insight into diverse aspects of the brain and also are able to use converging operations to begin to explain some of the phenomena they observe.

Thinking about Thinking: Analytical, Creative, and Practical Questions

1. Describe some of the evidence regarding the phenomena of priming and preconscious perception.
2. Why are habituation and dishabituation of particular interest to cognitive psychologists?
3. Compare and contrast the theories of visual search described in this chapter. Choose one of the theories of attention and explain how the evidence from signal detection, selective attention, or divided attention supports or challenges the theory.
4. Design one task likely to activate the posterior attentional system and another task likely to activate the anterior attentional system.
5. Design an experiment for studying divided attention.
6. How could advertisers use some of the principles of visual search or selective attention to increase the likelihood that people will notice their messages?
7. Describe some practical ways in which you can use forcing functions and other strategies for lessening the likelihood that automatic processes will have negative consequences for you in some of the situations you face.

Key Terms

arousal, *p. 169*
attention, *p. 137*
automatic processes, *p. 170*
automatization, *p. 170*
blindsight, *p. 181*
change blindness, *p. 165*
cocktail party problem, *p. 148*
conjunction search, *p. 144*
consciousness, *p. 138*
controlled processes, *p. 170*

dichotic presentation, *p. 149*
dishabituation, *p. 167*
distracters, *p. 143*
divided attention, *p. 138*
executive attention, *p. 161*
feature-integration theory, *p. 145*
feature search, *p. 144*
habituation, *p. 167*
priming, *p. 178*
search, *p. 143*

selective attention, *p. 138*
sensory adaptation, *p. 168*
signal, *p. 140*
signal detection, *p. 138*
signal-detection theory (SDT), *p. 140*
Stroop effect, *p. 174*
tip-of-the-tongue phenomenon, *p. 179*
vigilance, *p. 142*

Media Resources

Visit the companion website—**www.cengagebrain.com**—for quizzes, research articles, chapter outlines, and more.

CogLab

Explore CogLab by going to **http://coglab.wadsworth.com**. To learn more, examine the following experiments:

Prototypes

Absolute Identification

Implicit Learning

Memory: Models and Research Methods

Here are some of the questions we will explore in this chapter:

1. What are some of the tasks used for studying memory, and what do various tasks indicate about the structure of memory?
2. What has been the prevailing traditional model for the structure of memory?
3. What are some of the main alternative models for the structure of memory?
4. What have psychologists learned about the structure of memory by studying exceptional memory and the physiology of the brain?

■ BELIEVE IT OR NOT

MEMORY PROBLEMS? HOW ABOUT FLYING LESS?

Travel across time zones can actually get you more than just an annoying jet lag. Researchers have found that people who are subjected to jet lag frequently with less than two weeks of recovering time perform worse on spatial memory tests than people who have more time to recover (Cho, 2001). Twenty flight attendants who serve on flights across more than seven time zones at a regular basis had MRI analyses to measure the size of their brain. It turned out that those flight attendants who had only 5 days to recover from jet lag, as opposed to 14 days, had a smaller temporal lobe, which is important to memory functions, and performed worse on the spatial memory tests. But why would the temporal lobe be smaller? Cho presumes that this is the result of elevated stress hormones: Flight attendants had significantly higher salivary cortisol levels after repeated long-distance flights than after short-distance flights, and cortisol is known to cause harm to the temporal lobe. You need not worry, however, unless you travel repeatedly across many time zones with few days to recover. People who may be affected, however, are shift workers like doctors or nurses, because their day and night rhythms are frequently disrupted.

In this chapter, we will explore how our memory works and what factors improve or impair our memory performance.

Here are some questions. Try and see if you can answer them:

- Who is the president of the United States?
- What is today's date?
- What did you have for breakfast?
- What does your best friend look like, and what does your friend's voice sound like?
- What were some of your experiences when you first started college?
- How do you tie your shoelaces?

Those questions were pretty easy, right? Although retrieving the answers to these questions seemed easy, it is actually quite amazing that we can remember so many different facts and procedures without problems. In this chapter, we will see how we store information and retrieve it from memory.

As you age, your memory changes. As the author's grandmother got older, she gradually experienced a change in her memory. Memories from the grandmother's childhood and other details from her early and middle life were as vividly present as they had always been (your experiences when you started college), but she had more and more problems remembering anything that had happened in the recent past (what she had for breakfast earlier in the day). She would ask her grandchildren several times during a visit how they were doing and where they were currently working, but she was quick to recall events that had happened to her when she was a middle-aged adult.

Maybe you have seen symptoms like these in one of your older relatives? And what is memory exactly, anyway?

Memory is the means by which we retain and draw on our past experiences to use that information in the present (Tulving, 2000b; Tulving & Craik, 2000). As a process, memory refers to the dynamic mechanisms associated with storing, retaining, and retrieving information about past experience (Bjorklund, Schneider, & Hernández Blasi, 2003; Crowder, 1976). Specifically, cognitive psychologists have identified three common operations of memory: encoding, storage, and retrieval (Baddeley, 2002; Brebion, 2007; Brown & Craik, 2000). Each operation represents a stage in memory processing.

- In encoding, you transform sensory data into a form of mental representation.
- In storage, you keep encoded information in memory.
- In retrieval, you pull out or use information stored in memory. These memory processes are discussed at length in Chapter 6.

This chapter introduces some of the tasks that researchers use for studying memory. Then, we examine several models of how memory might work. First, we discuss the traditional model of memory. This model includes the sensory, short-term, and long-term storage systems. Although this model still influences current thinking about memory, we consider some interesting alternative perspectives and models of memory before moving on to discuss exceptional memory and insights provided by neuropsychology.

Tasks Used for Measuring Memory

In studying memory, researchers have devised various tasks that require participants to remember arbitrary information (e.g., numerals or letter strings) in different ways. Because this chapter includes many references to these tasks, we begin this section with a discussion of these tasks so that you will know how memory is studied. The tasks described fall into two major categories—recall versus recognition memory and implicit versus explicit memory.

Recall versus Recognition Tasks

In **recall**, you produce a fact, a word, or other item from memory. Fill-in-the-blank and most essay tests require that you recall items from memory. For example, suppose you want to measure people's memory for late-night comedians. You could ask people to name a TV comedian. In **recognition**, you select or otherwise identify an item as being one that you have been exposed to previously. (See also Table 5.1 for examples and explanations of each type of task.) For example, you could ask people which of the following is a late-night comic: Jennifer Lopez, Jay Leno, Guy Ritchie, Cameron Diaz. Multiple-choice and true-false tests involve some degree of recognition.

Three main types of recall tasks are used in experiments (Lockhart, 2000): serial recall, free recall, and cued recall. In *serial recall,* you recall items in the exact order in which they were presented. For example, you could ask people to remember the following list of comedians *in order*: Stephen Colbert, Jon Stewart, David

Table 5.1   Types of Tasks Used for Measuring Memory

Some memory tasks involve recall or recognition of explicit memory for declarative knowledge. Other tasks involve implicit memory and memory for procedural knowledge.

Memory Tasks	Description of What the Tasks Require	Example
Explicit-memory tasks	You must consciously recall particular information.	Who wrote *Hamlet?*
Declarative-knowledge tasks	You must recall facts.	What is your first name?
Recall tasks	You must produce a fact, a word, or other item from memory.	Fill-in-the-blank tests require that you recall items from memory. For example, "The term for persons who suffer severe memory impairment is _____."
Serial-recall task	You must repeat the items in a list in the exact order in which you heard or read them.	If you were shown the digits 2-8-7-1-6-4, you would be expected to repeat "2-8-7-1-6-4," in exactly that order.
Free-recall task	You must repeat the items in a list in any order in which you can recall them.	If you were presented with the word list "dog, pencil, time, hair, monkey, restaurant," you would receive full credit if you repeated "monkey, restaurant, dog, pencil, time, hair."
Cued-recall task	You must memorize a list of paired items; then when you are given one item in the pair, you must recall the mate for that item.	Suppose that you were given the following list of pairs: "time-city, mist-home, switch-paper, credit-day, fist-cloud, number-branch." Later, when you were given the stimulus "switch," you would be expected to say "paper," and so on.
Recognition tasks	You must select or otherwise identify an item as being one that you learned previously.	Multiple-choice and true-false tests involve recognition. For example, "The term for people with outstanding memory ability is (1) amnesics, (2) semanticists, (3) mnemonists, or (4) retrograders."
Implicit-memory tasks	You must draw on information in memory without consciously realizing that you are doing so.	Word-completion tasks tap implicit memory. You would be presented with a word fragment, such as the first three letters of a word; then you would be asked to complete the word fragment with the first word that comes to mind. For example, suppose that you were asked to supply the missing three letters to fill in these blanks and form a word: _e_or_. Because you had recently seen the word *memory*, you would be more likely to provide the three letters m-m-y for the blanks than would someone who had not recently been exposed to the word. (You have been "primed"; more on priming later in this chapter.)
Tasks involving procedural knowledge	You must remember learned skills and automatic behaviors, rather than facts.	If you were asked to demonstrate a "knowing-how" skill, you might be given experience in solving puzzles or in reading mirror writing, and then you would be asked to show what you remember of how to use those skills. Or you might be asked to master or to show what you already remember about particular motor skills (e.g., riding a bicycle or ice skating).

Letterman, Conan O'Brien, Jay Leno—and ask them then to repeat the list back in that order.

The second kind of task is *free recall,* in which you recall items in any order you choose (Golomb et al., 2008). In this case, you would ask people to remember the list of comedians above, in any order.

The third kind of task is *cued recall,* in which you are first shown items in pairs, but during recall you are cued with only one member of each pair and are asked to recall each mate. Cued recall is also called "paired-associates recall" (Lockhart, 2000). For example, you could ask people to learn the following pairings: Colbert–apple, Stewart–grape, Letterman–lemon, O'Brien–peach, Leno–orange, and then ask them to produce the pairing for Stewart (grape).

Psychologists also can measure *relearning,* which is the number of trials it takes to learn once again items that were learned in the past. Relearning has also been referred to as savings and can be observed in adults, children, and animals (Bauer, 2005; Sasaki, 2008). The relearning effect was also observed in fetal rats, whose limb movements were restrained by yokes and who were given kinesthetic feedback to influence their motor performance. These rats demonstrated shorter learning times for motor movements they had previously learned (Robinson, 2005). This effect is clearly extensively generalizable to many situations and participants. For example, suppose you studied Spanish in high school and then did not study it again in college. You now need it to succeed on your job in communicating with customers. If you relearn Spanish, you will experience a savings in time relative to what you experienced the first time you learned it.

Recognition memory is usually much better than recall (although there are some exceptions, which are discussed in Chapter 6). You may have experienced the superiority of recognition memory when you answered an exam question requiring you to remember a fact. You were not able to produce all the facts that were asked for, but when you discussed that particular question with a fellow student after the exam and he pointed out the correct answer, you immediately recognized it as correct and were annoyed with yourself for not coming up with the answer while taking the test.

A study by Standing and colleagues (1970) demonstrated that participants could recognize close to 2,000 pictures in a recognition-memory task. It is difficult to imagine anyone recalling 2,000 items of any kind they were just asked to memorize. As you will see later in the section on exceptional memory, even with extensive training, the best measured recall performance is typically around 80 items.

Informing participants of the type of future test they will take can influence the amount of learning that occurs. Specifically, anticipation of recall tasks generally elicits deeper levels of information processing than anticipation of recognition tasks. For example, if you are going to have a French vocabulary test, you may study differently (and more intensively) if you need to recall English meanings of French words than if you merely have to say whether a set of English definitions of French words are correct or incorrect (recognition).

Some psychologists refer to recognition-memory tasks as tapping *receptive* knowledge. Receptive means "responsive to a stimulus." In a recognition-memory task, you respond to stimuli presented to you and decide whether you have seen them before or not. Recall-memory tasks, in which you have to produce an answer, require *expressive* knowledge. Differences between receptive and expressive knowledge also are observed in areas other than that of simple memory tasks (e.g., language, intelligence, and cognitive development).

Implicit memory helps us to complete incomplete words we encounter without our even being consciously aware of it.

Implicit versus Explicit Memory Tasks

Memory theorists distinguish between explicit memory and implicit memory (Mulligan, 2003). Each of the tasks previously discussed involves **explicit memory,** in which participants engage in conscious recollection. For example, they might recall or recognize words, facts, or pictures from a particular prior set of items.

A related phenomenon is **implicit memory,** in which we use information from memory but are not consciously aware that we are doing so (Berry, 2008; McBride, 2007). You can read the word in the photo on the left without problems although a letter is missing.

Every day you engage in many tasks that involve your unconscious recollection of information. Even as you read this book, you unconsciously are remembering various things—the meanings of particular words, some of the cognitive-psychological concepts you read about in earlier chapters, and even how to read. These recollections are aided by implicit memory. There are differences in explicit memory over the life span; however, implicit memory does not show the same changes. Specifically, infants and older adults often tend to have relatively poor explicit memory but implicit memory that is comparable to that of young adults (Carver & Bauer, 2001; Murphy, McKone, & Slee, 2003). In certain patient groups, you also see deficiencies in explicit memory with spared implicit memory; these groups will be discussed later in the chapter.

In the following section, we will examine two tasks that involve implicit memory—priming tasks and tasks involving procedural knowledge. We will then have a look at the process-dissociation model, which postulates that only one task is needed to measure both implicit and explicit memory.

In the laboratory, implicit memory is sometimes examined by having people perform word-completion tasks that are based on the *priming* effect. In a word-completion task, participants receive a word fragment, such as the first three letters of a word. They then complete it with the first word that comes to mind. For example, suppose that you are asked to fill in the blanks with the five missing letters to form a word: imp_ _ _ _ _. Because you recently have seen the word *implicit*, you would be more likely to provide the five letters "l-i-c-i-t" for the blanks than would someone who had not recently been exposed to the word. You have been primed. Priming is the facilitation of your ability to utilize missing information. In general, participants perform better when they have seen the word on a recently presented list, although they have not been explicitly instructed to remember words from that list (Tulving, 2000a). Priming even works in situations where you are not aware that you have seen the word before—that is, if the word was presented for a fraction of a second or in some other degraded form.

Procedural memory, or memory for processes, can be tested in implicit-memory tasks as well. Examples of procedural memory include the procedures involved in riding a bike or driving a car. Consider when you drive to the mall: You probably put the car into gear, use your blinkers, and stay in your lane without actively thinking about the task. Nor do you consciously need to remember what you should do at a red light. Many of the activities that we do every day fall under the purview of procedural memory; these can range from brushing your teeth to writing.

In the laboratory, procedural memory is sometimes examined with the rotary pursuit task (Gonzalez, 2008; see Figure 5.1). The rotary pursuit task requires participants to maintain contact between an L-shaped stylus and a small rotating disk (Costello, 1967). The disk is generally the size of a nickel, less than an inch in diameter. This disk is placed on a quickly rotating platform. The participant must track the small disk with the wand as it quickly spins around on a platform. After learning with a specific disk and speed of rotation, participants are asked to complete the task again, either with the same disk and the same speed or with a new disk or speed. Verdolini-Marston and Balota (1994) noted that when a new disk or speed is used, participants do relatively poorly. But with the same disk and speed, participants do as well as they had after learning the task, even if they do not remember previously completing the task.

Another task used to examine procedural memory is mirror tracing. In the mirror-tracing task, a plate with the outline of a shape drawn on it is put behind a barrier where it cannot be seen. Beyond the barrier in the participant's line of sight is a mirror. When the participant reaches around the barrier, his or her hand and the plate with the shape are within view. Participants then take a stylus and trace the outline of the shape drawn on the plate. When first learning this task, participants have difficulty staying on the shape. Typically, there are many points at which

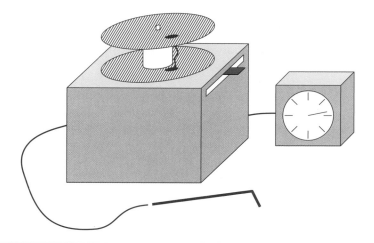

Figure 5.1   The Rotary Pursuit Task.

In the rotary pursuit task, subjects use an *L*-shaped stylus to track a small, rotating disk on a spinning platform.

the stylus leaves the outline. Moreover, it takes a relatively long time to trace the entire shape. With practice, however, participants become quite efficient and accurate with this task. Participants' retention of this skill gives us a way to study procedural memory (Rodrigue, Kennedy, & Raz, 2005).

The mirror-tracing task is also used to study the impact of sleep on procedural memory. Patients suffering from schizophrenia often have memory deficits as well as sleep problems. A study by Göder and colleagues (2008) found that when those patients received a medication that increased the duration of their slow-wave sleep, their procedural memory performance increased as well.

The methods for measuring both implicit and explicit memory described here and in Table 5.1 assume that implicit and explicit memory are separate and can be measured by different tasks. Some researchers have challenged this assumption. They assume that implicit and explicit memory both play a role in every response, even if the task at hand is intended to measure only one type of memory. Thus, cognitive psychologists have developed models that assume that both implicit and explicit memory influence almost all responses. One of the first and most widely recognized models in this area is the *process-dissociation model* (Daniels et al., 2006; Jacoby, 1991). The model assumes that implicit and explicit memory both have a role in virtually every response. Thus, only one task is needed to measure both these processes.

Although there are disagreements about exactly what the different measures show, there is agreement that both implicit and explicit memory are important in our everyday lives. Kaufman has also argued that implicit memory, like explicit memory, is an important part of human intelligence (Kaufman, 2010).

Intelligence and the Importance of Culture in Testing

In many cultures of the world, quickness is not at a premium. In these cultures, people may believe that more intelligent people do not rush into things. Even in our own culture, no one will view you as brilliant if you rush things that should not be rushed. For example, it generally is not smart to decide on a marital partner, a job, or a place to live in the 20 to 30 seconds you normally might have to solve an intelligence-test problem. Thus, there exist no perfectly culture-fair tests of intelligence, at least at present. How then should we consider context when assessing and understanding intelligence?

Several researchers have suggested that providing culture-relevant tests is possible (e.g., Baltes, Dittmann-Kohli, & Dixon, 1984; Jenkins, 1979; Keating, 1984). **Culture-relevant tests** measure skills and knowledge that relate to the cultural experiences of the test-takers. Baltes and his colleagues have designed tests measuring skill in dealing with the pragmatic aspects of everyday life. Designing culture-relevant tests requires creativity and effort, but it is probably not impossible. For example, one study investigated memory abilities—one aspect of intelligence as our culture defines it—in our culture versus the Moroccan culture (Wagner, 1978). The study found that the level of recall depended on the content that was being remembered. Culture-relevant content was remembered more effectively than non-relevant content. For example, when compared with Westerners, Moroccan rug merchants were better able to recall complex visual patterns on black-and-white photos of Oriental rugs. Sometimes tests are not designed to minimize the effects of cultural differences. In such cases, the key to culture-specific differences in memory may be the knowledge and use of metamemory strategies, rather than actual structural differences in memory (e.g., memory span and rates of forgetting) (Wagner, 1978).

Rural Kenyan school children have substantial knowledge about natural herbal medicines they believe fight illnesses. Western children, of course, would not be able to identify any of these medicines (Sternberg et al., 2001; Sternberg & Grigorenko, 1997). In short, making a test culturally relevant appears to involve much more than just removing specific linguistic barriers to understanding.

✔ CONCEPT CHECK

1. What is the difference between a recall task and a recognition task?
2. What is explicit memory?
3. What is implicit memory?
4. Why does it make sense to consider culture when doing research on memory in different countries?

Models of Memory

Researchers have developed several models to describe how our memory works. The traditional "three-store model" is not the only way to conceptualize memory. The following sections first present what we know about memory in terms of the three-store model. Then we examine the levels-of-processing model, and also consider an integrative model of working memory. Subsequently, we will explore some more conceptualizations of memory systems and lastly get to know a connectionist model. Let's begin with the traditional model of memory.

The Traditional Model of Memory

There are several major models of memory (McAfoose & Baune, 2009; Murdock, 2003). In the mid-1960s, based on the data available at the time, researchers proposed a model of memory distinguishing two structures of memory first proposed by William James (1890, 1970): primary memory, which holds temporary information currently in use, and secondary memory, which holds information permanently or at least for a very long time (Waugh & Norman, 1965). Three years later, Richard Atkinson and Richard Shiffrin (1968) proposed an alternative model that conceptualized memory in terms of three memory stores:

- a **sensory store**, capable of storing relatively limited amounts of information for very brief periods;
- a **short-term store**, capable of storing information for somewhat longer periods but of relatively limited capacity as well; and
- a **long-term store**, of very large capacity, capable of storing information for very long periods, perhaps even indefinitely (Richardson-Klavehn & Bjork, 2003).

The model differentiates among structures for holding information, termed *stores*, and the information stored in the structures, termed *memory*. Today, cognitive psychologists commonly describe the three stores as sensory memory, short-term memory, and long-term memory. Also, Atkinson and Shiffrin were not suggesting that the three stores are distinct physiological structures. Rather, the stores are **hypothetical constructs**— concepts that are not themselves directly measurable or observable but that serve as mental models for understanding how a psychological phenomenon works. Figure 5.2

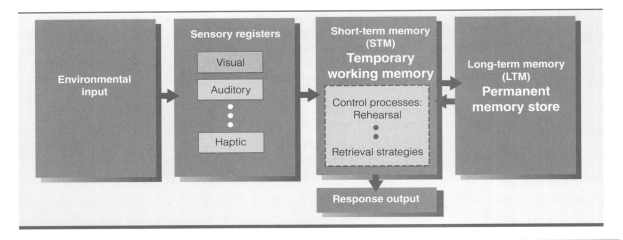

Figure 5.2   Atkinson and Shiffrin's Memory Model.

Richard Atkinson and Richard Shiffrin proposed a theoretical model for the flow of information through the human information processor.

Source: Illustration by Allen Beechel, adapted from "The Control of Short-Term Memory," by Richard C. Atkinson and Richard M. Shiffrin. Copyright © 1971 by Scientific American, Inc. All rights reserved. Reprinted with permission.

shows a simple information-processing model of these stores (Atkinson & Shiffrin, 1971). This Atkinson-Shiffrin model emphasizes the passive storage areas in which memories are stored; but it also alludes to some control processes that govern the transfer of information from one store to another. In the following sections, we take a closer look at the sensory store, the short-term store, and the long-term store.

Sensory Store

The *sensory store* is the initial repository of much information that eventually enters the short- and long-term stores. Strong (although not undisputed; see Haber, 1983) evidence argues in favor of the existence of an iconic store. The **iconic store** is a discrete visual sensory register that holds information for very short periods. Its name derives from the fact that information is stored in the form of icons. These in turn are visual images that represent something. Icons usually resemble whatever is being represented.

If you have ever "written" your name with a lighted sparkler (or stick of incense) against a dark background, you have experienced the persistence of a visual memory. You briefly "see" your name, although the sparkler leaves no physical trace. This visual persistence is an example of the type of information held in the iconic store.

Sperling's Discovery   The initial discovery regarding the existence of the iconic store came from a doctoral dissertation by a graduate student at Harvard University named George Sperling (1960). He addressed the question of how much information we can encode in a single, brief glance at a set of stimuli. Sperling flashed an array of letters and numbers on a screen for a mere 50 milliseconds (thousandths of a second). Participants were asked to report the identity and location of as many of the symbols as they could recall. Sperling could be sure that participants got only one glance because previous research had shown that 0.050 seconds is long enough for only a single glance at the presented stimulus.

Sperling found that when participants were asked to report on what they saw, they remembered only about four symbols. The finding confirmed an earlier one made by Brigden in 1933. The number of symbols recalled was pretty much the same, without regard to how many symbols had been in the visual display. Some of Sperling's participants mentioned that they had seen all the stimuli clearly. But while reporting what they saw, they forgot the other stimuli. Sperling then conceived an ingenious idea for how to measure what the participants saw. The procedure used by Brigden and in the first set of studies by Sperling is a *whole-report procedure*. In this procedure, participants report *every* symbol they have seen. Sperling then introduced a *partial-report procedure*. Here, participants need to report only part of what they see.

Sperling found a way to obtain a sample of his participants' knowledge. He then extrapolated from this sample to estimate their total knowledge. His logic was similar to that of school examinations, which also are used as samples of an individual's total knowledge of course material. Sperling presented symbols in three rows of four symbols each. Figure 5.3 shows a display similar to one that Sperling's participants might have seen. Sperling informed participants that they would have to recall only a single row of the display. The row to be recalled was signaled by a tone of high, medium, or low pitch. The pitches corresponded to the need to recall the top, middle, or bottom row, respectively.

To estimate the duration of iconic memory, Sperling manipulated the interval between the display and the tone. The range of the interval was from 0.10 seconds *before* the onset of the display to 1.0 second *after* the offset of the display. The partial-report procedure dramatically changed how much participants could recall. Sperling then multiplied the number of symbols recalled with this procedure by three. The reason was that participants had to recall only one third of the information presented but did not know beforehand which of the three lines they would be asked to report.

Using this partial-report procedure, Sperling found that participants had available roughly 9 of the 12 symbols if they were cued immediately before or immediately after the appearance of the display. However, when they were cued one second later, their recall was down to 4 or 5 of the 12 items. This level of recall was about the same as that obtained through the whole-report procedure. These data suggest that the iconic store can hold about 9 items. They also suggest that information in this store decays very rapidly (Figure 5.4). Indeed, the advantage of the partial-report procedure is

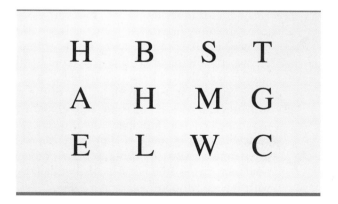

Figure 5.3   Display from a Visual-Recall Task.

This symbolic display is similar to the one used for George Sperling's visual-recall task.

Source: From *Psychology*, 2nd ed., by Margaret W. Matlin, Copyright © 1995 by Holt, Rinehart and Winston. Reproduced by permission of the publisher.

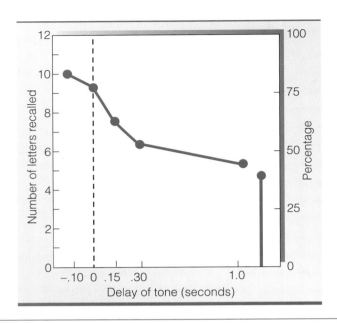

Figure 5.4 **Results of Sperling's Experiment.**
The figure shows the average number of letters recalled (left axis; percentage equivalents indicated on right axis) by a subject, based on using the partial-report procedure, as a function of the delay between the presentation of the letters and the tone signaling when to demonstrate recall. The bar at the lower-right corner indicates the average number of letters recalled when subjects used the whole-report procedure. (After Sperling, 1960.)

reduced drastically by 0.3 seconds of delay. It essentially is obliterated by 1 second of delay for onset of the tone.

Sperling's results suggest that information fades rapidly from iconic storage. Why are we subjectively unaware of such a fading phenomenon? First, we rarely are subjected to stimuli such as the ones in his experiment. They appeared for only 50 milliseconds and then disappeared before participants needed to recall them. Second and more important, however, we are unable to distinguish what we see in iconic memory from what we actually see in the environment. What we see in iconic memory is what we take to be in the environment. Participants in Sperling's experiment generally reported that they could still see the display up to 150 milliseconds after it actually had been terminated.

Elegant as it was, Sperling's use of the partial-report procedure was imperfect. It still suffered, at least to some small extent, from the problem inherent in the full-report procedure: Participants had to report multiple symbols. They may have experienced fading of memory during the report. Indeed, a distinct possibility of output interference exists. In this case, the production of output interferes with the phenomenon being studied. That is, verbally reporting multiple symbols may interfere with reports of iconic memory.

Subsequent Refinement In subsequent work, participants were shown displays of two rows of eight randomly chosen letters for a duration of 50 milliseconds (Averbach & Coriell, 1961). In this investigation, a small mark appeared just above one of the positions where a letter had appeared (or was about to appear). Its appearance was at varying time intervals before or after presentation of the letters. In this research, then, participants needed to report only a single letter at a time. The procedure thus minimized output interference. These investigators found that when the mark appeared immediately before or after the stimulus display, participants could report accurately on about 75% of the trials. Thus, they seemed to be holding about 12 items (75% of 16) in sensory memory. Sperling's estimate of the capacity of iconic memory, therefore, may have been conservative. The evidence in this study suggests that when output interference is greatly reduced, the estimates of the capacity of iconic memory may greatly increase. Iconic memory may comprise as many as 12 items.

A second experiment (Averbach & Coriell, 1961) revealed an additional important characteristic of iconic memory: It can be erased. The erasable nature of iconic memory definitely makes our visual sensations more sensible. We would be in serious trouble if everything we saw in our visual environment persisted for too long. For example, if we are scanning the environment at a rapid pace, we need the visual information to disappear quickly so that our memory does not get overloaded.

The investigators found that when a stimulus was presented after a target letter in the same position that the target letter had occupied, it could erase the visual icon (Averbach & Coriell, 1961). This interference is called backward visual masking. *Backward visual masking* is mental erasure of a stimulus caused by the placement of one stimulus where another one had appeared previously. If the mask stimulus is presented in the same location as a letter and within 100 milliseconds of the presentation of the letter, the mask is superimposed on the letter. For example, *F* followed by *L* would be *E*. At longer intervals between the target and the mask, the mask erases the original stimulus. For example, only the *L* would remain if *F* and then *L* had been presented. At still longer intervals between the target and the mask, the mask no longer interferes. This non-interference is presumably because the target information already has been transferred to more durable memory storage.

To summarize, visual information appears to enter our memory system through an iconic store. This store holds visual information for very short periods. In the normal course of events, this information may be transferred to another store. Or it may be erased. Erasure occurs if other information is superimposed on it before there is sufficient time for the transfer of the information to another memory store. Erasure or movement into another store also occurs with auditory information that is in echoic memory.

Short-Term Store

Most of us have little or no introspective access to our sensory memory stores. Nevertheless, we all have access to our short-term memory store. It holds memories for a few seconds and occasionally up to a couple of minutes. For example, can you remember the name of the researcher who discovered the iconic store? What about the names of the researchers who subsequently refined this work? If you can recall those names, you used some memory-control processes for doing so. According to the Atkinson-Shiffrin model, the short-term store does more than hold onto a few items. It also has some control processes available that regulate the flow of information to and from the long-term store, where we may hold information for longer periods. Typically, material remains in the short-term store for about 30 seconds, unless it is rehearsed to retain it. Information is stored acoustically (by the way it sounds) rather than visually (by the way it looks).

How many items of information can we hold in short-term memory at any one time? In general, our immediate (short-term) memory capacity for a wide range of items appears to be about seven items, plus or minus two (Miller, 1956). An item can be something simple, such as a digit, or something more complex, such as a word. If we chunk together a string of, say, 20 letters or numbers into 7 meaningful items, we can remember them. We could not, however, remember 20 items and repeat them immediately. For example, most of us cannot hold in short-term memory this string of 21 numbers: 101001000100001000100. However, if we chunk this string of numbers into larger units, such as 10, 100, 1,000, 10,000, 1,000, and 100. We probably will be able to reproduce easily the 21 numerals as 6 items (Miller, 1956).

Other factors also influence the capacity for temporary storage in memory. For example, the number of syllables we pronounce with each item affects the number of items we can recall. When each item has a larger number of syllables, we can recall fewer items (Hulme et al., 2006). In addition, any delay or interference can cause our seven-item capacity to drop to about three items. In general, the capacity limit may be closer to three to five than it is to seven (Cowan, 2001).

Most studies have used verbal stimuli to test the capacity of the short-term store, but people can also hold visual information in short-term memory. For example, they can hold information about shapes as well as their colors and orientations. What is the capacity of the short-term store of visual information? Is it less, the same, or perhaps greater?

A team of investigators set out to discover the capacity of the short-term store for visual information (Luck & Vogel, 1997; Vogel, Woodman, & Luck, 2001). They presented experimental participants with two visual displays. The displays were presented in sequence. The stimuli were of three types: colored squares, black lines at varying orientations, and colored lines at different orientations. Thus, the third kind of stimulus combined the features of the first two. The kind of stimulus was the same in each of the two displays. For example, if the first display contained colored squares, so did the second. The two displays could be either the same or different from each other. If they were different, then it was by only one feature. The participants needed to indicate whether the two displays were the same or different. The investigators found that participants could hold roughly four items in memory, which were within the estimates suggested by Cowan (2001). The results were the same whether just individual features were varied (i.e., colored squares, black lines at varying orientation) or pairs of features were varied (i.e., colored lines at different orientations). Thus, storage seems to depend on numbers of objects rather than numbers of features.

This work contained a possible confound (i.e., other responsible factors that cannot be easily disentangled from the supposed causal factor). In the stimuli with colored lines at different orientations, the added feature was at the same spatial location as the original one. That is, color and orientation were, with respect to the same object, in the same place in the display. A further study thus was done to separate the effects of spatial location from number of objects (Lee & Chun, 2001). In this research, stimuli comprising boxes and lines could be either at separate locations or at overlapping locations. The overlapping locations thus separated the objects from the fixed locations. The research would enable one to determine whether people can remember four objects, as suggested in the previous work, or four spatial locations. The results were the same as in the earlier research. Participants still could remember four objects, regardless of spatial locations. Therefore, memory was for objects, not spatial locations. Further, using American Sign Language, researchers have found that short-term memory can hold approximately four items for signed letters. This finding is consistent with earlier work on visual-spatial short-term memory. The finding makes sense, given the visual nature of these items (Bavelier et al., 2006; Wilson & Emmorey, 2006).

Long-Term Store

We constantly use short-term memory throughout our daily activities. When most of us talk about memory, however, we usually are talking about long-term memory. Here we keep memories that stay with us over long periods, perhaps indefinitely. All of us rely heavily on our long-term memory. We hold in it information we need to get us by in our day-to-day lives—people's names, where we keep things, how we schedule ourselves on different days, and so on.

How much information can we hold in long-term memory? How long does the information last? The question of storage capacity can be disposed of quickly because the answer is simple. We do not know. Nor do we know how we would find out. We can design experiments to tax the limits of short-term memory, but we do not know how to test the limits of long-term memory and thereby find out its capacity. Some theorists have suggested that the capacity of long-term memory is infinite, at least in practical terms (Bahrick, 2000; Brady, 2008). It turns out that the question of how long information lasts in long-term memory is not easily answerable. At present, we have no proof even that there is an absolute outer limit to how long information can be stored.

What is stored in the brain? Wilder Penfield addressed this question while performing operations on the brains of conscious patients afflicted with epilepsy. He used electrical stimulation of various parts of the cerebral cortex to locate the origins of each patient's problem. In fact, his work was instrumental in plotting the motor and sensory areas of the cortex, described in Chapter 3.

During the course of such stimulation, Penfield (1955, 1969) found that patients sometimes would appear to recall memories from their childhoods. These memories may not have been called to mind for many, many years. (Note that the patients could be stimulated to recall episodes such as events from their childhood, not facts such as the names of U.S. presidents.) These data suggested to Penfield that long-term memories might be permanent.

Some researchers have disputed Penfield's interpretations (e.g., Loftus & Loftus, 1980). For example, they have noted the small number of such reports in relation to the hundreds of patients on whom Penfield operated. In addition, we cannot be certain that the patients actually were recalling these events. They may have been inventing them. Other researchers, using empirical techniques on older participants, found contradictory evidence.

Some researchers tested participants' memory for names and photographs of their high-school classmates (Bahrick, Bahrick, & Wittlinger, 1975). Even after 25 years, there was little forgetting of some aspects of memory. Participants tended to recognize names as belonging to classmates rather than to outsiders. Recognition memory for matching names to graduation photos was quite high. As you might expect, recall of names showed a higher rate of forgetting.

The term *permastore* refers to the very long-term storage of information, such as knowledge of a foreign language (Bahrick, 1984a, 1984b; Bahrick et al., 1993) and of mathematics (Bahrick & Hall, 1991).

Schmidt and colleagues (2000) studied the permastore effect for names of streets near one's childhood homes. Indeed, the author just returned to his childhood home of more than 40 years ago and perfectly remembered the names of the nearby streets. These findings indicate that permastore can occur even for information that you have passively learned. Some researchers have suggested that permastore is a separate memory system. Others, such as Neisser (1999), have argued that one long-term memory system can account for both. There is to date no resolution of the issue.

In any case, research on the immense capacity of long-term memory has motivated researchers, instructors, and teachers to come up with new methods to help students memorize what they learn. Students do have great memory capacity, and ideally, they should leave school with both the ability to think critically and also a good knowledge base about which to think. To this end, new and motivating techniques are constantly being developed and include on-line quizzes that students can take to test their knowledge, or the use of clickers (remote control devices that allow students to communicate with their teacher in front via a computer system) with which students can answer multiple-choice questions during class and can give feedback to the teacher (Miller, 2009).

The Levels-of-Processing Model

A radical departure from the three-stores model of memory is the **levels-of-processing framework**, which postulates that memory does not comprise three or even any specific number of separate stores, but rather varies along a continuous dimension in terms of depth of encoding (Craik & Lockhart, 1972, 2008). In other words, there are theoretically an infinite number of levels of processing (LOP) at which items can be encoded through elaboration—or successively deeper understanding of material to be learned. There are no distinct boundaries between one level and the next. The emphasis in this model is on processing as the key to storage. The level at which information is stored will depend, in large part, on how it is encoded. Moreover, the deeper the level of processing, the higher, in general, is the probability that an item may be retrieved (Craik & Brown, 2000).

A set of experiments seems to support the LOP view (Craik & Tulving, 1975). Participants received a list of words. A question preceded each word. Questions were varied to encourage item elaboration on three different levels of processing. In progressive order of depth, they were *physical, phonological,* and *semantic.* Samples of the words and the questions are shown in Table 5.2. The results of the research were clear: The deeper the level of processing encouraged by the question, the higher the level of recall achieved. Similar results emerged independently in Russia (Zinchenko, 1962, 1981).

The levels-of-processing framework can also be applied to nonverbal stimuli. Melinda Burgess and George Weaver (2003) showed participants photos of faces and asked them questions about the persons of the photo to induce either deep or shallow processing. Faces that were deeply processed were better recognized on a subsequent test than those that were studied at a lower level of processing. A level-of-processing (or depth-of-processing) benefit can be seen for a variety of populations, including in people with schizophrenia. People suffering from schizophrenia often suffer from memory impairments because they do not process words semantically. Deeper processing helps them improve their memory (Ragland et al., 2003).

Table 5.2   Levels-of-Processing Framework

Among the levels of processing proposed by Fergus Craik and Endel Tulving are the physical, phonological, and semantic levels.

Level of Processing	Basis for Processing	Example	
Physical	Visually apparent features of the letters	Word:	TABLE
		Question:	Is the word written in capital letters?
Phonological	Sound combinations associated with the letters (e.g., rhyming)	Word:	CAT
		Question:	Does the word rhyme with "MAT"?
Semantic	Meaning of the word	Word:	DAFFODIL
		Question:	Is the word a type of plant?

An even more powerful inducement to recall has been termed the self-reference effect (Rogers, Kuiper, & Kirker, 1977). In the *self-reference effect*, participants show very high levels of recall when asked to relate words meaningfully to the participants by determining whether the words describe them. Even the words that participants assess as not describing themselves are recalled at high levels. This high recall is a result of considering whether the words do or do not describe the participants. However, the highest levels of recall occur with words that people consider self-descriptive. Similar self-reference effects have been found by many other researchers (e.g., Bower & Gilligan, 1979; Reeder, McCormick, & Esselman, 1987). Objects can be better remembered, for example, if they belong to the participant (Cunningham et al., 2008). Some researchers suggest that the self-reference effect is distinctive, but others suggest that it is explained easily in terms of the LOP framework or other ordinary memory processes (e.g., Mills, 1983). Specifically, each of us has a very elaborate self-schema. This self-schema is an organized system of internal cues regarding our attributes, our personal experiences, and ourselves. Thus, we can richly and elaborately encode information related to ourselves much more so than information about other topics (Bellezza, 1984, 1992).

Despite much supporting evidence, the LOP framework as a whole has its critics. For one thing, some researchers suggest that the particular levels may involve

INVESTIGATING COGNITIVE PSYCHOLOGY
Levels of Processing

Ask some friends or family members to help you with a memory experiment. Give half of them the instruction to count the number of letters in the words you are about to recite. Give the other half the instruction to think of three words related to the words you are about to recite. Recite the following words about 5 seconds apart: *beauty, ocean, competitor, bad, decent, happy, brave, beverage, artistic, dejected.* About 5 or 10 minutes later, ask your friends to write down as many of the 10 words as they can remember. In general, those who were asked to think of three related words to the words you read will remember more than those who were asked to count the number of letters in the words. This is a demonstration of levels of processing. Those friends who thought of three related words processed the words more deeply than those who merely counted up the number of letters in the words. Words that are processed more deeply are remembered better.

a circular definition. On this view, the levels are defined as deeper because the information is retained better. But the information is viewed as being retained better because the levels are deeper. In addition, some researchers noted some paradoxes in retention. For example, under some circumstances, strategies that use rhymes have produced better retention than those using just semantic rehearsal. That means, focusing on superficial sounds and not underlying meanings can result in better retention than focusing on repetition of underlying meanings. But now imagine two conditions—one in which participants encode the information acoustically (based on rhymes) and retrieve it based on acoustic cues as well; and one in which participants both encode and retrieve the information semantically. For example, participants are presented with a word and then have to determine whether that word rhymes with another word (acoustic encoding). For semantic encoding, they have to determine whether that word belongs to a given category or fits into a given sentence. Performance is greater for semantic retrieval than for acoustic retrieval (Fisher & Craik, 1977).

In light of these criticisms and some contrary findings, the LOP model has been revised. The sequence of the levels of encoding may not be as important as was thought before. Two other variables may be of more importance: the way people process (elaborate) the encoding of an item (e.g., phonological or semantic), and the way the item is retrieved later on. The better the match between the type of elaboration of the encoding and the type of task required for retrieval, the better the retrieval results (Morris, Bransford, & Franks, 1977).

Furthermore, there appear to be two kinds of strategies for elaborating the encoding. The first is within-item elaboration. It elaborates encoding of the particular item (e.g., a word or other fact) in terms of its characteristics, including the various levels of processing. The second kind of strategy is between-item elaboration. It elaborates encoding by relating each item's features (again, at various levels) to the features of items already in memory. Thus, suppose you wanted to be sure to remember something in particular. You could elaborate it at various levels for each of the two strategies.

 ## PRACTICAL APPLICATIONS OF COGNITIVE PSYCHOLOGY

ELABORATION STRATEGIES

Elaboration strategies have practical applications: In studying, you may wish to match the way in which you encode the material to the way in which you will be expected to retrieve it in the future, because the better the match between the way you encode the material and the way you will need to retrieve it later, the better you are able to retrieve items from memory. For example, if you are learning a new language and have a vocabulary test coming up, you will concentrate on learning the meaning of the words. If you have to write an essay, you will also need to concentrate on sentence structure and grammar.

Also, the more elaborately and diversely you encode material, the more readily you are likely to recall it later in a variety of task settings. Just looking over material again and again in the same way is less likely to be productive for learning the material than is finding more than one way in which to learn it. If the context for retrieval will require you to have a deep understanding of the information, you should find ways to encode the material at deep levels of processing, such as by asking yourself meaningful questions about the material.

Are there any circumstances under which elaboration might be problematic?

An Integrative Model: Working Memory

The working-memory model is probably the most widely used and accepted model to-day. Psychologists who use it view short-term and long-term memory from a different perspective (e.g., Baddeley, 2007, 2009; Unsworth, 2009). Table 5.3 shows the contrasts between the Atkinson-Shiffrin model and an alternative perspective. Note the semantic distinctions in how memory components are labeled, the differences in metaphorical representation, and the differences in emphasis for each view. The key feature of the alternative view is the role of working memory. **Working memory** holds only the most recently activated, or conscious, portion of long-term memory, and it moves these activated elements into and out of brief, temporary memory storage (Dosher, 2003).

The Components of Working Memory

Alan Baddeley has suggested an integrative model of memory (see Figure 5.5; Baddeley, 1990a, 1990b, 2007, 2009). It synthesizes the working-memory model with the LOP framework. Essentially, he views the LOP framework as an extension of, rather than as a replacement for, the working-memory model.

Baddeley originally suggested that working memory comprises five elements: the visuospatial sketchpad, the phonological loop, the central executive, subsidiary

Table 5.3 Traditional versus Nontraditional Views of Memory

Since Richard Atkinson and Richard Shiffrin first proposed their three-store model of memory (which may be considered a traditional view of memory), various other models have been suggested.

	Traditional Three-Store View	Alternative View of Memory
Terminology: definition of memory stores	Working memory is another name for short-term memory, which is distinct from long-term memory.	Working memory (active memory) is that part of long-term memory that comprises all the knowledge of facts and procedures that recently has been activated in memory, including the brief, fleeting short-term memory and its contents.
Metaphor for envisioning the relationships	Short-term memory may be envisioned as being distinct from long-term memory, perhaps either alongside it or hierarchically linked to it.	Short-term memory, working memory, and long-term memory may be envisioned as nested concentric spheres, in which working memory contains only the most recently activated portion of long-term memory, and short-term memory contains only a very small, fleeting portion of working memory.
Metaphor for the movement of information	Information moves directly from long-term memory to short-term memory and then back—never in both locations at once.	Information remains within long-term memory; when activated, information moves into long-term memory's specialized working memory, which actively will move information into and out of the short-term memory store contained within it.
Emphasis	Distinction between long- and short-term memory.	Role of activation in moving information into working memory and the role of working memory in memory processes.

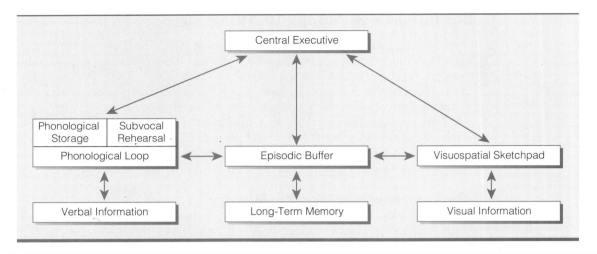

Figure 5.5 **Working Memory.**
The components of the working-memory model comprise the central executive, the phonological loop, the visuospatial sketchpad, and the episodic buffer, as well as several "subsidiary slave systems" (not pictured).

"slave systems," and the episodic buffer. The first element, the **visuospatial sketchpad**, briefly holds some visual images.

The **phonological loop** briefly holds inner speech for verbal comprehension and for acoustic rehearsal. We use the phonological loop for a number of everyday tasks, including sounding out new and difficult words and solving word problems. There are two critical components of this loop. One is *phonological storage*, which holds information in memory. The other is *subvocal rehearsal*, which is used to put the information into memory in the first place. The role of subvocal rehearsal can be seen in the following example. Try to memorize the following list of words while repeating the number *five* to yourself continuously:

Tree, pencil, marshmallow, lamp, sunglasses, computer, chocolate, noise, clock, snow, river, square, store.

Did you notice how hard it is to memorize these words? Try it again without repeating the number five to yourself—it should be much easier now! So what happens when you repeat the number five while memorizing words? In this case subvocal rehearsal is inhibited and you would be unable to rehearse the new words. When subvocal rehearsal is inhibited, the new information is not stored. This phenomenon is called *articulatory suppression*. Articulatory suppression is more pronounced when the information is presented visually versus aurally (e.g., by hearing). The amount of information that can be manipulated within the phonological loop is limited. Thus, we can remember fewer long words compared with short words (Baddeley, 2000b). Without this loop, acoustic information decays after about 2 seconds.

The third element is a **central executive**, which both coordinates attentional activities and governs responses. The central executive is critical to working memory because it is the gating mechanism that decides what information to process further and how to process this information. It decides what resources to allocate to memory and related tasks, and how to allocate them. It is also involved in higher-order reasoning and comprehension and is central to human intelligence.

The fourth element is a number of other *"subsidiary slave systems"* that perform other cognitive or perceptual tasks (Baddeley, 1989, p. 36). The fifth component is the **episodic buffer**. The episodic buffer is a limited-capacity system that is capable of binding information from the visuospatial sketchpad and the phonological loop as well as from long-term memory into a unitary episodic representation. This component integrates information from different parts of working memory—that is, visual-spatial and phonological—so that they make sense to us. This incorporation allows us to solve problems and re-evaluate previous experiences with more recent knowledge.

Whereas the three-store view emphasizes the structural receptacles for stored information (a relatively passive task), the working-memory model underscores the functions of working memory in governing the processes of memory. These processes include encoding and integrating information. Examples are integrating acoustic and visual information through cross-modality, organizing information into meaningful chunks, and linking new information to existing forms of knowledge representation in long-term memory.

We can conceptualize the differing emphases with contrasting metaphors. For example, we can compare the three-store view to a warehouse in which information is passively stored. The sensory store serves as the loading dock. The short-term store comprises the area surrounding the loading dock. Here, information is stored temporarily until it is moved to or from the correct location in the warehouse (long-term store).

A metaphor for the working-memory model might be a multimedia production house. It continuously generates and manipulates images and sounds. It also coordinates the integration of sights and sounds into meaningful arrangements. Once images, sounds, and other information are stored, they are still available for reformatting and reintegration in novel ways, as new demands and new information become available.

Neuroscience and Working Memory

Neuropsychological methods, and especially brain imaging, can be very helpful in understanding the nature of memory. Support for a distinction between working memory and long-term memory comes from neuropsychological research. Neuropsychological studies have shown abundant evidence of a brief memory buffer. The buffer is used for remembering information temporarily. It is distinct from long-term memory, which is used for remembering information for long periods (Rudner et al., 2007; Squire & Knowlton, 2000).

Furthermore, through some promising new research using positron emission tomography (PET) techniques, investigators have found evidence for distinct brain areas involved in the different aspects of working memory. The phonological loop, maintaining speech-related information, appears to involve activation in the left hemisphere of the lateral frontal and inferior parietal lobes as well as the temporal lobe (Gazzaniga et al., 2009; Baddeley, 2006).

It is interesting that the visuospatial sketchpad appears to activate slightly different areas. Which ones it activates depends on factors like task difficulty and the length of the retention interval (Logie & Della Sala, 2005). Shorter intervals activate areas of the occipital and right frontal lobes. Longer intervals activate areas of the parietal and left frontal lobes (Haxby et al., 1995).

Relatively little is known about the central executive. The central executive functions appear to involve activation mostly in the frontal lobes (Baddeley, 2006; Roberts, Robbins, & Weiskrantz, 1996).

Finally, the episodic buffer operations seem to involve the bilateral activation of the frontal lobes and portions of the temporal lobes, including the left hippocampus (Rudner et al., 2007). Different aspects of working memory are represented in the brain differently. Figure 5.6 shows some of these differences.

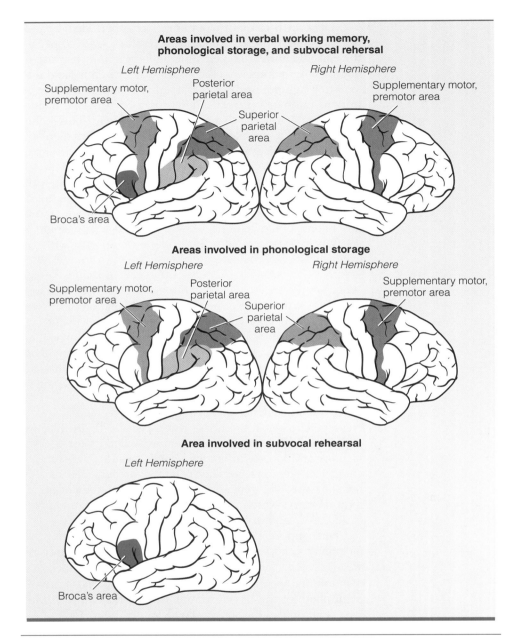

Figure 5.6 The Brain and Working Memory.

Different areas of the cerebral cortex are involved in different aspects of working memory. The figure shows those aspects involved primarily in the articulatory loop, including phonological storage and subvocal rehearsal.

Source: From E. Awh et al. (1996). Dissociation of storage and rehearsal in verbal working memory: Evidence from positron emission tomography. *Psychological Science*, 7, 25–31. Copyright © 1996 by Blackwell, Inc. Reprinted by permission.

Measuring Working Memory

Working memory can be measured through a number of different tasks. The most commonly used are shown in Figure 5.7.

Task (a) is a retention-delay task. It is the simplest task shown in the figure. An item is shown—in this case, a geometric shape. (The + at the beginning is merely a

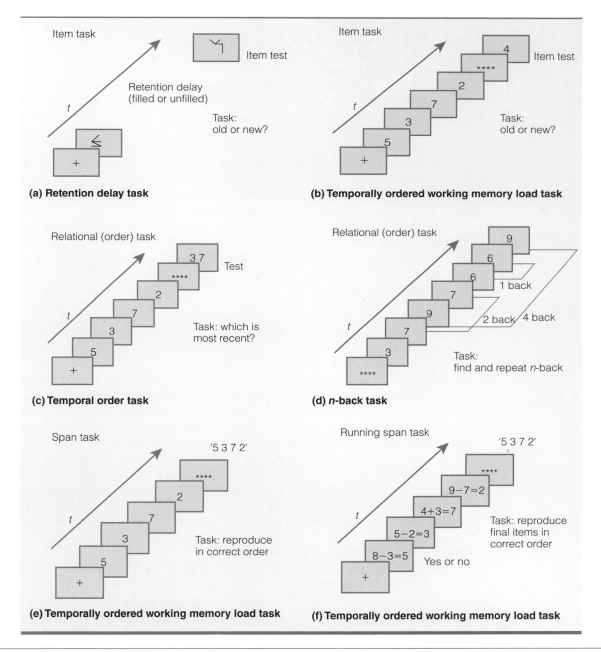

Figure 5.7 **Tasks to Assess Working Memory.**

Different kinds of tasks can be used to assess working memory.

Source: From *Encyclopedia of Cognitive Science, 4,* p. 571. Copyright © 2003. Reproduced with permission of B. Dosher.

focus point to indicate that the series of items is beginning.) There is then a retention interval, which may be filled with other tasks, or unfilled; in which case time passes without any specifically designed intervening activity. The participant is then presented with a stimulus and must say whether it is old or new. In the figure, the stimulus being tested is new. So "new" would be the correct answer.

Task (b) is a temporally ordered working memory load task. A series of items is presented. After a while, the series of asterisks indicates that a test item will be presented. The test item is presented, and the participant must say whether the item is old or new. Because "4," the number in the figure, has not been presented before, the correct answer is "new."

Task (c) is a temporal order task. A series of items is presented. Then the asterisks indicate a test item will be given. The test item shows two previously presented items, 3 and 7. The participant must indicate which of the two numbers, 3 or 7, appeared more recently. The correct answer is 7 because 7 occurred after 3 in the list.

Task (d) is an *n*-back task. Stimuli are presented. At specified points, one is asked to repeat the stimulus that occurred *n* presentations back. For example, one might be asked to repeat the digit that occurred 1 back—or just before (as with the 6). Or one might be asked to repeat the digit that occurred 2 back (as with the 7).

Task (e) is a temporally ordered working memory load task. It can also be referred to simply as a digit-span task (when digits are used). One is presented with a series of stimuli. After they are presented, one repeats them back in the order they were presented. A variant of this task has the participant repeat them back in the order opposite to that in which they were presented—from the end to the beginning.

Finally, Task (f) is a temporally ordered working memory load task. One is given a series of simple arithmetic problems. For each problem, one indicates whether the sum or difference is correct. At the end, one repeats the results of the arithmetic problems in their correct order.

Each of the tasks described here and in Figure 5.7 allows for the examination of how much information we can manipulate in memory. Frequently, these tasks are paired with a second task (called, appropriately, a *secondary task*) so that researchers can learn more about the central executive. The central executive is responsible for allocating attentional and other resources to ongoing tasks. By having participants do more than one task at once, we can examine how mental resources are assigned (Baudouin et al., 2006; D'Amico & Guarnera, 2005). A task that often is paired with those listed in Figure 5.7 is a random-number generation task. In this task, the participant must try to generate a random series of numbers while completing a working memory task (Rudkin, Pearson, & Logie, 2007).

Intelligence and Working Memory

Recent work suggests that a critical component of intelligence may be working memory. Indeed, some investigators have argued that intelligence may be little more than working memory (Kyllonen & Christal, 1990). In one study, participants read sets of passages and, after they had read the passages, tried to remember the last word of each passage (Daneman & Carpenter, 1983). Recall was highly correlated with verbal ability. In another study, participants performed a variety of working memory tasks. In one task, for example, the participants saw a set of simple arithmetic problems, each of which was followed by a word or a digit. An example would be

"Is $(3 \times 5) - 6 = 7$? TABLE" (Turner & Engle, 1989; see also Hambrick, Kane, & Engle, 2005). The participants saw sets of from two to six such problems and solved each one. After solving the problems in the set, they tried to recall the words that followed the problems. The number of words recalled was highly correlated with measured intelligence.

There are indications that a measure of working memory can provide almost perfect prediction of scores on tests of general ability (Colom et al., 2004; see also Kane, Hambrick, & Conway, 2005). Other researchers have demonstrated a significant but smaller relationship between working memory and general intelligence (e.g., Ackerman, Beier, & Boyle, 2005). Thus, it appears that the ability to store and manipulate information in working memory may be an important aspect of intelligence. It is probably not all there is to intelligence, however.

Multiple Memory Systems

The working-memory model is consistent with the notion that multiple systems may be involved in the storage and retrieval of information. Recall that when Wilder Penfield electrically stimulated the brains of his patients, the patients often asserted that they vividly recalled particular episodes and events. They did not, however, recall semantic facts that were unrelated to any particular event. These findings suggest that there may be at least two separate explicit memory systems. One would be for organizing and storing information with a distinctive time referent. It would address questions such as, "What did you eat for lunch yesterday?" or "Who was the first person you saw this morning?" The second system would be for information that has no particular time referent. It would address questions such as, "Who were the two psychologists who first proposed the three-stores model of memory?" and "What is a mnemonist?"

Based on such findings, Endel Tulving (1972) proposed a distinction between two kinds of explicit memory. **Semantic memory** stores general world knowledge. It is our memory for facts that are not unique to us and that are not recalled in any particular temporal context. **Episodic memory** stores personally experienced events or episodes. According to Tulving, we use episodic memory when we learn lists of words or when we need to recall something that occurred to us at a particular time or in a particular context. In either case, we have personally experienced the learning as associated with a given time. The list we learn in the experiment, for example, is associated with the experiment as the context for learning. For example, suppose I needed to remember that I saw Harrison Hardimanowitz in the dentist's office yesterday. I would be drawing on an episodic memory. But if I needed to remember the name of the person I now see in the waiting room ("Harrison Hardimanowitz"), I would be drawing on a semantic memory. There is no particular time tag associated with the name of that individual being Harrison. But there is a time tag associated with my having seen him at the dentist's office yesterday.

Tulving (1983, 1989) and others (e.g., Shoben, 1984) provide support for the distinction between semantic and episodic memory. It is based on both cognitive research and neurological investigation. The neurological investigations have involved electrical-stimulation studies, studies of patients with memory disorders, and cerebral blood flow studies. For example, lesions in the frontal lobe appear to affect recollection regarding *when* a stimulus was presented. But they do not affect recall or recognition memory *that* a particular stimulus was presented (Schacter, 1989a).

However, it is not clear that semantic and episodic memories are two distinct systems. They sometimes appear to function in different ways. But many cognitive psychologists question this distinction (e.g., Eysenck & Keane, 1990; Humphreys, Bain, & Pike, 1989). They point out that the boundary between these two types of memory is often fuzzy. They also note methodological problems with some of the supportive evidence. Perhaps episodic memory is merely a specialized form of semantic memory (Tulving, 1984, 1986).

Some neurological evidence suggests that these two types of memory are separate, however. Through neuropsychological methods, investigators found dissociations, which means that separate and distinct areas seem to be involved in semantic versus episodic memory retrieval (Prince, Tsukiura, & Cabeza, 2007). When researchers find neural substrates of particular brain functions, one speaks about *dissociation*. There are patients who suffer only from loss of semantic memory, but their episodic memory is not impaired, as well as vice versa (Temple & Richardson, 2004; Vargha-Khadem et al., 1997). A person with semantic memory loss may have trouble remembering what date it is or who the current president is; a person with episodic memory loss cannot remember personal events like where she met her spouse for the first time. These observations indicate that there is a dissociation between the two kinds of memory. These findings all support the conclusion that there are separate episodic and semantic memory systems.

A neuroscientific model called *HERA* (hemispheric encoding/retrieval asymmetry) attempts to account for differences in hemispheric activation for semantic versus episodic memories. According to this model, there is greater activation in the left than in the right prefrontal hemisphere for tasks requiring retrieval from semantic memory (Nyberg, Cabeza, & Tulving, 1996; Tulving et al., 1994). In contrast, there is more activation in the right than in the left prefrontal hemisphere for episodic-retrieval tasks. This model, then, proposes that semantic and episodic memories must be distinct because they draw on separate areas of the brain. For example, if one is asked to generate verbs that are associated with nouns (e.g., "*drive*" with "*car*"), this task requires semantic memory. It results in greater left-hemispheric activation (Nyberg, Cabeza, & Tulving, 1996). In contrast, if people are asked to freely recall a list of words—an episodic-memory task—they show more right-hemispheric activation. Some recent fMRI and ERP studies have not found the predicted frontal asymmetries during encoding and retrieval (Berryhill et al., 2007; Evans & Federmeier, 2009).

Other findings suggest that the neural processes involved in these memories overlap (Rajah & McIntosh, 2005). Although there is substantial behavioral and neurological evidence that there are differences between these two types of memory, most researchers agree that there is, at the very least, a great deal of interaction between these two types of memory. As a result, the question of whether these forms of memory are separate is still open.

A taxonomy of the memory system in terms of the dissociations described in the previous sections is shown in Figure 5.8 (Squire, 1986, 1993). It distinguishes declarative (explicit) memory from various kinds of nondeclarative (implicit) memory. Nondeclarative memory comprises procedural memory, priming effects, simple

IN THE LAB OF MARCIA K. JOHNSON

Memory and the Brain

MARCIA K. JOHNSON

A memory is a mental experience that is taken to be a veridical (truthful) representation of an event from one's past. Attributions we make about the origin of the active information that constitutes our mental experience are the result of cognitive processes that encode, revive, and monitor information from various sources or experiences. The integration of information across individual experiences is necessary for all higher order—complex thought. But this very capacity for creative integration of information from multiple events makes us vulnerable to false memories because we sometimes misattribute the sources of the information that comes to mind. Source monitoring errors include many types of confusions, for example, attributing something that was imagined to perception, an intention to an action, something only heard about to something one witnessed, something read in a tabloid to a television news program, or an incident that occurred in place *A* or at time *A* to place *B* or time *B*. Memories can be false in relatively minor ways (e.g., believing one last saw the car keys in the kitchen when they actually were in the living room) and in major ways that have profound implications for oneself and others (e.g., mistakenly believing one is the source or originator of an idea, or believing that one was sexually abused as a child when one was not).

Investigators from many labs are using neuroimaging (e.g., functional magnetic resonance imaging [fMRI]) to help identify the brain regions that encode different features of events (e.g., scenes [parahippocampal gyrus], faces [fusiform gyrus], lateral occipital cortex [objects]), and the regions involved in binding these features into representations of complex events (e.g., hippocampus). We have been particularly interested in the fact that the same regions are active when you perceptually process something (e.g., a visual scene) and when you think of it. This similarity between perception and reflection is one of the factors that sets the stage for false memories.

Several types of evidence indicate that the prefrontal cortex (PFC) plays a key role both in binding features of stimuli together during encoding and in later identifying the sources of mental experiences during remembering. Damage to PFC produces deficits in source memory. Source memory errors are more likely in children (whose frontal lobes are slow to develop) and in older adults (who are likely to show increased neuropathology in PFC with age). PFC dysfunction may also play a role in schizophrenia, which sometimes includes severe source monitoring deficits in the form of delusions or hallucinations. Neuroimaging is helping to clarify the specific functions of PFC in source memory.

For example, in one type of study, participants see a series of items of two types (e.g., pictures and words). Later they are given a memory test in which they are shown three kinds of words: words that correspond to the pictures seen earlier, words seen earlier as words, and new words that do not correspond to any of the items seen earlier (new items). They are asked to identify the source of some items (e.g., say "yes" to items previously seen as pictures), and for other items to simply decide if they are familiar (say "yes" to any previously presented ["old"] item). Typically there is greater brain activity in PFC in the source identification compared with the old/new test condition. Studies from our lab and other labs suggest that both right and left PFC contribute to evaluating the origin of mental experiences, possibly in different ways (e.g., engaging different processes or monitoring different types of information), and interactions between the right and left hemispheres are likely important. Thus, one goal for future research is to relate specific component processes of cognition to patterns of activity across various regions of the PFC and to specify how PFC regions interact with other brain regions (e.g., the hippocampus and various feature representational areas) in producing the subjective experiences we take to be memories.

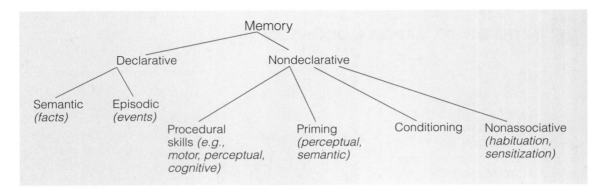

Figure 5.8   A Taxonomy of the Memory System.
Based on extensive neuropsychological research, Larry Squire has posited that memory comprises two fundamental types: declarative (explicit) memory and various forms of nondeclarative (implicit) memory, each of which may be associated with discrete cerebral structures and processes.

classical conditioning, habituation, sensitization, and perceptual aftereffects. In yet another view, there are five memory systems in all: episodic, semantic, perceptual (i.e., recognizing things on the basis of their form and structure), procedural, and working memory (Schacter, 2000).

A Connectionist Perspective

The network model provides the structural basis for the *connectionist* parallel distributed processing (PDP) model (see also Chapter 8; Frean, 2003; Sun, 2003). According to the PDP model, the key to knowledge representation lies in the connections among various *nodes*, or elements, stored in memory, not in each individual node (Feldman & Shastri, 2003). Activation of one node may prompt activation of a connected node. This process of spreading activation may prompt the activation of additional nodes (Figure 5.9). The PDP model fits nicely with the notion of working memory as comprising the activated portion of long-term memory. In this model, activation spreads through nodes within the network. This spreading continues as long as the activation does not exceed the limits of working memory.

A **prime** is a node that activates a connected node. A **priming effect** is the resulting activation of the node. The priming effect has been supported by considerable evidence. Examples are the aforementioned studies of priming as an aspect of implicit memory. In addition, some evidence supports the notion that priming is due to spreading activation (McClelland & Rumelhart, 1985, 1988). But not everyone agrees about the mechanism for the priming effect (see McKoon & Ratcliff, 1992b).

Connectionist models also have some intuitive appeal in their ability to integrate several contemporary notions about memory: *Working memory* comprises the *activated* portion of long-term memory and operates through at least some amount of *parallel processing*. *Spreading activation* involves the simultaneous (parallel) activation (*priming*) of multiple links among *nodes* within the *network*. Many cognitive psychologists who hold this integrated view suggest that part of the reason we humans are as efficient as we are in processing information is that we can handle many operations at once. Thus, the contemporary cognitive-psychological conceptions of working

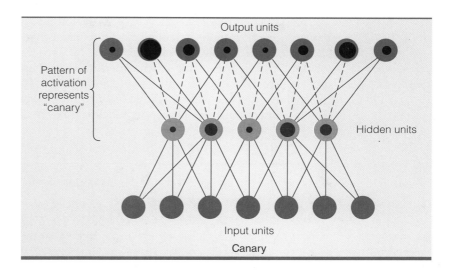

Figure 5.9   Connectionist Network.

A connectionist network consists of many different nodes. Unlike in semantic networks, it is not a single node that has a specific meaning, but rather the knowledge is represented in a combination of differently activated nodes. The size of the dots inside the nodes above indicates the amount of activation (with larger dots indicating more activation). The concept of a canary is represented by the overall pattern of activation.

Source: From *Cognitive Psychology,* 2nd ed., by E. Bruce Goldstein, Copyright © 2008.

memory, network models of memory, spreading activation, priming, and parallel processes mutually enhance and support one another.

Some of the research supporting this connectionist model of memory has come directly from experimental studies of people performing cognitive tasks in laboratory settings. Connectionist models effectively explain priming effects, skill learning (procedural memory), and several other phenomena of memory. Thus far, however, connectionist models have failed to provide clear predictions and explanations of recall and recognition memory that occurs following a single episode or a single exposure to semantic information.

In addition to using laboratory experiments on human participants, cognitive psychologists have used computer models to simulate various aspects of information processing. The three-store model is based on serial (sequential) processing of information. Serial processing can be simulated on individual computers that handle only one operation at a time. In contrast, the parallel-processing model of working memory, which involves simultaneous processing of multiple operations, cannot be simulated on a single computer. Parallel processing requires neural networks. In these networks, multiple computers are linked and operate in tandem. Alternatively, a single special computer may operate with parallel networks. Many cognitive psychologists now prefer a parallel-processing model to describe many phenomena of memory. The parallel-processing model was actually inspired by observing how the human brain seems to process information. Here, multiple processes go on at the same time. In addition to inspiring theoretical models of memory function, neuropsychological research has offered specific insights into memory processes. It also has provided evidence regarding various hypotheses of how human memory works.

Not all cognitive researchers accept the connectionist model. Some believe that human thought is more systematic and integrated than connectionist models seem to allow (Fodor & Pylyshyn, 1988; Matthews, 2003). They believe that complex behavior displays a degree of top-down orderliness and purposefulness that connectionist models, which are bottom-up, cannot incorporate. Connectionist modelers dispute this claim. The issue will be resolved as cognitive psychologists explore the extent to which connectionist models can reproduce and even explain complex behavior.

✔ CONCEPT CHECK

1. What is the difference between the sensory store and the short-term store?
2. What are levels of processing?
3. What are the components of the working-memory model?
4. Why do we need both semantic and episodic memories?
5. Describe a connectionist model of memory.

Exceptional Memory and Neuropsychology

Up to this point, the discussion of memory has focused on tasks and structures involving normally functioning memory. However, there are rare cases of people with exceptional memory (either enhanced or deficient) that provide some interesting insights into the nature of memory in general. The study of exceptional memory leads directly to neuropsychological investigations of the physiological mechanisms underlying memory.

Outstanding Memory: Mnemonists

Imagine what your life would be like if you were able to remember every word printed in this book. In this case, you would be considered a **mnemonist,** someone who demonstrates extraordinarily keen memory ability, usually based on using special techniques for memory enhancement. Perhaps the most famous of mnemonists was a man called "S."

Russian psychologist Alexander Luria (1968) reported that one day S. appeared in his laboratory and asked to have his memory tested. Luria tested him. He discovered that the man's memory appeared to have virtually no limits. S. could reproduce extremely long strings of words, regardless of how much time had passed since the words had been presented to him. Luria studied S. for over 30 years. He found that even when S.'s retention was measured 15 or 16 years after a session in which S. had learned words, S. still could reproduce the words. S. eventually became a professional entertainer. He dazzled audiences with his ability to recall whatever was asked of him.

What was S.'s trick? How did he remember so much? Apparently, he relied heavily on the mnemonic of visual imagery. He converted material that he needed to remember into visual images. For example, he reported that when asked to remember the word *green*, he would visualize a green flowerpot. For the word *red*, he visualized a man in a red shirt coming toward him. Numbers called up images. For example, *1* was a proud, well-built man. The number *3* was a gloomy person. The number 6 was a man with a swollen foot, and so on.

For S., much of his use of visual imagery in memory recall was not intentional. Rather, it was the result of a rare psychological phenomenon. This phenomenon, termed *synesthesia*, is the experience of sensations in a sensory modality different from the sense that has been physically stimulated. For example, S. automatically would convert a sound into a visual impression. He even reported experiencing a word's taste and weight. Each word to be remembered evoked a whole range of sensations that automatically would come to S. when he needed to recall that word.

Other mnemonists have used different strategies. "V. P.," a Russian immigrant, could memorize long strings of material, such as rows and columns of numbers (Hunt & Love, 1972). Whereas S. relied primarily on visual imagery, V. P. apparently relied more on verbal translations. He reported memorizing numbers by transforming them into dates. Then he would think about what he had done on that day.

Another mnemonist, "S. F.," remembered long strings of numbers by segmenting them into groups of three or four digits each. He then encoded them into running times for different races (Ericsson, Chase, & Faloon, 1980). An experienced long-distance runner, S. F. was familiar with the times that would be plausible for different races. S. F. did not enter the laboratory as a mnemonist. Rather, he had been selected to represent the average college student in terms of intelligence and memory ability.

S. F.'s original memory for a string of numbers was about seven digits, average for a college student. After 200 practice sessions distributed over a period of 2 years, however, S. F. had increased his memory for digits more than tenfold. He could recall up to about 80 digits. His memory was impaired severely, however, when the experimenters purposely gave him sequences of digits that could not be translated into running times. The work with S. F. suggests that a person with a fairly typical level of memory ability can, at least in principle, be converted into one with quite an extraordinary memory. At least, this is possible in some domains, following a great deal of concerted practice.

Many of us yearn to have memory abilities like those of S. or V. P. In this way, we may believe we could ace our exams virtually effortlessly. However, we should consider that S. was not particularly happy with his life, and part of the reason was his exceptional memory. He reported that his synesthesia, which was largely involuntary, interfered with his ability to listen to people. Voices gave rise to blurs of sensations. They in turn interfered with his ability to follow a conversation. Moreover, S.'s heavy reliance on imagery created difficulty for him when he tried to understand abstract concepts. For example, he found it hard to understand concepts such as *infinity* or *nothing*. These concepts do not lend themselves well to visual images. He also sometimes was overwhelmed when he read. Earlier memories also sometimes intruded on later ones. Of course, we cannot say how many of S.'s problems in life were caused by his exceptional memory. But clearly S. believed that his exceptional memory had a downside as well as an upside. It was often as likely to be a hindrance as a help.

These exceptional mnemonists offer some insight into processes of memory. Each of the three described here did more or less the same thing—consciously or almost automatically. Each translated arbitrary, abstract, meaningless information into more meaningful and often more concrete information, sometimes connected to the senses. Whether the translated information was racing times, dates and events, or visual images, the key was their meaning for the mnemonist.

Like the mnemonists, we more easily encode information into our long-term memory that is similar to the information already stored there. Because we have information in long-term memory that pertains to our interests, it is easier to learn

■ BELIEVE IT OR NOT

YOU CAN BE A MEMORY CHAMPION, TOO!!!

Have you ever heard about people who can effortlessly remember huge lists of words or numbers? Or would you already be satisfied if you could memorize your shopping list? Well, you can do this, too! How? The first thing you need to do is to come up with a nice system that helps you remember numbers. Then you connect the words you want to remember with those numbers. Sounds too complicated? Not really. The example below illustrates how you can imagine numbers as representations of objects (remember, you can create your own system!):

Once you are intimately familiar with your representations of numbers, you can start connecting them with words you would like to remember. Assume you want to buy beans, chopped tomatoes, and cereal. You'll create lively pictures that combine the numbers with the items you need to buy. For item #1, you can imagine beans growing up high on a flagpole, for example. For item #2, you can imagine a swan with red plumage because it is swimming in a pond of chopped tomatoes. And for item #3, you can imagine a nice plate of breakfast cereal shaped in the form of hearts. You get the idea? Once you are in the supermarket, you'll just work down your list from the first item to the last, imagining your created pictures. There are no rules except that the representations have to work for you. With a little bit of practice you'll soon be able to memorize long lists of words, even more complicated or abstract ones. This technique is one of many mnemonic techniques that belong to the group of association techniques.

Karin Sternberg

new information that is in line with these interests that we can relate to the old information (De Beni et al., 2007). Thus, you may be able to remember the lyrics of your favorite songs from years ago but not be able to recall the definitions of new terms that you have just learned. You can improve your memory for new information if you can relate the new information to old information already stored in long-term memory.

If you are unable to retrieve a memory that you need, does it mean that you have forgotten it? Not necessarily. Cognitive psychologists have studied a phenomenon called **hypermnesia**, which is a process of producing retrieval of memories that would seem to have been forgotten (Erdelyi & Goldberg, 1979; Holmes, 1991; Turtle & Yuille, 1994). Hypermnesia is sometimes loosely referred to as "unforgetting," although the terminology cannot be correct because, strictly speaking, the memories that are retrieved were never unavailable (i.e., forgotten), but rather, inaccessible (i.e., hard to retrieve). Hypermnesia is usually achieved by trying many and diverse retrieval cues to unearth a memory. Psychodynamic therapy, for example, is sometimes used to try to achieve hypermnesia. This therapy also points out the risk of trying to achieve hypermnesia. The individual may create a new memory, believing it is an old one, rather than retrieving a genuine old memory. In cases where there are accusations of abuse against a parent or other individual, newly created memories posing as old memories could pose a serious problem leading to false accusations.

We usually take for granted the ability to remember, much like the air we breathe. However, just as we become more aware of the importance of air when we do not have enough to breathe, we are less likely to take memory for granted when we observe people with serious memory deficiencies.

Deficient Memory

There are many syndromes associated with memory loss. Just as with the study of exceptionally good memory, the study of deficient memory provides us with many valuable insights into how memory works. In this section, we will have a look at two syndromes. The first and also most well known is amnesia. Afterwards, we will explore the symptoms and causes of Alzheimer's disease, which is another prominent disease that causes memory loss.

Amnesia

We begin this section on amnesia by looking at some case studies to gain a better understanding of what amnesia is and what different kinds of amnesia exist. Afterwards, we will consider what insights can be gained about the differences between implicit and explicit memory by studying amnesia, and have a look at neuropsychological findings in the context of amnesia.

If the patient uses hypermnesia to dredge up what has seemed to be a forgotten memory, we often cannot be certain that the memory is genuine, rather than one newly created by suggestion.

What Is Amnesia?   **Amnesia** is severe loss of explicit memory (Robbins, 2009). One type is retrograde amnesia, in which individuals lose their purposeful memory for events prior to whatever trauma induces memory loss (Levine et al., 2009; Squire, 1999). Mild forms of **retrograde amnesia** can occur fairly commonly when someone sustains a concussion. Usually, events immediately prior to the concussive episode are not well remembered.

W. Ritchie Russell and P. W. Nathan (1946) reported a more severe case of retrograde amnesia. A 22-year-old landscaper was thrown from his motorcycle in August of 1933. A week after the accident, the young man was able to converse sensibly. He seemed to have recovered. However, it quickly became apparent that he had suffered a severe loss of memory for events that had occurred prior to the trauma. On questioning, he gave the date as February 1922. He believed himself to be a schoolboy. He had no recollection of the intervening years. Over the next several weeks, his memory for past events gradually returned. The return started with the least recent event and proceeded toward more recent events. By 10 weeks after the accident, he had recovered his memory for most of the events of the previous years. He finally was able to recall everything that had happened up to a few minutes prior to the accident. In retrograde amnesia, the memories that return typically do so starting from the more distant past. They then progressively return up to the time of the trauma. Often events right before the trauma are never recalled.

One of the most famous cases of amnesia is the case of H. M. (Scoville & Milner, 1957). H. M. underwent brain surgery to save him from continual disruptions due to uncontrollable epilepsy. The operation took place on September 1, 1953. It was largely experimental. The results were highly unpredictable. At the time of the operation, H. M. was 29 years old. He was above average in intelligence. After the operation, his recovery was uneventful with one exception. He suffered severe **anterograde amnesia**, the inability to remember events that occur after a traumatic event. However, he had good (although not perfect) recollection of events that had occurred before his operation. H. M.'s memory loss severely affected his life. H. M. has been extensively studied through behavioral and neurological methods. On one occasion, he remarked, "Every day is alone in itself, whatever enjoyment I've had, and whatever sorrow I've had" (Milner, Corkin, & Teuber, 1968, p. 217). Many years after the surgery, H. M. still reported that the year was 1953. He also could not recall the name of any new person he met after the operation, regardless of the number of times they interacted. Apparently, H. M. lost his ability to recollect any new memories of the time following his operation. As a result, he lives suspended in an eternal present.

The examination of H. M.'s memory is ongoing, with recent work examining changes in H. M.'s memory and brain as he ages. These recent studies have noted additional memory and cognitive declines. In particular, H. M. exhibited new problems with comprehension and generation of new sentences (MacKay, 2006; MacKay et al., 2006; Salat et al., 2006; Skotko et al., 2004).

Another kind of "amnesia" that we all experience is **infantile amnesia**, the inability to recall events that happened when we were very young (Spear, 1979). (We place "amnesia" in quotation marks because some investigators question whether infantile amnesia is truly a form of amnesia at all.)

Amnesia and the Explicit-Implicit Memory Distinction   Why do researchers study amnesia patients? What kinds of insight can be gained from amnesia research? One of the general insights gained by studying amnesia victims highlights the distinction between explicit and implicit memories. Explicit memory is typically impaired in amnesia. Implicit memory, such as priming effects on word-completion tasks and procedural memory for skill-based tasks, is typically not impaired. This observation indicates that two kinds of abilities need to be distinguished. The first is the ability to reflect consciously on prior experience, which is required for tasks involving explicit memory. The second is the ability to demonstrate remembered learning in an apparently automatic way, without conscious recollection of the learning (implicit memory; Baddeley, 1989). Priming effects can be seen from about 250 to 500 milliseconds after exposure through positive brain potentials recorded in the frontal region of the brain. Explicit memory retrieval, however, is indicated by brain potentials that appear at a later time in the posterior regions (Voss & Paller, 2006).

Amnesia victims perform extremely poorly on most explicit memory tasks, but they may show normal or almost-normal performance on tasks involving implicit memory, such as cued-recall tasks (Warrington & Weiskrantz, 1970) and word-completion tasks (Baddeley, 1989). What do you think happens after word-completion tasks? When amnesics were asked whether they previously had seen the word they just completed, they were unlikely to remember the specific experience of having seen the word (Graf, Mandler, & Haden, 1982; Tulving, Schacter, & Stark, 1982). Furthermore, these amnesics do not explicitly recognize words they have seen at better than chance levels. Although the distinction between implicit memory and explicit memory has been readily observed in amnesics, both amnesics and normal participants show the presence of implicit memory.

Likewise, amnesia victims also show paradoxical performance in another regard. Consider two kinds of tasks. As previously described, *procedural-knowledge* tasks involve "knowing how." They involve skills such as how to ride a bicycle, whereas *declarative-knowledge* tasks involve "knowing that." They tap factual information, such as the terms in a psychology textbook. On the one hand, amnesia victims may perform extremely poorly on the traditional memory tasks requiring recall or recognition memory of declarative knowledge. On the other hand, they may demonstrate improvement in performance resulting from learning—remembered practice—when engaged in tasks that require procedural knowledge. Such tasks would include solving puzzles, learning to read mirror writing, or mastering motor skills (Baddeley, 1989).

Consider an example of procedural knowledge that is retained when a person suffers from amnesia. Patients with amnesia, when asked to drive in a normal situation, were able to operate and control the car as a normal driver would (Anderson et al., 2007). However, the investigators also exposed the patients to a simulation in which a complex accident sequence was experienced. In this situation, the patients with amnesia showed significant impairment. They could not recall the proper response to this situation. This finding is in line with the fact that in patients with amnesia, implicit, procedural knowledge is spared, while explicit knowledge is impaired. Most drivers do not have extensive experience with complex accident-avoidance scenarios and therefore would have to rely more on their declarative memory to make decisions about how to respond.

Amnesia and Neuropsychology Studies of amnesia victims have revealed much about the way in which memory depends on the effective functioning of particular structures of the brain. By looking for matches between particular lesions in the brain and particular deficits of function, researchers come to understand how normal

"I'm not losing my memory.
I'm living in the now."

memory functions. Thus, when studying cognitive processes in the brain, neuropsychologists frequently look for dissociations of function. In *dissociations*, normal individuals show the presence of a particular function (e.g., explicit memory). But people with specific lesions in the brain show the absence of that particular function. This absence occurs despite the presence of normal functions in other areas (e.g., implicit memory).

By observing people with disturbed memory function, we know that memory is volatile. A blow to the head, a disturbance in consciousness, or any number of other injuries to or diseases of the brain may affect it. We cannot determine, however, the specific cause-effect relationship between a given structural lesion and a particular memory deficit. The fact that a particular structure or region is associated with an interruption of function does not mean that the region is solely responsible for controlling that function. Indeed, functions can be shared by multiple structures or regions. A broad physiological analogy may help to explain the difficulty of determining localization based on an observed deficit. The normal functioning of a portion of the brain—the reticular activating system (RAS)—is essential to life. But life depends on more than a functioning brain. If you doubt the importance of other structures, ask a patient with heart or lung disease. Thus, although the RAS is essential to life, a person's death may be the result of malfunction in other structures of the body. Tracing a dysfunction within the brain to a particular structure or region poses a similar problem.

For the observation of simple dissociations, many alternative hypotheses may explain a link between a particular lesion and a particular deficit of function. Much more compelling support for hypotheses about cognitive functions comes from observing double dissociations. In *double dissociations*, people with different kinds of neuropathological conditions show opposite patterns of deficits. A double dissociation can be observed if a lesion in brain structure *1* leads to impairment in memory function A but not in memory function B; and a lesion in brain structure *2* leads to impairment in memory function B but not in memory function A.

For some functions and some areas of the brain, neuropsychologists have managed to observe the presence of a double dissociation. For example, some evidence for distinguishing brief memory from long-term memory comes from just such a double dissociation (Schacter, 1989b). People with lesions in the left parietal lobe of the brain show profound inability to retain information in short-term memory, but they show no impairment of long-term memory. They continue to encode, store, and retrieve information in long-term memory, apparently with little difficulty (Shallice & Warrington, 1970; Warrington & Shallice, 1972). In contrast, persons with lesions in the medial (middle) temporal regions of the brain show relatively normal short-term memory of verbal materials, such as letters and words, but they show serious inability to retain new verbal materials in long-term memory (Milner, Corkin, & Teuber, 1968; Shallice, 1979; Warrington, 1982).

Double dissociations offer strong support for the notion that particular structures of the brain play particular vital roles in memory (Squire, 1987). Disturbances or lesions in these areas cause severe deficits in memory formation. But we cannot say that memory—or even part of memory—resides in these structures. Nonetheless, studies of brain-injured patients are informative and at least suggestive of how memory works. At present, cognitive neuropsychologists have found that double dissociations support several distinctions. These distinctions are those between brief memory and long-term memory and between declarative (explicit) and nondeclarative (implicit) memory. There also are some preliminary indications of other distinctions.

Alzheimer's Disease

Although amnesia is the syndrome most associated with memory loss, it is often less devastating than a disease that includes memory loss as one of many symptoms. **Alzheimer's disease** is a disease of older adults that causes dementia as well as progressive memory loss (Kensinger & Corkin, 2003). Dementia is a loss of intellectual function that is severe enough to impair one's everyday life. The memory loss in Alzheimer's disease can be seen in comparative brain scans of individuals with and without Alzheimer's disease. Note in Figure 5.10 that as the disease advances, there is diminishing cognitive activity in the areas of the brain associated with memory function.

The disease was first identified by Alois Alzheimer in 1907. It is typically recognized on the basis of loss of intellectual function in daily life. Formally, a definitive diagnosis is possible only after death. Alzheimer's disease leads to an atrophy (decrease in size) of the brain; especially in the hippocampus and frontal and temporal brain regions (Jack et al., 2002). The brains of people with the disease show plaques and tangles that are not found in normal brains. Plaques are dense protein deposits found outside the nerve cells of the brain (Mirochnic et al., 2009). Tangles are pairs of filaments that become twisted around each other. They are found in the cell body and dendrites of neurons and often are shaped like a flame (Kensinger & Corkin, 2003). Alzheimer's disease is diagnosed when memory is impaired and there is at least one other area of dysfunction in the domains of language, motor, attention, executive function, personality, or object recognition. The symptoms are of gradual onset, and the progression is continuous and irreversible.

Although the progression of disease is irreversible, it can be slowed somewhat. The main drug currently being used for this purpose is Donepezil (Aricept). Research evidence is mixed (Fischman, 2004). It suggests that, at best, Aricept may slightly slow progression of the disease, but that it cannot reverse it. A more recent drug, memantine (sold as Namenda or Ebixa), can supplement Aricept and slow

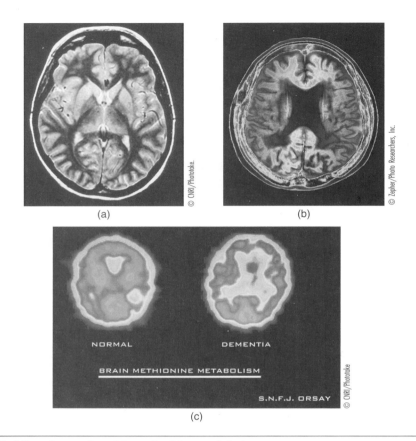

(a)   (b)

© CNRI/Phototake.   © Zephyr/Photo Researchers, Inc.

NORMAL   DEMENTIA

BRAIN METHIONINE METABOLISM

S.N.F.J. ORSAY

© CNRI/Phototake

(c)

Figure 5.10   The Brain with and without Alzheimer's.
Brain scans of (a) a normal individual and (b) an individual with early-stage Alzheimer's. You can see the atrophy (black space) in the brain of the Alzheimer's patient (b) compared with the healthy person (a). Image (c) depicts PET scans of an individual with late-stage Alzheimer's and a healthy person. The metabolism in the healthy brain is much more pronounced. As the disease progresses, cognitive activity in the brain associated with memory function decreases.

progression of the disease somewhat more. The two drugs have different mechanisms. Aricept slows destruction of the neurotransmitter acetylcholine in the brain. Memantine inhibits a chemical that overexcites brain cells and leads to cell damage and death (Fischman, 2004).

The incidence of Alzheimer's increases exponentially with age (Kensinger & Corkin, 2003). About 1% of people between 70 to 75 years of age experience an onset of Alzheimers. But between ages 80 and 85, the incidence is more than 6% a year.

A special kind of Alzheimer's disease is familial, known as early-onset Alzheimer's disease. It has been linked to a genetic mutation. People with the genetic mutation always develop the disease. It results in the disease exhibiting itself early, often before even 50 years of age and sometimes as early as the 20s (Kensinger & Corkin, 2003). Late-onset Alzheimer's, in contrast, appears to be complexly determined and related to a variety of possible genetic and environmental influences, none of which have been conclusively identified.

The earliest signs of Alzheimer's disease typically include impairment of episodic memory. People have trouble remembering things that were learned in a temporal or spatial context. As the disease progresses, semantic memory also begins to go. Whereas people without the disease tend to remember emotionally charged information better than they remember non-emotionally charged information, people with the disease show no difference in the two kinds of memory (Kensinger et al., 2002). Most forms of nondeclarative memory are spared in Alzheimer's disease until near the very end of its course. The end is inevitably death, unless the individual dies first of other causes.

Memory tests may be given to assess whether an individual has Alzheimer's disease. However, definitive diagnosis is possible only through analysis of brain tissue, which, as mentioned earlier, shows plaques and tangles in cases of disease. In one test, individuals see a sheet of paper containing four words (Buschke et al., 1999). Each word belongs to a different category. The examiner says the category name for one of the words. The individual must point to the appropriate word. For example, if the category is animal, the individual might point to a picture of a cow. A few minutes after the words have been presented, individuals make an attempt to recall all the words they saw. If they cannot recall a word, they are given the category to which the word belongs. Some individuals cannot remember the words, even when prompted with the categories. Alzheimer's patients score much worse on this test than do other individuals.

How Are Memories Stored?

Where in the brain are memories stored, and what structures and areas of the brain are involved in memory processes, such as encoding and retrieval? Many early attempts at localization of memory were unfruitful. For example, after literally hundreds of experiments, renowned neuropsychologist Karl Lashley (1950) reluctantly stated that he could find no specific locations in the brain for specific memories. In the decades since Lashley's admission, psychologists have located many cerebral structures involved in memory. For example, they know of the importance of the hippocampus and other nearby structures. However, the physiological structure may not be such that we will find Lashley's elusive localizations of specific ideas, thoughts, or events. Even Penfield's findings regarding links between electrical stimulation and episodic memory of events have been subject to question.

Some studies show encouraging, although preliminary, findings regarding the structures that seem to be involved in various aspects of memory. First, specific sensory properties of a given experience appear to be organized across various areas of the cerebral cortex (Squire, 1986). For example, the visual, spatial, and olfactory (odor) features of an experience may be stored discretely in each of the areas of the cortex responsible for processing each type of sensation. Thus, the cerebral cortex appears to play an important role in memory in terms of the long-term storage of information (Zola & Squire, 2000; Zola-Morgan & Squire, 1990).

In addition, the hippocampus and some related nearby cerebral structures appear to be important for explicit memory of experiences and other declarative information. The hippocampus also seems to play a key role in the encoding of declarative information (Manns & Eichenbaum, 2006; Thompson, 2000). Its main function appears to be in the integration and consolidation of separate sensory information as well as spatial orientation and memory (Ekstrom et al., 2003; Moscovitch, 2003;

Solstad et al., 2008). Most important, it is involved in the transfer of newly synthesized information into long-term structures supporting declarative knowledge. Perhaps such transfer provides a means of cross-referencing information stored in different parts of the brain (Reber, Knowlton, & Squire, 1996). Additionally, the hippocampus seems to play a crucial role in complex learning (Gupta et al., 2009; McCormick & Thompson, 1984). Finally, the hippocampus also has a significant role in the recollection of information (Gilboa et al., 2006).

In evolutionary terms, the aforementioned cerebral structures (chiefly the cortex and the hippocampus) are relatively recent acquisitions. Declarative memory also may be considered a relatively recent phenomenon. At the same time, other memory structures may be responsible for nondeclarative forms of memory. For example, the basal ganglia seem to be the primary structures controlling procedural knowledge (Shohamy et al., 2009). But they are not involved in controlling the priming effect (Heindel, Butters, & Salmon, 1988), which may be influenced by various other kinds of memory (Schacter, 1989b). Furthermore, the cerebellum also seems to play a key role in memory for classically conditioned responses and contributes to many cognitive tasks in general (Thompson & Steinmetz, 2009). Thus, various forms of nondeclarative memory seem to rely on differing cerebral structures.

The amygdala is often associated with emotional events, so a natural question to ask is whether, in memory tasks, there is involvement of the amygdala in memory for emotionally charged events. In one study, participants saw two video presentations presented on separate days (Cahill et al., 1996). Each presentation involved 12 clippings, half of which had been judged as involving relatively emotional content and the other half as involving relatively unemotional content. As participants watched the video clippings, brain activity was assessed by means of PET (see Chapter 3). After a gap of 3 weeks, the participants returned to the lab and were asked to recall the clips. For the relatively emotional clips, amount of activation in the amygdala was associated with recall; for the relatively unemotional clips, there was no association. This pattern of results suggests that when memories are emotionally charged, the level of amygdala activation is associated with recall. In other words, the more emotionally charged the emotional memory, the greater the probability the memory will later be retrieved. There also may be a gender difference with regard to recall of emotional memories. There is some evidence that women recall emotionally charged pictures better than do men (Canli et al., 2002). The amygdala also appears to play an important role in memory consolidation, especially where emotional experience is involved (Cahill & McGaugh, 1996; Roozendaal et al., 2008).

In addition to these preliminary insights regarding the macrolevel structures of memory, we are beginning to understand the microlevel structure of memory. For example, we know that repeated stimulation of particular neural pathways tends to strengthen the likelihood of firing. This is called *long-term potentiation* (where potentiation refers to an increase in activity). In particular, at a particular synapse, there appear to be physiological changes in the dendrites of the receiving neuron. These changes make the neuron more likely to reach the threshold for firing again. This finding is very important because it indicates that neurons in the hippocampus may be able to change their interactions (i.e., that they are *plastic*).

We also know that some neurotransmitters disrupt memory storage. Others enhance memory storage. Both serotonin and acetylcholine seem to enhance neural transmission associated with memory. Norepinephrine also may do so. High concentrations of acetylcholine have been found in the hippocampus of normal people (Squire, 1987), but low concentrations are found in people with Alzheimer's disease. In fact, Alzheimer's patients show severe loss of the brain tissue that secretes acetylcholine.

Serotonin also plays a role in another form of memory dysfunction, *Korsakoff syndrome*. Severe or prolonged abuse of alcohol can lead to this devastating form of anterograde amnesia. Alcohol consumption has been shown to disrupt the activity of serotonin. It thereby impairs the formation of memories (Weingartner et al., 1983). This syndrome is often accompanied by at least some retrograde amnesia (Clark et al., 2007). Korsakoff's syndrome has been linked to damage in the diencephalon (the region comprising the thalamus and the hypothalamus) of the brain (Postma et al., 2008). It also has been linked to dysfunction or damage in other areas, such as in the frontal and the temporal lobes of the cortex (Jacobson et al., 1990; Kopelman et al., 2009; Reed et al., 2003).

Other physiological factors also affect memory function. Some of the naturally occurring hormones stimulate increased availability of glucose in the brain, which enhances memory function. These hormones are often associated with highly arousing events. Examples of such events are traumas, achievements, first-time experiences (e.g., first passionate kiss), crises, or other peak moments (e.g., reaching a major decision). Hormones may play a role in remembering these events.

Some of the most fascinating research in cognitive psychology focuses on the strategies used in regard to memory. Memory strategies and memory processes are the subject of the following chapter.

✔ CONCEPT CHECK

1. Define amnesia and name three forms of amnesia.

2. What is Alzheimer's disease?

3. What is the role of the hippocampus in storing information?

Key Themes

This chapter illustrates some of the key themes noted in Chapter 1.

Applied versus basic research. Basic and applied research can interact. An example is research on Alzheimer's disease. Presently, the disease is not curable, but is treatable with drugs and with guidance provided in a structured living environment. Basic research into the biological structures (e.g., tangles and plaques) and cognitive functions (e.g., impaired memory) associated with Alzheimer's may one day help us better understand and treat the disease.

Biology versus behavioral methods. This chapter shows the interaction of biology with behavior. The hippocampus has become one of the most carefully studied parts of the brain. Current functional magnetic resonance imaging (fMRI) research is showing how the hippocampus and other parts of the brain, such as the amygdala (in the case of emotionally based memories) and the cerebellum (in the case of procedural memories) function to enable us to remember what we need to know. Biological processes have an impact on what we experience, how we behave, and what we remember.

Structures versus processes. Structure and function are both important to understanding human memory. The Atkinson-Shiffrin model proposed control processes that operate on three structures: a very short-term store, a short-term store, and a long-term store. The more recent working-memory model proposes how executive function controls and activates portions of long-term memory to provide the information needed to solve tasks at hand.

Summary

1. **What are some of the tasks used for studying memory, and what do various tasks indicate about the structure of memory?** Among the many tasks used by cognitive psychologists, some of the main ones have been tasks assessing explicit recall of information (e.g., free recall, serial recall, and cued recall) and tasks assessing explicit recognition of information. By comparing memory performance on these explicit tasks with performance on implicit tasks (e.g., word-completion tasks), cognitive psychologists have found evidence of differing memory systems or processes governing each type of task (e.g., as shown in studies of amnesics).

2. **What has been the prevailing traditional model for the structure of memory?** Memory is the means by which we draw on our knowledge of the past to use this knowledge in the present. According to one model, memory is conceived as involving three stores: a sensory store is capable of holding relatively limited amounts of information for very brief periods; a short-term store is capable of holding small amounts of information for somewhat longer periods; and a long-term store is capable of storing large amounts of information virtually indefinitely. Within the sensory store, the iconic store refers to visual sensory memory.

3. **What are some of the main alternative models for the structure of memory?** An alternative model uses the concept of working memory, usually defined as being part of long-term memory and also comprising short-term memory. From this perspective, working memory holds only the most recently activated portion of long-term memory. It moves these activated elements into and out of short-term memory.

A second model is the levels-of-processing framework, which hypothesizes distinctions in memory ability based on the degree to which items are elaborated during encoding.

A third model is the multiple memory systems model, which posits not only a distinction between procedural memory and declarative (semantic) memory but also a distinction between semantic and episodic memory.

In addition, psychologists have proposed other models for the structure of memory. They include a parallel distributed processing (PDP; connectionist) model. The PDP model incorporates the notions of working memory, semantic memory networks, spreading activation, priming, and parallel processing of information.

Finally, many psychologists call for a complete change in the conceptualization of memory, focusing on memory functioning in the real world. This call leads to a shift in memory metaphors from the traditional storehouse to the more modern correspondence metaphor.

4. **What have psychologists learned about the structure of memory by studying exceptional memory and the physiology of the brain?** Among other findings, studies of mnemonists have shown the value of imagery in memory for concrete information. They also have demonstrated the importance of finding or forming meaningful connections among items to be remembered. The main forms of amnesia are anterograde amnesia, retrograde amnesia, and infantile amnesia. The last form of amnesia is qualitatively different from the other forms and occurs in everyone.

Through the study of the memory function of people with each form of amnesia, it has been possible to differentiate various aspects of memory. These include long-term versus temporary forms of memory, procedural versus declarative memory processes, and explicit versus implicit memory.

Although specific memory traces have not yet been identified, many of the specific structures involved in memory function have been located. To date, the subcortical structures involved in memory appear to include the hippocampus, the thalamus, the hypothalamus, and even the basal ganglia, and the cerebellum. The cortex also governs much of the long-term storage of declarative knowledge.

The neurotransmitters serotonin and acetylcholine appear to be vital to memory function. Other physiological chemicals, structures, and processes also play important roles, although further investigation is required to identify these roles.

Thinking about Thinking: Analytical, Creative, and Practical Questions

1. Describe two characteristics each of sensory memory, short-term memory, and long-term memory.
2. What are double dissociations, and why are they valuable to understanding the relationship between cognitive function and the brain?
3. Compare and contrast the three-store model of memory with one of the alternative models of memory.
4. Critique one of the experiments described in this chapter (e.g., Sperling's 1960 experiment on the iconic store, or Craik and Tulving's 1975 experiment on the levels-of-processing model).

What problem do you see regarding the interpretation given? How could subsequent research be designed to enhance the interpretation of the findings?

5. How would you design an experiment to study some aspect of implicit memory?
6. Imagine what it would be like to recover from one of the forms of amnesia. Describe your impressions of and reactions to your newly recovered memory abilities.
7. How would your life be different if you could greatly enhance your own mnemonic skills in some way?

Key Terms

Alzheimer's disease, *p. 221*
amnesia, *p. 218*
anterograde amnesia, *p. 218*
central executive, *p. 204*
culture-relevant tests, *p. 192*
episodic buffer, *p. 205*
episodic memory, *p. 209*
explicit memory, *p. 190*
hypermnesia, *p. 216*
hypothetical constructs, *p. 193*

iconic store, *p. 194*
implicit memory, *p. 190*
infantile amnesia, *p. 218*
levels-of-processing framework, *p. 200*
long-term store, *p. 193*
memory, *p. 187*
mnemonist, *p. 214*
phonological loop, *p. 204*
prime, *p. 212*

priming effect, *p. 212*
recall, *p. 187*
recognition, *p. 187*
retrograde amnesia, *p. 218*
semantic memory, *p. 209*
sensory store, *p. 193*
short-term store, *p. 193*
visuospatial sketchpad, *p. 204*
working memory, *p. 203*

Media Resources

Visit the companion website—**www.cengagebrain.com**—for quizzes, research articles, chapter outlines, and more.

CogLab

Explore CogLab by going to **http://coglab.wadsworth.com**. To learn more, examine the following experiments:

Brain Asymmetry

Memory Span

Partial Report

Absolute Identification

Operation Span

Implicit Learning

Modality Effect

Position Error

Irrelevant Speech

Phonological Similarity

Levels of Processing

Memory Processes

Here are some of the questions we will explore in this chapter:

1. What have cognitive psychologists discovered regarding how we encode information for storing it in memory?

2. What affects our ability to retrieve information from memory?

3. How does what we know or what we learn affect what we remember?

■ BELIEVE IT OR NOT

THERE'S A REASON YOU REMEMBER THOSE ANNOYING SONGS

Having a song or part of a song stuck in your head is incredibly frustrating. We've all had the experience of the song from a commercial repeatedly running through our minds, even though we wanted to forget it. But sequence recall—remembering episodes or information in sequential order (like the notes to a song)—has a special and useful place in memory. We constantly have to remember sequences, from the movements involved in signing our name or making coffee in the morning, to the names of the exits that come before the motorway turn-off we take to drive home every day.

The ability to recall these sequences makes many aspects of everyday life possible. As you think about a snippet of song or speech, your brain may repeat a sequence that strengthens the connections associated with that phrase. In turn, this increases the likelihood that you will recall it, which leads to more reinforcement.

You could break this unending cycle of repeated recall and reinforcement—even though this is a necessary and normal process for the strengthening and cementing of memories—by introducing other sequences. Thinking of another song may allow a competing memory to crowd out the first one: Find another infectious song and hope that the cure doesn't become more annoying than the original problem.

In this chapter, we will learn more about how we store and recall information, as well as what makes us forget that information again.

Researchers John Bransford and Marcia Johnson (1972, p. 722) gave their participants the following procedure to follow. Are you able to recall the steps outlined in this procedure?

> *The procedure is actually quite simple. First, you arrange items into different groups. Of course one pile may be sufficient, depending on how much there is to do. If you have to go somewhere else due to lack of facilities that is the next step; otherwise, you are pretty well set. It is important not to overdo things. That is, it is better to do too few things at once than too many. In the short run this may not seem important but complications can easily arise. A mistake can be expensive as well. At first, the whole procedure will seem complicated. Soon, however, it will become just another facet of life. It is difficult to foresee any end to the necessity for this task in the immediate future, but then, one can never tell. After the procedure is completed one arranges the materials into different groups again. Then they can be put into their appropriate places. Eventually they will be used once more and the whole cycle will then have to be repeated. However, that is part of life.*

How easy or difficult is it for you to remember all the details? Bransford and Johnson's participants (and probably you, too) had a great deal of difficulty understanding this passage and recalling the steps involved. What makes this task so difficult? What are the mental processes involved in this task?

As mentioned in the previous chapter, cognitive psychologists generally refer to the main processes of memory as comprising three common operations: encoding, storage, and retrieval. Each one represents a stage in memory processing:

- **Encoding** refers to how you transform a physical, sensory input into a kind of representation that can be placed into memory.
- **Storage** refers to how you retain encoded information in memory.
- **Retrieval** refers to how you gain access to information stored in memory.

Our emphasis in discussing these processes will be on recall of verbal and pictorial material. Remember, however, that we have memories of other kinds of stimuli as well, such as odors (Herz & Engen, 1996; Olsson et al., 2009).

Encoding, storage, and retrieval often are viewed as sequential stages. You first take in information. Then you hold it for a while. Later you pull it out. However, the processes interact with each other and are interdependent. For example, you may have found the Bransford and Johnson procedure difficult to encode, thereby also making it hard to store and to retrieve the information. However, a verbal label can facilitate encoding and hence storage and retrieval.

Most people do much better with the passage if given its title, "Washing Clothes." Now, read the procedure again. Can you recall the steps described in the passage? The verbal label, "washing clothes" helps us to encode, and therefore to remember a passage that otherwise seems incomprehensible.

Encoding and Transfer of Information

Before information can be stored in memory, it first needs to be encoded for storage. Even if the information is held in our short-term memory, it is not always transferred to our long-term memory. So in order to remember events and facts over a long period of time, we need to encode and subsequently transfer them from short-term to long-term storage. These are the processes we will explore in the forthcoming section.

Forms of Encoding

We encode our memories to store them. However, do short-term and long-term storage use the same kind of code to store information, or do their codes differ? Let us have a look at some research to answer this question.

Short-Term Storage

When you encode information for temporary storage and use, what kind of code do you use? This is what Conrad and colleagues (1964) set out to discover with an experiment. Participants were visually presented with several series of six letters at the rate of 0.75 seconds per letter. The letters used in the various lists were B, C, F, M, N, P, S, T, V, and X. There were no vowels included in order to ensure that letter combinations did not result in any words or pronounceable combinations that could be memorized more easily. Immediately after the letters were presented, participants were asked to write down each list of six letters in the order given. What kinds of errors did participants make? Despite the fact that letters were presented visually, errors tended to be based on acoustic confusability. In other words, instead of recalling the letters they were supposed to recall, participants substituted letters that sounded like the correct letters. Thus, they were likely to confuse *F* for *S*, *B* for *V*, *P* for *B*, and so on.

Another group of participants simply listened to single letters in a setting that had noise in the background. They then immediately reported each letter as they heard it. Participants showed the same pattern of confusability in the listening task as in the visual memory task (Conrad, 1964). Thus, we seem to encode visually presented letters by how they sound, not by how they look.

The Conrad experiment shows the importance in short-term memory of an acoustic code rather than a visual code. But the results do not rule out the possibility that there are other codes. One such code would be a *semantic code*—one based on word meaning.

Baddeley (1966) argued that short-term memory relies primarily on an acoustic rather than a semantic code. He compared recall performance for lists of acoustically confusable words—such as *map, cab, mad, man,* and *cap*—with lists of acoustically distinct words—such as *cow, pit, day, rig,* and *bun.* He found that performance was much worse for the visual presentation of acoustically similar words. He also compared performance for lists of semantically similar words—such as *big, long, large, wide,* and *broad*—with performance for lists of semantically dissimilar words—such as *old, foul, late, hot,* and *strong.* There was little difference in recall between the two lists. If performance for the semantically similar words had been much worse, what would such a finding have meant? It would have indicated that participants were confused by the semantic similarities and hence were processing the words semantically. However, performance for the semantically similar words was only *slightly* worse than that for the semantically dissimilar words, meaning that semantics did not matter much for processing.

Subsequent work investigating how information is encoded in short-term memory has shown clear evidence, however, of at least some semantic encoding in short-term memory (Shulman, 1970; Wickens, Dalezman, & Eggemeier, 1976). Thus, encoding in short-term memory appears to be primarily acoustic, but there may be some secondary semantic encoding as well. In addition, we sometimes temporarily encode information visually as well (Posner, 1969; Posner et al., 1969; Posner & Keele, 1967). But visual encoding appears to be even more fleeting (about 1.5 seconds). We are more prone to forgetting visual information than acoustic information. Thus, initial encoding is primarily acoustic in nature, but other forms of encoding may be used under some circumstances. For example, when you remember a telephone number from long ago, you are more likely to remember how it sounds when you say it to yourself than to remember a visual image of it.

Long-Term Storage

As mentioned, information stored temporarily in working memory is encoded primarily in acoustic form. So, when we make errors in retrieving words from short-term memory, the errors tend to reflect confusions in sound. How is information encoded into a form that can be transferred into storage and available for subsequent retrieval?

Most information stored in long-term memory is primarily semantically encoded. In other words, it is encoded by the meanings of words. Consider some relevant evidence.

Participants in a research study learned a list of 41 words (Grossman & Eagle, 1970). Five minutes after learning took place, participants were given a recognition test. Included in the recognition test were distracters—items that appear to be legitimate choices but that are not correct alternatives. Nine of the distracters (words that were not in the list of 41 words) were semantically related to words on the list. Nine were not. The researchers were interested in "false alarm" responses in which the participants indicated that they had seen the distracters, even though those words weren't even on the list. Participants falsely recognized an average of 1.83 of the synonyms but only an average of 1.05 of the unrelated words. This result indicated a greater likelihood of semantic confusion.

Another way to show semantic encoding is to use sets of semantically related test words, rather than distracters. Participants learned a list of 60 words that included 15 animals, 15 professions, 15 vegetables, and 15 names of people (Bousfield, 1953). The words were presented in random order. Thus, members of the various categories were intermixed thoroughly. After participants heard the words, they were asked to use free recall to reproduce the list in any order they wished. The investigator then analyzed the order of output of the recalled words. Did participants recall successive words from the same category more frequently than would be expected by chance? Indeed, successive recalls from the same category did occur much more often than would be expected by chance occurrence. Participants were remembering words by clustering them into categories.

Levels of processing, discussed in Chapter 5, also influences encoding in long-term memory. When learning lists of words, participants move more information into long-term memory when using a semantic encoding strategy than when using a nonsemantic strategy. Interestingly, this advantage is not seen in people with autism. This finding suggests that, in persons with autism, information may not be encoded semantically, or at least, not to the same extent as in people who do not have autism (Toichi & Kamio, 2002). When engaged in semantic processing, people with autism show less activation in Broca's area than do healthy participants. This finding indicates that Broca's area may be related to the semantic deficits autistic patients often exhibit (Harris et al., 2006).

Encoding of information in long-term memory is not exclusively semantic. There also is evidence for visual encoding. Participants in a study received 16 drawings of objects, including four items of clothing, four animals, four vehicles, and four items of furniture (Frost, 1972). The investigator manipulated not only the semantic category but also the visual category. The drawings differed in visual orientation. Four were angled to the left, four angled to the right, four horizontal, and four vertical. Items were presented in random order. Participants were asked to recall them freely. The order of participants' responses showed effects of both semantic and visual categories. These results suggested that participants were encoding visual as well as semantic information. In fact, people are able to store thousands of images (Brady et al., 2008).

Functional Magnetic Resonance Imaging (fMRI) studies have found that the brain areas that are involved in encoding can be, but do not necessarily have to be, involved in retrieval. With respect to faces, the anterior medial prefrontal cortex and the right fusiform face area play an important role both in encoding and retrieval, whereas the left fusiform face area contributes mostly to encoding processes. Both encoding and retrieval of places activate the left parahippocampal place area (PPA); the left PPA is associated with encoding rather than retrieval. In addition, medial temporal and prefrontal regions are related to memory processes in general, no matter what kind of stimulus is used (Prince et al., 2009).

In addition to semantic and visual information, acoustic information can be encoded in long-term memory (Nelson & Rothbart, 1972). Thus, there is considerable flexibility in the way we store information that we retain for long periods. Those who seek to know the single correct way we encode information are seeking an answer to the wrong question. There is no one correct way. A more useful question involves asking, "In what *ways* do we encode information in long-term memory?" From a more psychological perspective, however, the most useful question to ask is, "*When* do we encode in *which* ways?" In other words, under what circumstances do we use one form of encoding, and under what circumstances do we use another? These questions are the focus of present and future research.

Transfer of Information from Short-Term Memory to Long-Term Memory

We encounter two key problems when we transfer information from short-term memory to long-term memory: interference and decay. When competing information interferes with our storing information, we speak of **interference**. Imagine you have watched two crime movies with the same actor. You then try to remember the

"The matters about which I'm being questioned, Your Honor, are all things I should have included in my long-term memory but which I mistakenly inserted in my short-term memory."

story line of one of the movies but mix it up with the second movie. You are experiencing interference. When we forget facts just because time passes, we speak of **decay**. These two concepts will be discussed in more detail later in this chapter.

Given the problems of decay and interference, how do we move information from short-term memory to long-term memory? The means of moving information depends on whether the information involves declarative or nondeclarative memory.

Some forms of nondeclarative memory are highly volatile and decay quickly. Examples are priming and habituation. Let's go back to our movie example and assume that one of the main protagonists in the movie was Tom Cruise. After the movie, you overhear a conversation in which the word "cruise" is mentioned. Automatically, Tom Cruise pops into your mind. If you hear the word "cruise" a few days later, however, Tom Cruise may not be so accessible in your mind, and you may rather think of a cruise you recently took, or would like to take, in the Caribbean. Other nondeclarative forms are maintained more readily, particularly as a result of repeated practice (of procedures) or repeated conditioning (of responses).

Entrance into long-term declarative memory may occur through a variety of processes. One method of accomplishing this goal is by deliberately attending to information to comprehend it. Another is by making connections or associations between the new information and what we already know and understand. We make connections by integrating the new data into our existing schemas of stored information. This process of integrating new information into stored information is called **consolidation**. In humans, the process of consolidating declarative information into memory can continue for many years after the initial experience (Squire, 1986). When you learn about someone or something, for example, you often integrate new information into your knowledge a long time after you have acquired that knowledge. For example, you may have met a friend many years ago and started organizing that knowledge at that time. But you still acquire new information about that friend—sometimes surprising information—and continue to integrate this new information into your knowledge base.

Stress generally impairs the memory functioning. However, stress also can help enhance the consolidation of memory through the release of hormones (Park et al., 2008; Roozendaal, 2002, 2003). The disruption of consolidation has been studied effectively in amnesics. Studies have particularly examined people who have suffered brief forms of amnesia as a consequence of electroconvulsive therapy (ECT; Squire, 1986). For these amnesics, the source of the trauma is clear. Confounding variables can be minimized. A patient history before the trauma can be obtained, and follow-up testing and supervision after the trauma are more likely to be available. A range of studies suggests that during the process of consolidation, our memory is susceptible to disruption and distortion.

We may use various metamemory strategies to preserve or enhance the integrity of memories during consolidation (Metcalfe, 2000; Waters & Schneider, 2010). **Metamemory** strategies involve reflecting on our own memory processes with a view to improving our memory. Such strategies are especially important when we are transferring new information to long-term memory by rehearsing it. Metamemory strategies are just one component of **metacognition**, our ability to think about and control our own processes of thought and ways of enhancing our thinking.

Rehearsal

One technique people use for keeping information active is **rehearsal**, the repeated recitation of an item. The effects of such rehearsal are termed *practice effects*. Rehearsal may be *overt*, in which case it is usually aloud and obvious to anyone watching. Or it may be *covert*, in which case it is silent and hidden.

Elaborative and Maintenance Rehearsal   To move information into long-term memory, an individual must engage in elaborative rehearsal. In *elaborative rehearsal*, the individual somehow elaborates the items to be remembered. Such rehearsal makes the items either more meaningfully integrated into what the person already knows or more meaningfully connected to one another and therefore more memorable.

In contrast, consider maintenance rehearsal. In *maintenance rehearsal*, the individual simply repetitiously rehearses the items to be repeated. Such rehearsal temporarily maintains information in short-term memory without transferring the information to long-term memory. Without any kind of elaboration, the information cannot be organized and transferred (Tulving, 1962). This finding is of immediate importance when you study for an exam. If you want to transfer facts to your long-term memory, you will need somehow to elaborate on the information and link it to what you already know. For example, if you meet a new acquaintance, you might encode not just the acquaintance's name but also other connections you have with the person, such as being members of a particular club or taking a particular course together. It will also be helpful to use mnemonic techniques like the ones discussed in the next section, but repeating words over and over again is not enough to achieve effective rehearsal.

The Spacing Effect   What is the best way to organize your time for rehearsing new information? More than a century ago, Hermann Ebbinghaus (1885, cited in Schacter, 1989a; see also Chapter 1) noticed that the distribution of study (memory rehearsal) sessions over time affects the consolidation of information in long-term memory. Much more recently, researchers have offered support for Ebbinghaus's observations as a result of their studies of people's recall of foreign language vocabulary, facts, and names of visual objects (Cepeda, 2009).

Much more recently, researchers have offered support for Ebbinghaus's observation as a result of their studies of people's long-term recall of Spanish vocabulary words the subjects had learned 8 years earlier (Bahrick & Phelps, 1987). People's memory for information depends on how they acquire it. Their memories tend to be good when they use **distributed practice**, learning in which various sessions are spaced over time. Their memories for information are not as good when the information is acquired through **massed practice**, learning in which sessions are crammed together in a very short space of time. The greater the distribution of learning trials over time, the more the participants remembered over long periods. To maximize the effect on long-term recall, the spacing should ideally be distributed over months, rather than days or weeks. This effect is termed the **spacing effect**. The research in this area is used by companies producing consumer products and advertising companies, among others. The goal of these companies is to anchor their products in your long-term memory so that you will remember them when you are in need of a particular product. The spacing in advertisements is varied to maximize the effect on your memory (Appleton-Knapp, 2005). That means that a company will not place ads for the same product on several papers of a given magazine, but rather that they will place one ad every month in that magazine.

The spacing effect is linked to the process by which memories are consolidated in long-term memory (Glenberg, 1977, 1979; Leicht & Overton, 1987). That is, the spacing effect may occur because at each learning session, the context for encoding may vary. The individuals may use alternative strategies and cues for encoding. They thereby enrich and elaborate their schemas for the information. The principle of the spacing effect is important to remember in studying. You will recall information longer, on average, if you distribute your learning of subject matter and you vary the context for encoding. Do not try to cram it all into a short period. Imagine studying for an

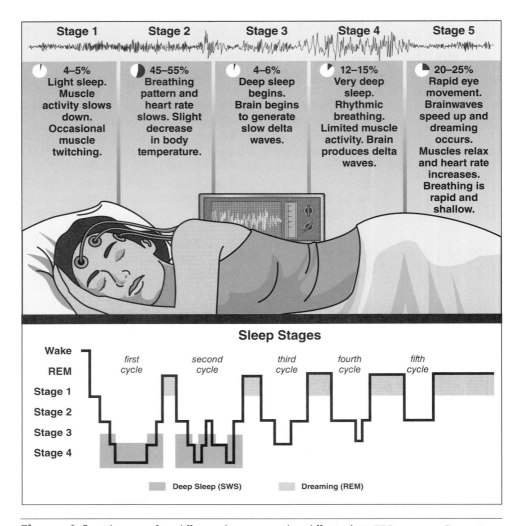

Figure 6.1   There are five different sleep stages that differ in their EEG patterns. Dreaming takes place during stage 5, the so-called REM sleep. REM sleep is particularly important for memory consolidation.

exam in several short sessions over a 2-week period. You will remember much of the material. However, if you try to study all the material in just one night, you will remember very little and the memory for this material will decay relatively quickly.

Why would distributing learning trials over days make a difference? One possibility is that information is learned in variable contexts. These diverse contexts help strengthen and begin to consolidate it. Another possible answer comes from studies of the influences of sleep on memory.

Sleep and Memory Consolidation   Of particular importance to memory is the amount of rapid eye movement (REM) sleep, a particular stage of sleep (see Figure 6.1) characterized by dreaming and increased brainwave activity (Karni et al., 1994), a person receives.

Specifically, disruptions in REM sleep patterns the night after learning reduced the amount of improvement on a visual discrimination task that occurred relative to normal sleep. Furthermore, this lack of improvement was not observed for disrupted stage-three or stage-four sleep patterns (Karni et al., 1994). Other research also shows better learning with increases in the proportion of REM-stage sleep after exposure to learning situations (Ellenbogen, Payne, & Stickgold, 2006; Smith, 1996). The positive influence of sleep on memory consolidation is seen across age groups (Hornung et al., 2007). People who suffer from insomnia, a disorder that deprives the sufferer of much-needed sleep, have trouble with memory consolidation (Backhaus et al., 2006). Research suggests that memory processes in the hippocampus are influenced by the production and integration of new cells into the neuronal network. Prolonged sleep deprivation seems to affect such cell development negatively (Meerlo et al., 2009). These findings highlight the importance of biological factors in the consolidation of memory. Thus, a good night's sleep, which includes plenty of REM-stage sleep, aids in memory consolidation.

Neuroscience and Memory Consolidation   Is there something special occurring in the brain that could explain why REM sleep is so important for memory consolidation? Neuropsychological research on animal learning may offer a tentative answer to this question. Recall that the hippocampus has been found to be an important structure for memory. In recording studies of rat hippocampal cells, researchers have found that cells of the hippocampus that were activated during initial learning are reactivated during subsequent periods of sleep. It is as if they are replaying the initial learning episode to achieve consolidation into long-term storage (Scaggs & McNaughton, 1996; Wilson & McNaughton, 1994). This effect has also been observed in humans. After learning routes within a virtual town, participants slept. Increased hippocampal activity was seen during sleep after the person had learned the spatial information. In the people with the most hippocampal activation, there was also an improvement in performance when they needed to recall the routes (Peigneux et al., 2004). During this increased activity, the hippocampus also shows extremely low levels of the neurotransmitter acetylcholine. When patients were given acetylcholine during sleep, they showed impaired memory consolidation, but only for declarative information. Procedural memory consolidation was not affected by acetylcholine levels (Gais & Born, 2004).

The hippocampus acts as a rapid learning system (McClelland, McNaughton, & O'Reilly, 1995). It temporarily maintains new experiences until they can be appropriately assimilated into the more gradual neocortical representation system of the brain. Such a complementary system is necessary to allow memory to more accurately represent the structure of the environment. McClelland and his colleagues have used connectionist models of learning to show that integrating new experiences too rapidly leads to disruptions in long-term memory systems. Thus, the benefits of distributed practice seem to occur because we have a relatively rapid learning system in the hippocampus that becomes activated during sleep. Repeated exposure on subsequent days and repeated reactivation during subsequent periods of sleep help learning. These rapidly learned memories become integrated into our more permanent long-term memory system.

Reconsolidation is a topic related to consolidation. The process of consolidation makes memories less likely to undergo either interference or decay. However, after a memory is called back into consciousness, it may return to a more unstable state. In this state, the memory that was consolidated may again fall victim to interference or

MEMORY STRATEGIES

You can use these memory strategies to help you study for exams:

1. Study throughout the course rather than cram the night before an exam. This distributes the learning sessions, which allows for consolidation into more permanent memory systems.
2. Link new information to what you already know by rehearsing new information in meaningful ways. Organize new information to relate it to other coursework or areas of your life.
3. Use the various mnemonic devices shown in Table 6.1.

How could mnemonic devices be helpful in memorizing the state capitals?

decay. To prevent this loss, a process of reconsolidation takes place. Reconsolidation has the same effect that consolidation does, but it is completed on previously encoded information. Reconsolidation does not necessarily occur with each memory we recall but does seem to occur with relatively newly consolidated material (Walker et al., 2003).

Organization of Information

Stored memories are organized. One way to show how memories are organized is by measuring subjective organization in free recall. This means that researchers measure the different ways that individuals organize their memories. Researchers do this by giving participants a list of unrelated words to recall in any order (free recall). Participants have multiple trials during which to learn to recall a list of unrelated words in any order they choose. Remember that if sets of test words can be divided into categories (e.g., names of fruits or of furniture), participants spontaneously will cluster their recall output by these categories. They do so even if the order of presentation is random (Bousfield, 1953). Similarly, participants will tend to show consistent patterns of word order in their recall protocols, even if there are no apparent relations among words in the list (Tulving, 1962). In other words, participants create their own consistent organization and then group their recall by the subjective units they create. Although most adults spontaneously tend to cluster items into categories, categorical clustering also may be used intentionally as an aid to memorization.

Mnemonic devices are specific techniques to help you memorize lists of words (Best, 2003). Essentially, such devices add meaning to otherwise meaningless or arbitrary lists of items. Even music can be used as a mnemonic device when a well-known or easy melody is used and connected with the material that needs to be learned. Music can even serve as a retrieval cue. For example, if you want to learn vocabulary words in a foreign language for body parts, sing those words to yourself in a melody that you like and know well (see, for example, Moore et al., 2008).

As Table 6.1 shows, a variety of methods—categorical clustering, acronyms, acrostics, interactive imagery among items, pegwords, and the method of loci—can help you to memorize lists of words and vocabulary items. Although the techniques described in Table 6.1 are not the only available ones, they are among the most frequently used.

Table 6.1   Mnemonic Devices

Of the many mnemonic devices available, the ones described here rely either on organization of information into meaningful chunks, such as categorical clustering, acronyms, and acrostics, or on visual images, such as interactive images, a pegword system, and the method of loci.

Technique	Explanation/Description	Example
Categorical clustering	Organize a list of items into a set of categories.	If you needed to remember to buy apples, milk, bagels, grapes, yogurt, rolls, Swiss cheese, grapefruit, and lettuce, you would be better able to do so if you tried to memorize the items by categories: *fruits*—apples, grapes, grapefruit; *dairy products*—milk, yogurt, Swiss cheese; *breads*—bagels, rolls; *vegetables*—lettuce.
Interactive images	Create interactive images that link the isolated words in a list.	Suppose you have to remember to buy socks, apples, and a pair of scissors. You might imagine using scissors to cut a sock that has an apple stuffed in it.
Pegword system	Associate each new word with a word on a previously memorized list and form an interactive image between the two words.	One such list is from a nursery rhyme: One is a bun. Two is a shoe. Three is a tree, and so on. To remember that you need to buy socks, apples, and a pair of scissors, you might imagine an apple between two buns, a sock stuffed inside a shoe, and a pair of scissors cutting a tree. When you need to remember the words, you first recall the numbered images and then recall the words as you visualize them in the interactive images.
Method of loci	Visualize walking around an area with distinctive landmarks that you know well, and then link the various landmarks to specific items to be remembered	Mentally walk past each of the distinctive landmarks, depositing each word to be memorized at one of the landmarks. Visualize an interactive image between the new word and the landmark. Suppose you have three landmarks on your route to school—a strange-looking house, a tree, and a baseball diamond. You might imagine a big sock on top of the house in place of the chimney, the pair of scissors cutting the tree, and apples replacing bases on the baseball diamond. When ready to remember the list, you would take your mental walk and pick up the words you had linked to each of the landmarks along the walk.
Acronym	Devise a word or expression in which each of its letters stands for a certain other word or concept (e.g., USA, IQ, and laser)	Suppose that you want to remember the names of the mnemonic devices described in this chapter. The acronym "IAM PACK" might prompt you to remember Interactive images, Acronyms, Method of loci, Pegwords, Acrostics, Categories, and Keywords. Of course, this technique is more useful if the first letters of the words to be memorized actually can be formed into a word phrase, or something close to one, even if the word or phrase is nonsensical, as in this example.
Acrostic	Form a sentence rather than a single word to help you remember the new words	Music students trying to memorize the names of the notes found on lines of the treble clef (the higher notes; specifically *E, G, B, D,* and *F* above middle *C*) learn that *"Every Good Boy Does Fine."*
Keyword system	Form an interactive image that links the sound and meaning of a foreign word with the sound and meaning of a familiar word.	Suppose that you needed to learn that the French word for butter is *beurre*. First, you would note that *beurre* sounds something like "bear." Next, you would associate the keyword bear with butter in an image or sentence. For instance, you might visualize a bear eating a stick of butter. Later, *bear* would provide a retrieval cue for *beurre*.

- In *categorical clustering*, organize a list of items into a set of categories.
- In *interactive images*, imagine (as vividly as possible) the objects represented by words you have to remember as if the objects are interacting with each other in some active way.
- In the *pegword system*, associate each word with a word on a previously memorized list and form an interactive image between the two words.
- In the *method of loci*, visualize walking around an area with distinctive, well-known landmarks and link the various landmarks to specific items to be remembered.
- In using *acronyms*, devise a word or expression in which each of its letters stands for a certain other word or concept.
- In using *acrostics*, form a sentence, rather than a single word, to help one remember new words.
- In using the *keyword system*, create an interactive image that links the sound and meaning of a foreign word with the sound and meaning of a familiar word.

What is the comparative effectiveness of the mnemonic strategies listed in Table 6.1? Henry Roediger (1980) conducted a study in which his participants used different strategies to memorize material. Table 6.2 shows how effective the different strategies were.

Henry Roediger's (1980) study of recall memory involved initial recall of a series of items compared with recall following brief training in each of several memory

Table 6.2 Mnemonic Devices: Comparative Effectiveness

Condition (type of mnemonic training)	Number of participants	Free Recall Criterion			Serial Recall Criterion		
		Average number of items recalled correctly following training			Average number of items recalled correctly following training		
		Number of correct items immediately recalled on practice list, prior to training	Immediate recall	Recall following a 24-hour delay	Number of correct items immediately recalled on practice list, prior to training	Immediate recall	Recall following a 24-hour delay
Elaborative rehearsal (verbal)	32	13.2	11.4	6.3	7.0	5.8	1.3
Isolated images of individual items	25	12.4	13.1	6.8	6.8	4.8	1.0
Interactive imagery (with links from one item to the next)	31	13.0	15.6	11.2	7.6	9.6	5.0
Method of loci	29	12.6	15.3	10.6	6.8	13.6	5.8
Pegword system	33	13.1	14.2	8.2	7.7	12.5	4.9
Mean performance across conditions	—	12.9	13.9	8.6	7.2	9.4	3.6

Source: H. L. Roediger (1980), "The Effectiveness of Four Mnemonics in Ordering Recall," *Journal of Experimental Psychology: HLM*, 6(5): 558–567. Copyright © 1980, by the American Psychological Association. Adapted with permission.

strategies. For both free recall and serial recall, training in interactive imagery, the method of loci, and the pegword system was more effective than either elaborative (verbal) rehearsal or imagery for isolated items. However, the beneficial effects of training were most pronounced for the serial recall condition. In the free recall condition, imagery of isolated items was modestly more effective than elaborative (verbal) rehearsal, but for serial recall, elaborative (verbal) rehearsal was modestly more effective than imagery for isolated items.

The relative effectiveness of the methods for encoding is influenced by the kind of task (free recall versus serial recall) required at the time of retrieval (Roediger, 1980). Thus, when choosing a method for encoding information for subsequent recall, you should consider the purpose for recalling the information. You should choose not only strategies that allow for effectively encoding the information (moving it into long-term memory), but strategies that offer appropriate cues for facilitating subsequent retrieval when needed. For example, using a strategy for retrieving an alphabetical list of prominent cognitive psychologists would probably be relatively ineffective prior to taking an exam in cognitive psychology. Using a strategy for linking particular theorists with the key ideas of their theories is likely to be more effective.

The use of mnemonic devices and other techniques for aiding memory involves metamemory (our understanding and reflection upon our memory and how to improve it). Because most adults spontaneously use categorical clustering, its inclusion in this list of mnemonic devices is actually just a reminder to use this common memory strategy. In fact, each of us often uses various kinds of *reminders*—external memory aids—to enhance the likelihood that we will remember important information. For example, by now you have surely learned the benefits of various external memory aids. These include taking notes during lectures, writing shopping lists for items to purchase, setting timers and alarms, and even asking other people to help you remember things. In addition, we can design our environment to help us remember important information through the use of *forcing functions* (Norman, 1988). These are physical constraints that prevent us from acting without at least considering the key information to be remembered. For example, to ensure that you remember to take your notebook to class, you might lean the notebook against the door through which you must pass to go to class.

So-called forcing functions are also used in professional settings, such as hospitals, to change behavior. Patients in emergency rooms sometimes have to be physically restrained, but that restraint also significantly increases their risk of dying. The computer systems physicians use can force the physicians to re-evaluate their decisions concerning the restraint orders by requiring them to renew the order and eventually blocking computer access if the renewal is not executed (Griffey et al., 2009). In effect, the physicians are forced to deal with the problem at hand.

Most of the time, we try to improve our *retrospective memory*—our memory for the past. At times we also try to improve our *prospective memory*—memory for things we need to do or remember in the future. For example, we may need to remember to call someone, to buy cereal at the supermarket, or to finish a homework assignment due the next day. We use a number of strategies to improve prospective memory. Examples are keeping a to-do list, asking someone to remind us to do something, or tying a string around our finger to remind us that we need to do something. Research suggests that having to do something regularly on a certain day does not necessarily improve prospective memory for doing that thing. However, being monetarily reinforced for doing the thing does tend to improve prospective memory (Meacham, 1982; Meacham & Singer, 1977).

Prospective memory, like retrospective memory, is subject to decline as we age. Over the years, we retain more of our prospective memory than of our retrospective memory. This retention is likely the result of the use of the external cues and strategies that can be used to bolster prospective memory. In the laboratory, older adults show a decline in prospective memory; however, outside the laboratory they show better performance than young adults. This difference may be due to greater reliance on strategies to aid in remembering as we age (Henry et al., 2004).

✔ CONCEPT CHECK

1. How does encoding differ in the short-term storage and the long-term storage?

2. What is rehearsal?

3. Name three mnemonic devices.

Retrieval

Once we have encoded and stored information in short-term memory, how do we retrieve it? If we have problems retrieving information, was the information even stored in the first place?

Retrieval from Short-Term Memory

In one study on memory scanning, Saul Sternberg presented participants with a short list including from one to six digits (Sternberg, 1966). They were expected to hold the list in short-term memory. After a brief pause, a test digit was flashed on a screen. Participants had to say whether this digit appeared in the set that they had been asked to memorize. Thus, if the list comprised the digits 4, 1, 9, 3, and the digit 9 flashed on the screen, the correct response would be "yes." If, instead, the test digit was 7, the correct response would be "no." The digits that were presented are termed the *positive set*. Those that were not presented are termed the *negative set*. Predictions of the possible results are shown in Figure 6.2.

Are items retrieved all at once (parallel processing) or sequentially (serial processing)? If retrieved serially, the question then arises: Are all items retrieved, regardless of the task (exhaustive retrieval), or does retrieval stop as soon as an item seems to accomplish the task (self-terminating retrieval)? In the next sections, we examine parallel and serial processing, and then exhaustive and self-terminating retrieval.

INVESTIGATING COGNITIVE PSYCHOLOGY
Test Your Short-Term Memory

Test your ability to retrieve information from your short-term memory. Try this memory scanning test that is similar to the S. Sternberg experiment described in the chapter. Use 10 index cards and write one number on each card (1–10). Have a friend quickly show you five of the index cards (e.g., 6, 3, 8, 2, 7). Then, have your friend hold up one of the index cards and ask, "Is this one of the numbers?" Have your friend repeat this procedure five times. How often were you correct? Now, switch roles and test your friend's short-term memory. How do people make decisions such as this one?

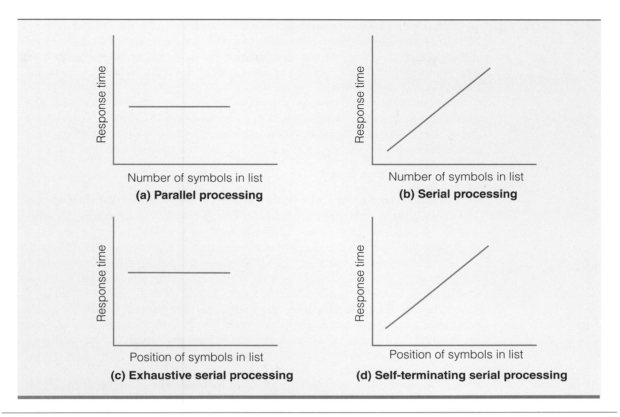

Figure 6.2 This figure shows the four possible predictions for retrieval from short-term memory of Saul Sternberg's experiment. Panel **(a)** illustrates findings suggestive of parallel processing; **(b)** illustrates serial processing; **(c)** shows exhaustive serial processing; and **(d)** shows self-terminating serial processing.

Source: Based on S. Sternberg (1966), "High Speed in S. Sternberg's Short-Term Memory-Scanning Task," *Science*, Vol. 153, pp. 652–654. Copyright © 1966 American Association for the Advancement of Science.

Let's think about these different options for retrieving memories and see what the research results say.

Parallel or Serial Processing?

Parallel processing refers to the simultaneous handling of multiple operations. As applied to short-term memory, the items stored in short-term memory would be retrieved all at once, not one at a time. The prediction in Figure 6.2(a) shows what would happen if parallel processing were the case in the Sternberg memory scanning task: Response times should be the same, regardless of the size of the positive set. This is because all comparisons would be done at once.

Serial processing refers to operations being done one after another. In other words, on the digit-recall task, the digits would be retrieved in succession, rather than all at once (as in the parallel model). According to the serial model, it should take longer to retrieve four digits than to retrieve two digits [as shown in Figure 6.2(b)].

Exhaustive or Self-Terminating Processing?

If information processing were serial, there would be two ways in which to gain access to the stimuli: exhaustive or self-terminating processing. *Exhaustive serial processing* implies that the participant always checks the test digit against *all* digits in the positive set, even if a match were found partway through the list.

Exhaustive processing would predict the pattern of data shown in Figure 6.2(c). Note that positive responses all would take the same amount of time, regardless of the serial position of a positive test probe. In other words, in an exhaustive search, you would take the same amount of time to find any digit. Where in the list it was located would not matter.

Self-terminating serial processing implies that the participant would check the test digit against only those digits needed to make a response. Consider Figure 6.2(d). It shows that response time now would increase linearly as a function of where a test digit was located in the positive set. The later the serial position, the longer is the response time.

The Winner—a Serial Exhaustive Model—with Some Qualifications

The actual pattern of data was crystal clear. The data looked like those in Figures 6.2(b) and (c). Response times increased linearly with set size, but they were the same, regardless of serial position. Later, this pattern of data was replicated (Sternberg, 1969). Moreover, the mean response times for positive and negative responses were essentially the same. This fact further supported the serial exhaustive model. Comparisons took roughly 38 milliseconds (0.038 seconds) apiece (Sternberg, 1966, 1969).

Although many investigators considered the question of parallel versus serial processing to have been answered decisively, in fact, a parallel model could account for the data (Corcoran, 1971). Imagine a horse race that involves parallel processing. The race is not over until the last horse passes the finish line. Now, suppose we add more horses to the race. The length of the race, from the start until the last of the horses crosses the finishing line, is likely to increase. For example, if horses are selected randomly, the slowest horse in an eight-horse race is likely to be slower than the slowest horse in a four-horse race. That is, with more horses, a wider range of speeds is more likely. So the entire race will take longer because the race is not complete until the slowest horse crosses the finish line.

Similarly, when applying a parallel model to a retrieval task involving more items, a wider range of retrieval speeds for the various items is also more likely. The entire retrieval process is not complete until the last item has been retrieved. Mathematically, it is impossible to distinguish parallel from serial models unequivocally (Townsend, 1971). Some parallel model always exists that will mimic any serial model in its predictions and vice versa. The two models may not be equally plausible, but they still exist. Moreover, it appears that which processes individuals use depends in part on the stimuli that are processed (e.g., Naus, 1974; Naus, Glucksberg, & Ornstein, 1972).

Some cognitive psychologists have suggested that we should seek not only to understand the *how* of memory processes but also the *why* of memory processes (e.g., Bruce, 1991). That is, what functions does memory serve for individual persons and for humans as a species? To understand the functions of memory, we must study memory for relatively complex information. We also need to understand the relationships between the information presented and other information available to the individual, both within the informational context and as a result of prior experience.

Retrieval from Long-Term Memory

It is difficult to separate storage from retrieval phenomena. Participants in one study were tested on their memory for lists of categorized words (Tulving & Pearlstone, 1966). Participants would hear words within a category together in the list. They even would be given the name of the category before the items within it were presented. For example, the participants might hear the category "article of clothing" followed by the words, "shirt, socks, pants, belt." Participants then were tested for their recall.

The recall test was done in one of two ways. In the free recall condition, participants merely recalled as many words as they could in any order they chose. In a cued recall condition, however, participants were tested category by category. They were given each category label as a cue. They then were asked to recall as many words as they could from that category. The critical result was that cued recall was far better, on average, than free recall. Had the researchers tested only free recall, they might have concluded that participants had not stored quite so many words. However, the comparison to the cued recall condition demonstrated that apparent memory failures were largely a result of retrieval, rather than storage failures.

Categorization dramatically can affect retrieval. Investigators had participants learn lists of categorized words (Bower et al., 1969). Either the words were presented in random order or they were presented in the form of a hierarchical tree that showed the organization of the words. For example, the category "minerals" might be at the top, followed by the categories of "metals and stones," and so on. Participants given hierarchical presentation recalled 65% of the words. In contrast, recall was just 19% by participants given the words in random order.

An interesting study by Khader and colleagues (2005) demonstrated that material that is processed in certain cortical areas during perception also activates those same areas again during long-term memory recall. Participants learned abstract words that were connected either with one or two faces or with one or two spatial positions (see Figure 6.3). A few days later in a cued recall task, they were presented with two words and were asked to decide whether those two words were connected by a common face or position, with their performance recorded by fMRI. Recall of

Experimental stimuli

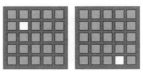

Spatial Information

Object information

Copyright © 2005, with permission from Elsevier.

Figure 6.3   In the experiment of Khader and colleagues (2005), participants were presented with abstract words like "concept," which were paired with either one or two spatial positions or faces.

Source: Reprinted from *Neuroimage*, *27*(4), Khader, P., Burke, M., Bien, S., Ranganath, C., & Roesler, F. (2005). Content-specific activation during associative long-term memory retrieval, 805–816.

spatial positions activated areas such as the parietal and precentral cortex, and faces activated areas such as the left prefrontal temporal cortex and the posterior cingulated cortex. Blood oxygen levels increased with the number of associations to be recalled.

Another problem that arises when studying memory is figuring out why we sometimes have trouble retrieving information. Cognitive psychologists often have difficulty finding a way to distinguish between availability and accessibility of items. **Availability** is the presence of information stored in long-term memory. **Accessibility** is the degree to which we can gain access to the available information. Memory performance depends on the accessibility of the information to be remembered. Ideally, memory researchers would like to assess the availability of information in memory. Unfortunately, they must settle for assessing the accessibility of such information.

Intelligence and Retrieval

Is there a link between age-related slowing of information processing and (1) initial encoding and recall of information and (2) long-term retention (Nettelbeck et al., 1996; see also Bors & Forrin, 1995)? It appears that the relation between inspection time and intelligence may not be related to learning. In particular, there is a difference between initial recall and actual long-term learning (Nettelbeck et al., 1996). Initial recall performance is mediated by processing speed. Older, slower participants showed deficits.

Longer-term retention of new information, preserved in older participants, is mediated by cognitive processes other than speed of processing. These processes include rehearsal strategies. Thus, speed of information processing may influence initial performance on recall and inspection time tasks, but speed is not related to long-term learning. Perhaps faster information processing aids participants in performance aspects of intelligence test tasks, rather than contributing to actual learning and intelligence. Clearly, this area requires more research to determine how information-processing speed relates to intelligence.

✔ CONCEPT CHECK

1. How do we retrieve data from short-term memory?

2. Why do we need to make a difference between the *availability* and the *accessibility* of information?

3. Does intelligence influence retrieval?

Processes of Forgetting and Memory Distortion

Why do we so easily and so quickly forget phone numbers we have just looked up or the names of people whom we have just met? Several theories have been proposed as to why we forget information stored in working memory. The two most well-known theories are interference theory and decay theory. Interference occurs when competing information causes us to forget something; decay occurs when simply the passage of time causes us to forget.

Interference Theory

Interference theory refers to the view that forgetting occurs because recall of certain words interferes with recall of other words. Evidence for interference goes back many years (Brown, 1958; Peterson & Peterson, 1959). In one study, participants were asked to recall *trigrams* (strings of three letters) at intervals of 3, 6, 9, 12, 15, or 18 seconds after the presentation of the last letter (Peterson & Peterson, 1959). The investigators used only consonants so that the trigrams would not be easily pronounceable—for example, "K B F." Figure 6.4 shows percentages of correct recalls after the various intervals of time.

Why does recall decline so rapidly? Because after the oral presentation of each trigram, participants counted backward by threes from a three-digit number spoken immediately after the trigram. The purpose of having the participants count backward was to prevent them from rehearsing during the *retention interval*. This is the time between the presentation of the last letter and the start of the recall phase of the experimental trial.

Clearly, the trigram is almost completely forgotten after just 18 seconds if participants are not allowed to rehearse it. Moreover, such forgetting also occurs when words rather than letters are used as the stimuli to be recalled (Murdock, 1961). So, counting backward interfered with recall from short-term memory, supporting the interference account of forgetting in short-term memory. At that time, it seemed surprising that counting backward with numbers would interfere with the recall of letters. The previous view had been that verbal information would interfere only with verbal (words) memory. Similarly, it was thought that quantitative (numerical) information would interfere only with quantitative memory.

At least two kinds of interference figure prominently in psychological theory and research: retroactive interference and proactive interference. **Retroactive interference** (or retroactive inhibition) occurs when newly acquired knowledge impedes the recall of older material. This kind of interference is caused by activity occurring *after* we learn something but *before* we are asked to recall that thing. The interference in the Brown-Peterson task appears to be retroactive because counting backward by threes occurs after learning the trigram. It interferes with our ability to remember information we learned previously.

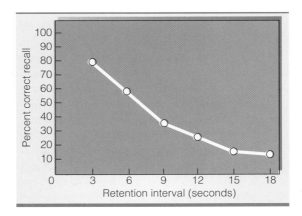

Figure 6.4   The percentage of recall of three consonants (a trigram) drops off quickly if participants are not allowed to rehearse the trigrams.

Source: G. Keppel and B. J. Underwood (1962), "Proactive Inhibition in Short-Term Retention of Single Items," *Journal of Verbal Learning and Verbal Behavior, 1*, pp. 153–161. Reprinted by permission of Elsevier.

Proactive interference (or proactive inhibition) occurs when material that was learned in the past impedes the learning of new material. In this case, the interfering material occurs *before*, rather than *after*, learning of the to-be-remembered material. If you have studied more than one foreign language, you may have experienced this effect quite intensely. The author studied French at school, and then started learning Spanish when she entered college. Unfortunately, French words found their way into her Spanish essays unnoticed, and it took her a while to eliminate those French words from her writing in Spanish (proactive interference). Later, she studied Italian, and because she had not practiced Spanish in a few years, when she formulated Spanish sentences in a conversation without much time to think, there was a good chance a mixture of Italian and Spanish would emerge (retroactive interference).

Proactive as well as retroactive interference may play a role in short-term memory (Keppel & Underwood, 1962; Makovski & Jiang, 2008). Thus, retroactive interference appears to be important (Reitman, 1971; Shiffrin, 1973; Waugh & Norman, 1965), but not the only factor impeding memory performance.

The amount of proactive interference generally climbs with increases in the length of time between when the information is presented (and encoded) and when the information is retrieved (Underwood, 1957). Also as you might expect, proactive interference increases as the amount of prior—and potentially interfering—learning increases (Greenberg & Underwood, 1950). Proactive interference generally has stronger effects in older adults than in younger people (Ebert & Anderson, 2009).

Proactive interference seems to be associated with activation in the frontal cortex. In particular, it activates Brodmann area 45 in the left hemisphere (Postle, Brush, & Nick, 2004). In alcoholic patients, proactive interference is seen to a lesser degree than in non-alcoholic patients. This finding suggests that the alcoholic patients have difficulty integrating past information with new information. Thus, alcoholic patients may have difficulty binding together unrelated items in a list (De Rosa & Sullivan, 2003). Taken together, these findings suggest that Brodmann area 45 is likely involved in the binding of items into meaningful groups. When more information is gathered, an attempt to relate them to one another can occupy much of the available resources, leaving limited processing ability for new items.

All information does not equally contribute to proactive interference. For instance, if you are learning a list of numbers, your performance in learning the list will gradually decline as the list continues. If, however, the list switches to words, your performance will rebound. This enhancement in performance is known as *release from proactive interference* (Bunting, 2006). The effects of proactive interference appear to dominate under conditions in which recall is delayed. However, proactive and retroactive interference now are viewed as complementary phenomena.

Some early psychologists recognized the need to study memory retrieval for connected texts and not just for unconnected strings of digits, words, or nonsense syllables. In one study, participants learned a text and then recalled it (Bartlett, 1932). British participants learned a North American Indian legend called "The War of the Ghosts," which to them was a strange and difficult-to-understand text. Read the legend in *Investigating Cognitive Psychology: Bartlett's Legend* and test yourself to see how much of the legend you can recall.

Participants distorted their recall to render the story more comprehensible to themselves. In other words, their prior knowledge and expectations had a substantial effect on their recall. Apparently, people bring into a memory task their already existing schemas, which affect the way in which they recall what they

INVESTIGATING COGNITIVE PSYCHOLOGY
Can You Recall Bartlett's Legend?

Read the following legend and then turn the page so you can not see the story. Now, try to recall the legend in its entirety by writing down what you remember.

(A) ORIGINAL INDIAN MYTH	(B) TYPICAL RECALL BY A STUDENT IN ENGLAND
The War of the Ghosts One night two young men from Egulac went down to the river to hunt seals, and while they were there it became foggy and calm. Then they heard war-cries, and they thought: "Maybe this is a war-party." They escaped to the shore, and hid behind a log. Now canoes came up, and they heard the noise of paddles, and saw one canoe coming up to them. There were five men in the canoe, and they said: "What do you think? We wish to take you along. We are going up the river to make war on the people." One of the young men said, "I have no arrows." "Arrows are in the canoe," they said. "I will not go along. I might be killed. My relatives do not know where I have gone. But you," he said, turning to the other, "may go with them." So one of the young men went, but the other returned home. And the warriors went on up the river to a town on the other side of Kalama. The people came down to the water, and they began to fight, and many were killed. But presently the young man heard one of the warriors say: "Quick, let us go home; that Indian has been hit." Now he thought: "Oh, they are ghosts." He did not feel sick, but they said he had been shot. So the canoes went back to Egulac, and the young man went ashore to his house, and made a fire. And he told everybody and said: "Behold I accompanied the ghosts, and we went to fight. Many of our fellows were killed, and many of those who attacked us were killed. They said I was hit, and I did not feel sick." He told it all, and then he became quiet. When the sun rose he fell down. Something black came out of his mouth. His face became contorted. The people jumped up and cried. He was dead.	*The War of the Ghosts* Two men from Edulac went fishing. While thus occupied by the river they heard a noise in the distance. "It sounds like a cry," said one, and presently there appeared some in canoes who invited them to join the party of their adventure. One of the young men refused to go, on the ground of family ties, but the other offered to go. "But there are no arrows," he said. "The arrows are in the boat," was the reply. He thereupon took his place, while his friend returned home. The party paddled up the river to Kaloma, and began to land on the banks of the river. The enemy came rushing upon them, and some sharp fighting ensued. Presently someone was injured, and the cry was raised that the enemy were ghosts. The party returned down the stream, and the young man arrived home feeling none the worse for his experience. The next morning at dawn he endeavored to recount his adventures. While he was talking something black issued from his mouth. Suddenly he uttered a cry and fell down. His friends gathered round him. But he was dead.

Source: "The War of the Ghosts," from *Remembering: A Study in Experimental and Social Psychology* by F. C. Bartlett. Copyright © 1932 by Cambridge University Press. Reprinted with permission of Cambridge University Press.

learn. **Schemas** are mental frameworks that represent knowledge in a meaningful way. The later work using the Brown-Peterson paradigm confirms the notion that prior knowledge has an enormous effect on memory, sometimes leading to interference or distortion.

INVESTIGATING COGNITIVE PSYCHOLOGY
The Serial-Position Curve

Get at least two or three friends or family members to help you with this experiment. Tell them that you are going to read a list of words and as soon as you finish, they are to write down as many words as they can remember in any order they wish. (Make sure everyone has paper and a pencil.) Read the following words to them about 1 second apart: *book, peace, window, run, box, harmony, hat, voice, tree, begin, anchor, hollow, floor, area, tomato, concept, arm, rule, lion, hope*. After giving them enough time to write down all of the words they can remember, total their number of recollections in the following groups of four:

(1) *book, peace, window, run;*
(2) *box, harmony, hat, voice;*
(3) *tree, begin, anchor, hollow;*
(4) *floor, area, tomato, concept;*
(5) *arm, rule, lion, hope.*

Most likely, your friends and family will remember more words from groups 1 and 5 than from groups 2, 3, and 4, with group 3 the least recalled group. This exercise demonstrates the serial-position curve. Save the results of this experiment for a demonstration in Chapter 7.

Another method often used for determining the causes of forgetting involves the serial-position curve. The **serial-position curve** represents the probability of recall of a given word, given its serial position (order of presentation) in a list. Suppose that you are presented with a list of words and are asked to recall them.

The **recency effect** refers to superior recall of words at and near the end of a list. The **primacy effect** refers to superior recall of words at and near the beginning of a list. As Figure 6.5 shows, both the recency effect and the primacy effect seem to influence recall. The serial-position curve makes sense in terms of interference theory. Words at the end of the list are subject to proactive but not to retroactive interference. Words at the beginning of the list are subject to retroactive but not to proactive interference. And words in the middle of the list are subject to both types of interference. Therefore, recall would be expected to be poorest in the middle of the list. Indeed, it is poorest.

Primacy and recency effects can also be encountered in everyday life. Have you noticed that when you meet someone and then get to know him or her better, it can sometimes be very hard to get over your first impressions? This difficulty may be a

INVESTIGATING COGNITIVE PSYCHOLOGY
Primacy and Recency Effects

Say the following list of words once to yourself, and then, immediately try to recall all the words, in any order, without looking back at them: *table, cloud, book, tree, shirt, cat, light, bench, chalk, flower, watch, bat, rug, soap, pillow*. If you are like most people, you will find that your recall of words is best for items at and near the end of the list. Your recall will be second best for items near the beginning of the list and poorest for items in the middle of the list. A typical serial-position curve is shown in Figure 6.5.

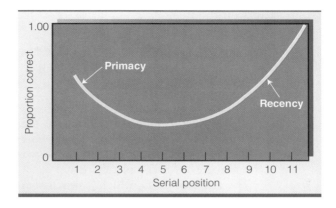

Figure 6.5 When asked to recall a list of words, we show superior recall of words close to the end of a list (the recency effect), pretty good recall of words close to the beginning of the list (primacy effect), and relatively poor recall of words in the middle of the list.

result of a primacy effect, which leads to your remembering your first impression particularly well. And if you are applying for a job and are doing interviews, you may be well served by being one of the first or last candidates that are interviewed in the hope that your interviewers will remember you better and more clearly than the candidates whose turns were in the middle.

Decay Theory

In addition to interference theory, there is another theory for explaining how we forget information—decay theory. **Decay theory** asserts that information is forgotten because of the gradual disappearance, rather than displacement, of the memory trace. Thus, decay theory views the original piece of information as gradually disappearing unless something is done to keep it intact. This view contrasts with interference theory, in which one or more pieces of information block recall of another.

Decay theory turns out to be exceedingly difficult to test because under normal circumstances, preventing participants from rehearsing is difficult. Through rehearsal, participants maintain the to-be-remembered information in memory. Usually participants know that you are testing their memory. They may try to rehearse the information or they may even inadvertently rehearse it to perform well during testing. However, if you do prevent them from rehearsing, the possibility of interference arises. The task you use to prevent rehearsal may interfere retroactively with the original memory.

For example, try not to think of white elephants as you read the next two pages. When instructed not to think about them, you actually find it quite difficult not to. The difficulty persists even if you try to follow the instructions. Unfortunately, as a test of decay theory, this experiment is itself a white elephant because preventing people from rehearsing is so difficult.

Despite these difficulties, it is possible to test decay theory. A research paradigm called the "recent-probes task" has been developed that does not encourage participants to rehearse the items presented (Berman et al., 2009; Monsell, 1978). It is based on the item-recognition task of S. Sternberg (1966) presented earlier in this chapter. Here is the recent-probes task:

- Participants are shown four target words.
- Next, participants are presented with a probe word.
- Participants decide whether or not the probe word is identical to one of the four target words.

If the probe word is not the same as the target words but is identical to a target word from a recent prior set of target words ("recent negative"), then it will take participants longer to decide that probe word and target words do not match than if the probe word is completely new.

The response delay, which is usually between 50–100 milliseconds, is a result of the high familiarity of the probe word. That is, the recent-probes task elicits clear interference effects. Of interest to researchers is the *intertrial interval* (the time between the presentation of one set of target words and subsequent probe), which can easily be varied. After each set of stimuli, participants have no incentive to rehearse the target words, so the longer the intertrial interval, the more time passes and the more are the target words subject to decay in memory. Thus, if there is memory decay just as a result of time passing by, then recent negative probes in trials with a longer intertrial interval should not be as interfering of memory performance as recent negative probes in trials with a shorter intertrial time. So even if both decay and interference contribute to forgetting, it can be argued that interference has the strongest effect (Berman et al., 2009).

And this is exactly what researchers have found:

- Decay only had a relatively small effect on forgetting in short-term memory.
- Interference accounted for most of the forgetting.
- So even if both decay and interference contribute to forgetting, it can be argued that interference has the strongest effect (Berman et al., 2009).

To conclude, evidence exists for both interference and decay, at least in short-term memory. There is some evidence for decay, but the evidence for interference is much stronger. For now, we can assume that interference accounts for most of the forgetting in short-term memory. However, the extent to which the interference is retroactive, proactive, or both is unclear. In addition, interference also affects material in long-term memory, leading to memory distortion.

✔ CONCEPT CHECK

1. Name and define two types of interference.
2. What is the recency effect?
3. What is the difference between interference and decay?

The Constructive Nature of Memory

An important lesson about memory is that memory retrieval is not just **reconstructive**, involving the use of various strategies (e.g., searching for cues, drawing inferences) for retrieving the original memory traces of our experiences and then rebuilding the original experiences as a basis for retrieval (see Kolodner, 1983, for an artificial-intelligence model of reconstructive memory). Rather, in real-life situations, memory is also **constructive**, in that prior experience affects how we recall things and what we actually recall from memory (Davis & Loftus, 2007; Grant & Ceci, 2000; Sutton, 2003). Think back to the Bransford and Johnson (1972) study, cited at the opening of this chapter. In this study, participants could remember a passage about washing clothes quite well but only if they realized that it was about washing clothes.

In a further demonstration of the constructive nature of memory, participants read an ambiguous passage that could be interpreted meaningfully in two ways (Bransford & Johnson, 1973). It could be viewed as being either about watching a peace march from the 40th floor of a building or about a space trip to an inhabited planet. Participants omitted different details, depending on what they thought the passage was about. Consider, for example, a sentence mentioning that the atmosphere did not require the wearing of special clothing. Participants were more likely to remember it when they thought the passage was about a trip into outer space than when they thought it was about a peace march.

Consider a comparable demonstration in a different domain (Bower, Karlin, & Dueck, 1975). Investigators showed participants 28 different *droodles*—nonsense pictures that can be given various interpretations (see also Chapter 10). Half of the participants in their experiment were given an interpretation by which they could label what they saw. The other half did not receive an interpretation prompting a label. Participants in the label group correctly reproduced almost 20% more droodles than did participants in the control group.

Autobiographical Memory

Autobiographical memory refers to memory of an individual's history. Autobiographical memory is constructive. One does not remember exactly what has happened. Rather, one remembers one's construction or reconstruction of what happened. People's autobiographical memories are generally quite good. Nevertheless, they are subject to distortions (as will be discussed later). They are differentially good for different periods of life. Middle-aged adults often remember events from their youthful and early-adult periods better than they remember events from their more recent past (Read & Connolly, 2007; Rubin, 1982, 1996).

One way of studying autobiographical memory is through diary studies. In such studies, individuals, often researchers, keep detailed autobiographies (e.g., Linton, 1982; Wagenaar, 1986). One investigator, for example, kept a diary for a 6-year period (Linton, 1982). She recorded at least two experiences per day on index cards. Then, each month she chose two cards at random and tried to recall the events she had written on the cards as well as the dates of the events. She further rated each memory for its salience and its emotional content. Surprisingly, her rate of forgetting of events was linear. It was not curvilinear, as is usually the case. In other words, a typical memory curve shows substantial forgetting over short time intervals and then a slowing in the rate of forgetting over longer time intervals. Linton's forgetting curve, however, did not show any such pattern. Her rate of forgetting was about the same over the entire 6-year interval. She also found little relationship between her ratings of the salience and emotionality of memories, on the one hand, and their memorability, on the other. Thus, she surprised herself in what she did and did not remember.

In another study of autobiographical memory, a researcher attempted to recall information regarding performances attended at the Metropolitan Opera over a period of 25 years (Sehulster, 1989). A total of 284 performances comprised the data for the study. The results were more in line with traditional expectations. Operas seen near the beginning and end of the 25-year period were remembered better (serial-position effect). Important performances also were better recalled than less important ones.

Recent work has illustrated the importance of self-esteem in the formation and recall of autobiographical memory. People with positive self-esteem remember more positive events, whereas people with negative self-esteem remember more negative events (Christensen, Wood, & Barrett, 2003). Likewise, depressed people recall more negative memories than people who are not depressed (Wisco & Nolen-Hoeksema, 2009). When people misremember, they usually tend to be wrong with regard to minor and marginal aspects, but remember the central characteristics

Events like the attacks of September 11, 2001, are often remembered in flashbulb memories that are experienced almost as vividly as a movie.

correctly. But if you think about it, this is not so surprising. If we would remember a large number of small details, those details would likely at some point start to interfere with our memories for important things. So it may be better to concentrate on what is really important (Bjork et al., 2005; Goldsmith et al., 2005).

An often-studied form of vivid memory is the **flashbulb memory**—a memory of an event so powerful that the person remembers the event as vividly as if it were indelibly preserved on film (Brown & Kulik, 1977). People old enough to recall the assassination of President John Kennedy may have flashbulb memories of this event. Some people also have flashbulb memories for the destruction of the World Trade Center, or momentous events in their personal lives. The emotional intensity of an experience may enhance the likelihood that we will recall the particular experience (over other experiences) ardently and perhaps accurately (Bohannon, 1988). A related view is that a memory is most likely to become a flashbulb memory under three circumstances: The memory trace is important to the individual, is surprising, and has an emotional effect on the individual (Conway, 1995).

Some investigators suggest that flashbulb memories may be more vividly recalled because of their emotional intensity. Other investigators, however, suggest that the vividness of recall may be the result of the effects of rehearsal. The idea here is that we frequently retell, or at least silently contemplate, our experiences of these momentous events. Perhaps our retelling also enhances the perceptual intensity of our recall (Bohannon, 1988). Other findings suggest that flashbulb memories may be perceptually rich (Neisser & Harsch, 1993). In this view, they may be recalled with relatively greater confidence in the accuracy of the memories (Weaver, 1993) but not actually be any more reliable or accurate than any other recollected memory (Neisser & Harsch, 1993; Weaver, 1993). Suppose flashbulb memories are indeed more likely to be the subject of conversation or even silent reflection. Then perhaps, at each retelling of the experience, we reorganize and construct our memories such that the accuracy of our recall actually diminishes, while the perceived vividness of recall increases over time.

A study examining the memories of more than 3,000 people of the September 11 attacks on the World Trade Center towers in New York City found that the rate of forgetting is faster in the first year and then slows down. This change in rate allows the content to become more stable later on. Furthermore, it seems that emotional reactions elicited by the flashbulb memories are not as well remembered as nonemotional features, such as where a person was at the time of the attack (Hirst et al., 2009).

Some interesting effects of flashbulb memory involve the role of emotion. The more a person is emotionally involved in an event, the better the person's memory is for that event. Also, over time, memory for the event degrades (Smith, Bibi, & Sheard, 2004). In one study, more than 70% of people who were questioned about the World Trade Center attacks on September 11, 2001, reported seeing the first plane hit the first tower. However, this footage was not available until the next day (Pezdek, 2003, 2006). These distortions illustrate the constructive nature of flashbulb memories. These findings further indicate that flashbulb memories are not immune to distortion, as once was thought.

Are different memory processes at work for flashbulb memories than for other kinds of memories? It appears not. Just as for other memories, the factors that influence encoding and retrieval are ones such as elaboration and the frequency of rehearsal (Neisser, 2003; Read & Connolly, 2007).

■ BELIEVE IT OR NOT

CAUGHT IN THE PAST!?

Have you ever been haunted by memories from your past? In a unique case of extraordinary autobiographical memory, a young woman named A. J. is able to recall the date and weekday of every day since she was 14 years old, as well as what she did that day. Conversations with other people, things she sees, and just about everything provides a cue for her to retrieve another memory from her past. She cannot let go of her memories and is caught thinking about it time and again while trying to live her life in the present. However, A. J. does not know how she retrieves her memories; she just "knows" what happened on any particular day in her life.

Researchers have examined her extraordinary ability and found that her superior memory is constrained to autobiographical events—she never was a particularly great student and does not fare well on memory tasks that ask her to recall word lists, for example. It is hypothesized she may have a rare neurodevelopmental, frontostriatal disorder that is related to other disorders like autism, schizophrenia, and attention deficit hyperactivity disorder. But whatever it is that distinguishes A. J. from the rest of us, it seems like for the foreseeable future she'll just have to keep remembering (Parker et al., 2006).

Which parts of the brain are involved in autobiographic memories? It seems that the medial temporal lobe is crucially involved in the recall of autobiographic memories. People with lesions in this area have trouble recalling memories from their recent past (but not from their more remote past; Kirwan et al., 2008).

Memory Distortions

People have tendencies to distort their memories (Aminoff et al., 2008; Roediger & McDermott, 2000; Schacter & Curran, 2000; Schnider, 2008). For example, just saying something has happened to you makes you more likely to think it really happened. This is true whether the event happened or not (Ackil & Zaragoza, 1998). These distortions tend to occur in seven specific ways, which Schacter (2001) refers to as the "seven sins of memory." Here are Schacter's "seven sins":

1. *Transience.* Memory fades quickly. For example, although most people know that O. J. Simpson was acquitted of criminal charges in the murder of his wife, they do not remember how they found out about his acquittal. At one time they could have said, but they no longer can.
2. *Absent-mindedness.* People sometimes brush their teeth after already having brushed them or enter a room looking for something only to discover that they have forgotten what they were seeking.
3. *Blocking.* People sometimes have something that they know they should remember, but they can't. It's as though the information is on the tip of their tongue, but they cannot retrieve it (see also the explanation of the tip-of-the-tongue phenomenon in Chapter 4). For example, people may see someone they know, but the person's name escapes them; or they may try to think of a synonym for a word, knowing that there is an obvious synonym, but are unable to recall it.
4. *Misattribution.* People often cannot remember where they heard what they heard or read what they read. Sometimes people think they saw things they did not see or heard things they did not hear. For example, eyewitness testimony is sometimes clouded by what we think we should have seen, rather than what we actually saw.
5. *Suggestibility.* People are susceptible to suggestion, so if it is suggested to them that they saw something, they may think they remember seeing it. For example,

in one study, when asked whether they had seen a television film of a plane crashing into an apartment building, many people said they had seen it. There was no such film.

6. *Bias*. People often are biased in their recall. For example, people who currently are experiencing chronic pain in their lives are more likely to remember pain in the past, whether or not they actually experienced it. People who are not experiencing such pain are less likely to recall pain in the past, again with little regard to their actual past experience.

7. *Persistence*. People sometimes remember things as consequential that, in a broad context, are inconsequential. For example, someone with many successes but one notable failure may remember the single failure better than the many successes.

What are some of the specific ways in which memory distortions are studied? We will consider two research areas next that investigate eyewitness testimony and repressed memories.

The Eyewitness Testimony Paradigm

A survey of U.S. prosecutors estimated that about 77,000 suspects are arrested each year after being identified by eyewitnesses (Dolan, 1995). Of the first 180 cases in the United States in which convicts were exonerated through the use of DNA evidence, more than three quarters involved eyewitness errors (Wells et al., 2006).

Eyewitness testimony may be the most common source of wrongful convictions in the United States (Modafferi et al., 2009). Generally, what proportion of eyewitness identifications are mistaken? The answer to that question varies widely ("from as low as a few percent to greater than 90%"; Wells, 1993, p. 554), but even the most conservative estimates of this proportion suggest frightening possibilities.

Consider the story of a man named Timothy. In 1986, Timothy was convicted of brutally murdering a mother and her two young daughters (Dolan, 1995). He was then sentenced to die, and for 2 years and 4 months, Timothy lived on death row. Although the physical evidence did not point to Timothy, eyewitness testimony placed him near the scene of the crime at the time of the murder. Subsequently, it was discovered that a man who looked like Timothy was a frequent visitor to the neighborhood of the murder victims. Timothy received a second trial and was acquitted.

What Influences the Accuracy of Eyewitness Testimonies?   There are serious potential problems of wrongful conviction when using eyewitness testimony as the sole, or even the primary, basis for convicting accused people of crimes (Loftus & Ketcham, 1991; Loftus, Miller, & Burns, 1987; Wells & Loftus, 1984). Moreover, eyewitness testimony is often a powerful determinant of whether a jury will convict an accused person. The effect is particularly pronounced if eyewitnesses appear highly confident of their testimony. This is true even if the eyewitnesses can provide few perceptual details or offer apparently conflicting responses. People sometimes even think they remember things simply because they have imagined or thought about them (Garry & Loftus, 1994). It has been estimated that as many as 10,000 people per year may be convicted wrongfully on the basis of mistaken eyewitness testimony (Cutler & Penrod, 1995; Loftus & Ketcham, 1991). In general, people are remarkably susceptible to mistakes in eyewitness testimony. They are generally prone to imagine that they have seen things they have not seen (Loftus, 1998).

Some of the strongest evidence for the constructive nature of memory has been obtained by those who have studied the validity of eyewitness testimony. In a

These are two slides that were shown to participants in the experiment of Loftus and colleagues (1978). Although the slides depicting the initial incident had featured a stop sign, participants who had been questioned about a yield sign often remembered having seen that yield sign in the original scene.
Source: From Loftus, E. F., Miller, D. G., & Burns, H. J. (1978). Semantic integration of verbal information into a visual memory. *Journal of Experimental Psychology: Human Learning and Memory, 4,* 19–31.

now-classic study, participants saw a series of 30 slides in which a red Datsun drove down a street, stopped at a stop sign, turned right, and then appeared to knock down a pedestrian crossing at a crosswalk (Loftus, Miller, & Burns, 1978). Afterwards, participants were asked a series of 20 questions, one of which referred either to correct information (the stop sign) or incorrect information (a yield sign instead of the stop sign). In other words, the information in the question given this second group was inconsistent with what the participants had seen. Later, after engaging in an unrelated activity, all participants were shown two slides and asked which they had seen. One had a stop sign, the other had a yield sign. Accuracy on this task was 34% better for participants who had received the consistent question (stop sign question) than for participants who had received the inconsistent question (yield sign question).

Loftus' eyewitness testimony experiment and other experiments (e.g., Loftus, 1975, 1977) have shown people's great susceptibility to distortion in eyewitness accounts. This distortion may be due, in part, to phenomena other than just constructive memory. But it does show that we easily can be led to construct a memory that is different from what really happened. As an example, you might have had a disagreement with a roommate or a friend regarding an experience in which both of you were in the same place at the same time. But what each of you remembers about the experience may differ sharply. And *both* of you may feel that you are truthfully and accurately recalling what happened.

Questions do not have to be suggestive to influence the accuracy of eyewitness testimony. Line-ups also can lead to faulty conclusions (Wells, 1993). Eyewitnesses assume that the perpetrator is in the line-up. This is not always the case, however. When the perpetrator of a staged crime was not in a line-up, participants were susceptible to naming someone other than the true perpetrator as the perpetrator. In this way, they believed they were able to recognize *someone* in the line-up as having committed the crime. The identities of the nonperpetrators in the line-up also can affect judgments (Wells, Luus, & Windschitl, 1994). In other words, whether a given person is identified as a perpetrator can be influenced simply by who the others are in the line-up. So the choice of the "distracter" individuals is important. Police may inadvertently affect the likelihood of whether or not an identification occurs and also whether a false identification is likely to occur.

Confessions also influence the testimony of eyewitnesses. A study by Hasel and Kassin (2009) had participants view a staged robbery. Afterwards, the participants were presented with a line-up of suspects and were given the opportunity to identify the robber (although the actual perpetrator was not among them). Sometime later, the participants were informed that one of the suspects in the lineup had made a confession. In all, 61% of those who had made a selection previously changed their identifications, and 50% of those who had not made an identification went on to positively identify the confessor. This finding shows what a grave impact a confession has on the identification of a perpetrator.

Likewise, feedback to eyewitnesses affected participants' testimony. Telling them that they had identified the perpetrator made them feel more secure in their choice, whereas the feedback that they had identified a filler person made them back away from their judgment immediately. This phenomenon is called *the post-identification feedback effect* (Wells, 2008; Wright & Skagerberg, 2007).

Eyewitness identification is particularly weak when identifying people of a racial or ethnic group other than that of the witness (e.g., Bothwell, Brigham, & Malpass, 1989; Brigham & Malpass, 1985; Pezdek, Blandon-Gitlin, & Moore, 2003; Shapiro & Penrod, 1986). Evidence suggests that this weakness is not a problem remembering stored faces of people from other racial or ethnic groups, but rather, a problem of accurately encoding their faces (Walker & Tanaka, 2003).

Eyewitness identification and recall are also affected by the witness's level of stress. As stress increases, the accuracy of both recall and identification declines (Deffenbacher et al., 2004; Payne et al., 2002). These findings further call into question the accuracy of eyewitness testimony because most crimes occur in highly stressful situations.

Not everyone views eyewitness testimony with such skepticism, however (e.g., see Zaragoza, McCloskey, & Jamis, 1987). It is still not clear whether the information about the original event actually is displaced by, or is simply competing with, the subsequent misleading information. Some investigators have argued that psychologists need to know a great deal more about the circumstances that impair eyewitness testimony before impugning such testimony before a jury (McKenna, Treadway, & McCloskey, 1992). At present, the verdict on eyewitness testimony is still not in.

Although there has been no ultimate verdict yet on eyewitness testimony, it is certainly important for all involved parties to know the limits of eyewitness statements. Research has shown, however, that although defense attorneys are moderately knowledgeable about the limitations of eyewitness testimony, prosecutors are less so. Indeed, prosecutors tend to overestimate the reliability of eyewitnesses' statements and to underestimate the role of eyewitness statements in wrongful convictions (Wise et al., 2009). These results show the importance of educating the public as well as the parties involved in court proceedings about the fallibility of eyewitness accounts.

Children as Eyewitnesses   Whatever may be the validity of eyewitness testimony for adults, it clearly is suspect for children (Ceci & Bruck, 1993, 1995). Children's recollections are particularly susceptible to distortion. Such distortion is especially likely when the children are asked leading questions, as in a courtroom setting.

Consider some relevant facts (Ceci & Bruck, 1995). First, the younger the child is, the less reliable the testimony of that child can be expected to be. In particular, children of preschool age are much more susceptible to suggestive questioning that tries to steer them to a certain response than are school-age children or adults.

Second, when a questioner is coercive or even just seems to want a particular answer, children can be quite susceptible to providing the adult with what he or

IN THE LAB OF ELIZABETH LOFTUS

Research on False Memories

Remember the time when you were a kid and your family went to Disneyland? The highlight of your trip was meeting Mickey Mouse, who shook your hand?

Remember that? Marketers use auto-biographical advertising like this to create nostalgia for their products. Several years ago, we wondered whether such referencing could cause people to believe that they had experiences as children that are mentioned in the ads (Braun, Ellis, & Loftus, 2002). In one study, participants viewed an ad for Disney that suggested that as a child they shook hands with Mickey Mouse. Later on they answered questions about their childhood experiences at Disney. Relative to controls, the ad increased their confidence that as a child they personally had shaken hands with Mickey at Disney.

A question came up as to whether the ad caused (1) a revival of a true memory, or (2) the creation of a new, false one. Because some people could have actually met Mickey at Disney, both are possibilities. So, we conducted another study in which people viewed a fake ad for Disney that suggested that they shook hands with an impossible character: Bugs Bunny. Of course, Bugs, a Warner Brothers character, would not be found at a Disney resort. Again, relative to controls, the ad increased confidence that they personally had shaken hands with the impossible character as a child at Disney. Although this could not possibly have happened because Bugs Bunny is a Warner Brothers character and would not be hanging around a Disney property, about 16% of the subjects later said

ELIZABETH LOFTUS

that this had actually happened to them. Many participants will freely supply details about this impossible experience such as remembering that they touched the ear or tail of Bugs or heard him say, "What's up Doc?"

It's one thing to plant a false memory of meeting Bugs Bunny, but quite another to plant a false memory of an unpleasant experience with another character. So with Shari Berkowitz and other colleagues, we tried to plant a false belief that people had had an unpleasant experience with the Pluto character while on a childhood trip to Disney (Berkowitz et al., 2008). We succeeded with about 30% of the subjects. Moreover, those who were seduced by the suggestion did not want to pay as much for a Pluto souvenir. This finding shows that false beliefs can have consequences that can affect later thoughts and behaviors.

A host of other studies show that false memories have repercussions. For example, we have shown that by planting false memories for food-related experiences (e.g., becoming ill after eating egg salad), we can affect how much people like particular foods and how much they actually eat (Bernstein & Loftus 2009).

These studies are part of a larger program of research on the malleability of human memory (Loftus, 2005). More specifically, they suggest that advertisements or other suggestive influences can tamper with our personal childhood memories. After decades of watching how easy it is to tamper with memory, I can't help but wonder how much of our vast store of memories reflects genuine experience, and how much is a product of suggestion, imagination, or some other mental process?

she wants to hear. Given the pressures involved in court cases, such forms of questioning may be unfortunately prevalent. For instance, when asked a yes-or-no question, even if they don't know the answer, most children will give an answer. If the question has an explicit "I don't know" option, most children, when they do not know an answer, will admit they do not know, rather than speculate (Waterman, Blades, & Spencer, 2001).

Third, children may believe that they recall observing things that others have said they observed. In other words, they hear a story about something that took place and then believe that they have observed what allegedly took place. If the child has some intellectual disability, memory for the event is even more likely to be distorted, at least when a significant delay has occurred between the time of the event and the time of recall (Henry & Gudjonsson, 2003).

A study in the United Kingdom has found that, when giving eyewitness testimony, children are also easily impressed by the presence of uniformed officers. When having to identify an individual in a line-up after having witnessed a staged incident, children made significantly more mistakes when a uniformed official was present (Lowenstein et al., 2010). Therefore, perhaps even more so than the eyewitness testimony of adults, the testimony of children must be interpreted with great caution.

Can Eyewitness Testimonies Be Improved?   Steps can be taken to enhance eyewitness identification (e.g., using methods to reduce potential biases, to reduce the pressure to choose a suspect from a limited set of options, and to ensure that each member of an array of suspects fits the description given by the eyewitness, yet offers diversity in other ways; described in Wells, 1993). Moreover, suggestive interviews can cause biases in memory (Melnyk & Bruck, 2004). This problem is especially likely to occur when these interviews take place close in time to the actual event. After a crime, witnesses are generally interviewed as soon as possible. Therefore, steps must be taken to ensure that the questions asked of witnesses are not leading questions, especially when the witness is a child. This caution can decrease the likelihood of distortion of memory.

Gary Wells (2006) made several suggestions to improve identification accuracy in line-ups. These suggestions include presenting only one suspect per line-up so that witnesses do not feel like they have to decide between several people they saw; making sure that all people in the line-up are reasonably similar to each other to decrease the chance that somebody is identified mistakenly, just because he or she happens to share one characteristic with the suspected perpetrator that no one else in the line-up shares; and cautioning witnesses that the suspect may not be in the line-up at all.

In addition, some psychologists (e.g., Loftus, 1993a, 1993b) and many defense attorneys believe that jurors should be advised that the degree to which the eyewitness feels confident of her or his identification does not necessarily correspond to the degree to which the eyewitness is actually accurate in her or his identification of the defendant as being the culprit. At the same time, some psychologists (e.g., Egeth, 1993; Yuille, 1993) and many prosecutors believe that the existing evidence, based largely on simulated eyewitness studies rather than on actual eyewitness accounts, is not strong enough to risk attacking the credibility of eyewitness testimony when such testimony might send a true criminal to prison, preventing the person from committing further crimes.

Repressed Memories

Might you have been exposed to a traumatic event as a child but have been so traumatized by this event that you now cannot remember it? Some psychotherapists have begun using hypnosis and related techniques to elicit from people what are alleged to be repressed memories. *Repressed memories* are memories that are alleged to have been pushed down into unconsciousness because of the distress they cause. Such memories, according to the view of psychologists who believe in their existence, are very inaccessible, but they can be dredged out (Briere & Conte, 1993). However, although people may be able to forget terrible events that happened to them, there is only dubious support for the notion that clients in psychotherapy often are unaware of their having been abused as a child (Loftus, 1996).

"First, we'll look for repressed memories of malpractice suits."

Do repressed memories actually exist? Many psychologists strongly doubt their existence (Ceci & Loftus, 1994; Pennebaker & Memon, 1996; Roediger & McDermott, 1995, 2000; Rofe, 2008). Others are at least highly skeptical (Bowers & Farvolden, 1996; Brenneis, 2000). There are many reasons for this skepticism, which are provided in the following section. First, some therapists may inadvertently plant ideas in their clients' heads. In this way, they may inadvertently create false memories of events that never took place. Indeed, creating false memories is relatively easy, even in people with no particular psychological problems. Such memories can be implanted by using ordinary, nonemotional stimuli (see below; Roediger & McDermott, 1995).

Second, showing that implanted memories are false is often extremely hard to do. Reported incidents often end up, as in the case of childhood sexual abuse, merely pitting one person's word against another (Schooler, 1994). At the present time, no compelling evidence points to the existence of such memories. But psychologists also have not reached the point where their existence can be ruled out definitively. Therefore, no clear conclusion can be reached at this time.

The Roediger-McDermott (1995) paradigm, which is adapted from the work of Deese (1959), is able to show the effects of memory distortion in the laboratory. Participants receive a list of 15 words strongly associated with a critical but nonpresented word. For example, the participants might receive 15 words strongly re-lated to the word *sleep* but never receive the word *sleep*. The recognition rate for the nonpresented word (in this case, *sleep*) was comparable to that for presented words. This result has been replicated multiple times (McDermott, 1996; Schacter, Verfaellie, & Pradere, 1996; Sugrue & Hayne, 2006). Even when shorter lists were used, there was an increased level of false recognition for nonpresented items. In one experiment, lists as short as three items revealed this effect, although to a lesser degree (Coane et al., 2007). Embedding the list in a story can increase this effect in young children. This strategy strengthens the shared context and increases the probability of a participant's falsely recognizing the nonpresented word (Dewhurst, Pursglove, & Lewis, 2007).

Why are people so weak in distinguishing what they have heard from what they have not heard? One possibility is a *source-monitoring error,* which occurs when a per-son attributes a memory derived from one source to another source. People frequently have difficulties in *source monitoring,* or figuring out the origins of a memory. They may believe they read an article in a prestigious newspaper, such as *The New York Times,* when in fact they saw it in a tabloid on a supermarket shelf while waiting to check out. When people hear a list of words not containing a word that is highly as-sociated with the other words, they may believe that their recall of that central word is from the list rather than from their minds (Foley et al., 2006; Johnson, 1996, 2002).

Another possible explanation of this increased false recognition is *spreading acti-vation.* In spreading activation, every time an item is studied, you think of the items related to that item. Imagine a metaphorical spider web with a word in the middle. Branching out from that word are all the words relating to that word. Of course there will be individual differences in the construction of these webs, but there will also be a lot of overlap. For instance, when you read the word *nap,* words like *sleep, bed,* and *cat* may be activated in your mind. In this way, activation branches out from the original word *nap.* If you see 15 words, all of which activate the word *sleep,* it is likely that, via a source-monitoring error, you may think you had been presented the word *sleep.* Some recent work supports the spreading-activation theory of errors in this paradigm (Dodd & MacLeod, 2004; Hancock et al., 2003; Roediger, Balota, & Watson, 2001). This theory is not, however, universally accepted (Meade et al., 2007.

The Effect of Context on Memory

A number of factors, such as emotions, moods, states of consciousness, schemas, and other features of our internal context, clearly affect memory retrieval. As studies of constructive memory show, our cognitive contexts for memory clearly influence our memory processes of encoding, storing, and retrieving information. Studies of exper-tise also show how existing schemas (frameworks for representing knowledge, see also Chapter 8) may provide a cognitive context for encoding, storing, and retriev-ing new information. Specifically, experts generally have more elaborated schemas than do novices in regard to their areas of expertise (e.g., Chase & Simon, 1973; Frensch & Sternberg, 1989). These schemas provide a cognitive context in which the experts can operate. The use of schemas makes integration and organization rel-atively easy. They fill in gaps when provided with partial or even distorted informa-tion and visualize concrete aspects of verbal information. They also can implement appropriate metacognitive strategies for organizing and rehearsing new information. Clearly, expertise enhances our confidence in our recollected memories.

Our moods and states of consciousness also may provide a context for encoding that affects later retrieval of semantic memories. Thus, when we encode semantic information during a particular mood or state of consciousness, we may more readily retrieve that information when in the same state again (Baddeley, 1989; Bower, 1983). Interestingly, an Australian study has found that weather-induced negative mood improves people's memory for everyday scenes (like a scene in a shopping mall; Forgas et al., 2009).

How does state of consciousness affect memory? Something that is encoded when we are influenced by alcohol or other drugs may be retrieved more readily while under those same influences again (Eich, 1980, 1995). On the whole, however, the "main effect" of alcohol and many drugs is stronger than the interaction. In other words, the depressing effect of alcohol and many drugs on memory is greater than the facilitating effect of recalling something in the same drugged state as when one encoded it.

Some investigators have suggested that persons in a depressed mood can more readily retrieve memories of previous sad experiences, which may further the continuation of the depression (Baddeley, 1989; see also Wisco & Nolen-Hoeksema, 2009). If psychologists or others can intervene to prevent the continuation of this vicious cycle, the person may begin to feel happier. As a result, other happy memories may be more easily retrieved, thus further relieving the depression, and so on. Perhaps the folk-wisdom advice to "think happy thoughts" is not entirely unfounded. In fact, under laboratory conditions, participants seem more accurately to recall items that have pleasant associations than they recall items that have unpleasant or neutral associations (Matlin & Underhill, 1979; Monnier & Syssau, 2008). Interestingly, people suffering from depression tend to have deficits in forming and recalling memories (Bearden et al., 2006).

Even our external contexts may affect our ability to recall information. We appear to be better able to recall information when we are in the same physical context as the one in which we learned the material (Godden & Baddeley, 1975). In one experiment, 16 underwater divers were asked to learn a list of 40 unrelated words. Learning occurred either while the divers were on shore or while they were 20 feet beneath the sea. Later, they were asked to recall the words when either in the same environment as where they had learned them or in the other environment. Recall was better when it occurred in the same place as did the learning.

Even infants demonstrate context effects on memory. Consider an operant-conditioning experiment in which the infants could make a crib mobile move in interesting ways by kicking it. Three-month-old infants (Butler & Rovee-Collier, 1989) and 6-month-old infants (Borovsky & Rovee-Collier, 1990) were given an opportunity to kick a distinctive crib mobile in the same context (i.e., surrounded by a distinctive bumper lining the periphery of the crib) in which they first learned to kick it or in a different context. They kicked more strongly in the same context. The infants showed much less kicking when in a different context or when presented with a different mobile.

From these results, such learning seems highly context dependent. However, in one set of studies, 3-month-old infants (Rovee-Collier & DuFault, 1991) and 6-month-old infants (Amabile & Rovee-Collier, 1991) were offered operant conditioning experiences in multiple contexts for kicking a distinctive mobile. They were soon thereafter placed in a novel context. It was unlike any of the contexts for conditioning. The infants retained the memory. They kicked the mobile at high rates in the novel context. Thus, when information is encoded in various contexts, the information also seems to be retrieved more readily in various contexts. This effect occurs at least when there is minimal delay between the conditioning contexts and the novel context. However, consider what happened when the novel context occurred after a long delay. The infants did not show increased kicking.

Nevertheless, they still showed context-dependent memory for kicking in the familiar contexts (Amabile & Rovee-Collier, 1991).

All of the preceding context effects may be viewed as an interaction between the context for encoding and the context for retrieval of encoded information. The results of various experiments on retrieval suggest that how items are encoded has a strong effect both on how, and on how well, items are retrieved. This relationship is called **encoding specificity**—what is recalled depends on what is encoded (Tulving & Thomson, 1973). Consider a rather dramatic example of encoding specificity. We know that recognition memory is virtually always better than recall. For example, recognizing a word that you have learned is easier than recalling it. After all, in recognition you have only to say whether you have seen the word. In recall, you have to generate the word and then mentally confirm whether it appeared on the list.

In one experiment, Watkins and Tulving (1975) had participants learn a list of 24 paired associates, such as *ground-cold* and *crust-cake*.

- Participants were instructed to learn to associate each response (such as *cold*) with its stimulus word (such as *ground*).
- After participants had studied the word pairs, they were given an irrelevant task.
- Then they were given a recognition test with distracters.
- Participants were asked simply to circle the words they had seen previously.

Participants recognized an average of 60% of the words from the list. Then, participants were provided with the 24 stimulus words. They were asked to recall the responses. Their cued recall was 73%. Thus, recall was better than recognition. Why? According to the encoding-specificity hypothesis, the stimulus was a better cue for the word than the word itself. The reason was that the words had been learned as paired associates.

As mentioned in Chapter 5, the link between encoding and retrieval also may explain the *self-reference effect* (Greenwald & Banaji, 1989). Specifically, the main cause of the self-reference effect is not due to unique properties of self-referent cues. Rather, it is due to a more general principle of encoding and retrieval: When individuals generate their own cues for retrieval, they are much more potent than when other individuals do so.

Other researchers have confirmed the importance of making cues meaningful to the individual to enhance memory. For example, consider what happened when participants made up their own retrieval cues. They were able to remember, almost without errors, lists of 500 and 600 words (Mantyla, 1986). For each word on a list, participants were asked to generate another word (the cue) that to them was an appropriate description or property of the target word. Later, they were given a list of their cue words. They were asked to recall the target word. Cues were most helpful when they were both *compatible* with the target word and *distinctive,* in that they would not tend to generate a large number of related words. For example, if you are given the word *coat*, then *jacket* might be both compatible and distinctive as a cue. However, suppose you came up with the word *wool* as a cue. That cue might make you think of a number of words, such as *fabric* and *sheep*, which are not the target word.

To summarize, retrieval interacts strongly with encoding. Suppose you are studying for a test and want to recall well at the time of testing. Organize the information you are studying in a way that appropriately matches the way in which you will be expected to recall it. Similarly, you will recall information better if the level of processing for encoding matches the level of processing for retrieval (Moscovitch & Craik, 1976).

✔ CONCEPT CHECK

1. What is autobiographical memory?
2. In what specific ways do memory distortions occur?
3. Do you think eyewitness accounts should be allowed in court?
4. What are repressed memories?
5. How does the context influence encoding and retrieval of information?

Key Themes

This chapter illustrates several of the key themes first presented in Chapter 1.

Rationalism versus empiricism. To what extent should courts rely on empirical evidence from psychological research to guide what they do? To what extent should the credibility of witnesses be determined by rational considerations (e.g., were they at the scene of a crime, or are they known to be trustworthy) and to what extent by empirical considerations revealed by psychological research (e.g., being at the scene of a crime does not guarantee credible testimony, and people's judgments of trustworthiness are often incorrect)? Court systems often work on the basis of rational considerations—of what should be. Psychological research reveals what is.

Domain generality versus domain specificity. Mnemonics discussed in this chapter work better in certain domains than they do in others. For example, you may be able to devise mnemonics better if you are highly familiar with a domain, such as was the case for the long-distance runner studied by Chase, Ericsson, and Faloon (discussed in Chapter 5). In general, the more knowledge you have about a domain, the easier it will be to chunk information in that domain.

Validity of causal inferences versus ecological validity. Some researchers, such as Mahzarin Banaji and Robert Crowder, have argued that laboratory research yields findings that maximize not only experimental control but also ecological validity. Ulric Neisser has disagreed, suggesting that if one wishes to study everyday memory, one must study it in everyday settings. Ultimately, the two kinds of research together are likely to maximize our understanding of memory phenomena. Typically, there is no one right way to do research. Rather, we learn the most when we use a variety of methods that converge on a set of common findings.

Summary

1. **What have cognitive psychologists discovered regarding how we encode information for storing it in memory?** Encoding of information in short-term memory appears to be largely, although not exclusively, acoustic in form. Information in short-term memory is susceptible to acoustic confusability—that is, errors based on sounds of words. But there is some visual and semantic encoding of information in short-term memory. Information in long-term memory appears to be encoded primarily in a semantic form. Thus, confusions tend to be in terms of meanings rather than in terms of the sounds of words. In addition, some evidence points to the existence of visual encoding, as well as of acoustic encoding, in long-term storage.

Transfer of information into long-term storage may be facilitated by several factors:

1. rehearsal of the information, particularly if the information is elaborated meaningfully;
2. organization, such as categorization of the information;
3. the use of mnemonic devices;
4. the use of external memory aids, such as writing lists or taking notes;
5. knowledge acquisition through distributed practice across various study sessions, rather than through massed practice.

However, the distribution of time during any given study session does not seem to affect transfer into long-term memory. The effects of distributed practice may be due to a hippocampal-based mechanism that results in rapid encoding of new information to be integrated with existing memory systems over time, perhaps during sleep.

2. **What affects our ability to retrieve information from memory?** Studying retrieval from long-term memory is difficult due to problems of differentiating retrieval from other memory processes.

It also is difficult to differentiate accessibility from availability. Retrieval of information from short-term memory appears to be in the form of serial exhaustive processing. This implies that a person always sequentially checks all information on a list. Nevertheless, some data may be interpreted as allowing for the possibility of self-terminating serial processing and even of parallel processing.

3. **How does what we know or what we learn affect what we remember?** Two of the main theories of forgetting in short-term memory are decay theory and interference theory. Interference theory distinguishes between retroactive interference and proactive interference. Assessing the effects of decay, while ruling out both interference and rehearsal effects, is much harder. However, some evidence of distinctive decay effects has been found.

Interference also seems to influence long-term memory, at least during the period of consolidation. This period may continue for several years after the initial memorable experience.

Memory appears to be not only reconstructive—a reproduction of what was learned, based on recalled data and on inferences from only those data. It is also constructive—influenced by attitudes, subsequently acquired information, and schemas based on past knowledge. As shown by the effects of existing schemas on the construction of memory, schemas affect memory processes. However, so do other internal contextual factors, such as emotional intensity of a memorable experience, mood, and even state of consciousness. In addition, environmental context cues during encoding seem to affect later retrieval. Encoding specificity refers to the fact that what is recalled depends largely on what is encoded. How information is encoded at the time of learning will greatly affect how it is later recalled.

One of the most effective means of enhancing recall is for the individual to generate meaningful cues for subsequent retrieval.

Thinking about Thinking: Analytical, Creative, and Practical Questions

1. In what forms do we encode information for brief memory storage versus long-term memory storage?
2. What is the evidence for encoding specificity? Cite at least three sources of supporting evidence.
3. What is the main difference between two of the proposed mechanisms by which we forget information?
4. Compare and contrast some of the views regarding flashbulb memory.
5. Suppose that you are an attorney defending a client who is being prosecuted solely on the basis of eyewitness testimony. How could you demonstrate to members of the jury the frailty of eyewitness testimony?
6. Use the chapter-opening example from Bransford and Johnson as an illustration to make up a description of a common procedure without

labeling the procedure (e.g., baking chocolate chip cookies or changing a tire). Try having someone read your description and then recall the procedure.

7. Make a list of 10 or more unrelated items you need to memorize. Choose one of the mnemonic devices mentioned in this chapter, and describe how you would apply the device to memorizing the list of items. Be specific.

8. What are three things you learned about memory that can help you to learn new information and effectively recall the information over the long term?

Key Terms

accessibility, *p. 246*
autobiographical memory, *p. 253*
availability, *p. 246*
consolidation, *p. 234*
constructive, *p. 253*
decay, *p. 234*
decay theory, *p. 251*
distributed practice, *p. 235*
encoding, *p. 230*
encoding specificity, *p. 265*

flashbulb memory, *p. 255*
interference, *p. 233*
interference theory, *p. 247*
massed practice, *p. 235*
metacognition, *p. 234*
metamemory, *p. 234*
mnemonic devices, *p. 238*
primacy effect, *p. 250*
proactive interference, *p. 248*
recency effect, *p. 250*

reconstructive, *p. 252*
rehearsal, *p. 234*
retrieval (memory), *p. 230*
retroactive interference, *p. 247*
schemas, *p. 249*
serial-position curve, *p. 250*
spacing effect, *p. 235*
storage (memory), *p. 230*

Media Resources

Visit the companion website—**www.cengagebrain.com**—for quizzes, research articles, chapter outlines, and more.

CogLab

Explore CogLab by going to **http://coglab.wadsworth.com**. To learn more, examine the following experiments:

Brown-Peterson

False Memory

Serial Position

Sternberg Research

Von Restorff Effect

Encoding Specificity

Forgot It All Along

Remember/Know

Representation and Manipulation of Knowledge in Memory: Images and Propositions

CHAPTER OUTLINE

Here are some of the questions we will explore in this chapter:

1. What are some of the major hypotheses regarding how knowledge is represented in the mind?
2. What are some of the characteristics of mental imagery?
3. How does knowledge representation benefit from both images and propositions?
4. How may conceptual knowledge and expectancies influence the way we use images?

■ BELIEVE IT OR NOT

CITY MAPS OF MUSIC FOR THE BLIND

How can a person who is blind find his or her way around in a new city? Well, not too far in the future they may be able to hear their way around by means of a translation of the landscape into music. Researchers are developing a handheld device that helps blind persons navigate their environment with their ears (Cronly-Dillon et al., 2000).

Just like a musical score is made up of black dots in a particular spatial distribution and are then transformed into music by a musician, the pixels in a digital image can be transformed into music as well. Listeners explore the musical landscape and create a mental image of what they see. The picture is read from the left to the right; a horizontal line is played as one continuous note, a vertical line is played as a fast chord of many notes, and a diagonal line from the top left to the bottom right can be heard as a

descending scale. Listeners can scan an entire scene or zoom in to see the details of an object. The resulting music sounds a little like modern music. However, this only works for people who were once able to see because they once developed the ability to create three-dimensional mental images.

For example, in one study, blind subjects were able to distinguish trees, different buildings (like Victorian or modern houses and churches), or various types of cars. The blind subjects communicated their mental images to the researchers by drawing. In Figure 7.1, you can see the original images of two cars, processed images that were analyzed by the blind subjects, and the pictures of the mental images they drew.

In this chapter, we will explore the representation of knowledge in our minds—in words as well as in images.

Figure 7.1   How People Who Are Blind Form Mental Images.
Source: Cronly-Dillon, J., Persaud, K. C., & Blore, R. (2000). Blind subjects construct conscious mental images of visual scenes encoded in musical form. *Proceedings of the Royal Society B: Biological Sciences, 267,* 2231–2238.

Look carefully at the photos depicted in Figure 7.2. Now cover the photos and describe to yourself what two of these people look like and sound like. Clearly, none of these people can truly exist in a physical form inside your mind. How are you able to imagine and describe them? You must have stored in your mind some form of *mental representation,* something that stands for these people-of what you know about them.

What you use to recall these celebrities is more generally called **knowledge representation**, the form for what you know in your mind about things, ideas, events, and so on, in the outside world.

This chapter explores how knowledge is stored and represented in our minds:

- First, we consider what representations are and in what form they can be stored.
- Second, we will look at theories that describe knowledge representation and suggest that we store our knowledge in images, symbols, or propositions.
- Third, we look more closely at images in our mind. How can we rotate or scan them; in short, how can we manipulate mental images?
- Fourth, we examine whether separate theories regarding images and propositions can be combined as one approach.
- Last, we look at mental maps.

Mental Representation of Knowledge

Ideally, cognitive psychologists would love to observe directly how each of us represents knowledge. It would be as if we could take a videotape or a series of snapshots of ongoing representations of knowledge in the human mind. Unfortunately, direct empirical methods for observing knowledge representations are not available at present. Also, such methods are unlikely to be available in the immediate future. When direct empirical methods are unavailable, several alternative methods remain. We can ask people to describe their own knowledge representations and knowledge-representation processes: What do they see in their minds when they think of the Statue of Liberty, for example? Unfortunately, none of us has conscious access to our own knowledge-representation processes and self-reported information about these processes is highly unreliable (Pinker, 1985). Therefore, an introspectionist approach goes only so far.

Another possibility for observing how we represent knowledge in our minds is the rationalist approach. In this approach, we try to deduce logically how people represent knowledge. For centuries, philosophers have done exactly that. In classic epistemology—the study of the nature, origins, and limits of human knowledge—philosophers distinguished between two kinds of knowledge structures. The first type of knowledge structure is **declarative knowledge**. Declarative knowledge refers to facts that can be stated, such as the date of your birth, the name of your best friend, or the way a rabbit looks. **Procedural knowledge** refers to knowledge of procedures that can be implemented. Examples are the steps involved in tying your shoelaces, adding a column of numbers, or driving a car. The distinction is between *knowing that* and *knowing how* (Ryle, 1949). These concepts will be used later in the chapter.

There are two main sources of empirical data on knowledge representation: standard laboratory experiments and neuropsychological studies. In experimental work, researchers indirectly study knowledge representation because they cannot look

Figure 7.2   Mental Representations.
Look at each of these photos carefully. Next, close your eyes, and picture two of the people represented—people whom you recognize from reports in the media. Without looking again at the photos, mentally compare the appearances of the two people you have chosen. To compare the people, you need to have a mental representation of them in your mind.

into people's minds directly. They observe how people handle various cognitive tasks that require the manipulation of mentally represented knowledge.

In neuropsychological studies, researchers typically use one of two methods: (1) they observe how the normal brain responds to various cognitive tasks involving knowledge representation, or (2) they observe the links between various deficits in knowledge representation and associated pathologies in the brain.

In the following sections, we explore some of the theories researchers have proposed to explain how we represent and store knowledge in our minds:

- First, we consider what the difference is between images and words when they are used to represent ideas in the outside world, such as in a book.
- Then we learn about mental images and the idea that we store some of our knowledge in the form of images.
- Next, we explore the idea that knowledge is stored in the form of both words and images (dual-code theory).
- Finally, we consider an alternative—propositional theory—which suggests that we actually use an abstract form of knowledge encoding that makes use of neither words nor mental images.

Communicating Knowledge: Pictures versus Words

Knowledge can be represented in different ways in your mind: It can be stored as a mental picture, or in words, or abstract propositions. In this chapter, we focus on the difference between those kinds of knowledge representation. Of course, cognitive psychologists chiefly are interested in our internal, mental representations of what we know. However, before we turn to our internal representations, let's look at external representations, like books. A book communicates ideas through words and pictures. How do external representations in words differ from such representations in pictures?

Some ideas are better and more easily represented in pictures, whereas others are better represented in words. For example, suppose someone asks you, "What is the shape of a chicken egg?" You may find drawing an egg easier than describing it. Many geometric shapes and concrete objects seem easier to represent in pictures rather than in words. However, what if someone asks you, "What is justice?" Describing such an abstract concept in words would already be very difficult, but doing so pictorially would be even harder.

As Figure 7.3(a) and Figure 7.3(b) show, both pictures and words may be used to represent things and ideas, but neither form of representation actually retains all the characteristics of what is being represented. For example, neither the word *cat* nor the picture of the cat actually eats fish, meows, or purrs when petted. Both the word *cat* and the picture of this cat are distinctive representations of "catness." Each type of representation has distinctive characteristics.

As you just observed, the picture is relatively *analogous* (i.e., similar) to the real-world object it represents. The picture shows concrete attributes, such as shape and relative size. These attributes are similar to the features and properties of the real-world object the picture represents. Even if you cover up a portion of the figure of the cat, what remains still looks like a part of a cat. Under typical circumstances, most aspects of the picture are grasped simultaneously; but you may scan the picture, zoom in for a closer look, or zoom out to see the big picture. Even when scanning or

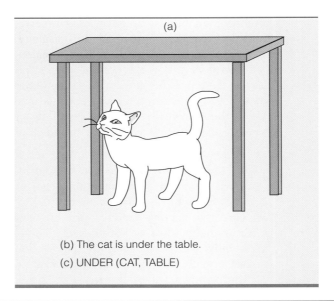

(a)

(b) The cat is under the table.

(c) UNDER (CAT, TABLE)

Figure 7.3   Different Kinds of Mental Representations.

We may represent things and ideas in pictures or in words. Neither pictures nor words capture all the characteristics of what they represent, and each more readily captures some kinds of information than other kinds. Some cognitive psychologists have suggested that we have (a) some mental representations that resemble pictorial, analogous images; (b) other mental representations that are highly symbolic, like words; and perhaps even (c) more fundamental propositional representations that are in a pure abstract "mentalese" that is neither verbal nor pictorial, which cognitive psychologists often represent in this highly simplified shorthand.

zooming, however, there are no arbitrary rules for looking at the picture—you may scan the picture from the left to the right, from the bottom to the top, or however it pleases you.

In contrast, the word *cat* is a **symbolic representation**, meaning that the relationship between the word and what it represents is simply arbitrary. There is nothing inherently catlike about the word. If you had grown up in another country like Germany or France, the word "Katze" or the word "chat," respectively, would instead symbolize the concept of a cat to you. Suppose you cover up part of the word "cat." The remaining visible part no longer bears even a symbolic relationship to any part of a cat.

Because symbols are arbitrary, their use requires the application of rules. For example, in forming words, the sounds or letters also must be sequenced according to rules (e.g., "c-a-t," not "a-c-t" or "t-c-a"). In forming sentences, the words also must be sequenced according to rules. For example, one can say "the cat is under the table," but not "table under cat the is."

Symbolic representations, such as the word *cat*, capture some kinds of information but not other kinds of information. The dictionary defines *cat* as "a carnivorous mammal (*Felis catus*) long domesticated as a pet and for catching rats and mice" (*Merriam-Webster's Online Dictionary*, 2010). Suppose our own mental representations for the meanings of words resemble those of the dictionary. Then the

INVESTIGATING COGNITIVE PSYCHOLOGY
Representations in Pictures and Words

Find a book or magazine with a photo of an animal, plant, or other object (house, car, airplane) and write down the word for that thing. What is the shape of the word? What is the shape of the picture? Cover part of the word and explain how what is left relates to the characteristics of that thing. Now cover part of the picture and explain how what is left relates to the characteristics of that thing.

word *cat* connotes an animal that eats meat ("carnivorous"), nurses its young ("mammal"), and so on. This information is abstract and general. It may be applied to any number of specific cats having any fur color or pattern. To represent additional characteristics, we must use additional words, such as *black*, *Persian*, or *calico*.

The picture of the cat does not convey any of the abstract information conveyed by the word regarding what the cat eats, whether it nurses its young, and so on. However, the picture conveys a great deal of concrete information about this specific cat. For example, it communicates the exact position of the cat's legs, the angle at which we are viewing the cat, the length of the cat's tail, whether both of its eyes are open, and so on.

Pictures and words also represent relationships in different ways. The picture in Figure 7.3(a) shows the spatial relationship between the cat and the table. For any given picture showing a cat and a table, the spatial (positional) relationship (e.g., beside, above, below, behind) will be represented concretely in the picture. In contrast, when using words, we must state spatial relationships between things explicitly by a discrete symbol, such as a preposition ("The cat is *under* the table."). More abstract relationships, however, such as class membership, often are implied by the meanings of the words. Cats are mammals or tables are items of furniture. But abstract relationships rarely are implied through pictures.

To summarize, pictures aptly capture concrete and spatial information in a manner analogous to whatever they represent. They convey all features simultaneously. In general, any rules for creating or understanding pictures pertain to the analogous relationship between the picture and what it represents. They help ensure as much similarity as possible between the picture and the object it represents. Words, on the contrary, handily capture abstract and categorical information in a manner that is symbolic of whatever the words represent. Representations in words usually convey information sequentially. They do so according to arbitrary rules that have little to do with what the words represent. Pictures and words are both well suited to some purposes but not to others. For example, blueprints and identification photos serve different purposes than essays and memos.

Now that we have some preliminary ideas about external representations of knowledge, let's consider internal representations of knowledge. Specifically, how do we represent what we know in our minds? Do we have mental scenarios (pictures) and mental narratives (words)? In subsequent chapters on information processing and language, we discuss symbolic mental representations. In this chapter, we focus on mental imagery.

Pictures in Your Mind: Mental Imagery

Imagery is the mental representation of things that are not currently seen or sensed by the sense organs (Moulton & Kosslyn, 2009; Thomas, 2003). In our minds we often have images for objects, events, and settings. For example, recall one of your first experiences on a college campus. What were some of the sights, sounds, and smells you sensed at that time—cut grass, tall buildings, or tree-lined paths? You do not actually smell the grass and see the buildings, but you still can imagine them. Mental imagery even can represent things that you have never experienced. For example, imagine what it would be like to travel down the Amazon River. Mental images even may represent things that do not exist at all outside the mind of the person creating the image. Imagine how you would look if you had a third eye in the center of your forehead!

Imagery may involve mental representations in any of the sensory modalities, such as hearing, smell, or taste. Imagine the sound of a fire alarm, your favorite song, or your nation's anthem. Now imagine the smell of a rose, of fried bacon, or of an onion. Finally, imagine the taste of a lemon, pickle, or your favorite candy. At least hypothetically, each form of mental representation is subject to investigation (e.g., Kurby et al., 2009; Palmieri et al., 2009; Pecenka & Keller, 2009).

Nonetheless, most research on imagery in cognitive psychology has focused on visual imagery, such as representations of objects or settings that are not presently visible to the eyes. When students kept a diary of their mental images, the students reported many more visual images than auditory, smell, touch, or taste images (Kosslyn et al., 1990). Most of us are more aware of visual imagery than of other forms of imagery.

We use visual images to solve problems and to answer questions involving objects (Kosslyn & Rabin, 1999; Kosslyn, Thompson & Ganis, 2006). Which is darker red—a cherry or an apple? How many windows are there in your house or apartment? How do you get from your home, apartment, or dormitory room to your first class of the day? How do you fit together the pieces of a puzzle or the component parts of an engine, a building, or a model? According to Kosslyn, to solve problems and answer questions such as these, we visualize the objects in question. In doing so, we mentally represent the images.

Many psychologists outside of cognitive psychology are interested in applications of mental imagery to other fields in psychology. Such applications include using guided-imagery techniques for controlling pain and for strengthening immune responses and otherwise promoting health. With such techniques, you could imagine being at a beautiful beach and feeling very comfortable, letting your pain fade into the background. Or you could imagine the cells of your immune system successfully destroying all the bad bacteria in your body. Such techniques are also helpful in overcoming psychological problems, such as phobias and other anxiety disorders. Design engineers, biochemists, physicists, and many other scientists and technologists use imagery to think about various structures and processes and to solve problems in their chosen fields.

Not everyone is equally skilled in creating and manipulating mental images, however. Research in applied settings and in the laboratory indicates that some of us are better able to create mental images than are others (Reisberg et al., 1986; Schienle et al., 2008). These differences are even measurable with functional magnetic resonance imaging (fMRI) (Cui et al., 2007). Research also indicates that the use of mental images can help to improve memory. In the case of persons with Down syndrome, the use of mental images in conjunction with hearing a story improved memory for the material as compared with just hearing the story (de la Iglesia, Buceta, & Campos, 2005; Kihara & Yoshikawa, 2001). Mental imagery also is used in other fields such as occupational therapy. Using this technique, patients with brain damage train themselves to complete complex tasks. For instance, by means of imagining the details of the tasks in the correct order so as to remember all the details involved, brain-damaged patients can wash dishes or take medication (Liu & Chan, 2009).

In what form do we represent images in our minds? According to an extreme view of imagery, all images of everything we ever sense may be stored as exact copies of physical images. But realistically, to store every observed physical image in the brain seems impossible. The capacity of the brain would be inadequate to such a task (Kosslyn, 2006; Kosslyn & Pomerantz, 1977). Note the simple example in *Investigating Cognitive Psychology: Can Your Brain Store Images of Your Face?*

Amazingly, learning can indeed take place just by using mental images. A study by Tartaglia and colleagues (2009) presented participants with a vertical parallel arrangement of three lines. The middle one was closer either to the right or left outer line. Practice using mental images resulted in participants becoming more sensitive to the asymmetry toward either the left or right side. A study with architects also showed the importance of mental images. Whether or not they were permitted to draw sketches in the early design phase of a project did not impact the design outcome and cognitive activity—if they were not allowed to draw sketches, they just used mental imaging (Bilda, 2006).

Dual-Code Theory: Images and Symbols

According to **dual-code theory**, we use both pictorial and verbal codes for representing information (Paivio, 1969, 1971) in our minds. These two codes organize information into knowledge that can be acted on, stored somehow, and later retrieved for subsequent use. According to Paivio, mental images are analog codes. **Analog codes** resemble the objects they are representing. For example, trees and rivers might be represented by analog codes. Just as the movements of the hands on an analog clock are analogous to the passage of time, the mental images we form in our minds are analogous to the physical stimuli we observe.

 INVESTIGATING COGNITIVE PSYCHOLOGY
Can Your Brain Store Images of Your Face?

Look at your face in a mirror. Gradually turn your head from far right (to see yourself out of your left peripheral vision) to far left. Now tilt your head as far forward as you can then tilt it as far back as you can. All the while, make sure you still are seeing your reflection. Now make a few different expressions, perhaps even talking to yourself to exaggerate your facial movements. Could your brain store this series of separate images of your face? Storing each of these images and every image you see every day for years likely is impossible for your brain. So how do we store images in our brains?

In contrast, our mental representations for words chiefly are represented in a symbolic code. A *symbolic code* is a form of knowledge representation that has been chosen arbitrarily to stand for something that does not perceptually resemble what is being represented. Just as a digital watch uses arbitrary symbols (typically, numerals) to represent the passage of time, our minds use arbitrary symbols (words and combinations of words) to represent many ideas. Sand can be used as well to represent the flow of time, as shown in the hourglass in Figure 7.4.

A symbol may be anything that is arbitrarily designated to stand for something other than itself. For example, we recognize that the numeral "9" is a symbol for the concept of "nineness." It represents a quantity of nine of something. But nothing about the symbol in any way would suggest its meaning. We arbitrarily have designated this symbol to represent the concept. But "9" has meaning only because we use it to represent a deeper concept. Concepts like *justice* and *peace* are best represented symbolically.

Paivio, consistent with his dual-code theory, noted that verbal information seems to be processed differently than pictorial information. For example, in one study, participants were shown both a rapid sequence of pictures and a sequence of words (Paivio, 1969). They then were asked to recall the words or the pictures in one of two ways. One way was at random, so that they recalled as many items as possible, regardless of the order in which the items were presented. The other way was in the correct sequence.

Participants more easily recalled the pictures when they were allowed to do so in any order. But they more readily recalled the sequence in which the words were presented than the sequence for the pictures, which suggests the possibility of two different systems for recall of words versus pictures.

Other researchers have found supporting evidence for dual-code theory as well. For example, it has been hypothesized that actual visual perception could interfere

Neustockimages./iStockphoto.com

Figure 7.4 Symbols Can Represent Ideas in Our Minds.
This hourglass illustrates that we can depict the passage of time in various ways. We do not necessarily need numbers.

INVESTIGATING COGNITIVE PSYCHOLOGY
Analogical and Symbolic Representations of Cats

To get an intuitive sense of how you may use each of the two kinds of representations, think about how you mentally represent all the facts you know about cats. Use your mental definition of the word *cat* and all the inferences you may draw from your mental image of a cat. Which kind of representation is more helpful for answering the following questions:

- Is a cat's tail long enough to reach the tip of the cat's nose if the cat is stretching to full length?
- Do cats like to eat fish?
- Are the back legs and the front legs of a cat exactly the same size and shape?
- Are cats mammals?
- Which is wider—a cat's nose or a cat's eye?

Which kinds of mental representations were the most valuable for answering each of these questions?

with simultaneous visual imagery. Similarly, the need to produce a verbal response could interfere with the simultaneous mental manipulation of words. If, however, an experiment found that visual and verbal tasks do not interfere with each other, this result would indicate that the two kinds of tasks draw on two different systems.

A classic investigation tested this notion (Brooks, 1968). Participants performed either a visual task or a verbal task. The visual task involved answering questions requiring judgments about a picture that was presented briefly. The verbal task involved answering questions requiring judgments about a sentence that was stated briefly. Participants expressed their responses verbally (saying "yes" or "no" aloud), visually (pointing to an answer), or manually (tapping with one hand to agree and the other to disagree). There were two conditions in which Brooks expected interference: a visual task requiring a visual (pointing) response and a verbal task requiring a verbal response. This prediction assumed that both task and response required the same system for completion. Interference was measured by slow-downs in

INVESTIGATING COGNITIVE PSYCHOLOGY
Dual Coding

Look at the list of words that your friends and family members recalled in the demonstration in Chapter 6. Add up the total number of recollections for every other word (i.e., book, window, box, hat, etc.—the words in odd-numbered positions in the list). Now add up the total number of recollections for the other words (i.e., peace, run, harmony, voice, etc.—the words in even-numbered positions in the list). Most people will recall more words from the first set than from the second set. This is because the first set is made up of words that are concrete, or those words that are easily visualized. The second set of words is made up of words that are abstract, or not easily visualized. This is a demonstration of the dual-coding hypothesis (or its more contemporary version, the functional-equivalence hypothesis).

IN THE LAB OF STEPHEN KOSSLYN

Seeing with the Mind's Eye

STEPHEN KOSSLYN

If asked to decide what shape Mickey Mouse's ears are, most people report that they visualize the cartoon figure's ears and "see" that the ears are circular. Visual mental imagery hinges on such "seeing with the mind's eye" and is used not only to recall information (often that one has not thought about previously, such as the shape of that rodent's ears), but also in various forms of reasoning. For example, when considering how best to fit a bunch of backpacks, suitcases, and duffle bags into a trunk of a car, you might visualize each of them, and "see" how best to move them around and pack them efficiently—all before lifting a finger to heft a single bag into the trunk.

My lab has studied the nature of visual mental imagery for more than three decades now and a considerable amount has been learned. First and foremost, visual mental imagery is a lot like visual perception, which occurs when one registers input from the eyes. That is, whereas imagery is a bit like playing a DVD and seeing the results on the screen, perception is more like seeing the input from a camera displayed on a screen (but this is just a metaphor; there's no little man in your head watching a screen—it's just signals being processed). In fact, when we asked participants to classify parts of visible (but degraded) objects and, in another part of the test, to close their eyes and classify parts of visualized objects, more than 90% of the same brain areas were activated in common.

However, there has been a controversy about which parts of the brain give rise to visual mental imagery. Specifically, are the first parts of the cortex to register input from the eyes during perception also used during visual mental imagery? (Just how similar is mental imagery to perception?) Some neuroimaging studies find that these portions of the brain are activated during visual imagery, but some do not. In an analysis of the results from more than 50 such studies, we found that the variations in results reflected three factors: (1) if the task required "seeing" parts with relatively high resolution (e.g., as is necessary to use imagery to classify the shape of an animal's ears from memory), then these parts of visual cortex are activated; (2) if the task is spatial (e.g., as required to decide in which arm the Statue of Liberty holds the torch), these parts of the brain are not activated; and (3) if a more powerful scanning technique is used (e.g., using a more powerful magnet in a magnetic resonance imaging machine), then it is more likely that activation in these areas will be detected.

In addition, in order to use imagery in reasoning—such as in packing the trunk of a car—one must be able to transform the image (rotating objects in it, sliding them around, bending them, etc.). We have found that there are several distinct ways in which such processes occur. For example, you can imagine physically moving the objects in the image (e.g., twisting them by hand) or can imagine some external force moving them (e.g., watching a motor spin them around). In the former case, parts of the brain used to control actual movements are activated during mental imagery, but not when the same movement is imagined as a result of an external force's being at work.

This research has shown that much of the brain is activated in comparable ways during visual imagery and perception. But imagery has turned out to be "not one thing"; rather, it is a collection of distinct abilities (such as those used to classify shapes versus those used to rotate objects). Each new discovery about mental imagery brings us a little closer toward understanding how we can "see" things that aren't there!

response times. Brooks confirmed his hypothesis. Participants did show slower response times in performing the pictorial task when asked to respond using a competing visual display, as compared with when they were using a noninterfering response medium (i.e., either verbal or manual).

Similarly, his participants showed more interference in performing the verbal task when asked to respond using a competing verbal form of expression, as compared with how they performed when responding manually or by using a visual display. Thus, a response involving visual perception can interfere with a task involving manipulations of a visual image. Similarly, a response involving verbal expression can interfere with a task involving mental manipulations of a verbal statement. These findings suggest the use of two distinct codes for mental representation of knowledge. The two codes are an imaginal (analogical) code and a verbal (symbolic) code.

Storing Knowledge as Abstract Concepts: Propositional Theory

Not everyone subscribes to the dual-code theory. Researchers have developed an alternative theory termed a conceptual-propositional theory, or propositional theory (Anderson & Bower, 1973; Pylyshyn, 1973, 1984; 2006). **Propositional theory** suggests that we do not store mental representations in the form of images or mere words. We may experience our mental representations as images, but these images are *epiphenomena*—secondary and derivative phenomena that occur as a result of other more basic cognitive processes. According to propositional theory, our mental representations (sometimes called "mentalese") more closely resemble the abstract form of a proposition. A proposition is the meaning underlying a particular relationship among concepts. Anderson and Bower have moved beyond their original conceptualization to a more complex model that encompasses multiple forms of mental representation. Others, such as Pylyshyn (2006), however, still hold to this position.

What Is a Proposition?

How would a propositional representation work? Consider an example. To describe Figure 7.3(a), you could say, "The table is above the cat." You also could say, "The cat is beneath the table." Both these statements indicate the same relationship as "Above the cat is the table." With a little extra work, you probably could come up with a dozen or more ways of verbally representing this relationship.

Logicians have devised a shorthand means, called "predicate calculus," of expressing the underlying meaning of a relationship. It attempts to strip away the various superficial differences in the ways we describe the deeper meaning of a proposition:

[Relationship between elements]([Subject element], [Object element])

The logical expression for the proposition underlying the relationship between the cat and the table is shown in Figure 7.3(c). This logical expression, of course, would need to be translated by the brain into a format suitable for its internal mental representation.

Using Propositions

It is easy to see why the hypothetical construct of propositions is so widely accepted among cognitive psychologists. Propositions may be used to describe any kind of relationship. Examples of relationships include actions of one thing on another, attributes of a thing, positions of a thing, class membership of a thing, and so on, as shown in Table 7.1. In addition, any number of propositions may be combined to represent more complex relationships, images, or series of words. An example would be "The furry mouse bit the cat, which is now hiding under the table." The

Table 7.1 Propositional Representations of Underlying Meanings

We may use propositions to represent any kind of relationship, including actions, attributes, spatial positions, class membership, or almost any other conceivable relationship. The possibility for combining propositions into complex propositional representational relationships makes the use of such representations highly flexible and widely applicable.

Type of Relationship	Representation in Words	Propositional Representation*	Imaginal Representation
Actions	A mouse bit a cat.	Bite [action] (mouse [agent of action], cat [object])	
Attributes	Mice are furry.	[external surface characteristic] (furry [attribute], mouse [object])	
Spatial positions	A cat is under the table.	[vertically higher position] (table, cat)	
Class or Category membership	A cat is an animal.	[categorical membership] (animal [category], cat [member])	

*In this table, propositions are expressed in a shorthand form (known as "predicate calculus") commonly used to express underlying meaning. This shorthand is intended only to give some idea of how the underlying meaning of knowledge might be represented. It is not believed that this form is literally the form in which meaning is represented in the mind. In general, the shorthand form for representing propositions is this: [Relationship between elements] ([subject element], [object element]).

key idea is that the propositional form of mental representation is neither in words nor in images. Rather, it is in an abstract form representing the underlying meanings of knowledge. Thus, a proposition for a sentence would not retain the acoustic or visual properties of the words. Similarly, a proposition for a picture would not retain the exact perceptual form of the picture (Clark & Chase, 1972).

According to the propositional view (Clark & Chase, 1972), both images [e.g., of the cat and the table in Figure 7.3(a)] and verbal statements [e.g., in Figure 7.3(b)] are mentally represented in terms of their deep meanings, and not as specific images or words. That is, they are represented as propositions. According to propositional theory, pictorial and verbal information are encoded and stored as propositions. Then, when we wish to retrieve the information from storage, the propositional representation is retrieved. From it, our minds re-create the verbal or the imaginal code relatively accurately.

Some evidence suggests that these representations need not be exclusive. People seem to be able to employ both types of representations to increase their performance on cognitive tests (Talasli, 1990).

Do Propositional Theory and Imagery Hold Up to Their Promises?

The controversy over whether we represent information in our memory by means of propositions or mental images continues today (see for example Kosslyn, 2006; Pylyshyn, 2006). Both theories have their limits. We explore these limits in the next section.

Limitations of Mental Images

What are the limits to analogical representation of images? For example, look quickly at Figure 7.5, then look away. Does Figure 7.5 contain a *parallelogram* (a four-sided figure that has two pairs of parallel lines of equal length)? Participants in one study looked at figures such as this one. They had to determine whether particular shapes (e.g., a parallelogram) were or were not part of a given whole figure (Reed, 1974). Overall performance was little better than chance. The participants appeared unable to call up a precise analogical mental image. They could not use a mental image to trace the lines to determine which component shapes were or were not part of a whole figure. To Reed, these findings suggested the use of a propositional code rather than an analogical one. Examples of a propositional code would be "a Star of David" or "two overlapping triangles, one of which is inverted." Another possible explanation is that people have analogical mental images that are imprecise in some ways.

There are additional limits to knowledge representation in mental images (Chambers & Reisberg, 1985, 1992).

- Look at Figure 7.6(a).
- Now cover the image and imagine the rabbit shown in the figure.

Actually, the figure shown here is an *ambiguous figure,* meaning that it can be interpreted in more than one way. Ambiguous figures often are used in studies of perception. But these researchers decided to use such figures to determine whether

Figure 7.5   Mental Images.

Quickly glance at this figure and then cover it with your hand. Imagine the figure you just saw. Does it contain a parallelogram?

Source: From *Cognition,* Third Edition, by Margaret W. Matlin. Copyright © 1994 by Holt, Rinehart and Winston. Reproduced by permission of the publisher.

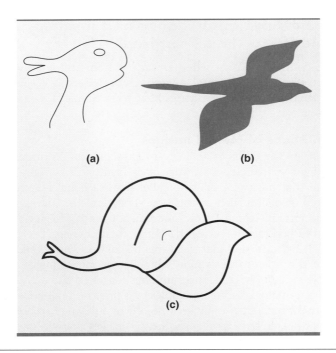

Figure 7.6 Can Mental Images Be Ambiguous?

(a) Look closely at the rabbit, then cover it with your hand and recreate it in your mind. Can you see a different animal in this image just by mentally shifting your perspective? (b) What animal do you observe in this figure? Create a mental image of this figure, and try to imagine the front end of this animal as the back end of another animal and the tail end of this animal as the front end of another animal. (c) Observe the animal in this figure, and create a mental image of the animal; cover the figure, and try to reinterpret your mental image as a different kind of animal (both animals probably are facing in the same direction).

Sources: From D. Chambers and D. Reisberg (1985), "Can Mental Images be Ambiguous?" *Journal of Experimental Psychology: Human Perception and Performance*, 11, 317–328. Copyright © 1985 by the American Psychological Association. Reprinted with permission. (b, c) Peterson, M. A., Kihlstrom, J. F., Rose, P. M., & Glisky, M. L. (1992). Mental images can be ambiguous: Reconstruals and reference-frame reversals. Memory & Cognition, 20, 107–123. Reprinted by permission of Psychonomic Society, Inc.

mental representations of images are truly analogical to perceptions of physical objects (i.e., if mental images are indeed representations similar to what our eyes see).

- Without looking back at the figure, can you determine the alternative interpretation of Figure 7.6(a)?

When the participants in Chambers and Reisberg's study had difficulty, the researchers offered cues. But even participants with high visualization skills often were unable to conjure the alternative interpretation.

Finally, the investigators suggested to participants that they should draw the figures out of their memory.

- Without looking again at the figure, briefly sketch Figure 7.6(a), based on your own mental representation of it.
- Once you have completed your sketch, try once more to see whether you can find an alternative interpretation of the figure.

If you are like most of Chambers and Reisberg's participants, you need to have an actual *percept* (object of perception) of the figure in front of you so you can guess at an alternative interpretation of the figure. These results indicate that mental representations of figures are not the same as percepts of these figures. In case you have not yet guessed it, the alternative interpretation of the rabbit is a duck. In this interpretation, the rabbit's ears are the duck's bill. One interpretation of Chambers and Reisberg's findings—an implausible one—is that people plainly do not use images to represent what they see. An alternative and more plausible explanation is that a propositional code may override the imaginal code in some circumstances.

Early studies have also suggested that visual images can be distorted through verbal information. Participants were asked to view figures that were labeled. When they recalled the images, they were distorted in the direction of the meaning of the images.

Much earlier work suggested that semantic (verbal) information (e.g., labels for figures) tends to distort recall of visual images in the direction of the meaning of the images (Carmichael, Hogan, & Walter, 1932). For example, for each of the figures in the center column of Figure 7.7, observe the alternative interpretations for the figures recalled. Recall differs based on the differing labels given for the figures.

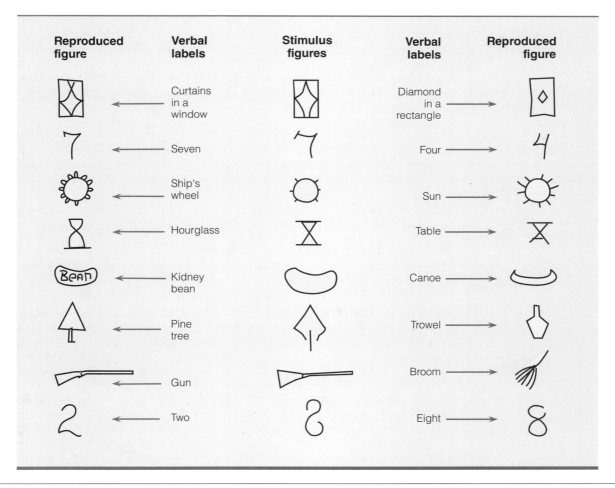

Figure 7.7 **The Influence of Semantic Labels.**
Semantic labels clearly influence mental images, as shown here in the differing drawings based on mental images of objects given differing semantic (verbal) labels. (After Carmichael, Hogan, & Walter, 1932.)

Limitations of Propositional Theory

In contrast to the work just discussed, there is some evidence that we do not necessarily need a propositional code to manipulate information, but can manipulate mental imagery directly.

Participants in a study by Finke and colleagues (Finke, Pinker, & Farah, 1989) manipulated mental images by combining two distinct images to form a different mental image altogether. This manipulation of mental images may be thought of as an imaginal Gestalt experience. In the combined image, the whole of the two combined images differed from the sum of its two distinct parts. The study showed that in some situations, mental images can be combined effectively (e.g., the letter *H* and the letter *X*) to create mental images. The images may be of geometric shapes (e.g., right triangles), of letters (e.g., M), or of objects (e.g., a bow tie).

It appears that propositional codes are less likely to influence imaginal ones when participants create their own mental images, rather than when participants are presented with a picture to be represented. However, propositional codes may influence imaginal ones. This influence is especially likely to occur when the picture used for creating an image is ambiguous [as in Figure 7.6(a)–(c)] or rather abstract (as in Figure 7.5).

Other investigators have built on Finke's work regarding the construction of mental images (Finke, Pinker, & Farah, 1989). They presented an alternative view of Chambers and Reisberg's findings regarding the manipulation of ambiguous figures (Peterson et al., 1992). They believe that the mental reinterpretation of ambiguous figures involves two manipulations.

1. The first is a mental *realignment* of the reference frame. This realignment would involve a shift in the positional orientations of the figures on the mental "page" or "screen" on which the image is displayed. In Figure 7.6(a), the shift would be of the duck's back to the rabbit's front, and the duck's front to the rabbit's back.
2. The second manipulation is a mental *reconstrual* (reinterpretation) of parts of the figure. This reconstrual would be of the duck's bill as the rabbit's ears.

Participants may be unlikely to manipulate mental images spontaneously to reinterpret ambiguous figures, but such manipulations occur when participants are given the right context.

Under what conditions do participants mentally reinterpret their image of the duck-rabbit figure [see Figure 7.6(a)] and of some other ambiguous figures (Peterson et al., 1992)? What are the supporting hints? Across experiments, 20% to 83% of participants were able to reinterpret ambiguous figures, using one or more of the following hints:

1. *Implicit reference-frame hint.* Participants first were shown another ambiguous figure involving realignment of the reference frame [e.g., see Figure 7.6(b); a hawk's head/a goose's tail, and a hawk's tail/a goose's head].
2. *Explicit reference-frame hint.* Participants were asked to modify the reference frame by considering either "the back of the head of the animal they had already seen as the front of the head of some other animal" (Peterson et al., 1992, p. 111; considered a conceptual hint) or "the front of the thing you were seeing as the back of something else" (p. 115; considered an abstract hint).

3. *Attentional hint*. Participants were directed to attend to regions of the figure where realignments or reconstruals were to occur.
4. *Construals from "good" parts*. Participants were asked to construe an image from parts determined to be "good" (according to both objective [geometrical] and empirical [inter-rater agreement] criteria), rather than from parts determined to be "bad" (according to similar criteria).

Additionally, some spontaneous reinterpretation of mental images for ambiguous figures may occur. This is particularly likely for images of figures that may be reinterpreted without realigning the reference frame. For example, see Figure 7.6(c), which may be a whole snail or an elephant's head, or possibly even a bird, a helmet, a leaf, or a seashell.

The investigators went on to suggest that the processes involved in constructing and manipulating mental images are similar to the processes involved in perceptual processes (Peterson et al., 1992). An example would be the recognition of forms (discussed in Chapter 2). Not everyone agrees with this view. Some support for their views has been found by cognitive psychologists who hold that mental imagery and visual perception are functionally equivalent. Here, *functional equivalence* refers to individuals using about the same operations to serve about the same purposes for their respective domains.

Overall, the weight of the evidence seems to indicate there are multiple codes rather than just a single code. But the controversy continues (Kosslyn, 2006; Pylyshyn, 2006).

✔ CONCEPT CHECK

> **1.** In what forms can knowledge be represented in our mind?
> **2.** What kinds of codes does dual-code theory comprise?
> **3.** What is a proposition?

Mental Manipulations of Images

According to the **functional-equivalence hypothesis**, although visual imagery is not identical to visual perception, it is functionally equivalent to it. Functionally equivalent things are strongly analogous to each other—they can accomplish the same goals. The functionally-equivalent images are thus analogous to the physical percepts they represent. This view essentially suggests that we use images rather than propositions in knowledge representation for concrete objects that can be pictured in the mind. This view has many advocates (e.g., Farah, 1988b; Finke, 1989; Jolicoeur & Kosslyn, 1985a, 1985b; Rumelhart & Norman, 1988; Shepard & Metzler, 1971).

Principles of Visual Imagery

One investigator has suggested some principles of how visual imagery may be functionally equivalent to visual perception (Finke, 1989). These principles may be used as a guide for designing and evaluating research on imagery. Table 7.2 offers an idea of some of the research questions that may be generated, based on Finke's principles.

Table 7.2   Principles of Visual Imagery: Questions

According to the functional-equivalence hypothesis, we represent and use visual imagery in a way that is functionally equivalent (strongly analogous) to that for physical percepts. Ronald Finke has suggested several principles of visual imagery that may be used to guide research and theory development.

Principle	Possible Questions Generated from Principles
1. Our mental transformations of images and our mental movements across images correspond to those of physical objects and percepts.	Do our mental images follow the same laws of motion and space that are observed in physical percepts? For example, does it take longer to manipulate a mental image at a greater angle of rotation than at a smaller one? Does it take longer to scan across a large distance in a mental image than across a smaller distance?
2. The spatial relations among elements of a visual image are analogous to those relations in actual physical space.	Are the characteristics of mental images analogous to the characteristics of percepts? For example, is it easier to see the details of larger mental images than of smaller ones? Are objects that are closer together in physical space also closer together in mental images of space?
3. Mental images can be used to generate information that was not explicitly stored during encoding.	After participants have been asked to form a mental image, can they answer questions that require them to infer information based on the image that was not specifically encoded at the time they created the image? For example, suppose that participants are asked to picture a tennis shoe. Can they later answer questions such as "How many lace-holes are there in the tennis shoe?"
4. The construction of mental images is analogous to the construction of visually perceptible figures.	Does it take more time mentally to construct a more complex mental image than a simpler one? Does it take longer to construct a mental image of a larger image than of a smaller one?
5. Visual imagery is functionally equivalent to visual perception in terms of the processes of the visual system used for each.	Are the same regions of the brain involved in manipulating mental imagery as are involved in manipulating visual percepts? For example, are similar areas of the brain activated when mentally manipulating an image, as compared with those involved when physically manipulating an object?

Neuroscience and Functional Equivalence

Evidence for functional equivalence can be found in neuroimaging studies. In one study, participants either viewed or imagined an image. Activation of similar brain areas was noted, in particular, in the frontal and parietal regions. However, there was no overlap in the areas associated with sensory processes, such as vision (Ganis, Thomspon, & Kosslyn, 2004).

Schizophrenia provides an interesting example of the similarities between perception and imagery. Many people who suffer from schizophrenia experience auditory hallucinations. Auditory hallucinations are experiences of "hearing" that occur in the absence of actual auditory stimuli. This "hearing" is the result of internally generated material. These patients have difficulty discriminating between many different types of self-produced and externally provided stimuli (Blakemore et al., 2000). Evidence from other researchers reveals that during auditory hallucinations there is abnormal activation of the auditory cortex (Lennox et al., 2000). Additionally, activation of brain areas involved with receptive language (i.e., hearing or reading as opposed to speaking or writing) is observed during auditory hallucinations (Ishii et al., 2000). In sum, it is believed that auditory hallucinations occur at least in part because of malfunctions of the auditory imaging system and problematic perception processes (Seal, Aleman, & McGuire, 2004). These challenges make it difficult for afflicted individuals to differentiate between internal images and the perception of external stimuli.

These results suggest that there is indeed functional equivalence between what our senses perceive and what we create in our minds. In the following section, we will explore the mental manipulation of images in more detail.

Mental Rotations

Mental images can be manipulated in many ways. They can be rotated just like physical objects. We can also zoom into mental images to see more details of a specific area, or we can scan across an image from one point to another. Keep in mind that studies about mental image manipulations also give us some indication of whether the functional-equivalence hypothesis is indeed correct; that is, of whether mental images and the images we see with our eyes work in the same way and adhere to the same principles.

How Does Mental Rotation Work?

Mental rotation involves rotationally transforming an object's visual mental image (Takano & Okubo, 2003; Zacks, 2008). Just like you can physically rotate a water bottle you hold in your hands, you can also imagine a water bottle in your mind and rotate it in the mind.

In a classic experiment, participants were asked to observe pairs of pictures showing three-dimensional (3-D) geometric forms (Shepard & Metzler, 1971). The forms were rotated from 0 to 180 degrees (Figure 7.8). The rotation was either in the picture plane [i.e., in 2-D space clockwise or counterclockwise; Figure 7.8(a)] or in depth [i.e., in 3-D space; Figure 7.8(b)].

In addition, participants were shown distracter forms. These forms were not rotations of the original stimuli [Figure 7.8(c)]. Participants then were asked to tell whether a given image was or was not a rotation of the original stimulus.

The response times for answering the questions about the rotation of the figures formed a *linear function* of the degree to which the figures were rotated (Figure 7.9). For each increase in the degree of rotation of the figures, there was a corresponding increase in the response times. Furthermore, there was no significant difference between rotations in the picture plane and rotations in depth. These findings are functionally equivalent to what we might expect if the participants had been rotating physical objects in space. To rotate objects at larger angles of rotation takes longer. Whether the objects are rotated clockwise, counterclockwise, or in the third dimension of depth, makes little difference. The finding of a relation between degree of angular rotation and reaction time has been replicated a number of times with a variety of stimuli (e.g., Gogos et al., 2010; Van Selst & Jolicoeur, 1994; see also Tarr, 1999).

To try your own hand at mental rotations, do the demonstration in the *Investigating Cognitive Psychology: Try Your Skills at Mental Rotations* box for yourself (based on Hinton, 1979).

Other researchers have supported these original findings in other studies of mental rotations. For example, they have found similar results in rotations of 2-D figures, such as letters of the alphabet (Gogos et al., 2010; Jordan & Huntsman, 1990),

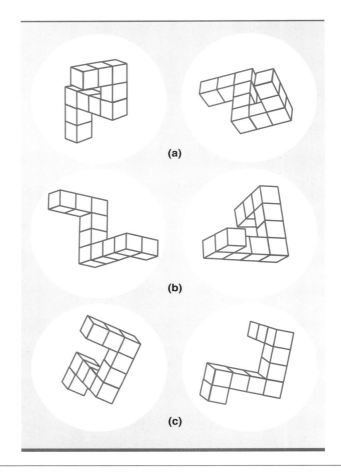

Figure 7.8 Mental Rotations.

For which of these pairs of figures does the figure on the right show an accurate rotation of the figure on the left?

Source: Reprinted with permission from "Mental Rotation," by R. Shepard and J. Metzler. *Science,* 171(3972), 701–703. Copyright © 1971, American Association for the Advancement of Science.

cubes (Just & Carpenter, 1985; Peters & Battista, 2008), and body parts, in particular hands (Fiorio, Tinazzi & Aglioti, 2006; Fiorio et al., 2007; Takeda et al., 2009). In addition, response times are longer for *degraded stimuli*—stimuli that are blurry, incomplete, or otherwise less informative (Duncan & Bourg, 1983)—than for intact stimuli. Response times are also longer for complex items compared with simple items (Bethell-Fox & Shepard, 1988) and for unfamiliar figures compared with familiar ones (Jolicoeur, Snow, & Murray, 1987). Older adults have more difficulty with this task than do younger adults (Band & Kok, 2000).

The benefits of increased familiarity also may lead to *practice effects*—improvements in performance associated with increased practice. When participants have practice in mentally rotating particular figures (increasing their familiarity), their performance improves (Bethell-Fox & Shepard, 1988). This improvement, however, appears not to carry over to rotation tasks for novel figures (Jolicoeur, 1985; Wiedenbauer, Schmid, & Jansen-Osmann, 2007).

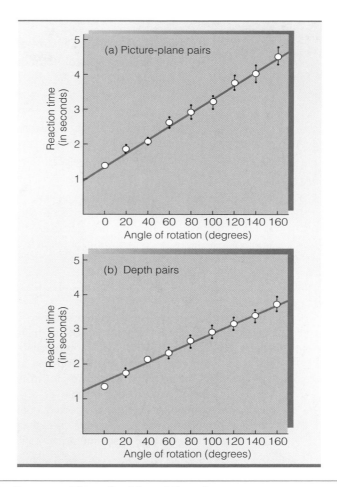

Figure 7.9 Response Times for Mental Rotation.

Response times to questions about mental rotations of figures show a linear relationship to the angle of rotation, and this relationship is preserved, whether the rotations are in the picture plane or are in depth.

Source: Reprinted with permission from "Mental Rotation," by R. Shepard and J. Metzler. *Science, 171*(3972), 701–703. Copyright © 1971, American Association for the Advancement of Science.

Moreover, children and young adults showed speedier response times in mental-rotation tasks when given opportunities for practice (Kail & Park, 1990). The performance of both school-aged children and young adults on mental-rotation tasks is not impaired as a function of their engaging in simultaneous tasks involving memory recall (Kail, 1991). These findings suggest that mental rotation may be an automatic process for school-aged children and adults. Given that familiarity with the items and practice with mental rotation appear to enhance response times, Robert Kail's work suggests that mental rotation may be an automatic process. Thus, enhanced response times may be the result of increasing automatization of the task across the years of childhood and adolescence. Furthermore, such automatic processes may be a sign of more effective visuospatial skills because increased speed is associated with increased accuracy in spatial memory (Kail, 1997).

INVESTIGATING COGNITIVE PSYCHOLOGY
Try Your Skills at Mental Rotation

Imagine a cube floating in the space in front of you. Now, mentally grasp the left front bottom corner of the cube with your left hand. Also grasp the right back top corner of the cube with your right hand. While mentally holding those corners, rotate the cube so that the corner in your left hand is directly below the corner in your right hand (as if to form a vertical axis around which the cube would spin). How many corners of the imaginary cube are in the middle (i.e., not being grasped by your hands)? Describe the positions of the corners.

How well did you do with this mental rotation? Very few people have experience with mental rotation of geometric shapes. Most people imagine that there are four remaining corners of the cube being held by the two corners in their hands. They further imagine that all four corners are aligned on a horizontal plane, parallel to the ground. In fact, six corners remain. Only two corners are aligned in a given horizontal plane (parallel to the ground) at any one time.

At the other end of the life span, two investigators studied whether processing speed or other factors may influence age-related changes in mental rotation by adults (Dror & Kosslyn, 1994). They found that older participants (55–71 years; mean 65 years) responded more slowly and less accurately than did younger participants (18–23 years; mean 20 years) on mental-rotation tasks, a finding that has been replicated (Band & Kok, 2000; Inagaki et al., 2002). However, they also found that older and younger participants showed comparable response times and error rates on tasks involving image scanning. Based on these and other findings, the authors concluded that aging affects some aspects of visual imagery more than others.

Intelligence and Mental Rotation

The work of Shepard and others on mental rotation provides a direct link between research in cognitive psychology and research on intelligence. The kinds of problems studied by Shepard and his colleagues are very similar to problems that can be found on conventional psychometric tests of spatial ability. For example, the Primary Mental Abilities test of Louis and Thelma Thurstone (1962) requires mental rotation of two-dimensionally pictured objects in the picture plane. Similar problems appear on other tests. Shepard's work points out a major contribution of cognitive research toward our understanding of intelligence: It has identified the mental representations and cognitive processes that underlie adaptations to the environment and thus, ultimately, that constitute human intelligence.

Neuroscience and Mental Rotation

Is there any physiological evidence for mental rotation? One type of study involves the brains of primates, animals whose cerebral processes seem most closely analogous to our own. Using single-cell recordings in the motor cortex of monkeys, investigators found some physiological evidence that monkeys can do mental rotations (Georgopoulos et al., 1989). Each monkey had been trained physically to move a handle in a specific direction toward a target light used as a reference point. Wherever the target light appeared, the monkeys were to use that point as a reference for the physical rotation of the handle. During these physical rotations, the monkey's cortical activity was recorded. Later, in the absence of the handle, the target light again was presented at various locations. The cortical activity again was recorded. During these presentations, activity in the motor cortex showed an interesting pattern. The same individual cortical cells tended to respond as if the monkeys were anticipating the particular rotations associated with particular locations of the target light. Another study examining mental rotation also indicates that the motor cortex (areas in the posterior frontal cortex) is activated during this task. The areas associated with hand movement were particularly active during the mental rotation task (Eisenegger, Herwig, & Jancke, 2007; Zacks, 2008).

Preliminary findings based on primate research suggest that areas of the cerebral cortex have representations that resemble the 2-D spatial arrangements of visual receptors in the retina of the eye (see Kosslyn, 1994b). These mappings may be construed as relatively depictive of the visual arrays in the real world (Cohen et al., 1996; Kosslyn et al., 1995). Perhaps if these same regions of the cortex are active in humans during tasks involving mental imagery, mental imagery may be similarly illustrative of the real world in mental representation.

Current brain-imaging techniques have allowed researchers to create images of human brain activity noninvasively to address such speculations. For example, in a study using functional magnetic resonance imaging, investigators found that the same brain areas involved in perception also are involved in mental rotation tasks (Cohen et al., 1996; see also Kosslyn & Sussman, 1995). Thus, not only are imagery and perception functionally equivalent in psychological studies, neuropsychological techniques also verify this equivalence by demonstrating overlapping brain activity.

Does mental imagery also involve the same mechanisms as memory processes because we have to recall those images from memory? If so, the functional-equivalence hypothesis for perception would lose some ground. If imagery is "functionally equivalent" to everything, then, in effect, it really is equivalent to nothing. A careful review cites many psychological studies that find differences between human-imagery and memory tasks so we can assume that these two kinds of tasks are not functionally equivalent (Georgopoulos & Pellizzer, 1995).

In sum, there is converging evidence, both from traditional and neuropsychological studies, to lend support to the hypothesis of functional equivalence between perception and mental imagery. Further neuropsychological work on images and propositions will be discussed later in the chapter.

Gender and Mental Rotation

Mental rotation has been extensively studied in addition to its application to the theories of imagery. A number of studies have highlighted an advantage for males over females in mental rotation tasks (Collins & Kimura, 1997; Roberts & Bell, 2000a, 2000b, 2003), but others have not (Beste et al., 2010; Jaencke & Jordan, 2007; Jansen-Osmann & Heil, 2007). A number of studies that have not found gender differences have used characters (like letters or numbers) for mental rotation; therefore, it is possible that the rotation of characters engages different processes than the mental rotation of other objects. Some researchers have speculated that this advantage has decreased since it was first observed. A number of other interesting features of this effect have been identified.

First, in young children, there is no gender difference either in performance or in neurological activation (Roberts & Bell, 2000a, 2000b). Second, there seem to be differences in the activation of the parietal regions between men and women. There is less parietal activation for women than for men completing the same mental rotation task. However, women exhibit additional inferior frontal activation (Hugdahl et al., 2006; Thomsen et al., 2000; Zack, 2008). Thus, in women, spatial tasks involve both sides of the brain, whereas in men, the right side dominates this function. The differences in brain activation may mean that men and women use different strategies to solve mental rotation problems (Blake, McKenzie, & Hamm, 2002; Hugdahl et al., 2006; Jordan et al., 2002). Additionally, women have a proportionally greater amount of gray matter in the parietal lobe than do men, which is associated with a performance disadvantage for mental rotation tasks for the women (as they need increased effort to complete the tasks) (Koscik et al., 2009). Training causes the gender difference to decrease or even to disappear (Bosco, Longoni, & Vecchi, 2004; Kass, Ahlers, & Dugger, 1998).

Zooming in on Mental Images: Image Scaling

The key idea underlying research on image size and scaling is that we represent and use mental images in ways that are functionally equivalent to our representations and uses of percepts. In other words, we use mental images the same way we use our actual perceptions.

For example, when you look at a building from afar, you won't be able to see as many details as when you are close by, and you may not be able to see things as clearly. Our *resolution* is limited. In general, seeing details of large objects is easier than seeing such details of small ones. We respond more quickly to questions about large objects we observe than to questions about small ones we observe. Now, if we assume that perception and mental representations are functionally equivalent, then participants should respond more quickly to questions about features of large imagined objects than to questions about features of small ones.

What happens when we zoom in closer to objects to perceive details? Sooner or later, we reach a point at which we can no longer see the entire object. To see the whole object once more, we must zoom out. See *Investigating Cognitive Psychology: Imaging Scaling* to observe perceptual zooming for yourself.

In research on visual perception, it is easy for researchers to control the sizes of the objects you see. However, for research on image size, controlling the sizes of people's mental images is more difficult. How do you know that the image of the elephant in your head is the same size as the image of the elephant in someone else's head? Fortunately, there are some ways to get around this problem (Kosslyn, 1975).

INVESTIGATING COGNITIVE PSYCHOLOGY
Image Scaling

Find a large bookcase (floor to ceiling, if possible; if not, observe the contents of a large refrigerator with an open door). Stand as close to the bookcase as you can while still keeping all of it in view. Now, read the smallest writing on the smallest book in the bookcase. Without changing your gaze, can you still see all of the bookcase? Can you read the title of the book farthest from the book on which you are focusing your perception? Depending on what you want to see (a detail like a book title or the whole shelf), you may have to zoom in and out of what you see. When you look at a small detail, it will be hard to perceive the whole shelf, and vice versa. The same is true for mental images.

One of the ways is to use relative size as a means of manipulating image size (Kosslyn, 1975). Participants imagine four pairs of animals—an elephant and a rabbit, a rabbit and a fly, a rabbit and an elephant-sized fly, and a rabbit and a fly-sized elephant (Figure 7.10 and *Investigating Cognitive Psychology: Image Scanning*). Then the participants answer specific questions about the features of the rabbit and are timed in their responses. It takes them longer to describe the details of smaller objects than to describe the details of the larger objects. That is, it takes longer to respond to rabbits paired with elephants or with elephant-sized flies than to respond to rabbits paired with flies or with fly-sized elephants. This result makes sense intuitively: Imagine we each have a mental screen for visual images and look at an elephant's eye. The larger the eye on the screen, the more details we can see (Kosslyn, 1983; Kosslyn & Koenig, 1992).

In another study, children in the first and fourth grades and adult college undergraduates were asked whether particular animals can be characterized as having various physical attributes (Kosslyn, 1976). Examples would be "Does a cat have claws?" and "Does a cat have a head?" In one condition, participants were asked to visualize each animal and to use their mental image in answering the questions. In the other condition, the participants were not asked to use mental images. It was presumed that they used verbal-propositional knowledge to respond to the verbal questions.

In the imagery condition, all participants responded more quickly to questions about physical attributes that were larger than to questions about attributes that were smaller. For example, they might have been asked about a cat's head (larger) and a cat's claws (smaller). Different results were found in the nonimagery condition. In the nonimagery condition, fourth graders and adults responded more quickly to questions about physical attributes based on the distinctiveness of the characteristic for the animal. For example, they responded more quickly to questions about whether cats have claws (which are distinctive) than to questions about whether cats have heads (which are not particularly distinctive to cats alone). The physical size of the features did not have any effect on performance in the nonimagery condition for either fourth graders or adults.

INVESTIGATING COGNITIVE PSYCHOLOGY
Image Scanning

Look at the rabbit and the fly in Figure 7.10. Close your eyes and picture them both in your mind. Now, in your imagination, look only at the fly and determine the exact shape of the fly's head. Do you notice yourself having to take time to zoom in to "see" the detailed features of the fly? If you are like most people, you are able to zoom in on your mental images to give the features or objects a larger portion of your mental screen, much as you might physically move toward an object you wanted to observe more closely.

Now, look at the rabbit and the elephant and picture them both in your mind. Next, close your eyes and look at the elephant. Imagine walking toward the elephant, watching it as it gets closer to you. Do you find that there comes a point when you can no longer see the rabbit or even all of the elephant? If you are like most people, you will find that the image of the elephant will appear to overflow the size of your image space. To "see" the whole elephant, you probably have to mentally zoom out again.

Figure 7.10 Zooming in on Details.
Stephen Kosslyn (1983) asked participants to imagine either a rabbit and a fly (to observe zooming in to "see" details) or a rabbit and an elephant (to observe whether zooming in may lead to apparent overflow of the image space).

Interestingly, first-graders constantly responded more quickly regarding larger attributes, not only in the imagery condition but also in the nonimagery condition. Many of these younger children indicated that they used imagery even when not instructed to do so. Furthermore, in both conditions, adults responded more quickly than did children. But the difference was much greater for the nonimagery condition than for the imagery condition. These findings support the functional-equivalence hypothesis: When we see something in front of our "mental eye," it takes children and adults about the same amount of time to perceive it, just as it would if we saw something in real life.

The findings also support the dual-code view in two ways. First, for adults and older children, responses based on the use of imagery (an imaginal code) differed from responses based on propositions (a symbolic code). Second, the development of propositional knowledge and ability does not occur at the same rate as the development of imaginal knowledge and ability. Children just did not have the propositional knowledge yet and therefore were slower than were adults in the nonimaginary condition. The distinction in the rate of development of each form of representation also seems to support Paivio's notion of two distinct codes.

Examining Objects: Image Scanning

Stephen Kosslyn has found additional support for his hypothesis that we use mental images in image scanning. The key idea underlying image scanning research is that images can be scanned in much the same way as physical percepts can be scanned. Furthermore, our strategies and responses for imaginal scanning should be the same as for perceptual scanning. A means of testing the functional equivalence of imaginal scanning is to observe some aspects of performance during perceptual scanning, and then compare that performance with performance during imaginal scanning.

For example, in perception, to scan across longer distances takes longer than to scan across shorter ones (Denis & Kosslyn, 1999). In one of Kosslyn's experiments, participants were shown a map of an imaginary island, which you can see in Figure 7.11 (Kosslyn, Ball, & Reiser, 1978). The map shows various objects on the island, such as a hut, a tree, and a lake. Participants studied the map until they could reproduce it accurately from memory. Once the memorization phase of the experiment was completed, the critical phase began:

- Participants were instructed that, on hearing the name of an object read to them, they should imagine the map and mentally scan to the mentioned object.
- As soon as they arrived at the location of that object, they should press a key.
- An experimenter then read to the participants the names of objects.
- The participants had to scan to the proper location and press the button once they had found it.

This procedure was repeated a number of times. In each case, the participants mentally moved between various pairs of objects on successive trials. For each trial, the experimenter kept track of the participants' response times, indicating the amount of time it took them to scan from one object to another.

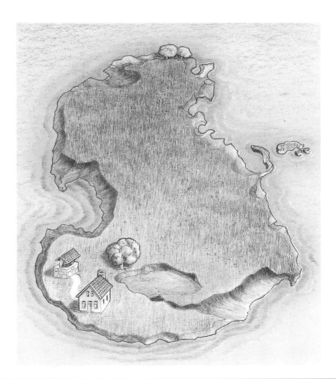

Figure 7.11   Mental Scanning: An Imaginary Island.
Stephen Kosslyn and his colleagues used a map of an imaginary island with various landmarks to determine whether mental scanning across the image of a map was functionally equivalent to perceptual scanning of a perceived map.

What did Kosslyn find? There was an almost perfect linear relation between the distances separating pairs of objects in the mental map and the amount of time it took participants to press the button. The further away from each other the objects were, the longer it took participants to scan from one object to the other. Participants seem to have encoded the map in the form of an image. They actually scanned that image as needed for a response, just as they would have scanned a real map.

These findings have been replicated using other objects as well. In one study, Borst and Kosslyn (2008) presented participants with dots on a screen for a short time. In the mental image scanning task, participants had to memorize the location of the dots before the trial. Once the dots had been presented, participants in the mental-image group were presented with an empty frame that contained only an arrow. They had to decide whether the arrow pointed at one of the dots they had seen previously. In another condition, the participants were presented with a frame that contained not only the arrow but also the dots. In all conditions, the time to make a judgment increased linearly, depending on the distance between the dot and the arrow.

This finding indicates that the same mechanisms were used, no matter whether participants looked at the actual dots presented with the arrow, or looked only at the arrow, needing to imagine the dots. If participants did not use a spatial representation but rather a code based on Pylyshyn's propositional theory (1973), then the distance between the points and the arrow should not have influenced reaction time, but it did. Recall that the experiment by Shepard and Metzler (1971) found linearly increasing reaction times for mental rotations as the angle of rotation increased.

Findings supporting an imaginal code have been shown in several other domains. For example, the same pattern of results has been obtained for scanning objects in three dimensions (Pinker, 1980). Specifically, participants observed and then mentally represented a 3-D array of objects—toys suspended in an open box—and then mentally scanned from one object to another.

Representational Neglect

Additional evidence for the similarity between perception and mental imagery can be seen in cases of representational neglect. Many patients suffering from spatial neglect (see Chapter 4) also suffer from a related impairment called representational neglect. As noted earlier, in *spatial neglect* a person ignores half of his or her visual field. In *representational neglect,* a person asked to imagine a scene and then describe it ignores half of the imagined scene. Although these two types of neglect often occur together, they can also occur independently. Peru and Zapparoli (1999) described a case of a woman who showed no evidence of spatial neglect while struggling with tasks that required the production of a mental image.

In another set of studies, an array was described to patients suffering from representational neglect. When the patients had to recall the array, they could not describe the left portion (Logie et al., 2005). Similarly, when subjects with representational neglect were presented with an image, they described the entire image. However, when the image was removed and they were asked to describe the image from memory, they failed to describe the left portion (Denis et al., 2002).

In scenes, representational neglect is present only when a vantage point is given (Rode et al., 2004). For example, if a person with representational neglect were asked to describe his or her kitchen, he or she would do so accurately. However, if the same person were asked to describe the kitchen from the refrigerator, then he or she would demonstrate neglect. It is likely that there exists complete knowledge of the scene, but that knowledge sometimes is not accessible when the patient generates a mental image.

✔ CONCEPT CHECK

1. What is mental rotation?
2. What is some of the neuropsychological evidence for mental rotation?
3. What is image scaling?
4. How do we mentally scan images?
5. What is representational neglect?

Synthesizing Images and Propositions

In this chapter, we have discussed two opposing views of knowledge representation. One is a dual-code theory, suggesting that knowledge is represented both in images and in symbols. The second is a propositional theory, suggesting that knowledge is represented only in underlying propositions, not in the form of images, words, or other symbols. Before we consider some proposed syntheses of the two hypotheses, let's review the findings described thus far. We do so in light of Finke's principles of visual imagery (see Table 7.3).

In our discussion, we addressed the first three of Finke's criteria for imaginal representations. Mental imagery appears functionally equivalent to perception in many ways. This conclusion is based on studies of mental rotations, image scaling (sizing), and image scanning. However, the studies involving ambiguous figures and unfamiliar mental manipulations suggest that there are limits to the analogy between perception and imagery.

Do Experimenters' Expectations Influence Experiment Outcomes?

Although there seems to be good evidence for the existence of both propositions and mental images (Borst, 2008; Kosslyn, 2006; Pylyshyn, 2006), the debate is not over. Perhaps some of the confirmatory results found in image research could be the result of demand characteristics (i.e., subjects' perceptions of what is expected of them when they participate in an experiment) (Intons-Peterson, 1983). Do experimenters' expectancies regarding the performance of participants on a particular task create an implicit demand for the participants to perform as expected?

Intons-Peterson (1983) set out to investigate just that question. She manipulated experimenter expectancies by suggesting to one group of experimenters that task performance would be expected to be better for perceptual tasks than for imaginal ones. She suggested the opposite outcome to a second group of experimenters. Would the different expectations of the experimenters lead to different performances

Table 7.3 Principles of Visual Imagery: Findings

How well did the studies reported in this chapter satisfy the criteria suggested by Ronald Finke's principles of visual imagery?

Principle	Study Findings
1. Our mental transformations of images and our mental movements across images correspond to similar transformations of and movements across physical objects and percepts.	Mental rotations generally conform to the same laws of motion and space that are observed in physical percepts (e.g., Shepard & Metzler, 1971), even showing performance decrements associated with degraded stimuli (Duncan & Bourg, 1983.) (See Chapter 2 for comparisons with perceptual stimuli). However, it appears that for some mental images, mental rotations of imaginal objects do not fully and accurately represent the physical rotation of perceived objects (e.g., Gogos et al., 2010; Hinton, 1979; Zacks, 2008). Therefore, some nonimaginal knowledge representations or cognitive strategies appear influential in some situations. In image scanning, it takes longer to scan across a large distance in a mental image than across a smaller distance (Borst & Kosslyn, 2008; Kosslyn, Ball, & Reiser, 1978).
2. The spatial relations among elements of a visual image are analogous to those relations in actual physical space.	It appears that cognitive manipulations of mental images are analogous to manipulations of percepts in studies involving image size. As in visual perception, there are limits to the resolution of the featural details of an image, as well as limits to the size of the image space (analogous to the visual field) that can be "observed" at any one time. To observe greater detail of individual objects or parts of objects, a smaller size or number of objects or parts of objects may be observed, and vice versa (Kosslyn, 1975). In related work (Kosslyn, 1976), it appears easier to see the details of larger mental images (e.g., a cat's head) than of smaller ones (e.g., a cat's claws). It appears also that, just as we perceive the physical proximity (closeness) of objects that are closer together in physical space, we also imagine the closeness of mental images in our mental image space (Kosslyn, Ball, & Reiser, 1978).
3. Mental images can be used to generate information that was not explicitly stored during encoding.	After participants have been asked to form a mental image, they can answer some questions that require them to infer information, based on the image, which was not specifically encoded at the time they created the image. The studies by Reed (1974) and by Chambers and Reisberg (1985) suggest that propositional representations may play a role. Studies by Finke (1989) and by Peterson and colleagues (1992) suggest that imaginal representations are sometimes sufficient for drawing inferences.
4. The construction of mental images is analogous to the construction of visually perceptible figures.	Studies of lifelong blind people suggest that mental imagery in the form of spatial arrangements may be constructed from haptic (touch-based), rather than visual, information. Based on the findings regarding cognitive maps (e.g., Friedmann & Montello, 2004; Louwerse & Zwaan, 2009; Saarinen, 1987b; Tversky, 1981; Wagner, 2006), it appears that both propositional and imaginal knowledge representations influence the construction of spatial arrangements.
5. Visual imagery is functionally equivalent to visual perception in terms of the processes of the visual system used for each.	It appears that some of the same regions of the brain that are involved in manipulating visual percepts may be involved in manipulating mental imagery (e.g., see Farah et al., 1988a, 1988b; see also Zacks, 2008). But it also appears that spatial and visual imagery may be represented differently in the brain.

of the participants? She found that experimenter expectancies did influence participants' responses in three tasks: image scanning, mental rotations, and another task comparing perceptual performance with imaginal performance.

When experimenters expected imaginal performance to be better than perceptual performance, participants responded accordingly, and vice versa. This result occurred even when the experimenters were not present while participants were responding and when the cues were presented via computer. Thus, experimental participants performing visualization tasks may be responding in part to the demand characteristics of the task. These demand characteristics result from the experimenters' expectations regarding the outcomes.

Other investigators responded to these findings (Jolicoeur & Kosslyn, 1985a, 1985b). In one experiment, participants were not asked to scan their mental images at all. However, they were asked two kinds of questions intermixed with each other: questions that involved responses requiring image scanning and questions that did not. Even when image scanning was not an implicit task demand, participants' responses to questions that required image scanning still showed a linear increase in response time if the subjects had to scan across a longer distance. When questions did not require image scanning, reaction time was always about the same, no matter what the focus of the question was.

In another set of experiments, Jolicoeur and Kosslyn used a map of an island, similar to the one presented in Figure 7.11, and again had participants imagine the map and scan from one location to another. They led their experimenters to expect a pattern of responses that would show a *U*-shaped curve, rather than a linear function. In this study, too, responses still showed a linear relation between distance and time. They did not show the *U*-shaped response pattern expected by the experimenters. Thus, the expectations of the experimenters did not influence the responses of the participants. The hypothesis regarding the functional equivalence of imagery and perception thus appears to have strong empirical support.

The debate between the propositional hypothesis and the functional-equivalence (analogical) hypothesis has been suggested to be intractable, based on existing knowledge (Keane, 1994). For each empirical finding that supports the view that imagery is analogous to perception, a rationalist reinterpretation of the finding may be offered. The reinterpretation offers an alternative explanation of the finding. Although the rationalist alternative may be a less parsimonious explanation than the empiricist explanation, the alternative cannot be refuted outright. Therefore, the debate between the functional-equivalence view and the propositional view may boil down to a debate between empiricism and rationalism.

Johnson-Laird's Mental Models

An alternative synthesis of the literature suggests that mental representations may take any of three forms: propositions, images, or mental models (Johnson-Laird, 1983, 1999; Johnson-Laird & Goldvarg, 1997). Here, propositions are fully abstracted representations of meaning that are verbally expressible. The criterion of the possibility of verbal expression distinguishes Johnson-Laird's view from that of other cognitive psychologists.

Mental models are knowledge structures that individuals construct to understand and explain their experiences (Brewer, 2003; Goodwin & Johnson-Laird, 2010; Johnson-Laird, 2001; Schaeken et al., 1996; Tversky, 2000). The models are constrained by the individuals' implicit theories about these experiences, which can be more or less accurate. For example, you may have a mental model to account for how planes fly into the air. But the model depends—not on physical or other laws but rather—on your beliefs about them. The same would apply to the creation of mental models from text or symbolic reasoning problems as from accounts of planes flying in the air (Byrne, 1996; Ehrlich, 1996; Garnham & Oakhill, 1996).

"The cat is under the table" may be represented in several ways: as a proposition (because it is verbally expressible); as an image (of a particular cat in a particular position under a particular table); or as a mental model (of any cat and table).

Is there any proof for the use of mental models? In an experiment by Mani and Johnson-Laird (1982), some participants received precise location information for each object in a spatial array (determinate descriptions). Other participants received ambiguous location information for objects in the array (indeterminate descriptions). As an analogy, consider a relatively determinate description of the location of Washington, D. C.: It lies between Alexandria, Virginia, and Baltimore, Maryland; an indeterminate description of the location is that it lies between the Pacific Ocean and the Atlantic Ocean. When participants were given detailed (determinate) descriptions for the spatial layout of objects, they inferred additional spatial information not included in the descriptions, but they did not recall the verbatim details well. For example, they could infer additional geographic information about Washington, D. C.'s location, but they could not remember the description word for word. Their having inferred additional spatial information suggests that the participants formed a mental model of the information. That they then did not recall the verbatim descriptions very well suggests that they relied on the mental models. They did not rely on the verbal descriptions for their mental representations.

What do you think happened when participants were given ambiguous (indeterminate) descriptions for the spatial layout of objects? They seldom inferred spatial information not given in the descriptions, but they remembered the verbatim descriptions better than did the other participants. The authors suggested that participants did not infer a mental model for the indeterminate descriptions because of the multitude of possibilities for mental models of the given information. Instead, the participants appear to have mentally represented the descriptions as verbally expressible propositions. The notion of mental models as a form of knowledge representation has been applied to a broad range of cognitive phenomena. These phenomena include visual perception, memory, comprehension of text passages, and reasoning (Johnson-Laird, 1983, 1989). Consider, for example, the statement: "Some dogs are poodles." How might you construct a mental model to represent this statement?

Perhaps the use of mental models may offer a possible explanation of some findings that cannot be fully explained in terms of visual imagery. A series of experiments studied people who were born blind (Kerr, 1983). Because these participants have never experienced visual perception, we may assume that they never have formed visual images (at least, they have not done so in the ordinary sense of the term). Some of Kosslyn's tasks were adapted to work comparably for sighted and for blind participants (Kerr, 1983). For example, for a map-scanning task, the experimenter used a board with topographical features and landmarks that could be detected by using touch. She then asked participants to form a mental image of the board.

Kerr asked participants to imagine various common objects of various sizes. The blind participants responded more slowly to all tasks than did the sighted participants. But Kerr's blind participants still showed similar response patterns to those of sighted participants. They showed faster response times when scanning shorter distances than when scanning longer distances. They also were faster when answering questions about images of larger objects than about images of smaller objects. At least in some respects, spatial imagery appears not to involve representations that are actual analogs to visual percepts.

The use of haptic (touch-based) "imagery" suggests alternative modalities for mental imagery. Haptic imagery has been explored further by a number of researchers. These researchers have found that haptic imagery shares a number of features with visual imagery. For instance, similar brain areas are active during both types of imagery (James et al., 2002; Zhang et al., 2004). Perhaps haptic imagery involves the formation of a mental model that is analogous, in some respects, to visual imagery.

Imaginal representation also may occur in an auditory modality (based on hearing). As an example, investigators found that participants seem to have auditory mental images, just as they have visual mental images (Intons-Peterson, Russell, & Dressel, 1992). Specifically, participants took longer mentally to shift a sound upward in pitch than downward. In particular, they were slower in going from the low-pitched purring of a cat to the high-pitched ringing of a telephone than in going from the cat's purring to a clock's ticking. The relative response times were analogous to the time needed physically to change sounds up or down in pitch. Consider what happened, in contrast, when individuals were asked to make psychophysical judgments involving discriminations between stimuli. Participants took longer to determine whether purring was lower-pitched than was ticking (two relatively close stimuli) than to determine whether purring was lower-pitched than was ringing (two relatively distant stimuli). As with haptic imagery, it is easier to conceptualize auditory imagery in terms of mental models than strictly in terms of the kinds of pictorial mental representations of which people speak when they think of visual imagery.

Psychophysical tests of auditory sensation and perception reveal findings analogous to the studies on auditory and haptic imagery. In another study, participants listened to either familiar or unfamiliar songs with pieces of the song replaced with silence. Examining the brains of these participants revealed that there was more activation of the auditory cortex during silence when the song was familiar than when the song was unfamiliar (Kraemer et al., 2005). These findings suggest that when one generates an auditory image, the same brain areas as those involved in hearing are engaged.

Faulty mental models are responsible for many errors in thinking. Consider several examples (Brewer, 2003). School children tend to think of heat and cold as moving through objects, much as fluids do. These children also believe that plants obtain their food from the ground, and that boats made of iron should sink. Even adults have trouble understanding the trajectory of an object dropped from a moving airplane.

Experience is a useful tool for the repair of faulty mental models (Greene & Azevedo, 2007). In one study, faulty mental models concerning the process of respiration were explored. A group of college students who made false predictions concerning the process of respiration participated in this study. These predictions were based on imprecise mental models. The experimenters set up a laboratory experience for the students to demonstrate and explore the process of respiration. One group stated their predictions before the experiment and another did not. Overall, participating in the activity improved the accuracy of the answers of participants to questions concerning respiration, compared with performance before the activity. However, when the students were required to state their predictions before the experiment, the improvement was even greater (Modell et al., 2000). This research can be applied to classroom teaching. For example, if a teacher asks students to explain how they think the respiratory system works and then offers an experiment or demonstration showing how respiration works, students who did not understand the process correctly are now more able, because of the activity, to correct their understanding and learn. Thus, experience can help correct faulty mental models. However, it is most helpful when the faulty models are made explicit.

In sum, mental models provide an additional means of representation in addition to propositions and visual images. They are not mutually exclusive with these other two forms of representation, but they are complementary to them. Mental models provide a way of explaining empirical findings, such as haptic and auditory forms of imagery, which seem quite different from visual images.

Neuroscience: Evidence for Multiple Codes

Participants involved in a research project involving cognitive tasks can be influenced by the expectations of the researcher. But it seems implausible that such factors would equally influence the results of neuropsychological research. For example, suppose you remembered every word in Chapter 3 regarding which particular parts of your brain govern which kinds of perceptual and cognitive functions. (This is, of course, an unlikely assumption for you or for most participants in neuropsychological research.) How would you go about conforming to experimenters' expectations? You would have to control directly your brain's activities and functions so that you would simulate what experimenters expected in association with particular perceptual or cognitive functions. Likewise, brain-damaged patients do not know that particular lesions are supposed to lead to particular kinds of deficits. Indeed, the patients rarely know where a lesion is until after deficits are discovered. Thus, neuropsychological findings may circumvent many issues of demand characteristics in resolving the dual-code controversy. However, this research does not eliminate experimenter biases regarding where to look for lesions or the deficits arising from them.

Left Brain or Right Brain: Where Is Information Manipulated?

Some investigators have followed the long-standing tradition of studying patterns of brain lesions and relating them to cognitive deficits. Initial neuropsychological research on imagery came from studies of patients with identified lesions and from split-brain patients. Recall the Chapter 3 studies of patients who underwent surgery that severed their right hemisphere from their left hemisphere. Researchers found that the right hemisphere appears to represent and manipulate visuospatial knowledge in a manner similar to perception (Gazzaniga & Sperry, 1967). In contrast, the left hemisphere appears to be more proficient in representing and manipulating verbal and other symbol-based knowledge.

Perhaps cerebral asymmetry has evolutionary origins (Corballis, 1989). The right hemisphere of the human brain represents knowledge in a manner that is analogous to our physical environment. This is also the case with the brains of other animals. Unlike the brains of other animals, however, the left hemisphere only of the human brain has the ability to manipulate imaginal components and symbols and to generate entirely new information (e.g., consonant and vowel sounds and geometric shapes). For example, the word "text" as a verb did not exist just a few years ago. Today it exists and most people know what it means, that is, to send a text message. According to Corballis, humans alone can conceive what they have never perceived. However, a review of the findings on lateralization has led to a modified view (Corballis, 1997). Specifically, recent neuropsychological studies of mental rotation in both animals and humans show that both hemispheres may be partially responsible for task performance. The apparent right-hemisphere dominance observed in humans may be the result of the overshadowing of left-hemisphere functions by linguistic abilities. Thus, it would be useful to have clear evidence of a cerebral-hemispheric dissociation between analog imagery functions and symbolic propositional functions. Scientists, however, will have to look deeper into brain functioning before this issue is resolved completely.

Two Kinds of Images: Visual versus Spatial

While examining visual imagery, researchers have found that images actually may be stored (represented) in different formats in the mind, depending on what kind of image is involved (Farah, 1988a, 1988b; Farah et al., 1988a). Here, *visual imagery* refers to the use of images that represent visual characteristics such as colors and shapes. *Spatial imagery* refers to images that represent spatial features such as depth dimensions, distances, and orientations.

Consider the case of L. H., a 36-year-old who had a head injury at age 18. The injury resulted in lesions in the right and the left temporo-occipital regions, the right temporal lobe, and the right inferior frontal lobe. L. H.'s injuries implicated possible impairment of his ability to represent and manipulate both visual and spatial images. Figure 7.12 shows those areas of L. H.'s brain where there was damage.

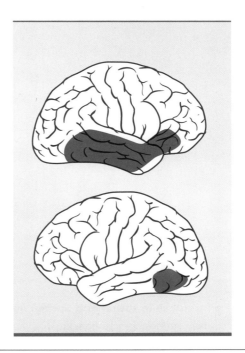

Figure 7.12 Damage to the Temporal Lobe.

Regions in which the brain of L. H. was damaged: the right temporal lobe and right inferior frontal lobe, as shown in the figure at the top; and the temporo-occipital region, as shown in the figure at the bottom.

Source: From Robert Solso, *Cognitive Psychology*, ed 6, p. 306. Copyright © 2000 Elsevier. Reprinted with permission.

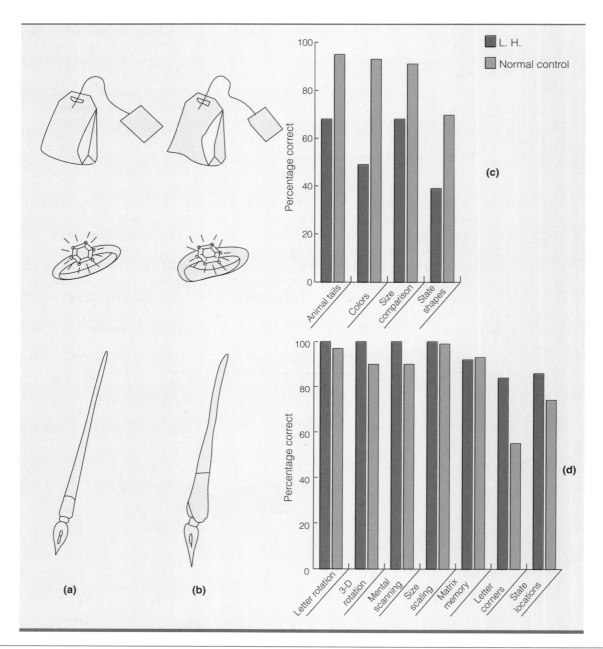

Figure 7.13 **L. H.'s Performance in Visual and Spatial Imagery.**

L. H. was able to draw accurately various objects. Panel (a) shows what he was shown, and panel (b) shows what he drew. However, he could not recognize the objects he copied. Despite L. H.'s severe deficits on visual-imagery tasks [panel (c), regarding colors, sizes, shapes, etc.], L. H. showed normal ability on spatial-imagery tasks [panel (d), regarding rotations, scanning, scaling, etc.].

Source: Reprinted from M. J. Farah, K. M. Hammond, D. N. Levine, & R. Calvanio. Visual and spatial mental imagery: Dissociable systems of representation. *Cognitive Psychology, 20,* 439–462, © 1988, with permission from Elsevier.

Despite L. H.'s injuries, L. H.'s ability to see was intact. He was able satisfactorily to copy various pictures [Figure 7.13(a) and (b)]. Nonetheless, he could not recognize any of the pictures he copied. In other words, he could not link verbal labels to the objects pictured. He performed very poorly when asked to respond verbally to questions requiring visual imagery, such as those regarding color or shape. Surprisingly, however, L. H. showed relatively normal abilities in several kinds of tasks. These involved: (1) rotations (2-D letters, 3-D objects); (2) mental scanning, size scaling, matrix memory, and letter corners; and (3) state locations [Figure 7.13(c) and (d)]. That is, his ability for several types of spatial imagery was not impaired. This finding indicates that spatial and visual imagery may indeed be different from each other.

Investigators have also used event-related potentials (ERP; see Chapter 3, Table 3.3) to study visual imagery. They thereby compared brain processes associated with visual perception to brain processes associated with visual imagery (Farah et al., 1988b). As you may recall, the primary visual cortex is located in the occipital region of the brain. During visual perception, ERPs generally are elevated in the occipital region. If visual imagery were analogous to visual perception, we could expect that, during tasks involving visual imagery, there would be analogous elevations of ERPs in the occipital region.

In Farah's study, ERPs were measured during a reading task. In one condition, participants were asked to read a list of concrete words (e.g., cat). In the other condition, participants were asked to read a comparable list of concrete words but were also asked to imagine the objects during reading. Each word was presented for 200 milliseconds. ERPs were recorded from the different sites in the occipital lobe and temporal lobe regions. The researchers found that the ERPs were similar across the two conditions during the first 450 milliseconds. After this time, however, participants in the imaginal condition showed greater neural activity in the occipital lobe than did participants in the nonimaginal (reading-only) condition.

"Neurophysiological evidence suggests that our cognitive architecture includes representations of both the visual appearance of objects in terms of their form, color, and perspective, and of the spatial structure of objects in terms of their three-dimensional layout in space" (Farah et al., 1988a, p. 459). Knowledge of object labels (recognizing the objects by name) and attributes (answering questions about the characteristics of the objects) taps propositional, symbolic knowledge about the pictured objects. In contrast, the ability to manipulate the orientation (rotation) or the size of images taps imaginal, analogous knowledge of the objects. Thus, both sforms of representation seem to answer particular kinds of questions for knowledge use.

✔ CONCEPT CHECK

1. Why are demand characteristics important when researchers design and interpret experiments?
2. What kind of mental model did Johnson-Laird propose?
3. What is the difference between visual and spatial imagery?

Spatial Cognition and Cognitive Maps

Most of the studies described thus far have involved the way in which we represent pictorial knowledge. The studies are based on what we have perceived by looking at and then imagining visual stimuli. Other research suggests that we may form imaginal maps based solely on our physical interactions with, and navigations through, our physical environment. This is true even when we never have a chance to "see the whole picture," as from an aerial photograph or a map. **Spatial cognition** deals with the acquisition, organization, and use of knowledge about objects and actions in two- and three-dimensional space.

Cognitive maps are internal representations of our physical environment, particularly centering on spatial relationships. Cognitive maps seem to offer internal representations that simulate particular spatial features of our external environment (Rumelhart & Norman, 1988; Wagner, 2006).

Of Rats, Bees, Pigeons, and Humans

Some of the earliest work on cognitive maps was done by Edward Tolman during the 1930s. At this time, it was considered almost unseemly for psychologists to try to understand cognitive processes that could not be observed or measured directly (you can't look into a person's head and "see" the image that person is thinking about). In one study, the researchers were interested in the ability of

PRACTICAL APPLICATIONS OF COGNITIVE PSYCHOLOGY

DUAL CODES

How do you benefit from having a dual code for knowledge representation? Although a dual code may seem redundant and inefficient, having a code for analog physical and spatial features that is distinct from a code for symbolic propositional knowledge actually can be very efficient. Consider how you learn material in your cognitive psychology course. Most people go to the lecture and obtain information from an instructor. They also read material from a textbook, as you are doing now. If you had only an analog code for knowledge representation, you would have a much harder time integrating the verbal information you received from your instructor in class with the printed information in your textbook. All your information would be in the form of auditory-visual images gleaned from listening to and watching your instructor in class and visual images of the words in your textbook. Thus, a symbolic code that is distinct from the analog features of encoding is helpful for integrating across different modes of knowledge acquisition.

Analog codes preserve important aspects of experience without interfering with underlying propositional information. For the purposes of performing well on a test, it is irrelevant whether the information was obtained in class or in the text, but later you may need to verify the source of information to prove that your answer is correct. In this case, analogical information might help.

Television used to be analog but is now largely digital. What are the advantages of digital television? Are there any potential disadvantages?

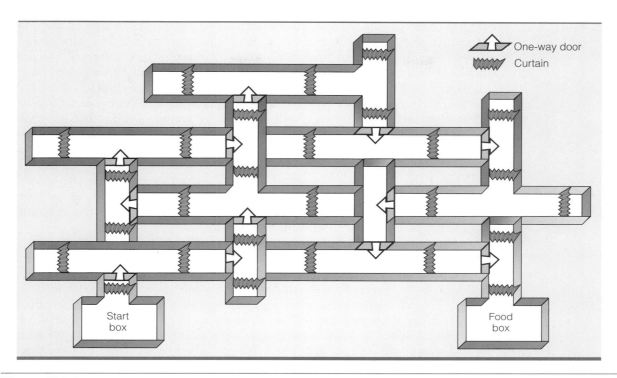

Figure 7.14   Research on Mental Imagery in Rats.

Edward Tolman found that rats seemed to have formed a mental map of a maze during behavioral experiments.

rats to learn a maze (Figure 7.14) (Tolman & Honzik, 1930). The rats were divided into three groups:

1. In the first group, the rats had to learn the maze. Their reward for getting from the start box to the end box was food. Eventually, these rats learned to run the maze without making any errors. In other words, they did not make wrong turns or follow blind alleys.

2. A second group of rats also was placed in the maze, but these rats received no reinforcement for successfully getting to the end box. Although their performance improved over time, they continued to make more errors than the reinforced group. These results are hardly surprising. We would expect the rewarded group to have more incentive to learn.

3. The third group of rats received no reward for 10 days of learning trials. On the 11th day, however, food was placed in the end box for the first time. With just one reinforcement, the learning of these rats improved dramatically. These rats ran the maze about as well in fewer trials as the rats in the first group.

What, exactly, were the rats in Tolman and Honzik's experiment learning? It seems unlikely that they were learning simply "turn right here, turn left there," and so on. According to Tolman, the rats were learning a cognitive map, an internal representation of the maze. Through this argument, Tolman became one of the earliest cognitive theorists. He argued for the importance of the mental representations that give rise to behavior.

Decades later, even very simple creatures were to appear able to form some cognitive maps. These creatures may be able to translate imaginal representations into a primitive, prewired, analogical, and perhaps even symbolic form. For example, a Nobel Prize–winning German scientist studied the behavior of bees when they return to their hive after having located a source of nectar (von Frisch, 1962, 1967).

Apparently, bees not only can form imaginal maps for getting to food sources, they also can use a somewhat symbolic form for communicating that information to other bees. Specifically, different patterns of dances can be used to represent different meanings. For example, a round dance indicates a source less than 100 yards from the hive. A figure-eight dance indicates a source at a greater distance. The details of the dance (e.g., in regard to wiggle patterns) differ from one species to another, but the basic dances appear to be the same across all species of bees. If the lowly bee appears able to imagine the route to nectar, what kinds of cognitive maps may be conceived in the minds of humans?

Homing pigeons are noted for their excellent cognitive maps. These birds are known for their ability to return to their home from distant locations. This quality made the birds useful for communication in ancient times and even in the 19th and 20th centuries. Extensive research has been completed on how pigeons form these maps. The left hippocampus plays a pivotal role in map formation. When the left hippocampus is lesioned, pigeons' ability to return to their homes is impaired. However, lesioning just any part of the hippocampus already impairs homing performance (Gagliardo et al., 2001, 2009). The left hippocampus is also crucial for the perception of landmarks within the environment (Bingman et al., 2003).

Other research suggests that the right hippocampus is involved in sensitivity to global features of the environment (e.g., geometry of the space). The hippocampus is involved in the formation of cognitive maps in humans as well (Iaria, 2008; Maguire, Frackowiak, & Frith, 1996).

Humans seem to use three types of knowledge when forming and using cognitive maps:

1. *Landmark* knowledge is information about particular features at a location and which may be based on both imaginal and propositional representations (Thorndyke, 1981).
2. *Route-road* knowledge involves specific pathways for moving from one location to another (Thorndyke & Hayes-Roth, 1982). It may be based on both procedural knowledge and declarative knowledge.
3. *Survey* knowledge involves estimated distances between landmarks, much as they might appear on survey maps (Thorndyke & Hayes-Roth, 1982). It may be represented imaginally or propositionally (e.g., in numerically specified distances).

Thus, people use both an analogical code and a propositional code for imaginal representations such as images of maps (McNamara, Hardy, & Hirtle, 1989; Russell & Ward, 1982).

Rules of Thumb for Using Our Mental Maps: Heuristics

When we use landmark, route-road, and survey knowledge, we sometimes use rules of thumb that influence our estimations of distance. These rules of thumb are cognitive strategies termed **heuristics**. For example, in regard to landmark knowledge, the density of the landmarks sometimes appears to affect our mental image of an area.

■ BELIEVE IT OR NOT

Memory Test? Don't Compete with Chimpanzees!

Can you believe that chimpanzees' working memory for numbers is actually better than that of humans? Japanese researchers taught chimpanzees the numerals from 1 to 9. Then they devised experiments that displayed a number scattered on a touch screen. After a particular time interval, the numbers were replaced by white squares. Then, chimpanzees and human subjects had to touch the white squares in ascending numerical sequence. Young chimpanzees outperformed humans, both in speed and accuracy, suggesting that chimpanzees might actually have what is often called a photographic memory (Inoue & Matsuzawa, 2007).

As the density of intervening landmarks increases, estimates of distances increase correspondingly. Using this rule of thumb distorts people's mental images, however. The more landmarks there are, the larger the distance they estimate (Thorndyke, 1981). It has also been shown that people estimate the distance between two places to be shorter when traveling to a landmark than when traveling to a nonlandmark. That is, if you're traveling from a small town to the major city, the distance may seem smaller to you than when you're traveling from the big city to the small town (Tversky, 2005; Wagner, 2006).

In estimations of distances between particular physical locations (e.g., cities), route-road knowledge appears often to be weighted more heavily than survey knowledge. This is true even when participants form a mental image based on looking at a map (McNamara, Ratcliff, & McKoon, 1984). Consider what happened when participants were asked to indicate whether particular cities had appeared on a map. They showed more rapid response times between names of cities when the two cities were closer together in route-road distance than when the two cities were physically closer together "as the crow flies" (Figure 7.15).

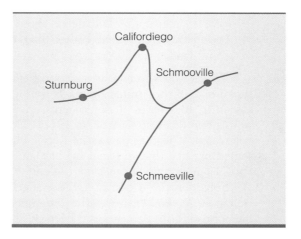

Figure 7.15   Mental Maps.

Which city is closer to Sturnburg, Schmeeville or Schmooville? It appears that our use of cognitive maps often emphasizes the use of route-road knowledge, even when it contradicts survey knowledge.

Source: Based on Timothy R. McNamara, Roger Ratcliff, and Gail McKoon (1984), "The Mental Representation of Knowledge Acquired from Maps," *Journal of Experimental Psychology: LMC, 10*(4), 723–732. Copyright © 1984 by the American Psychological Association.

The use of heuristics in manipulating cognitive maps suggests that propositional knowledge affects imaginal knowledge (Tversky, 1981). This is so at least when people are solving problems and answering questions about images. In some situations, conceptual information seems to distort mental images. In these situations, propositional strategies may better explain people's responses than strategies that are based on a mental image. For example, a study by Friedman and Brown (2000, see also Friedman et al., 2002 and Friedman & Montello, 2006) showed that when participants had to place cities on a map, those cities were clustered according to conceptual information like climate. The distortions seem to reflect a tendency to regularize features of mental maps. Thus, angles, lines, and shapes are represented as more like pure abstract geometric forms than they really are. Here are some examples:

1. *Right-angle bias:* People tend to think of intersections (e.g., street crossings) as forming 90-degree angles more often than the intersections really do (Moar & Bower, 1983; Smith & Cohen, 2008).
2. *Symmetry heuristic:* People tend to think of shapes (e.g., states or countries) as being more symmetrical than they really are (Montello et al., 2004; Tversky & Schiano, 1989).
3. *Rotation heuristic:* When representing figures and boundaries that are slightly slanted (i.e., oblique), people tend to distort the images as being either more vertical or more horizontal than they really are (Tversky, 1981, 1991; Wagner, 2006).
4. *Alignment heuristic:* People tend to represent landmarks and boundaries that are slightly out of alignment by distorting their mental images to be better aligned than they really are (i.e., we distort the way we line up a series of figures or objects; Tversky, 1981, 1991).
5. *Relative-position heuristic:* The relative positions of particular landmarks and boundaries is distorted in mental images in ways that more accurately reflect people's conceptual knowledge about the contexts in which the landmarks and boundaries are located, rather than reflecting the actual spatial configurations (Seizova-Cajic, 2003).

To see how the relative-position heuristic might work, close your eyes and picture a map of the United States. Is Reno, Nevada, west of San Diego, California, or east of it? In a series of experiments, investigators asked participants questions such as this one (Stevens & Coupe, 1978). They found that the large majority of people believe San Diego to be west of Reno. That is, for most of us, our mental map looks something like that in panel (a) of Figure 7.16. Actually, however, Reno is west of San Diego. See the correct map in panel (b) of Figure 7.16.

Some of these heuristics also affect our perception of space and of forms (Chapter 2). For example, the symmetry heuristic seems to be equally strong in memory and in perception (Tversky, 1991). Nonetheless, there are differences between perceptual processes and representational (imaginal or propositional) processes. For example, the relative-position heuristic appears to influence mental representation much more strongly than it does perception (Tversky, 1991).

Semantic or propositional knowledge (or beliefs) can also influence our imaginal representations of world maps (Saarinen, 1987b, see also Louwerse & Zwaan, 2009). Specifically, students from 71 sites in 49 countries were asked to draw a sketch map of the world. Most students (even Asians) drew maps showing a Eurocentric view of

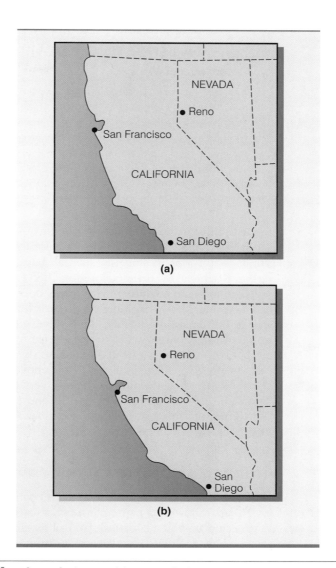

Figure 7.16   The Relative Position Heuristic.

Which of these two maps (a) or (b) more accurately depicts the relative positions of Reno, Nevada, and San Diego, California?

the world. Many Americans drew Americentric views. A few others showed views centered on and highlighting their own countries. (Figure 7.17 shows an Australian-centered view of the world.) In addition, most students showed modest distortions that enlarged the more prominent, well-known countries. They also diminished the sizes of less well-known countries (e.g., in Africa).

Finally, further work suggests that propositional knowledge about semantic categories may affect imaginal representations of maps. In one study, the researchers studied the influence of semantic clustering on estimations of distances (Hirtle & Mascolo, 1986). Hirtle's participants were shown a map of many buildings and then were asked to estimate distances between various pairs of buildings. They

INVESTIGATING COGNITIVE PSYCHOLOGY
Mental Maps

Which is larger in land area, India or Germany? If you are used to seeing the world in terms of the popular Mercator map, in which the map is flat and the equator is in the bottom half of the map, you might think that India and Germany are about the same size. In fact, you might think that Germany may be a bit larger than India.

Now look at a globe of the world. You will see that India is actually about five times as large as Germany. This is an example of how our cognitive maps may be based not in reality, but rather in our exposure to the topic and to our constructions and heuristics.

tended to distort the distances in the direction of guessing shorter distances for more similar landmarks and longer distances for less similar landmarks. Investigators found similar distortions in students' mental maps for the city in which they lived (Ann Arbor, Michigan) (Hirtle & Jonides, 1985).

The work on cognitive maps shows once again how the study of mental imagery can help elucidate our understanding of human adaptation to the environment—that is, of human intelligence. To survive, we need to find our way around the environment in which we live. We need to get from one place to another. Sometimes, to get between places, we need to imagine the route we will need to traverse. Mental imagery provides a key basis for this adaptation. In some societies (Gladwin, 1970), the ability to navigate with the help of very few cues is a life-or-death issue. If sailors cannot do so, they eventually get lost and potentially die of dehydration or starvation. Thus, our imagery abilities are potential keys to our survival and to what makes us intelligent in our everyday lives.

Creating Maps from What You Hear: Text Maps

We have discussed the construction of cognitive maps based on procedural knowledge (e.g., following a particular route, as a rat in a maze), propositional information (e.g., using mental heuristics), and observation of a graphic map. In addition, we may be able to create cognitive maps from a verbal description (Taylor & Tversky, 1992a, 1992b; Tversky, 2005). These cognitive maps may be as accurate as those created from looking at a graphic map. Others have found similar results in studies of text comprehension (Glenberg, Meyer, & Lindem, 1987).

Tversky noted that her research involved having the readers envision themselves in an imaginal setting as participants, not as observers, in the scene. She wondered whether people might create and manipulate images differently when envisioning themselves in different settings. Specifically, Tversky wondered whether propositional information might play a stronger role in mental operations when we think about settings in which we are participants, as compared with settings in which we are observers. As Item 4 in Table 7.3 indicates, the findings regarding cognitive maps suggest that the construction of mental imagery may involve both—processes analogous to perception, and processes relying on propositional representations.

Whether the debate regarding propositions versus imagery can be resolved in the terms in which it traditionally has been presented remains unclear. The various forms of mental representation sometimes are considered to be mutually exclusive. In other

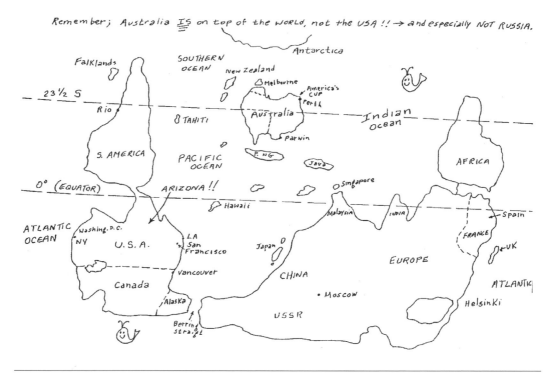

Figure 7.17 **Mental Representation of Maps.**

Based on this Australian student's map, can you infer that this student mentally represents the world in the same way you do?

Source: From Solso, Robert L., *Cognitive Psychology*, Eighth Edition. Published by Allyn and Bacon, Boston, MA. Copyright © 2008 by Pearson Education. Reprinted by permission of the publisher.

words, we think in terms of the question, "Which representation of information is correct?" Often, however, we create false dichotomies. We suggest that alternatives are mutually exclusive, when, in fact, they might be complementary. For example, models postulating mental imagery and those positing propositions can be seen as opposed to each other. However, this opposition is not necessary. Rather, it is in our construction of a relation. People possibly could use both representations. Propositional theorists might like to believe that all representations are fundamentally propositional. Quite possibly, though, both images and propositions are way stations toward some more basic and primitive form of representation in the mind of which we do not yet have any knowledge. A good case can be made in favor of both propositional and imaginal representations of knowledge. Neither is necessarily more basic than the other. The question we presently need to address is when we use which.

✔ CONCEPT CHECK

1. What is a cognitive map?
2. Name some heuristics that people use when manipulating cognitive maps.
3. What is a text map?

Key Themes

This chapter illustrates some of the key themes mentioned in Chapter 1.

Structures versus processes. The debate regarding whether images are phenomenal or epiphenomenal hinges upon what kinds of mental structures are used to process stimuli. For example, when people mentally rotate objects, is the structural representation imaginal or propositional? Either kind of mental representation could generate processes that would enable people to see objects at different angular viewpoints. But the kinds of processes would be different—either mental manipulation of images or mental manipulation of propositions. In order to understand cognition, we need to understand how structures and processes interact.

Validity of causal inferences versus ecological validity. Suppose you wish to hire air-traffic controllers. Can you assess their mental-imagery and spatial-visualization skills using paper-and-pencil tests of manipulation of geometric forms? Or do you need to test them in a setting that is more similar to that of air-traffic control, as through a simulation of the actual job? The paper-and-pencil test probably will yield more precise measurements, but will these measurements be valid? There is no final answer to the question. Researchers are studying this kind of question in order to understand how best to assess people's real-life skills.

Biological and behavioral methods. Early work by Stephen Kosslyn and his collaborators was all behavioral. The researchers investigated how people mentally manipulate various kinds of images. As time went by, the team started using biological techniques, such as fMRI to supplement their behavioral studies. But they never saw the two kinds of research as in opposition to each other. Rather, they viewed them as wholly complementary, and do even today.

Summary

1. **What are some of the major hypotheses regarding how knowledge is represented in the mind?** Knowledge representation comprises the various ways in which our minds create and modify mental structures that stand for what we know about the world outside our minds.

Knowledge representation involves both declarative (knowing that) and nondeclarative (knowing how) forms of knowledge. Through mental imagery, we create analog mental structures that stand for things that are not presently being sensed in the sense organs. Imagery may involve any of the senses, but the form of imagery most commonly reported by laypeople and most commonly studied by cognitive psychologists is visual imagery. Some studies (e.g., studies of blind participants and some studies of the brain) suggest that visual imagery itself may comprise two discrete systems of mental representation: One system involves nonspatial visual attributes, such as color and shape; another involves spatial attributes, such as location, orientation, and size or distance scaling.

According to Paivio's dual-code hypothesis, two discrete mental codes for representing knowledge exist. One code is for images and another for words and other symbols. Images are represented in a form analogous to the form we perceive through our senses. In contrast, words and concepts are encoded in a symbolic form, which is not analogical.

An alternative view of image representation is the propositional hypothesis. It suggests that both images and words are represented in a propositional form. The proposition retains the underlying meaning of either images or words, without any of the perceptual features of either. For example, the acoustic features of the sounds of the words are not stored, nor are the visual features of the colors or shapes of the images. Furthermore, propositional codes, more than imaginal codes, seem to influence mental representation when participants are shown ambiguous or abstract figures. Apparently, unless the context facilitates performance, the use of visual images does not always readily lead to successful performance on some tasks requiring mental manipulations of either abstract figures or ambiguous figures.

2. **What are some of the characteristics of mental imagery?** Based on a modification of the dual-code view, Shepard and others have espoused a functional-equivalence hypothesis. It asserts that images are represented in a form functionally equivalent to percepts, even if the images are not truly identical to percepts. Studies of mental rotations, image scaling, and image scanning suggest that imaginal task performance is functionally equivalent to perceptual task performance. Even performance on some tasks involving comparisons of auditory images seems to be functionally equivalent to performance on tasks involving comparisons of auditory percepts.

Propositional codes seem less likely to influence mental representation than imaginal ones when participants are given an opportunity to create their own mental images. For example, they might do so in tasks involving image sizing or mental combinations of imaginal letters.

Some researchers have suggested that experimenter expectancies may have influenced cognitive studies of imagery, but others have refuted these suggestions. In any case, neuropsychological studies are not subject to such influences. They seem to support the functional-equivalence hypothesis by finding overlapping brain areas involved in visual perception and mental rotation.

3. **How does knowledge representation benefit from both images and propositions?** Kosslyn has synthesized these various hypotheses to suggest that images may involve both analogous and propositional forms of knowledge representation. In this case, both forms influence our mental representation and manipulation of images. Thus, some of what we know about images is represented in a form that is analogous to perception. Other things we know about images are represented in a propositional form. Johnson-Laird has proposed an alternative synthesis. He has suggested that knowledge may be represented as verbally expressible propositions, as somewhat abstracted analogical mental models, or as highly concrete and analogical mental images.

Studies of split-brain patients and patients with lesions indicate some tendency toward hemispheric specialization. Visuospatial information may be processed primarily in the right hemisphere. Linguistic (symbolic) information may be processed primarily in the left hemisphere of right-handed individuals. A case study suggests that spatial imagery also may be processed in a different region of the brain than the regions in which other aspects of visual imagery are processed. Studies of normal participants show that visual-perception tasks seem to involve regions of the brain similar to the regions involved in visual-imagery tasks.

4. **How may conceptual knowledge and expectancies influence the way we use images?** People tend to distort their own mental maps in ways that regularize many features of the maps. For example, they may tend to imagine right angles, symmetrical forms, either vertical or horizontal boundaries (not oblique ones), and well-aligned figures and objects. People also tend to employ distortions of their mental maps in ways that support their propositional knowledge about various landmarks.

They tend to cluster similar landmarks, to segregate dissimilar ones, and to modify relative positions to agree with conceptual knowledge about the landmarks. In addition, people tend to distort their mental maps. They increase their estimates regarding the distances between endpoints as the density of intervening landmarks increases.

Some of the heuristics that affect cognitive maps support the notion that propositional information influences imaginal representations. The influence of propositional information may be particularly potent when participants are not shown a graphic map. Instead, they are asked to read a narrative passage and to envision themselves as participants in a setting described in the narrative.

Thinking about Thinking: Analytical, Creative, and Practical Questions

1. Describe some of the characteristics of pictures versus words as external forms of knowledge representation.
2. What factors might lead a person's mental model to be inaccurate with respect to how radio transmissions lead people to be able to hear music on a radio?
3. In what ways is mental imagery analogous (or functionally equivalent) to perception?
4. In what ways do propositional forms of knowledge representation influence performance on tasks involving mental imagery?
5. What are some strengths and weaknesses of ERP studies?
6. Some people report never experiencing mental imagery, yet they are able to solve mental-rotation problems. How might they solve such problems?
7. What are some practical applications of having two codes for knowledge representation? Give an example applied to your own experiences, such as applications to studying for examinations.
8. Based on the heuristics described in this chapter, what are some of the distortions that may be influencing your cognitive maps for places with which you are familiar (e.g., a college campus or your hometown)?

Key Terms

analog codes, *p. 277*
cognitive maps, *p. 308*
declarative knowledge, *p. 271*
dual-code theory, *p. 277*
functional-equivalence
    hypothesis, *p. 287*

heuristics, *p. 310*
imagery, *p. 276*
knowledge representation, *p. 271*
mental models, *p. 301*
mental rotation, *p. 289*
procedural knowledge, *p. 271*

propositional theory, *p. 281*
spatial cognition, *p. 308*
symbolic representation, *p. 274*

Media Resources

Visit the companion website—**www.cengagebrain.com**—for quizzes, research articles, chapter outlines, and more.

CogLab

Explore CogLab by going to **http://coglab.wadsworth.com**. To learn more, examine the following experiments:

Mental Rotation

Link Word

Mental Scanning

8 CHAPTER

Representation and Organization of Knowledge in Memory: Concepts, Categories, Networks, and Schemas

CHAPTER OUTLINE

Here are some of the questions we will explore in this chapter:

1. How are representations of words and symbols organized in the mind?
2. How do we represent other forms of knowledge in the mind?
3. How does declarative knowledge interact with procedural knowledge?

■ **BELIEVE IT OR NOT**

THERE IS A SAVANT IN ALL OF US

People with autism who have an extraordinary ability have been called autistic savants. Their abilities often leave us incredulous—they can multiply large numbers within a fraction of a second, remember huge amounts of data, or they can recall any detail with their photographic memory. But people who are autistic savants may actually not be that different from us.

Research suggests that we may all possess these talents, but they are part of low-level information processing that we normally do not use because we think at a higher level that is concept-driven and allows for multisensory comparisons. For people who are autistic savants, this low-level processing comes automatic and naturally. Although we usually cannot consciously control our brain activity, studies have shown that people can learn to become sensitive to low-level processing and gain access to those early states of processing that are usually unconscious. This opens new possibilities for behavior and self-awareness (Birbaumer, 1999).

In this chapter we'll learn about how we organize concepts in our minds and how these concepts help us think and to organize what we know.

John and Simon were college roommates and planned a trip to Arizona during spring break. They would be hiking through the remote Spikeleaf Canyon that hardly has been explored, was narrow, and had lots of pools in which the water collects and smooth rock slides that connect the pools. Once they arrived at the canyon, they parked their car and began the hike to the edge, and from there followed a steep path down to the bottom. When they were almost at the bottom of the canyon, Simon suddenly tripped, fell over, and tumbled down the remainder of the steep slope. He was unable to stand up and feared he may have broken his ankle. Simon was in excruciating pain. John could not help him climb back up the narrow path, and because they were in such a remote desert area, they did not have any cell phone reception. John raced back the way they had come, got in the car, and frantically drove about half an hour until his cell phone worked so he could call for help. Eventually, a rescue team arrived at the canyon and carried Simon back up the canyon so he could receive treatment in the nearest hospital.

This story, which sounds just like an adventure story, actually raises a number of questions relevant to cognitive psychology. John was panicked when he had to leave Simon behind and could not call for help immediately, and yet he managed to drive his car although his thoughts were completely elsewhere. How did he do that? Fortunately, his procedural knowledge of how to drive a car was so good that he was able to drive automatically and did not have to concentrate on any details. He also was worried because canyons can get flooded quickly if it rains in a distant area upriver. Such flooding would be very dangerous for his immobile friend. Therefore, John knew that he had to act fast, and he also knew how to make his cell phone work again and which number to call to get help when the phone started working.

Declarative versus Procedural Knowledge

The preceding chapter described how knowledge may be represented in the form of propositions and images. In this chapter, we explore how our knowledge can be organized so we can retrieve it when we need it. We expand this discussion to include various means of organizing declarative knowledge that can be expressed in words and other symbols (i.e., "knowing that"). John knew he had to call 9-1-1, and that to do so he would need to get into an area with cell phone reception. Consider your own knowledge of facts about cognitive psychology, about world history, about your personal history, and about mathematics. Your knowledge in these areas relies on your mental organization of declarative knowledge.

In addition, this chapter describes a few of the models for representing procedural knowledge. This is knowledge about how to follow procedural steps for performing actions (i.e., "knowing how"). For example, your knowledge of how to drive a car, how to write your signature, how to ride a bicycle to the nearest grocery store, and how to catch a ball depends on your mental representation of procedural knowledge. Some theorists even have suggested integrative models for representing both declarative and procedural knowledge.

To get an idea of how declarative and procedural knowledge may interact, get some scrap paper and a pen or pencil. Try the demonstration in *Investigating Cognitive Psychology: Testing Your Declarative and Procedural Knowledge*.

In addition to seeking to understand the *what* (the form or structure) of knowledge representation, cognitive psychologists also try to grasp the *how* (the processes) of knowledge representation and manipulation. Here are some of the questions we explore in this chapter:

- What are some of the general processes by which we select and control the disorganized array of raw data available to us through our sense organs?
- How do we relate that sensory information to the information we have available from internal sources of information (i.e., our memories and our thought processes)?
- How do we organize and reorganize our mental representations during various cognitive processes?

INVESTIGATING COGNITIVE PSYCHOLOGY
Testing Your Declarative and Procedural Knowledge

As quickly and as legibly as possible, write your normal signature, from the first letter of your first name to the last letter of your last name. Don't stop to think about which letters come next. Just write as quickly as possible.

Turn the paper over. As quickly and as legibly as possible, write your signature backward. Start with the last letter of your last name and work toward the first letter of your first name.

Now, compare the two signatures. Which signature was more easily and accurately created?

For both signatures, you had available extensive declarative knowledge of which letters preceded or followed one another. But for the first task, you also could call on procedural knowledge, based on years of knowing how to sign your name.

- Through what mental processes do we operate on the knowledge we have in our minds?
- To what extent are these processes domain general—common to multiple kinds of information, such as verbal and quantitative information?
- Conversely, to what extent are these processes domain specific—used only for particular kinds of information, such as verbal or quantitative information?

Knowledge representation and processing have been investigated by researchers from several disciplines. Among these researchers are cognitive psychologists, neuropsychologists, and computer scientists studying AI (artificial intelligence), which attempts to program machines to perform intelligently. The diverse approaches that researchers take when investigating knowledge representation promote exploration of a wide range of phenomena. They also encourage multiple perspectives of similar phenomena. Finally, they offer the strength of **converging operations**—the use of multiple approaches and techniques to address a problem.

Other than to satisfy their own idle curiosity, why do so many researchers want to understand how knowledge is represented? The way in which knowledge is represented profoundly influences how effectively knowledge can be manipulated for performing any number of cognitive tasks. To illustrate the influence of knowledge representation through a very crude analogy, try the following multiplication task using a representation in either Roman or Arabic numerals:

$$
\begin{array}{ll}
\text{CMLIX} & 959 \\
\underline{\times\,\text{LVIII}} & \underline{\times 58}
\end{array}
$$

The two multiplication tasks are exactly the same, but representation in Roman numerals probably makes it much harder for you to compute the solution, doesn't it?

In this chapter, we first have a closer look at how declarative knowledge (concepts) is organized in our minds. We consider theories of how concepts can be grouped into categories as well as how they can be organized by means of semantic networks and schemas. Then we move on to the representation of procedural knowledge. And finally, we will explore models that try to combine the representation of declarative and procedural knowledge.

Organization of Declarative Knowledge

The fundamental unit of symbolic knowledge (knowledge of correspondence between symbols and their meaning, for example, that the symbol "3" means *three*) is the **concept**—an idea about something that provides a means of understanding the world (Bruner, Goodnow, & Austin, 1956; Kruschke, 2003; Love, 2003). Often, a concept may be captured in a single word, such as *apple*. Each concept in turn relates to other concepts, such as *apple*, which relates to *redness, roundness,* or *fruit*.

As you can imagine, people amass a large number of concepts over the course of their lives. How do they organize all those concepts? One way to organize them is by means of categories. A **category** is a group of items into which different objects or concepts can be placed that belong together because they share some common features, or because they are all similar to a certain prototype. For example, the word *apple* can act as a category, as in a collection of different kinds of apples. But it also can act as a concept within the category *fruit*. In the following sections, we will discuss ways to organize concepts into categories. These ways include the use of defining features, prototypes, and exemplars.

Later, we will explore how concepts can be organized by means of hierarchically organized semantic **networks**, as well as **schemas**, which are mental frameworks of knowledge that encompass a number of interrelated concepts (Bartlett, 1932; Brewer, 1999).

Concepts and Categories

Concepts and categories can be divided in various ways. One commonly used distinction is between natural categories and artifact categories (Kalenine et al., 2009; Medin, Lynch, & Solomon, 2000). **Natural categories** are groupings that occur naturally in the world, like birds or trees. **Artifact categories** are groupings that are designed or invented by humans to serve particular purposes or functions. Examples of artifact categories are automobiles and kitchen appliances. The speed it takes to assign objects to categories seems to be about the same for both natural and artifact categories (VanRullen & Thorpe, 2001). Natural and artifact categories are relatively stable and people tend to agree on criteria for membership in them. A tiger is always a mammal, for example; and a knife is always an implement used for cutting.

Concepts, on the contrary, are not always stable but can change (Dunbar, 2003; Thagard, 2003). Some categories are created just for the moment or for a specific purpose, for example, "things you can write on." These categories are called *ad hoc categories* (Barsalou, 1983; Little, Lewandowsky, & Heit, 2006). They are described not in words but rather in phrases. Their content varies, depending on the context. People in rural Uganda will probably name different things that you can write on than will urban Americans or Inuit Eskimos.

Concepts are also used in other areas like computer science. Developers try to develop algorithms that define "spam" so that email programs can filter out unwanted messages and your mailbox is not flooded with them. However, spammers change the nature of their messages on a regular basis so that it is hard to create an algorithm that can catch all spam messages and can do so on a permanent basis (Fdez-Riverola, 2007).

Concepts appear to have a **basic level** (sometimes termed a natural level) of specificity, a level within a hierarchy that is preferred to other levels (Medin, Proffitt, & Schwartz, 2000; Rosch, 1978). Suppose I show you a red, roundish edible object that has a stem and that came from a tree. You might characterize it as a fruit, an apple, a delicious apple, a Red Delicious apple, and so on. Most people, however, would characterize the object as an apple. The basic, preferred level is *apple*. In general, the basic level is neither the most abstract nor the most specific. Of course, this basic level can be manipulated by context or expertise (Tanaka & Taylor, 1991). Suppose the object were held up at a fruit stand that sold only apples. You might describe it as a Red Delicious apple to distinguish it from the other apples around it.

How can we tell what the basic level is? Why is the basic level the *apple*, rather than *Red Delicious apple* or *fruit*? Or why is it *cow*, rather than *mammal* or *Guernsey*? Perhaps the basic level is the one that has the largest number of distinctive features that set it off from other concepts at the same level (Rosch et al., 1976). Thus, most of us would find more distinguishing features between an apple and a cow, say, than between a Red Delicious apple and a Pippin apple. Similarly, we would find few distinguishing features between a Guernsey cow and a Holstein cow. Again, not everyone necessarily would have the same basic level, as in the case of farmers. For our purposes, the basic level is the one that most people find to be maximally distinctive. By means of training, the basic level can be shifted to a more subordinate level (Scott et al., 2008). For example, the more a person learns about cars, the more he or she is likely to make elaborate distinctions among cars. Research suggests that the differences between experts and novices are not due to qualitatively different mechanisms but rather to quantitative differences in processing efficacy (Palmeri 2004; see also Mack et al., 2009).

When people are shown pictures of objects, they identify the objects at a basic level more quickly than they identify objects at higher or lower levels (Rosch et al., 1976). Objects appear to be recognized first in terms of their basic level. Only afterward are they classified in terms of higher- or lower-level categories. Thus, the picture of the roundish red, edible object from a tree probably first would be identified as an apple. Only then, if necessary, would it be identified as a fruit or a Red Delicious apple.

Now, how do people decide what objects to put into a category? There are several theories that try to explain this process. One theory suggests that we put an object only in one category if it has several defining features. Another approach proposes that we compare an object with an averaged representation (a prototype) to decide whether it fits into a category. Yet another is that people can categorize objects based on their own theories about those objects. We will explore these approaches in the next sections.

Feature-Based Categories: A Defining View

The classic view of categories disassembles a concept into a set of featural components. All those features are then necessary (and sufficient) to define the category (Katz, 1972; Katz & Fodor, 1963). This means that each feature is an essential element of the category. Together, the features uniquely define the category; they are **defining features** (or necessary attributes): For a thing to be an X, it must have that feature. Otherwise, it is not an "X."

Consider the term *bachelor*. In addition to being human, a bachelor can be viewed as comprising three features: *male*, *unmarried*, and *adult*. The features are each singly necessary. If one feature is absent, the object cannot belong to the category. Thus, an unmarried male who is not an adult would not be a bachelor. We would not refer to a 12-year-old unmarried boy as a bachelor, because he is not an adult. Nor would we refer to just any male adult as a bachelor. If he is married, he is out of the running. An unmarried female adult is not a bachelor, either.

Moreover, the three features are jointly sufficient. If a person has all three features, then he is automatically a bachelor. According to this view, you cannot be male, unmarried, and an adult, and at the same time not be a bachelor. The feature-based view applies to more than bachelorhood, of course. For example, the term *wife* is made up of the features *married*, *female*, and *adult*. *Husband* comprises the features *married*, *male*, and *adult*.

The feature-based view is especially common among linguists, those who study language (Clark & Clark, 1977; Finley & Badecker, 2009). This view is attractive because it makes categories appear so orderly and systematic. Unfortunately, it does not work as well as it appears to at first glance. Some categories do not readily lend themselves to featural analysis. *Game* is one such category. Finding anything at all that is a common feature of all games is actually difficult to do (Wittgenstein, 1953). Some are fun; some are not. Some involve multiple players; others, such as solitaire, do not. Some are competitive; others, such as children's circle games (e.g., ring-around-the-rosy), are not. The more you consider the concept of a game, the more you begin to wonder whether there is anything at all that holds the category together. It is not clear that there are any defining features of a game at all. Nonetheless, we all know what we mean, or think we do, by the word *game*.

Another problem with the feature-based view is that a violation of those defining features does not seem to change the category we use to define them. Consider a zebra (see Keil, 1989). Now suppose that someone painted a zebra all black. It would then be missing the critical attribute of stripes, but we still would call it a zebra. We run into the same problem with birds. We might think of the ability to fly as critical to being a bird. But certainly we would agree that a robin whose wings have been clipped is still a robin. So is an ostrich, which does not fly.

The examples of the robin and the ostrich point out another problem with the feature-based theory. Both a robin and an ostrich share the same defining features of birds. They are, therefore, birds. However, loosely speaking, a robin seems somehow to be a better example of a bird than is an ostrich. Indeed, when people are asked to rate the typicality of a robin versus an ostrich as a bird, the robin virtually always will get a higher rating than the latter (Malt & Smith, 1984; Mervis, Catlin, & Rosch, 1976; Rosch, 1975). Children learn typical instances of a category earlier than they learn atypical ones (Rosch, 1978). Table 8.1 shows some ratings of typicality for various instances of birds (Malt & Smith, 1984). Clearly, there are enormous differences, although the defining features are the same. On the 7-point scale used by Malt and Smith for ratings of the typicality of birds, *bat* received a rating of 1.53. This rating is despite the fact that a bat, strictly speaking, is not even a bird at all.

In sum, the feature-based theory has some attractive features, but it does not give a complete account of categories. Some specific examples of a category such as *bird* seem to be better examples than others. Yet, they all have the same defining features. However, the various examples may be differentially typical of the category of birds. Thus, we need a theory of knowledge representation that better characterizes how people truly represent knowledge.

Prototype Theory: A Characteristic View

Prototype theory takes a different approach: grouping things together not by their defining features but rather by their similarity to an averaged model of the category.

Table 8.1 Typicality Ratings for Birds

Barbara Malt and Edward Smith (1984) found enormous differences in the typicality ratings for various instances of birds (or bird-like animals). (After Malt & Smith, 1984.)

Bird	Rating*	Bird	Rating
Robin	6.89	Sandpiper	4.47
Seagull	6.26	Chicken	3.95
Swallow	6.16	Flamingo	3.37
Falcon	5.74	Albatross	3.32
Starling	5.16	Penguin	2.63
Owl	5.00	Bat	1.53

*Ratings were made on a 7-point scale, with 7 corresponding to the highest typicality.

Prototypes and Characteristic Features   A **prototype** is an abstract average of all the objects in the category we have encountered before. It is the prototype that objects are compared with in order to put them into a category. Crucial are **characteristic features**, which describe (characterize or typify) the prototype but are not necessary for it. Characteristic features commonly are present in typical examples of concepts, but they are not always present.

For example, consider the prototype of a game. It might include that it usually is enjoyable, has two or more players, and presents some degree of challenge. But a game does not have to be enjoyable. It does not have to have two or more players. And it does not have to be challenging. Similarly, a bird usually has wings and flies, but the prototype is just whatever game (or bird) represents the category best. This theory can handle the facts that (1) games seem to have no defining features at all and (2) a robin seems to be a better example of a bird than is an ostrich.

So what exactly is a characteristic feature? Whereas a defining feature is shared by every single object in a category, a characteristic feature need not be. Instead, many or most instances possess each characteristic feature. Thus, the ability to fly is typical of birds. But it is not a defining feature of a bird—an ostrich cannot fly. According to prototype theory, it thus seems less bird-like than a robin, which can fly. Similarly, a typical game may be enjoyable, but it need not be so. Indeed, when people are asked to list the features of a category, such as *fruit* or *furniture*, most list features like sweetness or "made out of wood." These features are characteristic rather than defining (Rosch & Mervis, 1975). You actually can compute a score that indicates how typical an instance is of its category by listing the properties typical of a category such as *fruit* and then assess how many of those properties a given instance has (Rosch & Mervis, 1975). This matters in our interactions with other people as well: Stereotypes of different groups of people (say, Italians or psychologists) consist of a conglomerate of average features (Medin, 1989; see also Dolderer et al., 2009).

Classical and Fuzzy Concepts   Psychologists differentiate two kinds of categories: *classical concepts* and *fuzzy concepts*. Classical concepts are categories that can be readily defined through defining features, such as *bachelor*. Fuzzy concepts are categories that cannot be so easily defined, such as *game* or *death*. Their borders are, as their name implies, fuzzy. Classical concepts tend to be inventions that experts have devised for arbitrarily labeling a class that has associated defining features. Fuzzy concepts tend to evolve naturally (Smith, 1988, 1995a; see also Brent et al., 1996). Thus, the concept of a bachelor is an arbitrary concept we invented. Some experts may suggest that we use the word *fruit* to describe any part of a plant that has seeds, pulp, and skin. But our natural, fuzzy concept of fruit usually does not easily extend to tomatoes, pumpkins, and cucumbers.

Classical concepts and categories may be built on defining features. Fuzzy concepts and categories are built around prototypes. According to the prototype view, an object will be classified as belonging to a category if it is sufficiently similar to the prototype. Exactly what is meant by similarity to a prototype can be a complex issue, however. There are actually different theories of how this similarity should be measured (Smith & Medin, 1981). For our purposes, we view similarity in terms of the number of features shared between an object and the prototype. Perhaps some features even should be weighed more heavily as being more central to the prototype than are other features (e.g., Komatsu, 1992).

Real-World Examples: Using Exemplars   Some psychologists suggest that instead of using a single abstract prototype for categorizing a concept, we use multiple, specific exemplars. **Exemplars** are typical representatives of a category (Ross, 2000; Ross & Spalding, 1994). For example, in considering birds, we might think not only of the prototypical songbird, which is small, flies, builds nests, sings, and so on. We also might think of exemplars for birds of prey, for large flightless birds, for medium-sized waterfowl, and so on. Some investigators use this approach in explaining how categories are both formed and used in speeded classification situations (Nosofsky & Palmeri, 1997; Nosofsky, Palmeri, & McKinley, 1994; see also Estes, 1994). In particular, categories are set up by creating a rule and then by storing examples as exemplars. Objects are then compared to the exemplars to decide whether or not they belong in the category the exemplars represent.

Exemplar theories of categorization have also been criticized. One notable criticism questions the number and types of exemplars that are stored for each category (Smith, 2005). Some theorists contend that there are not enough resources within the mind to store all the exemplars one would need to typify membership in a category (Collier, 2005).

A recent theory called VAM (varying abstraction model) suggests that prototypes and exemplars are just the two extremes on a continuum of abstraction. According to this theory, most of the time we use not just one abstract prototype nor a large number of concrete exemplars for categorization. Rather, we use a number of intermediate representations that represent subgroups within the category (Vanpaemel & Storms, 2008). For example, animals might be represented by specific exemplars of kinds of animals, such as finch or sparrow or whale, but also by higher-order categories, such as songbird or marine mammal.

Some researchers support neither an exclusive exemplar theory nor an exclusive rule-based theory (Rouder & Ratcliff, 2004, 2006). Rather, some combination of the two is thought to be more appropriate. This idea is discussed in the next section.

A Synthesis: Combining Feature-Based and Prototype Theories

A full theory of categorization can combine both defining and characteristic features (see also Hampton, 1997a; Poitrenaud et al., 2005; Smith et al., 1974, 1988; Wisniewski, 1997, 2000), so that each category has both a prototype and a core. A **core** refers to the defining features something must have to be considered an example of a category. The prototype encompasses the characteristic features that tend to be typical of an example (a bird can fly) but that are not necessary for being considered an example (an ostrich).

Consider the concept of a robber. The core requires that someone labeled as a robber be a person who takes things from others without permission. The prototype, however, tends to identify particular people as more likely to be robbers. Take, for example, white-collar criminals. Their crimes can include embezzling millions of dollars from their employers. These criminals are difficult to catch because they do not look like our prototypes of robbers, no matter how much they may steal from other people. In contrast, unkempt denizens of our inner cities sometimes are arrested for crimes they did not commit. In part, the reason is that they more closely match the commonly held prototype of a robber, regardless of whether or not they steal.

Two researchers tested the notion that we come to understand the importance of defining features only as we grow older (Keil & Batterman, 1984). Younger children, they hypothesized, view categories largely in terms of characteristic features.

The investigators presented children in the age range from 5 to 10 years with descriptions. Among them were two unusual individuals. The first was "a smelly, mean old man with a gun in his pocket who came to your house and took your TV set because your parents didn't want it anymore and told him he could have it." The second was "a very friendly and cheerful woman who gave you a hug, but then disconnected your toilet bowl and took it away without permission and with no intention to return it." Younger children often characterized the first description as a better depiction of a robber than the second description. It was not until close to age 10 that children began to shift toward characterizing the second individual as more robber-like. In other words, the younger children viewed someone as a robber even if the person did not steal anything. What mattered was that the person had the characteristic features of a robber. However, the transition is never fully complete. We might suspect that the first individual would be at least as likely to be arrested as the second. Thus, the issue of categorization itself remains somewhat fuzzy, but it appears to include some aspects of defining features and some aspects of prototypicality.

■ BELIEVE IT OR NOT

SOME NUMBERS ARE ODD, AND SOME ARE ODDER

Even classical concepts like that of an *odd number* seem to have prototypes (Armstrong, Gleitman, & Gleitman, 1983). The concept of an odd number is defined easily: An *odd number* is any integer not evenly divisible by 2. So how could one number be odder than another? People found different instances of this category to be more or less prototypical of odd numbers. For example, 7 and 13 are typical examples of odd numbers that are viewed as quite close to the prototype for an odd number. In contrast, 15 and 21 are not seen as so prototypically odd. In other words, people view 7 and 13 as better exemplars of odd numbers than 15 and 21. Nevertheless, all four numbers are actually odd.

Theory-Based View of Categorization

A departure from feature-based, prototype-based, and exemplar-based views of meaning is a theory-based view of meaning, also sometimes called an explanation-based view.

How Do People Use Their Theories for Categorization? A **theory-based view of meaning** holds that people understand and categorize concepts in terms of implicit theories, or general ideas they have regarding those concepts (Markman, 2003, 2007). For example, what makes someone a "good sport"?

- In the *componential view*, you would try to isolate features of a good sport.
- In the *prototype view*, you would try to find characteristic features of a good sport.
- In the *exemplar view*, you might try to find some good examples you have known in your life.
- In the *theory-based view*, you would use your experience to construct an explanation for what makes someone a good sport.

The theory-based view might go something like this: A good sport is someone who, when he or she wins, is gracious in victory and does not mock losers or otherwise make them feel bad about losing. It is also someone who, when he or she loses, loses graciously and does not blame the winner, the referee, or find excuses. Rather, he or she takes the defeat in stride, congratulates the winner, and then moves on. Note that in the theory-based view, it is difficult to capture the essence of the theory in a word or two. Rather, the view of a concept is more complex.

The theory-based view suggests that people can distinguish between essential and incidental, or accidental, features of concepts because they have complex mental representations of these concepts. One study showed how such theories might manifest themselves in judgments about newly learned concepts (Rips, 1989). Participants received stories about a hypothetical creature. The stimuli were presented under two experimental conditions.

In this study (Rips, 1989), one condition involved a bird-like creature called a sorp that, through an accident, came to look like an insect. It was never stated that the sorp was bird-like or insect-like. Rather, the circumstances of the transformation were described in some detail. The sorp was described as having a diet consisting of seeds and berries, as having two wings and two legs, and as nesting high in the branches of a tree. The nest, like that of a bird, was composed of twigs and similar materials. Moreover, the sorp was covered with bluish-gray feathers, like many birds. But a particular sorp had a misfortune: Its nest was near the burial place of hazardous chemicals. As the chemicals contaminated the vegetation that the sorp ate, its appearance gradually started to change. The sorp lost its feathers and instead grew a new pair of wings that had a transparent membrane. The sorp left its nest and developed an outer shell that was brittle and iridescent. It grew two more pairs of legs, so that it now had six legs in all. It came to be able to hold on to smooth surfaces, and it started sustaining itself solely on the nectar of flowers. In due course, the sorp mated with another sorp, a normal female. The female laid the fertilized eggs that resulted from the mating in her nest and incubated them. After three weeks, normal young sorps emerged from their shells. Note that in this description, the fact of the sorp's being able to mate with a normal sorp to produce normal sorps shows that the unfortunate sorp never really changed its basic biological makeup. It remained, in essence, a sorp.

The second condition involved an essential change in the nature of a creature. In other words, the change was one of essence rather than of accident and involved a creature known as a doon. During an early stage of the doon's life, it is known as a sorp. It has all the characteristics of a sorp (as previously described). But after a few months, the doon sheds its feathers and then develops the same characteristics that resulted from the unfortunate sorp's accident. Note that in this second condition there is a transformation identical to that of the sorp described in the first condition, but the transformation is represented as a natural biological change rather than an accidental one caused by proximity to hazardous chemicals.

Participants in the study were asked to provide two ratings after reading about the sorp and the doon. The first rating was of the degree to which the sorp (in the sorp condition) or the doon (in the doon condition) fit into the category of "bird." The second rating was the similarity of the sorp or doon to birds. Thus, one rating was for category membership and the other for similarity.

There was also a control group whose members read only the description of sorps. Control group participants were asked merely to rate the similarity of sorps to birds. They did not have to judge how well sorps fit into the category of "bird."

According to prototype and exemplar theories, there is no particular reason to expect the two sets of ratings from experimental participants to show different patterns. According to these theories, people categorize objects on the basis of their

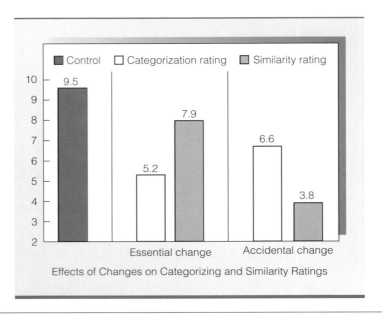

Figure 8.1   Similarity Ratings.

Control group participants clearly thought sorps are very similar to birds. When the sorp's features changed through an accident, the sorp was still rated relatively highly as belonging to the category of birds although its rating for similarity to birds was low. When the sorp transformed through a natural process, however, its rating for belonging to the category of birds went down although it was judged as being quite similar to birds.

Source: From L. J. Rips, "Similarity, Typicality, and Categorization," in Vosniadou & Ortony (Eds.), *Similarity and Analogical Reasoning,* pp. 21–59. Copyright © 1989 Cambridge University Press.

similarity to a prototype or an exemplar, so the results should be the same for both sets of ratings.

Now have a look at the results in Figure 8.1. The results for the categorization and similarity ratings are dramatically different! When the sorp's features changed through an accident, it was still rated highly as belonging to the category of birds, although participants did not perceive them as very similar to birds. However, when the doon changed through a natural process, it was rated less highly as belonging to the category of birds although it seemed relatively similar to birds.

Control group participants had no trouble recognizing the similarity of the sorp to a bird. The difference in patterns between the category-membership and similarity ratings is consistent with the theory-based view of meaning.

Finding the "Essence" of Things   Further support for the theory-based view comes from work with children. A number of investigators have studied a view of meaning called *essentialism*. This view holds that certain categories, such as those of "lion" or "female," have an underlying reality that cannot be observed directly (Gelman, 2003, 2004). For example, someone could be a female even if another individual were incapable in his or her observations on the street of detecting that femaleness. One instance is having short hair. Having short hair might be more typical of males than females, yet females can have short hair. Essentialist beliefs about the characteristics of groups are often associated with the devaluation of these groups and increased prejudice (Bastian & Haslam, 2006; Morton et al., 2009). These beliefs suggest that members of a particular group are intrinsically one way and can't change; therefore, they cannot ever really belong to another group.

Gelman (2004, 2009) showed that even young children look beyond obvious features to understand the essential nature of things. This view contradicts Piaget's theory of cognitive development. According to that theory, children in the age range from roughly 8 to 11 years are "concrete" thinkers. They cannot abstract features that are formal in nature. Yet, the work of psychologists studying essentialism suggest that young children can and do look for hidden features that are not obvious.

For example, in one study, 165 children ages 4 to 5 years were asked to make inferences about things like a tiger or gold (Gelman & Markman, 1986). The researchers found that even by age 4, children could make inferences using the abstract categories as opposed merely to perceptual similarity, even when these categories conflicted with appearances.

How people learn about concepts and categories depends, in part, on the tasks they need to do with those concepts and categories. For example, people learn about categories one way if they need to make classifications (e.g., "Is this particular animal a cat or a dog?") and another way if they need to make inferences (e.g., "If this animal is a dog, how many toes will it have?") (Yamauchi & Markman, 1998). Learning, therefore, is strategically flexible, depending on the task that the individual will have to do; it does not occur with a "one-size-fits-all" rigidity (Markman & Ross, 2003; Ross, 1997).

What all this means is that meaning is not just a matter of a set of features or exemplars. From the time children are very young, they start to form theories about the nature of objects. These theories develop with age. For example, you probably have a theory about what makes a car a car. You could see cars looking all kinds of strange ways. As long as they conformed to your theory, you nevertheless would label them as cars. Theories enable us to view meaning deeply rather than just to assign meaning on the basis of superficial features of objects.

Intelligence and Concepts in Different Cultures

Culture influences many cognitive processes, including intelligence (Lehman, Chiu, & Schaller, 2004). As a result, individuals in different cultures may construct concepts in quite different ways, rendering results of concept-formation or identification studies in a single culture suspect (Atran, 1999; Coley et al., 1999; Medin & Atran, 1999). Thus, groups may think about what appears superficially to be the same phenomenon—whether a concept or the taking of a test—differently. What appear to be differences in general intelligence may in fact be differences in cultural properties (Helms-Lorenz, Van de Vijver, & Poortinga, 2003). Helms-Lorenz and colleagues (2003) have argued that measured differences in intellectual performance may result from differences in cultural complexity; but complexity of a culture is extremely hard to define, and what appears to be simple or complex from the point of view of one culture may appear different from the point of view of another.

People in different cultures may have quite different ideas of what it means to be smart. For example, one of the more interesting cross-cultural studies of intelligence was performed by Michael Cole and his colleagues (Cole et al., 1971). These investigators asked adult members of the Kpelle tribe in Africa to sort terms representing concepts. Consider what happens in Western culture when adults are given a sorting task on an intelligence test. More intelligent people typically will sort hierarchically. For example, they may sort names of different kinds of fish together. Then they place the word *fish* over that. They place the name *animal* over *fish* and over *birds*, and so on. Less intelligent people will typically sort functionally. For example, they may sort *fish* with *eat*. Why? Because we eat fish. Or they may sort *clothes* with *wear* because we wear clothes. The Kpelle sorted functionally. They did so even after investigators unsuccessfully tried to get the Kpelle spontaneously to sort hierarchically.

Finally, in desperation, one of the experimenters (Glick) asked a Kpelle to sort as a foolish person would sort. In response, the Kpelle quickly and easily sorted hierarchically. The Kpelle were able to sort this way all along. They just had not done it because they viewed it as foolish. They probably also considered the questioners rather unintelligent for asking such stupid questions.

The Kpelle people are not the only ones who might question Western understandings of intelligence. In the Puluwat culture of the Pacific Ocean, for example, sailors navigate incredibly long distances. They use none of the navigational aids that sailors from technologically advanced countries would need to get from one place to another (Gladwin, 1970). Suppose Puluwat sailors were to devise intelligence tests for us and our fellow Americans. We and our compatriots might not seem very intelligent. Similarly, the highly skilled Puluwat sailors might not do well on American-crafted tests of intelligence. These and other observations have prompted quite a few theoreticians to recognize the importance of considering cultural context when intelligence is assessed.

Semantic-Network Models

Semantic-network models suggest that knowledge is represented in our minds in the form of concepts that are connected with each other in a web-like form. In the following, we consider a model developed by Collins and Quillian (1969) as well as another model that is based on a comparison of semantic features.

Collins and Quillian's Network Model

An older model still in use today is that knowledge is represented in terms of a hierarchical semantic (related to meaning as expressed in language—i.e., in linguistic symbols) network. A semantic network is a web of elements of meaning (nodes) that are connected with each other through links (Collins & Quillian, 1969). Organized knowledge representation takes the form of a hierarchical tree diagram. The elements are called **nodes**; they are typically concepts. The connections between the nodes are *labeled relationships*. They might indicate category membership (e.g., an "is a" relationship connecting "pig" to "mammal"), attributes (e.g., connecting "furry" to "mammal"), or some other semantic relationship. Thus, a network provides a means for organizing concepts. The exact form of a semantic network differs from one theory to another, but most networks look something like the highly simplified network shown in Figure 8.2. The labeled relationships form links that enable the individual to connect the various nodes in a meaningful way.

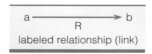

Figure 8.2 Structure of a Semantic Network.

In a simple semantic network, nodes serve as junctures representing concepts linked by labeled relationships: a basic network structure showing that relationship R links the nodes a and b.

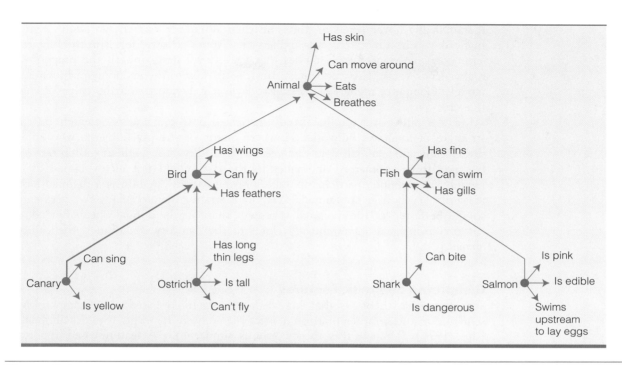

Figure 8.3 **Hierarchical Structure of a Semantic Network.**

A semantic network has a hierarchical structure. The concepts (represented through the nodes) are connected by means of relationships (arrows) like "is" or "has."

Source: From *In Search of the Human Mind*, by Robert J. Sternberg. Copyright © 1995 by Harcourt Brace & Company. Reproduced by permission of the publisher.

In a seminal study, the participants were given statements relating concepts, such as "A shark is a fish" and "A shark is an animal" (Collins & Quillian, 1969). They were asked to verify the truth of the statements. Some were true; others were not. As the object to be classified became more hierarchically remote from the category named in the statement, people generally took longer to verify a true statement. Thus, we could expect people to take longer to verify "A shark is an animal" than "A shark is a fish." The reason is that *fish* is an immediate superordinate category for *shark*. *Animal*, however, is a more remote superordinate category (see Figure 8.3). Collins and Quillian concluded that a hierarchical network representation, such as the one shown in Figure 8.3, adequately accounted for the response times in their study.

A hierarchical model seemed ideal to the investigators. Within a hierarchy, we can efficiently store information that applies to all members of a category at the highest possible level in the hierarchy. We do not have to repeat the information at all of the lower levels in the hierarchy. Therefore, a hierarchical model provides a high degree of cognitive economy. The system allows for maximally efficient capacity use with a minimum of redundancy. Thus, if you know that dogs and cats are mammals, you store everything you know about mammals at the mammal level. For example, you might store that mammals have fur and give birth to live young whom they nurse. You do not have to repeat that information again at the hierarchically lower level for dogs and cats. Whatever was known about items at higher levels in a hierarchy was applied to all items at lower levels in the hierarchy. This concept of *inheritance* implies that lower-level items inherit the properties of higher-level items. This concept, in turn, is the key to the economy of hierarchical models. Computer models of the network clearly demonstrated the value of cognitive economy.

The Collins and Quillian study instigated a whole line of research into the structure of semantic networks. However, many of the psychologists who studied the Collins and Quillian data disagreed with Collins and Quillian's interpretations. For one thing, numerous anomalies in the data could not be explained by the model. For example, participants take longer to verify "A lion is a mammal" than to verify "A lion is an animal." Yet, in a strictly hierarchical view, verification should be faster for the mammal statement than for the animal one. After all, the category *mammal* is hierarchically closer to the category *lion* than is the category *animal*.

Comparing Semantic Features

An alternative theory is that knowledge is organized based on a comparison of semantic features, rather than on a strict hierarchy of concepts (Smith, Shoben, & Rips, 1974). Though this theory sounds similar to the feature-based theory of categorization, it differs from it in a key way: Features of different concepts are compared directly, rather than serving as the basis for forming a category. Consider the categorization of different mammals. In the feature-based theory, each mammal would be described by its own set of defining features—a rabbit might be defined by its fur, long ears, hopping walk, etc. If features are compared directly, then you would compare all mammals on the basis of the same set of features. How does this work?

Let's stick with the mammal example. Mammal names can be represented in terms of a psychological space organized by three features: size, ferocity, and humanness (Henley, 1969). A lion, for example, would be high in all three. An elephant would be particularly high in size but not so high in ferocity. A rat would be small in size but relatively high in ferocity. Figure 8.4 shows how information might be organized within a nonhierarchical feature-based theory. Note that this representation, too, leaves a number of questions unanswered. For example, how does the word *mammal* itself fit in? It does not seem to fit into the space of mammal names. Where would other kinds of objects fit?

Neither of the preceding two theories of representation completely specifies how all information might be organized in a semantic network. For example, how are parts of a whole represented in the network? Perhaps some kind of combination of representations is used (e.g., Collins & Loftus, 1975). Other network models tend to emphasize mental relationships that we think about more frequently rather than just any hierarchical relationships. For example, they might emphasize the link between birds and robins or sparrows or the link between birds and flying. They would not emphasize the link between birds and turkeys or penguins or the link between birds and standing on two legs.

A common method for examining semantic networks involves the use of word-stem completion. In this task, participants are presented a prime for a very short amount of time and then given the first few letters of a word and told to complete the stem with the first word that comes to mind. The stems could be completed with

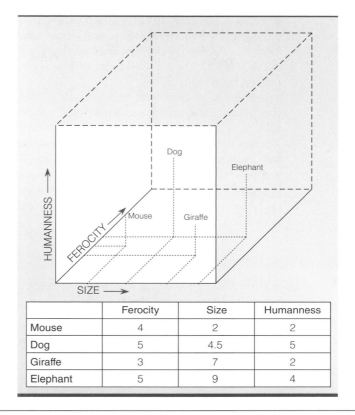

	Ferocity	Size	Humanness
Mouse	4	2	2
Dog	5	4.5	5
Giraffe	3	7	2
Elephant	5	9	4

Figure 8.4   Comparison of Semantic Features.

One alternative to hierarchical network models of semantic memory involves representations highlighting the comparison of semantic features. The features model, too, fails to explain all the data regarding semantic memory.

a semantically related word or any number of unrelated words. Normally, participants complete these stems with a semantically related item. For example, complete the following word:

s _ _ m

How did you complete it? Many people, after reading this paragraph, would complete it with "stem." But there are many other possibilities that were not primed, such as "spam," "slim," and "slum," and "sham," to name a few.

These findings are taken to mean that the activation of one node of the network increases the activation of related nodes. One study noted that, with the progression of Alzheimer's disease, the activation of related nodes is impaired. As a result, the word stems for patients with Alzheimer's disease more frequently are completed with words that are unrelated to the prime (Passafiume, Di Giacomo, & Carolei, 2006).

Semantic networks were also explored with the patient H. M. (see Chapter 5 for information on H. M). As you may recall, H. M.'s hippocampus was lesioned as a treatment for epilepsy. A side effect of this treatment was a great loss in the ability to form new memories. However, H. M. was capable of learning at least some new semantic information. Although performance on semantic tasks was impaired in H. M., clearly there was some semantic learning (O'Kane, Kensinger, & Corkin, 2004). These findings indicate that, although semantic learning can occur without the involvement of the hippocampus, such learning is greatly improved by its use.

We may broaden our understanding of concepts further if we consider not only the hierarchical and basic levels of a concept (Komatsu, 1992). We also should take into account other relational information the concept contains. Specifically, we may better understand the ways in which we derive meanings from concepts by considering their relations with other concepts, as well as the relations among attributes contained within a concept. For example, new multimedia learning and instruction devices that are based on semantic network models and use tools like mind-mapping can indeed increase knowledge acquisition (Zumbach, 2009).

Schematic Representations

Another way to organize the many concepts we have in our minds is by means of schemas. First we will discuss schemas in general and then have a look at scripts, which are a particular kind of schema.

Schemas

One main approach to understanding how concepts are related in the mind is through schemas. They are very similar to semantic networks, except that schemas are often more task-oriented. Recall that a schema is a mental framework for organizing knowledge. It creates a meaningful structure of related concepts. For example, we might have a schema for a kitchen that tells us the kinds of things one might find in a kitchen and where we might find them. Of course, both concepts and schemas may be viewed at many levels of analysis. It all depends on the mind of the individual and the context (Barsalou, 2000). Imagine your mother has a bad backache and you offer to give her a *massage*. Massage to you may mean rubbing her back and perhaps kneading her shoulders. For a massage therapist, *massage* may encompass much more. He distinguishes different muscles and tendons in the back and recognizes that a backache may also be related to a condition in the hips or elsewhere in the body. Thus, he targets his treatment much more specifically. Similarly, most people do not have an elaborate schema for *cognitive psychology*. However, for most cognitive psychologists, the schema for *cognitive psychology* is richly elaborated. It encompasses many subschemas, such as subschemas for attention, memory, and perception.

Schemas have several characteristics that ensure wide flexibility in their use (Rumelhart & Ortony, 1977; Thorndyke, 1984):

1. Schemas can include other schemas. For example, a schema for animals includes a schema for cows, a schema for apes, and so on.
2. Schemas encompass typical, general facts that can vary slightly from one specific instance to another. For example, although the schema for mammals includes a general fact that mammals typically have fur, it allows for humans, who are less hairy than most other mammals. It also allows for porcupines, which seem more prickly than furry, and for marine mammals like whales that have just a few bristly hairs.

3. Schemas can vary in their degree of abstraction. For example, a schema for *justice* is much more abstract than a schema for *apple* or even a schema for *fruit*.

Schemas also can include information about relationships (Komatsu, 1992). Some of this information includes relationships among the following:

- concepts (e.g., the link between trucks and cars);
- attributes within concepts (e.g., the height and the weight of an elephant);
- attributes in related concepts (e.g., the redness of a cherry and the redness of an apple);
- concepts and particular contexts (e.g., fish and the ocean); and
- specific concepts and general background knowledge (e.g., concepts about particular U.S. presidents and general knowledge about the U.S. government and about U.S. history).

Relationships within schemas that particularly interest cognitive psychologists are causal ("if-then") relationships. For example, consider our schema for *glass*. It probably specifies that if an object made of glass falls onto a hard surface, the object may break. Schemas also include information that we can use as a basis for drawing inferences in novel situations. For instance, suppose that a 75-year-old woman, a 45-year-old man, a 30-year-old nun, and a 25-year-old woman are sitting on park benches surrounding a playground. A young child falls from some playground equipment. He calls out "Mama!" To whom is the child calling? Chances are that, to determine your answer, you would be able to draw an inference by calling on various schemas. They would include ones for mothers, for men and women, for people of various ages, and even for people who join religious orders.

Researchers interested in artificial intelligence (AI) have adapted the notion of schemas to fit various computer models of human intelligence. These researchers devised computer models of how knowledge is represented and used. Schemas can be used, for example, when conducting searches in large and complex databases or to integrate masses of information (Do & Rahm, 2007; Fagin et al., 2009).

A problem with schemas is that they can give rise to stereotypes. For example, we might have a schema for the kind of person we believe was responsible for the destruction of the World Trade Center on September 11, 2001. This schema can easily generate a stereotype of certain groups of people as likely terrorists. For example, if you associate a certain type of clothing or a particular belief system with the terrorists, you may easily associate other people with the group of perpetrators just because they happen to wear the same kind of clothing or share some of the beliefs of the terrorists.

Scripts

One particular kind of schema is a script (Schank & Abelson, 1977). A **script** contains information about the particular order in which things occur. In general, scripts are much less flexible than schemas. However, scripts include default values for the actors, the props, the setting, and the sequence of events expected to occur. These values taken together compose an overview of an event.

Think about a restaurant script. The script may be applied to one particular kind of restaurant—for example, a coffee shop. A script has several features:

- *props*: tables, a menu, food, a check, and money
- *roles* to be played: a customer, a waiter, a cook, a cashier, and an owner

- *opening conditions* for the script: the customer is hungry, and he or she has money
- *scenes*: entering, ordering, eating, and exiting
- a set of *results*: the customer has less money; the owner has more money; the customer is no longer hungry; and sometimes the customer and the owner are pleased.

Various empirical studies have been conducted to test the validity of the script notion. In one, researchers presented their participants with 18 brief stories (Bower, Black, & Turner, 1979). You can read one of these, representing the doctor's office script, in *Investigating Cognitive Psychology: Scripts—The Doctor*.

In the research, participants were asked to read 18 stories similar to the one in the *Investigating Cognitive Psychology* box. Later, they were asked to perform one of two tasks. In a recall task, participants were asked to recall as much as they could about each of the stories. Here, participants showed a significant tendency to recall, as parts of the stories, elements that were not actually in the stories but that were parts of the scripts that the stories represented. In the recognition task, participants were presented with sentences. They were asked to rate, on a 7-point scale, their confidence that they had seen each of the sentences. Some of the sentences were from the stories, others were not. Of the sentences that were *not* from the stories, some were from the relevant scripts, and others were not from these scripts. Participants were more likely to characterize particular non-story sentences as having come from the stories if the non-story sentences were script-relevant than if the non-story sentences were not script relevant. The Bower, Black, and Turner research suggested that scripts seem to guide what people recall and recognize—ultimately, what people know.

In a related context, scripts also may come into play in regard to the ways in which experts converse with and write for one another. Certainly, experts share a **jargon**—specialized vocabulary commonly used within a group, such as a profession or a trade. You may overhear psychologists engrossed in a discussion about priming effects, but a layperson likely will not understand what they are talking about exactly.

 INVESTIGATING COGNITIVE PSYCHOLOGY
Scripts—The Doctor

John was feeling bad today and decided to go see the family doctor. He checked in with the doctor's receptionist and then looked through several medical magazines that were on the table by his chair. Finally, the nurse came and asked John to take off his clothes. The doctor was very nice to him. He eventually prescribed some pills for John. Then John left the doctor's office and headed home.

Did John take off his clothes?

This "scripted" description of a visit to a doctor's office is fairly typical. Notice that in this description, as would probably happen in any verbal description of a script, some details are missing. The speaker (or scriptwriter, in this case) may have omitted mentioning these details. Thus, we do not know for sure that John actually took off his clothes. Moreover, the nurse probably beckoned John at some point. She or he then escorted John to an examination room and probably took John's temperature and his blood pressure and weighed him. The doctor probably asked John to describe his symptoms, and so on. But we do not know any of these things for sure.

In addition, however, experts share a common understanding of scripts that are known by insiders to the field of expertise. For example, after reading Chapter 3, you have a basic understanding of positron emission tomography (PET) methods. Therefore, when someone mentions that a PET scan was used to examine the brain, you have an idea of what happened. People outside the area of expertise do not share this understanding. In the PET example, a person who has never read or learned about PETs might know that the result was an image of the brain but would not know that the procedure involved the injection of a slightly radioactive form of oxygen. When trying to understand technical manuals and technical conversations outside your own area of expertise, you may run into vocabulary difficulties and information gaps. You lack the proper script for interpreting the language being spoken.

Imaging studies reveal that the frontal and parietal lobes are involved in the generation of scripts (Godbout et al., 2004). The generation of scripts requires a great deal of working memory. Further script generation involves the use of both temporal and spatial information.

A number of patient populations experience impaired script use. For instance, people with schizophrenia frequently have trouble recalling and sequencing scripts. Also, these people add events to a script that should not be included. Research indicates a relationship between difficulties with script processing and the positive symptoms of schizophrenia (like hallucinations and illusions) on the one hand, and dysfunction of the frontal lobes, on the other hand (Matsui et al., 2006). People with attention deficit hyperactivity disorder (ADHD), people with autistic-spectrum disorders, and even people who are aging normally also may experience problems with scripts and may have trouble recalling the proper sequence of the steps involved in scripts (Allain et al., 2007; Braun et al., 2004; Loth et al., 2008). Again, the frontal lobes seem to play a central role in script generation and use.

The *typicality effect* is an interesting effect in script learning. In general, when a person is learning a script, if both typical and atypical actions are provided, the atypical information will be recalled more readily. This difference is likely due to the increased effort in processing required for atypical information as compared with typical information. When someone suffers from a closed-head injury, like a strong blow

PRACTICAL APPLICATIONS OF COGNITIVE PSYCHOLOGY

SCRIPTS IN YOUR EVERYDAY LIFE

Take a closer look at the scripts you use in your everyday life. Is your going-to-class script different from your going-to-meals script or other scripted activities? In what ways do your scripts differ—in structure or in details? Try making changes to your script, either in details or in structure and see how things work. For example, you may find that you rush in the morning to get to school or work and forget things or arrive late. Aside from the obvious adjustment of getting up earlier, analyze the structure of your script. See if you can combine or remove steps. You could try laying out your clothes and packing your backpack or briefcase the night before to simplify your morning routine. The bottom line? The best way to make your scripts work better for you is first to analyze what they are and then to correct them.

Are the scripts in your life always useful, or are there some that interfere with your getting things done?

to the head, the typicality effect disappears (Vakil et al., 2002). In other words, people then have roughly equal recall of typical and atypical information.

The script model has helped cognitive psychologists gain insight into knowledge organization. Scripts enable us to use a mental framework for acting in certain situations when we must fill in apparent gaps within a given context. Without access to mental scripts, we probably would be at a loss the first time we entered a new restaurant or a new doctor's office. Imagine what it would be like if the nurse at the doctor's office had to explain each step to you. When everyone in a given situation follows a similar script, the day flows much more smoothly.

Whether we subscribe to the notion of categories, semantic networks, or schemas, the important issue is that knowledge is organized. These forms of organization can serve different purposes. The most adaptive and flexible use of knowledge would allow us to use any form of organization, depending on the situation. We need some means to define aspects of the situation, to relate these concepts to other concepts and categories, and to select the appropriate course of action, given the situation. Next, we discuss theories about how the mind represents procedural knowledge.

✔ CONCEPT CHECK

1. What is a concept?
2. What is a category?
3. What is the difference between prototypes and examplars?
4. What is the theory-based view of meaning?
5. What are the components of a semantic network?
6. What is a schema?
7. Why do we need scripts?

Representations of How We Do Things: Procedural Knowledge

Some of the earliest models for representing procedural knowledge (how we do things) come from AI and computer-simulation research (see Chapter 1). Through these models, researchers try to get computers to perform tasks intelligently, particularly in ways that simulate intelligent performance of humans. In fact, cognitive psychologists have learned a great deal about representing and using procedural knowledge. They have had to because of the distinctive problems posed in getting computers to implement procedures based on a series of instructions compiled in programs. Through trial-and-error attempts at getting computers to simulate intelligent cognitive processes, cognitive psychologists have come to understand some of the complexities of human information processing. The next section will describe how psychologists believe procedural knowledge "works." Afterwards, we will have a look at some research on the brain and how it influenced theories and models.

The "Production" of Procedural Knowledge

Procedural knowledge representation is acquired through practicing the implementation of a procedure. It is not merely a result of reading, hearing, or otherwise acquiring information from explicit instructions. Once a mental representation of nondeclarative knowledge is constructed (proceduralization is complete), that knowledge is implicit. It is hard to make explicit by trying to put it in words. In fact, practice tends actually to decrease explicit access to that knowledge. For example, suppose you recently have learned how to drive a standard-shift car. You may find it easier to describe how to do so than someone who learned that skill long ago. As your explicit access to nondeclarative knowledge decreases, however, your speed and ease of gaining implicit access to that knowledge increases. Eventually, most nondeclarative knowledge can be retrieved for use much more quickly than declarative knowledge can be retrieved.

Psychologists have developed a variety of models for how procedural information is represented and processed. Each of these models involves the **serial processing** of information, in which information is handled through a linear sequence of operations, one operation at a time. One way in which computers can represent and organize procedural knowledge is in the form of sets of rules governing a **production**, which includes the generation and output of a procedure (Jones & Ritter, 2003). Computer simulations of productions follow production rules ("if-then" rules), comprising an "if" clause and a "then" clause (Newell & Simon, 1972). People may use this same form of organizing knowledge or something very close to it. For example, suppose your car is veering toward the left side of the road. Then you should steer toward the right side of the road if you wished to avoid hitting the curb. The "if" clause includes a set of conditions that must be met to implement the "then" clause. The "then" clause is an action or a series of actions that are a response to the "if" clause.

For a given "if-then" rule, each condition may contain one or more variables. For each of these conditions, there may be one or more possibilities. For example, *if* you want to go somewhere by car, and *if* you know how to drive a car, and *if* you are licensed and insured to drive, and *if* you have a car available to you, and *if* you do not have other constraints (e.g., no keys, no gas, broken engine, dead battery), *then* you may execute the actions for driving a car somewhere.

When the rules are described precisely and all the relevant conditions and actions are noted, a huge number of rules are required to perform even a very simple task. These rules are organized into a structure of *routines* (instructions regarding procedures for implementing a task) and *subroutines* (instructions for implementing a subtask within a larger task governed by a routine). Many of these routines and subroutines are *iterative*, meaning that they are repeated many times during the performance of a task.

If you want to complete a particular task or use a skill, you use a **production system** that comprises the entire set of rules (productions) for executing the task or using the skill (Anderson, 1983, 1993; Gugerty, 2007; Newell & Simon, 1972; Simon, 1999a, 1999b).

Consider an example of a simple production system for a pedestrian to cross the street at an intersection with a traffic light (Newell & Simon, 1972). It is shown here (with the "if" clauses indicated to the left of the arrows and the "then" clauses indicated to the right of the arrows):

traffic-light red → stop
traffic-light green → move
move and left foot on pavement → step with right foot
move and right foot on pavement → step with left foot

In this production system, the individual first tests to see whether the light is red. If it is red, the person stops and again tests to see whether the light is red. This sequence is repeated until the light turns green. At that point, the person starts moving. If the person is moving and the left foot is on the pavement, the person will step with the right foot. If the person is moving and the right foot is on the pavement, the person will step with the left foot.

Sometimes, production systems, like computer programs, contain bugs. *Bugs* are flaws in the instructions for the conditions or for executing the actions. For example, in the cross-the-street program, if the last line read "move and right foot on pavement → step with right foot," the individual executing the production system would get nowhere. According to the production-system model, human representations of procedural knowledge may contain some occasional bugs (Gugerty, 2007; VanLehn, 1990).

Until about the mid-1970s, researchers interested in knowledge representation followed either of two basic strands of research. AI and information-processing researchers were refining various models for representing procedural knowledge. Cognitive psychologists and other researchers were considering various alternative models for representing declarative knowledge. By the end of the 1970s, some integrative models of knowledge representation began to emerge.

Nondeclarative Knowledge

As mentioned previously, knowledge traditionally has been described as either declarative or procedural. One can expand the traditional distinction between declarative and procedural knowledge to suggest that nondeclarative knowledge may encompass a broader range of mental representations than just procedural knowledge (Squire, 1986; Squire et al., 1990). Specifically, in addition to declarative knowledge, we mentally represent the following forms of nondeclarative knowledge:

- perceptual, motor, and cognitive skills (procedural knowledge);
- simple associative knowledge (classical and operant conditioning);
- simple non-associative knowledge (habituation and sensitization); and
- priming (fundamental links within a knowledge network, in which the activation of information along a particular mental pathway facilitates the subsequent retrieval of information along a related pathway or even the same mental pathway; see Chapter 4).

INVESTIGATING COGNITIVE PSYCHOLOGY
Procedural Knowledge

Ask a friend if he or she would like to win $20. The $20 can be won if your friend can recite the months of the year within 30 seconds—in alphabetical order. Go! In the years that we have offered this cash to the students in our courses, not a single student has ever won, so your $20 is probably safe. This demonstration shows how something as common and frequently used as the months of the year is bundled together in a certain order. It is very difficult to rearrange their names in an order that is different from their commonly used or more familiar order.

All of these nondeclarative forms of knowledge are usually implicit. You are not aware of the different steps you carry out when you act, and it is hard for you to spell them out explicitly.

Squire's primary inspiration for his model came from three sources: his own work; a wide range of neuropsychological research done by others, including studies of amnesic patients and animal studies; and human cognitive experiments. Consider an example: Work with amnesic patients reveals clear distinctions between the neural systems for representing declarative knowledge versus neural systems for some of the nondeclarative forms of knowledge. For instance, amnesic patients often continue to show procedural knowledge even when they cannot remember that they possess such knowledge. They often they show improvements in performance on tasks requiring skills. These improvements indicate some form of new knowledge representation, despite an inability to remember ever having had previous experience with the tasks. For example, an amnesic patient who is given repeated practice in reading mirror writing will improve as a result of practice, but he or she will not recall ever having engaged in the practice (Baddeley, 1989).

Another paradox of human knowledge representation also is demonstrated by amnesics. Although amnesics do not show normal memory abilities under most circumstances, they do show the priming effect. Recall from Chapter 4 that, in priming, particular cues and stimuli seem to activate mental pathways, which in turn enhance the retrieval or cognitive processing of related information. For example, if someone asks you to spell the word *sight*, you will probably spell it differently, depending on several factors. These factors include whether you have been primed to think about sensory modalities ("s-i-g-h-t"), about locations for an archaeological dig ("s-i-t-e"), or about lists of references ("c-i-t-e"). When amnesic participants have no recall of the priming and cannot explicitly recall the experience during which priming occurred, priming still affects their performance.

Try the experiment on priming in *Investigating Cognitive Psychology: Priming*. It requires you to draw on your store of declarative knowledge.

The preceding examples illustrate situations in which an item may prime another item that is somehow related in meaning. We actually may differentiate two types of priming: semantic priming and repetition priming (Pesciarelli et al., 2007;

INVESTIGATING COGNITIVE PSYCHOLOGY
Priming

Recruit at least two (and preferably more) volunteers. Separate them into two groups. For one group, ask them to unscramble the following anagrams (puzzles in which you must figure out the correct order of letters to make a sensible word): ZAZIP, GASPETHIT, POCH YUSE, OWCH MINE, ILCHI, ACOT.

Ask the members of the other group to unscramble the following anagrams: TECKAJ, STEV, ASTEREW, OLACK, ZELBAR, ACOT.

For the first group, the correct answers are *pizza*, *spaghetti*, *chop suey*, *chow mein*, *chili*, and a sixth item. The correct answers for the second group are *jacket*, *vest*, *sweater*, *cloak*, *blazer*, and a sixth item. The sixth item in each group may be either *taco* or *coat*.

Did your volunteers show a tendency to choose one or the other answer, depending on the preceding list with which they were primed?

Posner et al., 1988). In semantic priming, we are primed by a meaningful context or by meaningful information. Such information typically is a word or cue that is meaningfully related to the target that is used. Examples are fruits or green things, which may prime *lime*. In repetition priming, a prior exposure to a word or other stimulus primes a subsequent retrieval of that information. For example, hearing the word *lime* primes subsequent stimulation for the word *lime*. Both types of priming have generated a great deal of research, but semantic priming often particularly interests cognitive psychologists.

According to spreading-activation theories, the amount of activation between a prime and a given target node is a function of two things: the number of links connecting the prime and the target, and the relative strengths of each connection. This view holds that increasing the number of intervening links tends to decrease the likelihood of the priming effect. But increasing the strength of each link between the prime and its target tends to increase the likelihood of the priming effect. This model has been well supported (e.g., McNamara, 1992). Furthermore, the occurrence of priming through spreading activation is taken by most psychologists as support for a network model of knowledge representation in memory processes. In particular, the notions of priming effects through spreading activation within a network model have led to the emergence of a newer model. It is called a connectionist model of knowledge representation and will be considered in more detail in the next section.

✔ CONCEPT CHECK

1. What is procedural knowledge?

2. What are the different kinds of nondeclarative knowledge?

3. What are two types of priming?

Integrative Models for Representing Declarative and Nondeclarative Knowledge

So far, we have considered models for the representation of either declarative or procedural knowledge. Next, we explore some models that attempt to explain both. The first model is the ACT-R model, which is based on semantic networks and production systems. Then we look at findings that are using the human brain, rather than computers, as a model. One such theory we will consider in detail: the connectionist model.

Last, we will discuss the question of whether psychologists should try to find models that explain all domains of knowledge representation (e.g., declarative *and* procedural knowledge), or whether it makes more sense to develop models that specialize in a particular domain.

Combining Representations: ACT-R

An excellent example of a theory that combines forms of mental representation is the **ACT** (adaptive control of thought) model of knowledge representation and information processing (Anderson, 1976, 1993; Anderson et al., 2001, 2004). In his ACT model, John Anderson synthesized some of the features of serial information-processing models and some of the features of semantic-network models. In ACT, procedural knowledge is represented in the form of production systems. Declarative knowledge is represented in the form of propositional networks. Anderson (1985) defined a proposition as being the smallest unit of knowledge that can be judged to be either true or false. Recall from Chapter 7 that propositions describe abstract relationships among elements. For example, "Bobby likes cheese sticks" is a proposition, but neither "Bobby" nor "cheese sticks" is a proposition. ACT is an evolved form of earlier models (Anderson, 1972; Anderson & Bower, 1973).

Anderson intended his model to be so broad in scope that it would offer an overarching theory regarding the entire architecture of cognition. In Anderson's view, individual cognitive processes such as memory, language comprehension, problem solving, and reasoning are merely variations on a central theme. They all reflect an underlying system of cognition. The most recent version of ACT, **ACT-R** (where the R stands for *rational*), is a model of information processing that integrates a network representation for declarative knowledge and a production-system representation for procedural knowledge (Anderson, 1983; Figure 8.5).

In ACT-R, networks include images of objects and corresponding spatial configurations and relationships. They also include temporal information, such as relationships involving the sequencing of actions, events, or even the order in which items appear. Anderson referred to the temporal information as "temporal strings." He noted that they contain information about the relative time sequence. Examples would be before/after, first/second/third, and yesterday/tomorrow. These relative time sequences can be compared with absolute time referents, such as 2 P.M., September 4, 2004. The model is under constant revision and currently includes information about statistical regularities in the environment (Anderson, 1991, 1996; Weaver, 2008). It is also used to examine learning processes that are reflected in the cortex (Anderson et al., 2004).

Declarative Knowledge within ACT-R

Anderson's declarative network model, like many other network models (e.g., Collins & Loftus, 1975), contains a mechanism by which information can be retrieved and also a structure for storing information. Recall that within a semantic network, concepts are stored at various nodes within the network. According to Anderson's model (and various other network models), the nodes can be either inactive or active at a given time. An active node is one that is, in a sense, "turned on." A node can be turned on—activated—directly by external stimuli, such as sensations, or it can be activated by internal stimuli, such as memories or thought processes. Also, it can be activated indirectly, by the activity of one or more neighboring nodes.

Given each node's receptivity to stimulation from neighboring nodes, there is **spreading activation** within the network from one node to another. But there are limits on the amount of information (number of nodes) that can be activated at any one time. (Danker et al., 2008; Shastri, 2003). Of course, as more nodes are activated and the spread of activation reaches greater distances from the initial source of the activation, the activation weakens. Therefore, the nodes closely related to the original node have a great deal of activation. However, nodes that are more remotely related are activated to a lesser degree. For instance, when the node for *mouse* is activated, the node for *cat* also is strongly activated. At the same time, the node for *deer* is activated (because a deer is an animal as well), but to a much lesser degree.

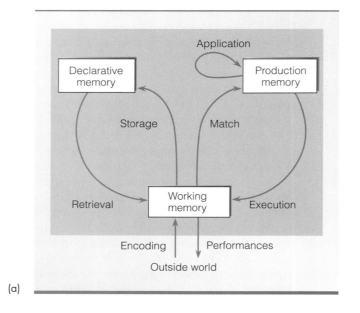

(a)

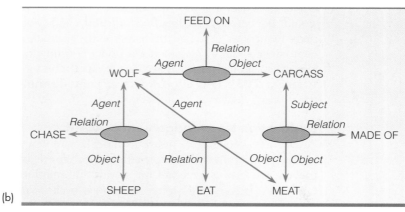

(b)

Figure 8.5 **Components of the ACT-R Model and a Propositional Network.**
(a) John Anderson's most recent version of ACT-R comprises declarative knowledge ("declarative memory"), procedural knowledge ("procedural memory"), and working memory (the activated knowledge available for cognitive processing, which has a limited capacity).
(b) The diagram shows a propositional network representing the facts that wolves feed on carcasses, eat meat, and chase sheep. The network can be extended arbitrarily to represent more information.
Sources: From *The Legacy of Solomon Asch: Essays in Cognition and Social Psychology,* by Irwin Rock. Copyright © 1990 by Lawrence Erlbaum Associates. Reprinted by permission; Reisberg, 2007 Cognition.

ACT-R also suggests means by which the network changes as a result of activation. For one thing, the more often particular links between nodes are used, the stronger the links become. In a complementary fashion, activation is likely to spread along the routes of frequently traveled connections. It is less likely to spread along infrequently used connections between nodes.

Consider an analogy. Imagine a complex set of water pipes interlinking various locations. When the water is turned on at one location, the water starts moving through various pipes. It is showing a sort of spreading activation. At various interconnections, a valve is either open or closed. It thus either permits the flow to continue through or diverts the flow (the activation) to other connections.

To carry the analogy a bit further, processes such as attention can influence the degree of activation throughout the system. Consider the water system again. The higher the water pressure in the system, the farther along the water will spread through the system of pipes. To relate this metaphor back to spreading activation, consider what happens when we are thinking about an issue and various associations seem to come to mind regarding that issue (for example, you think about tomorrow's dinner and that you have to make a shopping list, and then it occurs to you that you long promised to invite your parents for dinner, and so on). We are experiencing the spread of activation along the nodes that represent our knowledge of various aspects of the problem and, possibly, its solution.

To help explain some aspects of spreading activation, picture the pipes as being more flexible than normal pipes. These pipes gradually can expand or contract; it all depends on how frequently they are used. The pipes along routes that are traveled frequently may expand to enhance the ease and speed of travel along those routes. The pipes along routes that are seldom traveled gradually may contract. Similarly, in spreading activation, connections that frequently are used are strengthened. Connections that are seldom used are weakened. Thus, within semantic networks, declarative knowledge may be learned and maintained through the strengthening of connections as a result of frequent use. The theory of spreading activation has been applied to a number of other cognitive concepts. These concepts include social cognition and bilingualism (Dixon & Maddox, 2005; Green, 1998).

Procedural Knowledge within ACT-R

How does Anderson explain the acquisition of procedural knowledge? Such knowledge is represented in production systems rather than in semantic networks. Knowledge representation of procedural skills occurs in three stages: cognitive, associative, and autonomous (Anderson, 1980). See Table 8.2 for examples of each of these three stages.

Our progress through these stages is called proceduralization (Anderson et al., 2004; Oellinger et al., 2008). *Proceduralization* is the overall process by which we transform slow, explicit information about procedures ("knowing that") into speedy, implicit, implementations of procedures ("knowing how"). (Recall the discussion of *automatization* in Chapter 4. This is a term used by other cognitive psychologists to describe essentially the same process as proceduralization.) One means by which we make this transformation is through composition. During this stage, we construct a single production rule that effectively embraces two or more production rules. It thus streamlines the number of rules required for executing the procedure. For example, consider what happens when we learn to drive a standard-shift car. We may compose a single procedure for what were two separate procedures. One was for pressing down on the clutch. The other was for applying the brakes when we reach a stop sign. These multiple processes are combined together into the single procedure of driving.

Another aspect of proceduralization is "production tuning." It involves the two complementary processes of generalization and discrimination. We learn to generalize existing rules to apply them to new conditions. For example, we can generalize our use of the clutch, the brakes, and the accelerator to a variety of standard-shift cars.

Table 8.2 Three Stages of Acquisition of Procedural Knowledge Using the Example of Learning to Drive a Standard-Shift Car

Stage		Example
Cognitive stage	We think about explicit rules for implementing the procedure.	We must explicitly think about each rule for stepping on the clutch pedal, the gas pedal, or the brake pedal. Simultaneously, we also try to think about when and how to shift gears.
Associative stage	We consciously practice using the explicit rules extensively, usually in a highly consistent manner.	We carefully and repeatedly practice following the rules in a consistent manner. We gradually become more familiar with the rules. We learn when to follow which rules and when to implement which procedures.
Autonomous stage	We use these rules automatically and implicitly without thinking about them. We show a high degree of integration and coordination, as well as speed and accuracy.	At this time we have integrated all the various rules into a single, coordinated series of actions. We no longer need to think about what steps to take to shift gears. We can concentrate instead on listening to our favorite radio station. We simultaneously can think about going to our destination, avoiding accidents, stopping for pedestrians, and so on.

Finally, we learn to discriminate new criteria for meeting the conditions we face. For example, what happens after we have mastered driving a particular standard-shift car? If we drive a car with a different number of gears or with different positions for the reverse gear, we must discriminate the relevant information about the new gear positions from the irrelevant information about the old gear positions. Taatgen and Lee (2003) demonstrated that the learning of even extremely complex tasks—for instance, air-traffic controlling—can be described through these three processes.

Thus far, the models of knowledge representation presented in this chapter have been based largely on computer models of human intelligence. As the foregoing discussion shows, information-processing theories based on computer simulations of human cognitive processes have greatly advanced our understanding of human knowledge representation and information processing.

An alternative approach to understanding knowledge representation in humans has been to study the human brain itself. Much of the research in psychobiology has offered evidence that many operations of the human brain do not seem to process information step-by-step, bit-by-bit. Rather, the human brain seems to engage in multiple processes simultaneously. It acts on myriad bits of knowledge all at once. Such models do not necessarily contradict step-by-step models. First, people seem likely to use both serial and parallel processing. Second, different kinds of processes may be occurring at different levels. Thus, our brains may be processing multiple pieces of information simultaneously. They combine into each of the steps of which we are aware when we process information step by step.

Parallel Processing: The Connectionist Model

Computer-inspired information-processing theories assume that humans, like computers, process information serially. That is, information is processed one step after another. Some aspects of human cognition may indeed be explained in terms of serial processing, but psychobiological findings and other cognitive research seem to indicate other aspects of human cognition. These aspects involve **parallel processing**, in which multiple operations go on all at once. We have seen how the information processing of a computer has served as a metaphor for many models of cognition. Similarly, our increasing understanding of how the human brain processes information also serves as a metaphor for many of the recent models of knowledge representation in humans.

The human brain seems to handle many operations and to process information from many sources simultaneously—in parallel. In fact, it seems necessary that we are able to process information in parallel: A computer responds to an input within nanoseconds (millionths of a second), but an individual neuron may take up to 3 milliseconds to fire in response to a stimulus. Consequently, serial processing in the human brain would be far too slow to manage the amount of information the brain handles. For example, most of us can recognize a complex visual stimulus within about 300 milliseconds. If we processed the stimulus serially, only a few hundred neurons would have had time to respond, which is not enough for the perception of a complex stimulus. Therefore, the distribution of parallel processes better explains the speed and accuracy of human information processing.

As a result of these considerations, many contemporary models of knowledge representation emphasize the importance of parallel processing in human cognition. As a further result of interest in parallel processing, some computers have been made to simulate parallel processing, such as through so-called neural networks of interlinked computer processors.

At present, many cognitive psychologists are exploring the limits of parallel processing models. According to **parallel distributed processing (PDP) models** or **connectionist models**, we handle very large numbers of cognitive operations at once through a network distributed across incalculable numbers of locations in the brain (McClelland & Rogers, 2003; McClelland, Rumelhart, & the PDP Research Group, 1986; Rogers & McClelland, 2008).

How the PDP Model Works

The mental structure within which parallel processing is believed to occur is a network. In connectionist networks, all forms of knowledge are represented within the network structure. Recall that the fundamental element of the network is the node. Each node is connected to many other nodes. These interconnected patterns of nodes enable the individual to organize meaningfully the knowledge contained in the connections among the various nodes. In many network models, each node represents a concept.

The network of the PDP model is different in key respects from the semantic network described earlier. In the PDP model, the network comprises neuron-like units (McClelland & Rumelhart, 1981, 1985; Rumelhart & McClelland, 1982). They do not, in and of themselves, actually represent concepts, propositions, or any other type of information. Thus, the pattern of connections represents the knowledge, not the specific units. The same idea governs our use of language. Individual letters (or sounds) of a word are relatively uninformative, but the pattern of letters (or sounds) is highly informative. Similarly, no single unit is very informative, but the pattern of interconnections among units is highly informative. Figure 8.6 illustrates how just six units (dots) may be used to generate many more than six patterns of connections between the dots.

The PDP model demonstrates another way in which a brain-inspired model differs from a computer-inspired one. Differing cognitive processes are handled by differing patterns of activation, rather than as a result of a different set of instructions

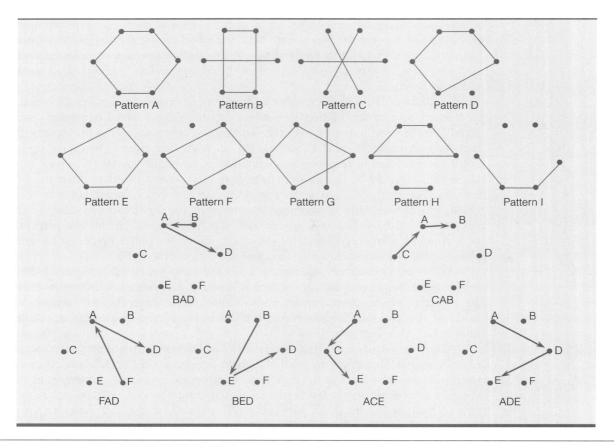

Figure 8.6 Knowledge Represented by Patterns of Connections.
Each individual unit (dot) is relatively uninformative, but when the units are connected into various patterns, each pattern may be highly informative, as illustrated in the patterns at the top of this figure. Similarly, individual letters are relatively uninformative, but patterns of letters may be highly informative. Using just three-letter combinations, we can generate many different patterns, such as DAB, FED, and other patterns shown in the bottom of this figure.

from a computer's central processing unit. In the brain, at any one time, a given neuron may be inactive, excitatory, or inhibitory.

- *Inactive* neurons are not stimulated beyond their threshold of excitation. They do not release any neurotransmitters into the synapse (the interneuronal gap).
- *Excitatory* neurons release neurotransmitters that stimulate receptive neurons at the synapse. They increase the likelihood that the receiving neurons will reach their threshold of excitation.
- *Inhibitory* neurons release neurotransmitters that inhibit receptive neurons. They reduce the likelihood that the receiving neurons will reach their threshold of excitation.

Furthermore, although the action potential of a neuron is all or none, the amounts of neurotransmitters and neuromodulators released may vary. (Neuromodulators are chemicals that can either increase or inhibit neural activation.) The frequency of firing also may vary. This variation affects the degree of excitation or inhibition of other neurons at the synapse.

Similarly, in the PDP model, individual units may be inactive, or they may send excitatory or inhibitory signals to other units. That is not to say that the PDP model actually indicates specific neural pathways for knowledge representation. We are still a long way from having more than a faint glimmer of knowing how to map specific neural information. Rather, the PDP model uses the physiological processes of the brain as a metaphor for understanding cognition. According to the PDP model, connections between units can possess varying degrees of potential excitation or inhibition. These differences can occur even when the connections are currently inactive. The more often a particular connection is activated, the greater is the strength of the connection, whether the connection is excitatory or inhibitory.

According to the PDP model, whenever we use knowledge, we change our representation of it. Thus, knowledge representation is not really a final product. Rather, it is a process or even a potential process. What is stored is not a particular pattern of connections. It is a pattern of potential excitatory or inhibitory connection strengths. The brain uses this pattern to re-create other patterns when stimulated to do so.

When we receive new information, the activation from that information either strengthens or weakens the connections between units. The new information may come from environmental stimuli, from memory, or from cognitive processes. The ability to create new information by drawing inferences and making generalizations allows for almost infinite versatility in knowledge representation and manipulation.

This versatility is what makes humans—unlike computers—able to accommodate incomplete and distorted information. Information that is distorted or incomplete is considered to be *degraded*. According to the PDP model, human minds are flexible. They do not require that all aspects of a pattern precisely match to activate a pattern. Thus, when enough distinctive (but not all) aspects of a particular pattern have been activated by other attributes in the description, we can re-create the correct pattern even though there is some degraded information. This cognitive flexibility also greatly enhances our ability to learn new information.

By using the PDP model, cognitive psychologists attempt to explain various general characteristics of human cognition. These characteristics include our ability to respond flexibly, dynamically, rapidly, and relatively accurately, even when we are given only partial or degraded information. In addition, cognitive psychologists attempt to use the model to explain specific cognitive processes. Examples of such processes are perception, reasoning, reading, language comprehension, priming, and the Stroop effect, as well as other memory processes (Elman et al., 1996; Kaplan et al., 2007; Rogers & McClelland, 2008; Smolensky, 1999; Welbourne & Ralph, 2007).

An example of the efforts to apply PDP models to specific cognitive processes can be seen through the exploration of dyslexia, or reading disability. A specific PDP model for the description of how we read was developed. This model involves pathways for both phonological and semantic representations (Plaut et al., 1996). Computer simulations with this model have been able to mimic normal reading. When one of these two pathways is damaged, these simulations are able to imitate the behavioral manifestations of dyslexia (Welbourne & Ralph, 2007). These simulations help researchers understand what processes are malfunctioning in people with reading disabilities.

Connectionist models of knowledge representation explain many phenomena of knowledge representation and processing, such as perception and memory. These processes may be learned gradually by our storing knowledge through the strengthening of patterns of connections within the network. But connectionist models are not flawless.

Criticisms of the Connectionist Models

One general criticism is that connectionist networks neglect properties that neural systems have, or that they propose properties that neural networks do not have. Furthermore, critics ask why any model should be more credible than another for explaining cognitive mechanisms just because it resembles the structure of the brain (Thomas & McClelland, 2008).

Many aspects of the connectionist models are not yet well defined. For example, a connectionist model is less effective in explaining how people can remember a single event (Schacter, 1989a). How do we suddenly construct a whole new interconnected pattern for representing what we know about a memorable event, such as graduation day?

Similarly, connectionist models do not satisfactorily explain how we often quickly can unlearn established patterns of connections when we are presented with contradictory information (Ratcliff, 1990; Treadway et al., 1992). For example:

1. Suppose that you are told that the criteria for classifying parts of plants as fruits are that they must have seeds, pulp, and skin.
2. You also are told that whether they are sweeter than other plant parts is not important.
3. Now you are given the task of sorting various photos of plant parts into groups that are or are not fruits.
4. What happens? You will sort tomatoes and pumpkins with apples and other fruits, even if you did not previously consider them to be fruits.

These shortcomings of connectionist systems can be bypassed. It may be that there are two learning systems in the brain (McClelland, McNaughton, & O'Reilly, 1995). One system corresponds to the connectionist model in resisting change and in being relatively permanent. The complementary system handles rapid acquisition of new information. It holds the information for a short time. It then integrates the newer information with information in the connectionist system. Evidence from neuropsychology and connectionist network modeling seem to corroborate this account (McClelland, McNaughton, & O'Reilly, 1995). Thus, the connectionist system is spared. But we still need a satisfactory account of the other learning system.

The preceding models of knowledge representation and information processing clearly have profited from technological advances in computer science, in brain imaging, and in the neuropsychological study of the human brain in action. These are techniques that few would have predicted to have been so promising 40 years ago. Thus, it would be foolish to predict that specific avenues of research will lead us in particular directions. Nonetheless, particular avenues of research do hold promise. For example, using powerful computers, researchers are attempting to create parallel-processing models via neural networks. Increasingly sophisticated techniques for studying the brain offer intriguing possibilities for research. Case studies, naturalistic studies, and traditional laboratory experiments in the field of cognitive psychology also offer rich opportunities for further exploration. Some researchers are trying to explore highly specific cognitive processes, such as auditory processing of speech sounds. Others are trying to investigate fundamental processes that underlie all aspects of cognition. Which type of research is more valuable?

Comparing Connectionist with Network Representations

How do connectionist models compare with network models? Figure 8.7 shows the concept of a robin as represented by both a network model and a connectionist model.

In the network representation, the nodes represent concepts. An individual builds up a knowledge base about a robin over time as more and more information is acquired about robins. Note that information about robins is embedded in a general network representation that goes beyond just robins. One's understanding of robins partly depends on the relationship of the robin to other birds and even other kinds of living things. Indeed, perhaps the most fundamental feature of the robin is that it is a living thing. So this information is represented at the top to show that it is an extremely general characteristic of a robin. Living things are living and can grow, so this information is also represented at a very general level. As one moves down the network, information gets more and more specific. For example, we learn that a robin is a bird and that it is partly red.

In contrast, the connectionist network represents patterns of activation. Here, too, the network shows knowledge that goes beyond just birds. But the knowledge is in the connections rather than in the nodes. Through activation of certain connections, knowledge about a robin is built up. A strong connection is one that is activated many times, whereas a weak one is activated only on rare occasions.

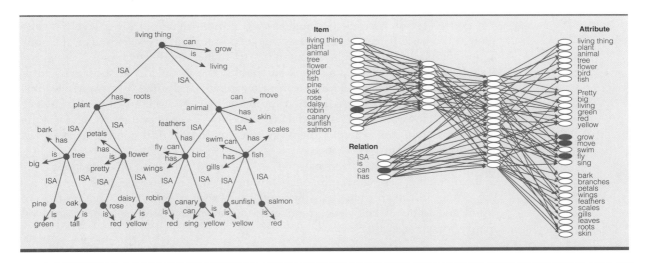

Figure 8.7 **Network and Connectionist Representations.**

Network and connectionist representations of concepts relating to birds. The network representation on the left illustrates how knowledge is built up like a tree with more superordinate concepts at the top. The connectionist representation on the right has three layers: item, relation, and attribute. Each unit in the relation layer restricts the information that can be retrieved—a "can" relation activates different attributes than a "has" relation, for example. Thus, the "robin can" constellation represents a situation in which one is presented with a bird and asked what that bird can do.

Source: From J. L. McClelland, "Connectionist Model of Memory," in E. Tulving & F. I. M. Craik (Eds.), *The Oxford Handbook of Memory*, pp. 583–596. Copyright © 2000 Oxford University Press. Reprinted by permission.

How Domain General or Domain Specific Is Cognition?

Should cognitive psychologists try to find a set of mental processes that is common across all domains of knowledge representation and processing? Or should they study mental processes specific to a particular domain? In early AI research, investigators believed that the ideal was to write programs that were as domain general as possible. Although none of the programs truly worked in all domains, they were a good start. Similarly, in the broader field of cognitive psychology, the trend in the 1960s through the mid-1970s was to strive for domain-general understandings of cognitive processes (Miller, Galanter, & Pribram, 1960; Simon, 1976).

Starting in the late 1970s, the balance shifted toward domain specificity. In part, this was because of striking demonstrations regarding the role of specific knowledge in chess playing (Chase & Simon, 1973; De Groot, 1965; see Chapter 12). A key book, *The Modularity of Mind*, presented an argument for extreme domain specificity (Fodor, 1983). In this view, the mind is **modular**, divided into discrete modules that operate more or less independently of each other. According to Fodor, each independently functioning module can process only one kind of input, such as language (e.g., words), visual percepts (e.g., faces), and so on.

Further evidence for the domain specificity of face recognition can be observed in studies employing functional magnetic resonance imaging (fMRI) methods. In one study, it was observed that when subjects viewed faces and houses, different brain areas were active. It thus appears that there are both specialized brain and cognitive processes for the processing of faces. This finding is taken to suggest that there is domain specificity for facial recognition (Yovel & Kanwisher, 2004). Studies have found domain specificity for other things like scenes and bodies as well (Downing et al., 2006).

Fodor (1983) asserted the modularity (distinct origins) of lower-level processes such as the basic perceptual processes involved in lexical access. However, the application of modularity has been extended to higher intellectual processes as well (Gardner, 1983). Also, Fodor's book emphasized the modularity of specific cognitive functions, such as lexical access to word meanings, as distinct from word meanings derived from context. These functions primarily have been observed in cognitive experiments. However, issues of modularity also have been important in neuropsychological research. For example, there are discrete pathological conditions associated with discrete cognitive deficits.

Recently, there has been more of an attempt to integrate domain-specific and domain-general perspectives in our thinking about knowledge representation and processing. In the chapters that follow, you may wish to reflect on whether the processes and forms of knowledge representation are primarily domain general or primarily domain specific.

✔ CONCEPT CHECK

1. What is the ACT-R model?
2. How is procedural knowledge represented in the ACT-R model?
3. What is parallel processing?
4. How does a connectionist network represent knowledge?
5. What is domain specificity?

IN THE LAB OF JAMES L. MCCLELLAND

Neural-Network Model

In my laboratory, we attempt to understand the implications of the idea that human cognitive processes arise from the interactions of neurons in the brain. We develop computational models that directly carry out some human cognitive task using simple, neuron-like processing units. We believe that the properties of the underlying hardware have important implications for the nature and organization of cognitive processes in the brain.

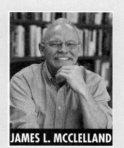

JAMES L. MCCLELLAND

An important case in point is the process of assigning the past tense to a word in English. Consider the formation of the past tense of *like, take,* and *gleat.* (*Gleat* is not a word in English, but it might be. For example, we might coin the word *gleat* to refer to the act of saluting in a particular way.) In any case, most people agree that the past tense of *like* is *liked;* the past tense of *take* is *took;* and the past tense of *gleat* is *gleated.*

Before the advent of neural network models, everyone in the field assumed that to form the past tense of a novel verb like *gleat,* one would need to use a rule (e.g., to form the past tense of a word, add -[e]d).

Also, developmental psychologists observed that young children occasionally made interesting errors like saying "taked" instead of "took," and they interpreted this as indicating that the children were (over)applying the past tense rule. They also assumed that to produce "took" a child would need to memorize this particular item. For familiar but regular words like *like,* either the rule or the look-up mechanism might be used.

In the brain, a single mechanism might be used to produce the past tenses of both regular and exceptional items. To explore this possibility, Rumelhart and I created a simple neural network model. The model takes as its input a pattern of activity representing the present tense form of a word and produces on its output another pattern of activity representing the past tense form of the word. The network operates by propagating activation from the input units to the output units. What determines whether a unit will be active is the pattern of incoming connection activation to each unit. The incoming connections are modulated by weights like synapses between neurons that modulate the effect of an input on an output. If the overall effect of the input is positive, the unit comes on; if negative, it goes off.

We trained this network with pairs of items representing the present and past tenses of familiar words. After we trained it with the 10 most frequent words (most of which are exceptions), the network could produce the past tenses of these words, but it did not know how to deal with other words. We then trained it with the 10 frequent words plus 400 more words, most of which were regular, and we found that early in training, it tended to overregularize most of the exceptions (e.g., it said "taked" instead of "took"), even for those words that it had previously produced correctly. After more training, it recovered its ability to produce exceptions correctly, while still producing regular past tenses for words like *like* and for many novel items like *gleat.* Thus, the model accounted for the developmental pattern in which children first deal correctly with exceptions, then learn how to deal with regular words and novel words and overregularize exceptions, and then deal correctly with regular words, novel words, and exceptions.

Our model illustrates that in a neural network, it is not necessary to have separate mechanisms to deal with rules and exceptions. This conclusion remains controversial but continues to gain ground. Other work in my lab and in other labs extends these ideas to reading, other aspects of language including grammar, and even to semantics, where there are many things like penguins and elephants that have exceptional properties.

Key Themes

This chapter brings out several of the key themes described in Chapter 1.

Rationalism versus empiricism. How do we assign meaning to concepts? The featural view is largely a rationalistic one. Concepts have sets of features that are largely a priori and that are the same from one person to another. The underlying notion is that one could understand a concept by a detailed dictionary definition, pretty much without reference to people's experience. The prototype, exemplar, and theory-based views are much more empirically based. They assign a major role to experience. For example, theories may change with experience. The theory of a concept such as a "dog" that a 3-year-old child has may be very different from that of a 10-year-old child.

Validity of causal inference versus ecological validity. Early research on concepts, such as that of Bruner, Goodnow, and Austin, used abstract concepts, such as geometric forms that could be of different colors, shapes, and sizes. But in her work, Eleanor Rosch called this approach into question. Rosch argued that natural concepts show few of the characteristics of artificial ones. Studying artificial concepts, therefore, might yield information that applied to those concepts but not necessarily to real-world ones. Modern researchers tend to study real-world concepts more than artificial ones.

Applied versus basic research. Basic research on concepts has generated a great deal of applied research. For example, market researchers are very interested in people's conceptualizations of commercial products. They use empirical and statistical techniques to understand how products are conceived. Often, then, advertising serves to reposition the products in customers' minds. For example, a car that is viewed as in the category of "economy cars" may be moved, through advertising, to a more "upscale car" category.

Summary

1. **How are representations of words and symbols organized in the mind?** The fundamental unit of symbolic knowledge is the concept. Concepts may be organized into categories, which may include other categories. They may be organized into schemas, which may include other schemas. They also may vary in application and in abstractness.

   Finally, they may include information about relationships between concepts, attributes, contexts, and general knowledge and information about causal relationships. There are different general theories of categorization. They include feature-based definitional categories, prototype-based categories, and exemplar-based approaches. One of the forms for schemas is the script. An alternative model for knowledge organization is a semantic network, involving a web of labeled relations between conceptual nodes. An early network model, based on the notion of cognitive economy, was strictly hierarchical. But subsequent ones have tended to emphasize the frequency with which particular associations are used.

2. **How do we represent other forms of knowledge in the mind?** Many cognitive psychologists have developed models for procedural knowledge. These are based on computer simulations of such representations. An example of such a model is the production system.

3. **How does declarative knowledge interact with procedural knowledge?** An important model in cognitive psychology is ACT, as well as its updated revision, ACT-R. It represents both procedural knowledge in the form of production systems and declarative knowledge in the form of a semantic network. In each of these models, the metaphor for understanding both knowledge representation and information processing is based on the way in which a computer processes information. For example, these models underscore the serial processing of information.

   Research on how the human brain processes information has shown that brains, unlike computers, use parallel processing of information. In addition, it appears that much of information processing is not localized only to particular areas of the brain. Instead it is distributed across various regions of the brain all at once. At a microscopic level of analysis, the neurons within the brain may be inactive, or they may be excited or inhibited by the actions of other neurons with which they share a synapse. Finally, studies of how the brain processes information have shown that some stimuli seem to prime a response to subsequent stimuli so that it becomes easier to process the subsequent stimuli.

A model for human knowledge representation and information processing based on what we know about the brain is the parallel distributed processing (PDP) model. It is also called a connectionist model. In such models, it is held that neuron-like units may be excited or inhibited by the actions of other units, or

they may be inactive. Further, knowledge is represented in terms of patterns of excitation or inhibition strengths, rather than in particular units. Most PDP models also explain the priming effect by suggesting the mechanism of spreading activation.

Many cognitive psychologists believe that the mind is at least partly modular. It has different activity centers that operate fairly independently of each other. However, other cognitive psychologists believe that human cognition is governed by many fundamental operations. According to this view, specific cognitive functions are merely variations on a theme. In all likelihood, cognition involves some modular, domain-specific processes and some fundamental, domain-general processes.

Thinking about Thinking: Analytical, Creative, and Practical Questions

1. Define *declarative knowledge* and *procedural knowledge*, and give examples of each.
2. What is a script that you use in your daily life? How might you make it work better for you?
3. Describe some of the attributes of schemas, and compare and contrast two of the schema models mentioned in this chapter.
4. In your opinion, why have many of the models for knowledge representation come from people with a strong interest in artificial intelligence?
5. What are some advantages and disadvantages of hierarchical models of knowledge representation?
6. How would you design an experiment to test whether a particular cognitive task was better

explained in terms of modular components, or in terms of some fundamental underlying domain-general processes?
7. What are some practical examples of the forms of nondeclarative knowledge in Squire's model? (For ideas on conditioning, see Chapter 1; for ideas on habituation or on priming, see Chapter 4.)
8. How might you use semantic priming to enhance the likelihood that a person will think of something you would like the person to think of (e.g., your birthday, a restaurant to visit, or a movie to view)?

Key Terms

ACT, *p. 344*
ACT-R, *p. 345*
artifact categories, *p. 323*
basic level, *p. 323*
category, *p. 322*
characteristic features, *p. 326*
concept, *p. 322*
connectionist models, *p. 349*
converging operations, *p. 322*
core, *p. 327*

defining features, *p. 324*
exemplars, *p. 327*
jargon, *p. 338*
modular, *p. 354*
natural categories, *p. 323*
networks, *p. 323*
nodes, *p. 332*
parallel distributed processing (PDP) models, *p. 349*
parallel processing, *p. 348*

production, *p. 341*
production system, *p. 341*
prototype, *p. 326*
prototype theory, *p. 325*
schemas, *p. 323*
script, *p. 337*
serial processing, *p. 341*
spreading activation, *p. 345*
theory-based view of meaning, *p. 328*

Media Resources

Visit the companion website—**www.cengagebrain.com**—for quizzes, research articles, chapter outlines, and more.

CogLab

Explore CogLab by going to **http://coglab.wadsworth.com**. To learn more, examine the following experiments:

Prototypes

Absolute Identification

Implicit Learning

Language: Nature and Acquisition

Here are some questions we will explore in this chapter:

1. What properties characterize language?
2. What are some of the processes involved in language?
3. How do perceptual processes interact with the cognitive processes of reading?
4. How does discourse help us understand individual words?

■ **BELIEVE IT OR NOT**

DO THE CHINESE THINK ABOUT NUMBERS DIFFERENTLY THAN AMERICANS ?

How languages name numbers and how they are pronounced differs widely. There are even significant differences between English and French. For example, in English, the number 80 is called "eighty," and in French it is "quatre-vingt" (literally, "four twenty," or 4 × 20).

Do those differences in language influence how our brain processes numbers and mathematics? This is what a Chinese research team set out to explore. Native Chinese speakers and native American speakers worked on numerical tasks while being monitored by an fMRI machine. The results found that for simple addition tasks, different areas of the brain were activated for Chinese and English speakers: English speakers used processes that involved the left perisylvian cortices, whereas Chinese speakers used a visuo-premotor network for the addition tasks. The results suggest that language influences the way non-language-related content is processed. It is also possible that the Chinese language's brevity for numbers (e.g., number words in Chinese generally contain fewer syllables than in English) increases working memory capacity, which in turn can result in more efficient processing (Tang et al., 2006).

In this chapter we will explore what language is, how we process language, and how it can influence our understanding of facts and the environment.

> *I stood still, my whole attention fixed upon the motions of her fingers. Suddenly, I felt a misty consciousness as of something forgotten—a thrill of returning thought; and somehow the mystery of language was revealed to me.*
>
> *I knew then that "w-a-t-e-r" meant the wonderful cool something that was flowing over my hand. That living word awakened my soul, gave it light, joy, set it free! … Everything had a name, and each name gave birth to a new thought. As we returned to the house every object which I touched seemed to quiver with life…. I learned a great many new words that day … words that were to make the world blossom for me.*
>
> —*Helen Keller*, Story of My Life

Helen Keller became both blind and deaf at 19 months of age after a severe childhood illness. She was first awakened to a sentient, thought-filled, comprehensible world through her teacher, Anne Sullivan. The miracle worker held one of Helen's hands under a spigot from which a stream of water gushed over Helen's hand. All the while she spelled with a manual alphabet into Helen's other hand the mind-awakening word "w-a-t-e-r."

Language is the use of an organized means of combining words in order to communicate with those around us. It also makes it possible to think about things and processes we currently cannot see, hear, feel, touch, or smell. These things include ideas that may not have any tangible form. As Helen Keller demonstrated, the words we use may be written, spoken, or otherwise signed (e.g., via American Sign

Language [ASL]). Even so, not all **communication**—exchange of thoughts and feelings—is through language. Communication encompasses other aspects—nonverbal communication, such as gestures or facial expressions, can be used to embellish or to indicate. Glances may serve many purposes. For example, sometimes they are deadly, other times, seductive. Communication can also include touches, such as handshakes, hits, and hugs. These are only a few of the means by which we can communicate.

Psycholinguistics is the psychology of our language as it interacts with the human mind. It considers both production and comprehension of language (Gernsbacher & Kaschak, 2003a, 2003b; Wheeldon, Meyer, & Smith, 2003). Four areas of study have contributed greatly to an understanding of psycholinguistics:

- *linguistics*, the study of language structure and change;
- *neurolinguistics*, the study of the relationships among the brain, cognition, and language;
- *sociolinguistics*, the study of the relationship between social behavior and language (Carroll, 1986); and
- *computational linguistics* and *psycholinguistics*, the study of language via computational methods (Coleman, 2003; Gasser, 2003; Lewis, 2003).

This chapter first briefly describes some general properties of language. The next sections discuss the processes of language. These processes include how we understand the meanings of particular words, and how we structure words into meaningful sentences. After our exploration of general language processes we turn to the question of how we read. And last but not least, we discuss how comprehension of larger language and text units, like essays or conversation, works. Chapter 10 describes the broader context within which we use language. This context includes the psychological and social contexts of language.

What Is Language?

There are almost 7,000 languages spoken in the world today (Lewis, 2009). New Guinea is the country with the most languages in the world—it has more than 850 indigenous languages, which means that on average, each language has just about 7,000 speakers. Surprisingly, there are still languages today that have not even been "discovered" and named by scientists. A linguist who traveled to southwestern China's Yunnan province in 2006 discovered 18 languages, spoken by members of the Phula ethnic group, that never before had been defined and named (Erard, 2009). It is to be expected that there are many more languages that linguists do not yet know about. Part of the reason for the Phula languages' not having been discovered earlier is that speakers of the language live in mountainous areas that are hard to access. What exactly constitutes a language, and are there some things that all languages have in common?

Properties of Language

Languages can be strikingly different, but they all have some commonalities (Brown, 1965; Clark & Clark, 1977; Glucksberg & Danks, 1975). No matter what language you speak, language is:

1. *communicative:* Language permits us to communicate with one or more people who share our language.

2. *arbitrarily symbolic:* Language creates an arbitrary relationship between a symbol and what it represents: an idea, a thing, a process, a relationship, or a description.
3. *regularly structured:* Language has a structure; only particularly patterned arrangements of symbols have meaning, and different arrangements yield different meanings.
4. *structured at multiple levels:* The structure of language can be analyzed at more than one level (e.g., in sounds, meaning units, words, and phrases).
5. *generative, productive:* Within the limits of a linguistic structure, language users can produce novel utterances. The possibilities for creating new utterances are virtually limitless.
6. *dynamic:* Languages constantly evolve.

Let's examine the six properties of language in more detail. The *communicative property* of language may be the most obvious feature, but it is also the most remarkable one. As an example, you can write what you are thinking and feeling so that others may read and understand your thoughts and feelings. Yet, as you may know from your own experience, there are occasional flaws in the communicative property of language. Despite the frustrations of miscommunications, however, for one person to be able to use language to communicate to another is impressive.

What may be more surprising is the second property of language. We communicate through our shared system of *arbitrary symbolic* reference to things, ideas, processes, relationships, and descriptions (Steedman, 2003). Words are symbols that were chosen arbitrarily to represent something else, such as a "tree," "swim," or "brilliant." The thing or concept in the real world that a word refers to is called **referent**. By consensual agreement, these combinations of letters or sounds may be meaningful to us. But the particular symbols themselves do not lead to the meaning of the word, which is why different languages use very different sounds to refer to the same thing (e.g., *Baum, árbol, tree*).

Symbols are convenient because we can use them to refer to things, ideas, processes, relationships, and descriptions that are not currently present, such as the Amazon River. We even can use symbols to refer to things that never have existed, such as dragons or elves. And we can use symbols to refer to things that exist in a form that is not physically tangible, such as calculus, truth, or justice. Without arbitrary symbolic reference, we would be limited to symbols that somehow resembled the things they are symbolizing (e.g., we would need a treelike symbol to represent a tree).

Two principles underlying word meanings are the *principle of conventionality* and the *principle of contrast* (Clark, 1993, 1995; Diesendruck, 2005). The principle of conventionality simply states that meanings of words are determined by conventions—they have a meaning upon which people agree. According to the principle of contrast, different words have different meanings. Thus, when you have two different words, they represent two things that are at least slightly different. Otherwise, what would be the point of having two different words for the same thing?

The third property is the *regular structure* of language: Particular patterns of sounds and of letters form meaningful words. Random sounds and letters, however, usually do not. Furthermore, particular patterns of words form meaningful sentences, paragraphs, and discourse. Most others make no sense. Later in this chapter, we will look more closely at the structure of language.

Signs that resemble the object they represent (i.e., their referent) are called icons. These pictographs are icons that were used in ancient Egyptian hieroglyphics. In contrast, most language involves the manipulation of symbols, which bear only an arbitrary relation to their referents.

The fourth property is that language is *structured at multiple levels*. Any meaningful utterance can be analyzed at more than one level. Let's see at what levels psycholinguists study language. They look at:

- sounds, such as *p* and *t;*
- words, such as "pat," "tap," "pot," "top," "pit," and "tip;"
- sentences, such as "Pat said to tap the top of the pot, then tip it into the pit;" and
- larger units of language, such as this paragraph or even this book.

A fifth property of language is *productivity* (sometimes termed *generativity*). *Productivity* refers here to our vast ability to produce language creatively. However, our use of language does have limitations. We have to conform to a particular structure and use a shared system of arbitrary symbols. We can use language to produce an infinite number of unique sentences and other meaningful combinations of words. Although the number of sounds (e.g., *s* as in "hiss") used in a language may be finite, the various sounds can be combined endlessly to form new words and new sentences. Among them are many novel utterances—linguistic expressions that are brand new and have never been spoken before by anyone. Thus, language is inherently creative. None of us possibly could have heard previously all the sentences we are capable of producing and that we actually produce in the course of our everyday lives. Any language appears to have the potential to express any idea in it that can be expressed in any other language. However, the ease, clarity, and succinctness of expression of a particular idea may vary greatly from one language to the next. Thus, the creative potential of different languages appears to be roughly the same.

Finally, the productive aspect of language quite naturally leads to the *dynamic*, evolutionary nature of language. Individual language users coin words and phrases and modify language usage. The wider group of language users either accepts or rejects the modifications. Each year, recently coined words are added to the dictionary, signifying the extensive acceptance of these new words. For example, you may be familiar with the words *netiquette* (a blend of "network" and "etiquette," referring to appropriate behavior on-line), *emoticon* (a blend of "emotion" and "icon," referring to punctuation symbols used in emails to indicate emotions), and *webinar* (referring to a seminar held on-line). All of these words have been created just in recent years. Can you think of other newly minted words that did not exist a decade ago?

Similarly, words that are no longer used are removed from the dictionary, further contributing to the evolution of language. To imagine that language would never change is almost as incomprehensible as to imagine that people and environments would never change. For example, the modern English we speak now evolved from Middle English, and Middle English evolved from Old English.

To give you an example of how English has evolved, here is a sample from the epic poem *Beowulf*, written in Old English around 900 A.D. On the right, you can see a translation in modern English.

Hwæt! We Gardena in geardagum,	Lo, praise of the prowess of people-kings
þeodcyninga, þrym gefrunon,	of spear-armed Danes, in days long sped,
hu ða æþelingas ellen fremedon.	we have heard, and what honor the athelings won!

And here is the beginning of the *Canterbury Tales* by Geoffrey Chaucer, written in Middle English in the 14th century:

Whan that aprill with his shoures soote	When April with his showers sweet with fruit
The droghte of march hath perced to the roote,	The drought of March has pierced unto the root
And bathed every veyne in swich licour	And bathed each vein with liquor that has power

Although we can delineate various properties of language, it is important always to keep in mind the main purpose of language: to construct a mental representation of a situation that enables us to understand the situation and communicate about it (Budwig, 1995; Radvansky & Dijkstra, 2007; Zwaan & Radvansky, 1998).

In other words, ultimately, language is primarily about use, not just about one set of properties or another. For example, it provides the basis for linguistic encoding in memory. You are able to remember things better because you can use language to help you recall or recognize them.

To conclude, many differences exist among languages. Nevertheless, there are some common properties. Among them are communication, arbitrary symbolic reference, regularity of structure, multiplicity of structure, productivity, and change. Next, we consider, in more detail how language is used. Then we observe some universal aspects of how we humans acquire our primary language.

The Basic Components of Words

Language can be broken down into many smaller units. It is much like the analysis of molecules into basic elements by chemists. The smallest unit of speech sound is the *phone*, which is simply a single vocal sound. A given phone may or may not be part of a particular language (Minagawa-Kawai at al., 2007; Munhall, 2003; Roca, 2003b). A click of your tongue, a pop of your cheek, or a gurgling sound are all phones. These sounds, however, are not used to form distinctive words in North American English. A **phoneme** is the smallest unit of speech sound that can be used to distinguish one utterance in a given language from another. In English, phonemes are made up of vowel or consonant sounds, like *a*, *i*, *s*, and *f*. For example, we can distinguish among "sit," "sat," "fat," and "fit," so the /s/ sound, the /f/ sound, the /i/ sound, and the /Æ/ sound are all phonemes in English (as is the /t/ sound). These sounds are produced by alternating sequences of opening and closing the vocal tract. Different languages use different numbers and combinations of phonemes. North American English has about 40 phonemes, as shown in Table 9.1. Hawaiian has about 13 phonemes. Some African dialects have up to 60.

In English, the difference between the /p/ and the /b/ sound is an important distinction. These sounds function as phonemes in English because they constitute the difference between different words. For example, English speakers distinguish between "they bit the buns from the bin" and "they pit the puns from the pin" (a well-structured but meaningless sentence). The study of the particular phonemes of a language is called *phonemics*.

Phonetics is the study of how to produce or combine speech sounds or to represent them with written symbols (Roca, 2003a). Whereas phonemes are relevant to a given language, phones, as studied in phonetics, are differentiable sounds irrespective of language. Linguists may travel to remote villages to observe, record, and analyze different languages. The study of phonetic inventories of diverse languages is one of the ways linguists gain insight into the nature of language (Hoff & Shatz, 2007; Ladefoged & Maddieson, 1996). In many cases, however, it is hard to explore a given language because many languages are going extinct: It is estimated that about two languages die each month (Crystal, 2002). Language death occurs for a variety of reasons, including members leaving tribal areas in favor of more urban areas, genocide, globalization, and the introduction of a new language to an area (Grimes, 2010; Mufwene, 2004). Language death is occurring at such an alarming rate that some estimates suggest that 90% of the world's languages will be extinguished within the next generation (Abrams & Strogatz, 2003).

At the next level of the hierarchy after the phoneme is the **morpheme**—the smallest unit of meaning within a particular language. The word *recharge* contains two morphemes, "re-" and "charge," where "re" indicates a repeated action. The word "cable" consists of only one morpheme although it is made up of two syllables; but the syllables "ca" and "ble" do not have any inherent meaning.

Table 9.1 North American English Phonetic Symbols

The phonemes of a language constitute the repertoire of the smallest units of sound that can be used to distinguish one meaningful utterance from another in the given language.

Consonants				Vowels	
[pʰ]	pit	[ð]	though	[ij]	fee
[p]	spit	[s]	sip	[ɪ]	fit
[tʰ]	tick	[z]	zap	[ej]	fate
[t]	stuck	[ʃ]	ship	[ɛ]	let
[kʰ]	keep	[ʒ]	azure	[æ]	bat
[k]	skip	[h]	hat	[uw]	boot
[tʃ]	chip	[j]	yet	[ʊ]	book
[ʤ]	judge	[w]	witch	[ow]	note
[b]	bib	[ʍ]	which	[ɔj]	boy
[d]	dip	[l]	leaf	[ɔ]	bore
[D]	butter	[r]	reef	[a]	pot
[g]	get	[r̩]	bird	[ə]	roses
[f]	fit	[m]	moat	[ʌ]	shut
[v]	vat	[n]	note	[aw]	crowd
[θ]	thick	[ŋ]	sing	[aj]	lies

Source: O'Grady, W., Archibald, J., Aronoff, M., and Rees-Miller, J. *Contemporary Linguistics*, 3rd ed., Bedford St. Martins.

English courses may have introduced you to two forms of morphemes—root words and affixes. Root words are the portions of words that contain the majority of meaning. These roots cannot be broken down into smaller meaningful units. They are the items that have entries in the dictionary (Motter et al., 2002). Examples of roots are the words "fix" and "active." We add the second form of morphemes, affixes, to these root words. Affixes include prefixes, which precede the root word, and suffixes, which follow the root word. Look at the word *affixes*. It contains three morphemes: *af-*, *-fix*, *-es*. Af- is a prefix variant of the prefix *ad-*, meaning "toward," "to," or "near." In contrast, *–fix* is the root word. Finally, *–es* is a suffix that indicates the plural of a noun. Similarly, the word *proactive* contains the prefix *pro-*, and the root word *-active*.

Linguists analyze the structure of morphemes and of words in general in a way that goes beyond the analysis of roots and affixes. **Content morphemes** are the words that convey the bulk of the meaning of a language. **Function morphemes** add detail and nuance to the meaning of the content morphemes or help the content morphemes fit the grammatical context. Examples are the suffix *-ist*, the prefix *de-*, the conjunction *and*, or the article *the*. For example, most American kindergartners know to add special suffixes to indicate the following:

- *Verb tense:* You study often. You stud**ied** yesterday. You are study**ing** now.
- *Verb and noun number:* The professor assign**s** homework. The teaching assistants assign homework.
- *Noun possession:* The student**'s** textbook is fascinating.

- *Adjective comparison:* The wis**er** of the two professors taught the wis**est** of the three students.

The **lexicon** is the entire set of morphemes in a given language or in a given person's linguistic repertoire. The average adult speaker of English has a lexicon of about 80,000 morphemes (Miller & Gildea, 1987). Children in grade 1 in the United States have approximately 10,000 words in their vocabularies. By grade 3, they have about 20,000. By grade 5, they have reached about 40,000, or half of their eventual adult level of attainment (Anglin, 1993). By combining morphemes, most adult English speakers have a vocabulary of hundreds of thousands of words. For example, by attaching just a few morphemes to the root content morpheme *study*, we have *student, studious, studied, studying,* and *studies.* Vocabulary is built up slowly. It develops through many diverse exposures to words and clues as to their meanings (Akhtar & Montague, 1999; Hoff & Naigles, 1999; Woodward & Markman, 1998). One of the ways in which English has expanded to embrace an increasing vocabulary is by combining existing morphemes in novel ways. Some suggest that a part of William Shakespeare's genius lay in his enjoying the creation of new words by combining existing morphemes. He is alleged to have coined more than 1,700 words—8.5 % of his written vocabulary—and countless expressions—including the word *countless* itself, but also other words like *inauspicious, pander,* and *dauntless* (Lederer, 1991).

The Basic Components of Sentences

Although we put together sentences so seemingly easy when we speak, a substantial framework of rules hides behind our creation of these sentences. **Syntax** refers to the way in which we put words together to form sentences. It plays a major role in our understanding of language. A sentence comprises at least two parts. The first is a **noun phrase**, which contains at least one noun (often the subject of the sentence) and includes all the relevant descriptors of the noun (like "big" or "fast"). The second is a **verb phrase** (*predicate*), which contains at least one verb and whatever the verb acts on, if anything. Linguists consider the study of syntax to be fundamental to understanding the structure of language. The syntactical structure of language specifically is addressed later in this chapter.

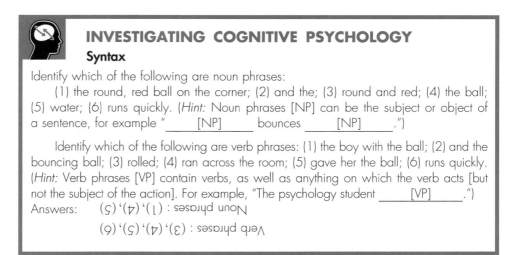

INVESTIGATING COGNITIVE PSYCHOLOGY
Syntax

Identify which of the following are noun phrases:
(1) the round, red ball on the corner; (2) and the; (3) round and red; (4) the ball; (5) water; (6) runs quickly. (*Hint:* Noun phrases [NP] can be the subject or object of a sentence, for example "_____[NP]_____ bounces _____[NP]_____.")

Identify which of the following are verb phrases: (1) the boy with the ball; (2) and the bouncing ball; (3) rolled; (4) ran across the room; (5) gave her the ball; (6) runs quickly. (*Hint:* Verb phrases [VP] contain verbs, as well as anything on which the verb acts [but not the subject of the action]. For example, "The psychology student _____[VP]_____.")
Answers: Noun phrases : (1), (4), (5)
Verb phrases : (3), (4), (5), (6)

Table 9.2 Summary Description of Language

All human languages can be analyzed at many levels. Here we analyze the sentence "It takes a heap of sense to write good nonsense."

Language Input ↓ Decoding ↓		Language Output ↑ Encoding ↑
	Phonemes Distinctive subset of all possible phones in a language	/t/ + /ā/ + /k/ + /s/ ...
	Morphemes From the distinctive lexicon of morphemes	... *take* (content morpheme) + *s* (plural function morpheme) ...
	Words From the distinctive vocabulary of words	*It* + *takes* + *a* + *heap* + *of* + *sense* + *to* + *write* + *good* + *nonsense.*
	Phrase Noun phrases (NP): a noun and its descriptors; Verb phrases (VP): a verb and whatever it acts on	NP + VP; *It* (NP) *takes a heap of sense to write good nonsense* (VP)
	Sentences Based on the language's syntax—syntactical structure	*It takes a heap of sense to write good nonsense.*
	Discourse	"It takes a heap of sense to write good nonsense" was first written by Mark Twain (Lederer, 1991, p. 131).
Comprehend Language		Produce Language

Understanding the Meaning of Words, Sentences, and Larger Text Units

When we read and speak, it is important not only to comprehend words and sentences but also to figure out the meaning of whole conversations or larger written pieces. **Semantics** is the study of meaning in a language. A semanticist would be concerned with how words and sentences express meaning. Discourse encompasses language use at the level beyond the sentence, such as in conversation, paragraphs, stories, chapters, and entire works of literature. (You will learn more about discourse later in this chapter.) Table 9.2 summarizes the various aspects of language. The next section discusses how we understand language through speech perception and further analysis.

✓ CONCEPT CHECK

1. What are some important properties of language?
2. What is the difference between phonemes and morphemes?
3. What is semantics?

Language Comprehension

Many processes are involved when we try to understand what somebody says. First of all, we need to perceive and recognize the words that are being said. Then we need to assign meaning to those words. In addition, we have to make sense of sentences we hear. These processes will be discussed in the next sections.

Understanding Words

Have you ever needed to communicate with someone over the phone, but the speech you heard was garbled because of faulty cell phone reception? If so, you will agree that speech perception is fundamental to language use in our everyday lives. Understanding speech is crucial to human communication. In this section, we investigate how we perceive speech. We also reflect on the question of whether speech is somehow special among all the various sounds we can perceive.

We are able to perceive speech with amazing rapidity. On the one hand, we can perceive as many as fifty phonemes *per second* in a language in which we are fluent (Foulke & Sticht, 1969). When confronted with non-speech sounds, on the other hand, we can perceive less than one phone per second (Warren et al., 1969). This limitation explains why foreign languages are difficult to understand (when we hear them), and sound like they are spoken quickly. The sounds of their letters and letter combinations are different from the sounds corresponding to the same letters and letter combinations in our native language. For example, the author's Spanish sounds "American" because he tends to reinterpret Spanish sounds in terms of the American English phonetic system, rather than the Spanish one.

Another problem we face when we try to understand what somebody else is saying is that no word sounds exactly the same when it is spoken across the various speakers who say the word. There is a lot of variability across people in the pronunciation of words. People speak faster or slower, or they may pronounce sounds differently depending on where they come from. For example, one of the author's elementary school teachers pronounced "get" in a way that sounded like "git." Speech sounds are very variable, but even if a word sounds different every time we hear it, we still need to be able to figure out what word it is. What makes it even more complicated is that often we pronounce more than one sound at the same time. This is called **coarticulation**. One or more phonemes begin while other phonemes still are being produced. For example, say the words "palace" and "pool." They both begin with a *p* sound. But can you notice a difference in the shape of your lips when you say the *p* of "pool" as compared to the *p* of "palace"? You are already preparing for the following vowel as you pronounce the *p* sound, and this impacts the sound you produce. Not only do phonemes within a word overlap, but the boundaries between words in continuous speech also tend to overlap.

The process of trying to separate the continuous sound stream into distinct words is called *speech segmentation*. Figure 9.1 shows a spectrogram that records physical sound patterns. As you can see, there is often no pause between words, while at the same time, there can be breaks within words. That is to say, the recording of speech sound waves poorly resembles what we hear.

This overlapping of speech sounds may seem to create additional problems for perceiving speech, but coarticulation is viewed as necessary for the effective transmission of speech information (Liberman et al., 1967). Thus, speech perception is viewed as different from other perceptual abilities because of both the linguistic nature of the information and the particular way in which information must be encoded for effective transmission.

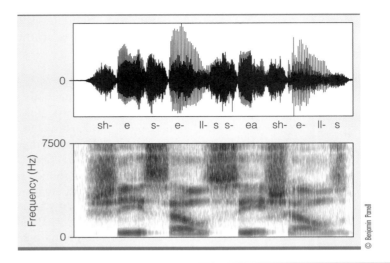

Figure 9.1 **Spectrogram.**

Spectrograms record physical sound patterns.

Coarticulation can be observed in nonverbal language as well. A number of studies have been completed that examine speech production in skilled signers (i.e., people who communicate in sign language). People who are skilled signers can convey many paragraphs worth of information in less than a minute (Lupton, 1998). A great deal of coarticulation occurs in skilled use of American Sign Language (ASL) (Grosvald & Corina, 2008; Jerde, Soechting, & Flanders, 2003). This coarticulation affects a number of aspects of the sign, both as it begins and as it leads into another sign. The affected aspects include hand shape, movement, and position (Yang & Sarkar, 2006). Coarticulation occurs more frequently with more informal forms of ASL (Emmorey, 1994). People who are just learning sign language are more likely to use the more formal form. Later, as people become more skillful, they typically begin to use the more informal forms. Therefore, as skill and fluency increase, so does the incidence of coarticulation. Coarticulation is a result of the anticipation of the next sign, much in the same way that verbal coarticulation is based on the anticipation of the next word. This coarticulation does not, however, typically impair understanding. These observations support the unique nature of language perception, regardless of whether its format is spoken or signed.

So, how do we perceive speech with such ease? There are many alternative theories of speech perception to explain our facility. These theories differ mainly as to whether speech perception is viewed as special, or ordinary, with respect to other types of auditory perception.

The View of Speech Perception as Ordinary

One approach to speech perception suggests that when we perceive speech, we use the same processes as when we perceive other sounds like the crowing of a rooster. These kinds of theories emphasize either template-matching or feature-detection processes. They suggest that there are different stages of neural processing: In one stage, speech sounds are analyzed into their components. In another stage, these components are analyzed for patterns and matched to a prototype or template (Kuhl,

1991; Massaro, 1987; Stevens & Blumstein, 1981). One theory of this kind is the *phonetic refinement theory* (Pisoni et al., 1985; see, for example, Hanson et al., 2010). It says that we start with an analysis of auditory sensations and shift to higher-level processing. We identify words on the basis of successively paring down the possibilities for matches between each of the phonemes and the words we already know from memory. In this theory, the initial sound that establishes the set of possible words we have heard need not be the first phoneme alone. You may have observed this phenomenon yourself on a conscious level. Have you ever been watching a movie or listening to a lecture when you heard only garbled sound? It takes you a few moments to figure out what the speaker must have said. To decide what you heard, you may have gone through a conscious process of phonetic refinement.

A similar theoretical idea is embodied by the TRACE model (McClelland & Elman, 1986; Mirman et al., 2008). According to this model, speech perception begins with three levels of feature detection: the level of acoustic features, the level of phonemes, and the level of words. According to this theory, speech perception is highly interactive. In Chapter 8, you were introduced to network theories, and the TRACE model works in a similar fashion of spreading activation. Phonemic information changes activation patterns in the network while information about words or their meaning can influence the analysis as well by prediction of which words are likely to appear next. Therefore, lower levels affect higher levels and vice versa.

One attribute these theories have in common is that they all require decision-making processes above and beyond feature detection or template matching. Thus, the speech we perceive may differ from the speech sounds that actually reach our ears. The reason is that cognitive and contextual factors influence our perception of the sensed signal. For example, the **phonemic-restoration effect** involves integrating what we know with what we hear when we perceive speech (Kashino, 2006; Samuel, 1981; Warren, 1970; Warren & Warren, 1970).

Suppose that you were in an experiment. You are listening to a sentence having the following pattern: "It was found that the *eel was on the _____." For the final word, one of the following words is inserted: *axle*, *shoe*, *table*, or *orange*. In addition, the speaker inserts a cough instead of the initial sound where the asterisk appeared in "*eel." Virtually all participants are unaware that a consonant has been deleted. The sound they recall having heard differs according to the context. The participants recall hearing "the *wheel* was on the axle," "the *heel* was on the shoe," "the *meal* was on the table," or "the *peel* was on the orange." In essence, they restore the missing phoneme that best suits the context of the sentence.

How well do we understand words that we hear without any context? Researchers recorded speech acts by different individuals and then presented individual words without any context to their participants. Depending on whether the speaker spoke at a slow, normal, or fast speed, the isolated words were only correctly identified 68% (slow speech) to 41% of the time (fast speech; Miller & Isard, 1963).

Phonemic restoration is similar to the visual phenomenon of closure, which is based on incomplete visual information. Indeed, one main approach to auditory perception attempts to extend to various acoustic events, including speech, the Gestalt principles of visual perception (Bregman, 1990; Shahin et al., 2009). These principles include, for example, symmetry, proximity, and similarity. Thus, theories that consider speech perception as ordinary use general perceptual principles of feature-detection and Gestalt psychology. They thereby attempt to explain how listeners understand speech. Other theorists, however, view speech perception as special.

The View of Speech Perception as Special

Some researchers suggest that speech-perception processes differ from the processes we use when we hear other sounds. We will explore this view further in the next sections by reviewing research on categorical perception and the motor theory of speech perception.

Categorical Perception   One phenomenon in speech perception that led to the notion of specialization was the finding of **categorical perception**—discontinuous categories of speech sounds. That is, although the speech sounds we actually hear comprise a continuum of variation in sound waves, we experience speech sounds categorically. This phenomenon can be seen in the perception of the consonant–vowel combinations *ba, da,* and *ga.* A speech signal would look different for each of these syllables. Some patterns in the speech signal lead to the perception of *ba.* Others lead to the perception of *da.* And still others lead to perception of *ga.*

Additionally, the sound patterns for each syllable may differ as a result of other factors like pitch. The *ba* that you said yesterday differs from the *ba* you say today. But it is not perceived as different: It is perceived as belonging to the same category as the *ba* you said a few days ago or will say tomorrow. However, a non-speech sound such as a tone would be perceived as different. Here, continuous differences in pitch (how high or low the tone is) are heard as continuous and distinct.

In a classic study, researchers used a speech synthesizer to mimic this natural variation in syllable acoustic patterns. By this means, they also were able to control the acoustic difference between the syllables (Liberman et al., 1957). They created a series of consonant–vowel sounds that changed in equal increments from *ba* to *da* to *ga.* People who listened to the synthesized syllables, however, heard a sudden switch. It was from the sound category of *ba* to the sound category of *da* (and likewise from the category of *da* to that of *ga*). Discrimination of differences within one sound category was relatively poor, whereas discrimination between categories (e.g., between *ba* and *da*) was enhanced. Although all the sounds differed from each other acoustically (and their acoustic distance was equal), people did not really perceive differences between the sounds that represented the same category. They only heard differences when the sounds represented different categories. That is, discrimination of two neighboring *ba*s was poor, whereas discrimination of *ba* from its neighboring *da* was preserved. Normal perceptual processing should discriminate equally between all equally spaced pairs of the different sounds along the continuum, however. The researchers thus concluded that speech is perceived via specialized processes.

A number of studies have further examined categorical perception in people with reading disabilities. In children with learning disabilities, the perceptual ability to discriminate *between* categories is impaired. Conversely, the perceptual ability to discriminate *within* categories is enhanced in these same children (Breier et al., 2005). That is, children at risk of reading disabilities, compared with children who are not at risk, use less phonological information even though they perceive more subtle acoustic (sound) differences when performing a categorical-perception task (Breier et al., 2004). These and other findings led the researchers to investigate the notion that speech perception relies on special processes.

The Motor Theory of Speech Perception   The findings described above also led to the early, but still influential, motor theory of speech perception (Galantucci, Fowler, & Turvey, 2006; Liberman et al., 1967; Liberman & Mattingly, 1985). According to the motor theory, we use the movements of the speaker's vocal tract to

INVESTIGATING COGNITIVE PSYCHOLOGY
Understanding Schemas

Ask a friend to do an experiment with you. Tell your friend that you are going to say a sentence and ask them what it means. Say the following sentence to your friend: "In mud eels are, in clay none are." Ask your friend the meaning of what you just said.

Chances are that your friend did not understand the sentence. Why? Your friend was not applying the appropriate schema to understand your utterance. Ask your friend to think of him- or herself as a fish who doesn't want to be eaten by eels. Now, repeat this sentence to your friend. Can your friend understand the sentence now? Many people can after they have the context. (Although, there are still some people who will not be able to understand this utterance, so you will have to give them stronger hints.)

perceive what he says. Observing that a speaker rounds his lips or presses his lips together provides the listener with phonetic information. Thus, the listener uses specialized processes involved in producing speech to perceive speech. In fact, there is substantial overlap between the parts of the cortex that are involved in speech production and speech perception.

So, how can the motor theory of speech perception be tested? In a recent study, researchers had participants listen to continuous acoustic signals. As we know from the section on categorical perception, people categorize continuous sounds as syllables like "ga" and "ba". With repetitive transcranial magnetic stimulation (rTMS), participants' lip representation in the primary motor cortex was then interrupted. With the motor cortex's lip representation impaired, participants had a much harder time distinguishing between speech sounds that involved the lips or tip of the tongue in their articulation (e.g., "ba" and "da"). However, differentiation between sounds that do not involve lip articulation (e.g., "ka" and "ga") was not impaired. These findings support the notion that motor parts of the cortex are not only involved in the production of speech but also in speech perception (Moettoenen & Watkins, 2009).

Since the early work of Liberman and colleagues, the phenomenon of categorical perception has been extended to the perception of other kinds of stimuli, such as color and facial emotion. This extension weakens the claim that speech perception is special (Galantucci, Fowler, & Turvey, 2006; Jusczyk, 1997). However, supporters of the speech-is-special position still maintain that other forms of evidence indicate that speech is perceived via specialized processes.

One such distinctive aspect of human speech perception can be seen in the so-called *McGurk effect* (McGurk & MacDonald, 1976). This effect involves the synchrony of visual and auditory perceptions: When watching a movie, an auditory syllable is perceived differently depending on whether you see the speaker make the sound that matches the pronunciation of the syllable or make another sound that does not match the syllable spoken. Imagine yourself watching a movie. As long as the soundtrack corresponds to the speakers' lip movements, you encounter no problems. However, suppose that the soundtrack indicates one thing, such as *da*. At the same time, the actor's lips clearly make the movements for another sound, such as *ba*. You are likely to hear a compromise sound, such as *tha*. It is neither what was said nor what was seen. You somehow synthesize the auditory and visual information. You thereby come up with a result that is unlike either. For this reason, poorly dubbed movies can be confusing. You are vaguely aware that the lips are saying one thing, and you are hearing something else entirely.

In one set of studies, Nicholls, Searle, and Bradshaw (2004) studied the McGurk effect with respect to lip reading. The experimenters covered half of the speaker's mouth, while either matching or mismatching auditory and visual information. The experimenters found that, when the left side of the mouth was covered, there was little change in the occurrence of the McGurk effect. However, when the right side of the mouth was covered, the occurrence of the McGurk effect dropped dramatically. Then the researchers used an inverted video of the left side of the mouth, such that it appeared to be the right side of the mouth, and saw the McGurk effect rebound (Nicholls, Searle, & Bradshaw, 2004). These findings suggest that the right side, or what is perceived as the right side of the mouth, is attended to more in lip reading. Hence, lack of correspondence between what the right side of the mouth says and what is heard are the more likely to lead to the McGurk effect.

The McGurk effect seems to have a physiological basis in the superior temporal sulcus (STS). Researchers presented their participants with stimuli like the ones described above that evoke the McGurk effect. However, when they used transcranial magnetic stimulation (TMS) to interrupt activity of the STS in their participants, the likelihood of the McGurk effect was significantly reduced (Beauchamp et al., 2010).

In normal conversation, we use lip reading to augment our perception of speech. It is particularly important in situations in which background noise may make speech perception more difficult. The motor theory accounts for this integration quite easily because articulatory information includes visual and auditory information. However, believers in other theories interpret these findings as support for more general perceptual processes. They believe these processes naturally integrate information across sensory modalities (Galantucci et al., 2006; Massaro, 1987; Massaro & Cohen, 1990).

Is a synthesis of these opposing views possible? Perhaps one reason for the complexity of this issue lies in the nature of speech perception itself. It involves both linguistic and perceptual attributes. From a purely perceptual perspective, speech is just a relatively complex signal that is not treated qualitatively differently from other signals. From a psycholinguistic perspective, speech is special because it lies within the domain of language, a special human ability. Indeed, cognitive psychology textbooks differ in terms of where speech perception is discussed. Sometimes it is discussed in the context of language, other times in the context of perception. Thus, the diversity of views on the nature of speech perception can be seen as reflecting the differences in how researchers treat speech. They view it either as regular acoustic signals or as more special phonetic messages (Remez, 1994).

Understanding Meaning: Semantics

Language is very difficult to put into words.
—Voltaire

The opening of this chapter quoted Helen Keller's description of her first awareness that words had meanings. You probably do not remember the moment that words first came alive to you, but your parents surely do. In fact, one of the greatest joys of being a parent is watching your children's amazing discovery that words have meanings. In semantics, **denotation** is the strict dictionary definition of a word.

Connotation is a word's emotional overtones, presuppositions, and other non-explicit meanings. Taken together, denotation and connotation form the meaning of a word. Because connotations may vary between people, there can be variation in the meaning formed. Imagine the word *snake*. For many people, the connotation of *snake* is negative or dangerous. Others, say a biologist specializing in snakes (called a herpetologist), would have a very different and probably much more positive connotation for the word *snake*.

How do we understand word meanings in the first place? Recall from previous chapters that we encode meanings into memory through concepts. These include ideas, to which we may attach various characteristics and with which we may connect various other ideas, such as through propositions (Rey, 2003). They also include images and perhaps motor patterns for implementing particular procedures. Here, we are concerned only with concepts, particularly in terms of words as arbitrary symbols for concepts.

Actually, when we think of words as representing concepts, words are economical ways in which to manipulate related information. For example, when you think about the single word *desk*, you also may conjure all these things:

- all the instances of desks in existence anywhere;
- instances of desks that exist only in your imagination;
- all the characteristics of desks;
- all the things you might do with desks; and
- all the other concepts you might link to desks (e.g., things you put on or in desks or places where you might find desks).

Having a word for something helps us to add new information to our existing information about that concept. For example, you have access to the word *desk*. When you have new experiences related to desks or otherwise learn new things about desks, you have a word around which to organize all this related information.

Recall, too, the constructive nature of memory. Having word labels (e.g., "washing clothes," "peace march") has several effects. First, it facilitates the ease of understanding and remembering a text passage. Second, it enhances subjects' recall of the shape of a droodle. (Recall that a droodle is essentially a doodle puzzle: You see a doodle and you have to guess what it is.) Third, it affects the accuracy of eyewitness testimony. Having words as concepts for things helps us in our everyday nonverbal

■ BELIEVE IT OR NOT

CAN IT REALLY BE HARD TO STOP CURSING?

In psychology, the involuntary utterance of socially inappropriate words or sentences is called *coprolalia*. There is a range of other coprophenomena, like making socially inappropriate gestures (copropraxia) and drawings (coprographia). Often, these utterances are related to obscene, religious, or ethnical content. They are not expressed out of anger but rather result from a kind of urge that the speaker cannot control and that can cause him or her considerable embarrassment. Coprolalia is often part of a neurological disorder called Tourette syndrome, which exhibits a widely variable pattern of tics (like suddenly and involuntarily kicking in the air or pulling one's earlobe). Tourette syndrome usually starts in childhood and stabilizes after adolescence. As of today, it is not entirely clear what causes tics, but studies indicate that generally the cortical-striatal-thalamocortical pathways are involved. Different tics seem to be caused by different brain mechanisms. Coprolalia, in particular, involves activation of the brain's language regions, caudate, thalamus, and cerebellum. It can also occur outside of Tourette syndrome in people who have suffered strokes or encephalitis, for example (Freeman et al., 2008). Indeed, even cases of Tourette syndrome patients swearing in sign language have been reported.

Published in *The New Yorker* 3/22/1993 by J.B. Handelsman/www.Cartoonbank.com

" 'Born in conservation,' if you don't mind. 'Captivity' has negative connotations."

interactions. For example, our concepts of *skunk* and of *dog* allow us more easily to recognize the difference between the two, even if we see an animal only for a moment (Ross & Spalding, 1994). Depending on which we saw, this rapid recognition enables us to respond appropriately. Clearly, being able to comprehend the conceptual meanings of words is important. But how do we retrieve the meanings of words?

All words are stored in our mental lexicon, which contains both the words and their meanings. One observation that hints at how we represent meaning comes from studies with people who once had normal language skills but at some point contracted lesions of the temporal lobes of the brain. When certain of those people were asked to indicate the meaning of a picture, their problems in naming objects were not arbitrary. One group of patients had trouble recognizing animate things, like animals and plants. Another group of patients was challenged in recognizing things that were manufactured, like tools. Warrington and colleagues (Warrington & McCarthy, 1987; Warrington & Shallice, 1984) have suggested criteria for determining the difference between manufactured and living things. Objects that are made by humans are mostly distinguished by means of their function. Do we use an object to get from one point to another, or to open something? Living things, in contrary, are mainly distinguished by means of their looks. A horse looks different than a donkey, and both differ from what a cow looks like. So when we retrieve the meaning of words from our memory, we may rely on their perceptual features and the function (as well as some other characteristics). This interpretation is in line with the findings of the lesion studies: People who had sustained damage in regions that are involved in perceptual processing have trouble recognizing living things. People with lesions in areas that are involved in the processing of functional information have more trouble recognizing man-made things.

As you may have noticed, many words in English have more than one meaning: Take the word "foot," for example. "I have a very wide foot," refers to the foot as a body part. "She lives at the foot of the hill," indicates that a person is living at the bottom part of a hill. Generally, words have a dominant meaning that is used more often, and one or more subordinate meanings. In the example with the word "foot," people typically think of a body part, which is the dominant meaning. The bottom part of a hill is a subordinate meaning. What meaning you ultimately ascribe to the word depends largely on the context in which it appears.

Understanding Sentences: Syntax

An equally important part of the psychology of language is the analysis of linguistic structure. Not only words convey meaning; the structure of sentences does as well. For example, "The man hunted the lion." has a different meaning from "The lion hunted the man." *Syntax* is the systematic way in which words can be combined and sequenced to make meaningful phrases and sentences (Carroll, 1986). Whereas studies of speech perception chiefly investigate the phonetic structure of language, syntax focuses on the study of the grammar of phrases and sentences. In other words, it considers the regularity of structure.

Although you have heard the word *grammar* before in regard to how people should structure their sentences, psycholinguists use the word *grammar* in a slightly different way. Specifically, **grammar** is the study of language in terms of noticing regular patterns. These patterns relate to the functions and relationships of words in a sentence. They extend as broadly to the level of discourse and narrowly to the pronunciation and meaning of individual words.

In your English courses, you may have been introduced to *prescriptive grammar*. This kind of grammar prescribes the "correct" ways in which to structure the use of written and spoken language. Of greater interest to psycholinguists is *descriptive grammar*, in which an attempt is made to describe the structures, functions, and relationships of words in language.

Consider an example of a sentence that illustrates the contrast between prescriptive and descriptive approaches to grammar: When Mario observes his father carrying upstairs an unappealing bedtime book, he responds, "Daddy, what did you bring that book that I don't want to be read to out of up for?" (Pinker, 1994, p. 97). Mario's utterance might shiver the spine of any prescriptive grammarian. But Mario's ability to produce such a complex sentence, with such intricate internal interdependencies, would please descriptive grammarians.

The study of syntax allows analysis of language in manageable—and therefore relatively easily studied—units. Also, it offers limitless possibilities for exploration. There are virtually no bounds to the possible combinations of words that may be used to form sentences. Earlier, we referred to this property as the productivity of language. In English, as in any language, we can take a particular set of words (or morphemes, to be more accurate) and a particular set of rules for combining the items and produce a breathtakingly vast array of meaningful utterances. Suppose you were to go to the U.S. Library of Congress and randomly select any sentence from any book. You then searched for an identical sentence in the vast array of sentences in the books therein. Barring intentional quotations, you would be unlikely to find the identical sentence.

People demonstrate a remarkable knack for understanding syntactical structure. Read through the following demonstration in the *Investigating Cognitive Psychology: Your Sense of Grammar* box and try to find the sentences that are not grammatical.

Fluent speakers of a language can recognize syntactical structure immediately. We can do so whether particular sentences and particular word orders are or are

INVESTIGATING COGNITIVE PSYCHOLOGY
Your Sense of Grammar

Mark an asterisk next to the sentences that are not grammatical, regardless of whether the sentences are meaningful or accurate:

1. The student the book.
2. Bought the book.
3. Bought the student the book.
4. The book was bought by the student.
5. By whom was the book bought?
6. By student the bought book.
7. The student was bought by the book.
8. Who bought the book?
9. The book bought the student.
10. The book bought.

Answers: 1, 2, 3, 6, 10

not grammatical (Bock, 1990; Pinker, 1994). We can do so even when the sentences are meaningless. For example, we can evaluate Chomsky's sentence, "Colorless green ideas sleep furiously." Or we can evaluate a sentence composed of nonsense words, as in Lewis Carroll's poem "Jabberwocky," "'Twas brillig and the slithy toves did gyre and gimble in the wabe."

In the following, we explore the properties and impact of syntax in more detail. We have a look at the phenomena of syntactical priming and speech errors and consider two approaches to analyzing sentences: phrase-structure grammar and transformational grammar. We will also explore the interaction between words and sentence structures.

Syntactical Priming

Just as we show semantic priming of word meanings in memory (that is, we react faster to words that are related in meaning to a prior presented word), we show syntactical priming of sentence structures. In other words, we spontaneously tend to use syntactical structures and read faster sentences that parallel the structures of sentences we have just heard (Bock, 1990; Bock, Loebell, & Morey, 1992; Sturt et al., 2010). For example, a speaker will be more likely to use a passive construction (e.g., "The student was praised by the professor") after hearing a passive construction. He or she will do so even when the topics of the sentences differ. Even children as young as age 3 described a series of new items with the same sentence structure used by an experimenter (Bencini & Valian, 2008).

Another example of syntactical priming is sentence priming. In this type of experiment, participants are presented with a sentence. Participants then are presented with new sentences and are asked to rate the degree to which they are grammatically correct. If a sentence has the same structure as the previously presented item, it is rated as more nearly grammatically correct (Luka & Barsalou, 2005), independent of its actual degree of grammatical correctness. Participants in the experimental group may have read the sentence, "Amanda carried Fernando the package," whereas control-group participants read the sentence, "Amanda carried the package to Fernando." Both groups were then asked to rate the test sentence, "Igor lugged Dr. Frankenstein the corpse." As you can see, this sentence is structurally similar to the first sentence that participants in the experimental group were asked to read; it does not resemble the structure of the first sentence that control-group participants read. And indeed, participants from the experimental group rated the test sentence as more grammatical than did control-group participants.

Speech Errors

Other evidence of our uncanny aptitude for syntax is shown in the *speech errors* we produce. Even when we accidentally switch the placement of two words in a sentence, we still form grammatical, if meaningless or nonsensical, sentences. We almost invariably switch nouns for nouns, verbs for verbs, prepositions for prepositions, and so on. For example, we may say, "I put the oven in the cake." But we will probably not say, "I put the cake oven in the." We usually even attach (and detach) appropriate function morphemes to make the switched words fit their new positions. For example, when meaning to say, "The butter knives are in the drawer," we may say, "The butter drawers are in the knife." Here, we change "drawer" to plural and "knives" to singular to preserve the grammaticality of the sentence. Even so-called agrammatic aphasics, who have extreme difficulties in both comprehending and producing language, preserve syntactical categories in their speech errors (Butterworth & Howard, 1987; Garrett, 1992). In Chapter 10, we consider slips of the tongue in more detail.

Analyzing Sentences: Phrase-Structure Grammar

The preceding examples seem to indicate that we humans have some mental mechanism for classifying words according to syntactical categories. This classification mechanism is separate from the meanings for the words (Bock, 1990). When we compose sentences, we seem to analyze and divide them into functional components. This process is called *parsing*. We assign appropriate syntactical categories (often called "parts of speech," e.g., noun, verb, article) to each component of the sentence. We then use the syntax rules for the language to construct grammatical sequences of the parsed components.

Early in the 20th century, linguists who studied syntax largely focused on how sentences could be analyzed in terms of sequences of phrases, such as noun phrases and verb phrases, which were mentioned previously. They also focused on how phrases could be parsed into various syntactical categories, such as nouns, verbs, and adjectives. Such analyses look at the **phrase-structure grammar**—they analyze the structure of phrases as they are used. Let's have a closer look at the sentence:

"The girl looked at the boy with the telescope."

First of all, the sentence can be divided into the noun phrase (NP) "The girl" followed by a verb phrase (VP) "looked at the boy with the telescope." The noun phrase can be further divided into a determiner ("the") and a noun ("girl"). Likewise, the verb phrase can be further subdivided. However, the analysis of how to divide the verb phrase depends on what meaning the speaker had in mind. You may have noticed that the sentence can have two meanings:

(a) The girl looked with a telescope at the boy, or
(b) The girl looked at a boy who had a telescope.

IN THE LAB OF STEVEN PINKER

The Psychology of Language

I have always thought of language as a window into human nature. Early in my career I tried to identify the mental mechanisms that children use to acquire their mother tongue as a way of shedding light on the nature-nurture debate. I then focused on the meaning and syntax of verbs—why you can pour water into a glass, but you can't pour a glass with water, and why you can fill a glass with water, but you can't fill water into a glass—to illuminate the basic concepts of human thought such as causation, agency, space, time, and substance. For a number of years I studied regular verbs, like *walk-walked* and *play-played* to get insight about the computational architecture of human cognition and how they differ from irregular verbs like *sing-sang* and *bring-brought* to understand the interaction between computation and memory.

STEVEN PINKER

Currently I am using "indirect speech"—innuendo, euphemism, doublespeak, shilly-shallying—as a window into social relationships. People often don't blurt out what they mean in so many words but veil their intentions in innuendo, counting on their listeners to "catch their drift" or "read between the lines." Here are some examples:

- If you could pass the guacamole, that would be awesome [a polite request].
- Gee, officer, is there some way we could take care of the ticket right here, without going to court or doing a lot of paperwork? [a bribe]
- Would you like to come up and see my etchings? [a sexual come-on]
- I hear you're the jury foreman in the *Soprano* trial. It's an important civic responsibility. You've got a wife and kids. We know you'll do the right thing. [a threat]

Why don't people just say what they mean? The reason, I believe, is that language has to do two things

at once: convey a proposition, and maintain social relationships. The anthropologist Alan Fiske has found that in every culture, the relationship between two people falls into a small number of types: communality (warmth and sharing), dominance, and reciprocity (tit-for-tat exchanges or equal distribution of resources). We distinguish these sharply: for example, everyone knows that good friends shouldn't engage in a business transaction, like one selling his car to the other, because the act of negotiating a price (reciprocity) clashes with the rules of a friendship (communal sharing), putting a strain on the relationship. The problem with language is that the very act of making a request in words can clash with the ongoing relationship type: an imperative like "Give me the guacamole" assumes a dominance relationship (you're bossing someone around) that clashes with friendship; a bribe like "If I give you $50, will you let me drive away?" treats the officer as a business customer rather than a superior. So, to treat your fellow diner as an equal, or to probe whether the officer is receptive to a bribe without challenging the current relationship, people use indirect speech. Basically, they are seeking plausible deniability of a transaction that presupposes a different relationship model than the one currently in force.

We test this idea by having people imagine themselves in the shoes of someone receiving a bribe, a threat, or a sexual come-on, which is posed either directly or with innuendo; and then to indicate how confident they are in what they think the speaker intends, whether they feel threatened or offended, how easy it would be to resume a normal relationship if the offer is rebuffed, and other questions. We also have people role-play these interactions while hooked up to electrophysiological recording equipment to measure their sense of threat and challenge in measures such as heart rate and blood pressure.

In case (a), the verb phrase contains a verb (V; "looked"), and two prepositional phrases (PP; "at the boy" and "with the telescope"). In case (b), the verb phrase would again contain the verb "looked," but there is just one prepositional phrase ("looked at the boy with the telescope"). You can then work your way further

INVESTIGATING COGNITIVE PSYCHOLOGY
Syntax

Using the following 10 words, create 5 strings of words that make grammatical sentences. Also create five sequences of words that violate the syntax rules of English grammar: *ball, basket, bounced, into, put, red, rolled, tall, the, woman.*

Finished? Now think about the steps involved in producing the sentences. To complete the preceding task, you mentally classified the words into syntactical categories, even if you did not know the correct labels for the categories. You then arranged the words into grammatical sequences according to the syntactical categories for the words and your implicit knowledge of English syntax rules. Most 4-year-olds can demonstrate the same ability to parse words into categories and to arrange them into grammatical sentences. Of course, most 4-year-olds probably cannot label the syntactical categories for any of the words.

down and divide the prepositional phrases further into prepositions, determiners, nouns, etc (see Figure 9.2 for details).

The rules governing the sequences of words are termed *phrase-structure rules*. Linguists often use tree diagrams, such as the ones shown in Figure 9.2, to observe the interrelationships of phrases within a sentence. Various other models also have been proposed (e.g., relational grammar, Farrell, 2005; Perlmutter, 1983a; lexical-functional grammar; Bresnan, 1982).

Tree diagrams help to reveal the interrelationships of syntactical classes within the phrase structures of sentences (Clegg & Shepherd, 2007; Wasow, 1989). In particular, such diagrams show that sentences are not merely organized chains of words, strung together sequentially. Rather, they are organized into hierarchical structures of embedded phrases. The use of tree diagrams helps to highlight many aspects of how we use language, including both our linguistic sophistication and our difficulties in using language. As you can see in Figure 9.2, our example sentence is depicted in two different ways, depending on its meaning. By observing tree diagrams of ambiguous sentences, psycholinguists can better pinpoint the source of confusion.

A New Approach to Syntax: Transformational Grammar

In 1957, Noam Chomsky revolutionized the study of syntax. He suggested that to understand syntax, we must observe not only the interrelationships among phrases within sentences. Additionally, we have to consider the syntactical relationships between sentences. Specifically, Chomsky observed that particular sentences and their tree diagrams show peculiar relationships.

For example, consider the following sentences:

S_1: Susie greedily ate the crocodile.

S_2: The crocodile was eaten greedily by Susie.

Oddly enough, a phrase-structure grammar would not show any particular relation at all between sentences S_1 and S_2. Indeed, phrase-structure analyses of S_1 and S_2 would look almost completely different (Figure 9.3). Yet, the two sentences differ only in voice. The first sentence is expressed in the active voice and the second in

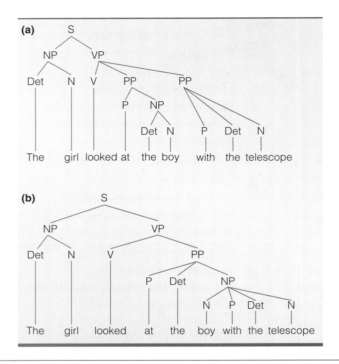

Figure 9.2 **Phrase-Structure Grammar (part 1).**

Phrase-structure grammars illustrate the hierarchies of phrases within sentences. Here you can see two possible ways to analyze the sentence "The girl looked at the boy with the telescope." The abbreviations used in the tree diagrams are: S (sentence), NP (noun phrase), VP (verb phrase), PP (prepositional phrase), N (noun), V (verb), Det (determiner), and P (preposition).

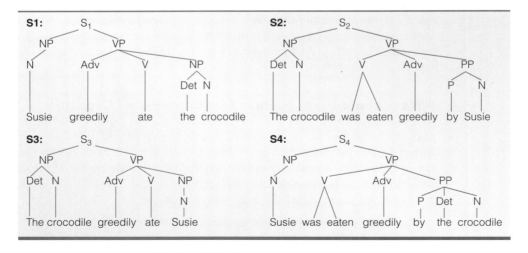

Figure 9.3 **Phrase-Structure Grammar (part 2).**

Phrase-structure grammars show surprising dissimilarities between sentences S_1 and S_2, yet surprising similarities between S_1 and S_3 or between S_2 and S_4. Noam Chomsky suggested that to understand syntax, we also must consider a way of viewing the interrelationships among various phrase structures.

the passive voice. But both sentences represent the same proposition "ate (greedily) (Susie, crocodile)." Recall from Chapter 7 that propositions may be used to illustrate that the same underlying meanings can be derived through alternative means of representation.

Consider another pair of sentences that have the same meaning:

S_3: The crocodile greedily ate Susie.

S_4: Susie was eaten greedily by the crocodile.

Again, the sentences have the same meaning, but phrase-structure grammar would show no relationship between S_3 and S_4. What's more, phrase-structure grammar would show some similarities of surface structure between S_1 and S_3 as well as S_2 and S_4. The pairs of sentences clearly have quite different meanings, particularly to Susie and the crocodile. Apparently, an adequate grammar would address the fact that sentences with similar surface structures can have very different meanings.

This observation and other observations of the interrelationships among various phrase structures led linguists to go beyond merely describing various individual phrase structures. They began to focus their attention on the relationships among different phrase structures. Linguists may gain deeper understanding of syntax by studying the relationships among phrase structures that involve transformations of elements within sentences (Chomsky, 1957). Specifically, Chomsky suggested a way to supplement the study of phrase structures. He proposed the study of **transformational grammar**, which involves transformational rules. These rules guide the ways in which an underlying proposition can be arranged into a sentence. There are obviously many different sentences that can express the same proposition.

A simple way of looking at Chomsky's transformational grammar is to say that "Transformations … are rules that map tree structures onto other tree structures" (Wasow, 1989, p. 170). For example, transformational grammar considers how the tree-structure diagrams in Figure 9.3 are interrelated. With application of transformational rules, the tree structure of S_1 can be mapped onto the tree structure of S_2. Similarly, the structure of S_3 can be mapped onto the tree structure of S_4.

In transformational grammar, **deep structure** refers to an underlying syntactical structure that links various phrase structures through various transformation rules. In contrast, **surface structure** refers to any of the various phrase structures that may result from such transformations. Many casual readers of Chomsky have misunderstood Chomsky's terms. They incorrectly inferred that deep structures refer to profound underlying meanings of sentences, whereas surface structures refer only to superficial interpretations of sentences. This is not the case. Chomsky meant only to show that differing phrase structures may have a relationship that is not immediately apparent by using phrase-structure grammar alone. For example, the sentences, "Susie greedily ate the crocodile," and "The crocodile was eaten greedily by Susie" have a relationship that cannot be seen just by looking at the phrase-structure grammar. For detection of the underlying relationship between two phrase structures, transformation rules must be applied.

Relationships between Syntactical and Lexical Structures

Chomsky (1965, cited in Wasow, 1989) also addressed how syntactical structures may interact with lexical structures, that is, words. He suggested that our mental lexicon contains more than the semantic meanings attached to each word (or morpheme). In addition, each lexical item also contains syntactical information. This syntactical information for each lexical item indicates three things:

- the syntactical category of the item, such as noun versus verb;
- the appropriate syntactical contexts in which the particular morpheme may be used, such as pronouns as subjects versus as direct objects; and
- any idiosyncratic information about the syntactical uses of the morpheme, such as the treatment of irregular verbs.

For example, there would be separate lexical entries for the word *spread* categorized as a noun and for *spread* as a verb. Each lexical entry also would indicate which syntactical rules to use for positioning the word. The rules that are applicable depend on which category is applicable in the given context. For example, as a verb, *spread* would not follow the article *the*. As a noun, however, spread would be allowed to do so. Even the peculiarities of syntax for a given lexical entry would be stored in the lexicon. For example, the lexical entry for the verb *spread* would indicate that this verb deviates from the normal syntactical rule for forming past tenses by adding *-ed* to the stem used for the present tense.

You may wonder why we would clutter up our mental lexicon with so much syntactical information. There is an advantage to attaching syntactical, context-sensitive, and idiosyncratic information to the items in our mental lexicon. If we add to the complexity of our mental lexicon, we can simplify drastically the number and complexity of the rules we need in our mental syntax. For example, by attaching information about the idiosyncratic treatment of irregular verbs (e.g., *spread* or *fall*) to our mental lexicon, we do not have to endure different syntactical rules for each verb. By making our lexicon more complex, we allow our syntax to be simpler. In this way, appropriate transformations may be simple and relatively context-free. Once we know the basic syntax of a language, we easily can apply the rules to all items in our lexicon. We then can gradually expand our lexicon to provide increasing complexity and sophistication.

Not all cognitive psychologists agree with all aspects of Chomsky's theories (e.g., Bock, Loebell, & Morey, 1992; Devitt, 2008; Garrett, 1992; Jackendoff, 1991). Many particularly disagree with his emphasis on syntax (form) over semantics (meaning). The suggestion that syntactic rules influence the creation of a deep structure, which is then transformed through the application of more rules into a surface structure, left psychologists wondering about the significance of meaning. A theory that put so much emphasis on syntax seemed insufficient to explain the processes of how we use language to express meaning. Nonetheless, several cognitive psychologists have proposed models of language comprehension and production that include key ideas of syntax.

How do we link the elements in our mental lexicon to the elements in our syntactical structures? Various models for such bridging have been proposed (Bock, Loebell, & Morey, 1992; Culicover & Jackendoff, 2005; Jackendoff, 1991). According to some of these models, when we parse sentences by syntactical categories, we create slots for each item in the sentence. Consider, for example, the sentence, "Juan gave María the book from the shelf." There is a slot for a noun used as: (1) a subject (Juan); (2) as a direct object (the book); (3) as an indirect object (María); and (4) as objects of prepositions (the shelf). There are also slots for the verb, the preposition, and the articles.

PRACTICAL APPLICATIONS OF COGNITIVE PSYCHOLOGY

SPEAKING WITH NON-NATIVE ENGLISH SPEAKERS

Given what you now know about processes of speech perception, semantics, and syntax, think about ways to make your speech production easier for others to perceive. If you are speaking to someone whose primary language differs from yours, try slowing down your speech, thus exaggerating the length of time between words. Be sure to enunciate consonant sounds carefully, without making your vowel sounds too long. Use simpler sentence constructions. Break down lengthy and involved sentences into smaller units. Insert longer pauses between sentences to give the person time to translate the sentence into propositional form. Communication may feel more effortful but will probably be more effective.

Think about conversations with people who suffer from hearing impairments. How can you help them understand you? Do you apply the same strategies as with foreigners, or maybe some others?

In turn, lexical items contain information regarding the kinds of slots into which the items can be placed. The information is based on the kinds of thematic roles the items can fill. **Thematic roles** are ways in which items can be used in the context of communication. Several roles have been identified. In particular, these are the roles of:

- the agent, the "doer" of any action;
- the patient, the direct recipient of the action;
- the beneficiary, the indirect recipient of the action;
- the instrument, the means by which the action is implemented;
- the location, the place where the action occurs;
- the source, where the action originated; and
- the goal, where the action is going (Bock, 1990; Fromkin & Rodman, 1988).

According to this view of how syntax and semantics are linked, the various syntactical slots can be filled by lexical entries with corresponding thematic roles. For example, the slot of subject noun might be filled by the thematic role of agent. Nouns that can fill agent roles can be inserted into slots for subjects of phrases. Patient roles correspond to slots for direct objects. Beneficiary roles fit with indirect objects, and so on. Nouns that are objects of prepositions may be filled with various thematic roles. These roles include location, such as "at the beach"; source, such as "from the kitchen"; and goal, such as "to the classroom."

✔ CONCEPT CHECK

1. What is coarticulation, and why is it important?
2. What does the view of speech perception as ordinary suggest?
3. What is categorical perception?
4. Describe a study that is evidence for the motor theory of speech perception.
5. What is syntactical priming?
6. What is the difference between phrase-structure grammar and transformational grammar?

Reading

Because reading is so complex, a discussion of how we engage in this process could be placed in any of a number of chapters in this book. At minimum, reading involves perception, language, memory, thinking, and intelligence (Adams, 1990, 1999; Garrod & Daneman, 2003; Smith, 2004): You have to recognize the letters on this page, put them together to form words that have meaning, keep their meaning in memory until you have finished reading the sentence or even paragraph, and think about what message the writer tried to communicate to you. Although there are so many different processes going on, we read with remarkable speed and accuracy: the average adult reads prose at about 250-300 words per minute.

In a typical day, we repeatedly encounter written language. Every day we see signs, billboards, labels, and notices. These items contain a wealth of information that helps us make decisions and understand situations. As a result, the ability to read is fundamental to our everyday lives.

When Reading Is a Problem—Dyslexia

To better understand what processes are involved in reading, let us first look at people who have trouble reading. People who have **dyslexia**—difficulty in deciphering, reading, and comprehending text—can suffer greatly in a society that puts a high premium on fluent reading (Sternberg & Spear-Swerling, 1999; Terras et al., 2009). Problems in phonological processing, and thus in word identification, pose "the major stumbling block in learning to read" (Pollatsek & Rayner, 1989, p. 403; see also Grodzinsky, 2003). Several different processes may be impaired in dyslexia:

- *Phonological awareness*, which refers to awareness of the sound structure of spoken language. A typical way of assessing phonological awareness is through a phoneme-deletion task. Children are asked to say, for example, "goat" without the "-t." Another task that is used is phoneme counting. Children might be asked how many different sounds there are in the word "fish." The correct answer is three.
- *Phonological reading*, which entails reading words in isolation. Teachers sometimes call this skill "word decoding" or "word attack." For measurement of the skill, children might be asked to read words in isolation. Some of the words might be quite easy; others, difficult. Individuals with dyslexia often have more trouble recognizing the words in isolation than in context. When given context, they use the context to figure out what the word means.
- *Phonological coding* in working memory. This process is involved in remembering strings of phonemes that are sometimes confusing. It might be measured by comparing working memory for confusable versus non-confusable phonemes. For example, a child might be assessed for how well he or she remembers the string t, b, z, v, g versus the string o, x, r, y, q. Most people will have more difficulty with the first string. But individuals with dyslexia, who have problems in phonological coding in working memory, will have particular trouble.
- *Lexical access* refers to one's ability to retrieve phonemes from long-term memory. The question here is whether one can quickly retrieve a word from long-term memory when it is seen. For example, if you see the word *pond*, do you immediately recognize the word as *pond*, or does it take you a while to retrieve it?

There are several different kinds of dyslexia. The most well-known kind is *developmental dyslexia*, which is difficulty in reading that starts in childhood and typically continues throughout adulthood. Most commonly, children with developmental dyslexia have difficulty in learning the rules that relate letters to sounds (Démonet, Taylor, & Chaix, 2004; Shaywitz & Shaywitz, 2005). A second kind of dyslexia is *acquired dyslexia*, which is typically caused by traumatic brain damage. A perfectly good reader who experiences a brain injury may acquire dyslexia (Coslett, 2003).

Developmental dyslexia is believed to have both biological and environmental causes. A major dispute in the field is the role of each. People with developmental dyslexia often have been found to have abnormalities in certain chromosomes, most notably, 3, 6, and 15 (Paracchini, Scerri, & Monaco, 2007). Neuropsychological studies suggest that readers with dyslexia exhibit hypoactivation (that is, too little activation) in their left temporo-parietal cortex as compared with regular readers. Other brain regions show atypical activation in dyslexic readers, for example, the left prefrontal region (linked with working memory), the left middle and superior temporal gyri (linked with receptive language), and the left occipito-temporal regions (associated with the visual analysis of letters; Gabrieli, 2009). However, educational interventions can help reduce the impairments in reading caused by dyslexia (Bakker, 2006).

In the following section, we examine three different processes that contribute to our ability to read: perceptual, lexical, and comprehension processes.

Perceptual Issues in Reading

A very basic but important step in reading is the activation of our ability to recognize letters. When you are reading, you somehow manage to perceive the correct letter when it is presented in a wide array of typestyles and typefaces. For example, you can perceive it correctly in capital and lowercase forms, and even in cursive forms. Such aspects are called *orthographic*. You then must translate the letter into a sound, creating a phonological code (relating to sound). This translation is particularly difficult in English because English does not always ensure a direct correspondence between a letter and a sound. George Bernard Shaw, playwright and lover of the English language, observed the illogicality of English spellings. He suggested that, in English, it would be perfectly reasonable to pronounce "ghoti" as "fish." You would pronounce the "gh" as in *rough*, the "o" as in *women*, and the "ti" as in *nation*. That brings up another perplexing "Englishism": How do you pronounce "ough"? Try the words *dough, bough, bought, through,* and *cough*—had *enough?*

After you somehow manage to translate all those visual symbols into sounds, you must sequence those sounds to form a word (Pollatsek & Miller, 2003). Then you need to identify the word and figure out what the word means. Ultimately you move on to the next word and repeat the process all over again. You continue this process with subsequent words to formulate a single sentence. You continue this process for as long as you read. Clearly, the normal ability to read is not at all simple. About 36 million American adults have not yet learned to read at an eighth-grade level (Conn & Silverman, 1991). There were no significant changes in literacy between 1992 and 2003 (http://nces.ed.gov/naal/kf_demographics.asp). On the one hand, the statistics on low literacy and illiteracy should alarm us and provoke us to action. On the other hand, we may need to reconsider our possibly less-than-favorable appraisal of those who have not yet mastered the task of reading. To undertake such a challenge—at any age—is difficult indeed.

When learning to read, novice readers must come to master two basic kinds of processes: lexical processes and comprehension processes. **Lexical processes** are used to identify letters and words. They also activate relevant information in memory about these words. **Comprehension processes** are used to make sense of the text as a whole (and are discussed later in this chapter). The separation and integration of both bottom-up and top-down approaches to perception can be seen as we consider the lexical processes of reading.

Lexical Processes in Reading

We are about to explore, in more detail, the lexical processes involved in reading. First, we take a closer look at fixations in our eye movements that help us read. Then, we discuss how we identify words so we can retrieve their meaning from our memory (lexical access); and finally, we consider what connection there is between lexical-access speed and intelligence.

Fixations and Reading Speed

When we read, our eyes do not move smoothly along a page or even along a line of text. Rather, our eyes move in *saccades*—rapid sequential movements—as they fixate on successive clumps of text. The fixations are like a series of "snapshots" (Pollatsek & Rayner, 1989), and are of variable length (Carpenter & Just, 1981). Readers fixate for a longer time on longer words than on shorter words. They also fixate longer on less familiar words (i.e., words that appear less frequently in the English language) than on more familiar words (i.e., words of higher frequency). The last word of a sentence also seems to receive an extra long fixation time. This can be called "sentence wrap-up time" (Carpenter & Just, 1981; Warren et al., 2009).

Although most words are fixated, not all of them are. Readers fixate up to about 80% of the content words in a text. These words include nouns, verbs, and other words that carry the bulk of the meaning. (Function words, such as *the* and *of*, serve a supporting role to the content words.) Just what is the visual span of one of these fixations? It appears that we can extract useful information from a perceptual window of characters about four characters to the left of a fixation point and about 14 or 15 characters to the right of it. These characters include letters, numerals, punctuation marks, and spaces. Saccadic movements leap an average of about seven to nine characters between successive fixations. So some of the information we extract may be preparatory for subsequent fixation (Pollatsek & Rayner, 1989; Rayner et al., 1995). When students speed-read, they show fewer and shorter fixations (Just, Carpenter, & Masson, 1982). But apparently their greater speed is at the expense of comprehension of anything more than just the gist of the passage (Homa, 1983).

Lexical Access

An important aspect of reading is **lexical access**—the identification of a word that allows us to gain access to the meaning of the word from memory. Most psychologists who study reading believe that lexical access is an interactive process. It combines information of different kinds, such as the features of letters, the letters themselves, and the words comprising the letters (Morton, 1969).

Investigators (McClelland et al., 2009; Rumelhart & McClelland 1981, 1982) developed an interactive-activation model suggesting that activation of particular lexical elements occurs at multiple levels. Moreover, activity at each of the levels is interactive (Figure 9.4).

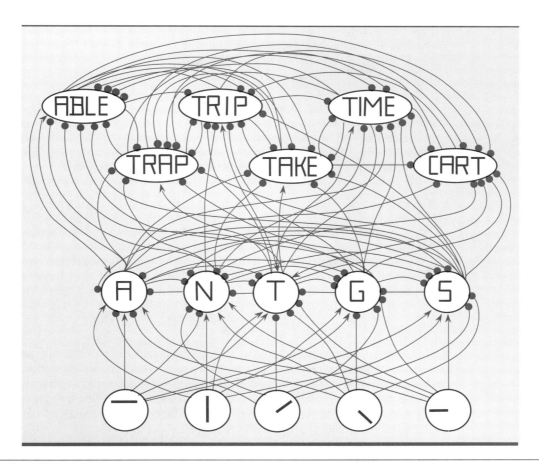

Figure 9.4 Word Recognition.

David Rumelhart and James McClelland used this figure to illustrate how activation at the feature level, the letter level, and the word level may interact during word recognition. In this figure, lines terminating in arrows prompt activation, and lines terminating in dots (blue circles) prompt inhibition. For example, the feature for a solid horizontal bar at the top of a letter leads to activation of the T character but to inhibition of the N character. Similarly, at the letter level, activation of T as the first letter leads to activation of TRAP and TRIP but to inhibition of ABLE. Going from the top down, activation of the word TRAP leads to inhibition of A, N, G, and S as the first letter but to activation of T as the first letter.

Source: From Richard E. Meyer, "The Search for Insight: Grappling with Gestalt Psychology's Unanswered Questions," in *The Nature of Insight*, edited by R. J. Sternberg and J. E. Davidson. Copyright © 1995 MIT Press. Reprinted with permission from MIT Press.

The interactive-activation model distinguishes among three levels of processing following visual input—the feature level, the letter level, and the word level. The model assumes that information at each level is represented separately in memory. Information passes from one level to another bidirectionally. In other words, processing occurs in each of two directions. First, it is bottom-up, starting with sensory data and working up to higher levels of cognitive processing. Second, it is top-down, starting with high-level cognition operating on prior knowledge and experiences related to a given context. The interactive view implies that not only do we use the visually or orally perceptible features of letters to help us identify words, but we also use the features we already know about words to help us identify letters. For this reason, the model is referred to as "interactive" (Plaut et al., 1996).

Other theorists have suggested alternatives to Rumelhart and McClelland's model (e.g., Meyer & Schvaneveldt, 1976; Paap et al., 1982), but the distinctions among interactive models go beyond the scope of this introductory text. Support for word-recognition models involving discrete levels of processing comes from studies of cerebral processing (Harley, 2008; Petersen et al., 1988; Posner et al., 1988, 1989). Studies that map brain metabolism indicate that different regions of the brain become activated during passive visual processing of word forms, as opposed to semantic analysis of words or even spoken pronunciation of the words. These studies involve the use of techniques such as positron emission tomography (PET) and functional magnetic resonance imaging (fMRI), discussed in Chapter 2.

In addition to neuropsychological support, a number of word-recognition models have been simulated on computers (e.g., Harm & Seidenberg, 2004). Both models aptly predicted a word-superiority effect as well as a pseudoword-superiority effect. The word-superiority effect is similar to the *configural-superiority effect* and the *object-superiority effect* (mentioned in regard to top-down influences on perception). In the **word-superiority effect**, letters are read more easily when they are embedded in words than when they are presented either in isolation or with letters that do not form words. People take substantially longer to read unrelated letters than to read letters that form a word (Cattell, 1886). This effect is sometimes called the Reicher-Wheeler effect, named for two researchers who did early investigations of this effect (Reicher, 1969; Wheeler, 1970).

To observe the word-superiority effect, researchers use an experimental paradigm called the *lexical-decision task*. In this paradigm, a string of letters is presented very briefly. It then is either removed or covered by a *visual mask*, a pattern that wipes out the previously presented stimulus from iconic memory (see Chapter 5 for more information about the iconic memory store). The participant then is asked to make a decision about whether the string of letters is a word.

To observe the word-superiority effect, the standard lexical-decision task is modified to examine the processing of letters. Participants are presented very briefly with either a word or a single letter, followed by a visual mask. Participants then are given a choice of two letters and have to decide which letter they just saw. For example, participants may be presented with the word "WORK" when the test stimulus is "K." The alternatives to choose from might be "D" and "K." They are presented as "_ _ _ D" and "_ _ _ K," which correspond to the target "WORK" and a similar word "WORD," respectively. Participants then are instructed to choose the letter they saw. Participants are more accurate in choosing the correct letter when it is presented in the context of a word than they are in choosing the correct letter when it is presented in isolation (Johnston & McClelland, 1973). Even letters in pronounceable pseudowords (e.g., "MARD") are identified more accurately than letters in isolation. However, strings of letters that cannot be pronounced as words (e.g., "ORWK") do not aid in identification (Grainger et al., 2003; Pollatsek & Rayner, 1989).

There is also a *sentence-superiority effect* (Cattell, 1886; Perfetti, 1985): People take about twice as long to read unrelated words as to read words in a sentence (Cattell, 1886). The sentence-superiority effect can be seen in other paradigms as well. For example, suppose that a reader very briefly sees a degraded stimulus. The word *window*, for example, might be shown but in degraded form (Figure 9.5). When the word is standing by itself in this form, it is more difficult to recognize than when it is preceded by a sentence context. An example of such a context would be, "There were several repair jobs to be done. The first was to fix the _____."

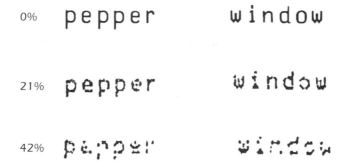

Figure 9.5 Word Degradation.
This figure shows instances of the word "window" and of the word "pepper," in which each word is clearly legible, somewhat legible, or almost completely illegible. Percentages indicate degree of degradation.

(Perfetti, 1985). Having a meaningful context for a stimulus helps the reader to perceive it.

Context effects work at both conscious and preconscious levels. At the conscious level, we have active control over the use of context to determine word meanings. At the preconscious level, the use of context is probably automatic and outside our active control. Participants seem to make lexical decisions more quickly when presented with strings of letters that commonly are associated pairs of words (e.g., "doctor" and "nurse" or "bread" and "butter"). They respond more slowly when presented with unassociated pairs of words, with pairs of non-words, or with pairs involving a word and a non-word (Hyoenae, J., & Lindeman, 2008; Meyer & Schvaneveldt, 1971; Schvaneveldt, Meyer, & Becker, 1976).

Intelligence and Lexical-Access Speed

Some investigations on information processing and intelligence have focused on *lexical-access speed*—the speed with which we can retrieve information about words (e.g., letter names) stored in our long-term memories (Hunt, 1978). This speed can be measured with a letter-matching, reaction-time task first proposed by Posner and Mitchell in 1967 (Hunt, 1978).

Participants are shown pairs of letters, such as "A A," "A a," or "A b." For each pair, they indicate whether the letters constitute a match in name (e.g., "A a" match in name of letter of the alphabet but "A b" do not). They also are given a simpler task where they are asked to indicate whether the letters match physically (e.g., "A A" are physically identical, whereas "A a" are not). The variable of interest is the difference between their speed for the first set of tasks, involving name-matching, and their speed for the second set, involving matching of physical characteristics. The difference in reaction time between the two kinds of tasks is said to provide a measure of speed of lexical access. This score is based on a *subtraction* of name-match minus physical-match reaction time. The subtraction controls for mere perceptual-processing time. Students with lower verbal ability take longer to gain access to lexical information than do students with higher verbal ability (Hunt, 1978). These results suggest that lexical access is a component of verbal ability.

✔ **CONCEPT CHECK**

1. Which processes can be impaired in dyslexia?
2. What is lexical access?
3. Give an example for the word-superiority effect.

Understanding Conversations and Essays: Discourse

The preceding sections discussed, at a general level, aspects of how we understand written and spoken language. However, in our understanding of language, not only do words and sentences play a role, but so does the greater context in which they appear. This section discusses more specifically the processes involved in understanding and using language in the greater context in which we encounter it. **Discourse** involves units of language larger than individual sentences—in conversations, lectures, stories, essays, and even textbooks (Di Eugenio, 2003). Just as grammatical sentences are structured according to systematic syntactical rules, passages of discourse are structured systematically (see *Investigating Cognitive Psychology: Discourse*).

By adulthood, most of us have a firm grasp of how sentences are sequenced into a greater whole (discourse structure). From our knowledge of discourse structure, we can derive meanings of sentence elements that are not apparent by looking at isolated sentences. To see how sentences influence the interpretation of other sentences, try out the *Investigating Cognitive Psychology: Deciphering Text* box.

INVESTIGATING COGNITIVE PSYCHOLOGY
Discourse

The following series of sentences is taken from a short story by O. Henry (William Sydney Porter, 1899–1953) titled "The Ransom of Red Chief." Actually, the following sequence of sentences is incorrect. Without knowing anything else about the story, try to figure out the correct sequence of sentences.

1. The father was respectable and tight, a mortgage financier and a stern, upright collection-plate passer and forecloser.

2. We selected for our victim the only child of a prominent citizen named Ebenezer Dorset.

3. We were down South in Alabama—Bill Driscoll and myself—when this kidnapping idea struck us.

4. Bill and me figured that Ebenezer would melt down for a ransom of two thousand dollars to a cent.

Hint: O. Henry was a master of irony, and by the end of the story the would-be kidnappers paid the father a hefty ransom to take back his son so that they could quickly escape from the boy.

The sequence used by O. Henry, ex-convict and expert storyteller, was 3, 2, 1, 4. Is that the order you chose? How did you know the correct sequence for these sentences?

INVESTIGATING COGNITIVE PSYCHOLOGY
Deciphering Text

Rita gave Thomas a book about problem solving. He thanked her for the book. She asked, "Is it what you wanted?" He answered enthusiastically, "Yes, definitely." Rita asked, "Should I get you the companion volume on decision making?" He responded, "Please do."

In the second and third sentences, who were the people and things being referred to with the pronouns "He," "her," "She," and "it"? Why was the noun "book" preceded by the article "a" in the first sentence and by the article "the" in the second one? How do you know what Thomas's answer, "Yes, definitely," means? What is the action being requested in the response, "Please do"?

Cognitive psycholinguists who analyze discourse particularly are intrigued by how we are able to answer the questions posed in the preceding example. When grasping the meanings of pronouns (e.g., *he, she, him, her, it, they, them, we, us*), how do we know to whom (or to what) the pronouns are pointing? How do we know the meanings of what could seem like cryptic utterances (e.g., "Yes, definitely")? What does the use of the definite article *the* (as opposed to the indefinite article *a*) signify to listeners regarding whether a noun was mentioned previously? How do you know what event is being referenced by the verb *do?* The meanings of pronouns, ellipses, definite articles, event references, and other local elements within sentences usually depend on the discourse structure within which these elements appear (Grosz, Pollack, & Sidner, 1989).

For understanding discourse, we often rely not only on our knowledge of discourse structure but also on our knowledge of a broad physical, social, or cultural context within which the discourse is presented (Cook & Gueraud, 2005; van Dijk, 2006). Our understanding of the meaning of a paragraph is influenced by our existing knowledge and expectations. For example, this cognitive psychology textbook will be easier to read if you have taken an introductory psychology course than if you have not taken such a course. When reading the sentences in the *Investigating Cognitive Psychology: Effects of Expectations in Reading* box, pause between sentences and think about what you know and what you expect, based on your knowledge.

The next sections explore in more detail how we comprehend larger units of language, like essays. We discuss how we retrieve known words from memory and how we infer the meaning of new words. We explore how we understand ideas communicated in text and how our interpretation depends on our point of view. Finally, we consider how we can represent text in mental models.

Comprehending Known Words: Retrieving Word Meaning from Memory

Semantic encoding is the process by which we translate sensory information (that is, the written words we see) into a meaningful representation. This representation is based on our understanding of the meanings of words. In lexical access, we identify words based on letter combinations. We thereby activate our memory in regard to the words. In semantic encoding, we take the next step and gain access to the

INVESTIGATING COGNITIVE PSYCHOLOGY
Effects of Expectations in Reading

1. Susan became increasingly anxious as she prepared for the upcoming science exam. (What do you know about Susan?)

2. She had never written an exam before, and she wasn't sure how to construct an appropriate test of the students' knowledge. (How have your beliefs about Susan changed?)

3. She was particularly annoyed that the principal had even asked her to write the exam.

4. Even during a teachers' strike, a school nurse should not be expected to take on the task of writing an examination. (How did your expectations change over the course of the four sentences?)

In the preceding example, your understanding at each point in the discourse was influenced by your existing knowledge and expectations based on your own experiences within a particular context. Thus, just as prior experience and knowledge may aid us in lexical processing of text, so may they also aid us in comprehending the text itself. What are the main reading-comprehension processes? The process of reading comprehension is so complex that many entire courses and myriad volumes are devoted exclusively to the topic, but we focus here on just a few processes. These include semantic encoding, acquiring vocabulary, comprehending ideas in text, creating mental models of text, and comprehending text based on context and point of view.

meaning of the word stored in memory. Sometimes we cannot semantically encode the word because its meaning does not already exist in memory. We then must find another way in which to derive the meanings of words, such as from noting the context in which we read them.

To engage in semantic encoding, the reader needs to know what a given word means. Knowledge of word meanings (vocabulary) very closely relates to the ability to comprehend text. People who are knowledgeable about word meanings tend to be good readers and vice versa. A reason for this relationship appears to be that readers simply cannot understand text well unless they know the meanings of the component words. For example, in one study, recall of the semantic content of a passage was much better when participants had a greater relevant vocabulary (Beck, Perfetti, & McKeown, 1982). In children, vocabulary size is positively related to performance on a number of semantic-understanding tasks, including retelling (both written and oral), decoding ability, and the ability to draw inferences across sentences (Hagtvet, 2003). A number of studies suggest that in order to grasp meaning of a sample of text with ease, one should know approximately 95% of the vocabulary (Nation, 2001; Read, 2000). Still other studies suggest that, for one to enjoy reading a text, one needs to understand about 98% of the vocabulary (Hu & Nation, 2000).

People with larger vocabularies are able to access lexical information more rapidly than are those with smaller vocabularies (Hunt, 1978). Verbal information often is presented rapidly—whether in listening or in reading. The individual who can gain access to lexical information rapidly is able to process more information per unit of time than can one who can only gain access to such information slowly.

Comprehending Unknown Words: Deriving Word Meanings from Context

Another way in which having a larger vocabulary contributes to text comprehension is through learning from context. Whenever we cannot semantically encode a word because its meaning is not already stored in memory, we must engage in some kind of strategy to derive meaning from the text. In general, we must either search for a meaning, using external resources, such as dictionaries or teachers, or formulate a meaning. Using context cues, we formulate the meaning based on the existing information stored in memory.

People learn most of their vocabulary indirectly. They do so not by using external resources but by figuring out the meanings of the flidges from the surrounding information (Werner & Kaplan, 1952).

For example, if you tried to look up the word *flidges* in the dictionary, you did not find it there. From the structure of the sentence you probably figured out that *flidges* is a noun. From the surrounding context you probably figured out that it is a noun having something to do with words or vocabulary. In fact, *flidges* is a nonsense word we used as a placeholder for the word *words* to show how you would gain a fairly good idea of a word's meaning from its context.

One study found that the ability to figure out meanings of words from context was impaired in children with low reading comprehension. If those children had good vocabularies, however, direct instruction could help them learn the meanings of new words just as well as did children with high reading comprehension (Cain, Oakhill, & Lemmon, 2004).

What happens when adults have to learn word meanings from sentence contexts? Studies have found that people with large or small vocabularies (high verbal/low verbal) learn word meanings differently. High-verbal participants perform a deeper analysis of the possibilities for a new word's meaning than do low-verbal participants. In particular, the high-verbal participants used a well-formulated strategy for figuring out word meanings. The low-verbal participants seemed to have no clear strategy at all (van Daalen-Kapteijns & Elshout-Mohr, 1981; see also Sternberg & Powell, 1983).

Comprehending Ideas: Propositional Representations

What factors influence our comprehension of what we read? Walter Kintsch has developed a model of text comprehension based on his observations (Kintsch, 1990, 2007; Kintsch & van Dijk, 1978). According to the model, as we read, we try to hold as much information as possible in working (active) memory to understand what we read. However, we do not try to store the exact words we read in working (active) memory. Rather, we try to extract the fundamental ideas from groups of words. We then store those fundamental ideas in a simplified representational form in working memory.

The representational form for these fundamental ideas is the proposition. Propositions were defined in more detail in Chapter 7. For now, it suffices to say that a proposition is the briefest unit of language that can be independently found to be true or false. For example, the sentence, "Penguins are birds, and penguins can fly" contains two propositions. You can verify independently whether penguins are birds and whether penguins can fly. In general, propositions assert either an action (e.g., flying) or a relationship (e.g., membership of penguins in the category of birds).

According to Kintsch, working memory holds propositions rather than words. Its limits are thus taxed by large numbers of propositions rather than by any particular number of words (Kintsch & Keenan, 1973). When a string of words in text requires us to hold a large number of propositions in working memory, we have difficulty comprehending the text. When information stays in working memory a longer time, it is better comprehended and better recalled subsequently. Because of the limits of working memory, however, some information must be moved out of working memory to make room for new information.

According to Kintsch, propositions that are thematically central to the understanding of the text will remain in working memory longer than propositions that are irrelevant to the theme of the text passage. Kintsch calls the thematically crucial propositions *macropropositions*. He further calls the overarching thematic structure of a passage of text the *macrostructure*. In an experiment testing his model, Kintsch and an associate asked participants to read a 1,300-word text passage (Kintsch & van Dijk, 1978). The participants then had to summarize the key propositions in the passage immediately, at one month, or at three months after reading the passage. What happened after three months? Participants recalled the macropropositions and the overall macrostructure of the passage about as well as could participants who summarized it immediately after reading it. However, the propositions providing nonthematic details about the passage were not recalled as well after one month and not at all well after three months.

Comprehending Text Based on Context and Point of View

What we remember from a given passage of text often depends on our point of view. For example, suppose that you were reading a text passage about the home of a wealthy family. It described many of the features of the house, such as a leaky roof, a fireplace, and a musty basement. It also described the contents of the house, such as valuable coins, silverware, and television sets. How might your encoding and comprehension of the text be different if you were reading it from the point of view of a prospective purchaser of the home as opposed to the viewpoint of a prospective cat burglar? In a study using just such a passage, people who read the passage from the viewpoint of a cat burglar remembered far more about the contents of the home. In contrast, those who read from the viewpoint of a homebuyer remembered more about the condition of the house (Anderson & Pichert, 1978). In fact, varying the retrieval situations or cues can cause different details to be remembered. Researchers found that differing retrieval instructions did not affect accuracy but did affect the specific details recalled (Gilbert & Fisher, 2006).

Representing the Text in Mental Models

Once words are semantically encoded or their meaning is derived from the use of context, the reader still must create a mental model of the text that is being read. This mental model simulates what is going on in the world (Craik, 1943; see Johnson-Laird, 1989, 2010). A mental model may be viewed as a sort of internal working model of the situation described in the text, as the reader understands it. In other words, the reader creates some sort of mental representation that contains the main elements of the text. These elements are represented in a way that is relatively easy to grasp or at least that is simpler and more concrete than the text itself.

For example, suppose that you read the sentence, "The loud bang scared Alice." You may form a picture of Alice becoming scared on hearing a loud noise. Or you may access propositions stored in memory regarding the effects of loud bangs.

A given passage of text or even a given set of propositions (to refer back to Kintsch's model) may lead to more than one mental model (Johnson-Laird, 1983). In fact, you may need to modify your mental model. Whether you do so depends on whether the next sentence is, "She tried to steer off the highway without losing control of the car," or "She ducked to avoid being shot." In representing the loud bang that scared Alice, more than one mental model is possible. If you start out with a different model than the one required in a given passage, your ability to comprehend the text depends on your ability to form a new mental model. You can hold in mind only a limited number of mental models at any given time (Johnson-Laird, Byrne, & Schaeken, 1992). Therefore, when one of the models is incorrect, it must be rejected to make room for new models.

To form mental models, you must make at least tentative inferences (preliminary conclusions or judgments) about what is meant but not said. In the first case, you are likely to assume that a tire blew out. In the second case, you may infer that someone is shooting a gun. Note that neither of these things is stated explicitly. The construction of mental models illustrates that, in addition to comprehending the words themselves, we also need to understand how words combine into meaningfully integrated representations of narratives or expositions. Passages of text that lead unambiguously to a single mental model are easier to comprehend than are passages that may lead to multiple mental models (Johnson-Laird, 1989).

Inferences can be of different kinds. One of the most important kinds is a bridging inference (Haviland & Clark, 1974; Mc Namara et al., 2006). This is an inference a reader or listener makes when a sentence seems not to follow directly from the sentence preceding it. In essence, what is new in the second sentence goes one step too far beyond what is given in the previous sentences. Consider, for example, two pairs of two sentences:

1. John took the picnic out of the trunk. The beer was warm.
2. John took the beer out of the trunk. The beer was warm.

Readers took about 180 milliseconds longer to read the first pair of sentences than the second. Haviland and Clark suggested a reason for this greater processing time. It was that, in the first pair, information needed to be inferred (the picnic included beer) that was directly stated in the second pair.

Although most researchers emphasize the importance of inference-making in reading and forms of language comprehension (e.g., Graesser & Kreuz, 1993; Cain & Oakhill, 2007), not all researchers agree. According to the minimalist hypothesis, readers make inferences based only on information that is easily available to them. They do so only when they need to make such inferences to make sense of adjoining sentences (McKoon & Ratcliff, 1992a; Ratcliff & McKoon, 2008). We believe that the bulk of the evidence regarding the minimalist position indicates that it is itself too minimalist. Readers appear to make more inferences than this position suggests (Suh & Trabasso, 1993; Trabasso & Suh, 1993).

To summarize, our comprehension of what we read depends on several abilities. First is gaining access to the meanings of words, either from memory or on the basis of context. Second is deriving meaning from the key ideas in what we read. Third is extracting the key information from the text, based on the contexts surrounding

INVESTIGATING COGNITIVE PSYCHOLOGY
Using Redundancy to Decipher Cryptic Text

Read the following passage:

Aoccdrnig to a rseearch at an Elingsh uinervtisy, it dseon't mttaer in waht oredr the ltteers in a wrod are; the olny iprmoatnt tihng is that the frist and lsat ltteres are at the rghit pclae. The rset can be a toatl mses and you can sitll raed it wouthit porbelm. Tihs is bcuseae we do not raed ervey lteter by itslef but the wrod as a wlohe.

Although most people cannot read the above passage as quickly as they can if all the letters are in the right order, they still can understand what the passage says.

what we read and on the ways in which we intend to use what we read. And fourth is forming mental models that simulate the situations about which we read.

✔ CONCEPT CHECK

1. What is discourse?
2. What technique can you apply when you come across a word you don't know in a text?
3. Does readers' point of view influence their text comprehension?
4. Is there a limit to the number or complexity of mental models one can have about a given text?

Key Themes

This chapter deals with a number of the major themes reviewed in Chapter 1.

Rationalism versus empiricism. Most psychologists emphasize empirical techniques in their research. But linguists such as Chomsky have emphasized more rationalistic techniques. They analyze language, typically without formally collecting empirical data at all, at least in the cognitive psychologists' sense of what constitutes such data. The stunning insights of Chomsky show that the two methods complement each other. Many insights can evolve from rationalism. They then can be tested by empirical methods.

Domain generality versus domain specificity. In particular, to what extent is language special? Is it a domain apart from other domains, or simply one more cognitive domain like any other? Many psychologists today believe that there is indeed something special about language. At the same time, cognitive processes operate on it so that people use their language in practically all the other domains in which they work. For example, many mathematical and physical problems are presented with words.

Summary

1. **What properties characterize language?** There are at least six properties of language, defined as the use of an organized means of combining words in order to communicate. (1) Language permits us to communicate with one or more people who share our language. (2) Language

creates an arbitrary relationship between a symbol and its referent—an idea, a thing, a process, a relationship, or a description. (3) Language has a regular structure; only particular sequences of symbols (sounds and words) have meaning. Different sequences yield different meanings. (4) The structure of language can be analyzed at multiple levels (e.g., phonemic and morphemic). (5) Despite having the limits of a structure, language users can produce novel utterances; the possibilities for generating new utterances are virtually limitless. (6) Languages constantly evolve.

Language involves verbal comprehension—the ability to comprehend written and spoken linguistic input, such as words, sentences, and paragraphs. It also involves verbal fluency—the ability to produce linguistic output. The smallest units of sound produced by the human vocal tract are phones. Phonemes are the smallest units of sound that can be used to differentiate meaning in a given language. The smallest semantically meaningful unit in a language is a morpheme. Morphemes may be either roots or affixes—prefixes or suffixes. Affixes in turn may be either content morphemes, conveying the bulk of the word's meaning, or function morphemes, augmenting the meaning of the word. A lexicon is the repertoire of morphemes in a given language (or for a given language user). The study of the meaningful sequencing of words within phrases and sentences in a given language is syntax. Larger units of language are embraced by the study of discourse.

2. **What are some of the processes involved in language?** In speech perception, listeners must overcome the influence of coarticulation (overlapping) of phonemes on the acoustic structure of the speech signal. Categorical perception is the phenomenon in which listeners perceive continuously varying speech sounds as distinct categories. It lends support to the notion that speech is perceived via specialized processes. The motor theory of speech perception attempts to explain these processes in relation to the processes involved in speech production. Those who believe speech perception is ordinary explain speech perception in terms of feature-detection, prototype, and Gestalt theories of perception.

Syntax is the study of the linguistic structure of sentences. Phrase-structure grammars analyze sentences in terms of the hierarchical relationships among words in phrases and sentences.

Transformational grammars analyze sentences in terms of transformational rules that describe interrelationships among the structures of various sentences. Some linguists have suggested a mechanism for linking syntax to semantics. By this mechanism, grammatical sentences contain particular slots for syntactical categories. These slots may be filled by words that have particular thematic roles within the sentences. According to this view, each item in a lexicon contains information regarding appropriate thematic roles, as well as appropriate syntactical categories.

3. **How do perceptual processes interact with the cognitive processes of reading?** The reading difficulties of people with dyslexia often relate to problems with the perceptual aspects of reading.

Reading comprises two basic kinds of processes: (1) lexical processes, which include sequences of eye fixations and lexical access; and (2) comprehension processes.

4. **How does discourse help us understand individual words?** Obviously, we can understand discourse only through analysis of words. But sometimes we understand words through discourse. For one example, sometimes in a conversation or watching a movie, we miss a word. The context of the discourse helps us figure out what the word was likely to be. As a second example, sometimes a word can have several meanings, such as "well." We use discourse to help us figure out which meaning is intended. As a third example, sometimes we realize, through discourse, that a word is intended to mean something different from its actual meaning, as in "Yeah, right!" Here, "right" is likely to be intended to mean "not really right at all." So discourse helps us understand individual words, just as the individual words help us understand discourse.

Thinking about Thinking: Analytical, Creative, and Practical Questions

1. Describe the six key properties of language.
2. In your opinion, why do some view speech perception to be special, whereas others consider speech perception to be ordinary?
3. Compare and contrast the speech-is-ordinary and speech-is-special views, particularly in reference to categorical perception and phonemic restoration.
4. How do phrase-structure diagrams reveal the alternative meanings of ambiguous sentences?
5. Write a noun phrase and a verb phrase. How are they different?

6. In this chapter, we saw that passive-voice sentences can be transformed into active-voice sentences using transformation rules. What are some other kinds of sentence structures that are related to one another? In your own words, state the transformation rules that would govern the changes from one form to another.
7. Based on the discussion of reading in this chapter, what practical suggestion could you recommend that might make reading easier for someone who is having difficulty reading?

Key Terms

categorical perception, *p. 372*
coarticulation, *p. 369*
communication, *p. 361*
comprehension processes, *p. 388*
connotation, *p. 375*
content morphemes, *p. 366*
deep structure, *p. 383*
denotation, *p. 374*
discourse, *p. 392*
dyslexia, *p. 386*
function morphemes, *p. 366*

grammar, *p. 377*
language, *p. 360*
lexical access, *p. 388*
lexical processes, *p. 388*
lexicon, *p. 367*
morpheme, *p. 365*
noun phrase, *p. 367*
phoneme, *p. 365*
phonemic-restoration effect, *p. 371*
phrase-structure grammar, *p. 379*

psycholinguistics, *p. 361*
referent, *p. 362*
semantics, *p. 368*
surface structure, *p. 383*
syntax, *p. 367*
thematic roles, *p. 385*
transformational grammar, *p. 383*
verb phrase, *p. 367*
word-superiority effect, *p. 390*

Media Resources

Visit the companion website—**www.cengagebrain.com**—for quizzes, research articles, chapter outlines, and more.

CogLab

Explore CogLab by going to **http://coglab.wadsworth.com**. To learn more, examine the following experiments:

Categorical Perception Identification

Discrimination

Suffix Effect

Lexical Decision

Word Superiority

Language in Context

Here are some of the questions we will explore in this chapter:

1. How does language affect the way we think?
2. How does our social context influence our use of language?
3. How can we find out about language by studying the human brain, and what do such studies reveal?

■ BELIEVE IT OR NOT

IS IT POSSIBLE TO COUNT WITHOUT WORDS FOR NUMBERS?

Not all cultures in the world have developed words for numbers. Even if they do have counting systems and words for numbers, those systems and words may be quite different. The Piraha tribe, which lives along the banks of the Amazon River in Brazil, has just three number words—one for the number 1, one for the number 2, and one that indicates "many." Does this lack of number words interfere with people's ability to deal with larger numerical quantities? Peter Gordon conducted experiments with members of the Piraha tribe and found that indeed, it does. He presented them with matching tasks where he lined up specific numbers of batteries and asked them to line up an equal amount. Although the Piraha were able to complete this task well for numbers of up to three, their performance declined as the numbers increased. This finding may indicate that we do not have an innate ability to count beyond small numbers. A lack of words for larger numbers may prevent people from thinking about those larger quantities (Gordon, 2004). In this chapter, we explore how people use language in a social context, and how the environment influences people's language and cognition.

"My surgeon was a butcher."

"His house is a rat's nest."

"Her sermons are sleeping pills."

"He's a real toad, and he always dates real dogs."

"Abused children are walking time bombs."

"My boss is a tiger in board meetings but a real pussycat with me."

"Billboards are warts on the landscape."

"My cousin is a vegetable."

"John's last girlfriend chewed him up and spit him out."

Not one of the preceding statements is literally true. Yet fluent readers of English have little difficulty comprehending these metaphors and other non-literal forms of language. How do we comprehend them? One of the reasons that we can understand non-literal uses of language is that we can interpret the words we hear within a broader linguistic, cultural, social, and cognitive context.

In this chapter, we first focus on the cognitive context of language—we look at how language and thought interact. Next, we discuss some uses of language in its social context. Then we explore animal language because it puts human language in perspective. Finally, we examine some neuropsychological insights into language. Although the topics in this chapter are diverse, they all have one element in common: They address the issue of how language is used in the everyday contexts in which we need it to communicate with others and to make our communications as meaningful as we possibly can.

Language and Thought

One of the most interesting areas in the study of language is the relationship between language and the thinking of the human mind (Harris, 2003). Many people believe that language shapes thoughts. It is for this reason that the *Publication Manual* of the American Psychological Association places big value on political correctness in researchers' writings. And for this reason politicians and media use labels like "freedom fighters" versus "terrorists," or "surgical strikes" versus "bombing raids" (Stapel & Semin, 2007).

Many different questions have been asked about the relationship between language and thought. We consider only some of them here. Studies comparing and contrasting users of differing languages and dialects form the basis of this section.

Differences among Languages

Why are there so many different languages around the world? And how does using any language in general and using a particular language influence human thought? As you know, different languages comprise different lexicons. They also use different syntactical structures. These differences often reflect variations in the physical and cultural environments in which the languages arose and developed. For example, in terms of lexicon, the Garo of Burma distinguish among many kinds of rice, which is understandable because they are a rice-growing culture. Nomadic Arabs have more than 20 words for camels. These peoples clearly conceptualize rice and camels more specifically and in more complex ways than do people outside their cultural groups. As a result of these linguistic differences, do the Garo think about rice differently than we do? And do the Arabs think about camels differently than we do? Consider the way we discuss computers. We differentiate between many aspects of computers, including whether the computer is a desktop or a laptop, a PC or a Mac, or uses Linux or Windows as an operating system. A person from a culture that does not have access to computers would not require so many words or distinctions to describe these machines. We expect, however, specific performance and features for a given computer based on these distinctions. Clearly, we think about computers in a way that is different than that of people who have never encountered a computer.

The syntactical structures of languages differ, too. Almost all languages permit some way in which to communicate actions, agents of actions, and objects of actions (Gerrig & Banaji, 1994). What differs across languages is the order of subject, verb, and object in a typical declarative sentence. Also differing is the range of grammatical inflections and other markings that speakers are obliged to include as key elements of a sentence. For example, in describing past actions in English, we indicate whether an action took place in the past by changing (inflecting) the verb form. For example, *walk* changes to *walked* in the past tense. In Spanish and German, the verb also must indicate whether the agent of action was singular or plural and whether it is being referred to in the first, second, or third person. In Turkish, the verb form must additionally indicate whether the action was witnessed or experienced directly by the speaker or was noted only indirectly. Do these differences and other differences in obligatory syntactical structures influence—or perhaps even constrain—the users of these languages to think about things differently because of the language they use while thinking? We will have a closer look at these questions in the next two sections, in which we explore the concepts of linguistic relativity and linguistic universals.

The Sapir-Whorf Hypothesis

The concept relevant to the question of whether language influences thinking is **linguistic relativity**. Linguistic relativity refers to the assertion that speakers of different languages have differing cognitive systems and that these different cognitive systems influence the ways in which people think about the world. Thus, according to the relativity view, the Garo would think about rice differently than we do. For example, the Garo would develop more cognitive categories for rice than would an English-speaking counterpart. What would happen when the Garo contemplated rice? They purportedly would view it differently—and perhaps with greater complexity of thought—than would English speakers, who have only a few words for rice. Thus, language would shape thought. There is some evidence that word learning may occur, in part, as a result of infants' mental differentiations among various kinds of concepts (Carey, 1994; Xu & Carey, 1995, 1996). So it might make sense that infants who encounter different kinds of objects might make different kinds of mental differentiations. These differentiations would be a function of the culture in which the infants grew up.

The linguistic-relativity hypothesis is sometimes referred to as the *Sapir-Whorf hypothesis*, named after the two men who were most forceful in propagating it. Edward Sapir (1941/1964) said that "we see and hear and otherwise experience very largely as we do because the language habits of our community predispose certain choices of interpretation" (p. 69). Benjamin Lee Whorf (1956) stated this view even more strongly:

> *We dissect nature along lines laid down by our native languages. The categories and types that we isolate from the world of phenomena we do not find there because they stare every observer in the face; on the contrary, the world is presented in a kaleidoscopic flux of impressions which has to be organized by our minds—and this means largely by the linguistic systems in our minds. (p. 213)*

The Sapir-Whorf hypothesis has been one of the most widely discussed ideas in all of the social and behavioral sciences (Lonner, 1989). However, some of its implications appear to have reached mythical proportions. For example, "many social scientists have warmly accepted and gladly propagated the notion that Eskimos have multitudinous words for the single English word *snow*. Contrary to popular beliefs, Eskimos do *not* have numerous words for snow (Martin, 1986). "No one who knows anything about Eskimo (or more accurately, about the Inuit and Yup'ik families of related languages spoken from Siberia to Greenland) has ever said they do" (Pullum, 1991, p. 160). Laura Martin, who has done more than anyone else to debunk the myth, understands why her colleagues might consider the myth charming. But she has been quite "disappointed" in the reaction of her colleagues when she pointed out the fallacy. Most, she says, took the position that true or not 'it's still a great example'" (Adler, 1991, p. 63). Apparently, we must exercise caution in our interpretation of findings regarding linguistic relativity.

Consider a milder form of linguistic relativism—it is that language may not determine thought, but that language certainly may influence thought. Our thoughts and our language interact in myriad ways, only some of which we now understand. Clearly, language facilitates thought; it even affects perception and memory. For some reason, we have limited means by which to manipulate non-linguistic images (Hunt & Banaji, 1988). Such limitations make desirable the use of language to facilitate mental representation and manipulation. Even nonsense pictures ("droodles")

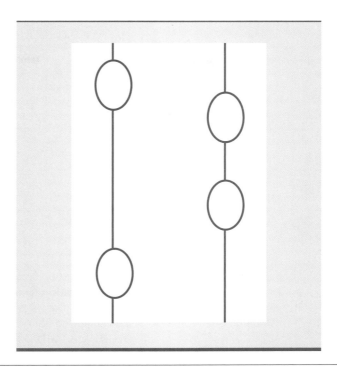

Figure 10.1   **Labels Affect Perception (part 1).**

How does your label for this image affect your perception, your mental representation, and your memory of the image?

Source: From *Psychology*, Fifth Edition, by John Darley, et al. Copyright © 1998, Pearson Education. Reprinted by permission of John Darley.

are recalled and redrawn differently, depending on the verbal label given to the picture (Bower, Karlin, & Dueck, 1975).

To see how this phenomenon might work, look at Figure 10.1. Suppose, instead of being labeled "beaded necklace," it had been titled "beaded curtain." You might have perceived it differently. However, once a particular label has been given, viewing the same figure from the alternative perspective is much harder (Glucksberg, 1988).

Psychologists have used other ambiguous figures (see Chapters 4 and 7) and have found similar results. Figure 10.2 illustrates three other figures that can be given alternative labels. When participants are given a particular label, they tend to draw their recollection of the figure in a way more similar to the given label. For example, after viewing a figure of two circles connected by a single line, they will draw a figure differently as a function of whether it is labeled "eyeglasses" or "dumbbells." Specifically, the connecting line will either be lengthened or shortened, depending on the label.

Language also affects how we encode, store, and retrieve information in memory. Remember the examples in Chapter 6 regarding the label "Washing Clothes"? That label enhanced people's responses to recall and comprehension questions about text passages (Bransford & Johnson, 1972, 1973). In a similar vein, eyewitness testimony is powerfully influenced by the distinctive phrasing of questions posed to

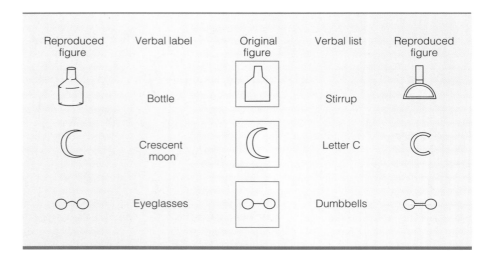

Figure 10.2 **Labels Affect Perception (part 2).**
When the original figures (in the center) are redrawn from memory, the new drawings tend to be distorted to be more like the labeled figures.
Source: From *Psychology*, Fifth Edition, by John Darley, et al. Copyright © 1998, Pearson Education. Reprinted by permission of John Darley.

eyewitnesses (Loftus & Palmer, 1974; see also Chapter 6 for more information on eyewitness testimony). In a famous study, participants viewed an accident (Loftus & Palmer, 1974). Participants then were asked to describe the speeds of the cars before the accident. The word indicating impact was varied across participants. These words included *smashed, collided, bumped,* and *hit.* When the word *smashed* was used, the participants rated speed as significantly higher than when any of the other words were used. The connotation of the word *smash* thereby seems to bias participants to estimate a higher speed. Similarly, when participants were asked if they saw broken glass (after a week's delay), the participants who were questioned with the word *smashed* said "yes" much more frequently than did any of the other participants (Loftus & Palmer, 1974). No other circumstances varied between participants, so the difference in the description of the accident is presumably the result of the word choice.

Even when participants generated their own descriptions, the subsequent accuracy of their eyewitness testimony declined (Schooler & Engstler-Schooler, 1990). Accurate recall actually declined following an opportunity to write a description of an observed event, a particular color, or a particular face. When given an opportunity to identify statements about an event—the actual color or a face—participants were less able to do so accurately if they previously had described it. Paradoxically, when participants were allowed to take their time in responding, their performance was even less accurate than when they were forced to respond quickly. In other words, given time to reflect on their answers, participants were more likely to respond in accord with what they had said or written than with what they had seen.

Is the Sapir-Whorf hypothesis relevant to everyday life? It almost certainly is. If language constrains our thought, then we may fail to see solutions to problems because we do not have the right words to express these solutions. Consider the misunderstandings we have with people who speak other languages. For example, one of the authors once was in Japan talking to a Japanese college student, who referred to the author as an "Aryan." The author explained that this concept has no basis in reality. It turned out that she meant to say "Alien," but in Japanese, there is not distinction between the "l" and "r" sounds. Even then, referring to him as an "alien" was not particularly comforting to him. According to the Sapir-Whorf view, the misunderstandings may result from the fact that other languages parse words differently than ours does, and may use different phonemes as well. One must be grateful that extreme versions of the Sapir-Whorf hypothesis do not appear to be justified. Such versions would suggest that we are, figuratively, slaves to the words available to us.

Linguistic Relativity or Linguistic Universals?

There has been some research that addresses **linguistic universals**—characteristic patterns across all languages of various cultures—and relativity. Recall from Chapter 9 that linguists have identified hundreds of linguistic universals related to phonology (the study of phonemes), morphology (the study of morphemes), semantics, and syntax. For example, Chomsky would argue that deep structure applies, in its own way, to the syntaxes of all languages.

Colors   An area that illustrates much of this research focuses on color names. These words provide an especially convenient way of testing for universals. Why? Because people in every culture can be expected to be exposed, at least potentially, to pretty much the same range of colors.

In actuality, different languages name colors quite differently. But the languages do not divide the color spectrum arbitrarily. A systematic pattern seems universally to govern color naming across languages. Consider the results of investigations of color terms across a large number of languages (Berlin & Kay, 1969; Kay, 1975). Two apparent linguistic universals about color naming have emerged across languages. First, all the languages surveyed took their basic color terms from a set of just 11 color names. These are *black, white, red, yellow, green, blue, brown, purple, pink, orange,* and *gray.* Languages ranged from using all 11 color names, as in English, to using just two of the names, as in the Dani tribe of Western New Guinea (Rosch Heider, 1972). Second, when only some of the color names are used, the naming of colors falls into a hierarchy of five levels. The levels are (1) black, white; (2) red; (3) yellow, green, blue; (4) brown; and (5) purple, pink, orange, gray. Thus, if a language names only two colors, they will be black and white. If it names three colors, they will be black, white, and red. A fourth color will be taken from the set of yellow, green, and blue. The fifth and sixth will be taken from this set as well. Selection will continue until all 11 colors have been labeled. The order of selection within the categories may, however, vary between cultures (Jameson, 2005).

Another study had participants name various colors that were shown to them on color plates. Participants also were asked to choose the best example for each color (e.g., out of the many color plates presented, which is the best "red"?). This procedure was done for many languages, and the results showed that the "best" colors tended to cluster around the colors that English speakers call red, yellow, green, and blue (Regier et al., 2005). This result indicates that there are some universals in color perception.

In contrast, several studies have shown that color categories vary, depending on the speaker's language. For example, Berinmo speakers from New Guinea tend to

■ **BELIEVE IT OR NOT**

Do You See Colors to Your Left Differently than Colors to Your Right?

The language center of the brain is located mostly in the left hemisphere. At the same time, light from objects on our right falls onto the left side of our retina and is then transmitted to the left hemisphere of the brain (and vice versa; for a graphical illustration of this, refer to Figure 3.8 in Chapter 3). Could this circumstance influence our perception of colors? Participants were shown a circle consisting of colored green squares. One of those squares was of a different color—either blue or a different shade of green—and it was located either in the lower right or lower left of the circle. The time it took people to pick the square with the different color was measured. If the square was located on the left (and the light therefore was transmitted to the right hemisphere), it did not make a difference whether its color was blue or a different shade of green. If the square was on the right, the blue square was detected faster than the green square. This is because the language center in the left hemisphere interacted with color recognition. If participants' language centers were kept busy with a memory task, the effect disappeared, making it indeed likely that the effect was a result of language (Gilbert et al., 2006).

aggregate colors together in one name (*nol*) that we call green and blue (Roberson et al., 2000, 2005). Other languages tend to see categorical differences where English speakers do not see any. For example, Russian speakers discriminate between light blue (*goluboy*) and dark blue (*siniy*) (Winawer et al., 2007). Various theories have been proposed of why color names differ in different cultures. It has been proposed, for example, that the sun's ultraviolet rays causes people's lenses to yellow, which makes it harder to discriminate between green and blue. The large sun exposure, then, in areas near the equator could be the reason for the relative scarcity of separate color terms for blue and green in some languages in this area (Lindsey & Brown, 2002). It also could be that color names are an evolutionary result of the most frequently occurring colors in the environment of members of a particular language group (Yendrikhovskij, 2001). But so far, none of the theories are consistent with each other.

So overall, while it seems that color naming is relatively universal in that it clusters worldwide around the same areas, color categories vary considerably and color names can have an impact on perception and cognition (Kay & Regier, 2006; Roberson & Hanley, 2007).

So, can we say that color perception is universal, or are there significant differences between cultures and languages? In the next section, we examine an interesting study that explored this question.

Verbs and Grammatical Gender   Syntactical as well as semantic structural differences across languages may affect thought. For example, Spanish has two forms of the verb "to be"—*ser* and *estar*. However, they are used in different contexts. One investigator studied the uses of *ser* and *estar* in adults and in children (Sera, 1992).

When "to be" indicated the identity of something (e.g., in English, "This is José.") or the class membership of something (e.g., "José is a carpenter."), both adults and children used the verb form *ser*. Moreover, both adults and children used different verb forms when "to be" indicated attributes of things. *Ser* was used to indicate permanent attributes (e.g., "Maria is tall."). *Estar* was also used to indicate temporary attributes (e.g., "Maria is busy."). Finally, when using forms of "to be" to describe the locations of objects, including people, animals, and other things, both adults and children used *estar* (e.g., "Marie is on the chair."). However, when using forms of "to be" to describe the locations of events (e.g., meetings or parties), adults used *ser*, whereas children continued to use *estar*.

Sera (1992) interprets these findings as indicating two things. First, *ser* seems to be used primarily for indicating permanent conditions, such as identity; class inclusion; and relatively permanent, stable attributes of things. *Estar* seems to be used primarily for indicating temporary conditions, such as short-term attributes of things and the location of objects. These things often are subject to change from one place to another. Moreover, children treat the location of events in the same way as the location of objects. They view it as temporary and hence use *estar*. Adults, in contrast, differentiate between events and objects. In particular, adults consider the locations of events to be unchanging. Because they are permanent, they require the use of *ser*.

Other researchers have also suggested that young children have difficulty distinguishing between objects and events (e.g., Keil, 1979). Young children also find it difficult to recognize the permanent status of many attributes (Marcus & Overton, 1978). Thus, the developmental differences regarding the use of *ser* to describe the location of events may indicate developmental differences in cognition. Sera's work suggests that differences in language use may indeed indicate differences in thinking. However, her work leaves open an important psychological question. Do native Spanish speakers have a more differentiated sense of the temporary and the permanent than do native English speakers, who use the same verb form to express both senses of "to be"? The answer is unclear.

Other languages also have been used in investigations of linguistic relativity. Some studies explore the relevance of different languages using different prepositions. In English, people use the prepositions "in" and "on" to describe putting a pear in a bowl or putting a cup on the table. "In" refers to containment of some sort, whereas "on" refers to support. Korean speakers differentiate between "tight fit" (*kkita*, like a DVD in its sleeve) and "loose fit" (*nehta*, like a pear in a bowl) in their prepositions. In one experiment, participants were shown several spatial actions and had to pick the one that seemed "odd" and not to fit the other actions. The spatial actions were performed with objects of different texture and material (e.g., wooden or made of sponge) and showed the objects either being put in a tight-fitting setting or a loose container. In all, 80% of the Korean speakers picked the odd scene on the basis of whether or not it involved tight/loose fit. In comparison, only 37% of English speakers did. The majority of English speakers picked out a scene where the material or shape of the object differed (McDonough et al., 2003).

Another experiment tested the effect of grammatical gender. The study was conducted in English, but participants were native German and Spanish speakers. They were presented with 24 noun words that they had to describe in three adjectives each. In all, 12 of the nouns were feminine in German and masculine in Spanish, and the other 12 nouns were masculine in German and feminine in Spanish. There were marked differences in how the objects were described, depending on their gender. For example, the word "key," which is feminine in Spanish (*la llave*), was described by the Spanish speakers as "golden, intricate, little, lovely." In German, the word "key" is masculine (*der Schluessel*) and was described as "hard, heavy, jagged, metal." The effect is especially impressive because the experiment was conducted in English and did not involve the participants speaking German or Spanish (Boroditsky et al., 2003).

Also consider some more facts:

- Children who learn Mandarin Chinese tend to use more verbs than nouns. In contrast, children acquiring English or Italian tend to use more nouns than verbs (Tardif, 1996; Tardif, Shatz, & Naigles, 1997).
- Korean-speaking children use verbs earlier than do English-speaking children. In contrast, English-speaking children have larger naming vocabularies earlier than do Korean-speaking children (Gopnik & Choi, 1995; Gopnik, Choi, & Baumberger, 1996).

What differences in thinking might such differences in acquisition imply? No one knows for sure.

Concepts   An intriguing experiment assessed the possible effects of linguistic relativity by studying people who speak more than one language (Hoffman, Lau, & Johnson, 1986). In Chinese, a single term, *shì gÈ,* specifically describes a person who is "worldly, experienced, socially skillful, devoted to his or her family, and somewhat reserved" (p. 1098). English clearly has no comparable single term to embrace these diverse characteristics. Hoffman and his colleagues composed text passages in English and in Chinese describing various characters. They included the *shì gÈ* stereotype, without, of course, specifically using the term *shì gÈ* in the descriptions. The researchers then asked participants who were fluent in both Chinese and English to read the passages either in Chinese or in English. Then they rated various statements about the characters, in terms of the likelihood that the statements would be true of the characters. Some of these statements involved a stereotype of a *shì gÈ* person.

Their results seemed to support the notion of linguistic relativity. The participants were more likely to rate the various statements in accord with the *shì gÈ* stereotype when they had read the passages in Chinese than when they had read the passages in English. Similarly, when participants were asked to write their own impressions of the characters, their descriptions conformed more closely to the *shì gÈ* stereotype if they previously read the passages in Chinese. These authors do not suggest that it would be impossible for English speakers to comprehend the *shì gÈ* stereotype. Rather, they suggest that having that stereotype readily accessible facilitates its mental manipulation.

Research on linguistic relativity is a good example of the dialectic in action. Before Sapir and Whorf, the issue of how language constrains thought was not salient in the minds of psychologists. Sapir and Whorf then presented a thesis that language largely controls thought. After they presented their thesis, a number of psychologists tried to show the antithesis. They argued that language does not control thought. Today, many psychologists believe in a synthesis: Language has some influence on thought but not nearly so extreme an influence as Sapir and Whorf believed.

The question of whether linguistic relativity exists, and if so, to what extent, remains open. There may be a mild form of relativity in the sense that language can influence thought. However, a stronger deterministic form of relativity is less likely. Based on the available evidence, language does not seem to determine differences in thought among members of various cultures. Finally, it is probably the case that language and thought interact with each other throughout the life span (Vygotsky, 1986).

IN THE LAB OF KEITH RAYNER

Eye Movements and Reading

Reading is a remarkable achievement of the human brain/mind. How do we understand written language on a moment-to-moment basis? This is the primary question that has driven my research for many years. We typically use eye movement measures as a reflection of moment-to-moment processing. A considerable amount of research from my lab (and others) clearly documents that how long

KEITH RAYNER

readers look at words in text is strongly influenced by cognitive processes and the ease or difficulty associated with processing a word. For example, readers look longer at low-frequency words (like "vituperative") than high-frequency words (like "house").

There are a number of critical issues that needed attention before one could safely assume that eye movements reflect moment-to-moment processing. In reading, our eyes pause on average for about 200–250 milliseconds. How much useful information do readers obtain on each fixation? To answer this question, George McConkie and I developed a gaze-contingent moving window paradigm in which we controlled how much information readers had available on each fixation. We found that the span of perception in reading extends about 3–4 letter spaces to the left of fixation to about 14–15 letters spaces to the right of fixation for readers of English.

In subsequent work, I developed a gaze-contingent boundary paradigm to determine what kind of information readers obtain from the word to the right of fixation. This work documented that readers obtain a preview benefit from having valid information to the right of fixation. In these types of experiments (which are quite popular these days), the type of information that is available in a target word location is manipulated (so for example, the preview might be the word *chest*), but during the eye movement to the word, the preview changes to the target word (*chart*). The amount of preview benefit depends on how far away the eyes were from the

target word when the saccade was launched and the relationship between the preview and the target.

A final type of gaze-contingent technique that we developed is the disappearing-text paradigm. Here, on each fixation, the word the reader is looking at disappears (or is masked) early in a fixation. One remarkable finding is that readers can read normally if they get to see the fixated word for 50–60 milliseconds (this doesn't mean that word recognition is completed in this time, just that the information has been entered into the processing system). Second, how long the eyes remain in place is strongly influenced by the frequency of the fixated word: If it is a low-frequency word, the eyes remain on it longer than if it is a high-frequency word. This is very good evidence that cognitive processing drives eye movements during reading.

Given these findings, eye movements can be used to study moment-to-moment processing. In my lab, we have taken advantage of the various types of ambiguity that exist in written English to strive to understand readers' moment-to-moment comprehension processes. Thus, we have studied how readers parse sentences that contain temporary syntactic ambiguities, as well as how they deal with lexically ambiguous words (words with two meanings, like *bank* and *straw*) and phonologically ambiguous words (that are spelled the same, but have two different pronunciations). We have also used eye movement data to study higher-level discourse processing, though the link between such processes and how long readers look at parts of the text is much more tenuous than is the case with lexical processes. Finally, given that we have learned so much about the relationship between eye movements and reading, we (Erik Reichle, Sandy Pollatsek, Don Fisher, and myself) developed a model of eye movement control in reading (called the E-Z Reader model) that does a good job of predicting where readers fixate and how long they fixate on words.

Bilingualism and Dialects

Suppose a person can speak and think in two languages. Does the person think differently in each language? Do **bilinguals**—people who can speak two languages—think differently from **monolinguals**—people who can speak only one language? (Multilinguals speak at least two and possibly more languages.) What differences, if any, emanate from the availability of two languages versus just one? Might bilingualism affect intelligence, positively or negatively?

Bilingualism—An Advantage or Disadvantage?

Does bilingualism make thinking in any one language more difficult, or does it enhance thought processes? The data are somewhat contradictory. Different participant populations, different methodologies, different language groups, and different experimenter biases may have contributed to the inconsistency in the literature. Consider what happens when bilinguals are balanced bilinguals, who are roughly equally fluent in both languages, and when they come from middle-class backgrounds. In these instances, positive effects of bilingualism tend to be found. Executive functions, which are located primarily in the prefrontal cortex and include abilities such as to shift between tasks or ignore distracters, are enhanced in bilingual individuals. Even the onset of dementia in bilinguals may be delayed by as much as four years (Andreou & Karapetsas, 2004; Bialystok & Craik, 2010; Bialystok et al., 2007). But negative effects may result as well. Bilingual speakers tend to have smaller vocabularies and their access to lexical items in memory is slower (Bialystok, 2001b; Bialystok & Craik, 2010). What might be the causes of this difference?

Let us distinguish between what might be called additive versus subtractive bilingualism (Cummins, 1976). In *additive bilingualism,* a second language is acquired in addition to a relatively well-developed first language. In *subtractive bilingualism,* elements of a second language replace elements of the first language. It appears that the additive form results in increased thinking ability. In contrast, the subtractive form results in decreased thinking ability (Cummins, 1976). In particular, there may be something of a threshold effect. Individuals may need to be at a certain relatively high level of competence in both languages for a positive effect of bilingualism. Classroom teachers often discourage bilingualism in children (Sook Lee & Oxelson, 2006). Either through letters requesting only English be spoken at home, or through subtle attitudes and methods, many teachers actually encourage subtractive bilingualism (Sook Lee & Oxelson, 2006). Additionally, children from backgrounds with lower socioeconomic status (SES) may be more likely to be subtractive bilinguals than are children from the middle SES. Their SES may be a factor in their being hurt rather than helped by their bilingualism.

Researchers also distinguish between *simultaneous bilingualism,* which occurs when a child learns two languages from birth, and *sequential bilingualism,* which occurs when an individual first learns one language and then another (Bhatia & Ritchie, 1999). Either form of language learning can contribute to fluency. It depends on the particular circumstances in which the languages are learned (Pearson et al., 1997). It is known, however, that infants begin babbling at roughly the same age. This happens regardless of whether they consistently are exposed to one or two languages (Oller et al., 1997). In the United States, many people make a big deal of bilingualism, perhaps because relatively few Americans born in the United States of non-immigrant parents learn a second language to a high degree of fluency. In other cultures, however, the learning of multiple languages is taken for granted. For example, in parts of India, people routinely may learn as many as four languages

(Khubchandani, 1997). In Flemish-speaking Belgium, many people learn at least some French, English, and/or German. Often, they learn one or more of these other languages to a high degree of fluency.

Factors That Influence Second Language Acquisition

A significant factor believed to contribute to acquisition of a language is age. Some researchers have suggested that native-like mastery of some aspects of a second language is rarely acquired after adolescence. Other researchers disagree with this view (Bahrick et al., 1994; Herschensohn, 2007). They found that some aspects of a second language, such as vocabulary comprehension and fluency, seem to be acquired just as well after adolescence as before. Furthermore, these researchers found that even some aspects of syntax seem to be acquired readily after adolescence. These results are contrary to prior findings. The mastery of native-like pronunciation often seems to depend on early acquisition. But individual differences are great and some learners attain native-like language abilities even at a later age (Birdsong, 2009). It may seem surprising that learning completely novel phonemes in a second language may be easier than learning phonemes that are highly similar to the phonemes of the first language (Flege, 1991). In any case, there do not appear to be critical periods for second-language acquisition (Birdsong, 1999, 2009). Adults may appear to have a harder time learning second languages because they can retain their native language as their dominant language. Young children, in contrast, who typically need to attend school in the new language, may have to switch their dominant language. So, they learn the new language to a higher level of mastery (Jia & Aaronson, 1999). A study on second language acquisition found that age and proficiency in a language are negatively correlated (Mechelli et al., 2004). This finding has been well documented (Birdsong, 2006). This does not mean that we cannot learn a new Flanguage later in life, but rather, that the earlier we learn it, the more likely we will become highly proficient in its use.

What kinds of learning experiences facilitate second-language acquisition? There is no single correct answer to that question (Bialystock & Hakuta, 1994). One reason is that each individual language learner brings distinctive cognitive abilities and knowledge to the language-learning experience. In addition, the kinds of learning experiences that facilitate second-language acquisition should match the context and uses for the second language once it is acquired.

For example, consider these individuals:

- Caitlin, a young child, may not need to master a wealth of vocabulary and complex syntax to get along well with other children. If she can master the phonology, some simple syntactical rules, and some basic vocabulary, she may be considered fluent.
- Similarly, José needs only to get by in a few everyday situations, such as shopping, handling routine family business transactions, and getting around town. He may be considered proficient after mastering some simple vocabulary and syntax, as well as some pragmatic knowledge regarding context-appropriate manners of communicating.
- Kim Yee must be able to communicate regarding her specialized technical field. She may be considered proficient if she masters the technical vocabulary, a primitive basic vocabulary, and the rudiments of syntax.
- Sumesh is a student who studies a second language in an academic setting. Sumesh may be expected to have a firm grasp of syntax and a rather broad, if shallow, vocabulary.

Each of these language learners may require different kinds of language experiences to gain the proficiency being sought. Different kinds of experiences may be needed to enhance their competence in the phonology, vocabulary, syntax, and pragmatics of the second language.

When speakers of one language learn other languages, they find the languages differentially difficult. For example, it is much easier, on average, for a native speaker of English to acquire Spanish as a second language than it is to acquire Russian. One reason is that English and Spanish share more roots than do English and Russian. Moreover, Russian is much more highly inflected than are English and Spanish. English and Spanish are more highly dependent on word order. The difficulty of learning a language as a second language, however, does not appear to have much to do with its difficulty as a first language. Russian infants probably learn Russian about as easily as U.S. infants learn English (Maratsos, 1998).

Bilingualism: One System or Two?

One way of approaching the study of bilingualism is to apply what we have learned from cognitive-psychological research to practical concerns regarding how to help with acquisition of a second language. Another approach is to study bilingual individuals to see how bilingualism may offer insight into the human mind. Some cognitive psychologists have been interested in finding out how the two languages are represented in the bilingual's mind. The **single-system hypothesis** suggests that two languages are represented in just one system or brain region (see Hernandez et al., 2001, for evidence supporting this hypothesis in early bilinguals). Alternatively, the **dual-system hypothesis** suggests that two languages are represented somehow in separate systems of the mind (De Houwer, 1995; Paradis, 1981). For instance, might German language information be stored in a physically different part of the brain than English language information? Figure 10.3 shows schematically the difference in the two points of view.

One way to address this question is through the study of bilinguals who have experienced brain damage. Suppose a bilingual person has brain damage in a particular part of the brain. According to the dual-system hypothesis, the individual would show different degrees of impairment in the two languages. The single-system view would suggest roughly equal impairment in the two languages. The logic of this kind of investigation is compelling, but the results are not. When recovery of language after trauma is studied, sometimes the first language recovers first; sometimes the second language recovers first. And sometimes recovery is about equal for the two languages (Albert & Obler, 1978; Marrero et al., 2002; Paradis, 1977). Recovery of one or both languages seems contingent on age of acquisition of the second language and on pre-incident language proficiency, among other factors (Marrero, Golden, & Espe Pfeifer, 2002).

A 32-year-old French-German bilingual who suffered from a stroke and subsequent aphasia was trained in German but was given no training in French. The researchers found significant recovery of German, but his German language abilities did not transfer to his French abilities (Meinzer et al., 2007).

The conclusions that can be drawn from all this research are ambiguous. Nevertheless, the results seem to suggest at least some duality of structure. A different method of study has led to an alternative perspective on bilingualism. Two investigators mapped the region of the cerebral cortex relevant to language use in two of their bilingual patients being treated for epilepsy (Ojemann & Whitaker, 1978).

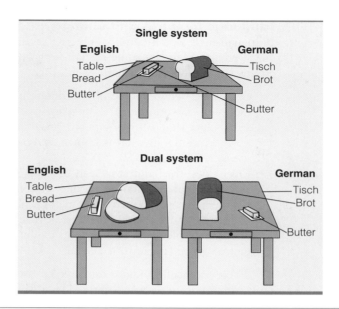

Figure 10.3 **Single-System and Dual-System Hypotheses.**
The single-system conceptualization hypothesizes that both languages are represented in a unified cognitive system. The dual-system conceptualization of bilingualism hypothesizes that each language is represented in a separate cognitive system.

Mild electrical stimulation was applied to the cortex of each patient. Electrical stimulation tends to inhibit activity where it is applied. It leads to a reduced ability to name objects for which the memories are stored at the location being stimulated. The results for both patients were the same. They may help explain the contradictions in the literature. Some areas of the brain showed equal impairments for object naming in both languages. But other areas of the brain showed differential impairment in one or the other language. The results also suggested that the weaker language was more diffusely represented across the cortex than was the stronger language. In other words, asking the question of whether two languages are represented singly or separately may be asking the wrong question. The results of this study suggest that some aspects of the two languages may be represented singly; other aspects may be represented separately.

To summarize, two languages seem to share some, but not all, aspects of mental representation. Learning a second language is often a plus, but it is probably most useful if the individual learning the second language is in an environment in which the learning of the second language adds to rather than subtracts from the learning of the first language. For beneficial effects to appear, the second language must be learned well. In the approach usually taken in schools, students may receive as little as two or three years of second-language instruction spread out over a few class periods a week. This approach probably will not be sufficient for the beneficial effects of bilingualism to appear. However, schooling does seem to yield beneficial effects on acquisition of syntax. This is particularly so when a second language is acquired after adolescence. Furthermore, whenever possible, individual learners should choose specific kinds of language-acquisition techniques that best fit their needs, abilities, preferences, and personal goals for using the second language.

Language Mixtures and Change

Bilingualism is not a certain outcome of linguistic contact between different language groups. Here are some scenarios of what can happen when different language groups come into contact with each other:

- Sometimes when people of two different language groups are in prolonged contact with one another, the language users of the two groups begin to share some vocabulary that is superimposed onto each group's language use. This superimposition results in what is known as a *pidgin*. It is a language that has no native speakers (Wang, 2009).
- Over time, this admixture can develop into a distinct linguistic form. It has its own grammar and hence becomes a *creole*. An example of a creole is the Haitian Creole language, spoken in Haiti. The Haitian Creole language is a combination of French and a number of West African languages.
- Modern creoles may resemble an evolutionarily early form of language, termed *protolanguage* (Bickerton, 1990).

The existence of pidgins and creoles, and possibly a protolanguage, supports the universality notion discussed earlier. That is, linguistic ability is so natural and universal that, given the opportunity, humans actually invent new languages quite rapidly.

Creoles and pidgins arise when two linguistically distinctive groups meet. The counterpart—a dialect—occurs when a single linguistic group gradually diverges toward somewhat distinctive variations. A **dialect** is a regional variety of a language distinguished by features such as vocabulary, syntax, and pronunciation. The study of dialects provides insights into such diverse phenomena as auditory discrimination and social discrimination. Many of the words we choose are a result of the dialect we use. The most well-known example is the word choice for a soft drink. Depending on the dialect you use, you may order a "soda," "pop," or a "Coke" (see Figure 10.4).

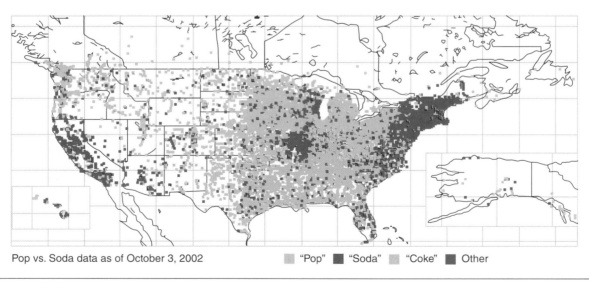

Pop vs. Soda data as of October 3, 2002   ▨ "Pop" ■ "Soda" ▨ "Coke" ■ Other

Figure 10.4 The Pop vs. Soda Controversy.
This map shows the distribution of different words used for "soft drink" across the United States. What word people use depends on the dialect they speak.

Source: http://popvssoda.com:2998/

Dialectical differences often represent harmless regional variations. They create few serious communication difficulties, but these difficulties can lead to some confusion. In the United States, for example, when national advertisers give toll-free numbers to call, they sometimes route the calls to the Midwest. They do so because they have learned that the Midwestern form of speech seems to be the most universally understood form within the country. Other forms, such as southern and northeastern ones, may be harder for people from diverse parts of the country to understand. And when calls are routed to other countries, such as India, there may be serious difficulties in achieving effective communication because of differences in dialect as well as accent. Many radio announcers try to learn something close to a standard form of English, often called "network English." In this way, they can maximize their comprehensibility to as many listeners as possible.

Sometimes, differing dialects are assigned different social statuses, such as *standard* forms having higher status than *non-standard* ones. The distinction between standard and non-standard forms of a language can become unfortunate when speakers of one dialect start to view themselves as speakers of a superior dialect. The view that one dialect is superior to another may lead one to make judgments about the speaker that are biased. This *linguicism*, or stereotype based on dialect, may be quite widespread and can cause many interpersonal problems (Phillipson, 2010; Zuidema, 2005). For example, we frequently make judgments about people's intelligence, competence, and morality based on the dialect they use. Specifically, a person who uses a non-standard form may be judged to be less educated or less trustworthy than a person who uses a more standard form. Usually, the standard dialect is that of the class in society that has the most political or economic power. Virtually any thought can be expressed in any dialect.

Neuroscience and Bilingualism

Learning a second language increases the gray matter in the left inferior parietal cortex (Mechelli et al., 2004). This density is positively correlated with proficiency. Thus, the more proficient a person is in a second language, the denser this area of the brain will be. Finally, a negative correlation exists between age of acquisition and the density in the left inferior parietal cortex (Mechelli et al., 2004)—the higher the age of acquisition, the less the density. These findings suggest that this area of the brain benefits from the learning of a second language and that the earlier this learning occurs, the better it is both for brain density and for overall proficiency.

Studies with aphasic patients suggest that first and second languages may be distributed in different anatomic regions of the brain. This assumption comes from the observation of a bilingual patient who suffered a stroke and subsequently had impaired language skills in his native language. His second language, however, was unaffected (Garcia et al., 2010). Other studies, however, suggest, that the brain regions activated by two languages may actually overlap (Gandour et al., 2007; Yokohama et al., 2006). Whether or not the same brain areas are involved likely depends on other factors, like the age of acquisition of the second language.

One study had bilingual persons complete a sentence-generation task (i.e., participants were asked to create sentences). The study showed that the centers of activation in the left inferior frontal gyrus are overlapping for early bilinguals. Late bilinguals, however, show separate centers of activation (Kim et al., 1997).

Slips of the Tongue

An area of particular interest to cognitive psychologists is how people use language incorrectly. Studying speech errors helps cognitive psychologists better understand normal language processing. One way of using language incorrectly is through **slips of the tongue**—inadvertent linguistic errors in what we say. They may occur at any level of linguistic analysis: phonemes, morphemes, or larger units of language (Crystal, 1987; McArthur, 1992). In such cases, what we think and what we mean to say do not correspond to what we actually do say. Freudian psychoanalysts have suggested that in Freudian slips, the verbal slips reflect some kind of unconscious processing that has psychological significance. The slips are alleged often to indicate repressed emotions. For example, a business competitor may say, "I'm glad to beat you," when what was overtly intended was, "I'm glad to meet you."

Most cognitive psychologists see things differently from the psychoanalytic view. They are intrigued by slips of the tongue because of what the lack of correspondence between what is thought and what is said may tell us about how language is produced. In speaking, we have a mental plan for what we are going to say. Sometimes, however, this plan is disrupted when our mechanism for speech production does not cooperate with our cognitive one. Often, such errors result from intrusions by other thoughts or by stimuli in the environment, such as a background noise from radio talk show or a neighboring conversation (Garrett, 1980; Saito & Baddeley, 2004).

Slips of the tongue may be taken to indicate that the language of thought differs somewhat from the language through which we express our thoughts (Fodor, 1975). Often we have the idea right, but its expression comes out wrong. Sometimes we are not even aware of the slip until it is pointed out to us. In the language of the mind, whatever it may be, the idea is right, although the expression represented by the slip is inadvertently wrong. This fact can be seen in the occasional slips of the tongue even in preplanned and practiced speech (Kawachi, 2002).

People tend to make various kinds of slips in their conversations (Fromkin, 1973; Fromkin & Rodman, 1988):

- In *anticipation*, the speaker uses a language element before it is appropriate in the sentence because it corresponds to an element that will be needed later in the utterance. For example, instead of saying, "an inspiring expression," a speaker might say, "an expiring expression."
- In *perseveration*, the speaker uses a language element that was appropriate earlier in the sentence but that is not appropriate later on. For example, a speaker might say, "We sat down to a bounteous beast" instead of a "bounteous feast."
- In *substitution*, the speaker substitutes one language element for another. For example, you may have warned someone to do something "after it is too late," when you meant "before it is too late."
- In *reversal* (also called "transposition"), the speaker switches the positions of two language elements. An example is the reversal that reportedly led "flutterby" to become "butterfly." This reversal captivated language users so much that it is now the preferred form. Sometimes, reversals can be fortuitously opportune.
- In *spoonerisms*, the initial sounds of two words are reversed and make two entirely different words. The term is named after the Reverend William Spooner, who was famous for them. Some of his choicest slips include, "You have hissed all my mystery lectures," [missed all my history lectures] and "Easier for a camel to go through the knee of an idol" [the eye of a needle] (Clark & Clark, 1977).

- In *malapropism*, one word is replaced by another that is similar in sound but different in meaning (e.g., furniture dealers selling "naughty pine" instead of "knotty pine").
- Additionally, slips may occur because of *insertions of sounds* (e.g., "mischievious" instead of "mischievous" or "drownded" instead of "drowned") or other linguistic elements. The opposite kind of slip involves deletions (e.g., sound deletions such as "prossing" instead of "processing"). Such deletions often involve blends (e.g., "blounds" for "blended sounds").

Each kind of slip of the tongue may occur at different hierarchical levels of linguistic processing (Dell, 1986). That is, it may occur at the acoustical level of phonemes, as in "bounteous beast" instead of "bounteous feast." It may occur at the semantic level of morphemes, as in "after it's too late" instead of "before it's too late." Or it may occur at even higher levels, as in "bought the bucket" instead of "kicked the bucket" or "bought the farm." The patterns of errors (e.g., reversals, substitutions) at each hierarchical level tend to be parallel (Dell, 1986). For example, in phonemic errors, initial consonants tend to interact with initial consonants, as in "tasting wime" instead of "wasting time." Final consonants tend to interact with final consonants, as in "bing his tut" instead of "bit his tongue." Prefixes often interact with prefixes, as in "expiring expression," and so on.

Also, errors at each level of linguistic analysis suggest particular kinds of insights into how we produce speech. Consider, for example, phonemic errors. A stressed word, which is emphasized through speech rhythm and tone, is more likely to influence other words than is an unstressed word (Crystal, 1987). Furthermore, even when sounds are switched, the basic rhythmic and tonal patterns usually are preserved. An example is the emphasis on "hissed" and the first syllable of "mystery" in the first spoonerism quoted here.

Even at the level of words, the same parts of speech tend to be involved in the errors we produce (e.g., nouns interfere with other nouns, and verbs with verbs; Bock, 1990; Bock, Loebell, & Morey, 1992). In the second spoonerism quoted here, Spooner managed to preserve the syntactical categories, the nouns *knee* and *idol*. He also preserved the grammaticality of the sentence by changing the articles from "*a* needle" to "*an* idol." Even in the case of word substitutions, syntactic categories are preserved. In speech errors, semantic categories, too, may be preserved. An example would be naming a category when intending to name a member of the category, such as "fruit" for "apple." Another example would be naming the wrong member of the category, such as "peach" for "apple." A last example would be naming a member of a category when intending to name the category as a whole, as in "peach" for "fruit" (Garrett, 1992).

People who are fluent in sign language and mouth at the same time they sign have slips of the tongue (or hand) occurring independently of each other, indicating that oral words and sign words are not stored together in that person's lexicon (Vinson et al., 2010).

Another aspect of language that offers us a distinctive view is the study of metaphorical language.

Metaphorical Language

Until now, we have discussed primarily the literal uses of language. At least as interesting to poets and to many others is the non-literal, figurative use of language.

A notable example is the use of metaphors as a way of expressing thoughts. **Metaphors** juxtapose two nouns in a way that positively asserts their similarities, while not disconfirming their dissimilarities (e.g., The house was a pigsty). Related to metaphors are similes. **Similes** introduce the words *like* or *as* into a comparison between items (e.g., The child was as quiet as a mouse).

Metaphors contain four key elements: Two are the items being compared, a tenor and a vehicle. And two are ways in which the items are related. The *tenor* is the topic of the metaphor (e.g., house). The *vehicle* is what the tenor is described in terms of (e.g., pigsty). For example, consider the metaphor, "Billboards are warts on the landscape." The tenor is "billboards." The vehicle is "warts." The *ground* of the metaphor is the set of similarities between the tenor and the vehicle (e.g., both are messy). The *tension* of the metaphor is the set of dissimilarities between the two (e.g., people do not live in pigsties but do live in houses). We may conjecture that a key similarity (ground) between billboards and warts is that they are both considered unattractive. The dissimilarities (tension) between the two are many, including that billboards appear on buildings, highways, and other impersonal public locations. But warts appear on diverse personal locations on an individual.

Various theories have been proposed to explain how metaphors work. The traditional views have highlighted either the ways in which the tenor and the vehicle are similar or the ways in which they differ.

- The traditional *comparison view* highlights the importance of the comparison. It underscores the comparative similarities and analogical relationship between the tenor and the vehicle (Malgady & Johnson, 1976; Miller, 1979; cf. also Sternberg & Nigro, 1983). As applied to the metaphor, "Abused children are walking time bombs," the comparison view underscores the similarity between the elements: their potential for explosion.

- In contrast, the *anomaly view* of metaphor emphasizes the dissimilarity between the tenor and the vehicle (Beardsley, 1962; Gerrig & Healy, 1983; Searle, 1979). The anomaly view would highlight the dissimilarities between abused children and time bombs.

- The *domain-interaction view* integrates aspects of each of the preceding views. It suggests that a metaphor is more than a comparison and more than an anomaly. According to this view, a metaphor involves an interaction of some kind between the domain (area of knowledge, such as animals, machines, plants) of the tenor and the domain of the vehicle (Black, 1962; Hesse, 1966). The exact form of this interaction differs somewhat from one theory to another. The metaphor often is more effective when two circumstances occur. First, the tenor and the vehicle share many similar characteristics (e.g., the potential explosiveness of abused children and time bombs). Second, the domains of the tenor and the vehicle are highly dissimilar (e.g., the domain of humans and the domain of weapons) (Tourangeau & Sternberg, 1981, 1982).

- Another view is that that metaphors are essentially a non-literal form of class-inclusion statements (Glucksberg & Keysar, 1990). According to this view, the tenor of each metaphor is a member of the class characterized by the vehicle of the given metaphor. That is, we understand metaphors not as statements of comparison but as statements of category membership, in which the vehicle is a prototypical member of the category. Suppose I say, "My colleague's partner is an iceberg." I am thereby saying that the partner belongs to the category of things that are characterized by an utter lack of personal warmth, extreme rigidity, and the ability to produce a massively chilling effect on anyone in the surrounding environment. For a metaphor to work well, the reader should find the salient features of the vehicle ("iceberg") to be unexpectedly relevant as features of the tenor ("my colleague's partner"). That is, the reader should be at least mildly surprised that prominent features of the vehicle may characterize the tenor. But after consideration, the reader should agree that those features do describe the tenor.

Metaphors enrich our language in ways that literal statements cannot match. Our understanding of metaphors seems to require not only some kind of comparison. It also requires that the domains of the vehicle and of the tenor interact in some way. Reading a metaphor can change our perception of both domains. It therefore can educate us in a way that is perhaps more difficult to transmit through literal speech.

A very prominent metaphor in cognitive psychology is that of humans as information processors. This metaphor highlights certain aspects of humans, such as our limited capacity for information processing. This limited capacity leads us to be selective in terms of what information to attend to in our environment (Newell & Broeder, 2008). Metaphors such as that of the human information processor guide scientific thinking and research.

Metaphors can enrich our speech in social contexts. For example, suppose we say to someone, "You are a prince." Chances are that we do not mean that the person is literally a prince. Rather, we mean that the person has characteristics of a prince. How, in general, do we use language to negotiate social contexts? We explore the social contexts of language in the next section.

✔ CONCEPT CHECK

1. What is linguistic relativity?
2. What impact can language have on the perception of color?
3. What is additive bilingualism?
4. Does age influence our ability to learn languages?
5. What are the single-system and dual-system hypotheses?
6. Name some kinds of slips of the tongue people make when they speak.
7. What are the key elements of metaphors?

Language in a Social Context

The study of the social context of language is a relatively new area of linguistic research. One aspect of context is the investigation of **pragmatics,** the study of how people use language. It includes sociolinguistics and other aspects of the social context of language.

Under most circumstances, you change your use of language in response to contextual cues without giving these changes much thought. Similarly, you usually unselfconsciously change your language patterns to fit different contexts.

For example, in speaking with a conversational partner, you seek to establish common ground, or a shared basis for engaging in a conversation (Clark & Brennan, 1991). When we are with people who share background, knowledge, motives, or

INVESTIGATING COGNITIVE PSYCHOLOGY
Language in Different Contexts

To get an idea of how you change your use of language in different contexts, suppose that you and your friend are going to meet right after work. Something comes up and you must call your friend to change the time or place for your meeting. When you call your friend at work, your friend's supervisor answers and offers to take a message. Exactly what will you say to your friend's supervisor to ensure that your friend will know about the change in time or location? Suppose, instead, that the 4-year-old son of your friend's supervisor answers. Exactly what will you say in this situation? Finally, suppose that your friend answers directly. How will you have modified your language for each context, even when your purpose (underlying message) in all three contexts was the same?

goals, establishing common ground is likely to be easy and scarcely noticeable. When little is shared, however, such common ground may be hard to find.

Gestures and vocal inflections, which are forms of nonverbal communication, can help establish common ground. One aspect of nonverbal communication is *personal space*—the distance between people in a conversation or other interaction that is considered comfortable for members of a given culture. *Proxemics* is the study of interpersonal distance or its opposite, proximity. It concerns itself with relative distancing and the positioning of you and your fellow conversants. In the United States, 2.45 feet to 2.72 feet are considered about right. In Mexico, the adequate distance ranges from 1.65 to 2.14 feet, whereas in Costa Rica it is between 1.22 and 1.32 feet (Baxter, 1970). Scandinavians expect more distance. Middle Easterners, southern Europeans, and South Americans expect less (Sommer, 1969; Watson, 1970).

When on our own familiar turf, we take our cultural views of personal space for granted. Only when we come into contact with people from other cultures do we notice these differences. For example, when the author was visiting Venezuela, he noticed his cultural expectations coming into conflict with the expectations of those around him. He often found himself in a comical dance: He would back off from the person with whom he was speaking; meanwhile, that person was trying to move closer. Within a given culture, greater proximity generally indicates one or more of three things. First, the people see themselves in a close relationship. Second, the people are participating in a social situation that permits violation of the bubble of personal space, such as close dancing. Third, the "violator" of the bubble is dominating the interaction.

Even within our own culture, there are differences in the amount of personal space that is expected. For instance, when two colleagues are interacting, the personal space is much smaller than when an employee and supervisor are interacting. When two women are talking, they stand closer together than when two men are talking (Dean, Willis, & Hewitt, 1975; Hall, 1966).

Does interpersonal distance also play a role in virtual-reality environments? When virtual worlds are created, a lot of factors matter in determining how believable the virtual worlds are. How people dress, how the streets look, and what sounds are in the background all facilitate or make it harder for people to immerse themselves in that environment. For example, when you visit a virtual place located in Latin America, you expect to see people who look Latin American. To create lifelike simulations, it also matters how people behave during interpersonal interactions. How close do they stand together, how often do they look at each other, and how long do they keep that gaze? Computational models are being developed to simulate the behavior of people from different cultures (Jan et al., 2007).

Violations of personal space, even in virtual environments, cause discomfort (Wilcox et al., 2006). When given the option, people whose personal space is violated in a virtual environment will move away (Bailenson et al., 2003). Physical space is also maintained in video conferencing (Grayson & Coventry, 1998).

These findings on proxemics indicate the importance of interpersonal space in all interactions. They also indicate that proxemics is important, even when one or more of the people are not physically present.

Speech Acts

When we communicate with others, we can use either direct or indirect speech. We will examine both kinds of speech acts in the next two sections.

Direct Speech Acts

When you speak, what kinds of things can you accomplish? **Speech acts** address the question of what you can accomplish with speech and fall into five basic categories, based on the purpose of the acts (Searle, 1975a; see also Harnish, 2003). There are essentially five things you can accomplish with speech. Table 10.1 identifies these categories and gives examples of each.

The appealing thing about Searle's taxonomy is that it classifies almost any statement that might be made. It shows the different kinds of things speech can accomplish. It also shows the close relationship between language structure and language function.

Indirect Speech Acts

Sometimes speech acts are indirect, meaning that we accomplish our goals in speaking in an oblique fashion. One way of communicating obliquely is through **indirect requests,** through which we make a request without doing so straightforwardly (Gordon & Lakoff, 1971; Searle, 1975b), for example, "Won't you please take out the garbage?"

Types of Indirect Speech Acts   There are four basic ways of making indirect requests:

- asking or making statements about abilities;
- stating a desire;
- stating a future action; and
- citing reasons.

Examples of these forms of indirect requests are illustrated in Table 10.2. In each case, the indirect request is aimed at having a waitress tell the speaker where to find the restroom in a restaurant.

When are indirect speech acts interpreted literally, and when is the indirect meaning understood by the listener? When an indirect speech act, such as "Must

Table 10.1 Searle's Taxonomy of Speech Acts

The five basic categories of speech acts encompass the various tasks that can be accomplished through speech (or other modes of using language).

Speech Act	Description	Example
Representative	A speech act by which a person conveys a belief that a given proposition is true. The speaker can use various sources of information to support the given belief. But the statement is nothing more, nor less, than a statement of belief. Qualifiers can be added to show the speaker's degree of certainty.	Mr. Smith has a son named Jack and a daughter named Jill. If Mr. Smith says, "It's important for Jack to learn responsibility. Asking him to help shovel the driveway is one way he can learn about responsibility," he is conveying that he believes it is important to teach children responsibility, and that having them participate in household tasks is one way to achieve this goal. He can use various sources of information to support his belief. Nonetheless, the statement is nothing more or less than a statement of belief. Similarly, he can make a statement that is more directly verifiable, such as, "As you can see on this thermometer, the temperature outside is 31 degrees Fahrenheit."
Directive	An attempt by a speaker to get a listener to do something, such as supplying the answer to a question. Sometimes a directive is quite indirect. For example, almost any sentence structured as a question probably is serving a directive function. Any attempt to elicit assistance of any kind, however indirect, falls into this category.	Mr. Smith wants Jack to help him shovel snow. He can request this in various ways, some of which are more direct than others, such as, "Please help me shovel the snow," or "It sure would be nice if you were to help me shovel the snow," or "Would you help me shovel the snow?" The different surface forms are all attempts to get Jack's help. Some directives are quite indirect. If Mr. Smith asks, "Has it stopped raining yet?" he is still uttering a directive, in this case seeking information rather than physical assistance. In fact, almost any sentence structured as a question probably serves a directive function.
Commissive	A commitment by the speaker to engage in some future course of action. Promises, pledges, contracts, guarantees, assurances, and the like all constitute commissives.	If Jack responds, "I'm busy now, but I'll help you shovel the snow later," he is uttering a commissive, in that he is pledging his future help. If Jill then says, "I'll help you," she too is uttering a commissive, because she is pledging her assistance now. Promises, pledges, contracts, guarantees, assurances, and the like all constitute commissives.
Expressive	A statement regarding the speaker's psychological state.	If Mr. Smith tells Jack later, "I'm really upset that you didn't come through in helping me shovel the snow," that would be an expressive. If Jack says, "I'm sorry I didn't get around to helping you out," he would be uttering an expressive. If Jill says, "Daddy, I'm glad I was able to help out," she is uttering an expressive.
Declaration (also termed *performative*)	A speech act by which the very act of making a statement brings about an intended new state of affairs. Declarations also are termed *performatives* (Clark & Clark, 1977).	Suppose that you are called into your boss's office and told that you are responsible for the company losing $50,000. Then your boss says, "You're fired." The speech act results in your being in a new state—that is, unemployed. You might then tell your boss, "That's fine, because I wrote you a letter yesterday saying that the money was lost because of your glaring incompetence, not mine, and I resign." You are making a declaration.

you open the window?" is presented in isolation, it usually first is interpreted literally, for example, as "Do you need to open the window?" (Gibbs, 1979). When the same speech act is presented in a story context that makes the indirect meaning clear, the sentence first is interpreted in terms of the indirect meaning. For instance,

Table 10.2 Indirect Speech Acts

Type of Indirect Speech Act	Example of an Indirect Request For Information
Abilities	If you say, "Can you tell me where the restroom is?" to a waitress at a restaurant, and she says, "Yes, of course I can," the chances are she missed the point. The question about her ability to tell you the location of the restroom was an indirect request for her to tell you exactly where it is.
Desire	"I would be grateful if you told me where the restroom is." Your statements of thanks in advance are really ways of getting someone to do what you want.
Future action	"Would you tell me where the restroom is?" Your inquiry into another person's future actions is another way to state an indirect request.
Reasons	You need not spell out the reasons to imply that there are good reasons to comply with the request. For example, you might imply that you have such reasons for the waitress to tell you where the restroom is by saying, "I need to know where the restroom is."

suppose a character in a story had a cold and asked, "Must you open the window?" It would be interpreted as an indirect request: "Do not open the window."

Subsequent work showed that indirect speech acts often anticipate what potential obstacles the respondent might pose. These obstacles are specifically addressed through the indirect speech act (Gibbs, 1986). For example:

- "May I have ... ?" addresses potential obstacles of permission.
- "Would you mind ... ?" addresses potential obstacles regarding a possible imposition on the respondent.
- "Do you have ... ?" addresses potential obstacles regarding availability.

Indirect requests that ask permission are judged to be the most polite (Clark & Schunk, 1980). Similarly, indirect requests that speak to an obligation (i.e., "Shouldn't you...?") are judged as the most impolite (Clark & Schunk, 1980). The responses to these requests typically match the requests in terms of politeness (Clark & Schunk, 1980).

Pinker's Theory of Indirect Speech Steven Pinker and his colleagues (2007) recently developed a three-part theory of indirect speech. Its basic assumption is that communication is always a mixture of cooperation and conflict. Indirect speech gives the speaker the chance to voice an ambiguous request that the listener can accept or decline without reacting adversely to it. According to the three-part theory, indirect speech can serve three purposes:

1. **Plausible deniability.** Imagine a policeman pulls you over when you are driving and wants to give you a traffic ticket. By saying, "Maybe the best thing is to take care of this right here," you can imply that you might be willing to pay a bribe to get off the ticket. If the policeman is inclined to accept, he can do so. If he is not interested in the bribe, he cannot arrest you for the attempted bribe (you hope!) because you never made an explicit offer. You purposely were indirect in order to ensure, to the extent possible, plausible deniability (in this case, of your attempt to bribe). Similarly, sexual overtures are often made in an indirect way in order to ensure deniability should the object of the overtures react negatively.

2. **Relationship negotiation**. This occurs when a person uses indirect language because the nature of a relationship is ambiguous. For example, one purpose of an indirect sexual overture may be plausible deniability (the first purpose). But the overture also may be indirect to avoid offending the targeted individual if he or she is not interested in a sexual relationship (relationship negotiation). In this case, indirectness is a way of helping two people mutually resolve the nature of their relationship.

3. **Language as a digital medium of indirect as well as direct communication.** Language can serve purposes other than direct communication. For example, suppose the emperor believes he is wearing fine robes when he is in fact naked. A boy shouts out, "The emperor has no clothes." The boy is not telling the others anything they do not know—they can see the emperor has no clothes. What he is telling them is that it is not just they as individuals who see no clothes—everyone sees the emperor wearing no clothes. The boy has communicated something digitally—that all know the emperor is naked—that before was ambiguous.

Both direct and indirect communication are part of what makes a conversation successful. What else leads to a successful conversation?

Characteristics of Successful Conversations

In speaking to each other, we implicitly set up a cooperative enterprise. Indeed, if we do not cooperate with each other when we speak, we often end up talking past rather than to each other. In other words, we fail to communicate what we intended. Conversations thrive on the basis of a **cooperative principle,** by which we seek to communicate in ways that make it easy for our listener to understand what we mean (Grice, 1967; Mooney, 2004). According to Grice, successful conversations follow four maxims: the maxim of quantity, the maxim of quality, the maxim of relation, and the maxim of manner. These are also called *conversational postulates.* Examples of these maxims are provided in Table 10.3.

To these four maxims noted by Grice, we might add an additional maxim: Only one person speaks at a time (Sacks, Schegloff, & Jefferson, 1974). Given that maxim, the situational context and the relative social positions of the speakers affect turn-taking (Keller, 1976). Sociolinguists have noted many ways in which speakers signal to one another when and how to take turns. Sometimes people flaunt the conversational postulates to make a point. For example, suppose one says, "My parents are wardens." One is not providing full information (what, exactly, does it mean for one's parents to be wardens?). But the ambiguity is intentional. Or sometimes when a conversation on a topic is becoming heated, one purposely may switch topics and bring up an irrelevant issue. One's purpose in doing so is to get the conversation to another, safer topic. When we flaunt the postulates, we are sending an explicit message by doing so: The postulates retain their importance because their absence is so notable.

People with autism have difficulty with both language and emotion. It is therefore not surprising that they have particular difficulty in detecting violations of the Gricean maxims (Eales, 1993; Surian, 1996). Further discussion of language impairments in people with autism are discussed later in the chapter.

Gender and Language

Within our own culture, do men and women speak a different language? Gender differences have been found in the content of what we say. Young girls are more

Table 10.3   Conversational Postulates

To maximize the communication that occurs during conversation, speakers generally follow four maxims.

Postulate	Maxim	Example
Maxim of quantity	Make your contribution to a conversation as informative as required but no more informative than is appropriate.	If someone asks you the temperature outside and you reply, "It's 31.297868086298 degrees out there," you are violating the maxim of quantity because you are giving more information than was probably wanted.
Maxim of quality	Your contribution to a conversation should be truthful; you are expected to say what you believe to be the case. Irony, sarcasm, and jokes might seem to be exceptions to the maxim of quality, but they are not. The listener is expected to recognize the irony or sarcasm and to infer the speaker's true state of mind from what is said. Similarly, a joke often is expected to accomplish a particular purpose. It usefully contributes to a conversation when that purpose is clear to everyone.	Clearly, there are awkward circumstances in which each of us is unsure of just how much honesty is being requested. Under most circumstances, however, communication depends on an assumption that both parties to the communication are being truthful.
Maxim of relation	You should make your contributions to a conversation relevant to the aims of the conversation.	Almost any large meeting we attend seems to have someone who violates this maxim. This someone inevitably goes into long digressions that have nothing to do with the purpose of the meeting and that hold up the meeting. "That reminds me of a story a friend once told me about a meeting he once attended, where ..."
Maxim of manner	You should try to avoid obscure expressions, vague utterances, and purposeful obfuscation of your point.	Nobel Prize–winning physicist Richard Feynman (1997) described how he once read a paper by a well-known scholar, and he found that he could not make heads or tails of it. One sentence went something like this: "The individual member of the social community often receives information via visual, symbolic channels" (p. 281). Feynman concluded, in essence, that the scholar was violating the maxim of manner when Feynman realized that the sentence meant, "People read."

likely to ask for help than are young boys (Thompson, 1999). Older adolescent and young adult males prefer to talk about political views, sources of personal pride, and what they like about the other person. In contrast, females in this age group prefer to talk about feelings toward parents, close friends, classes, and their fears (Rubin et al., 1980). Also, in general, women seem to disclose more about themselves than do men (Morton, 1978).

Conversations between men and women are sometimes regarded as cross-cultural communication (Tannen, 1986, 1990, 1994). Young girls and boys learn conversational communication in essentially separate cultural environments through their same-sex friendships. As men and women, we then carry over the conversational styles we have learned in childhood into our adult conversations.

Tannen has suggested that male–female differences in conversational style largely center on differing understandings of the goals of conversation. These cultural differences result in contrasting styles of communication. These in turn can lead to misunderstandings and even break-ups as each partner somewhat unsuccessfully tries to understand the other. Men see the world as a hierarchical social order in which the purpose of communication is to negotiate for the upper hand, to preserve independence, and to avoid failure (Tannen, 1990, 1994). Each man strives to one-up the other and to "win" the contest. Women, in contrast, seek to establish a connection between the two participants, to give support and confirmation to others, and to reach consensus through communication.

To reach their conversational goals, women use conversational strategies that minimize differences, establish equity, and avoid any appearances of superiority on the part of one or another conversant. Women also affirm the importance of and the commitment to the relationship. They handle differences of opinion by negotiating to reach a consensus that promotes the connection and ensures that both parties at least feel that their wishes have been considered. They do so even if they are not entirely satisfied with the consensual decision.

Men enjoy connections and rapport. But because men have been raised in a gender culture in which status plays an important role, other goals take precedence in conversations. Tannen has suggested that men seek to assert their independence from their conversational partners. In this way, they indicate clearly their lack of acquiescence to the demands of others, which would indicate lack of power. Men also prefer to inform (thereby indicating the higher status conferred by authority) rather than to consult (indicating subordinate status) with their conversational partners. The male partner in a close relationship thus may end up informing his partner of their plans. In contrast, the female partner expects to be consulted on their plans. When men and women engage in cross-gender communications, their crossed purposes often result in miscommunication because each partner misinterprets the other's intentions.

Tannen has suggested that men and women need to become more aware of their cross-cultural styles and traditions. In this way, they may at least be less likely to misinterpret one another's conversational interactions. They are also both more likely to achieve their individual aims, the aims of the relationship, and the aims of the other people and institutions affected by their relationship. Such awareness is important not only in conversations between men and women. It is also important in conversations among family members in general (Tannen, 2001).

Tannen may be right. But at present, converging operations are needed, in addition to Tannen's sociolinguistic case-based approach, to pin down the validity and generality of her interesting findings.

Gender differences in the written use of language have also been observed (Argamon et al., 2003). For example, a study that analyzed more than 14,000 text files from 70 separate studies found that women used more words that were related to psychological and social processes, whereas men related more to object properties and impersonal topics (Newman et al., 2008).

These findings are not conclusive. A study examining blogs noted that the type of blog, more than the gender of the author, dictated the writing style (Herring & Paolillo, 2006).

Thus far we have discussed the social and cognitive contexts for language. Language use interacts with, but does not completely determine, the nature of thought.

PRACTICAL APPLICATIONS OF COGNITIVE PSYCHOLOGY

IMPROVING YOUR COMMUNICATION WITH OTHERS

Think about how your gender influences your conversational style. Construct some ways to communicate more effectively with people of the opposite sex. How might your speech acts and conversational postulates differ? If you are a man, do you tend to use and prefer directives and declarations over expressives and commissives? If you are a woman, do you use and prefer expressives and commissives over directives and declarations? If so, speaking to people of the opposite sex can lead to misinterpretations of meaning based on differences in style. For example, when you want to get another person to do something, it may be best to use the style that more directly reflects the other person's style. In this case, you might use a directive with men ("Would you go to the store?") and an expressive with women ("I really enjoy going shopping."). Also, remember that your responses should match the other person's expectations regarding how much information to provide, honesty, relevance, and directness. The art of effective communication really involves listening carefully to another person, observing body language, and interpreting the person's goals accurately. This can be accomplished only with time, effort, and sensitivity.

Have you recently been in a situation where you felt communication was not ideal? Write down the communication and identify what you would do differently. How could you prevent such a situation, or at least improve it?

Social interactions influence the ways in which language is used and comprehended in discourse and reading. Next, we highlight some of the insights we have gained by studying the physiological context for language. Specifically, how do our brains process language? And do nonhuman animals have language?

✔ CONCEPT CHECK

1. What are the different categories of speech acts?
2. Name some advantages of indirect speech.
3. What are some maxims of successful conversations?
4. How does gender have an impact on language?

Do Animals Have Language?

Some cognitive psychologists specialize in the study of nonhuman animals. Why would they study such animals, when humans are so readily available? There are several reasons.

First, nonhuman animals often are presumed to have somewhat simpler cognitive systems. It is therefore easier to model their behavior. These models can then be bootstrapped to the study of humans, as has happened most notably in the study of learning. For example, a model of conditioning that originally was proposed for nonhuman animals such as white rats has proven to be extremely useful in understanding human learning (Rescorla & Wagner, 1972). The model, when first proposed, was unique in suggesting that nonhuman animal cognition is more complex than had previously been thought. Robert Rescorla and Allan Wagner showed that classical conditioning depends not just on simple contiguity of an unconditioned and conditioned stimulus, but rather on the contingency involved in the situation. In other words, classical conditioning occurs when animals reduce uncertainty in a learning situation—when they learn the relation between occurrences of two kinds of stimuli. In sum, research on simpler animals often leads to important insights about human learning.

Second, nonhuman animals can be subject to procedures that would not be possible for human ones. For example, a rat may be sacrificed at the end of a learning experiment to study changes that have occurred in the brain as a result of learning. A rat may also be injected with drugs to examine a compound's effects on functioning. Such experimentation clearly cannot be completed on humans. All such studies, of course, must be subject to institutional approval for the ethics of experimentation before they are conducted.

Third, nonhuman animals that are not in the wild can serve as full-time subjects, or at least, regularly available subjects. They are typically there when the experimenter needs them. In contrast, college students and other humans have many other obligations, such as classes, homework, jobs, and personal commitments. Moreover, sometimes, even when they sign up for research, they fail to show up.

Fourth, an understanding of the comparative and evolutionary as well as developmental bases of human behavior requires studies of nonhuman animals of various kinds (Rumbaugh & Beran, 2003). If cognitive psychologists want to understand the origins of human cognition in the distant past, they need to study other kinds of animals besides humans.

The philosopher René Descartes suggested that language is what qualitatively distinguishes human beings from other species. Was he right? Before we get into the particulars of language in nonhuman species, we should emphasize the distinction between communication and language. Few would doubt that nonhuman animals communicate in one way or another. What is at issue is whether they do so through what reasonably can be called a language. Whereas *language* is an organized means of combining words to communicate, *communication* more broadly encompasses not only the exchange of thoughts and feelings through language but also nonverbal expression. Examples include gestures, glances, distancing, and other contextual cues.

Primates—especially chimpanzees—offer our most promising insights into nonhuman language. Jane Goodall, the well-known investigator of chimpanzees in the wild, has studied diverse aspects of chimp behavior. One is vocalizations. Goodall considers many of them to be clearly communicative, although not necessarily indicative of language. For example, chimps have a specific cry indicating that they are about to be attacked. They have another for calling their fellow chimps together. Nonetheless, their repertoire of communicative vocalizations seems to be small, nonproductive (new utterances are not produced), limited in structure, lacking in structural complexity, and relatively non-arbitrary. It also is not spontaneously acquired. The chimps' communications thus do not satisfy our criteria for a language.

But can chimps be taught to use language by humans? Several researchers have had chimps and tried to teach them language skills. The vocal tract of chimpanzees is different from the one of humans, so by their very nature they are not able to reproduce the majority of human sounds. Instead, researchers have reverted to teaching them sign language.

Savage-Rumbaugh and her colleagues (Savage-Rumbaugh et al., 1986, 1993) have found the best evidence yet in favor of language use among chimpanzees. Their pygmy chimpanzees spontaneously combined the visual symbols (such as red triangles and blue squares) of an artificial language the researchers taught them. They even appear to have understood some of the language spoken to them. One pygmy chimp in particular (Greenfield & Savage-Rumbaugh, 1990) seemed to possess remarkable skill, even possibly demonstrating a primitive grasp of language structure. It may be that the difference in results across groups of investigators is due to the particular kind of chimp tested or to the procedures used. The chimp's language may not meet all the constraints posed by the properties of language described at the beginning of the chapter. For example, the language used by the chimps is not spontaneously acquired. Rather, they learn it only through very deliberate and systematic programs of instruction.

Another famous exploration of language in a nonhuman can be seen in the gorilla Koko. Koko can use approximately 1,000 signs and can communicate quite effectively with humans, expressing both desires and thoughts. Evidence also suggests that Koko is able to understand and use humor (Gamble, 2001). Koko also seems to be able to use language in a novel way, both combining signs in new ways and by forming entirely new signs. One of the most famous examples of this behavior was exhibited when Koko developed a new sign for "ring" by combining "finger" and "bracelet" (Hill, 1978).

A neuroanatomical study of chimpanzees found that when chimps use tools, the brain regions that were especially active corresponded to Broca's and Wernicke's areas in humans. Both of those areas are associated with language comprehension and production, and it has been hypothesized that the use of tools in early humans actually facilitated the development of language (Hopkins et al., 2007).

A less positive view of the linguistic capabilities of chimpanzees was taken by Herbert Terrace (1987), who raised a chimp named Nim Chimpsky, a takeoff on Noam Chomsky, the eminent linguist. Over the course of several years, Nim made more than 19,000 multiple-sign utterances in a slightly modified version of ASL. Most of his utterances consisted of two-word combinations. Terrace's careful analysis of these utterances, however, revealed that most of them were repetitions of what Nim had seen. Terrace concluded that, despite what appeared to be impressive accomplishments, Nim did not show even the rudiments of syntactical expression. The chimp could produce single- or even multiple-word utterances, but not in a syntactically organized way. For example, Nim would alternate signing, "Give Nim banana," "Banana give Nim," and "Banana Nim give," showing no preference for the grammatically correct form. Moreover, Terrace also studied films showing other chimpanzees supposedly producing language. He came to the same conclusion for them that he had reached for Nim. His position, then, is that although chimpanzees can understand and produce utterances, they do not have linguistic competence in the same sense that even very young humans do. Their communications lack structure, and particularly multiplicity of structure. At this point, we just cannot be sure if the chimps truly show the full range of language abilities.

Chimpanzees are not the only ones that can learn language to a certain extent—other species can as well. Take the example of Alex, an African Grey Parrot who died in 2007. Alex could produce more than 200 words and express a variety of complex concepts, including *present* and *absent* and a zero-like concept. Recent evidence also suggests that Alex was capable of novel combinations of words to form new ways of expressing concepts (Pepperberg, 1999, 2007; Pepperberg & Gordon, 2005).

Whether nonhuman species can use language, it seems almost certain that the language facility of humans far exceeds that of other species psychologists have studied. Noam Chomsky (1991) has stated the key question regarding nonhuman language quite eloquently: "If an animal had a capacity as biologically advantageous as language but somehow hadn't used it until now, it would be an evolutionary miracle, like finding an island of humans who could be taught to fly."

✔ CONCEPT CHECK

1. Why do psychologists conduct research with animals?

2. Do animals have the same potential for language as humans? Explain.

Neuropsychology of Language

In this part of the chapter, we will first explore which parts of the brain are involved in language production and comprehension. Afterwards, we will turn our attention to specific instances of language impairment. Recall from Chapter 3 that some of our earliest insights into brain localization related to an association between specific language deficits and specific organic damages to the brain, as first discovered by Marc Dax, Paul Broca, and Carl Wernicke (see also Brown & Hagoort, 1999; Garrett, 2003). Broca's aphasia and Wernicke's aphasia are particularly well-documented instances in which brain lesions affect linguistic functions.

Brain Structures Involved in Language

Through studies of patients with brain lesions, researchers have learned a great deal about the relations between particular areas of the brain (the areas of lesions observed in patients) and particular linguistic functions (the observed deficits in the brain-injured patients). For example, we can broadly generalize that many linguistic functions are located primarily in the areas identified by Broca and Wernicke. Damage to Wernicke's area, in the posterior of the cortex, is now believed to entail more grim consequences for linguistic function than does damage to Broca's area, closer to the front of the brain (Kolb & Whishaw, 1990). Also, lesion studies have shown that linguistic function is governed by a much larger area of the posterior cortex than just the area identified by Wernicke. In addition, other areas of the cortex also play a role. Examples are association-cortex areas in the left hemisphere and a portion of the left temporal cortex.

The Brain and Word Recognition

One avenue of research involves the study of the metabolic activity of the brain and the flow of blood in the brain during the performance of various verbal tasks. fMRI studies have found that the middle part of the superior temporal sulcus (STS) responds more strongly to speech sounds than to non-speech sounds. The response takes place in both sides of the STS, although it is usually stronger in the left hemisphere. Interestingly, it does not matter whether words or pseudo-words are presented. This means it is unlikely that processing of semantic information takes place here (Binder, 2009; Binder et al., 1996, 2000; Desai et al., 2005).

The Brain and Semantic Processing

Where does semantic processing take place then? Research shows a relatively consistent picture. The evidence comes from studies involving patients with Alzheimer's disease, aphasia, autism, and many other disorders.

There are five brain regions that are involved in the storage and retrieval of meaning (Binder, 2009):

- the *ventral temporal lobes*, including middle and inferior temporal, anterior fusiform, and anterior parahippocampal gyri;
- the *angular gyrus*;
- the anterior aspect (pars orbitalis) of the *inferior frontal gyrus*;
- the *dorsal prefrontal cortex*; and
- the *posterior cingulate gyrus*.

The activation of these areas takes place mostly in the left hemisphere, although there is some activation in the right hemisphere. It is suspected, however, that the right hemisphere does not play a significant role in word recognition (Binder, 2009; see also Binder et al., 2005, 2009; Ischebeck et al., 2004; Sabsewitz et al., 2005; Vandenbulcke, 2006).

Finally, some other subcortical structures (e.g., the basal ganglia and the posterior thalamus) also are involved in linguistic function. These structures remain poorly understood, however. Surgeons sometimes conduct brain surgery while patients are awake to map the language pathways and try to preserve the language capabilities of their patients after surgery (Duffau et al., 2008).

The Brain and Syntax

Event-related potentials, or ERPs (see Chapter 3), also can be used to study the processing of language in the brain. For one thing, a certain ERP called N400 (a negative potential 400 milliseconds after stimulus onset) typically occurs when individuals hear an anomalous sentence (Dambacher & Kliegl, 2007; Kutas & Hillyard, 1980). Thus, if people are presented a sequence of normal sentences but also anomalous sentences (such as "The leopard is a very good napkin"), the anomalous sentences will elicit the N400 potential. Moreover, the more anomalous a sentence is, the greater the response shown in another ERP, P600 (a positive potential 600 milliseconds after the stimulus onset; Kutas & Van Patten, 1994). The P600 effect seems to be more related to syntactic violations, whereas the N400 effect is more related to semantic violations (Friederici et al., 2004).

The Brain and Language Acquisition

There is some evidence that the brain mechanisms responsible for language learning are different from those responsible for the use of language by adults (Stiles et al., 1998). In general, the left hemisphere seems to be better at processing well-practiced routines. The right hemisphere is better at dealing with novel stimuli. A possibly related finding is that individuals who have learned language later in life show more right-hemisphere involvement (Neville, 1995; Polkczynska-Fiszer, 2008). Perhaps the reason is that language remains somewhat more novel for them than for others. These findings suggest that one cannot precisely map linguistic or other kinds of functioning to hemispheres in a way that works for all people. Rather, the mappings differ somewhat from one person to another (Zurif, 1995).

The Plasticity of the Brain

Recent imaging studies of the post-traumatic recovery of linguistic functioning find that neurological language functioning appears to redistribute to other areas of the brain. Thus, damage to the major left hemisphere areas responsible for language functioning sometimes can lead to enhanced involvement of other areas as language functioning recovers. It is as if previously dormant or overshadowed areas take over the duties left vacant (Rosenberg et a., 2008; Cappa, et al., 1997).

The Brain and Sex Differences in Language Processing

Another method used to examine brain functioning is fMRI. Through these methods, dominance of the left hemisphere is observed for most language users (Anderson et al., 2006; Gaillard et al., 2004). Men and women appear to process language differently, at least at the phonological level (Shaywitz, 2005). An fMRI study of men and women asked participants to perform one of four tasks:

1. indicate whether a pair of letters was identical;
2. indicate whether two words have the same meaning;
3. indicate whether a pair of words rhymes; and
4. compare the lengths of two lines (a control task).

The researchers found that when both male and female participants were performing the letter-recognition and word-meaning tasks, they showed activation in the left temporal lobe of the brain. When they were performing the rhyming task, however, different areas were activated for men versus women. Only the inferior (lower) frontal region of the left hemisphere was activated for men. The inferior frontal region of both the left and right hemispheres was activated in women. These results suggested that men localized their phonological processing more than did women.

Leo Cullum/www.Cartoonbank.com

Some intriguing sex differences emerge in the ways that linguistic function appears to be localized in the brain (Kimura, 1987). Men seem to show more left-hemisphere dominance for linguistic function than the women show. Women show more bilateral, symmetrical patterns of linguistic function. Furthermore, the brain locations associated with aphasia seemed to differ for men and women. Most aphasic women showed lesions in the anterior region, although some aphasic women showed lesions in the temporal region. In contrast, aphasic men showed a more varied pattern of lesions. Aphasic men were more likely to show lesions in posterior regions rather than in anterior regions. One interpretation of Kimura's findings is that the role of the posterior region in linguistic function may be different for women than it is for men.

Another interpretation relates to the fact that women show less lateralization of linguistic function. Women may be better able to compensate for any possible loss of function due to lesions in the left posterior hemisphere through functional offsets in the right posterior hemisphere. The possibility that there also may be subcortical sex differences in linguistic function further complicates the ease of interpreting Kimura's findings. (Recall also the earlier discussion of communication differences between men and women.) A recent meta-analysis, however, could not verify any sex differences in asymmetries of the Planum Temporale (which is at the center of Wernicke's area) or in functional imaging findings during language tasks (Sommer et al., 2008).

Despite the many findings that have resulted from studies of brain-injured patients, there are two key difficulties in drawing conclusions based only on studies of patients with lesions:

1. Naturally occurring lesions are often not easily localized to a discrete region of the brain, with no effects on other regions. For example, when hemorrhaging or insufficient blood flow (such as impairment due to clotting) causes lesions, the lesions also may affect other areas of the brain. Thus, many patients who show cortical damage also have suffered some damage in subcortical structures. This may confound the findings of cortical damage.
2. Researchers are able to study the linguistic function of patients only after the lesions have caused damage. Typically they are unable to document the linguistic function of patients prior to the damage.

Because it would be unethical to create lesions merely to observe their effects on patients, researchers are able to study the effects of lesions only in those areas where lesions happen to have occurred naturally. Other areas therefore are not studied.

Researchers also investigate brain localization of linguistic functions via electrical stimulation of the brain. Gender differences have been investigated this way as well (Ojemann, 1982; Spring et al., 2008). Through stimulation studies, researchers have found that stimulation of particular points in the brain seems to yield discrete effects on particular linguistic functions (such as the naming of objects) across repeated, successive trials. For example, in a given person, repeated stimulation of one particular point might lead to difficulties in recalling the names of objects on every trial. In contrast, stimulation of another point might lead to incorrect naming of objects. In addition, information regarding brain locations in a specific individual may not apply across individuals. Thus, for a given individual, a discrete point of stimulation may seem to affect only one particular linguistic function. But across individuals, these particular localizations of function vary widely.

The effects of electrical stimulation are transitory. Linguistic function returns to normal soon after the stimulation has ceased. These brain-stimulation studies also show that many more areas of the cortex are involved in linguistic function than was thought previously. One study examined electrical stimulation of the brains of bilingual speakers. The researchers found different areas of the brain were active when using the primary versus the secondary language to name items. There was, however, some overlap of active areas with the two languages (Lucas, McKhann, & Ojemann, 2004).

Using electrical-stimulation techniques, sex differences in linguistic function can be identified. There is a somewhat paradoxical interaction of language and the brain (Ojemann, 1982). Although females generally have superior verbal skills to males, males have a proportionately larger (more diffusely dispersed) language area in their brains than do females. Counterintuitively, therefore, the size of the language area in the brain may be inversely related to the ability to use language.

The Brain and Sign Language

Kimura (1981) also has studied hemispheric processing of language in people who use sign language rather than speech to communicate. She found that the locations of lesions that would be expected to disrupt speech also disrupt signing. Further, the hemispheric pattern of lesions associated with signing deficits is the same pattern shown with speech deficits. That is, all right-handers with signing deficits show left-hemisphere lesions, as do most left-handers. But some left-handers with signing deficits show right-hemisphere lesions (see also Newman et al., 2010; Pickell et al., 2005). This finding supports the view that the brain processes both signing and speech similarly in terms of their linguistic function. It refutes the view that signing involves spatial processing or some other non-linguistic form of cognitive processing.

Aphasia

Aphasia is an impairment of language functioning caused by damage to the brain (Caramazza & Shapiro, 2001; Garrett, 2003; Hillis & Caramazza, 2003). There are several types of aphasias (Figure 10.5).

Wernicke's Aphasia

Wernicke's aphasia is caused by damage to Wernicke's area of the brain (see Chapter 3). It is characterized by notable impairment in the understanding of spoken words and sentences. It also typically involves the production of sentences that have the basic structure of the language spoken but that make no sense. They are sentences that are empty of meaning. Two examples are "Yeah, that was the pumpkin furthest from my thoughts" and "the scroolish prastimer ate my spanstakes" (Hillis & Caramazza, 2003, p. 176). In the first case, the words make sense, but not in the context they are presented. In the second case, the words themselves are neologisms, or newly created words. Treatment for patients with this type of aphasia frequently involves supporting and encouraging non-language communication (Altschuler et al., 2006).

Broca's Aphasia

Broca's aphasia is caused by damage to Broca's area of the brain (see Chapter 3). It is characterized by the production of agrammatical speech at the same time that verbal

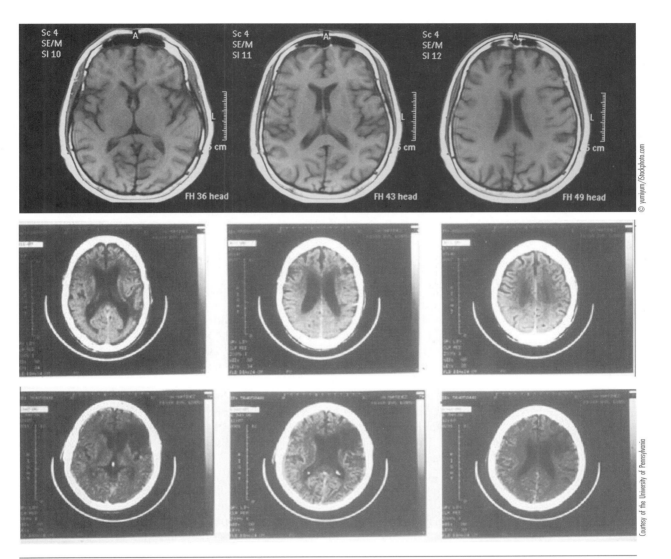

Figure 10.5   Healthy and Aphasic Brains.

Brain scans comparing the brain of (a) a normal patient with brains of patients with (b) Wernicke's aphasia and (c) Broca's aphasia.c

comprehension ability is largely preserved. It thus differs from Wernicke's aphasia in two key respects. First is that speech is agrammatical rather than grammatical (as in Wernicke's). Second is that verbal comprehension is largely preserved. An example of a production by a patient with Broca's aphasia is "Stroke … Sunday … arm, talking—bad" (Hillis & Caramazza, 2003, p. 176). The gist of the intended sentence is maintained, but the expression of it is badly distorted. Broca's area is important for speech production, regardless of the format of the speech. In particular, Broca's area is activated during imagined or actual sign production (Campbell, MacSweeney, & Waters, 2007; Horwitz et al., 2003).

Global Aphasia

Global aphasia is the combination of highly impaired comprehension and production of speech. It is caused by lesions to both Broca's and Wernicke's areas. Aphasia following a stroke frequently involves damage to both Broca's and Wernicke's areas. In one study, researchers found 32% of aphasias immediately following a stroke involved both Broca's and Wernicke's areas (Pedersen, Vinter, & Olsen, 2004).

Anomic Aphasia

Anomic aphasia involves difficulties in naming objects or in retrieving words. The patient may look at an object and simply be unable to retrieve the word that corresponds to the object. Sometimes, specific categories of things cannot be recalled, such as names of living things (Jonkers & Bastiaanse, 2007; Warrington & Shallice, 1984).

Autism

Autism is a developmental disorder characterized by abnormalities in social behavior, language, and cognition (Heinrichs et al., 2009; Pierce & Courchesne, 2003). It is biological in its origins, and researchers have already identified some of the genes associated with it (Wall et al., 2009). Children with autism show abnormalities in many areas of the brain, including the frontal and parietal lobes, as well as the cerebellum, brainstem, corpus callosum, basal ganglia, amygdala, and hippocampus. The disease was first identified in the middle of the 20th century (Kanner, 1943). It is five times more common in males than in females. The incidence of diagnosed autism has increased rapidly over recent years. Between the years of 2000 and 2004, the frequency of diagnosis of autism increased 14% (Chen et al., 2007). Autism has been diagnosed in recent years in approximately 60 out of every 10,000 children (Fombonne, 2003). This rate corresponds to about 1 out of every 165 children being diagnosed with an autism-spectrum disorder. The increase in recent times may be a result of a number of causes, including changes in diagnosing strategies or environmental pollution (Jick & Kaye, 2003; Windham et al., 2006).

Children with autism usually are identified by around 14 months of age, when they fail to show expected normal patterns of interactions with others. Children with autism display repetitive movements and stereotyped patterns of interests and activities (Pierce & Courchesne, 2003). Often they repeat the same motion, over and over again, with no obvious purpose to the movement. When they interact with someone, they are more likely to view their lips than their eyes. About half of children with autism fail to develop functional speech. What speech they do develop tends to be characterized by *echolalia,* meaning they repeat, over and over again, speech they have heard. Sometimes the repetition occurs several hours after the original use of the words by someone else (Pierce & Courchesne, 2003). People with autism also may have problems with the semantic encoding of language (Binder, 2009).

There are a variety of theories of autism. One recent theory suggests that autism can be understood in terms of sex differences in the wiring of the human brain. According to this theory (Baron-Cohen, 2003), male brains are, on average, stronger than female ones at understanding and building systems. These systems can be concrete ones, such as those involved in building machinery, or they can be abstract ones, such as those in politics or writing or music.

Females' brains, in contrast, are stronger at empathizing and communicating. According to Baron-Cohen, autism results from an extreme male brain. This brain is almost totally inept in empathy and communication but very strong in systematizing. As a result, individuals with autism sometimes can perform tasks that require a great deal of systematization, such as figuring out the day corresponding to a date well in the future. As it happens, autism is also much more common among males than among females. Although this theory has not been conclusively proven, it is intriguing and currently undergoing further investigation.

Another theory of autism is that of executive dysfunction (Chan et al., 2009; Ozonoff et al., 1994). Executive functions include abilities to control and regulate other abilities and behaviors. For example, when you initiate or terminate an action, or monitor your behavior to see if it helps you in achieving your goals, you are using executive functions. This theory describes the repetitive motion observed in autism, as well as difficulties in planning, mental flexibility, and self-monitoring (Hill, 2004). The executive dysfunction theory views autism as associated with dysfunction in the frontal lobes.

Much of this chapter has revealed the many ways in which language and thought interact. The following chapter focuses on problem solving and creativity. But it also further reveals the interconnectedness of the ways in which we use language and the ways in which we think.

✔ CONCEPT CHECK

1. Which parts of the brain are involved in semantic processing?
2. What does "plasticity" refer to with respect to the brain?
3. What are some difficulties when drawing conclusions from lesion studies?
4. What is the difference between Wernicke's aphasia and Broca's aphasia?

Key Themes

This chapter deals with several of the themes highlighted in Chapter 1.

Validity of causal inference versus ecological validity. Some researchers study language comprehension and production in controlled laboratory settings. For example, studies of phonology are likely to occur in a laboratory where it is possible to gain precise experimental control of stimuli. But work on language and thought often is done in remote parts of the world where tight experimental controls are only a dream. Studies of language usage in remote African villages, for example, typically cannot be done with tight controls, although some control is possible. As always, a combination of methodologies best enables cognitive psychologists to understand psychological phenomena to their fullest.

Biological versus behavioral methods. Lesion studies are a particularly good example of a combination of the two methodologies. On the one hand, they require a deep understanding of the nature of the brain and the parts of the brain affected by particular lesions. On the other hand, researchers examine behavior to understand how the particular lesions, and by inference, parts of the brain, are related to behavioral functioning.

Structure versus process. To understand any linguistic phenomena, one must analyze thoroughly the structure of the language under investigation. One can then investigate the processes that are used to comprehend and produce this language. Without an understanding of both structure and process, it would be impossible to fully understand language and thought.

Suppose you are on a camping trip and are sitting around the campfire at night, admiring the numerous stars in the sky. Imagine asking someone the following metaphorical question, "Would you like to see the sun paint a picture across the morning sky?" What does this question mean? Some people might say that it means that you are asking if they would like to wake up early to see how beautiful the sunrise will be the next morning. Others might say it means that it is getting late and that you should go to sleep to wake up early to see the beautiful sunrise. Now, suppose you ask this same question not on a camping trip but in a sleazy bar. What do you think the utterance will mean in that context?

Summary

1. **How does language affect the way we think?** According to the linguistic-relativity view, cognitive differences that result from using different languages cause people speaking the various languages to perceive the world differently. However, the linguistic-universals view stresses cognitive commonalities across different language users. No single interpretation explains all the available evidence regarding the interaction of language and thought.

Research on bilinguals seems to show that environmental considerations also affect the interaction of language and thought. For example, additive bilinguals have established a well-developed primary language. The second language adds to their linguistic and perhaps even their cognitive skills. In contrast, subtractive bilinguals have not yet firmly established their primary language when portions of a second language partially displace the primary language. This displacement may lead to difficulties in verbal skills. Theorists differ in their views as to whether bilinguals store two or more languages separately (dual-system hypothesis) or together (single-system hypothesis). Some aspects of multiple languages possibly could be stored separately and others unitarily. Creoles and pidgins arise when two or more distinct linguistic groups come into contact. A dialect appears when a regional variety of a language becomes distinguished by features such as distinctive vocabulary, grammar, and pronunciation.

Slips of the tongue may involve inadvertent verbal errors in phonemes, morphemes, or larger units of language. Slips of the tongue include anticipations, perseverations, reversals (including spoonerisms), substitutions, insertions, and deletions.

Alternative views of metaphor include the comparison view, the anomaly view, the domain-interaction view, and the class-inclusion view.

2. **How does our social context influence our use of language?** Psychologists, sociolinguists, and others who study pragmatics are interested in how language is used within a social context. Their research looks into various aspects of nonverbal as well as verbal communication. Speech acts comprise representatives, directives, commissives, expressives, and declarations. Indirect requests, ways of asking for something without doing so straightforwardly, may refer to abilities, desires, future actions, and reasons. Conversational postulates provide a means for establishing language as a cooperative enterprise. They comprise several maxims, including the maxims of quantity, quality, relation, and manner. Sociolinguists have observed that people engage in various strategies to signal turn-taking in conversations.

Sociolinguistic research suggests that male–female differences in conversational style center largely on men's and women's differing understandings of the goals of conversation. It has been suggested that men tend to see the world as a hierarchical social order in which their communication aims involve the need to maintain a high rank in the social order. In contrast, women tend to see communication as a means for establishing and maintaining their connection to their communication partners. To do so, they seek ways to demonstrate equity and support and to reach consensual agreement.

In discourse and reading comprehension, we use the surrounding context to infer the reference of pronouns and ambiguous phrases. The discourse context also can influence the semantic interpretation of unknown words in passages and aid in acquiring new vocabulary. Propositional representations of information in passages can be organized into mental models for text comprehension. Finally, a person's point of view likewise influences what will be remembered.

3. **How can we find out about language by studying the human brain, and what do such studies reveal?** Neuropsychologists, cognitive psychologists, and other researchers have managed to link quite a few language functions with specific areas or structures in the brain. They observe what happens when a particular area of the brain is injured, is electrically stimulated, or is studied in terms of its metabolic activity. For most people, the left hemisphere of the brain is vital to speech. It affects many syntactical aspects and some semantic aspects of linguistic processing. For most people, the right hemisphere handles a more limited number of linguistic functions. They include auditory comprehension of semantic information, as well as comprehension and expression of some non-literal aspects of language use. These aspects involve vocal inflection, gesture, metaphors, sarcasm, irony, and joke

Thinking about Thinking: Analytical, Creative, and Practical Questions

1. Why are researchers interested in the number of color words used by different cultures?
2. Describe the five basic kinds of speech acts proposed by Searle.
3. How should cognitive psychologists interpret evidence of linguistic universals when considering the linguistic-relativity hypothesis?
4. Compare and contrast the kinds of understandings that can be gained by studying speech errors made by healthy people with those that can be gained by studying the language produced by people who have particular brain lesions.
5. Write an example of a pidgin conversation between two people and a creole conversation, focusing on the differences between pidgins and creoles.
6. Draft an example of a brief dialogue between a male and a female in which each may misunderstand the other, based on their differing beliefs regarding the goals of communication.
7. Suppose that you are an instructor of English as a second language. What kinds of things will you want to know about your students to determine how much to emphasize phonology, vocabulary, syntax, or pragmatics in your instruction?
8. Give an example of a humorous violation of one of Grice's four maxims of successful conversation.

Key Terms

aphasia, *p. 436*
bilinguals, *p. 412*
cooperative principle, *p. 426*
dialect, *p. 416*
dual-system hypothesis, *p. 414*
indirect requests, *p. 423*

linguistic relativity, *p. 404*
linguistic universals, *p. 407*
metaphors, *p. 420*
monolinguals, *p. 412*
pragmatics, *p. 421*
similes, *p. 420*

single-system hypothesis, *p. 414*
slips of the tongue, *p. 418*
speech acts, *p. 423*

Media Resources

Visit the companion website—**www.cengagebrain.com**—for quizzes, research articles, chapter outlines, and more.

11 CHAPTER

Decision Making and Reasoning

CHAPTER OUTLINE

Here are some questions we will explore in this chapter:

1. What are some of the strategies that guide human decision making?
2. What are some of the forms of deductive reasoning that people may use, and what factors facilitate or impede deductive reasoning?
3. How do people use inductive reasoning to make causal inferences and to reach other types of conclusions?
4. Are there any alternative views of reasoning?

■ **BELIEVE IT OR NOT**

CAN A SIMPLE RULE OF THUMB OUTSMART A NOBEL LAUREATE'S INVESTMENT STRATEGY?

If you wanted to invest your money in the stock market, would you rather rely on a Nobel laureate's strategy or on a simple heuristic (which is kind of a rule of thumb)? Researchers (De Miguel, 2007) compared the levels of success of 14 portfolio management strategies and compared them with the success of the simple 1/N heuristic. This heuristic simply suggests that you distribute your assets evenly among a given number of options. That is, each of the N options receives 1/N of the total investment. Among the other strategies evaluated was Nobel laureate Harry Markowitz's mean-variance model, according to which investors should optimize the trade-off between the mean and variance of a portfolio return. Markowitz suggested you minimize your risk and maximize your return by considering several factors, such as that sometimes certain groups of stocks go up in price whereas others go down (e.g., if the oil price goes up, airline profits will go down). The researchers found that the simple 1/N heuristic actually outperformed all 14 other models. In this chapter, you will learn more about how humans make decisions and what shortcuts (heuristics) they use when they are faced with uncertainty or more information than they can process.

Let's start this chapter with a puzzle. Read the following description in *Investigating Cognitive Psychology: The Conjunction Fallacy*, and rate the likelihood of the presented statements.

 INVESTIGATING COGNITIVE PSYCHOLOGY
The Conjunction Fallacy

Linda is 31 years old, single, outspoken, and very bright. She majored in philosophy. As a student, she was deeply concerned with issues of discrimination and social justice and also participated in anti-nuclear demonstrations.

Based on the preceding description, list the likelihood that the following statements about Linda are true (with 0 meaning completely unlikely and 100 meaning totally likely):

(a) Linda is a teacher in elementary school.
(b) Linda works in a bookstore and takes yoga classes.
(c) Linda is active in the feminist movement.
(d) Linda is a psychiatric social worker.
(e) Linda is a member of the League of Women Voters.
(f) Linda is a bank teller.
(g) Linda is an insurance salesperson.
(h) Linda is a bank teller and is active in the feminist movement.

(Tversky & Kahneman, 1983, p. 297).

If you are like 85% of the people Tversky and Kahneman studied, you rated the likelihood of item (h) as greater than the likelihood of item (f). Imagine a huge convention hall filled with the entire population of bank tellers. Now think about how many of them would be at a hypothetical booth for feminist bank tellers—a subset of the entire population of bank tellers. If Linda is at the booth for feminist bank tellers, she must, by definition, be in the convention hall of bank tellers. Hence, the likelihood that she is at the booth (i.e., she is a feminist bank teller) cannot logically be greater than the likelihood that she is in the convention hall (i.e., she is a bank teller). Nonetheless, given the description of Linda, we intuitively feel more likely to find her at the booth within the convention hall than in the entire convention hall, which makes no sense. This intuitive feeling is an example of a **fallacy**—erroneous reasoning—in judgment and reasoning.

In this chapter, we consider many ways in which we make judgments and decisions and use reasoning to draw conclusions. The first section deals with how we make choices and judgments. **Judgment and decision making** are used to select from among choices or to evaluate opportunities. Afterward, we consider various forms of reasoning. The goal of reasoning is to draw conclusions, either deductively from principles or inductively from evidence.

Judgment and Decision Making

In the course of our everyday lives, we constantly are making judgments and decisions. One of the most important decisions you may have made is that of whether and where to go to college. Once in college, you still need to decide on which courses to take. Later on, you may need to choose a major field of study. You make decisions about friends, dates, how to relate to your parents, how to spend money, and countless other things. How do you go about making these decisions?

Classical Decision Theory

The earliest models of how people make decisions are referred to as *classical decision theory*. Most of these models were devised by economists, statisticians, and philosophers, not by psychologists. Hence, they reflect the strengths of an economic perspective. One such strength is the ease of developing and using mathematical models for human behavior.

The Model of Economic Man and Woman

Among the early models of decision making crafted in the 20th century was that of *economic man and woman*. This model assumed three things:

1. Decision makers are fully informed regarding all possible options for their decisions and of all possible outcomes of their decision options.
2. They are infinitely sensitive to the subtle distinctions among decision options.
3. They are fully rational in regard to their choice of options (Edwards, 1954; see also Slovic, 1990).

The assumption of infinite sensitivity means that people can evaluate the difference between two outcomes, no matter how subtle the distinctions among options may be. The assumption of rationality means that people make their choices to maximize something of value, whatever that something may be.

Consider an example of how this model works. Suppose that a decision maker is considering which of two smartphones to buy. The decision maker, according to this model, will consider every aspect of each phone. The shopper will next decide on some objective basis how favorable each phone is on each aspect. The shopper then will weigh objectively each of the aspects in terms of how important it is. The favorability ratings will be multiplied by the weights. Then an overall averaged rating will be computed, taking into account all of the data. The shopper then will buy the smartphone with the best score. A great deal of economic research has been based on this model.

Subjective Expected Utility Theory

An alternative model makes greater allowance for the psychological makeup of each individual decision maker. According to *subjective expected utility theory*, the goal of human action is to seek pleasure and avoid pain. According to this theory, in making decisions, people will seek to maximize pleasure (referred to as positive utility) and to minimize pain (referred to as negative utility). In doing so, however, each of us uses calculations of two things. One is **subjective utility,** which is a calculation based on the individual's judged weightings of utility (value), rather than on objective criteria. The second is **subjective probability,** which is a calculation based on the individual's estimates of likelihood, rather than on objective statistical computations. The difference between this model and the former one is that here the ratings and weights are subjective, whereas in the former model they are supposedly objective.

Scientists soon noticed that human decision making is more complex than even this modified theory implies. In particular, when have you seriously considered every aspect of a decision, rated each possible choice, weighted the choice, and then used your favorability ratings and weights to compute an averaged evaluation of each of the choices? Probably not recently.

Heuristics and Biases

The world is full of information and stimuli of different kinds. In order to function properly and not get overwhelmed, we need to filter out the information we need among the many different pieces of information available to us. The same holds true for decision making. In order to be able to make a decision within a reasonable time frame, we need to reduce the available information to a manageable amount. Heuristics help us achieve this goal and at the same time decrease our efforts by allowing us to examine fewer cues or deal with fewer pieces of information (Shah & Oppenheimer, 2008). However, sometimes our thinking also gets biased by our tendencies to make decisions more simply. The mental shortcuts of heuristics and biases lighten the cognitive load of making decisions, but they also allow for a much greater chance of error. We will explore both heuristics and biases in more detail in the next section.

Heuristics

In the following sections, we discuss several heuristics people use in their daily decision making. **Heuristics** are mental shortcuts that lighten the cognitive load of making decisions.

Satisficing   As early as the 1950s some researchers were beginning to challenge the notion of unlimited rationality. Not only did these researchers recognize that we humans do not always make ideal decisions and that we usually include subjective considerations in our decisions. But they also suggested that we humans are not entirely and boundlessly rational in making decisions. In particular, we humans are not necessarily irrational. Rather, we show **bounded rationality**—we are rational, but within limits (Simon, 1957).

Whereas classical decision theory suggested that people optimize their decisions, researchers began to realize that we have only limited resources and time to make a decision, so often we try to get as close as possible to optimizing, without actually optimizing.

One of the first heuristics that was formulated by researchers is termed satisficing (Simon, 1957). In **satisficing,** we consider options one by one, and then we select an option as soon as we find one that is satisfactory or just good enough to meet our minimum level of acceptability. When there are limited working-memory resources available, the use of satisficing for making decisions may be increased (Chen & Sun, 2003). Satisficing is also used in industrial contexts in which too much information can impair the quality of decisions, as in the selection of suppliers in electronic marketplaces (Chamodrakas, et al., 2010).

Of course, satisficing is only one of several strategies people can use. The appropriateness of this strategy will vary with the circumstance. For example, satisficing might be a reasonable strategy if you are in a hurry to buy a pack of gum and then catch a train or a plane, but a poor strategy for diagnosing a disease.

Elimination by Aspects   We sometimes use a different strategy when faced with far more alternatives than we feel that we reasonably can consider in the time we have available (Tversky, 1972a, 1972b). In such situations, we do not try to manipulate mentally all the weighted attributes of all the available options. Rather, we use a

According to Herbert Simon, people often satisfice when they make important decisions, such as which car to buy. They decide based on the first acceptable alternative that comes along.

process of **elimination by aspects**, in which we eliminate alternatives by focusing on aspects of each alternative, one at a time. If you are trying to decide which college to attend, the process of elimination by aspects might look like this:

- focus on one aspect (attribute) of the various options (the cost of going to college);
- form a minimum criterion for that aspect (tuition must be under $20,000 per year);
- eliminate all options that do not meet that criterion (e.g., Stanford University is more than $30,000 and would be eliminated);
- for the remaining options, select a second aspect for which we set a minimum criterion by which to eliminate additional options (the college must be on the West Coast); and
- continue using a sequential process of elimination of options by considering a series of aspects until a single option remains (Dawes, 2000).

Here is another example of elimination by aspects. In choosing a car to buy, we may focus on total price as an aspect. We may choose to dismiss factors, such as maintenance costs, insurance costs, or other factors that realistically might affect the money we will have to spend on the car in addition to the sale price. Once we have weeded out the alternatives that do not meet our criterion, we choose another aspect. We set a criterion value and weed out additional alternatives. We continue in this way. We weed out more alternatives, one aspect at a time, until we are left with a single option. In practice, it appears that we may use some elements of elimination by aspects or satisficing to narrow the range of options to just a few. Then we use more thorough and careful strategies. Examples would be those suggested by subjective expected utility theory. They can be useful for selecting among the few remaining options (Payne, 1976).

We often use mental shortcuts and even biases that limit and sometimes distort our ability to make rational decisions. One of the key ways in which we use mental shortcuts centers on our estimations of probability. Consider some of the strategies used by statisticians when calculating probability. They are shown in Table 11.1.

Another kind of probability is *conditional probability*, which is the likelihood of one event, given another. For example, you might want to calculate the likelihood

Table 11.1 Rules of Probability

Hypothetical Example	Calculation of Probability
Lee is one of 10 highly qualified candidates applying for one scholarship. What are Lee's chances of getting the scholarship?	Lee has a 0.1 chance of getting the scholarship.
If Lee is one of 10 highly qualified scholarship students applying for one scholarship, what are Lee's chances of not getting the scholarship?	$1 - 0.1 = 0.9$ Lee has a 0.9 chance of not getting the scholarship.
Lee's roommate and Lee are among 10 highly qualified scholarship students applying for one scholarship. What are the chances that one of the two will get the scholarship?	$0.1 + 0.1 = 0.2$ There is a 0.2 chance that one of the two roommates will get the scholarship.

of receiving an "A" for a cognitive psychology course, given that you receive an "A" on the final exam. The formula for calculating conditional probabilities in light of evidence is known as *Bayes's theorem*. It is quite complex, so most people do not use it in everyday-reasoning situations. Nonetheless, such calculations are essential to evaluating scientific hypotheses, forming realistic medical diagnoses, analyzing demographic data, and performing many other real-world tasks. (For a highly readable explanation of Bayes's theorem, see Eysenck & Keane, 1990, pp. 456–458.)

Representativeness Heuristic   Before you read about representativeness, try the following problem from Kahneman and Tversky (1972).

All the families having exactly six children in a particular city were surveyed. In 72 of the families, the exact order of births of boys and girls was G B G B B G (G, girl; B, boy).

What is your estimate of the number of families surveyed in which the exact order of births was B G B B B B?

Most people judging the number of families with the B G B B B B birth pattern estimate the number to be less than 72. Actually, the best estimate of the number of families with this birth order is 72, the same as for the G B G B B G birth order. The expected number for the second pattern would be the same because the gender for each birth is independent (at least, theoretically) of the gender for every other birth. For any one birth, the chance of a boy (or a girl) is one of two. Thus, any particular pattern of births is equally likely $(1/2)^6$, even B B B B B B or G G G G G G.

Why do many of us believe some birth orders to be more likely than others? In part, the reason is that we use the heuristic of representativeness. In **representativeness,** we judge the probability of an uncertain event according to:

1. how obviously it is similar to or representative of the population from which it is derived; and
2. the degree to which it reflects the salient features of the process by which it is generated (such as randomness) (see also Fischhoff, 1999; Johnson-Laird, 2000, 2004).

For example, people believe that the first birth order is more likely because: (1) it is more representative of the number of females and males in the population; and (2) it looks more like a random order than does the second birth order. In fact, of course, either birth order is equally likely to occur by chance.

Similarly, suppose people are asked to judge the probability of flips of a coin yielding the sequence H T H H T H (H, heads; T, tails). Most people will judge it as higher than they will if asked to judge the sequence H H H H T H. If you expect a sequence to be random, you tend to view as more likely a sequence that "looks random." Indeed, people often comment that the numbers in a table of random numbers "don't look random." The reason is that people underestimate the number of runs of the same number that will appear wholly by chance. We frequently reason in terms of whether something appears to represent a set of accidental occurrences, rather than actually considering the true likelihood of a given chance occurrence. This tendency makes us more vulnerable to the machinations of magicians, charlatans, and con artists. Any of them may make much of their having predicted the realistic probability of a non-random-looking event. For example, in one out of ten cases two people in a group of 40 (e.g., in a classroom or a small nightclub audience) will share a birthday (the same month and day). In a group of 14 people, there are better than even odds that two people will have birthdays within a day of each other (Krantz, 1992).

That we frequently rely on the representativeness heuristic may not be terribly surprising. It is easy to use and often works. For example, suppose we have not heard a weather report prior to stepping outside. We informally judge the probability that it will rain. We base our judgment on how well the characteristics of this day (e.g., the month of the year, the area in which we live, and the presence or absence of clouds in the sky) represent the characteristics of days on which it rains. Another reason that we often use the representativeness heuristic is that we mistakenly believe that small samples (e.g., of events, of people, of characteristics) resemble in all respects the whole population from which the sample is drawn (Tversky & Kahneman, 1971). We particularly tend to underestimate the likelihood that the characteristics of a small sample (e.g., the people whom we know well) of a population inadequately represent the characteristics of the whole population.

We also tend to use the representativeness heuristic more frequently when we are highly aware of anecdotal evidence based on a very small sample of the population. This reliance on anecdotal evidence has been referred to as a "man-who" argument (Nisbett & Ross, 1980). When presented with statistics, we may refute those data with our own observations of, "I know a man who . . ." For example, faced with statistics on coronary disease and high-cholesterol diets, someone may counter with, "I know a man who ate whipped cream for breakfast, lunch, and dinner, smoked two packs of cigarettes a day, and lived to be 110 years old. He would have kept going but he was shot through his perfectly healthy heart by a jealous lover."

One reason that people misguidedly use the representativeness heuristic is because they fail to understand the concept of base rates. **Base rate** refers to the prevalence of an event or characteristic within its population of events or characteristics. In everyday decision making, people often ignore base-rate information, but it is important to effective judgment and decision making. In many occupations, the use of base-rate information is essential for adequate job performance. For example, suppose a doctor was told that a 10-year-old boy was suffering chest pains. The doctor would be much less likely to worry about an incipient heart attack than if the doctor were told that a 60-year-old man had the identical symptom. Why? Because the base rate of heart attacks is much higher in 60-year-old men than in 10-year-old boys. Of course, people use other heuristics as well. People can be taught how to use base rates to improve their decision making (Gigerenzer, 1996; Koehler, 1996).

Availability Heuristic Most of us at least occasionally use the **availability heuristic,** in which we make judgments on the basis of how easily we can call to mind what we perceive as relevant instances of a phenomenon (Tversky & Kahneman, 1973; see also Fischhoff, 1999; Sternberg, 2000). For example, consider the letter *R*. Are there more words in the English language that begin with the letter *R* or that have *R* as their third letter? Most respondents say that there are more words beginning with the letter *R* (Tversky & Kahneman, 1973). Why? Because generating words beginning with the letter *R* is easier than generating words having *R* as the third letter. In fact, there are more English-language words with *R* as their third letter. The same happens to be true of some other letters as well, such as *K*, *L*, *N*, and *V*.

The availability heuristic also has been observed in regard to everyday situations. In one study, married partners individually stated which of the two partners performed a larger proportion of each of 20 different household chores (Ross & Sicoly, 1979). These tasks included mundane chores such as grocery shopping or preparing breakfast. Each partner stated that he or she more often performed about 16 of the 20 chores. Suppose each partner was correct. Then, to accomplish 100% of the work in a household, each partner would have to perform 80% of the work. Similar outcomes emerged from questioning members of college basketball teams and joint participants in laboratory tasks.

Although clearly 80% + 80% does not equal 100%, we can understand why people may engage in using the availability heuristic when it confirms their beliefs about themselves. However, people also use the availability heuristic when its use leads to a logical fallacy that has nothing to do with their beliefs about themselves. Two groups of participants were asked to estimate the number of words of a particular form that would be expected to appear in a 2,000-word passage. For one group the form was _ _ _ _ing (i.e., seven letters ending in -ing). For the other group the form was _ _ _ _ _n_ (i.e., seven letters with n as the second-to-the-last letter). Clearly, there cannot be more seven-letter words ending in -ing than seven-letter words with n as the second-to-the-last letter. But the greater availability of the former led to estimates of probability that were more than twice as high for the former, as compared with the latter (Tversky & Kahneman, 1983).

Anchoring   A heuristic related to availability is the *anchoring-and-adjustment heuristic*, by which people adjust their evaluations of things by means of certain reference points called *end-anchors*. Before you read on, quickly (in less than 5 seconds) calculate in your head the answer to the following problem:

$$8 \times 7 \times 6 \times 5 \times 4 \times 3 \times 2 \times 1$$

Now, quickly calculate your answer to the following problem:

$$1 \times 2 \times 3 \times 4 \times 5 \times 6 \times 7 \times 8$$

Two groups of participants estimated the product of one or the other of the preceding two sets of eight numbers (Tversky & Kahneman, 1974). The median (middle) estimate for the participants given the first sequence was 2,250. For the participants given the second sequence, the median estimate was 512. (The actual product is 40,320 for both.) The two products are the same, as they must be because the numbers are exactly the same (applying the commutative law of multiplication). Nonetheless, people provide a higher estimate for the first sequence than for the second because their computation of the anchor—the first few digits multiplied by each other—renders a higher estimate from which they make an adjustment to reach a final estimate. Furthermore, the adjustment people make in response to an anchor is bigger when the anchor is rounded than when it seems to be a precise value. For example, when the price of a TV set is given as $3,000, people adjust their estimate of its production costs more than when the price is given as $2,991 (Janiszewski & Uy, 2008). Anchoring effects occur in a variety of settings, for example at art auctions, where the price of paintings is anchored by the price the painting achieved in prior sales, or monthly economic forecasts, which are anchored toward the past month (Beggs & Graddy, 2009; Campbell & Sharpe, 2009).

Although riding a car is statistically much more risky than riding in a plane, people often feel less safe in a plane, in part because of the availability heuristic. People hear about every major U.S. plane crash that takes place, but they hear about relatively few car accidents.

Framing   Another consideration in decision theory is the influence of *framing effects*, in which the way that the options are presented influences the selection of an option (Tversky & Kahneman, 1981). For instance, we tend to choose options that demonstrate risk aversion when we are faced with an option involving potential gains. That is, we tend to choose options offering a small but certain gain rather

INVESTIGATING COGNITIVE PSYCHOLOGY
Framing Effects

Suppose that you were told that 600 people were at risk of dying of a particular disease. Vaccine A could save the lives of 200 of the people at risk. With Vaccine B, there is a 0.33 likelihood that all 600 people would be saved, but there is also a 0.66 likelihood that all 600 people will die. Which option would you choose? Explain how you made your decision.

We tend to choose options that demonstrate risk seeking when we are faced with options involving potential losses. That is, we tend to choose options offering a large but uncertain loss rather than a smaller but certain loss (as is the case for Vaccine B), unless the uncertain loss is either tremendously greater or only modestly less than certain. Here is an interesting example.

Suppose that for the 600 people at risk of dying of a particular disease, if Vaccine C is used, 400 people will die. However, if Vaccine D is used, there is a 0.33 likelihood that no one will die and a 0.66 likelihood that all 600 people will die. Which option would you choose?

In the preceding situations, most people will choose Vaccine A and Vaccine D.

Now, try this:

• Compare the number of people whose lives will be lost or saved by using Vaccines A or C.
• Compare the number of people whose lives will be lost or saved by using Vaccines B or D.

The expected value is identical for Vaccines A and C; it is also identical for Vaccines B and D. Our predilection for risk aversion versus risk seeking leads us to quite different choices based on the way in which a decision is framed, even when the actual outcomes of the choices are the same.

than a larger but uncertain gain, unless the uncertain gain is either tremendously greater or only modestly less than certain. The first example in *Investigating Cognitive Psychology: Framing Effects* is only slightly modified from one used by Tversky and Kahneman (1981).

Framing effects have public relevance. Messages from politicians, political parties, and other stakeholders can be framed in different ways and therefore take on a different connotation. A message about the Ku Klux Klan, for example, can be framed either as a free-speech issue or as a public-safety issue. Framing effects are less persuasive when they come from sources of low credibility (Druckman, 2001).

Biases

In the next section, we discuss several biases that frequently occur when people make decisions: illusory correlation, overconfidence, and hindsight bias.

Illusory Correlation   We are predisposed to see particular events or attributes and categories as going together, even when they do not. This phenomenon is called **illusory correlation** (Hamilton & Lickel, 2000). In the case of events, we may see spurious cause-effect relationships. In the case of attributes, we may use personal prejudices to form and use stereotypes (perhaps as a result of using the representativeness heuristic). For example, suppose we expect people of a given political party to show particular intellectual or moral characteristics. The instances in which people show those characteristics are more likely to be available in memory and recalled more easily than are instances that contradict our biased expectations. In other words, we perceive a correlation between the political party and the particular characteristics.

Illusory correlation even may influence psychiatric diagnoses based on projective tests such as the Rorschach and the Draw-a-Person tests (Chapman & Chapman, 1967, 1969, 1975). Researchers suggested a false correlation in which particular diagnoses would be associated with particular responses. For example, they suggested that people diagnosed with paranoia tend to draw people with large eyes more than do people with other diagnoses (which is not true). However, what happened when individuals expected to observe a correlation between a drawing with large eyes and the associated diagnosis of paranoia? They tended to see the illusory correlation, although no actual correlation existed.

Overconfidence   Another common error is **overconfidence**—an individual's overvaluation of her or his own skills, knowledge, or judgment. For example, people answered 200 two-alternative statements, such as "Absinthe is (a) a liqueur, (b) a precious stone." (Absinthe is a licorice-flavored liqueur.) People were asked to choose the correct answer and to state the probability that their answer was correct (Fischhoff, Slovic, & Lichtenstein, 1977). People were overconfident. For example, when people were 100% confident in their answers, they were right only 80% of the time. In general, people tend to overestimate the accuracy of their judgments (Kahneman & Tversky, 1996). Why are people overconfident? One reason is that people may not realize how little they know. Another is that they may not realize that their information comes from unreliable sources (Carlson, 1995; Griffin & Tversky, 1992).

People sometimes make poor decisions as a result of overconfidence. These decisions are based on inadequate information and ineffective decision-making strategies. Why we tend to be overconfident in our judgments is not clear. One simple explanation is that we prefer not to think about being wrong (Fischhoff, 1988).

Businesses sometimes use our tendencies toward overconfidence to their own advantage. Think about the American cell phone market, for example. Many contracts consist of a monthly fee that includes usage of a certain amount of air-time minutes. If a person exceeds this amount, he or she will incur steep charges. There are good reasons for such a contract model, but from the company's point of view, not from the consumer's point of view. Consumers tend to overestimate their usage of minutes, so they are willing to pay for a high-minute usage in advance. At the same time, they are confident they will not go over their limit, so they do not even realize the high costs they will incur if they exceed their free air-time minutes, until they actually discover they have gone over (Grubb, 2009).

Hindsight Bias   Finally, a bias that can affect all of us is **hindsight bias**—when we look at a situation retrospectively, we believe we easily can see all the signs and events leading up to a particular outcome (Fischhoff, 1982; Wasserman, Lempert, & Hastie, 1991). For example, suppose people are asked to predict the outcomes of psychological experiments in advance of the experiments. People rarely are able to predict the outcomes at better-than-chance levels. However, when people are told of the outcomes of psychological experiments, they frequently comment that these outcomes were obvious and could easily have been predicted in advance. Similarly, when intimate personal relationships are in trouble, people often fail to observe signs of the difficulties until the problems reach crisis proportions. By then, it may be too late to save the relationship. In retrospect, people may ask themselves, "Why didn't I see it coming? It was so obvious! I should have seen the signs."

Hindsight bias hinders learning because it impairs one's ability to compare one's expectations with the outcome—if one always expected the outcome that eventually happened, one thinks there is nothing to learn! And indeed, studies show that investment bankers' performance suffers when they exhibit a strong hindsight bias. Curiously, experience does not reduce the bias (Biais & Weber, 2009).

Fallacies

Heuristics and fallacies are often studied together because they go hand in hand. The application of a heuristic to make a decision may lead to fallacies in thinking. Therefore, when we discuss some fallacies, we refer back to some of the heuristics in association with which they often occur.

Gambler's Fallacy and the Hot Hand

Gambler's fallacy is a mistaken belief that the probability of a given random event, such as winning or losing at a game of chance, is influenced by previous random events. For example, a gambler who loses five successive bets may believe that a win is therefore more likely the sixth time. He feels that he is "due" to win. In truth, of course, each bet (or coin toss) is an independent event that has an equal probability of winning or losing. The gambler is no more likely to win on the 6th bet than on the 1st—or on the 1001st. Gambler's fallacy is an example of the representative heuristic gone awry: One believes that the pattern representative of past events is now likely to change.

A tendency opposite to that of gambler's fallacy is called the "hot hand" effect. It refers to a belief that a certain course of events will continue. Apparently, both professional and amateur basketball players, as well as their fans, believe that a player's chances of making a basket are greater after making a previous shot than after missing one. However, the statistical likelihoods (and the actual records of players) show no such tendency (Gilovich, Vallone, & Tversky, 1985; see also Roney & Trick, 2009). Shrewd players take advantage of this belief and closely guard opponents immediately after they have made baskets. The reason is that the opposing players will be more likely to try to get the ball to these perceived "streak shooters."

Conjunction Fallacy

Do you remember the experiment described in the section on the availability heuristic where people were asked to judge how often the form _ _ _ _ing (i.e., seven letters ending in –ing) or _ _ _ _ _n_ (i.e., seven letters with *n* as the second-to-the-last letter) appears in a passage? The availability heuristic might lead to the conjunction fallacy. In the *conjunction fallacy*, an individual gives a higher estimate for a subset of events (e.g., the instances of -ing) than for the larger set of events containing the given subset (e.g., the instances of *n* as the second-to-the-last letter). This fallacy also is illustrated in the chapter opening vignette regarding Linda.

People often mistakenly believe in the gambler's fallacy. They think that if they have been unlucky in their gambles, it is time for their luck to change. In fact, success or failure in past gambles has no effect on the likelihood of success in future ones.

The representativeness heuristic may also induce individuals to engage in the conjunction fallacy during probabilistic reasoning (Tversky & Kahneman, 1983; see also Dawes, 2000). Tversky and Kahneman asked college students:

> *Please give your estimate of the following values: What percentage of the men surveyed [in a health survey] have had one or more heart attacks?*

> *What percentage of the men surveyed both are over 55 years old and have had one or more heart attacks? (p. 308)*

The mean estimates were 18% for the former and 30% for the latter. In fact, 65% of the respondents gave higher estimates for the latter (which is clearly a subset of the former). However, people do not always engage in the conjunction fallacy. Only 25% of respondents gave higher estimates for the latter question than for the former when the questions were rephrased as frequencies rather than as percentages (e.g., "how many of the 1,000 men surveyed have had one or more heart attacks?"). The way statistical information is presented influences how likely it is that people draw the correct conclusions (see also Gigerenzer & Hoffrage, 1995).

Sunk-Cost Fallacy

An error in judgment that is quite common in people's thinking is the *sunk-cost fallacy* (Dupuy, 1998, 1999; Strough et al., 2008). This fallacy represents the decision to continue to invest in something simply because one has invested in it before and one hopes to recover one's investment. For example, suppose you have bought a car. It is a lemon. You already have invested thousands of dollars in getting it fixed. Now you have another major repair on it confronting you. You have no reason to believe that this additional repair really will be the last in the string of repairs. You think about how much money you have spent on repairs and reason that you need to do the additional repair to justify past amounts already spent. So you do the repair rather than buy a new car. You have just committed the sunk-cost fallacy. The problem is that you already have lost the money on those repairs. Throwing more money into the repairs will not get that money back. Your best bet may well be to view the money already spent on repairs as a "sunk cost" and then buy a new car.

Similarly, suppose you go on a two-week vacation. You are having a miserable time. Should you go home a week early? You decide not to, thereby attempting to justify the investment you have already made in the vacation. Again, you have committed the sunk-cost fallacy. Instead of viewing the money simply as lost on an unfortunate decision, you have decided to throw more money away. But you do so without any hope that the vacation will get any better.

The Gist of It: Do Heuristics Help Us or Lead Us Astray?

Heuristics do not always lead to wrong judgments or poor decisions (Cohen, 1981). Indeed, we use these mental shortcuts because they are so often right. Sometimes, they are amazingly simple ways of drawing sound conclusions. For example, a simple heuristic, *take-the-best,* can be amazingly effective in decision situations (Gigerenzer & Brighton, 2009; Gigerenzer & Goldstein, 1996; Marsh, Todd, & Gigerenzer, 2004). The rule is simple. In making a decision, identify the single most important criterion to you for making that decision. For example, when you choose a new automobile, the most important factor might be good gas mileage, safety, or appearance. Make your choice on the basis of that attribute.

On its face this heuristic would seem to be inadequate. In fact, it often leads to very good decisions. It produces even better decisions, in many cases, than far more complicated heuristics. Thus, heuristics can be used for good as well as for bad decision making. Indeed, when we take people's goals into account, heuristics often are amazingly effective (Evans & Over, 1996).

The take-the-best heuristic belongs to a class of heuristics called fast-and-frugal heuristics (FFH). As the name implies, this class of heuristics is based on a small fraction of information, and decisions using the heuristics are made rapidly. These heuristics set a standard of rationality that considers constraints including, time, information, and cognitive capacity (Bennis & Pachur, 2006; Gigerenzer, Todd, & the ABC Research Group, 1999). Furthermore, these models consider the lack of optimum solutions and environments in which the decision is taking place. As a result, these heuristics provide a good description of decision making during sports.

Fast-and-frugal heuristics can form a comprehensive description of how people behave in a variety of contexts. These behaviors vary from lunch selections to how physicians decide whether to prescribe medication for depression, to making business decisions (Goldstein & Gigerenzer, 2009; Scheibehenne, Miesler, & Todd, 2007; Smith & Gilhooly, 2006).

The work on heuristics and biases shows the importance of distinguishing between intellectual competence and intellectual performance as it manifests itself in daily life. Even experts in the use of probability and statistics can find themselves falling into faulty patterns of judgment and decision making in their everyday lives. People may be intelligent in a conventional, test-based sense. Yet they may show exactly the same biases and faulty reasoning that someone with a lower test score would show. People often fail to fully utilize their intellectual competence in their daily life. There can even be a wide gap between the two (Stanovich, 2010). Thus, if we wish to be intelligent in our daily lives and not just on tests, we have to be street smart. In particular, we must be mindful of applying our intelligence to the problems that continually confront us.

Opportunity Costs

Opportunity costs are the prices paid for availing oneself of certain opportunities. Taking opportunity costs into account is important when judgments are made. For example, suppose you see a great job offer in San Francisco. You always wanted to live there. You are ready to take it. Before you do, you need to ask yourself a question: What other things will you have to forego to take advantage of this opportunity? An example might be the chance, on your budget, of having more than 500 square feet of living space. Another might be the chance to live in a place where you probably do not have to worry about earthquakes. Any time you take advantage of an opportunity, there are opportunity costs. They may, in some cases, make what looked like a good opportunity look like not such a great opportunity at all. Ideally, you should try to look at these opportunity costs in an unbiased way.

Naturalistic Decision Making

Many researchers contend that decision making is a complex process that cannot be reproduced adequately in the laboratory because real decisions are frequently made in situations where there are high stakes. For instance, the mental state and cognitive pressure experienced by an emergency room doctor encountering a patient is difficult to reproduce outside a clinical setting.

This criticism has led to the development of a field of study that is based on decision making in natural environments (naturalistic decision making). Much of the research completed in this area is from professional settings, such as hospitals or nuclear plants (Carroll, Hatakenaka, & Rudolph, 2006; Galanter & Patel, 2005; Roswarski, & Murray, 2006). These situations share a number of features, including the challenges of ill-structured problems, changing situations, high risk, time pressure, and sometimes, a team environment (Orasanu & Connolly, 1993). A number of models are used to explain performance in these high-stakes situations. These models allow for the consideration of cognitive, emotional, and situational factors of skilled decision makers; they also provide a framework for advising future decision makers (Klein, 1997; Lipshitz et al., 2001). For instance, Orasanu (2005) developed recommendations for training astronauts to be successful decision makers by evaluating what makes current astronauts successful, such as developing team cohesion and managing stress. Naturalistic decision making can be applied to a broad range of behaviors and environments. These applications can include individuals as diverse as badminton players, railroad controllers, and NASA astronauts (Farrington-Darby et al., 2006; Macquet & Fleurance, 2007; Orasanu, 2005; Patel, Kaufman, & Arocha, 2002).

Group Decision Making

Groups form decisions differently than individuals. Often, there are benefits to making decisions in groups. However, a phenomenon called "groupthink" can occur that seriously impairs the quality of decisions made. In the next sections we will explore group decision making in more detail.

IN THE LAB OF GERD GIGERENZER

Making Decisions in an Uncertain World

GERD GIGERENZER

If you were in my lab, you would talk to pre-docs, post-docs, and researchers from ten different disciplines as well as nationalities. We investigate *bounded rationality*, that is, how humans make decisions in an *uncertain* world. This differs from the study of deductive reasoning, syllogisms, or classical decision theory, where all alternatives, consequences, and probabilities are known for certain. In the real world, omniscience is absent and surprises can happen; nevertheless, people have to make decisions, such as whom to trust, what medication to take, or how to invest money. How does this *rationality for mortals* work?

The first question we pose is descriptive: What heuristics do people rely on, consciously or unconsciously, to make decisions in an uncertain world? A heuristic is a strategy that focuses on the most relevant pieces of information and ignores the rest. We have investigated a number of these, including those relying on:

- recognition (the recognition and fluency heuristics),
- one good reason (such as *take-the-best*), and
- on the wisdom of others (such as *imitate-the-majority*).

The study of the *adaptive toolbox* investigates the heuristics used, their building blocks, and the core cognitive capacities they exploit.

Our second question is prescriptive: In what environment does a heuristic work, and where would it fail? To find answers, one needs to develop formal models of heuristics, using analysis and computer simulation. One surprising discovery we made is that simple heuristics that rely on only one good reason (such as take-the-best) can actually make more accurate predictions than can complex strategies such as multiple regression or neural networks. In contrast to what many textbooks still preach, this result shows that heuristics are not second-best, and that less information, computation, and time can lead to better decisions. In fact, unlike in certain worlds, in an uncertain world one needs to ignore part of the information to make good judgments.

The study of the *ecological rationality* of a given heuristic investigates in what world it succeeds.

The third question concerns intuitive design. Here we use the results of our research to design heuristics and environments that help experts and laypeople make better decisions. For instance, based on our work, physicians in Michigan hospitals use heuristics called *fast-and-frugal trees* when making ICU allocations. These simple heuristics mirror the sequential, intuitive thinking of doctors, are fast and frugal, and are nevertheless better than complex linear regression models at predicting heart attacks.

A particularly relevant aspect of intuitive design is risk communication. Consider the contraceptive pill scare in the United Kingdom. The media reported that third-generation pills increase the risk of potentially life-threatening blood clots (thrombosis) by 100%. Distressed by this news, many women stopped taking the pill, which led to unwanted pregnancies and an estimated 13,000 additional abortions in England and Wales. How big is 100%? The studies on which the warning was based had shown that out of every 7,000 women who took the earlier second-generation pill, about 1 had a thrombosis; this number increased to 2 among women who took third-generation pills. That is, the *absolute risk increase* was only 1 in 7,000 while the *relative risk increase* was indeed 100%. Had the media reported the absolute risks, few women would have panicked. The pill scare illustrates how citizens' fears are manipulated by framing numbers in a misleading and non-transparent way. We study and develop transparent representations—such as absolute risks and natural frequencies—that help people understand health statistics. During the last few years, I have trained some 1,000 physicians and dozens of U.S. federal judges in understanding risks, for instance when evaluating cancer screening or DNA tests. Few physicians and lawyers have been educated in risk communication, and this blind spot is an important area in which psychologists can apply their knowledge and help.

Benefits of Group Decisions

Working as a group can enhance the effectiveness of decision making, just as it can enhance the effectiveness of problem solving. Many companies combine individuals into teams to improve decision making. By forming decision-making teams, the group benefits from the expertise of each of the members. There is also an increase in resources and ideas (Salas, Burke, & Cannon-Bowers, 2000). Another benefit of group decision making is improved group memory over individual memory (Hinsz, 1990). Groups that are successful in decision making exhibit a number of similar characteristics, including the following:

- the group is small;
- it has open communication;
- members share a common mind-set;
- members identify with the group; and
- members agree on acceptable group behavior (Shelton, 2006).

In juries, members share more information during decision making when the group is made up of diverse members (Sommers, 2006). The juries are thereby in a position to make better decisions. Furthermore, in examining decision making in public policy groups, interpersonal influence is important (Jenson, 2007). Group members frequently employed tactics to affect other members' decisions (Jenson, 2007). The most frequently used and influential tactics were inspirational and rational appeals.

Groupthink

There can be disadvantages associated with group decision making, however. Of these disadvantages, one of the most explored is groupthink. *Groupthink* is a phenomenon characterized by premature decision making that is generally the result of group members attempting to avoid conflict (Janis, 1971). Groupthink frequently results in suboptimal decision making that avoids non-traditional ideas (Esser, 1998).

What conditions lead to groupthink? Janis cited three kinds:

(1) an isolated, cohesive, and homogeneous group is empowered to make decisions;
(2) objective and impartial leadership is absent, within the group or outside it; and
(3) high levels of stress impinge on the group decision-making process.

Another cause of groupthink is anxiety (Chapman, 2006). When group members are anxious, they are less likely to explore new options and will likely try to avoid further conflict.

The groups responsible for making foreign policy decisions are excellent candidates for groupthink. They are usually like-minded. Moreover, they frequently isolate themselves from what is going on outside their own group. They generally try to meet specific objectives and believe they cannot afford to be impartial. Also, of course, they are under very high stress because the stakes involved in their decisions can be tremendous.

But what exactly is groupthink? Janis (1971) delineated six symptoms of groupthink:

1. *Closed-mindedness*—the group is not open to alternative ideas.
2. *Rationalization*—the group goes to great lengths to justify both the process and the product of its decision making, distorting reality where necessary in order to be persuasive.

3. *Squelching of dissent*—those who disagree with the group are ignored, criticized, or even ostracized.
4. *Formation of a "mindguard"* for the group—one person appoints himself or herself the keeper of the group norm and ensures that people stay in line.
5. *Feeling invulnerable*—the group believes that it must be right, given the intelligence of its members and the information available to them.
6. *Feeling unanimous*—members believe that everyone unanimously shares the opinions expressed by the group.

Defective decision making results from groupthink, which in turn is due to examining alternatives insufficiently, examining risks inadequately, and seeking information about alternatives incompletely.

Consider how groupthink might arise in a decision when college students decide to damage a statue on the campus of a football rival to teach a lesson to the students and faculty in the rival university. The students rationalize that damage to a statue really is no big deal. Who cares about an old ugly statue anyway? When one group member dissents, other members quickly make him feel disloyal and cowardly. His dissent is squelched. The group's members feel invulnerable. They are going to damage the statue under the cover of darkness, and the statue is never guarded. They are sure they will not be caught. Finally, all the members agree on the course of action. This apparent feeling of unanimity convinces the group members that far from being out of line, they are doing what needs to be done.

Antidotes for Groupthink

Janis has prescribed several antidotes for groupthink. For example, the leader of a group should encourage constructive criticism, be impartial, and ensure that members seek input from people outside the group. The group should also form subgroups that meet separately to consider alternative solutions to a single problem. It is important that the leader take responsibility for preventing spurious conformity to a group norm.

In 1997, members of the Heaven's Gate cult in California committed mass suicide in the hope of meeting up with extraterrestrials in a spaceship trailing the Hale-Bopp comet. Although this group suicide is a striking example of conformity to a destructive group norm, similar events have occurred throughout human history, such as the suicide of more than 900 members of the Jonestown, Guyana, religious cult in 1978. In 2010, a series of incredibly bad decisions by a group of oil-rig operators on the Deepwater Horizon, situated in the Gulf of Mexico, led to the largest oil-well leak in history. And even in the 21st century, suicide bombers are killing themselves and others in carefully planned attacks.

Neuroscience of Decision Making

As in problem solving, the prefrontal cortex, and particularly the anterior cingulate cortex, is active during the decision-making process (Barraclough, Conroy, & Lee, 2004; Kennerley et al., 2006; Rogers et al., 2004). Explorations of decision making in monkeys have noted activation in the parietal regions of the brain (Platt & Glimcher, 1999). The amount of gain associated with a decision also affects the amount of activation observed in the parietal region (Platt & Glimcher, 1999).

Examination of decision making in drug abusers identified a number of areas involved in risky decisions. The researchers studied drug abusers because drug abuse,

In 1997, 39 members of the Heaven's Gate cult committed mass suicide in order to "evacuate" Earth and meet with a UFO that would lead them to a better existence.

by its very nature, produces risky decisions. They found decreased activation in the left pregenual anterior cingulate cortex of drug abusers (Fishbein et al., 2005). These findings suggest that during decision making, the anterior cingulate cortex is involved in the consideration of potential rewards.

Another study had healthy participants play the gambling game Blackjack. The researchers found that suboptimal decisions (too risky or too cautious) were associated with increased activity in the anterior cingulate cortex (Hewig et al., 2008).

Another interesting effect seen in this area is observed in participants who have difficulty with a decision. In one study, participants made decisions concerning whether an item was old or new and which of two items was larger (Fleck et al., 2006). Decisions that were rated lowest in confidence and that took the most time to answer were associated with higher activation of the anterior cingulate cortex.

These findings suggest that this area of the brain is involved in the comparison and weighing of possible solutions.

✔ CONCEPT CHECK

1. Why can the model of the economic man and woman not explain human decision making satisfactorily?
2. Why do we use heuristics?
3. What is the difference between overconfidence and hindsight bias?
4. Name and describe three fallacies.
5. What are the symptoms of groupthink?
6. Which parts of the brain play prominent roles in decision making?

Deductive Reasoning

Judgment and decision making involve evaluating opportunities and selecting one choice over another. A related kind of thinking is reasoning. **Reasoning** is the process of drawing conclusions from principles and from evidence (Leighton & Sternberg, 2004; Sternberg, 2004; Wason & Johnson-Laird, 1972). In reasoning, we move from what is already known to infer a new conclusion or to evaluate a proposed conclusion.

Reasoning is often divided into two types: deductive and inductive reasoning. We explore both kinds of reasoning in the remainder of this chapter.

What Is Deductive Reasoning?

Deductive reasoning is the process of reasoning from one or more general statements regarding what is known to reach a logically certain conclusion (Johnson-Laird, 2000; Rips, 1999; Williams, 2000). It often involves reasoning from one or more general statements regarding what is known to a specific application of the general statement.

Deductive reasoning is based on logical propositions. A **proposition** is basically an assertion, which may be either true or false. Examples are "Cognitive psychology students are brilliant," "Cognitive psychology students wear shoes," or "Cognitive psychology students like peanut butter." In a logical argument, **premises** are propositions about which arguments are made. Cognitive psychologists are interested particularly in propositions that may be connected in ways that require people to draw reasoned conclusions. That is, deductive reasoning is useful because it helps people connect various propositions to draw conclusions. Cognitive psychologists want to know how people connect propositions to draw conclusions. Some of these conclusions are well reasoned; others are not.

Much of the difficulty of reasoning is in even understanding the language of problems (Girotto, 2004). Some of the mental processes used in language understanding and the cerebral functioning underlying them are used in reasoning, too (Lawson, 2004).

Conditional Reasoning

One type of deductive reasoning is conditional reasoning. In the next sections, we will explore what conditional reasoning is and how it works.

What Is Conditional Reasoning?

One of the primary types of deductive reasoning is **conditional reasoning,** in which the reasoner must draw a conclusion based on an *if-then* proposition. The conditional if-then proposition states that if antecedent condition p is met, then consequent event q follows. For example, "If students study hard, then they score high on their exams." Under some circumstances, if you have established a conditional proposition, then you may draw a well-reasoned conclusion. The usual set of conditional propositions from which you can draw a well-reasoned conclusion is, "If p, then q. p. Therefore, q." This inference illustrates deductive validity. That is, it follows logically from the propositions on which it is based. The following is also logical:

"If students eat pizza, then they score high on their exams. They eat pizza. Therefore, they score high on their exams."

As you may have guessed, deductive validity does not equate with truth. You can reach deductively valid conclusions that are completely untrue with respect to the world. Whether the conclusion is true depends on the truthfulness of the premises. In fact, people are more likely mistakenly to accept an illogical argument as logical if the conclusion is factually true. For now, however, we put aside the issue of truth and focus only on the **deductive validity,** or logical soundness, of the reasoning.

One set of propositions and its conclusion is the argument:

"If p, then q. p.
Therefore, q,"

which is termed a *modus ponens* argument. In the *modus ponens* argument, the reasoner affirms the antecedent (p). For example, take the argument "If you are a husband, then you are married. Harrison is a husband. Therefore, he is married." The set of propositions for the *modus ponens* argument is shown in Table 11.2.

In addition to the *modus ponens* argument, you may draw another well-reasoned conclusion from a conditional proposition, given a different second proposition:

"If p, then q. Not q. Therefore, not p."

This inference is also deductively valid. This particular set of propositions and its conclusion is termed a *modus tollens* argument, in which the reasoner denies the consequent. For example, we modify the second proposition of the argument to deny the consequent:

"If you are a husband, then you are married. Harrison is not married. Therefore, he is not a husband."

Table 11.2 shows two conditions in which a well-reasoned conclusion can be reached. It also shows two conditions in which such a conclusion cannot be reached.

Table 11.2   Conditional Reasoning: Deductively Valid Inferences and Deductive Fallacies

Two kinds of conditional propositions lead to valid deductions, and two others lead to deductive fallacies; p is called the *antecedent*; q is called the *consequent*. $\rightarrow$ stands for *then*, and $\therefore$ stands for *therefore*.

Type of Argument		Conditional Proposition	Existing Condition	Inference
Deductively valid inferences	*Modus ponens—affirming the antecedent*	$p \rightarrow q$ If you are a mother, then you have a child.	p You are a mother.	$\therefore q$ Therefore, you have a child.
	Modus tollens—denying the consequent	$p \rightarrow q$ If you are a mother, then you have a child.	$\neg q$ You do not have a child.	$\therefore \neg p$ Therefore, you are not a mother.
Deductive fallacies	*Denying the antecedent*	$p \rightarrow q$ If you are a mother, then you have a child.	$\neg p$ You are not a mother.	$\therefore \neg q$ Therefore, you do not have a child.
	Affirming the consequent	$p \rightarrow q$ If you are a mother, then you have a child.	q You have a child.	$\therefore p$ Therefore, you are a mother.

As the examples illustrate, some inferences based on conditional reasoning are fallacies, which lead to conclusions that are not deductively valid. When using conditional propositions, we cannot reach a deductively valid conclusion based either on denying the antecedent condition or on affirming the consequent. Let's return to the proposition, "If you are a husband, then you are married." We would not be able to confirm or to refute the proposition based on denying the antecedent: "Joan is not a husband. Therefore, she is not married." Even if we ascertain that Joan is not a husband, we cannot conclude that she is not married. Similarly, we cannot deduce a valid conclusion by affirming the consequent: "Joan is married. Therefore, she is a husband." Even if Joan is married, her spouse may not consider her a husband.

The Wason Selection Task

Conditional reasoning can be studied in the laboratory using a "selection task" (Wason, 1968, 1969, 1983; Wason & Johnson-Laird, 1970, 1972). Participants are presented with a set of four two-sided cards. Each card has a number on one side and a letter on the other side. Face up are two letters and two numbers. The letters are a consonant and a vowel. The numbers are an even number and an odd number. For example, participants might be presented with the set of cards shown in Figure 11.1.

Each participant then is told a conditional statement. For example, "If a card has a consonant on one side, then it has an even number on the other side." The task is to determine whether the conditional statement is true or false. One does so by turning over the exact number of cards necessary to test the conditional statement. That is, the participant must not turn over any cards that are not valid tests of the statement. But the participant must turn over all cards that are valid tests of the conditional proposition. Which cards would you turn?

Table 11.3 illustrates the four possible tests participants might perform on the cards. Two of the tests (*modus ponens:* affirming the antecedent, and *modus tollens:* denying the consequent) are both necessary and sufficient for testing the conditional statement:

- That is, to evaluate the deduction, the participant must turn over the card showing a consonant to see whether it has an even number on the other side. He or she thereby affirms the antecedent (the *modus ponens* argument).
- In addition, the participant must turn over the card showing an odd number (i.e., not an even number) to see whether it has a vowel (i.e., not a consonant) on the other side. He or she thereby denies the consequent (the *modus tollens* argument).

The other two possible tests (denying the antecedent and affirming the consequent) are irrelevant. That is, the participant need not turn over the card showing a

Figure 11.1 Which two cards would you turn to confirm the rule, "If a card has a consonant on one side, then it has an even number on the other side"?

Table 11.3 Conditional Reasoning: Wason's Selection Task

In the Wason selection task, Peter Wason presented participants with a set of four cards, from which the participants were to test the validity of a given proposition. This table illustrates how a reasoner might test the conditional proposition ($p \rightarrow q$), "If a card has a consonant on one side (p), then it has an even number on the other side (q)."

Proposition based on what shows on the face of the card	Test	Type of Reasoning	
p A given card has a consonant on one side (e.g., "S," "F," "V," or "P")	**∴ q** Does the card have an even number on the other side?	Based on *modus ponens*	Deductively valid inferences
¬ q A given card does not have an even number on one side. That is, a given card has an odd number on one side (e.g., "3," "5," "7," or "9").	**∴ ¬ p** Does the card not have a consonant on the other side? That is, does the card have a vowel on the other side?	Based on *modus tollens*	
¬ p A given card does not have a consonant on one side. That is, a given card has a vowel on one side (e.g., "A," "E," "I," or "O").	**∴ ¬ q** Does the card not have an even number on the other side? That is, does the card have an odd number on the other side?	Based on denying the antecedent	Deductive fallacies
q A given card has an even number on one side (e.g., "2," "4," "6," or "8").	**∴ p** Does the card have a consonant on the other side?	Based on affirming the consequent	

vowel (i.e., not a consonant). To do so would be to deny the antecedent. He or she also need not turn over the card showing an even number (i.e., not a odd number). To do so would be to affirm the consequent.

Most participants knew to test for the *modus ponens* argument. However, many participants failed to test for the *modus tollens* argument. Some of these participants instead tried to deny the antecedent as a means of testing the conditional proposition.

Conditional Reasoning in Everyday Life

Most people of all ages (at least starting in elementary school) appear to have little difficulty in recognizing and applying the *modus ponens* argument. However, few people spontaneously recognize the need for reasoning by means of the *modus tollens* argument. Many people do not recognize the logical fallacies of denying the antecedent or affirming the consequent, at least as these fallacies are applied to abstract reasoning problems (Braine & O'Brien, 1991; O'Brien, 2004; Rips, 1988, 1994). In fact, some evidence suggests that even people who have taken a course in logic fail to demonstrate deductive reasoning across various situations (Cheng et al., 1986). Even training aimed directly at improving reasoning leads to mixed results. After training aimed at increasing reasoning, there is a significant increase in the use of mental models and rules. However, after this training, there may be only a moderate increase in the use of deductive reasoning (Leighton, 2006).

Why might both children and adults fallaciously affirm the consequent or deny the antecedent? Perhaps they do so because of invited inferences that follow from normal discourse comprehension of conditional phrasing (Rumain, Connell, & Braine, 1983). For instance, suppose that a textbook publisher advertises,

"If you buy the *Introduction to Ethics* textbook, then we will give you a $5 rebate."

You probably correctly infer that if you do not buy this textbook, the publisher will not give you a $5 rebate. However, formal deductive reasoning would consider this denial of the antecedent to be fallacious. The statement says nothing about what happens if you do *not* buy the textbook. Similarly, you may infer that you must have bought this textbook (affirm the consequent) if you received a $5 rebate from the publisher. But the statement says nothing about the range of circumstances that lead you to receive the $5 rebate. There may be other ways to receive it. Both inferences are fallacious according to formal deductive reasoning, but both are quite reasonably invited inferences in everyday situations. It helps when the wording of conditional reasoning problems either explicitly or implicitly disinvites these inferences. People are then much less likely to engage in these logical fallacies.

The demonstration of conditional reasoning also is influenced by the presence of contextual information that converts the problem from one of abstract deductive reasoning to one that applies to an everyday situation. For example, participants received both the Wason Selection Task and a modified version of the Wason Selection Task (Griggs & Cox, 1982). In the modified version, the participants were asked to suppose that they were police officers. As officers, they were attempting to enforce the laws applying to the legal age for drinking alcoholic beverages. The particular rule to be enforced was:

"If a person is drinking beer, then the person must be over 19 years of age."

Each participant was presented with a set of four cards:

(1) drinking a beer
(2) drinking a Coke
(3) 16 years of age
(4) 22 years of age.

The participant then was instructed to "Select the card or cards that you definitely need to turn over to determine whether or not the people are violating the rule" (p. 414). On the one hand, none of Griggs and Cox's participants had responded correctly on the abstract version of the Wason Selection Task. On the other hand, a remarkable 72% of the participants correctly responded to the modified version of the task; that is, they turned cards 1 and 3.

Influences on Conditional Reasoning

A more recent modification of the task based on drinking and age has shown that beliefs regarding plausibility influence whether people choose the *modus tollens* argument (denying the consequent—checking to see whether a person who is younger than 19 years of age is not drinking beer). When the test involves checking to see whether an 18-year-old is drinking beer, people are far more likely to try the *modus tollens* argument than when they have to check whether a 4-year-old is drinking beer. Nevertheless, the logical argument is the same in both cases (Kirby, 1994).

How do people use deductive reasoning in realistic situations? Two investigators have suggested that, rather than using formal inference rules, people often use pragmatic reasoning schemas (Cheng & Holyoak, 1985). **Pragmatic reasoning schemas** are general organizing principles or rules related to particular kinds of goals, such as permissions, obligations, or causations. These schemas sometimes are referred to as *pragmatic rules*. These pragmatic rules are not as abstract as formal logical rules. Yet, they are sufficiently general and broad so that they can apply to a wide variety of specific situations. Prior beliefs, in other words, matter in reasoning (Evans & Feeney, 2004).

Alternatively, one's performance may be affected by *perspective effects*—that is, whether one takes the point of view of the police officers or of the people drinking the alcoholic beverages (Almor & Sloman, 1996; Staller, Sloman, & Ben-Zeev, 2000). So it may not be permissions *per se* that matter. Rather, what may matter are the perspectives one takes when solving such problems.

Thus, consider situations in which our previous experiences or our existing knowledge cannot tell us all we want to know. Pragmatic reasoning schemas help us deduce what might reasonably be true. Particular situations or contexts activate particular schemas. For example, suppose that you are walking across campus and see someone who looks extremely young. Then you see the person walk to a car. He unlocks it, gets in, and drives away. This observation would activate your permission schema for driving: "If you are to be permitted to drive alone, then you must be at least 16 years old." You might now deduce that the person you saw is at least 16 years old. In one experiment, 62% of participants correctly chose *modus ponens* and *modus tollens* arguments when the conditional-reasoning task was presented in the context of permission statements. Only 11% did so when the task was presented in the context of arbitrary statements unrelated to pragmatic reasoning schemas (Cheng & Holyoak, 1985).

Researchers conducted an extensive analysis comparing the standard abstract Wason selection task with an abstract form of a permission problem (Griggs & Cox, 1993). The standard abstract form might be "If a card has an 'A' on one side, then it must have a '4' on the other side." The abstract permission form might be, "If one is to take action 'A,' then one must first satisfy precondition 'P.' " Performance on the abstract-permission task was still superior (49% correct overall) to performance on the standard abstract task (only 9% correct overall) (Griggs & Cox, 1993; Manktelow & Over, 1990, 1992).

Evolution and Reasoning

A different approach to conditional reasoning takes an evolutionary view of cognition (Cummins, 2004). This view asks what kinds of thinking skills would provide a naturally selective advantage for humans in adapting to our environment across evolutionary time (Cosmides, 1989; Cosmides & Tooby, 1996). To gain insight into human cognition, we should look to see what kinds of adaptations would have been most useful in the distant past. So we hypothesize on how human hunters and gatherers would have thought during the millions of years of evolutionary time that predated the relatively recent development of agriculture and the very recent development of industrialized societies.

How has evolution influenced human cognition? Humans may possess something like a schema-acquisition device (Cosmides, 1989). It facilitates our ability to quickly glean important information from our experiences. It also helps us to organize that information into meaningful frameworks. In Cosmides' view, these schemas are highly flexible. But they also are specialized for selecting and organizing the information that will most effectively aid us in adapting to the situations we face. One of the distinctive adaptations shown by human hunters and gatherers has been in the area of social exchange. There are two kinds of inferences in particular that social-exchange schemas facilitate: inferences related to cost-benefit relationships and inferences that help people detect when someone is cheating in a particular social exchange. In earlier times, detecting a cheater may have made the difference between life and death.

Syllogistic Reasoning: Categorical Syllogisms

In addition to conditional reasoning, the other key type of deductive reasoning is syllogistic reasoning, which is based on the use of syllogisms. **Syllogisms** are deductive arguments that involve drawing conclusions from two premises (Maxwell, 2005; Rips, 1994, 1999). All syllogisms comprise a major premise, a minor premise, and a conclusion. Unfortunately, sometimes the conclusion may be that no logical conclusion may be reached based on the two given premises.

What Are Categorical Syllogisms?

Probably the most well-known kind of syllogism is the categorical syllogism. Like other kinds of syllogisms, categorical syllogisms comprise two premises and a conclusion. In the case of the **categorical syllogism,** the premises state something about the category memberships of the terms. In fact, each term represents all, none, or some of the members of a particular class or category. As with other syllogisms, each premise contains two terms. One of them must be the middle term, common to both premises. The first and the second terms in each premise are linked through the categorical membership of the terms. That is, one term is a member of the class indicated by the other term. However the premises are worded, they state that some (or all or none) of the members of the category of the first term are (or are not) members of the category of the second term. To determine whether the conclusion follows logically from the premises, the reasoner must determine the category memberships of the terms. An example of a categorical syllogism would be as follows:

All cognitive psychologists are pianists.

All pianists are athletes.

Therefore, all cognitive psychologists are athletes.

Logicians often use circle diagrams to illustrate class membership. They make it easier to figure out whether a particular conclusion is logically sound. The conclusion for this syllogism does in fact follow logically from the premises. This is shown in the circle diagram in Figure 11.2. However, the conclusion is false because the premises are false. For the preceding categorical syllogism, the *subject* is cognitive psychologists, the *middle term* is pianists, and the *predicate* is athletes. In both premises, we asserted that all members of the category of the first term were members of the category of the second term.

There are four kinds of premises (see also Table 11.4):

1. Statements of the form "All A are B" sometimes are referred to as *universal affirmatives*, because they make a positive (affirmative) statement about all members of a class (universal).
2. *Universal negative statements* make a negative statement about all members of a class (e.g., "No cognitive psychologists are flutists.").
3. *Particular affirmative statements* make a positive statement about some members of a class (e.g., "Some cognitive psychologists are left-handed.").
4. *Particular negative statements* make a negative statement about some members of a class (e.g., "Some cognitive psychologists are not physicists.").

In all kinds of syllogisms, some combinations of premises lead to no logically valid conclusion. In categorical syllogisms, in particular, we cannot draw logically valid conclusions from categorical syllogisms with two particular premises or with two negative premises. For example, "Some cognitive psychologists are left-handed. Some

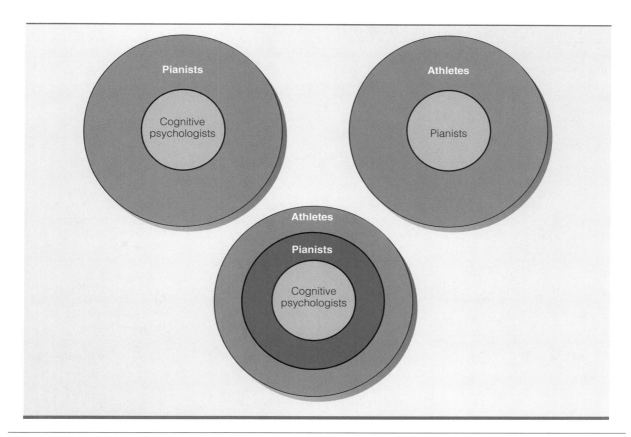

Figure 11.2   Circle Diagrams Representing a Categorical Syllogism.

Circle diagrams may be used to represent categorical syllogisms such as the one shown here: "All cognitive psychologists are pianists. All pianists are athletes. Therefore, all cognitive psychologists are athletes." It follows from the syllogism that all cognitive psychologists are athletes. However, if the premises are not true, a deduction that is logically valid still is not necessarily true, as is the case in this example.

Source: From In *Search of the Human Mind,* by Robert J. Sternberg. Copyright © 1995 by Harcourt Brace & Company. Reproduced by permission of the publisher.

left-handed people are smart." Based on these premises, you cannot conclude even that some cognitive psychologists are smart. The left-handed people who are smart might not be the same left-handed people who are cognitive psychologists. We just don't know. Consider a negative example: "No students are stupid. No stupid people eat pizza." We cannot conclude anything one way or the other about whether students eat pizza based on these two negative premises. As you may have guessed, people appear to have more difficulty (work more slowly and make more errors) when trying to deduce conclusions based on one or more particular premises or negative premises.

How Do People Solve Syllogisms?

Various theories have been proposed as to how people solve categorical syllogisms. One of the earliest theories was the atmosphere bias (Begg & Denny, 1969; Woodworth & Sells, 1935). There are two basic ideas of this theory:

Table 11.4 Categorical Syllogisms: Types of Premises

The premises of categorical syllogisms may be universal affirmatives, universal negatives, particular affirmatives, or particular negatives.

Type of Premise	Form of Premise Statements	Description	Examples	Reversibility*
Universal affirmative	All A are B.	The premise positively (affirmatively) states that all members of the first class (universal) are members of the second class.	All men are males.	All men are males ≠ All males are men. **Non-reversible** All A are B ≠ All B are A.
Universal negative	No A are B. (Alternative: All A are *not* B.)	The premise states that none of the members of the first class are members of the second class.	No men are females. *or* All men are not females.	No men are females = No females are men. ↔Reversible↔ No A are B = No B are A.
Particular affirmative	Some A are B.	The premise states that only some of the members of the first class are members of the second class.	Some females are women.	Some females are women ≠ Some women are females. **Non-reversible** Some A are B ≠ Some B are A.
Particular negative	Some A are not B.	The premise states that some members of the first class are not members of the second class.	Some women are not females.	Some women are not females ≠ Some females are not women. **Non-reversible** Some A are not B ≠ Some B are not A.

*In formal logic, the word *some* means "some and possibly all." In common parlance, and as used in cognitive psychology, *some* means "some and not all." Thus, in formal logic, the particular affirmative also would be reversible. For our purposes, it is not.

1. If there is at least one negative in the premises, people will prefer a negative solution.
2. If there is at least one particular in the premises, people will prefer a particular solution. For example, if one of the premises is "No pilots are children," people will prefer a solution that has the word *no* in it.

Nonetheless, the theory does not account very well for large numbers of responses.

Other researchers focused attention on the conversion of premises (Chapman & Chapman, 1959). Here, the terms of a given premise are reversed. People sometimes believe that the reversed form of the premise is just as valid as the original form. The idea is that people tend to convert statements like "If A, then B" into "If B, then A." They do not realize that the statements are not equivalent. These errors are made by children and adults alike (Markovits, 2004).

A more widely accepted theory is based on the notion that people solve syllogisms by using a semantic (meaning-based) process based on mental models (Ball & Quayle, 2009; Espino et al., 2005; Johnson-Laird & Savary, 1999; Johnson-Laird & Steedman, 1978). This view of reasoning as involving semantic processes based on mental models may be contrasted with rule-based ("syntactic") processes, such as those characterized by formal logic. A **mental model** is an internal representation of information that corresponds analogously with whatever is being represented (see Johnson-Laird, 1983). Some mental models are more likely to lead to a deductively valid conclusion than are others. In particular, some mental models may not be effective in disconfirming an invalid conclusion.

For example, in the Johnson-Laird study, participants were asked to describe their conclusions and their mental models for the syllogism, "All of the artists are beekeepers. Some of the beekeepers are clever. Are all artists clever?" One participant said, "I thought of all the little . . . artists in the room and imagined they all had beekeeper's hats on" (Johnson-Laird & Steedman, 1978, p. 77). Figure 11.3 shows two different mental models for this syllogism. As the figure shows, the choice of a mental model may affect the reasoner's ability to reach a valid deductive conclusion. Because some models are better than others for solving some syllogisms, a person is more likely to reach a deductively valid conclusion by using more than one mental model. In the figure, the mental model shown in (a) may lead to the

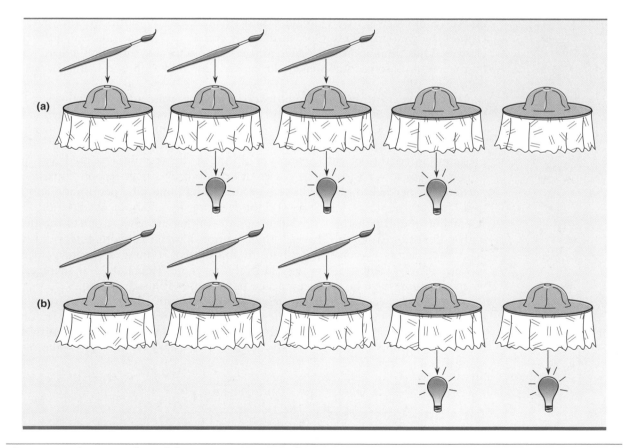

Figure 11.3   Mental Models Representing a Syllogism.

Philip Johnson-Laird and Mark Steedman hypothesized that people use various mental models analogously to represent the items within a syllogism. Some mental models are more effective than others, and for a valid deductive conclusion to be reached, more than one model may be necessary, as shown here. (See text for explanation.)

deductively invalid conclusion that some artists are clever. By observing the alternative model in (b), we can see an alternative view of the syllogism. It shows that the conclusion that some artists are clever may not be deduced on the basis of this information alone. Specifically, perhaps the beekeepers who are clever are not the same as the beekeepers who are artists.

As mentioned previously, circle diagrams are often used to represent categorical syllogisms. In circle diagrams, you can use overlapping, concentric, or non-overlapping circles to represent the members of different categories (see Figure 11.2). People can learn how to improve their reasoning by being taught how to draw circle diagrams (Nickerson, 2004). Amazingly, even congenitally blind persons are able to create spatial mental models to assist them in their reasoning processes (Fleming et al., 2006; Knauff & May, 2006).

The difficulty of many problems of deductive reasoning relates to the number of mental models needed for adequately representing the premises of the deductive argument (Johnson-Laird, Byrne, & Schaeken, 1992). Arguments that entail only one mental model may be solved quickly and accurately. However, to infer accurate conclusions based on arguments that may be represented by multiple alternative models is much harder. Such inferences place great demands on working memory (Gilhooly, 2004). In these cases, the individual must simultaneously hold in working memory each of the various models. Only in this way can he or she reach or evaluate a conclusion. Thus, limitations of working-memory capacity may underlie at least some of the errors observed in human deductive reasoning (Johnson-Laird, Byrne, & Schaeken, 1992).

In two experiments, the role of working memory was studied in syllogistic reasoning (Gilhooly et al., 1993). In the first, syllogisms were simply presented either orally or visually. Oral presentation placed a considerably higher load on working memory because participants had to remember the premises. In the visual-presentation condition, participants could look at the premises. As predicted, performance was lower in the oral-presentation condition. In a second experiment, participants needed to solve syllogisms while at the same time performing another task. Either the task drew on working-memory resources or it did not. The researchers found that the task that drew on working-memory resources interfered with syllogistic reasoning. The task that did not draw on these resources did not.

Other factors also may contribute to the ease of forming appropriate mental models. People seem to solve logical problems more accurately and more easily when the terms have high imagery value (Clement & Falmagne, 1986).

Some deductive reasoning problems comprise more than two premises. For example, transitive-inference problems, in which problem solvers must order multiple terms, can have any number of premises linking large numbers of terms. Mathematical and logical proofs are deductive in character and can have many steps as well.

Aids and Obstacles to Deductive Reasoning

In deductive reasoning, as in many other cognitive processes, we engage in many heuristic shortcuts. These shortcuts sometimes lead to inaccurate conclusions. In addition to these shortcuts, we often are influenced by biases that distort the outcomes of our reasoning. In this section, we examine heuristics and biases in deductive reasoning. Finally, we look at ways to enhance your deductive reasoning skills.

Heuristics in Deductive Reasoning

Heuristics in syllogistic reasoning include *overextension errors*. In these errors, we overextend the use of strategies that work in some syllogisms to syllogisms in which the strategies fail us. For example, although reversals work well with universal negatives, they do not work with other kinds of premises. We also experience *foreclosure effects* when we fail to consider all the possibilities before reaching a conclusion. In addition, *premise-phrasing effects* may influence our deductive reasoning, for example, the sequence of terms or the use of particular qualifiers or negative phrasing. Premise-phrasing effects may lead us to leap to a conclusion without adequately reflecting on the deductive validity of the syllogism.

Biases in Deductive Reasoning

Biases that affect deductive reasoning generally relate to the content of the premises and the believability of the conclusion. They also reflect the tendency toward **confirmation bias**. In confirmation bias, we seek confirmation rather than disconfirmation of what we already believe. Suppose the content of the premises and a conclusion seem to be true. In such cases, reasoners tend to believe in the validity of the conclusion, even when the logic is flawed (Evans, Barston, & Pollard, 1983).

Confirmation bias can be detrimental and even dangerous in some circumstances. For instance, in an emergency room, if a doctor assumes that a patient has condition X, the doctor may interpret the set of symptoms as supporting the diagnosis without fully considering all alternative interpretations (Pines, 2005). This shortcut can result in inappropriate diagnosis and treatment, which can be extremely dangerous. Other circumstances where the effects of confirmation bias can be observed are in police investigations, paranormal beliefs, and stereotyping behavior (Ask & Granhag, 2005; Biernat & Ma, 2005; Lawrence & Peters, 2004). To a lesser extent, people also show the opposite tendency to disconfirm the validity of the conclusion when the conclusion or the content of the premises contradicts the reasoner's existing beliefs (Evans, Barston, & Pollard, 1983; Janis & Frick, 1943).

Enhancing Deductive Reasoning

To enhance our deductive reasoning, we may try to avoid heuristics and biases that distort our reasoning. We also may engage in practices that facilitate reasoning. For example, we may take longer to reach or to evaluate conclusions. Effective reasoners also consider more alternative conclusions than do poor reasoners (Galotti, Baron, & Sabini, 1986). In addition, training and practice seem to increase performance on reasoning tasks. The benefits of training tend to be strong when the training relates to pragmatic reasoning schemas (Cheng et al., 1986) or to such fields as law and medicine (Lehman, Lempert, & Nisbett, 1987). The benefits are weaker for abstract logical problems divorced from our everyday life (see Holland et al., 1986; Holyoak & Nisbett, 1988).

One factor that affects syllogistic reasoning is mood. When people are in a sad mood, they tend to pay more attention to details (Schwarz & Skurnik, 2003). Perhaps surprisingly, they tend to do better in syllogistic reasoning tasks when they are in a sad mood than when they are in a happy mood (Fiedler, 1988; Melton, 1995). People in a neutral mood tend to show performance in between the two extremes.

IMPROVING YOUR DEDUCTIVE REASONING SKILLS

Even without training, you can improve your own deductive reasoning through developing strategies to avoid making errors. For example, an unscrupulous politician might state that, "We know that some suspicious-looking people are illegal aliens. We also know that some illegal aliens are terrorists. Therefore, we can be sure that some of those people whom we think are suspicious are terrorists, and that they are out to destroy our country!" The politician's syllogistic reasoning is wrong. If some A are B and some B are C, it is not necessarily the case that any A are C. This is obvious when you realize that some men are happy people and some happy people are women, but this does not imply that some men are women.

Make sure you are using the proper strategies in solving syllogisms. Remember that reversals only work with universal negatives. Sometimes translating abstract terms to concrete ones (e.g., the letter C to cows) can help. Also, take the time to consider contrary examples and create more mental models. The more mental models you use for a given set of premises, the more confident you can be that if your conclusion is not valid, it will be disconfirmed. Thus, the use of multiple mental models increases the likelihood of avoiding errors. The use of multiple mental models also helps you to avoid the tendency to engage in confirmation bias. Circle diagrams also can be helpful in solving deductive-reasoning problems.

Is the use of fingerprints in solving a crime an example of deductive reasoning? Why or why not?

✔ CONCEPT CHECK

1. Which are deductively valid inferences in conditional reasoning?
2. What are categorical syllogisms?
3. How can mental models be helpful when solving categorical syllogisms?
4. What does "reversibility" mean with respect to premises?
5. Name some biases that we are prone to in deductive reasoning.

Inductive Reasoning

We now consider inductive reasoning in more detail. First, we discuss what inductive reasoning is. Next, we will explore how we make causal inferences. Last, we will consider categorical inferences and reasoning by analogies.

What Is Inductive Reasoning?

Inductive reasoning is the process of reasoning from specific facts or observations to reach a likely conclusion that may explain the facts. The inductive reasoner then may use that probable conclusion to attempt to predict future specific instances (Johnson-Laird, 2000). The key feature distinguishing inductive from deductive reasoning is that, in inductive reasoning, we never can reach a logically certain conclusion. We only can reach a particularly well-founded or probable conclusion. With deductive reasoning, in contrast, reaching logically certain—deductively valid—conclusions is possible.

For example, suppose that you notice that all the people enrolled in your cognitive psychology course are on the dean's list (or honor roll). From these observations, you could reason inductively that all students who enroll in cognitive psychology are excellent students (or at least earn the grades to give that impression). However, unless you can observe the grade-point averages of all people who ever have taken or ever will take cognitive psychology, you will be unable to prove your conclusion. Furthermore, a single poor student who happened to enroll in a cognitive psychology course would disprove your conclusion. Still, after large numbers of observations, you might conclude that you had made enough observations to reason inductively.

The fundamental riddle of induction is how we can make any inductions at all. As the future has not happened, how can we predict what it will bring? There is also an important so-called new riddle of induction (Goodman, 1983). Given possible alternative futures, how do we know *which one* to predict? For example, in the number series problem 2, 4, 6, ?, most people would replace the question mark with an 8. But we cannot know for sure that the correct number is 8. A mathematical formula could be proposed that would yield any number at all as the next number. So why choose the pattern of ascending even numbers? Partly we choose it because it seems simple to us. It is a less complex formula than others we might choose. And partly we choose it because we are familiar with it. We are used to ascending series of even numbers. But we are not used to other complex series in which 2, 4, 6, may be embedded, such as 2, 4, 6, 10, 12, 14, 18, 20, 22, and so forth.

Inductive reasoning forms the basis of the empirical method (Holyoak & Nisbett, 1998). In it, we cannot logically leap from saying, "All observed instances to date of X are Y" to saying, "Therefore, all X are Y." It is always possible that the next observed X will not be a Y. For example, you may say that all swans that you have ever seen are white. However, you cannot form the conclusion then that all swans are white because the next swan you happen upon might be black. Indeed, black swans do exist.

In research, when we reject the null hypothesis (the hypothesis of no difference), we use inductive reasoning. We never know for sure whether we are correct in rejecting a null hypothesis.

Cognitive psychologists probably agree on at least two of the reasons why people use inductive reasoning. First, it helps them to become increasingly able to make sense out of the great variability in their environment. Second, it also helps them to predict events in their environment, thereby reducing their uncertainty. Thus, cognitive psychologists seek to understand the *how* rather than the *why* of inductive reasoning. We may (or may not) have some innate schema-acquisition device. But we certainly are not born with all the inferences we manage to induce.

We already have implied that inductive reasoning often involves the processes of generating and testing hypotheses. In addition, we reach inferences by generalizing some broad understandings from a set of specific instances. As we observe additional instances, we further broaden our understanding. Or, we may infer specialized exceptions to the general understandings. For example, after observing quite a few birds, we may infer that birds can fly. But after observing penguins and ostriches, we may add to our generalized knowledge specialized exceptions for flightless birds.

Causal Inferences

One approach to studying inductive reasoning is to examine **causal inferences**—how people make judgments about whether something causes something else (Cheng, 1997, 1999; Spellman, 1997). The philosopher David Hume observed that we are most likely to infer causality when we observe covariation over time: First one thing happens, then another. If we see the two events paired enough, we may come to believe that the first causes the second.

Perhaps our greatest failing is one that extends to psychologists, other scientists, and non-scientists: We demonstrate confirmation bias, which may lead us to errors such as illusory correlations (Chapman & Chapman, 1967, 1969, 1975). Furthermore, we frequently make mistakes when attempting to determine causality based on correlational evidence alone. Correlational evidence cannot indicate the direction of causation. Suppose we observe a correlation between Factor A and Factor B. We may find one of three things:

1. it may be that Factor A causes Factor B;
2. it may be that Factor B causes Factor A; or
3. some higher order, Factor C, may be causing both Factors A and B to occur together.

Based on the correlational data we cannot determine which of the three options indeed causes the observed phenomenon.

A related error occurs when we fail to recognize that many phenomena have multiple causes. For example, a car accident often involves several causes. It may have originated with the negligence of several drivers, rather than just one. Once we have identified one of the suspected causes of a phenomenon, we may commit what is known as a *discounting error*. We stop searching for additional alternative or contributing causes.

Confirmation bias can have a major effect on our everyday lives. For example, we may meet someone, expecting not to like her. As a result, we may treat her in ways that are different from how we would treat her if we expected to like her. She then may respond to us in less favorable ways. She thereby "confirms" our original belief that she is not likable. Confirmation bias thereby can play a major role in schooling. Teachers often expect little of students when they think them low in ability. The students then give the teachers little. The teachers' original beliefs are thereby "confirmed" (Sternberg, 1997). This effect is referred to as a *self-fulfilling prophecy* (Harber & Jussim, 2005).

Categorical Inferences

On what basis do people draw inferences? People generally use both bottom-up strategies and top-down strategies for doing so (Holyoak & Nisbett, 1988). That is, they use both information from their sensory experiences and information based on what they already know or have inferred previously. Bottom-up strategies are based on observing various instances and considering the degree of variability across instances. From these observations, we abstract a prototype (see Chapters 8 and 9). Once a prototype or a category has been induced, the individual may use focused sampling to add new instances to the category. He or she focuses chiefly on properties that have provided useful distinctions in the past. Top-down strategies include selectively searching for constancies within many variations and selectively combining existing concepts and categories.

Reasoning by Analogy

Inductive reasoning may be applied to a broader range of situations than those requiring causal or categorical inferences. For example, inductive reasoning may be applied to reasoning by analogy. Consider an example analogy problem:

Fire is to asbestos as water is to: (a) vinyl, (b) air, (c) cotton, (d) faucet.

In reasoning by analogy, the reasoner must observe the first pair of items ("fire" and "asbestos" in this example) and must induce from those two items one or more relations (in this case, surface resistance because surfaces coated with asbestos can resist fire). The reasoner then must apply the given relation in the second part of the analogy. In the example analogy, the reasoner chooses the solution to be "vinyl" because surfaces coated with vinyl can resist water.

Some investigators have used reaction-time methodology to figure out how people solve induction problems. For example, using mathematical modeling you might be able to break down the amounts of time participants spent on various processes of analogical reasoning. Most of the time spent in solving simple verbal analogies is spent in encoding the terms and in responding (Sternberg, 1977). Only a small part actually is spent in doing reasoning operations on these encodings.

The difficulty of encoding can become even greater in various puzzling analogies. For example, in the analogy:

RAT : TAR :: BAT : (a. CONCRETE, b. MAMMAL, c. TAB, d. TAIL),

the difficulty is in encoding the analogy as one involving letter reversal rather than semantic content for its solution. In a problematic analogy such as the following, the difficulty is in recognizing the meanings of the words:

AUDACIOUS : TIMOROUS :: MITIGATE :
(a. ADUMBRATE, b. EXACERBATE, c. EXPOSTULATE, d. EVISCERATE)

If reasoners know the meanings of the words, they probably will find it relatively easy to figure out that the relation is one of antonyms. (Did this example audaciously exacerbate your difficulties in solving problems involving analogies?)

An application of analogies in reasoning can be seen in politics. Analogies can help governing bodies come to conclusions (Breuning, 2003). These analogies also can be effectively used to conveying the justification of the decision to the public (Breuning, 2003). However, the use of analogies is not always successful. This highlights both the utility and possible pitfalls of using analogies in political deliberation. In 2010, opponents of the war in Afghanistan drew an analogy to Vietnam to argue for withdrawing from Afghanistan. They asserted that the failure of U.S. policies to lead to a conclusive victory were analogous between Vietnam and Afghanistan. Some members of government then turned the tables, using an analogy to Vietnam to argue that withdrawal from Afghanistan could lead to mass slaughter, as they asserted happened in Vietnam after the Americans left. Thus, analogies can end up being largely in the eye of the beholder rather than in the actual elements being compared.

Analogies are also used in everyday life as we make predictions about our environment. We connect our perceptions with our memories by means of analogies. The analogies then activate concepts and items stored in our mind that are similar to the current input. Through this activation, we can then make a prediction of what is likely in a given situation (Bar, 2007). For example, predictions about global warming are being guided in part by people drawing analogies to times in the past when the people believed either that the atmosphere warmed up or did not. Whether a given individual believes in global warming depends in part upon what analogy or analogies the individual decides to draw.

✔ CONCEPT CHECK

1. What is inductive reasoning?
2. Which strategies do people use to draw inferences?
3. What is an analogy?
4. What leads analogies to succeed or fail?

An Alternative View of Reasoning

By now you have reasonably inferred that cognitive psychologists often disagree—sometimes rather heatedly—about how and why people reason as they do. An alternative perspective on reasoning, *dual-process theory*, contends that two complementary systems of reasoning can be distinguished. The first is an *associative system*, which involves mental operations based on observed similarities and temporal contiguities (i.e., tendencies for things to occur close together in time). The second is a *rule-based system*, which involves manipulations based on the relations among symbols (Barrett, Tugade, & Engle, 2004; Sloman, 1996).

The associative system can lead to speedy responses that are highly sensitive to patterns and to general tendencies. Through this system, we detect similarities between observed patterns and patterns stored in memory. We may pay more attention to salient features (e.g., highly typical or highly atypical ones) than to defining features of a pattern. This system imposes rather loose constraints that may inhibit the selection of patterns that are poor matches to the observed pattern. It favors remembered patterns that are better matches to the observed pattern. An example of associative reasoning is use of the representativeness heuristic.

Another example is the *belief-bias effect* in syllogistic reasoning (Markovits et al., 2009; Tsujii et al., 2010). This effect occurs when we agree more with syllogisms that affirm our beliefs, whether or not these syllogisms are logically valid. An example of the workings of the associative system may be in the *false-consensus effect*. Here, people believe that their own behavior and judgments are more common and more appropriate than those of other people (Ross, Greene, & House, 1977). Suppose people have an opinion on an issue. They are likely to believe that because it is their opinion, it is likely to be shared and believed to be correct by others (Dawes & Mulford, 1996; Krueger, 1998). Associating others' views with our own simply because they are our own is a questionable practice, however.

The rule-based system of reasoning usually requires more deliberate, sometimes painstaking procedures for reaching conclusions. Through this system, we carefully analyze relevant features (e.g., defining features) of the available data, based on rules stored in memory. This system imposes rigid constraints that rule out possibilities that violate the rules. Evidence in favor of rule-based reasoning includes:

1. We can recognize logical arguments when they are explained to us.
2. We can recognize the need to make categorizations based on defining features despite similarities in typical features. For example, we can recognize that a coin with a 3-inch diameter, which looks exactly like a quarter, must be a counterfeit.

3. We can rule out impossibilities, such as cats conceiving and giving birth to puppies.
4. We can recognize many improbabilities. For example, it is unlikely that the U.S. Congress will pass a law that provides annual salaries to all full-time college students.

According to Sloman, we need both complementary systems. We need to respond quickly and easily to everyday situations, based on observed similarities and temporal contiguities. Yet we also need a means for evaluating our responses more deliberately.

The two systems may be conceptualized within a connectionist framework (Sloman, 1996). The associative system is represented easily in terms of pattern activation and inhibition, which readily fits the connectionist model. The rule-based system may be represented as a system of production rules (see Chapter 8).

An alternative connectionist view suggests that deductive reasoning may occur when a given pattern of activation in one set of nodes (e.g., those associated with a particular premise or set of premises) entails or produces a particular pattern of activation in a second set of nodes (Rips, 1994). Similarly, a connectionist model of inductive reasoning may involve the repeated activation of a series of similar patterns across various instances. This repeated activation then may strengthen the links among the activated nodes. It thereby leads to generalization or abstraction of the pattern for a variety of instances.

Connectionist models of reasoning and the other approaches described in this chapter offer diverse views of the available data regarding how we reason and make judgments. At present, no one theoretical model explains all the data well. But each model explains at least some of the data satisfactorily. Together, the theories help us understand human intelligence and cognition.

Consider a concrete example of the interface between intelligence and cognition in *Investigating Cognitive Psychology: When There Is No "Right" Choice*.

✔ CONCEPT CHECK

1. What are the two complementary systems of reasoning?

2. How does a connectionist model conceptualize deductive reasoning?

Neuroscience of Reasoning

As in both problem solving and decision making, the process of reasoning involves the prefrontal cortex (Bunge et al., 2004). Further, reasoning involves brain areas associated with working memory, such as the basal ganglia (Melrose, Poulin, & Stern, 2007). One would expect working memory to be involved because reasoning involves the integration of information (which needs to be held in working memory while it is being integrated).

The basal ganglia are involved in a variety of functions, including cognition and learning. This area is also associated with the prefrontal cortex through a variety of connections (Melrose, Poulin, & Stern, 2007).

However, when a person is presented with a statement that is either to be remembered, on the one hand, or to be used for reasoning, on the other, the processes

INVESTIGATING COGNITIVE PSYCHOLOGY
When There Is No "Right" Choice

Consider this passage from Shakespeare's *Macbeth*:

First Apparition: *Macbeth! Macbeth! Beware Macduff; Beware the thane of Fife. Dismiss me: enough....*

Second Apparition: *Be bloody, bold, and resolute; laugh to scorn the power of man, for none of woman born shall harm Macbeth.*

Macbeth: *Then live, Macduff: what need I fear of thee? But yet I'll make assurance double sure, and take a bond of fate: thou shalt not live; that I may tell pale-hearted fear it lies, and sleep in spite of thunder.*

In this passage, Macbeth mistakenly took the Second Apparition's vision to mean that no man could kill him, so he boldly decided to confront Macduff. However, Macduff was born by abdominal (Cesarean) delivery, so he did not fall into the category of men who could not harm Macbeth. Macduff eventually killed Macbeth because Macbeth came to a wrong conclusion based on the Second Apparition's premonition. The First Apparition's warning about Macduff should have been heeded.

Suppose you are trying to decide between buying an SUV or a subcompact car. You would like the room of the SUV, but you would like the fuel efficiency of the subcompact car. Whichever one you choose, did you make the right choice? This is a difficult question to answer because most of our decisions are made under conditions of uncertainty. Thus, let us say that you bought the SUV. You can carry a number of people, you have the power to pull a trailer easily up a hill, and you sit higher so your road vision is much better. However, every time you fill up the gas tank, you are reminded of how much fuel this vehicle takes. On the other hand, let us say that you bought the subcompact car. When picking up friends at the airport, you have difficulty fitting all of them and their luggage; you cannot pull trailers up hills (or at least, not very easily); and you sit so low that when there is an SUV in front of you, you can hardly see what is on the road. However, every time you fill up your gas tank or hear someone with an SUV complaining about how much it costs to fill up his or her tank, you see how little you have to pay for gas. Again, did you make the right choice? There are no "right" or "wrong" answers to most of the decisions we make. We use our best judgment at the time of our decisions and think that they are more nearly right than wrong as opposed to definitively right or wrong.

in the brain do differ somewhat. This means there may be more going on than encoding for recall when a person knows he or she will have to reason with a statement. In particular, for syllogistic reasoning, the left lateral frontal lobe (Broca's areas 44 and 45) is more active than when a statement just needs to be remembered. This activation cannot be found for processing of conditional premises.

While people were engaged in the integration of the information (solving the syllogistic and conditional reasoning problems), the left fronto-lateral cortex as well as the basal ganglia were activated for both conditional and syllogistic reasoning. However, syllogistic reasoning also involved activation in the lateral parietal cortex, precuneus, and left ventral fronto-lateral cortex (Reverberi et al., 2010). Thus, syllogistic and conditional reasoning seem to involve processing in different parts of the brain.

Exploration of conditional reasoning through event-related potential (ERP) methods revealed an increased negativity in the anterior cingulate cortex approximately 600 milliseconds and 2,000 milliseconds after task presentation (Qui et al., 2007). This negativity suggests increased cognitive control, as would be expected in a reasoning task.

In one study exploring moral reasoning in persons who show antisocial behaviors indicative of poor moral reasoning, malfunctions were noted in several areas within the prefrontal cortex, including the dorsal and ventral regions (Raine & Yang, 2006). Additionally, impairments in the amygdala, hippocampus, angular gyrus, anterior cingulate, and temporal cortex were also observed. Recall that the anterior cingulate is involved in decision making and the hippocampus is involved in working memory. Therefore, it is to be expected that malfunctions in these areas would result in deficiencies in reasoning.

✔ CONCEPT CHECK

1. Which parts of the brain are prominently involved in reasoning processes?

2. Why can we expect that the parts of the brain that are involved in working memory are also active during reasoning?

Key Themes

Several of the themes discussed in Chapter 1 are relevant to this chapter.

Rationalism versus empiricism. One way of understanding errors in syllogistic reasoning is in terms of the particular logical error made, independently of the mental processes the reasoner has used. For example, affirming the consequent is a logical error. One need do no empirical research to understand at the level of symbolic logic the errors that have been made. Moreover, deductive reasoning is itself based on rationalism. A syllogism such as, "All toys are chairs. All chairs are hot dogs. Therefore, all toys are hot dogs," is logically valid but factually incorrect. Thus, deductive logic can be understood at a rational level, independently of its empirical content. But if we wish to know psychologically why people make errors or what is factually true, then we need to combine empirical observations with rational logic.

Domain generality versus domain specificity. The rules of deductive logic apply equally in all domains. One can apply them, for example, to abstract or to concrete content. But research has shown that, psychologically, deductive reasoning with concrete content is easier than reasoning with abstract content. So although the rules apply in exactly the same way generally across domains, ease of application is not psychologically equivalent across those domains.

Nature versus nurture. Are people preprogrammed to be logical thinkers? Piaget, the famous Swiss cognitive developmental psychologist, believed so. He believed that the development of logical thinking follows an inborn sequence of stages that unfold over time. According to Piaget, there is not much one can do to alter either the sequence or timing of these stages. But research has suggested that the sequence Piaget proposed does not unfold as he thought. For example, many people never reach his highest stage, and some children are able to reason in ways he would not have predicted they would be able to reason until they were older. So once again, nature and nurture interact.

Summary

1. **What are some of the strategies that guide human decision making?** Early theories were designed to achieve practical mathematical models of decision making and assumed that decision makers are fully informed, infinitely sensitive to information, and completely rational. Subsequent theories began to acknowledge that humans often use subjective criteria for decision making, that chance elements often influence the outcomes of decisions, that humans often use subjective estimates for considering the outcomes, and that humans are not boundlessly rational in making decisions. People apparently often use satisficing strategies, settling for the first minimally acceptable option, and strategies involving a process of elimination by aspects to eliminate an overabundance of options.

   One of the most common heuristics most of us use is the representativeness heuristic. We fall prey to the fallacious belief that small samples of a population resemble the whole population in all respects. Our misunderstanding of base rates and other aspects of probability often leads us to other mental shortcuts as well, such as in the conjunction fallacy and the inclusion fallacy.

   Another common heuristic is the availability heuristic, in which we make judgments based on information that is readily available in memory, without bothering to seek less available information. The use of heuristics, such as anchoring and adjustment, illusory correlation, and framing effects, also often impairs our ability to make effective decisions.

   Once we have made a decision (or better yet, another person has made a decision) and the outcome of the decision is known, we may engage in hindsight bias, skewing our perception of the earlier evidence in light of the eventual outcome. Perhaps the most serious of our mental biases, however, is overconfidence, which seems to be amazingly resistant to evidence of our own errors.

2. **What are some of the forms of deductive reasoning that people may use, and what factors facilitate or impede deductive reasoning?** Deductive reasoning involves reaching conclusions from a set of conditional propositions or from a syllogistic pair of premises. Among the various types of syllogisms are linear syllogisms and categorical syllogisms. In addition, deductive reasoning may involve complex transitive-inference problems or mathematical or logical proofs involving large numbers of terms. Also, deductive reasoning may involve the use of pragmatic reasoning schemas in practical, everyday situations.

   In drawing conclusions from conditional propositions, people readily apply the *modus ponens* argument, particularly regarding universal affirmative propositions. Most of us have more difficulty, however, in using the *modus tollens* argument and in avoiding deductive fallacies, such as affirming the consequent or denying the antecedent, particularly when faced with propositions involving particular propositions or negative propositions.

   In solving syllogisms, we have similar difficulties with particular premises and negative premises and with terms that are not presented in the customary sequence. Frequently, when trying to draw conclusions, we overextend a strategy from a situation in which it leads to a deductively valid conclusion to one in which it leads to a deductive fallacy. We also may foreclose on a given conclusion before considering the full range of possibilities that may affect the conclusion. These mental shortcuts may be exacerbated by situations in which we engage in confirmation bias (tending to confirm our own beliefs).

   We can enhance our ability to draw well-reasoned conclusions in many ways, such as by taking time to evaluate the premises or propositions carefully and by forming multiple mental models of the propositions and their relationships. We also may benefit from training and practice in effective deductive reasoning. We are particularly likely to reach well-reasoned conclusions when such conclusions seem plausible and useful in pragmatic contexts, such as during social exchanges.

3. **How do people use inductive reasoning to reach causal inferences and to reach other types of conclusions?** Although we cannot reach logically certain conclusions through inductive reasoning, we can at least reach highly probable conclusions through careful reasoning. When

making categorical inferences, people tend to use both top-down and bottom-up strategies. Processes of inductive reasoning generally form the basis of scientific study and hypothesis testing as a means to derive causal inferences. In addition, in reasoning by analogy people often spend more time encoding the terms of the problem than in performing the inductive reasoning. Reasoning by analogy can lead to better conclusions, but also to worse ones if the analogy is weak or based on faulty assumptions. It appears that people sometimes may use reasoning based on formal-rule systems, such as by applying rules of formal logic, and sometimes use reasoning based on associations, such as by noticing similarities and temporal contiguities.

4. **Are there any alternative views of reasoning?** A number of scientists have suggested that people have two distinct systems of reasoning: an associative system that is sensitive to observed similarities and temporal contiguities and a rule-based system that involves manipulations based on relations among symbols. The two systems can work together to help us reach reasonable conclusions in an efficient way.

Thinking about Thinking: Analytical, Creative, and Practical Questions

1. Describe some of the heuristics and biases people use while making judgments or reaching decisions.
2. What are the two logical arguments and the two logical fallacies associated with conditional reasoning, as in the Wason Selection Task?
3. Which of the various approaches to conditional reasoning seems best to explain the available data? Give reasons for your answer.
4. Some cognitive psychologists question the merits of studying logical formalisms such as linear or categorical syllogisms. What do you think can be gained by studying how people reason in regard to syllogisms?
5. Based on the information in this chapter, design a way to help high school students more effectively apply deductive reasoning to the problems they face.

6. Design a question, such as the ones used by Kahneman and Tversky, which requires people to estimate subjective probabilities of two different events. Indicate the fallacies that you may expect to influence people's estimates, or tell why you think people would give realistic estimates of probability.
7. Suppose that you need to rent an apartment. How would you go about finding one that most effectively meets your requirements and your preferences? How closely does your method resemble the methods described by subjective expected utility theory, by satisficing, or by elimination by aspects?
8. Give two examples showing how you use rule-based reasoning and associative reasoning in your everyday experiences. In what kinds of instances do you believe each type of reasoning works better, or not as well?

Key Terms

availability heuristic, *p. 449*
base rate, *p. 449*
bounded rationality, *p. 446*
categorical syllogism, *p. 468*
causal inferences, *p. 476*
conditional reasoning, *p. 462*
confirmation bias, *p. 473*
deductive reasoning, *p. 462*
deductive validity, *p. 463*
elimination by aspects, *p. 447*

fallacy, *p. 444*
heuristics, *p. 445*
hindsight bias, *p. 453*
illusory correlation, *p. 452*
inductive reasoning, *p. 474*
judgment and decision making, *p. 444*
mental model, *p. 471*
overconfidence, *p. 453*

pragmatic reasoning schemas, *p. 466*
premises, *p. 462*
proposition, *p. 462*
reasoning, *p. 462*
representativeness, *p. 448*
satisficing, *p. 446*
subjective probability, *p. 445*
subjective utility, *p. 445*
syllogisms, *p. 468*

Media Resources —————————————————————————————

Visit the companion website—**www.cengagebrain.com**—for quizzes, research articles, chapter outlines, and more.

CogLab

Explore CogLab by going to **http://coglab.wadsworth.com**. To learn more, examine the following experiments:

Risky Decisions

Typical Reasoning

Wason Selection Task

Problem Solving and Creativity

Here are some of the questions we will explore in this chapter:

1. What are some key steps involved in solving problems?
2. What are the differences between problems that have a clear path to a solution versus problems that do not?
3. What are some of the obstacles and aids to problem solving?
4. How does expertise affect problem solving?
5. What is creativity, and how can it be fostered?

■ **BELIEVE IT OR NOT**

CAN NOVICES HAVE AN ADVANTAGE OVER EXPERTS?

An expert has invested countless hours into his field of study—be it playing a musical instrument, doing academic research, or playing chess. Does having this expertise always pay off? Research suggests that sometimes having less knowledge—being a novice—actually gives you an edge! In one experiment, researchers had expert and novice chess players briefly view a display of a chessboard with the chess pieces on it, and the players then had to recall the positions of the chess pieces on the board. As you might expect, the experts performed quite a bit better than the novices. However, the setup of the chess pieces on the board was then changed in a way that it did not make sense in terms of the actual game of chess. Suddenly, experts lost their advantage and performed no better, or even worse, than did the novices (Chase & Simon, 1973; see also Brockmole et al., 2008). We will explore possible reasons for this effect later in this chapter in the section on expertise.

Frensch and Sternberg (1989) found that when a strategic change was made in the rules for bridge, experts were hurt more than novices, presumably because the experts had become entrenched and somewhat stuck with the conventional set of rules.

How do you solve problems that arise in your relationships with other people? How do you solve the "two-string" problem illustrated in Figure 12.1? How does anyone solve any problem, for that matter? This chapter considers the process of solving problems, as well as some of the hindrances and aids to **problem solving**, an effort to overcome obstacles obstructing the path to a solution (Reed, 2000). At the conclusion of this chapter, we discuss creativity and its role in problem solving. Throughout the chapter, we discuss how people make the "mental leaps" that lead them from having a set of givens to having a solution to a problem (Holyoak & Thagard, 1995).

The focus of this chapter is on individual problem solving. It is worth remembering, however, that working in groups often facilitates problem solving. The solutions reached by groups often are better than those reached by individuals (Williams & Sternberg, 1988). This benefit is seen most notably when the group members represent a variety of ability levels (Hong & Page, 2004). We engage in problem solving when we need to overcome obstacles to answer a question or to achieve a goal. If we quickly can retrieve an answer from memory, we do not have a problem. If we cannot retrieve an immediate answer, then we have a problem to be solved.

How people solve problems depends partly on how they understand the problem (Whitten & Graesser, 2003). Consider an example of how understanding the nature of the problem matters.

Figure 12.1 **The String Problem.**

Imagine that you are the person standing in the middle of this room, in which two strings are hanging down from the ceiling. Your goal is to tie together the two strings, but neither string is long enough so that you can reach out and grab the other string while holding either of the two strings. You have available a few clean paintbrushes, a can of paint, and a heavy canvas tarpaulin. How will you tie together the two strings? If you have trouble finding a solution, look at Figure 12.7.

Source: From Richard E. Mayer, "The Search for Insight: Grappling with Gestalt Psychology's Unanswered Questions," in *The Nature of Insight*, edited by R. J. Sternberg and J. E. Davidson. © 1995 MIT Press. Reprinted with permission from MIT Press.

People are told the following about a drug (Stanovich, 2003; Stanovich & West, 1999):

- 150 people received the drug and were not cured.
- 150 people received the drug and were cured.
- 75 people did not receive the drug and were not cured.
- 300 people did not receive the drug and were cured.

Will they understand exactly what they were told? Many people believe that the drug in this instance is helpful. In fact, the drug described is not helpful at all. On the contrary, it is harmful. Only 50% of the people who received the drug were cured (i.e., 150 of 300). In contrast, 80% of the people who did not receive the drug were cured (300 of 375).

The Problem-Solving Cycle

The **problem-solving cycle** includes: problem identification, problem definition, strategy formulation, organization of information, allocation of resources, monitoring, and evaluation (shown in Figure 12.2; see Bransford & Stein, 1993; Pretz, Naples, & Sternberg, 2003; Sternberg, 1986).

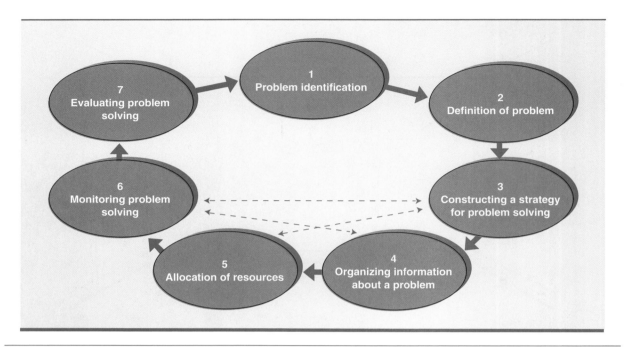

Figure 12.2 **The Problem-Solving Cycle.**
The steps of the problem-solving cycle include problem identification, problem definition, strategy formulation, organization of information, allocation of resources, monitoring, and evaluation.

In considering the steps, remember also the importance of flexibility in following the various steps of the cycle. Successful problem solving may involve occasionally tolerating some ambiguity regarding how best to proceed. Rarely can we solve problems by following any one optimal sequence of problem-solving steps. We may go back and forth through the steps. We can change their order, or even skip or add steps when it seems appropriate. Following is a description of each part of the problem-solving cycle.

1. *Problem identification:* Do we actually have a problem?
2. *Problem definition and representation:* What exactly is our problem?
3. *Strategy formulation:* How can we solve the problem? The strategy may involve **analysis**—breaking down the whole of a complex problem into manageable elements. Instead, or perhaps in addition, it may involve the complementary process of **synthesis**—putting together various elements to arrange them into something useful.

   Another pair of complementary strategies involves divergent and convergent thinking. In **divergent thinking**, you try to generate a diverse assortment of possible alternative solutions to a problem. Once you have considered a variety of possibilities, however, you must engage in **convergent thinking** to narrow down the multiple possibilities to converge on a single best answer.
4. *Organization of information:* How do the various pieces of information in the problem fit together?
5. *Resource allocation:* How much time, effort, money, etc., should I put into this problem?

"Relax, honey. Change is good."

Sometimes we don't recognize an important problem that confronts us.

Studies show that expert problem solvers (and better students) tend to devote more of their mental resources to global (big-picture) planning than do novice problem solvers. Novices (and poorer students) tend to allocate more time to local (detail-oriented) planning than do experts (Larkin et al., 1980; Sternberg, 1981). For example, better students are more likely than poorer students to spend more time in the initial phase, deciding how to solve a problem, and less time actually solving it (Bloom & Broder, 1950). By spending more time in advance deciding what to do, effective students are less likely to fall prey to false starts, winding paths, and all kinds of errors. When a person allocates more mental resources to planning on a large scale, he or she is able to save time and energy and to avoid frustration later on.

6. *Monitoring:* Am I on track as I proceed to solve the problem?
7. *Evaluation:* Did I solve the problem correctly?

Our emotions can influence how we implement the problem-solving cycle (Schwarz & Skurnik, 2003). In groups with participants with high measured emotional intelligence—that is, the ability to identify emotions in others and regulate emotions in oneself—emotional processing can positively influence problem solving (Jordan & Troth, 2004). In mathematicians, the ability to regulate their emotional state (among other factors) is related to higher problem-solving ability (Carlson & Bloom, 2005).

✔ CONCEPT CHECK

1. Why is the process of solving problems described as a cycle?
2. What are the different steps of the problem-solving cycle?

Types of Problems

Problems can be categorized according to whether they have clear paths to a solution (Davidson & Sternberg, 1984). **Well-structured problems** have clear paths to solutions. These problems also are termed *well-defined problems*. An example would be, "How do you find the area of a parallelogram?" **Ill-structured problems** lack clear paths to solutions (Shin et al., 2003). These problems are also termed *ill-defined problems*. An example is shown in Figure 12.1: "How do you tie together two suspended strings, when neither string is long enough to allow you to reach the other string while holding either of the strings?" Or how do you decide on which house to buy if each of the potential houses in which you are interested has advantages and disadvantages? Of course, in the real world of problems, these two categories may represent a continuum of clarity in problem solving rather than two discrete classes with a clear boundary between the two. Nonetheless, the categories are useful in understanding how people solve problems. Next, we consider each of these kinds of problems in more detail.

Well-Structured Problems

On tests in school, your teachers have asked you to tackle countless well-structured problems in specific content areas (e.g., math, history, geography). These problems had clear paths, if not necessarily easy paths, to their solutions—in particular, the application of a formula. In psychological research, cognitive psychologists might ask you to solve less content-specific kinds of well-structured problems. For example, cognitive psychologists often have studied a particular type of well-structured problem: the class of *move problems*, so termed because such problems require a series of moves to reach a final goal state. Perhaps the most well known of the move problems is one involving two antagonistic parties, whom we call "hobbits" and "orcs," in the *Investigating Cognitive Psychology: Move Problems* box.

 INVESTIGATING COGNITIVE PSYCHOLOGY
Move Problems

Three hobbits and three orcs are on a river bank. The hobbits and orcs need to cross over to the other side of the river. They have for this purpose a small rowboat that will hold just two people. There is one problem, however. If the number of orcs on either river bank exceeds the number of hobbits on that bank, the orcs will eat the hobbits on that bank. How can all six creatures get across to the other side of the river in a way that guarantees that they all arrive there with the forest intact? Try to solve the problem before reading on.

The solution to the problem is shown in Figure 12.3. The solution contains several features worth noting. First, the problem can be solved in a minimum of eleven steps, including the first and last steps. Second, the solution is essentially *linear* in nature. There is just one valid move (connecting two points with a line segment) at most steps of the problem solution. At all but two steps along the solution path, only one error can be made without violating the rules of the move problem: to go directly backward in the solution. At two steps, there are two possible forward-moving responses. But both of these lead toward the correct answer. Thus, again, the most likely error is to return to a previous state in the solution of the problem.

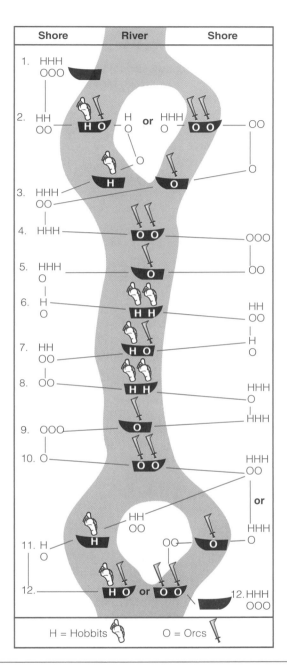

Figure 12.3   Solution to the Problem of the Hobbits and Orcs.

How can you get both the hobbits and the orcs to the other side of the river without any hobbits getting eaten? (For a more detailed description of the problem and its solution, refer to *Investigating Cognitive Psychology: Move Problems.*) What can you learn about your own methods of solving problems by seeing how you approached this particular problem?

Source: From *In Search of the Human Mind*, by Robert J. Sternberg. Copyright © 1995 by Harcourt Brace & Company. Reproduced by permission of the publisher.

People seem to make three main kinds of errors when trying to solve well-structured problems (Greeno, 1974; Simon & Reed, 1976; Thomas, 1974). These errors are:

(1) *Inadvertently moving backward*: They revert to a state that is further from the end goal, for instance, moving all of the "orcs" and "hobbits" back to the first side of the river.

(2) *Making illegal moves*: They make an illegal move—that is, a move that is not permitted according to the terms of the problem. For example, a move that resulted in having more than two individuals in the boat would be illegal.

(3) *Not realizing the nature of the next legal move*: They become "stuck"—they do not know what to do next, given the current stage of the problem. An example would be realizing that you must bring one "orc" or "hobbit" back across the river to its starting point before you can move any of the remaining characters.

One method for studying how to solve well-defined problems is to develop computer simulations. Here, the researcher's task is to create a computer program that can solve these problems. By developing the instructions a computer must execute to solve problems, the researcher may better understand how humans solve similar kinds of problems. According to one model of problem solving, the problem solver (which may be using human or artificial intelligence) must view the initial problem state and the goal state within a problem space (Wenke & Frensch, 2003). A **problem space** is the universe of all possible actions that can be applied to solving a problem, given any constraints that apply to the solution of the problem.

Algorithms are sequences of operations (in a problem space) that may be repeated over and over again and that, in theory, guarantee the solution to a problem (Hunt, 1975; Sternberg, 2000). Generally, an algorithm continues until it satisfies a condition determined by a program. Suppose a computer is provided with a well-defined problem and an appropriate hierarchy (program) of operations organized into procedural algorithms. The computer can readily calculate all possible operations and combinations of operations within the problem space. It also can determine the best possible sequence of steps to take to solve the problem.

Unlike computers, however, the human mind does not specialize in high-speed computations of numerous possible combinations. The limits of our working memory prohibit us from considering more than just a few possible operations at one time (Hambrick & Engle, 2003; Kintsch et al., 1999; see also Chapter 5). Newell and Simon recognized these limits and observed that humans must use mental shortcuts for solving problems. These mental shortcuts are termed **heuristics**—informal, intuitive, speculative strategies that sometimes lead to an effective solution and sometimes do not (see Chapter 11 for more on heuristics; Gilovich et al., 2002; Stanovich, 2003; Sternberg, 2000). Suppose we store, in long-term memory, several simple heuristics that we can apply to a variety of problems. We thereby can lessen the burden on our limited-capacity working memory. Studies suggest that when problem solvers are confronted with a problem for which they cannot immediately see an answer, effective problem solvers use the heuristic of means–ends analysis. In this strategy, the problem solver continually compares the current state and the goal state and takes steps to minimize the differences between the two states. Various other problem-solving heuristics include *working forward, working backward,* and *generate and test*. Table 12.1 illustrates how a problem solver might apply these heuristics to the aforementioned move problem (Greeno & Simon, 1988) and to a more common everyday problem (Hunt, 1994).

Table 12.1 Four Heuristics

These four heuristics may be used in solving the move problem illustrated in Figure 12.3.

Heuristic	Definition of Heuristic	Example of Heuristic Applied to the Move Problem (Greeno & Simon, 1988)	Example of Heuristic Applied to an Everyday Problem: How to Travel by Air from Your Home to Another Location Using the Most Direct Route Possible (Hunt, 1994)
Means–ends analysis	The problem solver analyzes the problem by viewing the end—the goal being sought—and then tries to decrease the distance between the current position in the problem space and the end goal in that space.	Try to get as many individuals on the far bank and as few people on the near bank as possible.	Try to minimize the distance between home and the destination.
Working forward	The problem solver starts at the beginning and tries to solve the problem from the start to the finish.	Evaluate the situation carefully with the six people on one bank and then try to move them step by step to the opposite bank.	Find the possible air routes leading from home toward the destination, and take the routes that seem most directly to lead to the destination.
Working backward	The problem solver starts at the end and tries to work backward from there.	Start with the final state—having all hobbits and all orcs on the far bank—and try to work back to the beginning state.	Find the possible air routes that reach the destination, and work backward to trace which of these routes can be most directly traced to originate at home.
Generate and test	The problem solver simply generates alternative courses of action, not necessarily in a systematic way, and then notices in turn whether each course of action will work.	This method works fairly well for the move problem because at most steps in the process, there is only one allowable forward move, and there are never more than two possibilities, both of which eventually will lead to the solution.	Find the various possible alternative routes leading from home, then see which of these routes might be used to end up at the destination. Choose the most direct route. Unfortunately, given the number of possible combinations of routes for air travel, this heuristic may not be very helpful.

Figure 12.4 shows a rudimentary problem space for the move problem. It illustrates that there may be any number of possible strategies for solving it.

Isomorphic Problems

Sometimes, two problems are **isomorphic**; that is, their formal structure is the same, and only their content differs. Sometimes, as in the case of the hobbits and orcs problem and a similar missionaries and cannibals problem, in which cannibals eat missionaries when they outnumber them, the isomorphism is obvious. Similarly, you can readily detect the isomorphism of many games that involve constructing words from jumbled or scrambled letters. Figure 12.5 also shows a different set of isomorphic problems. They illustrate some of the puzzles associated with isomorphic problems.

It often is extremely difficult to observe the underlying structural isomorphism of problems. It is also difficult to be able to apply problem-solving strategies from one

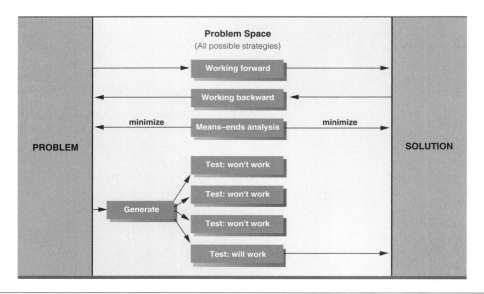

Figure 12.4 Problem Space.

A problem space contains all the possible strategies leading from the initial problem state to the solution (the goal state). This problem space, for example, shows four of the heuristics that might be used in solving the move problem illustrated in Figure 12.3.

Source: From *In Search of the Human Mind,* by Robert J. Sternberg. Copyright © 1995 by Harcourt Brace & Company. Reproduced by permission of the publisher.

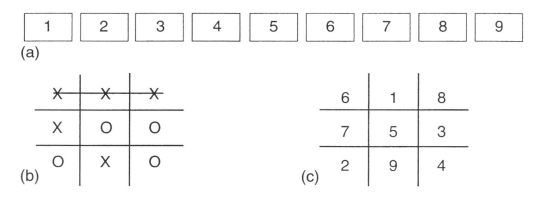

Figure 12.5 Isomorphic Problems.

Compare the problems illustrated in the games of (a) number scrabble, (b) tic-tac-toe, and (c) magic square. Number scrabble is based on equations. Which triples of numbers satisfy the equation $X + Y + Z = 15$? Tic-tac-toe requires one to produce three Xs or three Os in a row, column, or diagonal. The magic square requires one to place numbers in the tic-tac-toe board so that every row, column, and major diagonal adds up to 15. In what ways are these problems isomorphic? How do their differences in presentation affect the ease of representing and solving these problems? Although these problems seem different on their surface, they all require the same mental operations for their solution.

problem to another. For example, it may not be clear how an example from a text-book applies to another problem (e.g., one on a test). Problem solvers are particularly unlikely to detect isomorphisms when two problems are similar but not identical in structure. Furthermore, when the content or the surface characteristics of the problems differ sharply, detecting the isomorphism of the structure of problems is harder. For example, school-aged children may find it difficult to see the structural similarity between various word problems that are framed within different story situations. Similarly, physics students may have difficulty seeing the structural similarities among various physics problems when different kinds of materials are used. The problem of recognizing isomorphisms across varying contexts returns us to the recurring difficulties in problem representation.

Problem Representation Does Matter!

What is the key reason that some problems are easier to solve than others that are isomorphic to them? Consider the various versions of a problem known as the Tower of Hanoi. In this problem, the problem solver must use a series of moves to transfer a set of rings (usually three) from the first of three pegs to the third of the three pegs, using as few moves as possible (Figure 12.6). There are several electronic versions of the Tower of Hanoi on-line. You can find them by entering the search words "tower of Hanoi game" in a search engine. Try it out yourself!

Researchers presented this same basic problem in many different isomorphic forms, for example, as dots that have to be transferred between boxes (Kotovsky, Hayes, & Simon, 1985). They found that some forms of the problem took up to 16 times as long to solve as other forms. Although many factors influenced these findings, a major determinant of the relative ease of solving the problem was how the problem was represented. For example, in the form shown in Figure 12.6, the

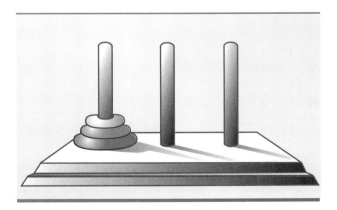

Figure 12.6   The Tower of Hanoi.

There are three discs of unequal sizes, positioned on the far-left side of three pegs so that the largest disc is at the bottom, the middle-sized disc is in the middle, and the smallest disc is on the top. Your task is to transfer all three discs to the peg on the far right, using the middle peg as a stationing area as needed. You may move only one disc at a time, and you may never move a larger disc on top of a smaller disc.

Source: From *Intelligence Applied: Understanding and Increasing Your Intellectual Skills*, by Robert J. Sternberg. Copyright © 1986 by Harcourt Brace & Company. Reproduced by permission of the publisher.

physically different sizes of the discs facilitated the mental representation of the restriction against moving larger discs onto smaller discs. Other forms of the problem
did not. There are many variations of this task, involving differing rules and restrictions (Chen, Tian, & Wang, 2007).

Problems such as the Tower of Hanoi challenge problem-solving skills, in
part through their demands on working memory. One study found that there is a
relationship between working-memory capacity and the ability to solve analytic
problems (Fleck, 2007). Other researchers had experimental participants do what
they called the "Tower of London" task, which is very similar to the Tower of
Hanoi (Welsh, Satterlee-Cartmell, & Stine, 1999). In this task, the goal was to
move a set of colored balls across different-sized pegs in order to match a target
configuration. As in the Tower of Hanoi, there were constraints on which balls
could be moved at a given time. The researchers also gave participants two tests
of working-memory capacity. They found that the measures of working-memory
capacity accounted for between 25% and 36% of the variance in how successful
participants were in solving the problem. Interestingly, mental-processing speed,
sometimes touted as a key to intelligence, showed no correlation with success in
solution. The brain areas that seem most involved in the Tower of Hanoi task are

Figure 12.7   Solution to the String Problem.

Many people assume that they must find a way to move themselves toward each string and then bring the two strings
together. They fail to consider the possibility of finding a way to get one of the strings to move toward them, such as by
tying something to one of the strings, then swinging the object as a pendulum, and grabbing the object when it swings
close to the other string. There is nothing in the problem that suggests that the person must move, rather than that the
string may move. Nevertheless, most people presuppose that the constraint exists. By placing an unnecessary and un-
warranted constraint on themselves, people make the problem insoluble.

Source: From Richard E. Mayer, "The Search for Insight: Grappling with Gestalt Psychology's Unanswered Questions," in *The Nature of
Insight*, edited by R. J. Sternberg and J. E. Davidson. Copyright © 1995 by MIT Press. Reprinted by permission.

the prefrontal cortex, bilateral parietal cortex, and bilateral premotor cortex (Fincham et al., 2002).

Recall the two-string problem, posed at the outset of this chapter. The solution to the two-string problem is shown in Figure 12.7. Many people find it extremely difficult to arrive at the solution. Many never do, no matter how hard they try. People who find the problem insoluble often err at Step 2 of the problem-solving cycle, after which they never recover. That is, by defining the problem as being one in which they must be able to move toward one string while holding another, they impose on themselves a constraint that makes the problem virtually insoluble.

Ill-Structured Problems and the Role of Insight

The two-string problem is an example of an ill-structured problem. In fact, although we occasionally may misrepresent well-structured problems, we are much more likely to have difficulty representing ill-structured problems. Before we explain the nature of ill-structured problems, try to solve a few more such problems. The following problems illustrate some of the difficulties created by the representation of ill-structured problems (after Sternberg, 1986). Be sure to try all three problems before you read about their solutions.

1. Haughty Harry has been asked to build a hat rack with a few given materials (see Figure 12.8). Can you help him construct the hat rack?

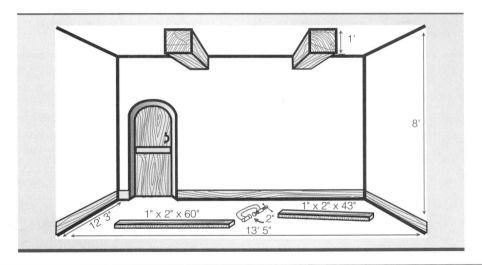

Figure 12.8 **Haughty Harry's Problem.**

Haughty Harry and several other job seekers were looking for work as carpenters. The site supervisor handed each applicant two sticks (a $1'' \times 2'' \times 60''$ stick and a $1'' \times 2'' \times 43''$ stick) and a $2''$ C-clamp. This situation is represented in Figure 12.8. The opening of the clamp is wide enough so that both sticks can be inserted and held together securely when the clamp is tightened. The supervisor ushered the job applicants into a room $12' 3'' \times 13' 5''$ with an $8'$ ceiling. Mounted on the ceiling were two $1' \times 1'$ beams, dividing the ceiling into thirds lengthwise. She told the applicants that she would hire the first applicant who could build a hat rack capable of supporting her hard hat, using just the two sticks and the C-clamp. She could hire only one person. So she recommended that the applicants not try to help one another. What should Harry do?

Source: From Richard E. Mayer, "The Search for Insight: Grappling with Gestalt Psychology's Unanswered Questions," in *The Nature of Insight*, edited by R. J. Sternberg and J. E. Davidson. Copyright © 1995 MIT Press. Reprinted with permission from MIT Press.

2. A woman who lived in a small town married 20 different men in that same town. All of them are still living, and she never divorced any of them. Yet she broke no laws. How could she do this?
3. You have loose black and brown socks in a drawer, mixed in a ratio of five black socks for every brown one. How many socks do you have to take out of that drawer to be assured of having a pair of the same color?

Both the two-string problem and each of the three preceding problems are ill-structured problems. There are no clear, readily available paths to solution. By definition, ill-structured problems do not have well-defined problem spaces. Problem solvers have difficulty constructing appropriate mental representations for modeling these problems and their solutions. For such problems, much of the difficulty is in constructing a plan for sequentially following a series of steps that inch ever closer to their solution. In one study, both domain knowledge and justification skills proved to be important for solving both ill- and well-structured problems. Justification skills are important because ill-structured problems can be represented in different ways and often have alternative solutions. Thus, problem solvers need to choose and justify their selection of a particular representation and solution. Additional cognitive and affective factors, including attitudes toward science and regulation of cognition, are also important for the solving of ill-structured problems (Shin, Jonassen, & McGee, 2003).

The preceding ill-structured problems are *insight problems* because you need to see the problem in a novel way. In particular, you need to see it differently from how you would probably see the problem at first, and differently from how you would probably solve problems in general. That is, you must restructure your representation of the problem to solve it.

Insight is a distinctive and sometimes seemingly sudden understanding of a problem or of a strategy that aids in solving the problem. Often, an insight involves reconceptualizing a problem or a strategy in a totally new way. Insight often involves detecting and combining relevant old and new information to gain a novel view of the problem or of its solution. Although insights may feel as though they are sudden, they are often the result of much prior thought and hard work. Without this work, the insight would never have occurred. Insight can be involved in solving well-structured problems, but it more often is associated with the rocky and twisting path to solution that characterizes ill-structured problems. For many years, psychologists interested in problem solving have been trying to figure out the true nature of insight.

What are the solutions to the insight problems we presented? Consider first the hat-rack problem. Harry was unable to solve the problem before Sally quickly whipped together a hat rack like the one shown in Figure 12.9. To solve the problem, Sally had to redefine her view of the materials in a way that allowed her to conceive of a C-clamp as a hat holder.

The woman who was involved in multiple marriages is a minister. The critical element for solving this problem is to recognize that the word *married* may be used to describe the performance of the marriage ceremony. So the minister married the 20 men but did not herself become wedded to any of them. To solve this problem, you had to redefine your interpretation of the term *married*. Others have suggested yet additional possibilities. For example, perhaps the woman was an actress and only married the men in her role as an actress. Or perhaps the woman's multiple marriages were annulled so she never technically divorced any of the men.

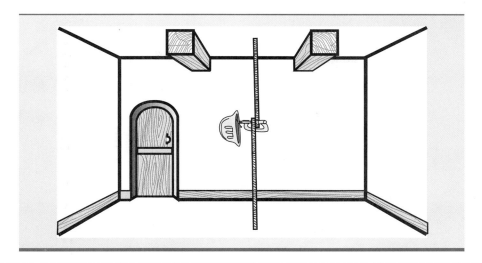

Figure 12.9 Solution to Haughty Harry's Problem.
Were you able to modify your definition of the materials available in a way that helped you solve the problem?
Source: From *Intelligence Applied: Understanding and Increasing Your Intellectual Skills,* by Robert J. Sternberg. Copyright © 1986 by Harcourt Brace & Company. Reproduced by permission of the publisher.

As for the socks, you need only to take out three socks to be assured of having a pair of the same color. The ratio information is irrelevant. Whether the first two socks you withdraw match in color, the third certainly will match at least one of the first two.

Early Gestaltist Views

Gestalt psychologists emphasized the importance of the whole as more than a collection of parts. In regard to problem solving, Gestalt psychologists held that insight problems require problem solvers to perceive the problem as a whole. Gestalt psychologist Max Wertheimer (1945/1959) wrote about **productive thinking**, which involves insights that go beyond the bounds of existing associations. He distinguished it from *reproductive thinking,* which is based on existing associations involving what is already known. According to Wertheimer, insightful (productive) thinking differs fundamentally from reproductive thinking. In solving the insight problems given in this chapter, you had to break away from your existing associations and see each problem in an entirely new light. Productive thinking also can be applied to well-structured problems.

Wertheimer's colleague Wolfgang Köhler (1927) studied insight in non-human primates, particularly a caged chimpanzee named Sultan. In Köhler's view, the ape's behavior illustrated insight (see Figure 12.10). To Köhler and other Gestaltists, insight is a special process. It involves thinking that differs from normal, linear information processing.

The Neo-Gestaltist View

Some researchers have found that insightful problem solving can be distinguished from non-insightful problem solving in two ways (Metcalfe, 1986; Metcalfe & Wiebe, 1987). For one thing, when given routine problems to solve, problem solvers show remarkable accuracy in their ability to predict their own success in solving a

Figure 12.10 **Insight Demonstrated by Chimpanzee.**

Gestalt psychologist Wolfgang Köhler placed an ape in an enclosure with a few boxes. At the top of the cage, just out of reach, was a bunch of bananas. After the ape unsuccessfully tried to jump and to stretch to reach the bananas, the ape showed sudden insight: The ape realized that the boxes could be stacked on top of one another to make a structure tall enough to reach the bunch of bananas.

problem prior to any attempt to solve it. In contrast, when given insight problems, problem solvers show poor ability to predict their own success prior to trying to solve the problems. Not only were successful problem solvers pessimistic about their ability to solve insight problems, but unsuccessful problem solvers were often optimistic about their ability to solve them.

In addition, the investigators used a clever methodology to observe the problem-solving process while participants were solving routine versus insight problems. Routine problems included algebra problems, such as "$(3x^2 + 2x + 10)(3x) = .$" Insight problems included problems such as "A prisoner was attempting escape from a tower. He found in his cell a rope which was half long enough to permit him to reach the ground safely. He divided the rope in half and tied the two parts together and escaped. How could he have done this?" At 15-second intervals, participants paused briefly to rate how close ("warm") versus far ("cold") they felt they were to reaching a solution. Consider first what happened for routine problems, such as algebra, or the Tower of Hanoi. Participants showed increases in their feelings of warmth as they drew closer to reaching a correct solution. For insight problems, however, participants showed no such increases. Figure 12.11 shows a comparison of participants' reported feelings of warmth for solving algebra problems versus insight problems. In solving insight problems, participants showed no increasing feelings of warmth until moments before abruptly realizing the solution and correctly solving the problem. Metcalfe's findings certainly seem to support the Gestaltist view that there is something special about insightful problem solving, as distinct from non-insightful, routine problem solving. The specific nature and underlying mechanisms of insightful problem solving have yet to be addressed by this research, however.

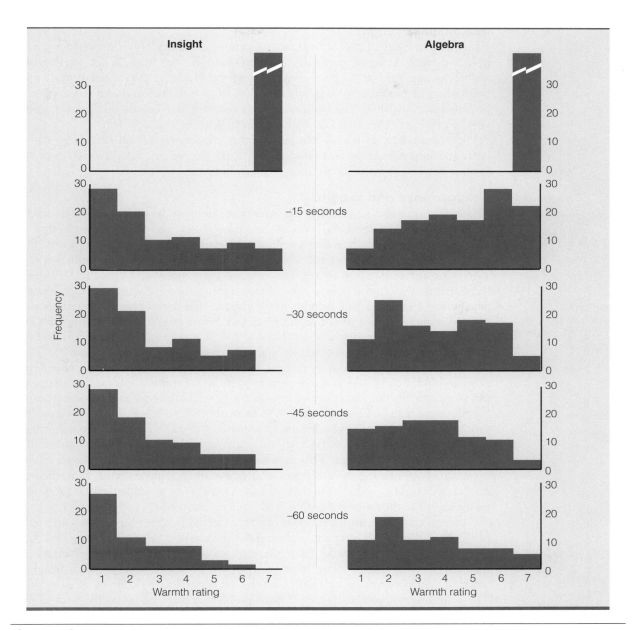

Figure 12.11   Feelings of Warmth in Insightful Problem Solving.

When Janet Metcalfe presented participants with routine problems and insight problems, they showed clear differences in their feelings of warmth as they approached a solution to the problems. These frequency histograms (bar graphs in which the area of each bar indicates the frequency for the given interval of time) show comparative feelings of warmth during the four 15-second intervals prior to solving the problems. When solving insight problems, participants showed no incremental increases in feelings of warmth, whereas when solving routine problems, participants showed distinct incremental increases in feelings of warmth. (From Metcalfe & Wiebe, 1987, pp. 242, 245.)

Insights into Insight

According to Smith (1995a), insights need not be sudden "a-ha" experiences. They may and often do occur gradually and incrementally over time. When an insightful solution is needed but not forthcoming, sleep may help produce a solution. In both mathematical problem solving and solution of a task that requires understanding underlying rules, sleep has been shown to increase the likelihood that an insight will be produced (Stickgold & Walker, 2004; Wagner et al., 2004).

Unfortunately, insights—like many other aspects of human thinking—can be both startlingly brilliant and dead wrong. How do we fall into mental traps that lead us down false paths as we try to reach solutions?

Neuroscience and Insight

Neuroimaging studies suggest that the activity of our brain during rest can be divided up into several different networks. Some of these networks are also active when we engage in problem solving. This indicates that at least portions of the thought processes are the same when we are problem solving and when we have thoughts during rest (Andreasen et al., 1995; Christoff et al., 2004; Damoiseaux et al., 2006; Kounios et al., 2008). fMRI studies show that activity in the right anterior superior-temporal gyrus increases when a person experiences an insight. Furthermore, EEGs also record a burst of high-frequency activity during insight (Jung-Beeman et al., 2004). In fact, before insights even become conscious, activity in the right hemisphere can be observed. It is therefore generally assumed that the right hemisphere has a special role in insight processes (Bowden et al., 2005).

The right hippocampus is critical in the formation of an insightful solution (Luo & Niki, 2003). (As you may remember from Chapters 2 and 5, the hippocampus is integral to the formation of new memories. Therefore it makes sense that the hippocampus would be involved in the formation of an insightful solution, as this process involves combining relevant information stored in memory.) Another study demonstrated a spike of activity in the right anterior temporal area immediately before an insight is formed. This area is active during all types of problem solving, as it involves making connections among distantly related items (Jung-Beeman et al., 2004). This spike in activity, however, suggests a sudden understanding of relationships within a problem that leads to a solution.

Neural correlates measured even before an individual sees a problem can predict if insight will occur. In one study, during the preparation prior to viewing of a problem, participants who would later generate an insightful solution had substantial activation in the frontal lobes, whereas those who would not generate an insightful solution had comparable activation in the occipital lobes (Kounios et al., 2006). These findings suggest, first, that certain problem solvers are more likely to use insight than others. Second, they suggest that insight involves some advanced planning that occurs before a problem is even presented.

✔ CONCEPT CHECK

1. What is the difference between well-structured and ill-structured problems?
2. When are two problems isomorphic?
3. What is insight?
4. According to Neo-Gestaltism, how can insightful problem solving and non-insightful problem solving be distinguished?
5. Are insights always sudden?

Obstacles and Aids to Problem Solving

Several factors can hinder or enhance problem solving. Among them are mental sets as well as positive and negative transfer. Incubation plays a role in problem solving as well. In the next sections, we will explore these factors in more detail.

Mental Sets, Entrenchment, and Fixation

One factor that can hinder problem solving is **mental set**—a frame of mind involving an existing model for representing a problem, a problem context, or a procedure for problem solving. Another term for mental set is *entrenchment*. When problem solvers have an entrenched mental set, they fixate on a strategy that normally works well in solving many problems but that does not work well in solving this particular problem. For example, in the two-string problem, you may fixate on strategies that involve moving yourself toward the string, rather than moving the string toward you. In the oft-marrying minister problem, you may fixate on the notion that to marry someone is to become wedded to the person.

Mental sets also can influence the solution of rather routine problems. For example, consider "water-jar" problems (Luchins, 1942). In water-jar problems, participants are asked how to measure out a certain amount of water using three different jars. Each jar holds a different amount of water. *Investigating Cognitive Psychology: Luchin's Water-Jar Problems* shows the problems used by Luchins. Look at the box and try to solve the problems yourself before you read on.

Problems 7 through 11 can be solved in a much simpler way. One need use just two of the jars. Problem 7 can be solved by $A - C$. Problem 8 can be solved by $A + C$, and so on. People who are given Problems 1 through 6 to solve generally continue to use the $B - A - 2C$ formula in solving Problems 7 through 11. Consider, in Luchins's original experiment, those participants who solved the first set of problems. Between 64% and 83% of them went on to solve the last set of problems by using the less simple strategy. What happened to the control participants who were not given the first set of problems? Only 1% to 5% failed to apply the simpler solutions to the last set of problems. They had no established mental set that interfered with their seeing things in a new and simpler way.

Another type of mental set involves fixation on a particular use (function) for an object. Specifically, **functional fixedness** is the inability to realize that something known to have a particular use may also be used for performing other functions (German & Barrett, 2005; Rakoczy et al., 2009). Functional fixedness prevents us from solving new problems by using old tools in novel ways. Becoming free of functional fixedness is what first allowed people to use a reshaped coat hanger to get into a locked car. It is also what first allowed thieves to pick simple spring door locks with a credit card.

Another type of mental set is considered an aspect of social cognition. **Stereotypes** are beliefs that members of a social group tend more or less uniformly to have particular types of characteristics. We seem to learn many stereotypes during childhood. For example, cross-cultural studies of children show their increasing knowledge about—and use of—gender stereotypes across the childhood years (Neto, Williams, & Widner, 1991; Seguino, 2007). Stereotype awareness, for a variety of groups, develops in most children between the ages of 6 and 10 (McKown & Weinstein, 2003). Stereotypes often arise in the same way that other kinds of mental sets develop. We observe a particular instance or set of instances of some pattern. We then may overgeneralize

INVESTIGATING COGNITIVE PSYCHOLOGY
Luchins's Water-Jar Problems

How do you measure out the right amount of water using Jars A, B, and C? You need to use up to three jars to obtain the required amounts of water (measured in numbers of cups) in the last column. Columns A, B, and C show the capacity of each jar. The first problem, for example, requires you to get 20 cups of water from just two of the jars, a 29-cup one (Jar A) and a 3-cup one (Jar B). Easy: Just fill Jar A, and then empty out 9 cups from this jar by taking out 3 cups three times, using Jar B. Problem 2 isn't too hard, either. Fill Jar B with 127 cups, then empty out 21 cups using Jar A, and then empty out 6 cups, using Jar C twice. Now try the rest of the problems yourself. (After Luchins, 1942.)

	Jars Available for Use			
Problem Number	A	B	C	Required Amount (CUPS)
1	29	3	0	20
2	21	127	3	100
3	14	163	25	99
4	18	43	10	5
5	9	42	6	21
6	20	59	4	31
7	23	49	3	20
8	15	39	3	18
9	28	76	3	25
10	18	48	4	22
11	14	36	8	6

Luchins, Abraham S. (1942). Mechanization in Problem Solving: The Effect of Einstellung, *Psychological Monographs*, 54(6), 248. © 1942, by Dr. Abraham S. Luchins. Reprinted by permission.

If you are like many people solving these problems, you will have found a formula that works for all the remaining problems. You fill up Jar B. Then you pour out of it the amount of water you can put into Jar A. Then you twice pour out of it the amount of water you can put into Jar C. The formula, therefore, is B − A − 2C.

from those limited observations. We may assume that all future instances similarly will demonstrate that pattern. For example, we may observe that some African Americans can run very fast. If we then conclude that every African American is a fast runner, we do have a stereotype because not every African American is a fast runner. Of course, when the stereotypes are used to target particular scapegoats for societal mistreatment, grave social consequences result for the targets of stereotypes. The targets are not the only ones to suffer from stereotypes, however. Like other kinds of mental sets, stereotypes hinder the problem-solving abilities of the individuals who used them. These people limit their thinking by using set stereotypes.

Negative and Positive Transfer

Often, people have particular mental sets that prompt them to fixate on one aspect of a problem or one strategy for problem solving to the exclusion of other possible relevant ones. They are carrying knowledge and strategies for solving one kind of problem to a different kind of problem. **Transfer** is any carryover of knowledge or skills from one problem situation to another (Detterman & Sternberg, 1993; Gentile, 2000). Transfer can be either negative or positive. **Negative transfer** occurs when solving an earlier problem makes it harder to solve a later one. Sometimes an early problem gets an individual on a wrong track. For example, police may have difficulty solving a political crime because such a crime differs so much from the kinds of crime that they typically deal with. Or when presented with a new tool, a person may operate it in a way similar to the way in which he or she operated a tool with which he or she was already familiar (Besnard & Cacitti, 2005). **Positive transfer** occurs when the solution of an earlier problem makes it easier to solve a new problem. That is, sometimes the transfer of a mental set can be an aid to problem solving. For instance, one may transfer early math skills, such as addition, to advanced math problems of the kinds found in algebra or physics (Bassok & Holyoak, 1989; Chen & Daehler, 1989; see also Campbell & Robert, 2008).

Transfer of Analogies

Researchers designed some elegant studies of positive transfer involving analogies (Gick & Holyoak, 1980, 1983). To appreciate their results, you need to become familiar with a problem first used by Karl Duncker (1945), often called the "radiation problem." It is described in the *Investigating Cognitive Psychology: Problems Involving Transfer*.

 INVESTIGATING COGNITIVE PSYCHOLOGY
Problems Involving Transfer

The Radiation Problem

Imagine that you are a doctor treating a patient with a malignant stomach tumor. You cannot operate on the patient because of the severity of the cancer. But unless you destroy the tumor somehow, the patient will die. You could use high-intensity X-rays to destroy the tumor. Unfortunately, the intensity of X-rays needed to destroy the tumor also will destroy healthy tissue through which the rays must pass. X-rays of lesser intensity will spare the healthy tissue, but they will be insufficiently powerful to destroy the tumor. What kind of procedure could you employ that will destroy the tumor without also destroying the healthy tissue surrounding the tumor?

Duncker had in mind a particular insightful solution as the optimal one for this problem. Figure 12.12 shows the solution pictorially.

Prior to presenting Duncker's radiation problem, participants received another, easier problem. This particular problem was called the "military problem" (Holyoak, 1984, p. 205).

The Military Problem

A general wishes to capture a fortress located in the center of a country. There are many roads radiating outward from the fortress. All have been mined. Although small groups of men can pass over the roads safely, any large force will detonate the mines. A full-scale direct attack is therefore impossible. What should the general do?

Think about this: What are the commonalities between the two problems, and what is an elemental strategy that can be derived by comparing the two problems?

Table 12.2 Correspondence between the Radiation and the Military Problems

What are the commonalities between the two problems, and what is an elemental strategy that can be derived by comparing the two problems? (After Gick & Holyoak, 1983.)

Military Problem

Initial State Goal: Use army to capture fortress

    Resources: Sufficiently large army

    Constraint: Unable to send entire army along one road

Solution Plan: Send small groups along multiple roads simultaneously

Outcome: Fortress captured by army

Radiation Problem

Initial State Goal: Use rays to destroy tumor

    Resources: Sufficiently powerful rays

    Constraint: Unable to administer high-intensity rays from one direction only

Solution Plan: Administer low-intensity rays from multiple directions simultaneously

Outcome: Tumor destroyed by rays

Convergence Schema

Initial State Goal: Use force to overcome a central target

    Resources: Sufficiently great force

    Constraint: Unable to apply full force along one path alone

Solution Plan: Apply weak forces along multiple paths simultaneously

Outcome: Central target overcome by force

M. L. Gick and K. J. Holyoak (1983), "Schema Induction and Analogical Transfer," *Cognitive Psychology*, Vol. 15, pp. 1–38. Reprinted by permission of Elsevier.

The correspondence between the radiation and military problems is actually quite close, although not perfect (see Table 12.2). The question is whether producing a group-convergence solution to the military problem helped participants in solving the radiation problem. Consider participants who received the military problem with the convergence solution and then were given a hint to apply it in some way to the radiation problem. About 75% of the participants reached the correct solution to the radiation problem. This figure compared with less than 10% of the participants who did not receive the military story first but instead received no prior story or only an irrelevant one.

In another experiment, participants were not given the convergence solution to the military problem. They had to figure it out for themselves. About 50% of the participants generated the convergence solution to the military problem. Of these, 41% went on to generate a parallel solution to the radiation problem. That is, positive transfer was *weaker* when participants produced the original solution themselves than when the solution to the first problem was given to them (41%, as compared with 75%).

The investigators found that the usefulness of the military problem as an analog to the radiation problem depended on the induced mental set with which the problem solver approached the problems. Consider what happened when participants were asked to memorize the military story under the guise that it was a story-recall experiment and then were given the radiation problem to solve.

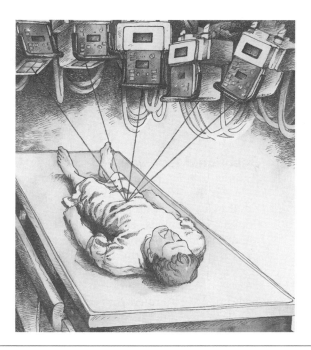

Figure 12.12   The Radiation Problem.

The solution to the X-ray problem involving the treatment of a patient with a tumor involves dispersion. The idea is to direct weak X-radiation toward the tumor from a number of different points outside the body. No single set of rays would be strong enough to destroy either the healthy tissue or the tumor. However, the rays would be aimed so that they all converged at one spot within the body—the spot that houses the tumor. This solution actually is used today in some X-ray treatments, except that a rotating source of X-rays is used for dispersing rays.

Source: From *In Search of the Human Mind,* by Robert J. Sternberg. Copyright © 1995 by Harcourt Brace & Company. Reproduced by permission of the publisher.

Only 30% of participants produced the convergence solution to the radiation problem. The investigators also found that positive transfer improved if two, rather than just one, analogous problems were given in advance of the radiation problem.

Researchers have expanded these findings to encompass problems other than the radiation problem. They found that when the domains or the contexts for the two problems were more similar, participants were more likely to see and apply the analogy (see Holyoak, 1990). Similar patterns of data were found with various types of problems involving electricity and mathematical insight (Davidson & Sternberg, 1984; Gentner & Gentner, 1983; Novick & Holyoak, 1991).

Perhaps the most crucial aspect of these studies is that people have trouble noticing analogies unless they explicitly are told to look for them. Consider studies involving physics problems. Positive transfer from solved examples to unsolved problems was more likely among students who specifically tried to understand *why* particular examples were solved as they were, as compared with students who sought only to understand *how* particular problems were solved as they were (Chi et al., 1989). Based on these findings, we generally need to be looking for analogies to find them. We often will not find them unless we explicitly seek them.

People sometimes do not recognize the surface similarities of problems (Bassok, 2003). Other times they are fooled by surface similarities into believing two different kinds of problems are the same (Bassok, Wu, & Olseth, 1995; Gentner, 2000). Sometimes even experienced problem solvers are led astray. They believe that similar surface structures indicate comparable deep structures. For example, problem solvers may use the verbal content rather than the mathematical operations required in a mathematical problem to classify the problem as being of a certain kind (Blessing & Ross, 1996).

Intentional Transfer: Searching for Analogies

In order to find analogies between two problems, one must perceive the relationships between them (Gentner, 1983, 2000). The actual content attributes of the problems are irrelevant. In other words, what matters in analogies is not the similarity of the content but how closely their structural systems of relationships match. Because we are accustomed to considering the importance of the content, we find it difficult to push the content to the background. It also is difficult to bring form (structural relationships) to the foreground. For example, the differing content makes the analogy between the military problem and the radiation problem hard to recognize and impedes positive transfer from one problem to the other.

The opposite phenomenon is **transparency**, in which people see analogies where they do not exist because of similarity of content. In making analogies, we need to be sure we are focusing on the relationships between the two terms being compared, not just their surface content attributes. For example, in studying for final exams in two psychology courses, you may need different strategies when studying for a closed-book essay exam than for an open-book, multiple-choice exam. Transparency of content may lead to negative transfer between non-isomorphic problems if care is not taken to avoid such transfer.

Incubation

For solving many problems, the chief obstacle is not the need to find a suitable strategy for positive transfer. Rather, it is to avoid obstacles resulting from negative transfer. **Incubation**—putting the problem aside for a while without consciously thinking about it—offers one way in which to minimize negative transfer. It involves taking a pause from the stages of problem solving. For example, suppose you find that you are unable to solve a problem. None of the strategies you can think of seem to work. Try setting the problem aside for a while to let it incubate. During incubation, you must not consciously think about the problem. You do, however, allow for the possibility that the problem will be processed subconsciously. Some investigators of problem solving have even asserted that incubation is an essential stage of the problem-solving process (e.g., Cattell, 1971; von Helmholtz, 1896). Others have failed to find experimental support for the phenomenon of incubation (e.g., Baron, 1988).

A recent meta–analysis (Sio & Ormerod, 2009) found that, as most of the time in psychological research, the state of affairs is complex. When people have more time to prepare for the solving of a problem, incubation periods are usually more fruitful. Likewise, being occupied with tasks that are highly cognitively demanding is detrimental to the effect of an incubation period. The effect of incubation furthermore depends on the kind of task, with performance on divergent-thinking tasks (where something has to be produced) benefiting more than performance on linguistic tasks, for example. Incubation seems to help because people continue to process, below consciousness, information about a problem on which they are incubating at the same time that they are attending to other matters.

Neuroscience and Planning during Problem Solving

One way to invest enough initial time in a problem is through the formation of a plan of action for the problem. As previously discussed, planning saves time and improves performance. In one study employing variants of the Tower of Hanoi, when participants became more familiar with this type of problem, they showed increased planning times, which resulted in a decrease in the total number of moves (Gunzelmann & Anderson, 2003). These results highlight the importance of planning for efficient problem solving.

Recall from Chapter 3 that the frontal lobes are involved in high-level cognitive processes. It is therefore not surprising that the frontal lobes and in particular the prefrontal cortex are essential for planning for complex problem-solving tasks (Unterrainer & Owen, 2006). A number of studies using a variety of neuropsychological methods, including functional magnetic resonance imaging (fMRI) and positron emission tomography (PET), have highlighted activation in this region of the brain during problem solving (Unterrainer & Owen, 2006). Additionally, both the left and right prefrontal areas are active during the planning stage of complex problem solving (Newman et al., 2003). When a participant gives an incorrect response in a problem-solving task and therefore has to continue working on the problem, he or she reveals greater bilateral prefrontal activation than is associated with a correct response (Unterrainer et al., 2004). This finding would suggest that if the initial plan fails, problem solvers must devise a new plan, thereby activating the prefrontal cortex.

Further evidence for the importance of the prefrontal regions in problem solving can be seen in cases of traumatic brain injury. Both problem solving and planning ability decline following traumatic brain injury (Catroppa & Anderson, 2006). In fact, with regard to the problem-solving ability of patients with traumatic brain injury, those patients who performed best were ones with limited damage to the left prefrontal regions (Cazalis et al., 2006).

In the Tower of London task, other areas, including the premotor cortex and the parietal regions, were also activated (Newman et al., 2003; Unterrainer & Owen, 2006). This additional activation is likely the result of the need for attention and planning for movement. In addition to the prefrontal regions, the same areas active during use of visual spatial working memory are also active during solution of the Tower of London (Baker et al., 1996).

Intelligence and Complex Problem Solving

Cognitive approaches for studying information processing can be applied to more complex problem-solving tasks, such as analogies, series problems (e.g., completing a numerical or figural series), and syllogisms (Sternberg, 1977, 1983, 1984; see Chapter 11). The idea is to take the kinds of tasks used on conventional intelligence tests and to isolate components of intelligence. *Components* are the mental processes used in performing these tasks, such as translating a sensory input into a mental representation, transforming one conceptual representation into another, or translating a conceptual representation into a motor output (Sternberg, 1982). Many investigators have elaborated on and expanded this basic approach (Lohman, 2000, 2005; Wenke, Frensch, & Funke, 2005). For example, in processing the analogy DOG : BOXER :: CAT : SIAMESE, one needs to encode the terms of the problem, infer the relation between DOG and BOXER, and then apply that relation from CAT to SIAMESE (see also Figure 12.13).

There are significant correlations between speed in executing these processes and performance on other, traditional intelligence tests. However, a more intriguing discovery is that participants who score higher on traditional intelligence tests take longer to encode the terms of the problem than do less intelligent participants. But they make up for the extra time by taking less time to perform the remaining components of the task. In general, more intelligent participants take longer during *global planning*—encoding the problem and formulating a general strategy for attacking the problem (or set of problems). But they take less time for *local planning*—forming and implementing strategies for the details of the task (Sternberg, 1981).

The advantage of spending more time on global planning is the increased likelihood that the overall strategy will be correct. Thus, when taking more time is advantageous, brighter people may take longer to do something than will less bright people. For example, the brighter person might spend more time researching and planning for writing a term paper but less time in the actual writing of it. This same differential in time allocation has been shown in other tasks as well. An example would be in solving physics problems (Larkin et al., 1980; see Sternberg, 1979, 1985a). That is, more intelligent people seem to spend more time planning for and encoding the problems they face. But they spend less time engaging in the other components of task performance. This may relate to the previously mentioned metacognitive attribute many include in their notions of intelligence.

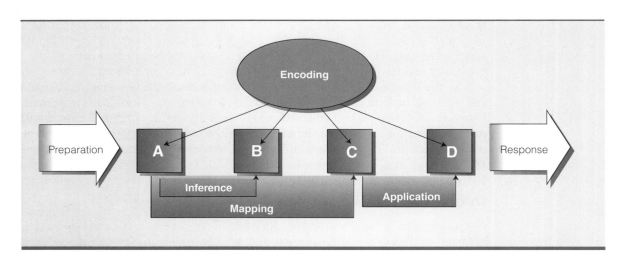

Figure 12.13 Mental Processes in Solving Analogies.

In the solution of an analogy problem, the problem solver must first encode the problem A is to B as C is to D. The problem solver then must infer the relationship between A and B. Next, the problem solver must map the relationship between A and B to the relationship between C and each of the possible solutions to the analogy. Finally, the problem solver must apply the relationship to choose which of the possible solutions is the correct solution to the problem.

Researchers have also studied information processing of people engaged in complex problem-solving situations, such as playing chess and performing logical derivations (Bilalic et al., 2008; Kiesel et al., 2009; Simon, 1976). For example, a simple, brief task might require the participants first to view an arithmetic or geometric series. Then they must figure out the rule underlying the progression. And finally they must guess what numeral or geometric figure might come next. More complex tasks might include some of the tasks mentioned before, like the water-jar problem.

✔ CONCEPT CHECK

1. How can mental sets impair our problem-solving ability?

2. What is negative transfer?

3. Are analogies always useful for problem solving?

4. What is the role of incubation in problem solving?

Expertise: Knowledge and Problem Solving

Even people who do not have expertise in cognitive psychology recognize that knowledge, particularly expert knowledge, greatly enhances problem solving. **Expertise** is superior skills or achievement reflecting a well-developed and well-organized knowledge base. What interests cognitive psychologists is the reason that expertise enhances problem solving. Why can experts solve problems in their field more successfully than can novices? Do experts know more problem-solving algorithms, heuristics, and other strategies? Do experts know better strategies? Or do they just use these strategies more often? What do experts know that makes the problem-solving process more effective for them than for novices in a field? Is it all talent or just acquired skill?

Organization of Knowledge

Do you think one can distinguish beers by their flavor? In one study, beer experts and beer novices experienced tasting a series of beers (Valentin et al., 2007). Both groups could sort the beers equally well. However, the beer experts performed better on subsequent recognition tasks (Valentin et al., 2007). These findings suggest that there was no difference in perceptual abilities between the experts and the novices, but there was a difference in memory between these two groups (Valentin et al., 2007). The researchers concluded that the beer experts had a superior framework for encoding and retrieving the new beer information (Valentin et al., 2007).

Knowledge can interact with understanding in problem solving as well (Whitten & Graesser, 2003). Consider a study investigating how knowledge interacts with coherence of a text. Investigators presented children with biology texts (McNamara et al., 1996). Half the children in the study had high levels of domain knowledge about biology and half had low levels. In addition, half the texts were highly coherent, meaning that they made clear how the various concepts in the text related to each other. The other half of the texts were of low coherence, meaning that they were more difficult to read because the ideas did not flow smoothly. Readers then had to do a variety of problem-solving tasks based on what they had read.

As the authors predicted, participants with low domain knowledge performed better when the texts were highly coherent. This finding suggests that, in general, learners do better when they are presented new material in a coherent way.

Surprisingly, however, the high-knowledge group performed better when the texts were of low rather than high coherence. The authors of the study suggested that high-knowledge readers may have been, essentially, on automatic pilot when reading the high-coherence texts, not paying much attention because they thought they knew what was in the texts. The low-coherence texts forced them to pay attention. These results point out the importance of attentional processes when people solve problems. This is particularly relevant in domains in which they are expert and in which they therefore may not feel they have to pay attention.

Elaboration of Knowledge

Do you remember the study with chess experts and novices described at the very beginning of this chapter in *Believe It or Not?* What differentiated the experts from the novices was the amount, organization, and use of knowledge. There were two tasks in the chess study: One involved a random array of pieces and the other a meaningful arrangement of pieces (Figure 12.14). For both chess tasks, the experts used heuristics for storing and retrieving information about the positions of the pieces on the chess-board. The novices, to the contrary, had not stored significant knowledge about positions. The key difference, therefore, was that chess experts had stored and organized in memory tens of thousands of particular board positions. When they saw sensible board positions, they could use the knowledge they had in memory to help them. They were able to remember the various board positions as integrated, organized chunks of information. As you may recall from Chapter 5, the ability to chunk information into meaningful units allows for superior memory and capacity. For random scatterings of pieces on the board, however, the knowledge of the experts was of no use. The experts had no advantage over the novices. Like the novices, they had to try to memorize the distinctive interrelations among many discrete pieces and positions. This memorization requires the storage of many more items, thus taxing one's memory abilities.

Retrieval processes involving recognition of board arrangements are instrumental in grand master–level chess players' success when compared with novices' play (Gobet & Simon, 1996a, 1996b, 1996c). Even when grand masters are time-constrained so that look-ahead processes are curtailed, their constrained performance does not differ substantially from their unconstrained playing. Thus, an organized knowledge system is relatively more important to experts' performance in chess than even the processes involved in predicting future moves.

Other studies have examined experts in other domains like radiology (Lesgold et al., 1988), physics (Larkin et al., 1980), and meditation (Brefczynski-Lewis et al., 2007). These studies revealed the same thing again and again. What differentiated experts from novices were their schemas for solving problems within their own domains of expertise (Glaser & Chi, 1988). The schemas of experts involve large, highly interconnected units of knowledge. They are organized according to underlying structural similarities among knowledge units. In contrast, the schemas of novices involve relatively small and disconnected units of knowledge. They are organized according to superficial similarities (Bryson et al., 1991).

Experts and novices also differ in how they classify various problems, describe the essential nature of problems, and how they determine and describe solutions (Chi, Glaser, & Rees, 1982; Larkin et al., 1980). One study exploring problem-solving strategies in both expert and novice mathematicians noted a difference in the use of

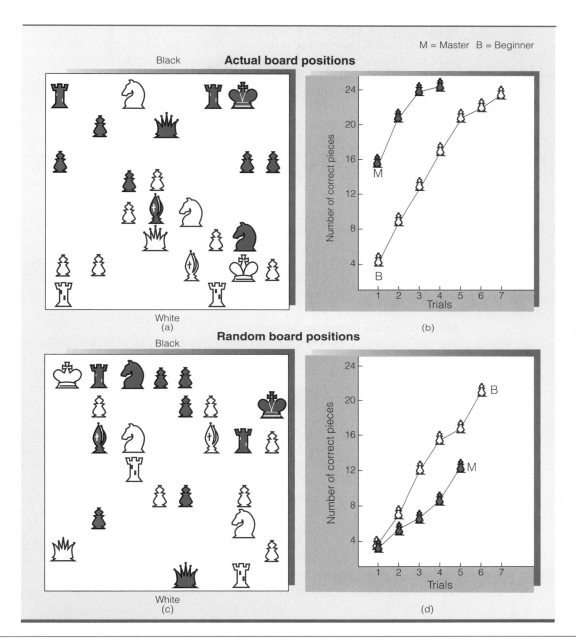

Figure 12.14   Experts Versus Novices in Playing Chess.

When experts and novices were asked to recall realistic patterns of chess pieces, as in panel (a), experts demonstrated much better performance, as shown in panel (b). However, when experts and novices were asked to recall random arrangements of chess pieces, as shown in panel (c), experts performed no better than novices, as shown in panel (d).

Source: From William G. Chase and Herbert A. Simon (1973), Copyright "The Mind's Eye in Chess," in *Visual Information Processing*, edited by William G. Chase. Reprinted by permission of Elsevier.

visual depictions. The researchers observed that novice problem solvers use a visual representation to solve problems that have an obvious spatial component, such as geometry problems. However, expert problem solvers used visual representations to solve a wide range of mathematical problems (Stylianou & Silver, 2004), whether or not they had an obvious spatial component. The ability to apply a visual representation to a variety of problems allows greater flexibility and an increased likelihood that a solution will be found.

An interesting study looked at the role of knowledge in understanding and interpreting a news broadcast regarding a baseball game (Hambrick & Engle, 2002). A total of 181 adults having a wide range of knowledge about baseball listened to radio broadcasts recorded by a professional baseball announcer. The announcements sounded like a real game. After each broadcast, memory for changes in the status of the game were measured. For example, participants would be asked questions about which bases were occupied after each player's turn at bat and about the numbers of outs and of runs scored during the inning. Baseball knowledge accounted for more than half the reliable variation in participants' performance. Working memory capacity also mattered, but not nearly so much as knowledge. Thus, people can remember things better and solve problems with what they remember better if they have a solid knowledge base with which to work.

Reflections on Problem Solving

Another difference between experts and novices can be observed by asking problem solvers to report aloud what they are thinking as they are attempting to solve various problems (Bilalic, 2008; Dew et al., 2009). Statements made by problem solvers are called *verbal protocols*. An interesting effect of verbal protocols is that they can lead to increased problem-solving ability. In one study, when participants spoke aloud or wrote about their problem-solving strategy in a way that centered on the objects of the problem, an improvement in quality of solutions was observed (Steif et al., 2006). In another study, problem-solving ability was enhanced when participants wrote a description of their problem-solving strategy as compared with when they spoke about their strategy (Pugalee, 2004). Thus, it seems that, for novice problem solvers, communicating problem-solving strategies improves performance.

Another difference between expert and novice problem solvers is the time spent on various aspects of problems, and the relationship between problem-solving strategies and the solutions reached. Experts appear to spend proportionately more time determining how to represent a problem than do novices (Lesgold, 1988; Lesgold et al., 1988), but they spend much less time than do novices actually implementing the strategy for solution.

The differences between experts and novices in their expenditure of time can be viewed in terms of the focus and direction of their problem solving. Experts seem to spend relatively more time than do novices figuring out how to match the given information in the problem with their existing schemas. In other words, they try to compare what they know about the problem with how the information they have matches what they already know, based on their expertise. Once experts find a correct match, they quickly can retrieve and implement a problem strategy. Thus, experts seem able to work forward from the given information ("What do I know?") to find the unknown information ("What do I need to find out?"). They implement the correct sequence of steps, based on the strategies they have retrieved from their schemas in long-term memory (Chi et al., 1982).

IN THE LAB OF K. ANDERS ERICSSON

Individual Differences in Problem Solving

For as long as I can remember I have been fascinated by individual differences in thinking and problem solving. In particular I wondered if it would be possible for regular persons, like myself, to learn from experts and exceptional thinkers, such as scientists and chess masters. Would it be possible to find out how they attained their performance so I could improve my abilities by adopting their methods of study and practice?

Most of the descriptions of the development of exceptional individuals' thinking come from informal interviews with these experts and contain subjective descriptions of events that happened many years ago. Scientists, however, have to be skeptical of this type of introspective description that cannot be verified or even reproduced with scientific methods.

In my research lab we have invited expert performers, such as musicians, chess players, and athletes, to reproduce their superior performance under controlled conditions, so we can compare their performance to those of less skilled individuals on the same tasks (Ericsson, 2009; Ericsson & Williams, 2007). We instruct the experts to give verbal expression to their thoughts as they perform, i.e. "think aloud," or report their thoughts immediately after their task performance is completed (see Ericsson, 2006a, for a description of the fundamental differences between "think aloud" and introspective analysis). Based on this type of verbal report, along with specially designed experiments, we and other colleagues have been able to uncover the complex skills and thought processes that mediate the superior performance in people with exceptional memory (for a recent study, see Hu, Ericsson, Yang, & Lu, 2009). We have been particularly interested in how experts, such as chess masters, musicians, athletes, and mental calculators, have acquired memory skills to allow them to plan, monitor, and evaluate complex sequences of actions (Ericsson, 2006a).

K. ANDERS ERICSSON

In my laboratory, we interview the experts about their current practice methods and how their performance in the domain developed—often their reported information can be verified by their parents and teachers or by public records from competitions. Perhaps the most general and intriguing finding is that experts' superior performance is closely linked to their massive amount of goal-directed practice activities. Future expert performers primarily differ from their peers in their engagement in special practice activities that help them to increase beyond their current performance by repetition and gradual refinement through problem solving (deliberate practice) (Ericsson, 2006b).

In domains such as music, sports and chess, the best performers start early and have spent up to four hours each day for many years engaged in deliberate practice, where the experts have accumulated more than 10,000 hours of deliberate practice (Ericsson, Krampe, & Tesch-Römer, 1993)—over a decade later Malcolm Gladwell's (2008) *Outliers: The Story of Success* made "the 10,000-hour rule" famous. Detailed analysis of the expert performers' deliberate practice in sports and music has also uncovered types of intense training activities that are capable of modifying physical characteristics of the body, such as increasing the degree of myelinization of nerve circuits in the brain, increasing number of capillaries supplying blood to critical muscles, and enlarging the chambers of the heart (Ericsson, 2006b).

Research on expert performance has produced new insights into the cognitive structures and physiological adaptations that are can be attained after thousands of hours of deliberate efforts to improve. The scientific study of the lives and practice methods of expert performers appears to be a very promising area to increase our knowledge about what is humanly possible when individuals are motivated to reach their highest levels of achievement.

Consider the ways an expert doctor and a novice medical student might handle a patient with a set of symptoms. The novice is not sure what to make of the symptoms. He somewhat haphazardly orders a long and expensive series of medical tests. He is hoping that with a more nearly complete set of symptomatic information, he may be able to make a correct diagnosis. The more experienced doctor, however, is more likely to immediately recognize the symptoms as fitting into a diagnostic pattern or one of a small number of patterns. This doctor orders only a small number of highly targeted tests. She is able to choose the correct diagnosis from among the limited number of possibilities. She then moves on to treat the diagnosed illness.

In contrast, novices seem to spend relatively little time trying to represent the problem. Instead, they choose to work backward from the unknown information to the given information. That is, they go from asking what they need to find out to asking what information is offered and what strategies do they know that can help them find the missing information. Often, novices use means–ends analysis (see Hunt, 1994). Thus, novices often consider more possible strategies than experts consider (see Holyoak, 1990). For experts, means–ends analysis of problems serves only as a backup strategy. They turn to it only if they are unable to retrieve an appropriate strategy, based on their existing schemas.

Thus, experts have not only more knowledge but also better-organized knowledge. They use their knowledge more effectively. Furthermore, the schemas of experts involve not only greater declarative knowledge about a problem domain. They also involve more procedural knowledge about strategies relevant to that domain. Perhaps because of their better grasp of the strategies required, experts more accurately predict the difficulty of solving problems than do novices. Experts also monitor their problem-solving strategies more carefully than do novices (Schoenfeld, 1981).

Automatic Expert Processes

Through practice in applying strategies, experts may automatize various operations. They can retrieve and execute these operations easily while working forward (see VanLehn, 1989). They use two important processes: One is *schematization*, which involves developing rich, highly organized schemas; the other is *automatization*, which involves consolidating sequences of steps into unified routines that require little or no conscious control. Through these two processes, experts may shift the burden of solving problems from limited-capacity working memory to infinite-capacity long-term memory. They thereby become increasingly efficient and accurate in solving problems. The freeing of their working-memory capacity may better enable them to monitor their progress and their accuracy during problem solving. Novices, in contrast, must use their working memory for trying to hold multiple features of a problem and various possible alternative strategies. This effort may leave novices with less working memory available for monitoring their accuracy and their progress toward solving the problem.

Automaticity can be seen in mathematics, for example, where low-level skills, such as counting and adding, become automatic (Tronsky, 2005). These skills reduce the working-memory load and allow for higher-level mathematical procedures to be complete.

However, the automaticity of experts actually may hinder problem solving by making them less flexible. This can occur when experts are tackling problems that differ structurally from the problems they normally encounter (Frensch & Sternberg, 1989). Initially, novices may perform better than experts when the problems appear structurally different from the norm. Eventually, however, the performance of experts generally catches up to and surpasses that of novices (Frensch & Sternberg, 1989; Lesgold, 1988). Perhaps this difference results from the experts' richly developed schemas and their enhanced self-monitoring skills. The highest level experts, however, are less vulnerable to falling prey to their own expertise (Bilalic et al., 2008). They have the wisdom to realize their own susceptibility to becoming entrenched and take this susceptibility into account.

Table 12.3 summarizes the various characteristics of expert problem solving.

Innate Talent and Acquired Skill

Although a richly elaborated knowledge base is crucial to expertise in a domain, there remain differences in performance that are not explainable in terms of knowledge level alone. There is considerable debate as to whether differences between novices and experts and among different experts themselves are due either to innate talent or to the quantity and quality of practice in a domain. Many espouse the "practice makes perfect" point of view (see for example Ericsson, 2003). The practice should be deliberate, or focused. It should emphasize acquisition of new skills and applications rather than mindless repetition of what the developing expert already knows how to do.

However, some take an alternative approach. This approach acknowledges the importance of practice in building a knowledge and skill base. It also underscores the importance of something like talent. Indeed, the interaction between innate abilities modified by experience is widely accepted in the domain of language acquisition as well as other domains. Certainly, some skill domains are heavily dependent on nurture. For example, wisdom is partly knowledge based. The knowledge one uses to make wise judgments is necessarily a result of experience (Baltes & Smith, 1990).

Experts in some domains perform at superior levels by virtue of prediction skills. For example, expert typists move their fingers toward keys corresponding to the letters they will need to type more quickly than do novice typists (Norman & Rumelhart, 1983). Indeed, the single best predictor of typing speed is how far ahead in the text a typist looks when typing (Ericsson, 2003). The farther ahead he or she looks, the better the typist is able to have fingers in position as needed. When typists are not allowed to look ahead in their typing, the advantage of expert typists is largely eliminated (Salthouse, 1984). Expert sign-language users show variations in sign production in preparation for the next sign (Yang & Sarkar, 2006). Rather than produce one sign in isolation, these signers are looking ahead. Looking ahead allows experts to produce signs more quickly than do novices. Expert musicians, too, are better able to sight-read than novices by virtue of their looking farther ahead in the music so they can anticipate what notes will be coming up (Sloboda, 1984). Even in sports, such as tennis, experts are superior to novices in part by virtue of their being able to predict the trajectory of an approaching ball more rapidly and accurately than novices (Abernethy, 1991).

Another characteristic of experts is that they tend to use a more systematic approach to difficult problems within their domain of expertise than do novices. For example, one study compared strategies used by problem solvers in a simulated biology laboratory (Vollmeyer, Burns, & Holyoak, 1996). The investigators found that better problem solvers were more systematic in their approach to the lab than were poorer problem solvers. For example, in seeking an explanation of a biological phenomenon, they were more likely to hold one variable constant while varying other variables.

Table 12.3   What Characterizes Expertise?

	Experts	Novices
Schemas	Have large, rich schemas containing a great deal of declarative knowledge about domain	Have relatively impoverished schemas containing relatively less declarative knowledge about domain
	Schemas contain a great deal of procedural knowledge about problem-solving strategies relevant to a given domain	Schemas contain relatively little procedural knowledge about problem strategies relevant to the given domain
Organization	Have well-organized, highly interconnected units of knowledge in schemas	Have poorly organized, loosely interconnected, scattered units of knowledge
Use of time	Spend proportionately more time determining how to represent a problem than in searching for and executing a problem strategy	Spend proportionately more time searching for and executing a problem strategy than in determining how to represent a problem
Representation of problems	Develop sophisticated representation of problems based on structural similarities among problems	Develop relatively poor and naive representation of problems based on superficial similarities among problems
Work direction	Work forward from given information to implement strategies for finding unknown information	Work backward from focusing on the unknown to finding problem strategies that make use of given information
Strategy	Generally choose a strategy based on elaborate schema of problem strategies; use means–ends analysis only as a backup strategy for handling unusual, atypical problems	Frequently use means–ends analysis as a strategy for handling most problems; sometimes choose a strategy based on knowledge of problem strategies
Automatization	Have automatized many sequences of steps within problem strategies	Show little or no automatization of any sequences of steps within problem strategies
Efficiency	Show highly efficient problem solving; when time constraints are imposed, solve problems more quickly than novices	Show relatively inefficient problem solving; solve problems less quickly than experts
Prediction of difficulty	Accurately predict the difficulty of solving particular problems	Do not accurately predict the difficulty of solving particular problems
Monitoring	Carefully monitor own problem-solving strategies and processes	Show poor monitoring of own problem-solving strategies and processes
Accuracy of solution	Show high accuracy in reaching appropriate solutions	Show much less accuracy than experts in reaching appropriate solutions
Confronting unusual problems	When confronting highly unusual problems with atypical structural features, take relatively more time than novices both to represent the problem and to retrieve appropriate problem strategies	When confronting highly unusual problems with atypical structural features, novices take relatively less time than experts both to represent the problem and to retrieve problem strategies
Handling contradictory information	When provided with new information that contradicts initial problem representation, show flexibility in adapting to a more appropriate strategy	Show less ability to adapt to new information that contradicts initial problem representation and strategy

Many scientists in the field of expertise prefer to minimize the contributions of talent to expertise by locking talent in the trunk of "folk" psychology (Sternberg, 1996a). This tendency is not surprising, given two factors. The first is the widespread use of the term *talent* outside the scientific community. The second is the lack of an adequate, testable definition of talent.

Genetic heritage seems to make some difference in the acquisition of at least some kinds of expertise. Studies of the heritability of reading disabilities, for example, seem to point to a strong role for genetic factors in people with a reading disability (see Haworth et al., 2009; Platko et al., 2008). Furthermore, differences in the phonological awareness required for reading ability could be a factor in reading for which individual differences are at least partially genetic (Wagner & Stanovich, 1996). In general, even if the role of practice is found to account for much of the expertise shown in a given domain, the contributions of genetic factors to the remaining portion of expertise could make some difference in a world of intense competition.

Artificial Intelligence and Expertise

Computer programs have been developed both to simulate human intelligence and to exceed it. In many ways, computer programs have been created with the intention of solving problems faster and more efficiently than humans. But can a computer be intelligent at all? How can it be tested? Where are systems used that mimic human expertise, and are they successful? These are some of the questions we explore in the next sections.

Can a Computer Be Intelligent?

Much of early information-processing research centered on work based on computer simulations of human intelligence as well as computer systems that use optimal methods to solve tasks. Programs of both kinds can be classified as examples of *artificial intelligence (AI)*, or intelligence in symbol-processing systems such as computers (see Schank & Towle, 2000). Computers cannot actually think; they must be programmed to behave as though they are thinking. That is, they must be programmed to simulate cognitive processes. In this way, they give us insight into the details of how people process information cognitively. Essentially, computers are just pieces of hardware—physical components of equipment—that respond to instructions. Other kinds of hardware (other pieces of equipment) also respond to instructions. For example, if you can figure out how to give the instructions, a DVR (digital video recorder) will respond to your instructions and will do what you tell it to do.

What makes computers so interesting to researchers is that they can be given highly complex instructions (computer programs, more commonly known as software). Programs tell the computer how to respond to new information.

Before we consider any intelligent programs, we need to consider seriously the issue of what, if anything, would lead us to describe a computer program as being "intelligent."

The Turing Test

Probably the first serious attempt to deal with the issue of whether a computer program can be intelligent was made by Alan Turing (1963). The basic idea behind the Turing Test is whether an observer can distinguish the performance of a computer

A common trait among experts in various skills is that they put in tremendous numbers of hours of deliberate practice to perfect their skills.

from that of a human. The test is conducted with a computer, a human respondent, and an interrogator. The interrogator has two different "conversations" with an interactive computer program. The goal of the interrogator is to figure out which of two parties is a person communicating through the computer, and which is the computer itself. The interrogator can ask the two parties any questions at all. However, the computer will try to fool the interrogator into believing that it is human. The human, in contrast, will be trying to show the interrogator that he or she truly is human. The computer passes the Turing Test if an interrogator is unable to distinguish the computer from the human.

Often, what researchers are interested in when assessing the "intelligence" of computers is not their reaction time, which is often much faster than that of humans. They are interested instead in patterns of reaction time, that is, whether the problems that take the computer relatively longer to solve also take human participants relatively longer.

Sometimes, the goal of a computer model is not to match human performance but to exceed it. In this case, maximum AI, rather than simulation of human intelligence, is the goal of the program. The criterion of whether computer performance matches that of humans is no longer relevant. Instead, the criterion of interest is that of how well the computer can perform the task assigned to it. Computer programs that play chess, for example, typically play in a way that emphasizes "brute force," or the consideration of all possible moves without respect to their quality. The programs evaluate extremely large numbers of possible moves. Many of them are moves humans would never even consider evaluating (Berliner, 1969; Bernstein, 1958). Using brute force, the IBM program, "Deep Blue," beat world champion Gary Kasparov in a 1997 chess match. The same brute-force method is used in programs that play checkers (Samuel, 1963). These programs generally are evaluated in terms of how well they can beat each other or, even more importantly, human contenders playing against them.

Expert Systems

Expert systems are computer programs that can perform the way an expert does in a fairly specific domain. They are not developed to model human intelligence, but to simulate performance in just one domain, often a narrow one. They are mostly based on rules that are followed and worked down like a decision tree.

Several programs were developed to diagnose various kinds of medical disorders, like cancer. Such programs are obviously of enormous potential significance, given the very high costs (financial and personal) of incorrect diagnoses. Not only are there expert systems for use by doctors, but there are even medical expert systems on-line for use by consumers who would like an analysis of their symptoms.

Expert systems are used in other areas as well, for example in banks. The processing of small mortgages is relatively expensive for banks because a lot of factors need to be considered. If the data are fed into a computer, however, an expert system makes a decision about the mortgage application based on rules it was programmed with. There is one expert system with which you may have made some experiences yourself: Microsoft Windows offers troubleshooting through the "help section" where you can enter into a dialogue with the system in order to figure out a solution to your particular problem. Reflecting on your own experiences with computerized troubleshooting processes, you can see the strengths but also weaknesses of expert systems.

One has to be cautious in the use of expert systems. Because patients generally do not have the knowledge their doctors have, their use of expert systems, such as on-line ones, may lead them to incorrect conclusions about what illnesses they suffer. In medicine, patient use of the Internet is no substitute for the judgment of a medical doctor.

The application of expertise to problem solving generally involves converging on a single correct solution from a broad range of possibilities. A complementary asset to expertise in problem solving involves creativity. Here, an individual extends the range of possibilities to consider never-before-explored options. In fact, many problems can be solved only by inventing or discovering strategies to answer a complex question. We will discuss the role of creativity in problem solving in the next section of this chapter.

✔ CONCEPT CHECK

1. How do the schemas of experts and novices differ?
2. Why does automatization help experts solve problems efficiently?
3. How does talent contribute to expertise?
4. What are expert systems?

Creativity

How can we possibly define creativity as a single construct that unifies the work of Leonardo da Vinci and Marie Curie, of Vincent Van Gogh and Isaac Newton, and of Toni Morrison and Albert Einstein? There may be about as many narrow definitions of creativity as there are people who think about creativity (Figure 12.15). However, most investigators in the field of creativity would broadly define **creativity** as the process of producing something that is both original and worthwhile (Csikszentmihalyi, 1999, 2000; Kozbelt, Beghetto, & Runco, 2010; Lubart & Mouchiroud, 2003; Sternberg & Lubart, 1996). The *something* could take many forms. It might be

CREATIVITY IS...

DIGGING DEEPER

CREATIVITY IS...

LOOKING TWICE

CREATIVITY IS...

LISTENING FOR SMELLS

CREATIVITY IS...

~~TALKING~~ LISTENING TO A CAT

CROSSING OUT MISTAKES

Figure 12.15   What Is Creativity?

Here are some original and worthwhile ways of defining creativity. How do you define creativity?

Source: From "The Nature of Creativity as Manifest in Its Testing," by E.P. Torrance in *The Nature of Creativity*, edited by Robert J. Sternberg. Copyright © 1988 by Cambridge University Press. Reprinted by permission of Cambridge University Press and E.P. Torrance.

a theory, a dance, a chemical, a process or procedure, a story, a symphony, or almost anything else.

What does it take to create something original and worthwhile? What are creative people like? Almost everyone would agree that creative individuals show creative productivity. They produce inventions, insightful discoveries, artistic works, revolutionary paradigms, or other products that are both original and worthwhile. Conventional wisdom suggests that highly creative individuals also have creative lifestyles. These lifestyles are characterized by flexibility, non-stereotyped behaviors, and non-conforming attitudes.

What Are the Characteristics of Creative People?

Some psychologists measure creativity through *divergent production*—the generation of a diverse assortment of appropriate responses, an approach originated by Guilford (1950) (see Runco & Albert, 2010, for a history of the field, and Plucker & Makel, 2010, for a discussion of assessment of creativity). For example, creative individuals often have high scores on assessments of creativity. An example of such an assessment is found in the Torrance Tests of Creative Thinking (Torrance, 1974, 1984). They measure the diversity, quantity, and appropriateness of responses to open-ended questions. An example of such a question is to think of all the possible ways in which to use a paper clip or a ballpoint pen. Torrance's test also assesses creative figural responses. For example, a person might be given a sheet of paper displaying some circles, squiggles, or lines. The test would assess how many different ways the person had used the given shapes to complete a drawing. Assessment of the Torrance test would consider particularly how much the person had used unusual or richly elaborated details in completing a figure.

Other psychological researchers have focused on creativity as a cognitive process by studying problem solving and insight (Finke, 1995; Ward & Kolomyts, 2010; Weisberg, 1988, 2009). Some of these researchers believe that what distinguishes remarkably creative individuals from less remarkable people is their expertise and commitment to their creative endeavor. Highly creative individuals work long and hard. They study the work of their predecessors and their contemporaries. They thereby become thoroughly expert in their fields. They then build on and diverge from what they know to create innovative approaches and products (Weisberg, 1988, 2009) and thereby change society (Moran, 2010). One study examined the creativity of projects completed by design students. The researchers found that the greater the knowledge amassed by a student, the greater, on average, the creativity of the project (Christiaans & Venselaar, 2007).

Some computer programs, such as those composing music or rediscovering scientific principles, can be viewed as creative. The question one always needs to ask with these programs is whether their accomplishments truly are comparable to those of creative humans, and whether the processes they use to be creative are the same as those used by humans (Boden, 1999). Langley and colleagues' (1987) programs of scientific discovery actually *re*discover scientific ideas rather than discover them for the first time. Even Deep Blue, the computer program that beat world-champion chess player Gary Kasparov, did so not by playing chess more creatively than Kasparov. Rather, it won through its enormous powers of rapid computation.

Personality and motivation play important roles in creativity (Barron, 1988; Feist, 2010; Hennessey, 2010; Runco, 2010). Often underlying creativity are flexible beliefs and broadly accepting attitudes toward other cultures, other races, and other

What do creative people such as Leonardo da Vinci, Albert Einstein, and Isaac Newton have in common?

religious creeds. Some investigators have focused on the importance of motivation in creative productivity (e.g., Amabile, 1996; Collins & Amabile, 1999).

One may differentiate intrinsic motivation, which is internal to the individual, from extrinsic motivation, which is external to the individual. For example, intrinsic motivators might include sheer enjoyment of the creative process or personal desire to solve a problem. Intrinsic motivation is essential to creativity. Extrinsic motivators might include a desire for fame or fortune. Extrinsic motivators actually may impede creativity under many but not all circumstances (Amabile, 1996; Prabhu et al., 2008). Curiously, in one experiment, extrinsic rewards for novel performance led to an increase in both creativity and intrinsic motivation. Conversely, extrinsic rewards for normal performance resulted in a decrease in both creativity and intrinsic motivation (Eisenberger & Shanock, 2003).

Certain traits seem consistently to be associated with creative individuals (Feist, 1998, 1999; Prabhu et al., 2008; Zhang & Sternberg, 2009). In particular, creative individuals tend to be more open to new experiences, self-confident, self-accepting, impulsive, ambitious, driven, dominant, and hostile than less creative individuals. They also are less conventional.

Creativity needs to be viewed in the contexts in which it occurs (Csikszentmihalyi, 1988, 1996; Moran, 2010). One can seek to understand creativity by going beyond the immediate social, intellectual, and cultural context to embrace the entire sweep of history (Simonton, 1988, 1994, 1997, 1999, 2010). Creative contributions, almost by definition, are unpredictable because they violate the norms established by the forerunners and the contemporaries of the creator. Among the many attributes of creative individuals are the abilities to make serendipitous discoveries and to pursue such discoveries actively (Simonton, 1994).

Evolutionary thinking also can be used to study creativity (Cziko, 1998; Gabora & Kaufman, 2010; Simonton, 2010). Underlying such models is the notion that creative ideas evolve much as organisms do. The idea is that creativity occurs as an outcome of a process of blind variation and selective retention (Campbell, 1960). In blind variation, creators first generate an idea. They have no real sense of whether the idea will be

■ **BELIEVE IT OR NOT**

DOES THE FIELD YOU'RE IN PREDICT WHEN YOU WILL DO YOUR BEST WORK?

Creative people often long to make a contribution that will change the world. What they may not realize is that the age at which they make such a contribution depends not only on them, but the field that they choose to enter. Dean Simonton (1988, 1991, 1994) has studied career trajectories for creative contributions. He has found that the age at which people make their outstanding creative

contributions varies somewhat widely by field. For example, in chemistry, the average age of one's greatest work is 38. In medicine, it is 42. Among composers, it is around 41. But notice this: Despite the variation, chances are pretty good that, on average, the best work will occur roughly around the age of 40. So if you view yourself as creative but have not yet had your great idea, and you are under 40, remember that the best is probably yet to come.

successful (selected for) in the world of ideas. As a result, their best bet for producing lasting ideas is to go for a large quantity of ideas. Some of these ideas then will be valued by their field. That is, they will be selectively retained by virtue of their being labeled as creative.

Creative individuals tended to have moderately supportive, but often strict and relatively chilly (i.e., not warmly affectionate and nurturing) early family lives. They have highly supportive mentors. Most showed an early interest in their chosen field, but many were not particularly noteworthy (Gardner, 1993a, Policastro & Gardner, 1999; see also Gruber, 1974/1981; Gruber & Davis, 1988). They generally tended to show an early interest in exploring uncharted territory; but only after gaining mastery of their chosen field, after about a decade of practicing their craft, did they have their initial revolutionary breakthrough. Most creators seemed to have obtained at least some emotional and intellectual support at the time of their breakthrough. However, following this initial breakthrough (and sometimes before), highly creative individuals generally dedicated all their energies to their work. They sometimes abandoned, neglected, or exploited close relationships during adulthood. About a decade after their initial creative achievement, most of the creators Gardner studied made a second breakthrough. It was more comprehensive and more integrative but less revolutionary. Whether a creator continued to make significant contributions depended on the particular field of endeavor. Poets and scientists were less likely to do so than musicians and painters.

An alternative integrative theory of creativity suggests that multiple individual and environmental factors must converge for creativity to occur (Sternberg & Lubart, 1991, 1996). What distinguishes the highly creative individual from the only modestly creative one is the confluence of multiple factors, rather than extremely high levels of any particular factor or even the possession of a distinctive trait. This theory is termed the *investment theory of creativity*. The theme unifying these various factors is that the creative individual takes a buy-low, sell-high approach to ideas (Sternberg & Lubart, 1995, 1996). In buying low, the creator initially sees the hidden potential of ideas that are presumed by others to have little value. The creative person then focuses attention on this idea. It is, at the time of the creator's interest, unrecognized or undervalued by contemporaries, but it has great potential for creative development. The creator then develops the idea into a meaningful, significant creative contribution until at last others also can recognize the merits of the idea. Some of these contributions may be stunning; others more modest (Sternberg, Kaufman, & Pretz, 2001, 2002). Once the idea has been developed and its value is recognized, the creator then sells high. He or she then moves on to other pursuits and looks for the hidden potential in other

INVESTIGATING COGNITIVE PSYCHOLOGY
Creativity in Problem Solving

Line up six toothpicks. Ask a friend to make four equilateral triangles with these six toothpicks without breaking the toothpicks into pieces. Most people will not be able to do this task because they will try to make the four triangles on a single plane. When they give up, make a single triangle flat on the table with three of the toothpicks; then with the other three toothpicks, make a pyramid by joining the three toothpicks at the top and having the sides connect with the intersections of the three toothpicks on the table. Your friend was fixated on the plane of the alignment of the toothpicks. See if any of your friends can figure out this problem if you give them the toothpicks standing up in a toothpick holder.

undervalued ideas. Thus, the creative person influences the field most by always staying a step ahead of the rest. In the ideal, students would develop not only a strong knowledge base, but the skills and attributes discussed here that are essential to creativity (Beghetto, 2010; Smith & Smith, 2010).

Neuroscience and Creativity

The examination of creative thought and production has led researchers to identify brain regions that are active during creativity (Kaufman, Kornilov, Bristol, Tan, & Grigorenko, 2010). The prefrontal regions are especially active during the creative process, regardless of whether the creative thought is effortful or spontaneous (Dietrich, 2004).

In addition to the prefrontal area, other regions have also been identified as important for creativity. In one study, participants were given a list of words that were either semantically related or unrelated (Bechtereva et al., 2004). The participants were then asked to make up a story using all of these words. Forming a story from a list of unrelated words should require more creativity than using a list of semantically related words. These researchers noted that Brodmann's area (BA) 39 was active during the unrelated-list story production but not during production of stories with the list of related words. Previous research has indicated that this and related Brodmann's areas are involved in verbal working memory, task switching, and imagination (Blackwood et al., 2000; Collette et al., 2001; Sohn et al., 2000; Zurowski et al., 2002).

A selective thinning of cortical areas seems to correlate with intelligence and creativity. In particular, a thinning of the left frontal lobe, lingual, cuneus, angular, inferior parietal, and fusiform gyri is connected with high scores on creativity measures. These areas include several Brodmann's areas, including BA 39. Additionally, a relative thickness of the right posterior cingulate gyrus and right angular gyrus was related to higher creativity as well. These variations in cortical thickness, and especially a thinning in various areas, probably influence information flow within the brain (Jung et al., 2010).

✔ CONCEPT CHECK

1. Name some ways how one can identify a creative individual.

2. What makes a contribution creative?

3. Which brain regions contribute to creative processes?

Key Themes

This chapter highlights several of the themes first presented in Chapter 1.

Domain generality versus domain specificity. Early work on problem solving, such as that by Allen Newell and Herbert Simon and their colleagues, emphasized the domain generality of problem solving. These investigators sought to write computer routines, such as the General Problem Solver, that would solve a broad array of problems. Later theorists have emphasized domain specificity in problem solving. They have especially called attention to the need for a broad knowledge base to solve problems successfully.

Validity of causal inference versus ecological validity. Most studies of creativity have occurred in laboratory settings. For example, Paul Torrance gave students paper-and-pencil tests of creative thinking administered in classrooms. In contrast, Howard Gruber has been interested only in creativity as it occurred in natural settings, such as when Darwin generated his many ideas behind the theory of evolution.

Applied versus basic research. The field of creativity has generated many insights regarding fundamental processes used in creative thought. But the field has also spawned a large industry of "creativity enhancement"—programs designed to make people more creative. Some of these programs use insights of basic research. Others represent little more than the intuitions of their inventors. When possible, training should be based on psychological theory and research, rather than guesswork.

Summary

1. **What are some key steps involved in solving problems?** Problem solving involves mentally working to overcome obstacles that stand in the way of reaching a goal. The key steps of problem solving are problem identification, problem definition and representation, strategy construction, organization of information, allocation of resources, monitoring, and evaluation. In everyday experiences, these steps may be implemented very flexibly. Various steps may be repeated, may occur out of sequence, or may be implemented interactively.

2. **What are the differences between problems that have a clear path to a solution versus problems that do not?** Although well-structured problems may have clear paths to solution, the route to solution still may be difficult to follow. Some well-structured problems can be solved using algorithms. They may be tedious to implement but are likely to lead to an accurate solution if applicable to a given problem. Computers are likely to use algorithmic problem-solving strategies. Humans are more likely to use rather informal heuristics (e.g., means–ends analysis, working forward, working backward, and generate and test) for solving problems. When ill-structured problems are solved, the choice of an appropriate problem representation powerfully influences the ease of reaching an accurate solution. Additionally, in solving ill-structured problems, people may need to use more than a heuristic or an algorithmic strategy; insight may be required.

   Many ill-structured problems cannot be solved without the benefit of insight. There are several alternative views of how insightful problem solving takes place. According to the Gestaltist and the neo-Gestaltist views, insightful problem solving is a special process. It comprises more than the sum of its parts and may be evidenced by the suddenness of realizing a solution.

3. **What are some of the obstacles and aids to problem solving?** A mental set (also termed entrenchment) is a strategy that has worked in the past but that does not work for a particular problem that needs to be solved in the present.

   A particular type of mental set is functional fixedness. It involves the inability to see that something that is known to have a particular use also may be used for serving other purposes.

Transfer may be either positive or negative. It refers to the carryover of problem-solving skills from one problem or kind of problem to another. Positive transfer across isomorphic problems rarely occurs spontaneously, particularly if the problems appear to be different in content or in context. Incubation follows a period of intensive work on a problem. It involves laying a problem to rest for a while and then returning to it. In this way, subconscious work can continue on the problem while the problem is consciously ignored.

4. **How does expertise affect problem solving?** Experts differ from novices in both the *amount* and the *organization of knowledge* that they bring to bear on problem solving in the domain of their expertise. For experts, many aspects of problem solving may be governed by automatic processes.

Such automaticity usually facilitates the expert's ability to solve problems in the given area of expertise. When problems involve novel elements requiring novel strategies, however, the automaticity of some procedures actually may impede problem solving, at least temporarily. Expertise in a given domain is viewed mostly from the practice-makes-perfect perspective. However, talent should not be ignored and probably contributes much to the differences among experts.

5. **What is creativity, and how can it be fostered?** Creativity involves producing something that is both original and worthwhile. Several factors characterize highly creative individuals. One is extremely high motivation to be creative in a particular field of endeavor (e.g., for the sheer enjoyment of the creative process). A second factor is both non-conformity in violating any conventions that might inhibit the creative work and dedication in maintaining standards of excellence and self-discipline related to the creative work. A third factor in creativity is deep belief in the value of the creative work, as well as willingness to criticize and improve the work. A fourth is careful choice of the problems or subjects on which to focus creative attention.

A fifth characteristic of creativity is thought processes characterized by both insight and divergent thinking. A sixth factor is risk taking. The final two factors in creativity are extensive knowledge of the relevant domain and profound commitment to the creative endeavor. In addition, the historical context and the domain and field of endeavor influence the expression of creativity.

Thinking about Thinking: Analytical, Creative, and Practical Questions

1. Describe the steps of the problem-solving cycle and give an example of each step.
2. What are some of the key characteristics of expert problem solvers?
3. What are some of the insights into problem solving gained through studying computer simulations of problem solving? How might a computer-based approach limit the potential for understanding problem solving in humans?
4. Compare and contrast the various approaches to creativity.
5. Design a problem that would require insight for its solution.
6. Design a context for problem solving that would enhance the ease of reaching a solution.
7. Given what we know about some of the hindrances to problem solving, how could you minimize those hindrances in your handling of the problems you face?
8. Given some of the ideas regarding creativity presented in this chapter, what can you do to enhance your own creativity?

Key Terms

algorithms, *p. 492*
analysis, *p. 488*
convergent thinking, *p. 488*
creativity, *p. 522*
divergent thinking, *p. 488*
expert systems, *p. 521*
expertise, *p. 511*
functional fixedness, *p. 503*
heuristics, *p. 492*

ill-structured problems, *p. 490*
incubation, *p. 508*
insight, *p. 498*
isomorphic, *p. 493*
mental set, *p. 503*
negative transfer, *p. 505*
positive transfer, *p. 505*
problem solving, *p. 486*
problem space, *p. 492*

problem-solving cycle, *p. 487*
productive thinking, *p. 499*
stereotypes, *p. 503*
synthesis, *p. 488*
transfer, *p. 505*
transparency, *p. 508*
well-structured problems, *p. 490*

Media Resources

Visit the companion website—**www.cengagebrain.com**—for quizzes, research articles, chapter outlines, and more.

CogLab

Explore CogLab by going to **http://coglab.wadsworth.com**. To learn more, examine the following experiments:

Monty Hall

Glossary

accessibility the degree to which we can gain access to the available information

ACT Adaptive Control of Thought. In his ACT model, John Anderson synthesized some of the features of serial information-processing models and some of the features of semantic-network models. In ACT, procedural knowledge is represented in the form of production systems. Declarative knowledge is represented in the form of propositional networks

ACT-R a model of information processing that integrates a network representation for declarative knowledge and a production-system representation for procedural knowledge

agnosia a severe deficit in the ability to perceive sensory information

algorithms sequences of operations that may be repeated over and over again and that, in theory, guarantee the solution to a problem

Alzheimer's disease a disease of older adults that causes dementia as well as progressive memory loss

amacrine cells along with horizontal cells, they make single lateral connections among adjacent areas of the retina in the middle layer of cells

amnesia severe loss of explicit memory

amygdala plays an important role in emotion, especially in anger and aggression

analog codes a form of knowledge representation that preserves the main perceptual features of whatever is being represented for the physical stimuli we observe in our environment

analysis breaking down the whole of a complex problem into manageable elements

anterograde amnesia the inability to remember events that occur after a traumatic event

aphasia an impairment of language functioning caused by damage to the brain

arousal a degree of physiological excitation, responsivity, and readiness for action, relative to a baseline

artifact categories groupings that are designed or invented by humans to serve particular purposes or functions

artificial intelligence (AI) the attempt by humans to construct systems that show intelligence and, particularly, the intelligent processing of information; intelligence in symbol-processing systems such as computers

associationism examines how events or ideas can become associated with one another in the mind to result in a form of learning

attention the active cognitive processing of a limited amount of information from the vast amount of information available through the senses, in memory, and through cognitive processes; focus on a small subset of available stimuli

autobiographical memory refers to memory of an individual's history

automatic processes involve no conscious control

automatization the process by which a procedure changes from being highly conscious to being relatively automatic; also termed proceduralization

availability the presence of information stored in long-term memory

availability heuristic cognitive shortcut that occurs when we make judgments on the basis of how easily we can call to mind what we perceive as relevant instances of a phenomenon

axon the part of the neuron through which intraneuronal conduction occurs (via the action potential) and at the terminus of which is located the terminal buttons that release neurotransmitters

base rate refers to the prevalence of an event or characteristic within its population of events or characteristics

basic level degree of specificity of a concept that seems to be a level within a hierarchy that is preferred to other levels; sometimes termed natural level

behaviorism a theoretical outlook that psychology should focus only on the relation between observable behavior, on the one hand, and environmental events or stimuli, on the other

bilinguals people who can speak two languages

binaural presentation presenting the same two messages, or sometimes just one message, to both ears simultaneously

binocular depth cues based on the receipt of sensory information in three dimensions from both eyes

bipolar cells make dual connections forward and outward to the ganglion cells, as well as backward and inward to the third layer of retinal cells

blindsight traces of visual perceptual ability in blind areas

bottleneck theories theories proposing a bottleneck that slows down information passing through

bottom-up theories data-driven (i.e., stimulus-driven) theories

bounded rationality belief that we are rational, but within limits

brain the organ in our bodies that most directly controls our thoughts, emotions, and motivations brainstem connects the forebrain to the spinal cord

categorical perception discontinuous categories of speech sounds

categorical syllogism a deductive argument in which the relationship among the three terms in the two premises involves categorical membership

category a concept that functions to organize or point out aspects of equivalence among other concepts based on common features or similarity to a prototype

causal inferences how people make judgments about whether something causes something else

central executive both coordinates attentional activities and governs responses

cerebellum controls bodily coordination, balance, and muscle tone, as well as some aspects of memory involving procedure-related movements; from Latin, "little brain"

cerebral cortex forms a 1- to 3-millimeter layer that wraps the surface of the brain somewhat like the bark of a tree wraps around the trunk

cerebral hemispheres the two halves of the brain

change blindness the inability to detect changes in objects or scenes that are being viewed

characteristic features qualities that describe (characterize or typify) the prototype but are not necessary for it

coarticulation occurs when phonemes or other units are produced in a way that overlaps them in time

cocktail party problem the process of tracking one conversation in the face of the distraction of other conversations

cognitive maps internal representations of our physical environment, particularly centering on spatial relationships

cognitive neuroscience the field of study linking the brain and other aspects of the nervous system to cognitive processing and, ultimately, to behavior

cognitive psychology the study of how people perceive, learn, remember, and think about information

cognitive science a cross-disciplinary field that uses ideas and methods from cognitive psychology, psychobiology, artificial intelligence, philosophy, linguistics, and anthropology

cognitivism the belief that much of human behavior can be understood in terms of how people think

communication exchange of thoughts and feelings

comprehension processes used to make sense of the text as a whole

concept an idea about something that provides a means of understanding the world

conditional reasoning occurs when the reasoner must draw a conclusion based on an if-then proposition

cones one of the two kinds of photoreceptors in the eye; less numerous, shorter, thicker, and more highly concentrated in the foveal region of the retina than in the periphery of the retina than are rods (the other type of photoreceptor); virtually nonfunctional in dim light, but highly effective in bright light and essential to color vision

confirmation bias the tendency to seek confirmation rather than disconfirmation of what we already believe

confounding variable a type of irrelevant variable that has been left uncontrolled in a study

conjunction search looking for a particular combination (conjunction: joining together) of features

connectionist models according to connectionist models, we handle very large numbers of cognitive operations at once through a network distributed across incalculable numbers of locations in the brain

connotation a word's emotional overtones, presuppositions, and other non-explicit meanings

consciousness includes both the feeling of awareness and the content of awareness

consolidation the process of integrating new information into stored information

constructive prior experience affects how we recall things and what we actually recall from memory

constructive perception the perceiver builds (constructs) a cognitive understanding (perception) of a stimulus; he or she uses sensory information as the foundation for the structure but also uses other sources of information to build the perception

content morphemes the words that convey the bulk of the meaning of a language

context effects the influences of the surrounding environment on perception

contextualism belief that intelligence must be understood in its real-world context

contralateral from one side to another

controlled processes accessible to conscious control and even require it

convergent thinking attempt to narrow down the multiple possibilities to converge on a single best answer

converging operations the use of multiple approaches and techniques to address a problem

cooperative principle principle in conversation that holds that we seek to communicate in ways that make it easy for our listener to understand what we mean

core refers to the defining features something must have to be considered an example of a category

corpus callosum a dense aggregate of neural fibers connecting the two cerebral hemispheres

creativity the process of producing something that is both original and worthwhile

culture-fair equally appropriate and fair for members of all cultures

culture-relevant tests measure skills and knowledge that relate to the cultural experiences of the test-takers

decay occurs when simply the passage of time causes an individual to forget

decay theory asserts that information is forgotten because of the gradual disappearance, rather than displacement, of the memory trace

declarative knowledge knowledge of facts that can be stated

deductive reasoning the process of reasoning from one or more general statements regarding what is known to reach a logically certain conclusion

deductive validity logical soundness

deep structure refers to an underlying syntactic structure that links various phrase structures through the application of various transformation rules

defining feature a necessary attribute

dendrites the branch-like structures of each neuron that extend into synapses with other neurons and that receive neurochemical messages sent into synapses by other neurons

denotation the strict dictionary definition of a word

dependent variable a response that is measured and is presumed to be the effect of one or more independent variables

depth the distance from a surface, usually using your own body as a reference surface when speaking in terms of depth perception

dialect a regional variety of a language distinguished by features such as vocabulary, syntax, and pronunciation

dichotic presentation presenting a different message to each ear

direct perception theory belief that the array of information in our sensory receptors, including the sensory context, is all we need to perceive anything

discourse encompasses language use at the level beyond the sentence, such as in conversation, paragraphs, stories, chapters, and entire works of literature

dishabituation change in a familiar stimulus that prompts us to start noticing the stimulus again

distracters nontarget stimuli that divert our attention away from the target stimulus

distributed practice learning in which various sessions are spaced over time

divergent thinking when one tries to generate a diverse assortment of possible alternative solutions to a problem

divided attention the prudent allocation of available attentional resources to coordinate the performance of more than one task at a time

dual-code theory belief suggesting that knowledge is represented both in images and in symbols

dual-system hypothesis suggests that two languages are represented somehow in separate systems of the mind

dyslexia difficulty in deciphering, reading, and comprehending text

ecological validity the degree to which particular findings in one environmental context may be considered relevant outside that context

electroencephalograms (EEGs) recordings of the electrical frequencies and intensities of the living brain, typically recorded over relatively long periods

elimination by aspects occurs when we eliminate alternatives by focusing on aspects of each alternative, one at a time

emotional intelligence the ability to perceive and express emotion, assimilate emotion in thought, understand and reason with emotion, and regulate emotion in the self and others

empiricist one who believes that we acquire knowledge via empirical evidence

encoding refers to how you transform a physical, sensory input into a kind of representation that can be placed into memory

encoding specificity what is recalled depends on what is encoded

episodic buffer a limited-capacity system that is capable of binding information from the subsidiary systems and from long-term memory into a unitary episodic representation

episodic memory stores personally experienced events or episodes

event-related potential an electrophysiological response to a stimulus, whether internal or external

executive attention a subfunction of attention that includes processes for monitoring and resolving conflicts that arise among internal processes

exemplars typical representatives of a category

expertise superior skills or achievement reflecting a well-developed and well-organized knowledge base

expert systems computer programs that can perform the way an expert does in a fairly specific domain

explicit memory when participants engage in conscious recollection

factor analysis a statistical method for separating a construct into a number of hypothetical factors or traits that the researchers believe form the basis of individual differences in test performance

fallacy erroneous reasoning

feature-integration theory explains the relative ease of conducting feature searches and the relative difficulty of conducting conjunction searches

feature-matching theories suggest that we attempt to match features of a pattern to features stored in memory

feature search simply scanning the environment for a particular feature or features

figure-ground what stands out from versus what recedes into the background

filter theories theories proposing a filter that blocks some of the information going through and thereby selects only a part of the total of information to pass through to the next stage

flashbulb memory a memory of an event so powerful that the person remembers the event as vividly as if it were indelibly preserved on film

flow chart a model path for reaching a goal or solving a problem

fovea a part of the eye located in the center of the retina that is largely responsible for the sharp central vision people use in activities such as reading or watching television or movies

frontal lobe associated with motor processing and higher thought processes, such as abstract reasoning

functional-equivalence hypothesis belief that although visual imagery is not identical to visual perception, it is functionally equivalent to it

functional fixedness the inability to realize that something known to have a particular use may also be used for performing other functions

functional magnetic resonance imaging (fMRI) a neuroimaging technique that uses magnetic fields to construct a detailed representation in three dimensions of levels of activity in various parts of the brain at a given moment

functionalism seeks to understand what people do and why they do it

function morphemes a morpheme that adds detail and nuance to the meaning of the content morphemes or helps the content morphemes fit the grammatical context

ganglion cells a kind of neuron usually situated near the inner surface of the retina of the eye; receive visual information from photoreceptors by way of bipolar cells and amacrine cells; send visual information from the retina to several different parts of the brain, such as the thalamus and the hypothalamus

Gestalt approach to form perception based on the notion that the whole differs from the sum of its individual parts

Gestalt psychology states that we best understand psychological phenomena when we view them as organized, structured wholes

"g" factor general ability

grammar the study of language in terms of noticing regular patterns

habituation involves our becoming accustomed to a stimulus so that we gradually pay less and less attention to it

heuristics informal, intuitive, speculative strategies that sometimes lead to an effective solution and sometimes do not

hindsight bias when we look at a situation retrospectively, we believe we easily can see all the signs and events leading up to a particular outcome

hippocampus plays an essential role in memory formation

horizontal cells along with amacrine cells, they make single lateral connections among adjacent areas of the retina in the middle layer of cells

hypermnesia a process of producing retrieval of memories that seem to have been forgotten

hypothalamus regulates behavior related to species survival: fighting, feeding, fleeing, and mating; also active in regulating emotions and reactions to stress

hypotheses tentative proposals regarding expected empirical consequences of the theory

hypothesis testing a view of language acquisition that asserts that children acquire language by mentally forming

tentative hypotheses regarding language, based on their inherited facility for language acquisition and then testing these hypotheses in the environment

hypothetical constructs concepts that are not themselves directly measurable or observable but that serve as mental models for understanding how a psychological phenomenon works

iconic store a discrete visual sensory register that holds information for very short periods

ill-structured problems problems that lack well-defined paths to solution

illusory correlation occurs when we tend to see particular events or particular attributes and categories as going together because we are predisposed to do so

imagery the mental representation of things that are not currently being sensed by the sense organs

implicit memory when we recollect something but are not consciously aware that we are trying to do so

incubation putting the problem aside for a while without consciously thinking about it

independent variable a variable that is varied or purposefully manipulated and that affects one or more dependent variables

indirect requests the making of a request without doing so straightforwardly

inductive reasoning the process of reasoning from specific facts or observations to reach a likely conclusion that may explain the facts

infantile amnesia the inability to recall events that happened when we were very young

insight a distinctive and sometimes seemingly sudden understanding of a problem or of a strategy that aids in solving the problem

intelligence the capacity to learn from experience, using metacognitive processes to enhance learning, and the ability to adapt to the surrounding environment

interference occurs when competing information causes an individual to forget something

interference theory refers to the view that forgetting occurs because recall of certain words interferes with recall of other words

introspection looking inward at pieces of information passing through consciousness

ipsilateral on the same side

isomorphic the formal structure is the same, and only the content differs

jargon specialized vocabulary commonly used within a group, such as a profession or a trade

judgment and decision making used to select from among choices or to evaluate opportunities

knowledge representation the form for what you know in your mind about things, ideas, events, and so on that exist outside your mind

Korsakoff's syndrome produces loss of memory function

language the use of an organized means of combining words in order to communicate

law of Prägnanz tendency to perceive any given visual array in a way that most simply organizes the disparate elements into a stable and coherent form

levels-of-processing framework postulates that memory does not comprise three or even any specific number of separate stores but rather varies along a continuous dimension in terms of depth of encoding

lexical access the identification of a word that allows us to gain access to the meaning of the word from memory

lexical processes used to identify letters and words

lexicon the entire set of morphemes in a given language or in a given person's linguistic repertoire

limbic system important to emotion, motivation, memory, and learning

linguistic relativity the assertion that speakers of different languages have differing cognitive systems and that these different cognitive systems influence the ways in which people speaking the various languages think about the world

linguistic universals characteristic patterns across all languages of various cultures

lobes divide the cerebral hemispheres and cortex into four parts

localization of function refers to the specific areas of the brain that control specific skills or behaviors

long-term store very large capacity, capable of storing information for very long periods, perhaps even indefinitely

magnetic resonance imaging (MRI) scan a technique for revealing high-resolution images of the structure of the living brain by computing and analyzing magnetic changes in the energy of the orbits of nuclear particles in the molecules of the body

magnetoencephalography (MEG) an imaging technique that measures the magnetic fields generated by electrical activity in the brain by highly sensitive measuring devices

massed practice learning in which sessions are crammed together in a very short space of time

medulla oblongata brain structure that controls heart activity and largely controls breathing, swallowing, and digestion

memory the means by which we retain and draw on our past experiences to use this information in the present

mental models knowledge structures that individuals construct to understand and explain their experiences; an internal representation of information that corresponds analogously with whatever is being represented

mental rotation involves rotationally transforming an object's visual mental image

mental set a frame of mind involving an existing model for representing a problem, a problem context, or a procedure for problem solving

metacognition our understanding and control of our cognition; our ability to think about and control our own processes of thought and ways of enhancing our thinking

metamemory strategies involve reflecting on our own memory processes with a view to improving our memory

metaphor two nouns juxtaposed in a way that positively asserts their similarities, while not disconfirming their dissimilarities

mnemonic devices specific techniques to help you memorize lists of words

mnemonist someone who demonstrates extraordinarily keen memory ability, usually based on the use of special techniques for memory enhancement

modular divided into discrete modules that operate more or less independently of each other

monocular depth cues can be represented in just two dimensions and observed with just one eye

monolinguals people who can speak only one language

morpheme the smallest unit that denotes meaning within a particular language

multimode theory proposes that attention is flexible; selection of one message over another message can be made at any of various different points in the course of information processing

myelin a fatty substance coating the axons of some neurons that facilitates the speed and accuracy of neuronal communication

natural categories groupings that occur naturally in the world

negative transfer occurs when solving an earlier problem makes it harder to solve a later one

nervous system the organized network of cells (neurons) through which an individual receives information from the environment, processes that information, and then interacts with the environment

networks a web of relationships (e.g., category membership, attribution) between nodes

neurons individual nerve cells

neurotransmitters chemical messengers used for interneuronal communication

nodes the elements of a network

nodes of Ranvier gaps in the myelin coating of myelinated axons

nominal kind the arbitrary assignment of a label to an entity that meets a certain set of prespecified conditions

noun phrase syntactic structure that contains at least one noun (often, the subject of the sentence) and includes all the relevant descriptors of the noun

object-centered representation the individual stores a representation of the object, independent of its appearance to the viewer

occipital lobe associated with visual processing, the primary motor cortex, which specializes in the planning, control, and execution of movement, particularly of movement involving any kind of delayed response

optic ataxia impaired visual control of the arm in reaching out to a visual target

optic nerve the nerve that transmits information from the retina to the brain

overconfidence an individual's overvaluation of her or his own skills, knowledge, or judgment

overregularization occurs when individuals apply the general rules of language to the exceptional cases that vary from the norm

parallel distributed processing (PDP) models or connectionist models the handling of very large numbers of cognitive operations at once through a network distributed across incalculable numbers of locations in the brain

parallel processing occurs when multiple operations are executed all at once

parietal lobe associated with somatosensory processing

perception the set of processes by which we recognize, organize, and make sense of the sensations we receive from environmental stimuli

perceptual constancy occurs when our perception of an object remains the same even when our proximal sensation of the distal object changes

phoneme is the smallest unit of speech sound that can be used to distinguish one utterance in a given language from another

phonemic-restoration effect sounds that are missing from a speech signal are constructed by the brain so it seems to the listener that he actually heard the missing sound

phonological loop briefly holds inner speech for verbal comprehension and for acoustic rehearsal

photopigments chemical substances that absorb light, thereby starting the complex transduction process that transforms physical electromagnetic energy into an electrochemical neural impulse; rods and cones contain different types of photopigments; different types of photopigments absorb differing amounts of light and may detect different hues

photoreceptors the third layer of the retina contains the photoreceptors, which transduce light energy into electrochemical energy

phrase-structure grammar syntactical analysis of the structure of phrases as they are used

pons serves as a kind of relay station because it contains neural fibers that pass signals from one part of the brain to another

positive transfer occurs when the solution of an earlier problem makes it easier to solve a new problem

positron emission tomography (PET) scans measure increases in glucose consumption in active brain areas during particular kinds of information processing

pragmatic reasoning schemas general organizing principles or rules related to particular kinds of goals, such as permissions, obligations, or causations

pragmatics the study of how people use language

pragmatists ones who believe that knowledge is validated by its usefulness

premises propositions about which arguments are made

primacy effect refers to superior recall of words at and near the beginning of a list

primary motor cortex region of the cerebral cortex that is chiefly responsible for directing the movements of all muscles

primary somatosensory cortex receives information from the senses about pressure, texture, temperature, and pain

prime a node that activates a connected node; this activation is known as the priming effect

priming the facilitation of one's ability to utilize missing information; occurs when recognition of certain stimuli is affected by prior presentation of the same or similar stimuli

priming effect the resulting activation of the node

proactive interference occurs when the interfering material occurs before, rather than after, learning of the to-be-remembered material

problem solving an effort to overcome obstacles obstructing the path to a solution

problem-solving cycle includes problem identification, problem definition, strategy formulation, organization of information, allocation of resources, monitoring, and evaluation

problem space the universe of all possible actions that can be applied to solving a problem, given any constraints that apply to the solution of the problem

procedural knowledge knowledge of procedures that can be implemented

production the generation and output of a procedure

production system an ordered set of productions in which execution starts at the top of a list of productions, continues until a condition is satisfied, and then returns to the top of the list to start anew

productive thinking involves insights that go beyond the bounds of existing associations

proposition basically an assertion, which may be either true or false

propositional theory belief suggesting that knowledge is represented only in underlying propositions, not in the form of images or of words and other symbols

prototype a sort of average of a class of related objects or patterns, which integrates all the most typical (most frequently observed) features of the class

prototype theory suggests that categories are formed on the basis of a (prototypical, or averaged) model of the category

psycholinguistics the psychology of our language as it interacts with the human mind

rationalist one who believes that the route to knowledge is through logical analysis

reasoning the process of drawing conclusions from principles and from evidence

recall to produce a fact, a word, or other item from memory

recency effect refers to superior recall of words at and near the end of a list

recognition to select or otherwise identify an item as being one that you learned previously

recognition-by-components (RBC) theory the belief that we quickly recognize objects by observing the edges of objects and then decomposing the objects into geons

reconstructive involving the use of various strategies (e.g., searching for cues, drawing inferences) for retrieving the original memory traces of our experiences and then rebuilding the original experiences as a basis for retrieval

referent the thing or concept in the real world that a word refers to

rehearsal the repeated recitation of an item

representativeness occurs when we judge the probability of an uncertain event according to (1) its obvious similarity to or representation of the population from which it is derived and (2) the degree to which it reflects the salient features of the process by which it is generated (such as randomness)

reticular activating system (RAS) a network of neurons essential to the regulation of consciousness (sleep, wakefulness, arousal, and even attention to some extent and to such vital functions as heartbeat and breathing); also called reticular formation

retina a network of neurons extending over most of the back (posterior) surface of the interior of the eye. The retina is where electromagnetic light energy is transduced—that is, converted—into neural electrochemical impulses

retrieval (memory) refers to how you gain access to information stored in memory

retroactive interference caused by activity occurring after we learn something but before we are asked to recall that thing; also called retroactive inhibition

retrograde amnesia occurs when individuals lose their purposeful memory for events prior to whatever trauma induces memory loss

rods light-sensitive photoreceptors in the retina of the eye that provide peripheral vision and the ability to see objects at night or in dim light; rods are not color sensitive

satisficing occurs when we consider options one by one, and then we select an option as soon as we find one that is satisfactory or just good enough to meet our minimum level of acceptability

schemas mental frameworks for representing knowledge that encompass an array of interrelated concepts in a meaningful organization

script a structure that describes appropriate sequences of events in a particular context

search refers to a scan of the environment for particular features—actively looking for something when you are not sure where it will appear

selective attention choosing to attend to some stimuli and to ignore others

selective-combination insight involves taking selectively encoded and compared snippets of relevant information and combining that information in a novel, productive way

selective-comparison insight involves novel perceptions of how new information relates to old information

selective-encoding insight involves distinguishing relevant from irrelevant information

semantic memory stores general world knowledge

semantic network a web of interconnected elements of meaning

semantics the study of meaning in a language

sensory adaptation a lessening of attention to a stimulus that is not subject to conscious control

sensory store capable of storing relatively limited amounts of information for very brief periods

septum is involved in anger and fear

serial-position curve represents the probability of recall of a given word, given its serial position (order of presentation) in a list

serial processing means by which information is handled through a linear sequence of operations, one operation at a time

short-term store capable of storing information for somewhat longer periods but also of relatively limited capacity

signal a target stimulus

signal detection the detection of the appearance of a particular stimulus

signal-detection theory (SDT) a theory of how we detect stimuli that involves four possible outcomes of the presence or absence of a stimulus and our detection or nondetection of a stimulus

simile introduces the word *like* or *as* into a comparison between items

single-system hypothesis suggests that two languages are represented in just one system

slips of the tongue inadvertent linguistic errors in what we say

soma the cell body of a neuron that is the part of the neuron essential to the life and reproduction of the cell

spacing effect refers to the fact that long-term recall is best when the material is learned over a longer period of time

spatial cognition refers to the acquisition, organization, and use of knowledge about objects and actions in two- and three-dimensional space

speech acts addresses the question of what you can accomplish with speech

split-brain patients people who have undergone operations severing the corpus callosum

spreading activation excitation that fans out along a set of nodes within a given network

statistical significance indicates the likelihood that a given set of results would be obtained if only chance factors were in operation

stereotypes beliefs that members of a social group tend more or less uniformly to have particular types of characteristics

storage (memory) refers to how you retain encoded information in memory

Stroop effect demonstrates the psychological difficulty in selectively attending to the color of the ink and trying to ignore the word that is printed with the ink of that color

structuralism seeks to understand the structure (configuration of elements) of the mind and its perceptions by analyzing those perceptions into their constituent components

structure-of-intellect (SOI) Guilford's model for a three-dimensional structure of intelligence, embracing various contents, operations, and products of intelligence

subjective probability a calculation based on the individual's estimates of likelihood, rather than on objective statistical computations

subjective utility a calculation based on the individual's judged weightings of utility (value), rather than on objective criteria

surface structure a level of syntactic analysis that involves the specific syntactical sequence of words in a sentence and any of the various phrase structures that may result

syllogisms deductive arguments that involve drawing conclusions from two premises

symbolic representation meaning that the relationship between the word and what it represents is simply arbitrary

synapse a small gap between neurons that serves as a point of contact between the terminal buttons of one or more neurons and the dendrites of one or more other neurons

syntax refers to the way in which users of a particular language put words together to form sentences

synthesis putting together various elements to arrange them into something useful

templates highly detailed models for patterns we potentially might recognize

temporal lobe associated with auditory processing

terminal buttons knobs at the end of each branch of an axon; each button may release a chemical neurotransmitter as a result of an action potential

thalamus relays incoming sensory information through groups of neurons that project to the appropriate region in the cortex

thematic roles ways in which items can be used in the context of communication

theory an organized body of general explanatory principles regarding a phenomenon

theory-based view of meaning holds that people understand and categorize concepts in terms of implicit theories, or general ideas they have regarding those concepts

theory of multiple intelligences belief that intelligence comprises multiple independent constructs, not just a single, unitary construct

tip-of-the-tongue phenomenon experience of trying to remember something that is known to be stored in memory but that cannot readily be retrieved

top-down theories driven by high-level cognitive processes, existing knowledge, and prior expectations

transcranial magnetic stimulation (TMS) technique that temporarily disrupts the normal activity of the brain in a limited area. This technique requires placing a coil on a person's head and then allowing an electrical current to pass though it. The current generates a magnetic field. This field disrupts the small area (usually no more than a cubic centimeter) beneath it. The researcher can then look at cognitive functioning when the particular area is disrupted

transfer any carryover of knowledge or skills from one problem situation to another

transformational grammar involves the study of transformational rules that guide the ways in which underlying propositions can be rearranged to form various phrase structures

transparency occurs when people see analogies where they do not exist because of similarity of content

triarchic theory of human intelligence belief that intelligence comprises three aspects, dealing with the relation of intelligence (1) to the internal world of the person, (2) to experience, and (3) to the external world

verbal comprehension the receptive ability to comprehend written and spoken linguistic input, such as words, sentences, and paragraphs

verbal fluency the expressive ability to produce linguistic output

verb phrase syntactic structure that contains at least one verb and whatever the verb acts on, if anything

viewer-centered representation an individual stores the way the object looks to him or her

vigilance refers to a person's ability to attend to a field of stimulation over a prolonged period, during which the person seeks to detect the appearance of a particular target stimulus of interest

visuospatial sketchpad briefly holds some visual images

well-structured problems problems that have well-defined paths to solution

word-superiority effect letters are read more easily when they are embedded in words than when they are presented either in isolation or with letters that do not form words

working memory holds only the most recently activated portion of long-term memory, and it moves these activated elements into and out of brief, temporary memory storage

References

Abernethy, B. (1991). Visual search strategies and decision-making in sport. *International Journal of Sport Psychology, 22*, 189–210.

Abrams, D. M., & Strogatz, S. H. (2003). Modeling the dynamics of language death. *Nature, 424*, 900.

Abler, B., Hahlbrock, R., Unrath, A., Groen, G., & Kassubek, J. (2009). At-risk for pathological gambling: imaging neural reward processing under chronic dopamine agonists. *Brain, 132*, 2396–2402.

Ackerman, P. L. (1996). A theory of adult intellectual development: Process, personality, interests, and knowledge. *Intelligence, 22*, 227–257.

Ackerman, P. L. (in press). Intelligence and expertise. In R. J. Sternberg & S. B. Kaufman (Eds.), *Cambridge Handbook of Intelligence.* New York: Cambridge University Press.

Ackerman, P. L., Beier, M. E., & Boyle, M. O. (2005). Working memory and intelligence: The same or different constructs? *Psychological Bulletin, 131*(1), 30–60.

Ackil, J. K., & Zaragoza, M. S. (1998). Memorial consequences of forced confabulation: Age differences in susceptibility to false memories. *Developmental Psychology, 34*, 1358–1372.

Acredolo, L. P., & Goodwyn, S. W. (1998). *Baby signs: How to talk with your baby before your baby can talk.* Chicago: NTB/Contemporary Publishers.

Adams, M. J. (1990). *Beginning to read: Thinking and learning about print.* Cambridge, MA: MIT Press.

Adams, M. J. (1999). Reading. In R. A. Wilson & F. C. Keil (Eds.), *The MIT encyclopedia of the cognitive sciences* (pp. 705–707). Cambridge, MA: MIT Press.

Adams, M. J., Treiman, R., & Pressley, M. (1997). Reading, writing and literacy. In I. Sigel & A. Renninger (Eds.), *Handbook of child psychology* (5th ed., vol. 4). *Child psychology in practice* (pp. 275–357). New York: Wiley.

Adler, J. (1991, July 22). The melting of a mighty myth. *Newsweek,* 63.

Adolphs, R. (2003). Amygdala. In L. Nadel (Ed.), *Encyclopedia of cognitive science* (Vol. 1, pp. 98–105). London: Nature Publishing Group.

Adolphs, R., Sears, L., & Piven, J. (2001). Abnormal processing of social information from faces in autism. *Journal of Cognitive Neuroscience, 13*, 232–240.

Adolphs, R., Tranel, D., Damasio, H., & Damasio, A. (1994). Impaired recognition of emotion in facial expressions following bilateral damage to the human amygdala. *Nature, 372*, 669–672.

Agulera, A., Selgas, R., Codoceo, R., & Bajo, A. (2000). Uremic anorexia: A consequence of persistently high brain serotonin levels? The tryptophan/serotonin disorder hypothesis. *Peritoneal Dialysis, 20*(6), 810–816.

Akhtar, N. & Montague, L. (1999). Early lexical acquisition: The role of cross-situational learning. *First Language, 19*, 347–358.

Al'bertin, S. V., Mulder, A. B., & Wiener, S. I. (2003). The advantages of electrophysiological control for the localization and selective lesioning of the nucleus accumbens in rats. *Neuroscience and Behavioral Physiology, 33*(8), 805–809.

Albert, M. L., & Obler, L. (1978). *The bilingual brain: Neuropsychological and neurolinguistic aspects of bilingualism.* New York: Academic Press.

Allain, P., Berrut, G., Etcharry-Bouyx, F., Barre, J., Dubas, F., & Le Gal, D. (2007). Executive functions in normal aging: An examination of script sequencing, script sorting, and script monitoring. *The Journals of Gerontology Series B: Psychological Sciences and Social Sciences, 62*, 187–190.

Almor, A., & Sloman, S. A. (1996). Is deontic reasoning special? *Psychological Review, 103*, 503–546.

Altschuler, E. L., Multari, A., Hirstein, W., & Ramachandran, V. S. (2006). Situational therapy for Wernicke's aphasia. *Medical Hypotheses, 67*(4), 713–716.

Amabile, T. M. (1996). *Creativity in context.* Boulder, CO: Westview.

Amabile, T. M., & Rovee-Collier, C. (1991). Contextual variation and memory retrieval at six months. *Child Development, 62*(5), 1155–1166.

Aminoff, E., Schacter, D. L., & Bar, M. (2008). The cortical underpinnings of context-based memory distortion. *Journal of Cognitive Neuroscience, 20*(12), 2226–2237.

American Psychiatric Association. (1994). *Diagnostic and statistical manual of mental disorders* (4th ed.). Washington, DC: Author.

Anaki, D., Kaufman, Y., Freedman, M., & Moscovitch, M. (2007). Associative (prosop) agnosia without (apparent) perceptual deficits: A case–study. *Neuropsychologia, 45*(8), 1658–1671.

Anderson, A. K., & Phelps, E. A. (2001). Lesions of the human amygdala impair enhanced perception of emotionally salient events. *Nature, 411*, 305–309.

Anderson, B. F. (1975). *Cognitive psychology.* New York: Academic Press.

Anderson, D. P., Harvey, A. S., Saling, M. M., Anderson, V., Kean, M., Abbott, D. F., et al. (2006). fMRI lateralization of expressive language in children with cerebral lesions. *Epilepsia 47*(6), 998–1008.

Anderson, J. R. (1972). FRAN: A simulation model of free recall. In G. H. Bower (Ed.), *The psychology of learning and motivation* (Vol. 5, pp. 315–378). New York: Academic Press.

Anderson, J. R. (1976). *Language, memory, and thought.* Hillsdale, NJ: Erlbaum.

Anderson, J. R. (1980). Concepts, propositions, and schemata: What are the cognitive units? *Nebraska Symposium on Motivation, 28*, 121–162.

Anderson, J. R. (1983). *The architecture of cognition.* Cambridge, MA: Harvard University Press.

Anderson, J. R. (1985). *Cognitive psychology and its implications.* New York: Freeman.

Anderson, J. R. (1991). The adaptive nature of human categorization. *Psychological Review, 98*, 409–429.

Anderson, J. R. (1993). *Rules of the mind.* Hillsdale, NJ: Erlbaum.

Anderson, J. R. (1996). ACT: A simple theory of complex cognition. *American Psychologist, 51*, 355–365.

Anderson, J. R., Bothell, D., Byrne, M. D., Douglass, S., Lebiere, C., & Qin, Y. (2004). An integrated theory of the mind. *Psychological Review, 111*(4),1036–1060.

Anderson, J. R., & Bower, G. H. (1973). *Human associative memory.* New York: Wiley.

Anderson, J. R., Budiu, R., & Reder, L. M. (2001). A theory of sentence memory as part of a general theory of memory. *Journal of Memory & Language, 45*, 277–367.

Anderson, M. (2005). Marrying intelligence and cognition. In R. J. Sternberg & J. E. Pretz (Eds.), *Cognition and intelligence* (pp. 268–287). New York: Cambridge University Press.

Anderson, R. C., & Pichert, J. W. (1978). Recall of previously unrecallable information following a shift in perspective. *Journal of Verbal Learning and Verbal Behavior, 17,* 1–12.

Anderson, S. W., Rizzo, M., Skaar, N., Stierman, L., Cavaco, S., Dawson, J., et al. (2007). Amnesia and driving. *Journal of Clinical and Experimental Neuropsychology, 29*(1), 1–12.

Andrade, J. (2010). What does doodling do? *Applied Cognitive Psychology, 24*(1), 100–106.

Andreasen, N. C., O'Leary, D. S., Cizadlo, T., Arndt, S., Rezai, K., Watkins, G. L., et al. (1995). Remembering the past: Two facets of episodic memory explored with positron emission tomography. *American Journal of Psychiatry, 152,* 1576–1585.

Andreou, G., & Karapetsas, A. (2004). Verbal abilities in low and highly proficient bilinguals. *Journal of Psycholinguistic Research, 33*(5), 357–364.

Andreou, P., Neale, B. M., Chen, W., Christiansen, H., Gabriel, I., Heise, A., et al. (2007). Reaction time performance in ADHD: improvement under fast-incentive condition and familial effects. *Psychological Medicine (2007), 37:*1703–1715.

Ang, S., Dyne, L. v., & Tan, M. L. (Eds.). (in press). *Cultural intelligence.* In R. J. Sternberg & S. B. Kaufman (Eds.), *Cambridge Handbook of Intelligence.* New York: Cambridge University Press.

Anglin, J. M. (1993). Vocabulary development: A morphological analysis. *Monographs of the Society for Research in Child Development, 58,* (No. 10).

Appel, L. F., Cooper, R. G., McCarrell, N., Sims-Knight, J., Yussen, S. R., & Flavell, J. H. (1972). The development of the distinction between perceiving and memorizing. *Child Development, 43,* 1365–1381.

Appleton-Knapp, S. L., Bjork, R. A., & Wickens, T. D. (2005). Examining the spacing effect in advertising: Encoding variability, retrieval processes, and their interaction. *Journal of Consumer Research, 32,* 266–276.

Ardekani, B. A., Nierenberg, J., Hoptman, M., Javitt, D., & Lim, K. O. (2003). MRI study of white matter diffusion anisotropy in schizophrenia. *Brain Imaging, 14*(16), 2025–2029.

Argamon, S., Koppel, M., Fine, J., & Shimoni, A. S. (2003). Gender, genre, and writing style in formal written texts. *Text, 23*(3), 321–346.

Armstrong, S. L., Gleitman, L. R., & Gleitman, H. (1983). What some concepts might not be. *Cognition, 13,* 263–308.

Ask, K., & Granhag, A. (2005). Motivational sources of confirmation bias in criminal investigations: The need for cognitive closure. *Journal of Investigative Psychology and Offender Profiling, 2*(1), 43–63.

Atkinson, R. C., & Shiffrin, R. M. (1968). Human memory: A proposed system and its control processes. In K. W. Spence & J. T. Spence (Eds.), *The psychology of learning and motivation: Vol. 2. Advances in research and theory.* New York: Academic Press.

Atkinson, R. C., & Shiffrin, R. M. (1971). The control of short-term memory. *Scientific American, 225,* 82–90.

Atran, S. (1999). Itzaj Maya folkbiological taxonomy: Cognitive universals and cultural particulars. In D. L. Medin & S. Atran (Eds.), *Folkbiology* (pp. 119–213). Cambridge, MA: MIT Press.

Attention deficit hyperactivity disorder. (http://www.nimh.nih.gov/Publicat/ADHD.cfm, retreived 6/01/10).

Averbach, E., & Coriell, A. S. (1961). Short-term memory in vision. *Bell System Technical Journal, 40,* 309–328.

Ayotte, J., Peretz, I., Rousseau, I., Bard, C., & Bojanowski, M. (2000). Patterns of music agnosia associated with middle cerebral artery infarcts. *Brain, 123,* 1926–1938.

Bachevalier, J., & Mishkin, M. (1986). Visual recognition impairment follows ventromedial but not dorsolateral frontal lesions in monkeys. *Behavioral Brain Research, 20*(3), 249–261.

Backhaus, J., Junghanns, K., Born, J., Hohaus, K., Faasch, F., & Hohagen, F. (2006). Impaired declarative memory consolidation during sleep in patients with primary insomnia: Influence of sleep architecture and nocturnal cortisol release. *Biological Psychiatry, 60*(12), 1324–1330.

Baddeley, A. (2007). *Working memory, thought, and action.* New York: Oxford University Press.

Baddeley, A. D. (1966). Short-term memory for word sequences as function of acoustic, semantic, and formal similarity. *Quarterly Journal of Experimental Psychology, 18,* 362–365.

Baddeley, A. D. (1989). The psychology of remembering and forgetting. In T. Butler (Ed.), *Memory: History, culture and the mind.* London: Basil Blackwell.

Baddeley, A. D. (1990a). *Human memory.* Hove, England: Erlbaum.

Baddeley, A. D. (1990b). *Human memory: Theory and practice.* Needham Heights, MA: Allyn & Bacon.

Baddeley, A. D. (2000). Short-term and working memory. In E. Tulving & F. I. M. Craik (Eds.), *The Oxford handbook of memory* (pp. 77–92). New York: Oxford University Press.

Baddeley, A. D. (2002). The psychology of memory. In A. D. Baddeley, M. D. Kopelman & B. A. Wilson (Eds.), *The handbook of memory disorders.* Chichester, UK: John Wiley & Sons.

Baddeley, A. D. (2006). Working memory: an overview. In S. J. Pickering (Ed.), *Working memory and education* (pp. 3–31). Burlington, MA: Elsevier.

Baddeley, A. D., Hitch, G. J., & Allen, R. J. (2009). Working memory and binding in sentence recall. *Journal of Memory and Language, 61,* 438–456.

Baddeley A. D., & Larsen J. D. (2007). The phonological loop unmasked? A comment on the evidence for a "perceptual-gestural" alternative. *The Quarterly Journal of Experimental Psychology, 60*(4), 497–504.

Baddeley, A. D., Thomson, N., & Buchanan, M. (1975). Word length and the structure of short-term memory. *Journal of Verbal Learning & Verbal Behavior, 14*(6), 575–589.

Badgaiyan, R. D., Schacter, D. L., & Alpert, N. M. (1999). Auditory priming within and across modalities: Evidence from positron emission tomography. *Journal of Cognitive Neuroscience, 11,* 337–348.

Bahrami, B., Carmel, D., Walsh, V., Rees, G., & Lavie, N. (2008). Unconscious orientation processing depends on perceptual load. *Journal of Vision, 8*(3), 1–10.

Bahrick, H. P. (1984a). Fifty years of second language attrition: Implications for programmatic research. *Modern Language Journal, 68*(2), 105–118.

Bahrick, H. P. (1984b). Semantic memory content in permastore: Fifty years of memory for Spanish learned in school. *Journal of Experimental Psychology: General, 113*(1), 1–29.

Bahrick, H. P. (2000). Long-term maintenance of knowledge. In E. Tulving & F. I. M. Craik (Eds.), *The Oxford handbook of memory* (pp. 347–362). New York: Oxford University Press.

Bahrick, H. P., & Hall, L. K. (1991). Lifetime maintenance of high school mathematics content. *Journal of Experimental Psychology: General, 120*(1), 20–33.

Bahrick, H. P., Bahrick, L. E., Bahrick, A. S., & Bahrick, P. E. (1993). Maintenance of foreign language vocabulary and the spacing effect. *Psychological Science, 4*(5), 316–321.

Bahrick, H. P., Bahrick, P. O., & Wittlinger, R. P. (1975). Fifty years of memory for names and faces: A cross-sectional approach. *Journal of Experimental Psychology: General, 104,* 54–75.

Bahrick, H. P., Hall, L. K., Goggin, J. P., Bahrick, L. E., & Berger, S. A. (1994). Fifty years of language maintenance and language dominance in bilingual Hispanic immigrants. *Journal of Experimental Psychology: General, 123*(3), 264–283.

Bahrick, H. P., & Phelps, E. A. (1987). Retention of Spanish vocabulary over eight years. *Journal of Experimental Psychology: Learning, Memory, & Cognition, 13,* 344–349.

Bailenson, J. N., Blascovich, J., Beall, A. C., & Loomis, J. M. (2003). Interpersonal distance in immersive virtual environments, *Personality and Social Psychology Bulletin, 29*(7), 819–833.

Baker, S. C., Rogers, R. D., Owen, A. M., Frith, C. D., Dolan, R. J., Frackowiak, R. S. J., et al. (1996). Neural systems engaged by planning: A PET study of the Tower of London task. *Neuropsychologia, 34,* 515–526.

Bakker, D. J. (2006). Treatment of developmental dyslexia: a review. *Developmental Neurorehabilitation, 9*(1), 3–13.

Baliki, M., Katz, J., Chialvo, D. R., & Apkarian, A. V. (2005). Single subject pharmacological-MRI (phMRI) study: Modulation of brain activity of psoriatic arthritis pain by cyclooxygenase-2 inhibitor. *Molecular Pain, 1,* 1–32.

Ball, L. J., & Quayle, J. D. (2009). Phonological and visual distinctiveness effects in syllogistic reasoning: Implications for mental models theory. *Memory & Cognition, 37*(6), 759–768.

Baltes, P. B., Dittmann-Kohli, F., & Dixon, R. A. (1984). New perspectives on the development of intelligence in adulthood: Toward a dual-process conception and a model of selective optimization with compensation. In P. B. Baltes & O. G. Brim, Jr. (Eds.), Life-span development and behavior (Vol. 6, pp. 33–76). New York: Academic Press.

Baltes, P. B., & Smith, J. (1990). Toward a psychology of wisdom and its ontogenesis. In R. J. Sternberg (Ed.), *Wisdom: Its nature, origins, and development* (pp. 87–120). New York: Cambridge University Press.

Banaji, M. R., & Crowder, R. G. (1989). The bankruptcy of everyday memory. *American Psychologist, 44,* 1185–1193.

Band, G. P. H., & Kok, A. (2000). Age effects on response monitoring in a mental-rotation task. *Biological Psychology, 51,* 201–221.

Bandler, R., & Shipley, M. T. (1994). Columnar organization in the midbrain periaqueductal gray: Modules for emotional expression? *Trends in Neuroscience, 17,* 379–389.

Bandura, A. (1977a). *Social learning theory.* Englewood Cliffs, NJ: Prentice-Hall.

Bandura, A. (1977b). *Social learning theory.* Englewood Cliffs, NJ: Prentice-Hall.

Bar, M. (2004). Visual objects in context. *Nature Reviews: Neuroscience, 5,* 617–629.

Bar, M. (2007). The proactive brain: using analogies and associations to generate predictions. *Trends in Neurosciences, 11*(7), 280–289.

Barker, B. A., & Newman, R. S. (2004). Listen to your mother! The role of talker familiarity in infant streaming. *Cognition, 94*(2), B45–B53.

Baron, J. (1988). *Thinking and deciding.* New York: Cambridge University Press.

Baron-Cohen, S. (2003). *The essential difference: The truth about the male and female brain.* New York: Basic Books.

Baron-Cohen, S., Leslie, A. M., & Frith, U. (1985). Does the autistic child have a "theory of mind"? *Cognition, 21,* 37–46.

Baron-Cohen, S., Ring, H. A., Bullmore, E. T., Wheelwright, S., Ashwin, C., & Williams, S. C. R. (2000). The amygdala theory of autism. *Neuroscience Biobehavior Review, 24,* 355–364.

Barraclough, D. J., Conroy, M. L., & Lee, D. (2004). Prefrontal cortex and decision making in a mixed-strategy game. *Nature Neuroscience, 7,* 404–410.

Barrett, L. F., Tugade, M. M., & Engle, R. W. (2004). Individual differences in working memory capacity and dual-process theories of the mind. *Psychological Bulletin, 130,* 553–573.

Barrett, P. T., & Eysenck, H. J. (1992). Brain evoked potentials and intelligence: The Hendrickson paradigm. *Intelligence, 16*(3, 4), 361–381.

Barron, F. (1988). Putting creativity to work. In R. J. Sternberg (Ed.), *The nature of creativity* (pp. 76–98). New York: Cambridge University Press.

Barsalou, L. W. (1983). Ad hoc categories. *Memory and Cognition, 11,* 211–227.

Barsalou, L. W. (1994). Flexibility, structure, and linguistic vagary in concepts: Manifestations of a compositional system of perceptual symbols. In A. F. Collins, S. E. Gathercole, M. A. Conway, & P. E. Morris (Eds.), *Theories of memory* (pp. 29–101). Hillsdale, NJ: Erlbaum.

Barsalou, L. W. (2000). Concepts: Structure. In A. E. Kazdin (Ed.), *Encyclopedia of psychology* (Vol. 2, pp. 245–248). Washington, DC: American Psychological Association.

Bartlett, F. C. (1932). Remembering: *A study in experimental and social psychology.* Cambridge, UK: Cambridge University Press.

Barton, J. J. S. (2008). Structure and function in acquired prosopagnosia: Lessons from a series of 10 patients with brain damage. *Journal of Neuropsychology, 2*(1), 197–225.

Bassok, M. (2003). Analogical transfer in problem solving. In J. E. Davidson & R. J. Sternberg (Eds.), *The psychology of problem solving* (pp. 343–369). New York: Cambridge University Press.

Bassok, M., & Holyoak, K. (1989). Interdomain transfer between isomorphic topics in algebra and physics. *Journal of Experimental Psychology: Learning,* 153–166.

Bassock, M., Wu, L., & Olseth, K. L. (1995). Judging a book by its cover: Interpretative effects of content on problem solving transfer. *Memory and Cognition, 23,* 354–367.

Bastian, B., & Haslam, N. (2006). Psychological essentialism and stereotype endorsement. *Journal of Experimental Social Psychology, 42,* 228–235.

Bastik, T. (1982). *Intuition: How we think and act.* Chichester, UK: Wiley.

Bates, E., & Goodman, J. (1999). On the emergence of grammar from the lexicon. In B. MacWhinney (Ed.), *The emergence of language* (pp. 29–80). Mahwah, NJ: Erlbaum.

Baudouin, A., Vanneste, S. Pouthas, V., & Isingrini, M. (2006). Age-related changes in duration reproduction: Involvement of working memory processes. *Brain and Cognition, 62*(1), 17–23.

Bauer, P. J. (2005). Developments in declarative memory. Decreasing susceptibility to storage failure over the second year of life. *Psychological Science 16*(1), 41–47.

Bauer, P. J., & Van Abbema, D. L. (2003). Memory, development of. In L. Nadel (Ed.), *Encyclopedia of cognitive science* (Vol. 2, pp. 1090–1095). London: Nature Publishing Group.

Baumgartner, C. (2000). Clinical applications of magnetoencephalography. *Journal of Clinical Neurophysiology, 17*(2), 175–176.

Bavelier, D., Newport, E. L., Hall, M. L., Supalla, T., & Boutla, M. (2006). Persistent difference in short-term memory span between sign and speech: Implications for cross-linguistic comparisons. *Psychological Science, 17*(12),1090–1092.

Baxter, J. C. (1970). Interpersonal spacing in natural settings. *Sociometry, 33*(4), 444–456.

Baylis, G., Driver, J., & McLeod, P. (1992). Movement and proximity constrain miscombinations of colour and form. *Perception, 21*(2), 201–218.

Bearden, C. E., Glahn, D. C., Monkul, E. S., Barrett, J., Najt, P., Villarreal, V., et al. (2006). Patterns of memory impairment in bipolar disorder and unipolar major depression. *Psychiatry Research, 142*(2–3), 139–150.

Beardsley, M. (1962). The metaphorical twist. *Philosophical Phenomenological Research, 22,* 293–307.

Beauchamp, M. S., Nath, A. R., & Pasalar, S. (2010). fMRI-guided transcranial magnetic stimulation reveals that the superior temporal sulcus is a cortical locus of the McGurk effect. *The Journal of Neuroscience, 30*(7), 2414–2417.

Bechtereva, N. P., Korotkov, A. D., Pakhomov, S. V., Roudas, M. S., Starchenko, M. G., Medvedev, S. V. (2004). PET study of brain maintenance of verbal creative activity. *International Journal of Psychophysiology, 53,* 11–20.

Beck, D. M., Muggleton, N., Walsh, V., & Lavie, N. (2006). Right parietal cortex plays a critical role in change blindness. *Cerebral Cortex, 16*(5), 712–717.

Beck, I. L., Perfetti, C. A., & McKeown, M. G. (1982). Effects of long-term vocabulary instruction on lexical access and reading comprehension. *Journal of Educational Psychology, 74,* 506–521.

Begg, I., & Denny, J. (1969). Empirical reconciliation of atmosphere and conversion interpretations of syllogistic reasoning. *Journal of Experimental Psychology, 81,* 351–354.

Bee, M. A., & Micheyl, C. (2008). The cocktail party problem: What is it? How can it be solved? And why should animal behaviorists study it? *Journal of Comparative Psychology, 122*(3), 235–251.

Beggs, A., & Graddy, K. (2009). Anchoring effects: Evidence from art auctions. *American Economic Review, 99*(3), 1027–1039.

Beghetto, R. A. (2010). Creativity in the classroom. In J. C. Kaufman & R. J. Sternberg (Eds.), *The Cambridge handbook of creativity* (pp. 447–463). New York: Cambridge University Press.

Behrmann, M., Kosslyn, S. M., & Jeannerod, M. (Eds.). (1996). *The neuropsychology of mental imagery.* New York: Pergamon.

Bellezza, F. S. (1984). The self as a mnemonic device: The role of internal cues. *Journal of Personality and Social Psychology, 47,* 506–516.

Bellezza, F. S. (1992). Recall of congruent information in the self-reference task. *Bulletin of the Psychonomic Society, 30*(4), 275–278.

Belmont, J. M., & Butterfield, E. C. (1971). Learning strategies as determinants of memory deficiencies. *Cognitive Psychology, 2,* 411–420.

Bencini, G., & Valian, V. (2008). Abstract sentence representations in 3-year-olds: Evidence from language production and comprehension. *A Journal of Memory and Language, 59*(1), 97–113.

Benjamin, L. T., Jr., & Baker, D. B. (2004). Science for sale: Psychology's earliest adventures in American advertising. In J. D. Williams, W. N. Lee, & C. P. Haugtvedt (Eds.), *Diversity in advertising: Broadening the scope of research directions* (pp. 22–39). Mahwah, NJ: Lawrence Erlbaum.

Bennis, W. M., & Pachur, T. (2006). Fast and frugal heuristics in sports. *Psychology of Sport and Exercise, 7*(6), 611–629.

Ben-Zeev, T. (1996). When erroneous mathematical thinking is just as "correct": The oxymoron of rational errors. In R. J. Sternberg & T. Ben-Zeev (Eds.), *The nature of mathematical thinking* (pp. 55–79). Mahwah, NJ: Erlbaum.

Beowulf from http://www8.georgetown.edu/departments/medieval/labyrinth/library/oe/texts/a4.1.html.

Bergerbest, D., Ghahremani, D. G., & Gabrieli, J. D. E. (2004). Neural correlates of auditory repetition priming: Reduced fMRI activation in the auditory cortex. *Journal of Cognitive Neuroscience, 16,* 966–977.

Berkow, R. (1992). *The Merck manual of diagnosis and therapy* (16th ed.). Rahway, NJ: Merck Research Laboratories.

Berkowitz, S. R., Laney, C., Morris, E. K., Garry, M., & Loftus, E. F. (2008). Pluto behaving badly: False beliefs and their consequences. *American Journal of Psychology, 121*(4), 643–660.

Berlin, B., & Kay, P. (1969). *Basic color terms: Their universality and evolution.* Los Angeles: University of California Press.

Berliner, H. J. (1969, August). Chess playing program. *SICART Newsletter, 19,* 19–20.

Berman, M. G., Jonides, J., & Lewis, R. L. (2009). In search of decay in verbal short-term memory. *Journal of Experimental Psychology: Learning, Memory, and Cognition, 35*(2), 317–333.

Bernstein, A. (1958, July). A chess-playing program for the IBM704. *Chess Review,* 208–209.

Bernstein, D. M., & Loftus, E. F. (2009). The consequences of false memories for food preferences and choices. *Perspectives on Psychological Science, 4,* 135–139.

Bernstein, M. J., Young, S. G., & Hugenberg, K. (2007). The cross-category effect: Mere social categorization is sufficient to elicit an own-group bias in face recognition. *Psychological Science, 18*(8), 706–712.

Berry, C. J., Shanks, D. R., & Henson, R. N. A. (2008). A unitary signal-detection model of implicit and explicit memory. *Trends in Cognitive Sciences, 12*(10), 367–373.

Berry, D. (2002). Donald Broadbent. *The Psychologist, 15*(8), 402–405.

Berryhill, M. E., Phuong, L., Picasso, L., Cabeza, R., & Olson, I. R. (2007). Parietal lobe and episodic memory: bilateral damage causes impaired free recall of autobiographical memory. *Journal of Neuroscience, 27,* 14415–14423.

Bertoncini, J. (1993). Infants' perception of speech units: Primary representation capacities. In B. B. De Boysson-Bardies, S. De Schonen, P. Jusczyk, P. MacNeilage, & J. Morton (Eds.), *Developmental neurocognition: Speech and face processing in the first year of life.* Dordrecht, Germany: Kluwer.

Bertsch, K., Böhnke, R., Kruk, M. R., & Naumann, E. (2009). Influence of aggression on information processing in the emotional Stroop task - an event-related potential study *Frontiers in Behavioral Neuroscience, 3,* 1–10.

Besnard, D., & Cacitti, L. (2005). Interface changes causing accidents. An empirical study of negative transfer. *International Journal of Human-Computer Studies, 62*(1), 105–125.

Bessman, P., Heider, T., Watten, V. P., & Watten, R. G. (2009). The tinnitus intensive therapy habituation program: a 2-year follow-up pilot study on subjective tinnitus. *Rehabilitation Psychology, 54*(2), 133–137.

Best, J. (2003). Memory mnemonics. In L. Nadel (Ed.), *Encyclopedia of cognitive science* (Vol. 2, pp. 1081–1084). London: Nature Publishing Group.

Beste, C., Heil, M., & Konrad, C. (2010). Individual differences in ERPs during mental rotation of characters: Lateralization, and performance level. *Brain and Cognition, 72,* 238–243.

Bethell-Fox, C. E., & Shepard, R. N. (1988). Mental rotation: Effects of stimulus complexity and familiarity. *Journal of Experimental Psychology: Human Perception and Performance, 14*(1), 12–23.

Beyer, J. L., Ranga, K., & Krishnan, R. (2002). Volumetric brain imaging findings mood disorders. *Bipolar Disorders, 4*(2), 89–104.

Bhatia, T. T., & Ritchie, W. C. (1999). The bilingual child: Some issues and perspectives. In W. C. Ritchie & T. K. Bhatia (Eds.), *Handbook of child language acquisition* (pp. 569–646). San Diego: Academic Press.

Biais, B., & Weber, M. (2009). Hindsight bias, risk perception, and investment performance. *Management Science, 55*(6), 1018–1029.

Bialystok, E., & Hakuta, K. (1994). *In other words: The science and psychology of second-language acquisition.* New York: Basic Books.

Bialystok, E., & Craik, F. I. M. (2010). Cognitive and linguistic processing in the bilingual mind. *Current Directions in Psychological Science, 19*(1), 19–23.

Bialystok, E., Craik, F. I. M., & Freedman, M. (2007). Bilingualism as a protection against the onset of symptoms of dementia. *Neuropsychologia, 45,* 459–464.

Bickerton, D. (1990). *Language and species.* Chicago: University of Chicago Press.

Biederman, I. (1972). Perceiving real-world scenes. *Science, 177*(4043), 77–80.

Biederman, I. (1987). Recognition-by-components: A theory of human image understanding. *Psychological Review, 94,* 115–147.

Biederman, I. (1993a). Geon theory as an account of shape recognition in mind and brain. *Irish Journal of Psychology, 14*(3), 314–327.

Biederman, I. (1993b). Visual object recognition. In A. I. Goldman (Ed.), *Readings in philosophy and cognitive science* (pp. 9–21). Cambridge, MA: MIT Press. (Original work published 1990)

Biederman, I. (2001). Recognizing depth-rotated objects: A review of results of research and theory. *Spatial Vision, 13,* 241–253.

Biederman, I., Glass, A. L., & Stacy, E. W. (1973). Searching for objects in real-world scenes. *Journal of Experimental Psychology, 97*(1), 22–27.

Biederman, I., Rabinowitz, J. C., Glass, A. L., & Stacy, E. W. (1974). On the information extracted from a glance at a scene. *Journal of Experimental Psychology, 103*(3), 597–600.

Biederman, J., & Faraone, S. V. (2005). Attention-deficit hyperactivity disorder. *The Lancet, 366*(9481), 237–248.

Biernat, M., & Ma, J. E. (2005). Stereotypes and the confirmability of trait concepts. *Personality and Social Psychology Bulletin, 31*(4), 483–495.

Bilalic, M., McLeod, P., & Gobet, F. (2008a). Expert and "novice" problem solving strategies in chess: Sixty years of citing de Groot (1946). *Thinking & Reasoning, 14*(4), 395–408.

Bilalic, M., McLeod, P., & Gobet, F. (2008b). Inflexibility of experts—Reality or myth? Quantifying the Einstellung effect in chess masters. *Cognitive Psychology, 56*, 73–102.

Bilda, Z., Gero, J. S., & Purcell, T. (2006). To sketch or not to sketch? That is the question. *Design Studies, 27*(5), 587–613.

Binder, J. R. (2009). fMRI of language systems. In M. Filippi (Ed.), *fMRI techniques and protocols* (pp. 323–351). New York: Humana Press.

Binder, J. R., Frost, J. A., Hammeke, T. A., Bellgowan, P. S. F., Springer, J. A., Kaufman, J. N., et al. (2000). Human temporal lobe activation by speech and nonspeech sounds. *Cerebral Cortex, 10*, 512–528.

Binder, J. R., Frost, J. A., Hammeke, T. A., Rao, S. M., & Cox, R. W. (1996). Function of the left planum temporale in auditory and linguistic processing. *Brain, 119*, 1239–1247.

Binder, J. R., Medler, D. A., Desai, R., Conant, L. L., & Liebenthal, E. (2005). Some neurophysiological constraints on models of word naming. *NeuroImage, 27*, 677–693.

Binder, J. R., Westbury, C. F., Possing, E. T., McKiernan, K. A., & Medler, D. A. (2005). Distinct brain systems for processing concrete and abstract concepts. *Journal of Cognitive Neuroscience, 17*, 905–917.

Bingman, V. P., Hough II, G. E., Kahn, M. C., & Siegel, J. J. (2003). The homing pigeon hippocampus and space: In search of adaptive specialization. *Brain, Behavior and Evolution, 62*(2), 117–127.

Birbaumer, N. (1999). Rain man's revelations. *Nature, 399*, 211–212.

Birdsong, D. (1999). Introduction: Whys and why nots of the critical period hypothesis for second language acquisition. In D. Birdsong (Ed.), *Second language acquisition and the critical period hypothesis* (pp. 1–22). Mahwah, NJ: Erlbaum.

Birdsong, D. (2006). Age and second language acquisition and processing: A selective overview. *Language Learning 56*(1), 9–49.

Birdsong, D. (2009). Age and the end state of second language acquistion. In W. C. Ritchie & T. K. Bhatia (Eds.), *The new handbook of second language acquisition* (pp. 401–424). Bingley, UK: Emerald Group.

Bisiach, E., & Luzzatti, C. (1978). Unilateral neglect of representational space. *Cortex, 14*(129–133).

Bjork, E. L., Bjork, R. A., & MacLeod, M. D. (2005). Types and consequences of forgetting: intended and unintended. In L.-G. Nilsson & N. Ohta (Eds.), *Memory and society: Psychological perspectives* (pp. 141–165). New York: Psychology Press.

Bjorklund, D. F., Schneider, W., & Hernández Blasi, C. (2003). Memory. In L. Nadel (Ed.), *Encyclopedia of cognitive science* (Vol. 2, pp. 1059–1065). London: Nature Publishing Group.

Black, M. (1962). *Models and metaphors.* Ithaca, NY: Cornell University Press.

Blackwood, N. J., Howard, R. J., Fytche, D. H., Simmons, A., Bentall, R. P., Murray, R. M. (2000). Imaging attentional and attributional bias: An fMRI approach to the paranoid delusion. *Psychological Medicine, 30*, 873–883.

Blake, R. (2000). Vision and sight: Structure and function. In A. E. Kazdin (Ed.), *Encyclopedia of psychology* (pp. 177–178). Washington, DC: American Psychological Association.

Blake, R., & Shiffrar, M. (2007). Perception of human motion. *Annual Review of Psychology, 58*, 47–73.

Blake, W. C. A., McKenzie, K. J., & Hamm, J. P. (2002). Cerebral asymmetry for mental rotation: Effects of response hand, handedness and gender. *NeuroReport, 13*(15), 1929–1932.

Blakemore, S.-J., Smith, J., Steel, R., Johnstone, E. C., & Frith, C. D. (2000). The perception of self-produced sensory stimuli in patients with auditory hallucinations and passivity experiences: Evidence for a breakdown in self-monitoring. *Psychological Medicine, 30*, 1131–1139.

Blakemore, S.-J., Wolpert, D. M., & Frith, C. D. (1998). Central cancellation of self-produced tickle sensation. *Nature Neuroscience, 1*(7), 635–640.

Blessing, S. B., & Ross, B. H. (1996). Content effects in problem categorization and problem solving. *Journal of Experimental Psychology: Learning, Memory, and Cognition, 22*, 792–810.

Bloom, B. S., & Broder, L. J. (1950). *Problem-solving processes of college students.* Chicago: University of Chicago Press.

Bloom, P. (2000). *How children learn the meanings of words.* Cambridge, MA: MIT Press.

Bock, K. (1990). Structure in language: Creating form in talk. *American Psychologist, 45*(11), 1221–1236.

Bock, K., Loebell, H., & Morey, R. (1992). From conceptual roles to structural relations: Bridging the syntactic cleft. *Psychological Review, 99*(1), 150–171.

Boden, M. A. (1999). Computer models of creativity. In R. J. Sternberg (Ed.), *Handbook of creativity* (pp. 351–372). New York: Cambridge University Press.

Bohannon, J. (1988). Flashbulb memories for the space shuttle disaster: A tale of two theories. *Cognition, 29*(2), 179–196.

Bolte, S., Hubl, D., Feineis-Matthews, S., Pruvulovic, D., Dierks, T., & Poustka, F. (2006). Facial affect recognition training in autism: Can we animate the fusiform gyrus? *Behavioral Neuroscience, 120*(1), 211–216.

Borges, B., Goldstein, D. G., Ortmann, A. & Gigerenzer, G. (1999). Can ignorance beat the stock market? In Gigerenzer, G., Todd, P. M., & the ABC Research Group (Eds.), *Simple heuristics that make us smart* (pp. 59–72). New York: Oxford University Press.

Boring, E. G. (1923, June 6). Intelligence as the tests test it. *New Republic*, 35–37.

Boring, E. G. (1929). *A history of experimental psychology.* New York: Appleton-Century-Crofts.

Boring, E. G. (1942). *Sensation and perception in the history of experimental psychology.* New York: Appleton-Century-Crofts.

Boring, E. G. (1950). *A history of experimental psychology.* New York: Appleton-Century-Crofts.

Boroditsky, L., Schmidt, L. A., & Phillips, W. (2003). Sex, syntax, and semantics. In D. Gentner & S. Goldin-Meadow (Eds.), *Language in mind: Advances in the studies of language and cognition.* Cambridge, MA: MIT Press.

Borovsky, D., & Rovee-Collier, C. (1990). Contextual constraints on memory retrieval at six months. *Child Development, 61*(5), 1569–1583.

Bors, D. A., & Forrin, B. (1995). Age, speed of information processing, recall, and fluid intelligence. *Intelligence, 20*, 229–248.

Bors, D. A., MacLeod, C. M., & Forrin, B. (1993). Eliminating the IQ–RT correlation by eliminating an experimental confound. *Intelligence, 17*(4), 475–500.

Borst, G., & Kosslyn, S. M. (2008). Visual mental imagery and visual perception: Structural equivalence revealed by scanning processes. *Memory & Cognition, 36*(4), 849–862.

Bortfeld, H., Morgan, J. L., Golinkoff, R. M., & Rathbun, K. (2005). Mommy and me: Familiar names help launch babies into speech-stream segmentation. *Psychological Science, 16*(4), 298–304.

Bosco, A., Longoni, A. M., & Vecchi, T. (2004). Gender effects in spatial orientation: Cognitive profiles and mental strategies. *Applied Cognitive Psychology, 18*(5), 519–532.

Bothwell, R. K., Brigham, J. C., & Malpass, R. S. (1989). Cross-racial identification. *Personality & Social Psychology Bulletin, 15*(1), 19–25.

Bourguignon, E. (2000). Consciousness and unconsciousness: Cross-cultural experience. In A. E. Kazdin (Ed.), *Encyclopedia of psychology* (pp. 275–277). Washington, DC: American Psychological Association.

Bousfield, W. A. (1953). The occurrence of clustering in the recall of randomly arranged associates. *Journal of General Psychology, 49*, 229–240.

Bower, G. H. (1983). Affect and cognition. *Philosophical Transaction: Royal Society of London* (Series B), *302*, 387–402.

Bower, G. H., Black, J. B., & Turner, T. J. (1979). Scripts in memory for texts. *Cognitive Psychology, 11*, 177–220.

Bower, G. H., Clark, M. C., Lesgold, A. M., & Winzenz, D. (1969). Hierarchical retrieval schemes in recall of categorized word lists. *Journal of Verbal Learning and Verbal Behavior, 8*, 323–343.

Bower, G. H., & Gilligan, S. G. (1979). Remembering information related to one's self. *Journal of Research in Personality, 13*, 420–432.

Bower, G. H., Karlin, M. B., & Dueck, A. (1975). Comprehension and memory for pictures. *Memory & Cognition, 3*, 216–220.

Bowers, K. S., & Farvolden, P. (1996). Revisiting a century-old Freudian slip: From suggestion disavowed to the truth repressed. *Psychological Bulletin, 119*, 355–380.

Bowers, K. S., Regehr, G., Balthazard, C., & Parker, K. (1990). Intuition in the context of discovery. *Cognitive Psychology, 22*, 72–110.

Brady, T. F., Konkle, T., Alvarez, G. A., & Oliva, A. (2008). Visual long-term memory has a massive storage capacity for object details. *Proceedings of the National Academy of Sciences of the United States of America, 105*(38), 14325–14329.

Braine, M. D. S., & O'Brien, D. P. (1991). A theory of if: A lexical entry, reasoning program, and pragmatic principles. *Psychological Review, 98*(2), 182–203.

Brambati, S. M., Termine, C., Ruffino, M., Danna, M., Lanzi, G., Stella, G., et al. (2006). Neuropsychological deficits and neural dysfunction in familial dyslexia. *Brain Research, 1113*(1), 174–185.

Bransford, J. D., & Johnson, M. K. (1972). Contextual prerequisites for understanding: Some investigations of comprehension and recall. *Journal of Verbal Learning and Verbal Behavior, 11*, 717–726.

Bransford, J. D., & Johnson, M. K. (1973). Considerations of some problems of comprehension. In W. G. Chase (Ed.), *Visual information processing* (pp. 383–438). New York: Academic Press.

Bransford, J. D., & Stein, B. S. (1993). *The ideal problem solver: A guide for improving thinking, learning, and creativity* (2nd ed.). New York: W. H. Freeman.

Braun, C. M. J., Godbout, L., Desbiens, C., Daigneault, S., Lussier, F., & Hamel-Hebert, I. (2004). Mental genesis of scripts in adolescents with attention deficit/hyperactivity disorder. *Child Neuropsychology, 10*(4), 280–296.

Braun, K. A., Ellis, R. & Loftus, E. F. (2002). Make my memory: How advertising can change our memories of the past. *Psychology and Marketing, 19*, 1–23.

Braun-LaTour, K. A., LaTour, M. S., Pickrell, J., & Loftus, E. F. (2004–05). How and when advertising can influence memory for consumer experience. *Journal of Advertising, 33*, 7–25.

Brebion, G., David, A. S., Bressan, R. A., & Pilowsky, L. S. (2007). Role of processing speed and depressed mood on encoding, storage, and retrieval memory functions in patients diagnosed with schizophrenia. *Journal of the International Neuropsychological Society, 13*, 99–107.

Brefczynski-Lewis, J. A., Lutz, A., Schaefer, H. S., Levinson, D. B., & Davidson, R. J. (2007). Neural correlates of attentional expertise in long-term meditation practitioners. *Proceedings of the National Academy of Sciences of the United States of America, 104*(27), 11483–11488.

Bregman, A. S. (1990). *Auditory scene analysis: The perceptual organization of sound.* Cambridge, MA: MIT Press.

Breier, J., Fletcher, J., Klaas, P., & Gray, L. (2004). Categorical perception of speech stimuli in children at risk for reading difficulty. *Journal of Experimental Child Psychology, 88*(2), 152–170.

Breier, J., Fletcher, J., Klaas, P., & Gray, L. (2005). The relation between categorical perception of speech stimuli and reading skills in children (A). *Journal of the Acoustical Society of America, 118*(3), 1963.

Brenneis, C. B. (2000). Evaluating the evidence: Can we find authenticated recovered memory? *Psychoanalytic Psychology, 17*, 61–77.

Brennen, T., Vikan, A., & Dybdahl, R. (2007). Are tip-of-the-tongue states universal? Evidence from the speakers of an unwritten language. *Memory, 15*(2), 167–176.

Brent, S. B., Speece, M. W., Lin, C., Dong, Q., et al. (1996). The development of the concept of death among Chinese and U.S. children 3–17 years of age: From binary to 'fuzzy' concepts? *Journal of Death and Dying, 33*(1), 67–83.

Bresnan, J. W. (Ed.). (1982). *The mental representation of grammatical relations.* Cambridge, MA: MIT Press.

Bressan, P., & Pizzighello, S. (2008). The attentional cost of inattentional blindness. *Cognition, 106*, 370–383.

Breuning, M. (2003). The role of analogies and abstract reasoning in decision-making: Evidence from the debate over Truman's proposal for development assistance. *International Studies Quarterly, 47*(2), 229–245.

Brewer, W. F. (1999). Schemata. In R. A. Wilson & F. C. Keil (Eds.), *The MIT encyclopedia of the cognitive sciences* (pp. 729–730). Cambridge, MA: MIT Press.

Brewer, W. F. (2003). Mental models. In L. Nadel (Ed.), *Encyclopedia of cognitive science* (Vol. 3, pp. 1–6). London: Nature Publishing Group.

Briere, J., & Conte, J. R. (1993). Self-reported amnesia for abuse in adults molested as children. *Journal of Traumatic Stress, 6*, 21–31.

Brigden, R. (1933). A tachistoscopic study of the differentiation of perception. *Psychological Monographs, 44*, 153–166.

Brigham, J. C., & Malpass, R. S. (1985). The role of experience and contact in the recognition of faces of own and other-race persons. *Journal of Social Issues, 41*(3), 139–155.

Broadbent, D. E. (1958). *Perception and communication.* Oxford, UK: Pergamon.

Brockmole, J. R., Hambrick, D. Z., Windisch, D. J., & Henderson, J. M. (2008). The role of meaning in contextual cueing: Evidence from chess expertise. *The Quarterly Journal of Experimental Psychology, 61*(12), 1886–1896.

Brooks, L. R. (1968). Spatial and verbal components of the act of recall. *Canadian Journal of Psychology, 22*(5), 349–368.

Brown, A. L. (1978). Knowing when, where, and how to remember: A problem of metacognition. In R. Glaser (Ed.), *Advances in instructional psychology* (Vol. 1, pp. 77–165). Hillsdale, NJ: Erlbaum.

Brown, A. L., & DeLoache, J. S. (1978). Skills, plans, and self-regulation. In R. Siegler (Ed.), *Children's thinking: What develops?* (pp. 3–35). Hillsdale, NJ: Erlbaum.

Brown, C., & Laland, K. (2001). Social learning and life skills training for hatchery reared fish. *Journal of Fish Biology, 59*(3), 471–493.

Brown, C. M., & Hagoort, P. (Eds.) (1999). *Neurocognition of language.* Oxford, UK: Oxford University Press.

Brown, J. A. (1958). Some tests of the decay theory of immediate memory. *Quarterly Journal of Experimental Psychology, 10*, 12–21.

Brown, R. (1965). *Social psychology.* New York: Free Press.

Brown, R. (1973). *A first language: The early stages.* Cambridge, MA: Harvard University Press.

Brown, R., Cazden, C. B., & Bellugi, U. (1969). The child's grammar from 1 to 3. In J. P. Hill (Ed.), *Minnesota Symposium on Child Psychology* (Vol. 2). Minneapolis: University of Minnesota Press.

Brown, R., & Kulik, J. (1977). Flashbulb memories. *Cognition, 5,* 73–99.

Brown, R., & McNeill, D. (1966). The "tip of the tongue" phenomenon. *Journal of Verbal Learning and Verbal Behavior, 5,* 325–337.

Brown, S. C., & Craik, F. I. M. (2000). Encoding and retrieval of information. In E. Tulving & F. I. M. Craik (Eds.), *The Oxford handbook of memory* (pp. 93–108). New York: Oxford University Press.

Bruce, D. (1991). Mechanistic and functional explanations of memory. *American Psychologist, 46*(1), 46–48.

Bruner, J. S. (1957). On perceptual readiness. *Psychological Review, 64,* 123–152.

Bruner, J. S., Goodnow, J. J., & Austin, G. A. (1956). *A study of thinking.* New York: Wiley.

Brungard, D. S., & Simpson, B. D. (2007). Cocktail party listening in a dynamic multitalker environment. *Perception & Psychophysics, 69*(1), 79–91.

Bryan, W. L., & Harter, N. (1899). Studies on the telegraphic language: The acquisition of a hierarchy of habits. *Psychological Review, 6,* 345–375.

Bryson, M., Bereiter, C., Scarmadalia, M., & Joram, E. (1991). Going beyond the problem as given: Problem solving in expert and novice writers. In R. J. Sternberg & P. A. Frensch (Eds.), *Complex problem solving: Principles and mechanisms* (pp. 61–84). Hillsdale, NJ: Erlbaum.

Buchanan, B. G., & Shortliffe, E. H. (1984). *Rule-based expert systems: The MYCIN experiments of the Stanford Heuristic Programming Project.* Reading, MA: Addison-Wesley.

Budak, F., & Topsever, T. M. F. P. (2005). Correlations between nonverbal intelligence and nerve conduction velocities in right-handed male and female subjects. *International Journal of Neuroscience, 115,* 613–623.

Budwig, N. (1995). *A developmental-functionalist approach to child language.* Mahwah, NJ: Erlbaum.

Bunge, S. A., Wendelken, C., Badre, D., & Wagner, A. D. (2004). Analogical reasoning and prefrontal cortex: Evidence for separable retrieval and integration mechanism. *Cerebral Cortex, 15*(3), 239–249.

Bunting, M. (2006). Proactive interference and item similarity in working memory. *Journal of Experimental Psychology: Learning, Memory and Cognition, 32*(2), 183–196.

Burgess, M. C. R, & Weaver, G. E. (2003). Interest and attention in facial recognition. *Perceptual and Motor Skills, 96*(2), 467–480.

Burgund, E. D., & Marsolek, C. J. (2000). Viewpoint-invariant and viewpoint-dependent object recognition in dissociable neural subsystems. *Psychonomic Bulletin & Review, 7,* 480–489.

Buschke, H., Kulansky, G., Katz, M., Stewart, W. F., Sliwinski, M. J., Eckholdt, H. M., et al. (1999). Screening for dementia with the Memory Impairment Screen. *Neurology, 52,* 231–238.

Butler, J., & Rovee-Collier, C. (1989). Contextual gating of memory retrieval. *Developmental Psychobiology, 22,* 533–552.

Butterfield, E. C., Wambold, C., & Belmont, J. M. (1973). On the theory and practice of improving short-term memory. *American Journal of Mental Deficiency, 77,* 654–669.

Butterworth, B., & Howard, D. (1987). Paragrammatisms. *Cognition, 26*(1), 1–37.

Byrne, R. M. J. (1996). A model theory of imaginary thinking. In J. Oakhill & A. Garnham (Eds.), *Mental models in cognitive science* (pp. 155–174). Hove, UK: Taylor & Francis.

Cabeza, R., Daselaar, S. M., Dolcos, F., Prince, S. E., Budde, M., & Nyberg, L. (2004). Task-independent and task-specific age effects on brain activity during working memory, visual attention and episodic retrieval. *Cerebral Cortex, 14,* 364–375.

Cabeza, R., & Kingstone, A. (Eds.). (2006). *Handbook of functional neuroimaging of cognition.* Cambridge, MA: MIT Press.

Cahill, L., Haier, R. J., Fallon, J., Alkire, M. T., Tang, C., Keator, D., Wu, J., & McGaugh, J. L. (1996). Amygdala activity at encoding correlated with long-term, free recall of emotional information. *Proceedings of the National Academy of Sciences, 93,* 8016–8021.

Cahill, L., & McGaugh, J. L. (1996). Modulation of memory storage. *Current Opinion in Neurobiology, 6,* 237–242.

Cain, D. P., Boon, F., & Corcoran, M. E. (2006). Thalamic and hippocampal mechanisms in spatial navigation: A dissociation between brain mechanisms for learning how versus learning where to navigate. *Brain Research, 170*(2), 241–256.

Cain, K., & Oakhill, J. (2007). Reading comprehension difficulties: Correlates, causes, and consequences. In K. Cain & J. Oakhill (Eds.), *Children's comprehension problems in oral and written language: A cognitive perspective.* New York: Guildford Press.

Cain, K., Oakhill, J., & Lemmon, K. (2004). Individual differences in the inference of word meanings from context: The influence of reading comprehension, vocabulary knowledge, and memory capacity. *Journal of Educational Psychology, 96*(4), 671–681.

Cameron, J., & Ritter, A. (2007). Contingency management: perspectives of Australian service providers. *Drug and Alcohol Review, 26,* 183–189.

Campbell, D. A. (1960). Blind variation and selective retention in creative thought as in other knowledge processes. *Psychological Review, 67,* 380–400.

Campbell, J. I. D., & Robert, N. D. (2008). Bidirectional associations in multiplication memory: Conditions of negative and positive transfer. *Journal of Experimental Psychology: Learning, Memory, and Cognition, 34*(3), 546–555.

Campbell, R., MacSweeney, M., & Waters, D. (2007). Sign language and the brain: A review. *Journal of Deaf Studies and Deaf Education.* Advance Access published online June 29, 2007.

Campbell, S. D., & Sharpe, S. A. (2009). Anchoring bias in consensus forecasts and its effect on market prices. *Journal of Financial and Quantitative Analysis, 44*(2), 369–390.

Campitelli, G., Gobet, F., Head, K., Buckley, M., & Parker, A. (2007). Brain localization of memory chunks in chessplayers. *International Journal of Neuroscience, 117,* 1641–1659.

Canli, T., Desmond, J. E., Zhao, Z., & Gabrieli, J. D. (2002). Sex differences in the neural basis of emotional memories. *Proceedings of the National Academies of Sciences, 99,* 10789–10794.

Cant, J. S., & Goodale, M. A. (2007). Attention to form or surface properties modulates different regions of human occipitotemporal cortex. *Cerebral Cortex, 17,* 713–731.

Cant, J. S., Large, M.-E., McCall, L., & Goodale, M. A. (2008). Independent processing of form, colour, and texture in object perception. *Perception, 37,* 57–78.

Cappa, S. F., Perani, D., Grassli, F., Bressi, S., Alberoni M., Franceschi M., et al. (1997). A PET follow-up study of recovery after stroke in acute aphasics. *Brain and Language, 56,* 55–67.

Caramazza, A., & Shapiro, K. (2001). Language categories in the brain: evidence from aphasia. In L. Rizzi & A. Belletti (Eds.), *Structures and beyond.* Oxford, UK: Oxford University Press.

Carey, S. (1987). *Conceptual change in childhood.* Cambridge, MA: Bradford Books.

Carey, S. (1994). Does learning a language require the child to reconceptualize the world? In L. Gleitman & B. Landau (Eds.), *The acquisition of the lexicon* (pp. 143–168). Cambridge, MA: Elsevier/MIT Press.

Carlson, E. R. (1995). Evaluating the credibility of sources: A missing link in the teaching of critical thinking. *Teaching of Psychology, 22*, 39–41.

Carlson, M. P., & Bloom, I. (2005). The cyclic nature of problem solving: An emergent multidimensional problem-solving framework. *Educational Studies in Mathematics, 58*(1), 45–75.

Carlson, N. R. (1992). *Foundations of physiological psychology* (2nd ed.). Boston: Allyn & Bacon.

Carlson, N. R. (2006). *Physiology of behavior* (9th ed.). Needham Heights, MA: Allyn-Bacon.

Carmichael, L., Hogan, H. P., & Walter, A. A. (1932). An experimental study of the effect of language on the reproduction of visually perceived form. *Journal of Experimental Psychology, 15*, 73–86.

Carpenter, M., Nagell, K., & Tomasello, M. (1998). Social cognition, joint attention, and communicative competence from 9 to 15 months of age. *Monographs of the Society for Research in Child Development, 63* (4, Serial No. 255).

Carpenter, P. A., & Just, M. A. (1981). Cognitive processes in reading: Models based on readers' eye fixations. In A. M. Lesgold & C. A. Perfetti (Eds.), *Interactive processes in reading* (pp. 177–213). Hillsdale, NJ: Erlbaum.

Carroll, D. W. (1986). *Psychology of language*. Monterey, CA: Brooks/Cole.

Carroll, J. B. (1993). *Human cognitive abilities: A survey of factor-analytic studies*. New York: Cambridge University Press.

Carroll, J. S., Hatakenaka, S., & Rudolph, J. W. (2006). Naturalistic decision making and organizational learning in nuclear power plants: negotiating meaning between managers and problem investigation teams. *Organization Studies, 27*(7), 1037–1057.

Carvalho, J. P., & Hopko, D. R. (2009). Treatment of a depressed breast cancer patient with problem-solving therapy. *Clinical Case Studies, 8*, 263–276.

Carver, L. J., & Bauer, P. J. (2001). The dawning of a past: The emergence of long-term explicit memory in infancy. *Journal of Experimental Psychology: General, 130*(4), 738–745.

Cassia, V. M., Simion, F., Milani, I., & Umiltà, C. (2002). Dominance of global visual properties at birth. *Journal of Experimental Psychology: General, 131*(3), 398–411.

Castelli, F., Happé, F., Frith, U., & Frith, C. (2005). Movement and mind: A functional imaging study of perception and interpretation of complex intentional movement patterns. In J. T. Cacioppo & G. G. Berntson (Eds.), *Social neuroscience: Key readings* (pp. 155–169). New York: Psychology Press.

Castellucci, V. F., & Kandel, E. R. (1976). Presynaptic facilitation as a mechanism for behavioral sensitization in *Aplysia. Science, 194*, 1176–1178.

Castle, L., Aubert, R. E., Verbrugge, R. R., Khalid, M., & Epstein, R. S. (2007). Trends in medication treatment for ADHD. *Journal of Attention Disorders, 10*(4), 335–342.

Catroppa, C., & Anderson, V. (2006). Planning, problem-solving and organizational abilities in children following traumatic brain injury: Intervention techniques. *Developmental Neurorehabilitation, 9*(2), 89–97.

Cattell, J. M. (1886). The influence of the intensity of the stimulus on the length of the reaction time. *Brain, 9*, 512–514.

Cattell, R. B. (1971). *Abilities: Their structure, growth, and action*. Boston: Houghton Mifflin.

Cave, K. R., & Wolfe, J. M. (1990). Modeling the role of parallel processing in visual search. *Cognitive Psychology, 22*(2), 225–271.

Cazalis, F., Feydy, A., Valabrègue, R., Pélégrini-Issac, M., Pierot, L., & Azouvi, P. (2006). fMRI study of problem-solving after severe traumatic brain injury. *Brain Injury, 20*(10), 1019–1028.

Ceci, S. J., & Bruck, M. (1993). Suggestibility of the child witness: A historical review and synthesis. *Psychological Bulletin, 113*(3), 403–439.

Ceci, S. J., & Bruck, M. (1995). *Jeopardy in the courtroom*. Washington, DC: American Psychological Association.

Ceci, S. J., & Loftus, E. F. (1994). "Memory work": A royal road to false memories? *Applied Cognitive Psychology, 8*, 351–364.

Cepeda, N. J., Coburn, N., Rohrer, D., Wixted, J. T., Mozer, M. C., & Pashler, H. (2009). Optimizing distributed practice: Theoretical analysis and practical implications. *Experimental Psychology, 56*(4), 236–246.

Chambers, D., & Reisberg, D. (1985). Can mental images be ambiguous? *Journal of Experimental Psychology: Human Perception & Performance, 11*(3), 317–328.

Chambers, D., & Reisberg, D. (1992). What an image depicts depends on what an image means. *Cognitive Psychology, 24*(2), 145–174.

Chamodrakas, I., Batis, D., & Martakos, D. (2010). Supplier selection in electronic marketplaces using satisficing and fuzzy AHP. *Expert Systems with Applications, 37*, 490–498.

Chan, A. S., Cheung, M.-c., Han, Y. M. Y., Sze, S. L., Leung, W. W., Man, H. S., et al. (2009). Executive function deficits and neural discordance in children with Autism Spectrum Disorders. *Clinical Neurophysiology, 120*, 1107–1115.

Chapman, J. P. (2006). Anxiety and defective decision making: An elaboration of the groupthink model. *Management Decision, 44*(10), 1391–1404.

Chapman, L. J., & Chapman, J. P. (1959). Atmosphere effect reexamined. *Journal of Experimental Psychology, 58*, 220–226.

Chapman, L. J., & Chapman, J. P. (1967). Genesis of popular but erroneous psychodiagnostic observations. *Journal of Abnormal Psychology, 72*(3), 193–204.

Chapman, L. J., & Chapman, J. P. (1969). Illusory correlation as an obstacle to the use of valid psychodiagnostic signs. *Journal of Abnormal Psychology, 74*, 271–280.

Chapman, L. J., & Chapman, J. P. (1975). The basis of illusory correlation. *Journal of Abnormal Psychology, 84*(5), 574–575.

Charltona, S. G. (2009). Driving while conversing: Cell phones that distract and passengers who react. *Accident Analysis and Prevention, 41*, 160–173.

Chase, W. G., & Simon, H. A. (1973). The mind's eye in chess. In W. G. Chase (Ed.), *Visual information processing* (pp. 215–281). New York: Academic Press.

Chechile, R. A. (2004). New multinomial models for the Chechile-Meyer task. *Journal of Mathematical Psychology, 48*(6), 364–384.

Chechile, R. A., & Soraci, S. A. (1999). Evidence for a multiple-process account of the generation effect, *Memory 7*, 483–508.

Cheesman, J., & Merikle, P. M. (1984). Priming with and without awareness. *Perception & Psychophysics, 36*, 387–395.

Chen, C.-Y., Liu, C.-Y., Su, W.-C., Huang, S.-L., & Lin, K.-M. (2007). Factors associated with the diagnosis of neurodevelopmental disorders: A population-based longitudinal study. *Pediatrics, 119*(2), 435–443.

Chen, X., Tian, B., & Wang, L. (2007). Santa Claus' towers of Hanoi. *Graphs and Combinatorics, 23*(1), 153–167.

Chen, Y., & Sun, Y. (2003). Age differences in financial decision-making: Using simple heuristics. *Educational Gerontology, 29*(7), 627–635.

Chen, Z. (2003). Worth one thousand words: Children's use of pictures in analogical problem solving. *Journal of Cognition and Development, 4*(4), 415–434.

Chen, Z., & Daehler, M. W. (1989). Positive and negative transfer in analogical problem solving. *Cognitive Development, 4*, 327–344.

Cheng, P. W. (1997). From covariation to causation: A causal power theory. *Psychological Review, 104*, 367–405.

Cheng, P. W. (1999). Causal reasoning. In R. A. Wilson & F. C. Keil (Eds.), *The MIT encyclopedia of the cognitive sciences* (pp. 106–108). Cambridge, MA: MIT Press.

Cheng, P. W., & Holyoak, K. J. (1985). Pragmatic reasoning schemas. *Cognitive Psychology, 17*, 391–416.

Cheng, P. W., Holyoak, K. J., Nisbett, R. E., & Oliver, L. M. (1986). Pragmatic versus syntactic approaches to training deductive reasoning. *Cognitive Psychology, 17*(3), 391–416.

Cherniss, C., Extein, M., Goleman, D., & Weissberg, R. P. (2006). Emotional intelligence: what does research really indicate? *Educational Psychologist, 41*(4), 239–245.

Cherry, E. C. (1953). Some experiments on the recognition of speech with one and two ears. *Journal of the Acoustical Society of America, 25*, 975–979.

Chi, M. T. H., Bassok, M., Lewis, M., Reimann, P., & Glaser, R. (1989). Self-explanations: How students study and use examples in learning to solve problems. *Cognitive Science, 13*, 145–182.

Chi, M. T. H., Glaser, R., & Rees, E. (1982). Expertise in problem solving. In R. J. Sternberg (Ed.), *Advances in the psychology of expertise* (Vol. 1, pp. 7–76). Hillsdale, NJ: Erlbaum.

Cho, K. (2001). Chronic 'jet lag' produces temporal lobe atrophy and spatial cognitive deficits. *Nature Neuroscience, 4*(6), 567–568.

Chomsky, N. (1957). *Syntactic structures*. The Hague, Netherlands: Mouton.

Chomsky, N. (1959). Review of the book *Verbal behavior*. *Language, 35*, 26–58.

Chomsky, N. (1965). *Aspects of the theory of syntax*. Cambridge, MA: MIT Press.

Chomsky, N. (1972). *Language and mind* (2nd ed.). New York: Harcourt Brace Jovanovich.

Chomsky, N. (1991, March). [Quoted in] *Discover, 12*(3), 20.

Christensen, B. T., & Schunn, C. D. (2005). Spontaneous access and analogical incubation effects. *Creativity Research Journal, 17*(2–3), 207–220.

Christensen, T. C., Wood, J. V., & Barrett, L. F. (2003). Remembering everyday experience through the prism of self-esteem. *Personality and Social Psychology Bulletin, 29*(1), 51–62.

Christiaans, H., & Venselaar, K. (2007). Creativity in design engineering and the role of knowledge: Modelling the expert. *International Journal of Technology and Design Education, 15*(3), 217–236.

Christoff, K., Ream, J. M., & Gabrieli, J. D. E. (2004). Neural basis of spontaneous thought processes. *Cortex, 40*, 623–630.

Chun, M. M., & Potter, M. C. (1995). A two-stage model for multiple target detection in rapid serial visual presentation. *Journal of Experimental Psychology: Human Perception and Performance, 21*, 109–127.

Churchland, P., & Sejnowski, T. (2004). *The computational brain*. Cambridge, MA: MIT Press.

Ciarrochi, J., Forgas, J. P., & Mayer, J. D. (Eds.) (2001). *Emotional intelligence in everyday life: A scientific inquiry*. Philadelphia: Psychology Press.

Cisler, J. M., Bacon, A. K., & Williams, N. L. (2007). Phenomenological characteristics of attentional biases towards threat: a critical review. *Cognitive Therapy and Research, 33*(2), 221–234.

Clark, A. (2003). Perception, philosophical issues about. In L. Nadel (Ed.), *Encyclopedia of cognitive science* (Vol. 3, pp. 512–517). London: Nature Publishing Group.

Clark, E. V. (1973). What's in a word? On the child's acquisition of semantics in his first language. In T. E. Moore (Ed.), *Cognitive development and the acquisition of language*. New York: Academic Press.

Clark, E. V. (1993). *The lexicon in acquisition*. Cambridge, UK: Cambridge University Press.

Clark, E. V. (1995). Later lexical development and word formation. In P. Fletcher & B. MacWhinney (Eds.), *The handbook of child language* (pp. 393–412). Oxford, UK: Blackwell.

Clark, H. H. (1969). Linguistic processes in deductive reasoning. *Psychological Review, 76*, 387–404.

Clark, H. H., & Brennan, S. E. (1991). Grounding in communication. In L. B. Resnick, J. M. Levine, & S. P. Tansley (Eds.), *Perspectives on socially shared cognition* (pp. 127–149). Washington, DC: American Psychological Association.

Clark, H. H., & Chase, W. G. (1972). On the process of comparing sentences against pictures. *Cognitive Psychology, 3*, 472–517.

Clark, H. H., & Clark, E. V. (1977). *Psychology and language: An introduction to psycholinguistics*. New York: Harcourt Brace Jovanovich.

Clark, H. H., & Schunk, D. H. (1980). Polite responses to polite requests. *Cognition, 8*, 111–143.

Clark, U. S., Oscar-Berman, M., Shagrin, B., & Pencina, M. (2007). Alcoholism and judgments of affective stimuli. *Neuropsychology, 21*(3), 346–362.

Clegg, A. B., & Shepherd, A. J. (2007). Benchmarking natural-language parsers for biological applications using dependency graphs. *BMC Bioinformatics, 8*(1), 24–41.

Clement, C. A., & Falmagne, R. J. (1986). Logical reasoning, world knowledge, and mental imagery: Interconnections in cognitive processes. *Memory & Cognition, 14*(4), 299–307.

Clinton, S. M., & Meador-Woodruff, J. H. (2004). Thalamic dysfunction in schizophrenia: Neurochemical, neuropathological, and in vivo imaging abnormalities. *Schizophrenia Research, 69*(2–3), 237–253.

Coane, J. H., McBride, D. M., Raulerson, B. A., & Jordan, J. S. (2007). False memory in a short-term memory task. *Experimental Psychology, 54*(1), 62–70.

Cohen, A. (2003). Selective attention. In L. Nadel (Ed.), *Encyclopedia of cognitive science* (Vol. 3, pp. 1033–1037). London: Nature Publishing Group.

Cohen, G. (1989). *Memory in the real world*. Hillsdale, NJ: Erlbaum.

Cohen, J. (1981). Can human irrationality be experimentally demonstrated? *Behavioral and Brain Sciences, 4*, 317–331.

Cohen, J. D., Romero, R. D., Servan-Schreiber, D., & Farah, M. J. (1994). Mechanisms of spatial attention: The relation of macrostructure to microstructure in parietal neglect. *Journal of Cognitive Neuroscience, 6*, 377–387.

Cohen, J. T., & Graham, J. D. (2003). A revised economic analysis of restrictions on the use of cell phones while driving. *Risk Analysis, 23*(1), 5–17.

Cohen, M. S., Kosslyn, S. M., Breiter, H. C., DiGirolamo, G. J., Thompson, W. L., Anderson, A. K., et al. (1996). Changes in cortical activity during mental rotation: A mapping study using functional MRI. *Brain, 119*, 89–100.

Cole, M., Gay, J., Glick, J., & Sharp, D. W. (1971). *The cultural context of learning and thinking*. New York: Basic Books.

Coleman, J. (2003). Phonology, computational. In L. Nadel (Ed.), *Encyclopedia of cognitive science* (Vol. 3, pp. 650–654). London: Nature Group Press.

Coley, J. D., Medin, D. L., Proffitt, J. B., Lynch, E., & Atran, S. (1999). Inductive reasoning in folkbiological thought. In D. L. Medin & S. Atran (Eds.), *Folkbiology* (pp. 205–232). Cambridge, MA: MIT Press.

Collette, F., Majerus, S., Van Der Linden, M., Dabe, P., Degueldre, C., Delfiore, G., et al. (2001). Contribution of lexico-semantic processes to verbal short-term memory tasks: A PET activation study. *Memory, 9*, 249–259.

Collie, A., Maruff, P., Shafiq-Antonacci, R., Smith, M., Hallup, M., Schofield, P. R., et al. (2001). Memory decline in healthy older people: Implications for identifying mild cognitive impairment. *Neurology, 56*, 1533–1538.

Collier, M. (2005). Hume and cognitive science: The current status of the controversy over abstract ideas. *Phenomenology and the Cognitive Sciences, 4*(2), 197–207.

Collins, A. M., & Loftus, E. F. (1975). A spreading-activation theory of semantic processing. *Psychological Review, 82*, 407–429.

Collins, A. M., & Quillian, M. R. (1969). Retrieval time from semantic memory. *Journal of Verbal Learning and Verbal Behavior, 8*, 240–248.

Collins, M. A., & Amabile, T. M. (1999). Motivation and creativity. In R. J. Sternberg (Ed.), *Handbook of creativity* (pp. 297–312). New York: Cambridge University Press.

Collins, D. W., & Kimura, D. (1997). A large sex difference on a two-dimensional mentalrotation task. *Behavioral Neuroscience, 111*, 845–849.

Colom, R., Haier, R. J., Head, K., Álvarez-Linera, J., Quiroga, M. Á., Shih, P. C., et al. (2009). Gray matter correlates of fluid, crystallized, and spatial intelligence: Testing the P-FIT model. *Intelligence, 37*, 124–135.

Colom, R., Rebollo, I., Palacios, A., Juan-Espinosa, M., & Kyllonen, P. C. (2004). Working memory is (almost) perfectly predicted by g. *Intelligence, 32*(3), 277–296.

Committeri, G., Galati, G., Paradis, A., Pizzamiglio, L., Berthoz, A., & LeBihan, D. (2004). Reference frames for spatial cognition: Different brain areas are involved in viewer-, object-, and landmark-centered judgments about object location. *Journal of Cognitive Neuroscience, 16*(9), 1517–1535.

Conn, C., & Silverman, I., (Eds.). (1991). *What counts: The complete Harper's index.* New York: Henry Holt.

Conrad, R. (1964). Acoustic confusions in immediate memory. *British Journal of Psychology, 55*, 75–84.

Conway, A. R. A., Cowan, N., & Bunting, M. F. (2001). The cocktail party phenomenon revisited: The importance of working memory capacity. *Psychonomic Bulletin & Review, 8*(2), 331–335.

Conway, M. A. (1995). *Flashbulb memories.* Hove, England: Erlbaum.

Cook, A. E., & Gueraud, S. (2005). What have we been missing? The role of general world knowledge in discourse processing. *Discourse Processes, 39*(2–3), 265–278.

Cooper, E. H., & Pantle, A. J. (1967). The total-time hypothesis in verbal learning. *Psychological Bulletin, 68*, 221–234.

Corballis, M. C. (1989). Laterality and human evolution. *Psychological Review, 96*(3), 49–50.

Corballis, M. C. (1997). Mental rotation and the right hemisphere. *Brain and Language, 57*, 100–121.

Corbetta, M., Miezin, F. M., Shulman, G. L., & Petersen, S. E. (1993). A PET study of visuospatial attention. *Journal of Neuroscience, 13*(3), 1202–1226.

Corcoran, D. W. J. (1971). *Pattern recognition.* Harmondsworth: Penguin.

Corcoran, J., & Dattalo, P. (2006). Parent involvement in treatment for ADHD: A meta-analysis of the published studies. *Research on Social Work Practice, 16*(6), 561–570.

Coren, S., & Girgus, J. S. (1978). *Seeing is deceiving: The psychology of visual illusions.* Hillsdale, NJ: Erlbaum.

Coslett, H. B. (2003). *Acquired dyslexia.* In K. M. Heilman & E. Valenstein (Eds.), *Clinical neuropsychology* (pp. 108–125). New York: Oxford University Press.

Cosmides, L. (1989). The logic of social exchange: Has natural selection shaped how humans reason? Studies with the Wason selection task. *Cognition, 31*, 187–276.

Cosmides, L., & Tooby, J. (1996). Are humans good intuitive statisticians after all? Rethinking some conclusions from the literature on judgment under uncertainty. *Cognition, 58*, 1–73.

Costello, C. G. (1967). The effects of an alien stimulus on reminiscence in pursuit rotor performance. *Psychonomic Science, 8*(8), 331–332.

Cowan, N. (1995). *Attention and memory: An integrated framework.* New York: Oxford University Press.

Cowan, N. (2001). The magical number 4 in short-term memory: A reconsideration of mental storage capacity. *Behavioral and Brain Sciences, 24.*

Cowan, N., Winkler, I., Teder, W., & Näätänen, R. (1993). Memory prerequisites of mismatch negativity in the auditory event-related potential (ERP). *Journal of Experimental Psychology: Learning, Memory, & Cognition, 19*(4), 909–921.

Cowey, A., & Heywood, C. A. (1997). Cerebral achromatopsia: colour blindness despite wavelength processing *Trends in Cognitive Science, 1*(4), 133–139.

Craik, F. I. M., & Brown, S. C. (2000). Memory: Coding processes. In A. E. Kazdin (Ed.), *Encyclopedia of psychology* (Vol. 5, pp. 162–166). Washington, DC: American Psychological Association.

Craik, F. I. M., & Lockhart, R. S. (1972). Levels of processing: A framework for memory research. *Journal of Verbal Learning and Verbal Behavior, 11*, 671–684.

Craik, F. I. M., & Lockhart, R. S. (2008). Levels of processing and Zinchenko's approach to memory research. *Journal of Russian and East European Psychology, 46*(6), 52–60.

Craik, F. I. M., & Tulving, E. (1975). Depth of processing and the retention of words in episodic memory. *Journal of Experimental Psychology: General, 104*, 268–294.

Craik, K. (1943). *The nature of exploration.* Cambridge, UK: Cambridge University Press.

Cronly-Dillon, J., Persaud, K. C., & Blore, R. (2000). Blind subjects construct conscious mental images of visual scenes encoded in musical form. *Proceedings of the Royal Society B: Biological Sciences, 267*, 2231–2238.

Crowder, R. G. (1976). *Principles of learning and memory.* Hillsdale, NJ: Erlbaum.

Cruz, N. V., & Bahna, S. L. (2006). Do food or additives cause behavior disorders? *Psychiatric Annals, 36*(10), 724–732.

Crystal, D. (Ed.). (1987). *The Cambridge encyclopedia of language.* New York: Cambridge University Press.

Crystal, D. (2002). *Language death.* Cambridge, UK: Cambridge University Press.

Csikszentmihalyi, M. (1988). Society, culture, and person: A systems view of creativity. In R. J. Sternberg (Ed.), *The nature of creativity* (pp. 325–339). New York: Cambridge University Press.

Csikszentmihalyi, M. (1996). *Creativity: Flow and the psychology of discovery and invention.* New York: HarperCollins.

Csikszentmihalyi, M. (1999). Creativity. In R. A. Wilson & F. C. Keil (Eds.), *The MIT encyclopedia of the cognitive sciences* (pp. 205–206). Cambridge, MA: MIT Press.

Csikszentmihalyi, M. (2000). Creativity: An overview. In A. E. Kazdin (Ed.), *Encyclopedia of psychology* (Vol. 2, p. 342). Washington, DC: American Psychological Association.

Cui, X., Jeter, C. B., Yang, D., Montague, P. R., & Eagleman, D. M. (2007). Vividness of mental imagery: Individual variability can be measured objectively. *Vision Research, 47*, 474–478.

Culham, J. C. (2003). Parietal cortex. In L. Nadel (Ed.), *Encyclopedia of cognitive science* (Vol. 3, pp. 451–457). London: Nature Publishing Group.

Culicover, P. W., & Jackendoff, R. (2005). *Simper syntax.* Oxford: Oxford University Press.

Cummings, A., & Ceponiene, R. (2010). Verbal and nonverbal semantic processing in children with developmental language impairment. *Neuropsychologia, 48*(1), 77–85.

Cummins, D. D. (2004). The evolution of reasoning. In J. P. Leighton & R. J. Sternberg (Eds.), *The nature of reasoning* (pp. 339–374). New York: Cambridge University Press.

Cummins, J. (1976). The influence of bilingualism on cognitive growth: A synthesis of research findings and explanatory hypothesis. *Working Papers on Bilingualism, 9*, 1–43.

Cummins, R., & Cummins, D. D. (Eds.). (2000). *Minds, brains, and computers: The foundations of cognitive science.* Singapore: Blackwell.

Cunningham, S. J., Turk, D. J., Macdonald, L. M., & Macrae, C. N. (2008). Yours or mine? Ownership and memory. *Consciousness and Cognition: An International Journal, 17*(1), 312–318.

Cutler, B. L., & Penrod, S. D. (1995). *Mistaken identification: The eyewitness, psychology, and the law.* New York: Cambridge University Press.

Cutting, J., & Kozlowski, L. (1977). Recognizing friends by their walk: Gait perception without familiarity cues. *Bulletin of the Psychonomic Society, 9*(5), 353–356.

Cziko, G. A. (1998). From blind to creative: In defense of Donald Campbell's selectionist theory of human creativity. *Journal of Creative Behavior, 32*, 192–208.

Dahlgren, A., Kecklund, G., Theorell, T., & Akerstedt, T. (2009). Day-to-day variation in saliva cortisol—Relation with sleep, stress and self-rated health. *Biological Psychology, 82*, 149–155.

D'Amico, A., & Guarnera, M. (2005). Exploring working memory in children with low arithmetical achievement. *Learning and Individual Differences, 15*(3),189–202.

Dakin, S. C., & Hess, R. F. (1999). Contour integration and scale combination processes in visual edge detection. *Spatial Vision, 12*, 309–327.

Damasio, A. R. (1985). Prosopagnosia. *Trends in Neurosciences, 8*, 132–135.

Damasio, A. R., Tranel, D., & Damasio, H. (1990). Face agnosia and the neural substrates of memory. *Annual Review of Neuroscience, 13*, 89–109.

Dambacher, M., & Kliegl, R. (2007). Synchronizing timelines: Relations between fixation durations and N400 amplitudes during sentence reading. *Brain Research, 1155*(25), 147–162.

Damoiseaux, J. S., Rombouts, S. A. R. B., Barkhof, F., Scheltens, P., Stam, C. J., Smith, S. M., et al. (2006). Consistent resting-state networks across healthy subjects. *Proceedings of the National Academy of Sciences of the United States of America, 103*, 13848–13853.

Daneman, M., & Carpenter, P. A. (1983). Individual differences in integrating information between and within sentences. *Journal of Experimental Psychology: Learning, Memory, and Cognition, 9*, 561–583.

Daniel, M. H. (1997). Intelligence testing: Status and trends. *American Psychologist, 52*, 1038–1045.

Daniel, M. H. (2000). Interpretation of intelligence test scores. In R. J. Sternberg (Ed.), *Handbook of intelligence* (pp. 477–491). New York: Cambridge University Press.

Daniels, K., Toth, J., & Jacoby, L. (2006). The aging of executive functions. In E. Bialystok & F. I. M. Craik (Eds.), *Lifespan cognition: Mechanisms of change* (pp. 96–111). New York: Oxford University Press.

Danker, J. F., Gunn, P., & Anderson, J. R. (2008). A rational account of memory predicts left prefrontal activation during controlled retrieval. *Cerebral Cortex, 18*, 2674–2685.

Darwin, C. J. (2008). Spatial hearing and perceiving sources. In W. A. Yost, R. R. Fay & A. N. Popper (Eds.), *Auditory perception of sound sources* (pp. 215–232). Berlin: Springer.

Das, J. P., Naglieri, J. A., & Kirby, J. R. (1994). *Assessment of cognitive processes: The PASS theory of intelligence.* Boston: Allyn and Bacon.

Davidson, J. E. (1995). The suddenness of insight. In R. J. Sternberg & J. E. Davidson (Eds.), *The nature of insight* (pp. 125–155). Cambridge, MA: MIT Press.

Davidson, J. E. (2003). Insights about insightful problem solving. In J. E. Davidson & R. J. Sternberg (Eds.), *The psychology of problem solving* (pp. 149–175). New York: Cambridge University Press.

Davidson, J. E., & Kemp, I. A. (in press). Contemporary models of intelligence. In R. J. Sternberg & S. B. Kaufman (Eds.), *The Cambridge handbook of intelligence.* New York: Cambridge University Press.

Davidson, J. E., & Sternberg, R. J. (Eds.). (2003). *The psychology of problem solving.* New York: Cambridge University Press.

Davidson, J. E., & Sternberg, R. J. (1984). The role of insight in intellectual giftedness. *Gifted Child Quarterly, 28*, 58–64.

Davidson, R. J., & Hugdahl, K. (Eds.) (1995). *Cerebral asymmetry.* Cambridge, MA: MIT Press.

Davies, M. (1999). Consciousness. In R. A. Wilson & F. C. Keil (Eds.), *The MIT encyclopedia of the cognitive sciences* (pp. 190–193). Cambridge, MA: MIT Press.

Davies, M., & Humphreys, G. W. (1993). *Consciousness: Psychological and philosophical essays.* Oxford, UK: Blackwell.

Davies, M., Stankov, L., & Roberts, R. D. (1998). Emotional intelligence: In search of an elusive construct. *Journal of Personality & Social Psychology, 75*, 989–1015.

Davis, D., & Loftus, E. F. (2007). Internal and external sources of misinformation in adult witness memory. In M. P. Toglia, J. D. Read, D. F. Ross & R. C. L. Lindsay (Eds.), *Handbook of eyewitness psychology* (Vol. 1, pp. 195–237). Mahwah, NJ: Erlbaum.

Davis, D., Loftus, E. F., Vanous, S., & Cucciare, M. (2008). 'Unconscious transference' can be an instance of 'change blindness'. *Applied Cognitive Psychology, 22*, 605–623.

Davis, M. P., Drecier, R., Walsh, D., Lagman, R., & LeGrand, S. B. (2004). Appetite and cancer-associated anorexia: A review. *Journal of Clinical Oncology, 22*(8), 1510–1517.

Dawes, R. (2000). Tversky, Amos. In A. Kazdin (Ed.), *Encyclopedia of psychology* (Vol. 8, pp. 127–128). Washington, DC: American Psychological Association.

Dawes, R. M., Mulford, M. (1996). The false consensus effect and overconfidence: Flaws in judgment or flaws in how we study judgment? *Organizational Behavior & Human Decision Processes, 65*(3), 201–211.

De Beni, R., Cornoldi, C., Larsson, M., Magnussen, S., & Ronnberg, J. (2007). Memory experts: Visual learning, wine tasting, orienteering and speech-reading. In S. Magnussen & T. Helstrup (Eds.), *Everyday memory* (pp. 201–227). New York: Psychology Press.

De Graef, P., Christiaens, D., & D'Ydewalle, G. (1990). Perceptual effects of scene context on object identification. *Psychological Research, 52*(4), 317–329.

De Groot, A. D. (1965). *Thought and choice in chess.* The Hague, Netherlands: Mouton.

De Houwer, A. (1995). Bilingual language acquisition. In P. Fletcher & B. MacWhinney (Eds.), *The handbook of child language* (pp. 219–250). Oxford, UK: Blackwell.

de la Iglesia, J. C. F., Buceta, M. J., & Campos, A. (2005). Prose learning in children and adults with Down syndrome: The use of visual and mental image strategies to improve recall. *Journal of Intellectual & Developmental Disability, 30*(4), 199–206.

De Renzi, E., Faglioni, P., Grossi, D., & Nichelli, P. (1991). Apperceptive and associative forms of prosopagnosia. *Cortex, 27*, 213–221.

De Rosa, E., & Sullivan, E. V. (2003). Enhanced release from proactive interference in nonamnesic alcoholic individuals: Implications for impaired associative binding. *Neuropsychology, 17*(3), 469–481.

De Weerd, P. (2003a). Attention, neural basis of. In L. Nadel (Ed.), *Encyclopedia of cognitive science* (Vol. 1, pp. 238–246). London: Nature Publishing Group.

De Weerd, P. (2003b). Occipital cortex. In L. Nadel (Ed.), *Encyclopedia of cognitive science* (Vol. 3, pp. 408–414). London: Nature Publishing Group.

De Yoe, E. A., & Van Essen, D. C. (1988). Concurrent processing streams in monkey visual cortex. *Trends in Neurosciences, 11*, 219–226.

Dean, L. M., Willis, F. N., & Hewitt K. (1975). Initial interaction distance among individuals equal and unequal in military rank. *Journal of Personality and Social Psychology, 32*, 294–299.

DeCasper, A. J., & Fifer, W. P. (1980). Of human bonding: Newborns prefer their mothers' voices. *Science, 208*, 1174–1176.

Dedeogle, A., Choi, J., Cormier, K., Kowall, N. W., & Jenkins, B. G. (2004). Magnetic resonance spectroscopic analysis of

Alzheimer's disease mouse brain that express mutant human APP shows altered neurochemical profile. *Brain Research, 1012*(1–2), 60–65.

Deeprose, C., Andrade, J., Harrison, D., & Edwards, N. (2005). Unconscious auditory priming during surgery with propofol and nitrous oxide anaesthesia: A replication. *British Journal of Anaesthesia, 94*(1), 57–62.

Deese, J. (1959). On the prediction of occurrence of particular verbal intrusions in immediate recall. *Journal of Experimental Psychology, 58*, 17–22.

Deffenbacher, J. L., Lynch, R. S., Filetti, L. B., Dahlen, E. R., & Oetting, E. R. (2003). Anger, aggression, risky behavior, and crash-related outcomes in three groups of drivers. *Behaviour Research and Therapy, 41*(3), 333–349.

Deffenbacher, K. A., Bornstein, B. H., Penrod, S. D., & McGorty, E. K. (2004). A meta-analytic review of the effects of high stress on eyewitness memory. *Law and Human Behavior, 28*(6), 697–706.

Dehaene-Lambertz, G., Hertz-Pannier, L., & Dubois, J. (2006). Nature and nurture in language acquisition: Anatomical and functional brain-imaging studies in infants. *Trends in Neuroscience, 29*(7), 367–373.

Dell, G. S. (1986). A spreading-activation theory of retrieval in sentence production. *Psychological Review, 93*(3), 283–321.

DeMiguel, V., Garlappi, L., & Uppal, R. (2007). Optimal versus naive diversification: How inefficient is the 1/N portfolio strategy? *The Review of Financial Studies, 22*(5), 1915–1953.

Démonet, J.-F., Taylor, M. J., & Chaix, Y. (2004). Developmental dyslexia. *The Lancet, 363*(9419), 1451–1460.

Dempster, F. N. (1991). Inhibitory processes: A neglected dimension of intelligence. *Intelligence, 15*(2), 157–173.

Denis, M., Beschin, N., Logie, R. H., & Della Sala, S. (2002). Visual perception and verbal descriptions as sources for generating mental representations: Evidence from representational neglect. *Cognitive Neuropsychology, 19*(2), 97–112.

Denis, M., & Kosslyn, S. M. (1999). Scanning visual mental images: A window on the mind. *Cahiers de Psychologie Cognitive, 18*(4), 409–616.

Derntl, B., Windischberger, C., Robinson, S., Kryspin-Exner, I., Gur, R. C., Moser, E., et al. (2009). Amygdala activity to fear and anger in healthy young males is associated with testosterone. *Psychoneuroendocrinology, 34*, 687–693.

Desai, R., Liebenthal, E., Possing, E. T., Waldron, E., & Binder, J. R. (2005). Volumetric vs. surface-based alignment for localization of auditory cortex activation. *NeuroImage, 26*, 1019–1029.

DeSoto, C. B., London, M., & Handel, S. (1965). Social reasoning and spatial paralogic. *Journal of Personality and Social Psychology, 2*, 513–521.

Detre, J. A. (2004). fMRI: Applications in epilepsy. *Epilepsia 45*(4), 26–31.

Detterman, D. K., & Sternberg, R. J. (Eds.) (1993). *Transfer on trial: Intelligence, cognition, and instruction.* Norwood, NJ: Ablex.

Deutsch, J. A., & Deutsch, D. (1963). Attention: Some theoretical considerations. *Psychological Review, 70*, 80–90.

DeValois, R. L., & DeValois, K. K. (1980). Spatial vision. *Annual Review of Psychology, 31*, 309–341.

Devitt, M. (2008). *Ignorance of language.* Oxford: Oxford University Press/Clarendon Press.

Dew, N., Read, S., Sarasvathy, S. D., & Wiltbank, R. (2009). Effectual versus predictive logics in entrepreneurial decision-making: Differences between experts and novices. *Journal of Business Venturing, 24*, 287–309.

Dewhurst, S. A., Pursglove, R. C., & Lewis, C. (2007). Story contexts increase susceptibility to the DRM illusion in 5-year-olds. *Developmental Science, 10*(3), 374–378.

Di Eugenio, B. (2003). Discourse processing. In L. Nadel (Ed.), *Encyclopedia of cognitive science* (Vol. 1, pp. 976–983). London: Nature Publishing Group.

Diesendruck, G. (2005). The principles of conventionality and contrast in word learning: an empirical examination. *Developmental Psychology, 41*(3), 451–463.

Dietrich, A. (2004). The cognitive neuroscience of creativity. *Psychonomic Bulletin & Review, 11*(6), 1011–1026.

DiGirolamo, G. J., & Griffin, H. J. (2003). Consciousness and attention. In L. Nadel (Ed.), *Encyclopedia of cognitive science* (Vol. 1, pp. 711–717). London: Nature Publishing Group.

Dijksterhuis, A., Bos, M. W., Norgdren, L. F., & Baaren, R. B. v. (2006). On making the right choice: the deliberation-without-attention effect. *Science, 31*, 1005–1007.

Ditchburn, R. W. (1980). The function of small saccades. *Vision Research, 20*, 271–272.

Dixon, T. L., & Maddox, K. B. (2005). Skin tone, crime news, and social reality judgments: Priming the stereotype of the dark and dangerous black criminal. *Journal of Applied Social Psychology, 35*(8), 1555–1570.

Do, H.-H., & Rahm, E. (2007). Matching large schemas: Approaches and evaluation. *Information Systems, 32*, 857–885.

Dodd, M. D., & MacLeod, C. M. (2004). False recognition without intention learning. *Psychonomic Bulletin & Review, 11*(1), 137–142.

Dolan, M. (1995, February 11). When the mind's eye blinks. *Los Angeles Times*, pp. A1, A24, A25.

Dolderer, M., Mummendey, A., & Rothermund, K. (2009). And yet they move: The impact of direction of deviance on stereotype change. *Personality and Social Psychology Bulletin, 35*(10), 1368–1381.

Donders, F. C. (1868/1869). Over de snelheid van psychische processen. Onderzoekingen gedaan in het Physiologisch Laboratorium der Utrechtsche Hoogeschool. [About the velocity of psychological processes: Studies done at the Physiological Laboratory of the University of Utrecht.] *Tweede reeks, II*, 92–120.

Dosher, B. A. (2003). Working memory. In L. Nadel (Ed.), *Encyclopedia of cognitive science* (Vol. 4, pp. 569–577). London: Nature Publishing Group.

Downing, P. E., Chan, A. W.-Y., Peelen, M. V., Dodds, C. M., & Kanwisher, N. (2006). Domain specificity in visual cortex. *Cerebral Cortex, 16*, 1453–1461.

Doyle, C. L. (2000). Psychology: Definition. In A. E. Kazdin (Ed.), *Encyclopedia of psychology* (Vol. 6, pp. 375–376). Washington, DC: American Psychological Association.

Drapier, D., Drapier, S., Sauleau, P., Derkinderen, P., Damier, P., Alain, H., et al. (2006). Pathological gambling secondary to dopaminergic therapy in Parkinson's disease. *Psychiatry Research, 144*(2–3), 241–244.

Drews, F. A., Pasupathi, M., & Strayer, D. L. (2008). Passenger and Cell Phone Conversations in Simulated Driving. *Journal of Experimental Psychology: Applied, 14*(4), 392–400.

Dror, I. E., & Kosslyn, S. M. (1994). Mental imagery and aging. *Psychology and Aging, 9*(1), 90–102.

Drubach, D. (1999). *The brain explained.* Upper Saddle River, NJ: Prentice-Hall.

Druckman, J. N. (2001). On the limits of framing effects: Who can frame? *The Journal of Politics, 63*(4), 1041–1066.

Duffau, H., Gatignol, P., Mandonnet, E., Capelle, L., & Taillandier, L. (2008). Intraoperative subcortical stimulation mapping of language pathways in a consecutive series of 115 patients with Grade II glioma in the left dominant hemisphere. *Journal of Neurosurgery, 109*, 461–471.

Dunbar, K. (2003). Scientific thought. In L. Nadel (Ed.), *Encyclopedia of cognitive science* (Vol. 3, pp. 1006–1009). London: Nature Publishing Group.

Duncan, E., & Bourg, T. (1983). An examination of the effects of encoding and decision processes on the rate of mental rotation. *Journal of Mental Imagery, 7*(2), 3–55.

Duncan, J., Burgess, P., & Emslie, H. (1995). Fluid intelligence after frontal lobe lesions. *Neuropsychologia, 33,* 261–268.

Duncan, J., & Humphreys, G. W. (1989). Visual search and stimulus similarity. *Psychological Review, 96*(3), 433–458.

Duncan, J., & Humphreys, G. W. (1992). Beyond the search surface: Visual search and attentional engagement. *Journal of Experimental Psychology: Human Perception & Performance, 18*(2), 578–588.

Duncker, K. (1945). On problem-solving. *Psychological Monographs, 58*(5, Whole No. 270).

Dupuy, J. P. (1998). Rationality and self-deception. In J. P. Dupuy (Ed.), *Self-deception and paradoxes of rationality* (pp. 113–150). Stanford, CA: CSLI Publications.

Dupuy, J. P. (1999). Rational choice theory. In R. A. Wilson & F. C. Keil (Eds.), *The MIT encyclopedia of the cognitive sciences* (pp. 699–701). Cambridge, MA: MIT Press.

Durgin, F. H. (2000). Visual adaptation. In A. E. Kazdin (Ed.), *Encyclopedia of psychology* (Vol. 8, pp. 183–187). Washington, DC: American Psychological Association.

Dye, M. W. G., Green, C. S., & Bavelier, D. (2009). The development of attention skills in action video game players. *Neuropsychologia, 47,* 1780–1789.

Eales, M. J. (1993). Pragmatic impairments in adults with childhood diagnoses of autism or developmental receptive language disorder. *Journal of Autism and Developmental Disorders, 23*(4), 593–617.

Eason, R., Harter, M., & White, C. (1969). Effects of attention and arousal on visually evoked cortical potentials and reaction time in man. *Physiology and Behavior, 4,* 283–289.

Easton, N., Marshall, F., Fone, K., & Marsden, C. (2007). Atomoxetine produces changes in cortico-basal thalamic loop circuits: Assessed by phMRI BOLD contrast. *Neuropharmacology, 52*(3), 812–826.

Ebbinghaus, H. (1885). *Uber das Gedächtnis.* Leipzig, Germany: Duncker and Humblot.

Ebert, P. L., & Anderson, N. D. (2009). Proactive and retroactive interference in young adults, healthy older adults, and older adults with amnestic mild cognitive impairment. *Journal of the International Neuropsychological Society, 15,* 83–93.

Edelman, S., & Weinshall, D. (1991). A self-organizing multiple-view representation of 3D objects. *Biological Cybernetics, 64,* 209–219.

Edwards, W. (1954). The theory of decision making. *Psychological Bulletin, 51,* 380–417.

Egeth, H. E. (1993). What do we not know about eyewitness identification? *American Psychologist, 48*(5), 577–580.

Ehrlich, K. (1996). Applied mental models in human-computer interaction. In J. Oakhill & A. Garnham (Eds.), *Mental models in cognitive science* (pp. 313–339). Hillsdale, NJ: Erlbaum.

Eich, E. (1995). Searching for mood dependent memory. *Psychological Science, 6,* 67–75.

Eich, J. E. (1980). The cue-dependent nature of state-dependent retrieval. *Memory & Cognition, 8,* 157–158.

Eichenbaum, H. (1997). Declarative memory: Insights from cognitive neurobiology. *Annual Review of Psychology, 48,* 547–572.

Eichenbaum, H. (1999). Hippocampus. In R. A. Wilson & F. C. Keil (Eds.), *The MIT encyclopedia of the cognitive sciences* (pp. 377–378). Cambridge, MA: MIT Press.

Eichenbaum, H. (2002). *The cognitive neuroscience of memory.* New York: Oxford University Press.

Eimas, P. D. (1985). The perception of speech in early infancy. *Scientific American, 252,* 46–52.

Eisenberger, R., & Shanock, L. (2003). Rewards, intrinsic motivation, and creativity: a case study of conceptual and methodological isolation. *Creativity Research Journal, 15*(2–3), 121–130.

Eisenegger, C., Herwig, U., & Jäncke, L. (2007). The involvement of primary motor cortex in mental rotation revealed by transcranial magnetic stimulation. *European Journal of Neuroscience, 25*(4), 1240–1244.

Ekstrom, A. D., Kahana, M. J., Caplan, J. B., Fields, T. A., Isham, E. A., Newman, E. L., et al. (2003). Cellular networks underlying human spatial navigation. *Nature, 425,* 184–188.

Eldridge, L. L., Knowlton, B. J., Furmanski, C. S., Bookheimer, S. Y., & Engel, S. A. (2000). Remembering episodes: A selective role for the hippocampus during retrieval. *Nature Neuroscience, 3*(11):1049–1052.

Ellenbogen, J. M., Payne, J. D., & Stickgold, R. (2006). The role of sleep in declarative memory consolidation: Passive, permissive, active or none? *Current Opinion in Neurobiology, 16*(6), 716–722.

Elman, J. L., Bates, E. A., Johnson, M. H., Karmiloff-Smith, A., Parisi, D., & Plunkett, K. (1996). *Rethinking innateness: A connectionist perspective on development.* Cambridge, MA: MIT Press.

Emmorey, K. (1994). Sign language: A window into the brain, language, and cognition. In S. Ramachandran (Ed.), *Encyclopedia of human behavior* (Vol. 4, pp. 193–204). San Diego: Academic Press.

Engel, A. S., Rumelhart, D. E., Wandell, B. A., Lee, A. T., Gover, G. H., Chichilisky, E. J., et al. (1994). MRI measurement of language lateralization in Wada-tested patients. *Brain, 118,* 1411–1419.

Engin, E., & Treit, D. (2008). The effects of intra-cerebral drug infusions on animals' unconditioned fear reactions: A systematic review. *Progress in Neuro-Psychopharmacology & Biological Psychiatry, 32,* 1399–1419.

Erard, M. (2009). How many languages? Linguists discover new tongues in China. *Science, 324*(5925), 332–333.

Erdelyi, M., & Goldberg, B. (1979). Let's now sweep repression under the rug: Toward a cognitive psychology of repression. In J. F. Kihlstrom & F. J. Evans (Eds.), *Functional disorders of memory.* Hillsdale, NJ: Erlbaum.

Ericsson, K. A. (2003). The acquisition of expert performance as problem solving: Construction and modification of mediating mechanisms through deliberate practice. In J. E. Davidson & R. J. Sternberg (Eds.), *The psychology of problem solving* (pp. 31–83). New York: Cambridge University Press.

Ericsson, K. A. (2006). The influence of experience and deliberate practice on the development of superior expert performance. In K. A. Ericsson, N. Charness, P. Feltovich, and R. R. Hoffman, R. R. (Eds.). *Cambridge handbook of expertise and expert performance* (pp. 685–706). Cambridge, UK: Cambridge University Press.

Ericsson, K. A. (2009). Enhancing the development of professional performance: Implications from the study of deliberate practice. In K. A. Ericsson (Ed.), *The development of professional expertise: Toward measurement of expert performance and design of optimal learning environments* (pp. 405–431). New York: Cambridge University Press.

Ericsson, K. A., Chase, W. G., & Faloon, S. (1980). Acquisition of a memory skill. *Science, 208,* 1181–1182.

Ericsson, K. A., Krampe, R. T., & Tesch-Römer, C. (1993). The role of deliberate practice in the acquisition of expert performance. *Psychological Review, 100,* 363–406.

Ericsson, K. A., & Simon, H. A. (1984). *Protocol analysis: Verbal reports as data.* Cambridge, MA: Bradford Books/MIT Press.

Ericsson, K. A., & Williams, A. M. (2007). Capturing naturally-occurring superior performance in the laboratory: Translational research on expert performance. *Journal of Experimental Psychology: Applied, 13,* 115–123.

Espino, O., Santamaria, C., Meseguer, E., & Carreiras, M. (2005). Early and late processes in syllogistic reasoning: Evidence from eye-movements. *Cognition, 98*(1), B1–B9.

Esser J. K. (1998). Alive and well after 25 years: A review of group-think research. *Organizational Behavioral and Human Decision Processes, 73*(23), 116–141.

Estes, W. K. (1982). Learning, memory, and intelligence. In R. J. Sternberg (Ed.), *Handbook of intelligence* (pp. 170–224). New York: Cambridge University Press.

Estes, W. K. (1994). *Classification and cognition*. New York: Oxford University Press.

Evans, J. St. B. T., Barston, J. I., & Pollard, P. (1983). On the conflict between logic and belief in syllogistic reasoning. *Memory and cognition, 11*(3), 295–306.

Evans, J. St. B. T., & Feeney, A. (2004). The role of prior belief in reasoning. In J. P. Leighton & R. J. Sternberg (Eds.), *The nature of reasoning* (pp. 78–102). New York: Cambridge University Press.

Evans, J. St. B. T., & Over, D. E. (1996). Rationality in the selection task: Epistemic utility versus uncertainty reduction. *Psychological Review, 103*, 356–363.

Evans, K. M., & Federmeier, K. D. (2009). Left and right memory revisited: Electrophysiological investigations of hemispheric asymmetries at retrieval. *Neuropsychologia, 47*, 303–313.

Eysenck, M., & Byrne, A. (1992). Anxiety and susceptibility to distraction. *Personality & Individual Differences, 13*(7), 793–798.

Eysenck, M., & Keane, M. T. (1990). *Cognitive psychology: A student's handbook*. Hove, UK: Erlbaum.

Fagin, R., Haas, L. M., Hernández, M., Miller, R. J., Popa, L., & Velegrakis, Y. (2009). Clio: Schema mapping creation and data exchange In *Lecture Notes in Computer Science* (pp. 198–236). Berlin: Springer.

Fahle, M. (2003). Perceptual learning. In L. Nadel (Ed.), *Encyclopedia of cognitive science* (Vol. 3, pp. 548–552). London: Nature Publishing Group.

Farah, M. J. (1988a). Is visual imagery really visual? Overlooked evidence from neuropsychology. *Psychological Review, 95*(3), 307–317.

Farah, M. J. (1988b). The neuropsychology of mental imagery: Converging evidence from brain-damaged and normal subjects. In J. Stiles-Davis, M. Kritchevsky, & U. Bellugi (Eds.), *Spatial cognition: Brain bases and development* (pp. 33–56). Hillsdale, NJ: Erlbaum.

Farah, M. J. (1990). *Visual agnosia: Disorders of object recognition and what they tell us about normal vision*. Cambridge, MA: MIT Press.

Farah, M. J. (1992). Is an object an object an object? Cognitive and neuropsychological investigations of domain specificity in visual object recognition. *Current Directions in Psychological Science, 1*, 164–169.

Farah, M. J. (1995). Dissociable systems for visual recogniiton: A cognitive neuropsychology approach. In S. M. Kosslyn & D. N. Osherson (Eds.), *Visual cognition: An invitation to cognitive science* (Vol. 2). Cambridge, MA: MIT Press.

Farah, M. J. (1999). Object recognition, human neuropsychology. In R. A. Wilson & F. C. Keil (Eds.), *The MIT encyclopedia of the cognitive sciences* (pp. 615–618). Cambridge, MA: MIT Press.

Farah, M. J. (2000a). *The cognitive neuroscience of vision*. Malden, MA: Blackwell.

Farah, M. J. (2000b). The neural bases of mental imagery. In M. S. Gazzaniga (Ed.), *The new cognitive neurosciences* (2nd ed., pp. 965–974). Cambridge, MA: MIT Press.

Farah, M. J. (2004). *Visual agnosia*. Cambridge, MA: MIT Press.

Farah, M. J., Hammond, K. M., Levine, D. N., & Calvanio, R. (1988a). Visual and spatial mental imagery: Dissociable systems of representation. *Cognitive Psychology, 20*(4), 439–462.

Farah, M. J., Levinson, K. L., & Klein, K. L. (1995). Face perception and within category discrimination in prosopagnosia. *Neuropsychologia, 33*, 661–674.

Farah, M. J., Peronnet, F., Gonon, M. A., & Giard, M. H. (1988b). Electrophysiological evidence for a shared representational medium for visual images and visual percepts. *Journal of Experimental Psychology: General, 117*(3), 248–257.

Farah, M. J., Wilson, K. D., Drain, H. M., & Tanaka, J. R. (1995). The inverted face inversion effect in prosopagnosia: Evidence for mandatory, face-specific, perceptual mechanisms. *Vision Research, 35*, 2089–2093.

Farah, M. J., Wilson, K. D., Drain, M., & Tanaka, J. (1998). What is "special" about face perception? *Psychological Review, 105*, 482–498.

Farrell, P. (2005). *Grammatical relations*. Oxford: Oxford University Press.

Farrington-Darby, T., Wilson, J. R., Norris, B. J., & Clarke, T. (2006). A naturalistic study of railway controllers. *Ergonomics, 49*(12–13), 1370–1394.

Farthing, G. W. (1992). *The psychology of consciousness*. Englewood Cliffs, NJ: Prentice-Hall.

Farthing, G. W. (2000). Consciousness and unconsciousness: An overview. In A. E. Kazdin (Ed.), *Encyclopedia of psychology* (Vol. 2, pp. 268–272). Washington, DC: American Psychological Association.

Fdez-Riverola, F., Iglesias, E. L., Diaz, F., Mende, J. R., & Corchado, J. M. (2007). Applying lazy learning algorithms to tackle concept drift in spam filtering. *Expert Systems with Applications, 33*, 36–48.

Federmeier, K. D., Kleim, J. A., & Greenough, W. T. (2002). Learning-induced multiple synapse formation in rat cerebellar cortex. *Neuroscience Letters, 332*, 180–184.

Feinberg, T. E., Schindler, R. J., Ochoa, E., Kwan, P. C., & Farah, M. H. (1994). Associative visual agnosia and alexia without prosopagnosia. *Cortex, 30*(3), 395–412.

Feist, G. J. (1998). A meta-analysis of personality in scientific and artistic creativity. *Personality and Social Psychology Review, 2*, 290–309.

Feist, G. J. (1999). The influence of personality on artistic and scientific creativity. In R. J. Sternberg (Ed.), *Handbook of creativity* (pp. 273–296). New York: Cambridge University Press.

Feist, G. J. (2010). The function of personality in creativity: The nature and nurture of the creative personality. In J. C. Kaufman & R. J. Sternberg (Eds.), *The Cambridge handbook of creativity* (pp. 113–130). New York: Cambridge University Press.

Feldman, J. A., & Shastri, L. (2003). Connectionism. In L. Nadel (Ed.), *Encyclopedia of cognitive science* (Vol. 1, pp. 680–687). London: Nature Publishing Group.

Fernald, A. (1985). Four-month-old infants prefer to listen to motherese. *Infant Behavior and Development, 8*, 118–195.

Fernald, A., Taeschner, T., Dunn, J., Papousek, M., De Boysson-Bardies, B., & Fukui, I. (1989). A cross-cultural study of prosodic modification in mothers' and fathers' speech to preverbal infants. *Journal of Child Language, 16*, 477–501.

Feynman, R. (1997). *Surely you're joking, Mr. Feynman: Adventures of a curious character*. New York: Norton.

Fiedler, K. (1988). Emotional mood, cognitive style, and behavior regulation. In K. Fiedler & J. Forgas (Eds.), *Affect, cognition, and social behavior* (pp.100–119). Toronto: Hogrefe International.

Field, T. (1978). Interaction behaviors of primary versus secondary caregiver fathers. *Developmental Psychology, 14*, 183–184.

Fincham, J. M., Carter, C. S., Veen, V. v., Stenger, V. A., & Anderson, J. R. (2002). Neural mechanisms of planning: A computational analysis using event-related fMRI. *Proceedings of the National Academy of Sciences of the United States of America, 99*(5), 3346–3351.

Finke, R. A. (1989). *Principles of mental imagery*. Cambridge, MA: MIT Press.

Finke, R. A. (1995). Creative insight and preinventive forms. In R. J. Sternberg & J. E. Davidson (Eds.), *The nature of insight* (pp. 255–280). Cambridge, MA: MIT Press.

Finke, R. A., Pinker, S., & Farah, M. J. (1989). Reinterpreting visual patterns in mental imagery. *Cognitive Science, 13*(3), 252–257.

Finley, S., & Badecker, W. (2009). Artificial language learning and feature-based generalization. *Journal of Memory and Language, 61*(3), 423–437.

Fiorio, M., Tinazzi, M., & Aglioti, S. M. (2006). Selective impairment of hand mental rotation in patients with focal hand dystonia. *Brain: A Journal of Neurology, 129*(1), 47–54.

Fiorio, M., Tinazzi, M., Ionta, S., Fiaschi, A., Moretto, G., Edwards, M. J., et al. (2007). Mental rotation of body parts and noncorporeal objects in patients with idiopathic cervical dystonia. *Neuropsychologia, 45*(10), 2346–2354.

Fischhoff, B. (1982). For those condemned to study the past: Heuristics and biases in hindsight. In D. Kahneman, P. Slovic, & A. Tversky (Eds.), *Judgment under uncertainty: Heuristics and biases* (pp. 335–351). Cambridge, UK: Cambridge University Press.

Fischhoff, B. (1988). Judgment and decision making. In R. J. Sternberg & E. E. Smith (Eds.), *The psychology of human thought* (pp. 153–187). New York: Cambridge University Press.

Fischhoff, B. (1999). Judgment heuristics. In R. A. Wilson & F. C. Keil (Eds.), *The MIT encyclopedia of the cognitive sciences* (pp. 423–425). Cambridge, MA: MIT Press.

Fischhoff, B., Slovic, P., & Lichtenstein, S. (1977). Knowing with certainty: The appropriateness of extreme confidence. *Journal of Experimental Psychology: Human Perception and Performance, 3,* 552–564.

Fischman, J. (2004, August 2). Vanishing minds: New research is helping Alzheimer's patients cope-and hope. *U.S. News & World Report, 137,* 3, 74–78.

Fishbein, D. H., Eldereth, D. L., Hyde, C., Matochik, J. A., London, E. D., Contoreggi, C., et al. (2005). Risky decision making and the anterior cingulate cortex in abstinent drug abusers and nonusers. *Brain Research Cognitive Brain Research, 23*(1), 119–136.

Fisher, D. L., & Pollatsek, A. (2007). Novice driver crashes: Failure to divide attention or failure to recognize risks. In A. F. Kramer, D. A. Wiegmann & A. Kirlik (Eds.), *Attention: from theory to practice* (pp. 134–153). New York: Oxford University Press.

Fisher, R. P., & Craik, F. I. M. (1977). Interaction between encoding and retrieval operations in cued recall. *Journal of Experimental Psychology: Human Learning & Memory, 3*(6), 701–711.

Fisher, R. P., & Craik, F. I. M. (1980). The effects of elaboration on recognition memory. *Memory & Cognition, 8*(5), 400–404.

Fisk, A. D., & Schneider, W. (1981). Control and automatic processing during tasks requiring sustained attention: A new approach to vigilance. *Human Factors, 23,* 737–750.

Fivush, R., & Hamond, N. R. (1991). Autobiographical memory across the preschool years: Toward reconceptualizing childhood memory. In R. Fivush & N. R. Hamond (Eds.), *Knowing and remembering in young children* (pp. 223–248). New York: Cambridge University Press.

Flavell, J. H., Flavell, E. R., & Green, F. L. (1983). Development of the appearance–reality distinction. *Cognitive Psychology, 15,* 95–120.

Flavell, J. H., & Wellman, H. M. (1977). Metamemory. In R. V. Kail, Jr., & J. W. Hagen (Eds.), *Perspectives on the development of memory and cognition* (pp. 3–33). Hillsdale, NJ: Erlbaum.

Fleck, J. I. (2007). Working memory demands in insight versus analytic problem solving. *European Journal of Cognitive Psychology, 19*(2), 187–212.

Fleck, M. S., Daselaar, S. M., Dobbins, I. G., & Cabeza, R. (2006). Role of prefrontal and anterior cingulate regions in decision-making processes shared by memory and nonmemory tasks. *Cerebral Cortex 16*(11), 1623–1630.

Flege, J. (1991). The interlingual identification of Spanish and English vowels: Orthographic evidence. *Quarterly Journal of Experimental Psychology: Human Experimental Psychology, 43,* 701–731.

Fleming, P., Ball, L. J., Ormerod, T. C., & Collins, A. F. (2006). Analogue versus propositional representation in congenitally blind individuals. *Psychonomic Bulletin & Review, 13,* 1049–1055.

Fodor, J. A. (1973). *The modularity of mind.* Cambridge, MA: MIT Press.

Fodor, J. A. (1975). *The language of thought.* New York: Crowell.

Fodor, J. A. (1983). *The modularity of mind.* Cambridge, MA: MIT Press.

Fodor, J. A. (1997). Do we have it in us? (Review of Elman et al., *Rethinking innateness*). *Times Literary Supplement,* May 16, pp. 3–4.

Fodor, J., & Pylyshyn, Z. (1988). Connectionism and cognitive architecture: A critical analysis. *Cognition, 28,* 3–71.

Foerde, K., Knowlton, B. J., & Poldrack, R. A. (2006). Modulation of competing memory systems by distraction. *Proceedings of the National Academy of Sciences of the United States of America, 103*(31), 11778–11783.

Fogel, A. (1991). *Infancy: Infant, family, and society* (2nd ed.). St. Paul, MN: West.

Foley, M. A., Foley, H. J., Durley, J. R., & Maitner, A. T. (2006). Anticipating partners' responses: Examining item and source memory following interactive exchanges. *Memory and Cognition, 34,* 1539–1547.

Fombonne, E. (2003). The prevalence of autism. *Journal of the American Medical Association, 289*(1), 87–89.

Forgas, J. P., Goldenberg, L., & Unkelbach, C. (2009). Can bad weather improve your memory? An unobtrusive field study of natural mood effects on real-life memory. *Journal of Experimental Social Psychology, 45*(1), 254–257.

Foulke, E., & Sticht, T. (1969). Review of research on the intelligibility and comprehension of accelerated speech. *Psychological Bulletin, 72,* 50–62.

Frackowiak, R. S. J., Friston, K. J., Frith, C. D., Dolan, R. J., & Mazziotta, J. C. (Eds.). (1997). *Human brain function.* San Diego: Academic Press USA.

Franks, J. J., & Bransford, J. D. (1971). Abstraction of visual patterns. *Journal of Experimental Psychology, 90*(1), 65–74.

Frean, M. (2003). Connectionist architectures: Optimization. In L. Nadel (Ed.), *Encyclopedia of cognitive science* (Vol. 1, pp. 691–697). London, England: Nature Publishing Group.

Freeman, R. D., Zinner, S. H., Mueller-Vahl, K. R., Fast, D. K., Burd, L. J., Kano, Y., et al. (2008). Coprophenomena in Tourette syndrome. *Developmental Medicine & Child Neurology, 51*(3), 218–227.

Frensch, P. A., & Sternberg, R. J. (1989). Expertise and intelligent thinking: When is it worse to know better? In R. J. Sternberg (Ed.), *Advances in the psychology of human intelligence* (Vol. 5, pp. 157–188). Hillsdale, NJ: Erlbaum.

Friederici, A. D., Gunter, T. C., Hahne, A., & Mauth, K. (2004). The relative riming of syntactic and semantic processes in sentence comprehension. *Cognitive Neuroscience and Neuropsychology, 15*(1), 165–169.

Friedman, A., & Brown, N. R. (2000). Reasoning about geography. *Journal of Experimental Psychology: General, 129,* 193–219.

Friedman, A., Kerkman, D. D., & Brown, N. (2002). Spatial location judgments: A cross-national comparison of estimation bias in subjective North American geography. *Psychonomic Bulletin & Review, 9,* 615–623.

Friedman, A., & Montello, D. R. (2006). Global-scale location and distance estimates: Common representations and strategies in absolute and relative judgments. *Journal of Experimental Psychology: Learning, Memory, & Cognition, 32,* 333–346.

Fromkin, V. A. (1973). *Speech errors as linguistic evidence.* The Hague, Netherlands: Mouton.

Fromkin, V. A., Krashen, S., Curtiss, S., Rigler, D., & Rigler, M. (1974). The development of language in Genie: A case of language acquisition beyond the "critical period," *Brain and Language, 1*(1), 81–107.

Fromkin, V. A., & Rodman, R. (1988). *An introduction to language* (4th ed.). Fort Worth, TX: Holt, Rinehart and Winston.

Frost, N. (1972). Encoding and retrieval in visual memory tasks. *Journal of Experimental Psychology, 95*, 317–326.

Funke, J. (1991). Solving complex problems: Exploration and control of complex social systems. In R. J. Sternberg & P. A. Frensch (Eds.), *Complex problem solving: Principles and mechanisms* (pp. 159–183). Hillsdale, NJ: Erlbaum.

Gabel, R. S., Dolan, S. L., & Cerdin, J. L. (2005). Emotional intelligence as predictor of cultural adjustment for success in global assignments. *Career Development International, 10*(5), 375–395.

Gabora, L., & Kaufman, S. B. (2010). Evolutionary approaches to creativity. In J. C. Kaufman & R. J. Sternberg (Eds.), *The Cambridge handbook of creativity* (pp. 279–300). New York: Cambridge University Press.

Gabrieli, J. D. E., Desmond, J. E., Demb, J. B., Wagner, A. D., Stone, M. V., Vaidya, C. J., et al. (1996). Functional magnetic resonance imaging of semantic memory processes in the frontal lobes. *Psychological Science, 7*, 278–283.

Gabrieli, J. D. E. (2009). Dyslexia: A new synergy between education and cognitive neuroscience. *Science, 325*, 208–283.

Gaillard, W. D., Balsamo, L., Xu, B., McKinney, C., Papero, P. H., Weinstein, S., et al. (2004). FMRI language task panel improves determination of language dominance. *Neurology, 63*, 1403–1408.

Gaillard, W. D., Sachs, B. C., Whitnah, J. R., Ahmad, Z., Balsamo, L. M., Petrella, J. R., et al. (2003). Developmental aspects of language processing: fMRI of verbal fluency in children and adults. *Human Brain Mapping, 18*(3), 176–185.

Gais, S., & Born, J. (2004). Low acetylcholine during slow-wave sleep is critical for declarative memory consolidation. *Proceedings of the National Academy of Sciences of the United States of America, 101*(7), 2140–2144.

Gagliardo, A., Ioalè, P., Savini, M., Dell'Omo, G., & Bingman, V. P. (2009). Hippocampal-dependent familiar area map supports corrective re-orientation following navigational error during pigeon homing: a GPS-tracking study. *European Journal of Neuroscience, 29*(12), 2389–2400.

Galaburda, A. M. (1999). Dyslexia. In R. A. Wilson & F. C. Keil (Eds.), *The MIT encyclopedia of the cognitive sciences* (pp. 249–251). Cambridge, MA: MIT Press.

Galaburda, A. M., & Rosen, G. D. (2003). Brain asymmetry. In L. Nadel (Ed.), *Encyclopedia of cognitive science* (Vol. 1, pp. 406–410). London: Nature Publishing Group.

Galanter, C. A., & Patel, V. L. (2005). Medical decision making: A selective review for child psychiatrists and psychologists. *Journal of Child Psychology and Psychiatry 46*(7), 675–689.

Galantucci, B., Fowler, C. A., & Turvey, M. T. (2006). The motor theory of speech perception reviewed. *Psychonomic Bulletin & Review, 13*(3), 361–377.

Galdo-Alvarez, S., Lindin, M., & Diaz, F. (2009). Age-related prefrontal over-recruitment in semantic memory retrieval: Evidence from successful face naming and the tip-of-the-tongue state. *Biological Psychology, 82*, 89–96.

Gallace, A., Auvray, M., Tan, H. Z., & Spence, C. (2006). When visual transients impair tactile change detection: A novel case of crossmodal change blindness? *Neuroscience Letters, 398*, 280–285.

Gallagher, S. (2008). Direct perception in the intersubjective context. *Consciousness and Cognition, 17*, 535–543.

Galotti, K. M., Baron, J., & Sabini, J. P. (1986). Individual differences in syllogistic reasoning: Deduction rules or mental models? *Journal of Experimental Psychology: General, 115*(1), 16–25.

Galpin, A., Underwood, G., & Crundall, D. (2009). Change blindness in driving scenes. *Transportation Research Part F, 12*, 179–185.

Gamble, J. (2001). Humor in apes. *Humor, 14*(2), 163–179.

Gandour, J., Tong, Y., Talavage, T., Wong, D., Dzemidzic, M., Xu, Y., et al. (2007). Neural basis of first and second language processing of sentence-level linguistic prosody. *Human Brain Mapping, 28*, 94–108.

Ganel, T., & Goodale, M. A. (2003). Visual control of action but not perception requires analytical processing of object shape. *Nature, 426*, 664–667.

Ganel, T., Valyear, K. F., Goshen-Gottstein, Y., & Goodale, M. A. (2005). The involvement of the "fusiform face area" in processing facial expression. *Neuropsychologia, 43*(11), 1645–1654.

Ganis, G, Thomspon, W. L., & Kosslyn, S. M. (2004). Brain areas underlying visual mental imagery and visual perception: An fMRI study. *Cognitive Brain Research, 20*, 226–241.

Garcia, A. M., Egido, J. A., & Barquero, M. S. (2010). Mother tongue lost while second language intact: insights into aphasia. *BMJ Case Reports*.

Gardner, H. (1983). *Frames of mind: The theory of multiple intelligences*. New York: Basic Books.

Gardner, H. (1985). *The mind's new science: A history of the cognitive revolution*. New York: Basic Books.

Gardner, H. (1993a). *Creating minds: An anatomy of creativity seen through the lives of Freud, Einstein, Picasso, Stravinsky, Eliot, Graham, and Gandhi*. New York: HarperCollins.

Gardner, H. (1993b). *Multiple intelligences: The theory in practice*. New York: Basic Books.

Gardner, H. (1999). *Intelligence reframed*. New York: Basic Books.

Gardner, H. (2006). *Multiple intelligences: New horizons*. New York: Basic Books.

Garnham, A. (1987). *Mental models as representations of discourse and text*. Chichester, UK: Ellis Horwood.

Garnham, A., & Oakhill, J. V. (1996). The mental models theory of language comprehension. In B. K. Britton & A. C. Graesser (Eds.), *Models of understanding text* (pp. 313–339). Hillsdale, NJ: Erlbaum.

Garrett, M. F. (1980). Levels of processing in sentence production. In B. Butterworth (Ed.), *Language production: Vol. 1. Speech and talk* (pp. 177–210). London: Academic Press.

Garrett, M. F. (1992). Disorders of lexical selection. *Cognition, 42*(1–3), 143–180.

Garrett, M. F. (2003). Language and brain. In L. Nadel (Ed.), *Encyclopedia of cognitive science* (Vol. 2, pp. 707–717). London: Nature Group Press.

Garrod, S., & Daneman, M. (2003). Reading, psychology of. In L. Nadel (Ed.), *Encyclopedia of cognitive science* (Vol. 3, pp. 848–854). London: Nature Publishing Group.

Garry, M., & Loftus, E. F. (1994). Pseudomemories without hypnosis. *International Journal of Clinical and Experimental Hypnosis, 42*, 363–378.

Gasser, M. (2003). Language learning, computational models of. In L. Nadel (Ed.), *Encyclopedia of cognitive science* (Vol. 2, pp. 747–753). London: Nature Group Press.

Gauthier, I., Curran, T., Curby, K. M., & Collins, D. (2003). Perceptual interference supports a non-modular account of face processing. *Nature Neuroscience, 6*, 428–432.

Gauthier, I., Skudlarski, P., Gore, J. C., & Anderson, A. W. (2000). Expertise for cars and birds recruits brain areas involved in face recognition. *Nature Neuroscience, 3*, 191–197.

Gauthier, I., Tarr, M. J., Anderson, A. W., Skudlarski, P., Gore, J. C. (1999). Activation of the middle fusiform "face area" increases with expertise in recognizing novel objects. *Nature Neuroscience, 2*(6), 568–573.

Gazzaniga, M. S. (1985). *The social brain: Discovering the networks of the mind.* New York: Basic Books.

Gazzaniga, M. S. (1995). Principles of human brain organization derived from split-brain studies. *Neuron, 14,* 217–228.

Gazzaniga, M. S. (Ed.). (1995b). *The cognitive neurosciences.* Cambridge, MA: MIT Press.

Gazzaniga, M. S. (Ed.). (2000). *The new cognitive neurosciences* (2nd ed.). Cambridge, MA: MIT Press.

Gazzaniga, M. S., & Hutsler, J. J. (1999). Hemispheric specialization. In R. A. Wilson & F. C. Keil (Eds.), *The MIT encyclopedia of the cognitive sciences* (pp. 369–372). Cambridge, MA: MIT Press.

Gazzaniga, M. S., Ivry, R. B., & Mangun, G. R. (2009). *Cognitive neuroscience. The biology of the mind.* New York: Norton.

Gazzaniga, M. S., Ivry, R. B., & Mangun, G. R. (2002). *Cognitive neuroscience: The biology of the mind* (2nd ed.). New York: Norton.

Gazzaniga, M. S., Ivry, R. B., & Mangun, G. R. (1998). *Cognitive neuroscience: The biology of the mind* (1st ed). New York: Norton.

Gazzaniga, M. S., & LeDoux, J. E. (1978). *The integrated mind.* New York: Plenum.

Gazzaniga, M. S., & Sperry, R. W. (1967). Language after section of the cerebral commissures. *Brain, 90*(1), 131–148.

Ge, L., Zhang, H., Wang, Z., Quinn, P. C., Pascalis, O., Kelly, D., et al. (2009). Two faces of the other-race effect: Recognition and categorisation of Caucasian and Chinese faces. *Perception, 38,* 1199–1210.

Gelman, S. A. (1985). Children's inductive inferences from natural kind and artifact categories. (Doctoral dissertation, Stanford University, 1984). *Dissertation Abstracts International, 45*(10B), 3351–3352.

Gelman, S. A. (1989). Children's use of categories to guide biological inferences. *Human Development, 32*(2), 65–71.

Gelman, S. A. (2003). *The essential child: Origins of essentialism in everyday thought.* New York: Oxford University Press.

Gelman, S. A. (2004). Psychological essentialism in children. *Trends in Cognitive Sciences, 8,* 404–409.

Gelman, S. A. (2009). Essentialist reasoning about the biological world. In *Neurobiology of "Umwelt"* (pp. 7–16). Berlin: Springer.

Gelman, S. A., & Kremer, K. E. (1991). Understanding natural causes: Children's explanations of how objects and their properties originate. *Child Development, 62*(2), 396–414.

Gelman, S. A., & Markman, E. M. (1986). Categories and induction in young children. *Cognition, 23,* 183–209.

Gelman, S. A., & Markman, E. M. (1987). Young children's inductions from natural kinds: The role of categories and appearances. *Child Development, 58*(6), 1532–1541.

Gelman, S. A., & O'Reilly, A. W. (1988). Children's inductive inferences within superordinate categories: The role of language and category structure. *Child Development, 59*(4), 876–887.

Gelman, S. A., & Wellman, H. M. (1991). Insides and essence: Early understandings of the non-obvious. *Cognition, 38*(3), 213–244.

Gentile, J. R. (2000). Learning, transfer of. In A. E. Kazdin (Ed.), *Encyclopedia of psychology* (Vol. 5, pp. 13–16). Washington, DC: American Psychological Association.

Gentner, D. (1983). Structure-mapping: A theoretical framework for analogy. *Cognitive Science, 7,* 155–170.

Gentner, D. (2000). Analogy. In R. A. Wilson & F. C. Keil (Eds.), *The MIT encyclopedia of the cognitive sciences* (pp. 17–20). Cambridge, MA: MIT Press.

Gentner, D., & Gentner, D. R. (1983). Flowing waters or teeming crowds: Mental models of electricity. In D. Gentner & A. Stevens (Eds.), *Mental models.* Hillsdale, NJ: Erlbaum.

Georgopoulos, A. P., Lurito, J. T., Petrides, M., & Schwartz, A. B., Massey, J. T. (1989). Mental rotation of the neuronal population vector. *Science, 243*(4888), 234–236.

Georgopoulos, A. P., & Pellizzer, G. (1995). The mental and the neural: Psychological and neural studies of mental rotation and memory scanning. *Neuropsychologia, 33,* 1531–1547.

German, T. P., & Barrett, H. C. (2005). Functional fixedness in a technologically sparse culture. *Psychological Science, 16*(1), 1–5.

Gernsbacher, M. A., & Kaschak, M. P. (2003a). Language comprehension. In L. Nadel (Ed.), *Encyclopedia of cognitive science* (Vol. 2, pp. 723–726). London: Nature Group Press.

Gernsbacher, M. A., & Kaschak, M. P. (2003b). Psycholinguistics. In L. Nadel (Ed.), *Encyclopedia of cognitive science* (Vol. 3, pp. 783–786). London: Nature Group Press.

Gerrig, R. J., & Banaji, M. R. (1994). Language and thought. In R. J. Sternberg (Ed.), *Thinking and problem solving* (pp. 235–261). New York: Academic Press.

Gerrig, R. J., & Healy, A. F. (1983). Dual processes in metaphor understanding: Comprehension and appreciation. *Journal of Experimental Psychology: Learning, Memory, & Cognition, 9,* 667–675.

Geschwind, N. (1970). The organization of language and the brain. *Science, 170,* 940–944.

Gibbs, R. W. (1979). Contextual effects in understanding indirect requests. *Discourse Processes, 2,* 1–10.

Gibbs, R. W. (1986). What makes some indirect speech acts conventional? *Journal of Memory and Language, 25,* 181–196.

Gibson, E. J. (1991). The ecological approach: A foundation for environmental psychology. In R. M. Downs, L. S. Liben, & D. S. Palermo (Eds.), *Visions of aesthetics, the environment & development: The legacy of Joachim F. Wohlwill* (pp. 87–111). Hillsdale, NJ: Erlbaum.

Gibson, E. J. (1992). How to think about perceptual learning: Twenty-five years later. In H. L. Pick, Jr., P. W. van den Broek, & D. C. Knill (Eds.), *Cognition: Conceptual and methodological issues* (pp. 215–237). Washington, DC: American Psychological Association.

Gibson, J. J. (1950). *The perception of the visual world.* Boston: Houghton Mifflin.

Gibson, J. J. (1966). *The senses considered as perceptual systems.* New York: Houghton Mifflin.

Gibson, J. J. (1979). *The ecological approach to visual perception.* Boston: Houghton Mifflin.

Gibson, J. J. (1994). The visual perception of objective motion and subjective movement. *Psychological Review, 101*(2), 318–323. (Original work published 1954)

Gick, M. L., & Holyoak, K. J. (1980). Analogical problem solving. *Cognitive Psychology, 12,* 306–355.

Gick, M. L., & Holyoak, K. J. (1983). Schema induction and analogical transfer. *Cognitive Psychology, 15,* 1–38.

Gigerenzer, G. (1996). On narrow norms and vague heuristics: A reply to Kahneman and Tversky. *Psychological Review, 103,* 592–596.

Gigerenzer, G. (2004). Dread risk, September 11, and fatal traffic accidents. *Psychological Science, 15*(4), 286–287.

Gigerenzer, G., & Brighton, H. (2009). Homo heuristicus: Why biased minds make better inferences. *Topics in Cognitive Science, 1,* 107–143.

Gigerenzer, G., & Goldstein, D. G. (1996). Reasoning the fast and frugal way: Models of bounded rationality. *Psychological Review, 103,* 650–669.

Gigerenzer, G., & Hoffrage, U. (1995). How to improve Bayesian reasoning without instruction: Frequency formats. *Psychological Review, 102,* 684–704.

Gigerenzer, G., Todd, P. M., & the ABC Research Group (1999). *Simple heuristics that make us smart.* New York: Oxford University Press.

Gignac, G., Vernon, P. A., & Wickett, J. C. (2003). Gignac, G., Vernon, P. A., & Wickett, J. C. In H. Nyborg (Ed.), *The scientific study of general intelligence* (pp. 93–106). Amsterdam: Pergamon.

Gilbert, A. L., Regier, T., Kay, P., & Ivry, R. B. (2006). Whorf hypothesis is supported in the right visual field but not the left. *Proceedings of the National Academy of Sciences of the United States of America, 103*(2), 489–494.

Gilbert, J. A. E., & Fisher, R. P. (2006). The effects of varied retrieval cues on reminiscence in eyewitness memory. *Applied Cognitive Psychology, 20*(6), 723–739.

Gilboa, A., Winocur, G., Rosenbaum, S., Poreh, A., Gao, F., Black, S., et al. (2006). Hippocampal contributions to recollection in retrograde and anterograde amnesia. *Hippocampus, 16*(11), 966–980.

Gilger, J. W. (1996). How can behavioral genetic research help us understand language development and disorders? In M. L. Rice (Ed.), *Toward a genetics of language* (pp. 77–110). Mahwah, NJ: Erlbaum.

Gilhooly, K. J. (2004). Working memory and reasoning. In J. P. Leighton & R. J. Sternberg (Eds.), *The nature of reasoning* (pp. 49–77). New York: Cambridge University Press.

Gilhooly, K. J., Logie, R. H., Wetherick, N. E., & Wynn, V. (1993). Working memory and strategies in syllogistic reasoning tasks. *Memory and Cognition, 21*, 115–124.

Gillam, B. (2000). Perceptual constancies. In A. E. Kazdin (Ed.), *Encyclopedia of psychology* (Vol. 6, pp. 89–93). Washington, DC: American Psychological Association.

Gilovich, T., Griffin, D., & Kahneman, D. (Eds.). (2002). *Heuristics and biases: The psychology of intuitive judgment*. New York: Cambridge University Press.

Gilovich, T., Vallone, R., & Tversky, A. (1985). The hot hand in basketball: On the misperception of random sequences. *Cognitive Psychology, 17*(3), 295–314.

Ginns, P. (2006). Integrating information: A meta-analysis of the spatial contiguity and temporal contiguity effects. *Learning and Instruction, 16*, 511–525.

Girelli, L., Sandrini, M., Cappa, S., & Butterworth, B. (2001). Number-Stroop performance in normal aging and Alzheimer's-type dementia. *Brain Cognition, 46*(1–2), 144–149.

Girotto, V. (2004). Task understanding. In J. P. Leighton & R. J. Sternberg (Eds.), *The nature of reasoning* (pp. 103–125). New York: Cambridge University Press.

Giuliodori, M. J., & DiCarlo, S. E. (2004). Myelinated vs. unmyelinated nerve conduction: a novel way of understanding the mechanisms. *Advances in Physiology Education, 28*, 80–81.

Givens, D. G. (2002). *The nonverbal dictionary of gestures, signs & body language cues*. Spokane, WA: Center for Nonverbal Studies Press.

Gladwin, T. (1970). *East is a big bird*. Cambridge, MA: Harvard University Press.

Glaescher, J., Tranel, D., Paul, L. K., Rudrauf, D., Rorden, C., Hornaday, A., et al. (2009). Lesion mapping of cognitive abilities linked to intelligence. *Neuron, 61*, 681–691.

Glaser, R., & Chi, M. T. H. (1988). Overview. In M. T. H. Chi, R. Glaser, & M. Farr (Eds.), *The nature of expertise* (pp. xv–xxxvi). Hillsdale, NJ: Erlbaum.

Glenberg, A. M. (1977). Influences of retrieval processes on the spacing effect in free recall. *Journal of Experimental Psychology: Human Learning & Memory, 3*(3), 282–294.

Glenberg, A. M. (1979). Component-levels theory of the effects of spacing of repetitions on recall and recognition. *Memory & Cognition, 7*(2), 95–112.

Glenberg, A. M. (1997). What memory is for. *Behavioral and Brain Sciences, 20*, 1–55.

Glenberg, A. M., Meyer, M., & Lindem, K. (1987). Mental models contribute to foregrounding during text comprehension. *Journal of Memory & Language, 26*(1), 69–83.

Glickstein, M., & Berlucchi, G. (2008). Classical disconnection studies of the corpus callosum. *Cortex, 44*, 914–927.

Gloor, P. (1997). *The temporal lobe and limbic system*. New York: Oxford University Press.

Gluck, M. A. (Ed.) (1996). Computational models of hippocampal function in memory. Special issue of *Hippocampus, 6*, 6.

Glucksberg, S. (1988). Language and thought. In R. J. Sternberg & E. E. Smith (Eds.), *The psychology of human thought* (pp. 214–241). New York: Cambridge University Press.

Glucksberg, S., & Danks, J. H. (1975). *Experimental psycholinguistics*. Hillsdale, NJ: Erlbaum.

Glucksberg, S., & Keysar, B. (1990). Understanding metaphorical comparisons: Beyond similarity. *Psychological Review, 97*(1), 3–18.

Gobet, F., & Jackson, S. (2002). In search of templates. *Cognitive Systems Research, 3*(1), 35–44.

Gobet, F., & Simon, H. A. (1996a). Recall of random and distorted chess positions: Implications for the theory of expertise. *Memory and Cognition, 24*, 493–503.

Gobet, F., & Simon, H. A. (1996b). Roles of recognition processes and look-ahead search in time-constrained expert problem solving: Evidence from grand-master-level chess. *Psychological Science, 7*, 52–55.

Gobet, F., & Simon, H. A. (1996c). Templates in chess memory: A mechanism for recalling several boards. *Cognitive Psychology, 31*, 1–40.

Godbout, L., Cloutier, P., Bouchard, C., Braun, C. M. J., & Gagnon, S. (2004). Script generation following frontal and parietal lesions. *Journal of Clinical and Experimental Neuropsychology, 26*(7), 857–873.

Godden, D. R., & Baddeley, A. D. (1975). Context-dependent memory in two natural environments: On land and underwater. *British Journal of Psychology, 66*, 325–331.

Göder, R., Fritzer, G., Gottwald, B., Lippmann, B., Seeck-Hirschner, M., Serafin, I., et al. (2008). Effects of olanzapine on slow wave sleep, sleep spindles and sleep-related memory consolidation in schizophrenia. *Pharmacopsychiatry, 41*, 92–99.

Gogos, A., Gavrilescu, M., Davison, S., Searle, K., Adams, J., Rossell, S. L., et al. (2010). Greater superior than inferior parietal lobule activation with increasing rotation angle during mental rotation: An fMRI study. *Neuropsychologia, 48*, 529–535.

Goldsmith, M., Koriat, A., & Pansky, A. (2005). Strategic regulation of grain size in memory reporting over time. *Journal of Memory and Language, 52*, 505–525.

Goldstein, D. G., & Gigerenzer, G. (2002). Models of ecological rationality: The recognition heuristic. *Psychological Review, 109*(1), 75–90.

Goldstein, D. G., & Gigerenzer, G. (2009). Fast and frugal forecasting. *International Journal of Forecasting, 25*, 760–772.

Goldstone, R. L. (2003). Perceptual organization in vision: Behavioral and neural perspectives. In R. Kimchi & M. Behrmann (Eds.), *Perceptual organization in vision: Behavioral and neural perspectives* (pp. 233–280). Mahwah, NJ: Erlbaum.

Goleman, D. (1995). *Emotional intelligence*. New York: Bantam.

Goleman, D. (1998). *Working with emotional intelligence*. New York: Bantam.

Goleman, D. (2007). *Social intelligence*. New York: Bantam.

Gollan, T. H., & Brown, A. S. (2006). From tip-of-the-tongue (TOT) data to theoretical implications in two steps: When more TOTs means better retrieval. *Journal of Experimental Psychology: General, 135*(3), 462–483.

Golomb, J. D., Peelle, J. E., Addis, K. M., Kahana, M. J., & Wingfield, A. (2008). Effects of adult aging on utilization of temporal and semantic associations during free and serial recall. *Memory & Cognition, 36*(5), 947–956.

Gonzalez, R., Jacobus, J., Amatya, A. K., Quartana, P. J., Vassileva, J., & Martin, E. M. (2008). Deficits in complex motor functions, despite no evidence of procedural learning deficits, among HIV+

individuals with history of substance dependence. *Neuropsychology, 22*(6), 776–786.

Goodale, M. A. (2000). Perception and action. In A. E. Kazdin (Ed.), *Encyclopedia of psychology* (Vol. 6, pp. 86–89). Washington, DC: American Psychological Association.

Goodale, M. A. (2000a). Perception and action. In A. E. Kazdin (Ed.), *Encyclopedia of psychology* (Vol. 6, pp. 86–89). Washington, DC: American Psychological Association.

Goodale, M. A. (2000b). Perception and action in the human visual system. In M. Gazzaniga (Ed.), *The new cognitive neurosciences* (pp. 365–378). Cambridge, MA: MIT Press.

Goodale, M. A., & Milner, A. D. (2004). *Sight unseen: An exploration of conscious and unconscious vision.* New York: Oxford University Press.

Goodale, M. A., & Westwood, D. A. (2004). An evolving view of duplex vision: Separate but interacting cortical pathways for perception and action. *Current Opinion in Neurobiology, 14,* 203–211.

Goodman, N. (1983). *Fact, fiction, and forecast* (4th ed). Cambridge, MA: Harvard University Press.

Goodwin, G. P., & Johnson-Laird, P. N. (2010). Conceptual illusions. *Cognition, 114,* 253–265.

Gopnik, A., & Choi, S. (1995). Names, relational words, and cognitive development in English and Korean speakers: Nouns are not always learned before verbs. In M. Tomasello & W. E. Merriman (Eds.), *Beyond names for things: Young children's acquisition of verbs* (pp. 83–90). Hillsdale, NJ: Erlbaum.

Gopnik, A., Choi, S., & Baumberger, T. (1996). Cross-linguistic differences in early semantic and cognitive development. *Cognitive Development, 11,* 197–227.

Gordon, D., & Lakoff, G. (1971). Conversational postulates. In *Papers from the Seventh Regional Meeting, Chicago Linguistic Society* (pp. 63–84). Chicago: Chicago Linguistic Society.

Gordon, P. (2004). Numerical cognition without words: Evidence from Amazonia. *Science, 306,* 496–499.

Graesser, A. C., & Kreuz, R. J. (1993). A theory of inference generation during text comprehension. *Discourse Processes, 16,* 145–160.

Graf, P., Mandler, G., & Haden, P. E. (1982). Simulating amnesic symptoms in normal subjects. *Science, 218*(4578), 1243–1255.

Grainger, J., Bouttevin, S., Truc, C., Bastien, M., & Ziegler, J. (2003). Word superiority, pseudoword superiority, and learning to read: A comparison of dyslexic and normal readers. *Brain and Language, 87*(3), 432–440.

Grant, E. R., & Ceci, S. J. (2000). Memory: Constructive processes. In A. E. Kazdin (Ed.), *Encyclopedia of psychology* (Vol. 5, pp. 166–169). Washington, DC: American Psychological Association.

Gray, J. A., & Wedderburn, A. A. I. (1960). Grouping strategies with simultaneous stimuli. *Quarterly Journal of Experimental Psychology, 12,* 180–184.

Gray, J. R., Chabris, C. F., & Braver, T. S. (2003). Neural mechanisms of general fluid intelligence. *Nature Neuroscience Reviews, 6,* 316–322.

Gray, J. R., & Thompson, P. M. (2004). Neurobiology of intelligence: Science and ethics. *Nature Neuroscience Reviews, 5,* 471–482.

Grayson, D., & Coventry, L. (1998). The effects of visual proxemic information in video mediated communication. *SIGCHI, 30*(3). In Y. Wilks (Ed.), *Machine conversations.* Amsterdam, Netherlands: Kluwer.

Green, D. W. (1998). Mental control of the bilingual lexico-semantic system. *Bilingualism: Language and Cognition, 1*(2), 67–81.

Greenberg, R., & Underwood, B. J. (1950). Retention as a function of stage of practice. *Journal of Experimental Psychology, 40,* 452–457.

Greene, J. A., & Azevedo, R. (2007). Adolescents' use of self-regulatory processes and their relation to qualitative mental model shifts while using hypermedia. *Journal of Educational Computing Research, 36*(2), 125–148.

Greenfield, P. M., & Savage-Rumbaugh, S. (1990). Grammatical combination in Pan paniscus: Processes of learning and invention in the evolution of language. In S. Parker & K. Gibson (Eds.), *"Language" and intelligence in monkeys and apes: Comparative developmental perspectives.* New York: Cambridge University Press.

Greeno, J. G. (1974). Hobbits and orcs: Acquisition of a sequential concept. *Cognitive Psychology, 6,* 270–292.

Greeno, J. G., & Simon, H. A. (1988). Problem solving and reasoning. In R. C. Atkinson, R. Herrnstein, G. Lindzey, & R. D. Luce (Eds.), *Stevens' handbook of experimental psychology* (Rev. ed., pp. 589–672). New York: Wiley.

Greenwald, A. G., & Banaji, M. (1989). The self as a memory system: Powerful, but ordinary. *Journal of Personality & Social Psychology, 57*(1), 41–54.

Gregory, R. L. (1980). Perceptions as hypotheses. *Philosophical Transactions of the Royal Society of London, Series B, 290,* 181–197.

Gregory, T., Nettelbeck, T., & Wilson, C. (2009). Inspection time and everyday functioning: A longitudinal study. *Personality and Individual Differences, 47*(8), 999–1002.

Grice, H. P. (1967). William James Lectures, Harvard University, published in part as "Logic and conversation." In P. Cole & J. L. Morgan (Eds.), *Syntax and semantics: Vol. 3. Speech acts* (pp. 41–58). New York: Seminar Press.

Griffey, R. T., Wittels, K., Gilboy, N., & McAfee, A. T. (2009). Use of a computerized forcing function improves performance in ordering restraints. *Annals of Emergency Medicine, 53*(4), 469–476.

Griffin, D., & Tversky, A. (1992). The weighing of evidence and the determinants of confidence. *Cognitive Psychology, 24,* 411–435.

Griggs, R. A., & Cox, J. R. (1982). The elusive thematic-materials effect in Wason's selection task. *British Journal of Psychology, 73,* 407–420.

Griggs, R. A., & Cox, J. R. (1993). Permission schemas and the selection task. *The Quarterly Journal of Experimental Psychology, 46A*(4), 637–651.

Grigorenko, E. L. (2000). Heritability and intelligence. In R. J. Sternberg (Ed.), *Handbook of intelligence* (pp. 53–91). New York: Cambridge University Press.

Grigorenko, E. L., Geissler, P. W., Prince, R., Okatcha, F., Nokes, C., Kenny, D. A., et al. (2001). The organization of Luo conceptions of intelligence: A study of implicit theories in a Kenyan village. *International Journal of Behavioral Development, 25,* 367–378.

Grigorenko, E. L., Jarvin, L., & Sternberg, R. J. (2002). School-based tests of the triarchic theory of intelligence: Three settings, three samples, three syllabi. *Contemporary Educational Psychology, 27,* 167–208.

Grimes, C. E. (2010). Digging for the roots of language death in Eastern Indonesia: The cases of Kayeli and Hukumina. In M. Florey (Ed.), *Endangered languages of Austronesia.* Oxford: Oxford University Press.

Grodzinsky, Y. (2003). Language disorders. In L. Nadel (Ed.), *Encyclopedia of cognitive science* (Vol. 2, pp. 740–746). London: Nature Group Press.

Groenholm, P., Rinne, J. O., Vorobyev, V., & Laine, M. (2005). Naming of newly learned objects: A PET activation study. *Cognitive Brain Research, 25,* 359–371.

Grossman, L., & Eagle, M. (1970). Synonymity, antonymity, and association in false recognition responses. *Journal of Experimental Psychology, 83,* 244–248.

Grossmann, T., Striano, T., & Friederici, A. D. (2006). Crossmodal integration of emotional information from face and voice in the infant brain. *Developmental Science*, 9(3), 309–315.

Grosvald, M., & Corina, D. (2008, 3–4 May). *Exploring the limits of long-distance vowel-to-vowel coarticulation*. Paper presented at the 24th Northwest Linguistics Conference, Seattle, Washington.

Grosz, B. J., Pollack, M. E., & Sidner, C. L. (1989). Discourse. In M. I. Posner (Ed.), *Foundations of cognitive science* (pp. 437–468). Cambridge, MA: MIT Press.

Grubb, M. D. (2009). Selling to overconfident consumers. *American Economic Review*, 99(5), 1770–1807.

Gruber, H. E. (1981). *Darwin on man: A psychological study of scientific creativity* (2nd ed.). Chicago: University of Chicago Press. (Original work published 1974.)

Gruber, H. E., & Davis, S. N. (1988). Inching our way up Mount Olympus: The evolving-systems approach to creative thinking. In R. J. Sternberg (Ed.), *The nature of creativity* (pp. 243–270). New York: Cambridge University Press.

Grunwald, M. (Ed.). (2008). *Human haptic perception: Basics and applications*. Basel, Switzerland: Birkhaeuser.

Gugerty, L. (2007). Cognitive components of troubleshooting strategies. *Thinking & Reasoning*, 13(2), 134–163.

Guilford, J. P. (1950). Creativity. *American Psychologist*, 5(9), 444–454.

Gunzelmann, G., & Anderson, J. R. (2003). Problem solving: Increased planning with practice. *Cognitive System Research*, 4(1), 57–76.

Gupta, R., Duff, M. C., Denburg, N. L., Cohen, N. J., Bechara, A., & Tranela, D. (2009). Declarative memory is critical for sustained advantageous complex decision-making. *Neuropsychologia*, 47, 1686–1693.

Haber, R. N. (1983). The impending demise of the icon: A critique of the concept of iconic storage in visual information processing. *Behavioral and Brain Sciences*, 6(1), 1–54.

Hagtvet, B. E. (2003). Listening comprehension and reading comprehension in poor decoders: Evidence for the importance of syntactic and semantic skills as well as phonological skills. *Reading and Writing: An Interdisciplinary Journal*, 16(6), 505–539.

Haier, R. J. (in press). Biological basis of intelligence: What does brain imaging show? In R. J. Sternberg & S. B. Kaufman (Eds.), *Cambridge handbook of intelligence*. New York: Cambridge University Press.

Haier, R. J., Chueh, D., Touchette, P., Lott, I., Buchbaum, M. S., MacMillan, D., et al. (1995). Brain size and cerebral glucose metabolic rate in nonspecific mental retardation and Down syndrome. *Intelligence*, 20, 191–210.

Haier, R. J., & Jung, R. E. (2007). Beautiful minds (i.e., brains) and the neural basis of intelligence. *Behavioral and Brain Sciences*, 30(2), 174–178.

Haier, R. J., Jung, R. E., Yeo, R. A., Head, K., & Alkire, M. T. (2004). Structural brain variation and general intelligence. *NeuroImage*, 23(1), 425–433.

Haier, R. J., Jung, R. E., Yeo, R. A., Head, K., & Alkire, M. T. (2005). The neuroanatomy of general intelligence: sex matters. *NeuroImage*, 25(1), 320–327.

Haier, R. J., Siegel, B., Tang, C., Abel, L., & Buchsbaum, M. S. (1992). Intelligence and changes in regional cerebral glucose metabolic rate following learning. *Intelligence*, 16(3–4), 415–426.

Hall, E. T. (1966). *The hidden dimension: Man's use of space in public and private*. Garden City, N.Y.: Doubleday.

Hall, G. B. C., Szechtman, H., & Nahmias, C. (2003). Enhanced salience and emotion recognition in autism: A PET study. *American Journal of Psychiatry*, 160, 1439–1441.

Hambrick, D. Z., & Engle, R. W. (2002). Effects of domain knowledge, working memory capacity, and age on cognitive performance: An investigation of the knowledge-is-power hypothesis. *Cognitive Psychology*, 44, 339–387.

Hambrick, D. Z., & Engle, R. W. (2003). The role of working memory in problem solving. In J. E. Davidson & R. J. Sternberg (Eds.), *The psychology of problem solving* (pp. 176–206). New York: Cambridge University Press.

Hambrick D. Z., Kane, M. J., & Engle, R. W. (2005). The role of working memory in higher-level cognition. In R. J. Sternberg & J. E. Pretz (Eds.), *Cognition and intelligence* (pp. 104–121). New York: Cambridge University Press.

Hamilton, D. L., & Lickel, B. (2000). Illusory correlation. In A. E. Kazdin (Ed.), *Encyclopedia of psychology* (Vol. 4, pp. 226–227). Washington, DC: American Psychological Association.

Hamm, A. O., Weike, A. I., Schupp, H. T., Treig, T., Dressel, A., & Kessler, C. (2003). Affective blindsight: Intact fear conditioning to a visual cue in a cortically blind patient. *Brain*, 126(2), 267–275.

Hampton, J. A. (1997). Emergent attributes of combined concepts. In T. B. Ward, S. M. Smith, & J. Vaid (Eds.), *Conceptual structures and processes: Emergence, discovery, and change* (pp. 83–110). Washington, DC: American Psychological Association.

Hancock, T. W., Hicks, J., Marsh, R. L., & Ritschel, L. (2003). Measuring the activation level of critical lures in the Deese-Roediger-McDermott paradigm. *American Journal of Psychology*, 116, 1–14.

Hanley, J. R., & Chapman, E. (2008). Partial knowledge in a tip-of-the-tongue state about two- and three-word proper names. *Psychonomic Bulletin & Review*, 15(1), 155–160.

Hanson, E. K., Beukelman, D. R., Heidemann, J. K., & Shutts-Johnson, E. (2010). The impact of alphabet supplementation and word prediction on sentence intelligiblity of electronically distorted speech. *Speech Communication*, 52, 99–105.

Harber, K. D., & Jussim, L. (2005). Teacher expectations and self-fulfilling prophecies: Knowns and unknowns, resolved and unresolved controversies. *Personality and Social Psychological Review*, 9(2), 131–155.

Harley, T. (2008). *The psychology of language: From data to theory* (3rd ed.). Hove, England: Psychology Press.

Harm, M. W., & Seidenberg, M. S. (2004). Computing the meanings of words in reading: Cooperative division of labor between visual and phonological processes. *Psychological Review*, 111(3), 662–720.

Harnish, R. M. (2003). Speech acts. In L. Nadel (Ed.), *Encyclopedia of cognitive science* (Vol. 4, pp. 150–156). London: Nature Publishing Group.

Harris, C. L. (2003). Language and cognition. In L. Nadel (Ed.), *Encyclopedia of cognitive science* (Vol. 2, pp. 717–722). London: Nature Group Press.

Harris, G. J., Chabris, C. F., Clark, J., Urban, T., Aharon, I., Steele, S., et al. (2006). Brain activation during semantic processing in autism spectrum disorders via functional magnetic resonance imaging. *Brain and Cognition*, 61, 54–68.

Hasel, L. E., & Kassin, S. M. (2009). On the Presumption of evidentiary independence: Can confessions corrupt eyewitness identifications? *Psychological Science*, 20(1), 122–126.

Hasselmo, M. E. (2006). The role of acetylcholine in learning and memory. *Current Opinion in Neurobiology*, 16(6), 710–715.

Hatfield, G. (2002). Psychology, philosophy, and cognitive science: Reflections on the history and philosophy of experimental psychology. *Mind & Language*, 17(3), 207–232.

Hausknecht, K. A., Acheson, A., Farrar, A. M., Kieres, A. K., Shen, R. Y., Richards, J. B., et al. (2005). Prenatal alcohol exposure causes attention deficits in male rats. *Behavioral Neuroscience*, 119(1), 302–310.

Haviland, S. E., & Clark, H. H. (1974). What's new? Acquiring new information as a process in comprehension. *Journal of Verbal Learning and Verbal Behavior, 13*, 512–521.

Haworth, C. M. A., Kovas, Y., Harlaar, N., Hayiou-Thomas, M. E., Petrill, S. A., Dale, P. S., et al. (2009). Generalist genes and learning disabilities: a multivariate genetic analysis of low performance in reading, mathematics, language and general cognitive ability in a sample of 8000 12-year-old twins. *Journal of Child Psychology and Psychiatry, 50*(10), 1318–1325.

Haxby, J. V., Gobbini, M. I., Furye, M. L., Ishai, A., Schouten, J. L., & Pietrini, P. (2001). Distributed and overlapping representations of faces and objects in ventral temporal cortex. *Science, 293*, 2425–2430.

Haxby, J. V., Gobbini, M. I., & Montgomery, K. (2004). Spatial and temporal distribution of face and object representations in the human brain. In M. S. Gazzaniga (Ed.), *The cognitive neurosciences* (3rd ed., pp. 889–904). Cambridge, MA: MIT Press.

Haxby, J. V., Ungerleider, L. G., Horwitz, B., Maisog, J. M., Rappaport, S. L., & Grady, C. L. (1996). Face encoding and recognition in the human brain. *Proceedings of the National Academy of Sciences of the United States, 98*, 922–927.

Haxby, J. V., Ungerleider, L. G., Horwitz, B., Rapoport, S., & Grady, C. L. (1995). Hemispheric differences in neural systems for face working memory: A PET-rCBF study. *Human Brain Mapping, 3*, 68–82.

Heaton, J. M. (1968). *The eye: Phenomenology and psychology of function and disorder*. London: Tavistock.

Hebb, D. O. (1949). *The organization of behavior: A neuropsychological theory*. New York: Wiley.

Hegarty, M. (1991). Knowledge and processes in mechanical problem solving. In R. J. Sternberg & P. A. Frensch (Eds.), *Complex problem solving: Principles and mechanisms* (pp. 159–183). Hillsdale, NJ: Erlbaum.

Hehir, A. (2006). The impact of analogical reasoning on U.S. foreign policy towards Kosova. *Journal of Peace Research, 43*(1), 67–81.

Heilman, K. M., Coenen, A., & Kluger, B. (2008). Progressive asymmetric apraxic agraphia. *Cognitive and Behavioral Neurology, 21*(1), 14–17.

Heindel, W. C., Butters, N., & Salmon, D. P. (1988). Impaired learning of a motor skill in patients with Huntington's disease. *Behavioral Neuroscience, 102*(1), 141–147.

Heinrichs, M., Dawansa, B. v., & Domes, G. (2009). Oxytocin, vasopressin, and human social behavior. *Frontiers in Neuroendocrinology, 30*(4), 548–557.

Helmes, E., & Velamoor, V. R. (2009). Long-term outcome of leucotomy on behaviour of people with schizophrenia. *International Journal of Social Psychiatry, 55*(1), 64–70.

Helms-Lorenz, M., Van de Vijver, F. J. R., & Poortinga, Y. H. (2003). Cross-cultural differences in cognitive performance and Spearman's hypothesis: g or c? *Intelligence, 31*, 9–29.

Henley, N. M. (1969). A psychological study of the semantics of animal terms. *Journal of Verbal Learning and Verbal Behavior, 8*, 176–184.

Hennessey, B. A. (2010). The creativity-motivation connection. In J. C. Kaufman & R. J. Sternberg (Eds.), *The Cambridge handbook of creativity* (pp. 342–365). New York: Cambridge University Press.

Hennessey, B. A., & Amabile, T. M. (1988). The conditions of creativity. In R. J. Sternberg (Ed.), *The nature of creativity* (pp. 11–38). New York: Cambridge University Press.

Henry, J. D., MacLeod, M. S., Phillips, L. H., & Crawford, J. R. (2004). A meta-analytic review of prospective memory and aging. *Psychology and Aging, 19*(1), 27–39.

Henry, L. A., & Gudjonsson, G. H. (2003). Eyewitness memory, suggestibility, and repeated recall sessions in children with mild and moderate intellectual disabilities. *Law and Human Behavior, 27*(5), 481–505.

Hernandez, A. E., Dapretto, M., Mazziotta, J., & Bookheimer, S. (2001). Language switching and language representation in Spanish-English bilinguals: An fMRI study. *Neuroimage, 14*, 510–520.

Herschensohn, J. (2007). *Language development and age*. Cambridge, UK: Cambridge University Press.

Herring, S. C., & Paolillo, J. C. (2006). Gender and genre variation in weblogs. *Journal of Sociolinguistics, 10*(4), 439–459.

Hertzog, C., Vernon, M. C., & Rypma, B. (1993). Age differences in mental rotation task performance: The influence of speed/accuracy tradeoffs. *Journal of Gerontology, 48*(3), 150–156.

Herz, R. S., & Engen, T. (1996). Odor memory: Review and analysis. *Psychonomic Bulletin and Review, 3*, 300–313.

Hesse, M. (1966). *Models and analogies in science*. South Bend, IN: University of Notre Dame Press.

Hewig, J., Straube, T., Trippe, R. H., Kretschmer, N., Hecht, H., Coles, M. G. H., et al. (2008). Decision-making under risk: An fMRI study. *Journal of Cognitive Neuroscience, 21*(8), 1642–1652.

Hickling, A. K., & Gelman, S. A. (1995). How does your garden grow? Early conceptualization of seeds and their place in the plant growth cycle. *Child Development, 66*, 856–867.

Hickok, G., & Poeppel, D. (2000). Towards a functional neuroanatomy of speech perception. *Trends in Cognitive Sciences, 4*, 131–138.

Hill, E. L. (2004). Evaluating the theory of executive dysfunction in autism. *Developmental Review, 24*, 189–233.

Hill, J. H. (1978). Apes and language. *Annual Review of Anthropology, 7*, 89–112.

Hillis, A. E. (2006). Neurobiology of unilateral spatial neglect. *Neuroscientist, 12*, 153–163.

Hillis, A. E., & Caramazza, A. (2003). Aphasia. In L. Nadel (Ed.), *Encyclopedia of cognitive science* (Vol. 1, pp. 175–184). London: Nature Publishing Group.

Hillis, A. E., Newhart, M., Heidler, J., Barker, P. B., Herskovits, E. H., & Degaonkar, M. (2005). Anatomy of spatial attention: Insights from perfusion imaging and hemispatial neglect in acute stroke. *Journal of Neuroscience, 25*, 3161–3167.

Hillix, W. A., & Rumbaugh, D. M. (2004). *Animal bodies, human minds: Ape, dolphin, and parrot language skills*. New York: Kluwer Academic/Plenum Publishers.

Hillyard, S. A., Hink, R. F., Schwent, V. L., & Picton, T. W. (1973). Electrical signs of selective attention in the human brain. *Science, 182*, 177–180.

Himmelbach, M., & Karnath, H. O. (2005). Dorsal and ventral stream interaction: Contributions from optic ataxia. *Journal of Cognitive Neuroscience, 17*, 632–640.

Himmelbach, M., Nau, M., Zündorf, I., Erb, M., Perenin, M.-T., & Karnath, H.-O. (2009). Brain activation during immediate and delayed reaching in optic ataxia. *Neuropsychologia, 47*, 1508–1517.

Hinsz, V. B. (1990). Cognitive and consensus processes in group recognition memory. *Journal of Personality and Social Psychology, 59*(4), 705–718.

Hinton, G. E. (1979). Some demonstrations of the effects of structural descriptions in mental imagery. *Cognitive Science, 3*, 231–251.

Hirsh-Pasek, K., Kemler Nelson, D. G., Jusczyk, P. W., Cassidy, K. W., Druss, B., & Kennedy, L. (1987). Clauses are perceptual units for young infants. *Cognition, 26*, 269–286.

Hirst, W., Phelps, E. A., Buckner, R. L., Budson, A. E., Cuc, A., Gabrieli, J. D. E., et al. (2009). Long-term memory for the terrorist attack of September 11: Flashbulb memories, event memories, and the factors that influence their retention. *Journal of Experimental Psychology: General, 138*(2), 161–176.

Hirtle, S. C., & Jonides, J. (1985). Evidence of hierarchies in cognitive maps. *Memory & Cognition, 13*(3), 208–217.

Hirtle, S. C., & Mascolo, M. F. (1986). Effect of semantic clustering on the memory of spatial locations. *Journal of Experimental Psychology: Learning, Memory, & Cognition, 12*(2), 182–189.

Hochberg, J. (1978). *Perception* (2nd ed.). Englewood Cliffs, NJ: Prentice-Hall.

Hoff, E., & Naigles, L. (1999). *Fast mapping is only the beginning: Complete word learning requires multiple exposures.* Paper presented at the VIIIth International Congress for the Study of Child Language. July 12–16. San Sebastian, Spain.

Hoff, E., & Shatz, M. (Eds.). (2007). *Blackwell handbook of language development.* Malden, MA: Blackwell.

Hoffding, H. (1891). *Outlines of psychology.* New York: Macmillan.

Hoffman, C., Lau, I., & Johnson, D. R. (1986). The linguistic relativity of person cognition: An English–Chinese comparison. *Journal of Personality and Social Psychology, 51*, 1097–1105.

Holden, C. (2009). Twins may think alike too, MRI brain study suggests. *Science, 323*, 1658.

Holland, J. H., Holyoak, K. J., Nisbett, R. E., & Thagard, P. R. (1986). *Induction processes of inference, learning, and discovery.* Cambridge, MA: MIT Press.

Holmes, D. (1991). The evidence for repression: an examination of sixty years of research. In J. L. Singer (Ed.), *Repression and dissociation: Implications for personality theory, psychopathology and health* (pp. 85–102). Chicago: University of Chicago Press.

Holt, J. (1964). *How children fail.* New York: Pitman.

Holyoak, K. J. (1984). Analogical thinking and human intelligence. In R. J. Sternberg (Ed.), *Advances in the psychology of human intelligence* (Vol. 2, pp. 199–230). Hillsdale, NJ: Erlbaum.

Holyoak, K. J. (1990). Problem solving. In D. N. Osherson & E. E. Smith (Eds.), *An invitation to cognitive science: Vol. 3. Thinking* (pp. 116–146). Cambridge, MA: MIT Press.

Holyoak, K. J., & Nisbett, R. E. (1988). Induction. In R. J. Sternberg & E. E. Smith (Eds.), *The psychology of human thought* (pp. 50–91). New York: Cambridge University Press.

Holyoak, K. J., & Thagard, P. (1995). *Mental leaps.* Cambridge, MA: MIT Press.

Homa, D. (1983). An assessment of two extraordinary speed-readers. *Bulletin of the Psychonomic Society, 21*, 115–118.

Honey, G., & Bullmore, E. (2004). Human pharmacological MRI. *Trends in Pharmacological Sciences, 2*(7), 366–374.

Hong, L., & Page, S. E. (2004). Groups of diverse problem solvers can outperform groups of high-ability problem solvers. *Proceedings of the National Academy of Sciences of the United States of America, 101*(46), 16385–16389.

Hopfinger, J. B., & Mangun, G. R. (1998). Reflexive attention modulates visual processing in human extrastriate cortex. *Psychological Science, 9*, 441–447.

Hopfinger, J. B., & Mangun, G. R. (2001). Tracking the influence of reflexive attention on sensory and cognitive processing. *Cognitive, Affective, and Behavioral Neuroscience, 1*, 56–65.

Hopkins, W. D., Russell, J. L., & Cantalupo, C. (2007). Neuroanatomical correlates of handedness for tool use in chimpanzees (pan troglodytes). Implication for theories on the evolution of language. *Psychological Science, 18*(11), 971–977.

Hornung, O. P., Regen, F., Danker-Hopfe, H., Schredl, M., & Heuser, I. (2007). The relationship between REM sleep and memory consolidation in old age and effects of cholinergic medication. *Biological Psychiatry, 61*(6), 750–757.

Horwitz, B., Amunts, K., Bhattacharyya, R., Patkin, D., Jeffries, K., Zilles, K., et al. (2003). Activation of Broca's area during the production of spoken and signed language: A combined cytoarchitectonic mapping and PET analysis. *Neuropsychologia, 41*, 1868–1876.

Howard, M., Cowell, P., Boucher, P., Broks, P., Mayes, A., Farrant, A., et al. (2000). Convergent neuroanatomical and behavioural evidence of an amygdala hypothesis of autism. *Neuroreport 11*, 2931–2935.

Howland, J. G., Harrison, R. A., Hannesson, D. K., & Phillips, A. G. (2008). Ventral hippocampal involvement in temporal order, but not recognition, memory for spatial information. *Hippocampus, 18*(3), 251–257.

Hu, M., & Nation, P. (2000). Unknown vocabulary density and reading comprehension. *Reading in a Foreign Language, 13*(1), 403–430.

Hubbard, T. L. (1995). Environmental invariants in the representation of motion: Implied and representational momentum, gravity, friction, and centripetal force. *Psychonomic Bulletin and Review, 2*, 322–338.

Hubel, D., & Wiesel, T. (1963). Receptive fields of cells in the striate cortex of very young, visually inexperienced kittens. *Journal of Neurophysiology, 26*, 994–1002.

Hubel, D., & Wiesel, T. (1968). Receptive fields and functional architecture of the monkey striate cortex. *Journal of Physiology, 195*, 215–243.

Hubel, D. H., & Wiesel, T. N. (1979). Brain mechanisms of vision. *Scientific American, 241*, 150–162.

Hugdahl, K., Thomsen, T., & Ersland, L. (2006). Sex differences in visuo-spatial processing: An fMRI study of mental rotation. *Neuropsychologia, 44*, 1575–1583.

Hulme, C., Neath, I., Stuart, G., Shostak, L., Surprenant, A. M., & Brown, G. D. A. (2006). The distinctiveness of the word-length effect. *Journal of Experimental Psychology: Applied Learning, Memory, and Cognition, 32*(3), 586–594.

Humphreys, M., Bain, J. D., & Pike, R. (1989). Different ways to cue a coherent memory system: A theory for episodic, semantic, and procedural tasks. *Psychological Review, 96*(2), 208–233.

Hunt, E. B. (1975). *Artificial intelligence.* New York: Academic Press.

Hunt, E. B. (1978). Mechanics of verbal ability. *Psychological Review, 85*, 109–130.

Hunt, E. B. (1994). Problem solving. In R. J. Sternberg (Ed.), *Handbook of perception and cognition: Vol. 12. Thinking and problem solving* (pp. 215–232). New York: Academic Press.

Hunt, E. B. (2005). Information processing and intelligence. In R. J. Sternberg & J. E. Pretz (Eds.), *Cognition and intelligence* (pp. 1–25). New York: Cambridge University Press.

Hunt, E. B., & Banaji, M. (1988). The Whorfian hypothesis revisited: A cognitive science view of linguistic and cultural effects on thought. In J. W. Berry, S. H. Irvine, & E. Hunt (Eds.), *Indigenous cognition: Functioning in cultural context.* Dordrecht, The Netherlands: Martinus Nijhoff Publishers.

Hunt, E. B., & Lansman, M. (1982). Individual differences in attention. In R. J. Sternberg (Ed.), *Advances in the psychology of human intelligence* (Vol. 1, pp. 207–254). Hillsdale, NJ: Erlbaum.

Hunt, E. B., & Love, T. (1972). How good can memory be? In A. W. Melton & E. Martin (Eds.), *Coding processes in human memory.* Washington, DC: V. H. Winston & Sons.

Hunt, E. B., Lunneborg, C., & Lewis, J. (1975). What does it mean to be high verbal? *Cognitive Psychology, 7*, 194–227.

Huttenlocher, J. (1968). Constructing spatial images: A strategy in reasoning. *Psychological Review, 75*, 550–560.

Huttenlocher, J., Hedges, L. V., & Duncan, S. (1991). Categories and particulars: Prototype effects in spatial location. *Psychological Review, 98*(3), 352–376.

Huttenlocher, J., & Presson, C. C. (1973). Mental rotation and the perspective problem. *Cognitive Psychology, 4*, 277–299.

Huttenlocher, J., & Presson, C. C. (1979). The coding and transformation of spatial information. *Cognitive Psychology, 11*(3), 375–394.

Hyoenae, J., & Lindeman, J. (2008). Syntactic context effects on word recognition: A developmental study. *Scandinavian Journal of Psychology, 35*(1), 27–37.

Iaria, G., Lanyon, L. J., Fox, C. J., Giaschi, D., & Barton, J. J. S. (2008). Navigational skills correlate with hippocampal fractional anisotropy in humans. *Hippocampus*, 18, 335–339.

Inagaki, H., Meguro, K., Shimada, M., Ishizaki, J., Okuzumi, H., & Yamadori, A. (2002). Discrepancy between mental rotation and perspective-taking abilities in normal aging assessed by Piaget's three-mountain task. *Journal of Clinical and Experimental Neuropsychology*, 24(1), 18–25.

Ingram, D. (1999). Phonological acquisition. In M. Barrett (Ed.), *The development of language* (pp. 73–98). East Sussex, UK: Psychology Press.

Inoue, S., & Matsuzawa, T. (2007). Working memory of numerals in chimpanzees. *Current Biology*, 17(23), R1004–R1005.

Intons-Peterson, M. J. (1983). Imagery paradigms: How vulnerable are they to experimenters' expectations? *Journal of Experimental Psychology: Human Perception & Performance*, 9(3), 394–412.

Intons-Peterson, M. J., Russell, W., & Dressel, S. (1992). The role of pitch in auditory imagery. *Journal of Experimental Psychology: Human Perception & Performance*, 18(1), 233–240.

Isaacowitz, D. M., Wadlinger, H. A., Goren, D., & Wilson, H. R. (2006a). Is there an age-related positivity effect in visual attention? A comparison of two methodologies. *Emotion*, 6, 511–516.

Isaacowitz, D. M, Wadlinger, H. A., Goren, D., & Wilson, H. R. (2006b). Selective preference in visual fixation away from negative images in old age? An eye-tracking study: Correction. *Psychology and Aging*, 21, 221.

Ischebeck, A., Indefrey, P., Usui, N., Nose, I., & Hellwig, F. (2004). Reading in a regular orthography: An fMRI study investigating the role of visual familiarity. *Journal of Cognitive Neuroscience*, 16, 727–741.

Ishii, R., Shinosaki, K., Ikejiri, Y., Ukai, S., Yamashita, K., Iwase, M., et al. (2000). Theta rhythm increase in left superior temporal cortex during auditory hallucinations in schizophrenia: A case report. *NeuroReport*, 28, 11–14.

Izquierdo, I., & Medina, J. H. (1997). Memory formation: The sequence of biochemical events in the hippocampus and its connection to activity in other brain structures. *Neurobiology of Learning and Memory*, 68, 285–316.

Jack, C. R., Dickson, D. W., Parisi, J. E., Xu, Y. C., Cha, R. H., O'Brien, P. C., et al. (2002). Antemortem MRI findings correlate with hippocampal neuropathology in typical aging and dementia. *Neurology*, 58, 750–757.

Jackendoff, R. (1991). Parts and boundaries. *Cognition*, 41(1–3), 9–45.

Jackson, S. R., Newport, R., Husain, M., Fowlie, J. E., O'Donoghue, M., & Bajaj, N. (2009). There may be more to reaching than meets the eye: Re-thinking optic ataxia. *Neuropsychologia*, 47, 1397–1408.

Jacobson, R. R., Acker, C., & Lishman, W. A. (1990). Patterns of neuropsychological deficit in alcoholic Korsakoff's syndrome. *Psychological Medicine*, 20, 321–334.

Jacoby, L. L. (1991). A process dissociation framework: Separating automatic from intentional uses of memory. *Journal of Memory and Language*, 30, 513–541.

Jacoby, L. L., Lindsay, D. S., & Toth, J. P. (1992). Unconscious influences revealed: Attention, awareness, and control. *American Psychologist*, 47, 802–209.

Jaffe, E. (2006). Sight for 'Saur Eyes. *Science News*, 170, 3–4.

James, T. W., Humphrey, G. K., Gati, J. S., Servos, P., Menon, R. S., & Goodale, M. A. (2002). Haptic study of three-dimensional objects activates extrastriate visual areas. *Neuropsychologia*, 40, 1706–1714.

James, W. (1970). *The principles of psychology* (Vol. 1). New York: Holt. (Original work published 1890.)

Jameson, K. A. (2005). Culture and cognition: What is universal about the representation of color experience. *Journal of Cognition and Culture*, 5(3), 293–347.

Jan, D., Herrera, D., Martinovski, B., Novick, D., & Traum, D. (2007). A computational model of culture-specific conversational behavior. In *Intelligent virtual agents*. Berlin: Springer.

Jäncke, L., & Jordan, K. (2007). Functional neuroanatomy of mental rotation, performance. In F. W. Mast & L. Jäncke (Eds.), S. p. i. n., & Springer, i. a. P. p. N. Y. (2007). Functional neuroanatomy of mental rotation performance. In F. W. M. L. Jäncke (Ed.), *Spatial processing in navigation imagery and perception* (pp. 183–207). New York: Springer.

Janis, I. L. (1971). Groupthink. *Psychology Today* 5(43–46), 74–76.

Janis, I. L., & Frick, F. (1943). The relationship between attitudes toward conclusions and errors in judging logical validity of syllogisms. *Journal of Experimental Psychology*, 33, 73–77.

Janiszewski, C., & Uy, D. (2008). Precision of the anchor influences the amount of adjustment. *Psychological Science*, 19(2), 121–127.

Jansen-Osmann, P., & Heil, M. (2007). Suitable stimuli to obtain (no) gender differences in the speed of cognitive processes involved in mental rotation. *Brain and Cognition*, 64(217-227).

Jansiewicz, E. M., Newschaffer, C. J., Denckla, M. B., & Mostofsky, S. H. (2004). Impaired habituation in children with attention deficit hyperactivity disorder. *Cognitive & Behavioral Neurology*, 17(1), 1–8.

Jarrold, C., Baddeley, A. D., & Hewes, A. K. (2000). Verbal short-term memory deficits in Down syndrome: A consequence of problems in rehearsal? *The Journal of Child Psychology and Psychiatry and Allied Disciplines*, 41, 233–244.

Jenkins, J. J. (1979). Four points to remember: A tetrahedral model of memory experiments. In L. S. Cermak & F. I. M. Craik (Eds.), *Levels of processing in human memory* (pp. 429–446). Hillsdale, NJ: Erlbaum.

Jensen, A. R. (1979). g: Outmoded theory or unconquered frontier? *Creative Science and Technology*, 2, 16–29.

Jensen, A. R. (1982). The chronometry of intelligence. In R. J. Sternberg (Ed.), *Advances in the psychology of human intelligence*. (Vol. 1, pp. 255–310). Hillsdale, NJ: Erlbaum.

Jenson, J. L. (2007). Getting one's way in policy debates: Influence tactics used in group decision-making settings. *Public Administration Review*, 67(2), 216–227.

Jerde, T. E., Soechting, J. F., & Flanders, M. (2003). Coarticulation in fluent fingerspelling. *The Journal of Neuroscience*, 23(3), 2383.

Jerison, H. J. (2000). The evolution of intelligence. In R. J. Sternberg (Ed.), *Handbook of intelligence* (pp. 216–244). New York: Cambridge University Press.

Jia, G., & Aaronson, D. (1999). Age differences in second language acquisition: The dominant language switch and maintenance hypothesis. In A. Greenhill, H. Littlefield, & C. Tano, *Proceedings of the 23rd Annual Boston University Conference on Language Development* (pp. 301–312). Somerville, MA: Cascadilla Press.

Jiang, Y., Boehler, C. N., Noennig, N., Duezel, E., Hopf, J.-M., Heinze, H.-J., et al. (2008). Binding 3-D object perception in the human visual cortex. *Journal of Cognitive Neuroscience*, 20(4), 553–562.

Jick, H., & Kaye, J. A. (2003). Epidemiology and possible causes of autism. *Pharmacotherapy*, 23(12), 1524–1530.

Johnson, E. K., & Jusczyk, P. W. (2001). Word segmentation by 8-month-olds: When speech cues count more than statistics. *Journal of Memory and Language*, 44(4), 548–567.

Johnson, M. K. (1996). Fact, fantasy, and public policy. In D. J. Herrmann, C. McEvoy, C. Hertzog, P. Hertel, & M. K. Johnson (Eds.), *Basic and applied memory research: Theory in context* (Vol. 1). Mahwah, NJ: Erlbaum.

Johnson, M. K. (2002). Reality monitoring: Varying levels of analysis. *APS Observer*, 15(8), 28–29.

Johnson, M. K., Foley, M. A., Suengas, A. G., & Raye, C. L. (1988). Phenomenal characteristics of memories for perceived and imagined autobiographical events. *Journal of Experimental Psychology: General*, 117(4), 371–376.

Johnson, M. K., Nolde, S. F., & De Leonardis, D. M. (1996). Emotional focus and source monitoring. *Journal of Memory and Language*, 35, 135–156.

Johnson, M. K., & Raye, C. L. (1981). Reality monitoring. *Psychological Review*, 88, 67–85.

Johnson-Laird, P. N. (1983). *Mental models*. Cambridge, MA: Harvard University Press.

Johnson-Laird, P. N. (1989). Mental models. In M. I. Posner (Ed.), *Foundations of cognitive science* (pp. 469–499). Cambridge, MA: MIT Press.

Johnson-Laird, P. N. (1999). Mental models. In R. A. Wilson & F. C. Keil (Eds.), *The MIT encyclopedia of the cognitive sciences* (pp. 525–527). Cambridge, MA: MIT Press.

Johnson-Laird, P. N. (2000). Thinking: Reasoning. In A. Kazdin (Ed.), *Encyclopedia of psychology* (Vol. 8, pp. 75–79). Washington, DC: American Psychological Association.

Johnson-Laird, P. N. (2001). Mental models and deduction. *Trends in Cognitive Sciences*, 5(10), 434–442.

Johnson-Laird, P. N. (2004). Mental models and reasoning. In J. P. Leighton & R. J. Sternberg (Eds.), *The nature of reasoning* (pp. 169–204). New York: Cambridge University Press.

Johnson-Laird, P. N. (2010). Mental models and language. In P. C. Hogan (Ed.), *Encyclopedia of language sciences*. Cambridge: Cambridge University Press.

Johnson-Laird, P. N., Byrne, R. M. J., & Schaeken, W. (1992). Propositional reasoning by model. *Psychological Review*, 99(3), 418–439.

Johnson-Laird, P. N., & Goldvarg, Y. (1997). How to make the impossible seem possible. In *Proceedings of the Nineteenth Annual Conference of the Cognitive Science Society* (pp. 354–357), Stanford, CA. Hillsdale, NJ: Erlbaum.

Johnson-Laird, P. N., & Savary, F. (1999). Illusory inference: A novel class of erroneous deductions. *Cognition*, 71, 191–229.

Johnson-Laird, P. N., & Steedman, M. (1978). The psychology of syllogisms. *Cognitive Psychology*, 10, 64–99.

Johnston, J. C., & McClelland, J. L. (1973). Visual factors in word perception. *Perception & Psychophysics*, 14, 365–370.

Johnston, W. A., & Heinz, S. P (1978). Flexibility and capacity demands of attention. *Journal of Experimental Psychology: General*, 107, 420–435.

Joiner, C., & Loken, B. (1998). The inclusion effect and category-based induction. *Journal of Consumer Psychology*, 7(2), 101–129.

Jolicoeur, P. (1985). The time to name disoriented natural objects. *Memory & Cognition*, 13(4), 289–303.

Jolicoeur, P., & Kosslyn, S. M. (1985a). Demand characteristics in image scanning experiments. *Journal of Mental Imagery*, 9(2), 41–49.

Jolicoeur, P., & Kosslyn, S. M. (1985b). Is time to scan visual images due to demand characteristics? *Memory & Cognition*, 13(4), 320–332.

Jolicoeur, P., Snow, D., & Murray, J. (1987). The time to identify disoriented letters: Effects of practice and font. *Canadian Journal of Psychology*, 41(3), 303–316.

Jones, G., & Ritter, F. E. (2003). Production systems and rule-based inference. In L. Nadel (Ed.), *Encyclopedia of cognitive science* (Vol. 3, pp. 741–747). London: Nature Publishing Group.

Jones, P. E. (1995). Contradictions and unanswered questions in the Genie case: A fresh look at the linguistic evidence. *Language & Communication*, 15(3), 261–280.

Jonkers, R., & Bastiaanse, R. (2007). Action naming in anomic aphasic speakers: Effects of instrumentality and name relation. *Brain and Language*, 102, 262–272.

Jordan, K., & Huntsman, L. A. (1990). Image rotation of misoriented letter strings: Effects of orientation cuing and repetition. *Perception & Psychophysics*, 48(4), 363–374.

Jordan, K., Wustenberg, T., Heinze, H. J., Peters, M., & Jänke, L. (2002). Women and men exhibit different cortical activation patterns during mental rotation tasks. *Neuropsychologia*, 40(13), 2397–2408.

Jordan, P. J., & Troth, A. C. (2004). Managing emotions during team problem solving: Emotional intelligence and conflict resolution. *Human Performance*, 17(2), 195–218.

Jung, R. E., & Haier, R. J. (2007). The parieto-frontal integration theory (P-FIT) of intelligence: Converging neuroimaging evidence. *Behavioral and Brain Sciences*, 30(2), 135–154.

Jung, R. E., Segall, J. M., Bockholt, H. J., Flores, R. A., Smith, S. M., Chavez, R. S., et al. (2010). Neuroanatomy of creativity. *Human Brain Mapping*, 31, 398–409.

Jung-Beeman, M., Bowden, E. M., Haberman, J., Frymiare, J. L., Arambel-Liu, S., Greenblatt, R., et al. (2004). Neural activity when people solve verbal problems with insight. *Public Library of Science Biology*, 2(4), e97.

Jusczyk, P. W. (1997). *The discovery of spoken language*. Cambridge, MA: MIT Press.

Just, M. A., & Carpenter, P. A. (1985). Cognitive coordinate systems: Accounts of mental rotation and individual differences in spatial ability. *Psychological Review*, 92(2), 137–172.

Just, M. A., Carpenter, P. A., & Masson, M. E. J. (1982). *What eye fixations tell us about speed reading and skimming* (EyeLab Tech. Rep.). Pittsburgh: Carnegie-Mellon University.

Kahneman, D. (1973). *Attention and effort*. Englewood Cliffs, NJ: Prentice-Hall.

Kahneman, D., & Tversky, A. (1996). On the reality of cognitive illusions. *Psychological Review*, 103, 582–591.

Kail, R. V. (1991). Controlled and automatic processing during mental rotation. *Journal of Experimental Child Psychology*, 51(3), 337–347.

Kail, R. V. (1997). Processing time, imagery, and spatial memory. *Journal of Experimental Child Psychology*, 64, 67–78.

Kail, R. V., & Bisanz, J. (1992). The information-processing perspective on cognitive development in childhood and adolescence. In R. J. Sternberg & C. A. Berg (Eds.), *Intellectual development* (pp. 229–260). New York: Cambridge University Press.

Kail, R. V., & Park, Y. S. (1990). Impact of practice on speed of mental rotation. *Journal of Experimental Child Psychology*, 49(2), 227–244.

Kail, R. V., Pellegrino, J. W., & Carter, P. (1980). Developmental changes in mental rotation. *Journal of Experimental Child Psychology*, 29, 102–116.

Kalénine, S., Peyrin, C., Pichat, C., Segebarth, C., Bonthoux, F., & Baciu, M. (2009). The sensory-motor specificity of taxonomic and thematic conceptual relations: A behavioral and fMRI study. *NeuroImage*, 44, 1152–1162.

Kalisch, R., Salome, N., Platzer, S., Wigger, A., Czisch, M., Sommer, W., et al. (2004). High trait anxiety and hyperreactivity to stress of the dorsomedial prefrontal cortex: A combined phMRI and Fos study in rats. *Neuroimage*, 23, 382–391.

Kalla, R., Muggleton, N. G., Cowey, A., & Walsh, V. (2009). Human dorsolateral prefrontal cortex is involved in visual search for conjunctions but not features: A theta TMS study. *Cortex*, 45, 1058–1090.

Kane, M. J., Hambrick, D. Z., & Conway, A. R. A. (2005). Working memory capacity and fluid intelligence are strongly related constructs: Comment on Ackerman, Beier, and Boyle (2005). *Psychology Bulletin, 131*(1), 66–71.

Kanner, L. (1943). Autistic disturbances of affective contact. *Nervous Child, 2*, 217–250.

Kanwisher, N., Chun, M. M., McDermott, J., & Ledden, P. J. (1996). Functional imaging of human visual recognition. *Cognitive Brain Research, 5*, 55–67.

Kanwisher, N., McDermott, J., & Chun, M. M. (1997). The fusiform face area: A module in human extrastriate cortex specialized for face perception. *Journal of Neuroscience, 17*, 4302–4311.

Kanwisher, N., Woods, R., Ioacoboni, M., & Mazziotta, J. (1997). A locus in human extrastriate cortex for visual shape analysis. *Journal of Cognitive Neuroscience, 9*, 133–142.

Kaplan, C. A., & Davidson, J. E. (1989). *Incubation effects in problem solving.* Unpublished manuscript.

Kaplan, G. B., Sengor, N. S., Gurvit, H., & Guzelis, C. (2007). Modelling the Stroop effect: A connectionist approach. *Neurocomputing, 70*(7–9), 1414–1423.

Karnath, H., Fruhmann Berger, M., Kueker, W., & Rorden, C. (2004). The anatomy of spatial neglect based on voxelwise statistical analysis: a study of 140 patients. *Cerebral Cortex, 14*, 1164–1172.

Karni, A., Tanne, D., Rubenstein, B. S., Askenasy, J. J. M., & Sagi, D. (1994). Dependence on REM sleep of overnight improvement of a perceptual skill. *Science, 265*, 679.

Karpicke, J. D. (2009). Metacognitive control and strategy selection: deciding to practice retrieval during learning. *Journal of Experimental Psychology: General, 138*(4), 469–486.

Kashino, M. (2006). Phonemic restoration: The brain creates missing speech sounds. *Acoustical Science and Technology, 27*(6), 318–321.

Kasper, B. S., Kerling, F., Graf, W., Stefan, H., & Pauli, E. (2009). Ictal delusion of sexual transformation. *Epilepsy & Behavior, 16*, 356–359.

Kass, S. J., Ahlers, R. H., & Dugger, M. (1998). Eliminating gender differences through practice in an applied visual spatial task. *Human Performance, 11*(4), 337–349.

Katz, A. N. (2000). Mental imagery. In A. E. Kazdin (Ed.), *Encyclopedia of psychology* (Vol. 5, pp. 187–191). Washington, DC: American Psychological Association.

Katz, J. J. (1972). *Semantic theory.* New York: Harper & Row.

Katz, J. J., & Fodor, J. A. (1963). The structure of a semantic theory. *Language, 39*, 170–210.

Kaufman, A. B., Kornilov, S. A., Bristol, A. S., Tan, M., & Grigorenko, E. L. (2010). The neurobiological foundation of creative cognition. In J. C. Kaufman & R. J. Sternberg (Eds.), *The Cambridge handbook of creativity* (pp. 216–232). New York: Cambridge University Press.

Kaufman, A. S. (2000). Tests of intelligence. In R. J. Sternberg (Ed.), *Handbook of intelligence* (pp. 445–476). New York: Cambridge University Press.

Kaufman, A. S., & Lichtenberger, E. O. (1998). Intellectual assessment. In C. R. Reynolds (Ed.), *Comprehensive clinical psychology: Vol. 4. Assessment* (pp. 203–238). Tarrytown, NY: Elsevier Science.

Kaufmann, L., & Nuerk, H. C. (2006). Interference effects in a numerical Stroop paradigm in 9- to 12-year-old children with ADHD-C. *Child Neuropsychology, 12*(3), 223–243.

Kaufman, S. B. (in press). Intelligence and the cognitive unconscious. In R. J. Sternberg & S. B. Kaufman (Eds.), *Cambridge handbook of intelligence.* New York: Cambridge University Press.

Kawachi, K. (2002). Practice effects on speech production planning: Evidence from slips of the tongue in spontaneous vs. preplanning speech in Japanese. *Journal of Psycholinguistic Research, 31*(4), 363–390.

Kay, P. (1975). Synchronic variability and diachronic changes in basic color terms. *Language in Society, 4*, 257–270.

Kay, P., & Regier, T. (2006). Language, thought and color: recent developments. *Trends in Cognitive Sciences, 10*(2), 51–54.

Keane, M. T. (1994). Propositional representations. In M. W. Eysenck (Ed.), *The Blackwell dictionary of cognitive psychology.* Cambridge, MA: Blackwell.

Kearins, J. M. (1981). Visual spatial memory in Australian aboriginal children of desert regions. *Cognitive Psychology, 13*(3), 434–460.

Keating, D. P. (1984). The emperor's new clothes: The "new look" in intelligence research. In R. J. Sternberg (Ed.), *Advances in the psychology of human intelligence* (Vol. 2, pp. 1–45). Hillsdale, NJ: Erlbaum.

Keating, D. P., & Bobbitt, B. L. (1978). Individual and developmental differences in cognitive-processing components of mental ability. *Child Development, 49*, 155–167.

Keil, F. C. (1979). *Semantic and conceptual development.* Cambridge, MA: Harvard University Press.

Keil, F. C. (1989). *Concepts, kinds, and cognitive development.* Cambridge, MA: MIT Press.

Keil, F. C. (1999). Cognition, content, and development. In M. Bennett (Ed.), *Developmental psychology: Achievements and prospects* (pp. 165–184). Philadelphia: Psychology Press.

Keil, F. C., & Batterman, N. (1984). A characteristic-to-defining shift in the development of word meaning. *Journal of Verbal Learning and Verbal Behavior, 23*, 221–236.

Keller, E. (1976). Gambits. *TESL Talk, 7*(2), 18–21.

Keller, H. (1988). *The story of my life.* New York: Signet. (Original work published 1902)

Kelly, S. W., Griffiths, S., & Frith, U. (2002). Evidence for implicit sequence learning in dyslexia. *Dyslexia, 8*(1), 43–52.

Kemple, V., Brooks, P. J., & Gills, S. (2005). Diminutives in child-directed speech supplement metric with distributional word segmentation cues. *Psychonomic Bulletin & Review, 12*(1), 145–151.

Kennerley, S. W., Walton, M. E., Behrens, T. E. J., Buckley, M. J., & Rushworth, M. F. S. (2006). Optimal decision making and the anterior cingulate cortex. *Nature Neuroscience, 9*, 940–947.

Kensinger, E. A., Brierley, B., Medford, N., Growdon, J. H., & Corkin, S. (2002). Effects of normal aging and Alzheimer's disease on emotional memory. *Emotion, 2*, 118–134.

Kensinger, E. A., & Corkin, S. (2003). Alzheimer's disease. In L. Nadel (Ed.), *Encyclopedia of cognitive science* (Vol. 1, pp. 83–89). London: Nature Publishing Group.

Kentridge, R. W. (2003). Blindsight. In L. Nadel (Ed.), *Encyclopedia of cognitive science* (Vol. 1, pp. 390–397). London: Nature Publishing Group.

Keppel, G., & Underwood, B. J. (1962). Proactive inhibition in short-term retention of single items. *Journal of Verbal Learning and Verbal Behavior, 1*, 153–161.

Kerr, N. (1983). The role of vision in "visual imagery" experiments: Evidence from the congenitally blind. *Journal of Experimental Psychology: General, 112*(2), 265–277.

Kessler Shaw, L. (1999). *Acquiring the meaning of know and think.* Unpublished doctoral dissertation. City University of New York Graduate Center.

Khader, P., Burke, M., Bien, S., Ranganath, C., & Roesler, F. (2005). Content-specific activation during associative long-term memory retrieval. *NeuroImage, 27*(4), 805–816.

Khubchandani, L. M. (1997). Bilingual education for indigenous groups in India. In J. Cummins & D. Corson (Eds.), *Encyclopedia of language and education: Vol. 5. Bilingual education* (pp. 67–76). Dordrecht, Netherlands: Kluwer.

Kiesel, A., Kunde, W., Pohl, C., Berner, M. P., & Hoffmann, J. (2009). Playing chess unconsciously. *Journal of Experimental Psychology: Learning, Memory, and Cognition, 35*(1), 292–298.

Kihara, K., & Yoshikawa, S. (2001). The comparison between mental image manipulation and distinctive feature scan on recognition memory of faces. *Japanese Journal of Psychology, 72*(3), 234–239.

Kihlstrom, J. F., & Cantor, N. (2000). Social intelligence. In R. J. Sternberg (Ed.), *Handbook of intelligence* (pp. 359–379). New York: Cambridge University Press.

Kilingberg, T. Forssberg, H., & Westerberg, H. (2002). Training of working memory in children with ADHD. *Journal of Clinical and Experimental Neuropsychology, 24*(6), 781–791.

Kim, K. H., Relkin, N. R., Lee, K. M., & Hirsch, J. (1997). Distinct cortical areas associated with native and second languages. *Nature, 388*, 171–174.

Kim, N. S., & Ahn, W. K. (2002). Clinical psychologists' theory-based representations of mental disorders predict their diagnostic reasoning and memory. *Journal of Experimental Psychology: General, 131*, 451–476.

Kimchi, R. (1992). Primacy of wholistic processing and global/local paradigm: A critical review. *Psychological Bulletin, 112*(1), 24–38.

Kimura, D. (1981). Neural mechanisms in manual signing. *Sign Language Studies, 33*, 291–312.

Kimura, D. (1987). Are men's and women's brains really different? *Canadian Psychology, 28*(2), 133–147.

Kintsch, W. (1990). The representation of knowledge and the use of knowledge in discourse comprehension. In C. Graumann & R. Dietrich (Eds.), *Language in the social context*. Amsterdam: Elsevier.

Kintsch, W. (2007). Meaning in context. In T. K. Landauer, D. McNamara, S. Dennis & W. Kintsch (Eds.), *Handbook of latent semantic analysis* (pp. 89–105). Mahwah, NJ: Erlbaum.

Kintsch, W., Healy, A. F., Hegarty, M., Pennington, B. F., & Salthouse, T. A. (1999). Models of working memory: Eight questions and some general issues. In A. Miyake & P. Shah (Eds.), *Models of working memory: Mechanisms of active maintenance and executive control* (pp. 412–441). New York: Cambridge University Press.

Kintsch, W., & Keenan, J. M. (1973). Reading rate and retention as a function of the number of propositions in the base structure of sentences. *Cognitive Psychology, 5*, 257–274.

Kintsch, W., & van Dijk, T. A. (1978). Toward a model of text comprehension and production. *Psychological Review, 85*(5), 363–394.

Kirby, K. N. (1994). Probabilities and utilities of fictional outcomes in Wason's selection task. *Cognition, 51*(1), 1–28.

Kirwan, C. B., Bayley, P. J., Galvan, V. V., & Squire, L. R. (2008). Detailed recollection of remote autobiographical memory after damage to the medial temporal lobe. *Proceedings of the National Academy of Sciences of the United States of America, 105*(7), 2676–2680.

Kitada, R., Johnsrude, I. S., Kochiyama, T., & Lederman, S. J. (2010). Brain networks involved in haptic and visual identification of facial expressions of emotion: An fMRI study. *Neuro-Image, 49*(2), 1677–1689.

Klein, G. (1997). Developing expertise in decision making. *Thinking & Reasoning, 3*(4), 337–352.

Klein, S. B., & Kihlstrom, J. F. (1986). Elaboration, organization, and the self-reference effect in memory. *Journal of Experimental Psychology: General, 115*(1), 26–38.

Kleinhans, N. M., Johnson, L. C., Richards, T., Mahurin, R., Greenson, J., Dawson, G., et al. (2009). Reduced neural habituation in the amygdala and social impairments in autism spectrum disorders. *American Journal of Psychiatry, 166*, 467–475.

Kloos, H., & Sloutsky, V. (2004). Are natural kinds psychologically distinct from nominal kinds? Evidence from learning and development. *Proceedings of the Meeting of the Cognitive Science Society*, Chicago, IL.

Knauff, M., & May, E. (2006). Mental imagery, reasoning, and blindness. *Quarterly Journal of Experimental Psychology, 59*, 161–177.

Koch, G., & Rothwell, J. C. (2009). TMS investigations into the task-dependent functional interplay between human posterior parietal and motor cortex. *Behavioural Brain Research, 202*, 147–152.

Koehler, J. J. (1996). The base rate fallacy reconsidered: Descriptive, normative, and methodological challenges. *Behavioral and Brain Sciences, 19*, 1–53.

Köhler, S., Kapur, S., Moscovitch, M., Winocur, G., & Houle, S. (1995). Dissociation of pathways for object and spatial vision in the intact human brain. *NeuroReport, 6*, 1865–1868.

Köhler, W. (1927). *The mentality of apes*. New York: Harcourt Brace.

Köhler, W. (1940). *Dynamics in psychology*. New York: Liveright.

Koivisto, M., & Revonsuo, A. (2007). How meaning shapes seeing. *Psychological Science, 18*(10), 845–849.

Kolb, B., & Whishaw, I. Q. (1985). *Fundamentals of human neuropsychology* (2nd ed.). New York: Freeman.

Kolb, B., & Whishaw, I. Q. (1990). *Fundamentals of human neuropsychology* (3rd ed.). New York: Freeman.

Kolb, I., & Whishaw, B. (1996). *Fundamentals of human neuropsychology*. New York: W. H. Freeman.

Kolodner, J. L. (1983). Reconstructive memory: A computer model. *Cognitive Science, 7*(4), 281–328.

Komatsu, L. K. (1992). Recent views on conceptual structure. *Psychological Bulletin, 112*(3), 500–526.

Kontogiannis, T., & Malakis, S. (2009). A proactive approach to human error detection and identification in aviation and air traffic control. *Safety Science, 47*, 693–706.

Kopelman, M. D., Thomson, A. D., Guerrini, I., & Marshall, E. J. (2009). The Korsakoff syndrome: clinical aspects, psychology and treatment. *Alcohol & Alcoholism, 44*(2), 148–154.

Kornblum, H. I., Araujo, D. M., Annala, A. J., Tatsukawa, K. J., Phelps, M. E., & Cherry, S. R. (2000). In vivo imaging of neuronal activation and plasticity in the rat brain by high resolution positron emission tomography (microPET). *Nature Biotechnology, 18*, 655–660.

Koscik, T., O'Leary, D., Moser, D. J., Andreasen, N. C., & Nopoulos, P. (2009). Sex differences in parietal lobe morphology: Relationship to mental rotation performance. *Brain and Cognition, 69*, 451–459.

Kosslyn, S. M. (1975). Information representation in visual images. *Cognitive Psychology, 7*(3), 341–370.

Kosslyn, S. M. (1976). Using imagery to retrieve semantic information: A developmental study. *Child Development, 47*(2), 434–444.

Kosslyn, S. M. (1981). The medium and the message in mental imagery: A theory. *Psychological Review, 88*(1), 46–66.

Kosslyn, S. M. (1983). *Ghosts in the mind's machine: Creating and using images in the brain*. New York: Norton.

Kosslyn, S. M. (1990). Mental imagery. In D. N. Osherson, S. M. Kosslyn, & J. M. Hollerbach (Eds.), *Visual cognition and action: Vol. 2. An invitation to cognitive science* (pp. 73–97). Cambridge, MA: MIT Press.

Kosslyn, S. M., Ball, T. M., & Reiser, B. J. (1978). Visual images preserve metric spatial information: Evidence from studies of image scanning. *Journal of Experimental Psychology: Human Perception and Performance, 4*, 47–60.

Kosslyn, S. M., & Koenig, O. (1992). *Wet mind: The new cognitive neuroscience*. New York: Free Press.

Kosslyn, S. M., & Osherson, D. N. (Eds.) (1995). *An invitation to cognitive science: Vol. 2. Visual cognition* (2nd ed.). Cambridge, MA: MIT Press.

Kosslyn, S. M., & Pomerantz, J. R. (1977). Imagery, propositions, and the form of internal representations. *Cognitive Psychology, 9*(1), 52–76.

Kosslyn, S. M., & Rabin, C. S. (1999). Imagery. In R. A. Wilson & F. C. Keil (Eds.), *The MIT encyclopedia of the cognitive sciences* (pp. 387–389). Cambridge, MA: MIT Press.

Kosslyn, S. M., Seger, C., Pani, J. R., & Hillger, L. A. (1990). When is imagery used in everyday life? A diary study. *Journal of Mental Imagery, 14*(3–4), 131–152.

Kosslyn, S. M., & Sussman, A. L. (1995). Roles of memory in perception. In M. S. Gazzaniga (Ed.), *The cognitive neurosciences* (pp. 1035–1042). Cambridge, MA: MIT Press.

Kosslyn, S. M., & Thompson, W. L. (2000). Shared mechanisms in visual imagery and visual perception: Insights from cognitive neuroscience. In M. S. Gazzaniga (Ed.), *The new cognitive neurosciences* (2nd ed., pp. 975–986). Cambridge, MA: MIT Press.

Kosslyn, S. M., Thompson, W. L., & Ganis, G. (2006). *The case for mental imagery.* New York: Oxford University Press.

Kosslyn, S. M., Thompson, W. L., Kim, J. J., & Alpert, N. M. (1995). Topographical representations of mental images in primary visual cortex. *Nature, 378,* 496–498.

Kotovsky, K., Hayes, J. R., & Simon, H. A. (1985). Why are some problems hard? Evidence from the tower of Hanoi. *Cognitive Psychology, 17,* 248–294.

Kounios, J., Fleck, J. I., Green, D. L., Payne, L., Stevenson, J. L., Bowden, E. M., et al. (2008). The origins of insight in resting-state brain activity. *Neuropsychologia, 46,* 281–291.

Kounios, J., Frymiare, J. L., Bowman, E. M., Fleck, J. I., Subramaniam, K., Parrish, T. B., et al. (2006). The prepared mind: Neural activity prior to problem presentation predicts subsequent solution by sudden insight. *Psychological Science, 17*(10), 882–890.

Koustanai, A., Boloix, E., Van Elslande, P., & Bastien, C. (2008). Statistical analysis of "looked-but-failed-to-see" accidents: Highlighting the involvement of two distinct mechanisms. *Accident Analysis and Prevention, 40,* 461–469.

Kozbelt, A., Beghetto, R. A., & Runco, M. A. (2010). Theories of creativity. In J. C. Kaufman & R. J. Sternberg (Eds.), *The Cambridge handbook of creativity* (pp. 20–47). New York: Cambridge University Press.

Kraemer, D. J. M., Macrae, C. N., Green, A. E., & Kelley, W. M. (2005). Musical imagery: Sound of silence activates auditory cortex. *Nature, 434*(7030), 158.

Krantz, L. (1992). *What the odds are: A-to-Z odds on everything you hoped or feared could happen.* New York: Harper Perennial.

Krueger, J. (1998, October). The bet on bias: A foregone conclusion? *Psychology, 9.*

Krieger, J. L. (2005). Shared mindfulness in cockpit crisis situations: an exploratory analysis. *Journal of Business Communication, 42*(2), 135–167.

Kringelbach, M. L., Jenkinson, N., Green, A. L., Owen, S. L. F., Hansen, P. C., Cornelissen, P. L., et al. (2007). Deep brain stimulation for chronic pain investigated with magnetoencephalography. *NeuroReport, 18* (3), 223–228.

Kruschke, J. K. (2003). Concept learning and categorization: Models. In L. Nadel (Ed.), *Encyclopedia of cognitive science* (Vol. 1, pp. 646–652). London: Nature Publishing Group.

Kuhl, P. K. (1991). Human adults and infants show a "perceptual magnet effect" for the prototypes of speech categories, monkeys do not. *Perception & Psycholinguistics, 50,* 93–107.

Kuhl, P. K., & Meltzoff, A. N. (1997). Evolution, nativism, and learning in the development of language and speech. In M. Gopnik (Ed.), *The inheritance and innateness of grammars* (pp. 7–44). New York: Oxford University Press.

Kunzendorf, R. (Ed.) (1991). *Mental imagery.* New York: Plenum.

Kurby, C. A., Magliano, J. P., & Rapp, D. N. (2009). Those voices in your head: Activation of auditory images during reading. *Cognition, 112,* 457–461.

Kutas, M., & Hillyard, S. A. (1980). Reading senseless sentences: Brain potentials reflect semantic incongruity. *Science, 207,* 203–205.

Kutas, M., & Van Patten, C. (1994). Psycholinguistics electrified: Event-related brain potential investigations. In M. A. Gernsbacher (Ed.), *Handbook of psycholinguistics* (pp. 83–143). San Diego: Academic Press.

Kyllonen, P. C., & Christal, R. E. (1990). Reasoning ability is (little more than) working-memory capacity?! *Intelligence, 14,* 389–433.

LaBerge, D. (1975). Acquisition of automatic processing in perceptual and associative learning. In P. M. A. Rabbit & S. Dornic (Eds.), *Attention and performance.* London: Academic Press.

LaBerge, D. (1990). Attention. *Psychological Science, 1*(3), 156–162.

LaBerge, D., Carter, M., & Brown, V. (1992). A network simulation of thalamic circuit operations in selective attention. *Neural Computation, 4*(3), 318–331.

Ladavas, E., del Pesce, M., Mangun, G. R., & Gazzaniga, M. S. (1994). Variations in attentional bias of the disconnected cerebral hemispheres. *Cognitive Neuropsychology, 11*(1), 57–74.

Ladefoged, P., & Maddieson, I. (1996). *The sounds of the world's languages.* Cambridge, UK: Blackwell.

Laland, K. N. (2004). Social learning strategies. *Learning & Behavior, 32*(1), 4–14.

Lamy, D., Mudrik, L., & Deouell, L. Y. (2008). Unconscious auditory information can prime visual word processing: A process-dissociation procedure study. *Consciousness and Cognition, 17,* 688–698.

Lander, K., & Metcalfe, S. (2007). The influence of positive and negative facial expressions on face familiarity. *Memory, 15*(1), 63–69.

Langer, E. J. (1989). *Mindfulness.* New York: Addison-Wesley.

Langer, E. J. (1997). *The power of mindful learning.* Needham Heights, MA: Addison-Wesley.

Langley, P., & Jones, R. (1988). A computational model of scientific insight. In R. J. Sternberg (Ed.), *The nature of creativity* (pp. 117–201). New York: Cambridge University Press.

Langley, P., Simon, H. A., Bradshaw, G. L., & Zytkow, J. M. (1987). *Scientific discovery: Computational explorations of the creative process.* Cambridge, MA: MIT Press.

Lanze, M., Weisstein, N., & Harris, J. R. (1982). Perceived depth versus structural relevance in the object-superiority effect. *Perception & Psychophysics, 31*(4), 376–382.

LaPointe, L. L. (2005). Feral children. *Journal of Medical Speech-Language Pathology, 13*(1), vii–ix.

Larkin, J. H., McDermott, J., Simon, D. P., & Simon, H. A. (1980). Expert and novice performance in solving physics problems. *Science, 208,* 1335–1342.

Larson, G. E., Haier, R. J., LaCasse, L. & Hazen, K. (1995). Evaluation of a "mental effort" hypothesis for correlation between cortical metabolism and intelligence. *Intelligence, 21,* 267–278.

Lashley, K. S. (1950). In search of the engram. *Symposia of the Society for Experimental Biology, 4,* 454–482.

Lawrence, E., & Peters, E. (2004). Reasoning in believers in the paranormal. *Journal of Nervous & Mental Disease, 192*(11), 727–733.

Lawson, A. E. (2004). Reasoning and brain function. In J. P. Leighton & R. J. Sternberg (Eds.), *The nature of reasoning* (pp. 12–48). New York: Cambridge University Press.

Leahey, T. H. (2003). *A history of psychology: Main currents in psychological thought.* Upper Saddle River, NJ: Prentice-Hall.

Lederer, R. (1991). *The miracle of language.* New York: Pocket Books.

Lee, D., & Chun, M. M. (2001). What are the units of visual short-term memory, objects or spatial locations? *Perception & Psychophysics, 63,* 253–257.

Lee, K. H., Choi, Y. Y., Gray, J. R., Cho, S. H., Chae, J.-H., Lee, S., et al. (2006). Neural correlates of superior intelligence: Stronger recruitment of posterior parietal cortex. *Neuroimage*, 29(2), 578–586.

Legg, S., & Hutter, M. (2007). A collection of definitions of intelligence. *Frontiers in Artificial Intelligence and Applications*, 157, 17–24.

Lehman, D. R., Chiu, C. Y. P., & Schaller, M. (2004). Psychology and culture. *Annual Review of Psychology*, 55, 689–714.

Lehman, D. R., Lempert, R., & Nisbett, R. E. (1987). *The effects of graduate education on reasoning: Formal discipline and thinking about everyday-life events*. Unpublished manuscript, University of British Columbia.

Leicht, K. L., & Overton, R. (1987). Encoding variability and spacing repetitions. *American Journal of Psychology*, 100(1), 61–68.

Leighton, J. P. (2006). Teaching and assessing deductive reasoning skills. *The Journal of Experimental Education*, 74(2), 107–136.

Leighton, J. P., & Sternberg, R. J. (Eds). (2004). *The nature of reasoning*. New York: Cambridge University Press.

Lennox, B. R., Park, S. B. G., Medley, I., Morris, P. G., & Jones, P. B. (2000). The functional anatomy of auditory hallucinations in schizophrenia. *Psychiatry Research: Neuroimaging*, 100(1), 13–20.

Leopold, D. A., O'Toole, A. J., Vetter, T., & Blanz, V. (2001). Prototype-referenced shape encoding revealed by high-level aftereffects. *Nature Neuroscience*, 4, 89–94.

Lerner, A. J., & Riley, D. (2008). Neuropsychiatric aspects of dementias associated with motor dysfunction. In S. C. Yudofsky & R. E. Hales (Eds.), *The American Psychiatric Publishing textbook of neuropsychiatry and behavioral neurosciences* (pp. 907–934). Arlington, VA: American Psychiatric Publishing.

Lesgold, A. M. (1988). Problem solving. In R. J. Sternberg & E. E. Smith (Eds.), *The psychology of human thought* (pp. 188–213). New York: Cambridge University Press.

Lesgold, A. M., Rubinson, H., Feltovich, P., Glaser, R., Klopfer, D., & Wang, Y. (1988). Expertise in a complex skill: Diagnosing x-ray pictures. In M. T. H. Chi, R. Glaser, & M. Farr (Eds.), *The nature of expertise*. Hillsdale, NJ: Erlbaum.

Levin, D. T. (Ed.). (2004). *Thinking and seeing: Visual metacognition in adults and children*. Cambridge, MA: MIT Press.

Levine, B., Svoboda, E., Turner, G. R., Mandic, M., & Mackey, A. (2009). Behavioral and functional neuroanatomical correlates of anterograde autobiographical memory in isolated retrograde amnesic patient M.L. *Neuropsychologia*, 47, 2188–2196.

Levy, J. (1974). Cerebral asymmetries as manifested in split-brain man. In M. Kinsbourne & W. L. Smith (Eds.), *Hemispheric disconnection and cerebral function*. Springfield, IL: Charles C. Thomas.

Levy, J. (2000). Hemispheric functions. In A. E. Kazdin (Ed.), *Encyclopedia of psychology* (Vol. 4, pp. 113–115). Washington, DC: American Psychological Association.

Levy, J., Trevarthen, C., & Sperry, R. W. (1972). Perception of bilateral chimeric figures following hemispheric deconnexion. *Brain*, 95(1), 61–78.

Lewis, M. P. (2009). *Ethnologue: Languages of the world* (16 ed.). Dallas, TX: SIL International.

Lewis, R. L. (2003). Psycholinguistics, computational. In L. Nadel (Ed.), *Encyclopedia of cognitive science* (Vol. 3, pp. 787–794). London: Nature Group Press.

Lewis, S. J. G., & Barker, R. A. (2009). A pathophysiological model of freezing of gait in Parkinson's disease. *Parkinsonism and Related Disorders*, 15, 333–338.

Liberman, A. M., Cooper, F. S., Shankweiler, D. P., & Studdert-Kennedy, M. (1967). Perception of the speech code. *Psychological Review*, 74, 431–461.

Liberman, A. M., Harris, K. S., Hoffman, H. S., & Griffith, B. C. (1957). The discrimination of speech sounds within and across phoneme boundaries. *Journal of Experimental Psychology*, 54, 358–368.

Liberman, A. M., & Mattingly, I. G. (1985). The motor theory of speech perception revised. *Cognition*, 21, 1–36.

Lightfoot, D. W. (2003). Language acquisition and language change. In L. Nadel (Ed.), *Encyclopedia of cognitive science* (Vol. 2, pp. 697–700). London: Nature Group Press.

Lindsey, D. T., & Brown, A. M. (2002). Color naming and the phototoxic effects of sunlight on the eye. *Psychological Science*, 13, 506–512.

Linton, M. (1982). Transformations of memory in everyday life. In U. Neisser (Ed.), *Memory observed: Remembering in natural contexts*. San Francisco: Freeman.

Lipshitz, R., Klein, G., Orasanu, J., & Salas, E. (2001). Taking stock of naturalistic decision making. *Journal of Behavioral Decision Making*, 14(5), 331–352.

Little, D. R., Lewandowsky, S., & Heit, E. (2006). Ad hoc category restructuring. *Memory & Cognition*, 34(7), 1398–1413.

Liu, K. P. Y., & Chan, C. C. H. (2009). Metacognitive mental imagery strategies for training of daily living skills for people with brain damage: The self-regulation and mental imagery program. In I. Soederback (Ed.), *International handbook of occupational therapy interventions*. New York: Springer.

Locke, J. L. (1994). Phases in the child's development of language. *American Scientist*, 82, 436–445.

Llinas, R. R., & Steriade, M. (2006). Bursting of thalamic neurons and states of vigilance. *Journal of Neurophysiology*, 95, 3297–3308.

Lockhart, R. S. (2000). Methods of memory research. In E. Tulving & F. I. M. Craik (Eds.), *The Oxford handbook of memory* (pp. 45–58). New York: Oxford University Press.

Lodi, R., Tonon, C., Vignatelli, L., Iotti, S., Montagna, P., Barbiroli, B., et al. (2004). In vivo evidence of neuronal loss in the hypothalamus of narcoleptic patients. *Neurology*, 63, 1513–1515.

Loftus, E. F. (1975). Leading questions and the eyewitness report. *Cognitive Psychology*, 7, 560–572.

Loftus, E. F. (1977). Shifting human color memory. *Memory & Cognition*, 5, 696–699.

Loftus, E. F. (1993a). Psychologists in the eyewitness world. *American Psychologist*, 48(5), 550–552.

Loftus, E. F. (1993b). The reality of repressed memories. *American Psychologist*, 48(5), 518–537.

Loftus, E. F. (1998). Imaginary memories. In M. A. Conway, S. E. Gathercole, & C. Cornoldi (Eds.), *Theory of memory II* (pp. 135–145). Hove, UK: Psychology Press.

Loftus, E. F. (1996). Memory distortion and false memory creation. *Bulletin of the American Academy of Psychiatry and the Law*, 24(3), 281–295.

Loftus, E. F. (2005). A 30-year investigation of the malleability of memory. *Learning and Memory*, 12, 361–366.

Loftus, E. F., & Davis, D. (2006). Recovered memories. *Annual Review of Clinical Psychology*, 2, 469–498.

Loftus, E. F., & Ketcham, K. (1991). *Witness for the defense: The accused, the eyewitness, and the expert who puts memory on trial*. New York: St. Martin's Press.

Loftus, E. F., & Loftus, G. R. (1980). On the permanence of stored information in the human brain. *American Psychologist*, 35, 409–420.

Loftus, E. F., Miller, D. G., & Burns, H. J. (1978). Semantic integration of verbal information into a visual memory. *Journal of Experimental Psychology: Human Learning and Memory*, 4, 19–31.

Loftus, E. F., Miller, D. G., & Burns, H. J. (1987). Semantic integration of verbal information into a visual memory. In L. S. Wrightsman, C. E. Willis, S. M. Kassin (Eds.), *On the witness stand: Vol. 2. Controversies in the courtroom* (pp. 157–177). Newbury Park, CA: Sage.

Loftus, E. F., & Palmer, J. C. (1974). Reconstruction of automobile destruction: An example of the interaction between language and memory. *Journal of Verbal Learning and Verbal Behavior, 13,* 585–589.

Logan, G. (1988). Toward an instance theory of automatization. *Psychological Review, 95*(4), 492–527.

Logie, R. H., & Della Sala, S. (2005). Disorders of visuospatial memory. In P. Shah & A. Miyaki (Eds.), *The Cambridge handbook of visuospatial thinking* (pp. 81–120). New York: Cambridge University Press.

Logie, R. H., Della Sala, S., Beschin, N., & Denis, M. (2005). Dissociating mental transformations and visuospatial storage in working memory: Evidence from representational neglect. *Memory, 13*(3–4), 430–434.

Logie, R. H., & Denis, M. (1991). *Mental images in human cognition.* Amsterdam: North Holland.

Logothetis, N. K. (2004). Functional MRI in monkeys: A bridge between human and animal brain research. In M. S. Gazzaniga (Ed.), *The cognitive neurosciences,* (Vol. 3, pp. 957–969). Cambridge, MA: MIT Press.

Logothetis, N. K., Pauls, J., & Poggio, T. (1995). Shape representation in the inferior temporal cortex of monkeys. *Current Biology, 5*(5), 552–563.

Lohman, D. F. (2000). Complex information processing and intelligence. In R. J. Sternberg (Ed.), *Handbook of intelligence* (pp. 285–340). New York: Cambridge University Press.

Lohman, D. F. (2005). Reasoning abilities. In R. J. Sternberg & J. E. Pretz (Eds.), *Cognition and intelligence* (pp. 225–250). New York: Cambridge University Press.

Lohr, S. (2007). Slow down, brave multitasker, and don't read this in traffic [Electronic Version]. *New York Times.* Retrieved December 12, 2009 from http://www.nytimes.com/2007/03/25/business/25multi.html?pagewanted=1&_r=1&en=f2&ex=1332475200

Lonner, W. J. (1989). The introductory psychology text: Beyond Ekman, Whorf, and biased IQ tests. In D. M. Keats, D. Munro, & L. Mann (Eds.), *Heterogeneity in cross-cultural psychology* (pp. 4–22). Amsterdam: Swets & Zeitlinger.

Loth, E., Gómez, J. C., & Happé, F. (2008). Event schemas in autism spectrum disorders: The role of theory of mind and weak central coherence. *Journal of Autism and Developmental Disorders, 38*(3), 449–463.

Lou, H. C., Henriksen, L., & Bruhn, P. (1984). Focal cerebral hypoperfusion in children with dyphasia and/or attention deficit disorder. *Archives of Neurology, 41*(8), 825–829.

Louwerse, M. M., & Zwaan, R. A. (2009). Language encodes geographical information. *Cognitive Science, 33,* 51–73.

Love, B. C. (2003). Concept learning. In L. Nadel (Ed.), *Encyclopedia of cognitive science* (Vol. 1, pp. 646–652). London: Nature Publishing Group.

Lowenstein, J. A., Blank, H., & Sauer, J. D. (2010). Uniforms affect the accuracy of children's eyewitness identification decisions. *Journal of Investigative Psychology and Offender Profiling, 7,* 59–73.

Luaute, J., Halligan, P., Rode, G., Rossetti, Y., & Boisson, D. (2006). Visuo-spatial neglect: A systematic review of current interventions and their effectiveness. *Neuroscience & Biobehavioral Reviews, 30*(7), 961–982.

Lubart, T. I., & Mouchiroud, C. (2003). Creativity: A source of difficulty in problem solving. In J. E. Davidson & R. J. Sternberg (Eds.), *The psychology of problem solving* (pp. 127–148). New York: Cambridge University Press.

Lucas, T. H., McKhann, G. M., & Ojemann, G. A. (2004). Functional separation of languages in the bilingual brain: A comparison of electrical stimulation language mapping in 25 bilingual patients and 117 monolingual control patients. *Journal of Neurosurgery, 101,* 449–457.

Luchins, A. S. (1942). Mechanization in problem solving. *Psychological Monographs, 54*(6, Whole No. 248).

Luck, S. J., Hillyard, S. A., Mangun, G. R., & Gazzaniga, M. S. (1989). Independent hemispheric attentional systems mediate visual search in split-brain patients. *Nature, 342*(6249), 543–545.

Luck, S. J., & Vogel, E. K. (1997). The capacity of visual working memory for features and conjunctions. *Nature, 390,* 279–281.

Luka, B. J., & Barsalou, L. W. (2005). Structural facilitation: Mere exposure effects for grammatical acceptability as evidence for syntactic priming in comprehension. *Journal of Memory and Language, 52*(3), 436–459.

Luo, J., & Niki, K. (2003). Function of hippocampus in "insight" of problem solving. *Hippocampus, 13*(3), 316–323.

Lupton, L. (1998). Fluency in American sign language. *Journal of Deaf Studies and Deaf Education, 3*(4), 320–328.

Luria, A. R. (1968). *The mind of a mnemonist.* New York: Basic Books.

Luria, A. R. (1973). *The working brain.* London: Penguin.

Luria, A. R. (1976). *Basic problems of neurolinguistics.* The Hague, Netherlands: Mouton.

Luria, A. R. (1984). *The working brain: An introduction to neuropsychology* (B. Haigh, Trans.). Harmondsworth, UK: Penguin. (Original work published 1973)

Lycan, W. (2003). Perspectival representation and the knowledge argument. In Q. Smith & A. Jokic (Eds.), *Consciousness. New philosophical perspectives.* Oxford, UK: Oxford University Press.

Mace, W. M. (1986). J. J. Gibson's ecological theory of information pickup: Cognition from the ground up. In T. J. Knapp & L. C. Robertson (Eds.), *Approaches to cognition: Contrasts and controversies* (pp. 137–157). Hillsdale, NJ: Erlbaum.

Mack, M. L., Wong, A. C.-N., Gauthier, I., Tanaka, J. W., & Palmeri, T. J. (2009). Time course of visual object categorization: Fastest does not necessarily mean first. *Vision Research, 49*(15), 1961–1968.

MacKay, D., James, L., Taylor, J., & Marian, D. (2006). Amnesic H. M. exhibits parallel deficits and sparing in language and memory: Systems versus binding theory accounts. *Language and Cognitive Processes, 21.*

MacKay, D. G. (2006). Aging, memory, and language in amnesic H. M. *Hippocampus, 16*(5), 491–494.

Mackworth, N. H. (1948). The breakdown of vigilance during prolonged visual search. *Quarterly Journal of Experimental Psychology, 1,* 6–21.

MacLean, K. A., Aichele, S. R., Bridwell, D. A., Mangun, G. R., Wojciulik, E., & Saron, C. D. (2009). Interactions between endogenous and exogenous attention during vigilance. *Attention, Perception, & Psychophysics, 71*(5), 1042–1058.

MacLeod, C. (1991). Half a century of research on the Stroop effect: An integrative review. *Psychological Bulletin, 109*(2), 163–203.

MacLeod, C. M. (1996). How priming affects two-speeded implicit tests of remembering: Naming colors versus reading words. *Consciousness and Cognition: An International Journal, 5,* 73–90.

MacLeod, C. M. (2005). The Stroop task in cognitive research. In A. Wenzel & D. C. Rubin (Eds.), *Cognitive methods and their application to clinical research* (pp. 17–40). Washington, DC: American Psychological Association.

MacLin, O. H., & Malpass, R. S. (2001). Racial categorization of faces: The ambiguous-race face effect. *Psychology, Public Policy, and Law, 7,* 98–118.

MacLin, O. H., & Malpass, R. S. (2003). The ambiguous-race face illusion. *Perception, 32,* 249–252.

Macquet, A. C., & Fleurance, P. (2007). Naturalistic decision-making in expert badminton players. *Ergonomics, 50*(9), 1433–1450.

MacWhinney, B. (1999). *The emergence of language.* Mahwah, NJ: Erlbaum.

Madden, D. J. (2007). Aging and visual attention. *Current Directions in Psychological Science, 16*(2), 70–74.

Madden, D. J., Spaniol, J. Whiting, W. L., Bucur, B., Provenzale, J. M., Cabeza, R., et al. (2007). Adult age differences in the functional neuroanatomy of visual attention: A combined fMRI and DTI study. *Neurobiology of Aging, 28*(3), 459–476.

Madden, D. J., Turkington, T. G., Provenzale, J. M., Denny, L. L., Langley, L. K., Hawk, T. C., et al. (2002). Aging and attentional guidance during visual search: Funtional neuroanatomy by positron emission tomography. *Psychology and Aging, 17*(1), 24–43.

Maguire, E. A., Frackowiak, S. J., & Frith, C. D. (1996). Learning to find your way: A role for the human hippocampal formation. *Proceedings: Biological Sciences, 263*(1377), 1745–1750.

Makovski, T., & Jiang, Y. V. (2008). Proactive interference from items previously stored in visual working memory. *Memory & Cognition, 36*(1), 43–52.

Malgady, R., & Johnson, M. K. (1976). Modifiers in metaphors: Effects of constituent phrase similarity on the interpretation of figurative sentences. *Journal of Psycholinguistic Research, 5*, 43–52.

Malsbury, C. W. (2003). Hypothalamus. In L. Nadel (Ed.), *Encyclopedia of cognitive science* (Vol. 2, pp. 445–451). London: Nature Publishing Group.

Malt, B. C., & Smith, E. E. (1984). Correlated properties in natural categories. *Journal of Verbal Learning and Verbal Behavior, 23*, 250–269.

Mandonnet, E., Nouet, A., Gatignol, P., Capelle, L., & Duffau, H. (2007). Does the left inferior longitudinal fasciculus play a role in language? A brain stimulation study. *Brain, 130*, 623–629.

Mani, K., & Johnson-Laird, P. N. (1982). The mental representation of spatial descriptions. *Memory & Cognition, 10*(2), 181–187.

Manktelow, K. I., & Over, D. E. (1990). Deontic thought and the selection task. In K. J. Gilhooly, M. T. G. Keane, & G. Erdos (Eds.), *Lines of thinking* (Vol. 1, pp. 153–164). London: Wiley.

Manktelow, K. I., & Over, D. E. (1992). Obligation, permission, and mental models. In V. Rogers, A. Rutherford, & P. Bibby (Eds.), *Models in the mind* (pp. 249–266). London: Academic Press.

Manns, J. R., & Eichenbaum, H. (2006). Evolution of declarative memory. *Hippocampus, 16*(9), 795–808.

Mantyla, T. (1986). Optimizing cue effectiveness: Recall of 500 and 600 incidentally learned words. *Journal of Experimental Psychology: Learning, Memory, & Cognition, 12*, 66–71.

Maratsos, M. P. (1998). The acquisition of grammar. In D. Kuhn & R. S. Siegler (Eds.), *Handbook of child psychology: Vol. 2: Cognition, perception, and language* (5th ed., pp. 421–466). New York: Wiley.

Maratsos, M. P. (2003). Language acquisition. In L. Nadel (Ed.), *Encyclopedia of cognitive science* (Vol. 2, pp. 691–696). London: Nature Group Press.

Marcel, A. J. (1983a). Conscious and unconscious perception: An approach to the relations between phenomenal experience and perceptual processes. *Cognitive Psychology, 15*(2), 238–300.

Marcel, A. J. (1983b). Conscious and unconscious perception: Experiments on visual masking and word recognition. *Cognitive Psychology, 15*(2), 197–237.

Marcel, A. J. (1986). Consciousness and processing: Choosing and testing a null hypothesis. *Brain and Behavioral Sciences, 9*, 40–41.

Marcus, D., & Overton, W. (1978). The development of gender constancy and sex role preferences. *Child Development, 49*, 434–444.

Marcus, G. F. (1998). Rethinking eliminative connectionism. *Cognitive Psychology, 37*, 243–282.

Marcus, G. F., Vijayan, S., Bandi Rao, S., & Vishton, P. M. (1999). Rule learning by seven-month-old infants. *Science, 283*, 77–80.

Marewski, J. N., Gaissmaier, W., & Gigerenzer, G. (2010). Good judgments do not require complex cognition. *Cognitive Processing, 11*, 103–121.

Maril, A., Wagner, A. D., & Schacter, D. L. (2001). On the tip of the tongue: An event-related fMRI study of semantic retrieval failure and cognitive conflict. *Neuron, 31*(4), 653–660.

Markman, A. B. (2003). Conceptual representations in psychology. In L. Nadel (Ed.), *Encyclopedia of cognitive science* (Vol. 1, pp. 670–673). London: Nature Publishing Group.

Markman, A. B., Maddox, W. T., Worthy, D. A., & Baldwin, G. C. (2007). Using regulatory focus to explore implicit and explicit processing in concept learning. *Journal of Consciousness Studies, 14*(9-10), 132–155.

Markman, A. B., & Ross, B. H. (2003). Category use and category learning. *Psychological Bulletin, 129*, 592–613.

Markman, E. M. (1977). Realizing that you don't understand: A preliminary investigation. *Child Development, 48*, 986–992.

Markman, E. M. (1979). Realizing that you don't understand: Elementary school children's awareness of inconsistencies. *Child Development, 50*, 643–655.

Markovits, H. (2004). The development of deductive reasoning. In J. P. Leighton & R. J. Sternberg (Eds.), *The nature of reasoning* (pp. 313–338). New York: Cambridge University Press.

Markovits, H., Saelen, C., & Forgues, H. L. (2009). An inverse belief–bias effect: More evidence for the role of inhibitory processes in logical reasoning. *Experimental Psychology, 56*(2), 112–120

Marmor, G. S. (1975). Development of kinetic images: When does the child first represent movement in mental images? *Cognitive Psychology, 7*, 548–559.

Marmor, G. S. (1977). Mental rotation and number conservation: Are they related? *Developmental Psychology, 13*, 320–325.

Marr, D. (1982). *Vision*. San Francisco: Freeman.

Marrero, M. Z., Golden, C. J., & Espe Pfeifer, P. (2002). Bilingualism, brain injury, and recovery: Implications for understanding the bilingual and for therapy. *Clinical Psychology Review, 22*(3), 465–480.

Marsh, B., Todd, P. M., & Gigerenzer, G. (2004). Cognitive heuristics: Reasoning the fast and frugal way. In J. P. Leighton & R. J. Sternberg (Eds.), *The nature of reasoning* (pp. 273–287). New York: Cambridge University Press.

Marsh, R. L., Cook, G. I., Meeks, J. T., Clark-Foos, A., & Hicks, J. L. (2007). Memory for intention-related material presented in a to-be-ignored channel. *Memory and Cognition, 35*(6), 1197–1204.

Martin, J. A. (1981). A longitudinal study of the consequences of early mother–infant interaction: A microanalytic approach. *Monographs of the Society for Research in Child Development, 46* (203, Serial No. 190).

Martin, L. (1986). Eskimo words for snow: A case study in the genesis and decay of an anthropological example. *American Psychologist, 88*, 418–423.

Martin, M. (1979). Local and global processing: The role of sparsity. *Memory & Cognition, 7*, 476–484.

Martinez-Conde, S., Macknik, S. L., & Hybel, D. (2004). The role fixational eye movements in visual perception. *Nature Reviews: Neuroscience, 5*, 229–240.

Massaro, D. W. (1987). *Speech perception by ear and eye: A paradigm for psychological inquiry*. Hillsdale, NJ: Erlbaum.

Massaro, D. W., & Cohen, M. M. (1990). Perception of synthesized audible and visible speech. *Psychological Science, 1*, 55–63.

Masuda, T., & Nisbett, R. E. (2006). Culture and change blindness. *Cognitive Science: A Multidisciplinary Journal, 20*(2), 381–399.

Matarazzo, J. D. (1992). Biological and physiological correlates of intelligence. *Intelligence, 16*(3, 4), 257–258.

Matlin, M. W., & Underhill, W. A. (1979). Selective rehearsal and selective recall. *Bulletin of the Psychonomic Society, 14*(5), 389–392.

Matsui, M., Sumiyoshi, T., Yuuki, H., Kato, K., & Kurachi, M. (2006). Impairment of event schema in patients with schizophrenia: Examination of script for shopping at supermarket. *Psychiatry Research, 143*(2–3), 179–187.

Matthews, R. J. (2003). Connectionism and systematicity. In L. Nadel (Ed.), *Encyclopedia of cognitive science* (Vol. 1, pp. 687–690). London: Nature Publishing Group.

Maunsell, J. H. (1995). The brain's visual world: Representation of visual targets in cerebral cortex. *Science, 270,* 764–769.

Maxwell, R. J. (2005). Expanding the universe of categorical syllogisms: A challenge for reasoning researchers. *Behavior Research Methods, 37*(4), 560–580.

Mayer, J. D., & Salovey, P. (1997). What is emotional intelligence? In P. Salovey & D. Sluyter (Eds.), *Emotional development and emotional intelligence: Implications for educators* (pp. 3–31). New York: Basic.

Mayer, J. D., Salovey, P., & Caruso, D. (2000). Emotional intelligence. In R. J. Sternberg (Ed.), *Handbook of intelligence* (pp. 396–420). New York: Cambridge University Press.

McAfoose, J., & Baune, B. T. (2009). Exploring visual–spatial working memory: A critical review of concepts and models. *Neuropsychology Review, 19*(1), 130–142.

McAlister, A., & Peterson, C. (2007). A longitudinal study of child siblings and theory of mind development. *Cognitive Development, 22*(2), 258–270.

McArthur, T. (Ed.). (1992). *The Oxford companion to the English language.* New York: Oxford University Press.

McBride, D. (2007). Methods for measuring conscious and automatic memory: A brief review. *Journal of Consciousness Studies, 14*(1–2), 198–215.

McCann, R. S., & Johnston, J. C. (1992). Locus of single-channel bottleneck in dual-task interference. *Journal of Experimental Psychology: Human Perception & Performance, 18*(2), 471–484.

McCarthy, G., Blamire, A. M., Puce, A., Nobe, A. C., Bloch, G., Hyder, F., et al. (1994). Functional magnetic resonance imaging of human prefrontal cortex activation during a spatial working memory task. *Proceedings of the National Academy of Sciences, USA, 90,* 4952–4956.

McCarthy, G., Puce, A., Gore, J. C., & Allison, T. (1997). Facespecific processing in the human fusiform gyrus. *Journal of Cognitive Neuroscience, 9,* 605–610.

McClelland, J. L., & Elman, J. L. (1986). The TRACE model of speech perception. *Cognitive Psychology, 18,* 1–86.

McClelland, J. L., McNaughton, B. C., & O'Reilly, R. C. (1995). Why there are complementary learning systems in the hippocampus and neocortex: Insights from the successes and failures of connectionist models of learning and memory. *Psychological Review, 102,* 419–457.

McClelland, J. L., Mirman, D., & Holt, L. L. (2009). Are there interactive processes in speech perception? *Trends in Cognitive Science, 10*(8), 363–369.

McClelland, J. L., & Rogers, T. T. (2003). The parallel distributed processing approach to semantic cognition. *Nature Reviews: Neuroscience, 4,* 1–14.

McClelland, J. L., & Rumelhart, D. E. (1981). An interactive activation model of context effects in letter perception: Part 1. An account of basic findings. *Psychological Review, 88,* 483–524.

McClelland, J. L., & Rumelhart, D. E., (1985). Distributed memory and the representation of general and specific information. *Journal of Experimental Psychology: General, 114*(2), 159–188.

McClelland, J. L., & Rumelhart, D. E. (1988). *Explorations in parallel distributed processing: A handbook of models, programs, and exercises.* Cambridge, MA: MIT Press.

McClelland, J. L., Rumelhart, D. E., & the PDP Research Group (1986). *Parallel distributed processing: Explorations in the microstructure of cognition: Vol. 2. Psychological and biological models.* Cambridge, MA: MIT Books.

McCormick, D. A., & Thompson, R. F. (1984). Cerebellum: Essential involvement in the classically conditioned eyelid response. *Science, 223,* 296–299.

McDaniel, M. A. (2005). Big-brained people are smarter: A meta-analysis of the relationship between in vivo brain volume and intelligence. *Intelligence, 33*(4), 337–346.

McDermott, J., & Hauser, M. D. (2007). Nonhuman primates prefer slow tempos but dislike music overall. *Cognition, 104,* 654–668.

McDermott, K. B. (1996). The persistence of false memories in list recall. *Journal of Memory and Language, 35,* 212–230.

McDonough, L., Choi, S., & Mandler, J. M. (2003). Understanding spatial relations: Flexible infants, lexical adults. *Cognitive Psychology, 46,* 229–259.

McDowd, J. M. (2007). An overview of attention: behavior and brain. *Journal of Neurologic Physical Therapy, 31,* 98–103.

McEwen, F., Happe, F., Bolton, P., Rijsdijk, F., Ronald, A., Dworzynski, K., et al. (2007). Origins of individual differences in imitation: Links with language, pretend play, and social insightful behavior in two-year-old twins. *Child Development, 78*(2), 474–492.

McGarry-Roberts, P. A., Stelmack, R. M., & Campbell, K. B. (1992). Intelligence, reaction time, and event-related potentials. *Intelligence, 16*(3, 4), 289–313.

McGarva, A. R., Ramsey, M., & Shear, S. A. (2006). Effects of driver cell phone use on driver aggression. *Journal of Social Psychology, 146*(2), 133–146.

McGurk, H., & MacDonald, J. (1976). Hearing lips and seeing voices. *Nature, 264,* 746–748.

McIntyre, C. K., Pal, S. N., Marriott, L. K., & Gold, P. E. (2002). Competition between memory systems: acetylcholine release in the hippocampus correlates negatively with good performance on an amygdala-dependent task. *The Journal of Neuroscience, 22*(3), 1171–1176.

McKenna, J., Treadway, M., & McCloskey, M. E. (1992). Expert psychological testimony on eyewitness reliability: Selling psychology before its time. In P. Suedfeld & P. E. Tetlock (Eds.), *Psychology and social policy* (pp. 283–293). New York: Hemisphere.

McKoon, G., & Ratcliff, R. (1980). Priming in item recognition: The organization of propositions in memory for text. *Journal of Verbal Learning and Verbal Behavior, 19,* 369–386.

McKoon, G., & Ratcliff, R. (1992a). Inference during reading. *Psychological Review, 99,* 440–464.

McKoon, G., & Ratcliff, R. (1992b). Spreading activation versus compound cue accounts of priming: Mediated priming revisited. *Journal of Experimental Psychology: Learning, Memory, & Cognition, 18*(6), 1155–1172.

McKown, C., & Weinstein, R. S. (2003). The development and consequences of stereotype consciousness in middle childhood. *Child Development 74*(2), 498–515.

McLeod, P., Plunkett, K., & Rolls, E. T. (1998). *Introduction to connectionist modelling of cognitive processes.* Oxford, UK: Oxford University Press.

McMullen, P. A., & Farah, M. J. (1991). Viewer-centered and object-centered representations in the recognition of naturalistic line drawings. *Psychological Science, 2*(4), 275–277.

McNamara, D. S., Kintsch, E., Songer, N. B., & Kintsch, W. (1996). Learning from text: Effect of prior knowledge and text coherence. *Discourse Processes, 30,* 201–236.

McNamara, D. S., O'Reilly, T., Best, R. M., & Ozuru, Y. (2006). Improving adolescent students' reading comprehension with iStart. *Journal of Educational Computing Research, 34*(2), 147–171.

McNamara, T. P. (1992). Theories of priming: I. Associative distance and lag. *Journal of Experimental Psychology: Learning, Memory, & Cognition, 18*(6), 1173–1190.

McNamara, T. P., Hardy, J. K., & Hirtle, S. C. (1989). Subjective hierarchies in spatial memory. *Memory & Cognition, 17*(4), 444–453.

McNamara, T. P., Ratcliff, R., & McKoon, G. (1984). The mental representation of knowledge acquired from maps. *Journal of Experimental Psychology: Learning, Memory, & Cognition, 10*(4), 723–732.

McNeil, J. E., & Warrington, E. K. (1993). Prosopagnosia: A face specific disorder. *Quarterly Journal of Experimental Psychology: Human Experimental Psychology, 46*, 1–10.

McRorie, M., & Cooper, C. (2001). Neural transmission and general mental ability. *Learning and Individual Differences, 13*(4), 335–338.

Meacham, J. (1982). A note on remembering to execute planned actions. *Journal of Applied Developmental Psychology, 3*, 121–133.

Meacham, J. A., & Singer, J. (1977). Incentive in prospective remembering. *Journal of Psychology, 97*, 191–197.

Meade, M. L., Watson, J. M., Balota, D. A., & Roediger, H. L. (2007). The roles of spreading activation and retrieval mode in producing false recognition in the DRM paradigm. *Journal of Memory and Language, 56*(3), 305–320.

Mechelli, A., Crinion, J. T., Nippeney, U., O'Doherty, J., Ashburner, J., Frackowiak, R. S., et al. (2004). Neurolinguistics: Structural plasticity in the bilingual brain. *Nature, 431*(7010), 757.

Medin, D. L. (1989). Concepts and conceptual structure. *American Psychologist, 44*, 1469–1481.

Medin, D. L., & Atran, S. (Eds.) (1999). *Folkbiology*. Cambridge, MA: MIT Press.

Medin, D. L., Lynch, J., & Solomon, H. (2000). Are there kinds of concepts? *Annual Review of Psychology, 51*, 121–147.

Medin, D. L., Proffitt, J. B., & Schwartz, H. C. (2000). Concepts: An overview. In A. E. Kazdin (Ed.), *Encyclopedia of psychology* (Vol. 2, pp. 242–245). Washington, DC: American Psychological Association.

Meerlo, P., Mistlberger, R. E., Jacobs, B. L., Heller, H. C., & McGinty, D. (2009). New neurons in the adult brain: The role of sleep and consequences of sleep loss. *Sleep Medicine Reviews, 13*, 187–194.

Mehler, J., Dupoux, E., Nazzi, T., & Dahaene-Lambertz, G. (1996). Coping with linguistic diversity: The infant's viewpoint. In J. L. Morgan & K. Demuth (Eds.), *Signal to Syntax: Bootstrapping from speech to grammar in early acquisition* (pp. 101–116). Mahwah, NJ: Erlbaum.

Meier, R. P. (1991). Language acquisition by deaf children. *American Scientist, 79*, 60–76.

Meinzer, M., Obleser, J., Flaisch, T., Eulitz, C., & Rockstroh, B. (2007). Recovery from aphasia as a function of language therapy in an early bilingual patient demonstrated by fMRI. *Neuropsychologia, 45*(6), 1247–1256.

Mejia-Arauz, R., Rogoff, B., & Paradise, R. (2005). Cultural variation in children's observation during a demonstration. *International Journal of Behavioral Development, 29*(4), 282–291.

Melnyk, L., & Bruck, M. (2004). Timing moderates the effects of repeated suggestive interviewing on children's eyewitness memory. *Applied Cognitive Psychology, 18*(5), 613–631.

Melrose, R. J., Poulin, R. M., & Stern, C. E. (2007). An fMRI investigation of the role of the basal ganglia in reasoning. *Brain Research, 1142*, 146–158.

Melton, R. J. (1995). The role of positive affect in syllogism performance. *Personality and Social Psychology Bulletin, 21*, 788–794.

Merikle, P. (2000). Consciousness and unconsciousness: Processes. In A. E. Kazdin (Ed.), *Encyclopedia of psychology* (Vol. 2, pp. 272–275). Washington, DC: American Psychological Association.

Merriam-Webster's Collegiate Dictionary (Ed.) (Eds.). (2003). Springfield, MA: Merriam-Webster.

Merriam-Webster's Online Dictionary. (2010). from www.merriam-webster.com.

Mervis, C. B., Catlin, J., & Rosch, E. (1976). Relationships among goodness-of-example, category norms, and word frequency. *Bulletin of the Psychonomic Society, 7*, 268–284.

Metcalfe, J. (1986). Feeling of knowing in memory and problem solving. *Journal of Experimental Psychology: Learning, Memory, & Cognition, 12*(2), 288–294.

Metcalfe, J. (2000). Metamemory: Theory and data. In E. Tulving & F. I. M. Craik (Eds.), *The Oxford handbook of memory* (pp. 197–211). New York: Oxford University Press.

Metcalfe, J., & Wiebe, D. (1987). Intuition in insight and noninsight problem solving. *Memory & Cognition, 15*(3), 238–246.

Metzinger, T. (Ed.) (1995). *Conscious experience*. Paderborn: Schoningh.

Metzger, W. (1930). Optische Untersuchungen am Ganzfeld. II: Zur Phaenomenologie des homogenen Ganzfelds. *Psychologische Forschung, 13*, 6–29.

Meyer, D. E., & Schvaneveldt, R. W. (1971). Facilitation in recognizing pairs of words: Evidence of a dependence between retrieval operations. *Journal of Experimental Psychology, 90*(2), 227–234.

Meyer, D. E., & Schvaneveldt, R. W. (1976). Meaning, memory structure, and mental processes. *Science, 192*(4234), 27–33.

Middleton, F. A., & Helms Tillery, S. I. (2003). Cerebellum. In L. Nadel (Ed.), *Encyclopedia of cognitive science* (Vol. 1, pp. 467–475). London: Nature Publishing Group.

Mignot, E., Taheri, S., & Nishino, S. (2002). Sleep with the hypothalamus: Emerging therapeutic targets for sleep disorders. *Nature Neuroscience 5*, 1071–1075.

Mill, J. S. (1887). *A system of logic*. New York: Harper & Brothers.

Miller, G. A. (1956). The magical number seven, plus or minus two: Some limits on our capacity for processing information. *Psychological Review, 63*, 81–97.

Miller, G. A. (1979). Images and models, similes and metaphors. In A. Ortony (Ed.), *Metaphor and thought* (pp. 202–250). New York: Cambridge University Press.

Miller, G. A., Galanter, E. H., & Pribram, K. H. (1960). *Plans and the structure of behavior*. New York: Holt, Rinehart and Winston.

Miller, G. A., & Gildea, P. M. (1987). How children learn words. *Scientific American, 257*(3), 94–99.

Miller, G. A. & Isard, S. (1963). Some perceptual consequences of linguistic rules. *Journal of Verbal Learning and Verbal Behavior, 2*, 217–228.

Miller, J., Ulrich, R., & Rolke, B. (2009). On the optimality of serial and parallel processing in the psychological refractory period paradigm: Effects of the distribution of stimulus onset asynchronies. *Cognitive Psychology, 58*, 273–310.

Miller, M. D. (2009). What the science of cognition tells us about instructional technology. *Change, 41*(2), 16–17.

Mills, C. J. (1983). Sex-typing and self-schemata effects on memory and response latency. *Journal of Personality & Social Psychology, 45*(1), 163–172.

Milner, A. D., Dijkerman, H. C., McIntosh, R. D., Rossetti, Y., & Pisella, L. (2003). Delayed reaching and grasping in patients with optic ataxia. *Progress in Brain Research, 142*, 225–242.

Milner, A. D., & Goodale, M. A. (2008). Two visual systems re-viewed. *Neuropsychologia, 46*, 774–785.

Milner, B. (1968). Disorders of memory loss after brain lesions in man: Preface-material-specific and generalized memory loss. *Neuropsychologia, 6*(3), 175–179.

Milner, B., Corkin, S., & Teuber, H. L. (1968). Further analysis of the hippocampal amnesic syndrome: 14-year follow-up study of H. M. *Neuropsychologia, 6*, 215–234.

Milner, B., Squire, L. R., & Kandel, E. R. (1998). Cognitive neuroscience and the study of memory. *Neuron, 20*(3), 445–468.

Minagawa-Kawai, Y., Mori, K., Naoi, N., & Kojima, S. (2007). Neural attunement processes in infants during the acquisition of a language-specific phonemic contrast. *The Journal of Neuroscience, 27*(2), 315–321.

Mirman, D., McClelland, J. L., Holt, L. L., & Magnuson, J. S. (2008). Effects of attention on the strength of lexical influences on speech perception: Behavioral experiments and computational mechanisms. *Cognitive Science, 32*(2), 398–417.

Mirochnic, S., Wolf, S., Staufenbiel, M., & Kempermann, G. (2009). Age effects on the regulation of adult hippocampal neurogenesis by physical activity and environmental enrichment in the APP23 mouse model of Alzheimer disease. *Hippocampus, 19*, 1008–1018.

Mishkin, M., & Appenzeller, T. (1987). The anatomy of memory. *Scientific American, 256*(6), 80–89.

Mishkin, M., & Petri, H. L. (1984). Memories and habits: Some implications for the analysis of learning and retention. In L. R. Squire & N. Butters (Eds.), *Neurophysiology of memory* (pp. 287–296). New York: Guilford.

Mishkin, M., Ungerleider, L. G., & Macko, K. A. (1983). Object vision and spatial vision: Two cortical pathways. *Trends in Neurosciences, 6*(10), 414–417.

Moar, I., & Bower, G. H. (1983). Inconsistency in spatial knowledge. *Memory & Cognition, 11*(2), 107–113.

Modafferi, P. A., Corley, M., Green, R., & Perkins, C. (2009). Eyewitness identification: Views from the trenches. *Police Chief, 76*(10), 78–87.

Modell, H. I., Michael, J. A., Adamson, T., Goldberg, J., Horwitz, B. A., Bruce, D. S., et al. (2000). Helping undergraduates repair faulty mental models in the student laboratory. *Advances in Physiological Education, 23*, 82–90.

Moettoenen, R., & Watkins, K. E. (2009). Motor representations of acrticulators contribute to categorical perception of speech sounds. *The Journal of Neuroscience, 29*(31), 9819–9825.

Mohammed, A. K., Jonsson, G., & Archer, T. (1986). Selective lesioning of forebrain noradrenaline neurons at birth abolishes the improved maze learning performance induced by rearing in complex environment. *Brain Research, 398*(1), 6–10.

Monnier, C., & Syssau, A. (2008). Semantic contribution to verbal short-term memory: Are pleasant words easier to remember than neutral words in serial recall and serial recognition? *Memory and Cognition, 36*(1), 35–42.

Monsell, S. (1978). Recency, immediate recognition memory, and reaction time. *Cognitive Psychology, 10*(4), 465–501.

Montello, D. R., Waller, D., Hegarty, M., & Richardson, A. E. (2004). Spatial memory of real environments, virtual environments, and maps. In G. L. Allen (Ed.), *Human spatial memory: Remembering where* (pp. 251–285). Mahwah, NJ: Erlbaum.

Mooney, A. (2004). Co-operation, violations and making sense. *Journal of Pragmatics, 36*(5), 899–920.

Moore, K. S., Peterson, D. A., O'Shea, G., McIntosh, G. C., & Thaut, M. H. (2008). The effectiveness of music as a mnemonic device on recognition memory for people with multiple sclerosis. *Journal of Music Therapy, 45*(3), 307–329.

Moran, S. (2010). The roles of creativity in society. In J. C. Kaufman & R. J. Sternberg (Eds.), *The Cambridge handbook of creativity* (pp. 74–90). New York: Cambridge University Press.

Morawski, J. (2000). Psychology: Early twentieth century. In A. E. Kazdin (Ed.), *Encyclopedia of psychology* (Vol. 6, pp. 403–410). Washington, DC: American Psychological Association.

Moray, N. (1959). Attention in dichotic listening: Affective cues and the influence of instructions. *Quarterly Journal of Experimental Psychology, 11*, 56–60.

Morris, C. D., Bransford, J. D., & Franks, J. (1977). Levels of processing versus transfer appropriate processing. *Journal of Verbal Learning & Verbal Behavior, 16*(5), 519–533.

Morton, J. (1969). Interaction of information in word recognition. *Psychological Review, 76*, 165–178.

Morton, T. A., Hornsey, M. J., & Postmes, T. (2009). Shifting ground: The variable use of essentialism in contexts of inclusion and exclusion. *British Journal of Social Psychology, 48*, 35–59.

Morton, T. U. (1978). Intimacy and reciprocity of exchange: A comparison of spouses and strangers. *Journal of Personality and Social Psychology, 36*, 72–81.

Moscovitch, M. (2003). Memory consolidation. In L. Nadel (Ed.), *Encyclopedia of cognitive science* (Vol. 2, pp. 1066–1081). London: Nature Publishing Group.

Moscovitch, M., & Craik, F. I. M. (1976). Depth of processing, retrieval cues, and uniqueness of encoding as factors in recall. *Journal of Verbal Learning and Verbal Behavior, 15*, 447–458.

Moscovitch, M., Winocur, G., & Behrmann, M. (1997). What is special about face recognition? Nineteen experiments on a person with visual object agnosia but normal face recognition. *Journal of Cognitive Neuroscience, 9*, 555–604.

Motter, A. E., de Moura, A. P. S., Lai, Y. C., & Dasgupta, P. (2002). Topology of the conceptual network of language. *Physical Review E: Statistical, Nonlinear, and Soft Matter Physics, 65*, 065102.

Motter, B. (1999). Attention in the animal brain. In R. A. Wilson & F. C. Keil (Eds.), *The MIT encyclopedia of the cognitive sciences* (pp. 41–43). Cambridge, MA: MIT Press.

Moulton, S. T., & Kosslyn, S. M. (2009). Imagining predictions: mental imagery as mental emulation. *Philosophical Transactions of the Royal Society: B, 364*, 1273–1280.

MSNBC. (2005). Rosemary Kennedy, JFK's sister, dies at 86 [Electronic Version] from http://www.msnbc.msn.com/id/6801152/.

Mufwene, S. S. (2004). Language birth and death. *Annual Review of Anthropology, 33*, 201–222.

Mulligan, N. W. (2003). Memory: Implicit versus explicit. In L. Nadel (Ed.), *Encyclopedia of cognitive science* (Vol. 2, pp. 1114–1120). London: Nature Publishing Group.

Munhall, K. G. (2003). Phonology, neural basis of. In L. Nadel (Ed.), *Encyclopedia of cognitive science* (Vol. 3, pp. 655–658). London: Nature Group Press.

Münte, T. F., Altenmüller, E., & Jäncke, L. (2002). The musician's brain as a model of neuroplasticity. *Nature Reviews: Neuroscience, 3*, 473–478.

Münte, T. F., Spring, D. K., Szycik, G. R., & Noesselt, T. (2010). Electrophysiological attention effects in a virtual cocktail-party setting. *Brain Research, 1307*, 78–88.

Murdock, B. B. (2003). Memory models. In L. Nadel (Ed.), *Encyclopedia of cognitive science* (Vol. 2, pp. 1084–1089). London: Nature Publishing Group.

Murdock, B. B., Jr. (1961). Short-term retention of single paired-associates. *Psychological Reports, 8*, 280.

Murphy, K., McKone, E., & Slee, J. (2003). Dissociations between implicit and explicit memory in children: The role of strategic processing and the knowledge base. *Journal of Experimental Child Psychology, 84*(2), 124–165.

Murray, E. A. (2003). Temporal cortex. In L. Nadel (Ed.), *Encyclopedia of cognitive science* (Vol. 4, pp. 353–360). London: Nature Publishing Group.

Nadel, L. (Ed.). (2005). *Encyclopedia of cognitive science.* Hoboken, NJ: Wiley.

Naglieri, J. A., & Kaufman, J. C. (2001). Understanding intelligence, giftedness and creativity using PASS theory. *Roeper Review, 23*(3), 151–156.

Nairne, J. S., & Crowder, R. G. (1982). On the locus of the stimulus suffix effect. *Memory & Cognition, 10*, 350–357.

Nakayama, Y. (1978). Role of visual perception in driving. *IATSS Research, 2*, 64–73.

Nation, P. (2001). *Learning vocabulary in another language.* Cambridge, UK: Cambridge University Press.

National Research Council. (1998). *Preventing reading difficulties in young children.* Washington, DC: National Academy Press.

National Center for Injury Prevention and Control. (2009a). Signs and symptoms [Electronic Version]. Retrieved October 25, 2009 from http://www.cdc.gov/ncipc/tbi/Signs_and_Symptoms.htm.

National Center for Injury Prevention and Control. (2009b). What is traumatic brain injury? [Electronic Version]. Retrieved October 25, 2009 from http://www.cdc.gov/ncipc/tbi/TBI.htm.

National Institute of Mental Health. (2009). Attention deficit hyperactivity disorder (ADHD) [Electronic Version]. Retrieved 11/30/2009 from http://www.nimh.nih.gov/health/publications/attention-deficit-hyperactivity-disorder/complete-index.shtml.

Naus, M. J. (1974). Memory search of categorized lists: A consideration of alternative self-terminating search strategies. *Journal of Experimental Psychology, 102*, 992–1000.

Naus, M. J., Glucksberg, S., & Ornstein, P. A. (1972). Taxonomic word categories and memory search. *Cognitive Psychology, 3*, 643–654.

Naveh-Benjamin, M., & Ayres, T. J. (1986). Digit span, reading rate, and linguistic relativity. *Quarterly Journal of Experimental Psychology: Human Experimental Psychology, 38*(4), 739–751.

Navalpakkam, V., & Itti, L. (2007). Search goal tunes visual features optimally. *Neuron, 53*, 605–617.

Navon, D. (1977). Forest before trees: The precedence of global features in visual perception. *Cognitive Psychology, 9*, 353–383.

Navon, D. (1984). Resources—a theoretical soupstone? *Psychological Review, 91*, 216–234.

Navon, D., & Gopher, D. (1979). On the economy of the human-processing system. *Psychological Review, 86*, 214–255.

Neely, J. H. (2003). Priming. In L. Nadel (Ed.), *Encyclopedia of cognitive science* (Vol. 3, pp. 721–724). London: Nature Publishing Group.

Neisser, U. (1967). *Cognitive psychology.* New York: Appleton-Century-Crofts.

Neisser, U. (1978). Memory: What are the important questions? In M. M. Gruneberg, P. Morris, & R. Sykes (Eds.), *Practical aspects of memory* (pp. 3–24). London: Academic Press.

Neisser, U. (1982). Snapshots or benchmarks? In U. Neisser (Ed.), *Memory observed: Remembering in natural contexts.* San Francisco: Freeman.

Neisser, U. (1999). *Memory observed* (rev. ed.). New York: Worth.

Neisser, U. (2003). New directions for flashbulb memories: Comments on the ACP special issue. *Applied Cognitive Psychology, 17*, 1149–1155.

Neisser, U., & Becklen, R. (1975). Selective looking: Attending to visually specified events. *Cognitive Psychology, 7*(4), 480–494.

Neisser, U., & Harsch, N. (1993). Phantom flashbulbs: False recollections of hearing the news about Challenger. In E. Winograd & U. Neisser (Eds.), *Affect and accuracy in recall: Studies of "flashbulb" memories* (pp. 9–31). New York: Cambridge University Press.

Nelson, K. (1973). Structure and strategy in learning to talk. *Monograph of the Society for Research in Child Development, 38*(Serial No. 149).

Nelson, K. (1999). Language and thought. In M. Bennett (Ed.), *Developmental psychology* (pp. 185–204). Philadelphia: Psychology Press.

Nelson, K., & Fivush, R. (2004). The emergence of autobiographical memory: A social cultural *Neuropsychologia, 40*, 964–969.

Nelson, T. O., & Rothbart, R. (1972). Acoustic savings for items forgotten from long-term memory. *Journal of Experimental Psychology, 93*, 357–360.

Neto, F., Williams, J. E., & Widner, S. C. (1991). Portuguese children's knowledge of sex stereotypes: Effects of age, gender, and socioeconomic status. *Journal of Cross-Cultural Psychology, 22*(3), 376–388.

Nettelbeck, T. (1987). Inspection time and intelligence. In P. A. Vernon (Ed.), *Speed of information-processing and intelligence* (pp. 295–346). Norwood, NJ: Ablex.

Nettelbeck, T., Rabbitt, P. M. A., Wilson, C., & Batt, R. (1996). Uncoupling learning from initial recall: The relationship between speed and memory deficits in old age. *British Journal of Psychology, 87*, 593–607.

Nettelbeck, T., & Young, R. (1996). Intelligence and savant syndrome: Is the whole greater than the sum of the fragments? *Intelligence, 22*, 49–67.

Neubauer, A. C., & Fink, A. (2005). Basic information processing and the psychophysiology of intelligence. In R. J. Sternberg & J. E. Pretz (Eds.), *Cognition and intelligence* (pp. 68–87). New York: Cambridge University Press.

Neumann, P. G. (1977). Visual prototype formation with discontinuous representation of dimensions of variability. *Memory & Cognition, 5*(2), 187–197.

Neville, H. J. (1995). Developmental specificity in neurocognitive development in humans. In M. S. Gazzaniga (Ed.), *The cognitive neurosciences* (pp. 219–231). Cambridge, MA: MIT Press.

New, A. S., Hazlett, E. A., Newmark, R. E., Zhang, J., Triebwasser, J., Meyerson, D., et al. (2009). Laboratory induced aggression: a positron emission tomography study of aggressive individuals with Borderline Personality Disorder [Electronic Version]. *Biological Psychiatry, 66*, 1107–1114.

Newell, A., Shaw, J. C., & Simon, H. A. (1957). Problem solving in humans and computers. *Carnegie Technical, 21*(4), 34–38.

Newell, A., & Simon, H. A. (1972). *Human problem solving.* Englewood Cliffs, NJ: Prentice-Hall.

Newell, B. R., & Bröder, A. (2008). Cognitive processes, models and metaphors in decision research. *Judgment and Decision Making, 3*(3), 195–204.

Newman, A. J., Supalla, T., Hauser, P., Newport, E., & Bavelier, D. (2010). Prosodic and narrative processing in American Sign Language: An fMRI study. *NeuroImage, 52*(2), 669–676.

Newman, E. J., & Lindsay, D. S. (2009). False memories: What the hell are they for? *Applied Cognitive Psychology, 23*, 1105–1121.

Newman, M. L., Groom, C. J., Groom, L. J., & Pennebaker, J. W. (2008). Gender differences in language use: An analysis of 14,000 text samples. *Discourse Processes, 45*, 211–236.

Newman, R. S. (2005). The cocktail party effect in infants revisited: Listening to one's name in noise. *Developmental Psychology, 41*(2), 352–362.

Newman, S. D., Carpenter, P. A., Varma, S., & Just, M. A. (2003). Frontal and parietal participation in problem solving in the Tower of London: fMRI and computational modeling of planning and high-level perception. *Neuropsychologia, 41*, 1668–1682.

Newman, S. D., & Just, M. A. (2005). The neural bases of intelligence. In R. J. Sternberg & J. E. Pretz (Eds.), *Cognition and intelligence* (pp. 88–103). New York: Cambridge University Press.

Newport, E. L. (1991). Constraining concepts of the critical period of language. In S. Carey & R. Gelman (Eds.), *The epigenesis of mind: Essays on biology and cognition* (pp. 111–130). Hillsdale, NJ: Erlbaum.

Newport, E. L. (2003). Language development, critical periods in. In L. Nadel (Ed.), *Encyclopedia of cognitive science* (Vol. 2, pp. 737–740). London: Nature Group Press.

Newton, M. (2004). *Savage girls and wild boys: A history of feral children.* London: Faber and Faber.

Nicholls, M. E. R., Searle, D. A., & Bradshaw, J. L. (2004). Read my lips. Asymmetries in the visual expression and perception of speech revealed through the McGurk effect. *Psychological Science, 15*(2), 138–141.

Nickerson, R. S. (2004). Teaching reasoning. In J. P. Leighton & R. J. Sternberg (Eds.), *The nature of reasoning* (pp. 410–442). New York: Cambridge University Press.

Nickerson, R. S. (2005). Technology and cognition amplification. In R. J. Sternberg & D. Preiss (Eds), *Intelligence and technology: The impact of tools on the nature and development of human abilities* (pp. 3–27). Mahwah, NJ: Erlbaum.

Nigg, J. T., Knottnerus, G. M., Martel, M. M., Nikolas, M., Cavanagh, K., Karmaus, W., et al. (2008). Low blood lead levels associated with clinically diagnosed attention-deficit/hyperactivity disorder and mediated by weak cognitive control. *Biological Psychiatry, 63,* 325–331.

Nijboer, T. C. W., van der Smagt, M., van Zandvoort, M. J. E., & de Haan, E. H. F. (2007). Colour agnosia impairs the recognition of natural but not of non-natural scenes. *Cognitive Neuropsychology, 24*(2), 152–161.

Nijboer, T. C. W., van Zandvoort, M. J. E., & de Haan, E. H. F. (2007). A familial factor in the development of colour agnosia. *Neuropsychologia, 45*(8), 1961–1965.

NINDS stroke information page. Retrieved June 1, 2010, from http://www.ninds.nih.gov/disorders/stroke/stroke.html

Nisbett, R. E. (2003). *The geography of thought: Why we think the way we do.* New York: The Free Press.

Nisbett, R. E., & Masuda, T. (2003). Culture and point of view. *Proceedings of the National Academy of Sciences of the United States of America, 100*(19), 11163–11170.

Nisbett, R. E., & Miyamoto, Y. (2005). The influence of culture: Holistic versus analytic perception. *Trends in Cognitive Science, 9*(10), 467–473.

Nisbett, R. E., & Ross, L. (1980). *Human inference: Strategies and shortcomings of social judgment.* Englewood Cliffs, NJ: Prentice-Hall.

Nisbett, R. E., & Wilson, T. D. (1977). Telling more than we can know: Verbal reports on mental processes. *Psychological Review, 84,* 231–259.

Norman, D. A. (1968). Toward a theory of memory and attention. *Psychological Review, 75,* 522–536.

Norman, D. A. (1976). *Memory and attention: An introduction to human information processing* (2nd ed.). New York: Wiley.

Norman, D. A. (1988). *The design of everyday things.* New York: Doubleday.

Norman, D. A., & Rumelhart, D. E. (1975). *Explorations in cognition.* San Francisco: Freeman.

Norman, D. A., & Rumelhart, D. E. (1983). Studies of typing from the LNR research group. In W. E. Cooper (Ed.), *Cognitive aspects of skilled typing* (pp. 45–65). New York: Springer-Verlag.

Nosofsky, R. M., & Palmeri, T. J. (1997). An exemplar-based random walk model of speeded classification. *Psychological Review, 104,* 266–300.

Nosofsky, R. M., Palmeri, T. J., & McKinley, S. C. (1994). Rule-plus-exception model of classification learning. *Psychological Review, 101,* 53–79.

Novick, L. R., & Holyoak, K. J. (1991). Mathematical problem solving by analogy. *Journal of Experimental Psychology: Learning, Memory and Cognition, 17*(3), 398–415.

Nyberg, L., Cabeza, R. & Tulving, E. (1996). PET studies of encoding and retrieval: The HERA model. *Psychonomic Bulletin and Review, 3,* 135–148.

O'Brien, D. P. (2004). Mental-logic theory: What it proposes, and reasons to take this proposal seriously. In J. P. Leighton & R. J. Sternberg (Eds.), *The nature of reasoning* (pp. 205–233). New York: Cambridge University Press.

O'Kane, G., Kensinger, E. A., & Corkin, S. (2004). Evidence for semantic learning in profound amnesia: An investigation with patient H.M. *Hippocampus, 14*(4), 417–425.

O'Keefe, J. (2003). Hippocampus. In L. Nadel (Ed.), *Encyclopedia of cognitive science* (Vol. 1, pp. 336–347). London: Nature Publishing Group.

O'Keefe, J. A., & Nadel, L. (1978). *The hippocampus as a cognitive map.* New York: Oxford University Press.

O'Leary, D. S., Block, R. I., Koeppel, J. A., Schultz, S. K., Magnotta, V. A., Ponto, L. B., et al. (2007). Effects of smoking marijuana on focal attention and brain blood flow. *Human Psychopharmacology: Clinical and Experimental, 22*(3), 135–148.

O'Regan, J. K. (2003). Change blindness. In L. Nadel (Ed.), *Encyclopedia of cognitive science* (Vol. 1, pp. 486–490). London: Nature Publishing Group.

O'Toole, A. J., Jiang, F., Abdi, H., & Haxby, J. V. (2005). Partially distributed representations of objects and faces in ventral temporal cortex. *Journal of Cognitive Neuroscience, 17,* 580–590.

Obel, C., Linnet, K. M., Henriksen, T. B., Rodriguez, A., Järvelin, M. R., Kotimaa, A., et al. (2009). Smoking during pregnancy and hyperactivity-inattention in the offspring—comparing results from three Nordic cohorts. *International Journal of Epidemiology, 38*(3), 698–705.

Ojemann, G. A. (1982). Models of the brain organization for higher integrative functions derived with electrical stimulation techniques. *Human Neurobiology, 1,* 243–250.

Ojemann, G. A., & Whitaker, H. A. (1978). The bilingual brain. *Archives of Neurology, 35,* 409–412.

Oken, B. S., Salinsky, M. C., & Elsas, S. M. (2006). Vigilance, alertness, or sustained attention: physiological basis and measurement. *Clinical Neurophysiology, 117,* 1885–1901.

Olesen, P. J., Schendan, H. E., Amick, M. M., & Cronin-Golomb, A. (2007). HIV infection affects parietal-dependent spatial cognition: Evidence from mental rotation and hierarchical pattern perception. *Behavioral Neuroscience, 121*(6), 1163–1173.

Olivers, C. N. L., & Meeter, M. (2008). A boost and bounce theory of temporal attention. *Psychological Review 115, 115*(4), 836–863.

Oller, D. K., & Eilers, R. E. (1998). Interpretive and methodological difficulties in evaluating babbling drift. *Parole, 7/8,* 147–164.

Oller, D. K., Eilers, R. E., Urbano, R., & Cobo-Lewis, A. B. (1997). Development of precursors to speech in infants exposed to two languages. *Journal of Child Language, 24,* 407–425.

Öllinger, M., Jones, G., & Knoblich, G. (2008). Investigating the effect of mental set on insight problem solving. *Experimental Psychology, 55*(4), 269–282.

Olshausen, B., Andersen, C., & Van Essen, D. C. (1993). A neural model of visual attention and invariant pattern recognition. *Journal of Neuroscience, 13,* 4700–4719.

Olsson, M. J., Lundgren, E. B., Soares, S. C., & Johansson, M. (2009). Odor memory performance and memory awareness: A comparison to word memory across orienting tasks and retention intervals. *Chemosensory Perception, 2,* 161–171.

Orasanu, J. (2005). Crew collaboration in space: A naturalistic decision-making perspective. *Aviation, Space and Environmental Medicine, 76*(Suppl 6), B154–B163.

Orasanu, J., & Connolly, T. (1993). The reinvention of decision making. In G. E. Klein, J. Orasanu, R. Calderwood, & C. E. Zsambok (Eds.), *Decision making in action: Models and methods* (pp. 3–20). Norwood, NJ: Ablex.

Orban, G. A., Fize, D., Peuskens, H., Denys, K., Nelissen, K., Sunaert, S., et al. (2003). Similarities and differences in motion processing between the human and macaque brain: Evidence from fMRI. *Neuropsychologia, 41,* 1757–1768.

Osherson, D. N. (1990). Judgment. In D. N. Osherson & E. E. Smith (Eds.), *An invitation to cognitive science: Vol. 3. Thinking* (pp. 55–87). Cambridge, MA: MIT Press.

Otapowicz, D., Sobaniec, W., Kulak, W., & Okurowska-Zwada, B. (2005). Time of cooing appearance and further development of speech in children with cerebral palsy. *Annales Academiae Medicae Bialostocensis, 50*(1), 78–81.

Oxford English Dictionary (2nd ed.). (1989). Oxford, England: Clarendon Press.

Ozonoff, S., Strayer, D. L., McMahon, W. M., & Filloux, F. (1994). Executive function abilities in autism and Tourette syndrome: An information-processing approach. *Journal of Child Psychology and Psychiatry, 35*, 1015–1032.

Paap, K. R., Newsome, S. L., McDonald, J. E., & Schvaneveldt, R. W. (1982). An activation-verification model for letter and word recognition: The word-superiority effect. *Psychological Review, 89*(5), 573–594.

Paavilainen, P., Tiitinen, H., Alho, K., & Näätänen R. (1993). Mismatch negativity to slight pitch changes outside strong attentional focus. *Biological Psychology, 37*(1), 23–41.

Paivio, A. (1969). Mental imagery in associative learning and memory. *Psychological Review, 76*(3), 241–263.

Paivio, A. (1971). *Imagery and verbal processes.* New York: Holt, Rinehart and Winston.

Palermo, R., & Rhodes, G. (2007). Are you always on my mind? A review of how face perception and attention interact. *Neuropsychologia, 2007*, 75–92.

Pallanti, S., & Bernardi, S. (2009). Neurobiology of repeated transcranial magnetic stimulation in the treatment of anxiety: a critical review. *International Clinical Psychopharmacology, 24*(4), 163–173.

Palmer, S. E. (1975). The effects of contextual scenes on the identification of objects. *Memory & Cognition, 3*, 519–526.

Palmer, S. E. (1977). Hierarchical structure in perceptual representation. *Cognitive Psychology, 9*, 441–474.

Palmer, S. E. (1992). Modern theories of Gestalt perception. In G. W. Humphreys (Ed.), *Understanding vision: An interdisciplinary perspective-readings in mind and language* (pp. 39–70). Oxford, UK: Blackwell.

Palmer, S. E. (1999a). Gestalt perception. In R. A. Wilson & F. C. Keil (Eds.), *The MIT encyclopedia of the cognitive sciences* (pp. 344–346). Cambridge, MA: MIT Press.

Palmer, S. E. (1999b). *Vision science: Photons to phenomenology.* Cambridge, MA: MIT Press.

Palmer, S. E. (2000). Perceptual organization. In A. E. Kazdin (Ed.), *Encyclopedia of psychology* (Vol. 6, pp. 93–97). Washington, DC: American Psychological Association.

Palmer, S. E., & Rock, I. (1994). Rethinking perceptual organization: The role of uniform connectedness. *Psychonomic Bulletin & Review, 1*, 29–55.

Palmeri, T. J. (2003). Automaticity. In L. Nadel (Ed.), *Encyclopedia of cognitive science* (Vol. 1, pp. 290–301). London: Nature Publishing Group.

Palmeri, T. J., Wong, A. C.-N., & Gauthier, I. (2004). Computational approaches to the development of perceptual expertise. *Trends in Cognitive Sciences, 8*(8), 378–386.

Palmiero, M., Belardinelli, M. O., Nardo, D., Sestieri, C., Matteo, R. D., D'Ausilio, A., et al. (2009). Mental imagery generation in different modalities activates sensory-motor areas. *Cognitive Processing, 10*(2), S268–S271.

Paracchini, S., Scerri, T., & Monaco, A. P. (2007). The genetic lexicon of dyslexia. *Annual Review of Genomics and Human Genetics, 8*, 57–79.

Paradis, M. (1977). Bilingualism and aphasia. In H. A. Whitaker & H. Whitaker (Eds.), *Studies in neurolinguistics* (Vol. 3). New York: Academic Press.

Paradis, M. (1981). Neurolinguistic organization of a bilingual's two languages. In J. E. Copeland & P. W. Davis (Eds.), *The seventh LACUS forum.* Columbia, SC: Hornbeam Press.

Park, C. R., Phillip R. Zoladz, Conrad, C. D., Fleshner, M., & Diamond, D. M. (2008). Acute predator stress impairs the consolidation and retrieval of hippocampus-dependent memory in male and female rats. *Learning and Memory, 15*, 271–280.

Parker, A. J. (2007). Binocular depth perception and the cerebral cortex. *Nature Reviews: Neuroscience, 8*(6), 379–391.

Parker, A. J., Cumming, B. G., & Dodd, J. V. (2000). Binocular neurons and the perception of depth. In M. Gazzaniga (Ed.), *The new cognitive neurosciences* (pp. 263–278). Cambridge, MA: MIT Press.

Parker, E. S., Cahill, L., & McGaugh, J. L. (2006). A case of unusual autobiographical remembering. *Neurocase, 12*, 35–49.

Parker, J. D. A., Duffy, J. M., Wood, L. M., Bond, B. J., & Hogan, M. J. (2006). Academic achievement and emotional intelligence: Predicting the successful transition from high school to university. *Journal of The First-Year Experience & Students in Transition, 17*(1), 67–78.

Parron, C., & Fagot, J. (2007). Comparison of grouping abilities in humans (homo sapiens) and baboons (papio papio) with the Ebbinghaus illusion. *Journal of Comparative Psychology, 121*(4), 405–411.

Parsons, O. A., & Nixon, S. J. (1993). Neurobehavioral sequelae of alcoholism. *Neurologic Clinics, 11*(1), 205–218.

Pashler, H. (1994). Dual-task interference in simple tasks: Data and theory. *Psychological Bulletin, 116*(2), 220–244.

Passafiume, D., Di Giacomo, D., & Carolei, A. (2006). Word-stem completion task to investigate semantic network in patients with Alzheimer's disease. *European Journal of Neurology, 13*(5), 460–464.

Patel, V. L., Kaufman, D. R., & Arocha, J. F. (2002). Methodological review: Emerging paradigms of cognition in medical decision-making. *Journal of Biomedical Informatics, 35*, 52–75.

Patterson, J. C., Lilien, D. L., Takalkar, A., Kelley, R. E., & Minagar, A. (2009). Potential value of quantitative analysis of cerebral PET in early cognitive decline. *American Journal of Alzheimer's Disease & Other Dementias, 23*(6), 586–592.

Pavlov, I. P. (1955). *Selected works.* Moscow: Foreign Languages Publishing House.

Payne, J. (1976). Task complexity and contingent processing in decision making: An information search and protocol analysis. *Organizational Behavior and Human Performance, 16*, 366–387.

Payne, J. D., Nadel, L., Allen, J. J. B., Thomas, K. G. F., & Jacobs, W. J. (2002). The effects of experimentally induced stress on false recognition. *Memory, 10*(1), 1–6.

Pearson, B. Z., Fernandez, S. C., Lewedeg, V., & Oller, D. K. (1997). The relation of input factors to lexical learning by bilingual infants. *Applied Psycholinguistics, 18*, 41–58.

Pecenka, N., & Keller, P. E. (2009). Auditory pitch imagery and its relationship to musical synchronization. *Annals of the New York Academy of Sciences 1169*, 282–286.

Pedersen, P. M., Vinter, K., & Olsen, T. S. (2004). Aphasia after stroke: Type, severity and prognosis—the Copenhagen aphasia study. *Cerebrovascular Disease, 17*(1), 35–43.

Peigneux, P., Laureys, S., Fuchs, S., Collette, F., Perrin, F. Reggers, J., et al. (2004). Are spatial memories strengthened in the human hippocampus during slow wave sleep? *Neuron, 44*(3), 535–545.

Penfield, W. (1955). The permanent record of the stream of consciousness. *Acta Psychologica, 11*, 47–69.

Penfield, W. (1969). Consciousness, memory, and man's conditioned reflexes. In K. H. Pribram (Ed.), *On the biology of learning* (pp. 129–168). New York: Harcourt, Brace & World.

Pennebaker, J. W., & Memon, A. (1996). Recovered memories in context: Thoughts and elaborations on Bowers and Farvolden. *Psychological Bulletin, 119*, 381–385.

Pepperberg, I. M. (1999). *The Alex Studies: Cognitive and communicative abilities of grey parrots.* Cambridge, MA: Harvard University Press.

Pepperberg, I. M. (2007). Grey parrots do not always 'parrot': The roles of imitation and phonological awareness in the creation of new labels from existing vocalizations. *Language Sciences, 29*(1), 1–13.

Pepperberg, I. M., & Gordon, J. D. (2005). Number comprehension by a grey parrot *(Psittacus erithacus)*, including a zero-like concept. *Journal of Comparative Psychology, 119*(2), 197–209.

Peretz, I. (1996). Can we lose memories for music? A case of music agnosia in a nonmusician. *Journal of Cognitive Neuroscience, 8*(6), 481–496.

Peretz, I., Kolinsky, R., Tramo, M., Labrecque, R., Hublet, C., Demeurisse, G., & Belleville, S. (1994). Functional dissociations following bilateral lesions of auditory cortex. *Brain, 117*, 1283–1301.

Perfetti, C. A. (1985). *Reading ability.* New York: Oxford University Press.

Perkins, D. N. (1981). *The mind's best work.* Cambridge, MA: Harvard University Press.

Perlmutter, D. (Ed.). (1983). *Studies in relational grammar* (Vol. 1). Chicago: University of Chicago Press.

Perner, J. (1998). The meta-intentional nature of executive functions and theory of mind. In P. Carruthers & J. Boucher (Eds.), *Language and thought* (pp. 270–283). Cambridge, UK: Cambridge University Press.

Perner, J. (1999). Theory of mind. In M. Bennett (Ed.), *Developmental psychology: Achievements and prospects* (pp. 205–230). Philadelphia: Psychology Press.

Peru, A., & Zapparoli, P. (1999). A new case of representational neglect. The Italian *Journal of Neurological Sciences, 20*(4), 392–461.

Pesciarelli, F., Kutas, M., Dell'Acqua, R., Peressotti, F., Job, R., & Urbach, T. P. (2007). Semantic and repetition priming within the attentional blink: An event-related brain potential (ERP) investigation study. *Biological Psychology, 76*, 21–30.

Peters, M., & Battista, C. (2008). Applications of mental rotation figures of the Shepard and Metzler type and description of a mental rotation stimulus library. *Brain and Cognition, 66*, 260–264.

Petersen, S. E., Fox, P. T., Posner, M. I., Mintun, M., & Raichle, M. E. (1988). Positron emission tomographic studies of the cortical anatomy of single-word processing. *Nature, 331*(6157), 585–589.

Peterson, L. R., & Peterson, M. J. (1959). Short-term retention of individual verbal items. *Journal of Experimental Psychology, 58*, 193–198.

Peterson, M. A. (1999). What's in a stage name? *Journal of Experimental Psychology: Human Perception and Performance, 25*, 276–286.

Peterson, M. A., Kihlstrom, J. F., Rose, P. M., & Glisky, M. L. (1992). Mental images can be ambiguous: Reconstruals and reference-frame reversals. *Memory & Cognition, 20*(2), 107–123.

Petitto, L., & Marentette, P. F. (1991). Babbling in the manual mode: Evidence for the ontogeny of language. *Science, 251*(5000), 1493–1499.

Petitto, L. A., Holowka, S., Sergio, L. E., Levy, B., & Ostry, D. J. (2004). Baby hands that move to the rhythm of language: Hearing babies acquiring sign language babble silently on the hands. *Cognition, 93*(1), 43–73.

Pezdek, K. (2003). Event memory and autobiographical memory for the events of September 11, 2001. *Applied Cognitive Psychology, 17*(9), 1033–1045.

Pezdek, K. (2006). Memory for the events of September 11, 2001. In L.-G. Nilsson & N. Ohta (Eds.), *Memory and society: Psychological perspectives* (pp. 73–90). New York: Psychology Press.

Pezdek, K., Blandon-Gitlin, I., & Moore, C. M. (2003). Children's face recognition memory: More evidence for the cross-race effect. *Journal of Applied Psychology, 88*(4), 760–763.

Phaf, R. H., & Kan, K. J. (2007). The automaticity of emotional Stroop: A meta-analysis. *Journal of Behavior Therapy and Experimental Psychiatry, 38*(2), 184–199.

Phelps, E. A. (1999). Brain versus behavioral studies of cognition. In R. J. Sternberg (Ed.), *The nature of cognition* (pp. 295–322). Cambridge, MA: MIT Press.

Phelps, E. A. (2004). Human emotion and memory: Interactions of the amygdala and the hippocampal complex. *Current Opinions in Neurobiology, 14*, 198–202.

Phelps, E. A. (2006). Emotion and cognition: Insights from studies of the human amygdala. *Annual Review of Psychology, 57*, 27–53.

Phillipson, R. (in press). English: from British empire to corporate empire. *Sociolinguistic Studies.*

Pickell, H., Klima, E., Love, T., Krichevsky, M., Bellugi, U., & Hickok, G. (2005). Sign language aphasia following right hemisphere damage in a left-hander: A case of reversed cerebral dominance in a deaf signer? *Neurocase, 11*(3), 194–203.

Picton, T. W., & Mazaheri, A. (2003). Electroencephalography. In L. Nadel (Ed.), *Encyclopedia of cognitive science* (Vol. 1, pp. 1083–1087). London: Nature Publishing Group.

Pierce, K., & Courchesne, E. (2003). Austism. In L. Nadel (Ed.), *Encyclopedia of cognitive science* (Vol. 1, pp. 278–283). London: Nature Publishing Group.

Piercy, M. (1964). The effects of cerebral lesions on intellectual function: A review of current research trends. *British Journal of Psychiatry 110*, 310–352.

Pillemer, D., & White, S. H. (1989). Childhood events recalled by children and adults. In H. W. Reese (Ed.), *Advances in child development and behavior,* (Vol. 22, pp. 297–340). New York: Academic Press.

Pines, J. M. (2005). Profiles in patient safety: Confirmation bias in emergency medicine. *Academic Emergency Medicine, 13*(1), 90–94.

Pinker, S. (1980). Mental imagery and the third dimension. *Journal of Experimental Psychology: General, 109*(3), 354–371.

Pinker, S. (1985). Visual cognition: An introduction. In S. Pinker (Ed.), *Visual cognition* (pp. 1–63). Cambridge, MA: MIT Press.

Pinker, S. (1994). *The language instinct.* New York: William Morrow.

Pinker, S. (1997a). *How the mind works.* New York: Norton.

Pinker, S. (1997b). Letter to the editor. *Science, 276*, 1177–1178.

Pinker, S. (1999). *Words and rules.* New York: Basic Books.

Pinker, S., Nowak, M. A., & Lee, J. J. (2008). The logic of indirect speech. *Proceedings of the National Academy of Sciences of the United States of America, 105*(3), 833–838.

Pisoni, D. B., Nusbaum, H. C., Luce, P. A., & Slowiaczek, L. M. (1985). Speech perception, word recognition and the structure of the lexicon. *Speech Communication, 4*, 75–95.

Pizzorusso, T. (2009). Erasing fear memories. *Science, 325*, 1214–1215.

Platek, S. M., Keenan, J. P., Gallup, G. G., & Geroze, B. M. (2004). Where am I? The neurological correlates of self and other. *Cognitive Brain Research, 19*, 114–122.

Platko, J. V., Wood, F. B., Pelser, I., Meyer, M., Gericke, G. S., O'Rourke, J., et al. (2008). Association of reading disability on chromosome 6p22 in the Afrikaner population. *Volume 147B Issue 7, Pages 1278 – 1287, 147B*(7), 1278–1287.

Platt, M. L., & Glimcher, P. W. (1999). Neural correlates of decision variables in parietal cortex. *Nature, 400*, 233–238.

Plaut, D. C., McClelland, J. L., Seidenberg, M. S., & Patterson, K. (1996). Understanding normal and impaired word reading: Computational principles in quasi-regular domains. *Psychological Review, 103*, 56–115.

Plucker, J. A., & Makel, M. C. (2010). Assessment of creativity. In J. C. Kaufman & R. J. Sternberg (Eds.), *The Cambridge handbook of creativity* (pp. 47–73). New York: Cambridge University Press.

Plunkett, K. (1998). Language acquisition and connectionism. *Language and Cognitive Processes, 13*, 97–104.

Poggio, T., & Edelman, S. (1990). A network that learns to recognize three-dimensional objects. *Nature, 343*, 263–266.

Poincaré, H. (1913). *The foundations of science*. New York: Science Press.

Poitrenaud, S., Richard, J.-F., & Tijus, C. (2005). Properties, categories, and categorisation. *Thinking & Reasoning, 11*(2), 151–208.

Polanczyk, G., & Jensen, P. (2008). Epidemiologic considerations in attention deficit hyperactivity disorder: a review and update. *Child and Adolesccent Psychiatric Clinics of North America, 17*, 245–260.

Policastro, E., & Gardner, H. (1999). From case studies to robust generalizations: An approach to the study of creativity. In R. J. Sternberg (Ed.), *Handbook of creativity* (pp. 213–225). New York: Cambridge University Press.

Polk, T. A., Stallcup, M., Aguirre, G. K., Alsop, D. C., D'Esposito, M., Detre, J. A., et al. (2002). Neural specialization for letter recognition. *Journal of Cognitive Neuroscience, 14*(2), 145–159.

Polkczynska-Fiszer, M., & Mazaux, J. M. (2008). Second language acquisition after traumatic brain injury: A case study *Disability and Rehabilitation, 30*(18), 1397–1407.

Pollack, I., & Pickett, J. M. (1964). Intelligibility of excerpts from fluent speech: auditory vs. structural context. *Journal of Verbal Learning and Verbal Behavior, 3*, 79–84.

Pollatsek, A., & Miller, B. (2003). Reading and writing. In L. Nadel (Ed.), *Encyclopedia of cognitive science* (Vol. 3, pp. 841–847). London: Nature Publishing Group.

Pollatsek, A., & Rayner, K. (1989). Reading. In M. I. Posner (Ed.), *Foundations of cognitive science* (pp. 401–436). Cambridge, MA: MIT Press.

Pomerantz, J. R. (1981). Perceptual organization in information processing. In M. Kubovy & J. R. Pomerantz (Eds.), *Perceptual organization* (pp. 141–180). Hillsdale, NJ: Erlbaum.

Pomerantz, J. R. (2003). Perception: Overview. In L. Nadel (Ed.), *Encyclopedia of cognitive science* (Vol. 3, pp. 527–537). London: Nature Publishing Group.

Posner, M., & Keele, S. W. (1968). On the genesis of abstract ideas. *Journal of Experimental Psychology, 77*(3, Pt. 1), 353–363.

Posner, M. I. (1969). Abstraction and the process of recognition. In G. H. Bower & J. T. Spence (Eds.), *The psychology of learning and motivation: Vol. 3. Advances in learning and motivation*. New York: Academic Press.

Posner, M. I. (1992). Attention as a cognitive and neural system. *Current Directions in Psychological Science, 1*(1), 11–14.

Posner, M. I. (1995). Attention in cognitive neuroscience: An overview. In M. Gazzaniga (Ed.), *The cognitive neurosciences* (pp. 615–624). Cambridge, MA: MIT Press.

Posner, M. I., Boies, S., Eichelman, W., & Taylor, R. (1969). Retention of visual and name codes of single letters. *Journal of Experimental Psychology, 81*, 10–15.

Posner, M. I., & Dehaene, S. (1994). Attentional networks. *Trends in Neurosciences, 17*(2), 75–79.

Posner, M. I., & DiGirolamo, G. J. (1998). Conflict, target detection and cognitive control. In R. Parasuraman (Ed.), *The attentive brain*. Cambridge, MA: MIT Press.

Posner, M. I., Goldsmith, R., & Welton, K. E., Jr. (1967). Perceived distance and the classification of distorted patterns. *Journal of Experimental Psychology, 73*(1), 28–38.

Posner, M. I., & Keele, S. W. (1967). Decay of visual information from a single letter. *Science, 158*(3797), 137–139.

Posner, M. I., & Petersen, S. E. (1990). The attention system of the human brain. *Annual Review of Neuroscience, 13*, 25–42.

Posner, M. I., Petersen, S. E., Fox, P. T., & Raichle, M. E. (1988). Localization of cognitive operations in the human brain. *Science, 240*(4859), 1627–1631.

Posner, M. I., & Raichle, M. E. (1994). *Images of mind*. New York: Freeman.

Posner, M. I., & Rothbart, M. K. (2007). Research on attention networks as a model for the integration of psychological science. *Annual Review of Psychology, 58*, 1–23.

Posner, M. I., Sandson, J., Dhawan, M., & Shulman, G. L. (1989). Is word recognition automatic? A cognitive-anatomical approach. *Journal of Cognitive Neuroscience, 1*, 50–60.

Posner, M. I., & Snyder, C. R. R. (1975). Attention and cognitive control. In R. Solso (Ed.), *Information processing and cognition: The Loyola Symposium* (pp. 55–85). Hillsdale, NJ: Erlbaum.

Postle, B. R., Brush, L. N., & Nick, A. M. (2004). Prefrontal cortex and the mediation of proactive interference in working memory. *Cognitive Affective Behavioral Neuroscience, 4*(4), 600–608.

Postma, A., Wester, A. J., & Kessels, R. P. C. (2008). Spared unconscious influences of spatial memory in diencephalic amnesia. *Experimental Brain Research, 190*(2), 125–133.

Pouget, A. & Bavelier, D. (2007). Paying attention to neurons with discriminative taste. *Neuron. Neuron Previews, 53*(4), 473–475.

Prabhu, V., Sutton, C., & Sauser, W. (2008). Creativity and certain personality traits: Understanding the mediating effect of intrinsic motivation. *Creativity Research Journal, 20*(1), 53–66.

Pretz, J. E., Naples, A. J., & Sternberg, R J. (2003). Recognizing, defining, and representing problems. In J. E. Davidson & R. J. Sternberg (Eds.), The *psychology of problem solving* (pp. 3–30). New York: Cambridge University Press.

Prince, S. E., Dennis, N. A., & Cabeza, R. (2009). Encoding and retrieving faces and places: Distinguishing process- and stimulus-specific differences in brain activity. *Neuropsychologia, 47*, 2282–2289.

Prince, S. E., Tsukiura, R., & Cabeza, R. (2007). Distinguishing the neural correlates of episodic memory encoding and semantic memory retrieval. *Psychological Science, 18*(2), 144–151.

Prinzmetal, W. P. (1995). Visual feature integration in a world of objects. *Current Directions in Psychological Science, 4*, 90–94.

Proffitt, D. R., Stefanucci, J., Banton, T., & Epstein, W. (2003). The role of effort in perceiving distance. *Psychological Science, 14*, 106–112.

Proffitt, D. R., Stefanucci, J., Banton, T., & Epstein, W. (2006). Reply to Hutchinson & Loomis. *Spanish Journal of Psychology, 9*, 340–342.

Pugalee, D. K. (2004). A comparison of verbal and written descriptions of students' problem solving processes. *Educational Studies in Mathematics, 55*(1–3), 27–47.

Pullum, G. K. (1991). *The Great Eskimo vocabulary hoax and other irreverent essays on the study of language*. Chicago: University of Chicago Press.

Pyers, J. E., Gollan, T. H., & Emmorey, K. (2009). Bimodal bilinguals reveal the source of tip-of-the-tongue states. *Cognition, 112*, 323–329.

Pylyshyn, Z. (1973). What the mind's eye tells the mind's brain: A critique of mental imagery. *Psychological Bulletin, 80*, 1–24.

Pylyshyn, Z. (1984). *Computation and cognition*. Cambridge, MA: MIT Press.

Pylyshyn, Z. W. (2006). *Seeing and visualizing: It's not what you think.* Cambridge, MA: MIT Press.

Qui, J., Li, H., Huang, X., Zhang, F., Chen, A., Luo, Y., et al. (2007). The neural basis of conditional reasoning: An event-related potential study. *Neuropsychologia, 45*(7), 1533–1539.

Quinn, P. C., Bhatt, R. S., & Hayden, A. (2008). Young infants readily use proximity to organize visual pattern information. *Acta Psychologica, 127*(2), 289–298.

Radvansky, G. A., & Dijkstra, K. (2007). Aging and situation model processing. *Psychonomic Bulletin & Review, 14*(6), 1027–1042.

Ragland, J. D., Moelter, S. T., McGrath, C., Hill, S. K., Gur, R. E., Bilker, W. B., et al. (2003). Levels-of-processing effect on word recognition in schizophrenia. *Biological Psychiatry, 54*(11), 1154–1161.

Raichle, M. E. (1998). Behind the scenes of function brain imaging: A historical and physiological perspective. *Proceedings of the National Academy of Sciences, 95*, 765–772.

Raichle, M. E. (1999). Positron emission tomography. In R. A. Wilson & F. C. Keil (Eds.), *The MIT encyclopedia of the cognitive sciences* (pp. 656–659). Cambridge, MA: MIT Press.

Raine, A., & Yang, Y. (2006). Neural foundations to moral reasoning and antisocial behavior. *Social Cognitive and Affective Neuroscience, 1*(3), 203–213.

Rajah, M. N., & McIntosh, A. R. (2005). Overlap in the functional neural systems involved in semantic and episodic memory retrieval. *Journal of Cognitive Neuroscience, 17*(3), 470–482.

Rakoczy, H., Warneken, F., & Tomasello, M. (2009). Young children's selective learning of rule games from reliable and unreliable models. *Cognitive Development, 24*, 61–69.

Ramachandra, P., Tymmala, R. M., Chu, H. L., Charles, L., & Truwit, W. A. H. (2003). Application of diffusion tensor imaging to magnetic-resonance-guided brain tumor resection. *Pediatric Neurosurgery, 39*(1), 39–43.

Ramírez-Esparza, N., Mehl, M. R., Álvarez-Bermúdez, J., & Pennebaker, J. W. (2009). Are Mexicans more or less sociable than Americans? Insights from a naturalistic observation study. *Journal of Research in Personality, 43*, 1–7.

Ramus, F., Rosen, S., Dakin, S., Day, B. L., Castellote, J. M., White, S., et al. (2003). Theories of developmental dyslexia: Insights from a multiple case study of dyslexic adults. *Brain, 126*(4), 841–865.

Rao, R. P. N. (2003). Attention, models of. In L. Nadel (Ed.), *Encyclopedia of cognitive science* (Vol. 1, pp. 231–237). London: Nature Publishing Group.

Ratcliff, R. (1990). Connectionist models of recognition memory: Constraints imposed by learning and forgetting functions. *Psychological Review, 97*(2), 285–308.

Ratcliff, R., & McKoon, G. (2008). Passive parallel automatic minimalist processing. In C. Engel & W. Singer (Eds.), *Better than Conscious? Decision making, the human mind, and implications for institutions.* Cambridge, MA: MIT Press.

Raymond, J. E., Shapiro, K. L., Arnell, K. M. (1992). Temporary suppression of visual processing in an RSVP task: an attentional blink? *Journal of experimental psychology. Human perception and performance 18* (3): 849–60.

Rayner, K., & Pollatsek, A. (2000). Reading. In A. E. Kazdin (Ed.), *Encyclopedia of psychology* (Vol. 7, pp. 14–18). Washington, DC: American Psychological Association.

Rayner, K., Sereno, S. C., Lesch, M. F., & Pollatsek, A. (1995). Phonological codes are automatically activated during reading: Evidence from an eye movement priming paradigm. *Psychological Science, 6*, 26–31.

Raz, A., Moreno-Iniguez, M., Martin, L., & Zhu, H. (2007). Suggestion overrides the Stroop effect in highly hypnotizable individuals. *Consciousness and Cognition, 16*, 331–338.

Read, J. D. (2000). *Assessing vocabulary.* Cambridge, UK: Cambridge University Press.

Read, J. D., & Connolly, D. A. (2007). The effects of dealy on long-term memory for witnessed events. In M. P. Toglia, J. D. Read, D. F. Ross & R. C. L. Lindsay (Eds.), *Handbook of eyewitness psychology* (Vol. 1, pp. 117–155). Mahwah, NJ: Erlbaum.

Reason, J. (1990). *Human error.* New York: Cambridge University Press.

Reber, P. J., Knowlton, B. J, & Squire, L. R. (1996). Dissociable properties of memory systems: Differences in the flexibility of declarative and nondeclarative knowledge. *Behavioral Neurosciences, 110*, 861–871.

Reed, L. J., Lasserson, D., Marsden, P., Stanhope, N., Stevens, T., Bello, F., et al. (2003). 18FDG-PET findings in the Wernicke–Korsakoff syndrome. *Cortex, 39*, 1027–1045.

Reed, S. (1972). Pattern recognition and categorization. *Cognitive Psychology, 3*(3), 382–407.

Reed, S. (1974). Structural descriptions and the limitations of visual images. *Memory & Cognition, 2*(2), 329–336.

Reed, S. K. (1987). A structure-mapping model for word problems. *Journal of Experimental Psychology: Learning, Memory, & Cognition, 13*(1), 125–139.

Reed, S. K. (2000). Thinking: Problem solving. In A. E. Kazdin (Ed.), *Encyclopedia of psychology* (Vol. 8, pp. 71–75). Washington, DC: American Psychological Association.

Reed, T. E., & Jensen, A. R. (1991). Arm nerve conduction velocity (NCV), brain NCV, reaction time, and intelligence. *Intelligence, 15*, 33–47.

Reed, T. E., & Jensen, A. R. (1993). Choice reaction time and visual pathway nerve conduction velocity both correlate with intelligence, but appear not to correlate with each other: Implications for information processing. *Intelligence, 17*, 191–203.

Reeder, G. D., McCormick, C. B., & Esselman, E. D. (1987). Self-referent processing and recall of prose. *Journal of Educational Psychology, 79*, 243–248.

Rees, G. (2008). The anatomy of blindsight. *Brain, 131*, 1414–1415.

Regier, T., Kay, P., & Cook, R. S. (2005). Focal colors are universal after all. *Proceedings of the National Academy of Sciences of the United States of America, 102*, 8386–8391.

Reicher, G. M. (1969). Perceptual recognition as a function of meaningfulness of stimulus material. *Journal of Experimental Psychology, 81*, 275–280.

Reines, M. F., & Prinz, J. (2009). Reviving Whorf: The return of linguistic relativity. *Philosophy Compass, 4/6*, 1022–1032.

Reinholdt-Dunne, M. L., Mogg, K., & Bradley, B. P. (2009). Effects of anxiety and attention control on processing pictorial and linguistic emotional information. *Behaviour Research and Therapy, 47*, 410–417.

Reisberg, D., Culver, L. C., Heuer, F., & Fischman, D. (1986). Visual memory: When imagery vividness makes a difference. *Journal of Mental Imagery, 10*(4), 51–74.

Reitman, J. S. (1971). Mechanisms of forgetting in short-term memory. *Cognitive Psychology, 2*, 185–195.

Reitman, J. S. (1974). Without surreptitious rehearsal, information in short-term memory decays. *Journal of Verbal Learning and Verbal Behavior, 13*, 365–377.

Reitman, J. S. (1976). Skilled perception in Go: Deducing memory structures from inter-response times. *Cognitive Psychology, 8*, 336–356.

Remez, R. E. (1994). A guide to research on the perception of speech. In M. A. Gernsbacher (Ed.), *Handbook of psycholinguistics* (pp. 145–172). San Diego: Academic Press.

Repacholi, B. M., & Meltzoff A. N. (2007). Emotional eavesdropping: Infants selectively respond to indirect emotional signals. *Child Development, 78*(2), 503–521.

Resches, M., & Perez Pereira, M. (2007). Referential communication abilities and Theory of Mind development in preschool children. *Journal of Child Language, 34*(1), 21–52.

Rescorla, R. A. (1967). Pavlovian conditioning and its proper control procedures. *Psychological Review, 74*, 71–80.

Rescorla, R. A., & Wagner, A. R. (1972). A theory of Pavlovian conditioning: Variations in the effectiveness of reinforcement and non-reinforcement. In A. H. Black & W. F. Prokasy (Eds.), *Classical conditioning: Vol. 2. Current research and theory.* New York: Appleton-Century-Crofts.

Reverberi, C., Cherubini, P., Frackowiak, R. S. J., Caltagirone, C., Paulesu, E., & Macaluso, E. (2010). Conditional and syllogistic deductive tasks dissociate functionally during premise integration. *Human Brain Mapping, 31*(9), 1430–1445.

Rey, G. (2003). Language of thought. In L. Nadel (Ed.), *Encyclopedia of cognitive science* (Vol. 2, pp. 753–760). London: Nature Group Press.

Rhodes, G., Byatt, G., Michie, P. T., & Puce, A. (2004). Is the fusiform face area specialized for faces, individuation, or expert individuation? *Journal of Cognitive Neuroscience, 16*(2), 189–203.

Rice, M. L. (1989). Children's language acquisition. *American Psychologist, 44*, 149–156.

Richardson-Klavehn, A., & Bjork, R. A. (1988). Measures of memory. *Annual Review of Psychology, 39*, 475–543.

Richardson-Klavehn, A. R., & Bjork, R. A. (2003). Memory, long-term. In L. Nadel (Ed.), *Encyclopedia of cognitive science* (Vol. 2, pp. 1096–1105). London: Nature Publishing Group.

Riedel, G., Platt, B., & Micheau, J. (2003). Glutamate receptor function in learning and memory. *Behavioural Brain Research, 140*, 1–47.

Riggs, L. A., Ratliff, F., Cornsweet, J. C., & Cornsweet, T. N. (1953). The disappearance of steadily fixated visual test objects. *Journal of the Optical Society of America, 43*, 495–501.

Rinck, F., Rouby, C., & Bensafi, M. (2009). Which format for odor images? *Chemical Senses, 34*, 11–13.

Rips, L. J. (1988). Deduction. In R. J. Sternberg & E. E. Smith (Eds.), *The psychology of human thought* (pp. 116–152). New York: Cambridge University Press.

Rips, L. J. (1989). Similarity, typicality, and categorization. In S. Vosniadou & A. Ortony (Eds.), *Similarity and analogical reasoning* (pp. 21–59). New York: Cambridge University Press.

Rips, L. J. (1994). Deductive reasoning. In R. J. Sternberg (Ed.), *Handbook of perception and cognition: Thinking and problem solving* (pp. 149–178). New York: Academic Press.

Rips, L. J. (1999). Deductive reasoning. In R. A. Wilson & F. C. Keil (Eds.), *The MIT Encyclopedia of the cognitive sciences* (pp. 225–226). Cambridge, MA: MIT Press.

Ro, T., & Rafal, R. (2006). Visual restoration in cortical blindness: Insights from natural and TMS-induced blindsight. *Neuropsychological Rehabilitation, 16*(4), 377–396.

Robbins, S. E. (2009). The COST of explicit memory. *Phenomenology and the Cognitive Sciences, 8*, 33–66.

Roberson, D., Davidoff, J., Davies, I. R. L., & Shapiro, L. R. (2005). Color categories: Evidence for the cultural relativity hypothesis. *Cognitive Psychology, 50*(4), 378–411.

Roberson, D., Davies, I., & Davidoff, J. (2000). Color categories are not universal: replications and new evidence from a stone age culture. *Journal of Experimental Psychology: General, 129*, 369–398.

Roberson, D., & Hanley, J. (2007). Color vision: Color categories vary with language after all. *Current Biology, 17*(15), R605–R607.

Roberson-Nay, R., McClure, E. B., Monk, C. S., Nelson, E. E., Guyer, A. E., Fromm, S. J., et al. (2006). Increased amygdala activation during successful memory encoding in adolescent major depressive disorder: An fMRI study. *Biological Psychiatry, 60*(9), 966–973.

Roberts, A. C., Robbins, T. W., & Weiskrantz, L. (1996). Executive and cognitive functions of the prefrontal cortex. *Philosophical Transactions of the Royal Society (London), B, 351*, (1346).

Roberts, J. E., & Bell, M. A. (2000a). Sex differences on a computerized mental rotation task disappear with computer familiarization. *Perceptual and Motor Skills, 91*, 1027–1034.

Roberts, J. E., & Bell, M. A. (2000b). Sex differences on a mental rotation task: Variations in electroencephalogram hemispheric activation between children and college students. *Developmental Neuropsychology, 17*(2), 199–223.

Roberts, J. E., & Bell, M. A. (2003). Two- and three-dimensional mental rotation tasks lead to different parietal laterality for men and women. *International Journal of Psychophysiology, 50*, 235–246.

Robinson, S. R. (2005). Conjugate limb coordination after experience with an interlimb yoke: Evidence for motor learning in the rat fetus. *Developmental Psychobiology, 47*(4), 328–344.

Roca, I. M. (2003a). Phonetics. In L. Nadel (Ed.), *Encyclopedia of cognitive science* (Vol. 3, pp. 619–625). London: Nature Group Press.

Roca, I. M. (2003b). Phonology. In L. Nadel (Ed.), *Encyclopedia of cognitive science* (Vol. 3, pp. 637–645). London: Nature Group Press.

Rock, I. (1983). *The logic of perception.* Cambridge, MA: MIT Press.

Rockland, K. S. (2000). Brain. In A. E. Kazdin (Ed.), *Encyclopedia of psychology* (Vol. 1, pp. 447–455). Washington, DC: American Psychological Association.

Rode, G., Rossetti, Y., Perenin, M.-T., & Boisson, D. (2004). Geographic information has to be spatialised to be neglected: a representational neglect case. *Cortex, 40*(2), 391–397.

Rodrigue, K. M., Kennedy, K. M., & Raz, N. (2005). Aging and longitudinal change in perceptual-motor skill acquisition in healthy adults. *Journals of Gerontology: Series B: Psychological Sciences and Social Sciences, 60*(4), 174–181.

Rodriguez, A., & Bohlin, G. (2005) Are maternal smoking and stress during pregnancy related to ADHD symptoms in children? *Journal of Child Psychology and Psychiatry, 46*(3), 246–254.

Roediger, H. L. (1980). The effectiveness of four mnemonics in ordering recall. *Journal of Experimental Psychology: Human Learning & Memory, 6*(5), 558–567.

Roediger, H. L. & Karpicke, J. D. (2006). The power of testing memory: Basic research and implications for educational practice. *Perspectives on Psychological Science, 1*, 181–210.

Roediger, H. L., & McDermott, K. B. (2000). Distortions of memory. In E. Tulving & F. I. M. Craik (Eds.), *The Oxford handbook of memory* (pp. 149–162). New York: Oxford University Press.

Roediger, H. L., McDermott, K. B., & McDaniel, M. A. (2011). Using testing to improve learning and memory. In M. A. Gernsbacher, R. Pew, L. Hough, & J. R. Pomerantz (Eds.), *Psychology and the real world: Essays illustrating fundamental contributions to society.* (pp. 65–74). New York: Worth Publishing Co.

Roediger, H. L., III, Balota, D. A., & Watson, J. M. (2001). Spreading activation and arousal of false memories. In H. L. Roediger III, J. S. Nairne, I. Neath, & A. M. Surprenant (Eds.), *The nature of remembering* (pp. 95–115). Washington, DC: American Psychological Association.

Roediger, H. L., III., & McDermott, K. B. (1995). Creating false memories: Remembering words not presented in lists. *Journal of Experimental Psychology: Learning, Memory, and Cognition, 21*, 803–814.

Rofe, Y. (2008). Does repression exist? Memory, pathogenic, unconscious and clinical Evidence. *Review of General Psychology, 12*(1), 63–85.

Rogers, R. D., Ramnani, N., Mackay, C., Wilson, J. L., Jezzard, P., Carter, C. S., et al. (2004). Distinct portions of anterior cingulate cortex and medial prefrontal cortex are activated by reward processing in separable phases of decision-making cognition. *Biological Psychiatry, 55*(6), 594–602.

Rogers, T. B., Kuiper, N. A., & Kirker, W. S. (1977). Self-reference and the encoding of personal information. *Journal of Personality & Social Psychology*, 35(9), 677–688.

Rogers, T. T., & McClelland, J. L. (2008). Precis of semantic cognition: A parallel distributed processing approach. *Behavioral and Brain Sciences*, 31, 689–749.

Rogers, W. A., Pak, R., & Fisk, A. D. (2007). Applied cognitive psychology in the context of everyday living. In F. T. Durso, R. S. Nickerson, S. T. Dumais, S. Lewandowsky & T. J. Perfect (Eds.), *Handbook of applied cognition* (pp. 3–27). Hoboken, NJ: John Wiley & Sons.

Rogers, Y., Rutherford, A, & Bibby, P. A. (Eds.) (1992). *Models in the mind: Theory, perspective and application*. London: Academic Press.

Rogoff, B. (1986). The development of strategic use of context in spatial memory. In M. Perlmutter (Ed.), *Perspectives on intellectual development*. Hillsdale, NJ: Erlbaum.

Rohde, D. L. T., & Plaut, D. C. (1999). Language acquisition in the absence of explicit negative evidence: How important is starting small? *Cognition*, 72, 67–109.

Roney, C. J. R., & Trick, L. M. (2009). Sympathetic magic and perceptions of randomness: The hot hand versus the gambler's fallacy. *Thinking & Reasoning*, 15(2), 197–210.

Roozendaal, B. (2002). Stress and memory: Opposing effects of glucocorticoids on memory consolidation and memory retrieval. *Neurobiology of Learning and Memory*, 78, 578–595.

Roozendaal, B. (2003). Systems mediating acute glucocorticoid effects on memory consolidation and retrieval. *Progress in Neuro-Psychopharmacology and Biological Psychiatry*, 27(8), 1213–1223.

Roozendaal, B., Barsegyan, A., & Lee, S. (2008). Adrenal stress hormones, amygdala activation, and memory for emotionally arousing experiences. *Progress in Brain Research*, 167, 79–97.

Rosch, E. H. (1975). Cognitive representations of semantic categories. *Journal of Experimental Psychology: General*, 104, 192–233.

Rosch, E. H. (1978). Principles of categorization. In E. Rosch & B. B. Lloyd (Eds.), *Cognition and categorization*. Hillsdale, NJ: Erlbaum.

Rosch, E. H., & Mervis, C. B. (1975). Family resemblances: Studies in the internal structure of categories. *Cognitive Psychology*, 7, 573–605.

Rosch, E. H., Mervis, C. B., Gray, W. D., Johnson, D. M., & Boyes-Braem, P. (1976). Basic objects in natural categories. *Cognitive Psychology*, 8, 382–439.

Rosch Heider, K. G. (1972). Universals in color naming and memory. *Journal of Experimental Psychology*, 93(1), 10–20.

Rosenberg, K., Liebling, R., Avidan, G., Perry, D., Siman-Tov, T., Andelman, F., et al. (2008). Language related reorganization in adult brain with slow growing glioma: fMRI prospective case-study. *Neurocase*, 14(6), 465–473.

Rosenzweig, M. R., & Leiman, A. L. (1989). *Physiological psychology* (2nd ed.). New York: Random House.

Ross, B. H. (1997). The use of categories affects classification. *Journal of Memory and Language*, 37, 165–192.

Ross, B. H. (2000). Concepts: Learning. In A. E. Kazdin (Ed.), *Encyclopedia of psychology* (Vol. 2, pp. 248–251). Washington, DC: American Psychological Association.

Ross, B. H., & Spalding, T. L. (1994). Concepts and categories. In R. J. Sternberg (Ed.), *Handbook of perception and cognition: Vol. 12. Thinking and problem solving* (pp. 119–148). New York: Academic Press.

Ross, L., Greene, D., & House, P. (1977). The false consensus effect: An egocentric bias in social perception and attribution processes. *Journal of Experimental Social Psychology*, 13(3), 279–301.

Ross, M., & Sicoly, F. (1979). Egocentric biases in availability and attribution. *Journal of Personality and Social Psychology*, 37, 322–336.

Rostad, K., Mayer, A., Fung, T. S., & Brown, L. N. (2007). Sex-related differences in the correlations for tactile temporal thresholds, interhemispheric transfer times, and nonverbal intelligence. *Personality and Individual Differences*, 43, 1733–1743.

Rostain, A. L., & Tamsay, J. R. (2006). A combined treatment approach for adults with ADHD—results of an open study of 43 patients. *Journal of Attention Disorders*, 10(2), 150–159.

Roswarski, T. E., & Murray, M. D. (2006). Supervision of students may protect academic physicians from cognitive bias: A study of decision making and multiple treatment alternatives in medicine. *Medical Decision Making*, 26(2), 154–161.

Rouder, J. N., & Ratcliff, R. (2004). Comparing categorization models. *Journal of Experimental Psychology: General*, 133(1), 63–82.

Rouder, J. N., & Ratcliff, R. (2006). Comparing exemplar- and rule-based theories of categorization. *Current Directions in Psychological Science*, 15(1), 9–13.

Rovee-Collier, C., & DuFault, D. (1991). Multiple contexts and memory retrieval at three months. *Developmental Psychobiology*, 24(1), 39–49.

Rubin, D. C. (1982). On the retention function for autobiographical memory. *Journal of Verbal Learning and Verbal Behavior*, 19, 21–38.

Rubin, D. C. (Ed.). (1996). *Remembering our past: Studies in autobiographical memory*. New York: Cambridge University Press.

Rubin, Z., Hill, C. T., Peplau, L. A., & Dunkel-Schetter, C. (1980). Self-disclosure in dating couples: Sex roles and the ethic of openness. *Journal of Marriage and the Family*, 42, 305–317.

Rudkin, S. J., Pearson, D. G., & Logie, R. H. (2007). Executive processes in visual and spatial working memory tasks. *Quarterly Journal of Experimental Psychology*, 60(1), 79–100.

Rudner, M., Fransson, P., Ingvar, M., Nyberg, L., & Rönnberg J. (2007). Neural representation of binding lexical signs and words in the episodic buffer of working memory. *Neuropsychologia*, 45(10), 2258–2276.

Ruffman, T., Perner, J., Naito, M., Parkin, L., & Clements, W. A. (1998). Older (but not younger) siblings facilitate false belief understanding. *Developmental Psychology*, 34, 161–174.

Rugg, M. D. (Ed.) (1997). *Cognitive neuroscience*. Hove East Sussex, UK: Psychology Press.

Rumain, B., Connell, J., & Braine, M. D. S. (1983). Conversational comprehension processes are responsible for reasoning fallacies in children as well as adults: If is not the biconditional. *Developmental Psychology*, 19(4), 471–481.

Rumbaugh, D. M., & Beran, M. J. (2003). Language acquisition by animals. In L. Nadel (Ed.), *Encyclopedia of cognitive science* (Vol. 2, pp. 700–707). London: Nature Group Press.

Rumelhart, D. E., & McClelland, J. L. (1981). Interactive processing through spreading activation. In A. M. Lesgold & C. A. Perfetti (Eds.), *Interactive processes in reading* (pp. 37–60). Hillsdale, NJ: Erlbaum.

Rumelhart, D. E., & McClelland, J. L. (1982). An interactive activation model of context effects in letter perception: Part 2. The contextual enhancement effect and some tests and extensions of the model. *Psychological Review*, 89, 60–94.

Rumelhart, D. E., & Norman, D. A. (1988). Representation in memory. In R. C. Atkinson, R. J. Herrnstein, G. Lindzey, R. D. Luce (Eds.), *Stevens' handbook of experimental psychology: Vol. 2. Learning and cognition* (2nd ed., pp. 511–587). New York: Wiley.

Rumelhart, D. E., & Ortony, A. (1977). The representation of knowledge in memory. In R. C. Anderson, R. J. Spiro, & W. E. Montague (Eds.), *Schooling and the acquisition of knowledge* (pp. 99–135). Hillsdale, NJ: Erlbaum.

Runco, M. A. (2010). Divergent thinking, creativity, and ideation. In J. C. Kaufman & R. J. Sternberg (Eds.), *The Cambridge handbook of creativity* (pp. 413–446). New York: Cambridge University Press.

Runco, M. A., & Albert, R. S. (2010). Creativity research: A historical view. In J. C. Kaufman & R. J. Sternberg (Eds.), *The Cambridge handbook of creativity* (pp. 3–19). New York: Cambridge University Press.

Russell, J. A., & Ward, L. M. (1982). Environmental psychology. *Annual Review of Psychology, 33*, 651–688.

Russell, W. R., & Nathan, P. W. (1946). Traumatic amnesia. *Brain, 69*, 280–300.

Rychkova, S. I., & Ninio, J. (2009). Paradoxical fusion of two images and depth perception with a squinting eye. *Vision Research, 49*, 530–535.

Rychlak, J. E., & Struckman, A. (2000). Psychology: Post-World War II. In A. E. Kazdin (Ed.), *Encyclopedia of psychology* (Vol. 6, pp. 410–416). Washington, DC: American Psychological Association.

Ryle, G. (1949). *The concept of mind*. London: Hutchinson.

Saarinen, J. (1987a). Perception of positional relationships between line segments in eccentric vision. *Perception, 16*(5), 583–591.

Saarinen, T. F. (1987b). *Centering of mental maps of the world* (discussion paper). University of Arizona, Tucson: Department of Geography and Regional Development.

Sabsevitz, D. S., Medler, D. A., Seidenberg, M., & Binder, J. R. (2005). Modulation of the semantic system by word imageability. *NeuroImage, 27*, 188–200.

Sacks, H., Schegloff, E. A., & Jefferson, G. (1974). A simplest systematics for the organization of turn-taking for conversation. *Language, 50*, 696–735.

Saffran, J. R. (2001). Words in a sea of sounds: The output of infant statistical learning. *Cognition, 81*, 149–169.

Saffran, J. R., Newport, E. L., & Aslin, R. N. (1996). Word segmentation: The role of distributed cues. *Journal of Memory and Language, 35*, 606–621.

Saito, S., & Baddeley, A. D. (2004). Irrelevant sound disrupts speech production: Exploring the relationship between short-term memory and experimentally induced slips of the tongue. *The Quarterly Journal of Experimental Psychology Section A: Human Experimental Psychology, 57A*(7), 1309–1340.

Salas, E., Burke, C. S., & Cannon-Bowers, J. A. (2000). Teamwork: Emerging principles. *International Journal of Management Reviews, 2*(4), 305–379.

Salat, D. H., Van der Kouwe, A. J. W., Tuch, D. S., Quinn, B. T., Fischl, B., Dale, A. M., et al. (2006). Neuroimaging H. M.: A 10-year follow-up examination. *Hippocampus, 16*(11), 936–945.

Salovey, P., & Sluyter, D. J. (Eds.) (1997). *Emotional development and emotional intelligence: Implications for educators*. New York: Basic Books.

Salthouse, T. A. (1984). Effects of age and skill in typing. *Journal of Experimental Psychology: General, 113*, 345–371.

Salthouse, T. A., & Somberg, B. L. (1982). Skilled performance: Effects of adult age and experience on elementary processes. *Journal of Experimental Psychology: General, 111*(2), 176–207.

Samanez-Larkin, G. R., Robertson, E. R., Mikels, J. A., Carstensen, L. L., & Gotlib, I. H. (2009). Selective attention to emotion in the aging brain. *Psychology and Aging, 24*(3), 519–529.

Samuel, A. G. (1981). Phonemic restoration: Insights from a new methodology. *Journal of Experimental Psychology: General, 110*, 474–494.

Samuel, A. L. (1963). Some studies in machine learning using the game of checkers. In E. A. Feigenbaum & J. Feldman (Eds.), *Computers and thought* (pp. 71–105). New York: McGraw-Hill.

Samuels, J. J. (1999). Developing reading fluency in learning disabled students. In R. J. Sternberg & L. Spear-Swerling (Eds.), *Perspectives on learning disabilities: Biological, cognitive, contextual* (pp. 176–189). Boulder, CO: Westview Press.

Sapir, E. (1964). *Culture, language and personality*. Berkeley, CA: University of California Press. (Original work published 1941)

Sarter, M., Bruno, J. P., & Berntson, G. G. (2003). Reticular activating system. In L. Nadel (Ed.), *Encyclopedia of cognitive science* (Vol. 3, pp. 963–967). London: Nature Publishing Group.

Sasaki, T. (2008). Working memory load in the initial learning phase facilitates relearning: A study of vocabulary learning. *Perceptual and Motor Skills, 106*(1), 317–327.

Savage-Rumbaugh, S., McDonald, K., Sevcik, R. A., Hopkins, W. D., & Rubert, E. (1986). Spontaneous symbol acquisition and communicative use by pygmy chimpanzees *(Pan paniscus)*. *Journal of Experimental Psychology: General, 115*, 211–235.

Savage-Rumbaugh, S., Murphy, J., Sevcik, R., Brakke, K., Williams, S., & Rumbaugh, D. M. (1993). Language comprehension in ape and child. *Monographs of the Society for Research in Child Development, 58*(3–4, Serial No. 233).

Scaggs, W. E., & McNaughton, B. L. (1996). Replay of neuronal firing sequences in rat hippocampus during sleep following spatial experience. *Science, 271*, 1870–1873.

Schacter, D. L. (1989). On the relation between memory and consciousness: Dissociable interactions and conscious experience. In H. L. Roediger & F. I. M. Craik (Eds.), *Varieties of memory and consciousness: Essays in honor of Endel Tulving*. Hillsdale, NJ: Erlbaum.

Schacter, D. L. (2000). Memory: Memory systems. In A. E. Kazdin (Ed.), *Encyclopedia of psychology* (Vol. 5, pp. 169–172). Washington, DC: American Psychological Association.

Schacter, D. L. (2001). *The seven sins of memory: How the mind forgets and remembers*. Boston: Houghton Mifflin.

Schacter, D. L., & Curran, T. (2000). Memory without remembering and remembering without memory: Implicit and false memories. In M. S. Gazzaniga (Ed.), *The new cognitive neurosciences* (2nd ed., pp. 829–840). Cambridge, MA: MIT Press.

Schacter, D. L., Verfaellie, M., & Pradere, D. (1996). The neuropsychology of memory illusions: False recall and recognition in amnesic patients. *Journal of Memory and Language, 35*, 319–334.

Schaeken, W., Johnson-Laird, P. N., & D'Ydewalle, G. (1996). Mental models and temporal reasoning. *Cognition, 60*, 205–234.

Schaffer, H. R. (1977). *Mothering*. Cambridge, MA: Harvard University Press.

Schank, R. C., & Abelson, R. P. (1977). *Scripts, plans, goals, and understanding*. Hillsdale. NJ: Erlbaum.

Schank, R. C., & Towle, B. (2000). Artificial intelligence. In R. J. Sternberg (Ed.), *Handbook of intelligence* (pp. 341–356). New York: Cambridge University Press.

Scheck, P., & Nelson, T. O. (2003). Metacognition. In L. Nadel (Ed.), *Encyclopedia of cognitive science* (Vol. 3, pp. 11–15). London: Nature Publishing Group.

Scheibehenne, B., Miesler, L., & Todd, P. M. (2007). Fast and frugal food choices: Uncovering individual decision heuristics. *Appetite, 49*(3), 578–589.

Schienle, A., Schaefer, A., & Vaitl, D. (2008). Individual differences in disgust imagery: a functional magnetic resonance imaging study. *Brain Imaging, 19*(5), 527–530.

Schindler, I., Clavagnier, S., Karnath, H. O., Derex, L., & Perenin, M. T. (2006). A common basis for visual and tactile exploration deficits in spatial neglect? *Neuropsychologia, 44*(8), 1444–1451.

Schirduan, V., & Case, K. (2004). Mindful curriculum leadership for students with attention deficit hyperactivity disorder: Leading in elementary schools by using multiple intelligences theory (SUMIT). *Teachers College Record, 106*(1), 87–95.

Schmidt, H. G., Peech, V. H., Paas, F., & Van Breukelen, G. J. P. (2000). Remembering the street names of one's childhood neighbourhood: A study of very long-term retention. *Memory, 8*(1), 37–49.

Schmiedek, F., MacLean, K. A., Oberauer, K., Wilhelm, O., Suess, H.-M., & Wittmann, W. W. (2007). Individual Differences in Components of Reaction Time Distributions and Their Relations to Working Memory and Intelligence. *Journal of Experimental Psychology: General, 136*(3), 414–429.

Schneider, W., & Bjorklund, D. F. (1998). Memory. In W. Damon (Ed.-in-Chief), D. Kuhn, & R. S. Siegler (Vol. Eds.), *Handbook of child psychology: Vol. 2. Cognitive development* (pp. 467–521). New York: Wiley.

Schneider, W., & Shiffrin, R. M. (1977). Controlled and automatic human information processing. *Psychological Review, 84,* 1–66.

Schnider, A. (2008). *The confabulating mind: How the brain creates reality.* New York: Oxford University Press.

Schoenfeld, A. H. (1981). *Episodes and executive decisions in mathematical problem solving.* Paper presented at the annual meeting of the American Educational Research Association, Los Angeles, CA.

Schonbein, W., & Bechtel, W. (2003). History of computational modeling and cognitive science. *Encyclopedia of Cognitive Science.* London, England: Nature Publishing Group.

Schooler, J. W. (1994). Seeking the core: The issues and evidence surrounding recovered accounts of sexual trauma. *Consciousness and Cognition, 3,* 452–469.

Schooler, J. W., & Engstler-Schooler, T. Y. (1990). Verbal overshadowing of visual memories: Some things are better left unsaid. *Cognitive Psychology, 22,* 36–71.

Schvaneveldt, R. W., Meyer, D. E., & Becker, C. A. (1976). Lexical ambiguity, semantic context, and visual word recognition. *Journal of Experimental Psychology: Human Perception & Performance, 2*(2), 243–256.

Schwartz, D. L. (1996). Analog imagery in mental model reasoning: Depictive models. *Cognitive Psychology, 30,* 154–219.

Schwartz, D. L., & Black, J. B. (1996). Analog imagery in mental model reasoning: Depictive models. *Cognitive Psychology, 30,* 154–219.

Schwarz, N., & Skurnik, I. (2003). Feeling and thinking: Implications for problem solving. In J. E. Davidson & R. J. Sternberg (Eds.), *The psychology of problem solving* (pp. 263–290). New York: Cambridge University Press.

Schweickert, R., & Boruff, B. (1986). Short-term memory capacity: Magic number or magic spell? *Journal of Experimental Psychology: Learning, Memory, & Cognition, 12*(3), 419–425.

Scott, L. S., Tanaka, J. W., Sheinberg, D. L., & Curran, T. (2008). The role of category learning in the acquisition and retention of perceptual expertise: A behavioral and neurophysiological study. *Brain Research, 1210,* 204–215.

Scovel, T. (2000). A critical review of the critical period research. *Annual Review of Applied Linguistics, 20,* 213–223.

Scoville, W. B., & Milner, B. (1957). Loss of recent memory after bilateral hippocampal lesions. *Journal of Neurology, Neurosurgery, and Psychiatry, 20,* 11–19.

Seal, M. L., Aleman, A., & McGuire, P. K. (2004). Compelling imagery, unanticipated speech and deceptive memory: Neurocognitive models of auditory verbal hallucinations in schizophrenia. *Cognitive Neuropsychiatry, 9*(1–2), 43–72.

Searle, J. R. (1975a). Indirect speech acts. In P. Cole & J. L. Morgan (Eds.), *Syntax and semantics: Speech acts* (Vol. 3, pp. 59–82). New York: Seminar Press.

Searle, J. R. (1975b). A taxonomy of elocutionary acts. In K. Gunderson (Ed.), *Minnesota studies in the philosophy of language* (pp. 344–369). Minneapolis: University of Minnesota Press.

Searle, J. R. (1979). *Expression and meaning: Studies in the theory of speech acts.* Cambridge, UK: Cambridge University Press.

Seguino, S. (2007). *Plus ça change?* Evidence on global trends in gender norms and stereotypes. *Feminist Economics, 13*(2), 1–28.

Sehulster, J. R. (1989). Content and temporal structure of autobiographical knowledge: Remembering twenty-five seasons at the Metropolitan Opera. *Memory and Cognition, 17,* 290–606.

Seifert, C. M., Meyer, D. E., Davidson, N., Palatano, A. L., & Yaniv, I. (1995). Demystification of cognitive insight: Opportunistic assimilation and the prepare-mind perspective. In R. J. Sternberg & J. E. Davidson (Eds.), *The nature of insight* (pp. 65–124). Cambridge, MA: MIT Press.

Seizova-Cajic, T. (2003). The role of perceived relative position in pointing to objects apparently shifted by depth-contrast. *Spatial Vision, 6*(3–4), 325–346.

Selfridge, O. G. (1959). Pandemonium: A paradigm for learning. In D. V. Blake & A. M. Uttley (Eds.), *Proceedings of the Symposium on the Mechanization of Thought Processes* (pp. 511–529). London: Her Majesty's Stationery Office.

Selfridge, O. G., & Neisser, U. (1960). Pattern recognition by machine. *Scientific American, 203,* 60–68.

Selkoe, D. J. (2002). Alzheimer's disease is a synaptic failure. *Science, 298,* 789–791.

Seo, D. C., & Torabi, M. R. (2004). The impact of in-vehicle cell-phone use on accidents or near-accidents among college students. *Journal of American College Health, 53*(3), 101–107.

Sera, M. D. (1992). To be or to be: Use and acquisition of the Spanish copulas. *Journal of Memory and Language, 31,* 408–427.

Serpell, R. (2000). Intelligence and culture. In R. J. Sternberg (Ed.), *Handbook of intelligence* (pp. 549–577). New York: Cambridge University Press.

Shafir, E. B., Osherson, D. N., & Smith, E. E. (1990). Typicality and reasoning fallacies. *Memory & Cognition, 18*(3), 229–239.

Shah, A. K., & Oppenheimer, D. M. (2008). Heuristics made easy: An effort-reduction framework. *Psychological Bulletin, 134*(2), 207–222.

Shahin, A. J., Bishop, C. W., & Miller, L. M. (2009). Neural mechanisms for illusory filling-in of degraded speech. *NeuroImage, 44*(3), 1133–1143.

Shallice, T. (1979). Neuropsychological research and the fractionation of memory systems. In L. G. Nilsson (Ed.), *Perspectives on memory research.* Hillsdale, NJ: Erlbaum.

Shallice, T., & Warrington, E. (1970). Independent functioning of verbal memory stores: A neuropsychological study. *Quarterly Journal of Experimental Psychology, 22*(2), 261–273.

Shankweiler, D., Crain, D. S., Katz, L., Fowler, A. E., Liberman, A. M., Brady, S. A., et al. (1995). Cognitive profiles of reading-disabled children: Comparison of language skills in phonology, morphology, and syntax. *Psychological Science, 6,* 149–156.

Shannon, C., & Weaver, W. (1963). *The mathematical theory of communication.* Urbana, IL: University of Illinois Press.

Shapiro, P., & Penrod, S. (1986). Meta-analysis of facial identification studies. *Psychological Bulletin, 100*(2), 139–156.

Shapley, R., & Lennie, P. (1985). Spatial frequency analysis in the visual system. *Annual Review of Neuroscience, 8,* 547–583.

Shastri, L. (2003). Spreading-activation networks. In L. Nadel (Ed.), *Encyclopedia of cognitive science* (Vol. 4, pp. 211–218). London: Nature Publishing Group.

Shaywitz, S. E. (2005). *Overcoming dyslexia.* New York: Knopf.

Shaywitz, S. E., & Shaywitz, B. A. (2005). Dyslexia (specific reading disability). *Biological Psychiatry, 57*(11), 1301–1309.

Shear, J. (Ed.) (1997). *Explaining consciousness: The hard problem.* Cambridge, MA: MIT Press.

Shelton, S. T. (2006). Jury decision making: Using group theory to improve deliberation. *Politics & Policy, 34*(4), 706–725.

Shepard, R. N. (1984). Ecological constraints on internal representation. Resonant kinematics of perceiving, imaging, thinking, and dreaming. *Psychological Review, 91*, 417–447.

Shepard, R. N., & Metzler, J. (1971). Mental rotation of three-dimensional objects. *Science, 171*(3972), 701–703.

Shepherd, G. (Ed.) (1998). *The synaptic organization of the brain*. New York: Oxford University Press.

Shepherd, G. M. (2004). *The synaptic organization of the brain* (5th ed.). New York: Oxford University Press.

Shiffrin, R. M. (1973). Information persistence in short-term memory. *Journal of Experimental Psychology, 100*, 39–49.

Shiffrin, R. M. (1996). Laboratory experimentation on the genesis of expertise. In K. A. Ericsson (Ed.), *The road to excellence* (pp. 337–347). Mahwah, NJ: Erlbaum.

Shiffrin, R. M., & Schneider, W. (1977). Controlled and automatic human information processing: II. Perceptual learning, automatic attending, and a general theory. *Psychological Review, 84*, 127–190.

Shin, N., Jonassen, D. H., & McGee, S. (2003). Predictors of well-structured and ill-structured problem solving in astronomy simulation. *Journal of Research in Science Teaching, 40*(1), 6–33.

Shinoura, N., Suzukib, Y., Yamada, R., Tabeia, Y., Saitoa, K., & Yagib, K. (2009). Damage to the right superior longitudinal fasciculus in the inferior parietal lobe plays a role in spatial neglect. *Neuropsychologia, 47*, 2600–2603.

Shoben, E. J. (1984). Semantic and episodic memory. In R. W. Wyer, Jr., & T. K. Srull (Eds.), *Handbook of social cognition* (Vol. 2, pp. 213–231). Hillsdale, NJ: Erlbaum.

Shohamy, D., Myers, C. E., Kalanithi, J., & Gluck, M. A. (2009). Basal ganglia and dopamine contributions to probabilistic category learning. *Neuroscience & Biobehavioral Reviews, 32*(2), 219–236.

Shortliffe, E. H. (1976). *Computer-based medical consultations: MYCIN*. New York: American Elsevier.

Shulman, H. G. (1970). Encoding and retention of semantic and phonemic information in short-term memory. *Journal of Verbal Learning and Verbal Behavior, 9*, 499–508.

Siegler, R. S. (1986). *Children's thinking*. Englewood Cliffs, NJ: Prentice-Hall.

Siegler, R. S. (1988). Individual differences in strategy choices: Good students, not-so-good students, and perfectionists. *Child Development, 59*(4), 833–851.

Simon, H. A. (1957). *Administrative behavior* (2nd ed.). Totowa, NJ: Littlefield, Adams.

Simon, H. A. (1976). Identifying basic abilities underlying intelligent performance of complex tasks. In L. B. Resnick (Ed.), *The nature of intelligence* (pp. 65–98). Hillsdale, NJ: Erlbaum.

Simon, H. A. (1999a). Problem solving. In R. A. Wilson & F. C. Keil (Eds.), *The MIT encyclopedia of the cognitive sciences* (pp. 674–676). Cambridge, MA: MIT Press.

Simon, H. A. (1999b). Production systems. In R. A. Wilson & F. C. Keil (Eds.), *The MIT encyclopedia of the cognitive sciences* (pp. 676–678). Cambridge, MA: MIT Press.

Simon, H. A., & Reed, S. K. (1976). Modeling strategy shifts in a problem-solving task. *Cognitive Psychology, 8*, 86–97.

Simons, D. J. (1996). In sight, out of mind: When object representations fail. *Psychological Science, 5*, 301–305.

Simons, D. J. (2007). Inattentional blindness [Electronic Version]. *Scholarpedia, 2*, 3244 from www.scholarpedia.org/article/Inattentional_blindness.

Simons, D. J., & Ambinder, M. S. (2005). Change blindness: Theory and consequences. *Current Directions in Psychological Science, 14*(1), 44–48.

Simons, D. J, & Levin, D. T. (1997). Change blindness. *Trends in Cognitive Science, 1*, 261–267.

Simons, D. J., & Levin, D. T. (1998). Failure to detect changes to people during a real-world interaction. *Psychonomic Bulletin & Review, 5*, 644–649.

Simons, D. J., & Rensink, R. A. (2005). Change blindness: Past, present, and future. *Trends in Cognitive Science, 9*(1), 16–20.

Simonton, D. K. (1988a). Age and outstanding achievement: What do we know after a century of research? *Psychological Bulletin, 104*, 251–267.

Simonton, D. K. (1988b). Creativity, leadership, and chance. In R. J. Sternberg (Ed.), *The nature of creativity* (pp. 386–426). New York: Cambridge University Press.

Simonton, D. K. (1991). Career landmarks in science: Individual differences and interdisciplinary contrasts. *Developmental Psychology, 27*, 119–130.

Simonton, D. K. (1994). *Greatness: Who makes history and why*. New York: Guilford.

Simonton, D. K. (1997). Creativity in personality, developmental, and social psychology: Any links with cognitive psychology? In T. B. Ward, S. M. Smith, & J. Vaid (Eds.), *Creative thought: Conceptual structures and processes* (pp. 309–324). Washington, DC: American Psychological Association.

Simonton, D. K. (1998). Donald Campbell's model of the creative process: Creativity as blind variation and selective retention. *Journal of Creative Behavior, 32*, 153–158.

Simonton, D. K. (1999). Creativity from a historiometric perspective. In R. J. Sternberg (Ed.), *Handbook of creativity* (pp. 116–133). New York: Cambridge University Press.

Simonton, D. K. (2009). Genius, creativity, and leadership. In T. Rickards, M. A. Runco & S. Moger (Eds.), *The Routledge companion to creativity* (pp. 247–255). New York: Routledge.

Simonton, D. K. (2010). Creativity in highly eminent individuals. In J. C. Kaufman & R. J. Sternberg (Eds.), *The Cambridge handbook of creativity* (pp. 174–188). New York: Cambridge University Press.

Simonton, D. K. (2010). Creative thought as blind-variation and selective-retention: Combinatorial models of exceptional creativity. *Physics of Life Reviews, 7*(2), 190–194.

Sincoff, J. B., & Sternberg, R. J. (1988). Development of verbal fluency abilities and strategies in elementary-school-age children. *Developmental Psychology, 24*, 646–653.

Sio, U. N., & Ormerod, T. C. (2009). Does incubation enhance problem solving? A meta-analytic review. *Psychological Bulletin, 135*(1), 94–120.

Skinner, B. F. (1957). *Verbal behavior*. New York: Appleton-Century-Crofts.

Skotko, B. G., Kensinger, E. A., Locascio, J. J., Einstein, G., Rubin, D. C., Tupler, L. A., et al. (2004). Puzzling thoughts for H. M.: Can new semantic information be anchored to old semantic memories? *Neuropsychology, 18*(4), 756–769.

Slobin, D. I. (1971). Cognitive prerequisites for the acquisition of grammar. In C. A. Ferguson & D. I. Slobin (Eds.), *Studies of child language development*. New York: Holt, Rinehart and Winston.

Slobin, D. I. (Ed.). (1985). *The cross-linguistic study of language acquisition*. Hillsdale, NJ: Erlbaum.

Sloboda, J. A. (1984). Experimental studies in music reading: A review. *Music Perception, 22*, 222–236.

Sloman, S. A. (1996). The empirical case for two systems of reasoning. *Psychological Bulletin, 119*, 3–22.

Slovic, P. (1990). Choice. In D. N. Osherson & E. E. Smith (Eds.), *An invitation to cognitive science: Vol. 3. Thinking* (pp. 89–116). Cambridge, MA: MIT Press.

Smith, A. D. (2009). On the use of drawing tasks in neuropsychological assessment. *Neuropsychology 23*(2), 231–239.

Smith, A. D., & Cohen, G. (2008). Memory for places: Routes, maps, and object locations. In G. Cohen & M. A. Conway

(Eds.), *Memory in the real world* (pp. 173–206). New York: Psychology Press.

Smith, C. (1996). Sleep states, memory phases, and synaptic plasticity. *Behavior and Brain Research, 78,* 49–56.

Smith, C., Bibi, U., & Sheard, D. E. (2004). Evidence for the differential impact of time and emotion on personal and event memories for September 11, 2001. *Applied Cognitive Psychology, 17*(9), 1047–1055.

Smith, E. E. (1988). Concepts and thought. In R. J. Sternberg & E. E. Smith (Eds.), *The psychology of human thought* (pp. 19–49). New York: Cambridge University Press.

Smith, E. E. (1995). Concepts and categorization. In E. E. Smith & D. N. Osherson (Eds.), *An invitation to cognitive science: Vol. 3. Thinking* (2nd ed., pp. 3–33). Cambridge, MA: MIT Press.

Smith, E. E., & Medin, D. L. (1981). *Categories and concepts.* Cambridge, MA: Harvard University Press.

Smith, E. E., Osherson, D. N., Rips, L. J., & Keane, M. (1988). Combining prototypes: A modification model. *Cognitive Science, 12,* 485–527.

Smith, E. E., Shoben, E. J., & Rips, L. J. (1974). Structure and process in semantic memory: A featural model for semantic decisions. *Psychological Review, 81,* 214–241.

Smith, F. (2004). *Understanding reading* (6th ed.). Mahwah, NJ: Lawrence Erlbaum.

Smith, J. D. (2005). Wanted: A new psychology of exemplars. *Canadian Journal of Experimental Psychology, 59*(1), 47–53.

Smith, J. K., & Smith, L. F. (2010). Educational creativity. In J. C. Kaufman & R. J. Sternberg (Eds.), *The Cambridge handbook of creativity* (pp. 250–264). New York: Cambridge University Press.

Smith, L. B., & Gilhooly, K. (2006). Regression versus fast and frugal models of decision-making: The case of prescribing for depression. *Applied Cognitive Psychology, 20*(2), 265–274.

Smolensky, P. (1999). Connectionist approaches to language. In R. A. Wilson & F. C. Keil (Eds.), *The MIT encyclopedia of the cognitive sciences* (pp. 188–190). Cambridge, MA: MIT Press.

Snow, C. (1999). Social perspectives on the emergence of language. In B. MacWhinney (Ed.), *The emergence of language* (pp. 257–276). Mahwah, NJ: Erlbaum.

Snow, C. E. (1977). The development of conversation between mothers and babies. *Journal of Child Language, 4,* 1–22.

Snow, J. C., & Mattingley, J. B. (2003). Perception, unconscious. In L. Nadel (Ed.), *Encyclopedia of cognitive science* (Vol. 3, pp. 517–526). London: Nature Publishing Group.

Snowdon, C. T., & Teie, D. (2009). Affective responses in tamarins elicited by species-specific music [Electronic Version]. *Biology Letters.*

Sobel, D. M., & Kirkham, N. Z. (2006). Blickets and babies: The development of causal reasoning in toddlers and infants. *Developmental Psychology, 42*(6), 1103–1115.

Sodian, B., Zaitchik, D., & Carey, S. (1991). Young children's differentiation of hypothetical beliefs from evidence. *Child Development, 62*(4), 753–766.

Sohn, M. H., Ursu, S., Anderson, J. R., Stenger, V. A., & Carter, C. S. (2000). Inaugural article: The role of prefrontal cortex and posterior parietal cortex in task switching. *Proceedings of the National Academy of Sciences, 97,* 13448–13453.

Solso, R., & McCarthy, J. E. (1981). Prototype formation of faces: A case of pseudomemory. *British Journal of Psychology, 72,* 499–503.

Solstad, T., Boccara, C. N., Kropff, E., Moser, M. B., & Moser, E. I. (2008). Representation of geometric borders in the entorhinal cortex. *Science, 322,* 1865–1868.

Sommer, I. E., Aleman, A., Somers, M., Boks, M. P., & Kahna, R. S. (2008). Sex differences in handedness, asymmetry of the Planum Temporale and functional language lateralization. *Brain Research, 1206,* 76–88.

Sommer, R. (1969). *Personal space.* Englewood Cliffs, NJ: Prentice-Hall.

Sommers, S. R. (2006). On racial diversity and group decision making: Identifying multiple effects of racial composition on jury deliberations. *Journal of Personality and Social Psychology, 90*(4), 597–612.

Sook Lee, J., & Oxelson, E. (2006). "It's not my job": K–12 teacher attitudes towards students' heritage language maintenance. *Bilingual Research Journal, 30*(2), 453–477.

Sotak, C. (2002). Diffusion tensor imaging and axonal mapping—state of the art. *NRM in Biomedicine, 15*(7–8), 561–569.

Spang, M. (2005). Your own hall of memories. *Scientific American Mind, 16*(2), 60–65.

Sparing, R., Dafotakis, M., Meister, I. G., Thirugnanasambandam, N., & Fink, G. R. (2008). Enhancing language performance with non-invasive brain stimulation—A transcranial direct current stimulation study in healthy humans. *Neuropsychologia, 46,* 261–268.

Sparr, S. A., Jay, M., Drislane, F. W., & Venna, N. (1991). A historical case of visual agnosia revisited after 40 years. *Brain, 114*(2), 789–790.

Spear, N. E. (1979). Experimental analysis of infantile amnesia. In J. E. Kihlstrom & F. J. Evans (Eds.), *Functional disorders of memory.* Hillsdale, NJ: Erlbaum.

Spear-Swerling, L., & Sternberg, R. J. (1996). *Off-track: When poor readers become learning disabled.* Boulder, CO: Westview.

Spelke, E., Hirst, W., & Neisser, U. (1976). Skills of divided attention. *Cognition, 4,* 215–230.

Spellman, B. A. (1997). Crediting causality. *Journal of Experimental Psychology: General, 126,* 1–26.

Sperling, G. (1960). The information available in brief visual presentations. *Psychological Monographs: General and Applied, 74,* 1–28.

Sperry, R. W. (1964). The great cerebral commissure. *Scientific American, 210*(1), 42–52.

Squire, L. R. (1982). The neuropsychology of human memory. *Annual Review of Neuroscience, 5,* 241–273.

Squire, L. R. (1986). Mechanisms of memory. *Science, 232*(4578), 1612–1619.

Squire, L. R. (1987). *Memory and the brain.* New York: Oxford University Press.

Squire, L. R. (1992). Memory and the hippocampus: A synthesis of findings with rats, monkeys, and humans. *Psychological Review, 99,* 195–231.

Squire, L. R. (1993). The organization of declarative and nondeclarative memory. In T. Ono, L. R. Squire, M. E. Raichle, D. I. Perrett, & M. Fukuda (Eds.), *Brain mechanisms of perception and memory: From neuron to behavior* (pp. 219–227). New York: Oxford University Press.

Squire, L. R., (1999). Memory, human neuropsychology. In R. A. Wilson & F. C. Keil (Eds.), *The MIT encyclopedia of the cognitive sciences* (pp. 521–522). Cambridge, MA: MIT Press.

Squire, L. R., Cohen, N. J., & Nadel, L. (1984). The medial temporal region and memory consolidations: A new hypothesis. In H. Weingardner & E. Parker (Eds.), *Memory consolidation.* Hillsdale, NJ: Erlbaum.

Squire, L. R., & Knowlton, B. J. (2000). The medial temporal lobe, the hippocampus, and the memory systems of the brain. In M. Gazzaniga (Ed.), *The new cognitive neurosciences* (2nd ed., pp. 765–780). Cambridge, MA: MIT Press.

Squire, L. R., Zola-Morgan, S., Cave, C. B., Haist, F., Musen, G., & Suzuki, W. P. (1990). Memory: Organization of brain systems and cognition. In D. E. Meyer & S. Kornblum (Eds.), *Attention and performance: Vol. 14. Synergies in experimental psychology, artificial intelligence, and cognitive neuroscience* (pp. 393–424). Cambridge, MA: MIT Press.

Srinivasan, N. (2008). Interdependence of attention and consciousness. *Progress in Brain Research, 168*, 65–75.

Staller, A., Sloman, S. A., & Ben-Zeev, T. (2000). Perspective effects in non-deontic version of the Wason selection task. *Memory and Cognition, 28*, 396–405.

Standing, L., Conezio, J., & Haber, R. N. (1970). Perception and memory for pictures: Single-trial learning of 2500 visual stimuli. *Psychonomic Science, 19*, 73–74.

Stankiewicz, B. J. (2003). Perceptual systems: The visual model. In L. Nadel (Ed.), *Encyclopedia of cognitive science* (Vol. 3, pp. 552–560). London: Nature Publishing Group.

Stankov, L. (2005). Reductionism versus charting. In R. J. Sternberg & J. E. Pretz (Eds.), *Cognition and intelligence* (pp. 51–67). New York: Cambridge University Press.

Stanovich, K. E. (2003). The fundamental computational biases of human cognition: Heuristics that (sometimes) impair decision making and problem solving. In J. E. Davidson & R. J. Sternberg (Eds.), *The psychology of problem solving* (pp. 291–342). New York: Cambridge University Press.

Stanovich, K. E. (2010). *What intelligence tests miss: The psychology of rational thought.* New Haven, CT: Yale University Press.

Stanovich, K. E., & West, R. F. (1999). Individual differences in reasoning and the heuristics and biases debate. In P. L. Ackerman, P. C. Kyllonen, & R. D. Roberts (Eds.), *Learning and individual differences: Process, trait, and content determinants* (pp. 389–411). Washington, DC: American Psychological Association.

Stapel, D. A., & Semin, G. R. (2007). The magic spell of language: Linguistic categories and their perceptual consequences. *Journal of Personality and Social Psychology, 93*(1), 23–33.

Starr, C., Evers, C. A., & Starr, L. (2007). *Biology: concepts and applications*: Cengage Learning.

Starr, M S., & Rayner, K. (2003). Language comprehension, methodologies for studying. In L. Nadel (Ed.), *Encyclopedia of cognitive science* (Vol. 2, pp. 730–736). London: Nature Group Press.

Steedman, M. (2003). Language, connectionist and symbolic representations of. In L. Nadel (Ed.), *Encyclopedia of cognitive science* (Vol. 2, pp. 765–771). London: Nature Group Press.

Steffanaci, L. (1999). Amygdala, primate. In R. A. Wilson & F. C. Keil (Eds.), *The MIT encyclopedia of the cognitive sciences* (pp. 15–17). Cambridge, MA: MIT Press.

Steif, P. S., Fay, A. L., Kara, L. B., & Spencer, S. E. (2006). Work in progress: Improving problem solving performance in statics through body-centric talk. *ASEE/IEEE Frontiers in Education Conference.*

Stein, M., Federspiel, A., Koenig, T., Wirth, M., Lehmann, C., Wiest, R., et al. (2009). Reduced frontal activation with increasing 2nd language proficiency. *Neuropsychologia, 47*(13), 2712–2720.

Stein, S. J., & Book, H. E. (2006). *The EQ Edge: Emotional intelligence and your success.* Mississuaga, Ontario, Canada: John Wiley & Sons.

Steriade, M., Jones, E. G., & McCormick, D. A. (1997). *Thalamus, organization and function* (Vol. 1). New York: Elsevier.

Stern, D. (1977). *The first relationship: Mother and infant.* Cambridge, MA: Harvard University Press.

Sternberg, R. J. (1977). *Intelligence, information processing, and analogical reasoning: The componential analysis of human abilities.* Hillsdale, NJ: Erlbaum.

Sternberg, R. J. (1979, September). Beyond IQ: Stalking the IQ quark. *Psychology Today,* pp. 42–54.

Sternberg, R. J. (1980). Representation and process in linear syllogistic reasoning. *Journal of Experimental Psychology: General, 109,* 119–159.

Sternberg, R. J. (1981). Intelligence and nonentrenchment. *Journal of Educational Psychology, 73,* 1–16.

Sternberg, R. J. (Ed.). (1982). *Handbook of human intelligence.* New York: Cambridge University Press.

Sternberg, R. J. (1983). Components of human intelligence. *Cognition, 15,* 1–48.

Sternberg, R. J. (Ed.). (1984). *Human abilities: An information-processing approach.* San Francisco: Freeman.

Sternberg, R. J. (1985). *Beyond IQ: A triarchic theory of human intelligence.* New York: Cambridge University Press.

Sternberg, R. J. (1986). *Intelligence applied: Understanding and increasing your intellectual skills.* San Diego: Harcourt Brace Jovanovich.

Sternberg, R. J. (1988). *The triarchic mind.* New York: Viking.

Sternberg, R. J. (1996a). Costs of expertise. In K. A. Ericsson (Ed.), *The road to excellence* (pp. 347–355). Mahwah, NJ: Erlbaum.

Sternberg, R. J. (1996b). Myths, countermyths, and truths about human intelligence. *Educational Researcher, 25*(2), 11–16.

Sternberg, R. J. (1997). *Successful intelligence.* New York: Simon & Schuster.

Sternberg, R. J. (1998). Abilities are forms of developing expertise. *Educational Researcher, 27*(3), 11–20.

Sternberg, R. J. (1999). A dialectical basis for understanding the study of cognition. In R. J. Sternberg (Ed.), *The nature of cognition* (pp. 51–78). Cambridge, MA: MIT Press.

Sternberg, R. J. (2000). Thinking: An overview. In A. Kazdin (Ed.), *Encyclopedia of psychology* (Vol. 8, pp. 68–71). Washington, DC: American Psychological Association.

Sternberg, R. J. (2004). What do we know about the nature of reasoning? In J. P. Leighton & R. J. Sternberg (Eds.), *The nature of reasoning* (pp. 443–455). New York: Cambridge University Press.

Sternberg, R. J., & Detterman, D. K. (Eds.). (1986). *What is intelligence? Contemporary viewpoints on its nature and definition.* Norwood, NJ: Ablex.

Sternberg, R. J., & Grigorenko, E. L. (1997, Fall). The cognitive costs of physical and mental ill health: Applying the psychology of the developed world to the problems of the developing world. *Eye on Psi Chi, 2*(1), 20–27.

Sternberg, R. J., & Grigorenko, E. L. (2004). Successful intelligence in the classroom. *Theory into Practice, 43*(4), 274–280.

Sternberg, R. J., & Grigorenko, E. L. (2006). Cultural intelligence and successful intelligence. *Group & Organization Management, 31*(1), 27–39.

Sternberg, R. J., & Kaufman, J. C. (1996). Innovation and intelligence testing: The curious case of the dog that didn't bark. *European Journal of Psychological Assessment, 12,* 175–182.

Sternberg, R. J., & Kaufman, J. C. (1998). Human abilities. *Annual Review of Psychology, 49,* 479–502.

Sternberg, R. J., Kaufman, J. C., & Pretz, J. E. (2001). The propulsion model of creative contributions applied to the arts and letters. *Journal of Creative Behavior, 35,* 75–101.

Sternberg, R. J., Kaufman, J. C., & Pretz, J. E. (2002). *The creativity conundrum: A propulsion model of kinds of creative contributions.* New York: Psychology Press.

Sternberg, R. J., & Lubart, T. I. (1991). An investment theory of creativity and its development. *Human Development, 34,* 1–31.

Sternberg, R. J., & Lubart, T. I. (1995). *Defying the crowd.* New York: Free Press.

Sternberg, R. J., & Lubart, T. I. (1996). Investing in creativity. *American Psychologist, 51,* 677–688.

Sternberg, R. J., & Nigro, G. (1980). Developmental patterns in the solution of verbal analogies. *Child Development, 51,* 27–38.

Sternberg, R. J., & Nigro, G. (1983). Interaction and analogy in the comprehension and appreciation of metaphors. *Quarterly Journal of Experimental Psychology, 35A,* 17–38.

Sternberg, R. J., & Powell, J. S. (1983). Comprehending verbal comprehension. *American Psychologist, 38,* 878–893.

Sternberg, R. J., & The Rainbow Project Collaborators (2006). The Rainbow Project: Enhancing the SAT through assessments of analytical, practical and creative skills. *Intelligence, 34*(4), 321–350.

Sternberg, R. J., & Spear-Swerling, L. (Eds.) (1999). *Perspectives on learning disabilities*. Boulder, CO: Westview.

Sternberg, R. J., Torff, B., & Grigorenko, E. L. (1998). Teaching for successful intelligence raises school achievement. *Phi Delta Kappan, 79*(9), 667–669.

Sternberg, R. J., & Wagner, R. K. (Eds.). (1994). *Mind in context: Interactionist perspectives on human intelligence*. New York: Cambridge University Press.

Sternberg, R. J., & Weil, E. M. (1980). An aptitude–strategy interaction in linear syllogistic reasoning. *Journal of Educational Psychology, 72*, 226–234.

Sternberg, S. (1966). High-speed memory scanning in human memory. *Science, 153*, 652–654.

Sternberg, S. (1969). Memory-scanning: Mental processes revealed by reaction-time experiments. *American Scientist, 4*, 421–457.

Stevens, A., & Coupe, P. (1978). Distortions in judged spatial relations. *Cognitive Psychology, 10*, 422–437.

Stevens, C., Lauinger, B., & Neville, H. (2009). Differences in the neural mechanisms of selective attention in children from different socioeconomic backgrounds: an event-related brain potential study. *Developmental Science, 12*(4), 634–646.

Stevens, K. A. (2006). Binocular vision in theropod dinosaurs. *Journal of Vertebrate Paleontology, 26*(2), 321–330.

Stevens, K. N., & Blumstein, S. E. (1981). The search for invariant acoustic correlates of phonetic features. In P. K. Eimas & J. L. Miller (Eds.), *Perspectives on the study of speech* (pp. 1–38). Hillsdale: Erlbaum.

Stickgold, R., & Walker, M. (2004). To sleep, perchance to gain creative insight? *Trends in Cognitive Science, 8*(5), 191–192.

Stiles, J., Bates, E. A., Thal, D., Trauner, D., & Reilly, J. (1998). Linguistic, cognitive, and affective development in children with pre- and perinatal focal brain injury: A ten-year overview from the San Diego longitudinal project. In C. Rovee-Collier, L. Lipsitt, & H. Hayne (Eds.), *Advances in infancy research* (Vol. 12, pp. 131–164). Stamford, CT: Ablex.

Strayer, D. L., Drews, F. A., & Crouch, D. J. (2006). A comparison of the cell phone driver and the drunk driver. *Human Factors, 48*(2), 381–391.

Strayer, D. L., & Johnston, W. A. (2001). Driven to distraction: Dual-task studies of simulated driving and conversing on a cellular telephone. *Psychological Science, 12*, 462–466.

Stromswold, K. (1998). The genetics of spoken language disorders. *Human Biology, 70*, 297–324.

Stromswold, K. (2000). The cognitive neuroscience of language acquisition. In M. Gazzaniga (Ed.), *The new cognitive neurosciences* (2nd ed., pp. 909–932). Cambridge, MA: MIT Press.

Stroop, J. R. (1935). Studies of interference in serial verbal reactions. *Journal of Experimental Psychology, 18*, 624–643.

Strough, J., Mehta, C. M., McFall, J. P., & Schuller, K. L. (2008). Are older adults less subject to the sunk-cost fallacy than younger adults? *Psychological Science, 19*(7), 650–652.

Structuralism [Electronic Version]. *Encyclopedia Britannica*. Retrieved November 7, 2009 from http://www.britannica.com/EBchecked/topic/569652/structuralism.

Sturt, P., Keller, F., & Dubey, A. (2010). Syntactic priming in comprehension: Parallelism effects with and without coordination. *Journal of Memory and Language, 62*, 333–351.

Stuss, D. T., & Floden, D. (2003). Frontal cortex. In L. Nadel (Ed.), *Encyclopedia of cognitive science* (Vol. 2, pp. 163–169). London: Nature Publishing Group.

Stuss, D. T., Shallice, T., Alexander, M. P., & Picton, T. W. (1995). A multidisciplinary approach to anterior attention functions. In J. Grafman, K. J. Holyoak, & F. Boller (Eds.), *Structure and functions of the human prefrontal cortex*. New York: New York Academy of Sciences.

Styles, E. A. (2006). *The psychology of attention*. East Sussex, Great Britain: Psychology Press.

Stylianou, D. A., & Silver, E. A. (2004). The role of visual representations in advanced mathematical problem solving: An examination of expert–novice similarities and differences. *Mathematical Thinking and Learning, 6*(4), 353–387.

Sugrue, K., & Hayne, H. (2006). False memories produced by children and adults in the DRM paradigm. *Applied Cognitive Psychology, 20*(5), 625–631.

Suh, S., & Trabasso, T. (1993). Inferences during reading: Converging evidence from discourse analysis, talk-aloud protocols, and recognition priming. *Journal of Memory and Language, 32*, 279–300.

Sun, R. (2003). Connectionist implementation and hybrid systems. In L. Nadel (Ed.), *Encyclopedia of cognitive science* (Vol. 1, pp. 697–703). London: Nature Publishing Group.

Sundgren, P. C., Dong, Q., Gómez-Hassan, D., Mukherji, S. K., Maly, P., & Welsh, R. (2004). Diffusion tensor imaging of the brain: Review of clinical applications. *Neuroradiology, 46*(5), 339–350.

Surian, L. (1996). Are children with autism deaf to Gricean maxims? *Cognitive Neuropsychiatry, 1*(1), 55–72.

Sutton, J. (2003). Memory, philosophical issues about. In L. Nadel (Ed.), *Encyclopedia of cognitive science* (Vol. 2, pp. 1109–1113). London: Nature Publishing Group.

Swanson, J. M., Volkow, N. D., Newcorn, J., Casey, B. J., Moyzis, R., Grandy, D., & Posner, M. (2003). Attention deficit hyperactivity disorder. In L. Nadel (Ed.), *Encyclopedia of cognitive science* (Vol. 1, pp. 226–231). London: Nature Publishing Group.

Szentagotai, A. (2005). Cognitive psychology as a tool for developing new techniques in cognitive behavioral therapy: a clinical example. *Journal of Cognitive and Behavioral Psychotherapies, 5*(1), 83–94.

Taatgen, N. A., & Lee, F. L. (2003). Production compilation: A simple mechanism to model complex skill acquisition. *Human Factors, 45*(1), 61–77.

Takano, Y., & Okubo, M. (2003). Mental rotation. In L. Nadel (Ed.), *Encyclopedia of cognitive science* (Vol. 3, pp. 7–10). London: Nature Publishing Group.

Takeda, K., Shimoda, N., Sato, Y., Ogano, M., & Kato, H. (2009). eaction time differences between left- and right-handers during mental rotation of hand pictures. *Laterality, 8*, 1–11.

Talasli, U. (1990). Simultaneous manipulation of propositional and analog codes in picture memory. *Perceptual and Motor Skills, 70*(2), 403–414.

Tanaka, J. W., & Taylor, M. (1991). Object categories and expertise: Is the basic level in the eye of the beholder? *Cognitive Psychology, 23*, 457–482.

Tanaka, K. (1993). Neural mechanisms of object recognition. *Science, 262*(5134), 685–688.

Tang, Y., Zhang, W., Chen, K., Feng, S., Ji, Y., Shen, J., et al. (2006). Arithmetic processing in the brain shaped by cultures. *Proceedings of the National Academy of Sciences of the United States of America, 103*(28), 10775–10780.

Tannen, D. (1986). *That's not what I meant! How conversational style makes or breaks relationships*. New York: Ballantine.

Tannen, D. (1990). *You just don't understand: Women and men in conversation*. New York: Ballantine.

Tannen, D. (1994). *Talking from 9 to 5: How women's and men's conversational styles affect who gets heard, who gets credit, and what gets done at work*. New York: Morrow.

Tannen, D. (2001). *I only say this because I love you: How the way we talk can make or break family relationships throughout our lives.* New York: Random House.

Tardif, T. (1996). Nouns are not always learned before verbs: Evidence from Mandarin speakers' early vocabularies. *Developmental Psychology, 32,* 492–504.

Tardif, T., Shatz, M., & Naigles, L. (1997). Caregiver speech and children's use of nouns versus verbs: A comparison of English, Italian, and Mandarin. *Journal of Child Language, 24,* 535–565.

Tarr, M. J. (1995). Rotating objects to recognize them: a case study on the role of viewpoint dependency in the recognition of three-dimensional objects. *Psychonomic Bulletin and Review, 2,* 55–82.

Tarr, M. J. (1999). Mental rotation. In R. A. Wilson & F. C. Keil (Eds.), *The MIT encyclopedia of the cognitive sciences* (pp. 531–533). Cambridge, MA: MIT Press.

Tarr, M. J. (2000). Pattern recognition. In A. Kazdin (Ed.), *Encyclopedia of psychology* (Vol. 6, pp. 66–71). Washington, DC: American Psychological Association.

Tarr, M. J., & Bülthoff, H. H. (1995). Is human object recognition better described by geon structural descriptions or by multiple views? Comment on Biederman and Gerhardstein (1993). *Journal of Experimental Psychology: Human Perception and Performance, 21,* 1494–1505.

Tarr, M. J., & Bülthoff, H. H. (1998). Image-based object recognition in man, monkey, and machine. *Cognition, 67,* 1–20.

Tarr, M. J., & Cheng, Y. D. (2003). Learning to see faces and objects. *Trends in Cognitive Sciences, 7,* 23–30.

Tartaglia, E. M., Bamert, L., Mast, F. W., & Herzog, M. H. (2009). Human perceptual learning by mental imagery. *Current Biology, 19,* 2081–2085.

Taylor, H., & Tversky, B. (1992a). Descriptions and depictions of environments. *Memory & Cognition, 20*(5), 483–496.

Taylor, H., & Tversky, B. (1992b). Spatial mental models derived from survey and route descriptions. *Journal of Memory & Language, 31*(2), 261–292.

Taylor, J. (2002). Paying attention to consciousness. *Trends in Cognitive Science, 6*(5), 206–210.

Taylor, M. J., & Baldeweg, T. (2002). Application of EEG, ERP and intracranial recordings to the investigation of cognitive functions in children. *Developmental Science, 5*(3), 318–334.

Temple, C. M., & Richardson, P. (2004). Developmental amnesia: A new pattern of dissociation with intact episodic memory. *Neuropsychologia 42*(6), 764–781.

Terrace, H. (1987). *Nim.* New York: Columbia University Press.

Terras, M. M., Thompson, L. C., & Minnis, H. (2009). Dyslexia and ssycho-social functioning: An exploratory study of the role of self-esteem and understanding. *Dyslexia, 15,* 304–327.

Thagard, P. (2003). Conceptual change. In L. Nadel (Ed.), *Encyclopedia of cognitive science* (Vol. 1, pp. 666–670). London: Nature Publishing Group.

Thiessen, E. D., Hill, E. A., & Saffran, J. R. (2005). Infant-directed speech facilitates word segmentation. *Infancy, 7*(1), 53–71.

Thomas, J. C., Jr. (1974). An analysis of behavior in the hobbits-orcs problem. *Cognitive Psychology, 6,* 257–269.

Thomas, M. S. C., & McClelland, J. L. (2008). Connectionist models of cognition. In R. Sun (Ed.), *The Cambridge handbook of computational psychology* (pp. 23–58). New York: Cambridge University Press.

Thomas, N. J. T. (2003). Mental imagery, philosophical issues about. In L. Nadel (Ed.), *Encyclopedia of cognitive science* (Vol. 2, pp. 1147–1153). London: Nature Publishing Group.

Thomas, S. J., Johnstone, S. J., & Gonsalvez, C. J. (2007). Event-related potentials during an emotional Stroop task. *International Journal of Psychophysiology, 63*(3), 221–231.

Thompson, R. B. (1999). Gender differences in preschoolers' help-eliciting communication. *The Journal of Genetic Psychology, 160,* 357–368.

Thompson, R. F. (1987). The cerebellum and memory storage: A response to Bloedel. *Science, 238,* 1729–1730.

Thompson, R. F. (2000). Memory: Brain systems. In A. E. Kazdin (Ed.), *Encyclopedia of psychology* (Vol. 5, pp. 175–178). Washington, DC: American Psychological Association.

Thompson, R. F., & Steinmetz, J. E. (2009). The role of the cerebellum in classical conditioning of discrete behavioral responses. *Neuroscience, 162,* 732–755.

Thomsen, T., Hugdahl, K., Ersland, L., Barndon, R., Lundervold, A., Smievoll, A. I., et al. (2000). Functional magnetic resonance imaging (fMRI) study of sex differences in a mental rotation task. *Medical Science Monitor, 6*(6), 1186–1196.

Thorndike, E. L. (1905). *The elements of psychology.* New York: Seiler.

Thorndyke, P. W. (1981). Distance estimation from cognitive maps. *Cognitive Psychology, 13,* 526–550.

Thorndyke, P. W. (1984). Applications of schema theory in cognitive research. In J. R. Anderson & S. M. Kosslyn (Eds.), *Tutorials in learning and memory* (pp. 167–192). San Francisco: Freeman.

Thorndyke, P. W., & Hayes-Roth, B. (1982). Differences in spatial knowledge acquired from maps and navigation. *Cognitive Psychology, 14,* 580–589.

Thurstone, L. L. (1938). *Primary mental abilities.* Chicago: University of Chicago Press.

Thurstone, L. L., & Thurstone, T. G. (1962). *Tests of primary abilities* (Rev. ed.). Chicago: Science Research Associates.

Titchener, E. B. (1910). *A textbook of psychology.* New York: Macmillan.

Toichi, M., & Kamio, Y. (2002). Long-term memory and levels-of-processing in autism. *Neuropsychologia 7*(40), 964–969.

Tolman, E. C. (1932). *Purposive behavior in animals and men.* New York: Appleton-Century-Crofts.

Tolman, E. C., & Honzik, C. H. (1930). "Insight" in rats. *University of California Publications in Psychology, 4,* 215–232.

Tomasello, M. (1999). *The cultural origins of human cognition* (hardback). Cambridge, MA: Harvard University Press.

Tomlinson, T. D., Huber, D. E., Rieth, C. A., & Davelaar, E. J. (2009). An interference account of cue-independent forgetting in the no-think paradigm. *Proceedings of the National Academy of Sciences of the United States of America, 106*(37), 15588–15593.

Torgesen, J. K. (1997). The prevention and remediation of reading disabilities: Evaluating what we know from research. *Journal of Academic Language Therapy, 1,* 11–47.

Toro, R., Perron, M., Pike, B., Richer, L., Veillette, S., Pausova, Z., et al. (2008). Brain size and folding of the human cerebral cortex. *Cerebral Cortex, 18,* 2352–2357.

Torrance, E. P. (1974). *The Torrance tests of creative thinking: Technical-norms manual.* Bensenville, IL: Scholastic Testing Services.

Torrance, E. P. (1984). *Torrance tests of creative thinking: Streamlined (revised) manual, Figural A and B.* Bensenville, IL: Scholastic Testing Services.

Torregrossa, M. M., Quinn, J. J., & Taylor, J. R. (2008). Impulsivity, compulsivity, and habit: the role of orbitofrontal cortex revisited. *Biological Psychiatry, 63*(3), 253–255.

Tottenham, N., Hare, T. A., & Casey, B. J. (2009). A developmental perspective on human amygdala function. In P. J. Whalen & E. A. Phelps (Eds.), *The human amygdala* (pp. 107–171). New York: Guilford Press.

Tourangeau, R., & Sternberg, R. J. (1981). Aptness in metaphor. *Cognitive Psychology, 13,* 27–55.

Tourangeau, R., & Sternberg, R. J. (1982). Understanding and appreciating metaphors. *Cognition, 11,* 203–244.

Townsend, J. T. (1971). A note on the identifiability of parallel and serial processes. *Perception and Psychophysics, 10,* 161–163.

Trabasso, T., & Suh, S. (1993). Understanding text: achieving explanatory coherence through on-line inferences and mental operations in working memory. *Discourse Processes, 16(1&2),* 3–34.

Treadway, M., McCloskey, M., Gordon, B., & Cohen, N. J. (1992). Landmark life events and the organization of memory: Evidence from functional retrograde amnesia. In S. A. Christianson (Ed.), *The handbook of emotion and memory: Research and theory* (pp. 389–410). Hillsdale, NJ: Erlbaum.

Treisman, A. M. (1960). Contextual cues in selective listening. *Quarterly Journal of Experimental Psychology, 12,* 242–248.

Treisman, A. M. (1964a). Monitoring and storage of irrelevant messages in selective attention. *Journal of Verbal Learning and Verbal Behavior, 3,* 449–459.

Treisman, A. M. (1964b). Selective attention in man. *British Medical Bulletin, 20,* 12–16.

Treisman, A. M. (1986). Features and objects in visual processing. *Scientific American, 255(5),* 114B–125.

Treisman, A. M. (1990). Visual coding of features and objects: Some evidence from behavioral studies. In National Research Council (Ed.), *Advances in the modularity of vision: Selections from a symposium on frontiers of visual science* (pp. 39–61). Washington, DC: National Academy Press.

Treisman, A. M. (1991). Search, similarity, and integration of features between and within dimensions. *Journal of Experimental Psychology: Human Perception & Performance, 17,* 652–676.

Treisman, A. M. (1992). Perceiving and re-perceiving objects. *American Psychologist, 47,* 862–875.

Treisman, A. M. (1993). The perception of features and objects. In A. Baddeley & C. L. Weiskrantz (Eds.), *Attention: Selection, awareness, and control* (pp. 5–35). Oxford, UK: Clarenden.

Treue, S. (2003). Visual attention: The where, what, how and why of saliency. *Current Opinion in Neurobiology, 13,* 428–432.

Triandis, H. C. (2006). Cultural intelligence in organizations. *Group & Organization Management, 31(1),* 20–26.

Troche, S. J., Houlihan, M. E., Stelmack, R. M., & Rammsayer, T. H. (2009). Mental ability, P300, and mismatch negativity: Analysis of frequency and duration discrimination. *Intelligence, 37,* 365–373.

Tronsky, L. N. (2005). Strategy use, the development of automaticity, and working memory involvement in complex multiplication. *Memory & Cognition, 33(5),* 927–940.

Tsujii, T., Masuda, S., Akiyama, T., & Watanabe, S. (2010). The role of inferior frontal cortex in belief-bias reasoning: An rTMS study. *Neuropsychologia, 48(7),* 2005–2008.

Tsushima, T., Takizawa, O., Saski, M., Siraki, S., Nishi, K., Kohno, M., et al. (1994). Discrimination of English /r-l/ and w-y/ by Japanese infants at 6–12 months: Language specific developmental changes in speech perception abilities. Paper presented at International Conference on Spoken Language Processing, 4. Yokohama, Japan.

Tulving, E. (1962). Subjective organization in free recall of "unrelated" words. *Psychological Review, 69,* 344–354.

Tulving, E. (1972). Episodic and semantic memory. In E. Tulving & W. Donaldson (Eds.), *Organization of memory.* New York: Academic Press.

Tulving, E. (1983). *Elements of episodic memory.* New York: Oxford University Press.

Tulving, E. (1984). Precis: Elements of episodic memory. *Behavioral and Brain Sciences, 7,* 223–268.

Tulving, E. (1986). What kind of a hypothesis is the distinction between episodic and semantic memory? *Journal of Experimental Psychology: Learning, Memory, & Cognition, 12(2),* 307–311.

Tulving, E. (1989, July/August). Remembering and knowing the past. *American Scientist, 77,* 361–367.

Tulving, E. (2000a). Concepts of memory. In E. Tulving & F. I. M. Craik (Eds.), *The Oxford handbook of memory* (pp. 33–44). New York: Oxford University Press.

Tulving, E. (2000b). Memory: An overview. In A. E. Kazdin (Ed.), *Encyclopedia of psychology* (Vol. 5, pp. 161–162). Washington, DC: American Psychological Association.

Tulving, E., & Craik, F. I. M. (Eds.) (2000). *The Oxford handbook of memory.* New York: Oxford University Press.

Tulving, E., Kapur, S., Craik, F. I. M., Moscovitch, M., & Houle, S. (1994). Hemispheric encoding/retrieval asymmetry in episodic memory: Positron emission tomography findings. *Proceedings of the National Academy of Sciences, 91,* 2016–2020.

Tulving, E., & Pearlstone, Z. (1966). Availability versus accessibility of information in memory for words. *Journal of Verbal Learning and Verbal Behavior, 5,* 381–391.

Tulving, E., & Schacter, D. L. (1994). *Memory systems 1994.* Cambridge, MA: MIT Press.

Tulving, E., Schacter, D. L., & Stark, H. A. (1982). Priming effects in word-fragment completion are independent of recognition memory. *Journal of Experimental Psychology: Learning, Memory, & Cognition, 8(4),* 336–342.

Tulving, E., & Thomson, D. M. (1973). Encoding specificity and retrieval processes in episodic memory. *Psychological Review, 80,* 352–373.

Tunney, N., Taylor, L. F., Higbie, E. J., & Haist, F. (2002). Declarative memory and motor learning in the older adult. *Physical & Occupational Therapy in Geriatrics, 20(2),* 21–42.

Turing, A. (1950). Computing machinery and intelligence. *Mind, 59,* 433–460.

Turing, A. M. (1963). Computing machinery and intelligence. In E. A. Feigenbaum & J. Feldman (Eds.), *Computers and thought.* New York: McGraw-Hill.

Turner, M. L., & Engle, R. W. (1989). Is working-memory capacity task dependent? *Journal of Memory and Language, 28,* 127–154.

Turtle, J., & Yuille, J. (1994). Lost but not forgotten details: Repeated eyewitness recall leads to reminiscence but not hypermnesia. *Journal of Applied Psychology, 79,* 260–271.

Turvey, M. T. (2003). Perception: The ecological approach. In L. Nadel (Ed.), *Encyclopedia of cognitive science* (Vol. 3, pp. 538–541). London: Nature Publishing Group.

Tversky, A. (1972a). Choice by elimination. *Journal of Mathematical Psychology, 9(4),* 341–367.

Tversky, A. (1972b). Elimination by aspects: A theory of choice. *Psychological Review, 79,* 281–299.

Tversky, A., & Kahneman, D. (1971). Belief in the law of small numbers. *Psychological Bulletin, 76(2),* 105–110.

Tversky, A., & Kahneman, D. (1973). Availability: A heuristic for judging frequency and probability. *Cognitive Psychology, 5,* 207–232.

Tversky, A., & Kahneman, D. (1974). Judgment under uncertainty: Heuristics and biases. *Science, 185,* 1124–1131.

Tversky, A., & Kahneman, D. (1981). The framing of decisions and the psychology of choice. *Science, 211,* 453–458.

Tversky, A., & Kahneman, D. (1983). Extensional versus intuitive reasoning: The conjunction fallacy in probability judgment. *Psychological Review, 90(4),* 293–315.

Tversky, B. (1981). Distortions in memory for maps. *Cognitive Psychology, 13(3),* 407–433.

Tversky, B. (1991). Distortions in memory for visual displays. In S. R. Ellis, M. Kaiser, & A. Grunewald (Eds.), *Spatial instruments and spatial displays* (pp. 61–75). Hillsdale, NJ: Erlbaum.

Tversky, B. (1992). Distortions in cognitive maps. *Geoforum, 23,* 131–138.

Tversky, B. (2000a). Remembering spaces. In E. Tulving & F. I. M. Craik (Eds.), *The Oxford handbook of memory* (pp. 363–378). New York: Oxford University Press.

Tversky, B. (2000b). Mental models. In A. E. Kazdin (Ed.), *Encyclopedia of psychology* (Vol. 5, pp. 191–193). Washington, DC: American Psychological Association.

Tversky, B. (2005). Functional significance of visuospatial representations. In P. Shah & A. Miyake (Eds.), *The Cambridge handbook of visuospatial thinking* (pp. 1–34). New York: Cambridge University Press.

Tversky, B., & Schiano, D. J. (1989). Perceptual and conceptual factors in distortions in memory for graphs and maps. *Journal of Experimental Psychology: General, 118*, 387–398.

Underwood, B. J. (1957). Interference and forgetting. *Psychological Review, 64*, 49–60.

Ungerleider, L., & Mishkin, M. (1982). Two cortical visual systems. In D. J. Ingle, M. A. Goodale, & R. J. W. Mansfield (Eds.), *Analysis of visual behavior* (pp. 549–586). Cambridge, MA: MIT Press.

Ungerleider, L. G., & Haxby, J. V. (1994). "What" and "where" in the human brain. *Current Opinion in Neurobiology, 4*, 157–165.

Unsworth, N., Redick, T. S., Heitz, R. P., Broadway, J. M., & Engle, R. W. (2009). Complex working memory span tasks and higher-order cognition: A latent-variable analysis of the relationship between processing and storage. *Memory, 17*(6), 635–654.

Unsworth, N., Schrock, J. C., & Engle, R. W. (2004). Working memory capacity and the antisaccade task: Individual differences in voluntary saccade control. *Journal of Experimental Psychology: Learning, Memory, and Cognition, 30*, 1302–1321.

Unterrainer, J. M., & Owen, A. M. (2006). Planning and problem solving: From neuropsychology to functional neuroimaging. *Journal of Physiology Paris, 99*(4–6), 308–317.

Unterrainer, J. M., Rahm, B., Kaller, C. P., Ruff, C. C., Spreer, J., Krause, B. J., et al. (2004). When planning fails: Individual differences and error-related brain activity in problem solving. *Cerebral Cortex, 14*(12), 1390–1397.

Usher, J. A., & Neisser, U. (1993). Childhood amnesia and the beginnings of memory for four early life events. *Journal of Experimental Psychology: General, 122*(2), 155–165.

Vakil, S., Sharot, T., Markowitz, M., Aberbuch, S., & Groswasser, Z. (2002). Script memory for typical and atypical actions: Controls versus patients with severe closed-head injury. *Brain Injury, 17*(10), 825–833.

Valentin, D., Chollet, S., Beal, S., & Patris, B. (2007). Expertise and memory for beers and beer olfactory compounds. *Food Quality and Preference, 18*, 776–785.

van Daalen-Kapteijns, M., & Elshout-Mohr, M. (1981). The acquisition of word meanings as a cognitive learning process. *Journal of Verbal Learning & Verbal Behavior, 20*(4), 386–399.

van der Leij, A., de Jong, P. F., & Rijswijk-Prins, H. (2001). Characteristics of dyslexia in a Dutch family. *Dyslexia, 7*(3), 105–123.

van Dijk, T. A. (2006). Discourse, context and cognition. *Discourse Studies, 8*(1), 159–177.

Van Garderen, D. (2006). Spatial visualization, visual imagery, and mathematical problem solving of students with varying abilities. *Journal of Learning Disabilities, 39*(6), 496–506.

van Heuven, W. J. B., & Dijkstra, T. (2010). Language comprehension in the bilingual brain: fMRI and ERP support for psycholinguistic models. *Brain Research Reviews, 64*(1), 104–122.

van Marle, H. J. F., Hermans, E. J., Qin, S., & Fernández, G. (2009). From specificity to sensitivity: How acute stress affects amygdala processing of biologically salient stimuli. *Biological Psychiatry, 66*(7), 649–655.

Van Selst, M., & Jolicoeur, P. (1994). Can mental rotation occur before the dual-task bottleneck? *Journal of Experimental Psychology: Human Perception and Performance, 20*, 905–921.

Van Voorhis, S., & Hillyard, S. A. (1977). Visual evoked potentials and selective attention to points in space. *Perception and Psychophysics, 22*(1), 54–62.

van Zoest, W., & Donk, M. (2004). Bottom-up and top-down control in visual search. *Perception, 33*, 927–937.

Vandenbulcke, M., Peeters, R., Fannes, K., & Vandenberghe, R. (2006). Knowledge of visual attributes in the right hemisphere. *Nature Neuroscience, 9*, 964–970.

VanLehn, K. (1989). Problem solving and cognitive skill acquisition. In M. I. Posner (Ed.), *Foundations of cognitive science* (pp. 526–579). Cambridge, MA: MIT Press.

VanLehn, K. (1990). *Mind bugs: The origins of procedural misconceptions.* Cambridge, MA: MIT Press.

Vanpaemel, W., & Storms, G. (2008). In search of abstraction: The varying abstraction model of categorization. *Psychonomic Bulletin & Review, 15*(4), 732–749.

VanRullen R., & Thorpe S. J. (2001). Is it a bird? Is it a plane? Ultra-rapid visual categorisation of natural and artifactual objects. *Perception 30*(6), 655–668.

Vargha-Khadem, F., Gadian, D. G., Watkins, K. E., Connelly, A., Van Paesschen, W., & Mishkin, M. (1997). Differential effects of early hippocampal pathology on episodic and semantic memory. *Science, 277*(5324), 376–380.

Vellutino, F. R., Scanlon, D. M., Sipay, E., Small, S., Pratt, A., Chen, R., et al. (1996). Cognitive profiles of difficult-to-remediate and readily remediated poor readers: Early intervention as a vehicle for distinguishing between cognitive and experiential deficits as basic causes of specific reading disability. *Journal of Educational Psychology, 88*, 601–638.

Verdolini-Marston, K., & Balota, D. A. (1994). Role of elaborative and perceptual integrative processes in perceptual–motor performance. *Journal of Experimental Psychology: Learning, Memory and Cognition, 20*(3), 739–749.

Vernon, P. A., & Mori, M. (1992). Intelligence, reaction times, and peripheral nerve conduction velocity. *Intelligence, 16*(3–4), 273–288.

Vernon, P. A., Wickett, J. C., Bazana, P. G., & Stelmack, R. M. (2000). The neuropsychology and psychophysiology of human intelligence. In R. J. Sternberg (Ed.), *Handbook of intelligence* (pp. 245–264). New York: Cambridge University Press.

Vignal, J., Maillard, L., McGonigal, A., & Chauvel, P. (2007). The dreamy state: Hallucinations of autobiographic memory evoked by temporal lobe stimulation and seizures. *Brain, 130*(1), 88–99.

Vignolo, L. A. (2003). Music agnosia and auditory agnosia: Dissociation in stroke patients. *The Neuroscience and Music, 999*(50), 50–57.

Vinson, D. P., Thompson, R. L., Skinner, R., Fox, N., & Vigliocco, G. (2010). The hands and mouth do not always slip together in British sign language: Dissociating articulatory channels in the lexicon. *Psychological Science, 21*, 1158–1167.

Visual disabilities: Color-blindness. Retrieved December 28, 2004, from http://www.webaim.org/techniques/visual/colorblind

Vitevitch, M. S. (2003). Change deafness: The inability to detect changes between two voices. *Journal of Experimental Psychology: Human Perception and Performance, 29*(2), 333–342.

Vogel, E. K., Woodman, G. F., & Luck, S. J. (2001). Storage of features, conjunctions, and objects in visual working memory. *Journal of Experimental Psychology: Human Perception and Performance, 27*, 92–114.

Vogel, J. J., Bowers, C. A., & Vogel, D. S. (2003). Cerebral lateralization of spatial abilities: A meta-analysis. *Brain Cognition, 52*(2), 197–204.

Vogels, R., Biederman, I., Bar, M., & Lorincz, A. (2001). Inferior temporal neurons show greater sensitivity to nonaccidental than to metric shape differences. *Journal of Cognitive Neuroscience, 13*(4), 444–453.

Vogels, T. P., Rajan, K., & Abbott, L. E. (2005). Neural network dynamics. *Annual Review of Neuroscience, 28,* 357–376.

Vollmeyer, R., Burns, B. D., & Holyoak, K. J. (1996). The impact of goal specificity on strategy use and the acquisition of problem structure. *Cognitive Science, 20,* 75–100.

von Bohlen und Halbach, O., & Dermietzel, R. (2006). *Neurotransmitters and neuromodulators: Handbook of receptors and biological effects.* New York: Wiley.

Von Eckardt, B. (2005). *What is cognitive science?* Cambridge, MA: Bradford.

von Frisch, K. (1962). Dialects in the language of the bees. *Scientific American, 207,* 79–87.

von Frisch, K. (1967). Honeybees: Do they use direction and distance information provided by their dances? *Science, 158,* 1072–1076.

von Helmholtz, H. (1896). *Vorträge und Reden.* Braunschweig, Germany: Vieweg und Sohn.

von Helmholtz, H. L. F. (1962). *Treatise on physiological optics* (3rd ed., J. P. C. Southall, Ed. and Trans.). New York: Dover. (Original work published 1909)

Voon, V., Thomsen, T., Miyasaki, J. M., de Souza, M., Shafro, A., Fox, S. H., et al. (2007). Factors associated with dopaminergic drug-related pathological gambling in Parkinson disease. *Archives of Neurology, 64*(2), 212–216.

Voss, J. L., & Paller, K. A. (2006). Fluent conceptual processing and explicit memory for faces are electrophysiologically distinct. *Journal of Neuroscience, 26*(3), 926–933.

Vygotsky, L. S. (1986). *Thought and language.* Cambridge, MA: MIT Press.

Wackermann, J., Puetz, P., & Allefeld, C. (2008). Ganzfeld-induced hallucinatory experience, its phenomenology and cerebral electrophysiology. *Cortex, 44,* 1364–1378.

Wagenaar, W. (1986). My memory: A study of autobiographic memory over the past six years. *Cognitive Psychology, 18,* 225–252.

Wagner, A. R., & Rescorla, R. A. (1972). Inhibition in Pavlovian conditioning: Application of a theory. In R. A. Boakes & M. S. Halliday (Eds.), *Inhibition and learning.* New York: Academic Press.

Wagner, D. A. (1978). Memories of Morocco: The influence of age, schooling, and environment on memory. *Cognitive Psychology, 10,* 1–28.

Wagner, M. (2006). *The geometries of visual space.* Mahwah, NH: Erlbaum.

Wagner, R. K. (2000). Practical intelligence. In R. J. Sternberg (Ed.,), *Practical intelligence in everyday life.* New York: Cambridge University Press.

Wagner, R. K., & Stanovich, K. E. (1996). Expertise in reading. In K. A. Ericsson (Ed.), *The road to excellence* (pp. 159–227). Mahwah, NJ: Erlbaum.

Wagner, U., Gais, S., Haider, H., Verleger, R., & Born, J. (2004). Sleep inspires insight. *Letters to Nature, 427,* 352–355.

Walker, M. P., Brakefield, T., Hobson, J. A., & Stickgold, R. (2003). Dissociable stages of human memory consolidation and reconsolidation. *Nature, 425*(6958), 616–620.

Walker, P. M., & Tanaka, J. W. (2003). An encoding advantage for own-race versus other-race faces. *Perception, 32,* 1117–1125.

Wall, D. P., Estebana, F. J., DeLuca, T. F., Huycka, M., Monaghana, T., Mendizabala, N. V. d., et al. (2009). Comparative analysis of neurological disorders focuses genome-wide search for autism genes. *Genomics, 93*(2), 120–129.

Walpurger, V., Hebing-Lennartz, G., Denecke, H., & Pietrowsky, R. (2003). Habituation deficit in auditory event-related potentials in tinnitus complainers. *Hearing Research, 181*(1–2), 57–64.

Walsh, V., & Pascual-Leone, A. (2005). *Transcranial magnetic stimulation: A neurochronometrics of mind.* Cambridge, MA: MIT Press.

Wang, C. (2009). On linguistic environment for foreign language acquisition. *Asian Culture and History, 1*(1), 58–62.

Ward, T. B., & Kolomyts, Y. (2010). Cognition and creativity. In J. C. Kaufman & R. J. Sternberg (Eds.), *The Cambridge handbook of creativity* (pp. 93–112). New York: Cambridge University Press.

Warner, J. (2004). Rubbernecking distracts more than phone. Retrieved August 11, 2004, from http://content.health.msn.com/content/article/62/71477.html

Warren, R. M. (1970). Perceptual restoration of missing speech sounds. *Science, 167,* 392–393.

Warren, R. M. (2008). *Auditory perception: An analysis and synthesis.* New York: Cambridge University Press.

Warren, R. M., Obusek, C. J., Farmer, R. M., & Warren, R. P. (1969). Auditory sequence: Confusion of patterns other than speech or music. *Science, 164,* 586–587.

Warren, R. M., & Warren, R. P. (1970). Auditory illusions and confusions. *Scientific American, 223,* 30–36.

Warren, T., White, S. J., & Reichle, E. D. (2009). Investigating the causes of wrap-up effects: Evidence from eye movements and E–Z Reader. *Cognition, 111,* 132–137.

Warrington, E. (1982). The double dissociation of short- and long-term memory deficits. In L. S. Cermak (Ed.), *Human memory and amnesia.* Hillsdale, NJ: Erlbaum.

Warrington, E. K., & McCarthy, R. A. (1987). Categories of knowledge. Further fractionations and an attempted integration. *Brain, 110,* 1273–1296.

Warrington, E., & Shallice, T. (1984). Category specific semantic impairments. *Brain, 107,* 829–853.

Warrington, E., & Weiskrantz, L. (1970). Amnesic syndrome: Consolidation or retrieval? *Nature, 228*(5272), 628–630.

Warrington, E. K, & Shallice, T. (1972). Neuropsychological evidence of visual storage in short-term memory tasks. *The Quarterly Journal of Experimental Psychology, 24,* 30–40.

Wason, P. C. (1968). Reasoning about a rule. *Quarterly Journal of Experimental Psychology, 20*(3), 273–281.

Wason, P. C. (1969). Regression in reasoning? *British Journal of Psychology, 60*(4), 471–480.

Wason, P. C. (1983). Realism and rationality in the selection task. In J. St. B. T. Evans (Ed.), *Thinking and reasoning: Psychological approaches* (pp. 44–75). Boston: Routledge & Kegan Paul.

Wason, P. C., & Johnson-Laird, P. (1970). A conflict between selecting and evaluating information in an inferential task. *British Journal of Psychology, 61*(4), 509–515.

Wason, P. C., & Johnson-Laird, P. N. (1972). *Psychology of reasoning: Structure and content.* London: B. T. Batsford.

Wasow, T. (1989). Grammatical theory. In M. I. Posner (Ed.), *Foundations of cognitive science* (pp. 208–243). Cambridge, MA: MIT Press.

Wasserman, D., Lempert, R. O., & Hastie, R. (1991). Hindsight and causality. *Personality & Social Psychology Bulletin, 17*(1), 30–35.

Waterhouse, L. (2006). Multiple intelligences, the Mozart effect, and emotional intelligence: A critical review. *Educational Psychologist, 41*(4), 207–225.

Waterman, A. H., Blades, M., & Spencer, C. (2001) Interviewing children and adults: The effect of question format on the tendency to speculate. *Applied Cognitive Psychology, 15*(5), 521–531.

Waters, G. S., & Caplan, D. (2003). Language comprehension and verbal working memory. In L. Nadel (Ed.), *Encyclopedia of cognitive science* (Vol. 2, pp. 726–730). London: Nature Group Press.

Waters, H. S., & Schneider, W. (Eds.). (2010). *Metacognition, strategy use, and instruction.* New York: Guilford Press.

Watkins, M. J., & Tulving, E. (1975). Episodic memory: When recognition fails. *Journal of Experimental Psychology: General, 104,* 5–29.

Watson, D. G., Maylor, E. A., Allen, G. E. J., & Bruce, L. A. M. (2007). Early visual tagging: Effects of target–distractor similarity and old age on search, subitization, and counting. *Journal of Experimental Psychology: Human Perception and Performance, 33*(3), 549–569.

Watson, O. M. (1970). *Proxemic behavior: A cross-cultural study.* The Hague, Netherlands: Mouton.

Waugh, N. C., & Norman, D. A. (1965). Primary memory. *Psychological Review, 72,* 89–104.

Weaver, C. A. (1993). Do you need a "flash" to form a flashbulb memory? *Journal of Experimental Psychology: General, 122*(1), 39–46.

Weaver, K. E., & Stevens, A. A. (2007). Attention and sensory interactions within the occipital cortex in the early blind: An fMRI study. *Journal of Cognitive Neuroscience, 19*(2), 315–330.

Weaver, R. (2008). Parameters, Predictions, and Evidence in Computational Modeling: A Statistical View Informed by ACT-R. *Cognitive Science, 32*(8), 1349–1375.

Webster, M. A., Kaping, D., Mizokami, Y., & Duhamel, P. (2004). Adaptation to natural face categories. *Nature, 428,* 557–561.

Wegner, D. M. (1997a). When the antidote is the poison: Ironic mental control processses. *Psychological Science, 8,* 148–153.

Wegner, D. M. (1997b). Why the mind wanders. In J. D Cohen & J. W. Schooler (Eds.), *Scientific approaches to consciousness* (pp. 295–315). Mahwah, NJ: Erlbaum.

Wegner, D. M. (2002). *The illusion of conscious will.* Cambridge, MA: Bradford Books.

Weidner, R., & Fink, G. R. (2007). The neural mechanisms underlying the Mueller-Lyer illusion and its interaction with visuospatial judgments. *Cerebral Cortex, 17,* 878–884.

Weidner, R., & Mueller, H. J. (2009). Dimensional weighting of primary and secondary target-defining dimensions in visual search for singleton conjunction targets. *Psychological Research, 73,* 198–211.

Weinberger, D. R., Mattay, V., Callicott, J. Kotrla, K., Santha, A., van Gelderen, P., et al. (1996). fMRI applications in schizophrenia research. *Neuroimage, 4*(3), 118–126.

Weingartner, H., Rudorfer, M. V., Buchsbaum, M. S., & Linnoila, M. (1983). Effects of serotonin on memory impairments produced by ethanol. *Science, 221,* 442–473.

Weisberg, R. W. (1986). *Creativity: Genius and other myths.* New York: Freeman.

Weisberg, R. W. (1988). Problem solving and creativity. In R. J. Sternberg (Ed.), *The nature of creativity* (pp. 148–176). New York: Cambridge University Press.

Weisberg, R. W. (2009). On "out-of-the-box" thinking in creativity. In A. B. Markman & K. L. Wood (Eds.), *Tools for innovation.* Oxford: Oxford University Press.

Weiskrantz, L. (1994). Blindsight. In M. W. Eysenck (Ed.), *The Blackwell dictionary of cognitive psychology.* Cambridge, MA: Blackwell.

Weiskrantz, L. (2007). The case of blindsight. In M. Velmans & S. Schneider (Eds.), *The Blackwell companion to consciousness.* Malden, MA: Blackwell.

Weiskrantz, L. (2009). Is blindsight just degraded normal vision? *Experimental Brain Research, 192,* 413–416.

Weisstein, N., & Harris, C. S. (1974). Visual detection of line segments: An object-superiority effect. *Science, 186,* 752–755.

Welbourne, S. R., & Ralph, M. A. L. (2007). Using parallel distributed processing models to simulate phonological dyslexia: The key role of plasticity-related recovery. *Journal of Cognitive Neuroscience, 19,* 1125–1139.

Wellman, H. M., & Gelman, S. A. (1998). Knowledge acquisition in foundational domains. In W. Damon (Ed.-in-Chief), D. Kuhn, & R. S. Siegler (Vol. Eds.), *Handbook of child psychology: Vol. 2. Cognitive development* (pp. 523–573). New York: Wiley.

Wells, G. L. (1993). What do we know about eyewitness identification? *American Psychologist, 48,* 553–571.

Wells, G. L. (2006). Eyewitness identification: systemic reforms. *Wisconsin Law Review,* 615–643.

Wells, G. L. (2008). Field experiments on eyewitness identification: Towards a better understanding of pitfalls and prospects. *Law and Human Behavior, 32*(1), 6–10.

Wells, G. L., & Loftus, E. G. (1984). *Eyewitness testimony: Psychological perspectives.* New York: Cambridge University Press.

Wells, G. L., Luus, C. A. E., & Windschitl, P. D. (1994). Maximizing the utility of eyewitness identification evidence. *Current Directions in Psychological Science, 6,* 194–197.

Wells, G. L., Memon, A., & Penrod, S. D. (2006). Eyewitness evidence: Improving its probative value. *Psychological Science in the Public Interest, 7,* 43–75.

Welsh, M. C., Satterlee-Cartmell, T., & Stine, M. (1999). Towers of Hanoi and London: Contribution of working memory and inhibition to performance. *Brain & Cognition, 41,* 231–242.

Wenke, D., & Frensch, P. A. (2003). Is success or failure at solving complex problems related to intellectual ability? In J. E. Davidson & R. J. Sternberg (Eds.), *The psychology of problem solving* (pp. 87–126). New York: Cambridge University Press.

Wenke, D., Frensch, P. A., & Funke, J. (2005). Complex problem solving and intelligence. In R. J. Sternberg & J. E. Pretz (Eds.), *Cognition and intelligence* (pp. 160–187). New York: Cambridge University Press.

Werker, J. F. (1989). Becoming a native listener. *American Scientist, 77,* 54–59.

Werker, J. F. (1994). Cross-language speech perception: Developmental change does not involve loss. In J. C. Goodman & H. L. Nusbaum (Eds.), *The development of speech perception: The transition from speech sounds to spoken words* (pp. 93–120). Cambridge, MA: MIT Press.

Werker, J. F., & Tees, R. L. (1984). Cross-language speech perception: Evidence for perceptual reorganization during the first year of life. *Infant Behavior and Development, 7,* 49–63.

Werner, H., & Kaplan, E. (1952). The acquisition of word meanings: A developmental study. *Monographs of the Society for Research in Child Development,* No. 51.

Wertheimer, M. (1959). *Productive thinking* (Rev. ed.). New York: Harper & Row. (Original work published 1945)

Wexler, K. (1996). The development of inflection in a biologically based theory of language acquisition. In M. L. Rice (Ed.), *Toward a genetics of language* (pp. 113–144). Mahwah, NJ: Erlbaum.

Whalen, P. J. (1998). Fear, vigilance, and ambiguity: Initial neuroimaging studies of the human amygdala. *Current Directions in Psychological Science, 7*(6), 177–188.

What is achromatopsia? Retrieved March 21, 2007, from http://www.achromat.org/what_is_achromatopsia.html

What you need to know about brain tumors. Retrieved June 1, 2010, from http://www.cancer.gov/cancertopics/wyntk/brain

Wheeldon, L. R., Meyer, A. S., & Smith, M. (2003). Language production, incremental. In L. Nadel (Ed.), *Encyclopedia of cognitive science* (Vol. 2, pp. 760–764). London: Nature Group Press.

Wheeler, D. D. (1970). Processes in word recognition. *Cognitive Psychology, 1,* 59–85.

Whitten, S., & Graesser, A. C. (2003). Comprehension of text in problem solving. In J. E. Davidson & R. J. Sternberg (Eds.), *The psychology of problem solving* (pp. 207–229). New York: Cambridge University Press.

Whorf, B. L. (1956). In J. B. Carroll (Ed.), *Language, thought and reality: Selected writings of Benjamin Lee Whorf.* Cambridge, MA: MIT Press.

Wickens, D. D., Dalezman, R. E., & Eggemeier, F. T. (1976). Multiple encoding of word attributes in memory. *Memory & Cognition, 4*(3), 307–310.

Wickett, J. C., & Vernon, P. (1994). Peripheral nerve conduction velocity, reaction time, and intelligence: An attempt to replicate Vernon and Mori. *Intelligence, 18,* 127–132.

Wiedenbauer, G., Schmid, J., & Jansen-Osmann, P. (2007). Manual training of mental rotation. *European Journal of Cognitive Psychology, 19*(1), 17–36.

Wilcox, L. M., Allison, R. S., Elfassy, S., & Grelik, C. (2006). Personal space in virtual reality. *ACM Transactions on Applied Perception (TAP), 3*(4), 412–428.

Williams, M. (1970). *Brain damage and the mind.* London: Penguin.

Williams, R. N. (2000). Epistemology. In A. E. Kazdin (Ed.), *Encyclopedia of psychology* (Vol. 3, pp. 225–232). Washington, DC: American Psychological Association.

Williams, S. E., Turley, C., Nettelbeck, T., & Burns, N. R. (2009). A measure of inspection time in 4-year-old children: The Benny Bee IT task. *British Journal of Developmental Psychology, 27,* 669–680.

Williams, W. M., & Sternberg, R. J. (1988). Group intelligence: Why some groups are better than others. *Intelligence, 12,* 351–377.

Wilson, B. A. (2003). Brain damage, treatment and recovery from. In L. Nadel (Ed.), *Encyclopedia of cognitive science* (Vol. 1, pp. 410–416). London: Nature Publishing Group.

Wilson, D. A., & Stevenson, R. J. (2006). *Learning to smell: Olfactory perception from neurobiology to behavior.* Baltimore, MD: Johns Hopkins University Press.

Wilson, M. A., & Emmorey, K. (2006). No difference in short–term memory span between sign and speech. *Psychological Science, 17*(12), 1093–1094.

Wilson, M. A., & McNaughton, B. L. (1994). Reactivation of hippocampal ensemble memories during sleep. *Science, 265,* 676–679.

Wilson, R. A., & Keil, F. C. (Eds.). (2001). *The MIT encyclopedia of cognitive sciences.* Cambridge, MA: MIT Press.

Wilson, T. D. (2002). *Strangers to ourselves: Discovering the adaptive unconscious.* Cambridge, MA: Belknap.

Wilt, J. K., & Proffitt, D. R. (2005). See the ball; hit the ball: Apparent ball size is correlated with batting average. *Psychological Science, 16,* 937–938.

Wilt, J. K., Proffitt, D. R., & Epstein, W. (2004). Perceiving distance: A role of effort and intent. *Perception, 33,* 577–590.

Windham, G. C., Zhang, L., Gunier, R., Croen, L. A., & Grether, J. K. (2006). Autism spectrum disorders in relation to distribution of hazardous air pollutants in the San Francisco Bay Area. *Environmental Health Perspective, 114*(9), 1438–1444.

Winawer, J., Witthoft, N., Frank, M. C., Wu, L., & Boroditsky, L. (2007). Russian blues reveal effects of language on color discrimination. *Proceedings of the National Academy of Sciences of the United States of America, 104,* 7780–7785.

Winograd, T. (1972). *Understanding natural language.* New York: Academic Press.

Wisco, B. E., & Nolen-Hoeksema, S. (2009). The interaction of mood and rumination in depression: effects on mood maintenance and mood-congruent autobiographical memory. *Journal of Rational-Emotive & Cognitive-Behavior Therapy 27*(3), 144–159.

Wise, R. A., Pawlenko, N. B., Safer, M. A., & Meyer, D. (2009). What U.S. prosecutors and defence attorneys know and believe about eyewitness testimony. *Applied Cognitive Psychology, 23,* 1266–1281.

Wisniewski, E. J. (1997). When concepts combine. *Psychonomic Bulletin and Review, 4,* 167–183.

Wisniewski, E. J. (2000). Concepts: Combinations. In A. E. Kazdin (Ed.), *Encyclopedia of psychology* (Vol. 2, pp. 251–253). Washington, DC: American Psychological Association.

Wissler, C. (1901). The correlation of mental and physical tests. *Psychological Review, Monograph Supplement 3*(6).

Witelson, S. F., Beresh, H., & Kiga, D. L. (2006). Intelligence and brain size in 100 postmortem brains: Sex, lateralization and age factors. *Brain, 129*(2), 386–398.

Witelson, S. F., Kigar, D. L., & Walter, A. (2003). Cerebral commissures. In L. Nadel (Ed.), *Encyclopedia of cognitive science* (Vol. 1, pp. 476–485). London: Nature Publishing Group.

Wittgenstein, L. (1953). *Philosophical investigations.* New York: Macmillan.

Wittgenstein, L. (1980). *Remarks on the philosophy of psychology* (C. J. Luckhardt & M. A. E. Aue, Trans. Vol. 2). Chicago: University of Chicago Press.

Woldorff, M. G., Gallen, C. C., Hampson, S. A., Hillyard, S. A., Pantev, C., Sobel, D., et al. (1993). Modulation of early sensory processing in human auditory cortex during auditory selective attention. *Proceedings of the National Academy of Sciences of the United States of America, 90,* 8722–8726.

Woldorff, M. G., & Hillyard, S. A. (1993). Modulation of early auditory processing during selective listening to rapidly presented tones. *Electroencephalography and Clinical Neurophysiology, 79,* 170–191.

Wolf, O. T. (2009). Stress and memory in humans: Twelve years of progress? *Brain Research, 1293,* 142–154.

Wolfe, J. M. (2005). Watching single cells pay attention. *Science, 308,* 503–504.

Wolfe, J. M. (2007). Guided Search 4.0: Current progress with a model of visual search. In W. D. Gray (Ed.), *Integrated models of cognitive systems* (pp. 99–119). New York: Oxford University Press.

Wolfe, J. M., Butcher, S. J., Lee, C., & Hyle, M. (2003). Changing your mind: On the contributions of top-down and bottom-up guidance in visual search for feature singletons. *Journal of Experimental Psychology: Human Perception and Performance, 29*(2), 483–502.

Wolford, G., Miller, M. B., & Gazzaniga, M. (2000) The left hemisphere's role in hypothesis formation. *The Journal of Neuroscience, 20*(64), 1–4.

Wolkowitz, O. M., Tinklenberg, J. R., & Weingartner, H. (1985). A psychopharmacological perspective of cognitive functions: II. Specific pharmacologic agents. *Neuropsychobiology, 14*(3), 133–156.

Wood, N., & Cowan, N. (1995). The cocktail party phenomenon revisited: How frequent are attention shifts to one's name in an irrelevant auditory channel? *Journal of Experimental Psychology: Learning, Memory, and Cognition, 21,* 255–260.

Woodward, A. L., & Markman. E. M. (1998). Early word learning. In D. Kuhn & R. S. Siegler (Eds.), *Handbook of child psychology: Vol. 2. Cognition, perception, and language* (5th ed., pp. 371–420). New York: Wiley.

Woodward, T. S., Dixon, M. J., Mullen, K. T. Christensen, K. M., & Bub, D. N. (1999). Analysis of errors in color agnosia: a single-case study. *Neurocase, 5*(2), 95–108.

Woodworth, R. S., & Sells, S. B. (1935). An atmosphere effect in formal syllogistic reasoning. *Journal of Experimental Psychology, 18,* 451–460.

Wright, D. B., & Skagerberg, E. M. (2007). Post-identification feedback affects real eyewitnesses. *Psychological Science, 18,* 172–178.

Xu, F., & Carey, S. (1995). Do children's first object names map onto adult-like conceptual representations? In D. MacLaughlin & S. McEwen (Eds.), *Proceedings of the 19th Annual Boston University Conference on Language Development* (pp. 679–688). Somerville, MA: Cascadilla Press.

Xu, F., & Carey, S. (1996). Infants' metaphysics: The case of numerical identity. *Cognitive Psychology, 30,* 111–153.

Xu, Y. (2005). Revisiting the role of the fusiform face area in visual expertise. *Cerebral Cortex. 15*(8), 1234–1242.

Yamashita, K.-i., Hirose, S., Kunimatsu, A., Aoki, S., Chikazoe, J., Jimura, K., et al. (2009). Formation of long-term memory representation in human temporal cortex related to pictorial paired associates. *Journal of Neuroscience, 29*(33), 10335–10340.

Yamauchi, T., & Markman. A. B. (1998). Category learning by inference and classification. *Journal of Memory and Language, 39,* 124–148.

Yang, R., & Sarkar, S. (2006). Detecting coarticulation in sign language using conditional random fields. *Proceedings of the 18th International Conference on Pattern Recognition, 2,* 108–112.

Yang, S. Y., & Sternberg, R. J. (1997). Taiwanese Chinese people's conceptions of intelligence. *Intelligence, 25,* 21–36.

Yantis, S. (1993). Stimulus-driven attentional capture. *Current Directions in Psychological Science, 2*(5), 156–161.

Yendrikhovskij, S. N. (2001). Computing color categories from statistics of natural images. *Journal of Imaging Science and Technology, 45,* 409–417.

Yi, D.-J. & Chun, M. M. (2005). Attentional modulation of learning-related repetition attenuation effects in human parahippocampal cortex. *Journal of Neuroscience, 25,* 3593–3600.

Yokoyama, S., Okamoto, H., Miyamoto, T., Yoshimoto, K., Kim, J., Iwata, K., et al. (2006). Cortical activation in the processing of passive sentences in L1 and L2: an fMRI study. *NeuroImage, 30,* 570–579.

Young, A. W. (2003). Prosopagnosia. In L. Nadel (Ed.), *Encyclopedia of cognitive science* (Vol. 3, pp. 768–771). London: Nature Publishing Group.

Yovel, G., & Kanwisher, N. (2004). Face perception: Domain specific, not process specific. *Neuron, 44*(5), 889–898.

Yu, V. L., Fagan, L. M., Bennet, S. W., Clancey, W. J., Scott, A. C., Hannigan, J. F., et al. (1984). An evaluation of MYCIN's advice. In B. G. Buchanan & E. H. Shortliffe (Eds.), *Rule-based expert systems.* Reading, MA: Addison-Wesley.

Yuille, J. C. (1993). We must study forensic eyewitnesses to know about them. *American Psychologist, 48*(5), 572–573.

Zacks, J. M. (2008). Neuroimaging studies of mental rotation: A meta-analysis and review. *Journal of Cognitive Neuroscience 20:1, pp. 1–19, 20*(1), 1–19.

Zaragoza, M. S., McCloskey, M., & Jamis, M. (1987). Misleading post-event information and recall of the original event: Further evidence against the memory impairment hypothesis. *Journal of Experimental Psychology: Learning, Memory, & Cognition, 13*(1), 36–44.

Zaromb, F. & Roediger, H. L. (2011). The testing effect in free recall and enhanced organization during retrieval. *Memory & Cognition,* in press.

Zhang, L. F., & Sternberg, R. J. (2009). Intellectual styles and creativity. In T. Rickards, M. A. Runco & S. Moger (Eds.), *The Routledge companion to creativity* (pp. 256–266). New York: Routledge.

Zhang, M., Weisser, V. D., Stilla, R., Prather, S. C., & Sathian, K. (2004). Multisensory cortical processing of object shape and its relation to mental imagery. *Cognitive, Affective, & Behavioral Neuroscience, 4*(2), 251–259.

Zhao, L., & Chubb, C. (2001). The size-tuning of the face-distortion after-effect. *Vision Research, 41,* 2979–2994.

Zigler, E., & Berman, W. (1983). Discerning the future of early childhood intervention. *American Psychologist, 38,* 894–906.

Zihl, J., von Cramon, D., & Mai, N. (1983). Selective disturbance of movement vision after bilateral brain damage. *Brain, 106,* 313–340.

Zimmerman, B. J., & Campillo, M. (2003). Motivating self-regulated problem solvers. In J. E. Davidson & R. J. Sternberg (Eds.), *The psychology of problem solving* (pp. 233–262). New York: Cambridge University Press.

Zinchenko, P. I. (1962). *Neproizvol'noe azpominanie* [Involuntary memory] (pp. 172–207). Moscow: USSR APN RSFSR.

Zinchenko, P. I. (1981). Involuntary memory and the goal-directed nature of activity. In J. V. Wertsch, *The concept of activity in Soviet psychology.* Armonk, NY: Sharpe.

Zola, S. M., & Squire, L. R. (2000). The medial temporal lobe and the hippocampus. In E. Tulving & F. I. M. Craik (Eds.), *The Oxford handbook of memory* (pp. 485–500). New York: Oxford University Press.

Zola-Morgan, S. M., & Squire, L. R. (1990). The primate hippocampal formation: Evidence for a time-limited role in memory storage. *Science, 250,* 228–290.

Zoltan, B. (1996). *Vision, perception, & cognition: A manual for the evaluation and treatment of the neurologically impaired adult* (pp. 109–111). Thorofare, NJ: Slack Incorporated.

Zuidema, L. A. (2005). Myth education: Rationale and strategies for teaching against linguistic prejudice: Literacy educators must work to combat prejudice by dispelling linguistic myths. *Journal of Adolescent & Adult Literacy, 48*(8), 666–675.

Zumbach, J. (2009). The role of graphical and text based argumentation tools in hypermedia learning. *Computers in Human Behavior, 25,* 811–817.

Zurif, E. B. (1990). Language and the brain. In D. N. Osherson & H. Lasnik (Eds.), *Language* (pp. 177–198). Cambridge, MA: MIT Press.

Zurif, E. B. (1995). Brain regions of relevance to syntactic processing. In L. R. Gleitman & M. Liberman (Eds.), *Language: An invitation to cognitive science* (Vol. 1, 2nd ed., pp. 381–398). Cambridge, MA: MIT Press.

Zurowski, B., Gostomzyk, J., Gron, G., Weller, R., Schirrmeister, H., Neumeier, B., et al. (2002). Dissociating a common working memory network from different neural substrates of phonological and spatial stimulus processing. *Neuroimage, 15,* 45–57.

Zwaan, R. A., & Radvansky, G. A. (1998). Situation models in language comprehension and memory. *Psychological Bulletin, 123,* 62–185.

Name Index

Page numbers followed by F indicate figures; T, tables.

Subject Index

Page numbers followed by F indicate figures; T, tables.

A

ACT-R (adaptive control of thought-rational) model, 344–48, 346F

Adaptation to environment. *See also* ADHD (attention deficit hyperactivity disorder); Cognitive errors; Flexibility; Habituation; Nervous system; Sensory adaptation
by animals, 69
and brainstem, 101
and change blindness, 165
as evolutionary advantage, 467
in expertise, 515, 518T
intelligence as, 17, 18, 131, 292, 314
knowledge organization as, 340
by limbic systems, 97
via conscious attention, 138, 142

ADHD (attention deficit hyperactivity disorder), 163–65, 169, 182

Agnosia. *See* Visual agnosia

Alzheimer's disease
acetylcholine deficit in, 115, 133
applied vs. basic research in, 225
cognitive dysfunction in, 113, 161, 335
diagnosis of, 221–23
and hippocampus, 117, 133, 221
PET scans for, 123–24

Amnesia, 171, 217–21, 226, 343

Amygdala
and anger and aggression, 96, 97, 100
and emotion, 26, 224, 225
and fear, 75
vigilance regulation by, 142

Analogical codes, 281, 310

Angiograms, 119, 120–21

Animal research, 11, 117, 429–32

Aphasia, 103, 379, 436–38, 437F

Apraxia, 105

Arousal response, 115, 160, 161, 169

Artificial intelligence (AI), 14, 33, 337, 519–20

Associationism, 9–10, 38, 54. *See also* Functionalism; Structuralism

Attention. *See also* Attentional-resources theory; Schizophrenia; Selective attention theories; Task-specific attention theories
automatic vs. controlled processes in, 169–70, 172–75, 172T
and brain areas, 108, 160–61
consciousness compared to, 138, 160, 177–81, 182–83
deficits in, 163–66
defined, 137, 137F
functions of, 138, 139T
influences on, 159–60
and intelligence, 161–62
and learning, 76

Attentional blink phenomena, 76, 155

Attentional-resources theory, 155–57, 156F, 183

Attention deficit hyperactivity disorder. *See* ADHD (attention deficit hyperactivity disorder)

Attentive processes. *See* Controlled processes

Attenuation model. *See* Treisman's model

Autism
emotional impairment in, 77, 97
language impairment in, 232, 426
orienting dysfunction in, 161
savant ability in, 320
theories of, 438–39

Automatic processes. *See also* ACT-R (adaptive control of thought-rational) model; Habituation; Preconscious processing; Unconscious processing
and attention, 172–75
vs. controlled processes, 169–70, 172T

defined, 183
by experts, 516, 518T, 528
mental rotation as, 291
as preattentive, 152, 169–70
and slips, 175, 176T
and task types, 173

Automatization. *See* Automatic processes

Axons, 112–13

B

Base-rate information, 449, 482

Behaviorism, 11–13, 15, 38

Beowulf (epic poem), 364

Biases, 452–54, 469–70, 473, 478, 482. *See also* Expectations, influence of; Heuristics

Bilingualism
advantages vs. disadvantages, 412, 415
and age factors, 413, 417
and brain studies, 436
single- vs. dual-system hypotheses, 414–15, 415F

Binocular depth cues. *See* Depth cues

Blindsight phenomenon, 181, 182

Boredom. *See* Habituation

Bottom-up perception theories, 53–54, 67, 90. *See also* Direct perception theory; Feature-matching theories; Recognition-by-components (RBC) theory; Template theories

Brain. *See also* Brain lesions; Brain research; Cerebral cortex; Cerebral hemispheres; Localization of brain functions; Neurons; Prefrontal cortex (PFC); Primary motor cortex; Primary visual cortex; Visual pathways in brain
as cognition metaphor, 351
death determination of, 101
development of, 95F, 102
disorders of, 97, 115, 126–29
energy used by, 93
and intelligence, 16, 129–31

nurturance effect on, 98
views of, 94F

Brain lesions. *See also* Lesioning techniques
and attentional dysfunction, 165–66
and behavioral dysfunction, 116, 117
in blindsight phenomenon, 181
and cognitive deficits, 30, 97, 304
and color perception deficits, 87
and inconclusiveness of study findings, 435
and memory, 209, 256
MRI detection of, 122
and object recognition, 376
and speech dysfunction, 103, 104F, 432

Brain mapping. *See* Localization of brain functions

Brain research, 117, 121T, 126, 132–33, 161, 179. *See also* Brain; Brain lesions; Research methods; Split-brain patients; Treatment methods; *individual techniques*

Brainstem, 101

Brain tumors, 127–28

Broadbent's model, 150–51, 150F

Broca's area
and *aphasia*, 436–38, 437F
and autism, 232
defined, 103
and language, 124, 431
and speech, 104F, 117

Brodmann's areas, 526

C

Canterbury Tales (Chaucer), 364

Capacity models of attention. *See* Attentional-resources theory

Car accidents
and attention deficits, 136, 157
cell phone use in, 159, 160F
change blindness in, 88
cognitive research on, 34
head injuries from, 128
perceptual distortion in, 3